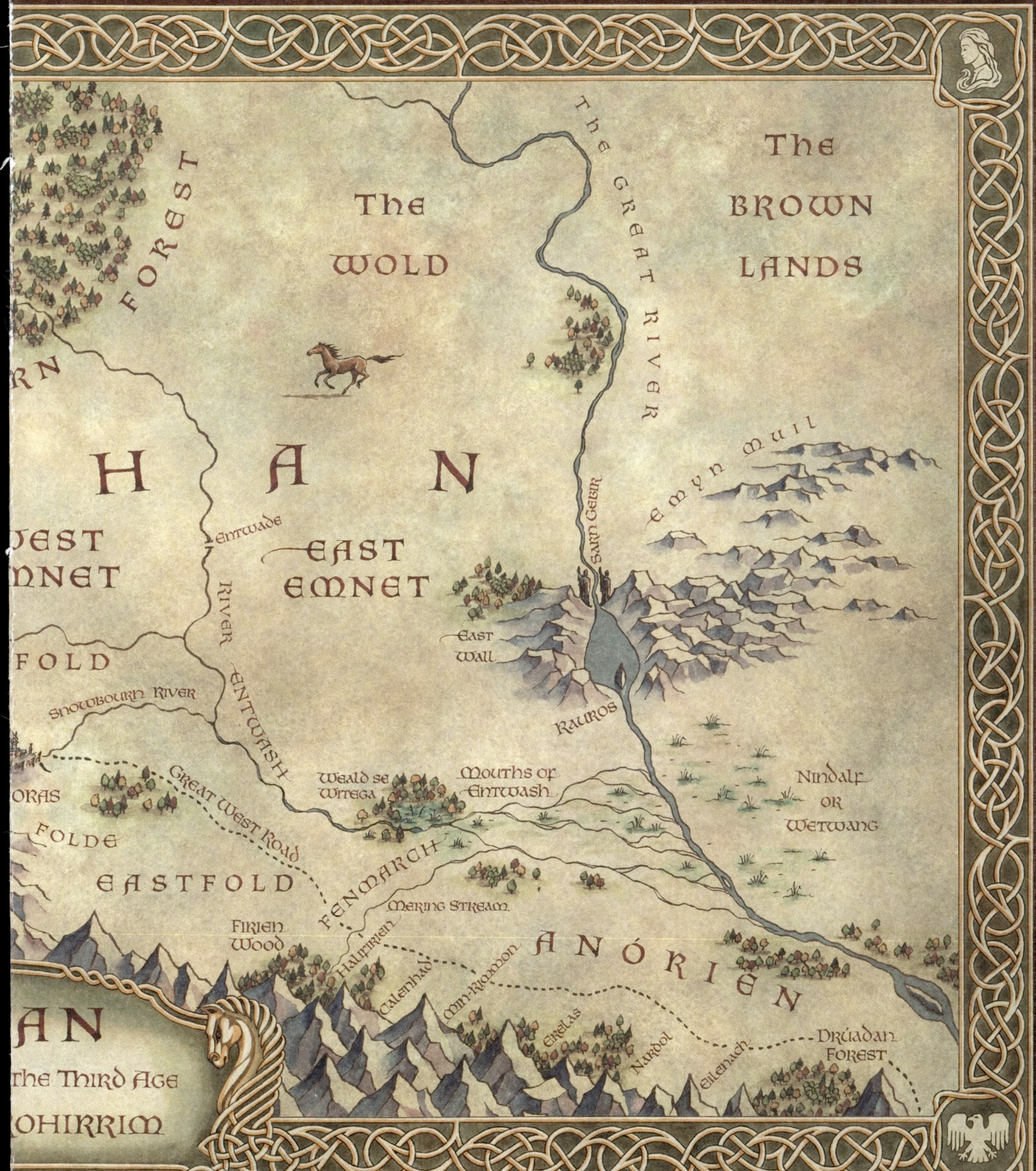

AF251118

FOREST
The WOLD
The GREAT RIVER
The BROWN LANDS
HAN
WEST EMNET
EAST EMNET
Entwade
River Entwash
Emyn Muil
Sarn Gebir
East Wall
FOLD
Snowbourn River
Great West Road
Weald se Witega
Mouths of Entwash
Nindalf or Wetwang
Rauros
ORAS FOLDE
EASTFOLD
FENMARCH
Mering Stream
Firien Wood
Halifirien
Calenhad
Min-Rimmon
ANÓRIEN
Erelas
Nardol
Eilenach
Drúadan Forest
AN
the Third Age
OHIRRIM

THE ART OF
THE LORD OF THE RINGS
THE WAR OF THE ROHIRRIM

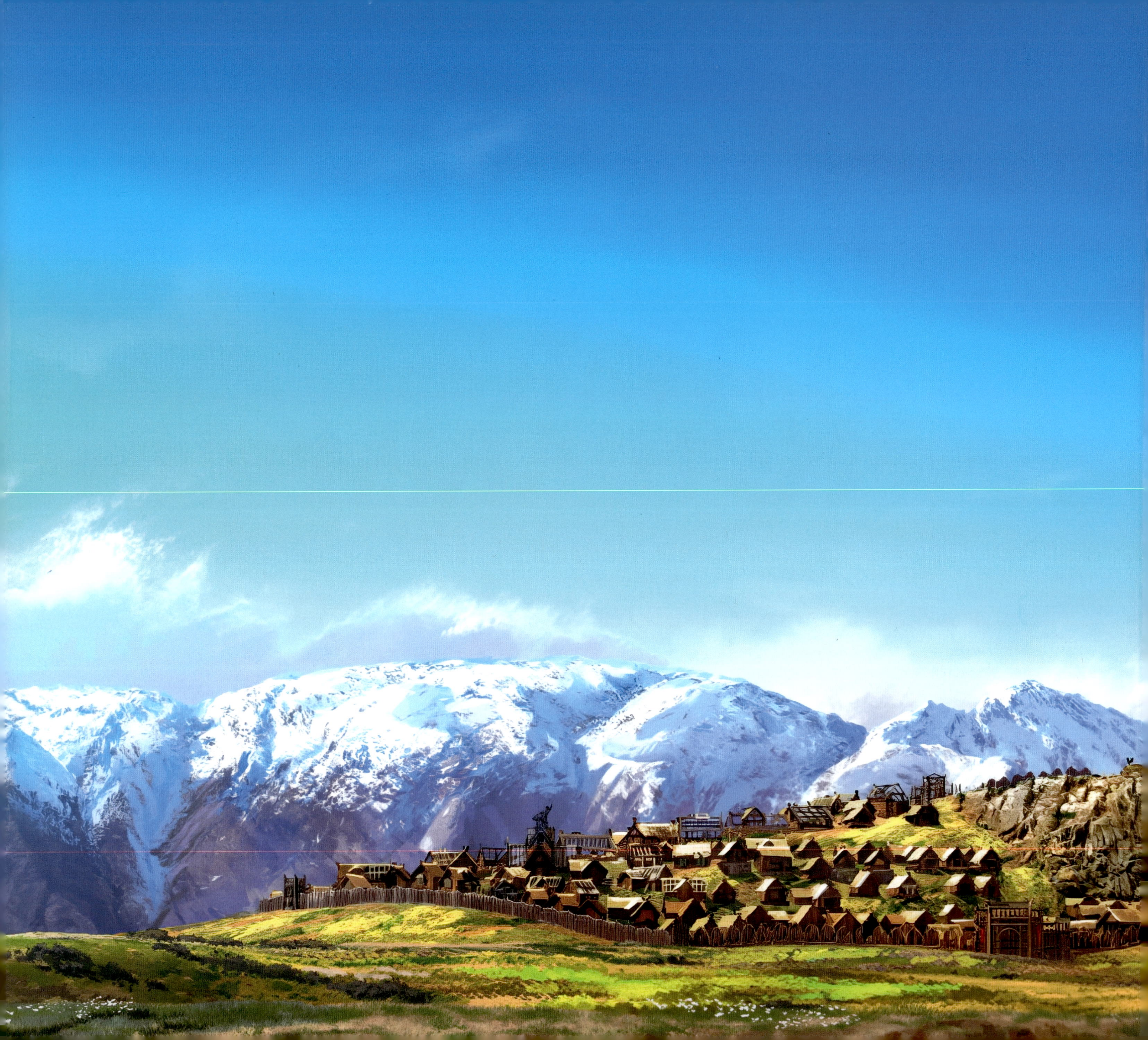

THE ART OF
THE LORD OF THE RINGS
THE WAR OF THE ROHIRRIM

DANIEL FALCONER

FOREWORD BY KENJI KAMIYAMA   ✦   INTRODUCTION BY PHILIPPA BOYENS

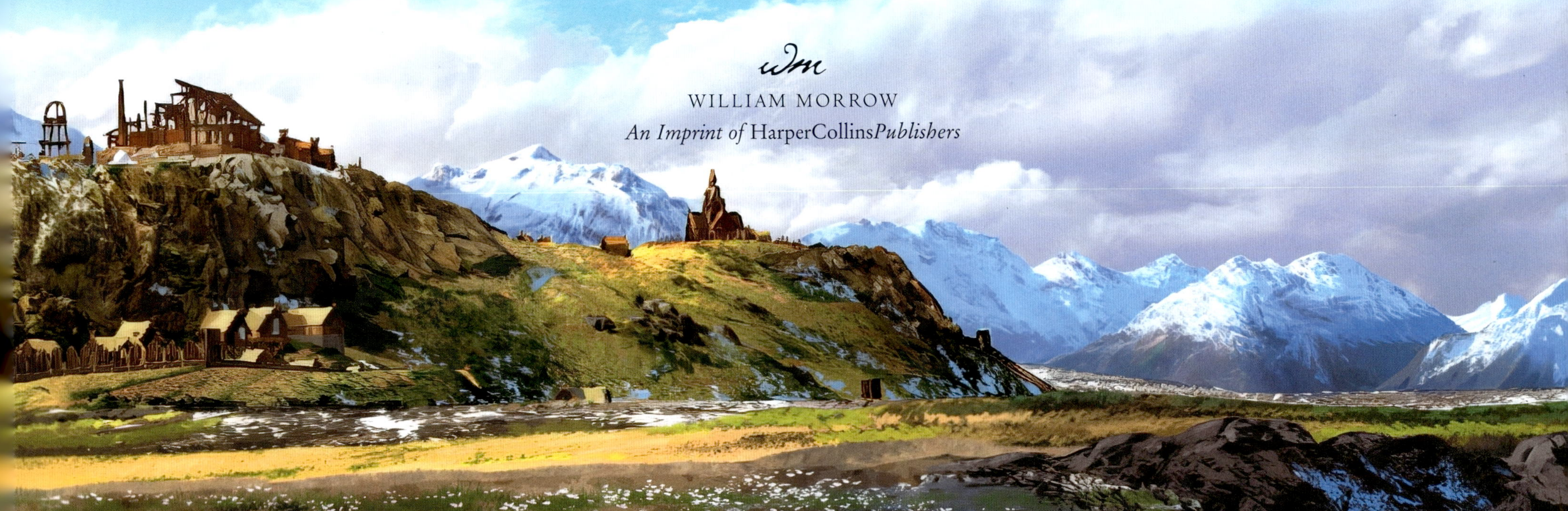

WILLIAM MORROW

An Imprint of HarperCollins*Publishers*

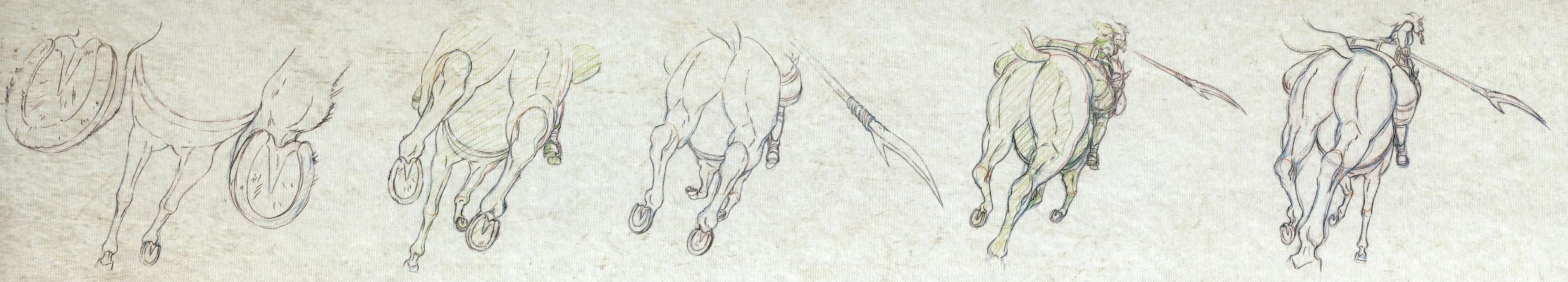

HarperCollins*Publishers*
195 Broadway
New York, NY 10007
www.tolkienestate.com

Published by HarperCollins*Publishers* 2025
1

Text by Daniel Falconer © HarperCollins*Publishers* 2025
Artwork, Film Logos, Script Extracts © 2024 Warner Bros.
Entertainment Inc.
All rights reserved

Quotation by J.R.R. Tolkien from *The Letters of J.R.R. Tolkien* © The Tolkien
Estate Limited 1981
Reproduced with permission.

Compilation © HarperCollins*Publishers* 2025

THE LORD OF THE RINGS: THE WAR OF THE ROHIRRIM and all
characters and elements © & ™ Middle-earth Enterprises, LLC under
license to Warner Bros. Entertainment Inc. (s25)

THE LORD OF THE RINGS, THE FELLOWSHIP OF THE RING,
THE TWO TOWERS and THE RETURN OF THE KING and the
characters, events, items and places therein are trademarks of The Saul
Zaentz Company d/b/a Middle-earth Enterprises under license to New
Line Productions Inc.
All rights reserved.

Unit photographs from THE LORD OF THE RINGS motion picture
trilogy on pages 6, 48, 51, 59, 116, 117, 121, 131 & 143: Pierre Vinet,
Chris Coad, Ken George, Grant Maiden

'Tolkien'® is a registered trademark of The Tolkien Estate
Limited.

The Art of The Lord of the Rings: The War of the Rohirrim is a
companion to the film *The Lord of the Rings: The War of the
Rohirrim* and it is published with the permission, but not the
approval, of the Estate of the late J.R.R. Tolkien. Dialogue
quotations are from the film, not *The Lord of the Rings* novel.

Daniel Falconer asserts the moral right to be identified as the
author of his text and compiler of the work.

Design: Terence Caven
Production: Megan Donaghy

Library of Congress Cataloging-in-Publication Data has been
applied for.

ISBN 978-0-06-342224-7

Printed and bound in Italy by Rotolito S.p.A.

All rights reserved. No part of this publication may be
reproduced, stored in a retrieval system, or transmitted, in any
form or by any means, electronic, mechanical, photocopying,
recording or otherwise, without the prior permission of the
publishers.

Previous Page [PP]: Edoras background art. 1: Animation key frames, MT.

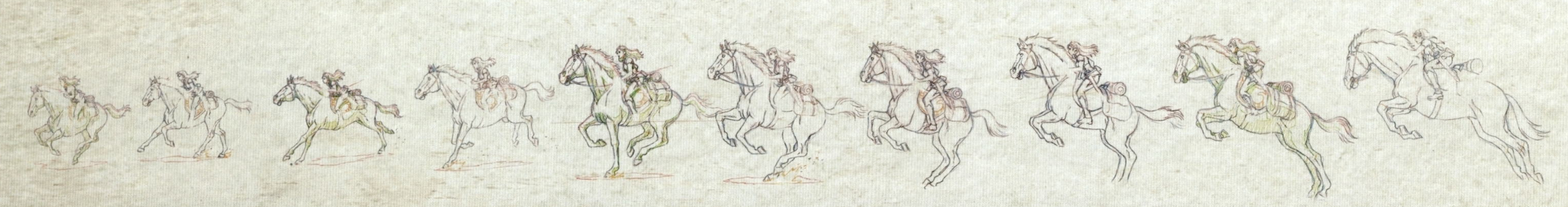

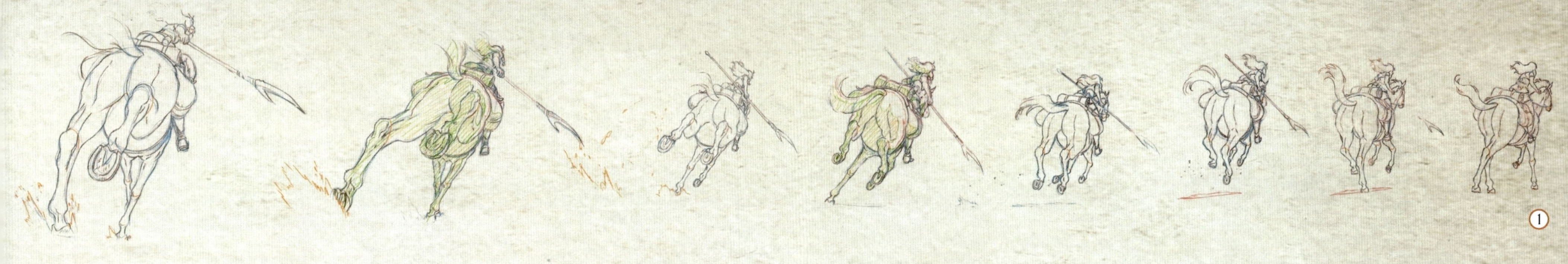

CONTENTS

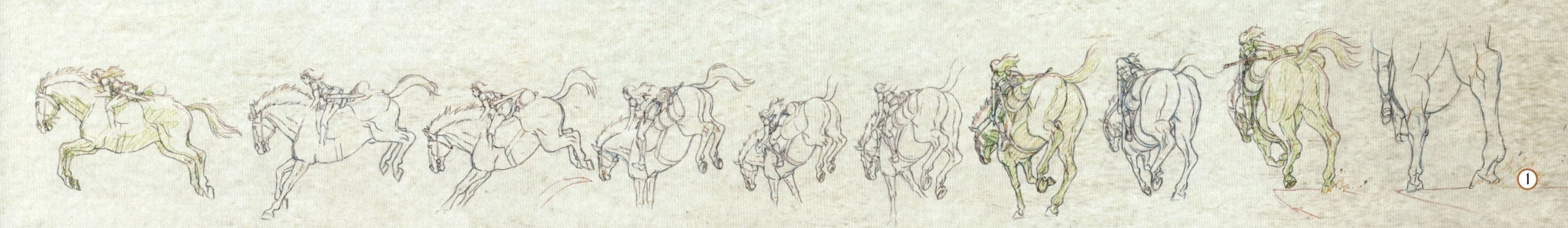

ACKNOWLEDGEMENTS

Profound thanks are due many people for their unwavering support and encouragement in producing this book. None more so than to Takenari Maeda and Hinako Okasora, who were my eyes, ears and hands in Japan, always so generous with their time, so quick to help with advice, assets, interview requests, and invaluable translations. It's a cliché to say so, but this book really could never have happened without them.

Thank you to Philippa Boyens for her faith and advocacy, and to Phoebe Gittins and Arty Papageorgiou for their thoughtfulness, generosity and friendship. It was such a pleasure helping to share their story. Grateful thanks to Jo Clarke for helping to facilitate it happening.

Sincerest appreciations to Joseph Chou, Jason DeMarco and Kenji Kamiyama for their insights, encouragement and time, without which this task would have been impossible.

Many thanks to the amazing artists who so patiently shared their creativity, ideas, and time with me.

The support and enthusiasm of the team at Warner Bros. has been nothing short of amazing. I am very grateful to Jill Benscoter, Logan Nash, Melanie Swartz and Victoria Selover for their tireless help.

Sincerest thanks to my good friends and teammates in this endeavour at HarperCollins, Chris Smith, Terence Caven and David Brawn, who were always so affirming and collaborative.

Finally, thanks to my family for their understanding, and tolerating my absences when I had to put book deadlines ahead of home responsibilities! It has been fun!

DANIEL FALCONER

Final film frame (LOTR trilogy).

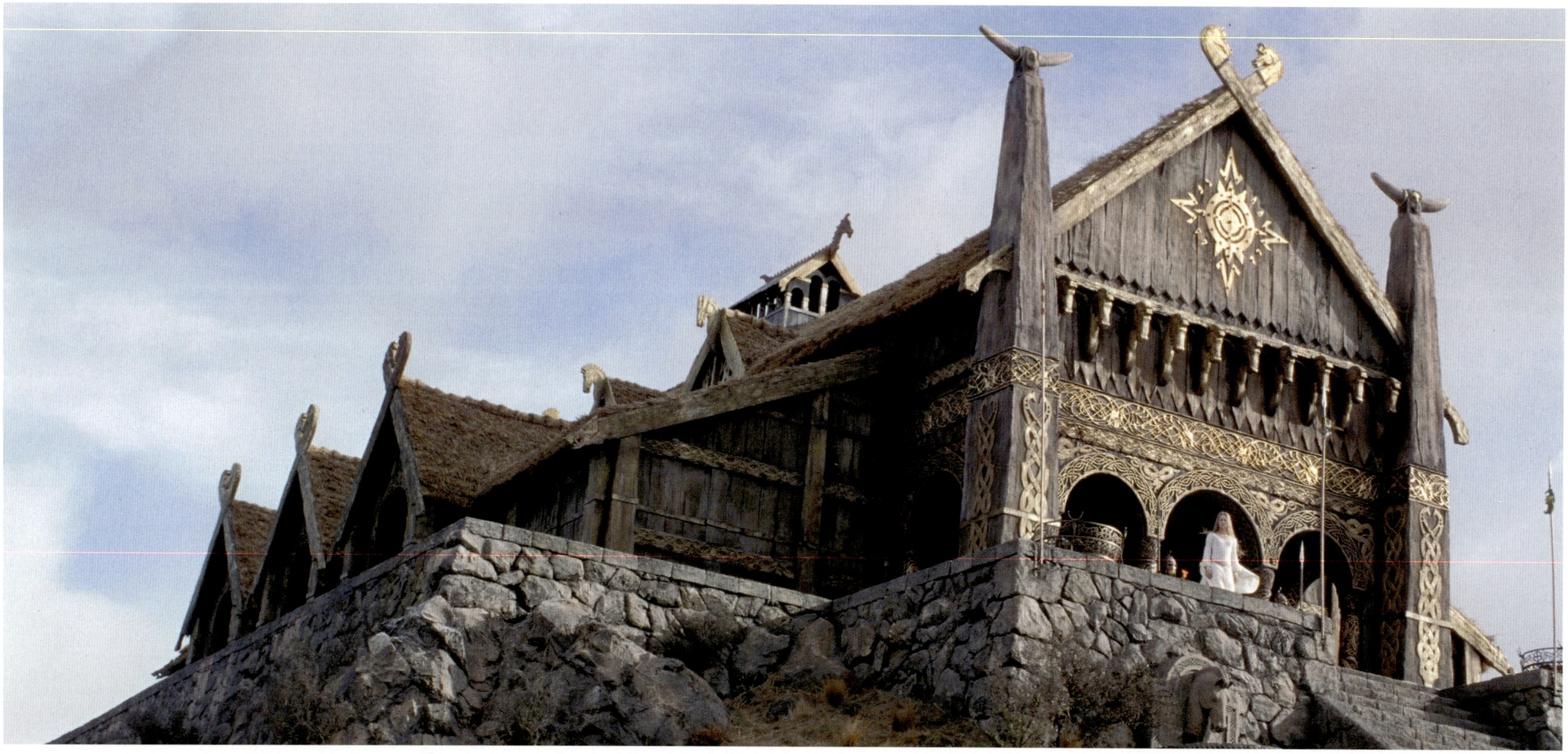

FOREWORD

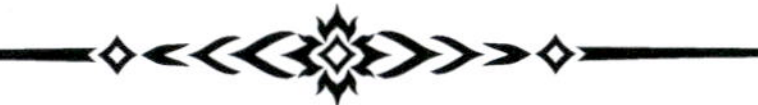

I loved Peter Jackson's *The Lord of the Rings* films, so when the call came from Los Angeles it was an almost instant, 'Yes!'

The idea of reinterpreting that world in anime was very interesting to me, so then the question became, which story do we adapt? There were lots of possibilities in J.R.R. Tolkien's tome; so many potential stories that could be expanded, but all of them quite challenging to create as animated features. When I heard about the story of Helm Hammerhand and his three children – two sons and a daughter we knew nothing about – I thought that sounded very interesting. The story held so many dramatic possibilities. I was immediately intrigued and excited.

Normally I write my own scripts, even if it's a story I am adapting, but in this instance the script was being written by other creatives, so it was a much more collaborative process than I had been used to. I had worked on the *Blade Runner: Black Lotus* series scripts, but this was the first time that I had really left the crafting of the language, the dialogue, entirely to someone else. It was very new, and I was placing all my trust in other writers, but with that also comes the opportunity for a rich exchange of ideas and discussion.

We were in the middle of the pandemic, so everyone was in different locations and time zones around the world. We worked together via video calls, which was itself quite challenging at times. Everything was translated for me to look at and provide commentary on, which in turn was translated and sent back. There was a lot of massaging of the material, so it was a very involved process.

Getting to grips with making a film in a different language was one of the more significant challenges to overcome at every stage of the project. It's difficult for a director to make a film in a language that isn't your own – English in this case – and the nuances of the dialogue are not in your control. How do I stage scenes without relying on the dialogue? How do I direct these scenes? It was a whole new challenge, but what it meant was that I could focus almost entirely on the tools and tasks of staging and directing of sequences to convey how I felt about the story, using visual and dramatic cues without relying on dialogue. Those are things a director thinks about for any project, and I have directed anime feature films before, but on this movie it was particularly important. It really became the heart of the filmmaking process.

Just like Helm and Héra, it was about finding a different way.

KENJI KAMIYAMA, DIRECTOR

Final film frame.

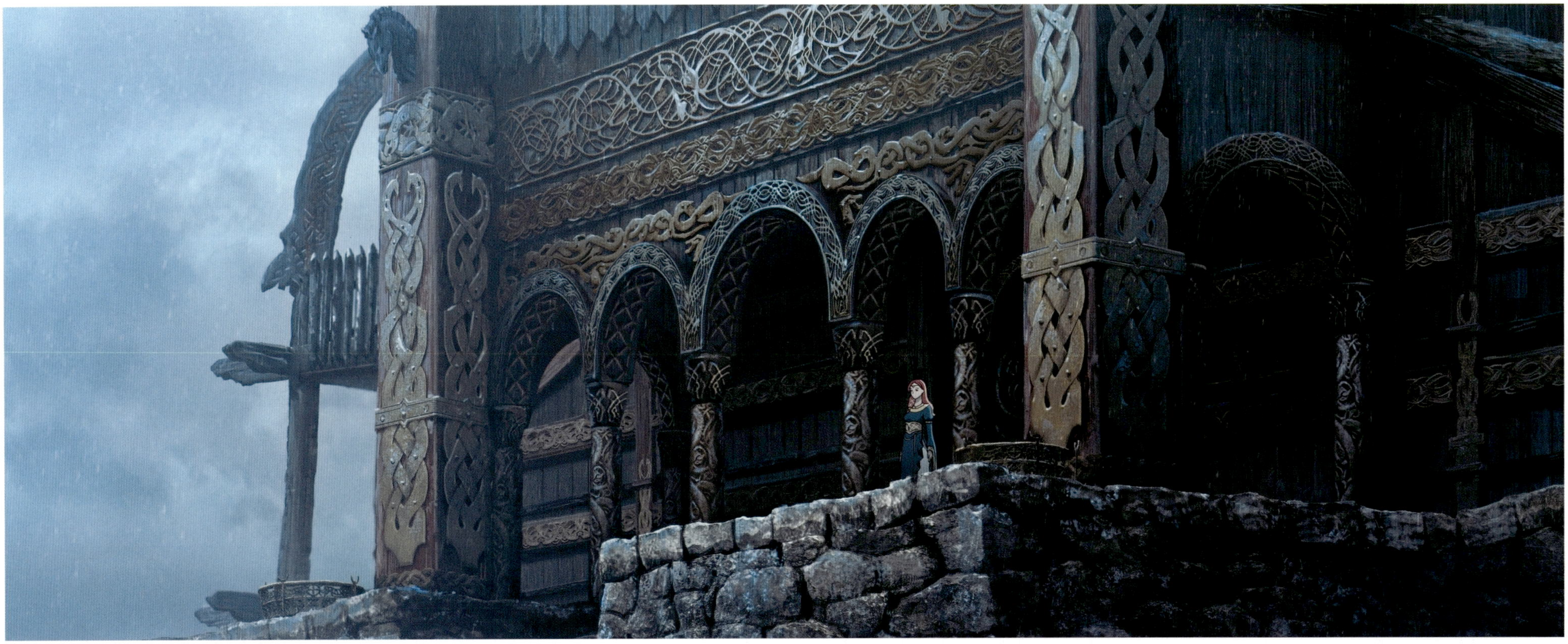

"A story must be told or there'll be no story, yet it is the untold stories that are most moving. . . mountains seen far away, never to be climbed. . ." J.R.R. Tolkien, Letter to Christopher Tolkien, 30 January 1945.

In 2021 New Line Cinema was looking for a story from *The Lord of the Rings* that could be realized as an animated feature film. The appendices at the back of *The Return of the King* hold a rich history of the events that shaped Middle-earth. There are many interesting threads of – as yet – untold stories that we could have delved into. But from the first mention of film being anime, I knew what our story had to be – the tale of Helm Hammerhand and the war for the throne of Rohan.

I had a sense that – whatever story we chose to tell – it needed to be self-contained. Ideally it would not be something that required us to create potentially jarring animated versions of our live-action main characters, nor depend on a Dark Lord or Rings of Power. It could be set against the context of those bigger events and histories, but I felt this needed to be its own complete story.

Given those constraints, we faced the choice of either going much further back into the histories of Middle-earth, or find our tale in the comfort of something familiar, yet unique. To me the choice was obvious; we had to tell the story of the fall of Helm Hammerhand.

Returning to Rohan with new characters held a lot of value for us and for fans of *The Lord of the Rings*, but thinking about it as an anime film, there were other reasons why this tale felt right. Rohirrim history and culture held elements that I thought would play well with the tradition of anime storytelling; warring families, the examination of the concept of honour, the nature of leadership and what makes a good ruler. Looking at a potential structure for the story, it struck me that the great battle in the film would come at the end of the first act rather than at the climax of the film. Which meant that this could be a film – not just about war – but about the wreckage it creates. Thematically, this felt like something that would not be out of place within the great tradition of Japanese filmmaking.

There is a starkness and an honesty to the way in which Japanese filmmakers approach all human emotions, and the way those relationships engage with each other in Japanese cinema. I felt it would be a good fit for Tolkien, and particularly for this story.

Never having made an anime movie myself, I hadn't considered the challenge of animating so many horses. I recall my first conversation with Kenji Kamiyama and Joseph Chou. I was relating the potential battle scene on the plains before Edoras and they interrupted me – looking a bit shocked – and asked 'How many horses?!' Thankfully for everyone involved, in Kenji Kamiyama, we are dealing with a master of anime cinema. He overcame this challenge along with many others to create countless stunning visual tableaux.

But I think the element of this story which was most attractive to me was the chance to tell the story of Helm's unnamed daughter, whom we would eventually call Héra. In many ways, Tolkien's story about Helm Hammerhand is centred around her – it is her rejection of the hand of Wulf that sets in motion the conflict that follows. Beyond that, though, we know very little about her, which gave us some freedom in relating her part of the story. It became a shared story; a father-daughter story. The tale begins as one thing but becomes something else as it shifts with the choices that the characters make, and that is exactly what you look for when writing for cinema.

Professor Tolkien only sketched his idea in the Appendices, but I feel that, given the chance, he might have fleshed it out, one day, as he did for so many other stories. As written, it stands outside of the narrative of Sauron and the One-Ring; the events that unfold don't have a profound effect on the War of the Ring, so, for him, at the time, there probably wasn't the need to tell it in full. But that being the case, why include it unless there was something about the story that he found interesting, perhaps to revisit at a later date? I feel strongly that it was the germ of another story that he might have told, but never got back to.

In adapting this tale for the screen, it is our responsibility to build around the threads of story that Professor Tolkien had sketched, but we always aspired to be thoughtful and studied in our approach. We tried never to do anything that would add to the pot or the soup, as the professor would say, without making sure that it felt authentic to that world, or to his intentions.

It is my great hope that in doing so we honoured the story he had in mind.

PHILIPPA BOYENS, PRODUCER

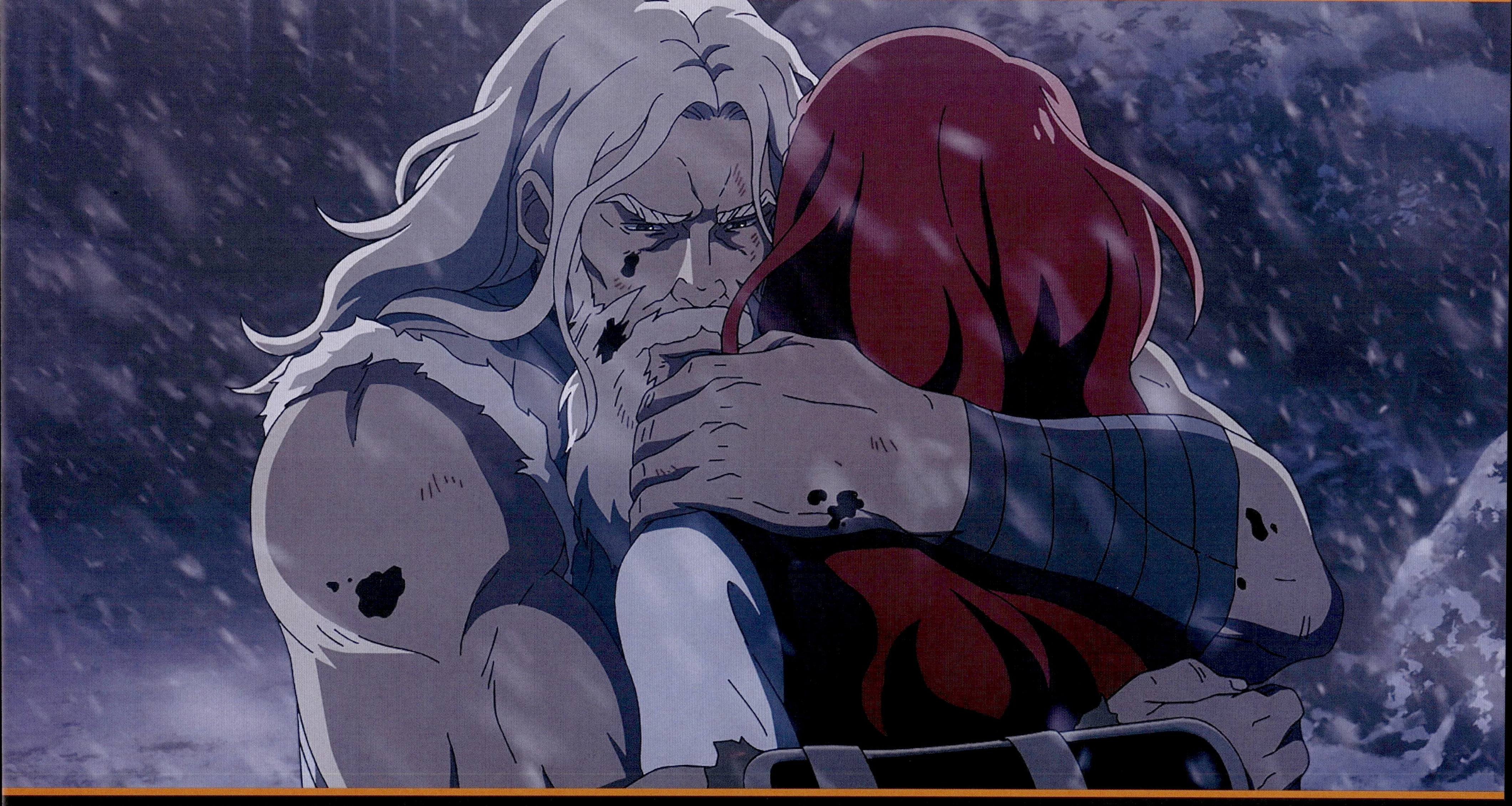

THE MAKING OF AN ANIME EPIC

There had been discussions at New Line Cinema for some time about making a new *The Lord of the Rings* movie, and it was proposed to be CG-animated. There was a story that they had been exploring with Sir Peter Jackson, but for whatever reason it didn't happen. Carolyn Blackwood ran New Line at the time. She was still excited by the idea of making an animated Middle-earth film and was open to trying something different that perhaps wasn't going to be as significant an investment. She spoke to Tom Ascheim, who was the head of animation for all of Warner Bros., and he in turn brought Sam Register into the conversation.

Sam proposed an anime film. Anime is well suited to projects with fantasy elements and does action very well. Knowing that I had been producing anime for Warner Bros. for twenty-five years and was also a huge fan of *The Lord of the Rings*, Sam asked me whether I thought it

could be done. Of course I told him, yes! It would come down to time and money.

The challenge was that New Line wanted the film in two and a half years, and was not keen to spend a lot. Anime is cheaper to produce than some other forms of animation, but it is time-consuming. The average anime film takes five years to make from beginning to end, and we didn't have that time. Anime studios of the quality that we would want to work with are typically booked up for years in advance. We couldn't just pick up the phone and say, "Congratulations, you're going to do a *Lord of the Rings* film!"

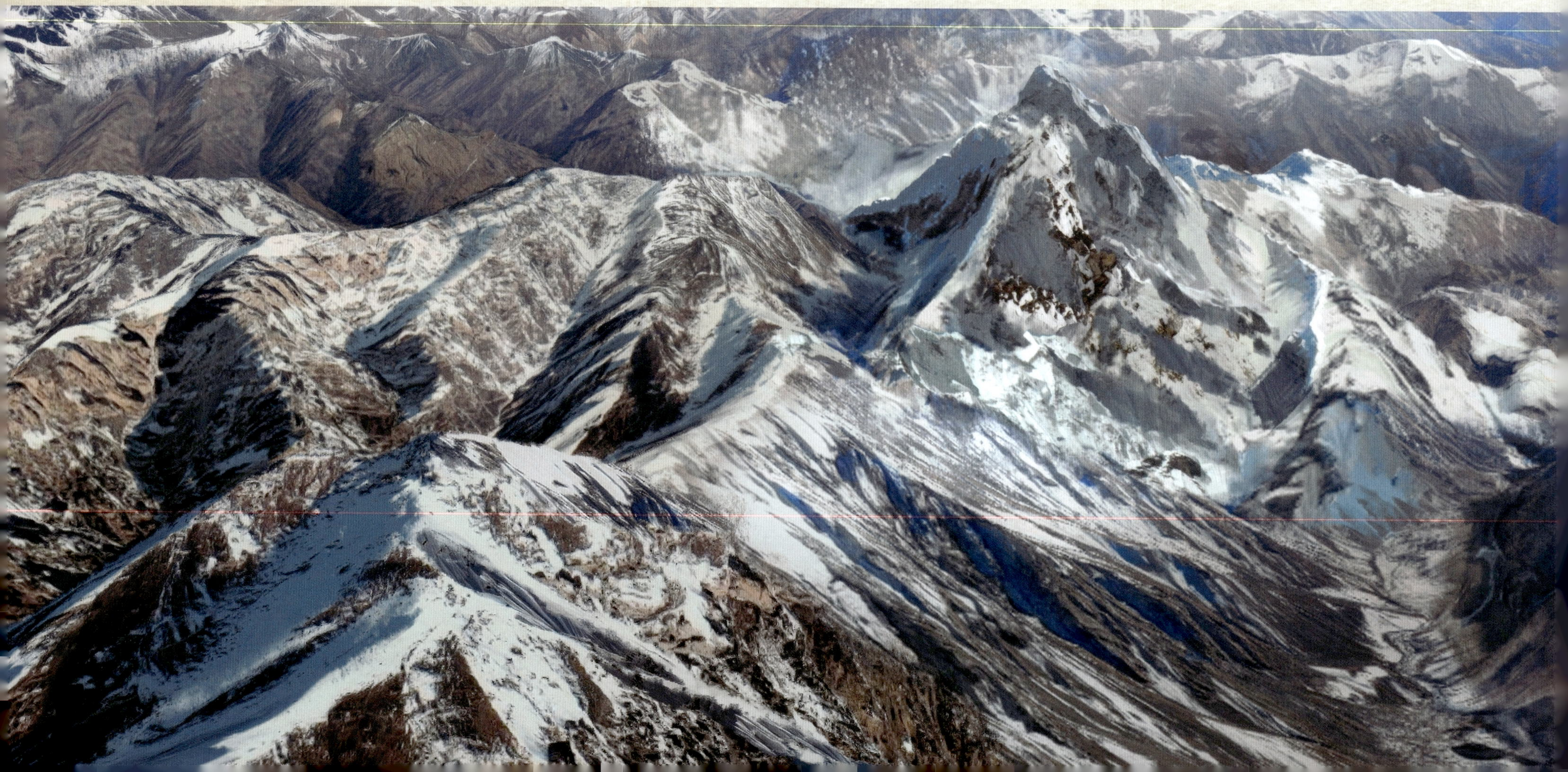

The second challenge was figuring out a story that felt achievable, given the time and budget. We had to be clever in our choices and not bite off more than we could chew, so I spent some time researching possible stories derived from the Appendices of *The Lord of the Rings* which might work for our purposes. Anime studios are very good at using limited animation creatively in a cinematic way that doesn't feel cheap or compromised. If we kept things tightly managed and were mindful of scale, saving heavy, complex animation for only those key sequences that really needed it, then it seemed like perhaps this might be doable. In many ways, anime was the perfect choice for a two-dimensional animated adaptation of Middle-earth because anime artists are so good at the kind of fluid, gorgeous hand-drawn animation that needs to shine in important scenes.

New Line put me in touch with Philippa Boyens, who wrote the original *Lord of the Rings* films with Peter Jackson and Fran Walsh. Sam was putting my nerd credibility to the test! Philippa was enthusiastic about the various stories we were talking about, but it was her who first proposed the story of Helm Hammerhand and his family as a strong standalone film. I reread those pages in the book and immediately agreed. The siege setting would work well for us, it had emotional weight, and we wouldn't necessarily need to animate lots of huge battle sequences.

I then reached out to Joseph Chou, who ran Sola. He had produced several projects that we worked on together and used to work for Warner Bros. many years ago. As one of the original producers of *The Animatrix*, I knew he was somebody who understood how to uniquely bridge Western IP with anime, was well connected in the industry and might know which directors would be interested in something like this.

Not only did Joseph like the idea, but he wanted to be part of the project. We talked about directors, and the name of Kenji Kamiyama, with whom I had worked on *Bladerunner, Black Lotus*, came up. I knew him from his time at Production IG. Kamiyama san had directed *Ghost in the Shell: Stand Alone Complex*, one of my favourite shows, and the excellent animated fantasy series *Moribito: Guardian of the Spirit*. He was both a very strong director and writer, a steady hand, and he could himself also draw. I knew he would be a great choice, if we could get him. . .

Joseph called Kamiyama right after I hung up the phone, and to our great relief he agreed! It was a phenomenal leap of faith on Kamiyama's part; one of many that were made on this project. We knew that we probably didn't have the time or money to do this, but we were going to make the best film that we could. We had faith that, once we started, we could prove how worthy the film was, and maybe New Line might give

White Mountains background setting art, TK.

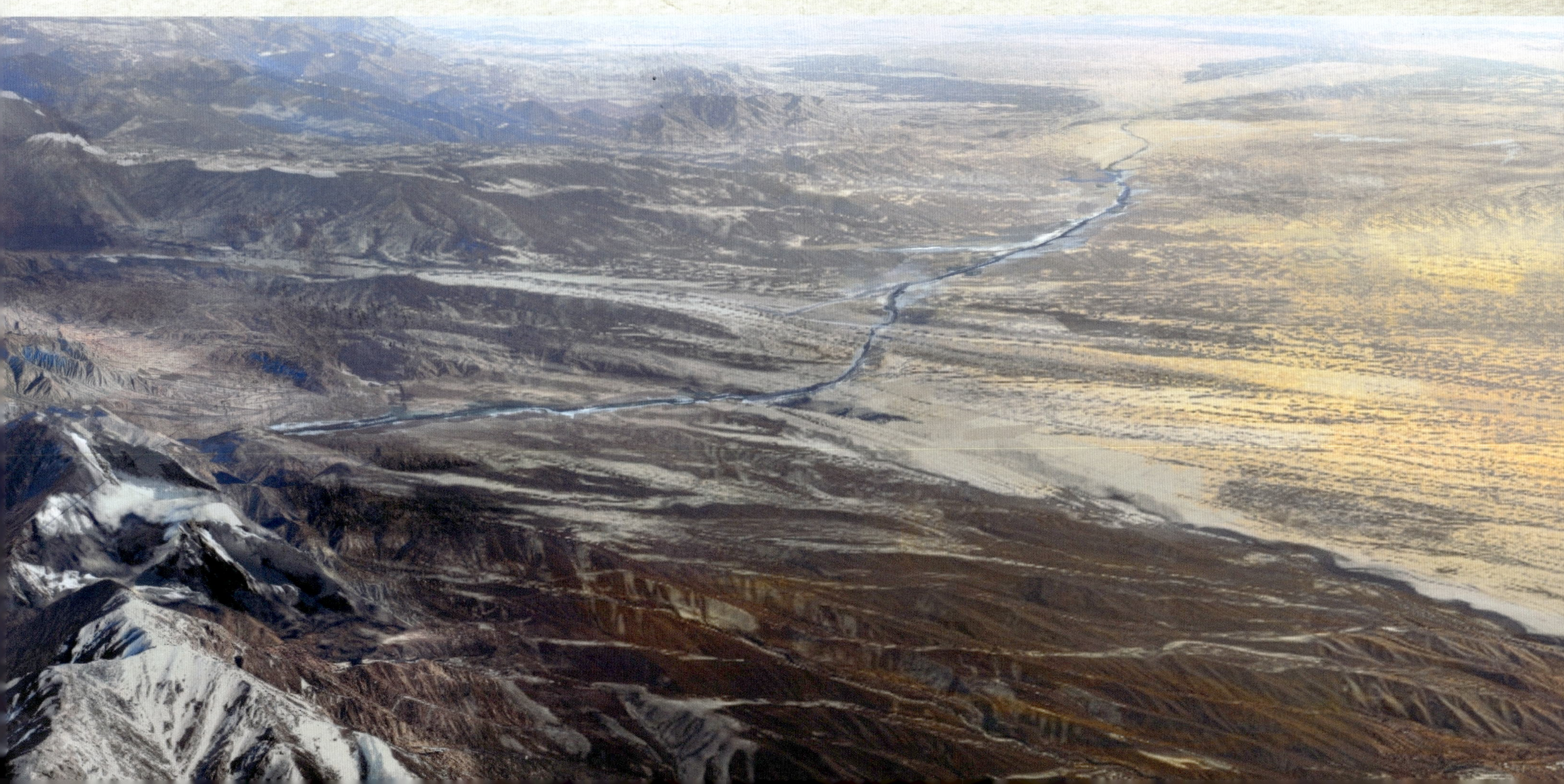

us more to take it to the level that it deserved. In talking to those people who helped make the original live-action films, that was just how these movies got made. When you are playing in this epic world, even the smallest of films, like ours, is going to be a huge undertaking.

With our director secured, we needed an anime studio. That was going to be difficult, given our timeline, and we didn't have the budget to be able to throw money at them until they said yes. We quickly came to the realization that we would need to build our own crew. Finding the high-level animators that we needed who weren't already working was challenging. The project demanded incredible attention to detail. Animation houses usually have their own full-time, in-house animators who help integrate those rotating in and out on contracts. That stability helps ensure consistent animation results when you have hundreds of different people drawing frames.

We had thought about importing animators from France, because France has a tradition of incredible 2D anime artists, but unfortunately the pandemic hitting made that unfeasible. Japan's borders were shut down for two years and this just wasn't a project that could be done remotely, let alone with the extra language challenges. We hired freelancers and we trained people. Joseph did an amazing job cutting deals to beg or borrow key people from other productions, and Kamiyama san was instrumental in helping to elevate the expectation of the art being produced from television to feature film quality, because many of those whom we found had TV backgrounds. He was a great teacher.

Sola produced CG animation, so Joseph had to adapt their way of working to integrate a fully 2D, hand-drawn pipeline on top of or in parallel with that. We used motion capture to help us where we could, and Kamiyama came up with an innovative way of using CG animation to help us block out sequences, which certainly brought efficiencies, but it would take the crew a while to get used to working this way and, in the end, every frame still had to be drawn. It couldn't be rotoscoped or traced.

We did everything that we would to manage the project as tightly as possible but, as Tolkien said, the tale grew in the telling. We needed an epic battle in the middle of the film, with hundreds of soldiers on horseback, and we needed things like *mûmakil*, the Watcher, and a Troll. This was a Middle-earth film and there are things that you just had to have.

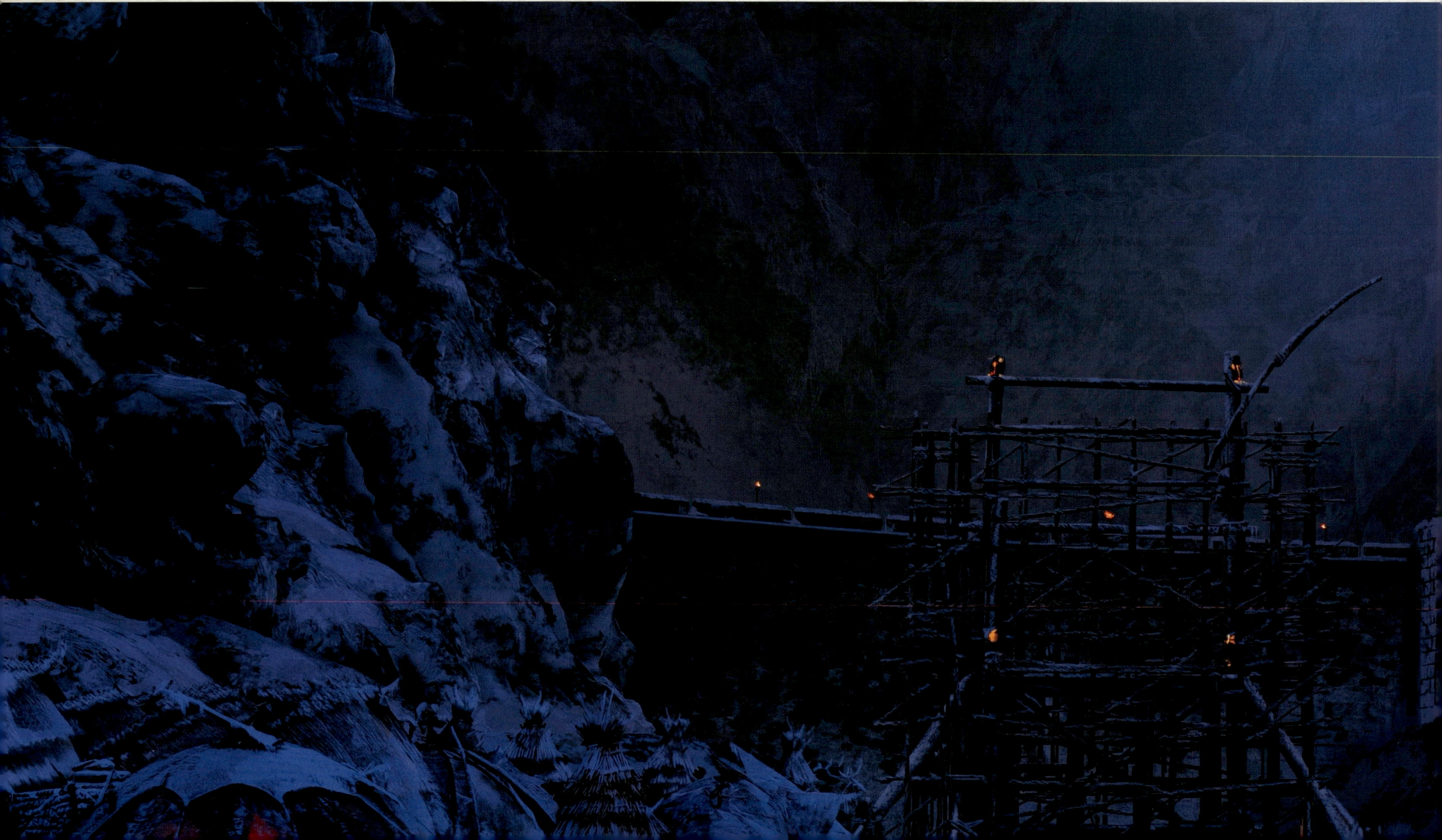

Horses are one of the most difficult things to draw, and we had whole armies galloping and fighting.

We were embraced by the New Zealand team that had made the two film trilogies. They understood the potential of this project as a worthy successor to the work they had done. They believed that it belonged in the same world, with the same design choices and colours, and they supported our efforts to create an original stylistic interpretation of their vision of Middle-earth.

A big moment for us came when we screened our first rough cut of the film to New Line. There was almost no finished animation, but even without it, there was a key moment when they realized the full potential of what we were creating and said that they would give us more money. That helped a lot. It gave us the comfort to know that we might actually achieve this.

Six months later the strikes in Hollywood threw release schedules into chaos. Movies couldn't be promoted properly due to talent being on strike, so theatre dates changed. Another film was pushed into our original mid-year 2024 slot, so *The War of the Rohirrim* was pushed back by six months. We already had our dialogue recorded and our animators were working in Japan, so it didn't negatively impact us; in fact, it bought us an additional six months to finish the film, which was a blessing. We ended up with three and a half years to make a film that probably should have taken five, but we did it.

It came together the way it needed to, but it was definitely a leap of faith for us all. I have such a love for this world; I didn't want to be the guy that screwed it up! I think we were incredibly lucky to get Joseph as producer and Kamiyama as director. It was an incredibly difficult and unusual project for a Japanese director. He brought his own very strong voice to the film and made it his own, but also always respected the many other voices in the room who had been working with J.R.R. Tolkien's world for so long. I can't think of anyone else who could have done it.

JASON DEMARCO, PRODUCER
SENIOR VICE PRESIDENT OF ANIME, ACTION FOR WARNER BROS.

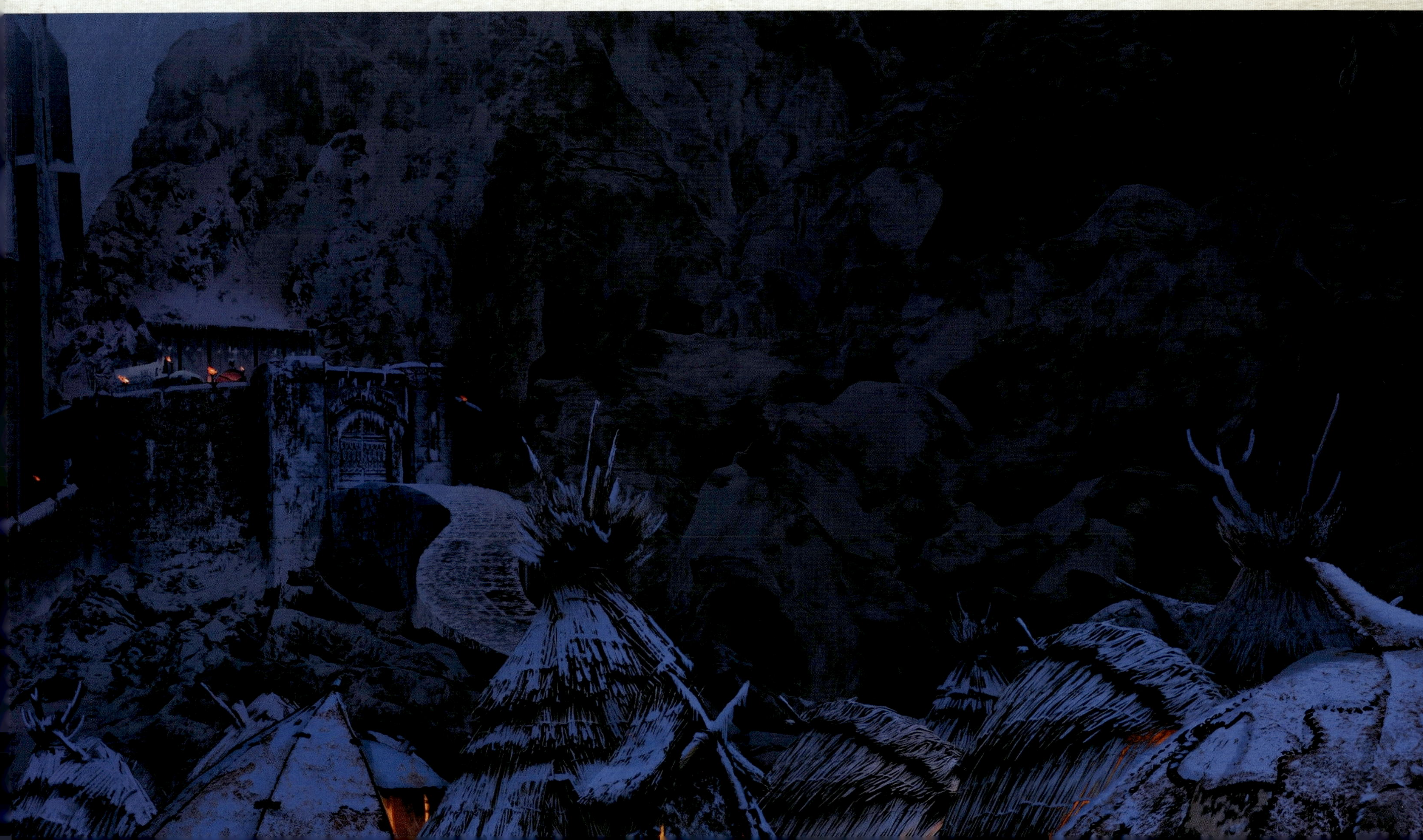

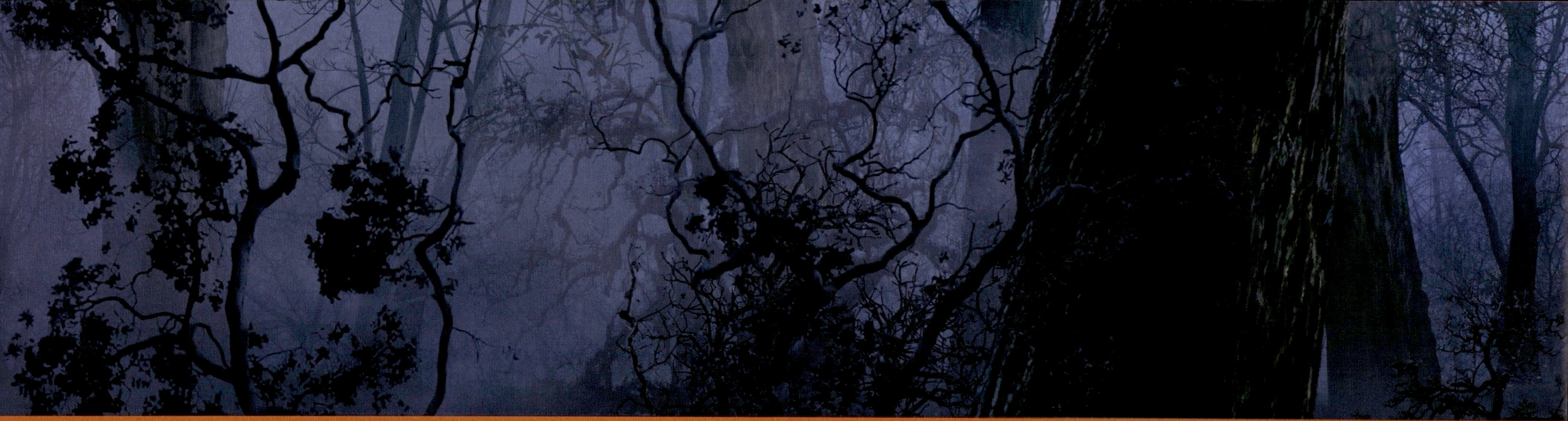

ARTISTS AND CONTRIBUTORS

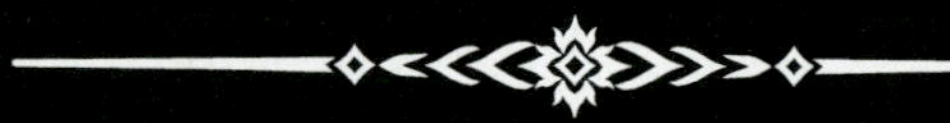

Director KENJI KAMIYAMA (KK)
Producer PHILIPPA BOYENS
Writers PHOEBE GITTINS & ARTY PAPAGEORGIOU
Producer JASON DEMARCO
Producer JOSEPH CHOU (Founder of Sola Entertainment)

SOLA ENTERTAINMENT
Based in Tokyo, Japan, Sola Entertainment was the film's main animation studio.

Original Character Designer STATO (S)
Conceptual Designers ALAN LEE (AL) & JOHN HOWE (JH)
Additional Concept Designs DANIEL FALCONER (DF)

Character Designer & Chief Animation Supervisor MIYAKO TAKASU (MT)
Prop Designer KENJI MASUDA (KM)
Creature Designer MASAHIKO SUZUKI (MS)
Senior Animation Supervisors WANQIAN XIA (SH; Additional Character Designs), AI SATAKE (AS; Additional Character Designs)
Assistant Director IORI MIURA (IM; Additional Creature Designs)
Scene Coordinator YU AOKI (YA)
Senior Key Animators KAZUHIDE TOMONAGA (KT) & HISAO YOKOBORI (HY)
Key Animators ASAMI TAGUCHI (AT; Additional Character Designs),
In-Between Animation Supervisors AISHA ARI HAGIWARA (AAH; Additional Creature Designs) &

Color Designers OSAMU MIKASA (OM), KUMIKO NARUKE & YUKO NOJIRI
Background Art Supervisors YASUHIRO YAMANE (YY) & TAMIKO KANAMORI (TK; also Set Design & Image Board)
Set Design & Image Board KEIICHIRO SHIMIZU (KS)

Background artists
YUHAO OU, NANAMI SAKATA, RIO TAKEDA, NAO YOSHIDA, ANRI ISHIDA, YUJI OHNUKI, ARISA MATSUZAWA, JEAN-MARC POIRIAULT, ATTACHAI BOONSMAI, ADITEP MEECHAIJREONYING, PARINYA PHETWIPHAT, AUTTAPON BOONSMAI, YOSANANN RUJICHAYAKHUN, WATCHARA HORTHONG, SUPAKORN KUNPRATUM, THEERANAN TAEJAROENKUL, PALIN THONGSANTHIN, PICHET CHAIYARIN, ERI SODEYAMA, SHINSUKE KINOSHITA, HARUKA MASUO, YURI ISHIKAWA, ANNA TAKAHASHI, ONOO FUJII, MAYU HIGUCHI, WONG BOKI, SHUNSUKE NEGISHI, TASUKU WATANABE, AKIRA HIROSAWA, YANN LE GALL, AYMERIC GESBERT, RAVENEL M RIECK, YUTO MURATA, HARUKA FUKAGAWA

CGI & Background Supervision SANKAKU (SHUNSUKE WATANABE) (SS)

Associate Producer TAKENARI MAEDA
Line Producer HINAKO OKASORA
Post Production Supervisor JOEY GOUBEAUD
CGI Producer KENTARO TOMINAGA

WĒTĀ WORKSHOP (WW)
The Design Studio at Wētā Workshop, based in Wellington, New Zealand, was commissioned to produce concept and key scene art for the film.

Design Studio Art Director & Senior Concept Artist ADAM MIDDLETON (AM)
Design Studio Senior Concept Artists GUS HUNTER (GH), CHRIS GUISE (CG) & ADAM ANDERSON (AA)
Design Studio Concept Artists IONA BRINCH (IB), THOMAS OATES (TO) & KEN SAMONTE (KSa)
Design Studio Junior Concept Artists JOSHUA DAMIAN (JD) & JEROME MORRIS (JM)
Design Studio Supervising Production Manager TALEI SEARELL
Design Studio Production Manager MEGAN TREZISE

HARPERCOLLINS PUBLISHERS
Editor and Publishing Director CHRIS SMITH
Design Manager TERENCE CAVEN
Senior Production Controller MEGAN DONAGHY
Publisher DAVID BRAWN

WARNER BROS.
Vice President, Integrated Marketing JILL BENSCOTER
Administrator, Integrated Marketing LOGAN NASH
Director, Global Publishing MELANIE SWARTZ
Director, Editorial Publishing VICTORIA SELOVER

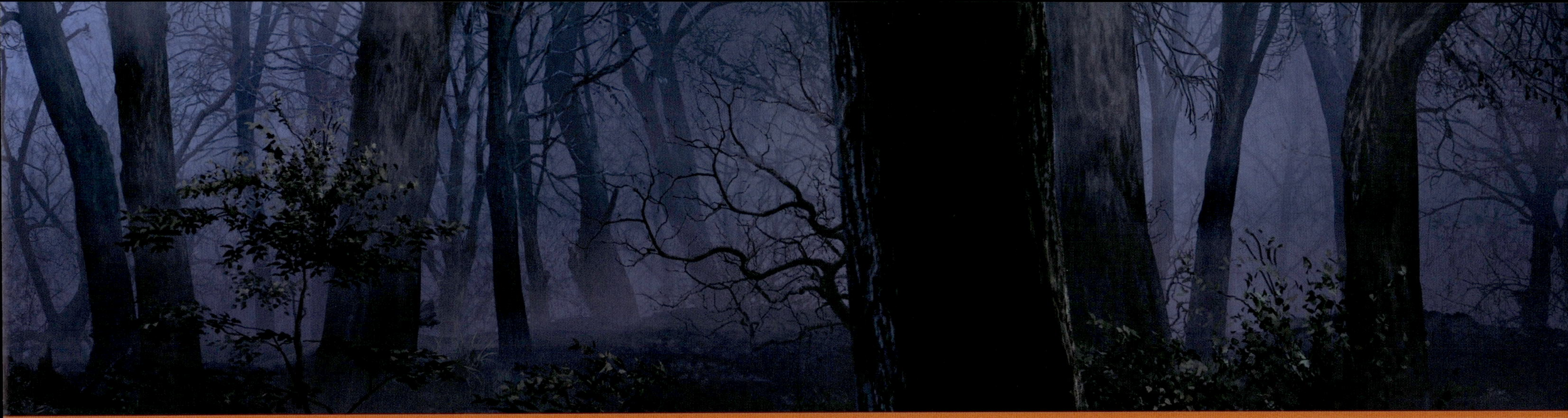

AUTHOR'S NOTE

In mid-2021 I was lucky enough to join the team working on *The War of the Rohirrim*. As someone who had worked on *The Lord of the Rings* and *The Hobbit* film trilogies, the idea was that I could help offer connectivity between the films. *The War of the Rohirrim* was being produced as an anime feature, but it was always intended to be part of the same visual canon as Peter Jackson's films. It was my job to help bridge them by being a sounding board for designs produced by the Asia-based artists and help guide new artwork being produced elsewhere.

I was very excited when I learned that both John Howe and Alan Lee would be returning to Middle-earth. My own apprenticeship as a professional artist had been under these two extraordinary men, when we were designing for *The Lord of the Rings* trilogy. The look of those films owes everything to their imaginations and wisdom.

It was also great to be revisiting Middle-earth with so many new artists bringing their creative vision to bear. My friends in the Wētā Workshop Design Studio were asked to provide concepts; both veterans of the trilogies and brand-new designers. The film's character designs were also already well underway before I came on board, under the pencil of Korean artist STATO. I was unfamiliar with him, but quickly became a fan. There was an amazing team of background artists, prop, character and creature designers in Japan, with whom I would get to work closely as the world of the *War of the Rohirrim* took shape in their hands over the following months. This was one of the most exciting aspects of the project for me. The mix of returning and new artists from East and West imbued the film with the best of all worlds, where experience and legacy could blend with fresh ideas and complementary perspectives to build something beautiful together.

Having no professional experience with hand-drawn animation, I was initially hesitant about what I could offer, beyond reference and anecdotes, but this anxiety was quickly laid to rest. The artistic direction we Jackson movie alumni received from the production was not to worry about the anime aspect or second guess the process when designing; we were to treat the film as if it was an extension of the live-action world that we had known and worked in over the last twenty years. The team in Japan would handle the translation of designs into anime. Our task was simply to think about Middle-earth elements, and in fact we were expressly asked to provide our concepts in a realistic style.

I began by sharing original reference and research materials, and providing briefs and feedback to other artists, but my role quickly expanded, and I had the opportunity to offer new concepts of my own. It was such a pleasure to be back in Middle-earth again, and have the chance to work with friends old and new, jamming together like a bunch of musicians composing an album.

In due course my time on the project came to an end and the world of our Rohirrim heroes was passed into the hands of other artists. I was lucky to occasionally see some of the breathtaking work being done by the animation team. I had great appreciation for the astonishing animators and production crew, so it was with great delight that I jumped at the chance to help share their stories with the world when I was offered authorship of *The Art of The Lord of the Rings: The War of the Rohirrim*.

The wealth of imagery and stories produced could fill a tome this size many times over, so the hardest part of putting this book together was undoubtedly having to cut material. Nevertheless, I hope that all of the artists involved can be proud of the work, even if only a small portion of it is presented here.

For my part, I am deeply grateful for the opportunity and hope I have done them justice.

DANIEL FALCONER

Weald se Witega background art.

- 1 -

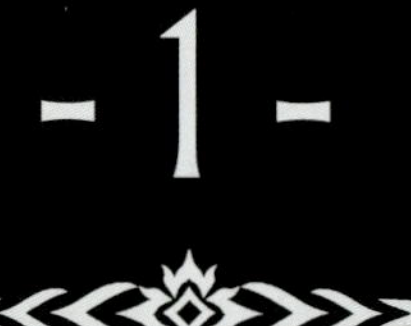

WESTFOLD HIGH PLAINS

Over the White Mountains of Middle-earth soar two Great Eagles, diving and wheeling; free and wild. On the plains below they are watched by Héra, daughter of Helm, princess of Rohan. Climbing to a promontory she calls to the giant birds, and hurling a lure she draws the white-plumed fledgling eagle to her. For a moment they are eye to eye, before the connection is broken and he wheels and ascends once more to the unreachable sky.

Héra is called home and gallops on her white horse Ashere back toward Edoras, capital of Rohan.

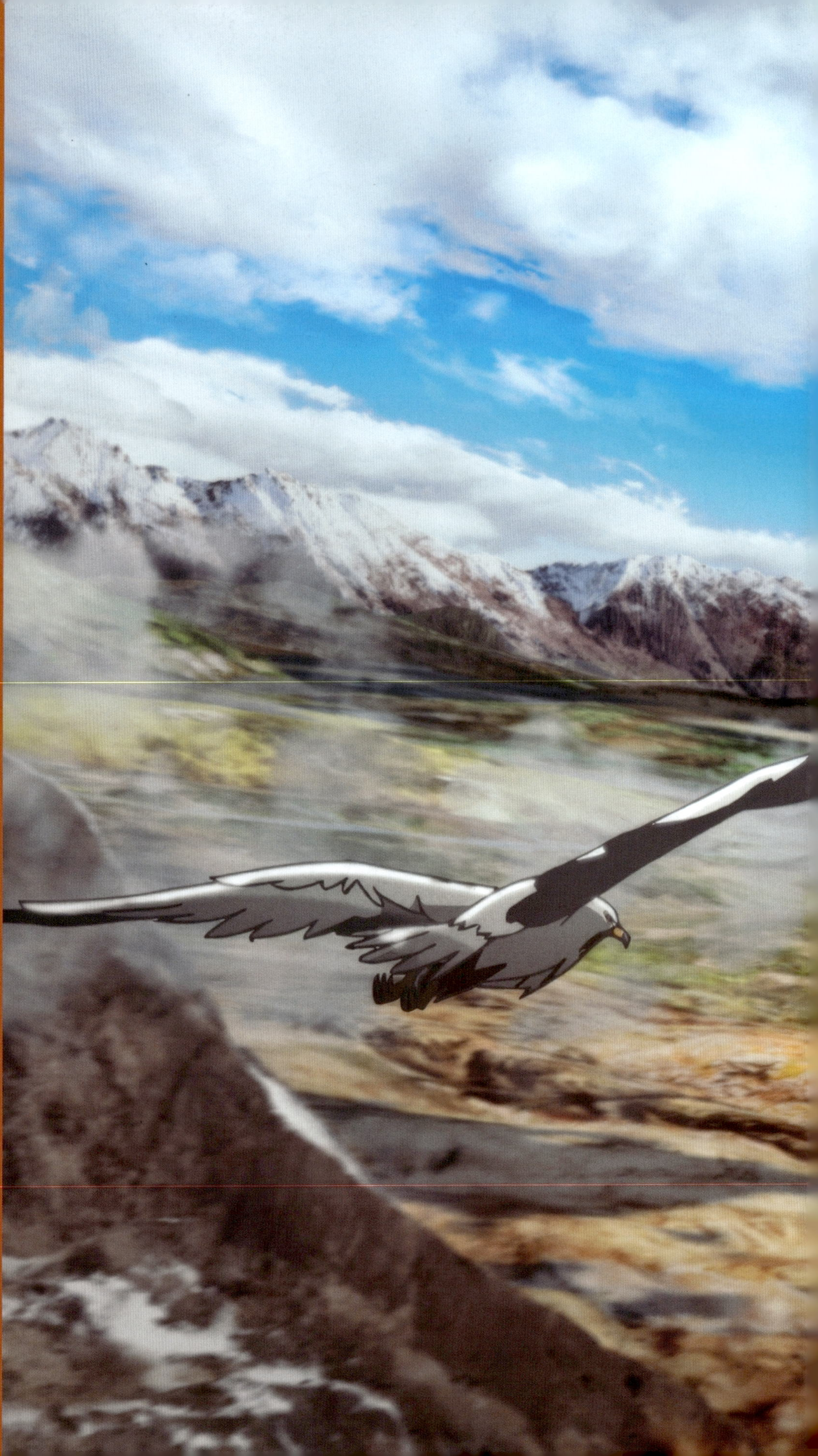

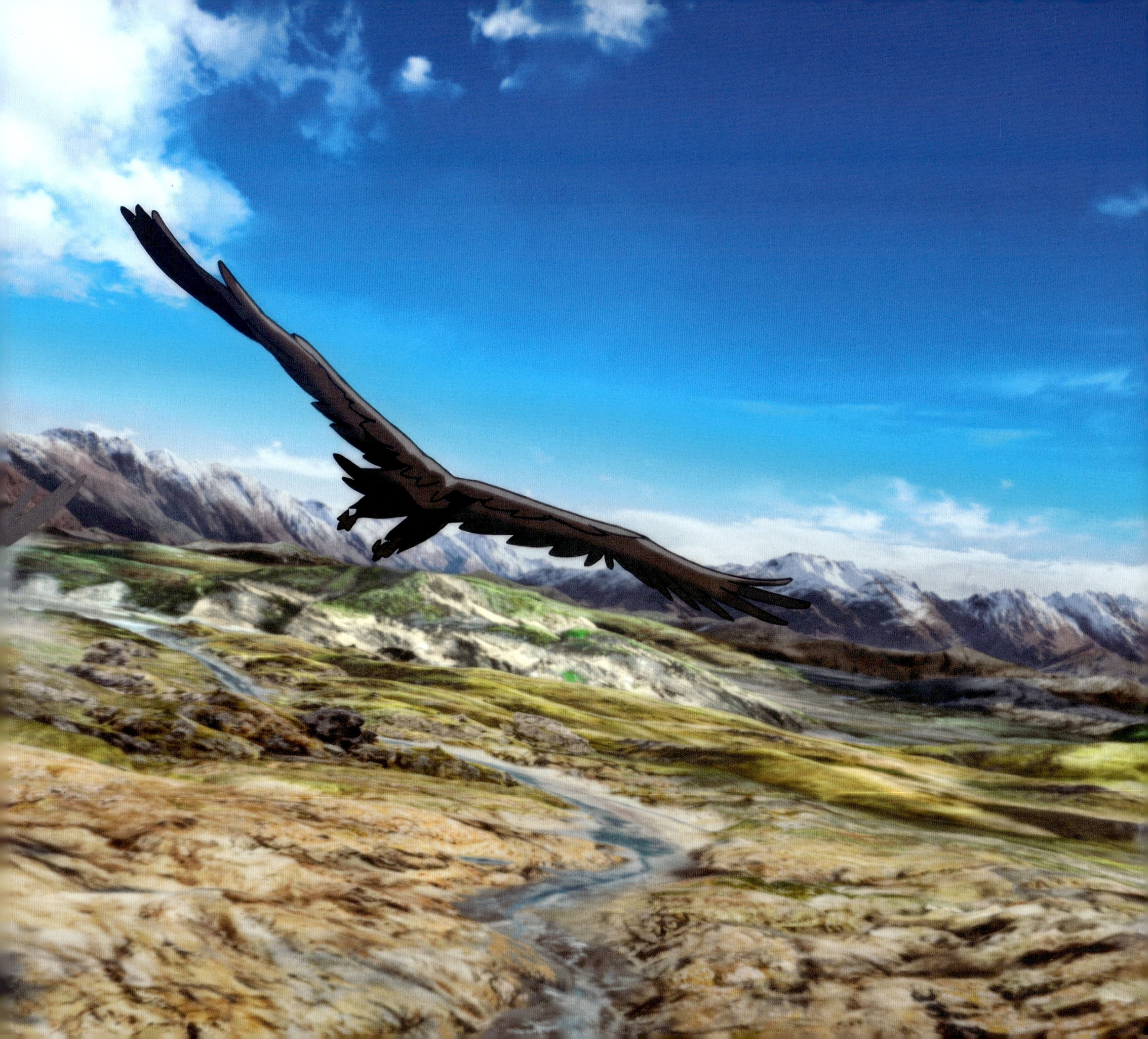

STORYBOARDS

Storyboarding is an important part of the filmmaking process, especially on an animated feature. The boards are the backbone of the project, informing the composition and storytelling of every scene in the film, breaking it down into shots, which in turn generates a list of the background art and animation defining the needs of the film.

Kamiyama san is very visual in his processes. Often, he has a strong visual idea for a scene or shot in his head, which is written into a script and then storyboarded, but the idea originated with him in visual form. – JOSEPH CHOU, PRODUCER

On a television series I might share the work with other people, because there is simply too much for one person to do, but on a film I like to do all the storyboarding myself. They are a critical reference for everyone working on the film. Many directors stick to them very closely and don't deviate from what is drawn, but I like to remain open to incorporating new ideas and make changes as key art is drawn and we progress further into the production. The storyboards are an important roadmap; they are a blueprint for the film, but they're not a textbook that can't be added to or changed.

On this film the process was a bit different to what I am used to because I didn't write the script. Normally the essence of a character is something that I would find or form myself, through the scripting process, so it is very easy to translate from script to storyboards. This time that was harder to get hold of because I was interpreting someone else's ideas. Why a character might react a certain way in a scene, or what their motivation was, were not always things that I immediately understood, because I had not conceived the character or the interaction myself. Additionally, it was written in English, so it had to be translated. There are nuances that are important. It was an involved process that I worked through in close partnership with Philippa Boyens. – KENJI KAMIYAMA, DIRECTOR

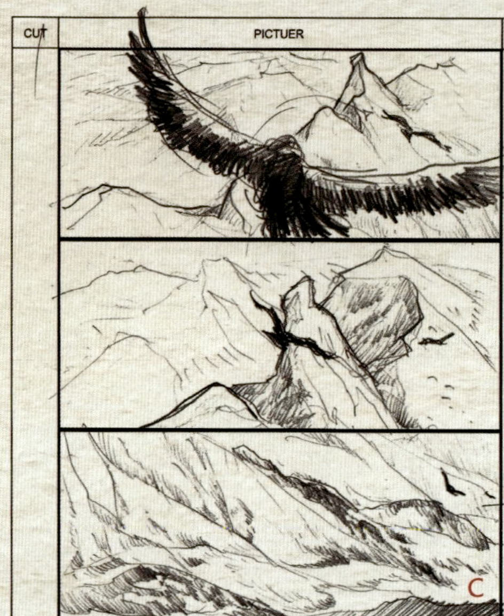

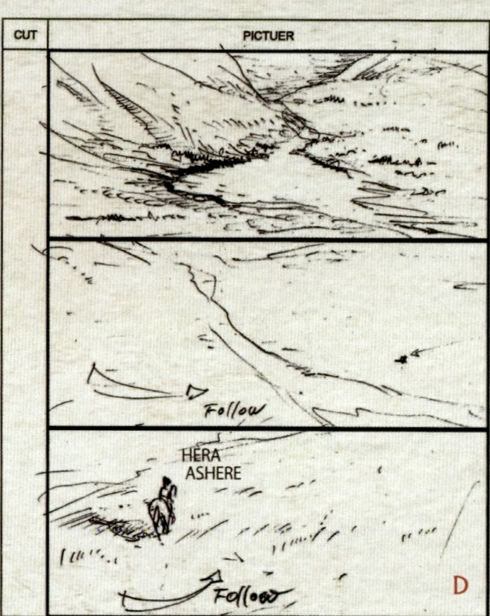

PP: Final film frame. Storyboard frames, KK.

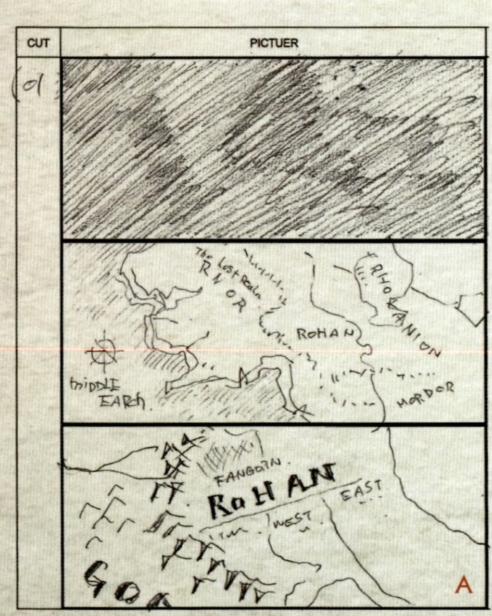

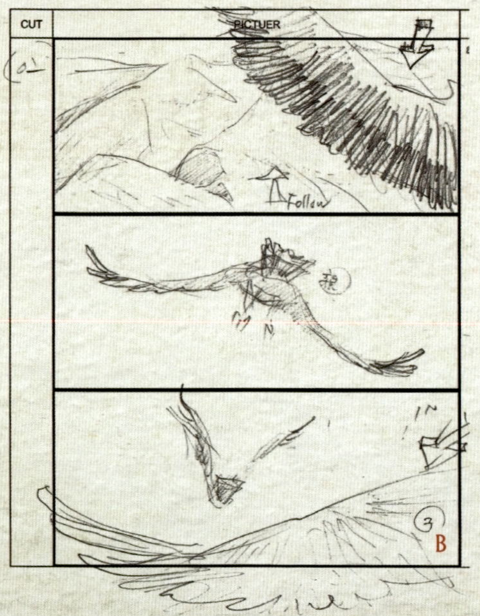

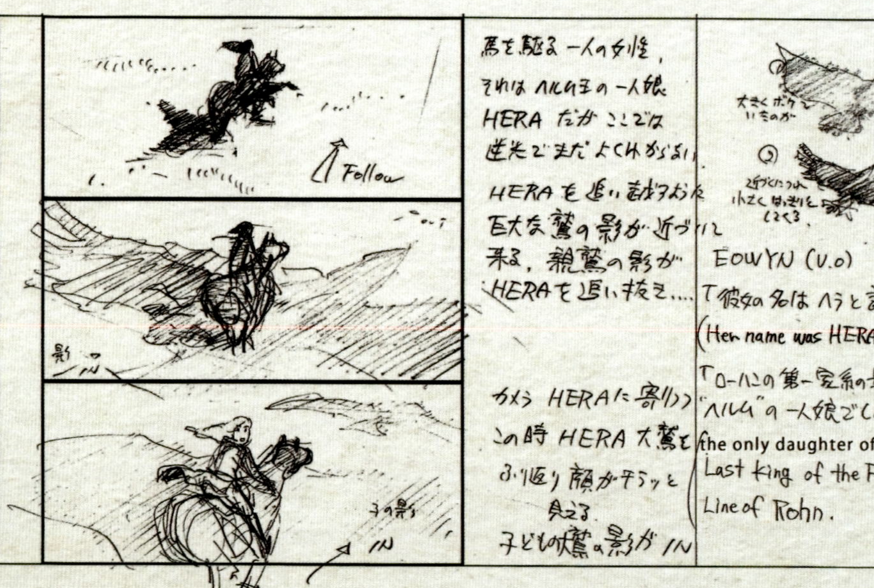

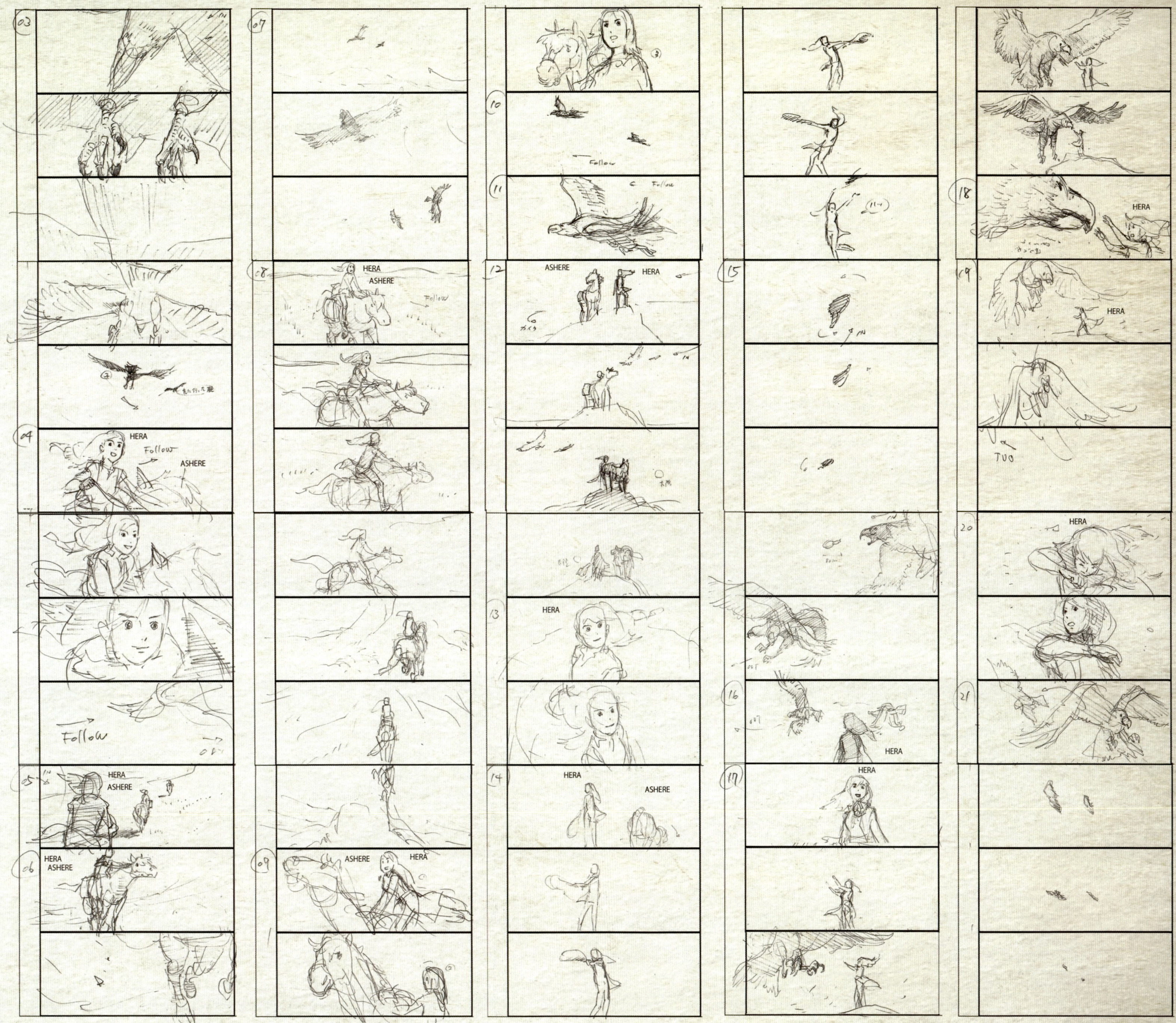

THE WESTFOLD

The background art briefs for the film were more specific than other anime because they had to reflect geography that was often very thoroughly described in detail in Tolkien's writings or visually established in the live-action films. They depended on lots of film, book and real-world location reference being gathered and sifted for the artists to draw upon.

Background artists for anime generally have quite a lot of freedom to make up their imagery, but in this instance we looked for artists who could work closely with the director to create artwork with very specific needs. They had to understand where everything within the fictional landscape of Middle-earth should be and be able to interpret live-action reference in a way that felt like anime, but also unmistakably of this world versus any other animated fantasy world. – JASON DEMARCO, PRODUCER

Everyone working on this film was very conscious of the fact that it was part of *The Lord of the Rings*, and part of the world that Tolkien so richly developed in his books. That influenced every creative choice. When developing backgrounds for locations in our story we would begin

by consulting with people who worked on the film trilogy and were familiar with the original texts. We sought to understand the facts of the landscapes: this is where we are, this is the geography, this is the climate, this is what is nearby. Once they understood that, we could begin to think about the needs of our specific scene or shot. For the opening sequence of the film, we needed to have the Eagles flying over mountains, and Héra needed somewhere to be, riding on her horse. We also needed an elevated place where she could throw the meat to the Eagle. Once we understood all those elements, I could begin to stage the scene within those boundaries, knowing that where it is and what the geography looks like were informed by the text and the original films. Then imagination comes into play and it becomes about how it is staged and how we can make it filmic. – KENJI KAMIYAMA, DIRECTOR

To create the mountain scenery, our 3D team first generated the terrain, and I drew along with it. When drawing, we used footage and photos from the film trilogy, as well as the scenery of New Zealand as reference to ensure it looked and felt like Middle-earth.

It was sometimes difficult to get the right sense of scale while matching the shapes of the 3D model. – TAMIKO KANAMORI, ART DIRECTOR

As well as Aoraki Mount Cook in New Zealand, mountain ranges in Islamabad and Switzerland provided inspiration. The scene was created using a pseudo-3D technique of camera mapping. The terrain model was made at Sankaku Studio. The shapes of the mountains and terrain began quite simple, but we worked on it for more than a year to get it to the level we wanted. The camera altitude and angle both change in the scene, so as to make it look natural, like a live-action movie, we then added clouds, shadows, and 3D objects, and refined the texture details many times.

At the director's suggestion, the rocky area where Héra stands was inspired by imagery of the Mongolian grasslands. It's dry and not much grass grows there. – YASUHIRO YAMANE, ART DIRECTOR

1: White Mountains and Rohan landscapes background setting art, YY.
2: Rohan landscape concepts, TK.

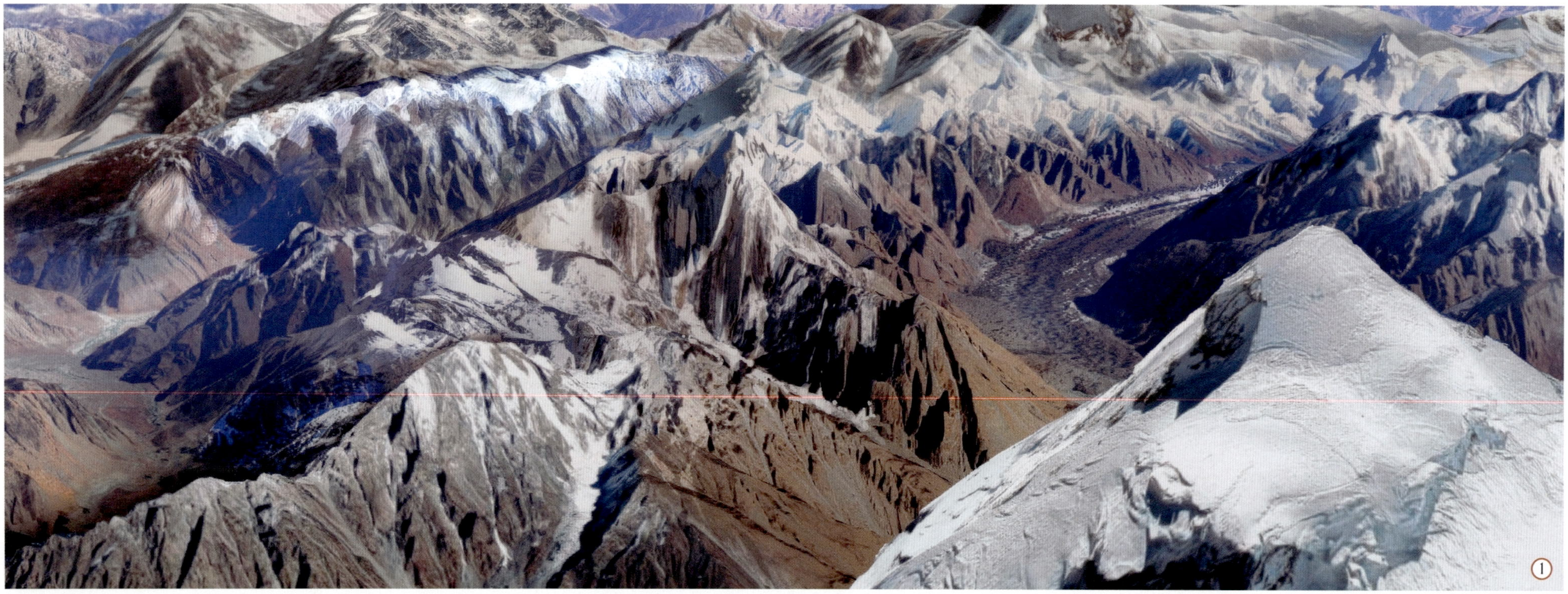

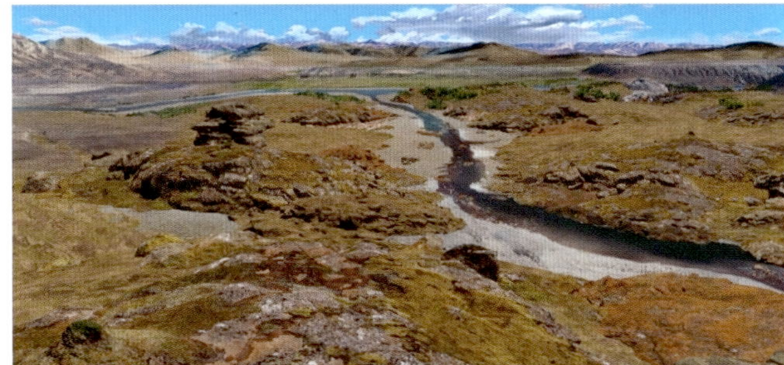
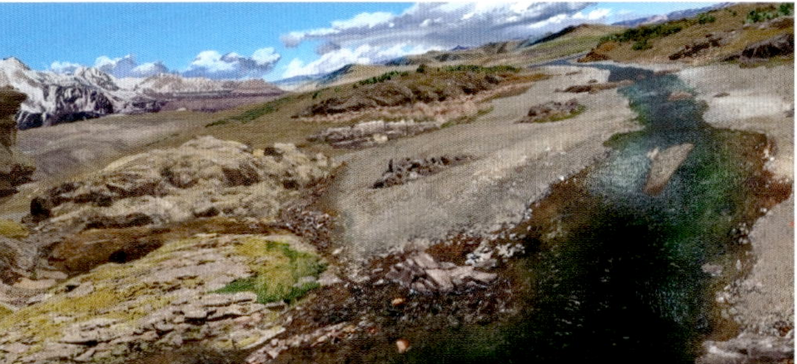
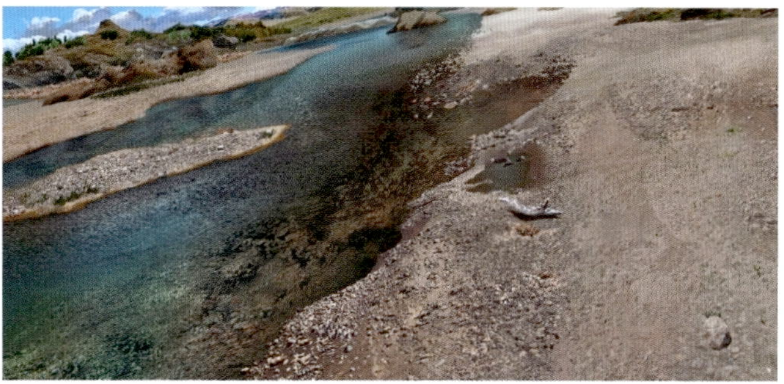

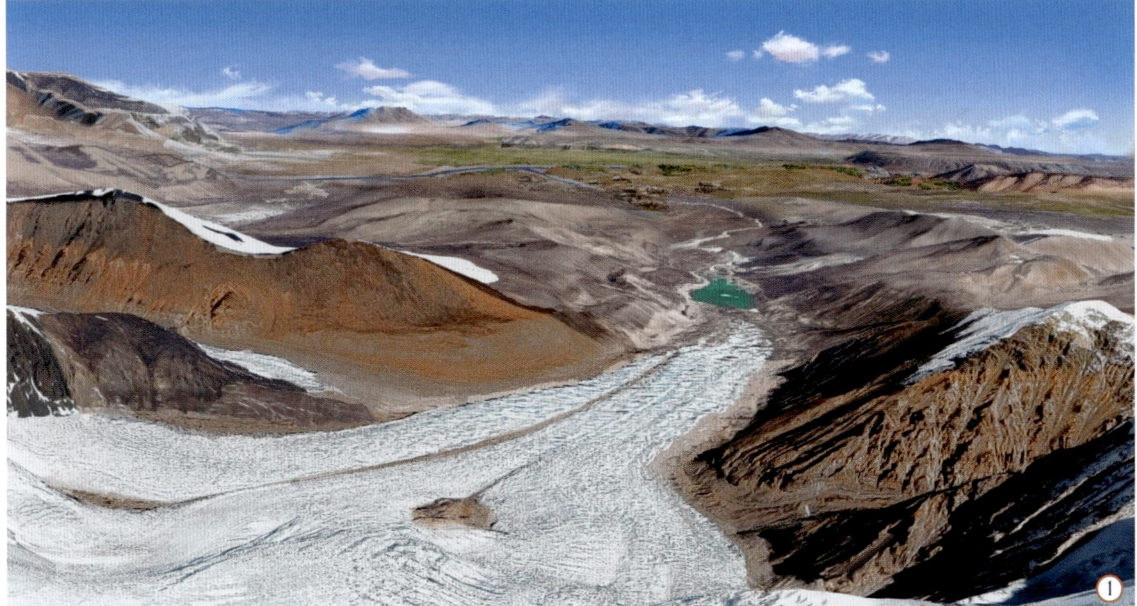

From my point of view, the opening sequence was probably the most difficult of the film to achieve. The camera swoops, following Ashere and Héra galloping across the plains from an Eagle's point of view. It was a key shot that showcased the hand-drawn look of the animation and sets the scene for the story.

For the backgrounds, we divided the massive amount of material into hundreds of layers and processed them on the CG side, then added further detail to create the spectacular image of the Eagle in hand-drawn animation gliding over the landscape.

The shot was created with the cooperation of artists from every department – direction, animation, colour, CGI, compositing, and background art – and, consequently, left the deepest impression on me.
– SHUNSUKE WATANABE, CG/COMPOSITE DIRECTOR, SANKAKU STUDIO

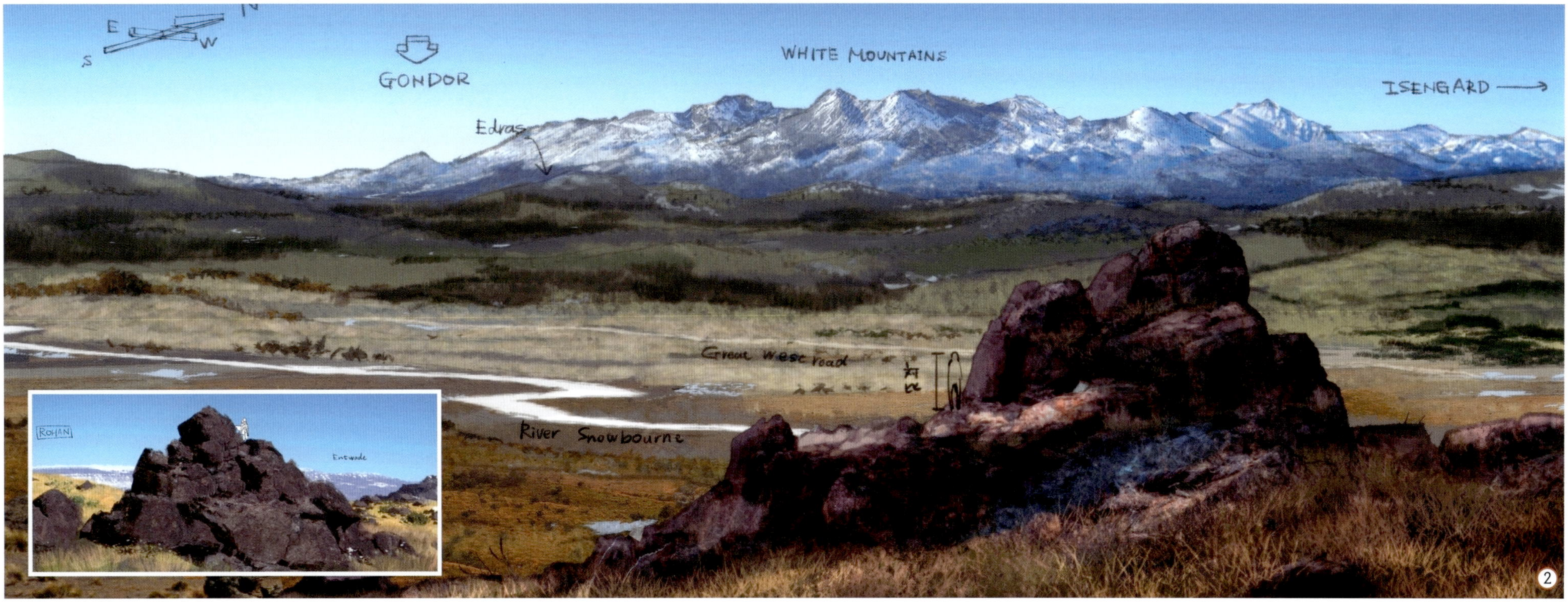

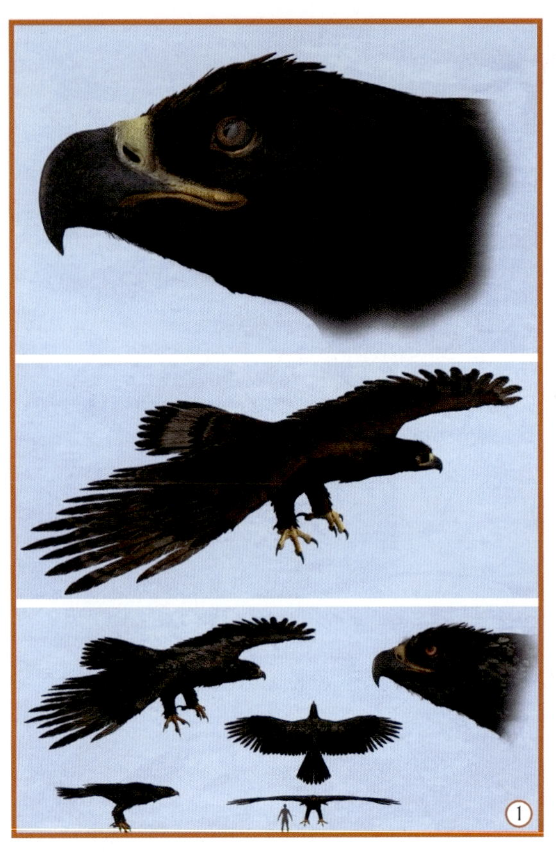

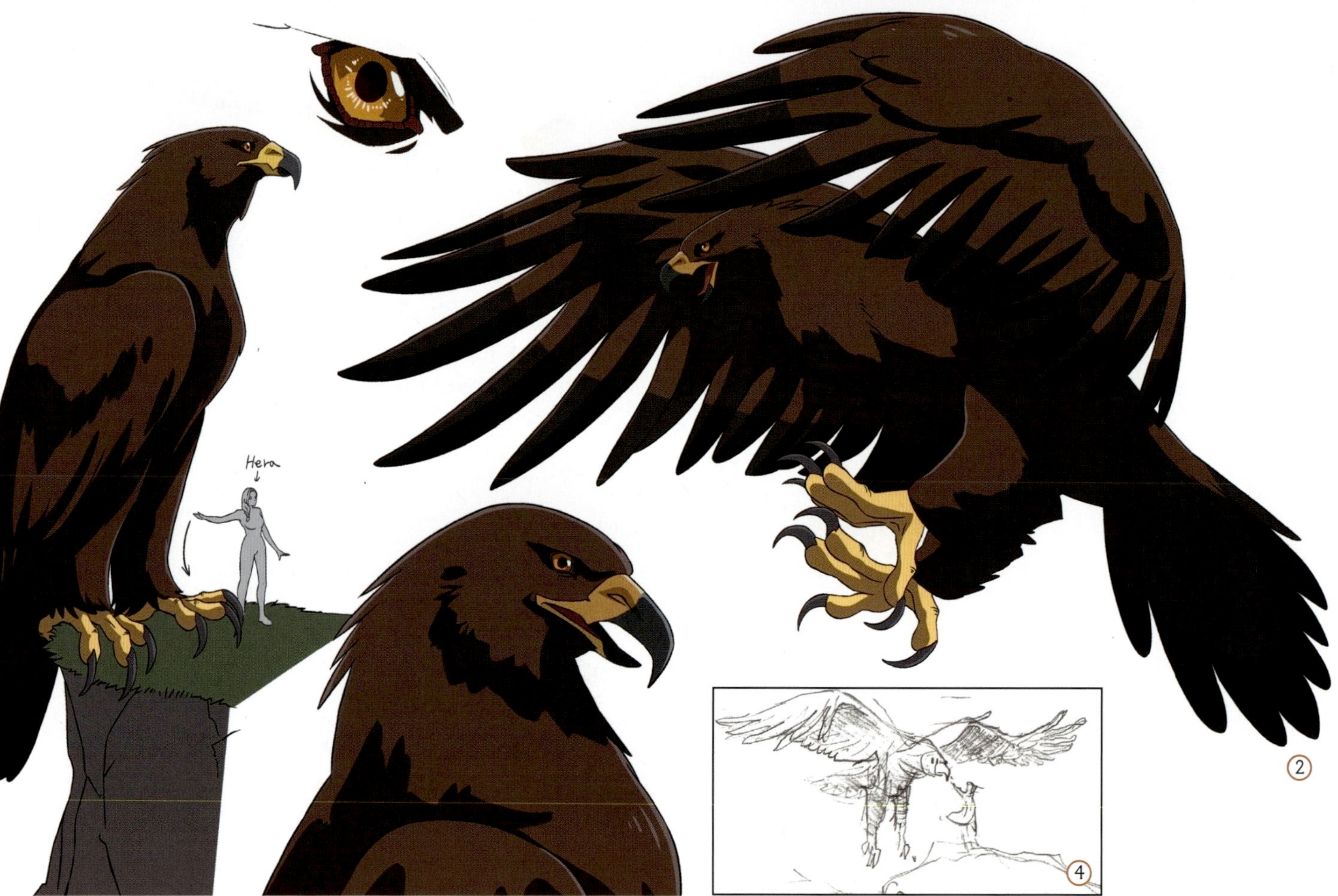

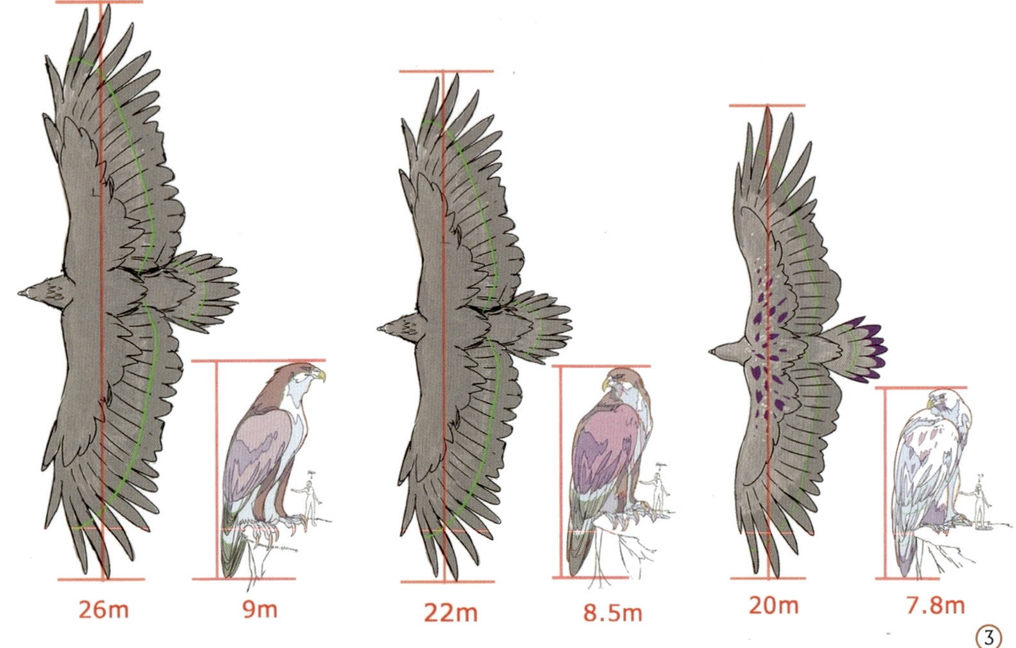

26m   9m   22m   8.5m   20m   7.8m

THE GREAT EAGLES

Héra feeding the Eagle demonstrates her love for the wildness of nature and her adventurous spirit, but it also hints at her awareness of the landscape and creatures of her world, which will become important later in the story. As she tells us, she knows that Eagles can speak the common tongue of men. She is inquisitive; she has curiosity.

The Eagles represent freedom, and that freedom is so important to Héra – the freedom to choose, to be wild and unbound. – PHILIPPA BOYENS, PRODUCER

There is an obvious connection between Héra and the Fledgling Eagle. They're both fledglings, at a similar point in their lives. – ARTY PAPAGEORGIOU, WRITER

There are two Eagles in the scene. One is an adult, while the other is a fledgling. Later in the film, we wanted audiences to be able to recognize the Eagle that Héra interacts with as the grown fledgling we met at the beginning, so it needed a distinctive appearance. The other factor that drove us to choose to make it white was that it was the colour image that I had for the character of Héra. Every character has a colour associated with them and for Héra it linked her costumes throughout the film. Choosing white was a way of connecting them visually. – KENJI KAMIYAMA, DIRECTOR

1: Great Eagle concepts, WW. 2: Great Eagle creature setting art, AAH. 3: Great Eagle size comparisons, AAH. 4: Storyboard frame, KK. 5: Final film frame. 6: Fledgling Great Eagle creature setting art, AAH. 7: Chai.

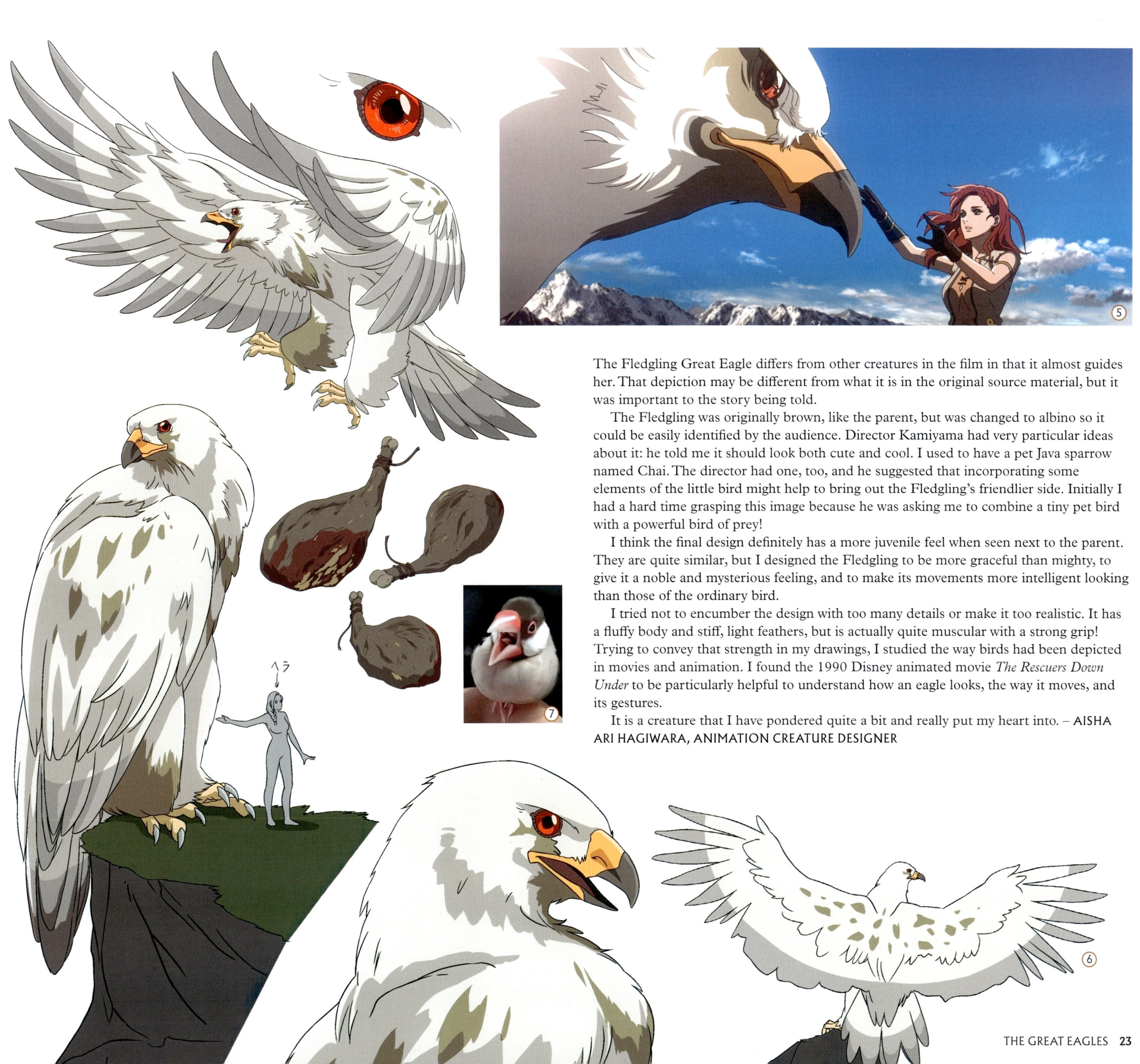

The Fledgling Great Eagle differs from other creatures in the film in that it almost guides her. That depiction may be different from what it is in the original source material, but it was important to the story being told.

The Fledgling was originally brown, like the parent, but was changed to albino so it could be easily identified by the audience. Director Kamiyama had very particular ideas about it: he told me it should look both cute and cool. I used to have a pet Java sparrow named Chai. The director had one, too, and he suggested that incorporating some elements of the little bird might help to bring out the Fledgling's friendlier side. Initially I had a hard time grasping this image because he was asking me to combine a tiny pet bird with a powerful bird of prey!

I think the final design definitely has a more juvenile feel when seen next to the parent. They are quite similar, but I designed the Fledgling to be more graceful than mighty, to give it a noble and mysterious feeling, and to make its movements more intelligent looking than those of the ordinary bird.

I tried not to encumber the design with too many details or make it too realistic. It has a fluffy body and stiff, light feathers, but is actually quite muscular with a strong grip! Trying to convey that strength in my drawings, I studied the way birds had been depicted in movies and animation. I found the 1990 Disney animated movie *The Rescuers Down Under* to be particularly helpful to understand how an eagle looks, the way it moves, and its gestures.

It is a creature that I have pondered quite a bit and really put my heart into. – AISHA
ARI HAGIWARA, ANIMATION CREATURE DESIGNER

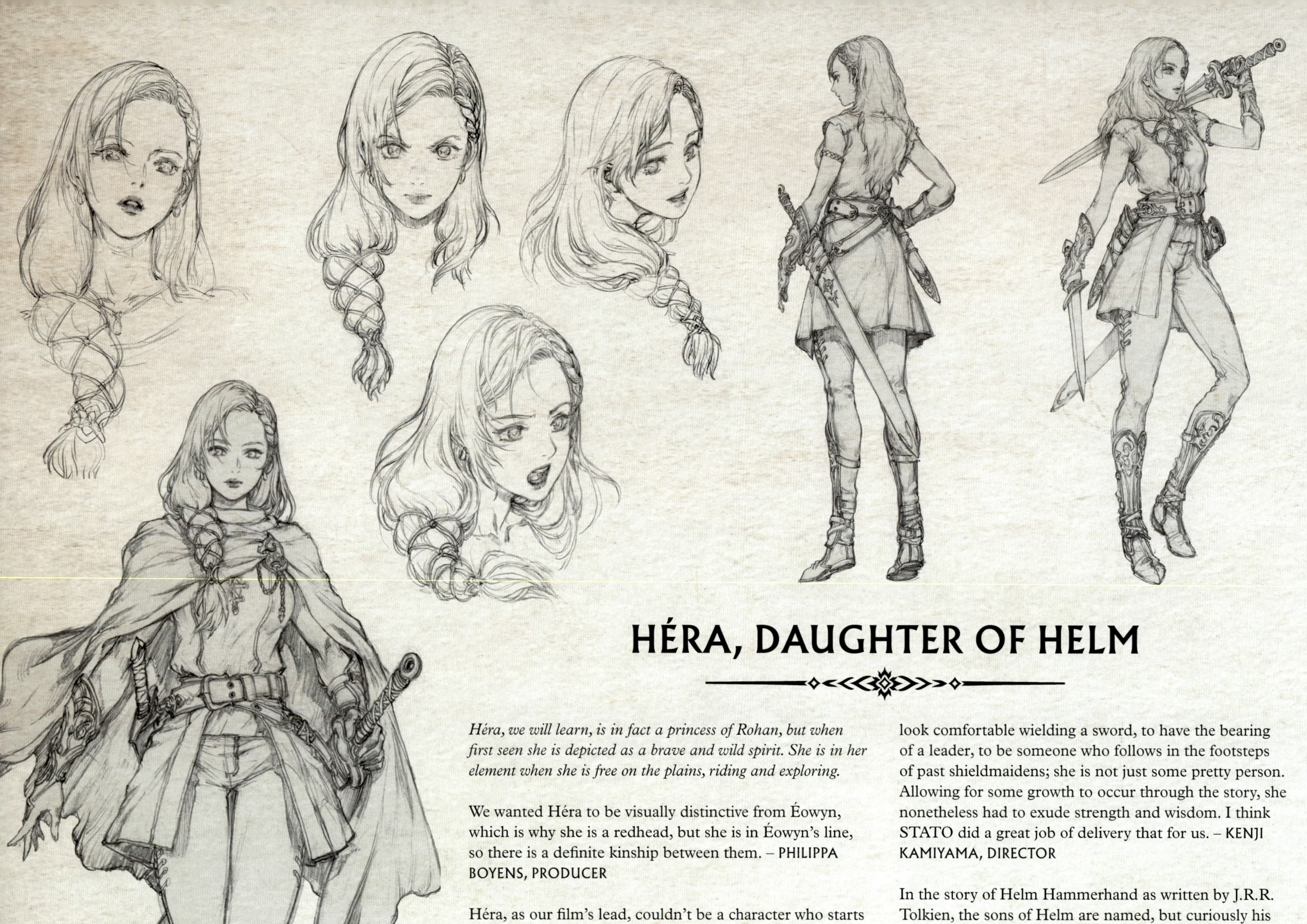

HÉRA, DAUGHTER OF HELM

Héra, we will learn, is in fact a princess of Rohan, but when first seen she is depicted as a brave and wild spirit. She is in her element when she is free on the plains, riding and exploring.

We wanted Héra to be visually distinctive from Éowyn, which is why she is a redhead, but she is in Éowyn's line, so there is a definite kinship between them. – PHILIPPA BOYENS, PRODUCER

Héra, as our film's lead, couldn't be a character who starts from zero, meaning a character who is just learning the ropes, how to fight, etc. She needed to be in a certain place to begin with, so in terms of the background and setting, she had to exhibit an obvious strength of character. If she had been born a son, she could have been the favourite to inherit Helm's kingship. Because of the world that she was born into, that is not to be, but it shapes who she is.

    In briefing character designer STATO, I told him that Héra's capability needed to be evident in her design from the very beginning of the film, so that audiences would accept what she rose to become by the end. She had to

look comfortable wielding a sword, to have the bearing of a leader, to be someone who follows in the footsteps of past shieldmaidens; she is not just some pretty person. Allowing for some growth to occur through the story, she nonetheless had to exude strength and wisdom. I think STATO did a great job of delivery that for us. – KENJI KAMIYAMA, DIRECTOR

In the story of Helm Hammerhand as written by J.R.R. Tolkien, the sons of Helm are named, but curiously his daughter is not. Nonetheless, a close reading of the story shows that it all starts with her and Freca's proposal of the marriage of Helm's unnamed daughter to his son Wulf, so she is central to the tale.

    There were lots of names for her that were suggested. I was determined that it had to begin with an 'H', given the rest of the names in her family. That led us to names like Helga, or Hilda, but it was Fran Walsh who said, 'What about our Viking, Hera Helmer?' Hera played the character of Hester in *Mortal Engines*. We used to call her, 'Our Viking'.

If we did that, then her name couldn't be the Greek 'Hera'. Tolkien's source for Rohirrim names and language was Old English, so I spoke to scholars. They told me that the name didn't exist, but if we were making it up it would mean, 'One-who-is-forever-noble', or if we accented the 'a' then it would mean 'forever-strong'. Technically, to be correct, it should be spelled with an 'h' on the end, as 'Hérâh', but we couldn't get clearance for that spelling. So, in the end, the name of Héra is one that we made up, but it is based on Old English.

Gaia Wise voiced Héra in our film, and she was just the best. We had some really good reads from many young actors, but she was the stand-out. We all landed separately on her as the right person. I thought I had discovered this incredible young talent but, of course, it turns out she was Emma Thompson's daughter! We had no idea. We cast her without knowing that, but Gaia *is* the character of Héra. She grew up a tomboy who spent her childhood roaming in the Scottish Highlands. She works her ass off, and she is funny; so confident one moment and then a complete goofball another. She gave it everything as an actor, and it was actually very physical. I have photographs of her in mid-air. She would throw herself around to produce the vocal performance that we needed for such an active character. – PHILIPPA BOYENS, PRODUCER

Who could we ask to design these characters? Initially it was tough to find someone in Japan who could pick this up, understand the genre of fantasy, and appreciate what we needed. Kamiyama san was a fan of STATO's work and had been following him on social media, so one day, having come to the conclusion that this guy might be it, he had me cold e-mail STATO. We couldn't mention *The Lord of the Rings*, yet, but I explained that Kamiyama san was interested in meeting him to talk about designing characters for a new film, and we discussed his past work. Thankfully, STATO was intrigued.

Working with him, there wasn't the normal back and forth, asking for fixes and changes. Most of the time he got it in one shot. The director doesn't usually give his okay so quickly; STATO just got it, and it went that way with so many of the characters. – JOSEPH CHOU, PRODUCER

A project like *The War of the Rohirrim* could be daunting, but I was confident that I could deliver if I kept three guiding principles in mind as I designed; firstly, the aesthetics of *The Lord of the Rings* live-action films; secondly, the director's instructions; and, finally, relying on my experience designing costumes inspired by the Middle Ages for fantasy games. – STATO, ORIGINAL CHARACTER DESIGNER

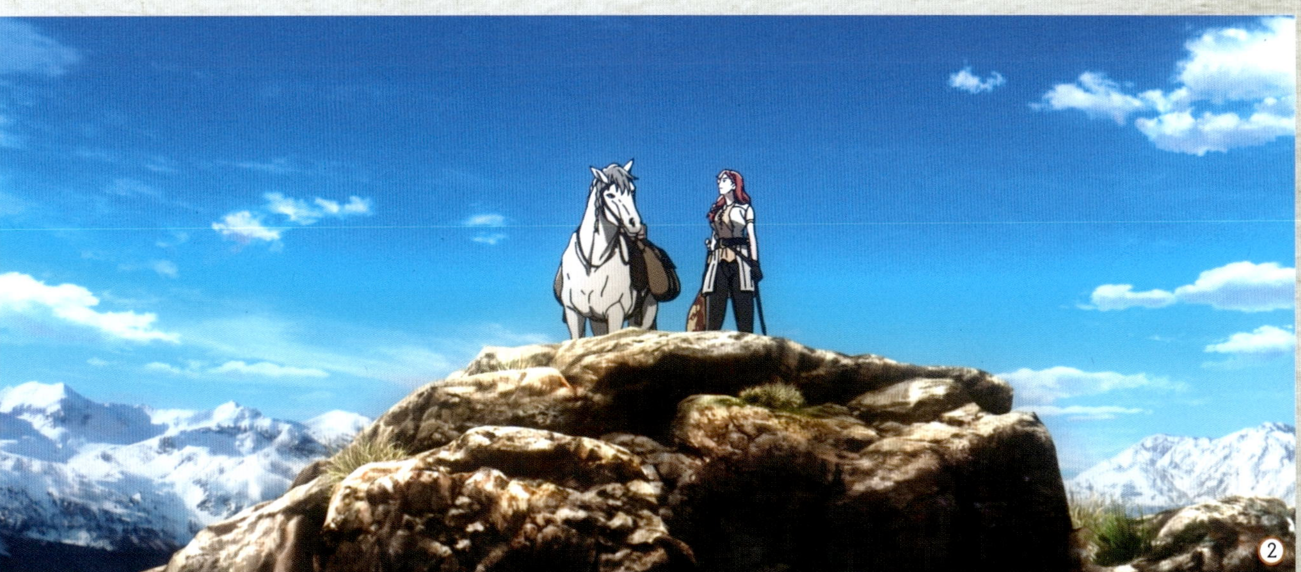

1: Héra concepts, S. 2: Final film frame.

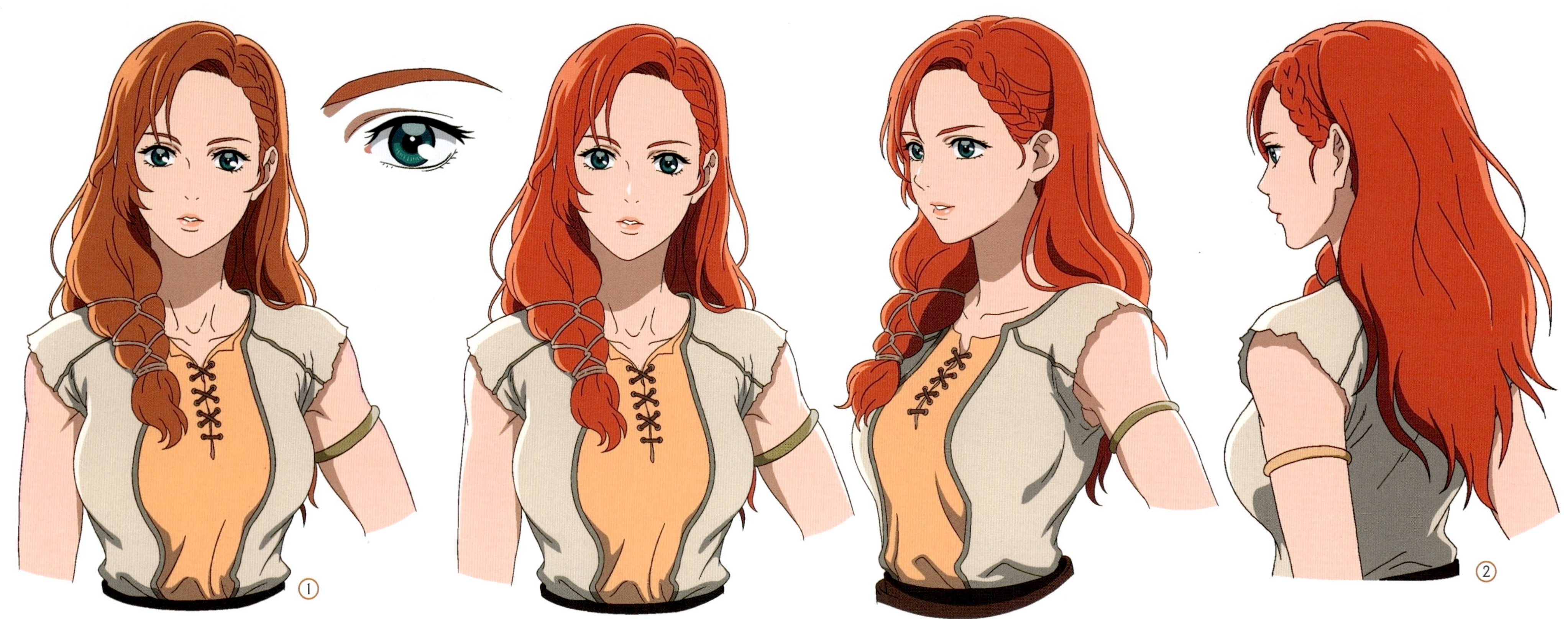

STATO's designs were beautiful, but they are what we would consider as original design. To be able to use them in the film, we had to have them refined into what we considered to be anime character design, a process of refinement and simplification. The challenge was taking a very sophisticated piece of art and translating it to something that could be drawn repeatedly, consistently and efficiently, by many people. That had to be handled by someone familiar enough with the animation process, who understood how far we could go with certain details, and how much to reduce the line-work without it becoming too simple.

Film and television differ in their needs, but this being a film, Kamiyama san worked very closely with Miyako Takasu, who is our animation designer and chief animation director. She would oversee all of the animation going forward, so she and the director spent a lot of time going back and forth to refine the designs together. Takasu san created character setting art which would be the primary reference every artist drawing these characters would refer to. Similar setting art was generated for every prop or creature in the film by prop and creature designers.

Once we had found the right level to take the characters to, it became easier, but getting to this point was a process. Takasu san understood how to interpret the designs into

something fit for animation without losing the essence of the character in the original art. Héra had to be able to move, for example, so things like limb lengths and proportions were important questions to resolve. Only someone with experience and understanding could do that well.

Even then, the final designs are still very ambitious, with a lot of intricate linework and detail. – JOSEPH CHOU, PRODUCER

The overall vision for the film was yet to be defined when I began designing characters for *The War of the Rohirrim*. A designer's job is to help realize the director's vision, but in the beginning that was still being developed, so there was a period of exploring without clear boundaries or guidelines. I spent many sessions working very closely with the director, gradually coming to grasp what his vision for the film was.

The atmosphere and world of *The Lord of the Rings* was already established in live-action, but determining how it would translate to animation was very challenging. How to represent the complexity of armour, horses, creatures, crowds, were hugely difficult undertakings, and caused a lot of headaches!

When designing characters based on STATO's original

artwork, we tried to make as few changes to designs as possible. Rather, we tried to keep to the original character and design concepts and concentrated on how to implement them as animation. It may be different from what people might think of as character design, but coming up with a practical blueprint for the animation, based on your intuition and experience, has as much importance as the creative design work itself. A character like Héra would be drawn tens of thousands of times before the film is finished. This is very different from a one-off illustration. The blueprint effectively determines the animation staff's ability to get through the production. The amount of visual information in a design needs to be reorganized to allow it to move and express emotion. So many different animators would be drawing it so it needs to be reproducible.

As the lead and one of the first to be defined, Héra's design process also helped to establish the visual rules that would influence all the other characters in the production. It took about six months of work and many iterations to decide on the final design for her. – MIYAKO TAKASU, ANIMATION CHARACTER DESIGNER & KEY ANIMATION SUPERVISOR

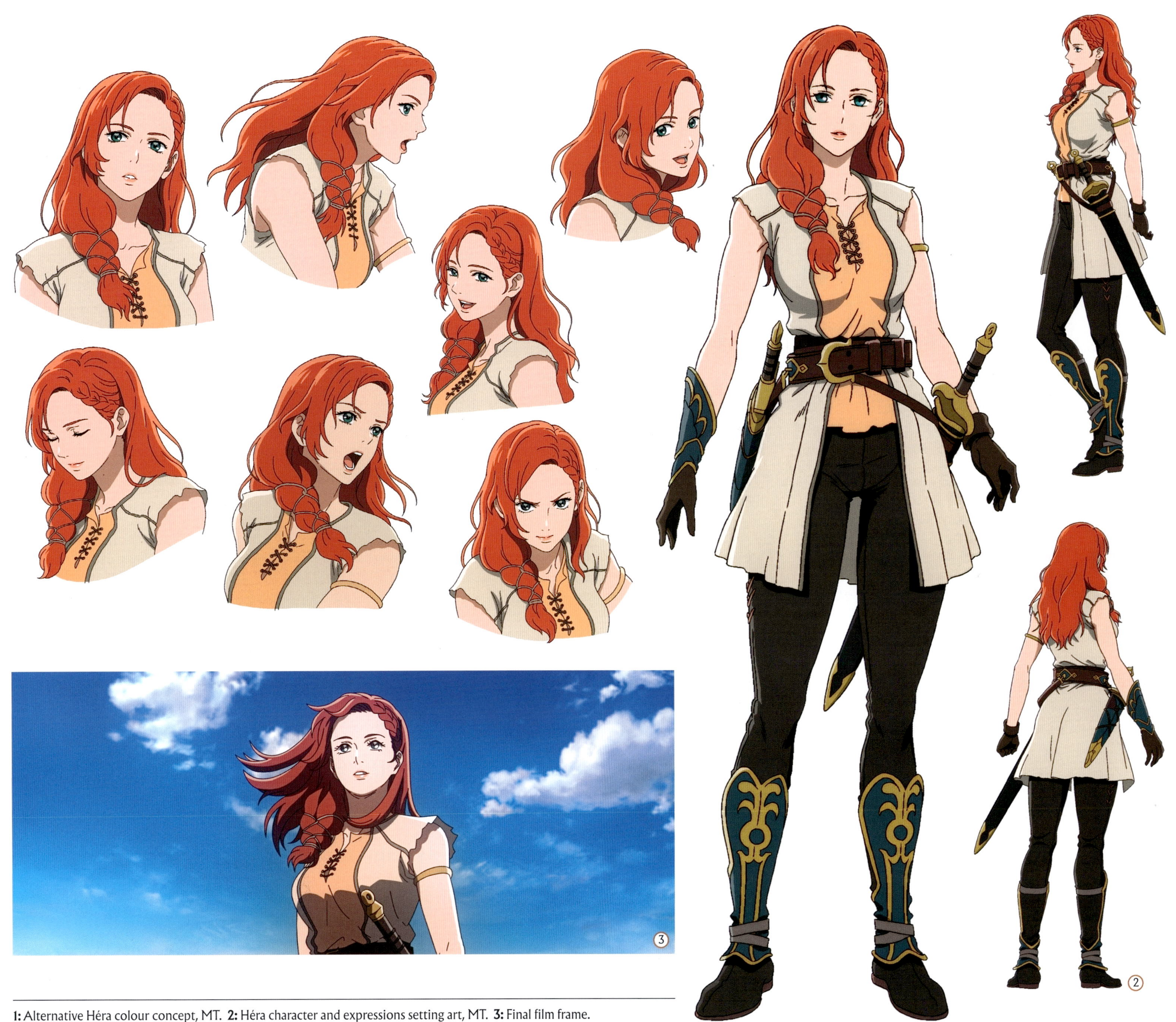

1: Alternative Héra colour concept, MT. **2:** Héra character and expressions setting art, MT. **3:** Final film frame.

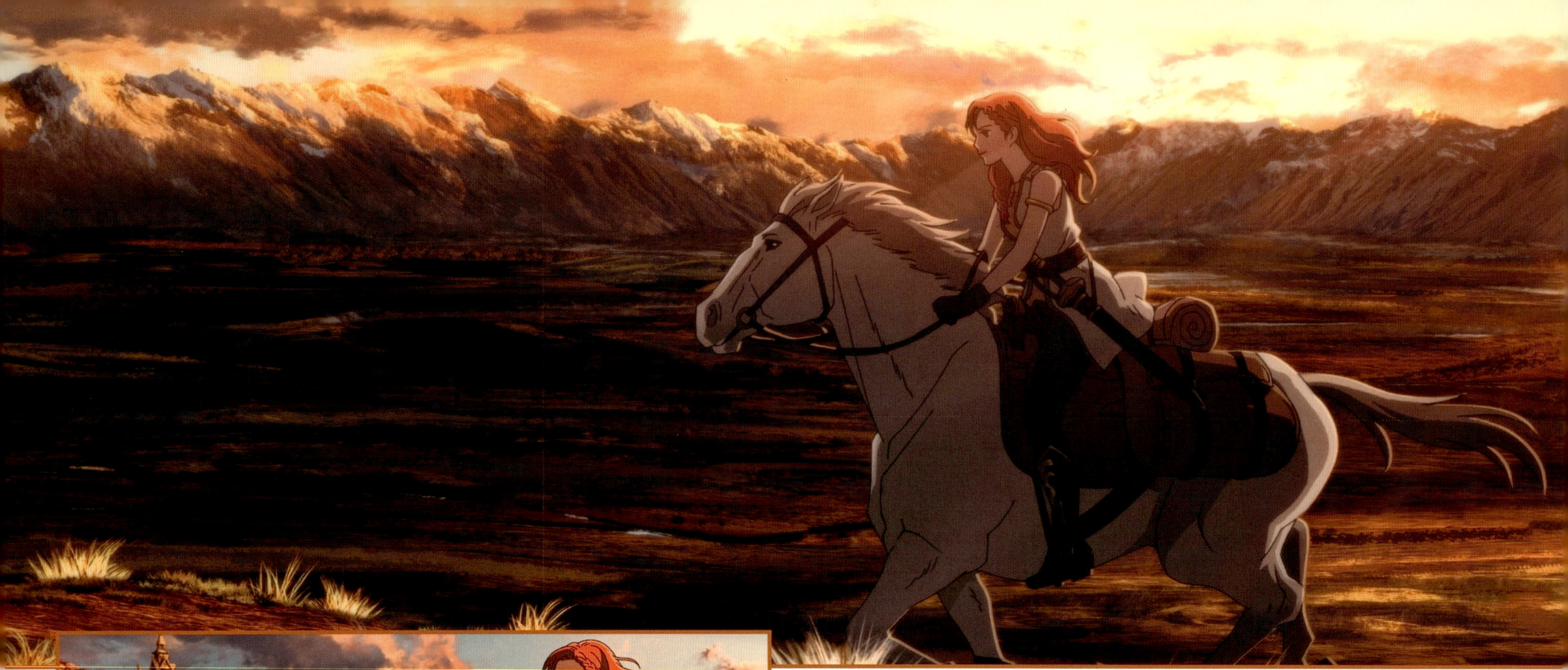

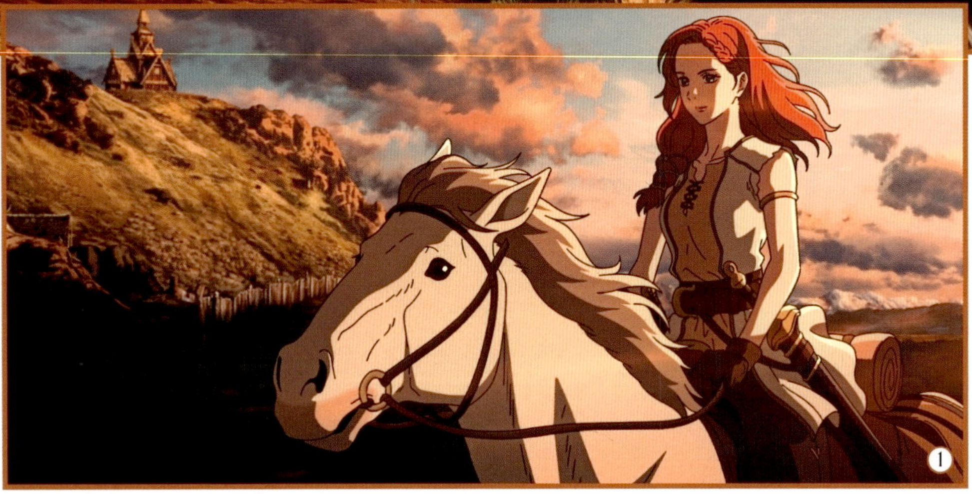

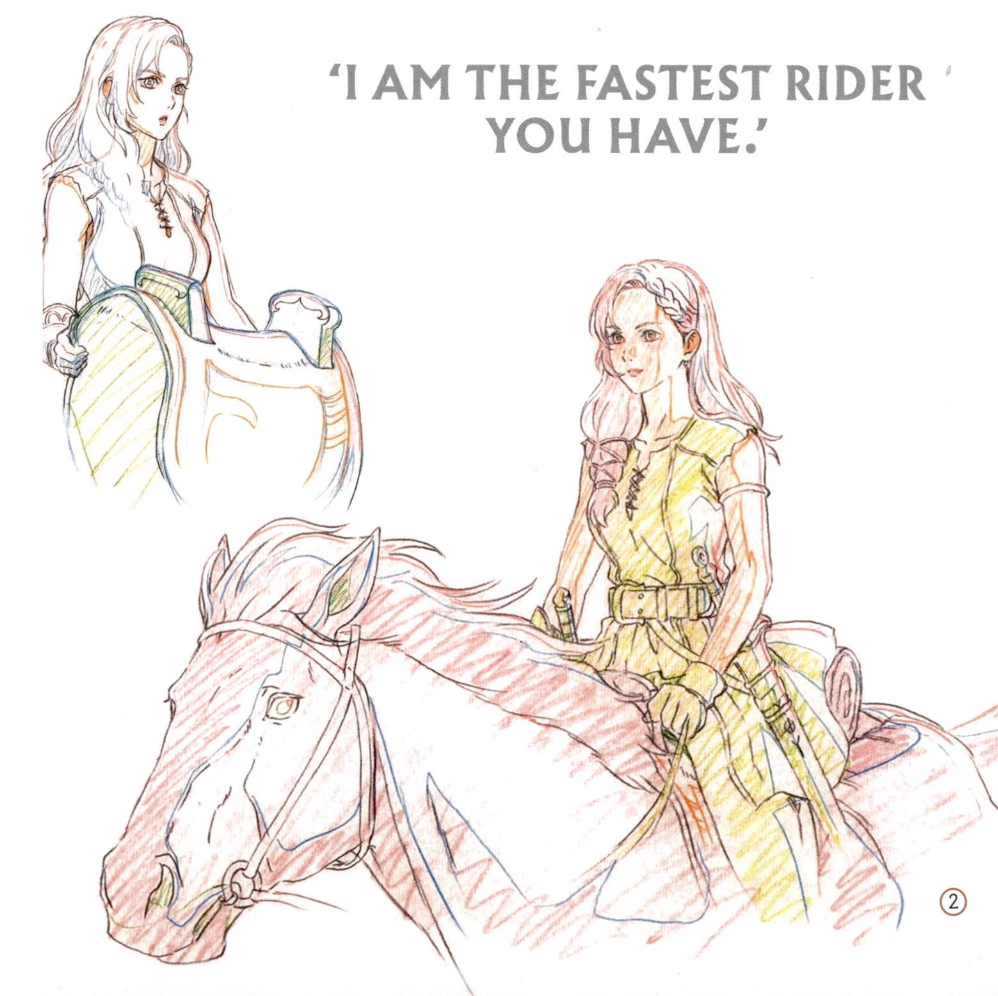

Although Héra is a princess, she is an active and tomboyish character, not at all demure
or weak. That is as the director requested. Personally, I wanted the main character to
be someone who would be attractive to both men and women, so I wanted her to retain
some of her princess quality as well. That part is expressed in the silhouette of her hair:
thick, curved and full. There is liveliness, but it's not rough or hard; and has a supple
feel to it. – MIYAKO TAKASU, ANIMATION CHARACTER DESIGNER & KEY ANIMATION
SUPERVISOR

1: Final film frames. 2: Animation key frames, MT. 3: Héra's sword hilt concept, JH. 4: Héra's sword concept,
JH & DF. 5: Héra's sword and dagger concepts, S. 6: Héra's sword and dagger prop setting art, KM.

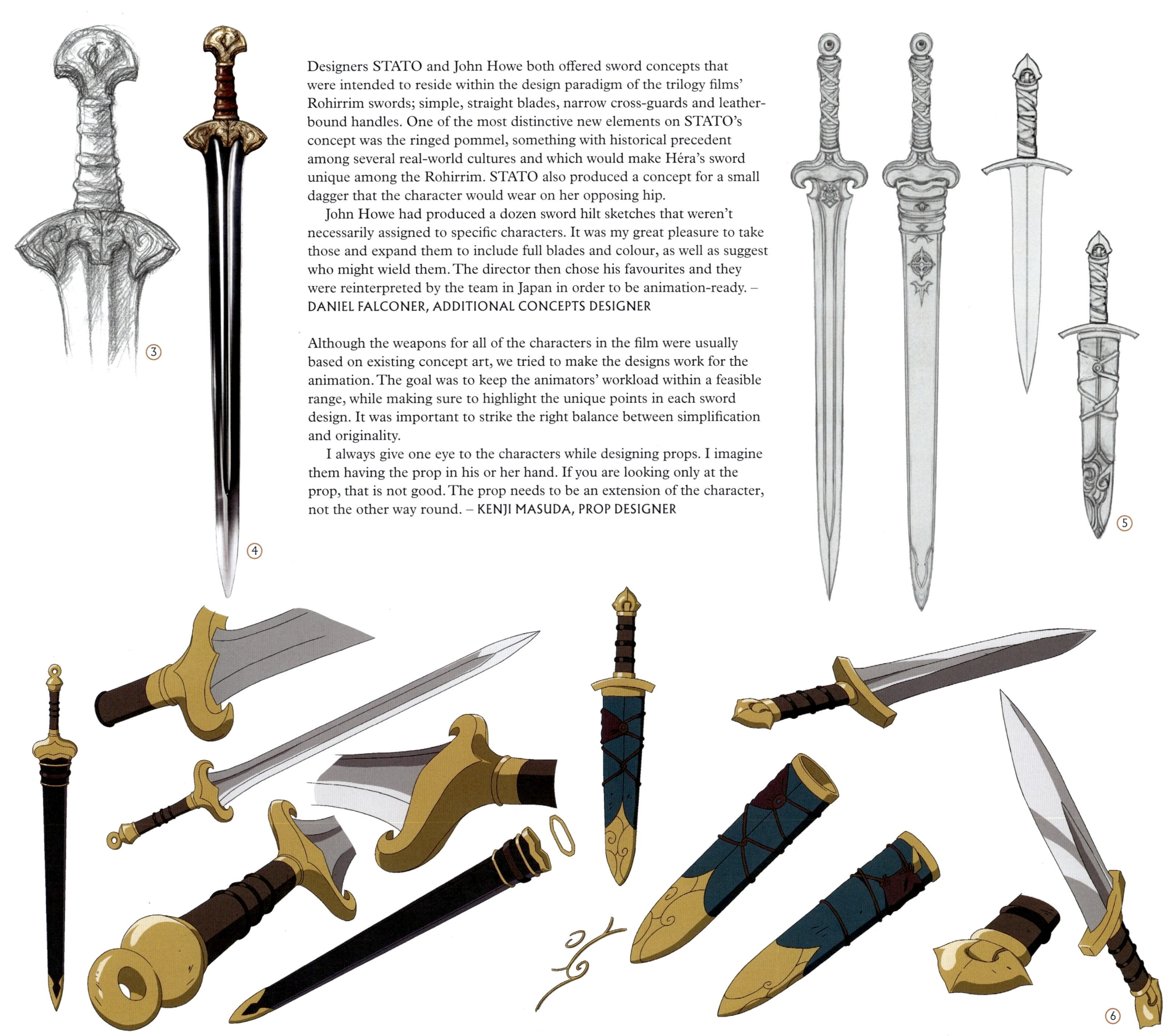

Designers STATO and John Howe both offered sword concepts that were intended to reside within the design paradigm of the trilogy films' Rohirrim swords; simple, straight blades, narrow cross-guards and leather-bound handles. One of the most distinctive new elements on STATO's concept was the ringed pommel, something with historical precedent among several real-world cultures and which would make Héra's sword unique among the Rohirrim. STATO also produced a concept for a small dagger that the character would wear on her opposing hip.

John Howe had produced a dozen sword hilt sketches that weren't necessarily assigned to specific characters. It was my great pleasure to take those and expand them to include full blades and colour, as well as suggest who might wield them. The director then chose his favourites and they were reinterpreted by the team in Japan in order to be animation-ready. – DANIEL FALCONER, ADDITIONAL CONCEPTS DESIGNER

Although the weapons for all of the characters in the film were usually based on existing concept art, we tried to make the designs work for the animation. The goal was to keep the animators' workload within a feasible range, while making sure to highlight the unique points in each sword design. It was important to strike the right balance between simplification and originality.

I always give one eye to the characters while designing props. I imagine them having the prop in his or her hand. If you are looking only at the prop, that is not good. The prop needs to be an extension of the character, not the other way round. – KENJI MASUDA, PROP DESIGNER

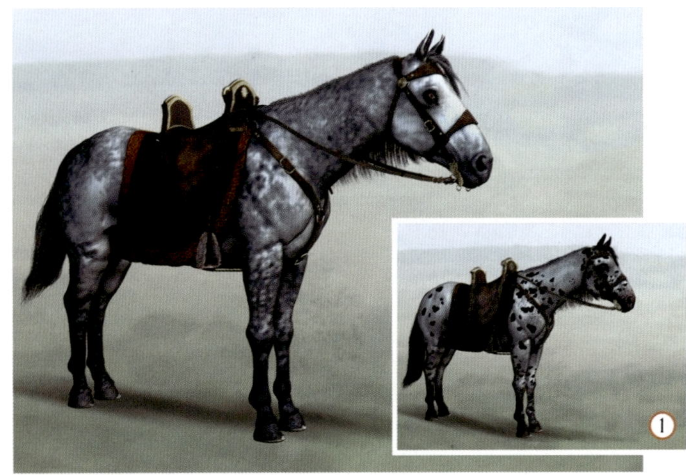

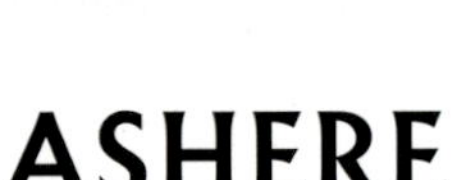

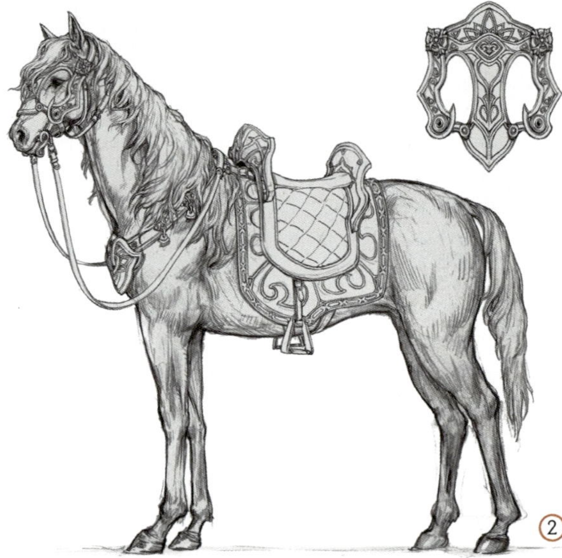

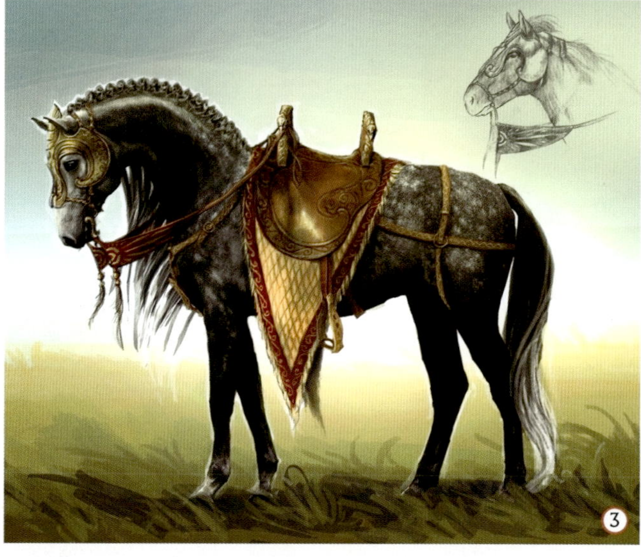

ASHERE

Ashere, Héra's horse, was named by Will Matthews and Jeffrey Addiss, who wrote the first version of the screenplay. It's not far from the name of Æschere, who was Hrothgar's most trusted advisor in the story of *Beowulf*.

There is an element of, 'a girl and her horse,' in our story. The connection between horse and rider is such an important part of who the Rohirrim are, and it is incredibly tight between them. At a critical point, Héra tells her brother Háma, 'Take Ashere,' but then Háma replies, 'Ashere will have no one but you.' That could be read as a nod to Shadowfax, and to the fact that the *Mearas* would suffer to be ridden only by wizards or kings. Whether Ashere is one of the *Mearas*, I am not sure. We haven't made that connection explicitly. – PHILIPPA BOYENS, PRODUCER

In one way this is a coming-of-age story, so it feels appropriate that there was an element of 'a teen and their car'. Short of giving Héra James Dean's leather jacket or Marlon Brando's motorbike, her relationship with Ashere

can be seen as a symbol for that youthful yearning for freedom. – ARTY PAPAGEORGIOU, WRITER

As a princess of Rohan, we imagined Héra grew up with a certain level of isolation from her peers… so I always thought of Ashere as her best friend. They have that kind of bond, loyal and playful. They're with each other through thick and thin, they always have each other's backs. – PHOEBE GITTINS, WRITER

What colour would Ashere be? Would he have distinctive patterning that might help him stand out in the film? The initial description in the script described him as a dark bay Thuringian stallion, but the character of the horse would evolve as different design options were explored at Wētā Workshop and Telecom Animation Film. Ultimately, Ashere would be pale cream and grey, aligning with the director's vision of Héra's signature colour being white.

As the hero's horse, it was important that Ashere look distinctive, so I imagined saddlery and tack that might be unique. I recalled some cool harness elements that looked a bit like miniature banners that my friend and former

colleague at Wētā Workshop, Warren Mahy, had drawn twenty years ago, when we were first coming up with ideas for the Rohirrim for the *Lord of the Rings* trilogy. They weren't used, so I included them in my concept for Ashere. I also suggested a pointed saddle blanket, which isn't necessarily practical, but it was pretty! Ashere did end up with something similar towards the end of the film. – DANIEL FALCONER, ADDITIONAL CONCEPTS DESIGNER

I envisioned Ashere as a girl and so I added a braided mane on the right side of her face, matching the one that Héra has. I like to think that Héra must have woven it herself. – MIYAKO TAKASU, ANIMATION CHARACTER DESIGNER & KEY ANIMATION SUPERVISOR

1: Ashere concepts, WW. **2:** Ashere concept, S. **3:** Ashere concept, DF, & inset, Rohirrim horse concept (LOTR trilogy), Warren Mahy (WW Designer). **4:** Animation key frames, MT. **5:** Ashere colour concepts. **6:** Ashere creature setting art, MT.

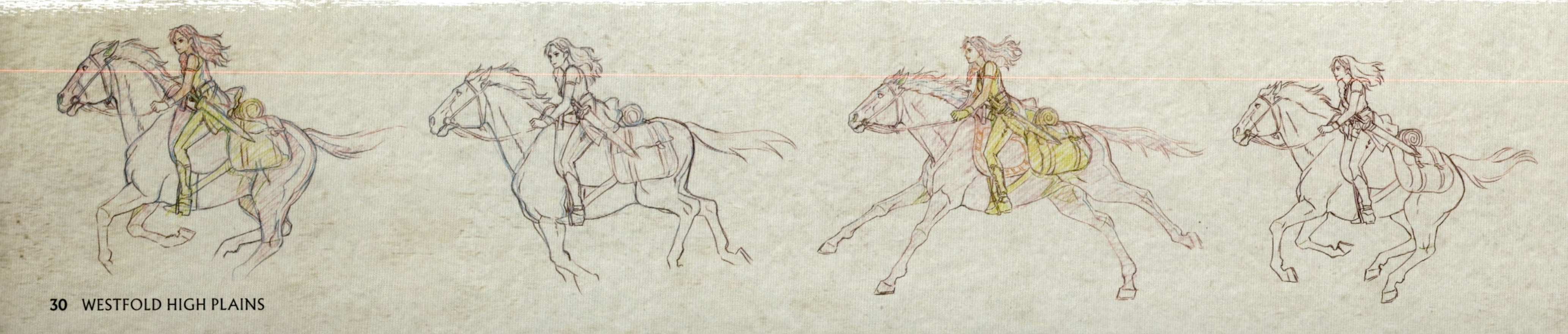

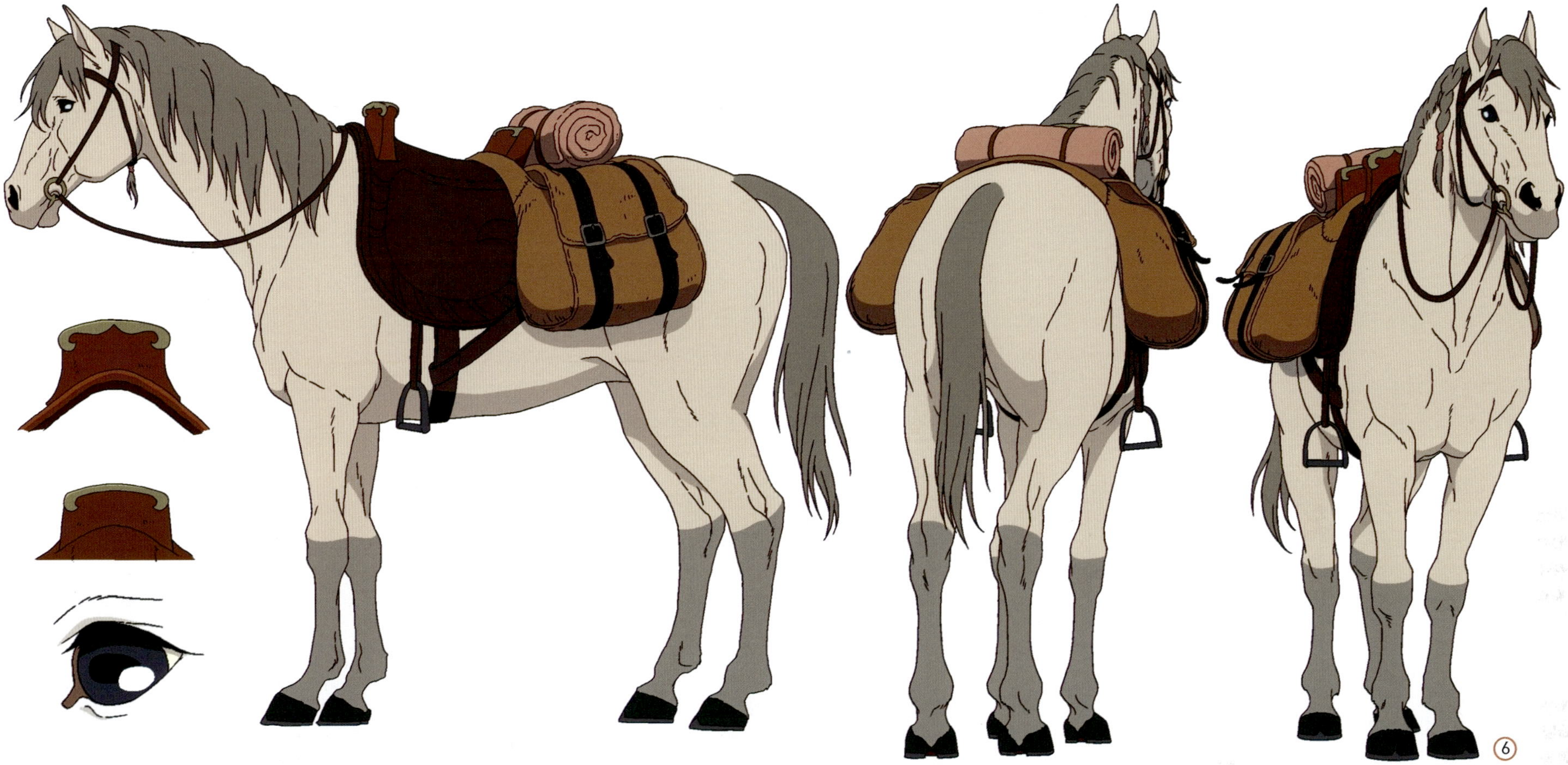

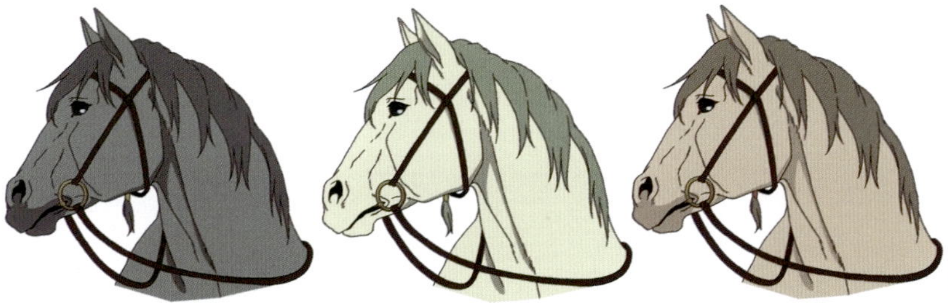

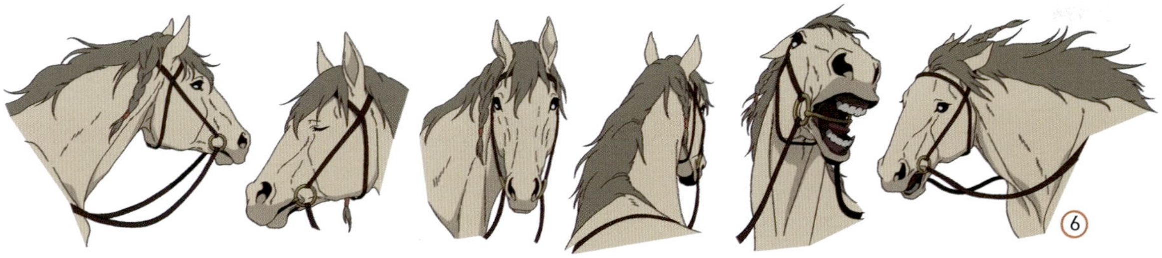

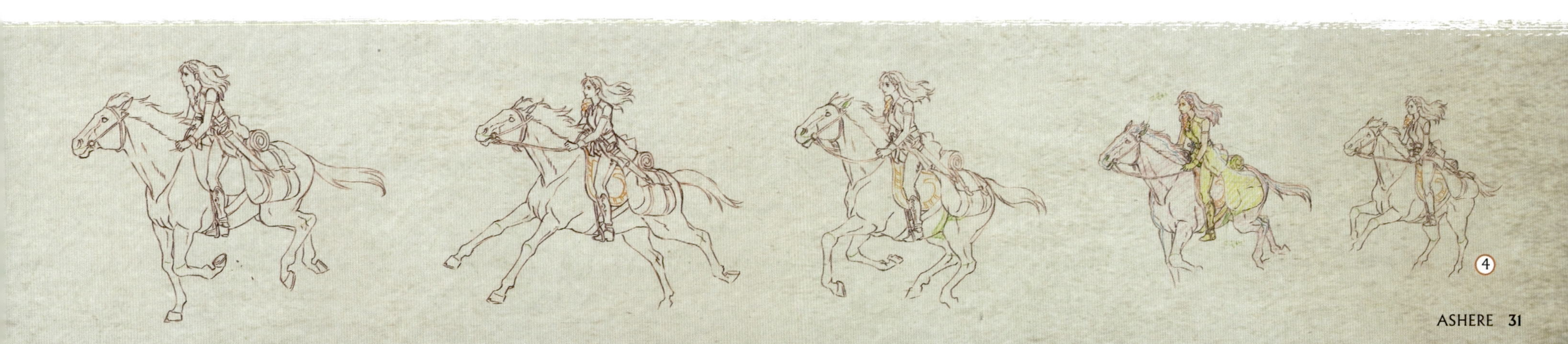

- 2 -

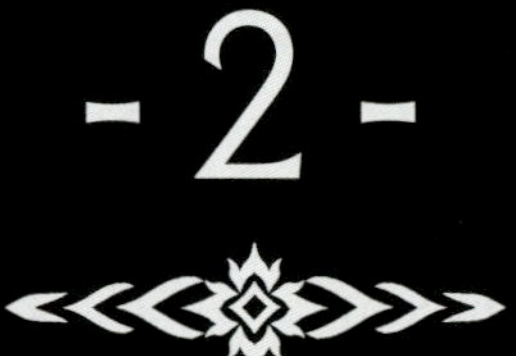

EDORAS

Edoras is a stockaded city of wooden homes, stables and smithies draped over a steep hill. Here dwells King Helm of the line of Eorl, lord of the Riddermark. As his daughter, Héra is required to attend a witan, a gathering of the lords of the wide lands Rohan, called in this case not by the king himself, but by Freca, lord of Rohan's most westerly domain, the West-march.

Edoras's dominion of the West-march is strained by past conflict with the Dunlending people who have long called it home. The ambitious Freca covets Helm's throne, and under pretence of uniting their households to bury old enmities, he proffers his son Wulf's hand in marriage to Héra.

Helm sees through the scheme and rebukes Freca, insulting and calling him out. Outside the Golden Hall of Meduseld the two men seek to settle their quarrel with fists, but Helm strikes Freca with a single blow, killing him.

Wulf swears revenge for his father and rides from Edoras in a rage, an exile now banished from the kingdom of Rohan.

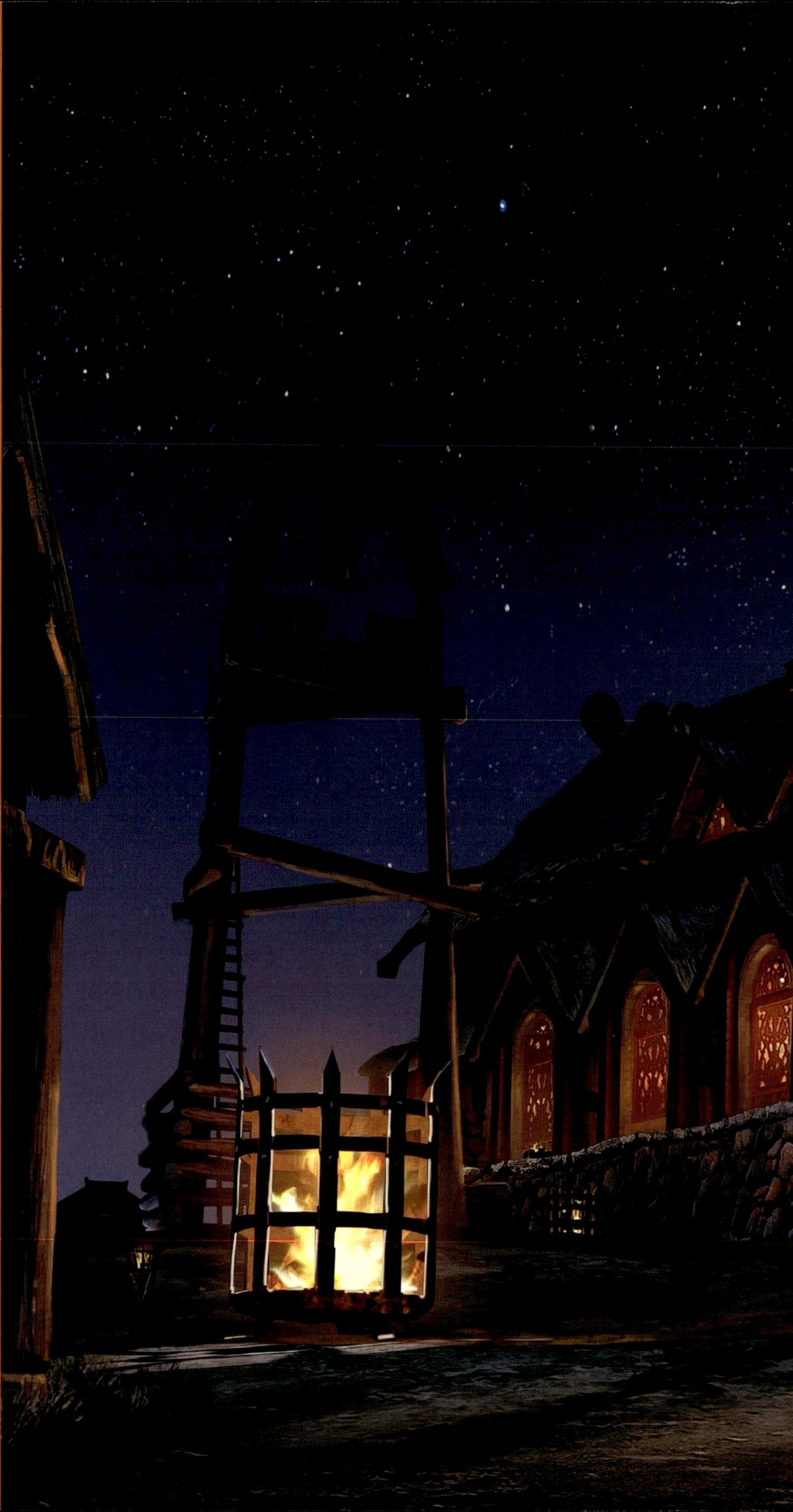

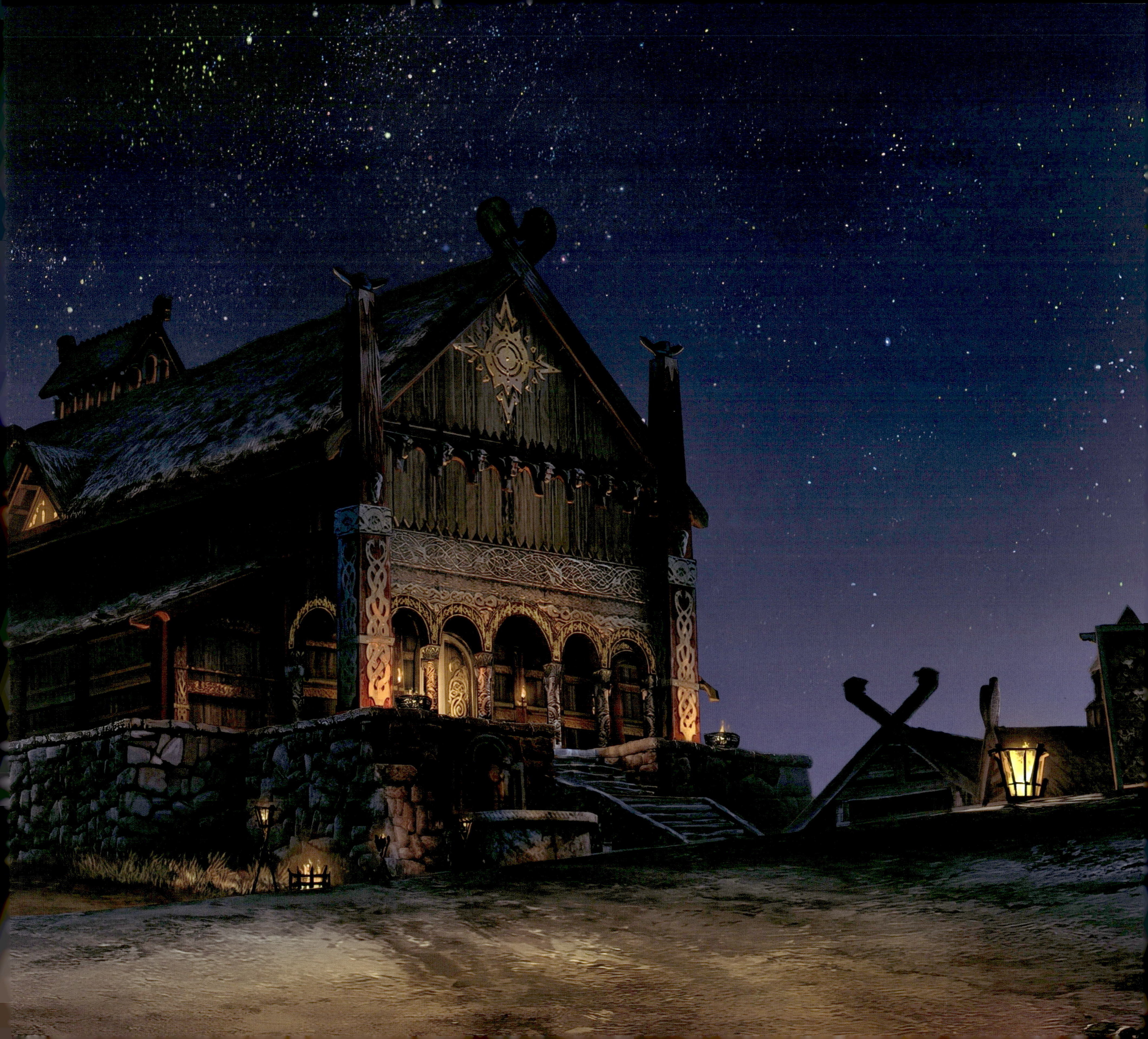

EDORAS

Edoras presented a two-stage challenge: the first being to understand and reconstruct the city as it appeared in the film trilogy, and then to reimagine it as it might have appeared almost two centuries earlier. This began with research into the original set design and physical build. The exterior set had been built at Mount Sunday, a striking location in the heart of Te Waipounamu, Aotearoa, New Zealand's South Island, featuring a front gate and nearby homes, plus a larger cluster of buildings on the summit, with a second gate and stockade, stables, a bell tower, and the Golden Hall of Meduseld. The remainder of the city was digitally painted in for shots that revealed its sprawl. At the end of the shoot everything was removed, and the site was restored to its original state in accordance with the production's agreement with the New Zealand government allowing it to utilize conservation land.

We looked at satellite scan data of Mount Sunday and used camera-mapping satellite imagery to recreate the geography of the hill as accurately as we could in 3D. Using that as guide to the landforms, I built a higher resolution version based on photographs and screen shots. The cliff face in particular is quite distinctive, so I referenced plate photos from the trilogy to get it as close as possible. That became the base onto which I built a virtual set of Edoras, just as if we were building it as a real place on that actual hill. It was perhaps a little bit fanatical, but to me that was the most important thing because of my love for it.

I had already researched and built a 3D model of the Golden Hall, purely for my own enjoyment, so that was easy to drop in. Once that was positioned correctly, it was like the keystone for the rest, and we could begin filling in all of the other structures to recreate what was built all those years ago. I love that my act of fan devotion has been useful to an actual production, that something I had made for fun was now being used as part of the movie-making process, becoming part of that world. – ADAM MIDDLETON, WĒTĀ WORKSHOP ART DIRECTOR & SENIOR CONCEPT ARTIST

The filmmakers wanted the city to be bigger in Helm's time. Rohan suffered terribly during the Long Winter and much of the city would be destroyed during Wulf's attack, so it was reasoned that it was home to a much larger population than when Théoden was king. – DANIEL FALCONER, ADDITIONAL CONCEPTS DESIGNER

Our design had to be recognizable as the Edoras in the trilogy, so that meant not altering the silhouette of the city by adding too many buildings that would change that iconic visual. The establishing shots from *The Two Towers* are very distinctive, with the Golden Hall being clearly visible atop the hill, above the front gate, and we wanted to preserve that. We generally only saw the city from this angle, so that left the entire back side of the city for us to explore and expand without interfering with the iconic front.

As we fleshed it out, I wanted to ensure it was done thoughtfully and that buildings were neither haphazardly placed or too evenly scattered. I thought we could include nods to the farming side of Rohan's culture, and other aspects of their lifestyle. I tried to imagine clusters of buildings that served purposes. I painted roads where

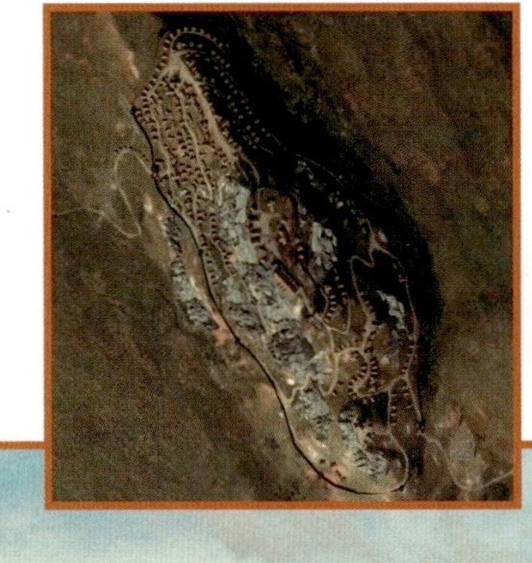
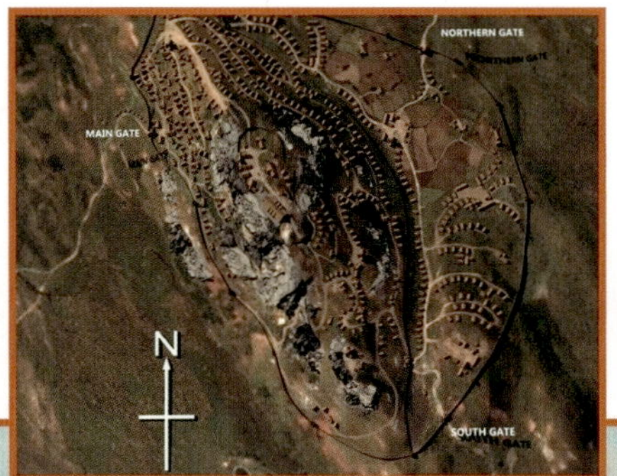

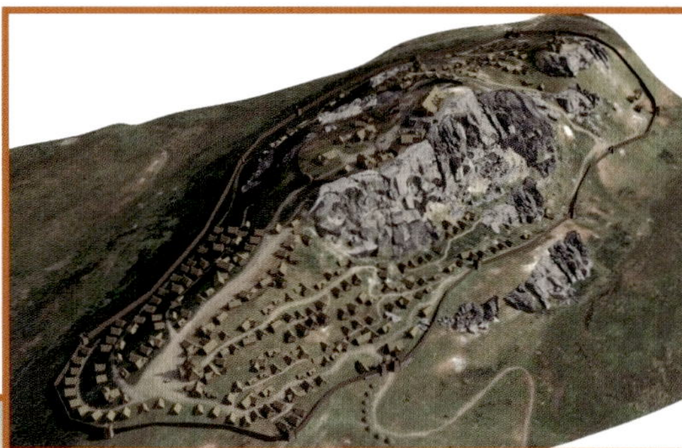

"

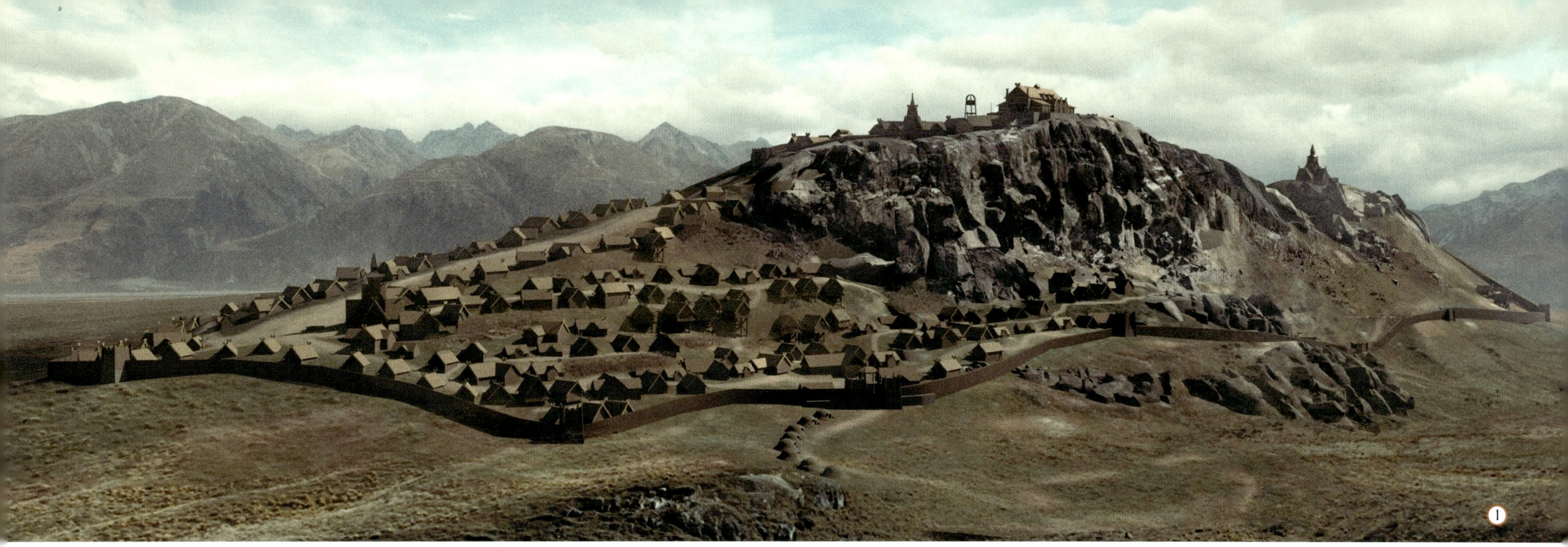

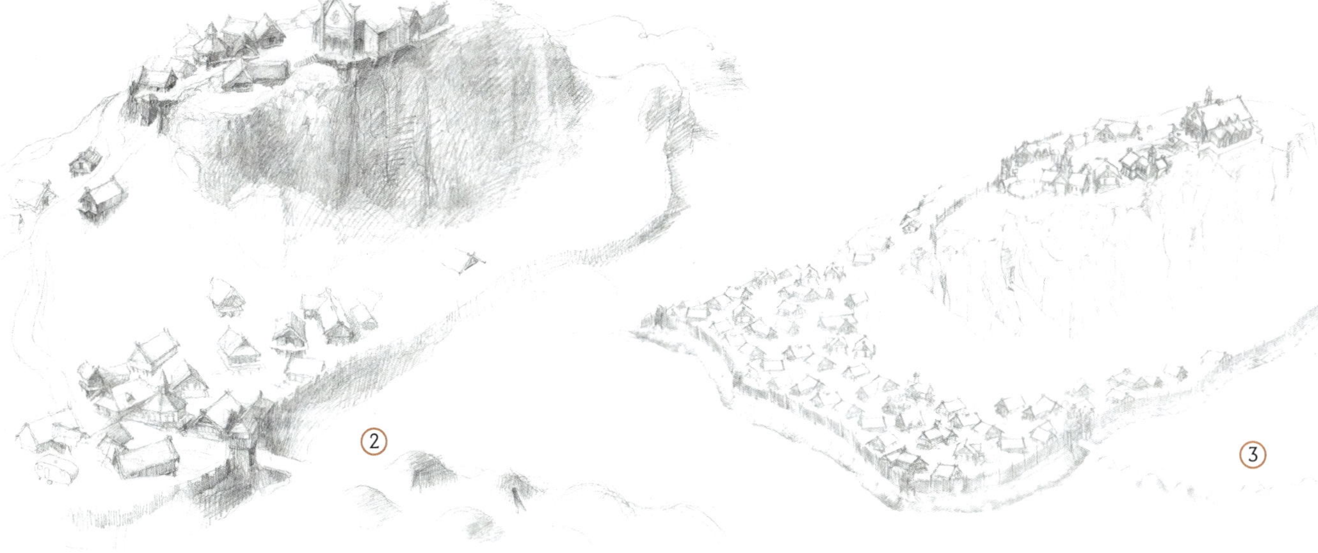

I imagined they might go in relation to the topology on the downloaded satellite imagery, and then projected that back onto the 3D model. Houses and stables, smithies and other structures could be placed along those roads in a considered way.

Once we had gone through a few rounds of design, all of that 3D work was provided to the production for their use, as well. – ADAM MIDDLETON, WĒTĀ WORKSHOP ART DIRECTOR & SENIOR CONCEPT ARTIST

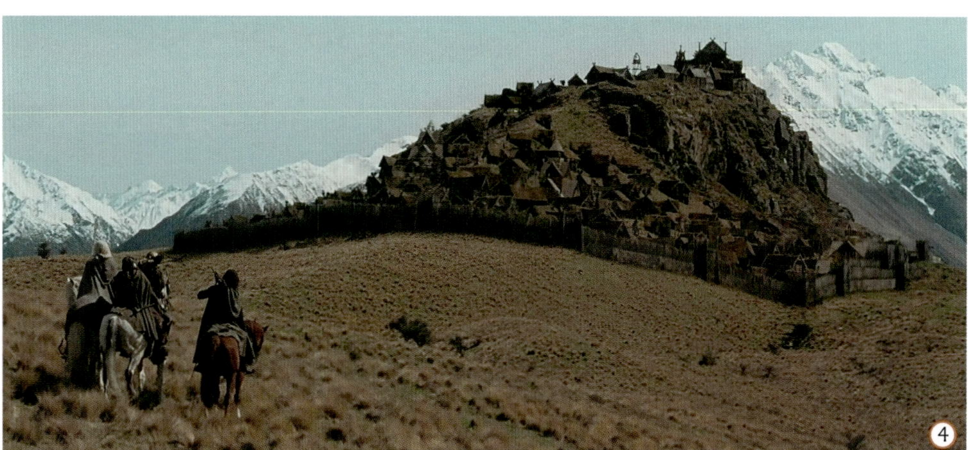

PP: Meduseld background art. **1:** Edoras concepts, AM. **2:** Edoras concept (LOTR trilogy), AL. **3:** Edoras concept, DF. **4:** Edoras, Film frame (LOTR trilogy).

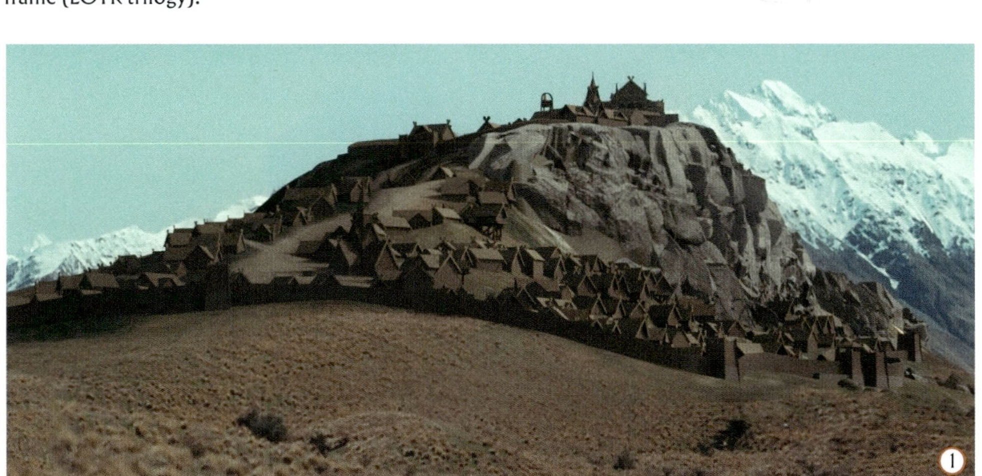

There are a lot of 2D renditions of Edoras, but a fully 3D version was built to assist with animation. We consulted to discuss how the city might look two-hundred years prior to *The Lord of the Rings*, and what might be different. The overall impression was to be similar, but with some important differences. For example, Meduseld looks very much like the one in the trilogy, but in our film it burns down, so it could afford to be a little different. We imagined to be quite a bit bigger and more colourful. It shows a Rohan that was once more prosperous and thriving than it later became. – JOSEPH CHOU, PRODUCER

Kamiyama san paid such reverent and strong homage to Edoras as we saw it in the trilogy. There are certainly ghosts of the trilogy in our film – our characters tread many of the same paths, mind you, they were there first! I love the shot of Héra standing where we have seen Éowyn stand before the hall. You can tell from the attention to detail in every beam, every element, how meticulous and careful the team has been in their crafting of these spaces. – PHOEBE GITTINS, WRITER

Saying that, the artists of this film also made it their own. We see Edoras in ways that we never did in the original films; new parts of it, or new angles, and the director was masterful in his lighting. His is an artist, himself, so he has that eye. – PHILIPPA BOYENS, PRODUCER

There were two background art directors that we worked with: Tamiko Kamamori and Yasuhiro Yamane, who are top artists. It was very important to me that this background art not simply feel like live-action images; it had to have a certain artistic quality, while still being very convincing, and be thoughtfully and beautifully lit. If it was evening,

for example, the light had to have the right colour, depth, temperature and direction. I challenged them to achieve this, and they almost always got it right in just one try. – KENJI KAMIYAMA, DIRECTOR

Projects of this sort are rare in Japan. You don't get to draw backgrounds of this quality very often in Japanese anime, so I think the art directors were highly motivated and very happy to work on this. It was the chance of a lifetime to produce this level of background artwork. – JOSEPH CHOU, PRODUCER

The live-action movies were the primary reference for our depictions of Rohan's capital, but one of the key differences the director asked for was for Edoras to look prosperous. I tried to make it feel like a place of life and vitality. You can see the people smiling and waving as Héra rides through Edoras. I think this was a good way to let the audience know that the place was doing well. – TAMIKO KANAMORI, ART DIRECTOR

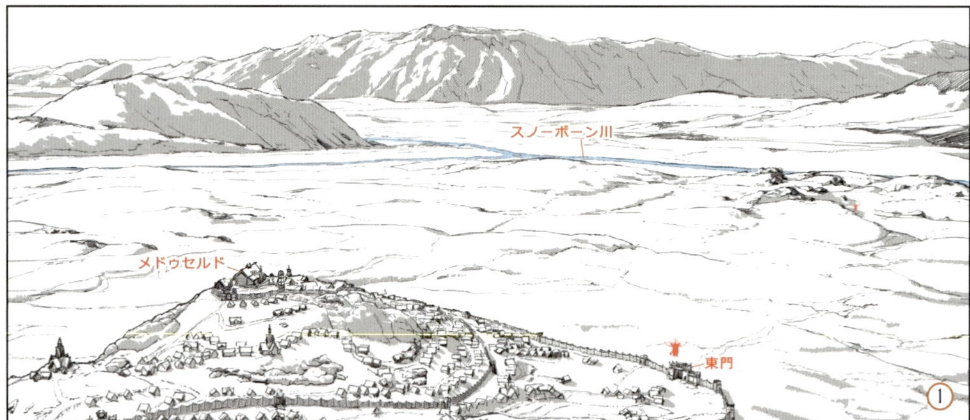

1: Edoras and Snowbourn River concept, TK. **2**: Edoras and Snowbourn River background setting art, TK. **3**: Edoras background art.

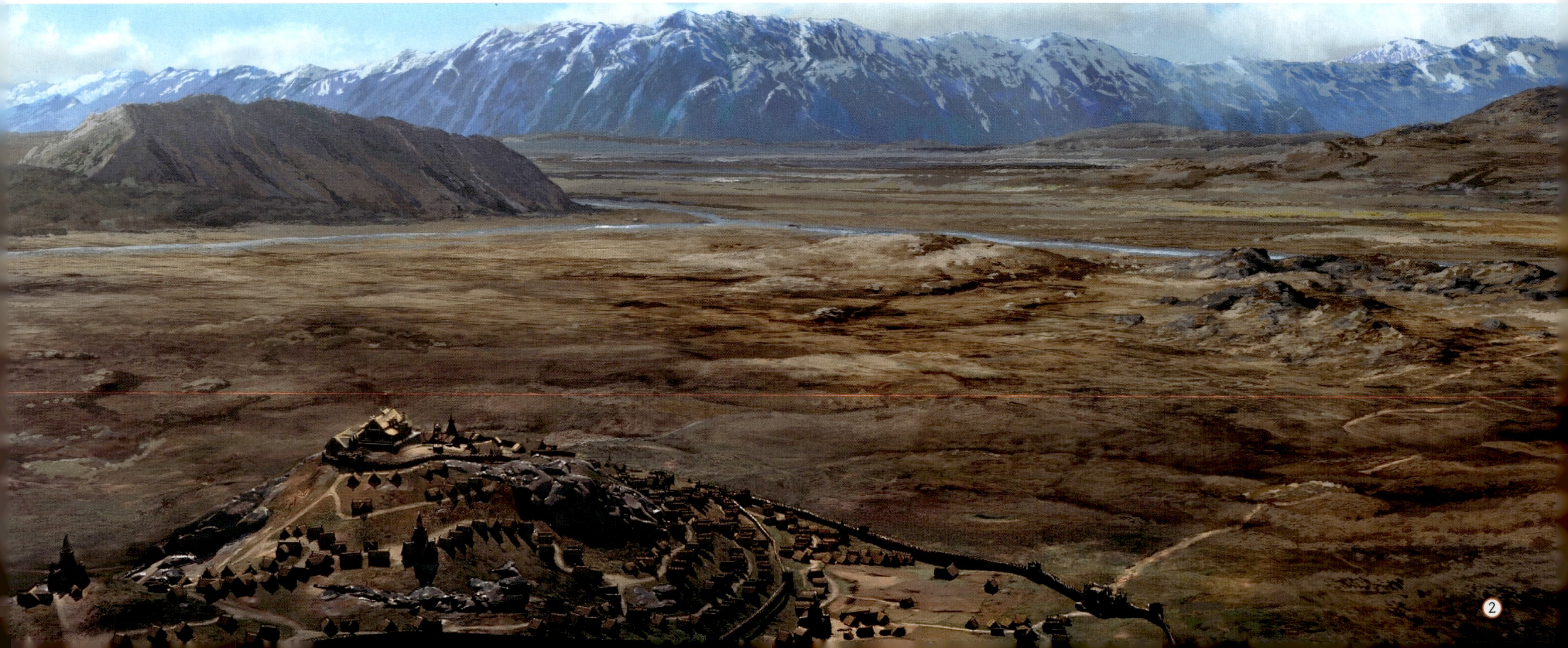

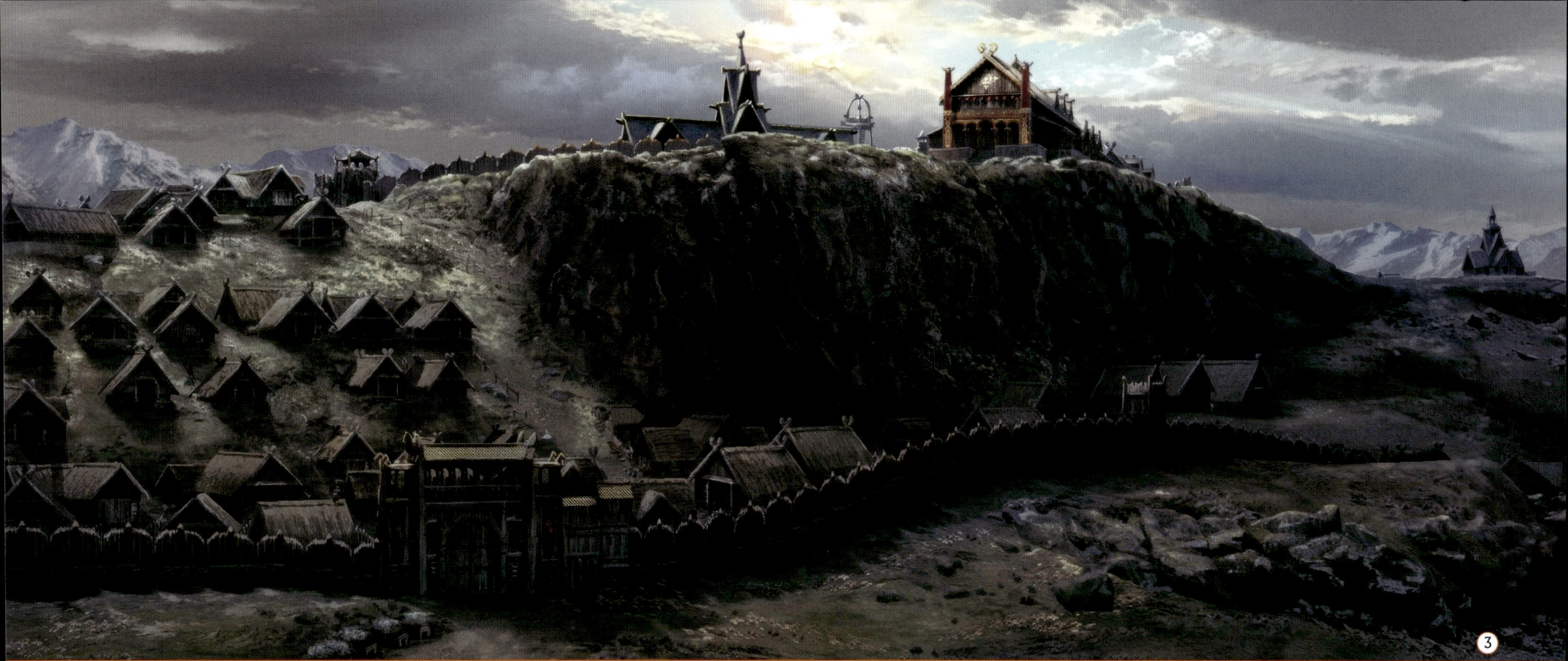

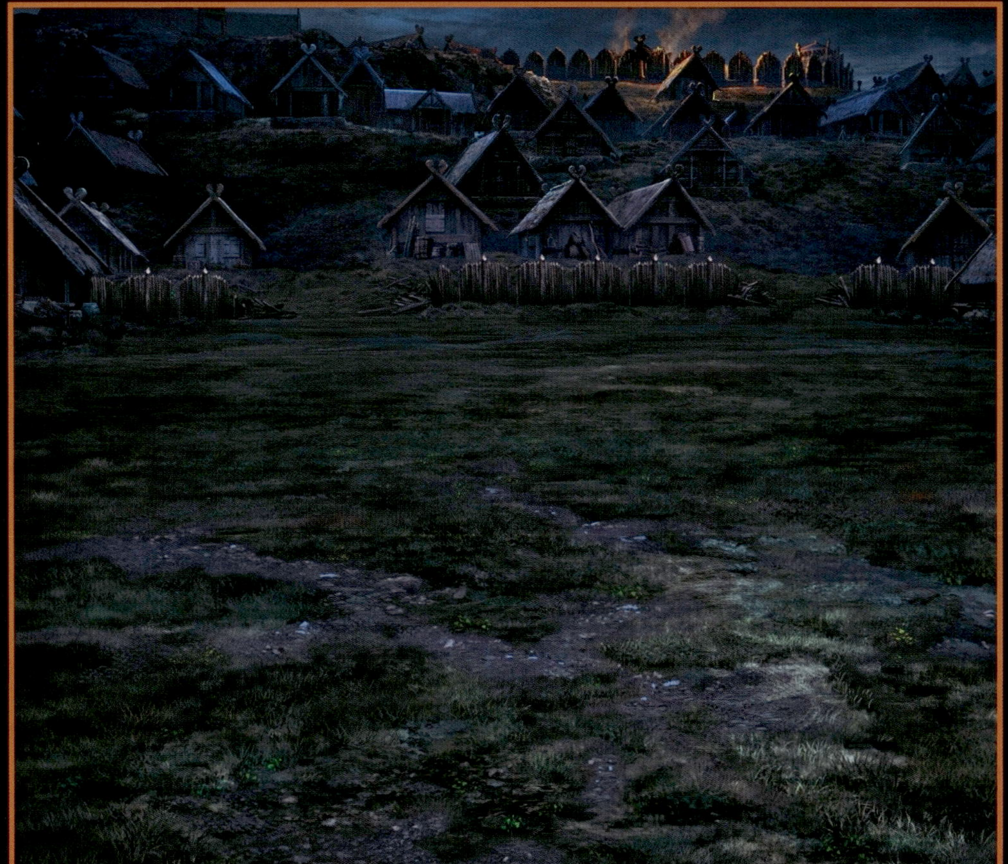

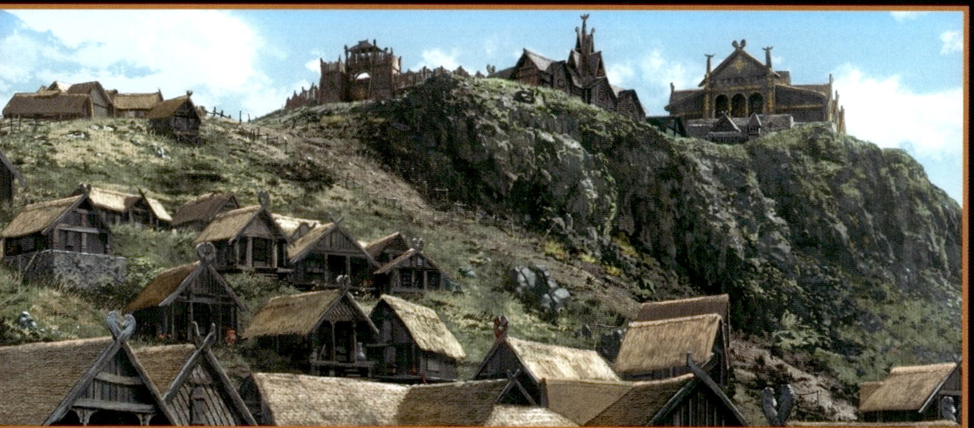

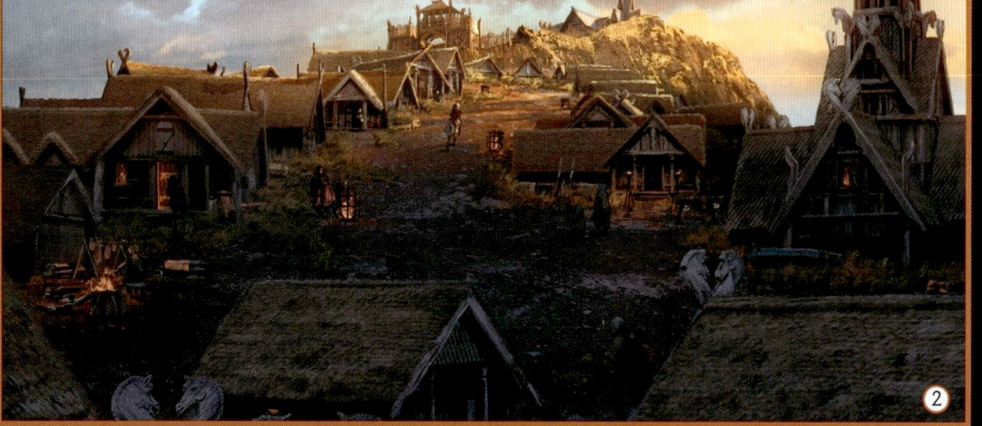

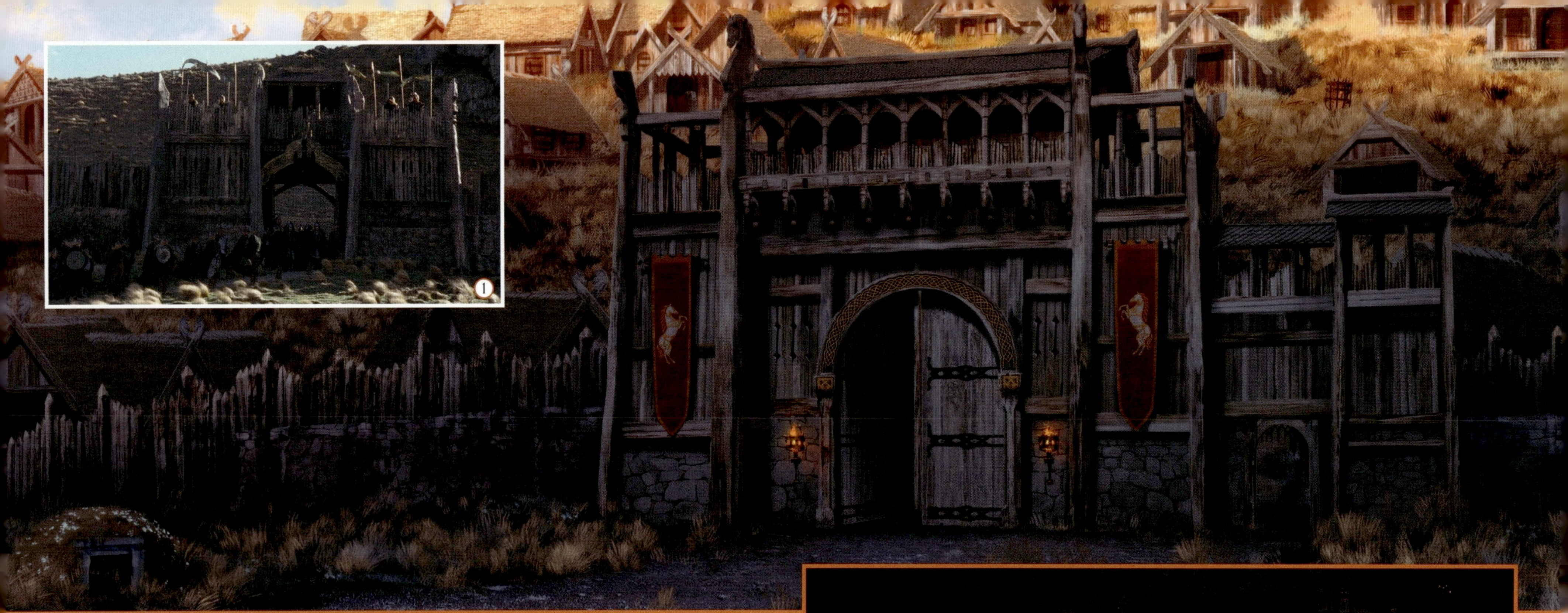

Caption 1 image

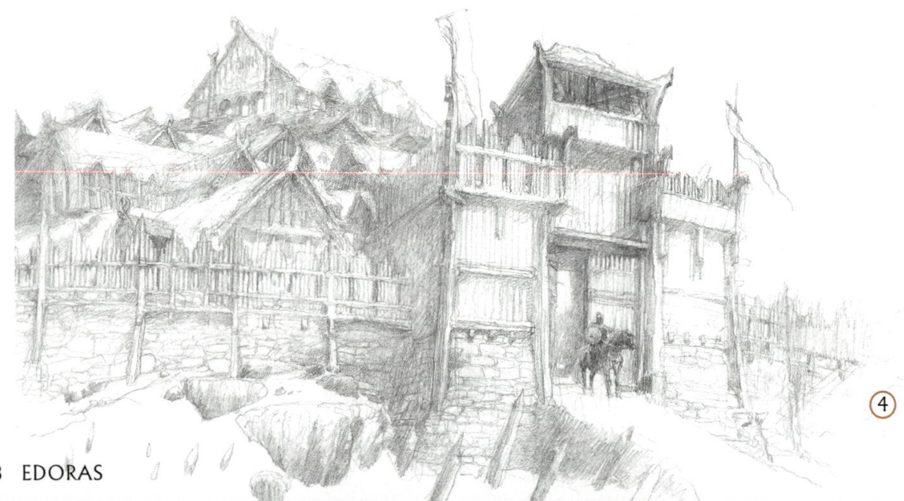

EDORAS FRONT GATE

◆ ⟨⟨◆⟩⟩ ◆

We looked for a balance between what was the same and what was different between our version of Edoras and the way it looked in the trilogy films. It couldn't be a shining city, two centuries earlier, nor could it appear to be ancient. We tried to find what would be an appropriate difference in appearance while still looking like it had stood for many generations. The front gate was a good example of trying to find this balance. – KENJI KAMIYAMA, DIRECTOR

1: Edoras front gate set (LOTR trilogy). 2: Edoras front gate background art, TK. 3: Edoras front gate concept TK. 4: Edoras front gate concept (LOTR trilogy), AL.

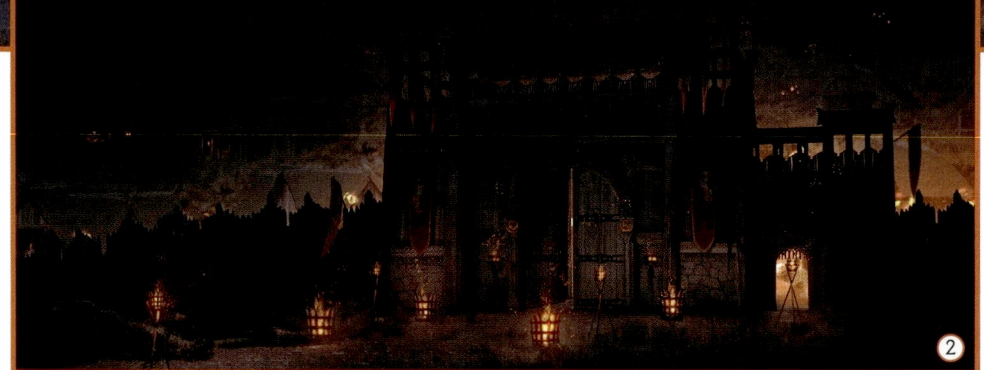

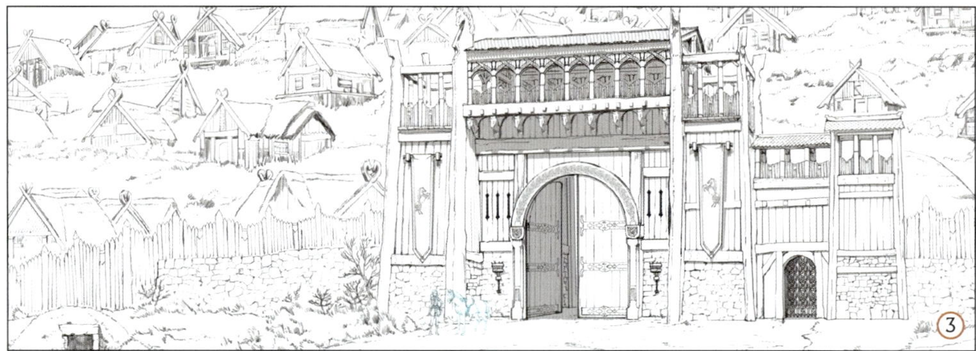

The main gate was made bigger and more impressive than it appeared in the trilogy to show that Edoras was thriving. Helm's Rohirrim would ride through the gateway to meet Wulf's forces in battle, later in the film. While retaining the same design details, we significantly altered the structure. Next to the main entryway we included a small door. Although there were no scenes in which we saw it used, I think Héra probably used the small door to come and go on her rides in the countryside. – TAMIKO KANAMORI, ART DIRECTOR

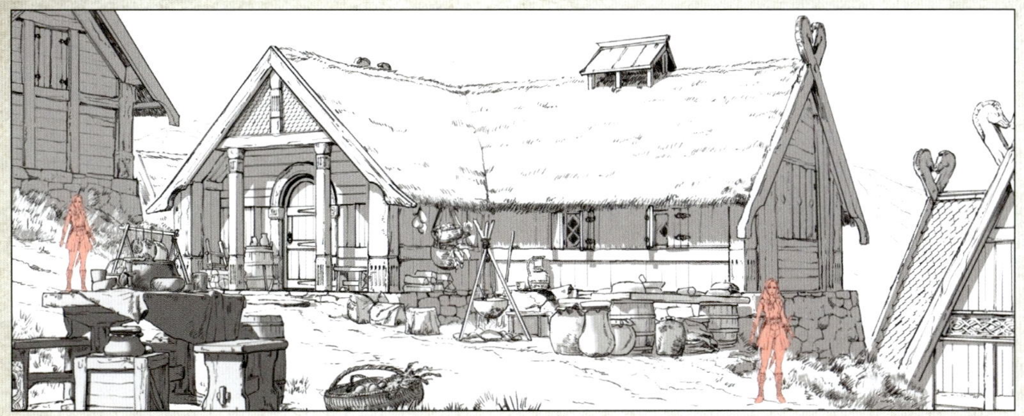

EDORAS SUMMIT BUILDINGS

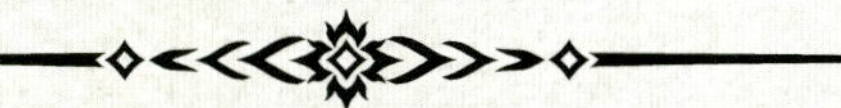

The structures clustered about Meduseld and built on location on the summit of Mount Sunday for the trilogy were painstakingly researched and recreated. Similar in spirit, small changes were folded into the designs to reflect the two hundred years between Helm and Théoden's reign. Among them were quirky structures like the belltower and food stores.

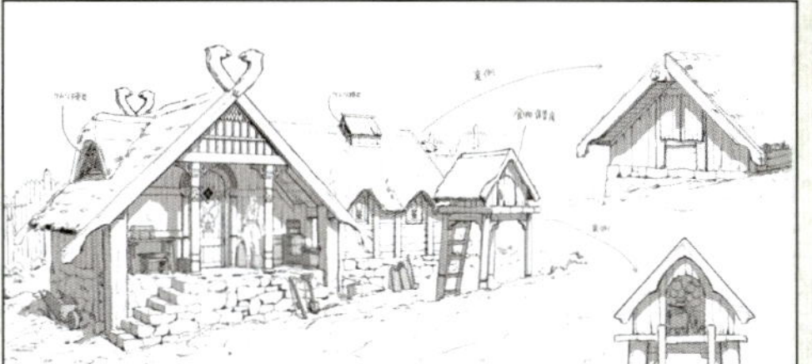
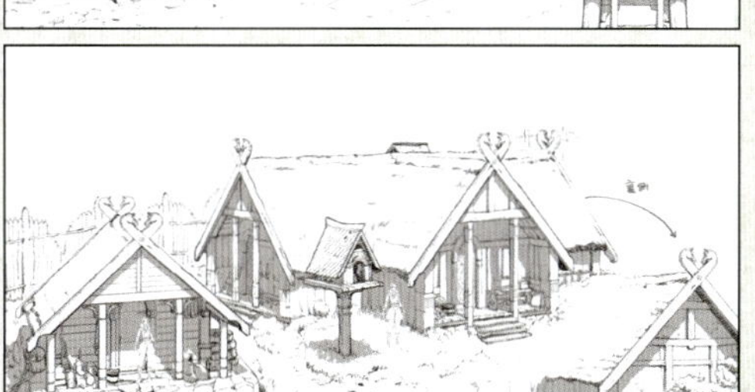
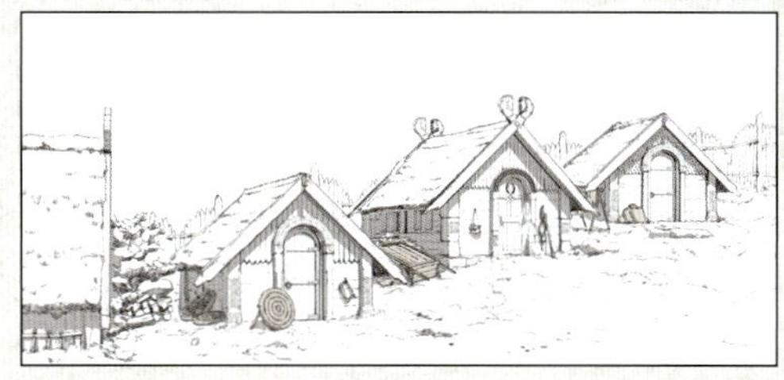
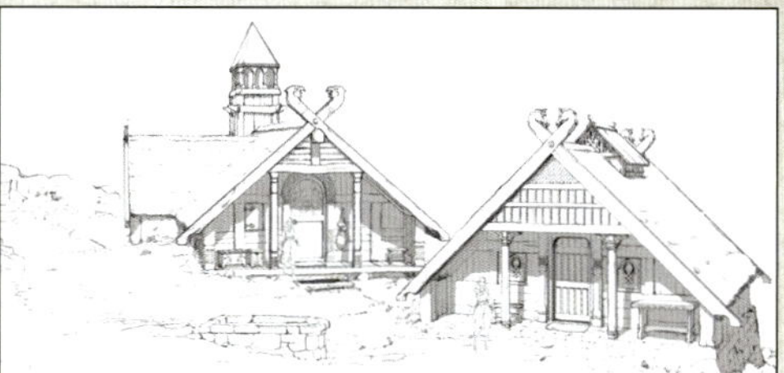
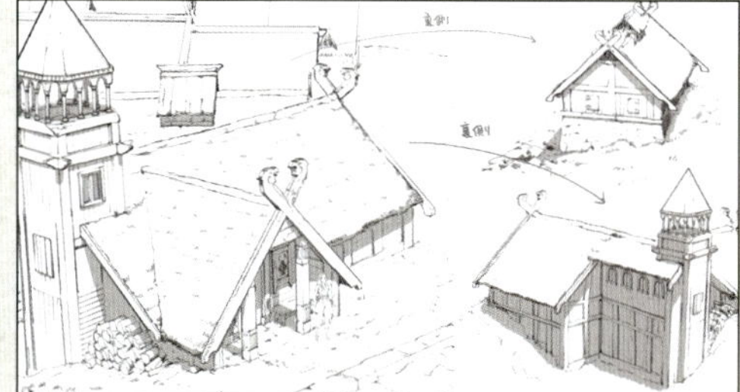
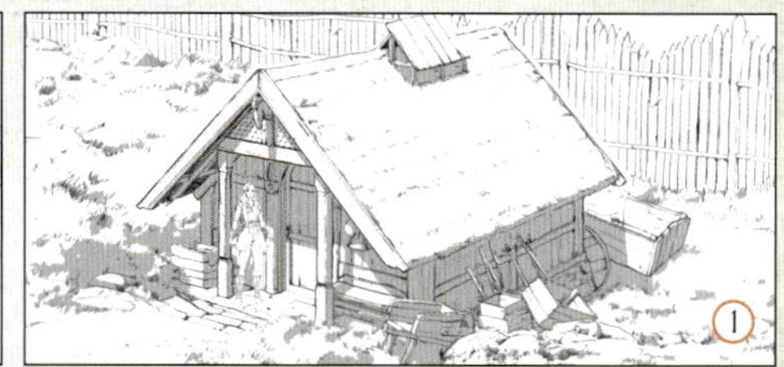

1: Edoras summit buildings concepts, TK. **2:** Meduseld background art, TK.

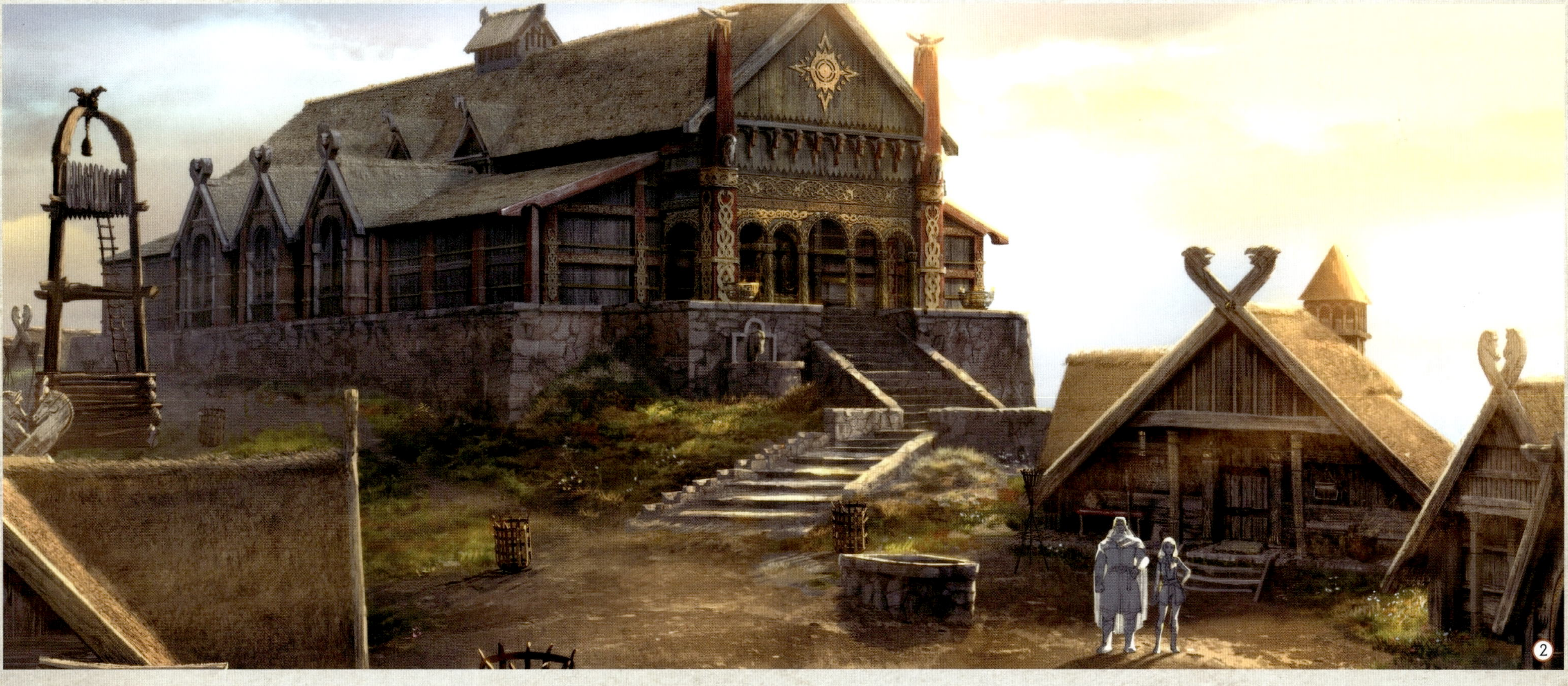

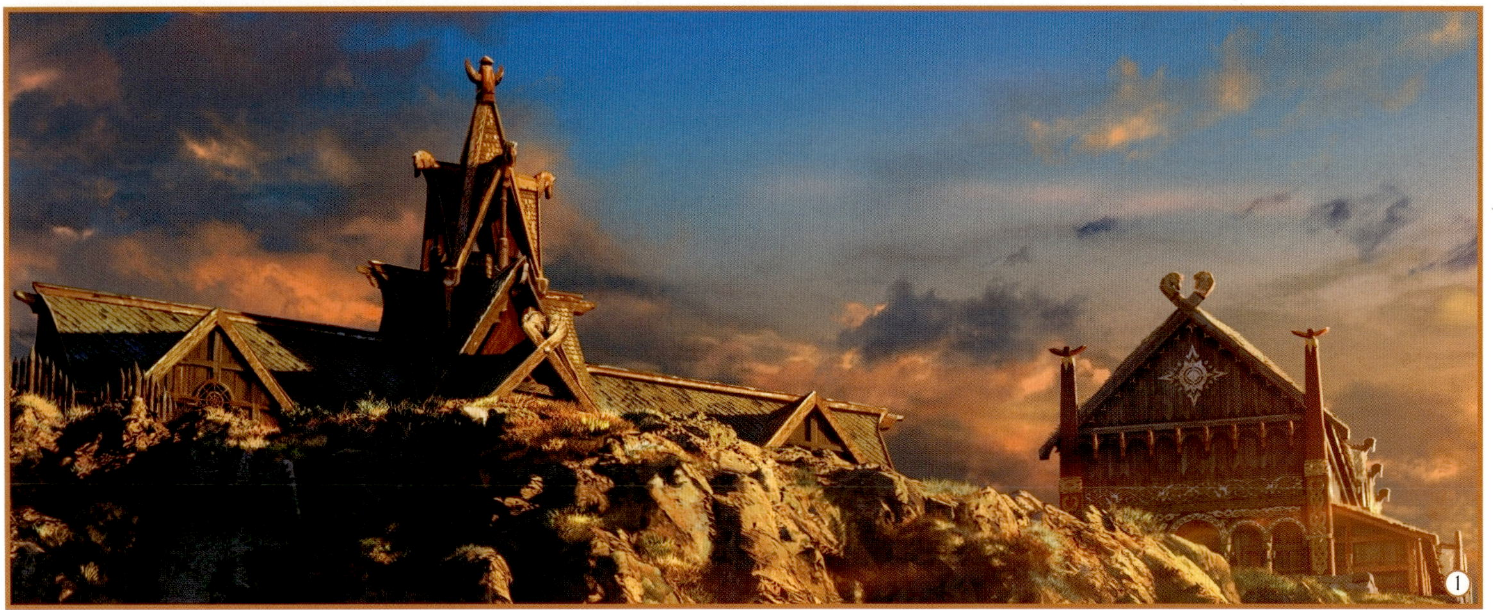

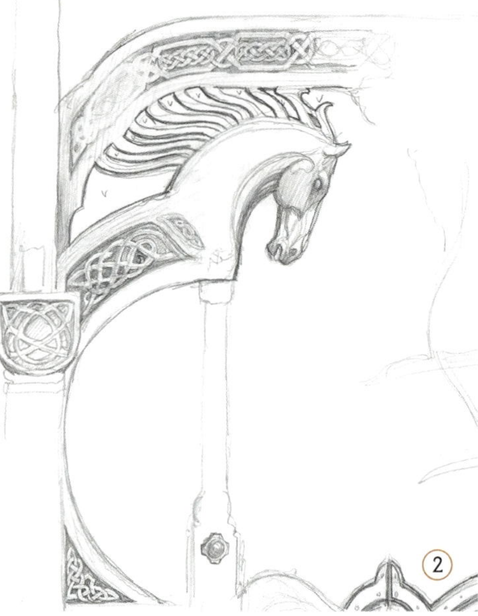

EDORAS STABLES

The stables closely match what was designed and built for the trilogy. We made them slightly larger overall, because Helm is quite large, and to provide more space for storing hay. The low-angled beams of golden light in the stable interior were the director's idea, while we painted the dark, night scenes to look like they were shot with a smaller aperture, capturing the feeling of a city lit only by torches. – TAMIKO KANAMORI, ART DIRECTOR

1: Edoras stable background art. **2:** Edoras stable concept (LOTR trilogy), AL. **3:** Edoras stable interior background setting art, TK. **4:** Edoras stable interior background art. **5:** Final film frame.

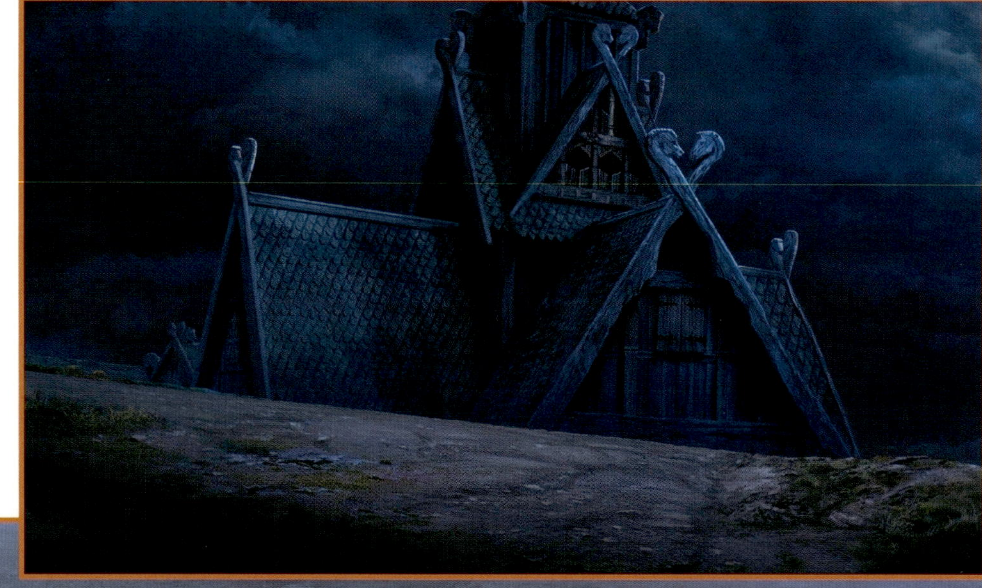

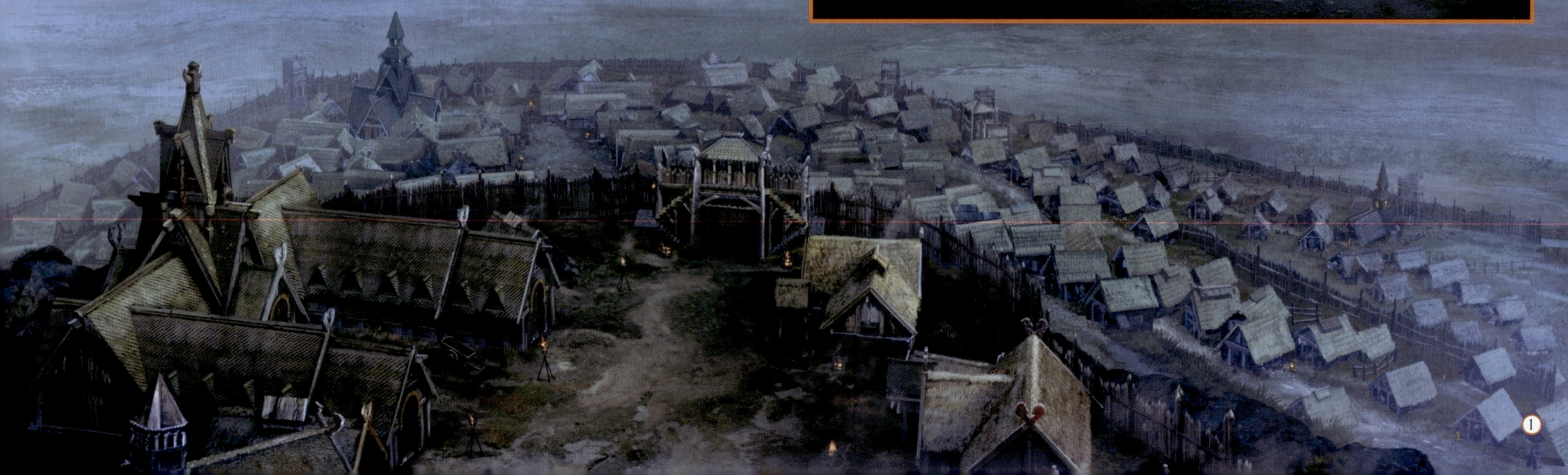

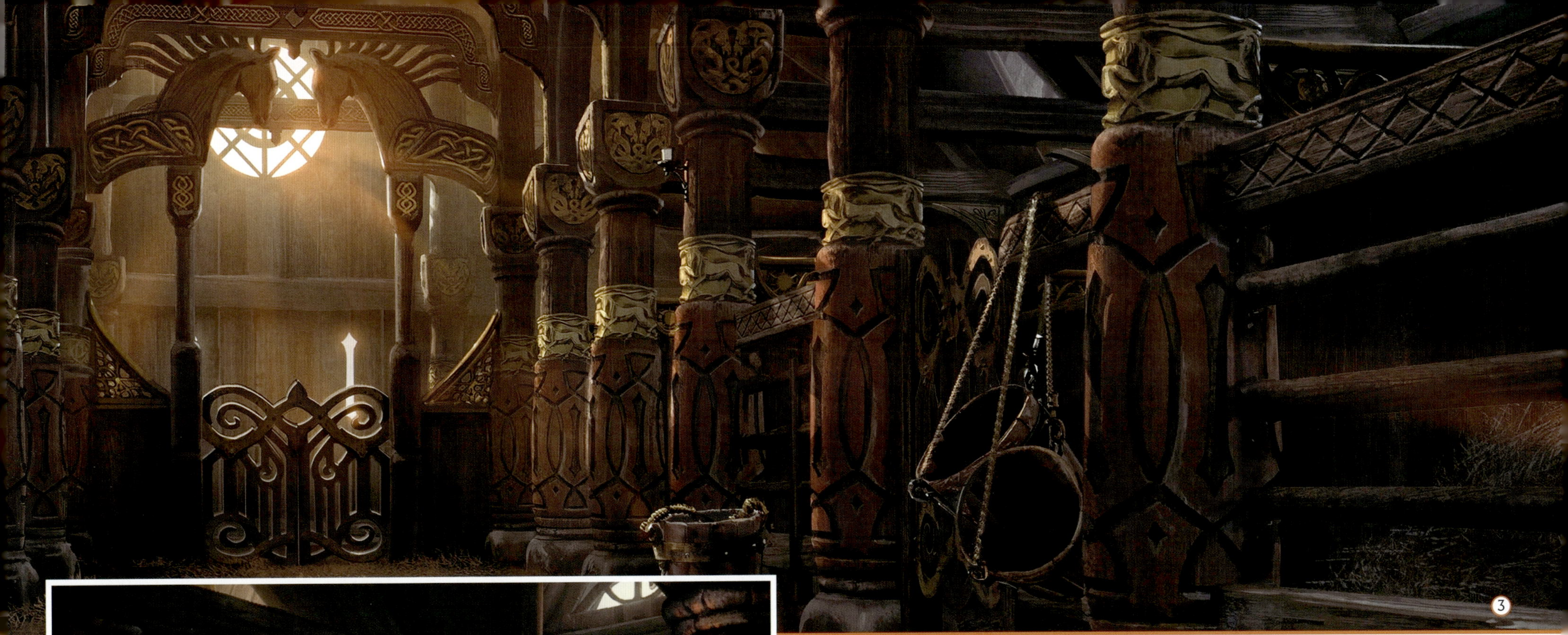

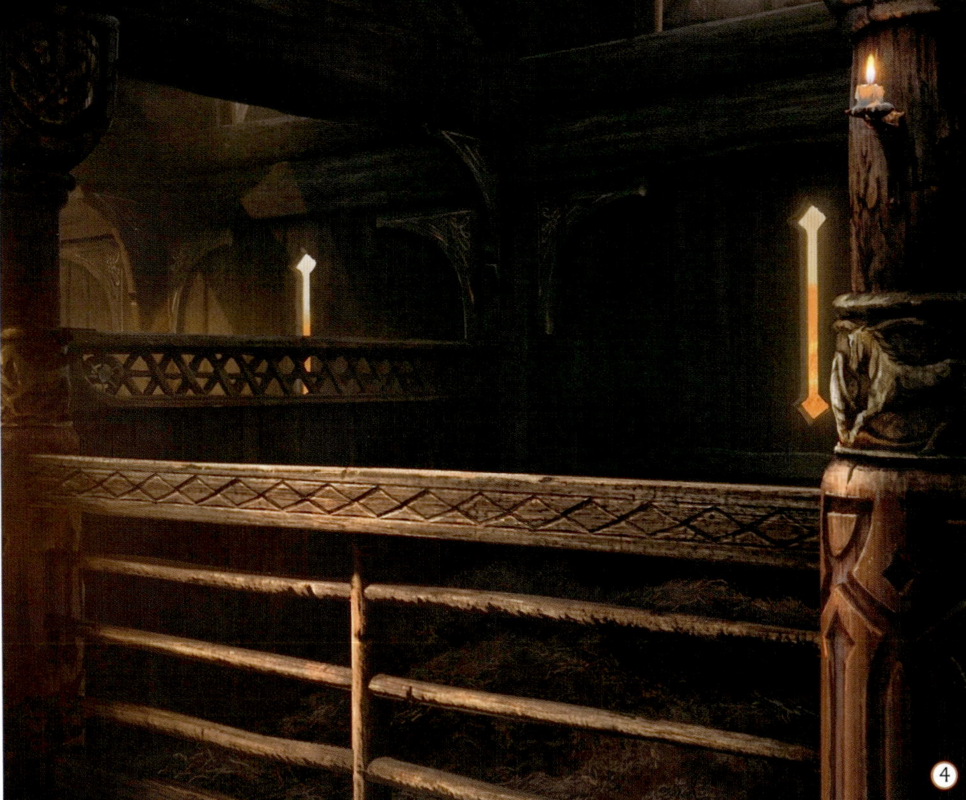

The stable is the first structure that we spend time in, so it had to set the tone for Rohan in this time of peace. It was important that it feel comfortable and warm, clean and bright. This is a place where Héra attends her horse, Ashere, with whom she is very close. The Horse-lords of Rohan care for their animals deeply, so the stables are a beautiful, uplifting place, bathed in this warm light. Here, the king and his family keep their horses and look after them, themselves; it's not full of servants. We meet Háma here, just relaxing, playing his lyre. This is a place where both characters spend a lot of their time. – JASON DEMARCO, PRODUCER

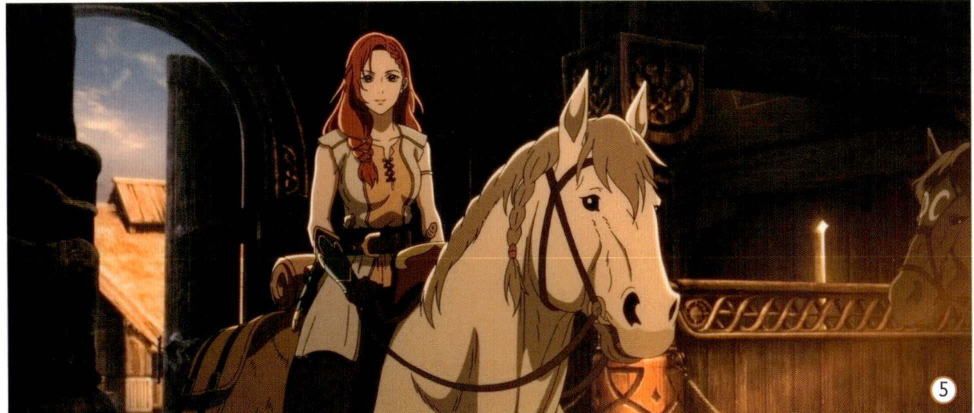

'RAISED ALONGSIDE TWO BROTHERS BY A WARRIOR KING,
THE GIRL COULD RIDE A HORSE BEFORE SHE COULD WALK.'

HÁMA, SON OF HELM

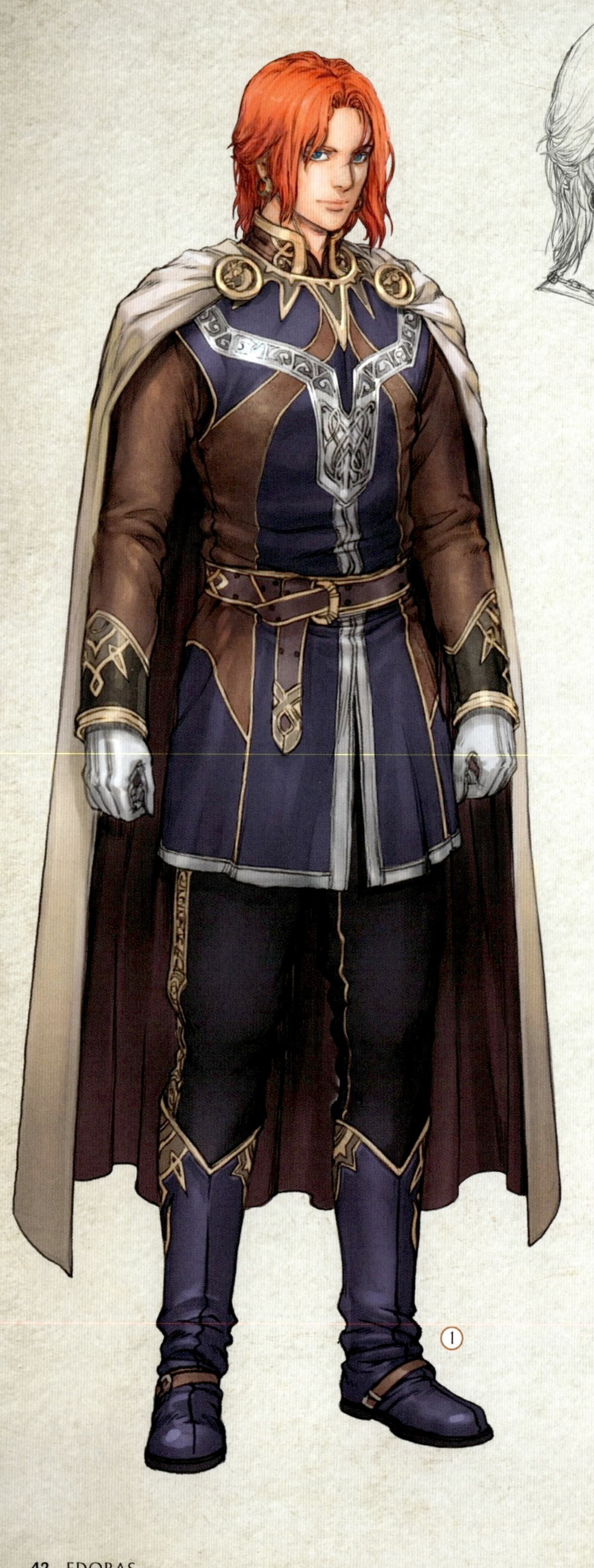

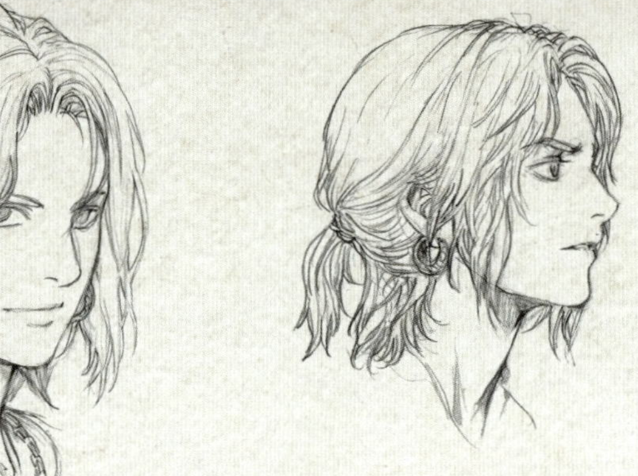

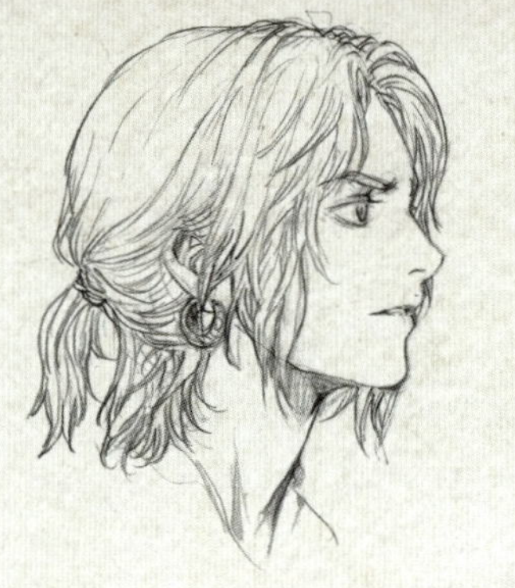

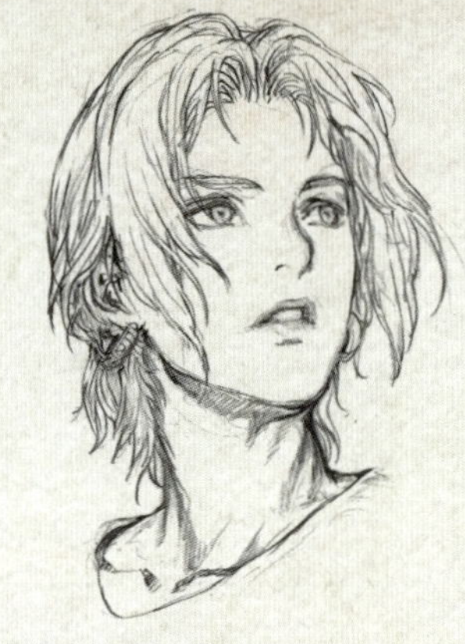

Háma is the contrast to his powerfully built brother, Haleth. Kamiyama san had drawn Háma with a lyre to highlight his softer, more poetic nature. So then we thought, if he's been given this instrument, he ought to play it! Arty and I turned to Tolkien for lyric inspiration and wrote what ended up being called 'Háma's song'. It's a melody he sings in the stables and which is reprised several times throughout the film to evoke his character, even after he is gone. His lyre also becomes a bit of a symbol in the film - a passing down of the stories in keeping with the Rohirrim culture. – PHOEBE GITTINS, WRITER

As the second son of Helm, Háma was not burdened with following in his father's footsteps as warrior or leader. He is probably aware and ready, if that burden were to fall to him by circumstances, but his nature is to be a more sensitive character who reads, sings and plays music. Giving him an instrument to pluck helped audiences to differentiate him from Haleth and immediately identified him as perhaps more studious and artistically expressive. – KENJI KAMIYAMA, DIRECTOR

Háma was a softer, gentler character than Helm or Haleth. They told me that he was popular with the production staff, but not necessarily easy to animate. They took pains to reproduce the hairstyle from the concept art in the final animation character design. – STATO, ORIGINAL CHARACTER DESIGNER

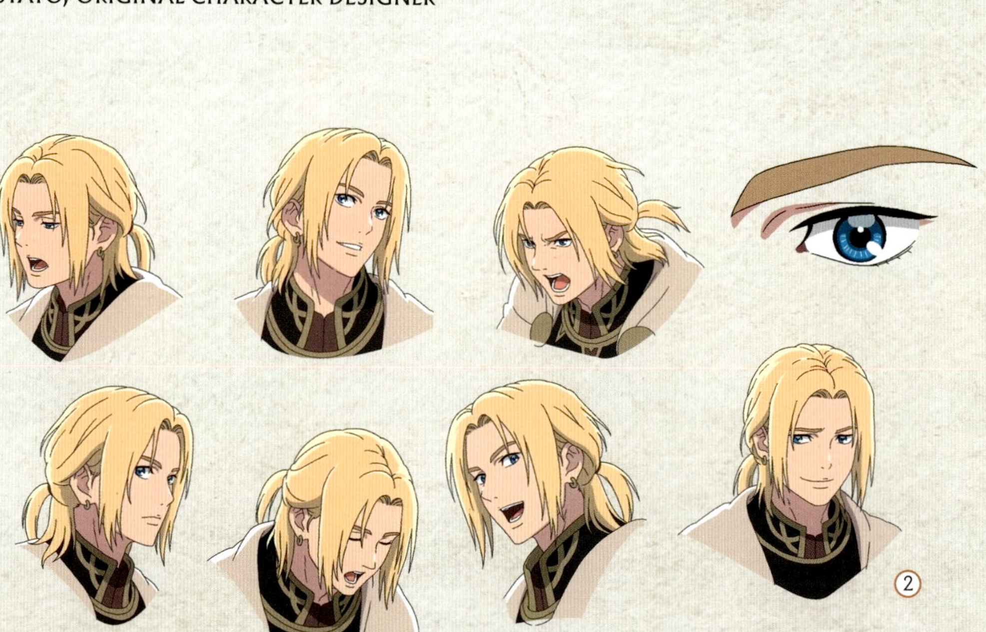

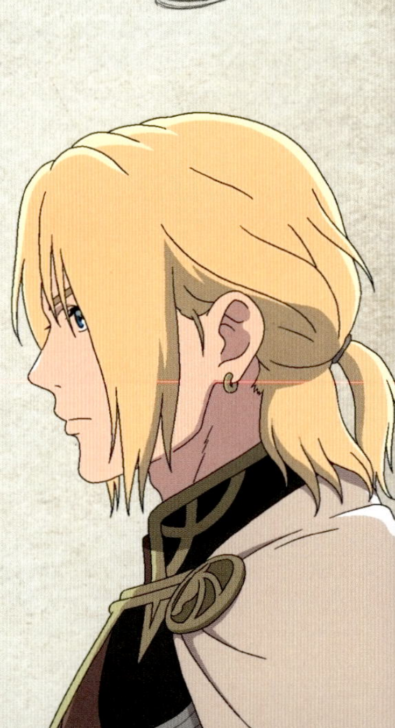

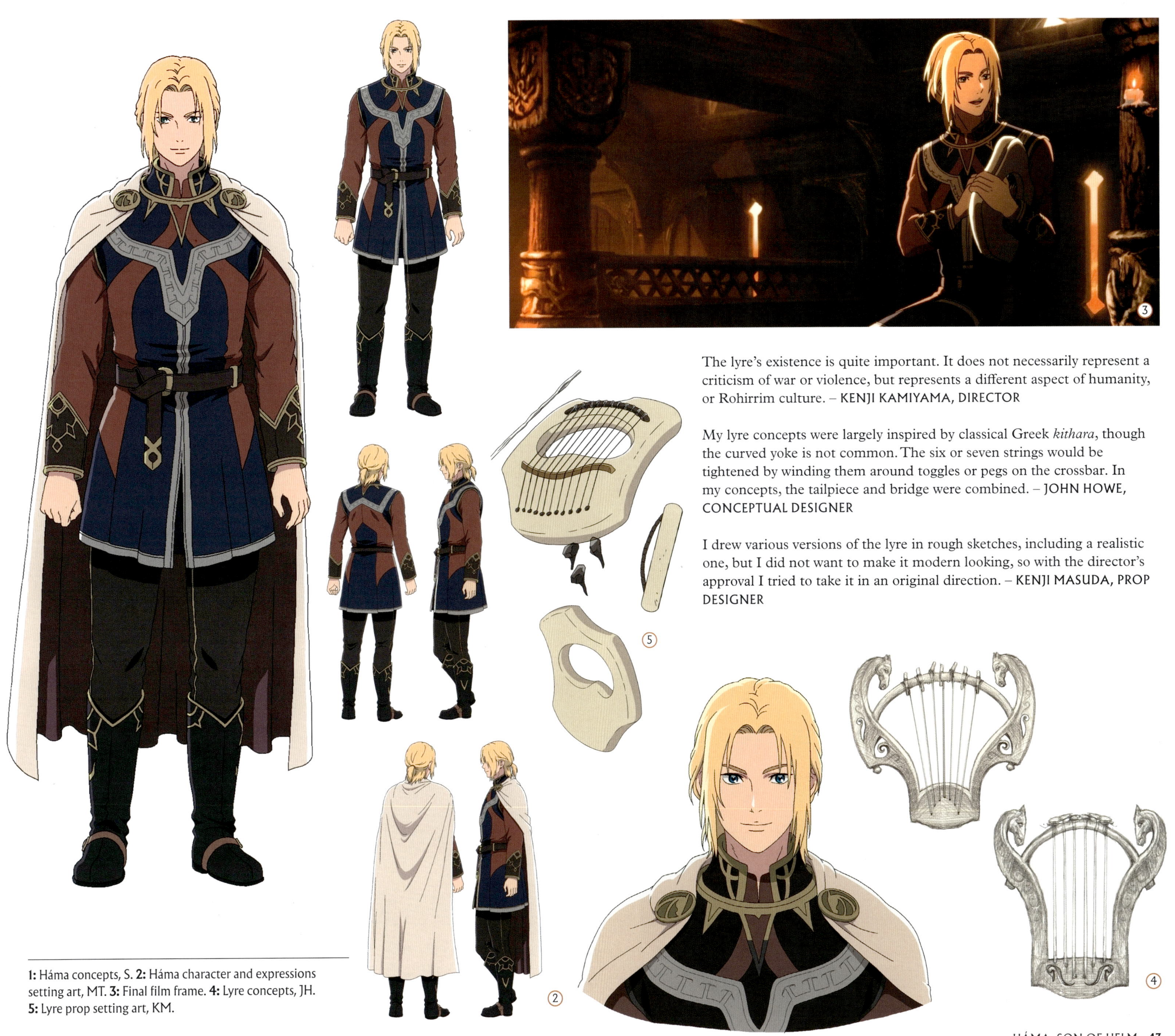

The lyre's existence is quite important. It does not necessarily represent a criticism of war or violence, but represents a different aspect of humanity, or Rohirrim culture. – KENJI KAMIYAMA, DIRECTOR

My lyre concepts were largely inspired by classical Greek *kithara*, though the curved yoke is not common. The six or seven strings would be tightened by winding them around toggles or pegs on the crossbar. In my concepts, the tailpiece and bridge were combined. – JOHN HOWE, CONCEPTUAL DESIGNER

I drew various versions of the lyre in rough sketches, including a realistic one, but I did not want to make it modern looking, so with the director's approval I tried to take it in an original direction. – KENJI MASUDA, PROP DESIGNER

1: Háma concepts, S. 2: Háma character and expressions setting art, MT. 3: Final film frame. 4: Lyre concepts, JH. 5: Lyre prop setting art, KM.

OLWYN, LADY'S MAID

Olwyn, originally named 'Solwyn' in earlier versions of the script, is Héra's lady in waiting. Having lost her birth mother as an infant, Héra was also nursed by Olwyn, so Olwyn is both mother and mentor to the young princess. Helm chose her for his daughter, knowing of her capabilities as a protector as well as a caregiver.

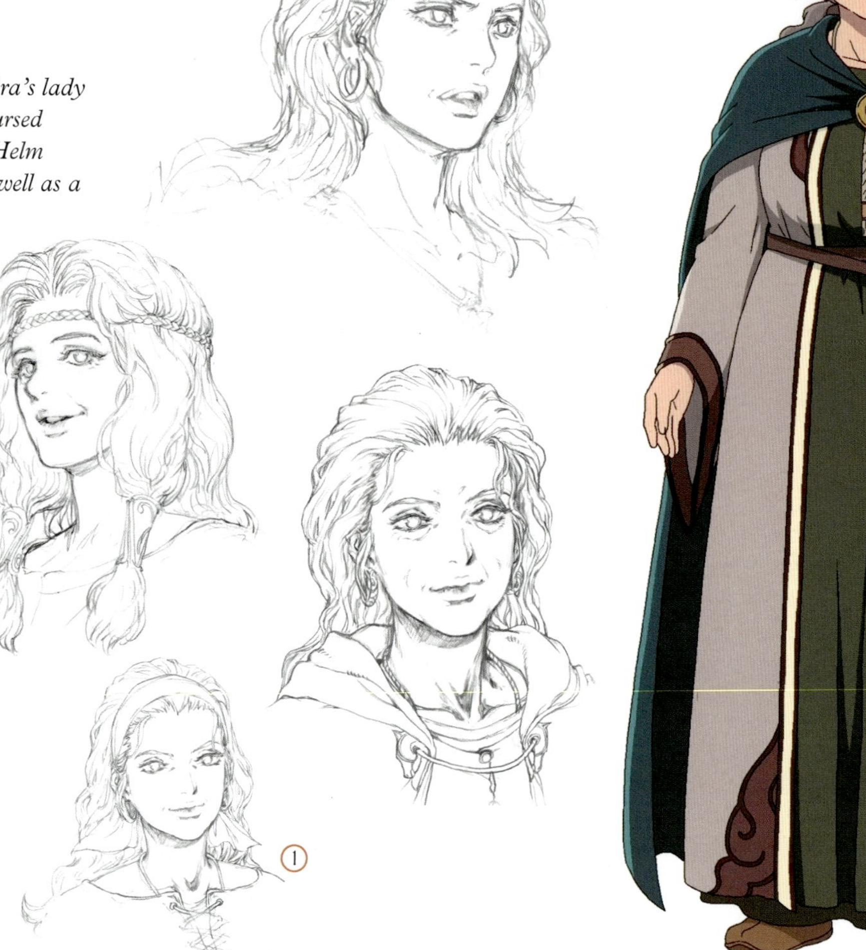

Lorraine Ashbourne plays Olwyn. Early on, Philippa mentioned Lorraine and that's where the character just came to life. We wrote her for Lorraine, really, and so we were lucky that she then said yes! – PHOEBE GITTINS, WRITER

Lorraine is smart and clever, with a very dry sense of humour, but so strong. It's something that you get immediately when you meet her. She was perfect for this role. – PHILIPPA BOYENS, PRODUCER

Always by Héra's side, Olwyn had to look dependable. A little shorter than Héra, but not heavy set, I imagined her as a character who might not impress you at first glance, but later you would find her strong-willed and reliable.

I wanted to give her a charming and likable demeanour as a woman of middle age, but also wanted people to be able to tell that she must have been an even greater beauty when she was Héra's age. – MIYAKO TAKASU, ANIMATION CHARACTER DESIGNER & KEY ANIMATION SUPERVISOR

1: Olwyn concepts, S. 2: Olwyn character setting art, MT. 3: Final film frame.

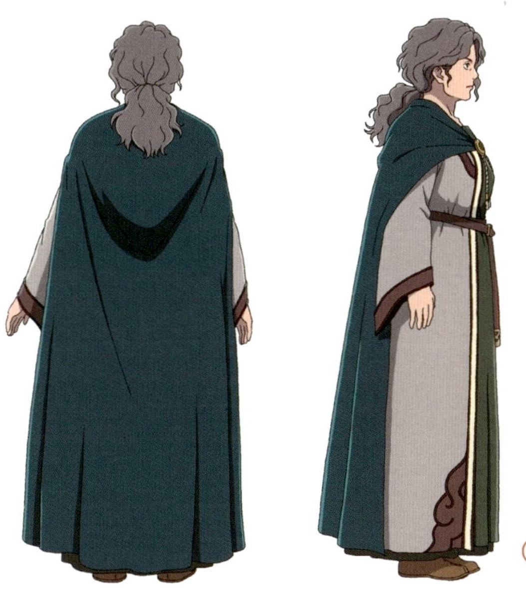

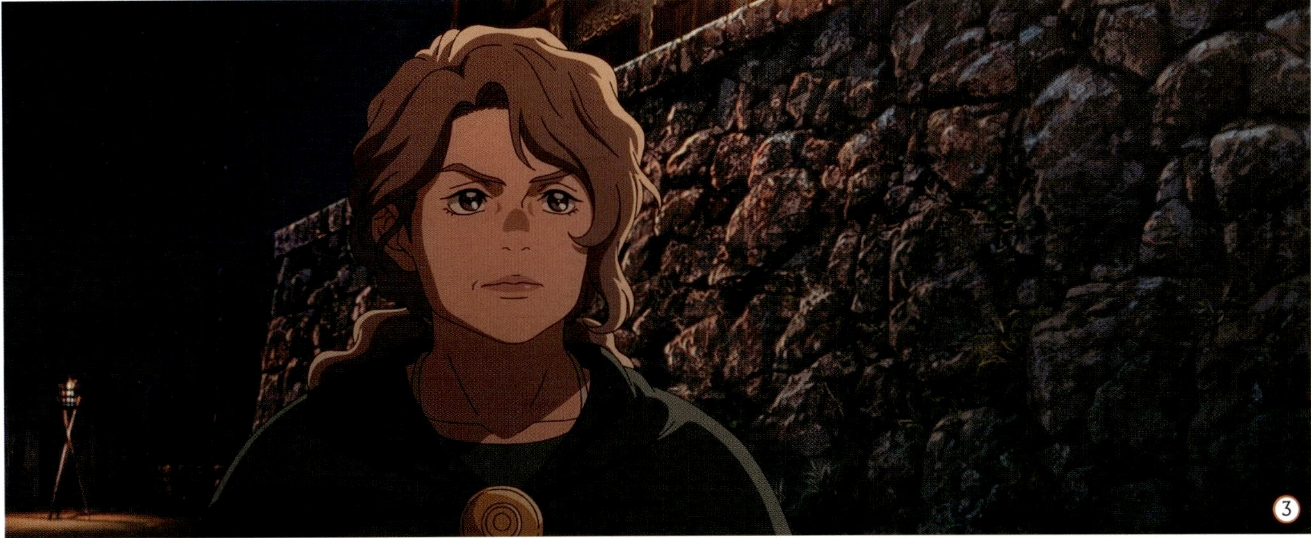

LIEF, ROYAL PAGE

To me, Lief embodies all that is good about the Rohirrim: he is so brave and loyal even in the most dire of circumstances. Lief always tries his best… even though he doesn't always get it right, and Héra loves him for it. – PHOEBE GITTINS, WRITER

We chose the name 'Lief' because if its softness, in contrast to some of the Rohirrim names. Lief carries a horn as Helm's page. He is the herald, and it is his role to call the banners. – PHILIPPA BOYENS, PRODUCER

Initially Lief wasn't a very developed character. He wasn't that important in early passes of the script and didn't have that big of a presence. As we progressed through the production of the film, and especially when we were recording, Lief grew in our imaginations. I think it was also probably in response to the first drawings. He was growing into such a lovely character, so naturally his prominence and importance increased. We started finding ways to add to his character in small ways. You'll notice that he even has a little moment in the film when we introduce a possible girlfriend among the servants of the other Rohirrim lords! That wasn't scripted. It was something that happened along the way. – KENJI KAMIYAMA, DIRECTOR

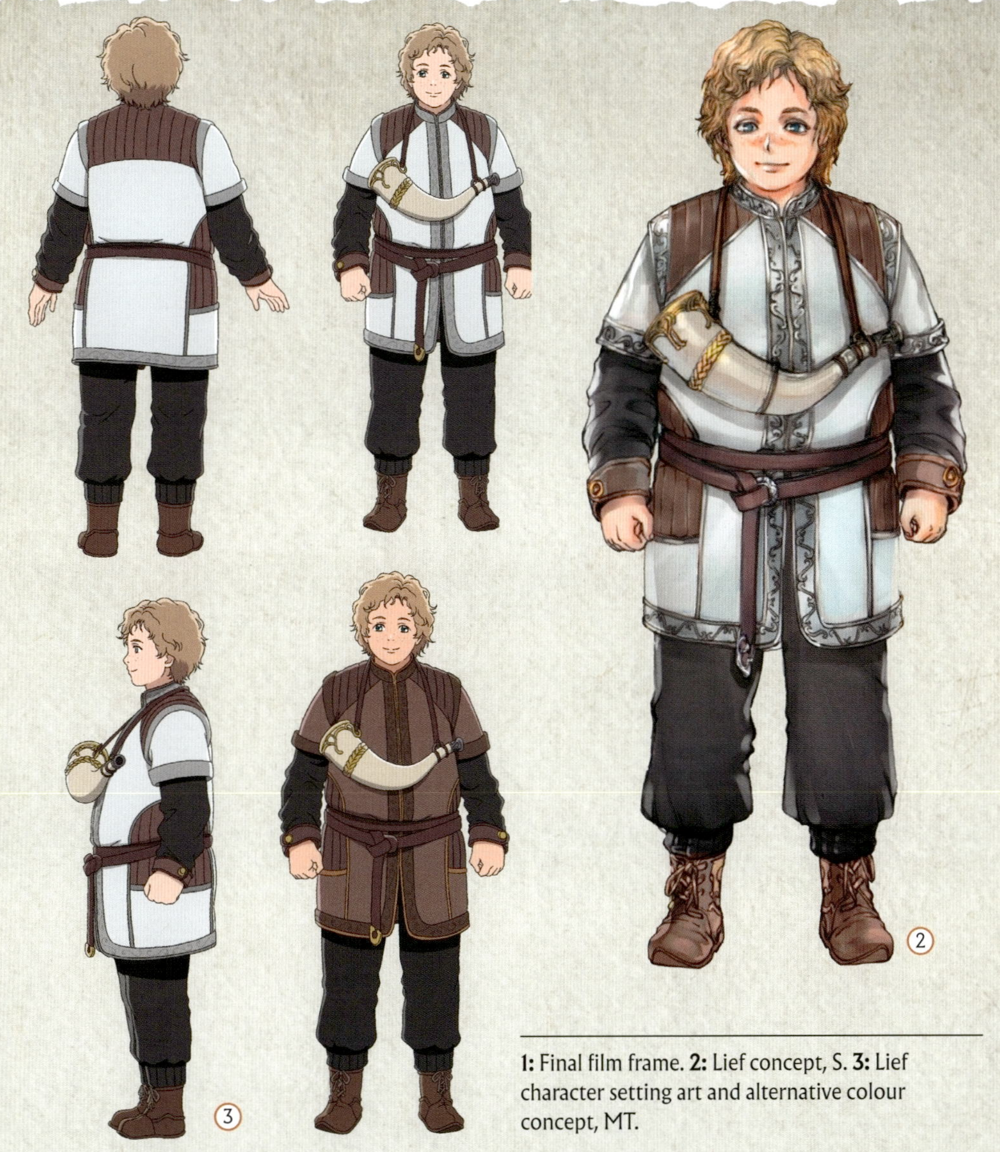

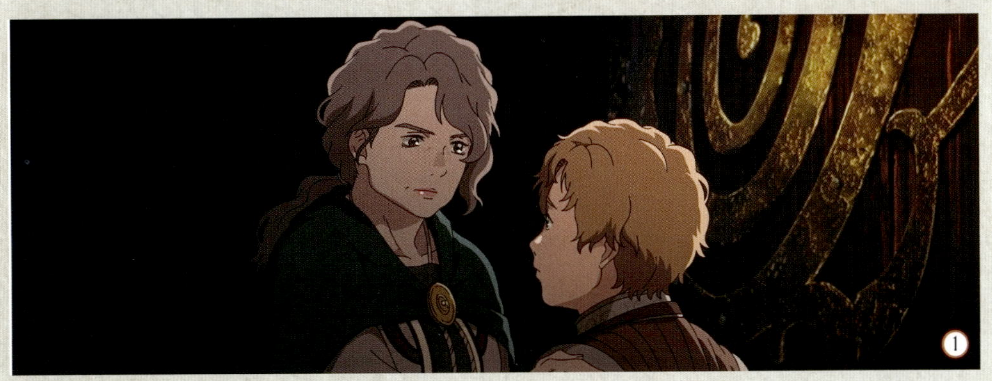

1: Final film frame. 2: Lief concept, S. 3: Lief character setting art and alternative colour concept, MT.

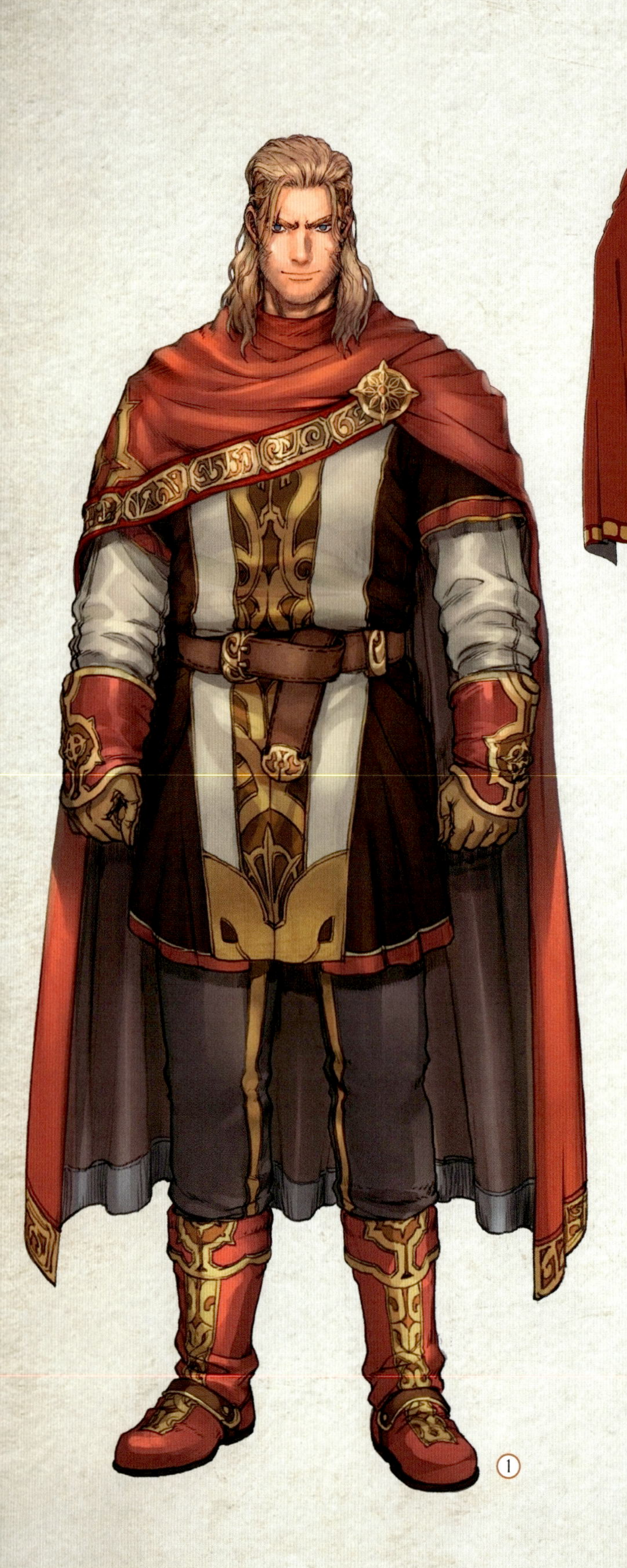

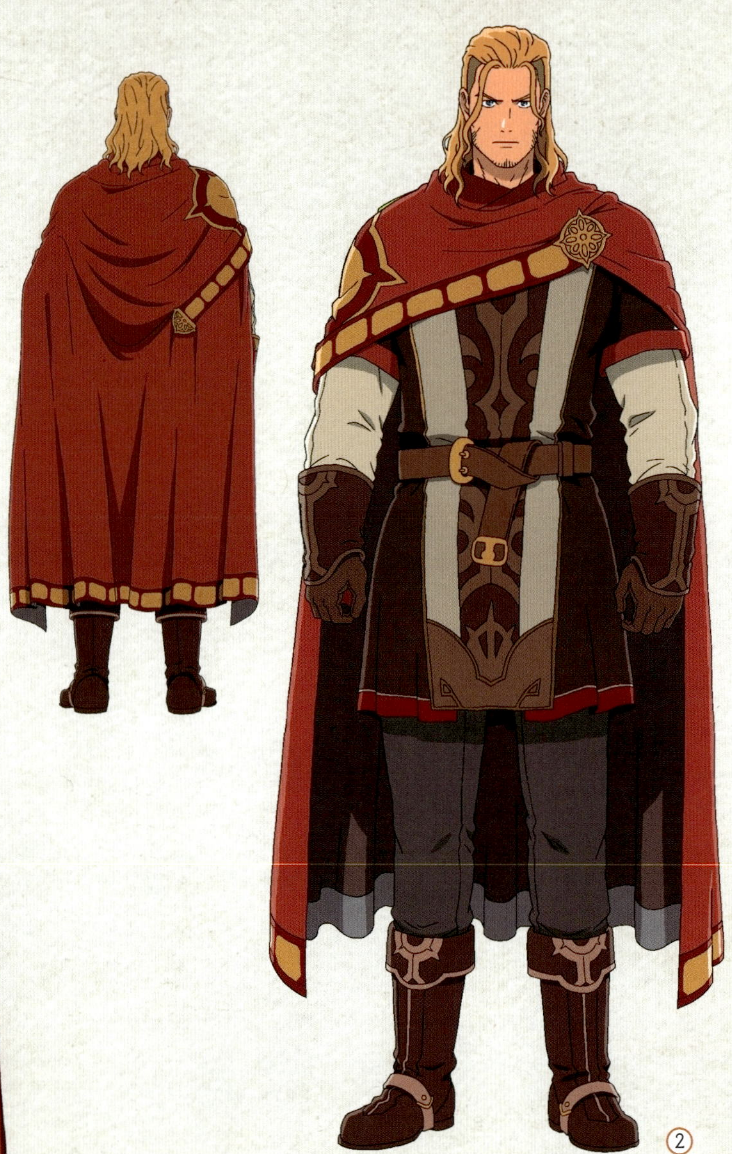

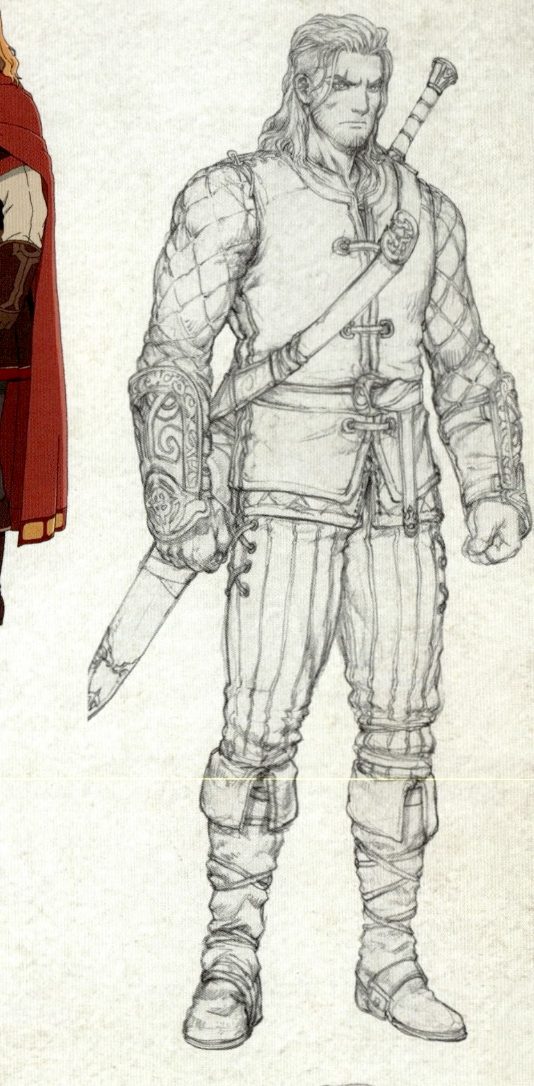

HALETH, SON OF HELM

As someone who is supposed to follow in Helm's footsteps, Haleth needed to be something of a warrior; physically powerful. His body type, size, even hair, bore an intentional similarity to Helm.

Unfortunately, we don't get to spend a lot of time with the character on screen, but in his few scenes we tried to use Haleth to demonstrate the very strong side of Helm; the warrior, the defender, his fierceness; qualities reflected in his son. – KENJI KAMIYAMA, DIRECTOR

Haleth has a belligerent streak, much like his father. He is someone who is trying to follow in Helm's footsteps, so I designed Haleth to look like him. – STATO, ORIGINAL CHARACTER DESIGNER

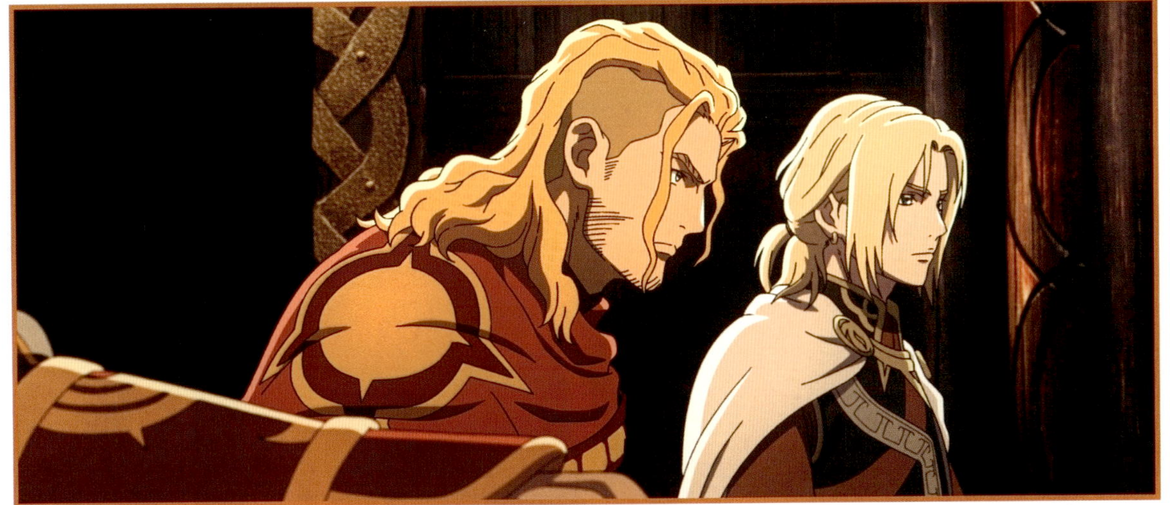

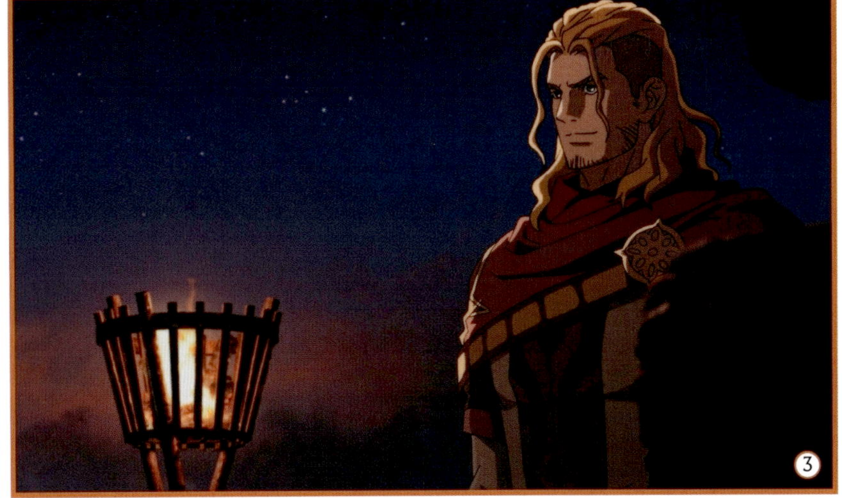

Haleth is the son who was always going to be the obvious choice to succeed Helm, and probably would have made a good king. He's a hothead, but he would have learnt, and he was built for it, like his father.
– PHILIPPA BOYENS, PRODUCER

Haleth admires and respects his father deeply. When originally designing him, I used to think of Haleth as the muscle man or strong-arm type. I didn't initially think of him as smart, but later, while drawing him in the production phase, I came to realize that he is much more thoughtful than that. Haleth has the dependable quality of an eldest son, destined to follow his father as king. He is very physically capable, like Helm, but he is also more than just that. I think audiences will be able to see his more serious side in the film. – MIYAKO TAKASU, ANIMATION CHARACTER DESIGNER & KEY ANIMATION SUPERVISOR

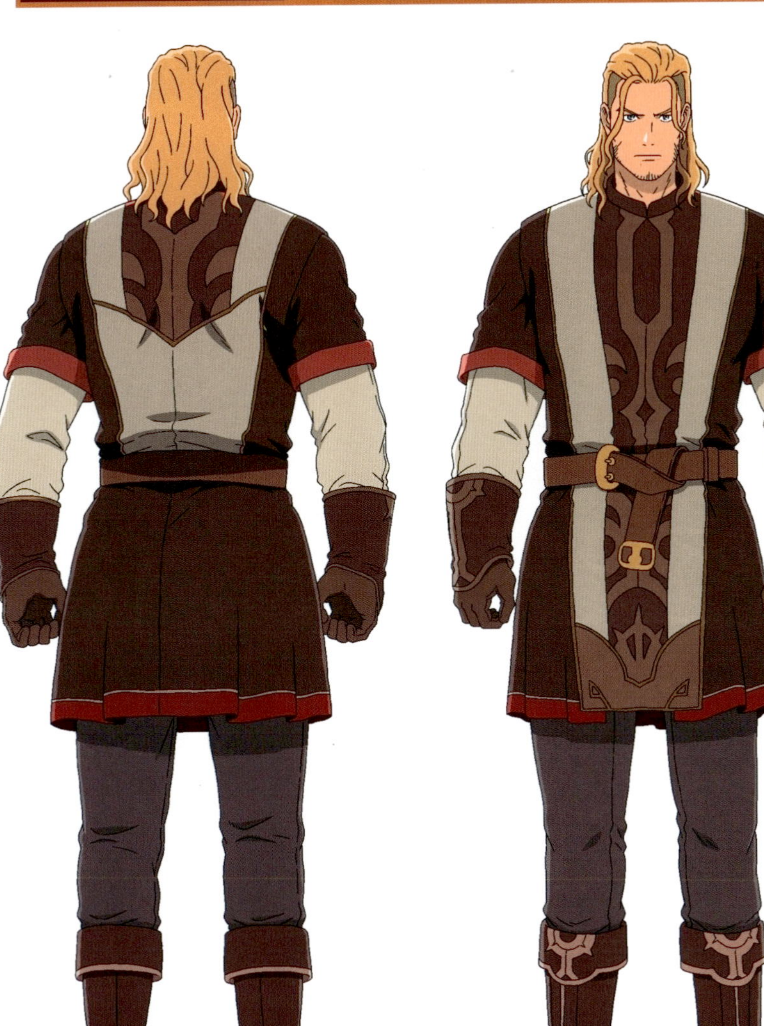

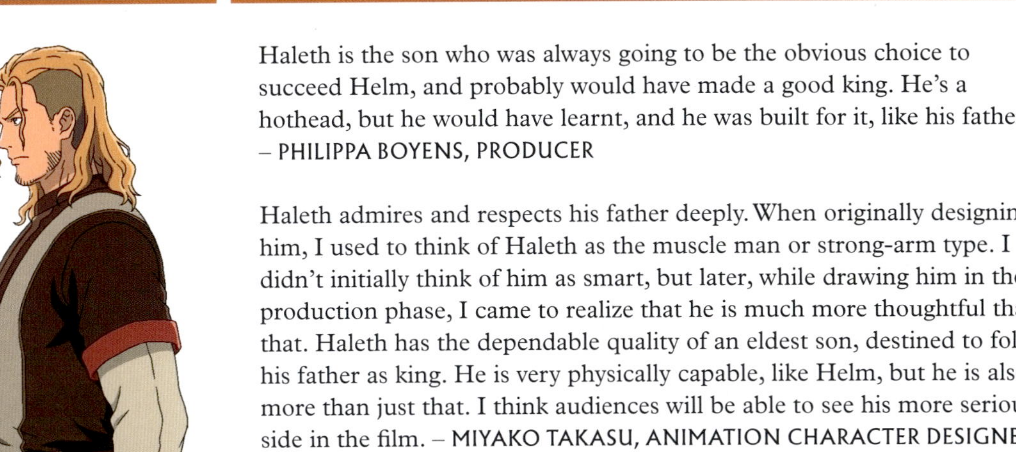

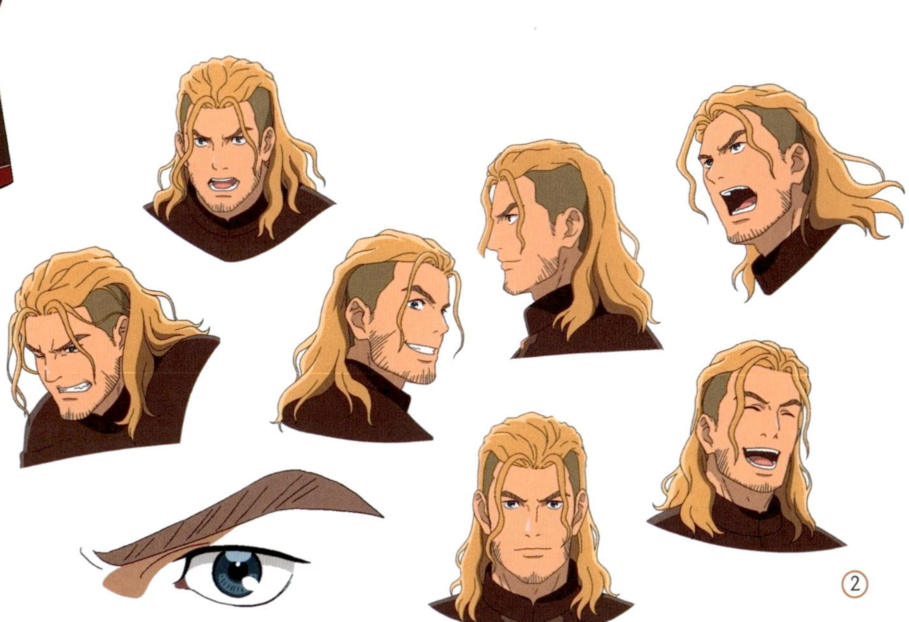

1: Haleth concepts, S. 2: Haleth character and expressions setting art, T MT. 3: Final film frames.

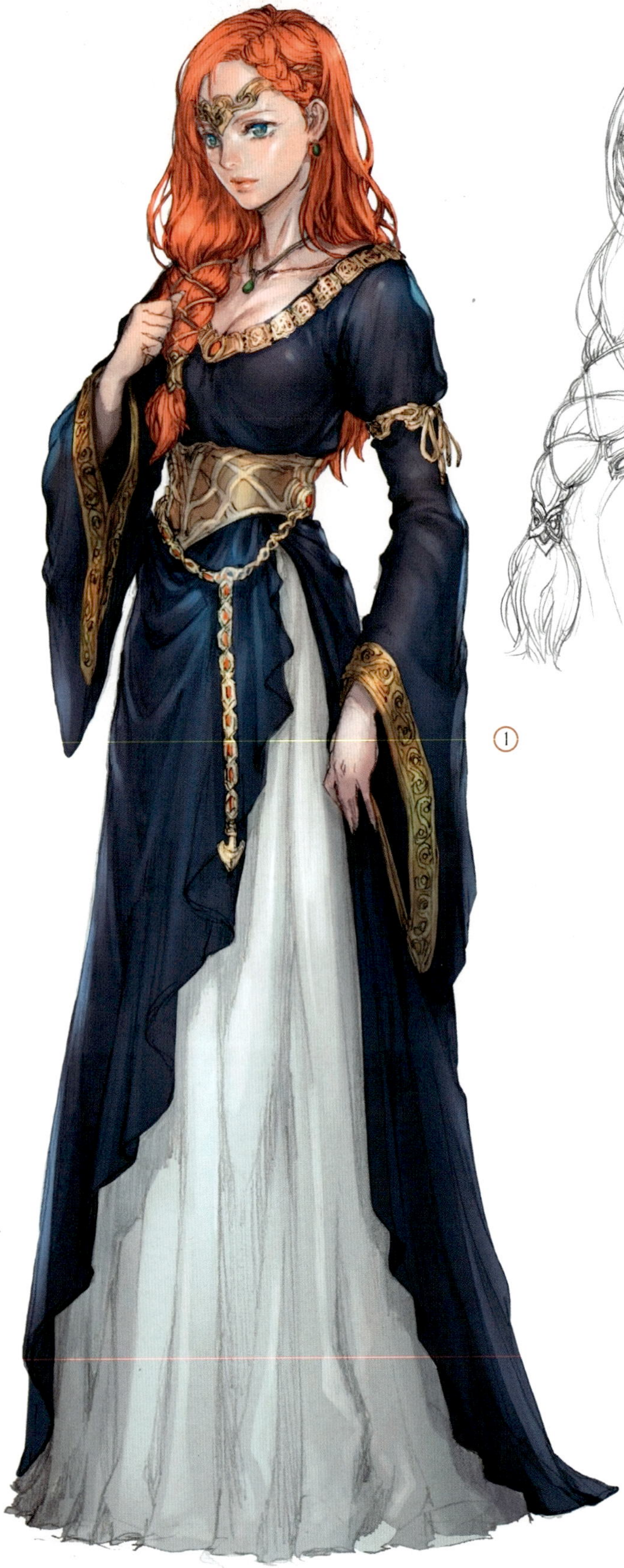

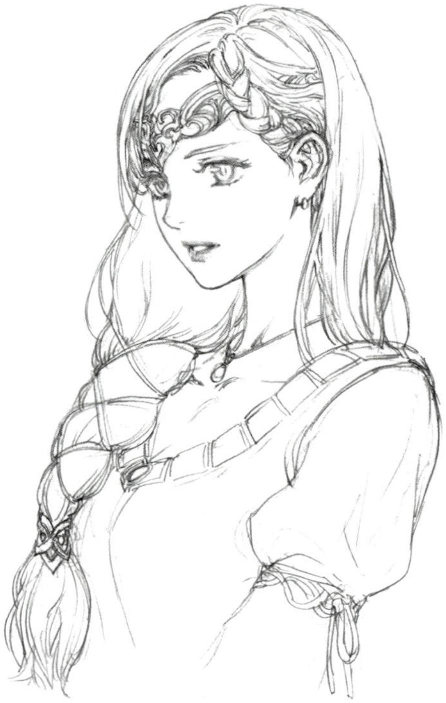

HÉRA, PRINCESS OF ROHAN

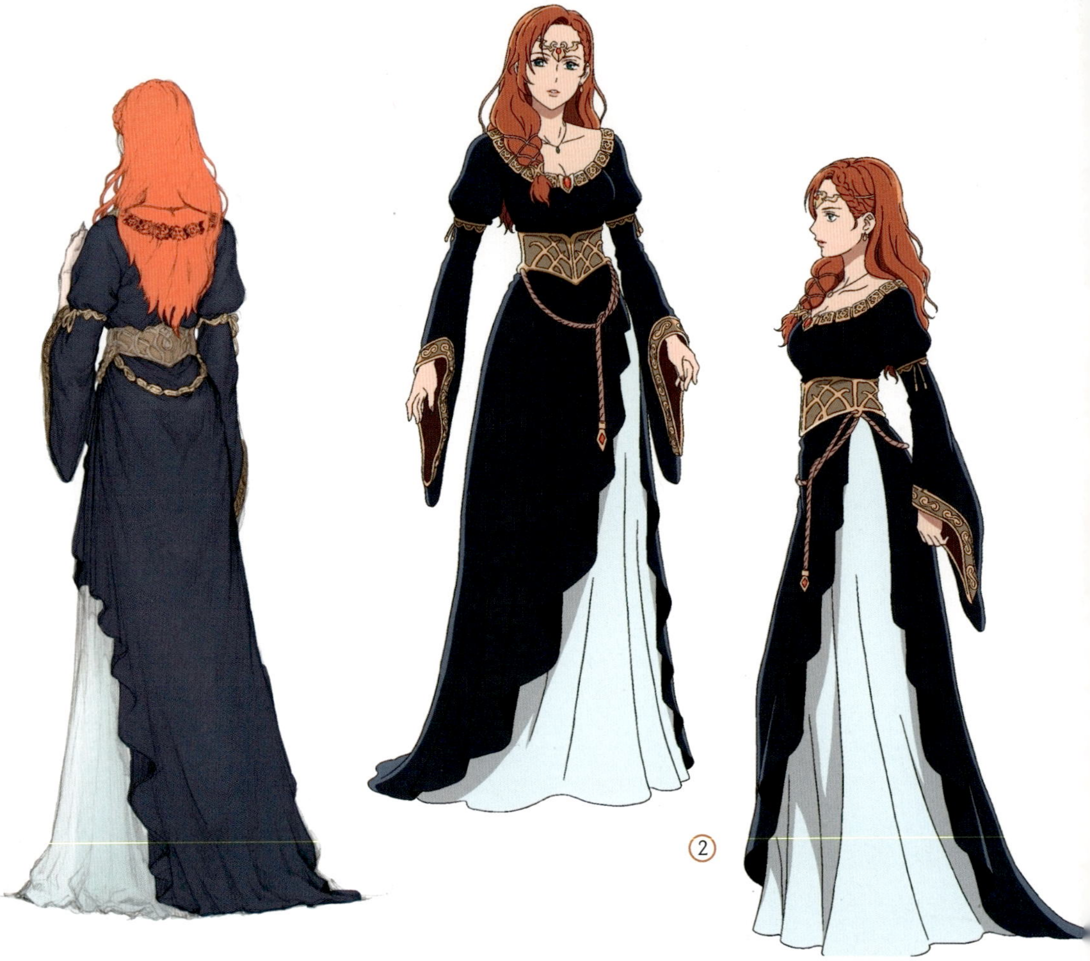

Héra is a princess of Rohan, and her future would have been to be married off, but she is not comfortable in her courtly dress; it's not her natural state. We liked the idea that she had messy hair – that it was wild and not perfect. Phoebe was adamant that she had to feel real and not some perfect superhero chick. – PHILIPPA BOYENS, PRODUCER

Fréaláf has a line when Héra is coming into council. He makes a little joke about how she normally presents herself, 'No twigs in your hair, cousin?'. It shows that everyone who knows Héra knows that she is more at home in her riding gear. Héra never tries to be something she is not; we felt it was important that despite the expectations placed upon her, she is always honest and true to herself. – PHOEBE GITTINS, WRITER

Concepts for Héra's dress drew inspiration from Éowyn's dresses seen in The Two Towers, *designed by Ngila Dickson. The character was always intended to exhibit kinship with Éowyn, given they are related, but not look exactly like her.*

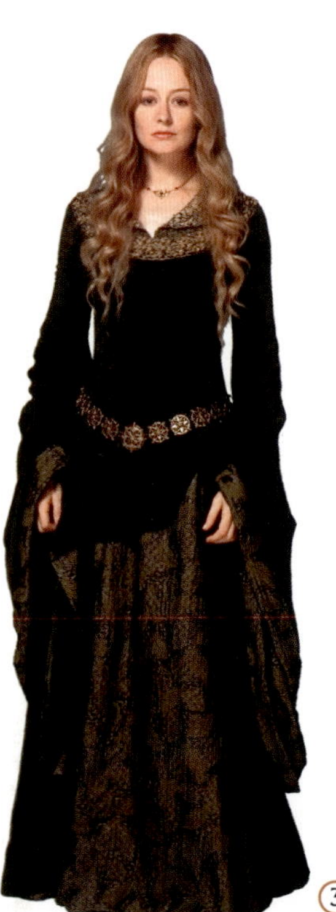

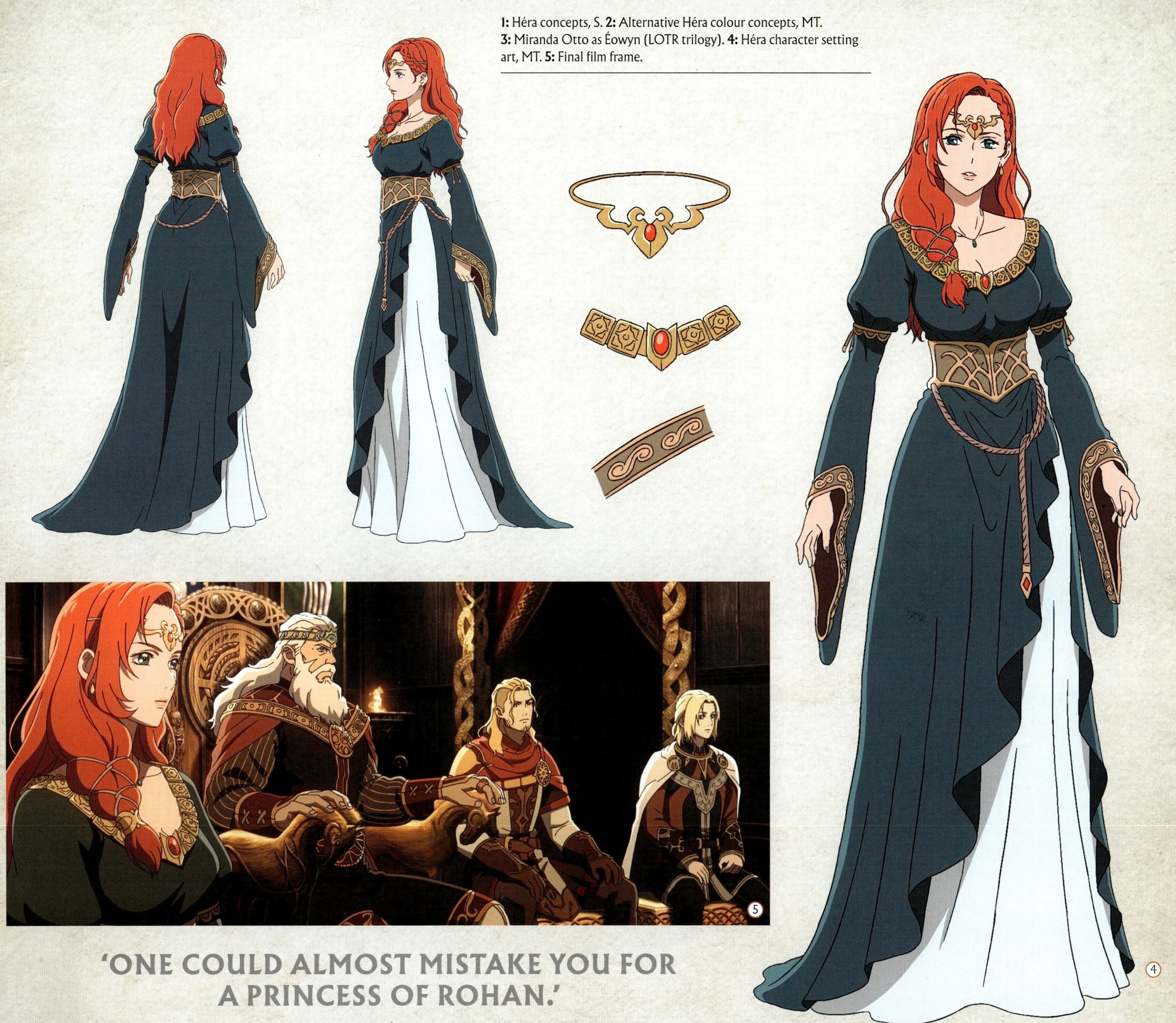

'ONE COULD ALMOST MISTAKE YOU FOR
A PRINCESS OF ROHAN.'

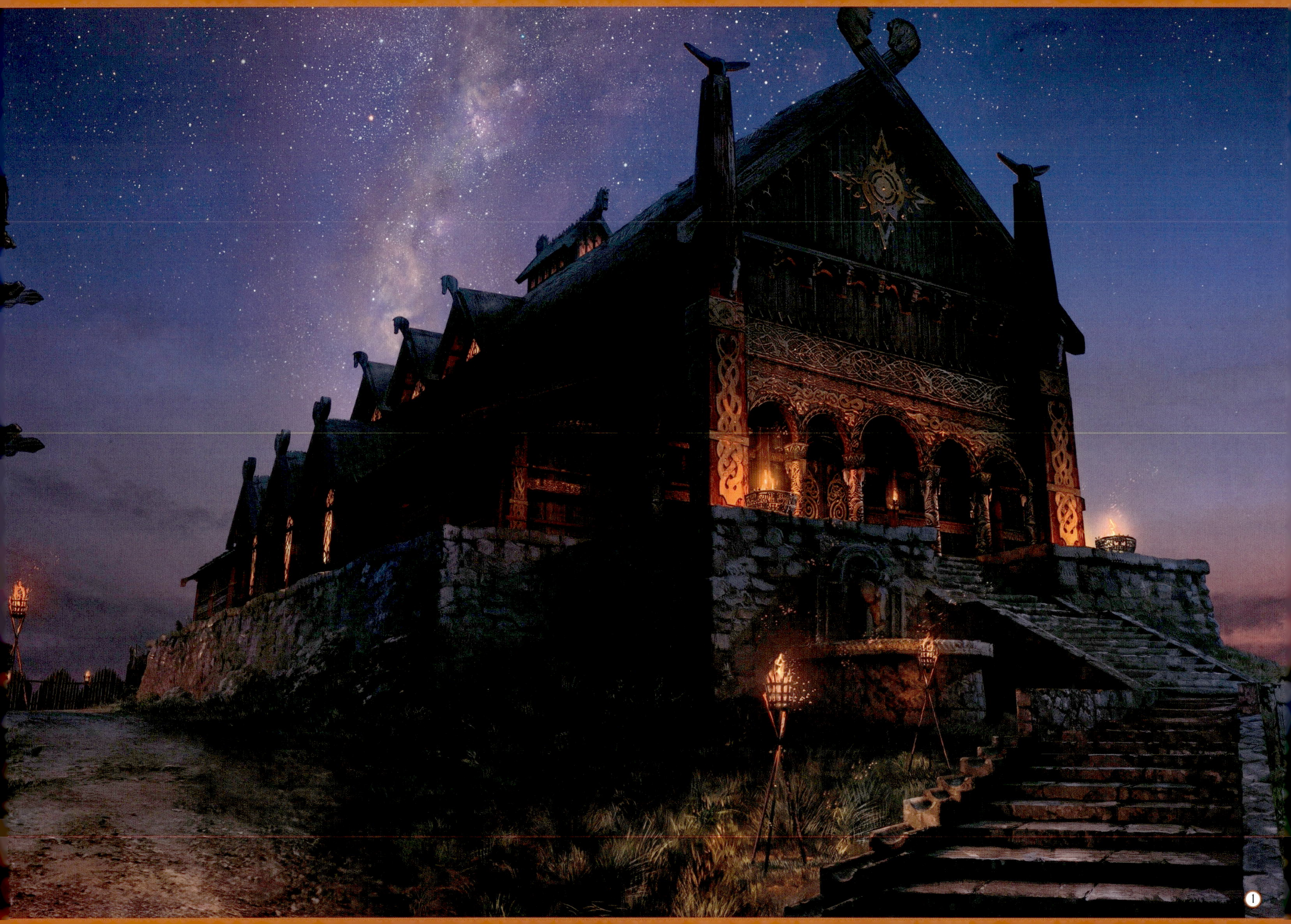

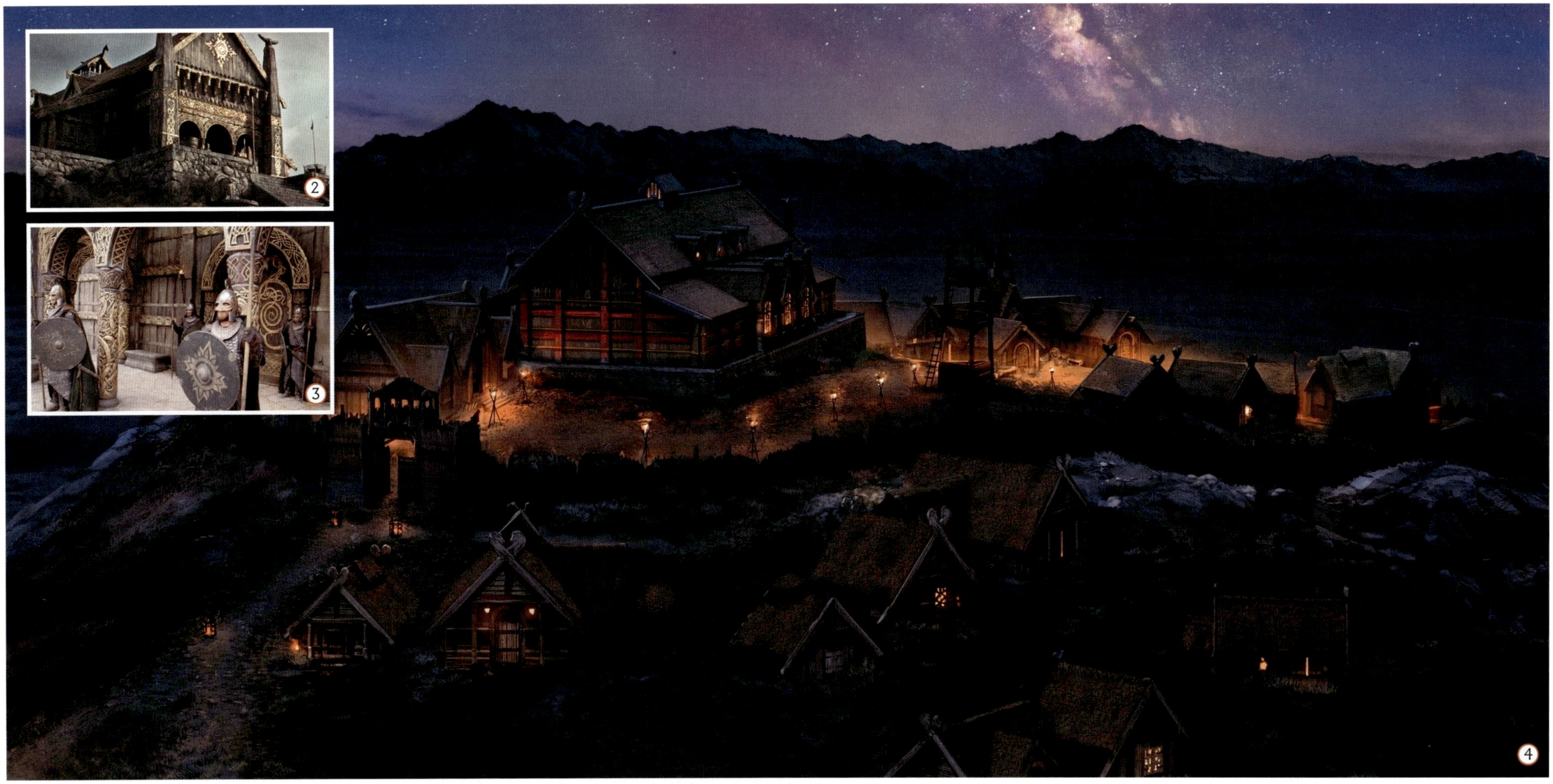

MEDUSELD

At the heart of Rohan stood the Golden Hall of Meduseld, where Helm, Ninth King of the Mark, dwelt and held court. Built by Helm's ancestor Brego, the Second King, its thatched roof and metallic decoration gleamed in the sunlight and could be seen from miles away.

The wooden buildings of Rohan are based on structures that would have existed in northern Europe during the Dark Ages. The description of Hrothgar's hall, Heorot, in the Anglo-Saxon poem Beowulf was probably as useful as Tolkien's own words in evoking the kind of place we wanted to create. When designing it for the original films, we wanted it to feel ancient and strong, bound with iron and heavily decorated. We adopted the sunburst motif as something that felt appropriate for a plains-dwelling, semi-nomadic people, and, of course, we used lots of carvings of horses on gables and gateways.
We used weighted ropes on the thatched roofs of our buildings, following examples that we'd seen on farmhouses in remote and equally windswept areas of northern Europe.
– ALAN LEE, CONCEPT ARTIST

We made our version of Meduseld a little larger than it was in the trilogy but were careful to preserve the overall impression of the hall. The stone foundation remained the same size, but the wooden structure was expanded. We increased the amount of decoration, and added red to the exterior pillars to look more vibrant in this time when the realm was thriving under Helm. The differences can be reconciled by the fact that Wulf burns Meduseld in our film. When later rebuilt it would not be constructed exactly the same way.

While we wanted it to seem more prosperous, we didn't want the hall to appear too shiny and new. It would still be centuries old and look like Héra and the others actually lived there.

For night scenes, the director thought it would enhance the splendour of the scene if the hall was set against a backdrop of the beautiful starry sky with the arc of a galaxy in view. – TAMIKO KANAMORI, ART DIRECTOR

1: Meduseld background art. **2:** Final film frame (LOTR trilogy). **3:** Meduseld set (LOTR trilogy).
4: Meduseld background setting art, TK.

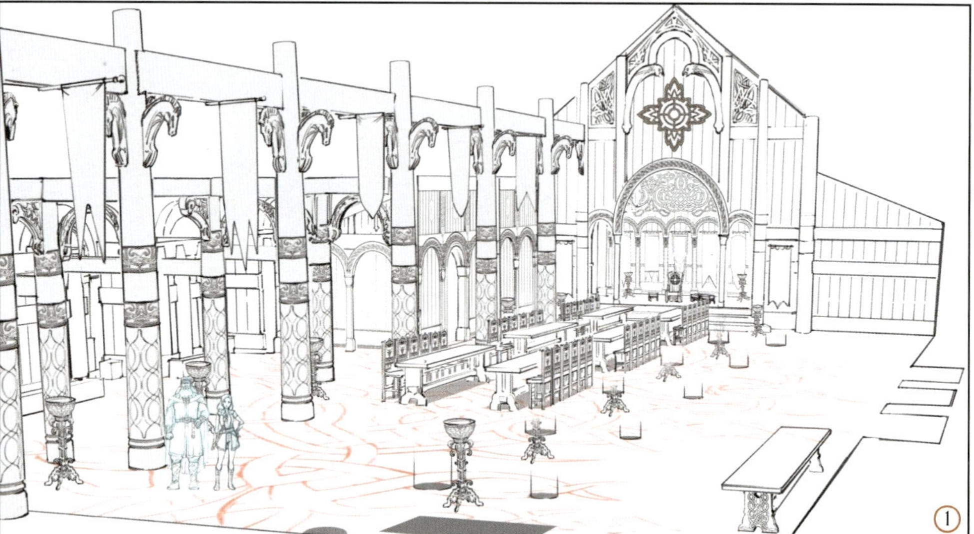

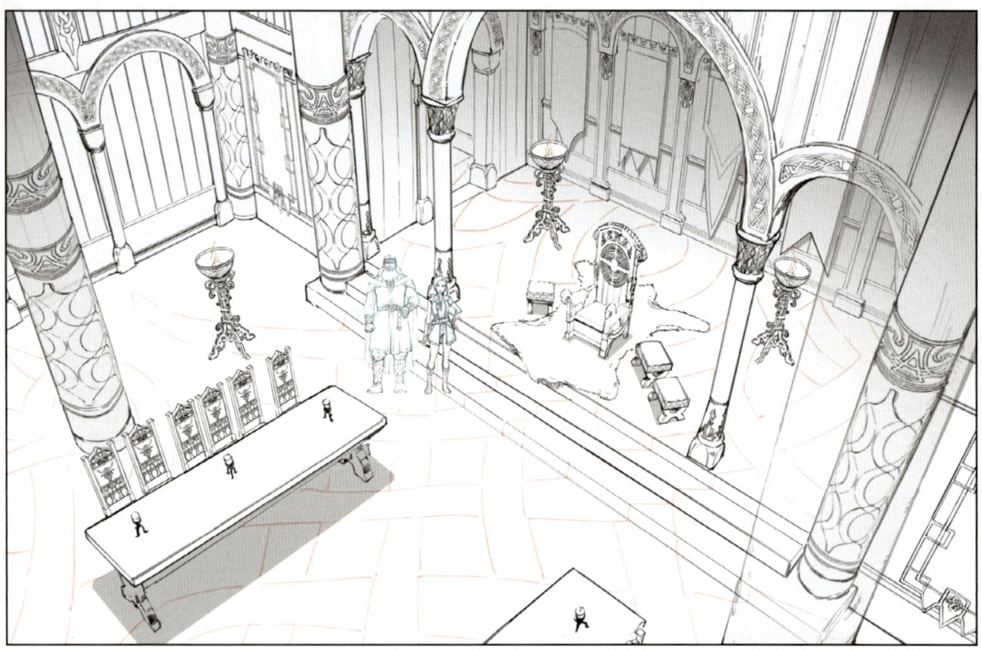

We spend the first ten to fifteen minutes of our film inside Meduseld, which is probably longer than we have spent there in any of the films without cutting away. We are seeing it at the height of Helm's power. The challenge was to make it look as ornate and colourful and beautiful as a king's castle would be, but at the same time reflecting the original design and feel of the live-action Meduseld.

We didn't see a lot of the interior in the trilogy. The camera did not take us into the shadowy recesses and corners of the hall. It was a dark, sombre place, where King Théoden had fallen into decline under Saruman's spell, and Gríma Wormtongue had clearly neglected it. This meant we had to flesh out the interior and draw the whole thing as one big location, figure out where everyone would be standing, and know what it all looked like in every direction We couldn't hide anything in darkness: that was not the character of Meduseld in this time.

We did a lot of research into the original sets and were careful to accurately recreate what was done before, but also fold in new elements that reflect the time that we're in, like the new banners. We did not want to modernize it, but we did need to peel away the patina of years of neglect seen in the trilogy, without losing the character. – JASON DEMARCO, PRODUCER

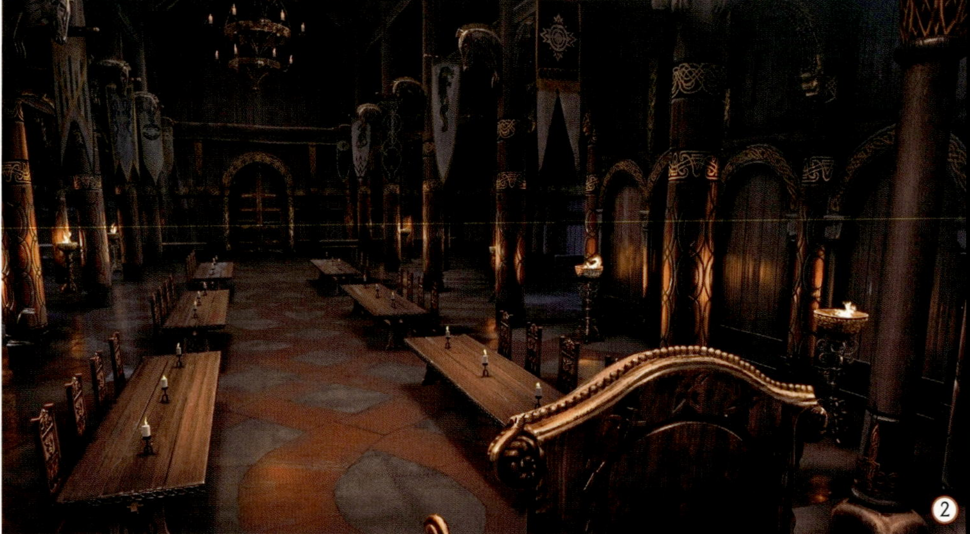

1: Meduseld interior concepts, TK. 2: Meduseld interior background setting art, TK. 3: Meduseld interior concepts (LOTR trilogy), AL. 4: Meduseld interior background art.

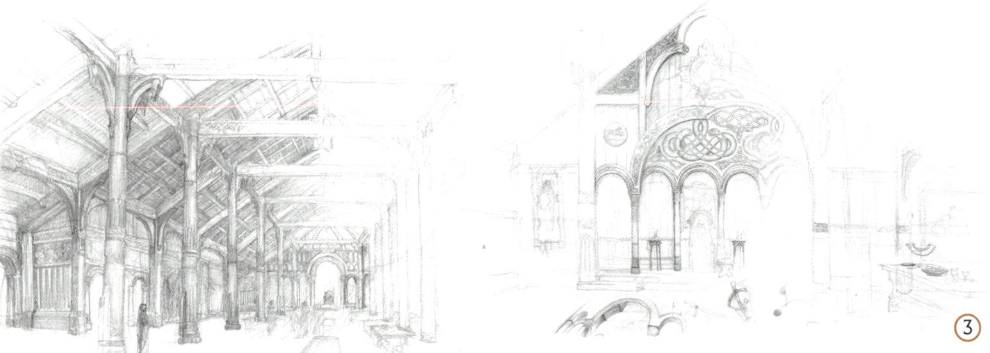

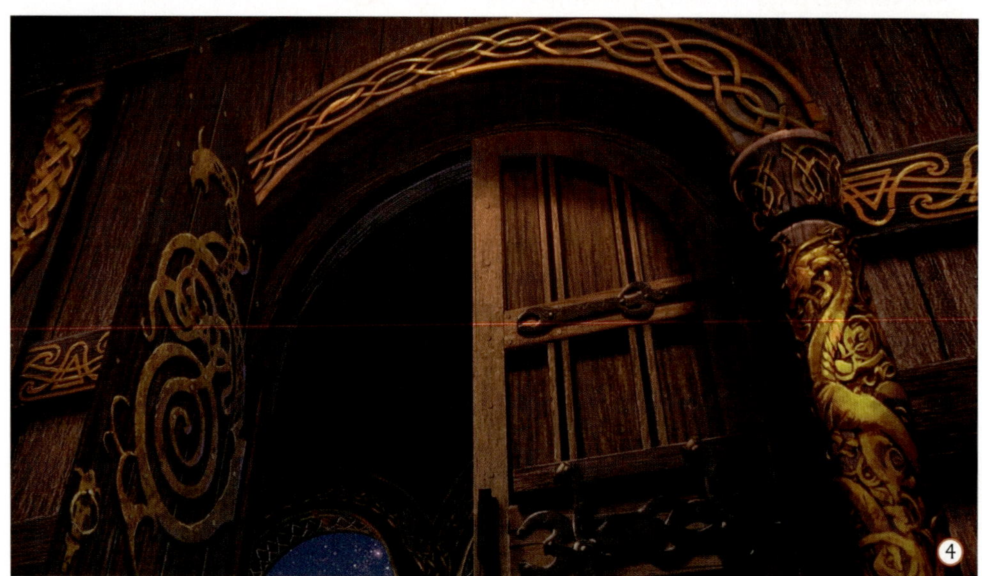

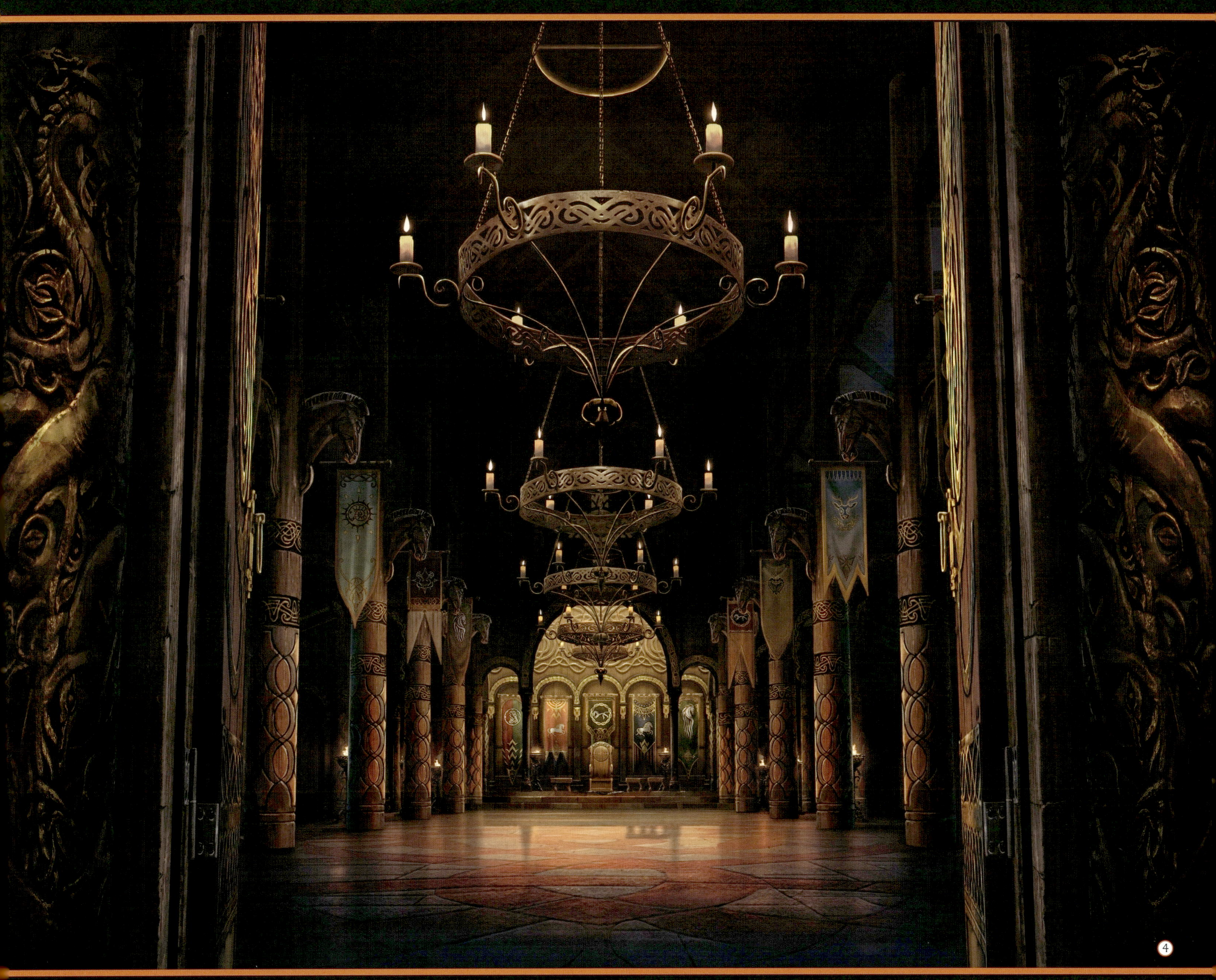

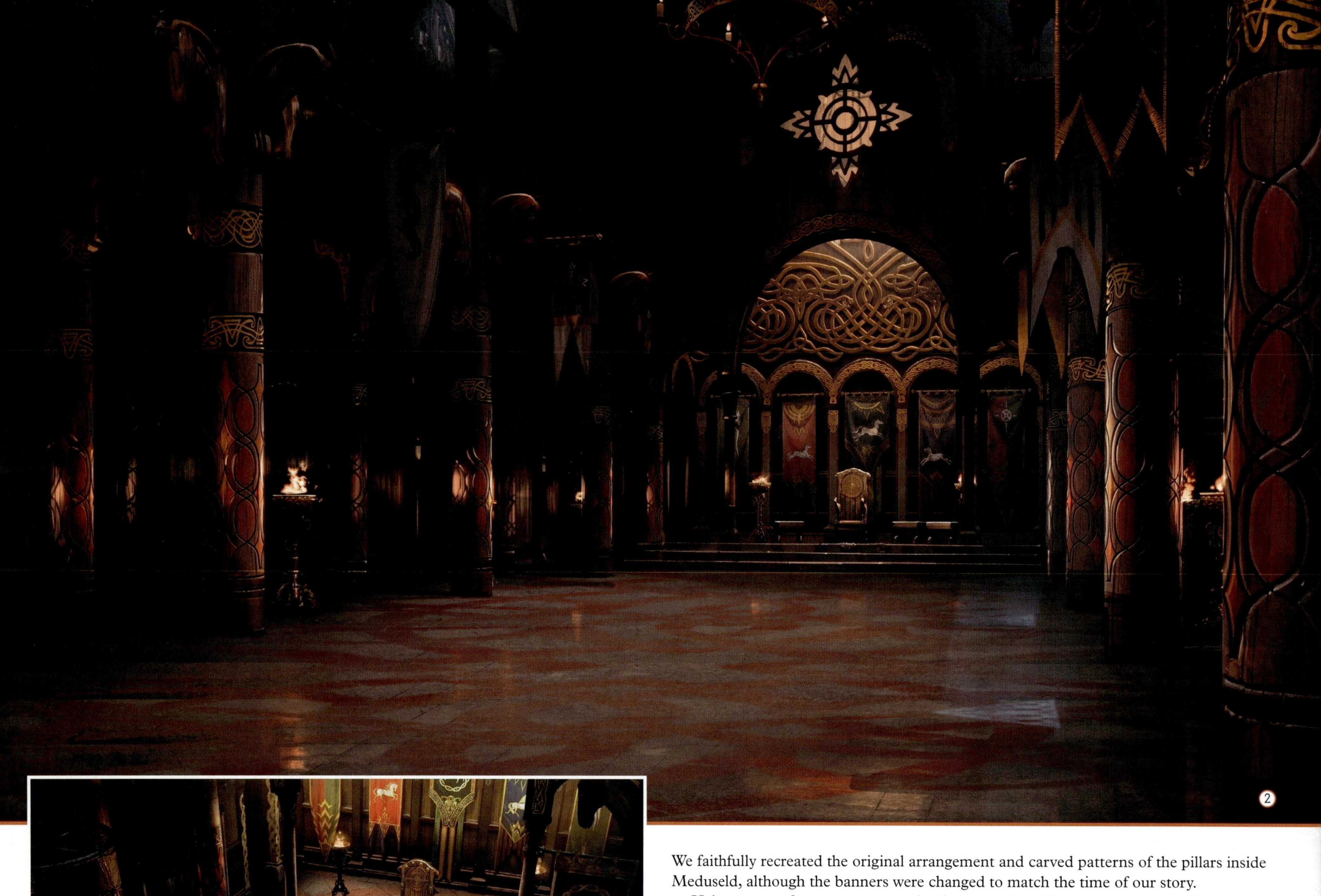

We faithfully recreated the original arrangement and carved patterns of the pillars inside Meduseld, although the banners were changed to match the time of our story.

Helm appears from a room near the throne, so the adjacent area was modified to accommodate the needs of this scene. Because it is difficult to draw the back sides of things in animation, the design of the throne's base was also changed slightly to close the gaps beneath.

We were careful to create a mood that was neither too dark nor too bright, and I lit the area where Helm and his family sat so that it was the brightest, as if they were being hit by a spotlight. – TAMIKO KANAMORI, ART DIRECTOR

1: Meduseld interior background art. **2:** Meduseld interior background setting art, TK. **3:** Final film frame.
4: Throne of Rohan concepts (LOTR trilogy), AL.

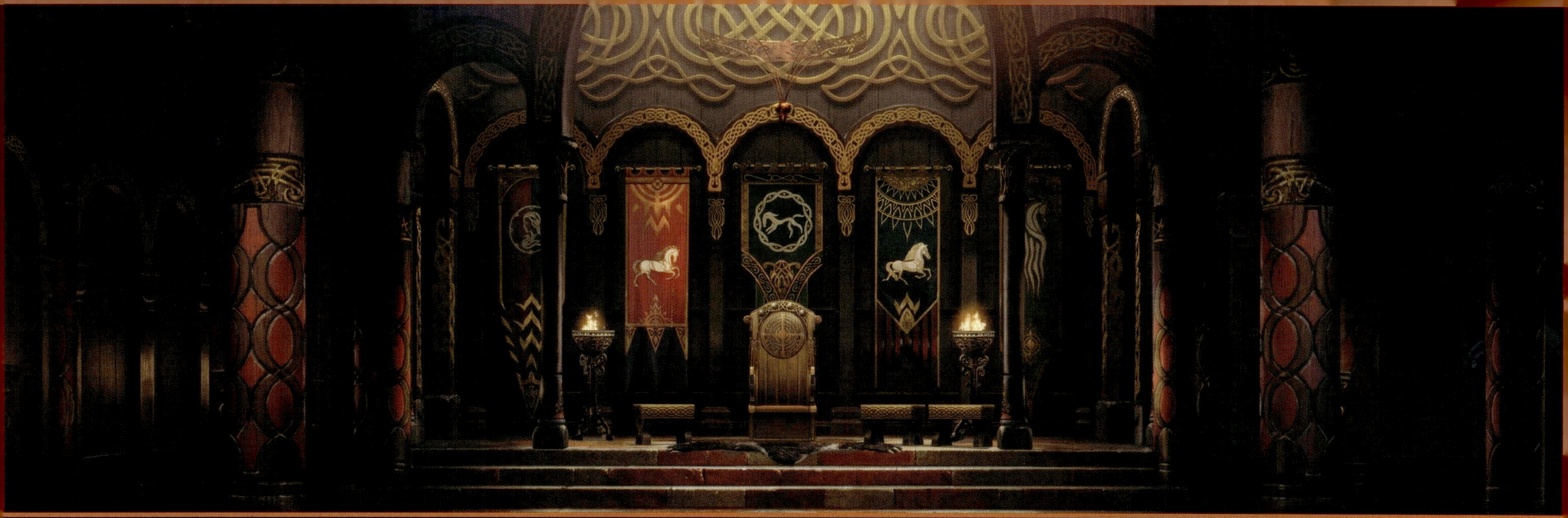

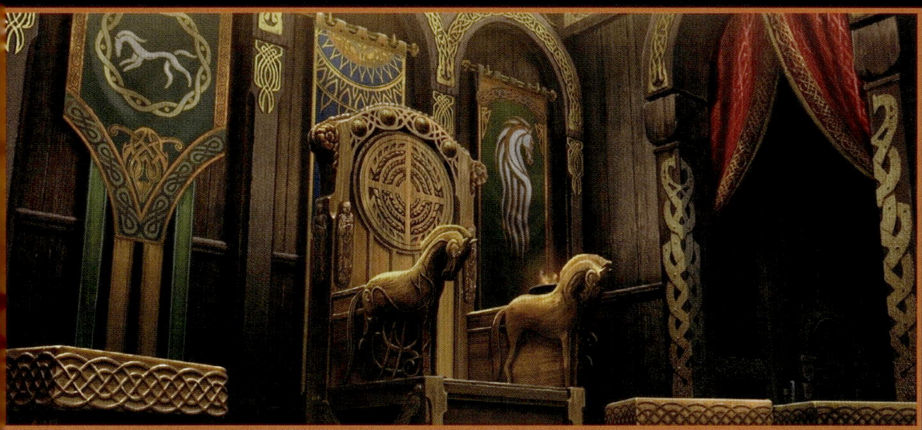

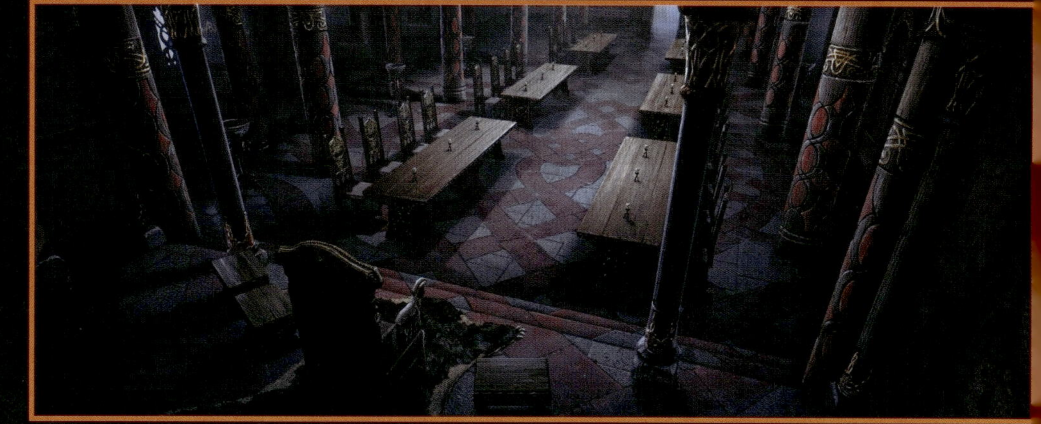

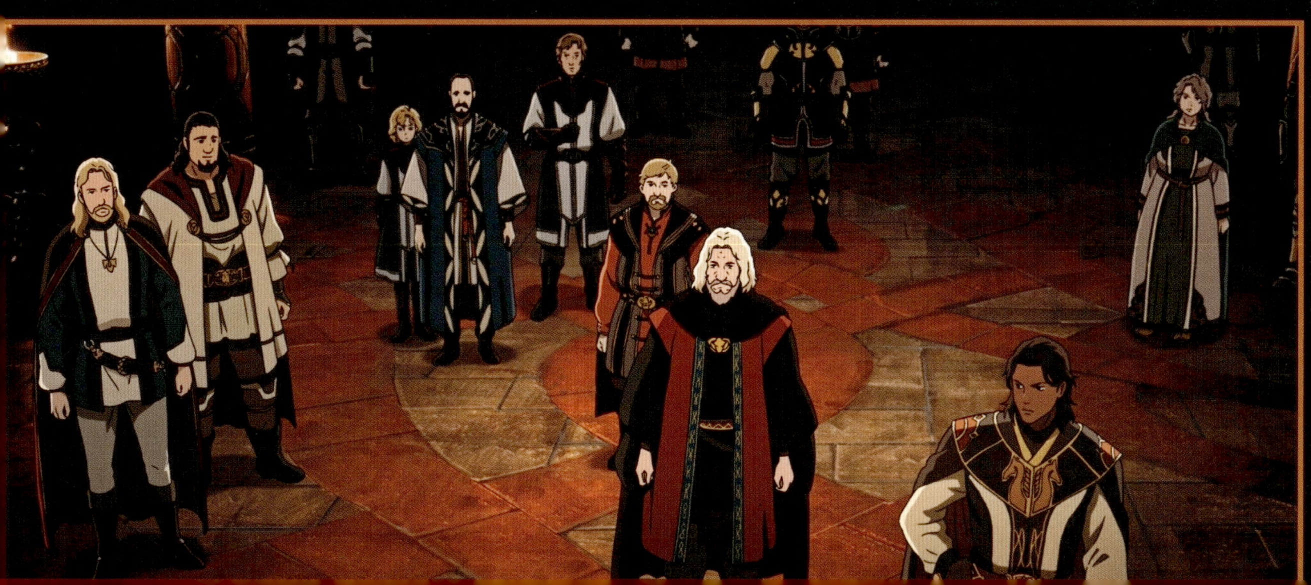

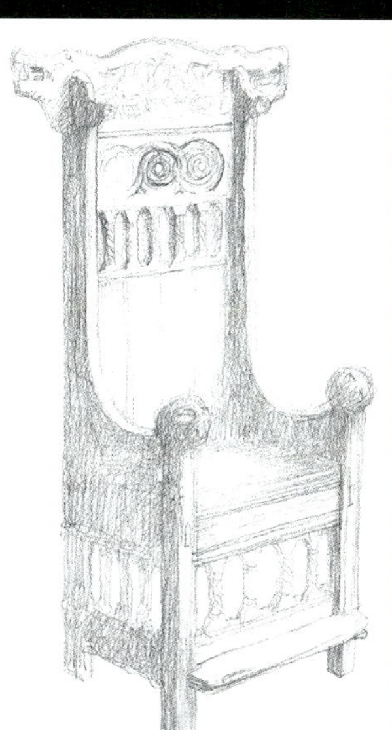

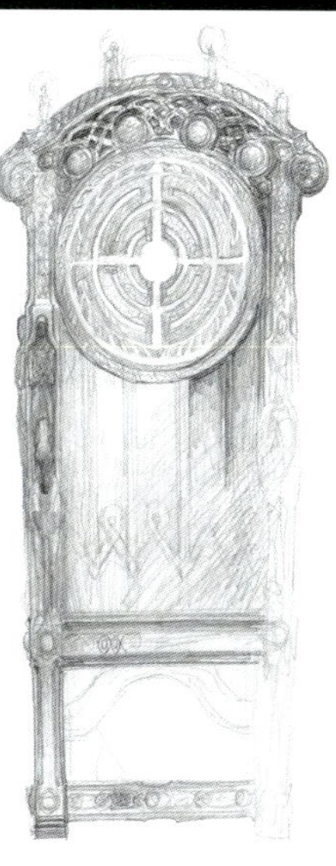

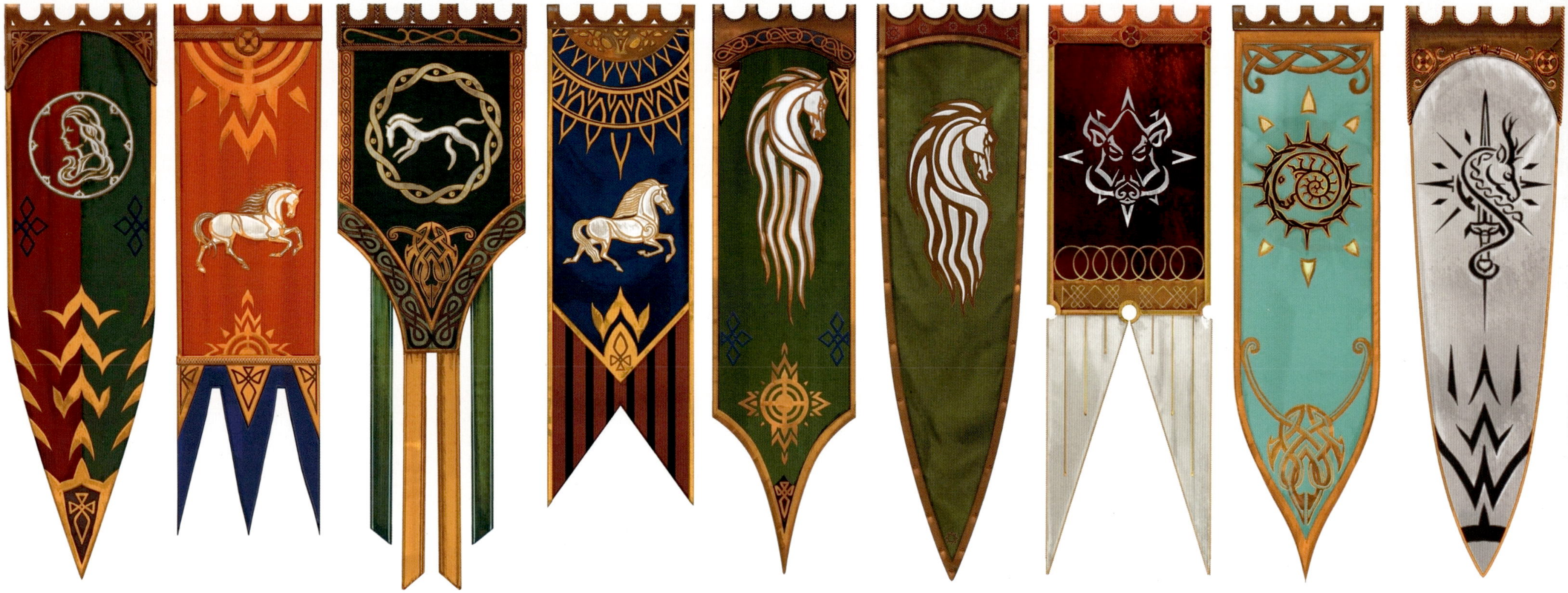

HERALDRY OF ROHAN

As we learned more about how much detail went into creating everything for *The Lord of the Rings* trilogy it was quite a revelation. There were many things that wouldn't necessarily be obvious from watching the films, but became clear as soon as you looked deeper and began to make connections. An example would be the stylized horses used throughout to reflect the relationship between the Rohirrim and their horses, or the banners and painted imagery inside Meduseld, full of references to their history that J.R.R. Tolkien had written. It was moving to find out about all the creativity, research and reverence that went into making those films.
– KENJI KAMIYAMA, DIRECTOR

The art department at 3Foot6 had decorated the interior of Meduseld with heraldic banners. Some bore different versions of the golden sun, the emblem of Rohan, and the white horse, sigil of the House of Eorl to which both Helm and Théoden belonged, but there were also other symbols. Many of these banners were recreated for *The War of the Rohirrim*, and because of the importance of heraldry to the story there was the opportunity to go back in and both add new imagery as well as assign meaning to some of the previously established livery.

For example, there were a number of stylistically distinct interpretations of the white horse. We needed to design unique heraldry for Helm and Fréaláf, both of whom were of the line of Eorl, so I suggested that we could define one particular style of white horse as representing Helm's reign, and choose one of the others to perhaps be a newer variant adopted by Fréaláf as Lord of Harrowdale.

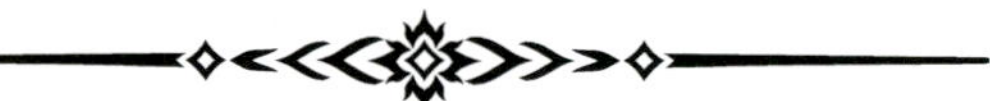

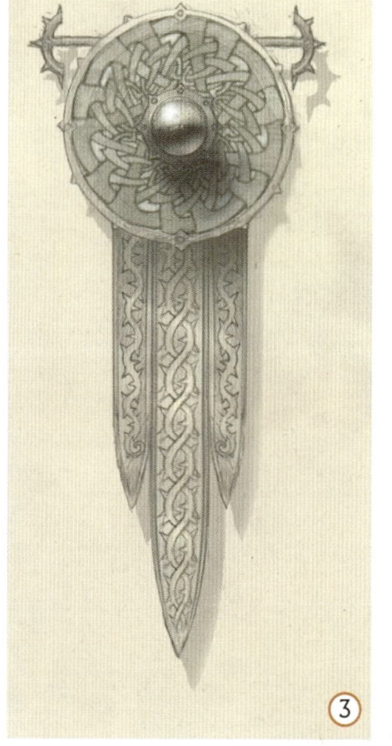

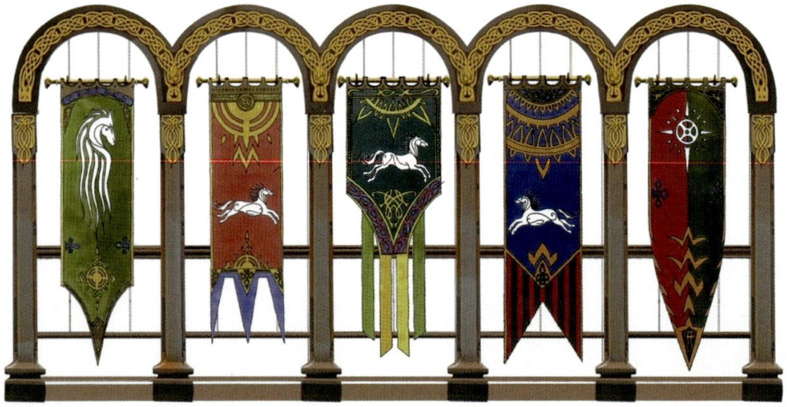

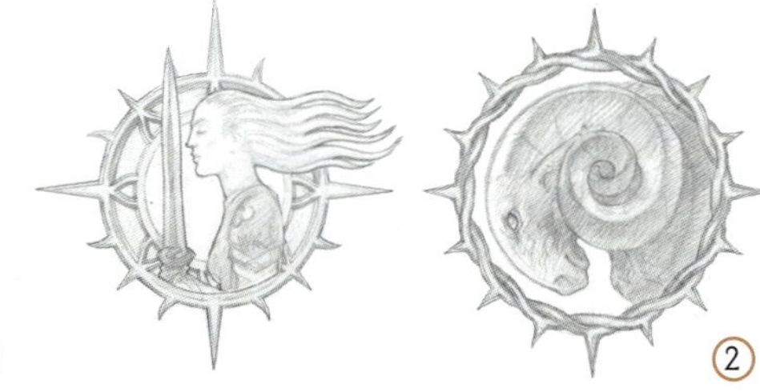

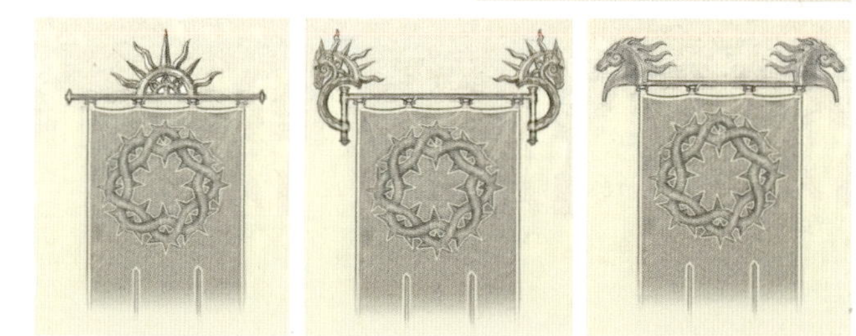

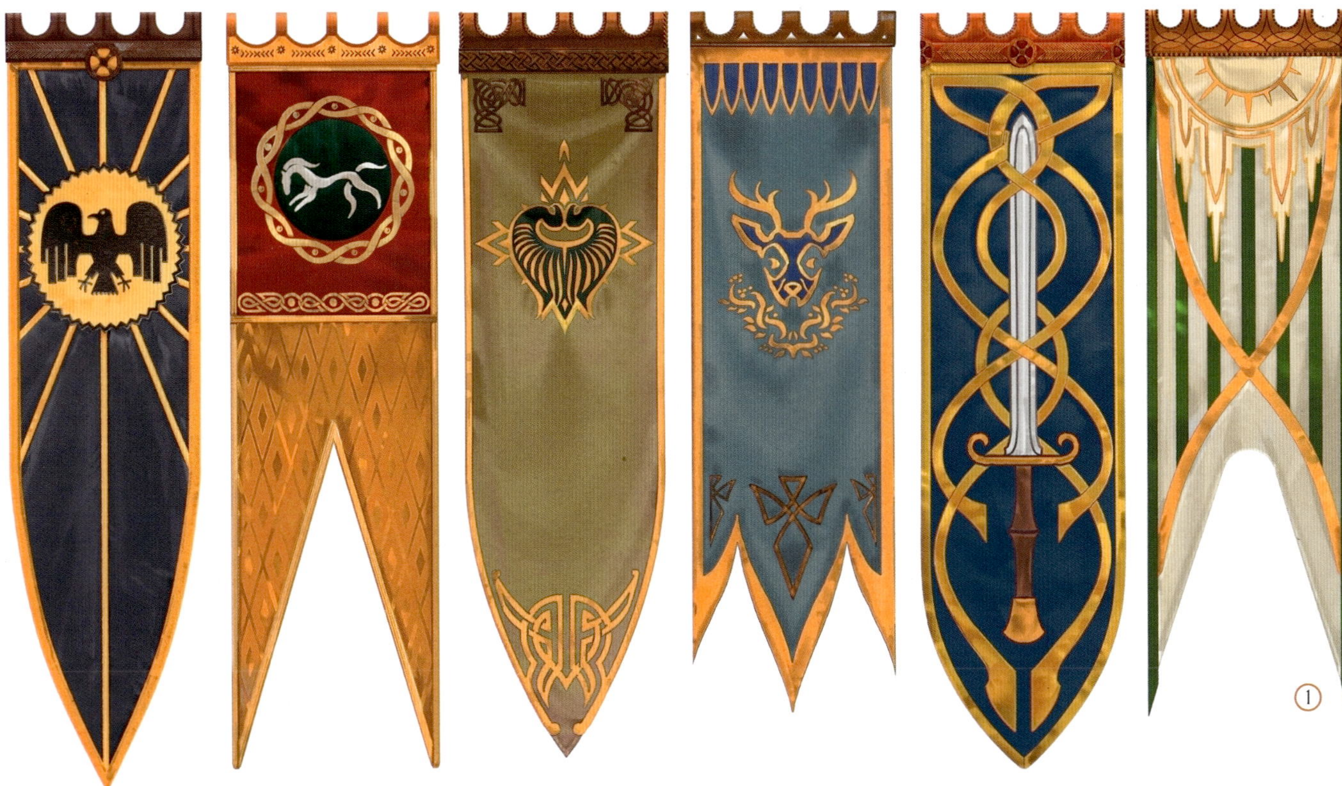

1: Meduseld banner concepts, TK.

For the other lords of Rohan who we would meet in our new film, we looked at the additional banners designed by Gareth Jensen more than twenty years ago and pulled inspiration from some of these. The director specifically asked for badge-like crests associated with animals, which the audience could quickly and easily recognize where associations existed with these characters. A crebain symbol had been designed for Freca and Wulf's household, but we needed crests for the remaining lords of Rohan and the shieldmaidens. John Howe took the lead on the shieldmaiden and Thorne designs. – DANIEL FALCONER, ADDITIONAL CONCEPTS DESIGNER

There is a Joan of Arc feel to the shieldmaiden's sigil: an almost mystical dedication to battle, not unlike entering a religious order, although, in this case, hardly a life of contemplation and silence. Thorne's seal evolved from a circle of twisted brambles to the ram's head ringed by thorns, summing up his keenness for confrontation.

Most of my suggested heraldry designs included the frames to hold the standards, which are often afterthoughts to the banners themselves. Holding to the idea of early decorative arts –interiors made of unadorned natural materials, with highly detailed artistry limited to specific features – the Rohan metalsmiths might have expressed here some of their finest work. – JOHN HOWE, CONCEPTUAL DESIGNER

Lords Pryme and Fryght were named in the script and needed heraldry of their own, but we also needed symbols for unnamed lords, and names. I enjoyed the opportunity to suggest some for these background characters and submitted a long list, from which the filmmakers selected Everbrand and Gramhere. Of the many animalistic crest concepts offered, they chose falcon, deer and boar emblems, which also shared imagery with the sword hilts and pommels designed for those characters. – DANIEL FALCONER, ADDITIONAL CONCEPTS DESIGNER

I sketched some additional stringed instrument concepts that Rohirrim other than Háma might play. These were reminiscent of both the *psalterion* and African instruments, where the strings traverse holes pierced in the skin stretched over a hollowed-out base. – JOHN HOWE, CONCEPTUAL DESIGNER

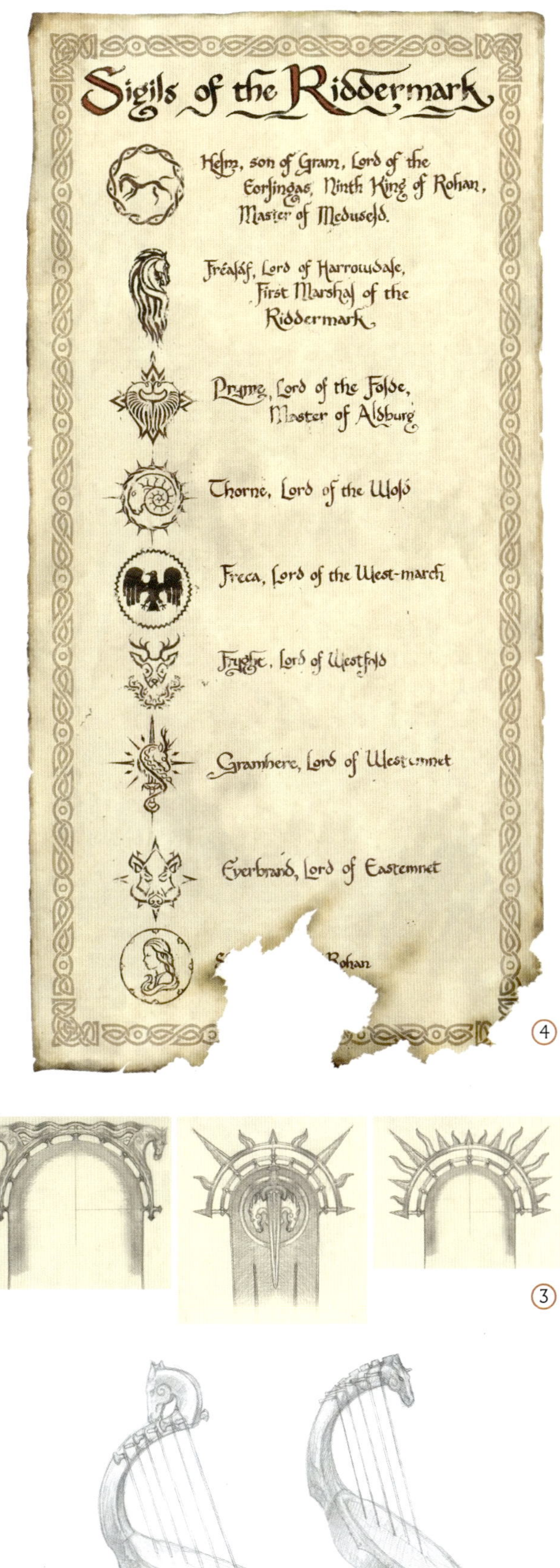

Sigils of the Riddermark

Helm, son of Gram, Lord of the Eorlingas, Ninth King of Rohan, Master of Meduseld.

Fréaláf, Lord of Harrowdale, First Marshal of the Riddermark

Pryme, Lord of the Folde, Master of Aldburg

Thorne, Lord of the Wold

Freca, Lord of the West-march

Fryght, Lord of Westfold

Gramhere, Lord of Westemnet

Everbrand, Lord of Eastemnet

[...] Rohan

4

1: Meduseld banner concepts, TK. 2: Lord Thorne and Shieldmaiden sigil concepts, JH. 3: Rohirrim banner and standard concepts, JH. 4: Lief's scroll, DF. 5: Lyre concepts, JH.

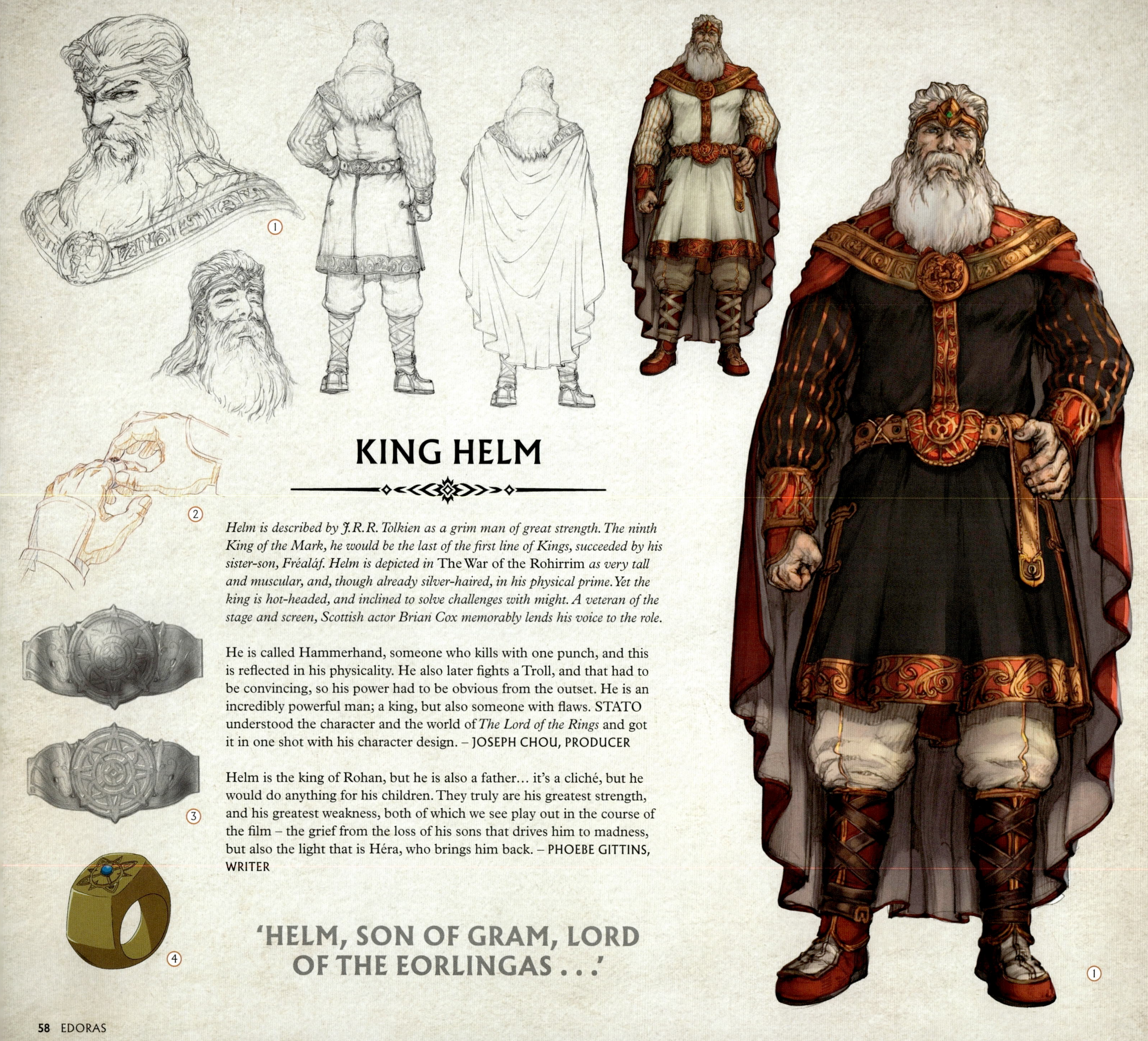

KING HELM

—◆—◆—◆—

Helm is described by J.R.R. Tolkien as a grim man of great strength. The ninth King of the Mark, he would be the last of the first line of Kings, succeeded by his sister-son, Fréaláf. Helm is depicted in The War of the Rohirrim *as very tall and muscular, and, though already silver-haired, in his physical prime. Yet the king is hot-headed, and inclined to solve challenges with might. A veteran of the stage and screen, Scottish actor Brian Cox memorably lends his voice to the role.*

He is called Hammerhand, someone who kills with one punch, and this is reflected in his physicality. He also later fights a Troll, and that had to be convincing, so his power had to be obvious from the outset. He is an incredibly powerful man; a king, but also someone with flaws. STATO understood the character and the world of *The Lord of the Rings* and got it in one shot with his character design. – JOSEPH CHOU, PRODUCER

Helm is the king of Rohan, but he is also a father… it's a cliché, but he would do anything for his children. They truly are his greatest strength, and his greatest weakness, both of which we see play out in the course of the film – the grief from the loss of his sons that drives him to madness, but also the light that is Héra, who brings him back. – PHOEBE GITTINS, WRITER

'HELM, SON OF GRAM, LORD OF THE EORLINGAS . . .'

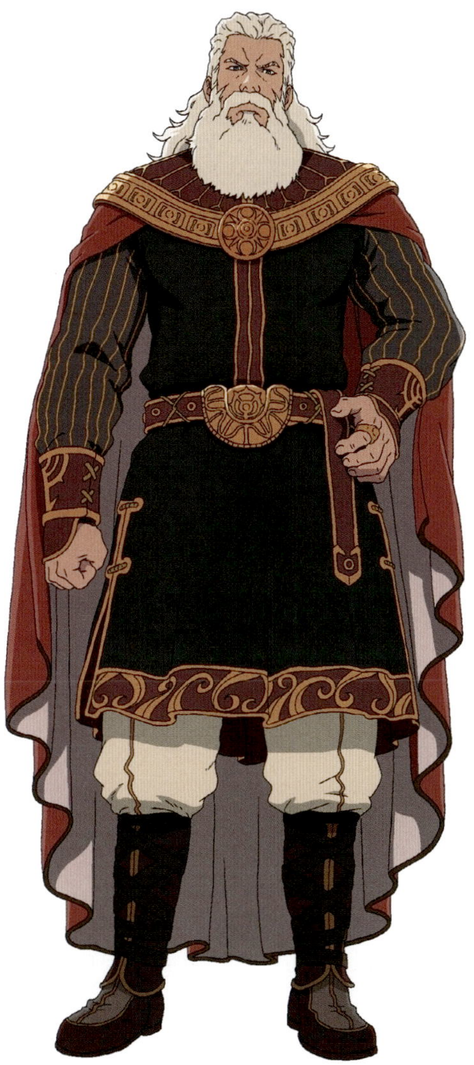

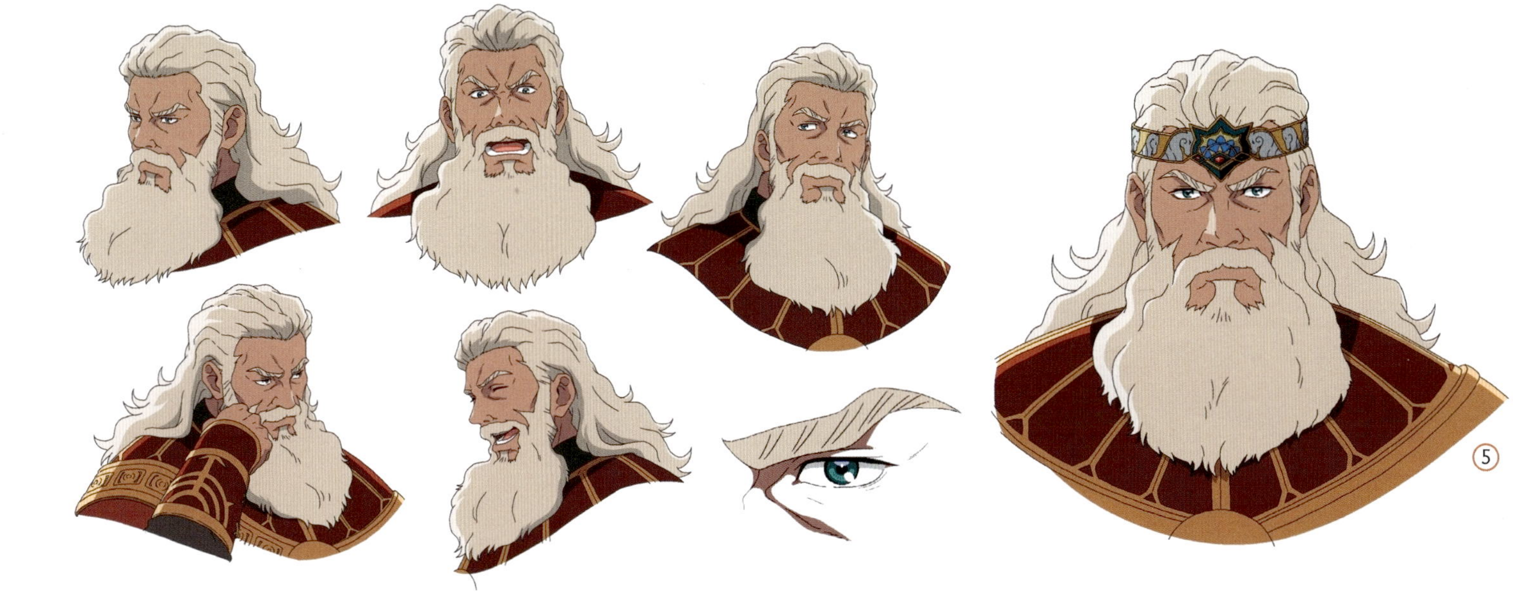

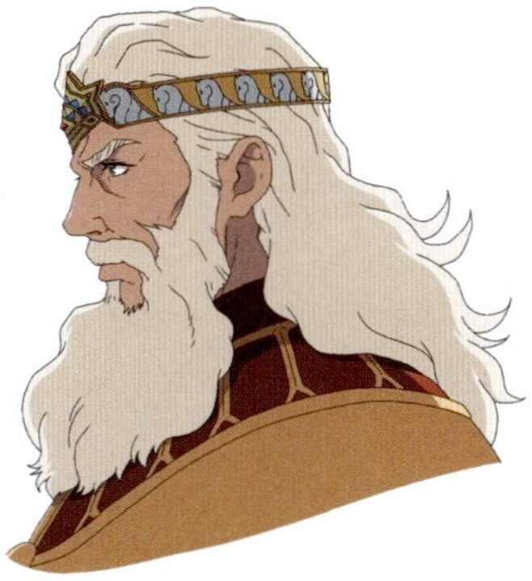

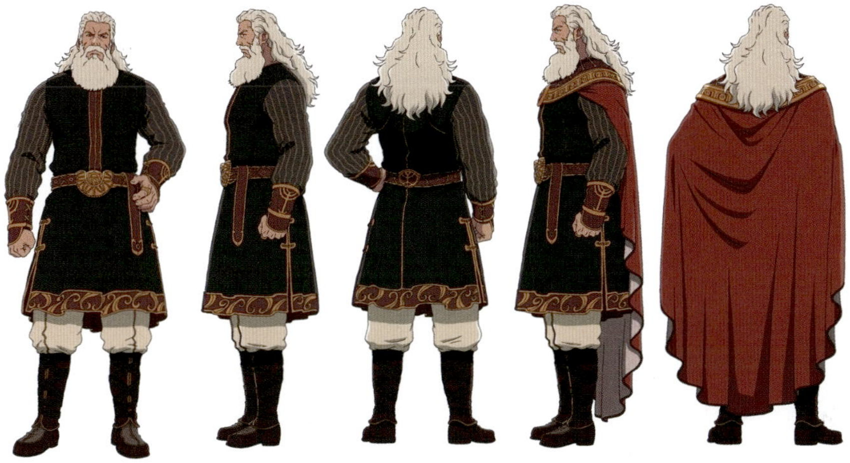

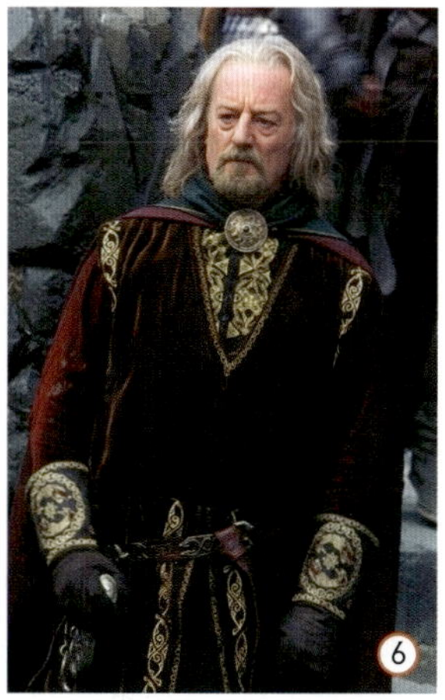

I had initially imagined Helm dressed in white but the director rightly opted for a darker costume as a light colour would have given him a somewhat softer impression. – STATO, ORIGINAL CHARACTER DESIGNER

In the process of refining his design, I think Helm became even more aggressive looking. The impression I had of him while drawing was of a dignified and powerful person, but also a bit scary. I was conscious of creating a certain air of unapproachability about him and keeping him unfamiliar.

We also took care with his facial expressions that his sternness was never eroded, and that, regardless of his expression, he never appeared too weak. – MIYAKO TAKASU, ANIMATION CHARACTER DESIGNER & KEY ANIMATION SUPERVISOR

I proposed a fairly traditional design for Helm's signet ring, featuring a full sun motif flanked by equine profiles. The full sun, as opposed to the rising sun often seen in Rohan heraldry, symbolizes the bright but ultimately brief power of the king of the Rohirrim. – JOHN HOWE, CONCEPTUAL DESIGNER

1: Helm concepts, S. 2: Animation key frame, MT. 3: Helm's signet ring concepts, JH. 4: Helm's signet ring prop setting art, KM. 5: Helm character and expression setting art, MT. 6: Bernard Hill as King Théoden (LOTR trilogy). 7: Final film frame.

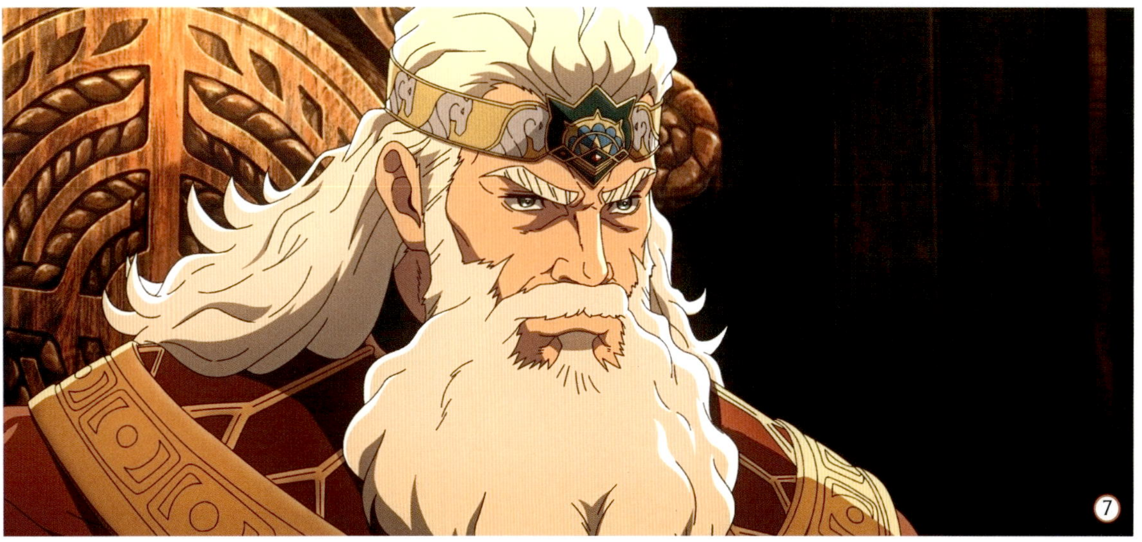

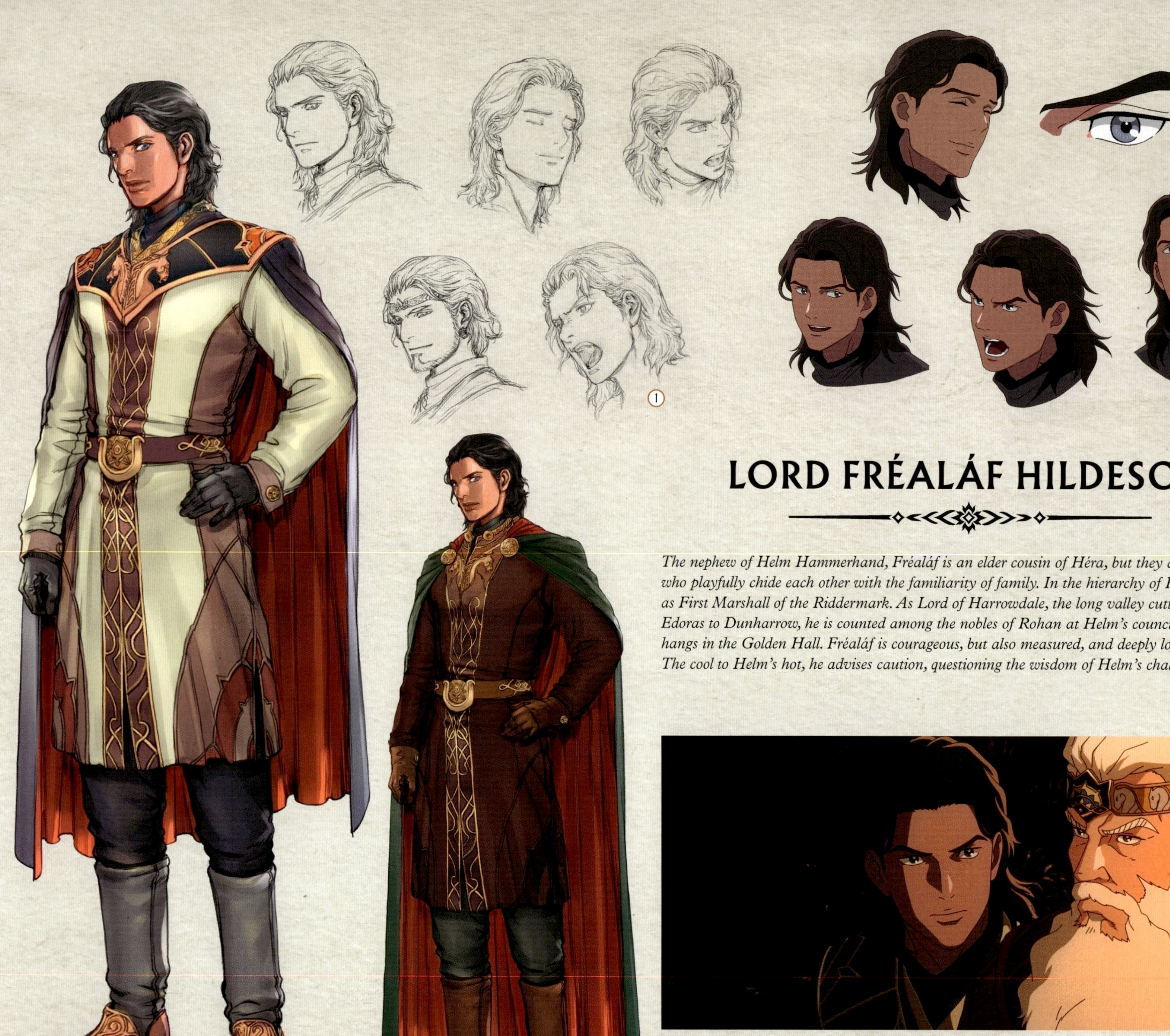

LORD FRÉALÁF HILDESON

The nephew of Helm Hammerhand, Fréaláf is an elder cousin of Héra, but they are also friends who playfully chide each other with the familiarity of family. In the hierarchy of Rohan, he serves as First Marshall of the Riddermark. As Lord of Harrowdale, the long valley cutting south from Edoras to Dunharrow, he is counted among the nobles of Rohan at Helm's council and his banner hangs in the Golden Hall. Fréaláf is courageous, but also measured, and deeply loyal to his king. The cool to Helm's hot, he advises caution, questioning the wisdom of Helm's challenge to Freca.

'COUSIN, NO MUD, NO TWIGS
IN YOUR HAIR . . .'

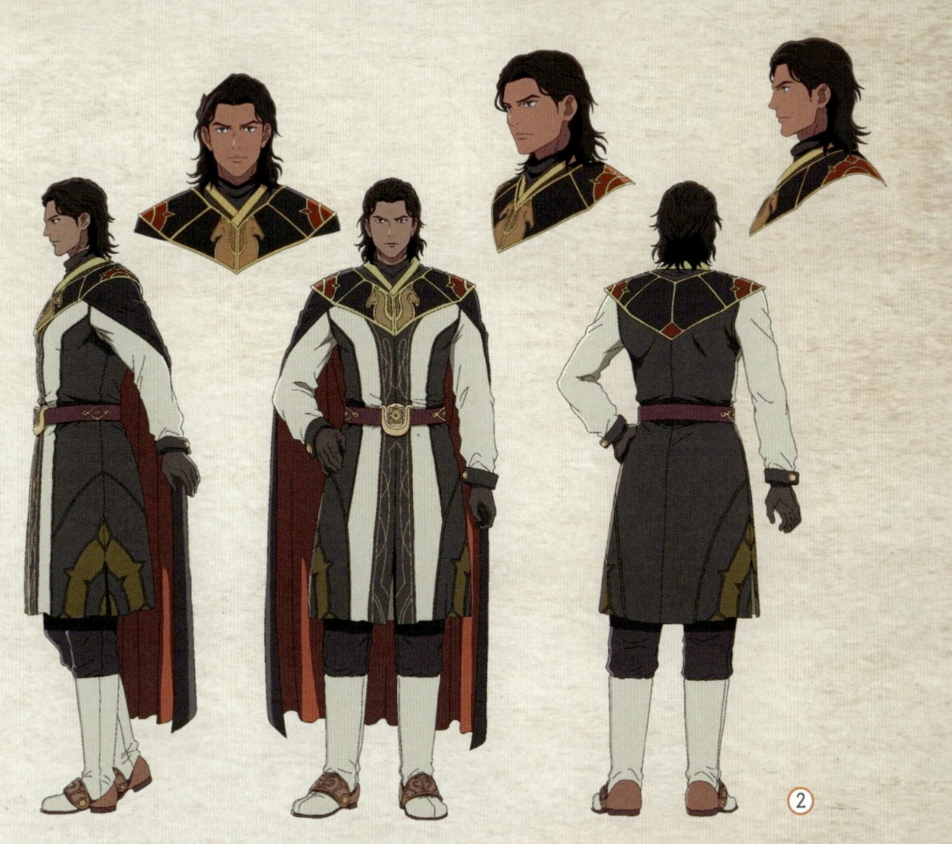

②

It is telling that Helm gives his ring to Fréaláf when he steps outside with Freca. It's a subtle signal, not only of the trust he places in his nephew, but also foreshadows Fréaláf's eventual succession.

In terms of design, we wanted to respect the lineage of the people of Rohan as defined by Tolkien. They were clearly based somewhat on the Vikings or Anglo-Saxons, but at the same time there would be some diversity of appearance within the world that our characters inhabit. Rohan does not exist in isolation: marriages happen.

It's not established in the book who Fréaláf's father was. Recognizing the close relationship between Rohan and Gondor, we liked the idea that his father might have been from the south. Perhaps he was from Dol Amroth on the coast, where the people would have been darker complexioned than the ancestors of the Rohirrim, who came from the north? Actor Lawrence Ubong Williams, who plays our Fréaláf, is also dark, so it felt like a natural fit for the character to have that heritage. It gave him a difference that we liked, showing that while he was part of Helm and Héra's family, he was also just a little bit different, with a different perspective.

Ultimately, he would have led his people to the south for safety, to the lands of his father. – PHILIPPA BOYENS, PRODUCER

Fréaláf was designed to be a visual embodiment of the concept of justice. – STATO, ORIGINAL CHARACTER DESIGNER

Fréaláf was drawn as a serious, formal person. He was usually seen with a calm expression on his face, reflecting his level-headed nature. – MIYAKO TAKASU, ANIMATION CHARACTER DESIGNER & KEY ANIMATION SUPERVISOR

1: Fréaláf concepts, S. 2: Fréaláf character and expression setting art, MT. 3: Fréaláf concept, S & DF. 4: Final film frame.

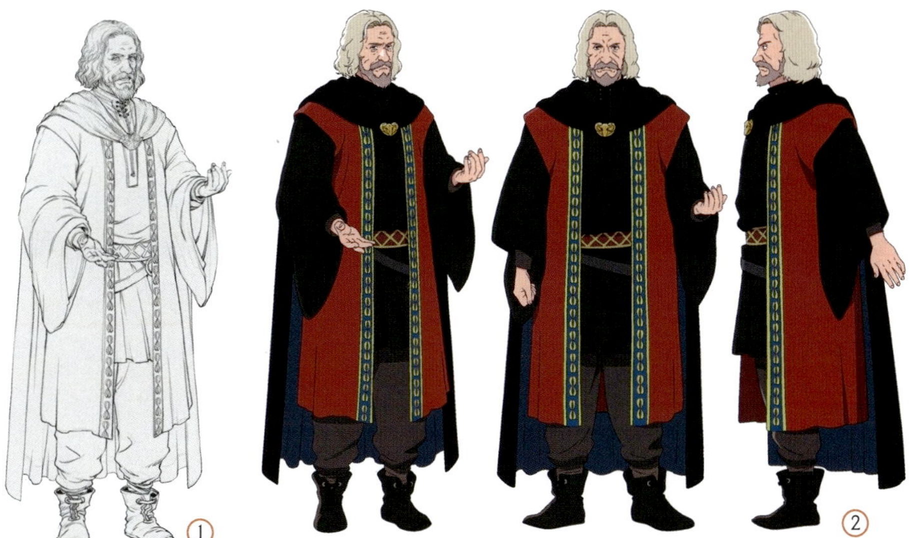

① ②

LORD THORNE

'Thorne' is an old English name, and its meaning is quite literal. – PHILIPPA BOYENS, PRODUCER

The story called for a Wormtongue-type of character, and in Thorne we find someone solely motivated by greed: he sells out Helm to fuel his desire for more. – ARTY PAPAGEORGIOU, WRITER

Freca teases early in the film that there's a turncoat when he says, 'You do not command the loyalty you think you do.' When pieced together, that's a reference to Thorne, who he has already turned. Jude Akuwudike, who plays Thorne, does a marvellous dance of toeing that villainous line without giving too much away. – PHOEBE GITTINS, WRITER

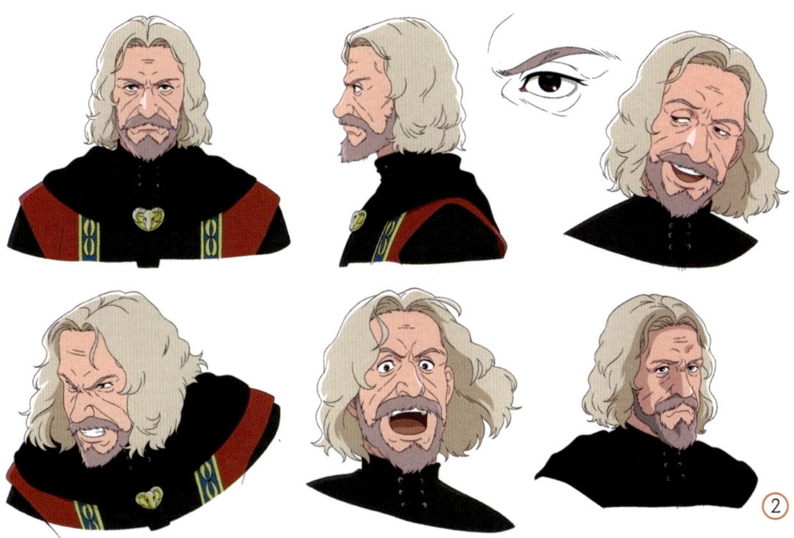

②

1: Thorne concept, S. 2: Thorne character and expression setting art, AT.

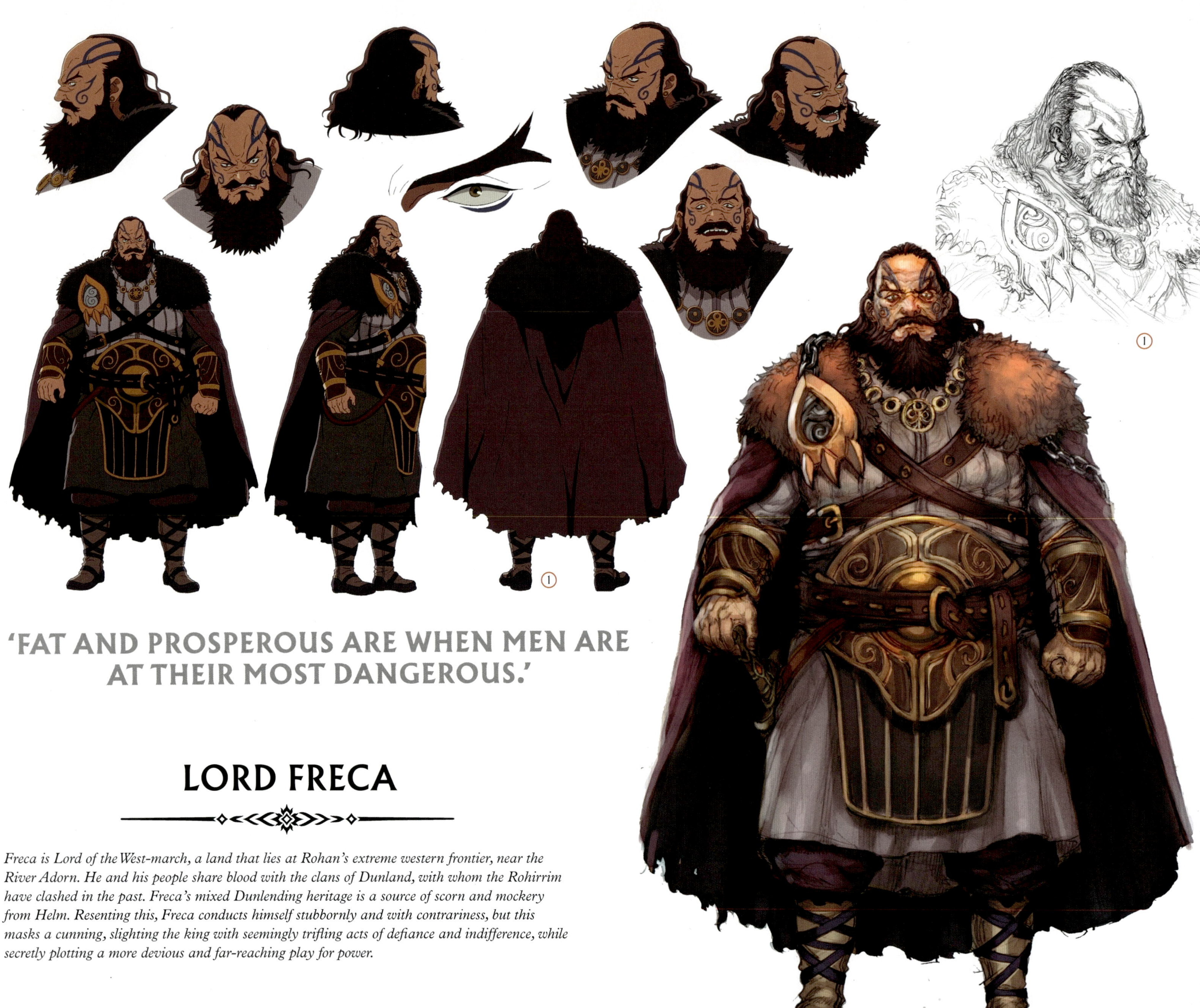

'FAT AND PROSPEROUS ARE WHEN MEN ARE
AT THEIR MOST DANGEROUS.'

LORD FRECA

—◆◆‹‹›◆›◆—

*Freca is Lord of the West-march, a land that lies at Rohan's extreme western frontier, near the
River Adorn. He and his people share blood with the clans of Dunland, with whom the Rohirrim
have clashed in the past. Freca's mixed Dunlending heritage is a source of scorn and mockery
from Helm. Resenting this, Freca conducts himself stubbornly and with contrariness, but this
masks a cunning, slighting the king with seemingly trifling acts of defiance and indifference, while
secretly plotting a more devious and far-reaching play for power.*

1: Freca character and expression setting art, MT . **2:** Freca concept, S. **3:** Final film frames. **4:** Animation key
frames, MT.

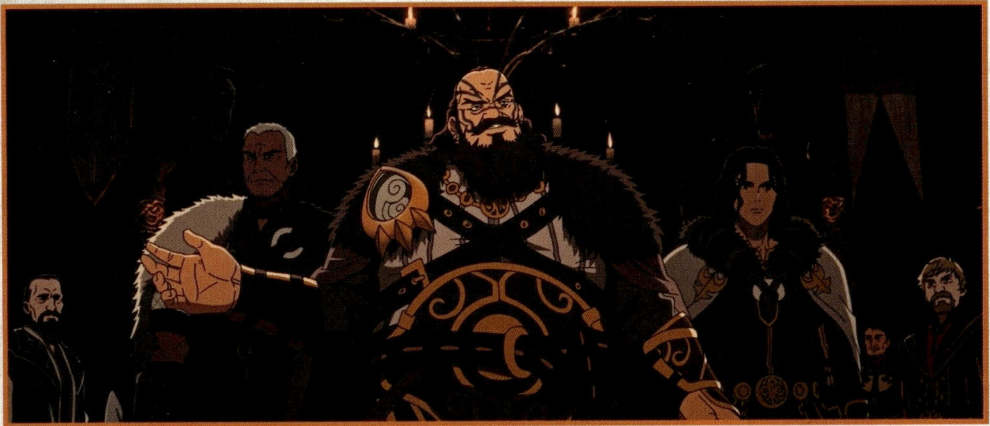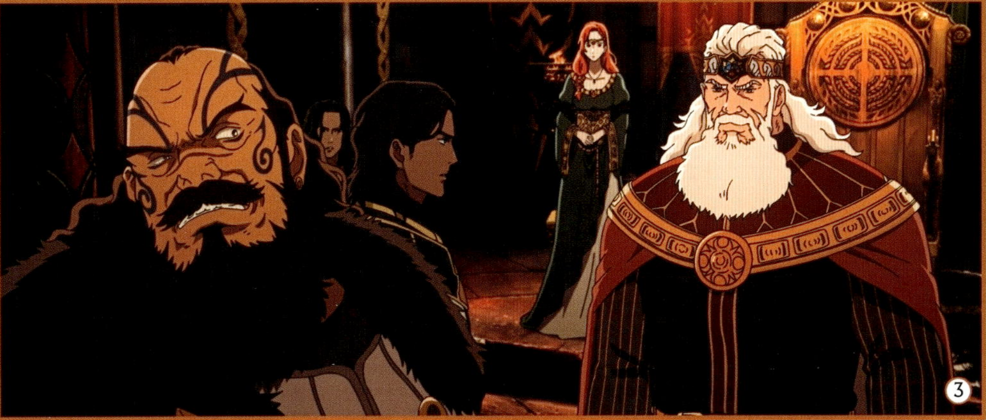

Helm is angered by Freca, but he also perceives the dark political motive behind it. We used Fréaláf here, to question the wisdom of engaging Freca in a brawl, so that Helm can explain what this proposition of marriage is really about. He knows Freca – this isn't an honest attempt at uniting peoples; it's a power-hungry move. The moment needed that weight behind it because Helm's actions ultimately lead to a death and to war. It was a challenge to get that stuff right. The othering of the Dunlendings is a legitimate grievance, so it underscored how important it was to also show that Helm understood Freca's true motive and aspirations. On the surface Freca's pledge to unite their families would seem almost noble, but of course the real plan is to lay the groundwork for him to seize the throne for his son. Without that revelation of Freca's villainy, the Rohirrim could easily lose audience sympathy. – PHOEBE GITTINS, WRITER

Freca is a very insolent character and not one to be trusted. I designed his costume and the accessory on his shoulder with a bear motif. He also has a tattoo on his face, which visually connects him to the Dunlendings. – STATO, ORIGINAL CHARACTER DESIGNER

While he has a sense of anger at sharing the lands with the Rohirrim, who are not his culture, Freca also dresses in a way that emulates them. His pride causes him to crave acknowledgement by the royalty of Rohan as their equal. We dressed the Dunlending characters in darker hues. There are wilder elements to their garb, like fur and claws, but in Freca there are also elements of finery that he thinks make him look regal. – KENJI KAMIYAMA, DIRECTOR

Kamiyama san knew exactly what he wanted for the look of Freca and it was great. I loved how he rolled when he walked. He has such a swagger. – PHILIPPA BOYENS, PRODUCER

Helm's jabs at Freca's weight are straight out of Tolkien's text, and meant our character had to be this heavyset guy. Shaun Dooley is nowhere near as wide in the belt, but his voice fit the character like a glove. In fact, we hear Freca before we really see him and Shaun's voice effortlessly takes command of the entire hall from the moment he enters – we loved that he was able to pose a true threat, even up against the great Helm Hammerhand.

And being in the room with Shaun was honestly such a privilege, his process is fascinating to watch. He would take his time absorbing everything, talk to himself about what he was doing and then just go, and the result was always amazing! – PHOEBE GITTINS, WRITER

In one of the most important scenes early in the film, this character's particular expressiveness is something to behold. We generally adopted more subdued, realistic facial expressions for the characters throughout the film, but Freca was one of the exceptions. He has a heightened, sarcastic way about him, and I feel it turned out very well. I think he's one of the more fascinating characters. – MIYAKO TAKASU, ANIMATION CHARACTER DESIGNER & KEY ANIMATION SUPERVISOR

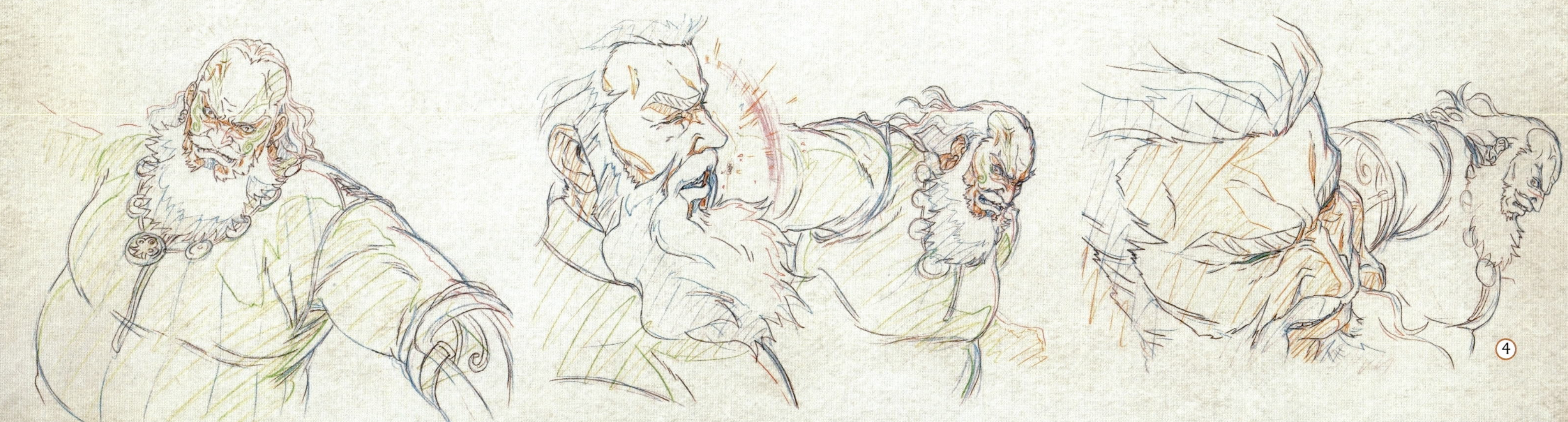

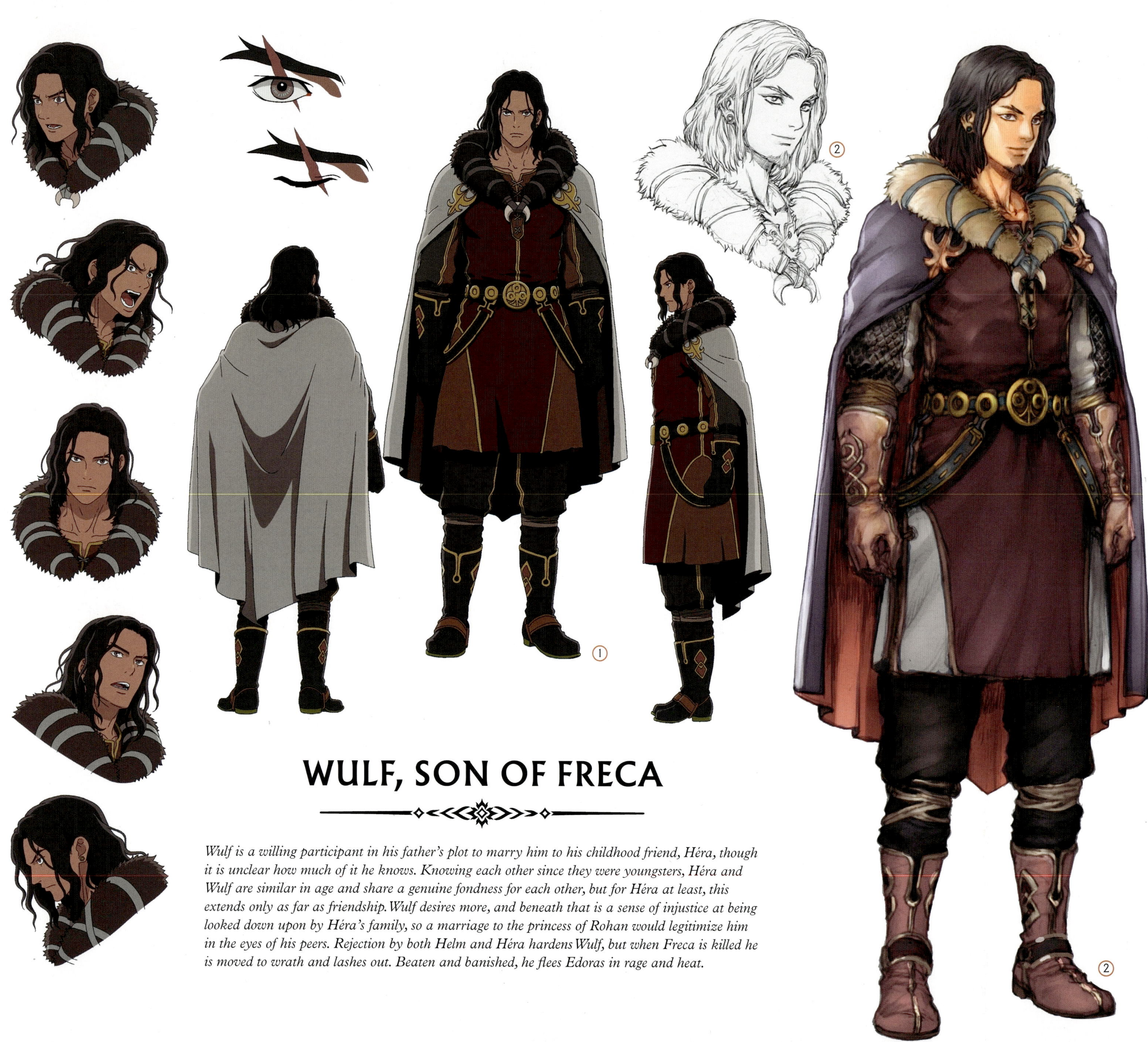

WULF, SON OF FRECA

Wulf is a willing participant in his father's plot to marry him to his childhood friend, Héra, though it is unclear how much of it he knows. Knowing each other since they were youngsters, Héra and Wulf are similar in age and share a genuine fondness for each other, but for Héra at least, this extends only as far as friendship. Wulf desires more, and beneath that is a sense of injustice at being looked down upon by Héra's family, so a marriage to the princess of Rohan would legitimize him in the eyes of his peers. Rejection by both Helm and Héra hardens Wulf, but when Freca is killed he is moved to wrath and lashes out. Beaten and banished, he flees Edoras in rage and heat.

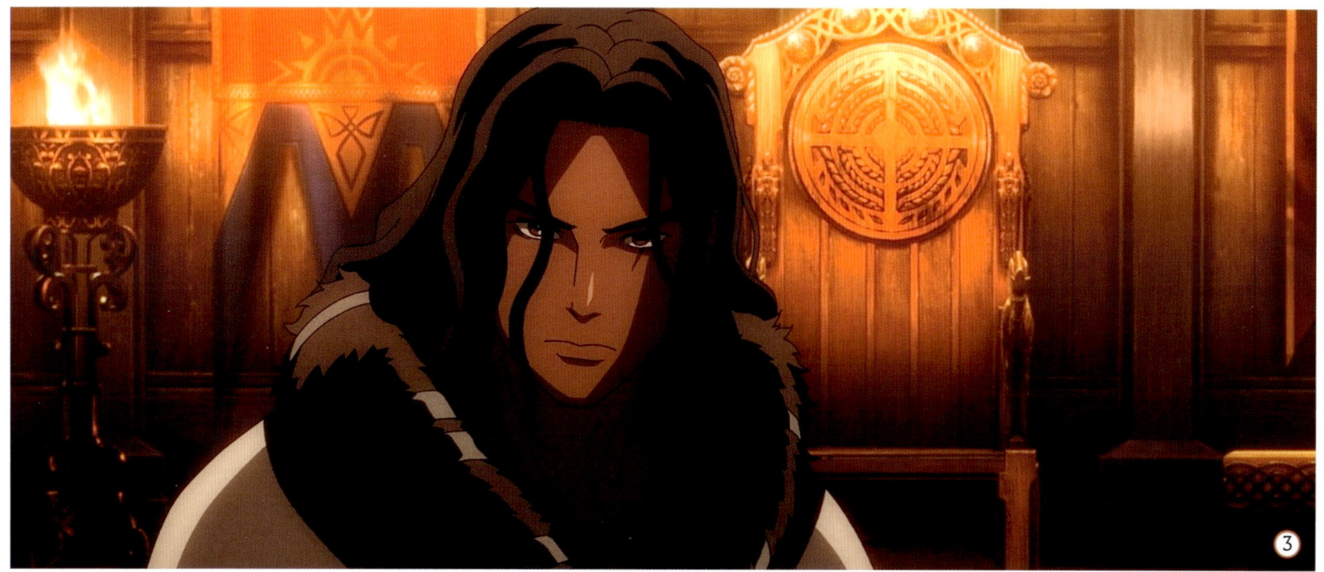

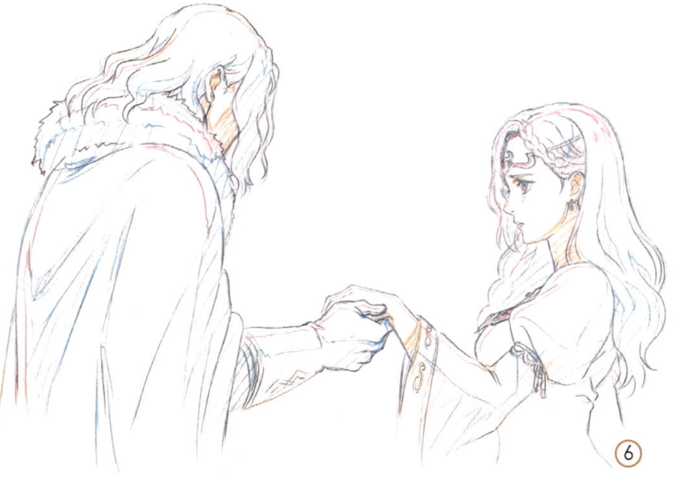

'WE WERE INSEPARABLE ONCE.'
'WE WERE CHILDREN.'

Wulf is the most complex character in the film, which also made him one of the most difficult. He couldn't be a simple villain. He goes through the most change throughout the film and it was important that there was real depth to his motivation.

We see that in Wulf's design. He begins like his father, exhibiting a certain longing for acceptance within Rohirrim court culture. He might be a Dunlending lord's son, but he presents himself in Edoras almost like a Rohan wannabe, yet with the death of his father that turns. At its simplest, he goes from being a boy who was in love with a girl to a very vengeful character, but it couldn't be that he just wanted to wage war because of the death of his father. He feels his people have been marginalized and denied and he directs that anger towards Rohan, but there is also the personal wound that he bears, which he directs at Héra. – KENJI KAMIYAMA, DIRECTOR

Wulf becomes the main villain, but after talking with the director, I also wanted him to be likable as well, especially in the beginning. The story presents him as having a twisted personality, so figuring out how to show him in an appealing light was difficult. He had good looks at the beginning, and even later there is enough of that left in him, but they are marred by his madness. – MIYAKO TAKASU, ANIMATION CHARACTER DESIGNER & KEY ANIMATION SUPERVISOR

Originally a short-sword, or a long knife, Wulf's blade eventually lengthened to be a full sword. It features an offset grip, aligned with the back of the blade, perhaps made of black horn, carved to evoke the profile of a crebain. The blade is single-edged for half its length, then double-edged to the point. The crow motif seemed to spontaneously associate itself with Wulf. – JOHN HOWE, CONCEPTUAL DESIGNER

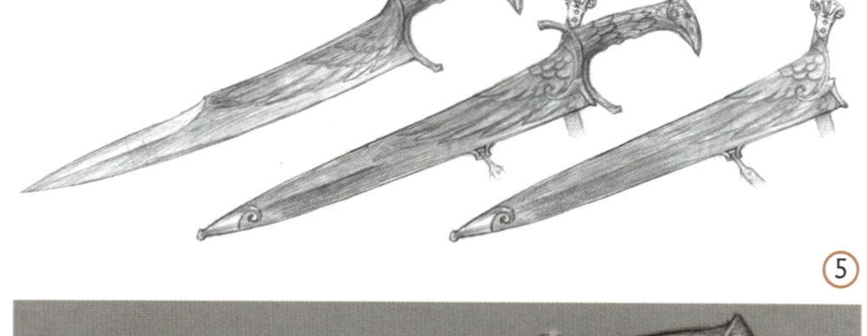

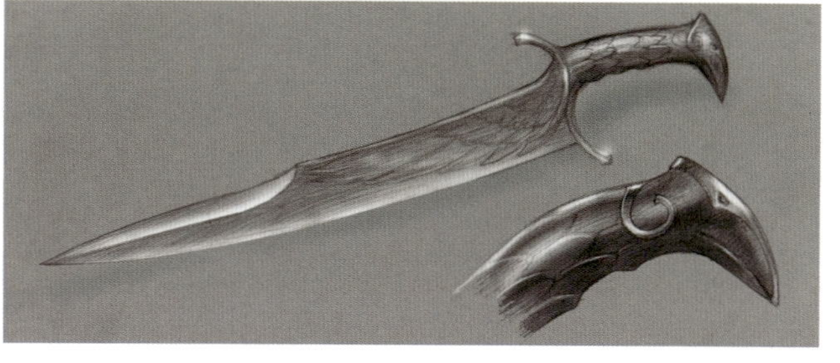

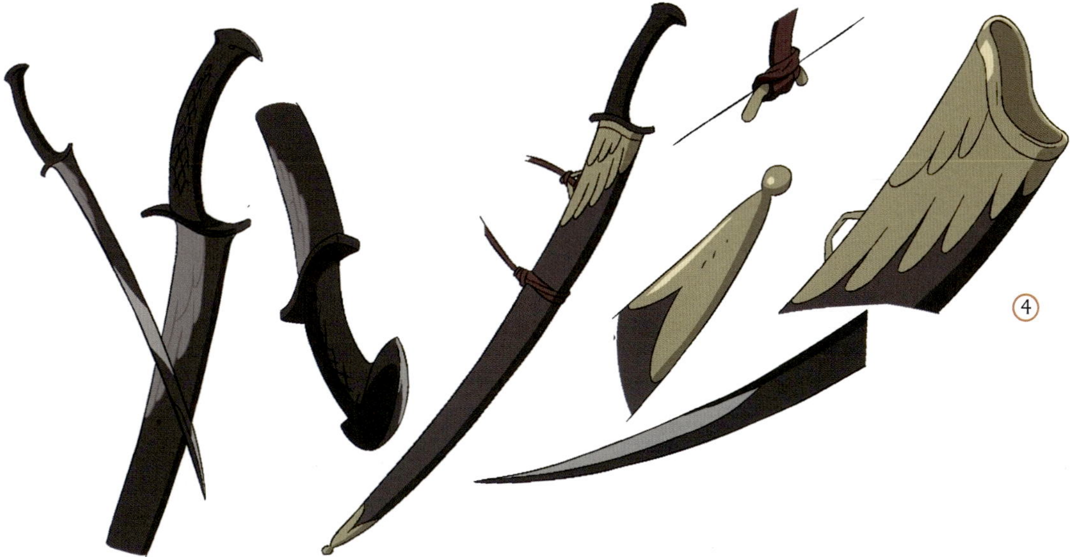

1: Wulf character and expression setting art, MT. 2: Wulf concepts, S. 3: Final film frame. 4: Wulf's sword prop setting art, KM. 5: Wulf's sword concepts, JH. 6: Animation key frame, MT.

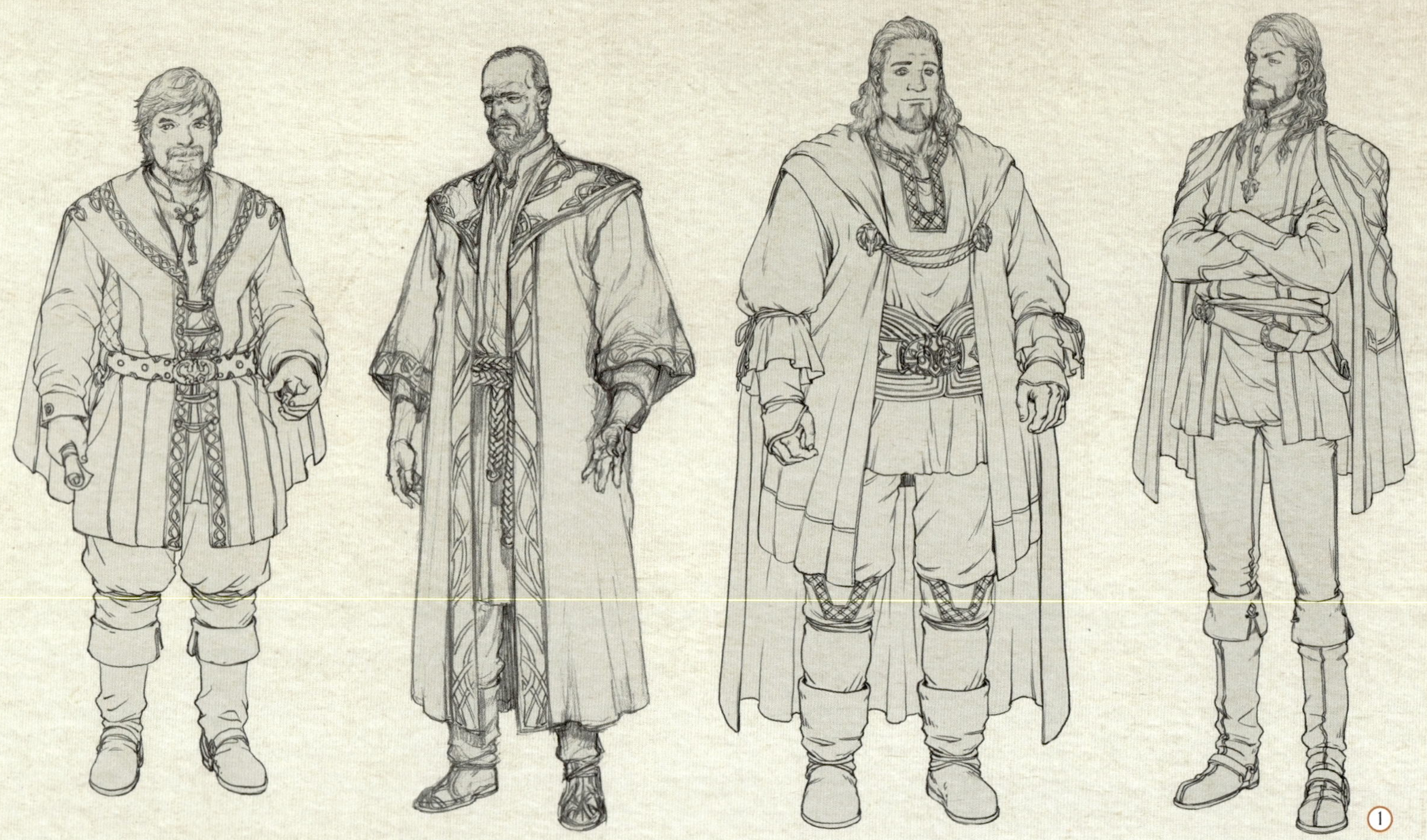

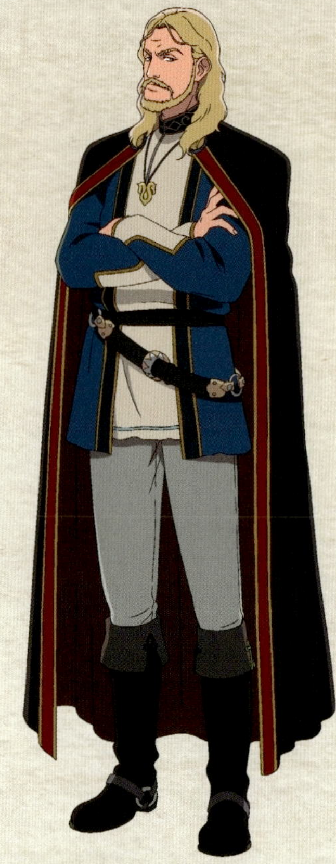

THE LORDS OF ROHAN

Fréaláf and Thorne both hold lordship over smaller fiefs within Rohan while Helm rules as king, but there are other lords as well. Each represents a different region, but all answer the call when a witan, a meeting of the lords, is convened at Meduseld. Lords Pryme and Fryght are named in the script, but all of the lords were given distinctive designs so as to be distinguishable on screen.

Unlike in Gondor, the divine right of kings does not exist in Rohan. The most powerful lord will rule. People will be loyal to that family as long as they are strong. That's why Freca calls for a *witan*, which he has every right to do. 'I thought only the king could do that?' asks Héra, to which Olwyn replies, 'That is the custom, but not the law.' – PHILIPPA BOYENS, PRODUCER

The lords of Rohan began without names, but as they became more important in the story we felt they needed them. In some cases, they are quite literal. Fryght, for example, grew from simply being referred to as 'Anxious Lord', a reflection of his character, constantly worrying about everything. – PHOEBE GITTINS, WRITER

1: Rohirrim Lord concepts (from left, Fryght, Pryme, Everbrand, Gramhere), S.
2: Rohirrim Lords character and expressions setting art, AT.

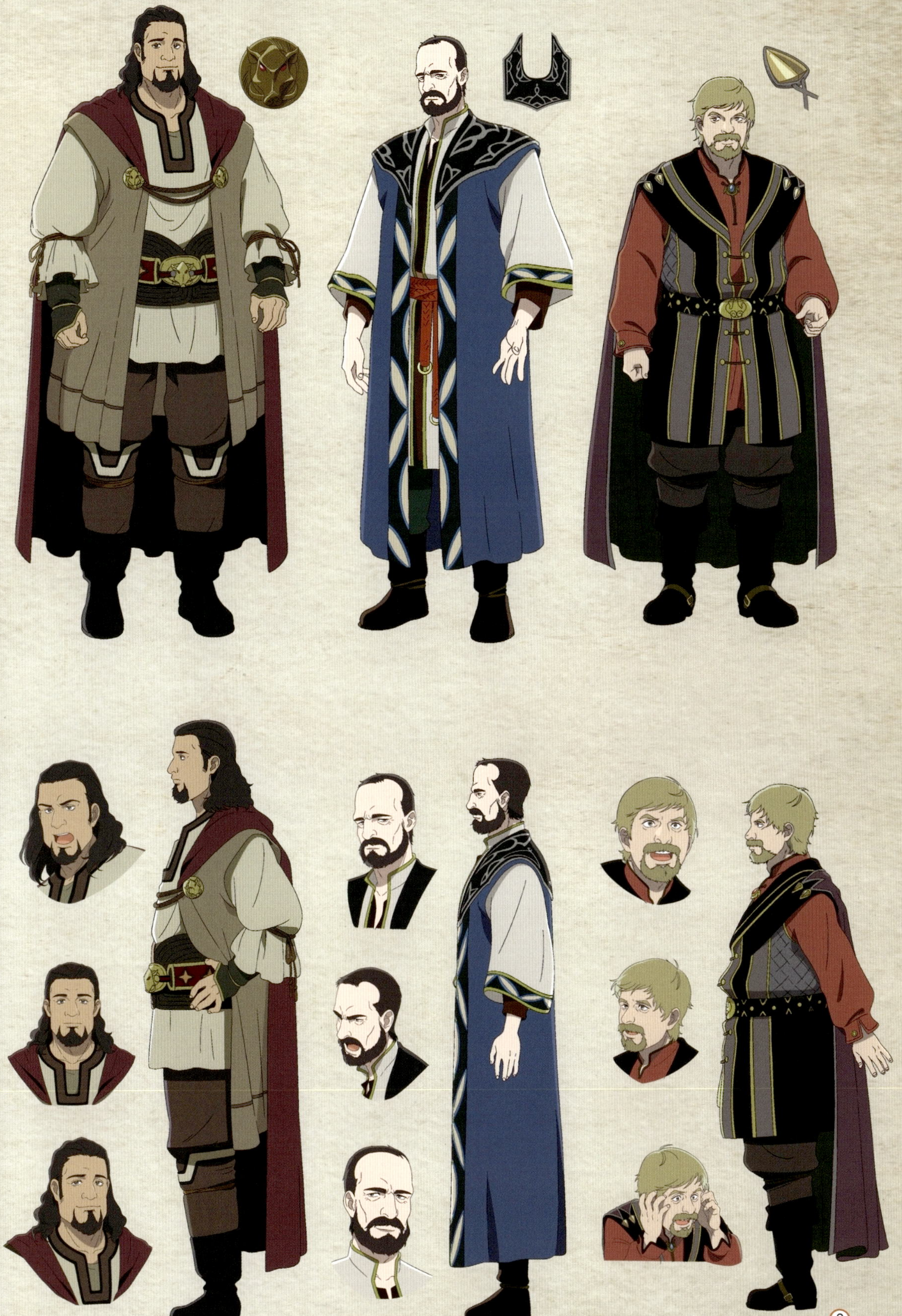

FRECA'S MEN

I loved the design of Freca's lieutenants, who eventually become Wulf's lieutenants. They were such interesting looking characters. The one-eyed guy gets a lot of screen time, but you never hear him speak, or even hear his name. I always wondered what his deal was.
— JASON DEMARCO, PRODUCER

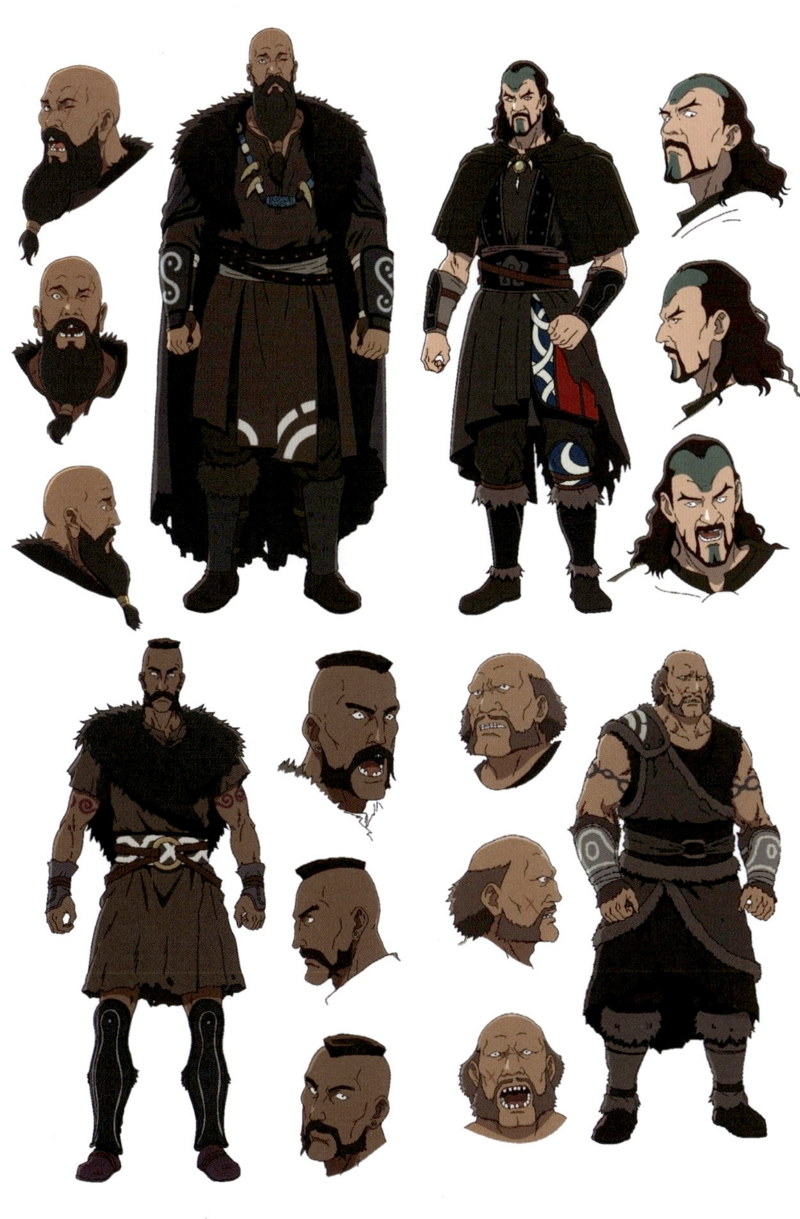

Freca's men character and expressions setting art, MT.

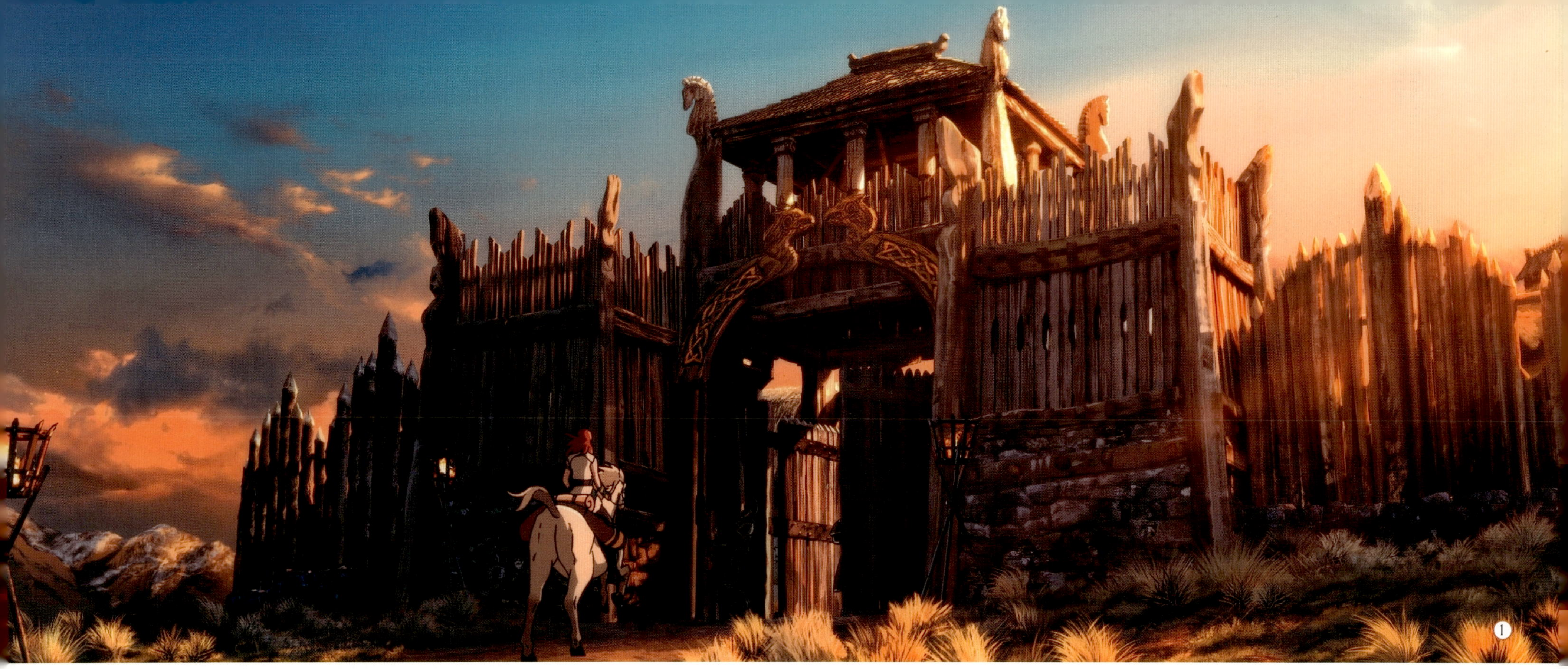

EDORAS INNER GATE

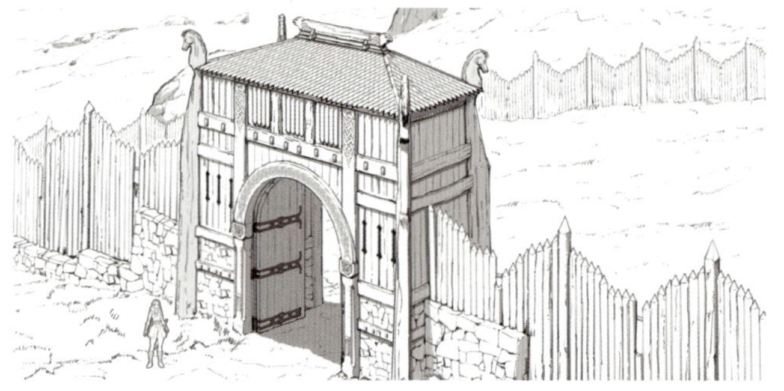
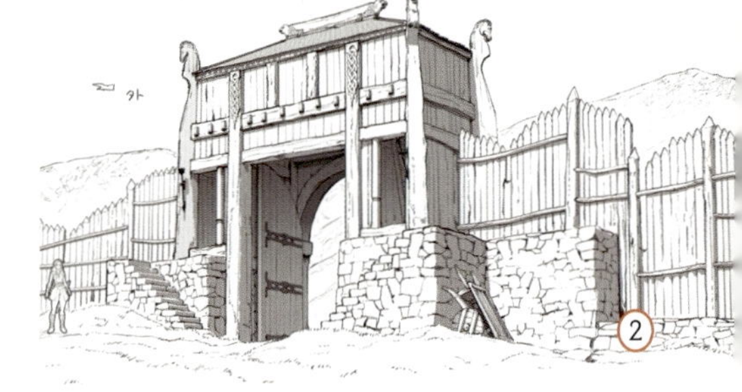

The design of Edoras's main gate was changed significantly from the original films, so the inner gate that guarded the summit buildings was also re-envisioned. It ended up looking much closer to the main gate of the trilogy. To show prosperity here as well, we designed the entryway to be double-doored and decorated with a sun symbol. – TAMIKO KANAMORI, ART DIRECTOR

1. Final film frame. **2.** Edoras summit gate concepts, TK. **3.** Edoras summit gate background art.

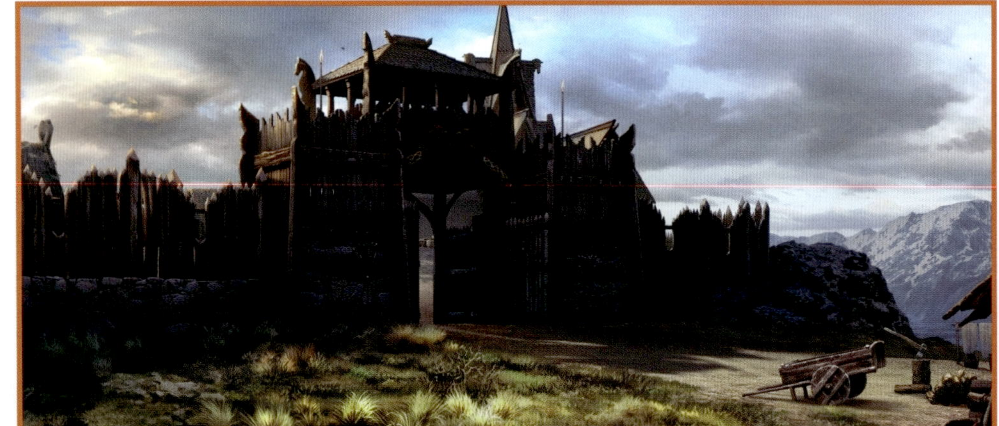
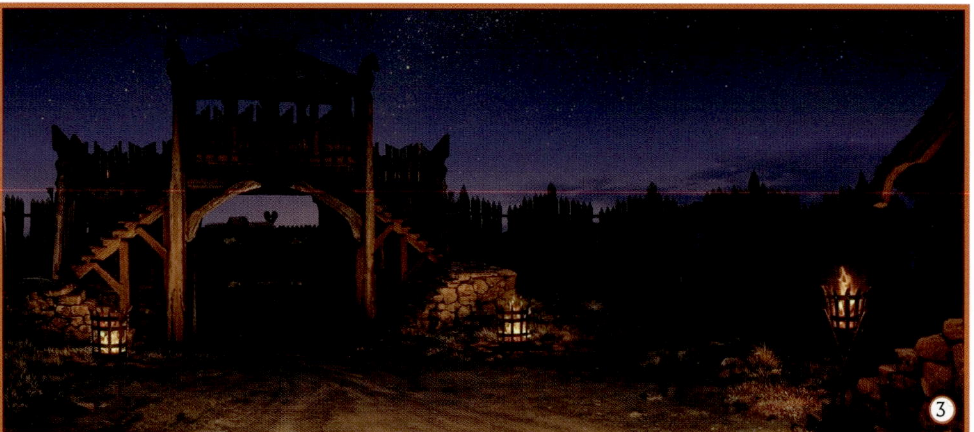

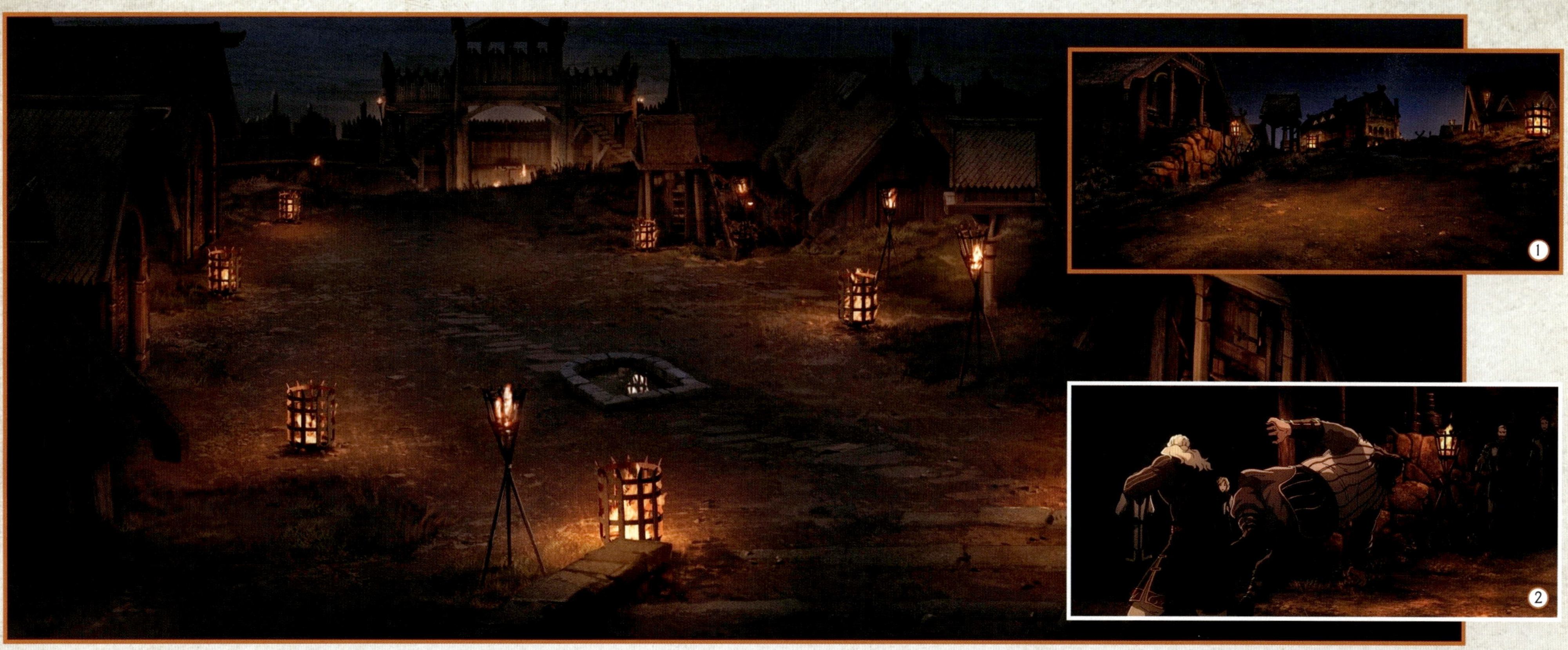

FRECA'S DEATH

Freca's death was something that Tolkien himself described and it's probably one of the most important scenes in the tale. Fans of the book would be looking forward to seeing it portrayed on screen, but for most audience members who are not familiar with the text, the death of Freca needed to be a shock. It needed to feel like a fight between relative equals, so that the shock was preserved, but when it happened you had to buy it and understand, 'Yeah, that's the hammer-hand.' When that fist comes flying in, you feel it! The sound team also helped make it work. Kamiyama's direction to them was, 'More!'

There was a lot of discussion about the hit; was it a backhand slap, a punch, or an uppercut? Everyone had a mental image of what it might be. – JOSEPH CHOU, PRODUCER

We staged Helm and Freca's fight between the inner gate and Meduseld. It takes place at night, surrounded by torches, but the director requested that the torch-lights be made larger to avoid it looking too desolate or empty. I think the fiery illumination enhances the excitement and tension of the battle. – TAMIKO KANAMORI, ART DIRECTOR

The scene in which Wulf shed tears after his father's death was a very memorable one to draw for that character. Even being anime, I think that this emotional state makes him seem very human. – MIYAKO TAKASU, ANIMATION CHARACTER DESIGNER & KEY ANIMATION SUPERVISOR

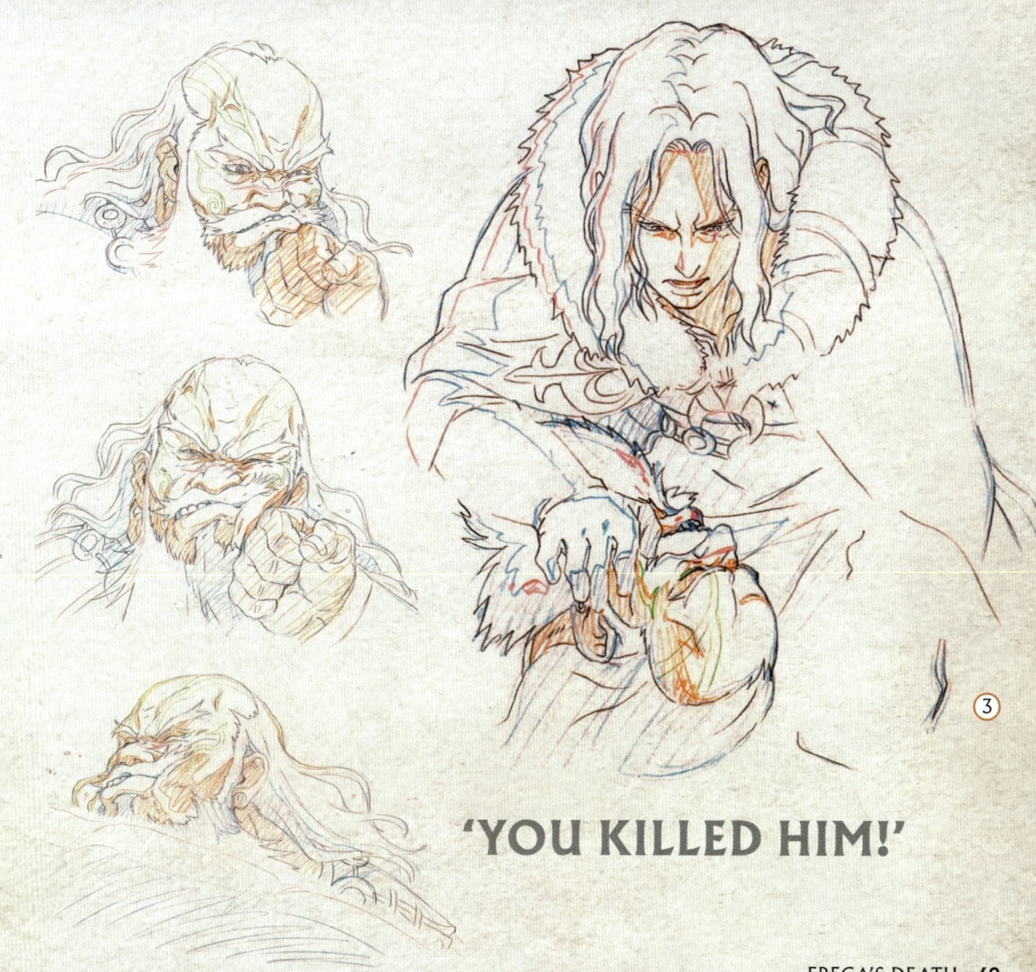

'YOU KILLED HIM!'

1: Edoras courtyard background setting art, TK. 2: Final film frame. 3: Animation key frames, MT.

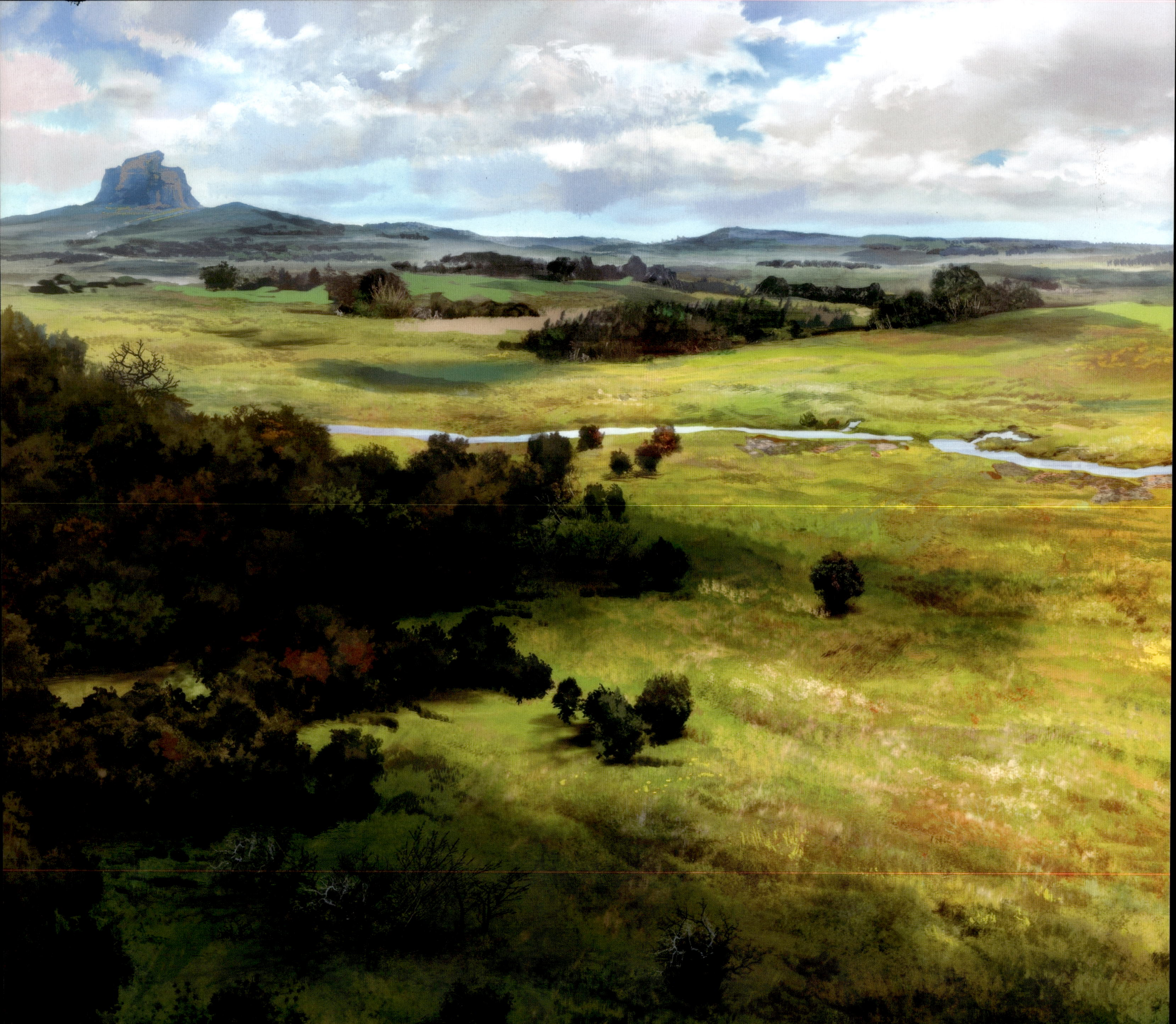

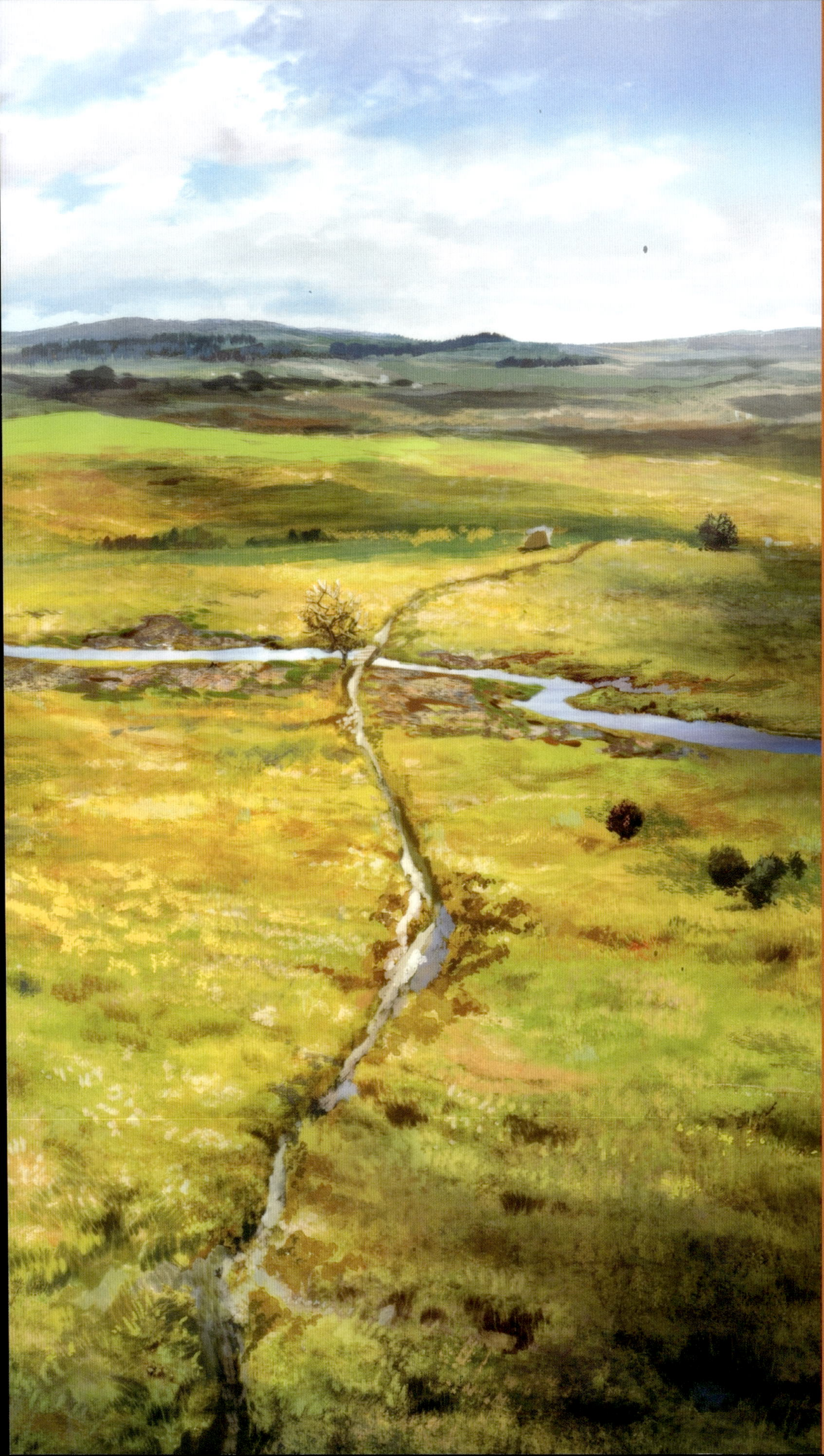

- 3 -

THE GREAT WEST ROAD

Years pass and while Héra seeks Wulf, he and his men have seemingly vanished from Rohan. The threat of war looms as word comes of attacks upon Rohan's ally Gondor in the east and south. Héra is no longer permitted to ride alone upon the plains, and must be escorted wherever she goes.

On one such ride with her lady-in-waiting, Olwyn, royal page Lief and cousin Lord Fréaláf, Héra finds a dead warrior in the grass, being picked at by crows. A Southron mercenary they name him, and his presence in Rohan is concerning, but before they can act the party is attacked by a huge and rabid beast.

Héra quickly takes the measure of the monster, a towering mûmak from the hot lands of the south. She knows they cannot defeat it and lures the maddened beast away from her friends. The mûmak gives chase, and Héra leads it through a dense woodland to the edge of a stagnant pool. The beast charges, but writhing arms burst from the greenish waters and ensnare it, dragging the mûmak into a deadly embrace as a many tentacled creature rises from the murk to consume it.

Héra is saved, but only for a moment, as General Tarrg of the West-march, who once served Lord Freca, appears and kidnaps the princess.

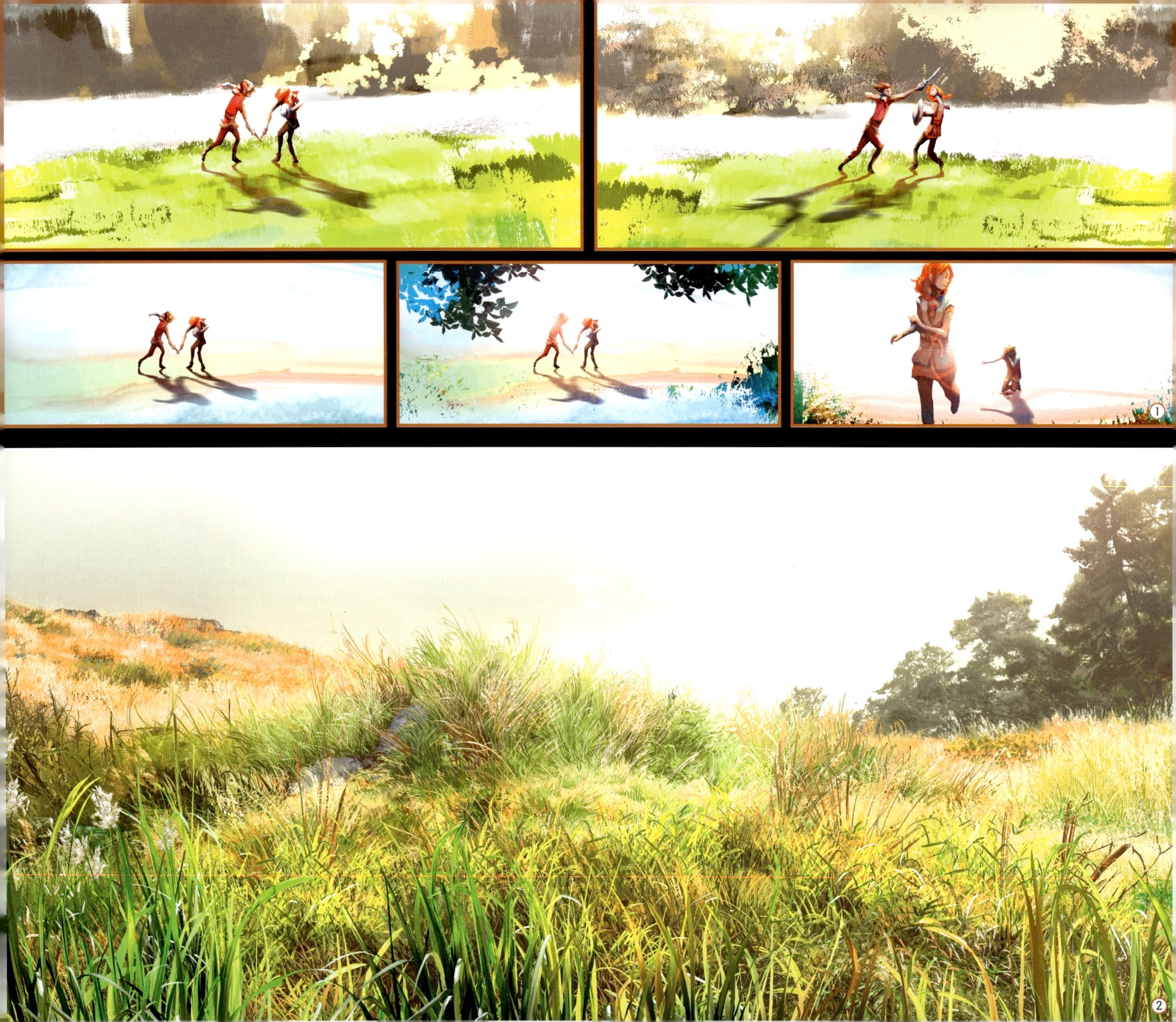

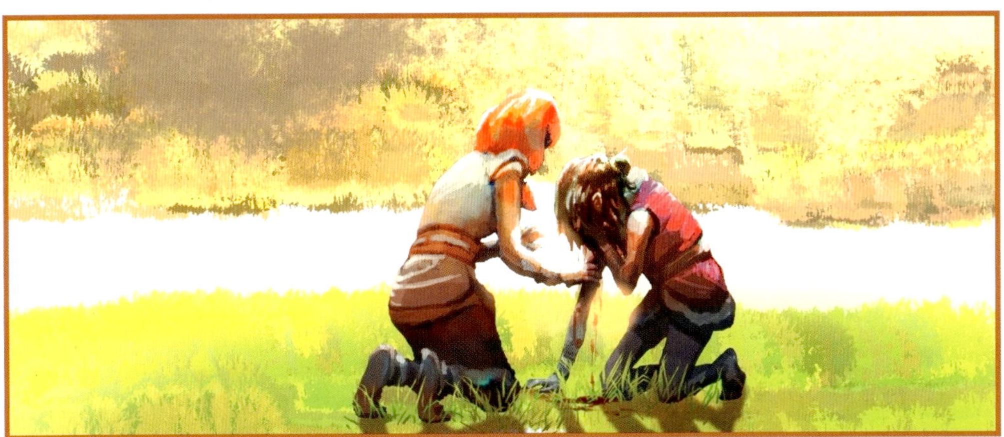

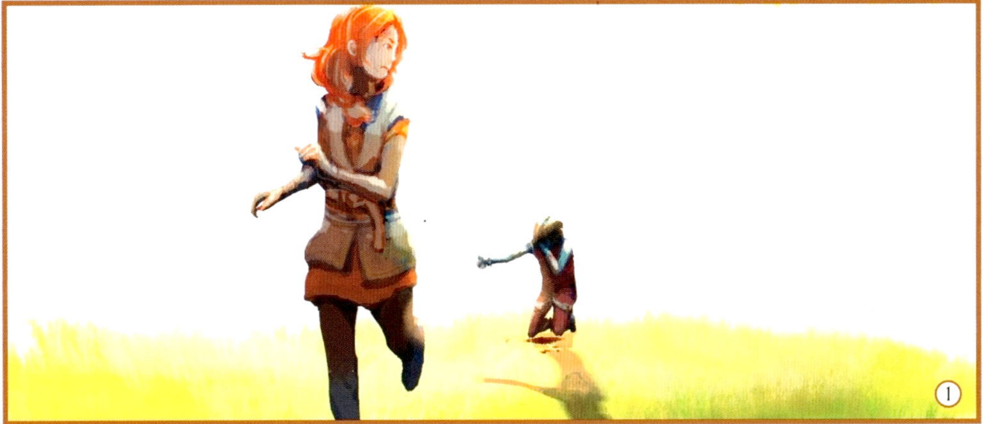

YOUNG HÉRA AND WULF

In a golden-hued childhood memory, Héra and Wulf practice their sword-fighting skills together, but getting carried away, Héra cuts Wulf, leaving him with a scar that he will carry for the rest of his life.

The flashback between Wulf and Héra as children wasn't originally in the script. It showed they were once friends, and that they had both been raised with blades in their hands, but I thought it was also important to build in an element of love denied. The humiliation that comes from it is also a motivation that drives Wulf's anger. Along with Héra, Wulf carries the most weight in the film. His complexity had to be reflected in his appearance, which is why he has the scar from a childhood spar with Héra.

It's not depicted in the film, but something that I imagined was that not only did Héra scar Wulf, but in fact it cost him his sight in that eye. His history with her has literally affected the way he sees the world and he has hidden it from everyone. Later, when he has her captive, Wulf holds his own knife at Héra's face, and it is to the same eye, in effect saying: 'This is how much I have thought of you, and you have completely denied me.'

I would have loved to dig even deeper into Wulf in the film, but at some point you have to stop. There are so many characters and only so much time! – KENJI KAMIYAMA, DIRECTOR

The scene in which Wulf and Héra were seen in flashback went through some changes in construction. The character designs could not be finalized in advance, so we ended up finishing them directly in the key animation stage. I'm glad that the scene was included, as it provides a sensitive insight into their relationship. The film is set in the time of King Helm, but it is also a story about Héra and Wulf. – MIYAKO TAKASU, ANIMATION CHARACTER DESIGNER & KEY ANIMATION SUPERVISOR

I based the environment and lighting of the flashback scene on photographs provided by the director. It wasn't a specific location, but I first created a sketch based on the image of a little stream I saw in France. For the finished shot, the image was further enriched by adding in composited elements. – YASUHIRO YAMANE, ART DIRECTOR

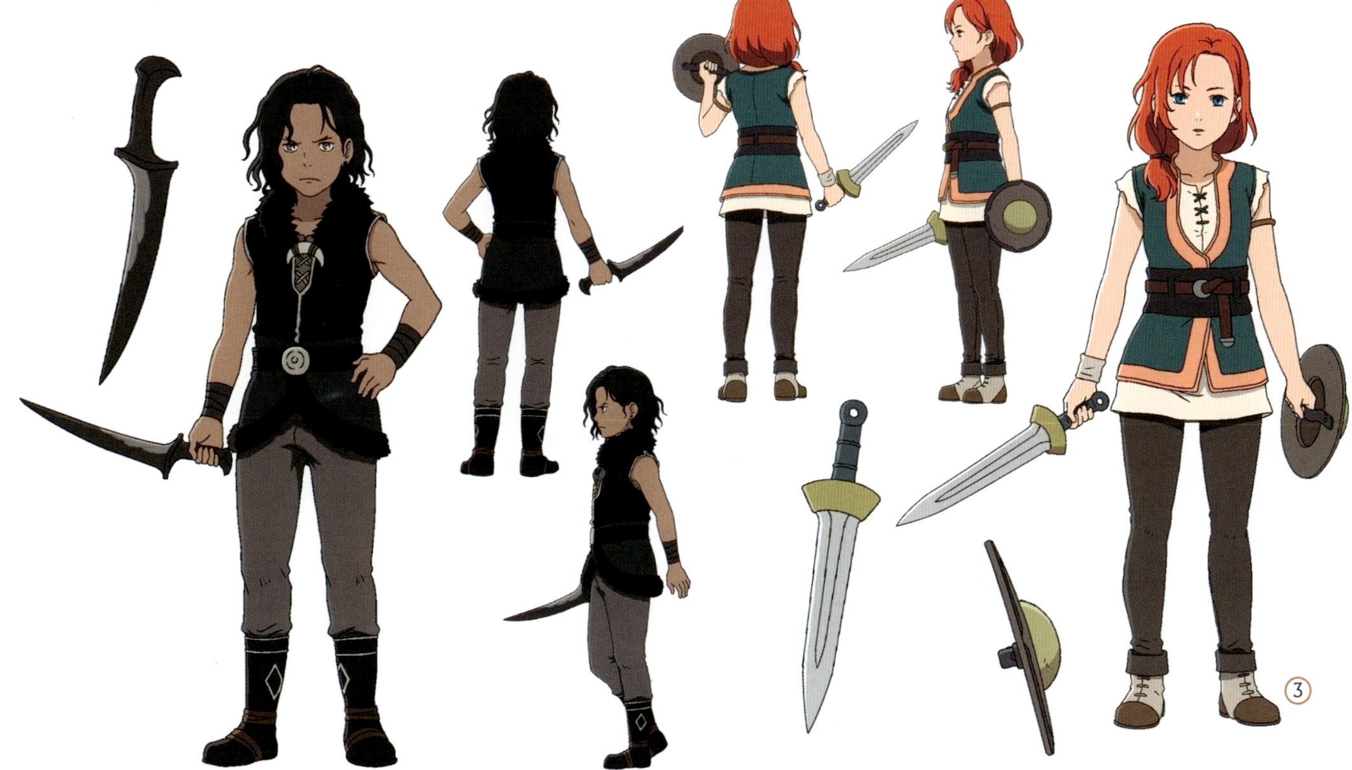

PP: Great West Road background setting art, YY. **1:** Flashback concepts, YY. **2:** Great West Road background art. **3:** Young Wulf and Héra character and prop setting art, MT.

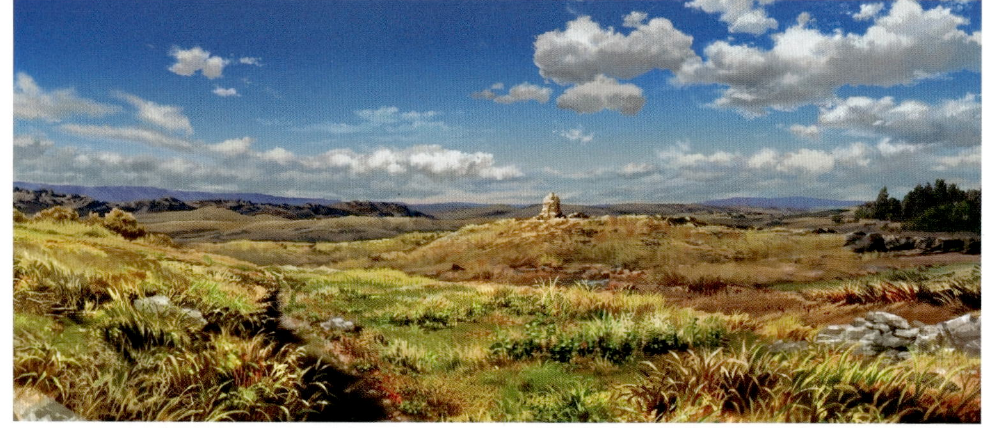

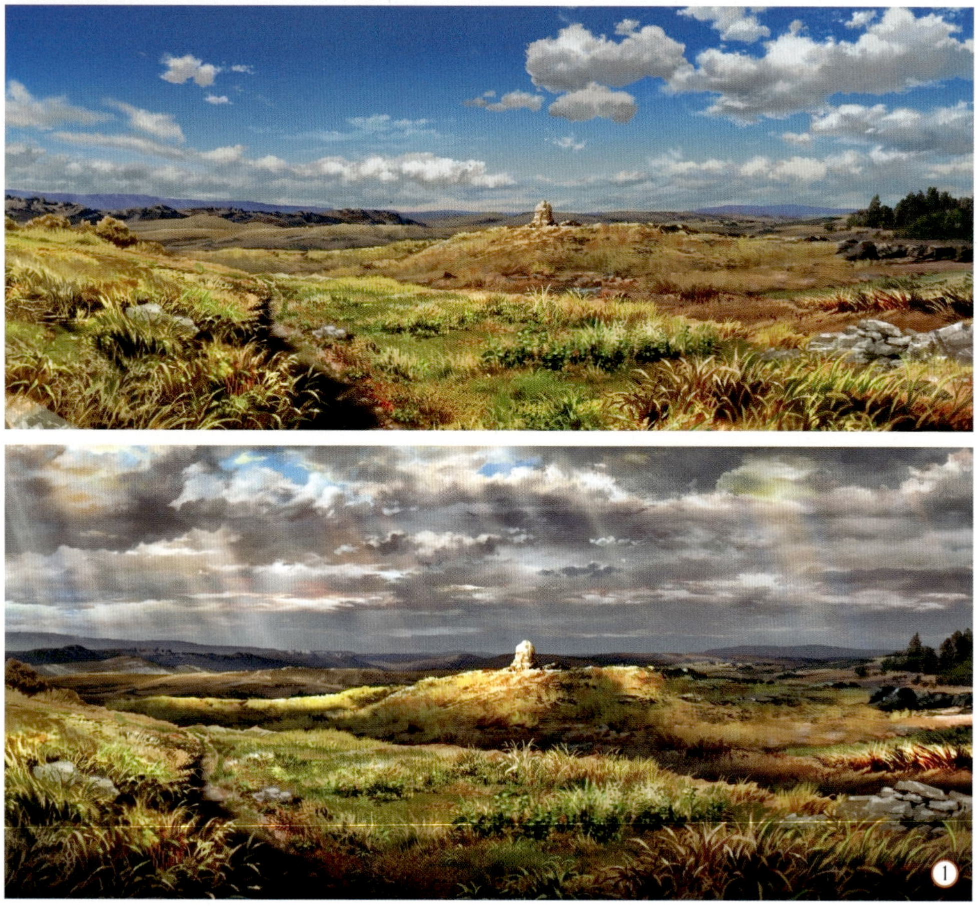

THE GREAT WEST ROAD

The Great West Road was a well-trod trail traversing the lands of Rohan, connecting Eriador to Anorien. Years after the death of Freca and disappearance of his son, Héra and her party explored the rolling plains north and south of the road. There may be no word of Wulf, but rumours of other strange things being seen have reached their ears.

The setting for Héra's confrontation with a rabid mûmak, Rohan's grass sea took shape as a series of background paintings. The artists drew inspiration from the plains of Otago and Canterbury, in Aotearoa, New Zealand, where filming took place for the live-action films' Rohan sequences, but also elsewhere in the world, including the Eurasian Steppe.

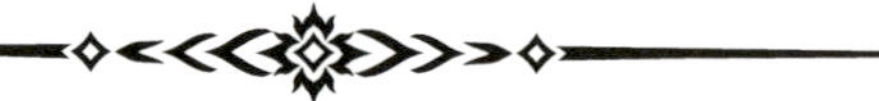

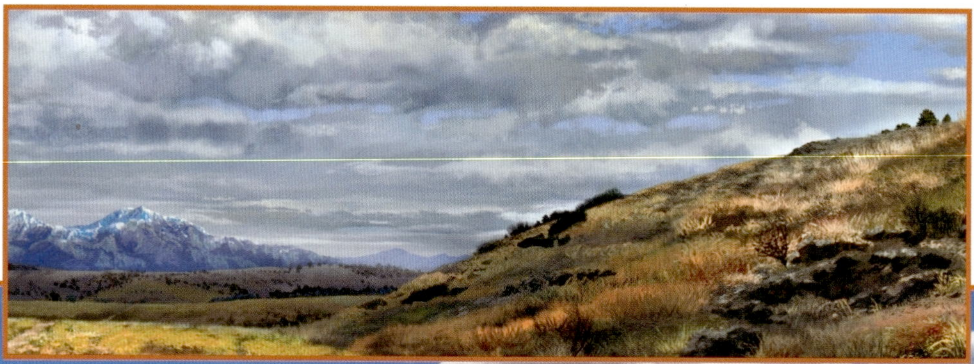

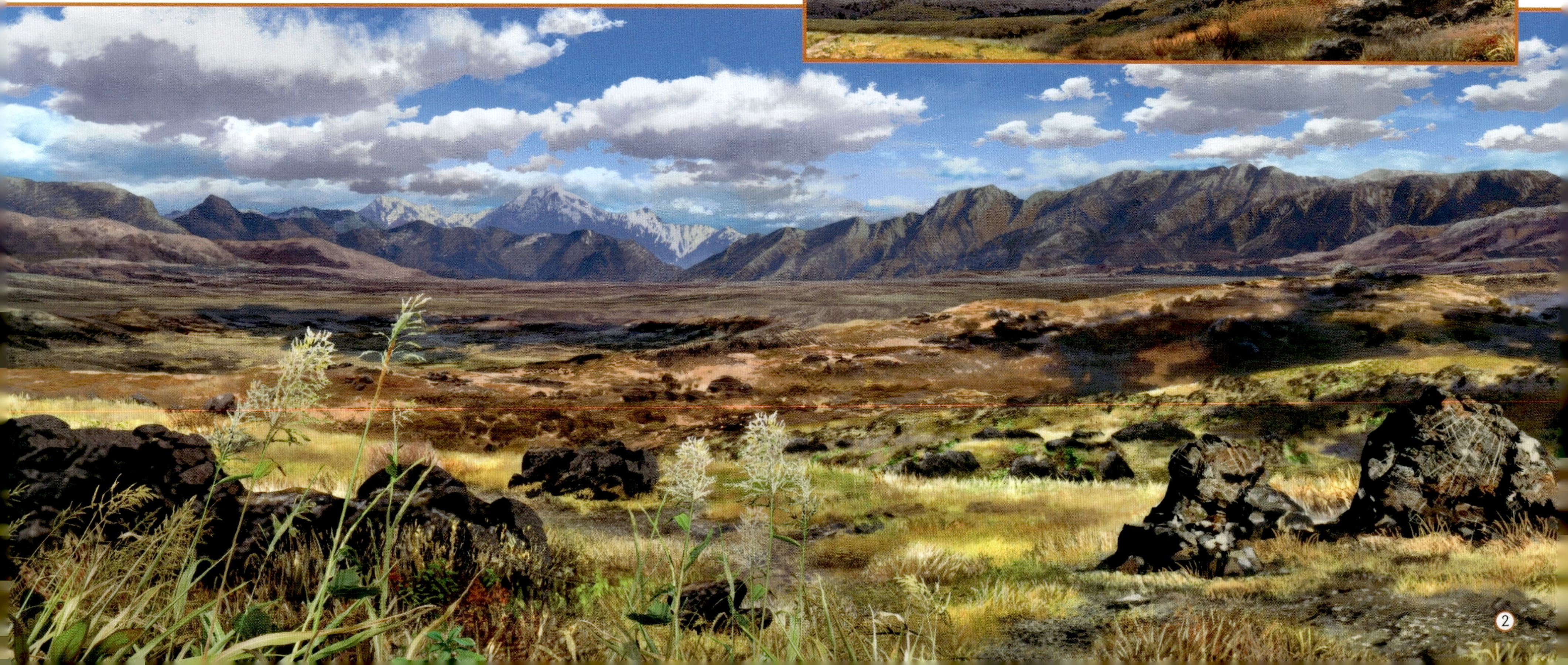

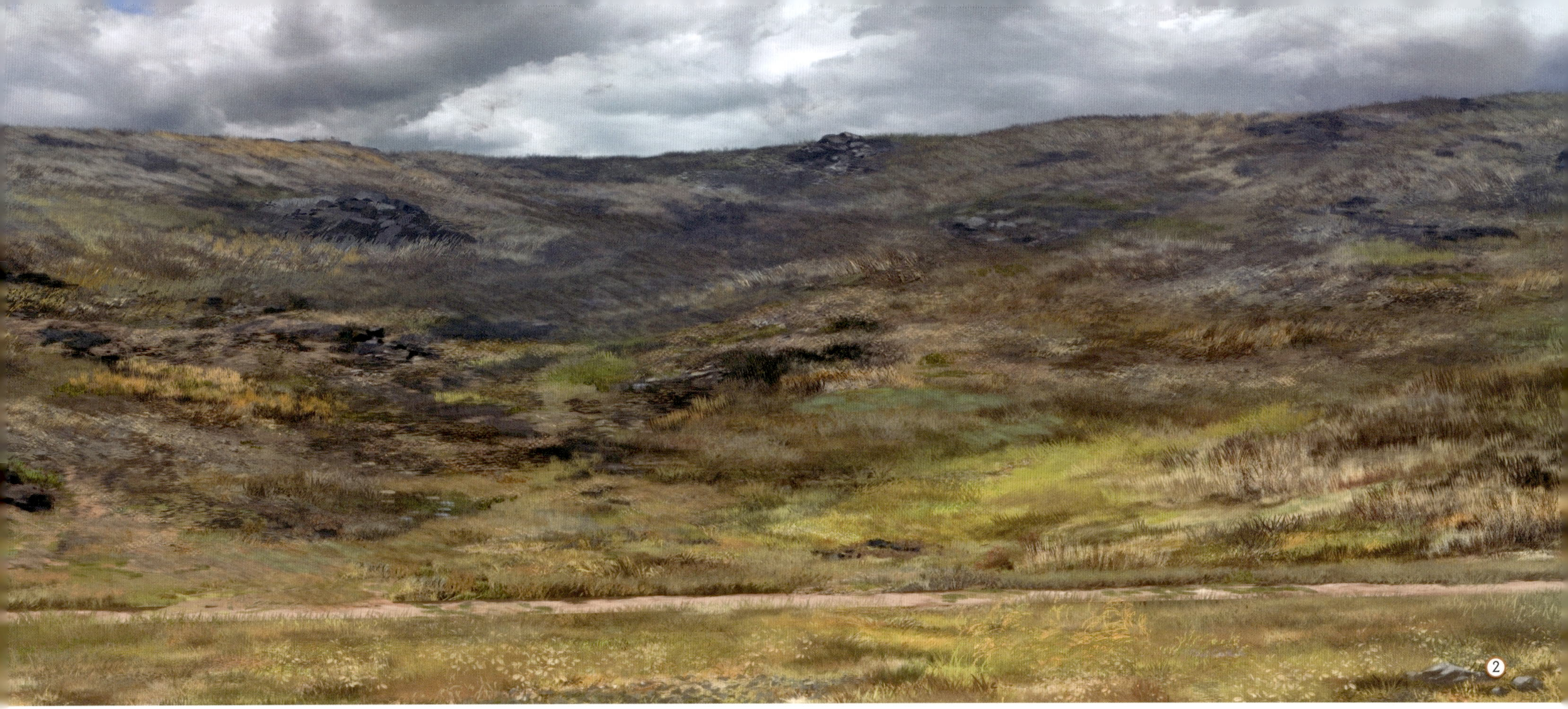

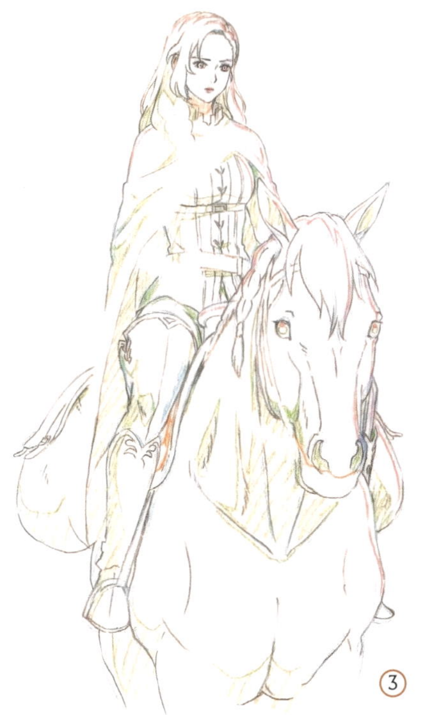

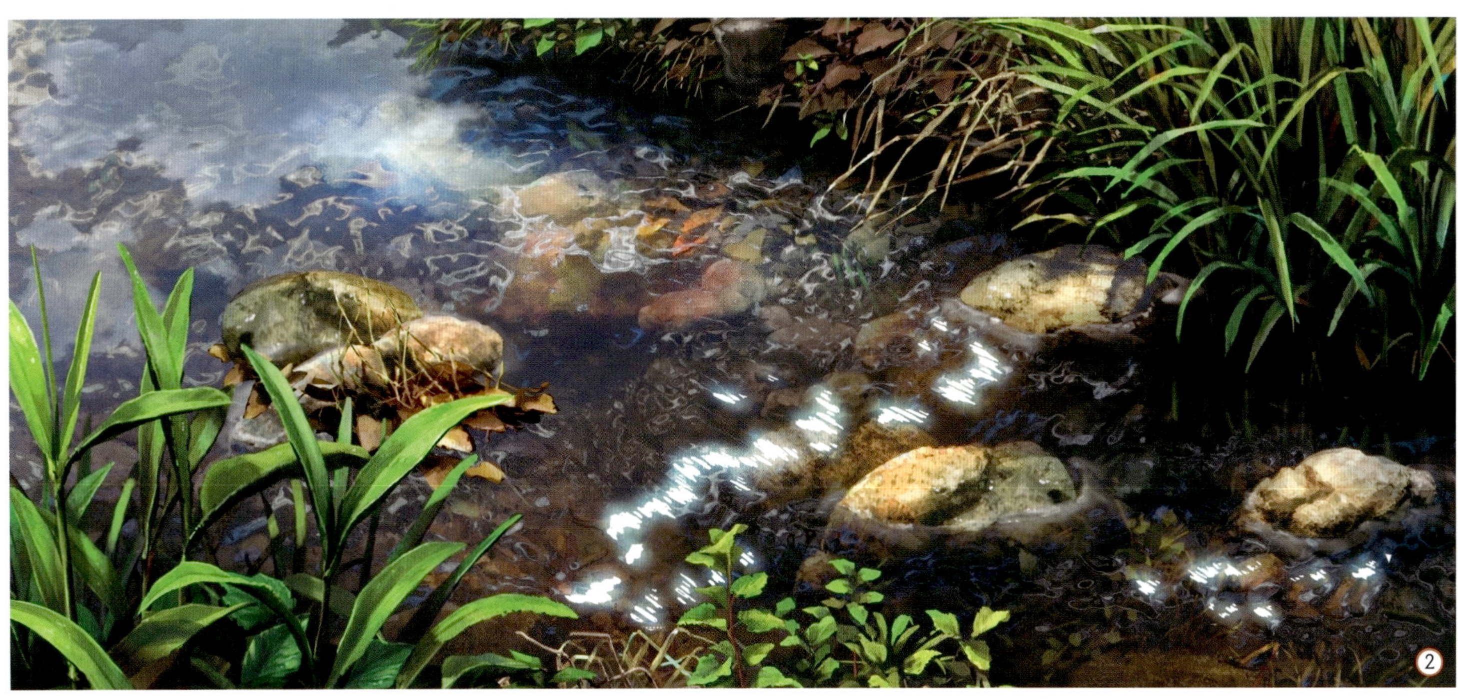

1: Great West Road background setting art, YY.
2: Great West Road background art. 3: Animation key frame, MT.

'WULF'S FATE WEIGHED HEAVY ON HÉRA'S MIND.'

HÉRA, THE RIDER

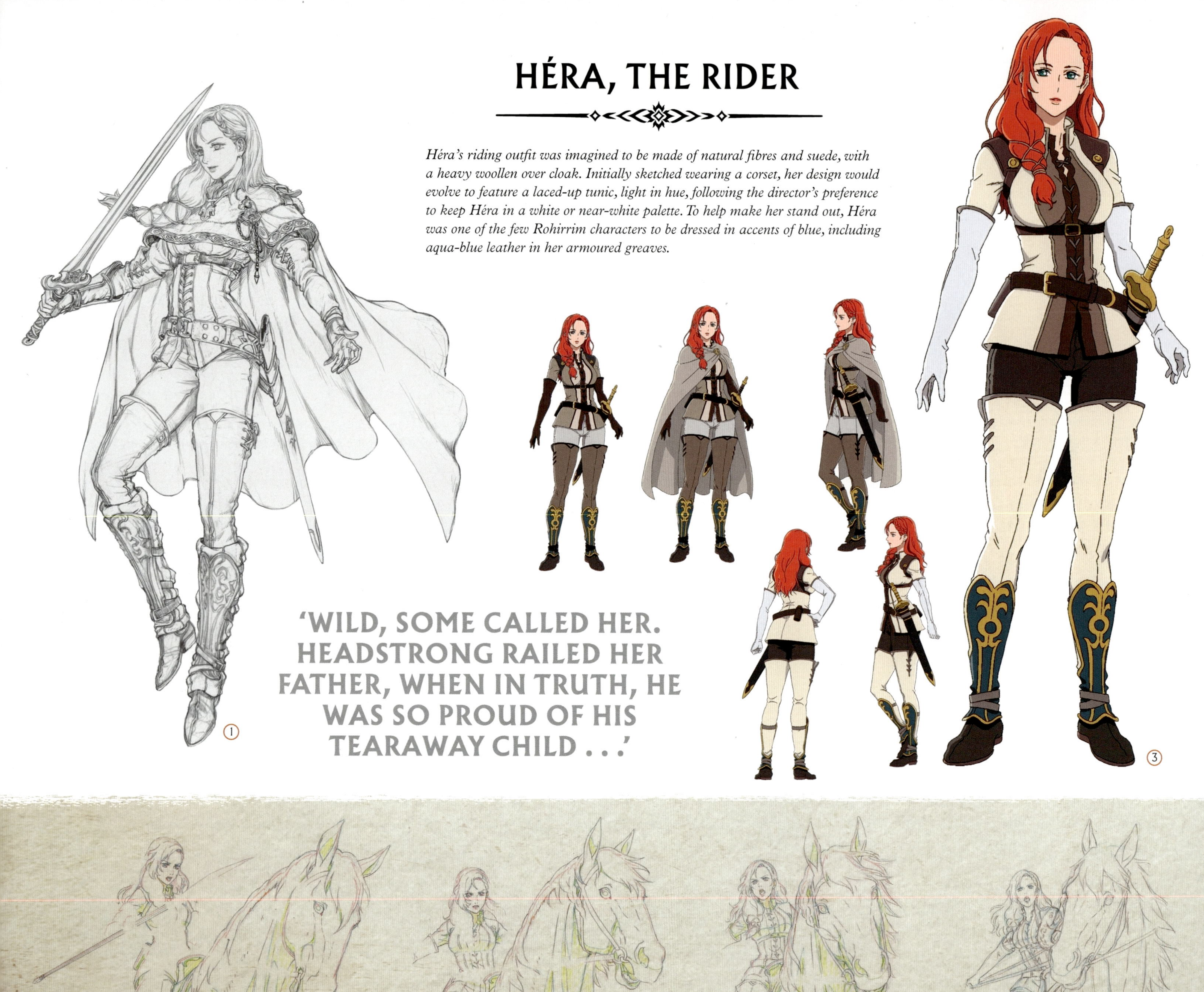

Héra's riding outfit was imagined to be made of natural fibres and suede, with a heavy woollen over cloak. Initially sketched wearing a corset, her design would evolve to feature a laced-up tunic, light in hue, following the director's preference to keep Héra in a white or near-white palette. To help make her stand out, Héra was one of the few Rohirrim characters to be dressed in accents of blue, including aqua-blue leather in her armoured greaves.

'WILD, SOME CALLED HER. HEADSTRONG RAILED HER FATHER, WHEN IN TRUTH, HE WAS SO PROUD OF HIS TEARAWAY CHILD . . .'

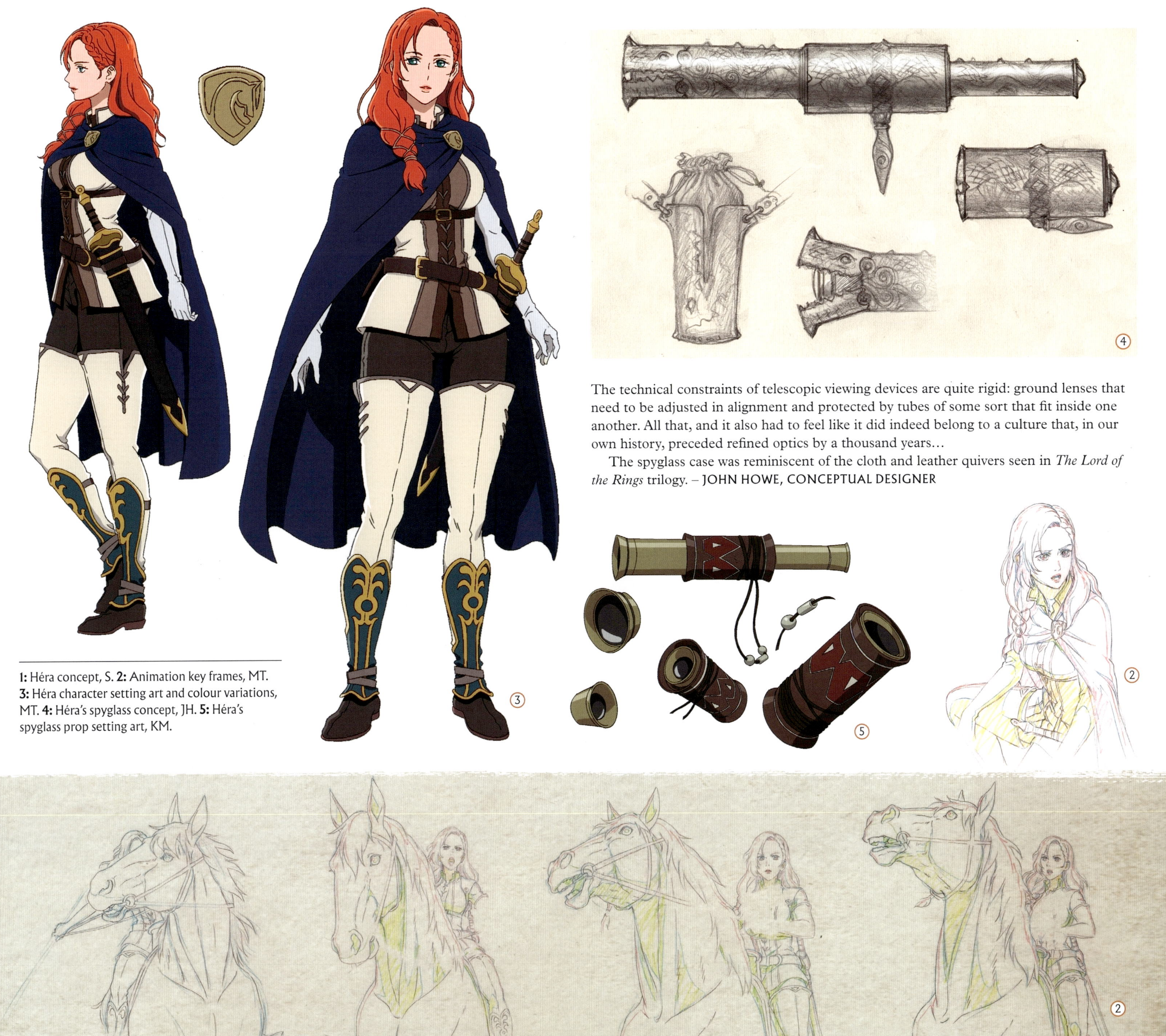

The technical constraints of telescopic viewing devices are quite rigid: ground lenses that need to be adjusted in alignment and protected by tubes of some sort that fit inside one another. All that, and it also had to feel like it did indeed belong to a culture that, in our own history, preceded refined optics by a thousand years…

The spyglass case was reminiscent of the cloth and leather quivers seen in *The Lord of the Rings* trilogy. – JOHN HOWE, CONCEPTUAL DESIGNER

1: Héra concept, S. 2: Animation key frames, MT. 3: Héra character setting art and colour variations, MT. 4: Héra's spyglass concept, JH. 5: Héra's spyglass prop setting art, KM.

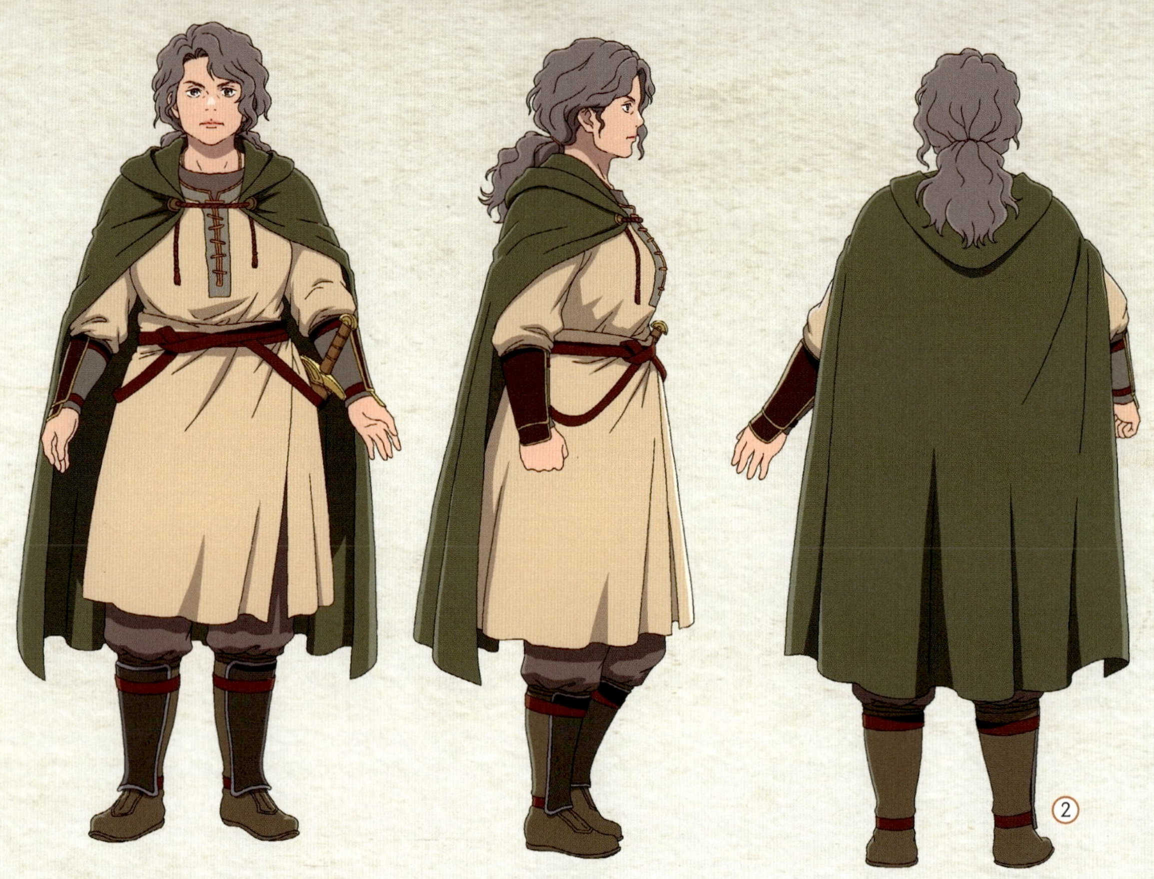

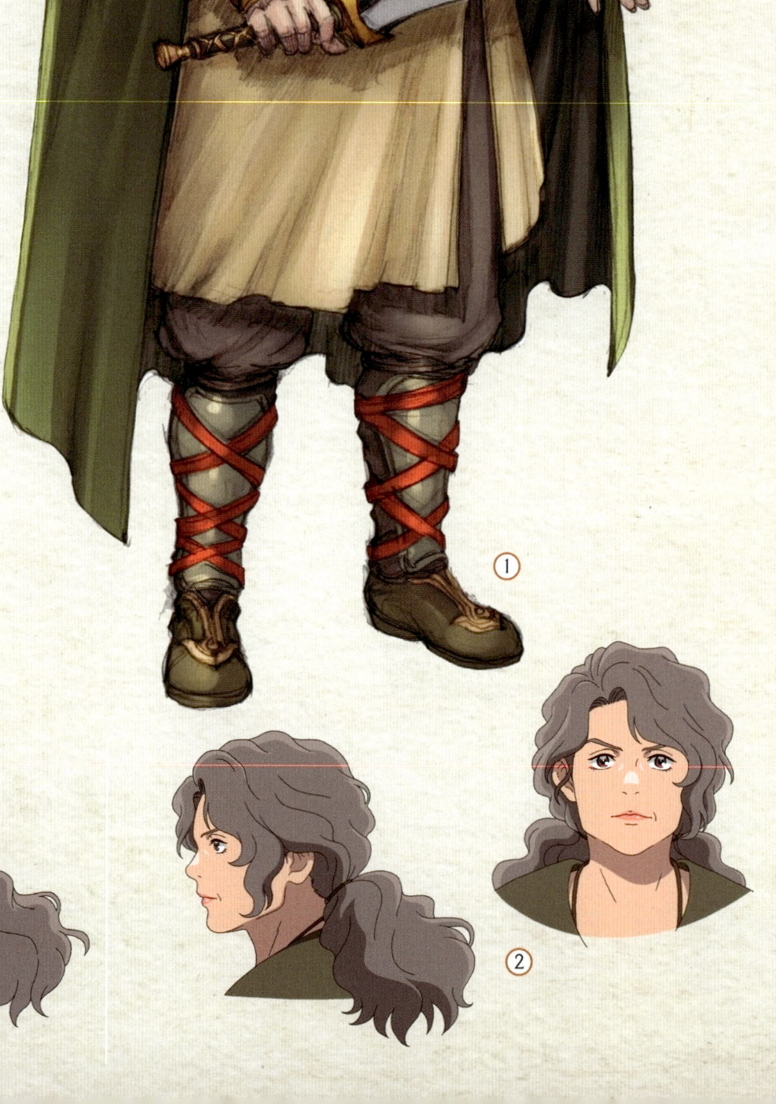

OLWYN, SHIELDMAIDEN

For the costume that Olwyn wore when riding, and later when she rescues Héra, our goal was to present her as a character with surprising power and agility. – MIYAKO TAKASU, ANIMATION CHARACTER DESIGNER & KEY ANIMATION SUPERVISOR

Olwyn was, for various reasons, probably the most difficult character to design, mostly because she had to both exhibit and hide her capabilities as a warrior at the same time. Olwyn embodies the shieldmaiden legacy, but her past had to be hidden from the audience. It couldn't be too obvious in the beginning, or it would give away what was later supposed to be a reveal. Yet she still had to seem strong and capable, so when her moment came it would be believable. Her costume progression through the film also helps to peel back the layers of her character. We went through a number of design iterations to arrive at her final look. – KENJI KAMIYAMA, DIRECTOR

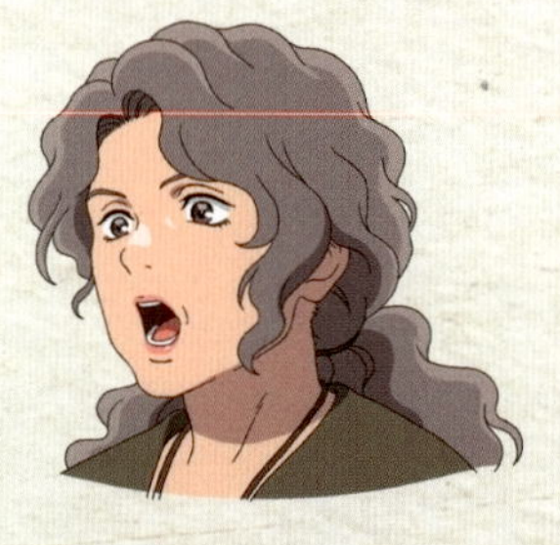

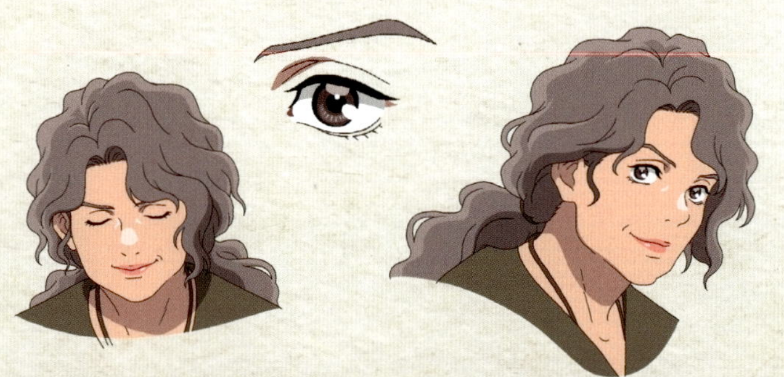

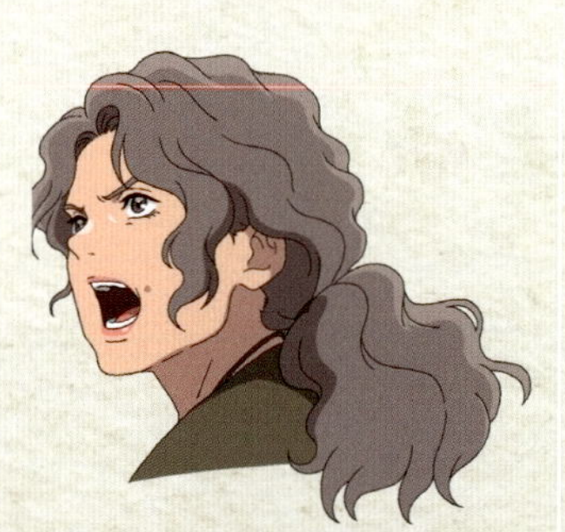

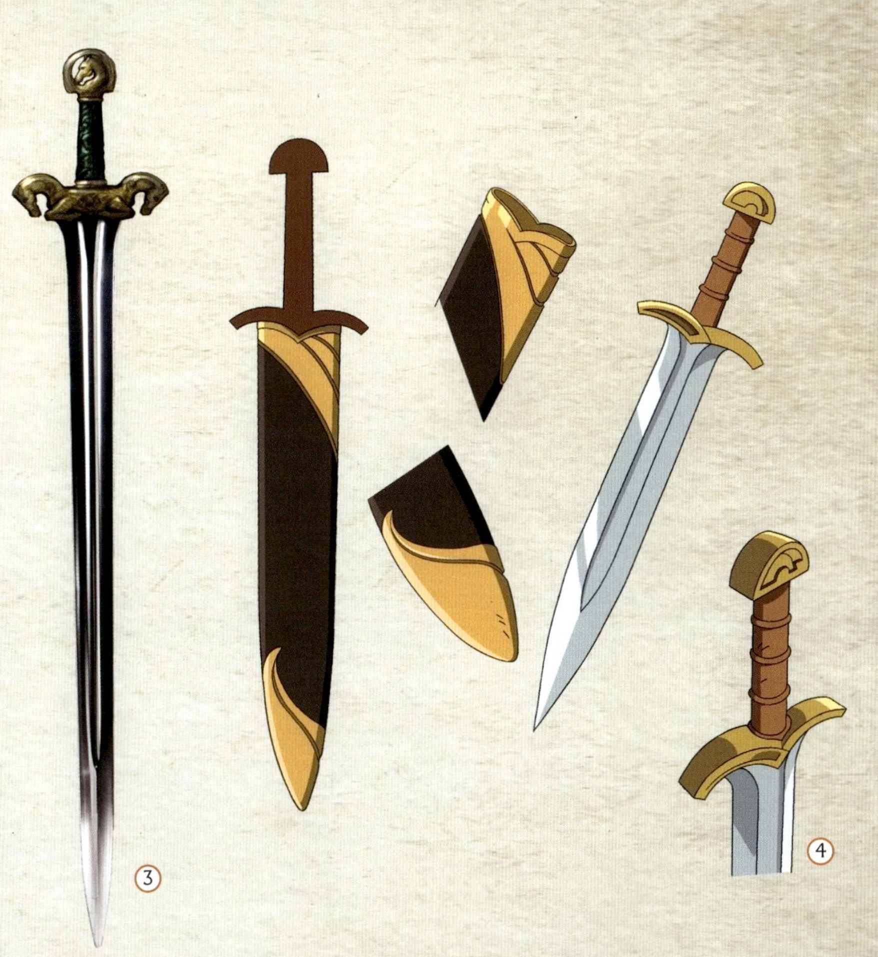

Héra's nursemaid, as we come to find out, was a shieldmaiden, and she can handle a sword. – PHILIPPA BOYENS, PRODUCER

Olwyn has fought beside Helm. She was from the borderlands and her village was overrun. That was the conceit; that when Héra's mother died, Helm knew he needed help in raising his daughter. He remembered this brave young shieldmaiden: her strength and courage. Olwyn is only too happy to put her fighting days behind her to care for Héra, in the hopes that she may pass on those skills and traits that Helm so valued. But with Héra's adventuring spirit, Olwyn quickly realized that she was going to need to keep her shield close at hand after all. – PHOEBE GITTINS, WRITER

Olwyn's final sword design mixed elements of traditional Rohirrim weapons with some shapes inspired by Frodo's sword, Sting, although, in-world, these were intended to be coincidentally similar rather than implying any direct link between the weapons.

1: Olwyn concept, S. 2: Olwyn character and expressions setting art, MT. 3: Olwyn's sword concept, JH & DF. 4: Olwyn's sword prop setting art, KM.

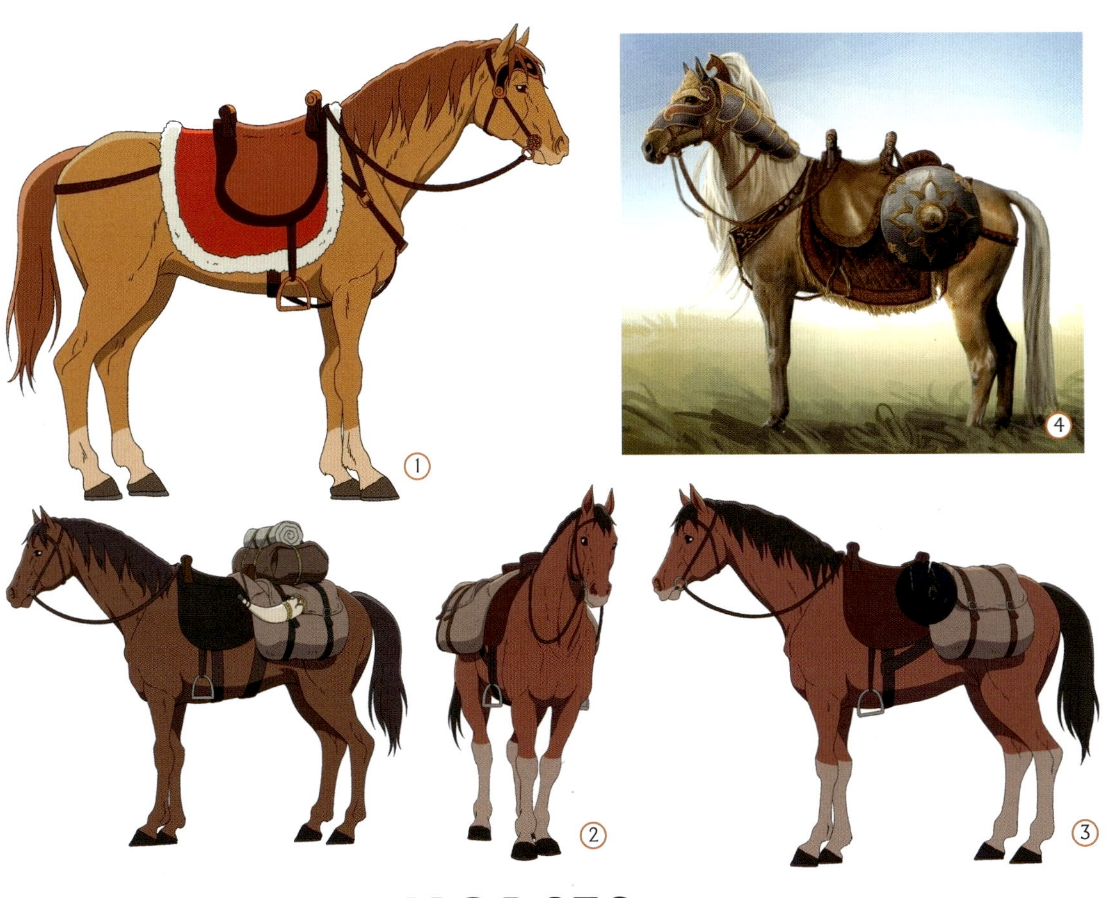

HORSES

Olwyn, Lief and Fréaláf accompany Héra on her ride. Each character's horse was designed to match its rider in personality and have saddlery and bags appropriate to their station. Fréaláf, as a lord, had a large, striking honey-hued horse with a richly trimmed saddle blanket, whereas Lief and Olwyn's mounts were humbler in appearance.

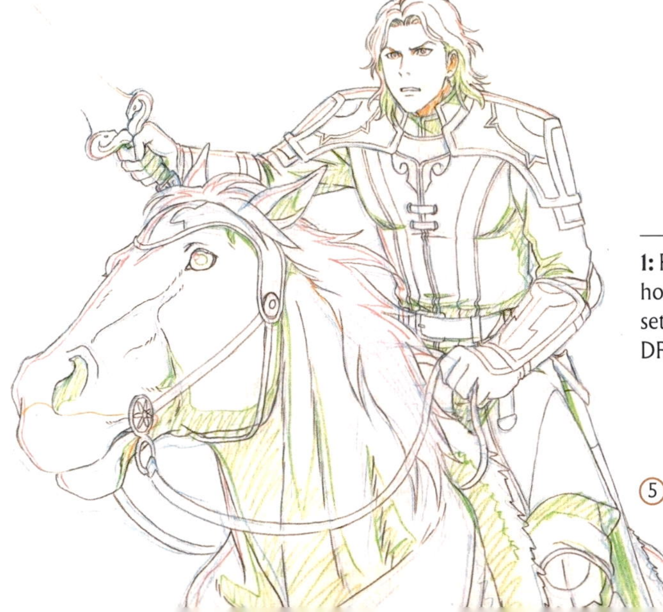

1: Fréaláf's horse setting art, MT. 2: Lief's horse setting art. MT. 3: Olwyn's horse setting art, MT. 4: Fréaláf's horse concept, DF. 5: Animation key frame, MT.

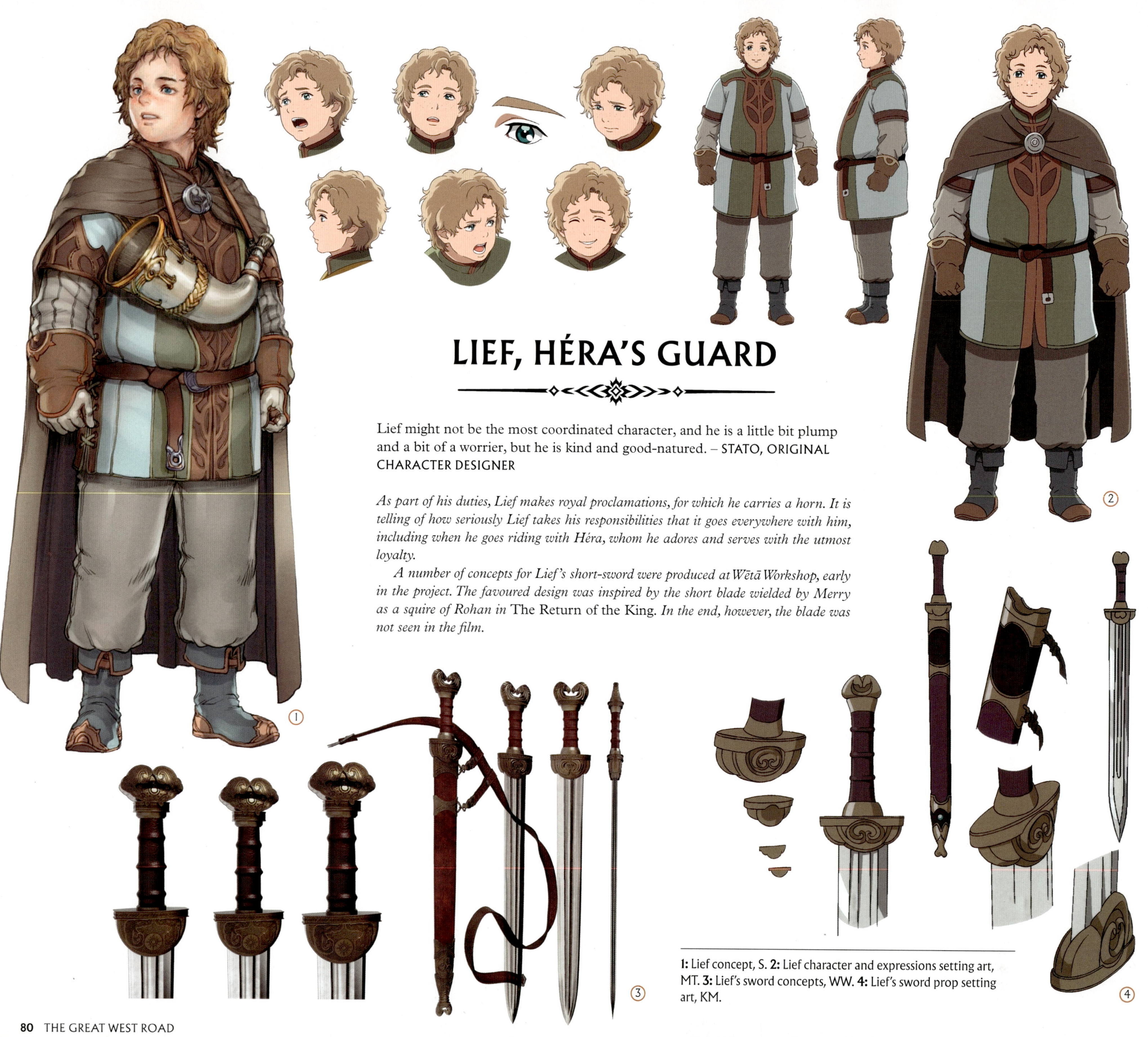

LIEF, HÉRA'S GUARD

Lief might not be the most coordinated character, and he is a little bit plump and a bit of a worrier, but he is kind and good-natured. – STATO, ORIGINAL CHARACTER DESIGNER

As part of his duties, Lief makes royal proclamations, for which he carries a horn. It is telling of how seriously Lief takes his responsibilities that it goes everywhere with him, including when he goes riding with Héra, whom he adores and serves with the utmost loyalty.

A number of concepts for Lief's short-sword were produced at Wētā Workshop, early in the project. The favoured design was inspired by the short blade wielded by Merry as a squire of Rohan in The Return of the King. *In the end, however, the blade was not seen in the film.*

1: Lief concept, S. 2: Lief character and expressions setting art, MT. 3: Lief's sword concepts, WW. 4: Lief's sword prop setting art, KM.

DUNLAND CREBAIN

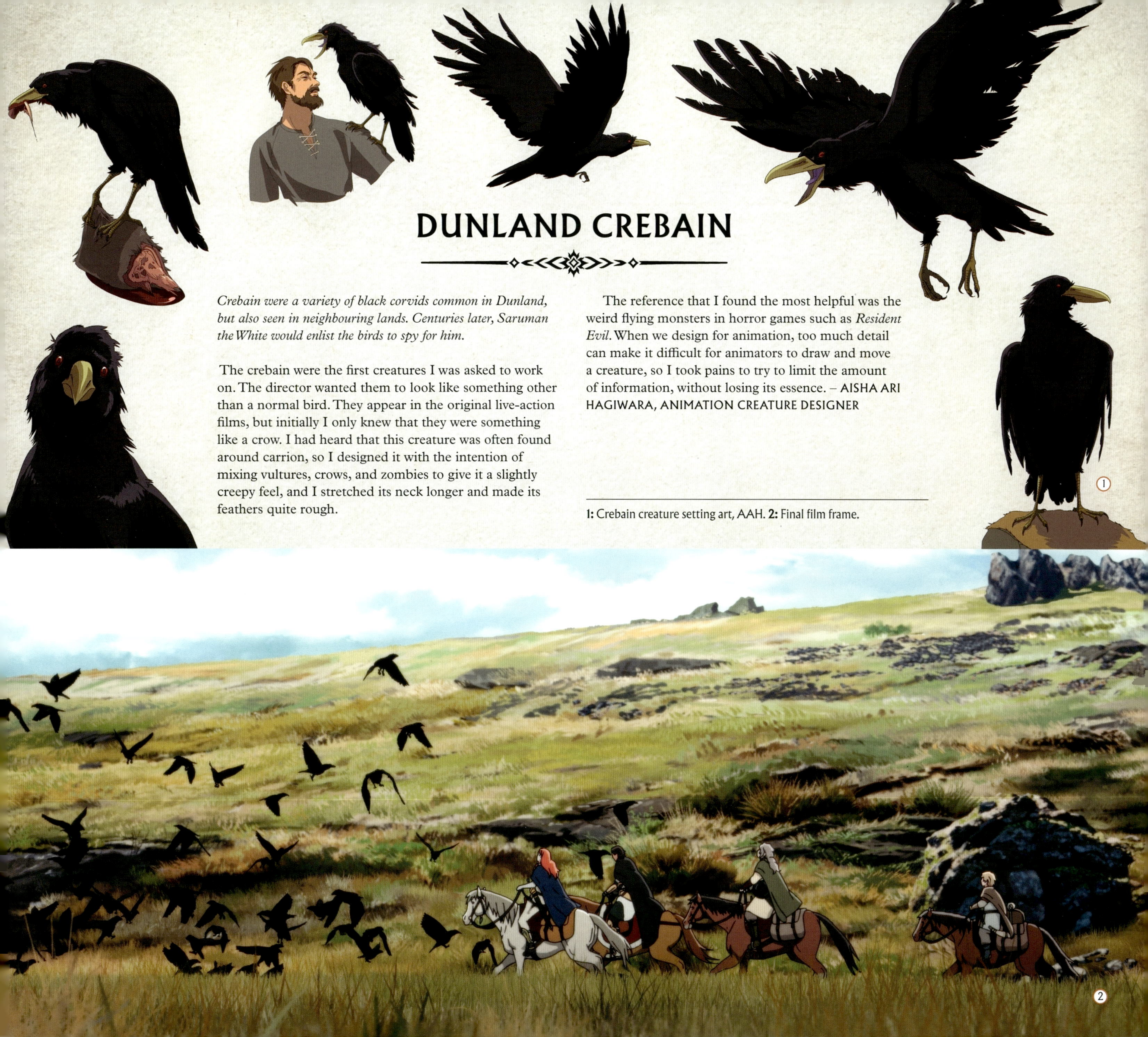

Crebain were a variety of black corvids common in Dunland, but also seen in neighbouring lands. Centuries later, Saruman the White would enlist the birds to spy for him.

The crebain were the first creatures I was asked to work on. The director wanted them to look like something other than a normal bird. They appear in the original live-action films, but initially I only knew that they were something like a crow. I had heard that this creature was often found around carrion, so I designed it with the intention of mixing vultures, crows, and zombies to give it a slightly creepy feel, and I stretched its neck longer and made its feathers quite rough.

The reference that I found the most helpful was the weird flying monsters in horror games such as *Resident Evil*. When we design for animation, too much detail can make it difficult for animators to draw and move a creature, so I took pains to try to limit the amount of information, without losing its essence. – AISHA ARI HAGIWARA, ANIMATION CREATURE DESIGNER

1: Crebain creature setting art, AAH. 2: Final film frame.

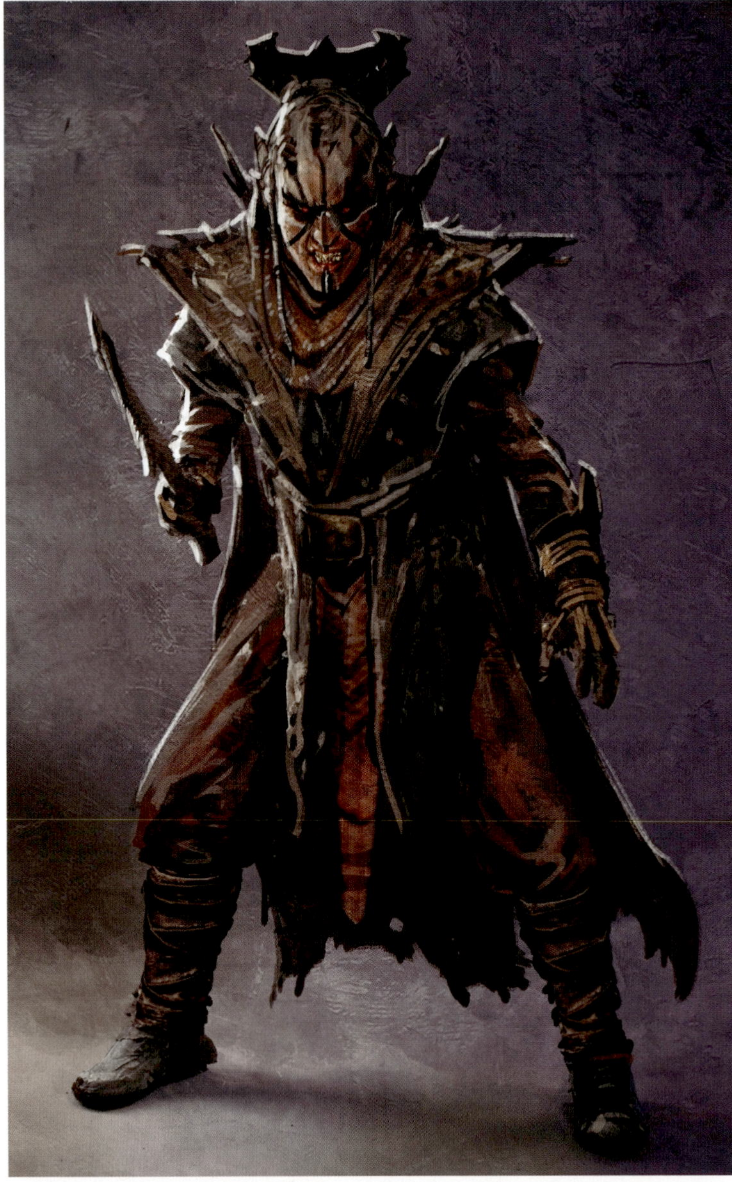

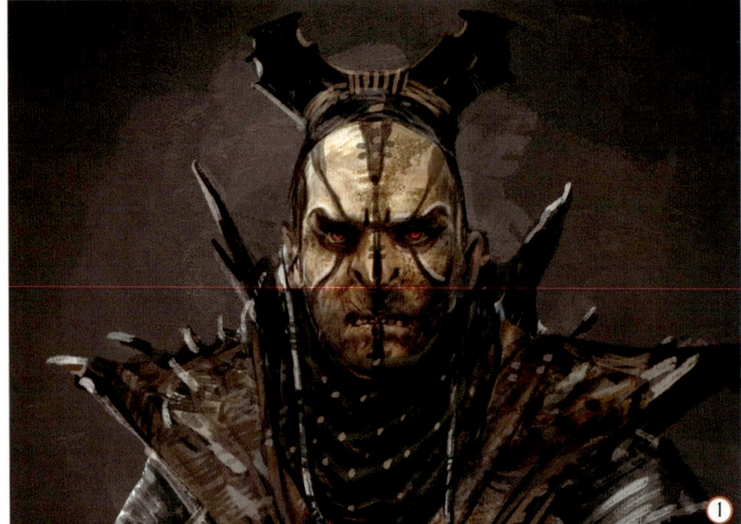

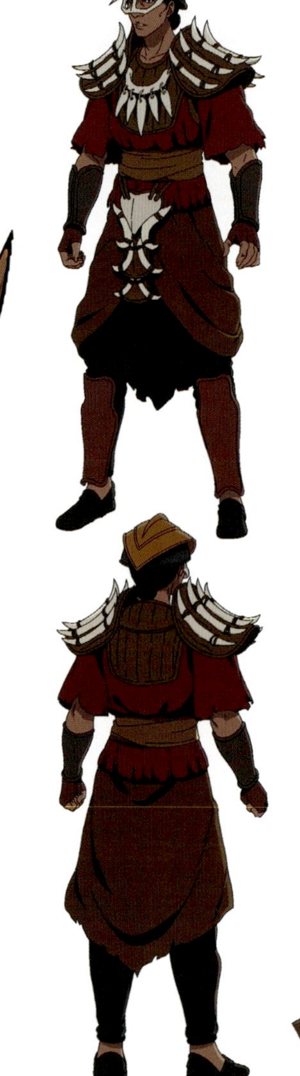

SOUTHRON MERCENARY

Wulf, as we will come to find out, has hired mercenaries from the south. Haleth will later call them 'variags'. That owes to the notion of them being mercenaries, which is what the word means to Haleth in the same way that we might call someone a vandal. 'Variag' to the Rohirrim means mercenaries, but there are a people called the Variags elsewhere in Middle-earth. They're not fighting out of belief in Wulf's cause; they are fighting because he is paying them. – PHILIPPA BOYENS, PRODUCER

As mentioned in Tolkien's Appendices to The Lord of the Rings, *enemies of Gondor entered Rohan from the east and southwest, seemingly in coordination with that realm coming under attack itself. Héra finds a dead mercenary on the plains. In the earliest versions of the script, the notion of Wulf's hirelings from the south being Half-Orcs was explored. This took the form of pointed ears, sharpened teeth and fiery eyes in some of the first concept art produced. The idea was dropped, but costume and war-paint elements from those concepts were carried through into the final designs.*

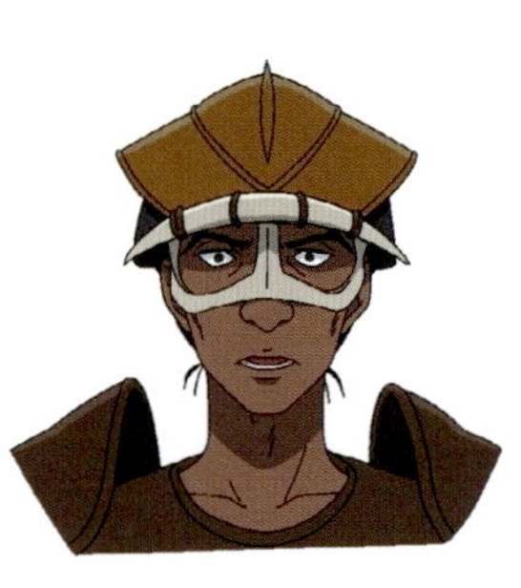

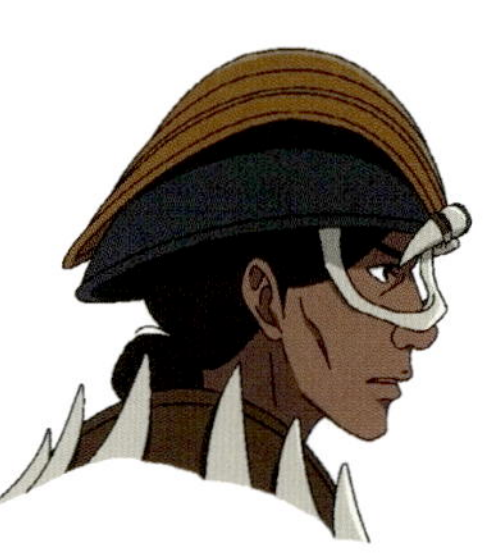

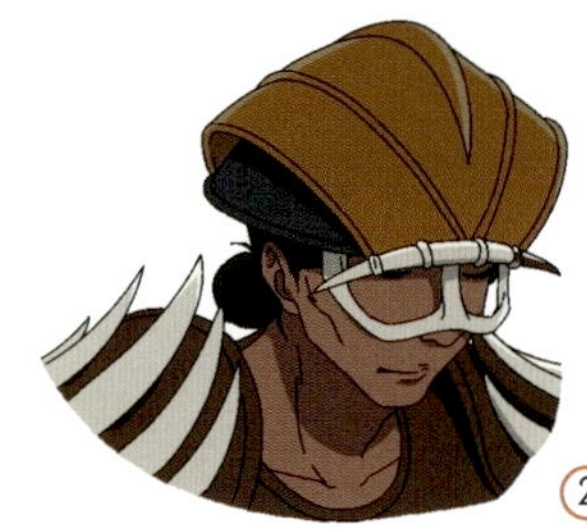

'IT'S A SOUTHRON. THE ARMOUR MARKS HIM AS A MERCENARY.'

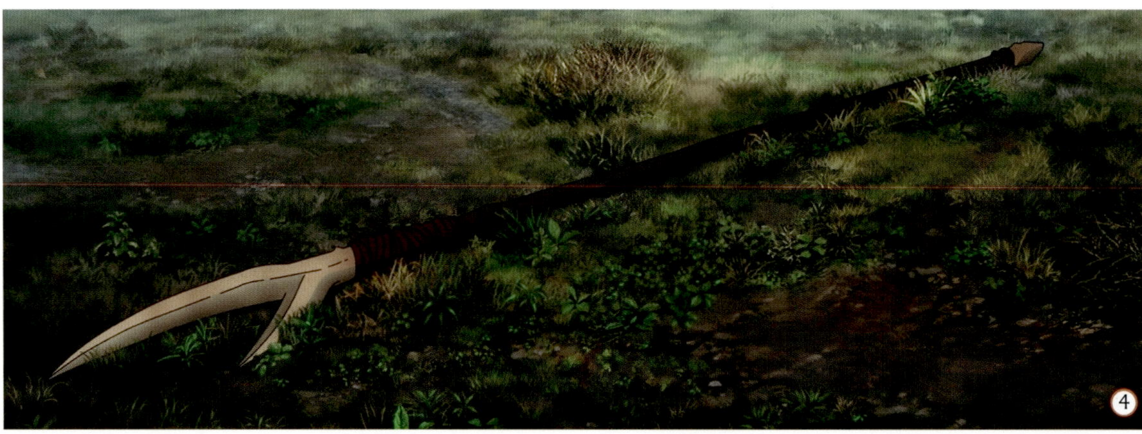

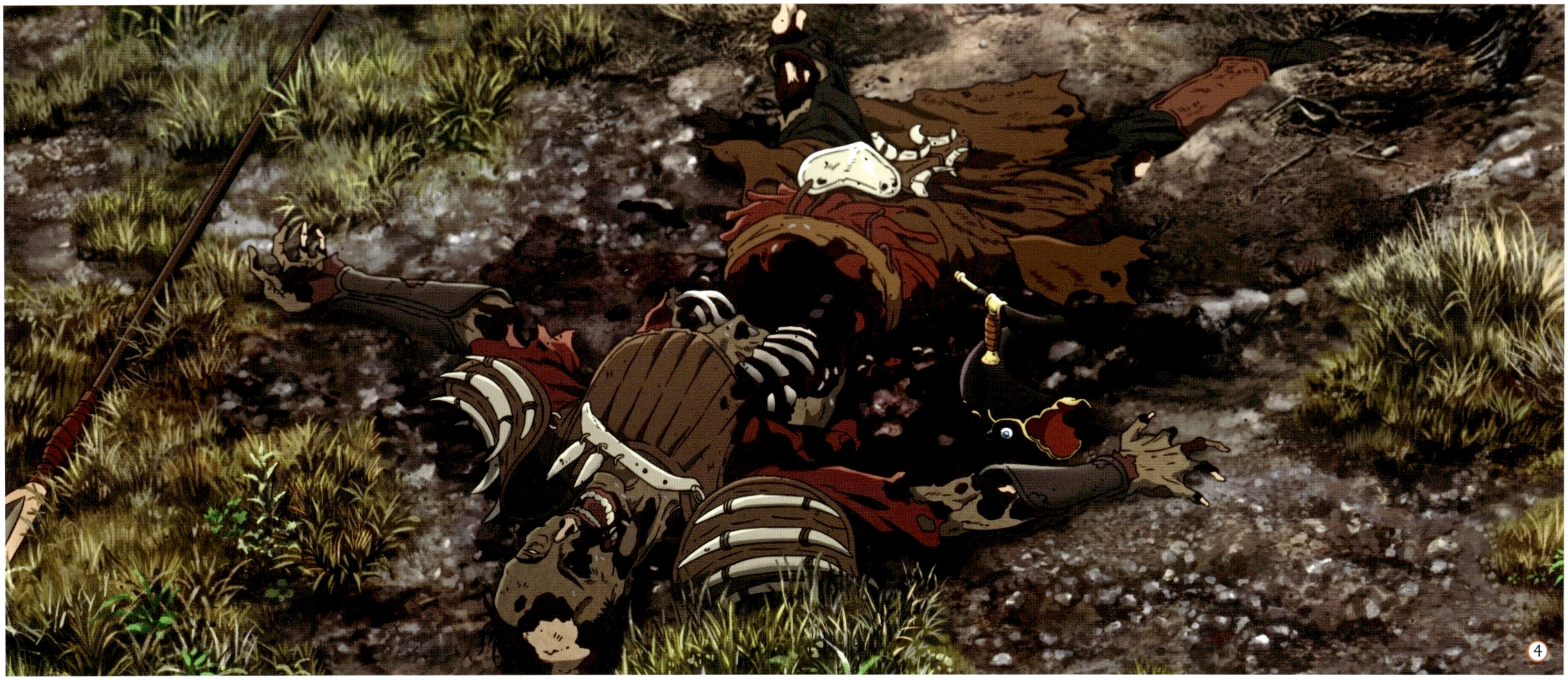

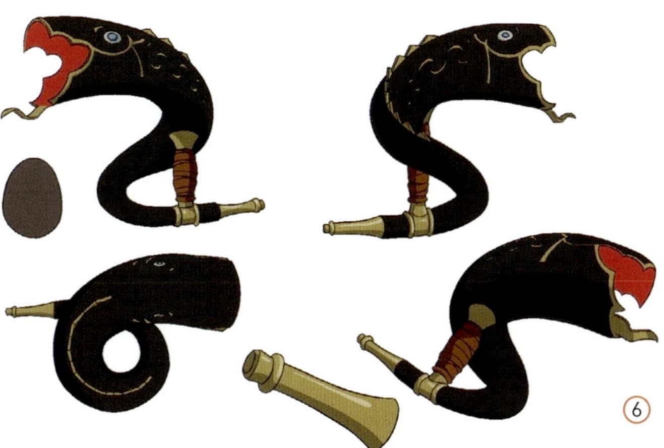

Spiral and serpentine motifs predominate in my spear designs, with openwork inlays of a different metal. There were even traces of Númenórean motifs, holdovers from another Age.

As for the war horns or battle trumpets, they might be fashioned from the horns of some gigantic beast unknown in western Middle-earth. – JOHN HOWE, CONCEPTUAL DESIGNER

The Southron horn had a very unique design. Unique shapes are not a problem in live action, but in animation they may or may not be viable at certain angles and require careful consideration. In the end it was used for a scene in a shot with a 360-degree turn. – KENJI MASUDA, PROP DESIGNER

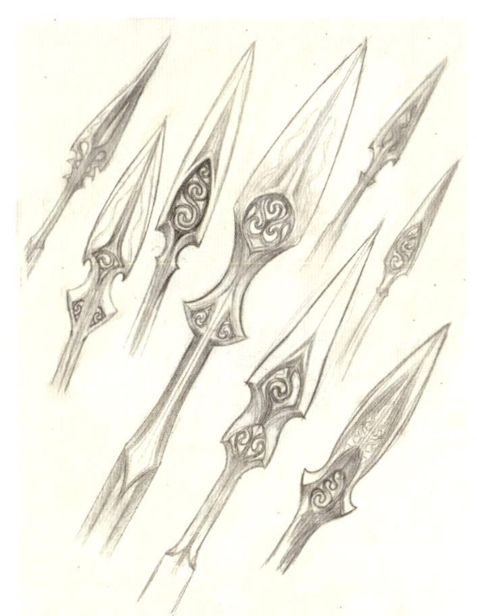

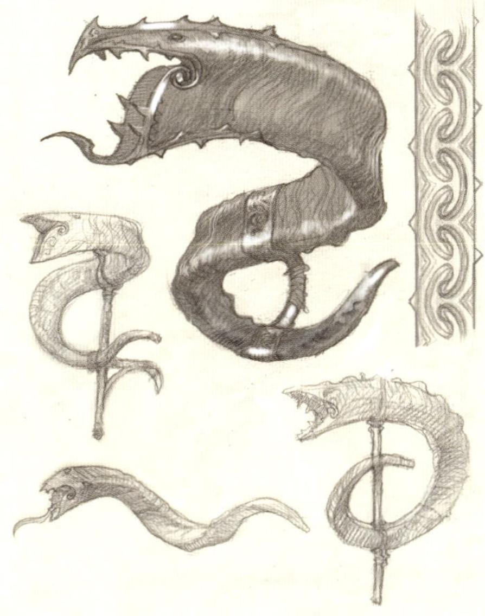

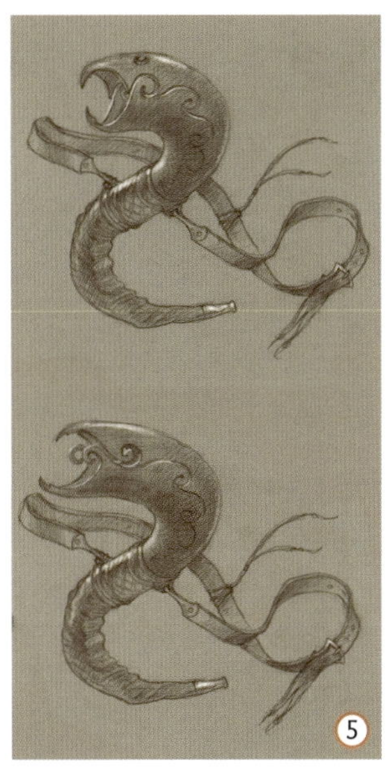

1: Southron mercenary concepts, GH. 2: Southron mercenary character setting art, SH. 3: Southron spear prop setting art, KM. 4: Final film frames. 5: Southron spear and horn concepts, JH. 6: Southron horn prop setting art, KM.

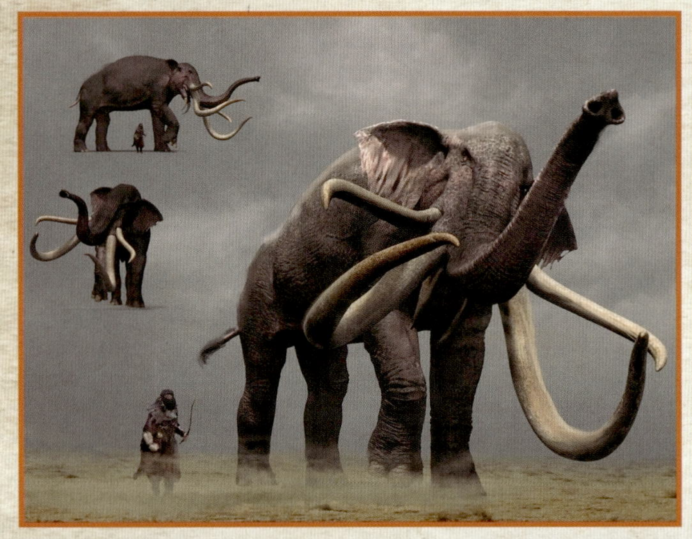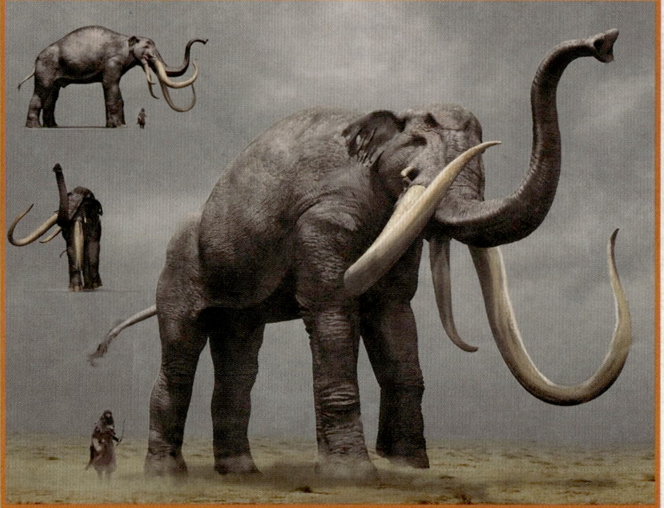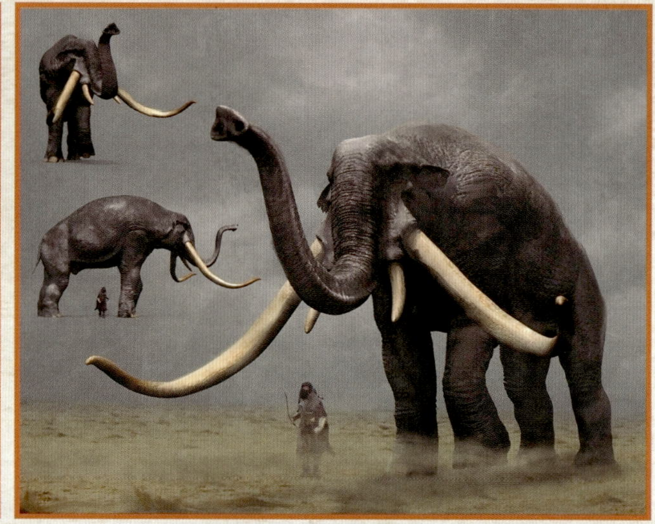

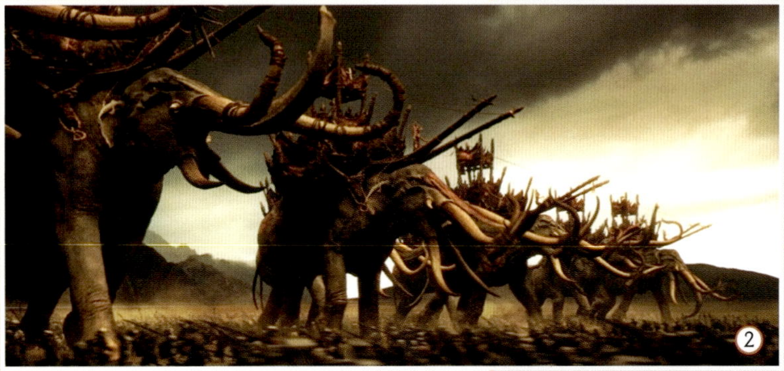

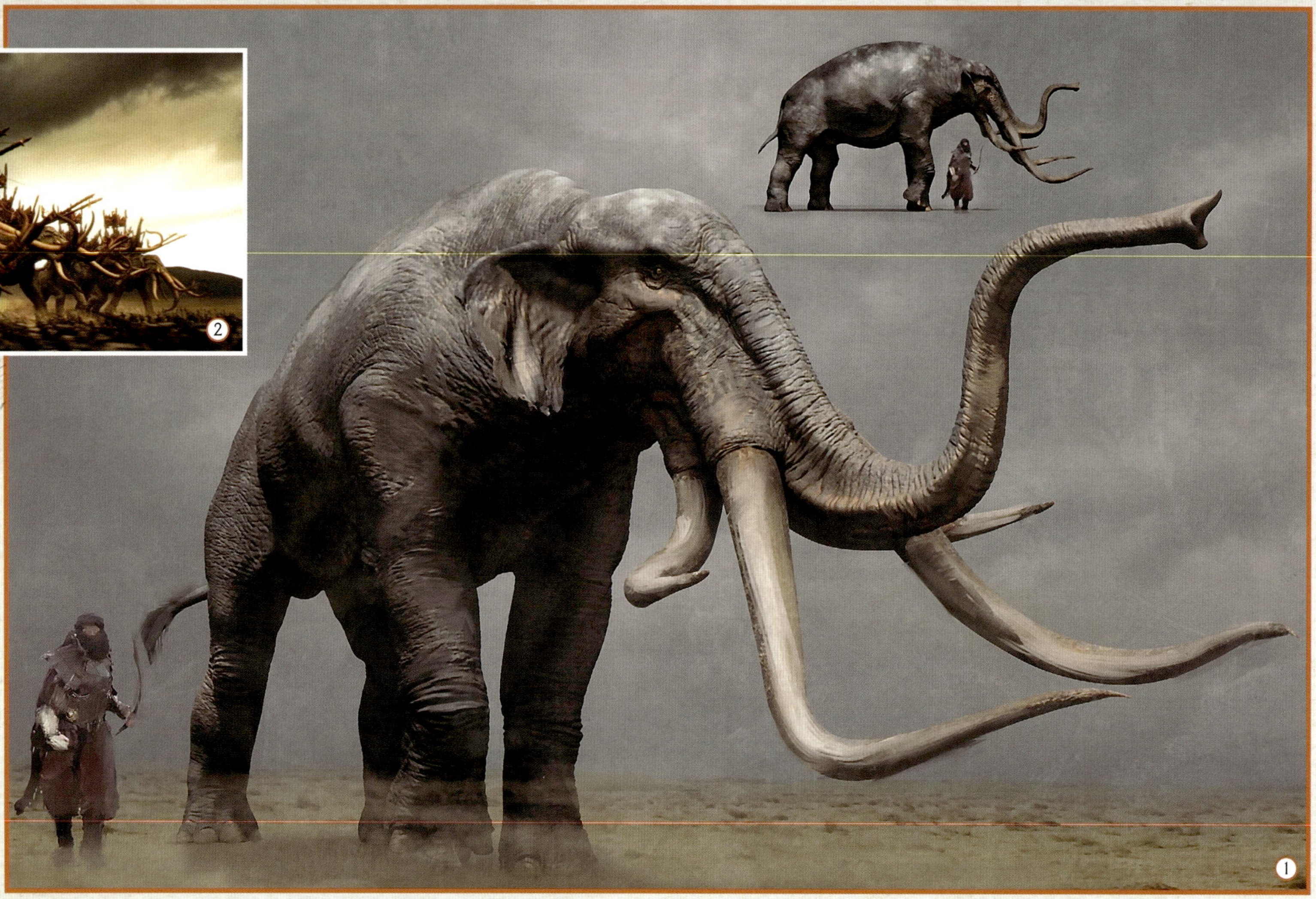

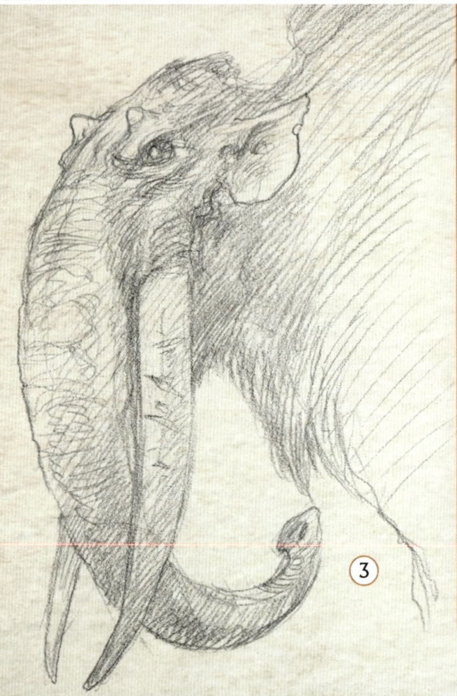

'WHAT WAS THE OLD POEM YOU USED TO RECITE TO ME AS A CHILD?
SOMETHING ABOUT MAKING THE EARTH SHAKE?'

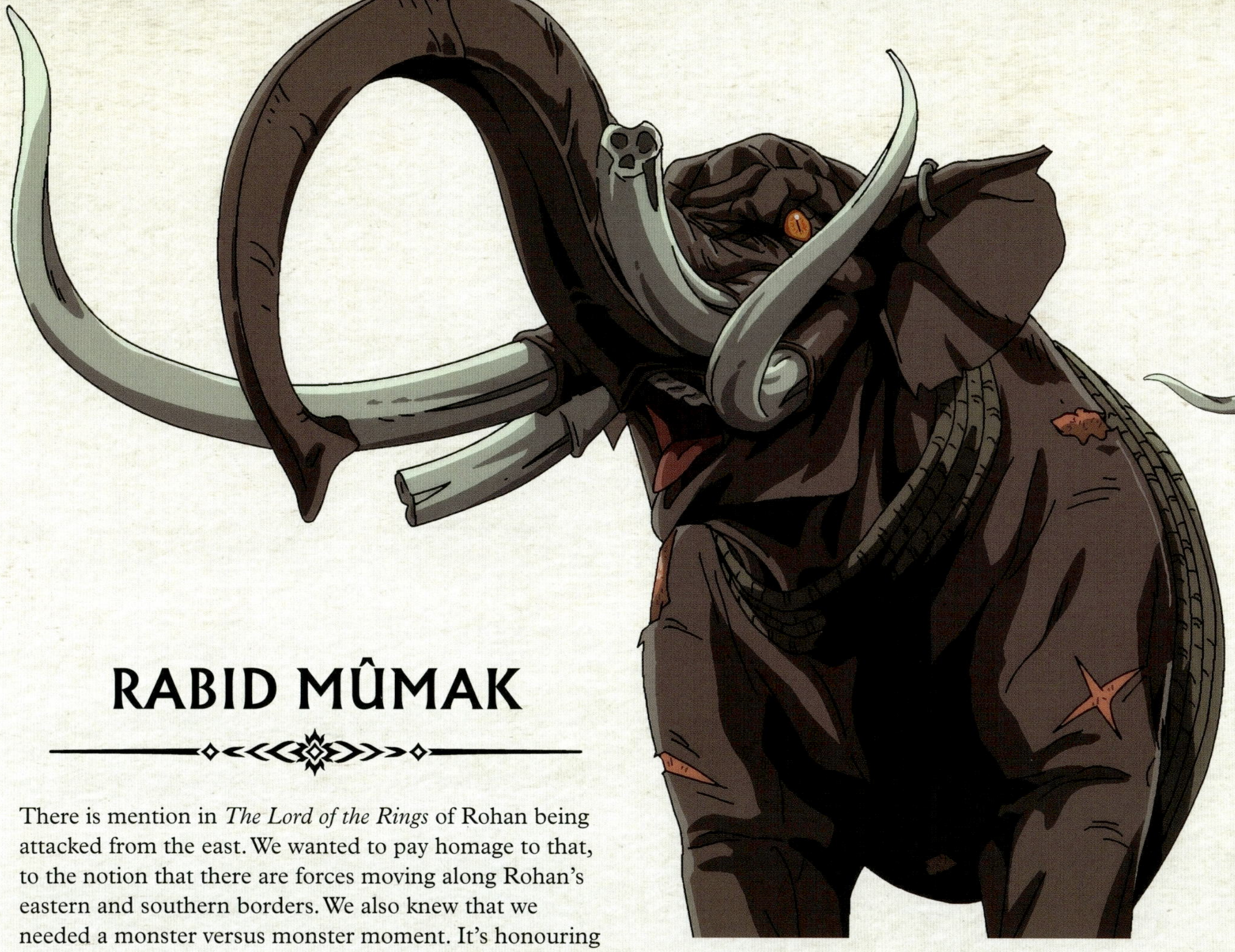

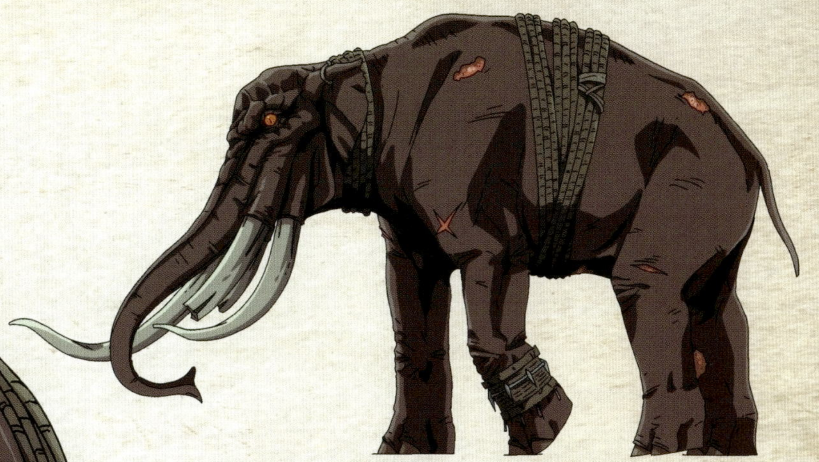

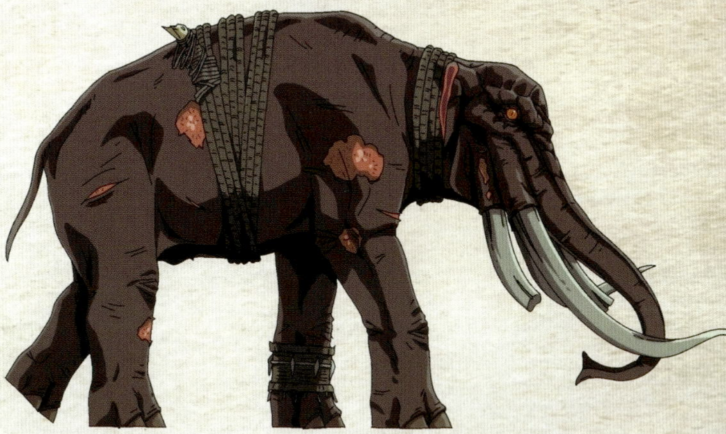

RABID MÛMAK

There is mention in *The Lord of the Rings* of Rohan being attacked from the east. We wanted to pay homage to that, to the notion that there are forces moving along Rohan's eastern and southern borders. We also knew that we needed a monster versus monster moment. It's honouring an anime tradition, which was important to us. How do we do that using monsters that are established in Middle-earth lore, without inventing something new?

The *mûmak* being rabid made it more monstrous and different to what had been seen in the previous films, and even more frightening. It has broken its chains and turned on its masters. That was how the Watcher came to be in the film, too, to fight the *mûmak*. – PHILIPPA BOYENS, PRODUCER

The idea of the rabid *mûmak* being a perversion of its natural form appeals to me, because Wulf has also been corrupted into a twisted, deviant version of himself. Wulf's life is derailed from its natural path, the journey he should have been on. It's fitting then, that before we even see him again, the very first hint of what Wulf has become and the army he has amassed is through this depraved, deadly beast. – ARTY PAPAGEORGIOU, WRITER

Wētā Workshop's artists led the charge on the mûmak *design, imagining a related breed that was at first glance the same as those that had been conceived for the trilogy, but with a few key differences, such as number and configuration of tusks, and overall size. Just as it had twenty years before, inspiration came from prehistoric relatives of modern-day elephants.*

Compared to the live-action version, our *mûmak* was a little smaller. We realized that it needed to be of a size that the Rohirrim soldiers could potentially take it on. The ones in the trilogy were simply too big for the purposes of our action, and especially when it came to the rabid *mûmak* that attacked Héra's party. Being a little bit smaller than the very large war *mûmakil* from the trilogy also meant we could have it move in an interesting way to help demonstrate that it is crazy.

This creature was drawn entirely in 2D and it was quite a demanding process! We had one of the very best animators there is working on it. – KENJI KAMIYAMA, DIRECTOR

1: Mûmak concepts, WW. **2:** Final film frame (LOTR trilogy). **3:** Mûmak concept, JH. **4:** Rabid mûmak creature setting art, IM.

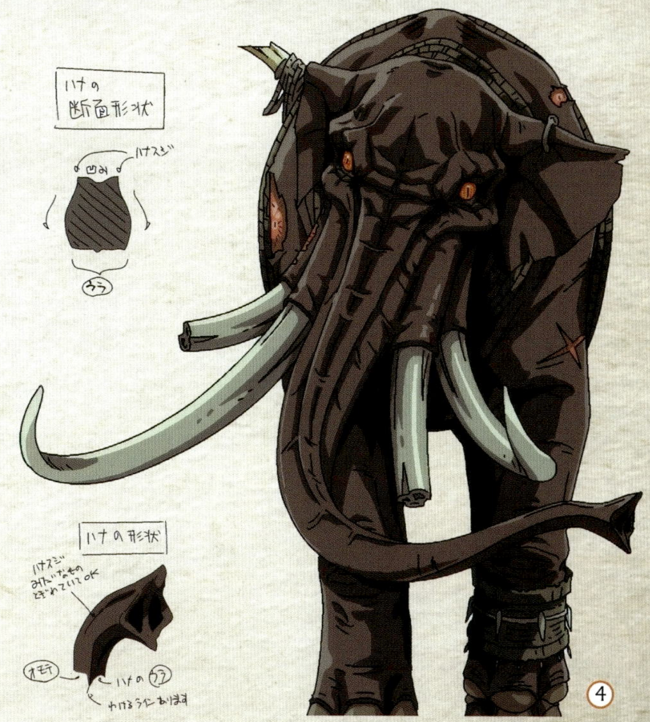

MÛMAK PURSUIT

At first glance it would seem Héra is acting rashly to save Fréaláf – but far from it. Olwyn later points out she knows exactly what she is doing in that moment. Héra is aware that she can't pierce the *mûmak*'s hide, so fighting the creature is useless. Instead, she makes a quick analysis by drawing on her deep knowledge of nature and the land and concocts a completely mad but calculated plan. – PHOEBE GITTINS, WRITER

This moment builds on Héra's use of a lure during the film's opening, with the Fledgling Eagle. Showing Héra's use of lures with these ferocious and wild creatures not only reinforces her bravery and deep understanding of nature, but also proves to be the inspiration for her daring and desperate plan to save her people. We witness Héra willing to sacrifice herself, becoming the lure that sends Wulf's final assault into disarray. – ARTY PAPAGEORGIOU, WRITER

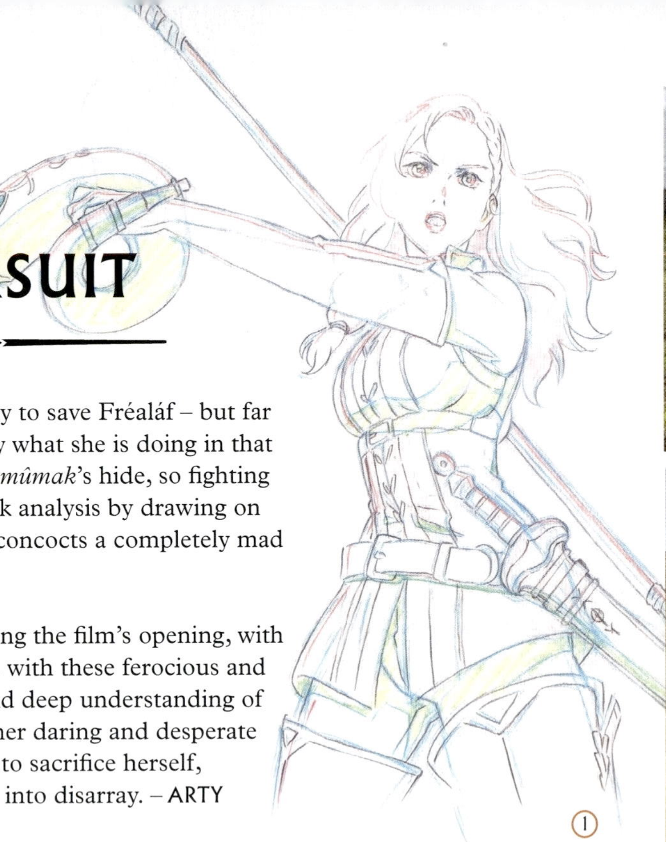

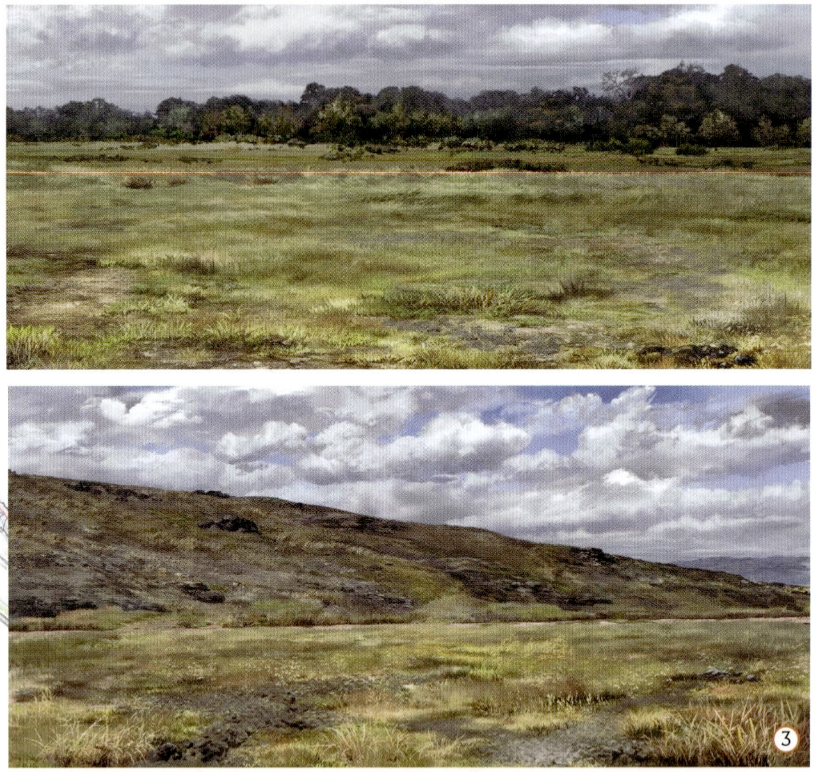

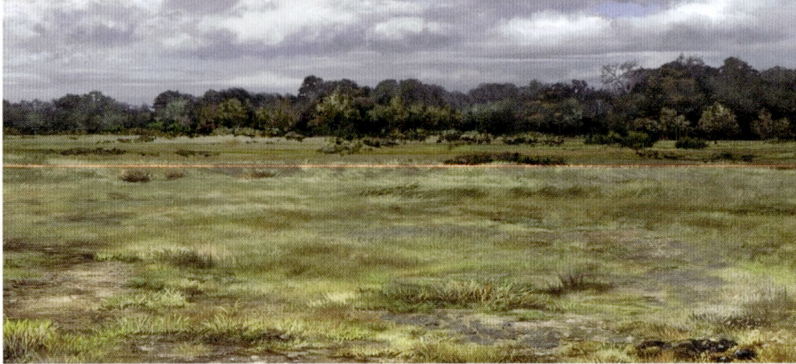

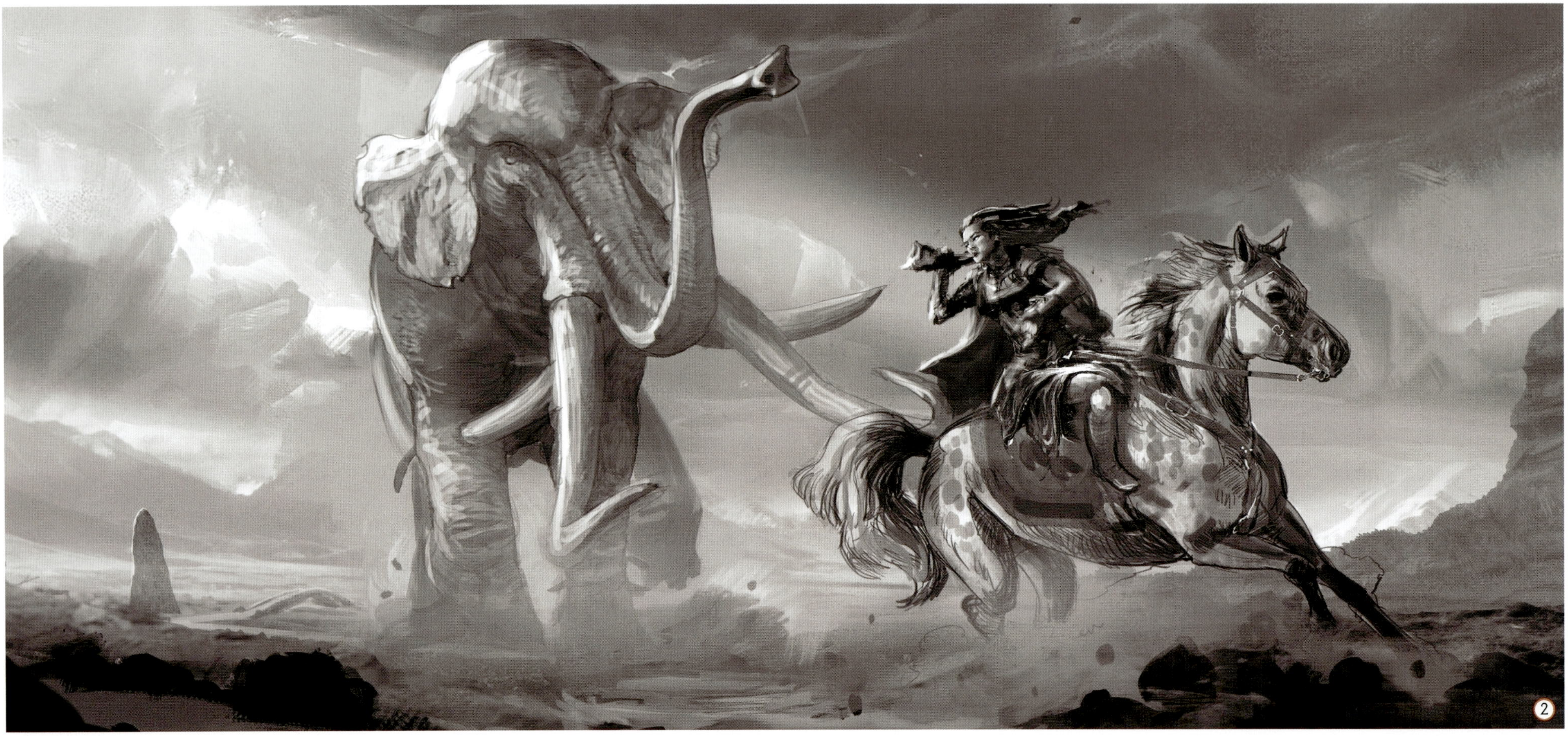

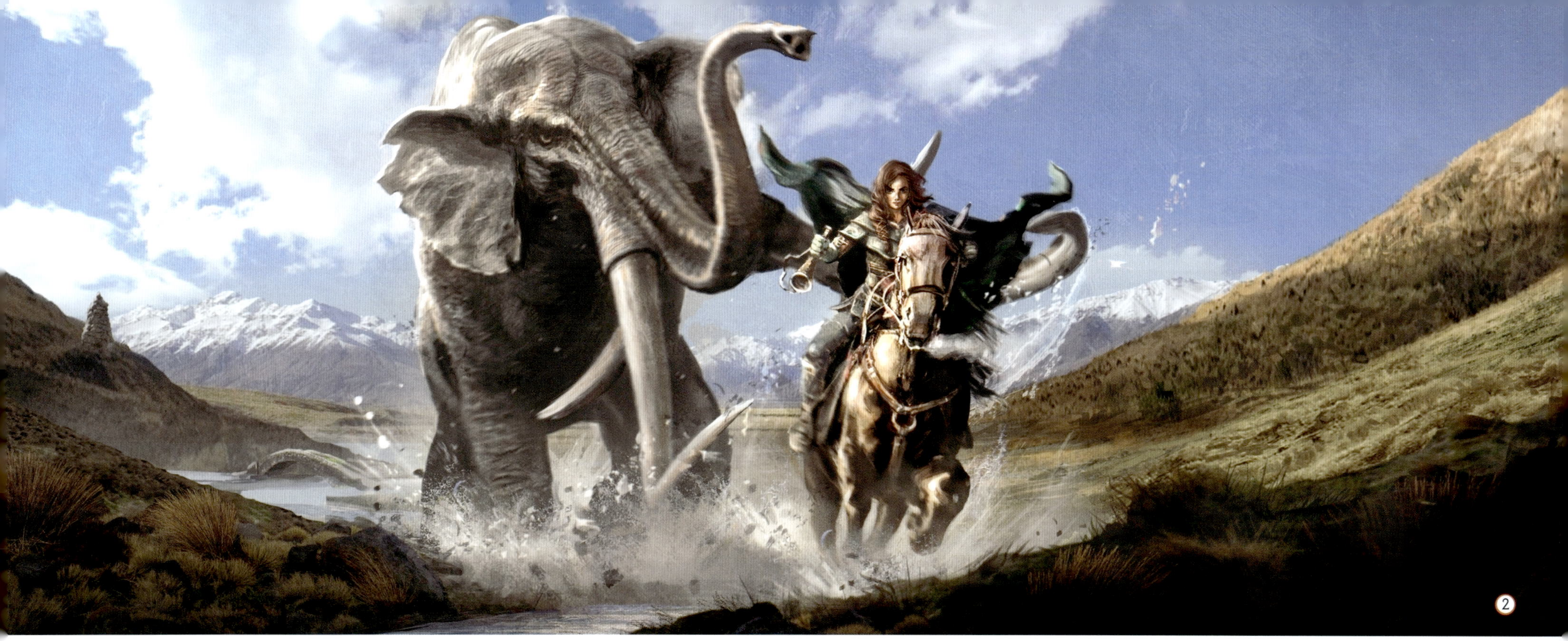

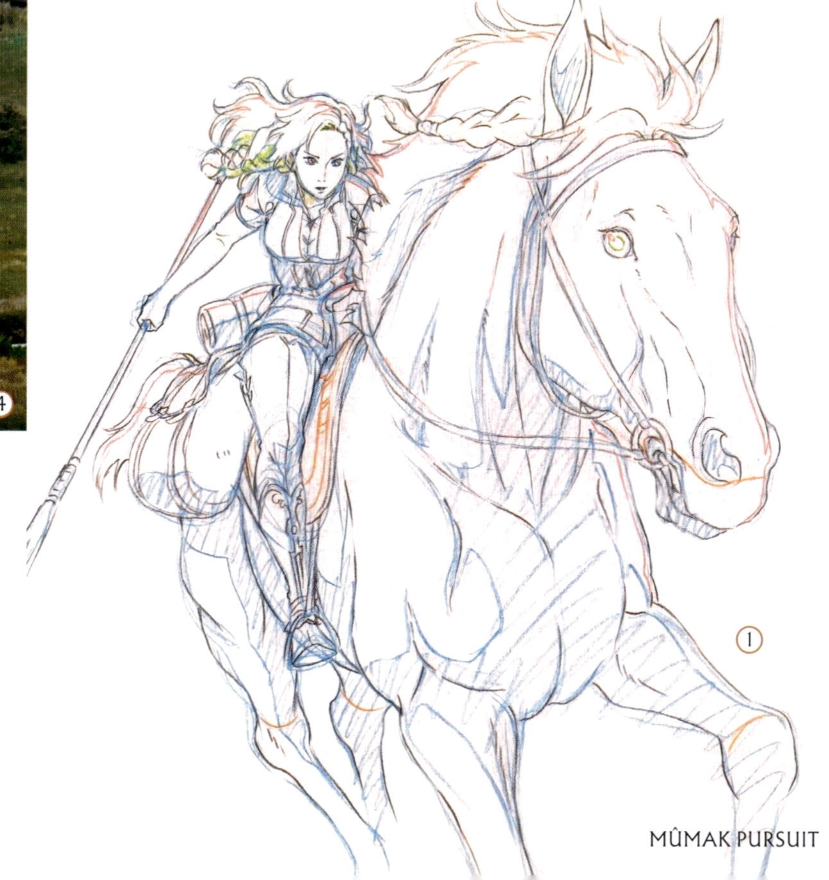

2

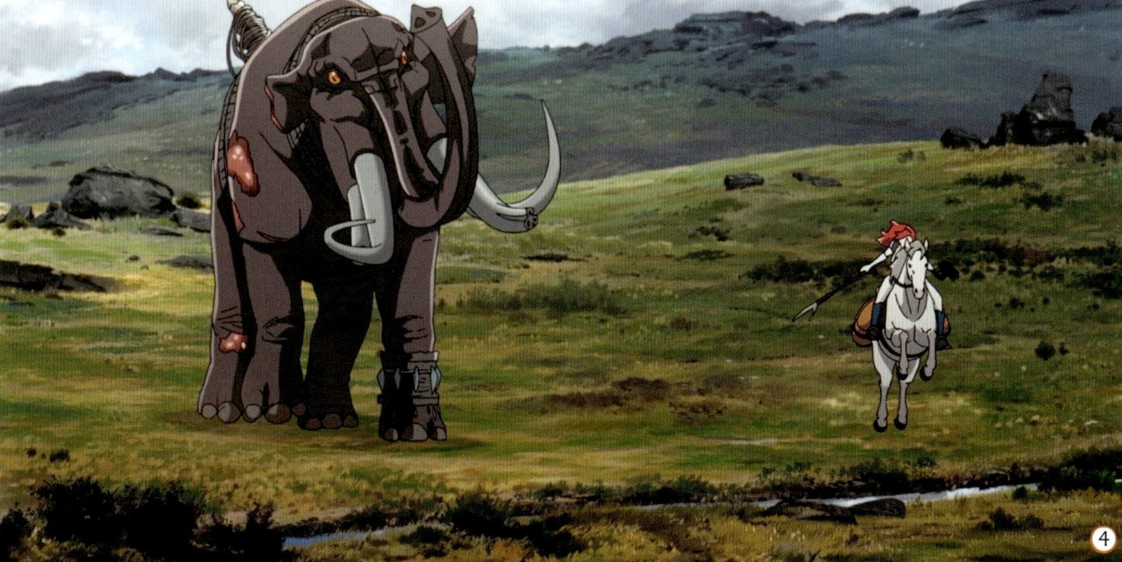

4

1

Problem-solving key scene artwork is all about composing it so that it looks cool and dramatic, trying to capture a concentrated snapshot of the drama of the entire scene in just one image. In this sequence Héra is racing towards the camera, pursued by the *mûmak*. They are the focus, but the other elements in the shot, including the environment, the mountains, the horn, all complement the action in composition and placement, helping to tell the story. Dark going to light and back to dark again, creates a sense of depth. – GUS HUNTER, WĒTĀ WORKSHOP SENIOR CONCEPT ARTIST

1: Animation key frames, MT. **2:** Mûmak pursuit key scene concepts, GH. **3:** Plains of Rohan background art. **4:** Final film frame.

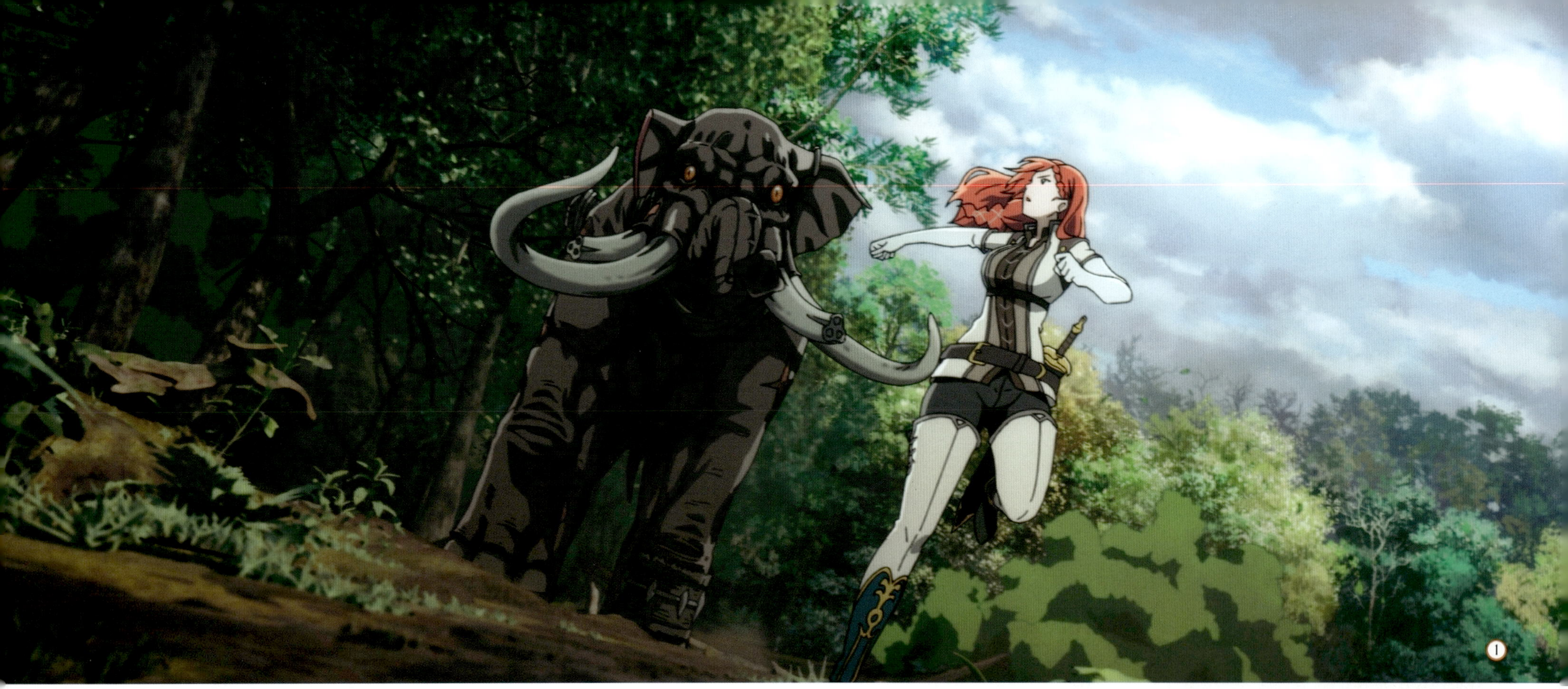

WEALD SE WITEGA

Rohan is a region of rolling plains, but threading the golden grasslands are streams and rivers, and punctuating its expanses are small lakes and patches of woods. Days spent riding far from home and nights sleeping under the stars have taught Héra about many of Rohan's secret places. Among them is the Weald se Witega, a small patch of tangled woodland reputedly haunted by some unsavoury thing. Héra knows what lurks in the waters at the centre of the wood, and counts on it to save her from the beast pursuing her.

Cartographer Daniel Reeve and I were talking about what to call the forest. We were trying to find something that would hint at the creature lurking there, without giving too much away. *Weald se Witega*; the Forest of the Guardian; the guardian being a reference to the Watcher, in Old English. – PHILIPPA BOYENS, PRODUCER

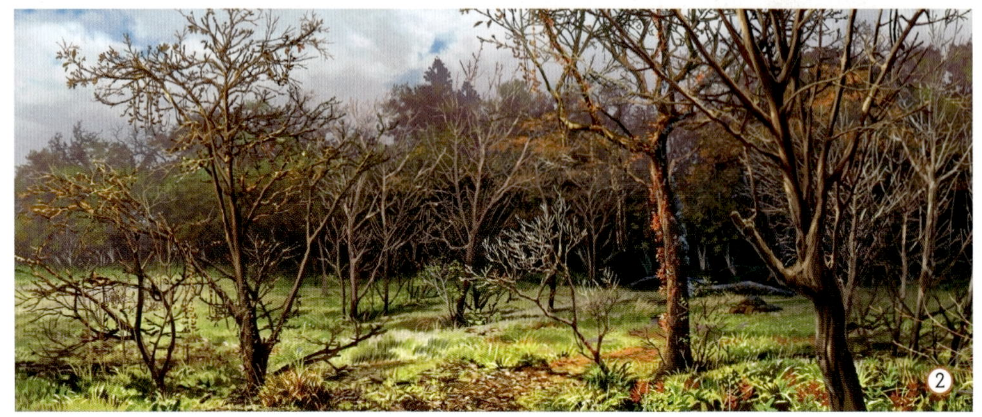

'DOES SHE KNOW WHAT KIND OF CREATURE LIVES IN THOSE WOODS?!'

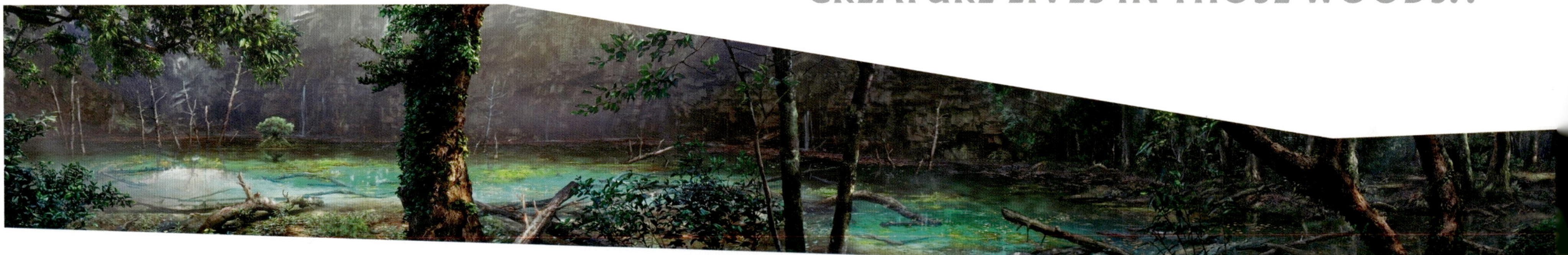

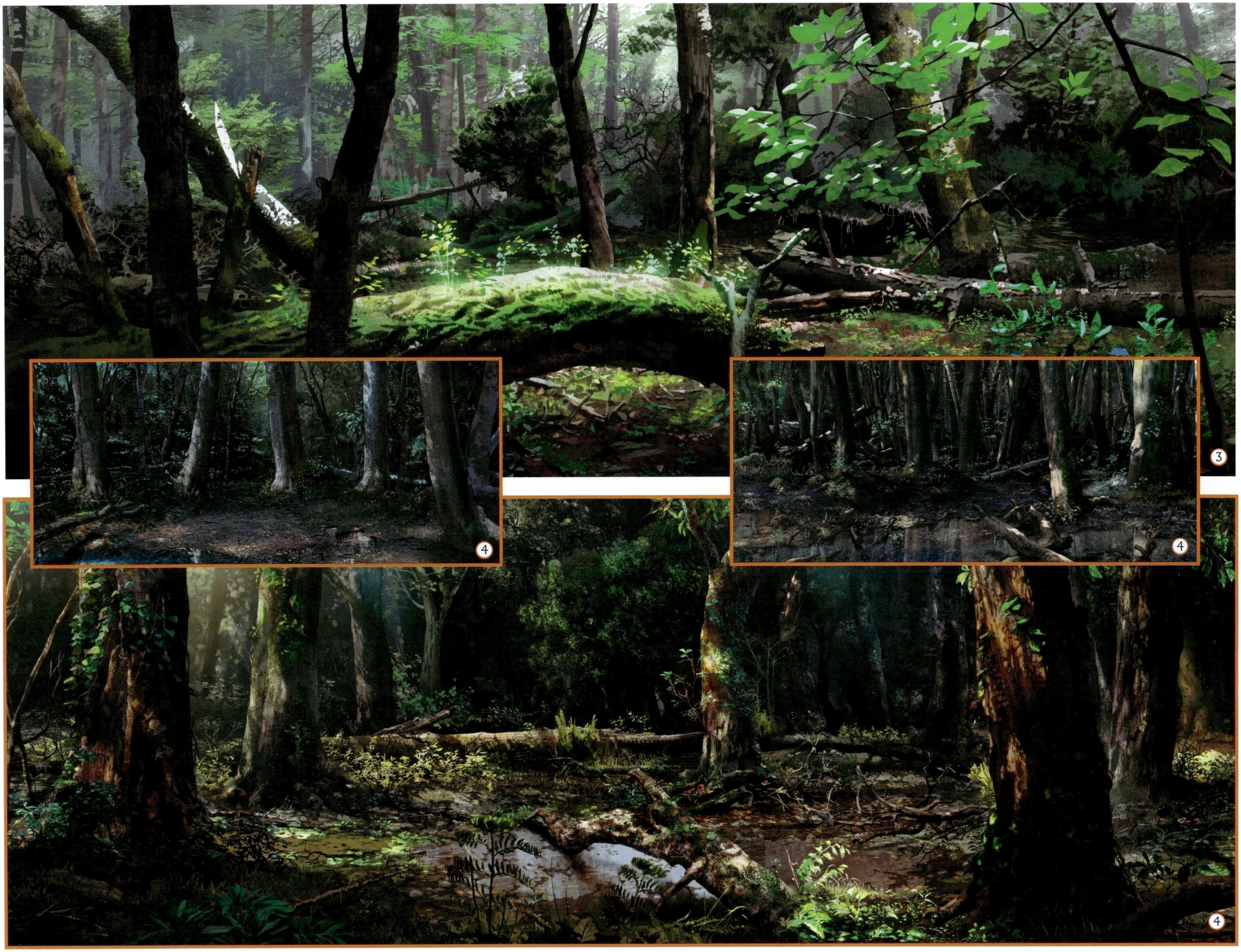

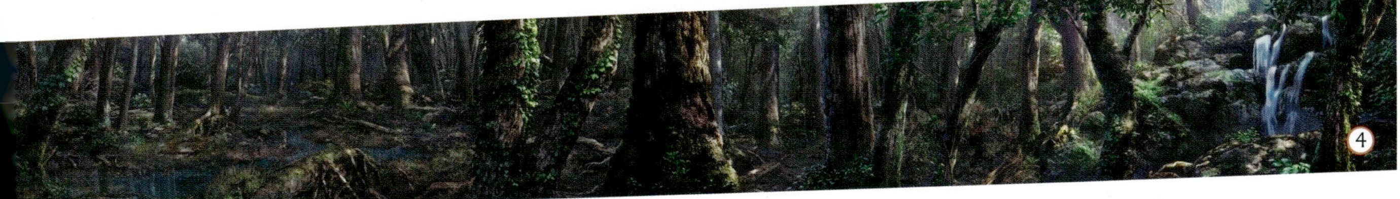

1: Final film frame. **2:** Woodland border background setting art, KS.
3: Weald se Witega background setting art, YY. **4:** Weald se Witega background art.

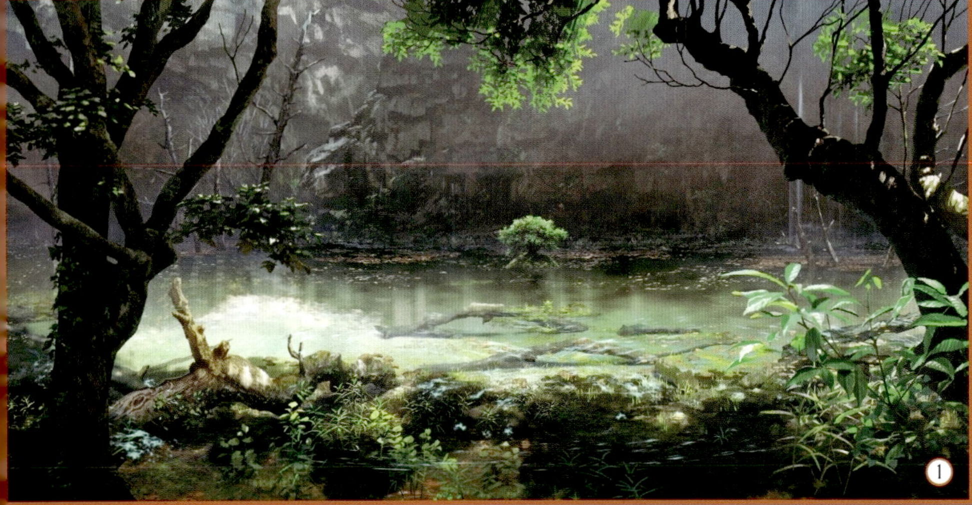

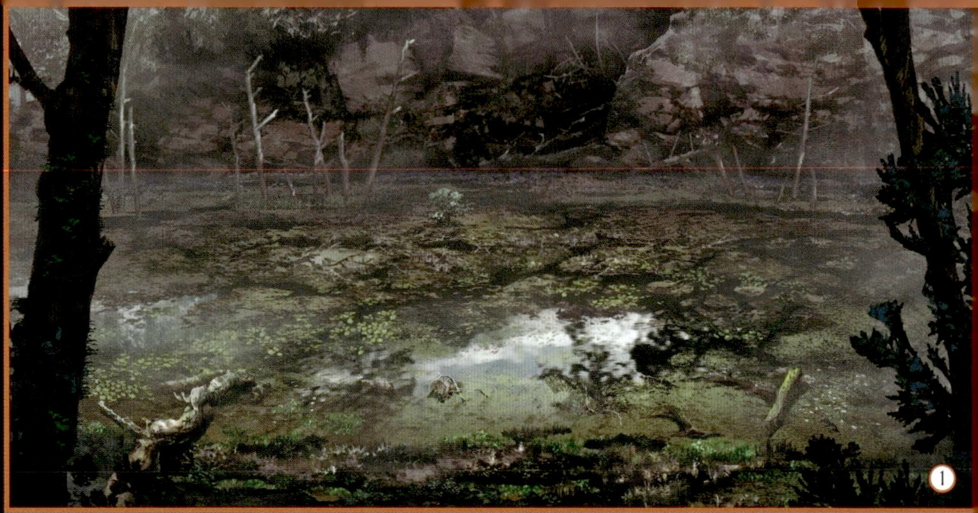

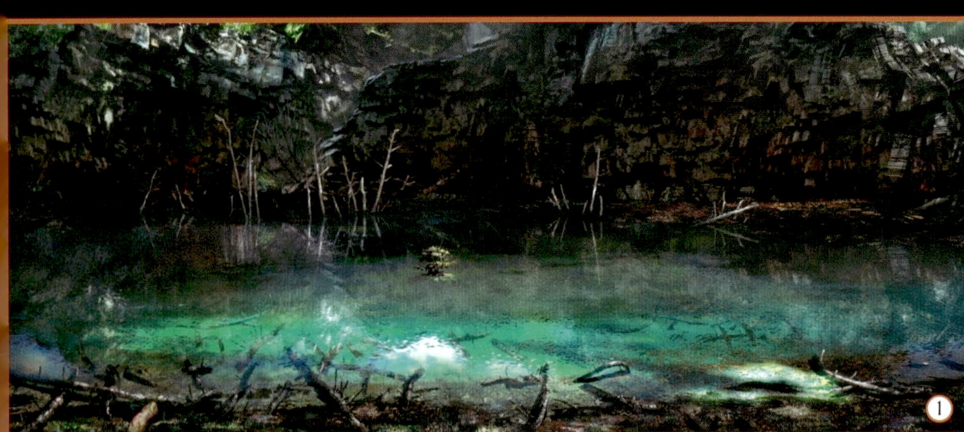

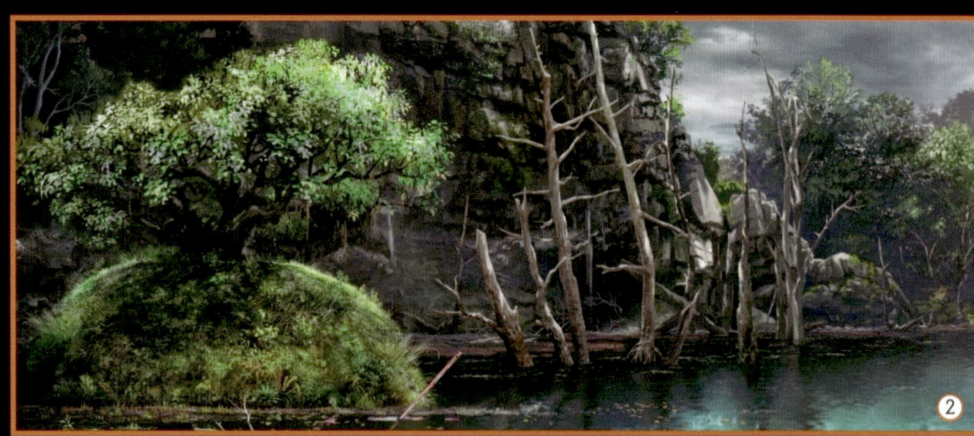

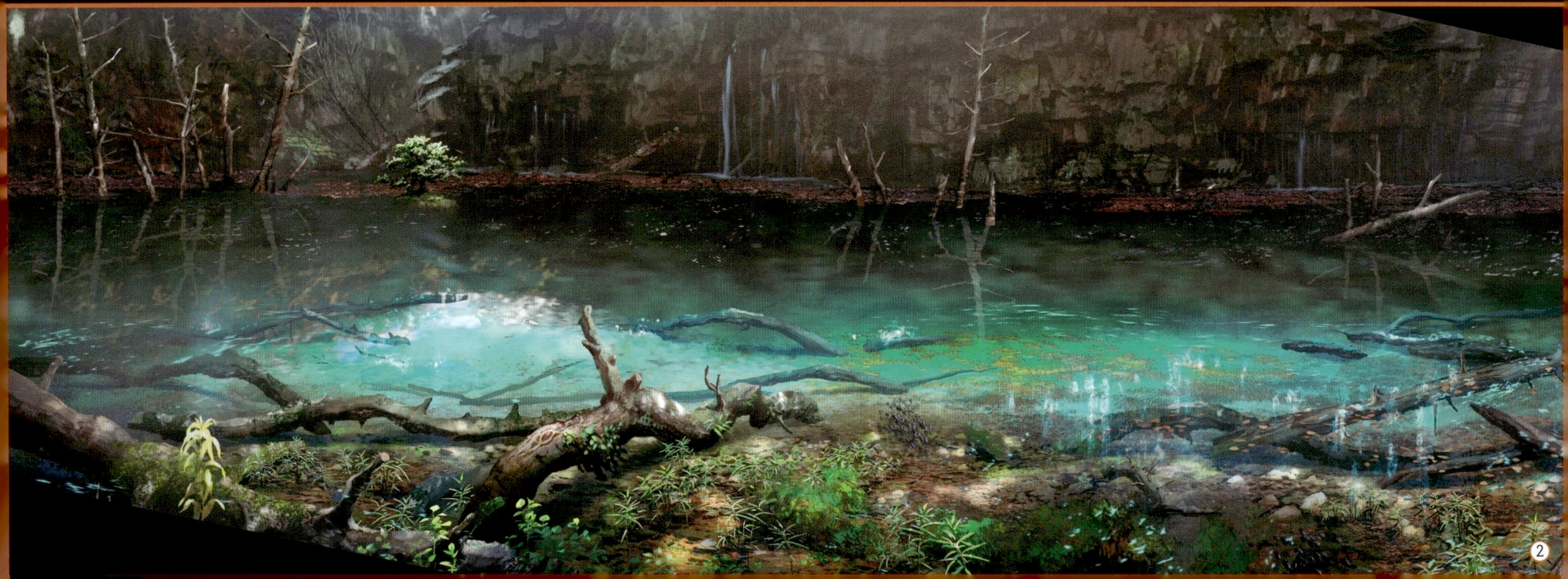

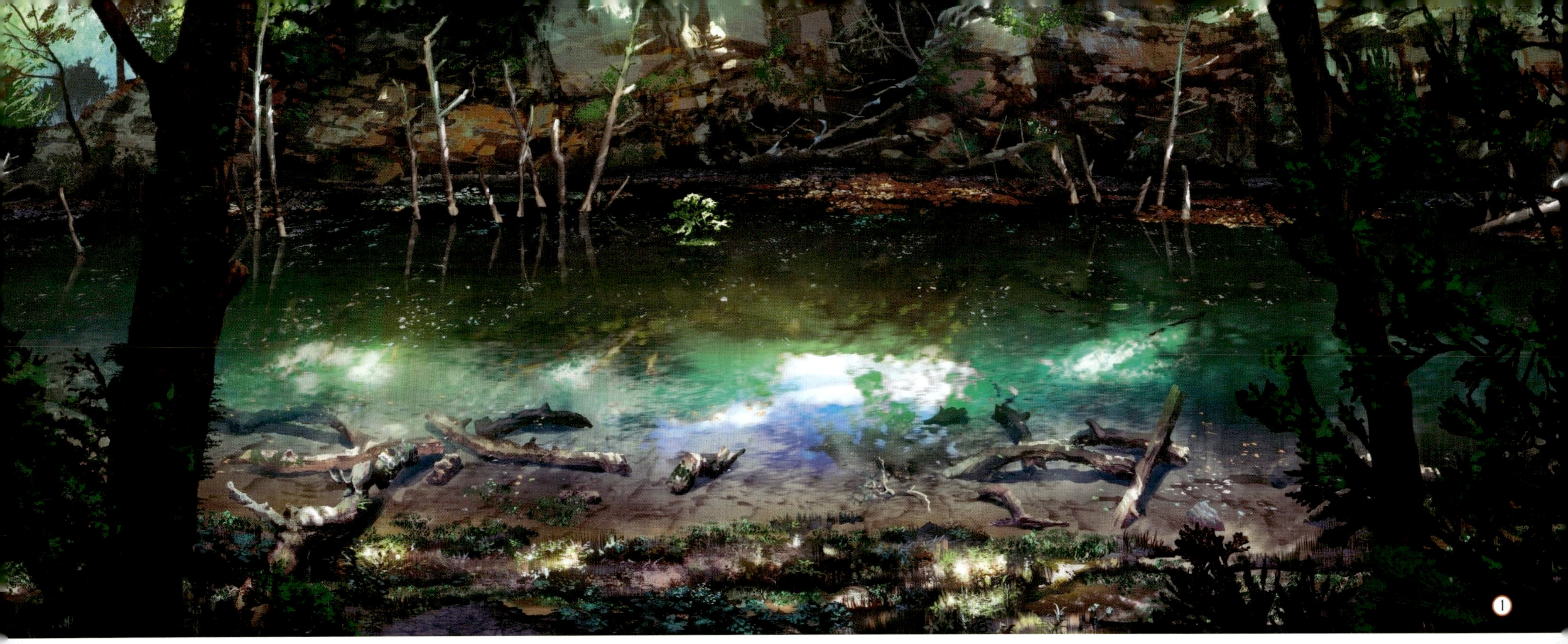

The Wētā Workshop artists had produced some imagery of the Watcher and *mûmak* fighting which had a misty grey colour scheme. That was a reference point for us as we began designing the look of the gloomy forest. The shadows of the tangled trees kept the forest in darker hues, but when Héra comes to the edge of the lake it becomes lighter and the sky is visible. – YASUHIRO YAMANE, ART DIRECTOR

In *The Fellowship of the Ring* the Watcher was seen at night, so the audience didn't get a good look at it. In *The War of the Rohirrim*, the scene with the Watcher takes place during the day and is one of the film's spectacles. When Héra arrives, it's a beautiful little lake. The intent was to suggest that it's a very nice, pretty place. Why would she come here? We were trying to mislead the audience and then surprise them when the creature appeared, so the point for Kamiyama was to make it a serene rather than scary or dark place. – JOSEPH CHOU, PRODUCER

The forest scene is the only one in the entire film in which there are trees. At first, I was going for a more autumnal, withered forest, but it ended up looking a little creepy. We thought it might be better to lull the audience into false ease by making the strange lake in the middle of the forest quite beautiful, setting them up to be surprised when suddenly a tentacled creature erupts from it.

I hope that the lush forest scene is an accent for the film. The fact that many different artists contributed to the scene accounts for some variation in style. The landscape is the most familiar to me of all the film's environments. I was inspired by local vegetation, so it probably has a vaguely Asian feeling to it. – YASUHIRO YAMANE, ART DIRECTOR

1: Weald se Witega background setting art, TK. 2: Weald se Witega background art.

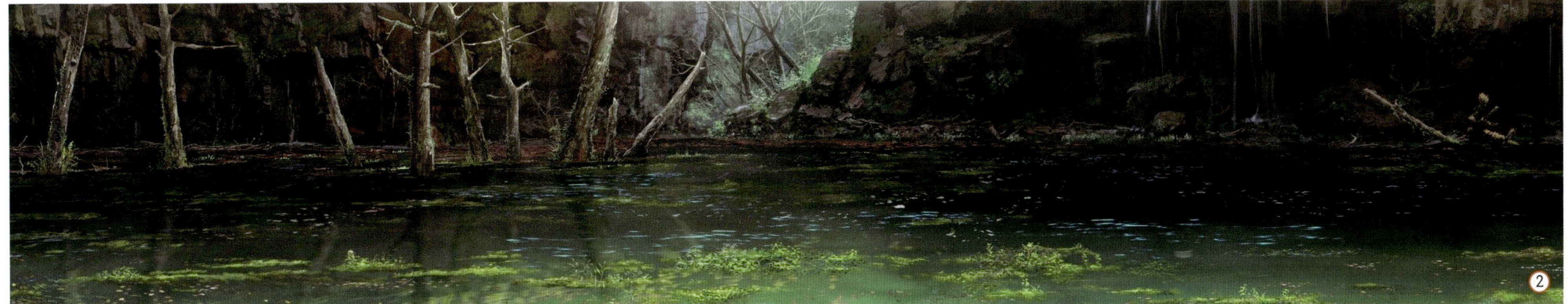

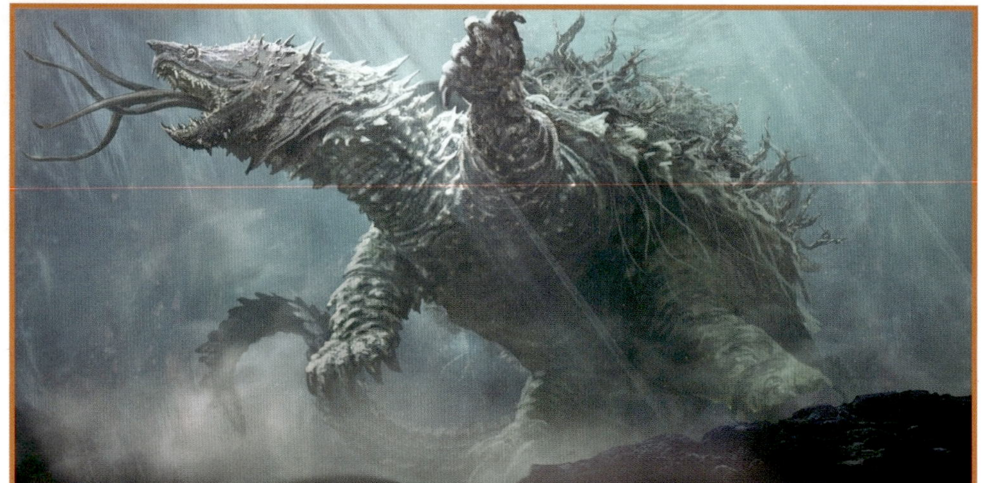

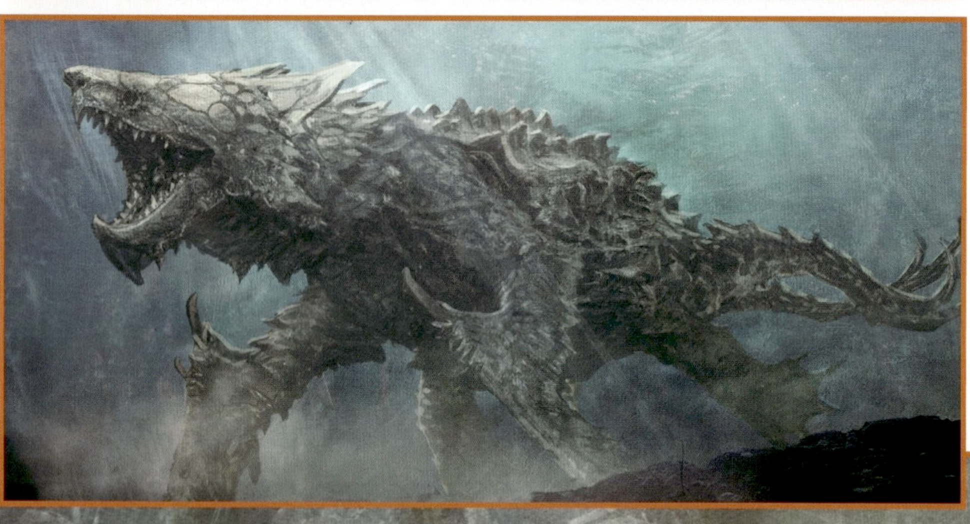

THE WATCHER IN THE WOOD

The murky pond in the middle of the old wood hides a secret, one that Héra hopes she can turn to her advantage. While the script had always identified it as a Watcher, or guardian, like the one we saw outside the West-gate of Moria, we briefly experimented with the notion of the creature lurking there being something we hadn't seen before. We were wary of inventing monsters. Tolkien's creatures tend to recall those of our own world, but with a unique Middle-earth twist, or scaled up.

In one of Tolkien's poems he describes a giant sea turtle-like creature, so I felt that something along the lines of a huge freshwater turtle might not be too big a conceptual leap. It is evocative of something ancient and forgotten from the First Age, and on a practical level I imagined that it might be significantly simpler to animate than a creature with lots of tentacles! Gus Hunter illustrated the concept and did an amazing job with his matamata/snapping turtle-inspired designs! – DANIEL FALCONER, ADDITIONAL CONCEPTS DESIGNER

1: Swamp creature concepts, GH. 2: Swamp creature concept, DF. 3: Watcher concept, AL.

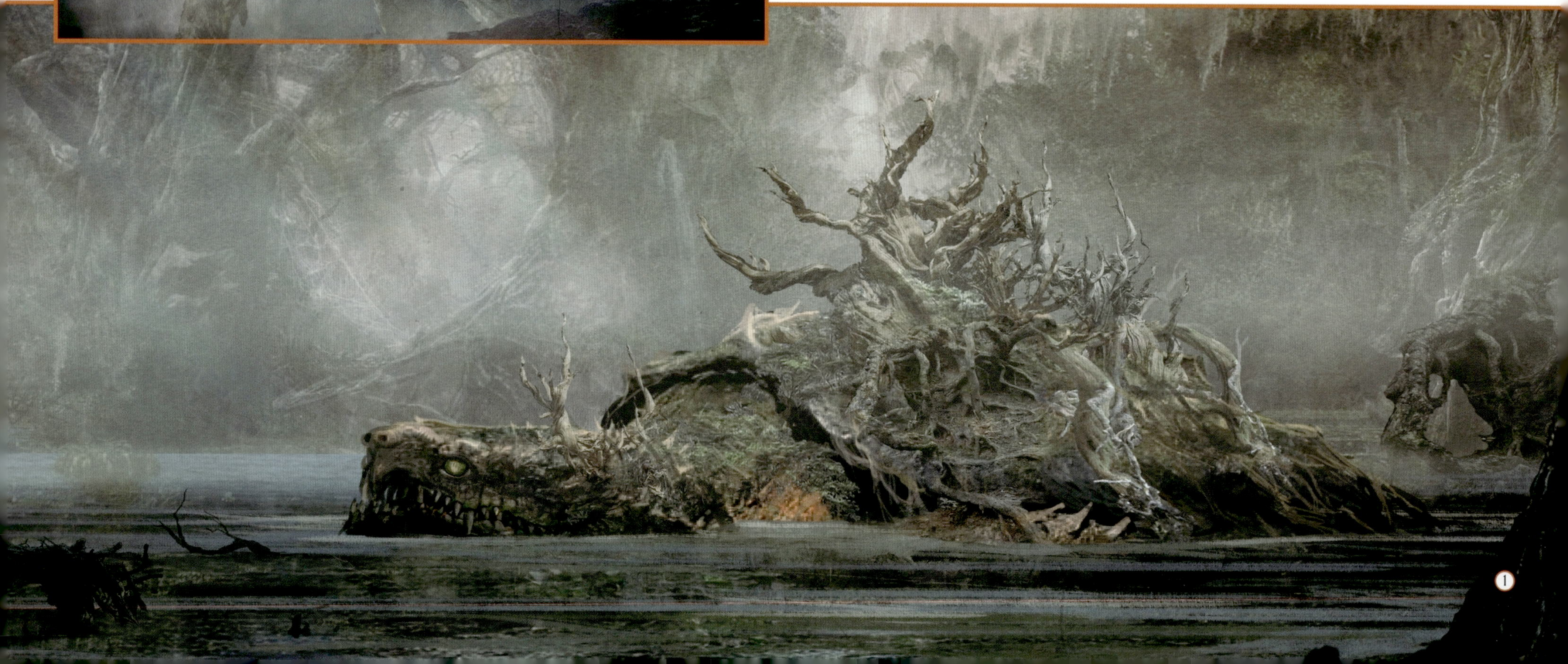

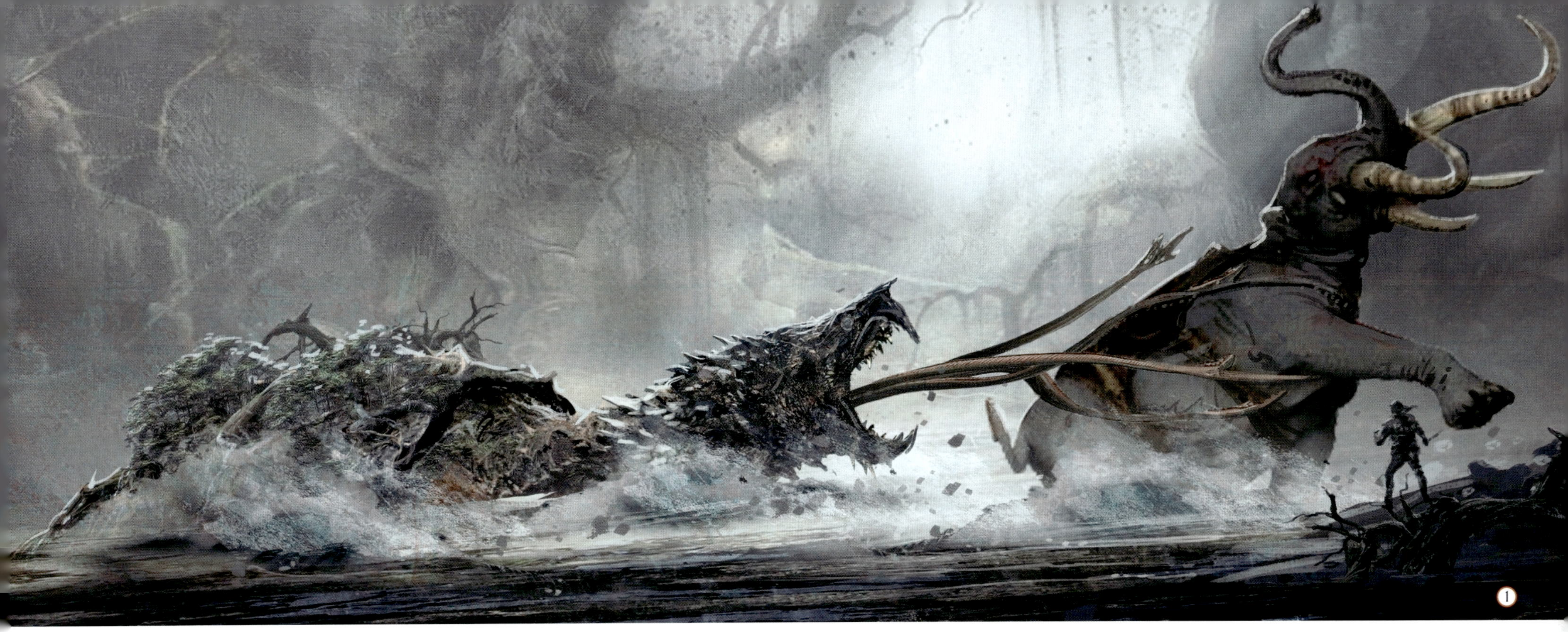

'BEWARE DARK WATERS, THAT HIDE OLD SECRETS . . .'

There are lots of precedents in Tolkien's writings for malevolent and dangerous trees. We were imagining what might lurk in the forest, if it wasn't a Watcher like the one outside Moria. How about a creature with tentacle-like roots – a sort of vegetable swamp-thing – that bind around the *mûmak* and drag it under? I thought that might be a striking piece of animation. – ALAN LEE, CONCEPTUAL DESIGNER

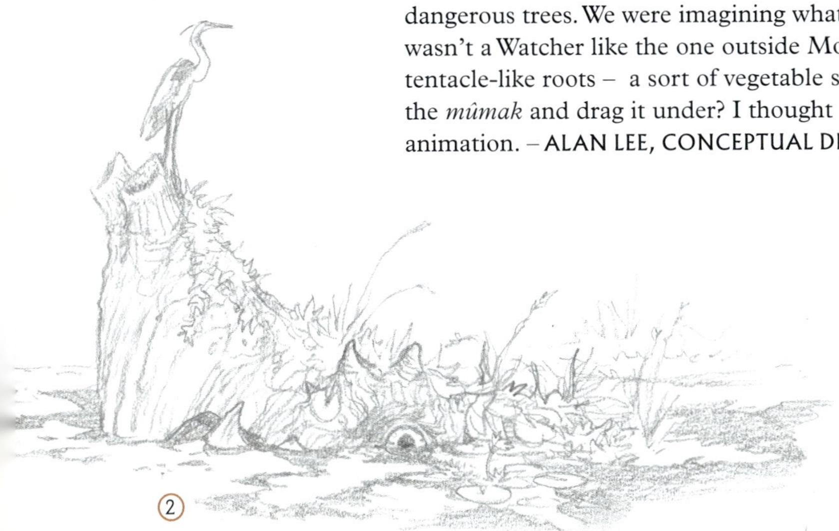

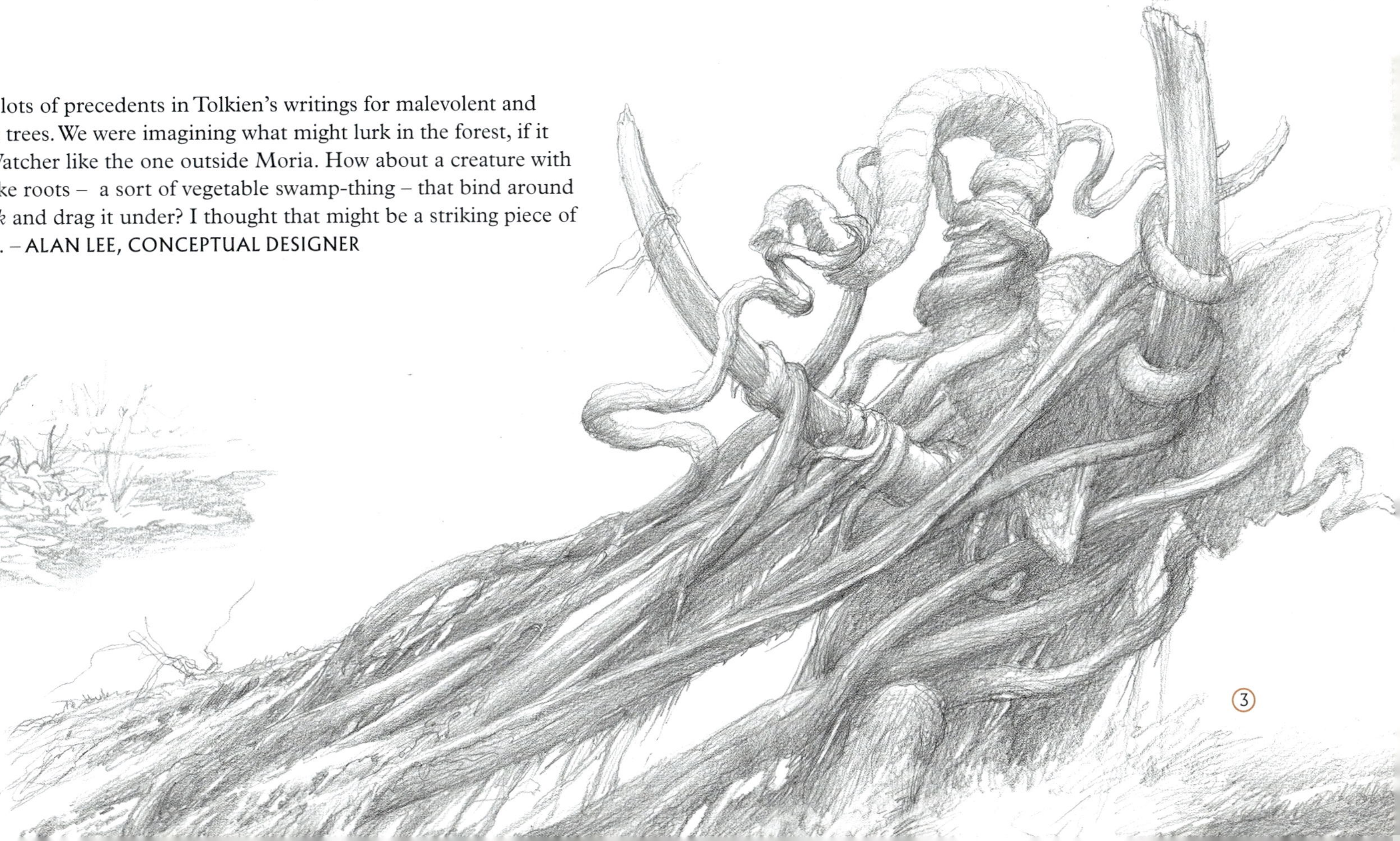

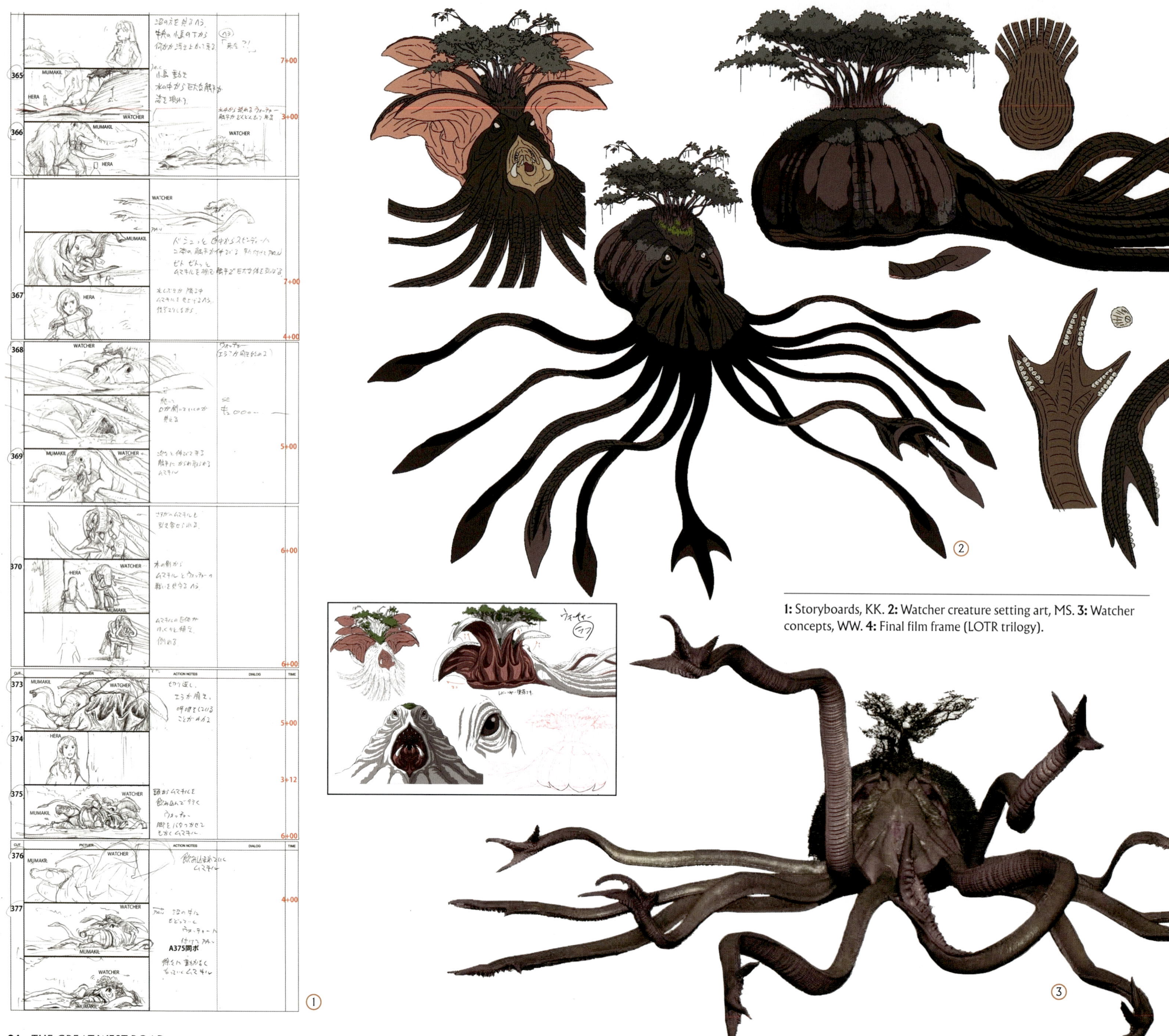

1: Storyboards, KK. 2: Watcher creature setting art, MS. 3: Watcher concepts, WW. 4: Final film frame (LOTR trilogy).

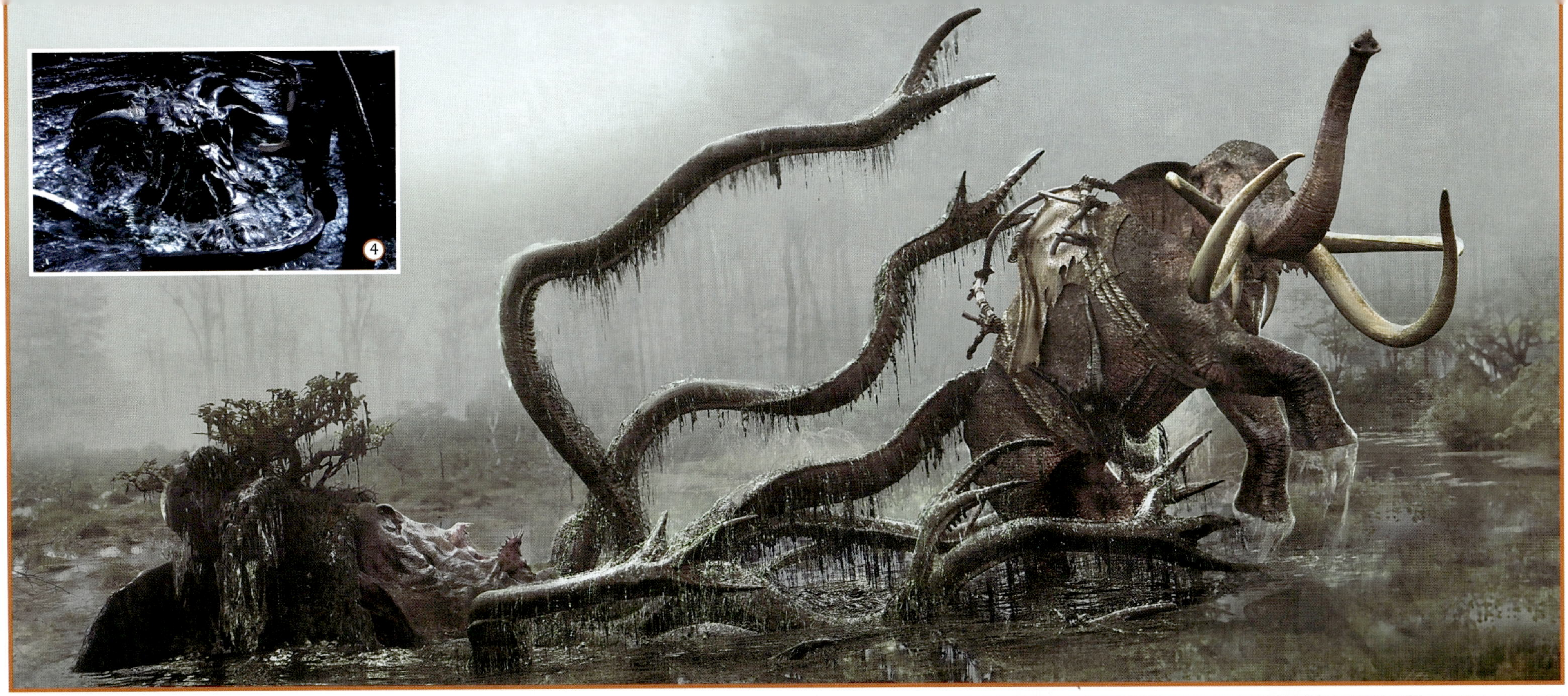

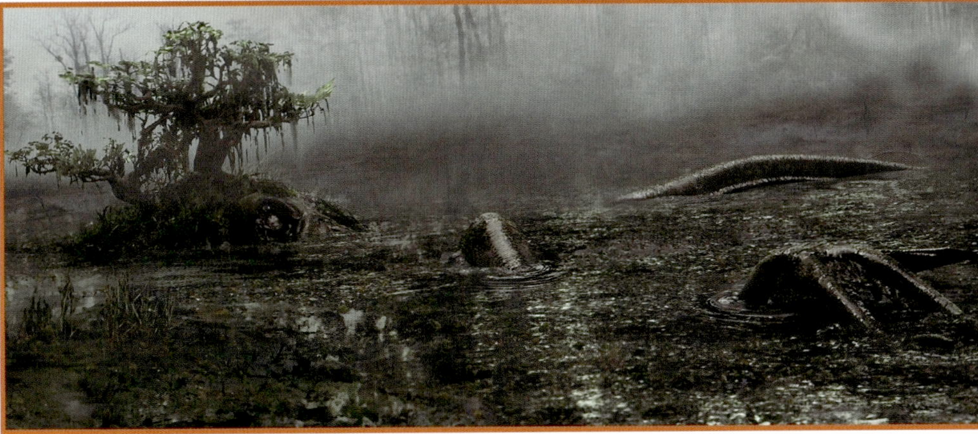 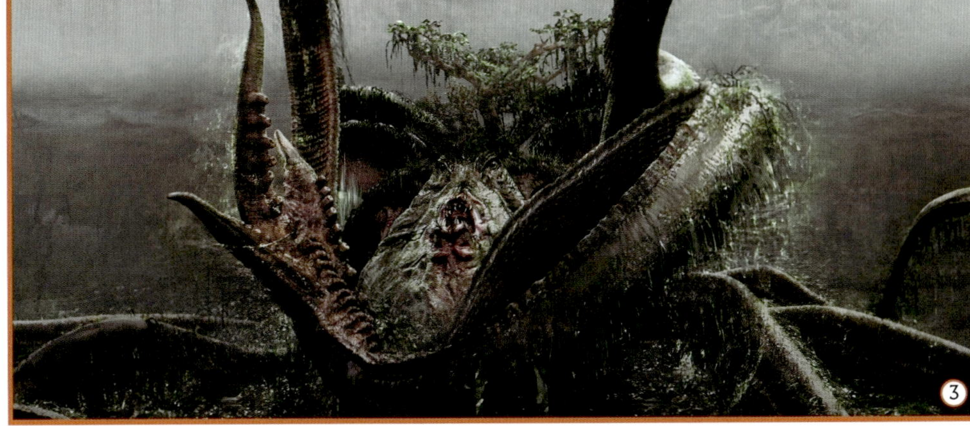

In the end, our Watcher ended up a big squid-like critter that called back to the nameless thing outside the West-gate of Moria, which was what the writers had in mind and were honouring when they wrote the scene. The cool thing was how the new context in which it appeared changed the creature and made it feel fresh. That's where the thought of putting a tree on its back came from. This is a creature left over from a different time. I imagined the stagnant mire in which it lives is shrinking. It can't even fully submerge any more, so there's stuff growing on it. Eventually, as the world changes, it will be gone and all that will remain of this beast is the myth of it, and a tree. – DANIEL FALCONER, ADDITIONAL CONCEPTS DESIGNER

I loved the design of the Watcher, with its tree on the top. I thought it was really interesting and fun. I liked the idea of the tree being a way to lure and confuse prey. It creates an interesting setting for us because it really doesn't move at all until something comes close enough to be snatched. It feels like it has been here for a very long time. – KENJI KAMIYAMA, DIRECTOR

I was very happy that we got to have the Watcher in our film. It was hugely important to me that we have some more fantastical elements like the *mûmak* and Watcher fight in what was otherwise a story about two tribes of Horse-lords going to war. There was some talk of cutting it, but I put my foot down. I felt that we had to be mindful of audience expectations to see creatures in a fantasy movie. We might not have Elves or hobbits, but we could have these.

Tolkien never explained the creature's presence in *The Fellowship of the Ring* in detail, so we felt it gave us the freedom to have another one living somewhere else in Middle-earth. They're probably not common, but maybe there are more out there? – JASON DEMARCO, PRODUCER

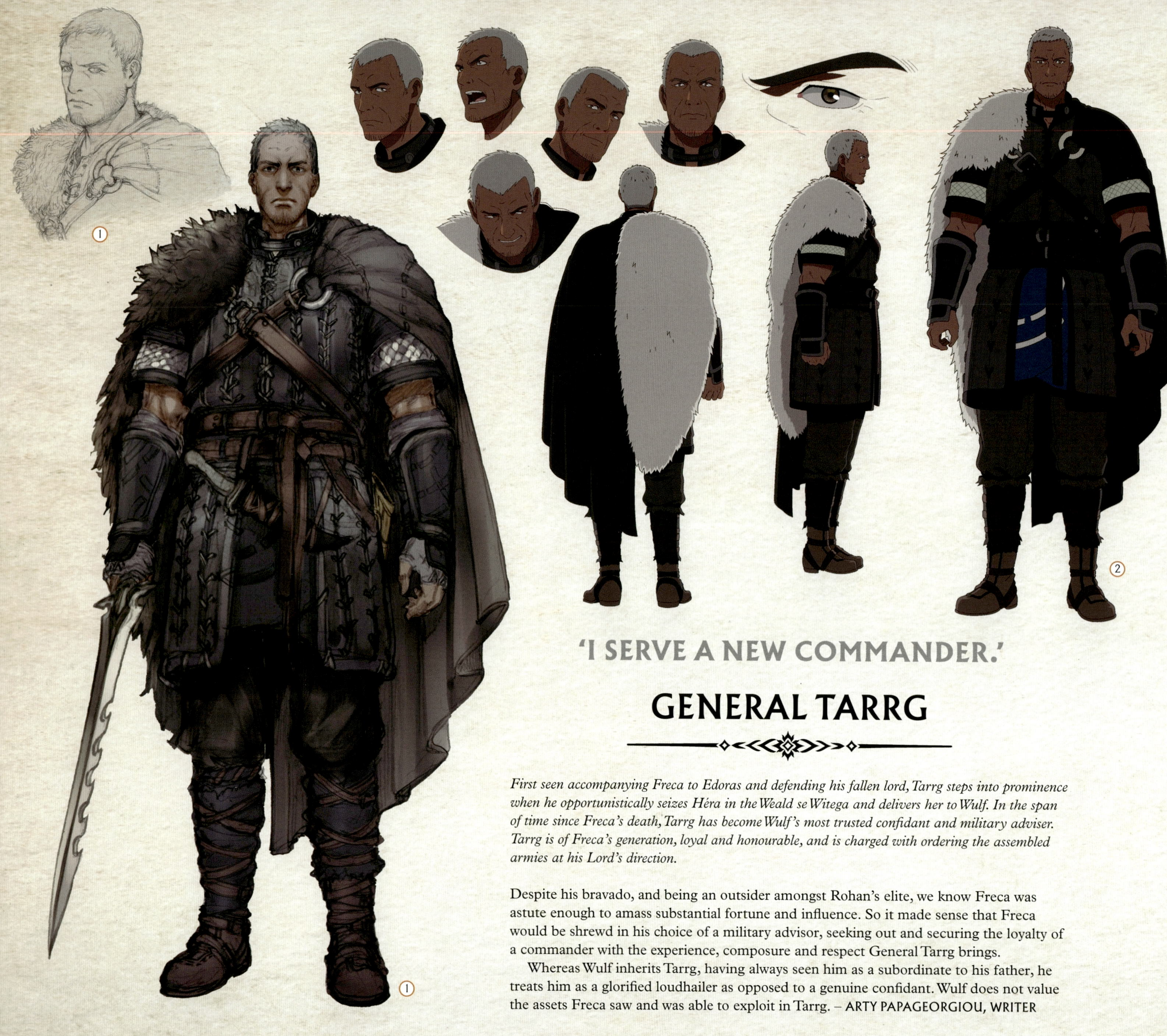

'I SERVE A NEW COMMANDER.'

GENERAL TARRG

First seen accompanying Freca to Edoras and defending his fallen lord, Tarrg steps into prominence when he opportunistically seizes Héra in the Weald se Witega and delivers her to Wulf. In the span of time since Freca's death, Tarrg has become Wulf's most trusted confidant and military adviser. Tarrg is of Freca's generation, loyal and honourable, and is charged with ordering the assembled armies at his Lord's direction.

Despite his bravado, and being an outsider amongst Rohan's elite, we know Freca was astute enough to amass substantial fortune and influence. So it made sense that Freca would be shrewd in his choice of a military advisor, seeking out and securing the loyalty of a commander with the experience, composure and respect General Tarrg brings.

Whereas Wulf inherits Tarrg, having always seen him as a subordinate to his father, he treats him as a glorified loudhailer as opposed to a genuine confidant. Wulf does not value the assets Freca saw and was able to exploit in Tarrg. – ARTY PAPAGEORGIOU, WRITER

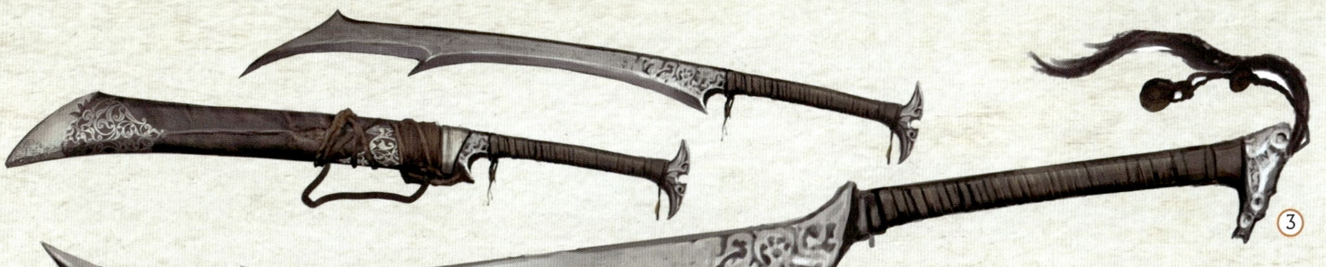

My idea for Tarrg's horse was all about offering something that was the exact opposite of the sleek, swift mounts of the Rohirrim. I loved the idea of him sitting astride a huge, black Shire horse, powerful and imposing. To try to make it seem more threatening, my concept included a cowl, emulating an executioner's mask, and jagged edging intended to evoke the black feathers of crebain wings. – DANIEL FALCONER, ADDITIONAL CONCEPTS DESIGNER

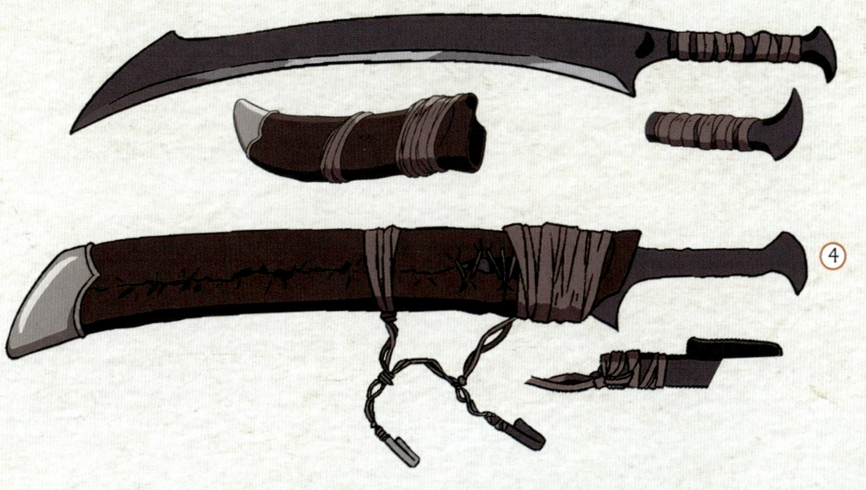

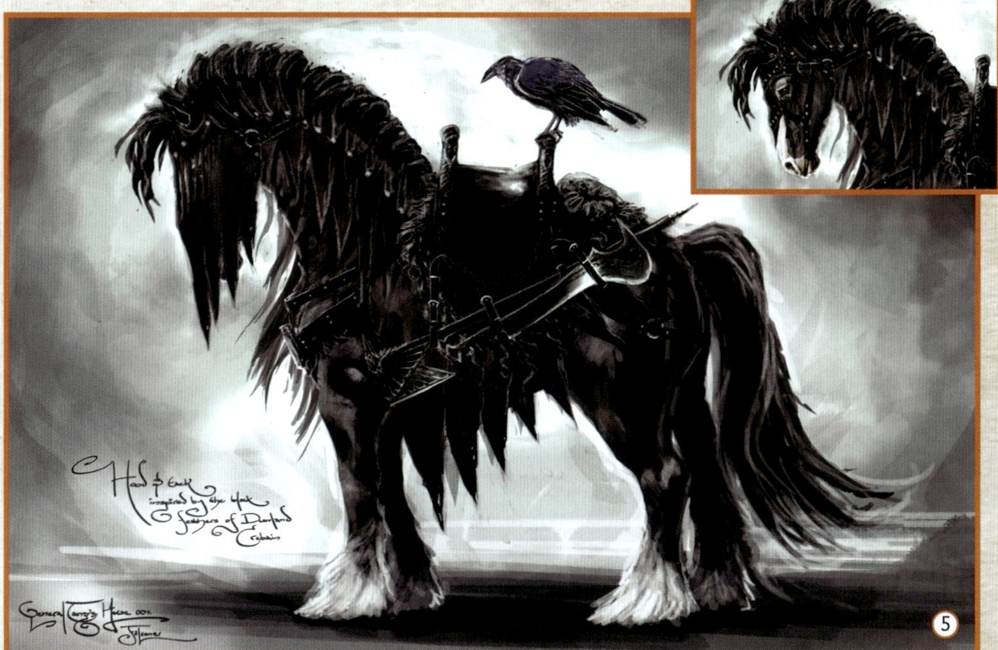

Tarrg is an interesting character because he serves Freca and Wulf, who act without honour in the film, but Tarrg himself is honourable. When drawing his face, I tried to show there is a sense of justice in him, and that he has principles. His cape is a mix of dark cloth and white animal hide, a visual representation of this inner conflict between good and evil, duty and honour. – STATO, ORIGINAL CHARACTER DESIGNER

Based on the idea that perhaps the Dunlendings cobbled their armour together from different sources, I thought maybe Tarrg's sword could be forged out of two blades that had been fused together. I figured that these guys were not as well-resourced as the Rohirrim, so maybe they didn't have the same quality of forges for making weapons. They would get their fires as hot as they could and just do whatever they could to quickly turn out usable weapons.

Though crude in nature, and doing only as much as they needed to the Dunlendings were efficient and inventive. So, for Tarrg's weapon, despite being two swords forged into one, there's still filigree showing from one blade; though the points don't line up, there's beauty and originality that has come out of this unusual combination.

The shape of the combined blades was also made to resemble a deer's antlers, because that motif was emerging in the Dunlending designs and I thought it was striking. – JOSHUA DAMIAN, WĒTĀ WORKSHOP JUNIOR CONCEPT ARTIST

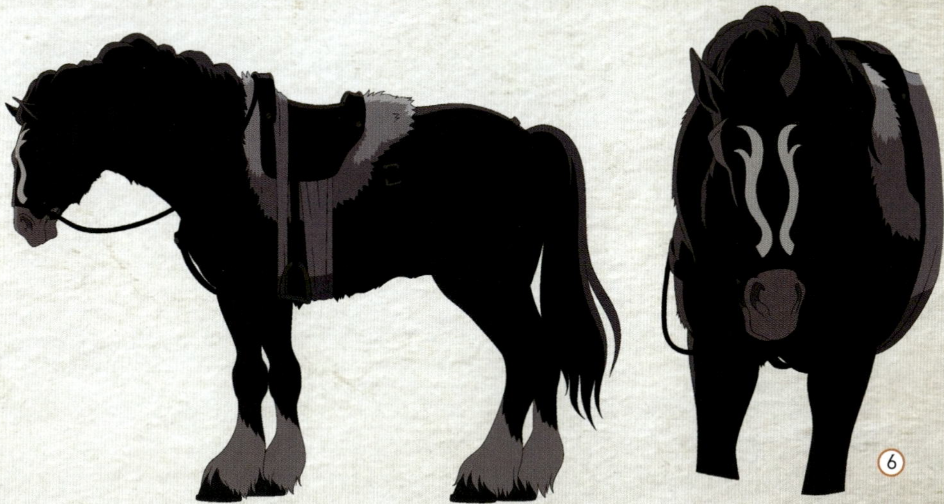

- 4 -

ISENGARD

Héra awakens at night in a crumbling structure where Wulf has taken up residence; but is she a guest or prisoner? The building is an old guard tower erected within the grounds of the abandoned fortress of Isengard. Here, Wulf has mustered an army of some kind, and Héra sees plans and parchments upon his desk, including one bearing a distinctive thorn and ram's head seal.

Wulf confronts Héra. Friends they had been as children, and Héra tries to reach the boy she once knew, but Wulf is bitter and vengeful. He rebukes her for the arrogance of her house, and pinning her to a wall, cuts her cheek in reprisal for the wound she once accidentally gave him when they playfully sparred as children.

Olwyn leads a rescue, and surprising Wulf she buys Héra the chance to escape. The two recover their horses and flee Isengard with the help of Lief and Fréaláf, making for home with news of the invasion to come.

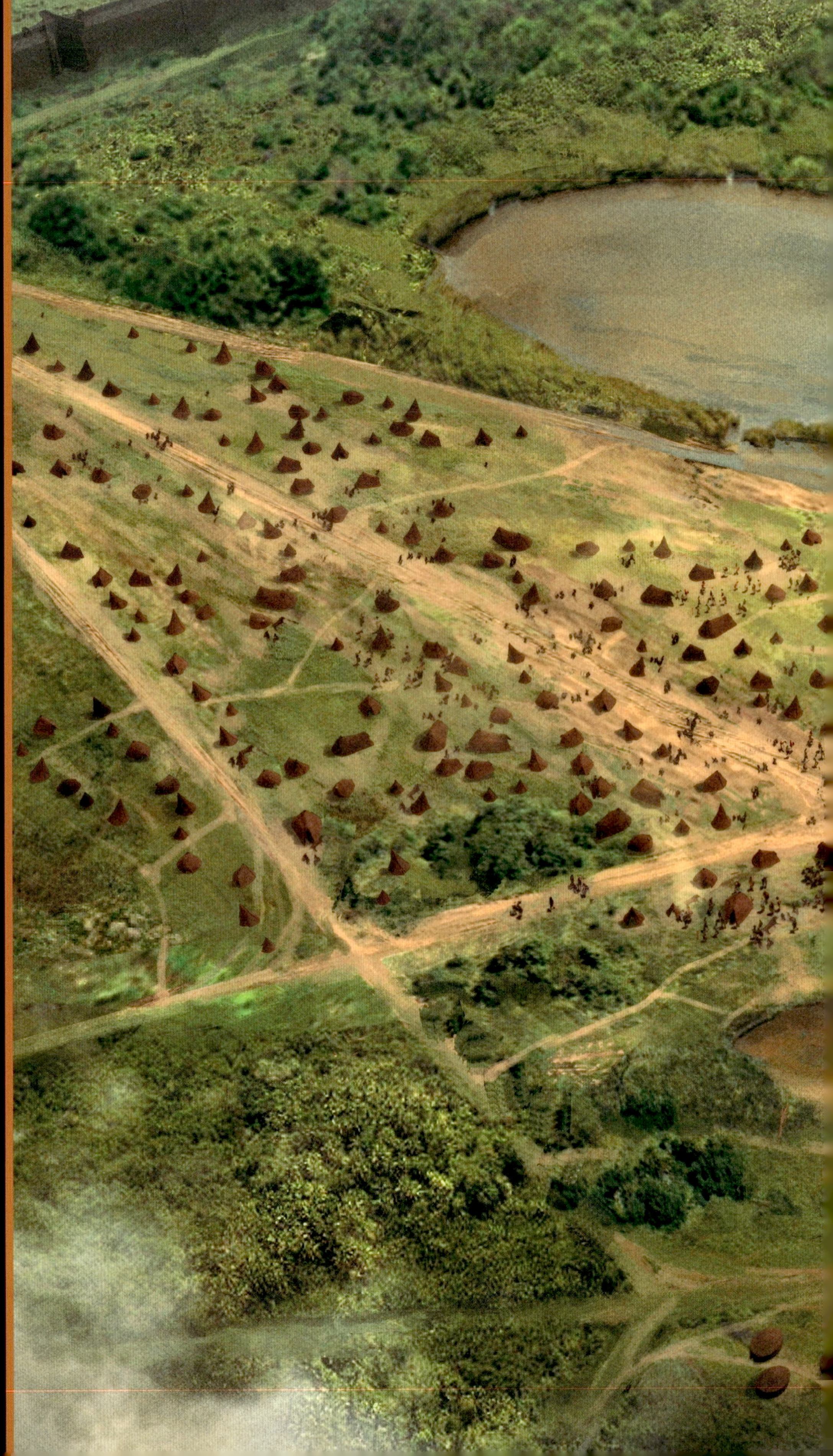

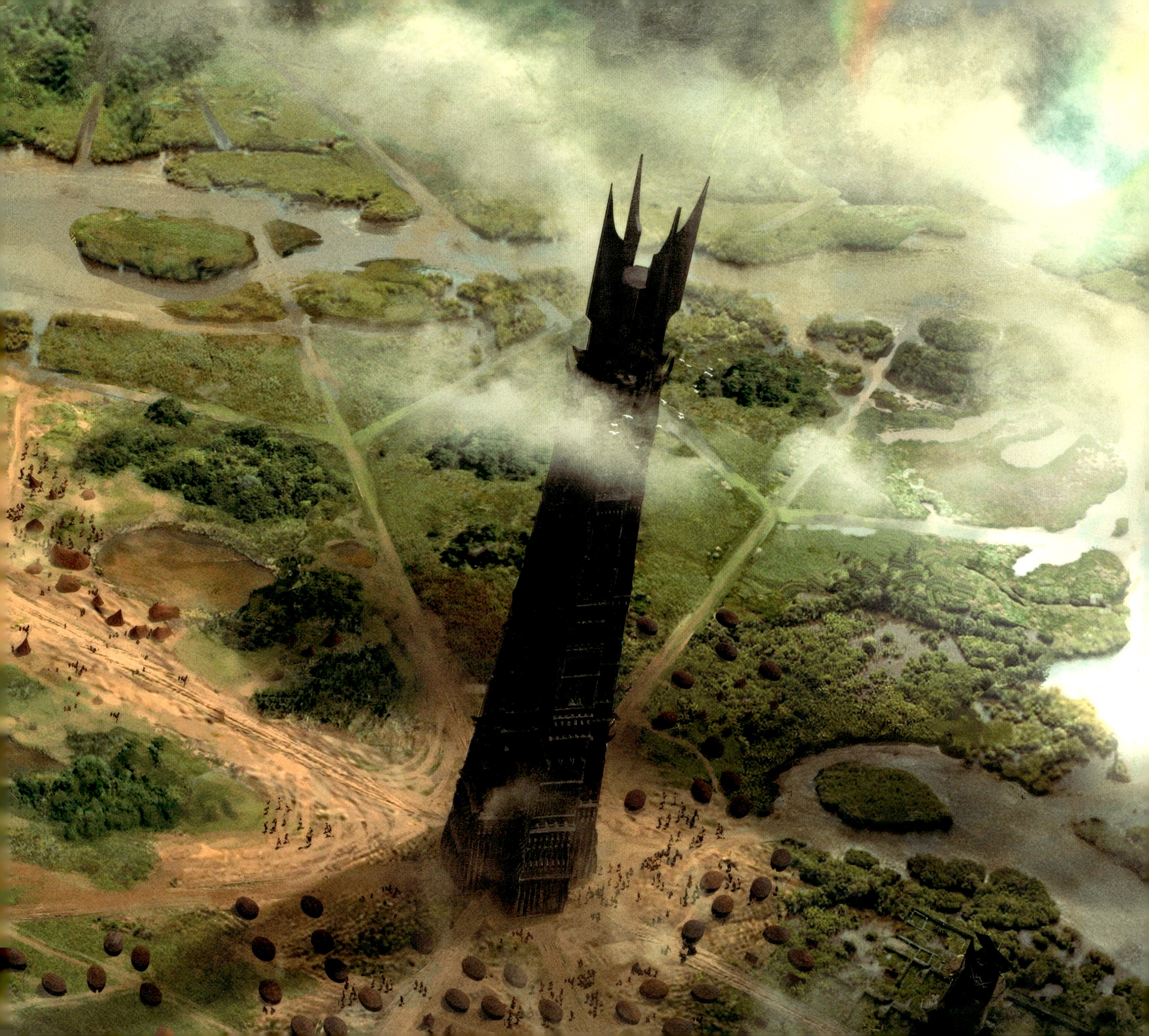

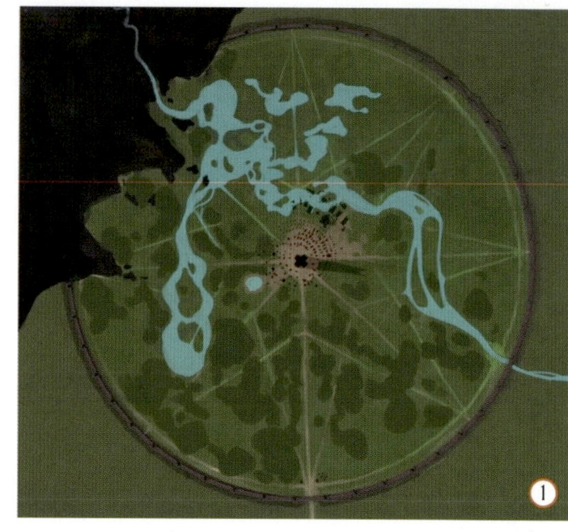

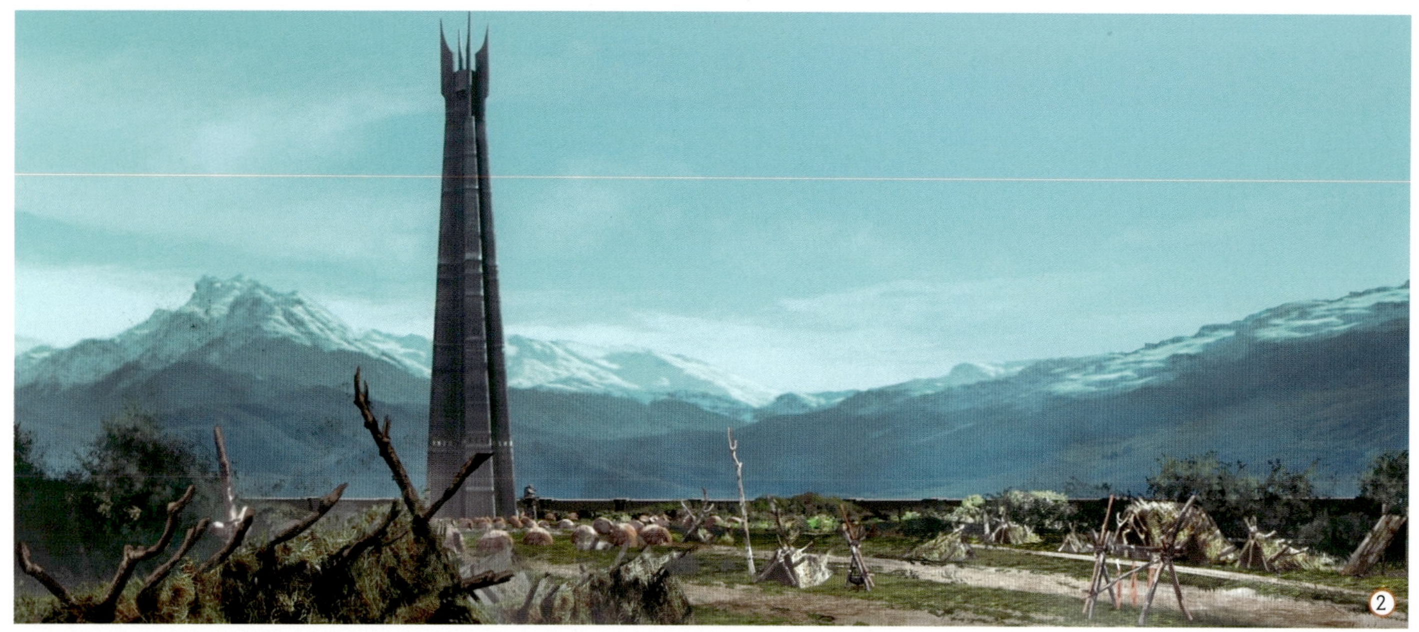

PP & 1: Isengard concepts, AM. 2: Isengard concept, TK. 3: Isengard background art. 4: Final film frames (LOTR trilogy).

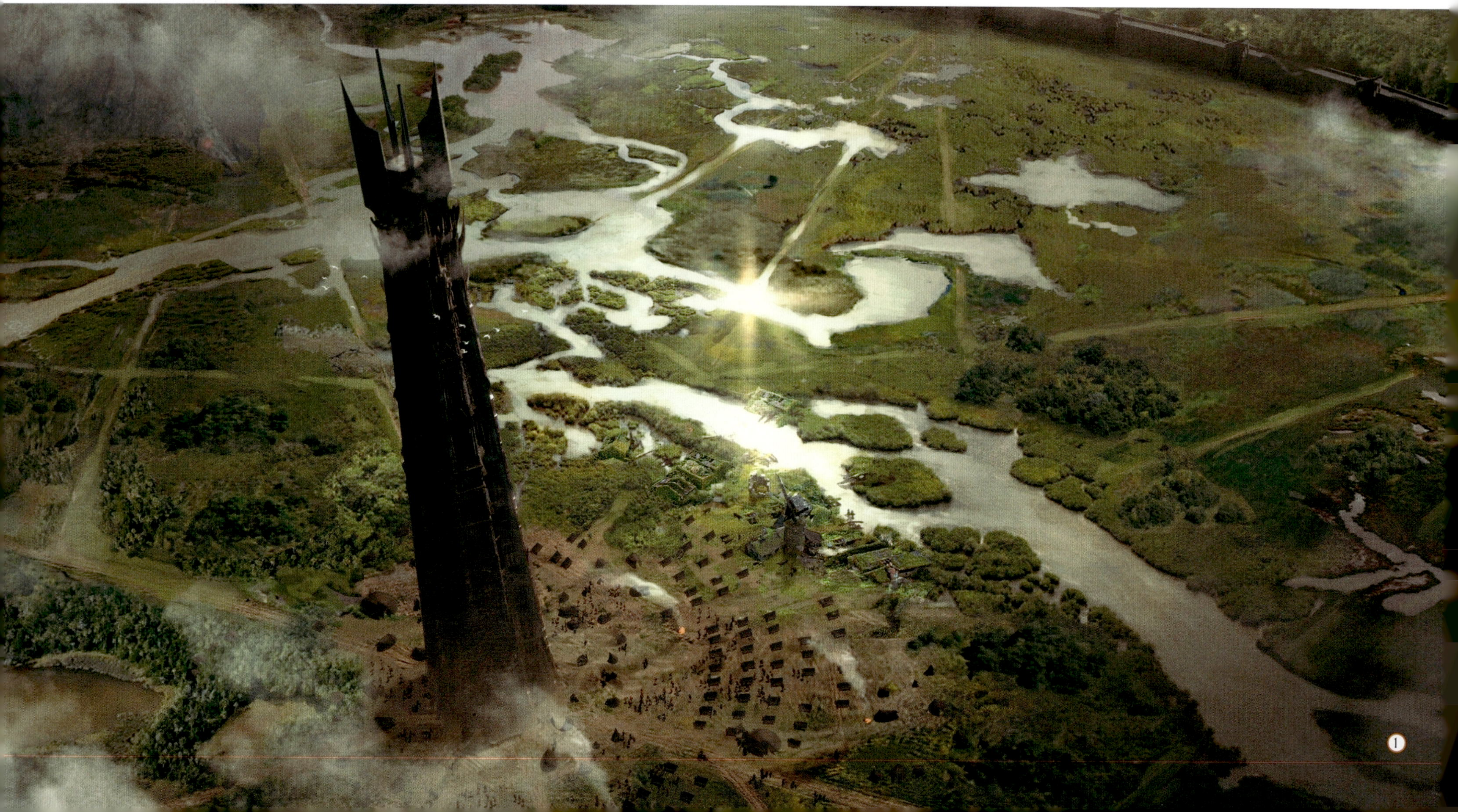

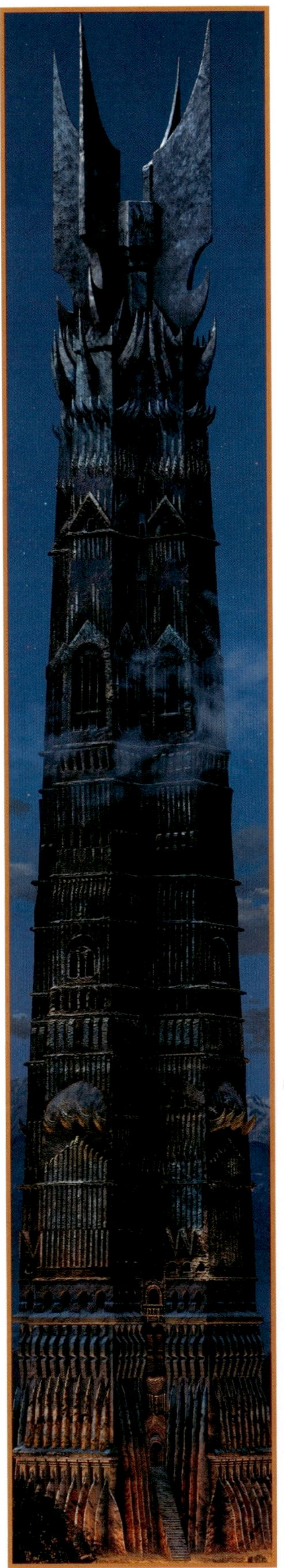

ISENGARD

At the centre of the ringed fortress of Isengard looms the gleaming black stone tower of Orthanc. Carved centuries ago by the Númenóreans of the Second Age, Orthanc now stands sealed and empty, silent witness to the forces that Wulf has secretly gathered behind Isengard's crumbling ring wall to make war upon Rohan. Lacking the key and unable to break the tower's locks, he has reluctantly installed himself in an ancillary structure.

The tower of Orthanc is locked. Wulf can't get in. It's a source of frustration; a visual symbol of his situation, being on the outside, denied what he feels is his due, perhaps fairly. The people of Gondor would have had someone stationed here in the past, and Rohan since taken up the watch, but over the centuries it has fallen away into disrepair. – PHILIPPA BOYENS, PRODUCER

It is perfect that Wulf can't take control of Isengard the way he wants to. He is set up there as lord of the place, but he doesn't have the keys to the tower. It's a great expression of how he finds himself. – ARTY PAPAGEORGIOU, PRODUCER

Isengard in this time is in an abandoned, dilapidated state. No one is looking after the grounds, so I thought it was important that its appearance be in strong contrast to the pristine state we saw it in in *The Fellowship of the Ring*, with maintained paths, manicured gardens, lawns and trees. Taking inspiration from the epic set piece at the end of *The Two Towers*, when the dam was broken and the ring of Isengard was flooded by the Ents, the obvious choice for me was to put a river in it, but in keeping with the state of disrepair, the waterway is meandering and threaded. I imagined there is no dam, so the river has flowed into some of the areas where there were once roadways, creating an overgrown, scrubby, marsh-like environment. I liked how great the black tower looked when set against a green environment.

There are still hints of roads crisscrossing the grounds to form a star-shaped sigil, suggesting it having been something very beautiful in the past. It also conveys the idea that this place has existed for a long time, even before we see it in this prequel. We only visit Isengard for a small period of time, yet it has and will exist for a long time either side of when this story takes place. Orthanc looks much the same, but everything else changes through the centuries. – ADAM MIDDLETON, WĒTĀ WORKSHOP ART DIRECTOR & SENIOR CONCEPT ARTIST

The complexity of painting Orthanc's shape was a challenge made even harder because it was black and seen at night. Fortunately, there were not many shots of the tower, and shots from the original movies were a great source of reference. – YASUHIRO YAMANE, ART DIRECTOR

'WHO WOULD DARE OCCUPY ISENGARD?'

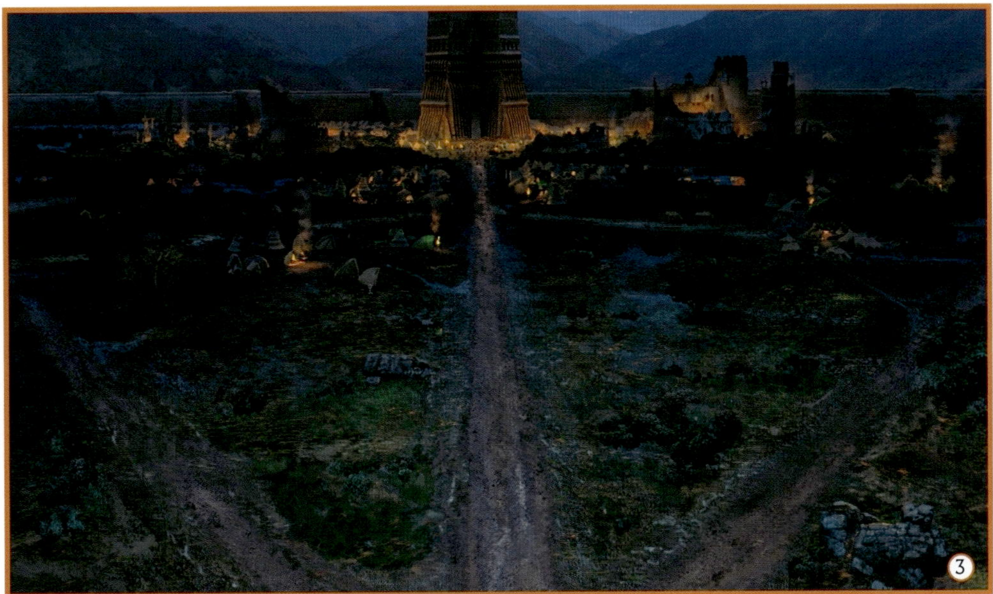

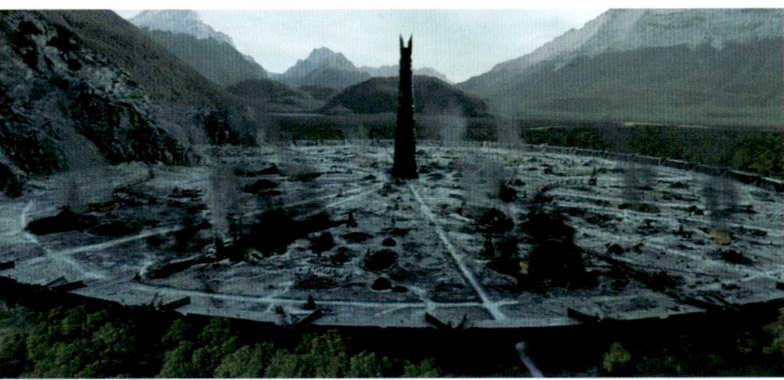

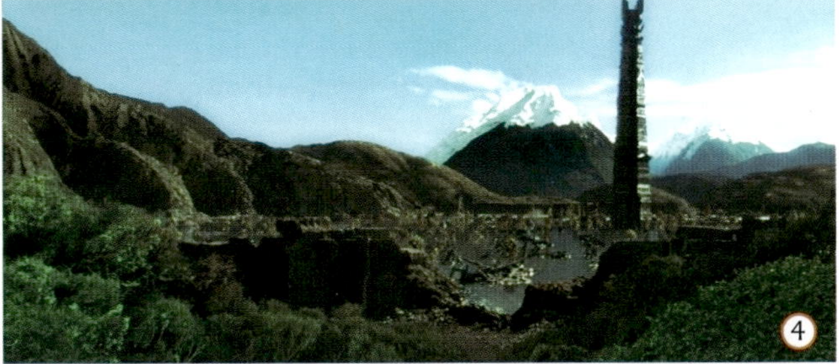

DUNLENDING AND WILD MEN CAMP

Spread out around the tower of Orthanc is Wulf's army, a force comprised of Dunlending warriors and men of the Hill Tribes, bolstered by Southron mercenaries. Their makeshift shelters and tents dot the landscape as they gather, readying to make war upon Edoras.

It was actually scary to be drawing ideas for the Dunlendings' camp, knowing that Alan Lee was also working on it. I had barely started my career in this field and here was this legend. But it occurred to me, 'This guy is having fun! I'm overthinking everything.' I decided to just approach it as an opportunity to play and not get too precious with it all. It made such a difference! – JOSHUA DAMIAN, WĒTĀ WORKSHOP JUNIOR CONCEPT ARTIST

Some of the shelters might have moss on them, some might be made with bone, or leather, or built against a tree; a pagan vibe was at the core of what I was trying to express. This can encompass so many things, but what I mean is pagan from the point of view of the Rohirrim, because we see the Dunlendings from their perspective in the film. While it may not matter to the Rohirrim, antlers on a shelter might mean something to the Dunlendings. – JOSHUA DAMIAN, WĒTĀ WORKSHOP JUNIOR CONCEPT ARTIST

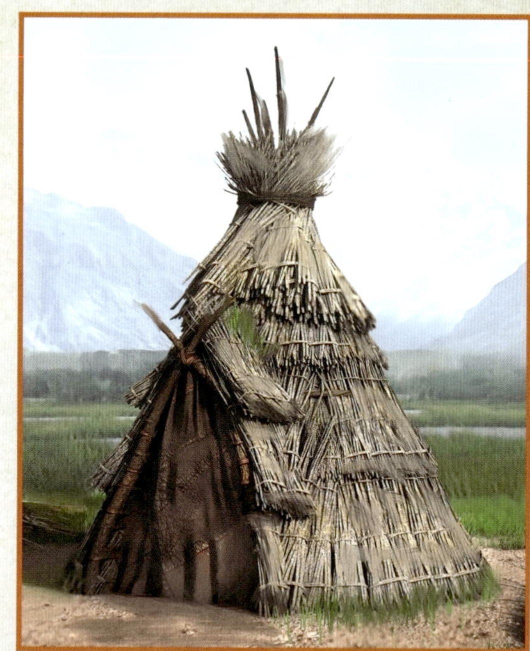

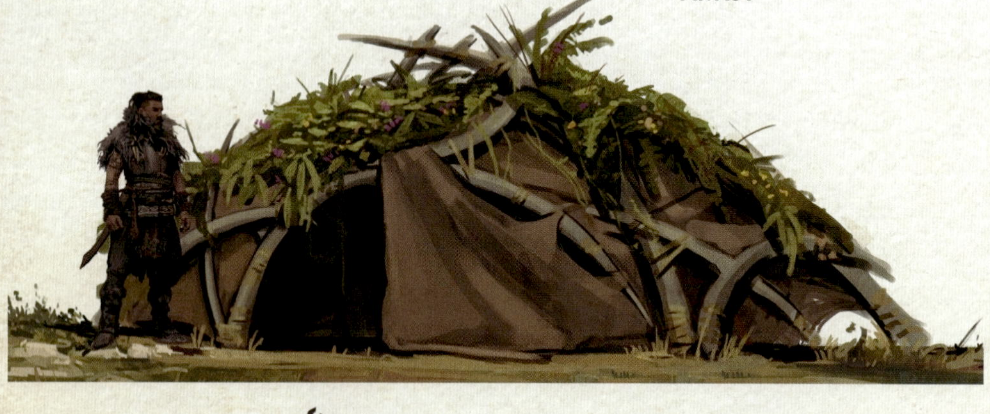

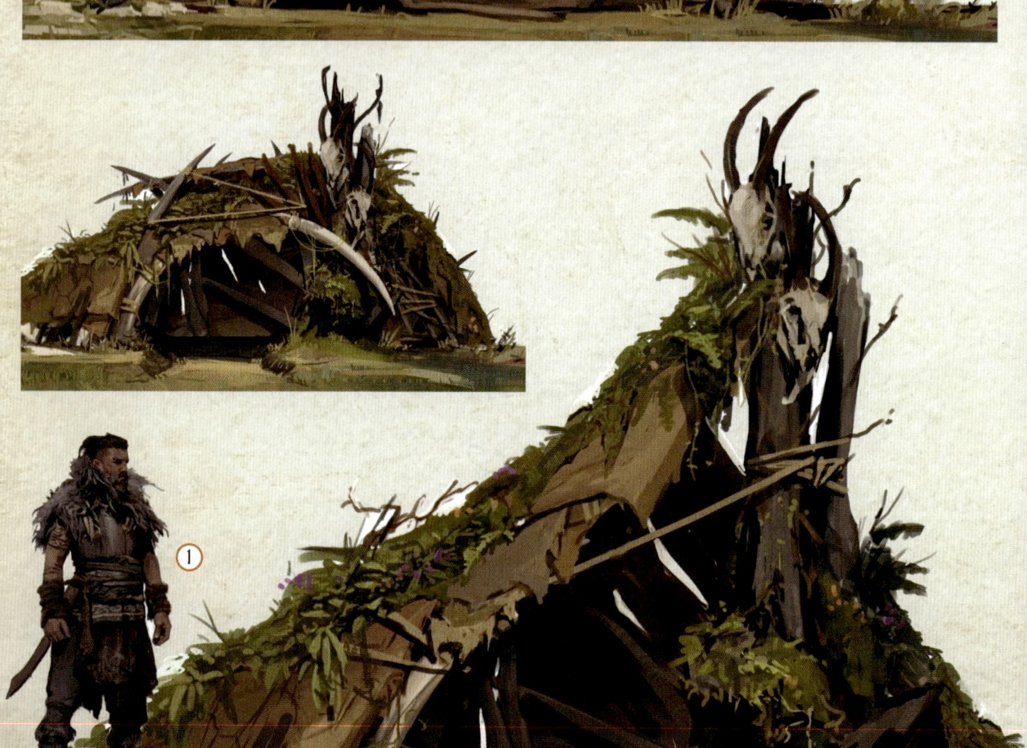

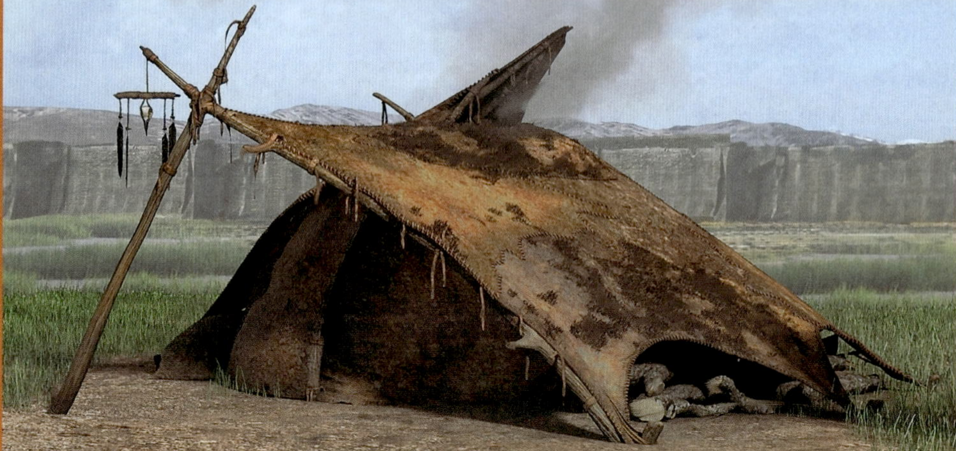

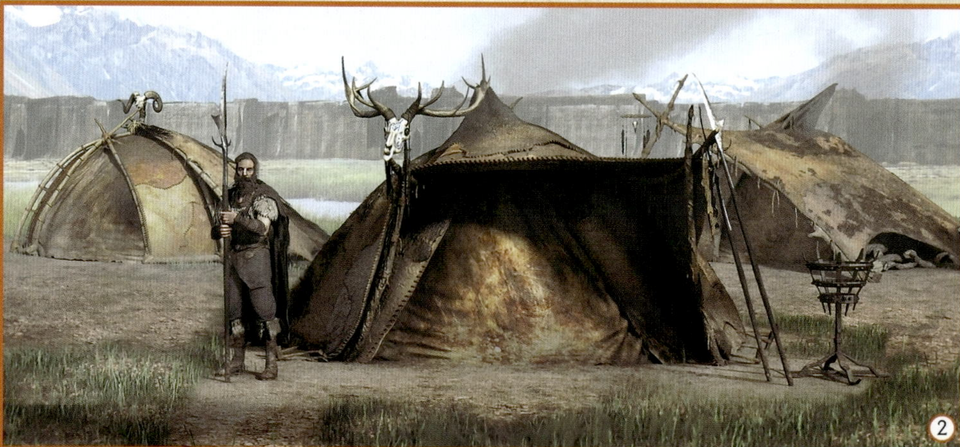

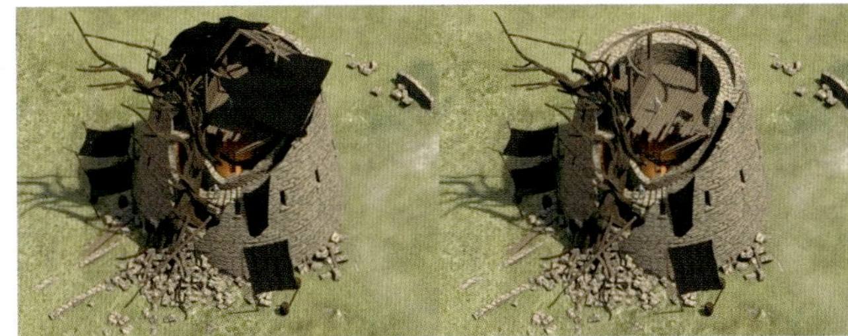

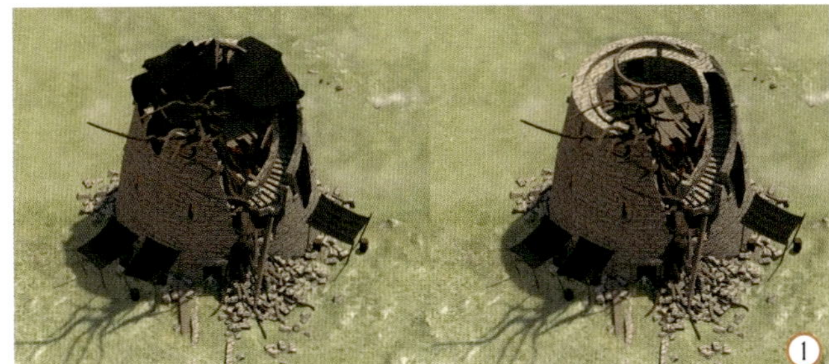

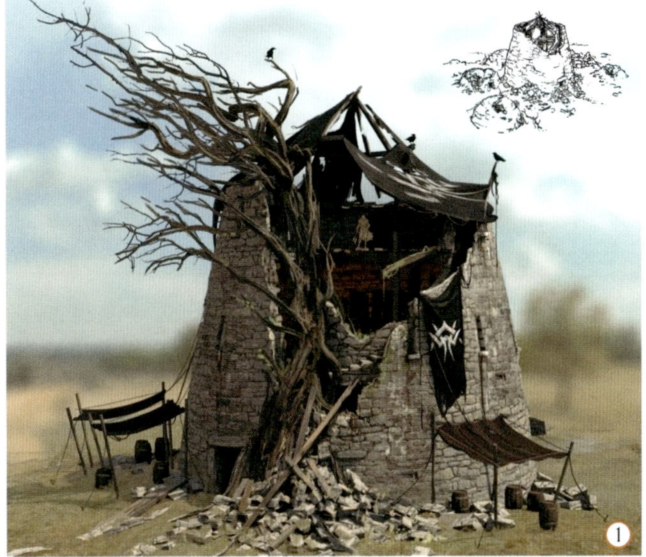

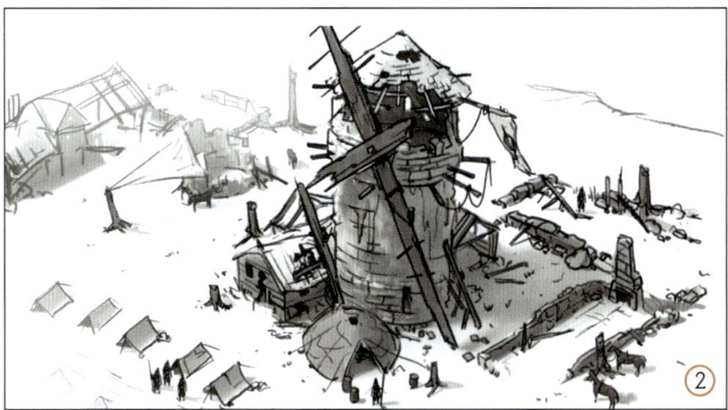

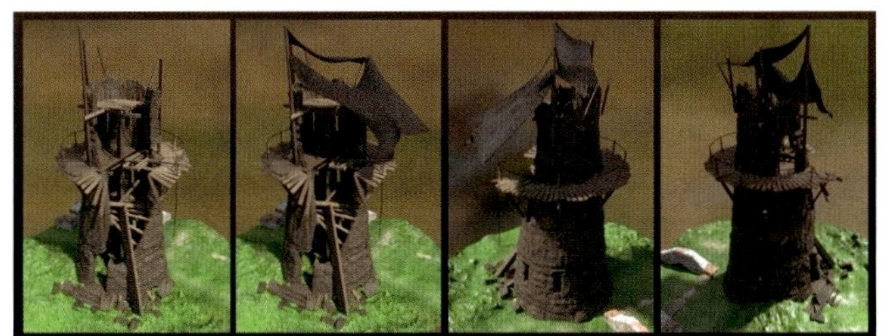

GUARD TOWER

The tower in which Héra awakens presented a conceptual challenge for the designers. Other than Orthanc itself and some wooden Orc structures erected later, there were no buildings to be seen. Wulf has set himself up in an ancillary structure of some kind, described in the early script as 'a crumbling tower.' The ambiguity and novelty of the concept of a small ruin being present near to this great tower became a fun puzzle to be solved.

While later defined as a guard tower, initially we had no idea what this might be. The first concepts proceeded from the idea of it being built by some transitory civilization that might have lived in the grounds for a brief time between Isengard's construction many centuries ago by the ancient Númenóreans and the time of our story. Not being of Númenórean make, it would be prone to rapid decline. The conscious design choice then became to make something that was unmistakably distinct and inferior.

What then might its function have been? Perhaps it was a windmill? One aspect of that idea that appealed was we could include the rotting sail arms of the mill as a feature that Héra could slide down when making her escape. – DANIEL FALCONER, ADDITIONAL CONCEPTS DESIGNER

An aspect of Middle-earth that I always liked was the presence of hints at past cultures and civilizations. We saw an abandoned farmhouse in *The Hobbit* just before the Dwarves' encounter with the Trolls, and there were ruins and broken statues throughout the background of scenes in *The Lord of the Rings*. It almost doesn't matter whether we know anything about them, but their presence builds history and adds to the worldbuilding.

The script mentioned a ruined tower where Wulf would hold Héra captive. I imagined that maybe it was left over from an old human settlement that had been erected within the walls of Isengard. Maybe they had farmed the grounds and used the river, but long ago they had been run out and their settlement had rotted away. – ADAM MIDDLETON, WĒTĀ WORKSHOP ART DIRECTOR & SENIOR CONCEPT ARTIST

The mill idea didn't catch, so I suggested something akin to a real-world Iron Age *broch*. *Brochs* are broad, conical structures with spiral staircases that run between their outer and inner walls. Their precise function seems to be a matter of debate among archaeologists, but in Middle-earth it could be a number of things. What was cool about them was the construction was somewhat similar to the Wall of Isengard, so maybe the builders used rocks pulled from the wall. I did a very hasty drawing and Wētā Workshop's Adam Middleton worked it up in 3D and Photoshop as a full concept. I loved that he added a windblown tree growing up through it. That felt very Middle-earthy to me. – DANIEL FALCONER, ADDITIONAL CONCEPTS DESIGNER

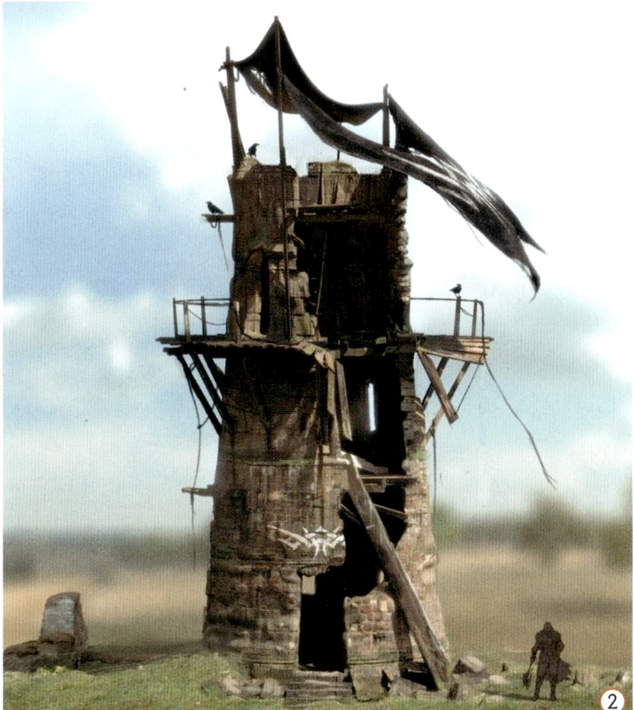

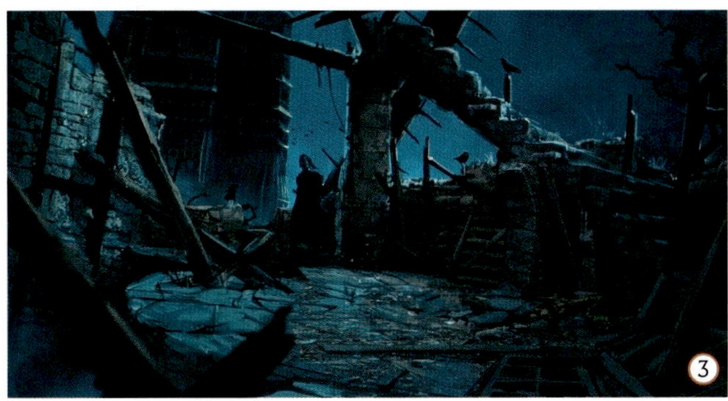

1: Broch tower concepts, AM (inset, DF). **2:** Windmill tower concepts, AM . **3:** Tower interior concept, AM.

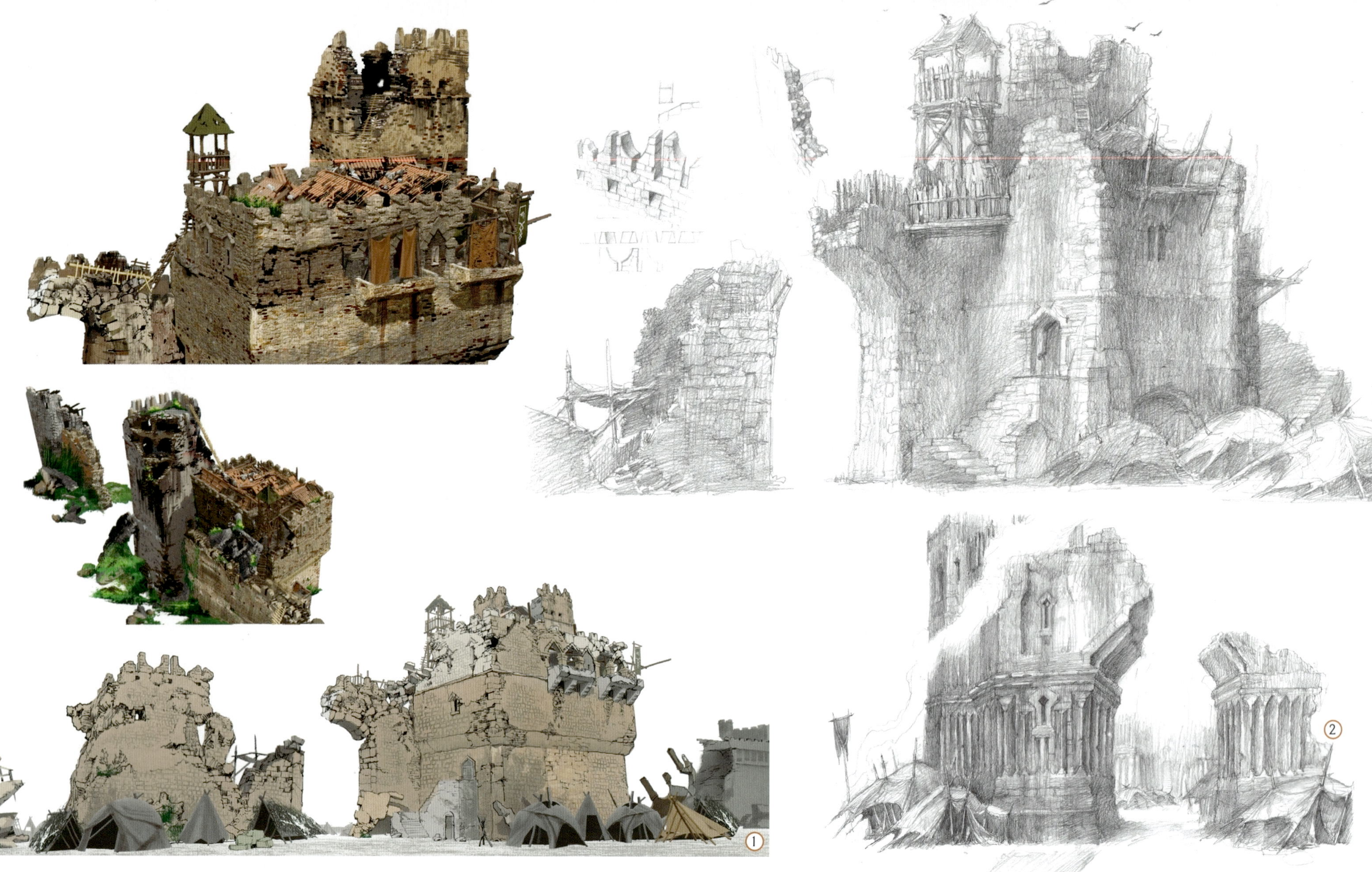

The methodology of designing the crumbling tower speaks more broadly to how the Wētā Workshop design studio approached the project. We were directed not to second-guess the anime medium, but instead to design as if we were doing so for a live-action film, and leave the translation into anime to the Japanese team. They understand their medium better than we could, so they would put their spin on it and do a much better job than if we tried to emulate their style, ourselves.

When designing for live-action films we would often incorporate 3D methodology to explore the space in a full 360 degrees to ensure that we were delivering something plausible, fully considered and which could exist. We treated this no differently, and it was particularly appropriate because the tower had an interior and exterior that had to seamlessly match. Approaching it in 3D meant we were able to examine both at the same time. – ADAM MIDDLETON, WĒTĀ WORKSHOP ART DIRECTOR & SENIOR CONCEPT ARTIST

Isengard and the tower of Orthanc were places that had featured in my book illustrations. Peter Jackson was happy with the look of the tower, and asked that I complete the design in the same style for *The Lord of the Rings* films. He also asked for the interiors, gardens and walls, followed by another pass at the industrialized caverns and forges, and its flooded and ruined final appearance.

The War of the Rohirrim is set at a period before Saruman took up residence there and was a garrison and encampment for other armies. I was asked to provide designs for some less permanent structures, which would look as though they were the work of a different culture but not be out of keeping with the established environment. I loved the meandering streams and marshes that Adam Middleton added into the environment, which would help to make the place look as though it had been neglected for hundreds of years, adding to the sense of desolation. Perhaps there might be a few more ruinous buildings scattered around, and perhaps even some attached to the inside of the outer wall? If Isengard was essentially a fortress, and Orthanc the keep, there would be guardhouses, barracks, storehouses, and other infrastructure servicing the residents. The idea was basically that there was at one time a second gateway nearer the central tower, with an adjacent guardroom with access to what remained of the gate tower and walls. Wulf could have set up his headquarters there.

The Dunlending camp would be mainly tents, or

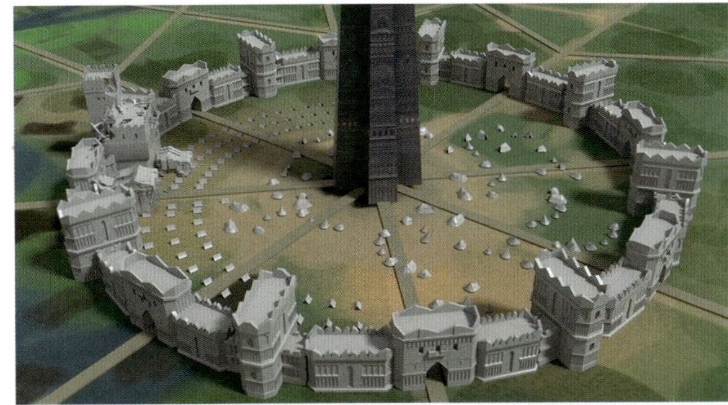

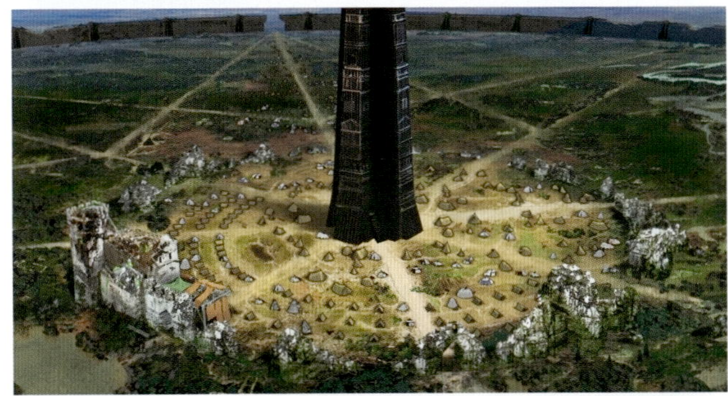

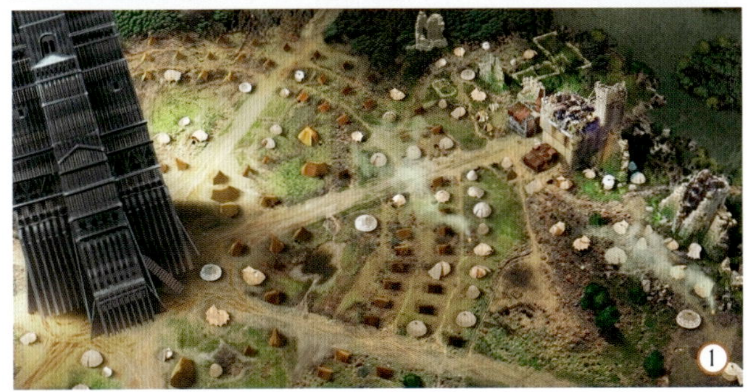

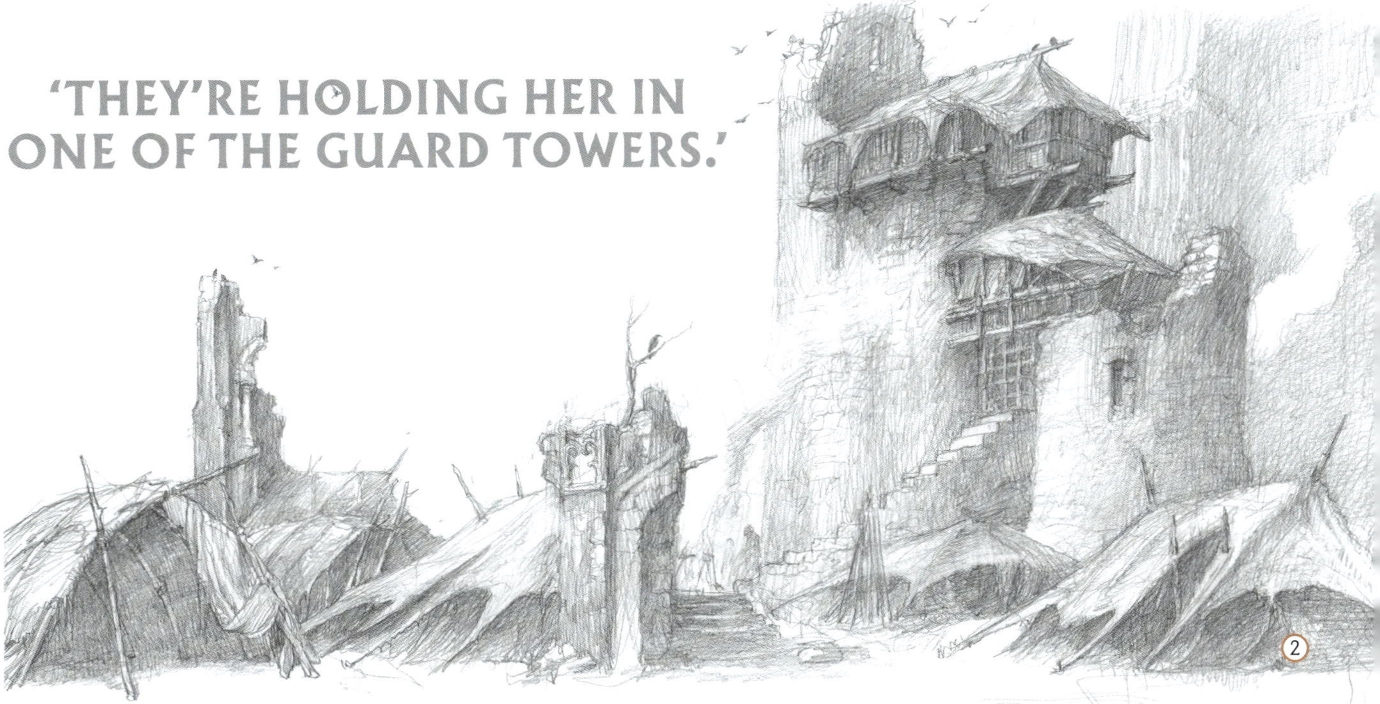

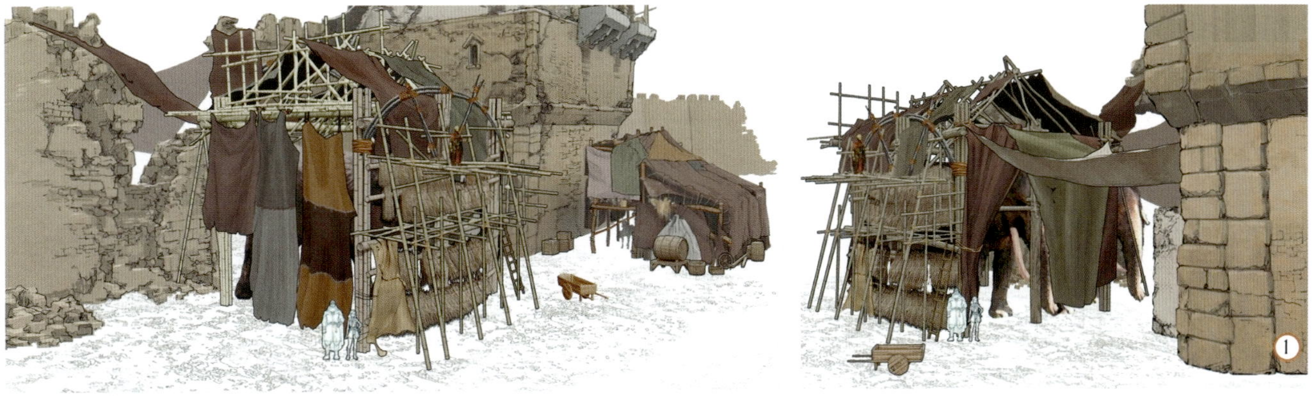

perhaps a variety of tent/yurt/bender hybrids, mainly covered by skins and supported by lashed-together poles. They would make a nice soft and springy landing for Héra when she jumped from the tower. – ALAN LEE, CONCEPTUAL DESIGNER

I developed the general layout of the buildings and crumbling tower, and then Sankaku Studio developed the entire space as a 3D environment. Next to the guard tower is a tent to house *mûmakil*, only a part of which was visible in the film. This is a Southron-style structure built mostly of bamboo, which they most likely brought with them. I used southeast Asian buildings as a reference in coming up with ideas for the construction. – YASUHIRO YAMANE, ART DIRECTOR

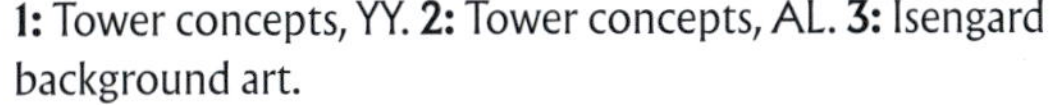

1: Tower concepts, YY. 2: Tower concepts, AL. 3: Isengard background art.

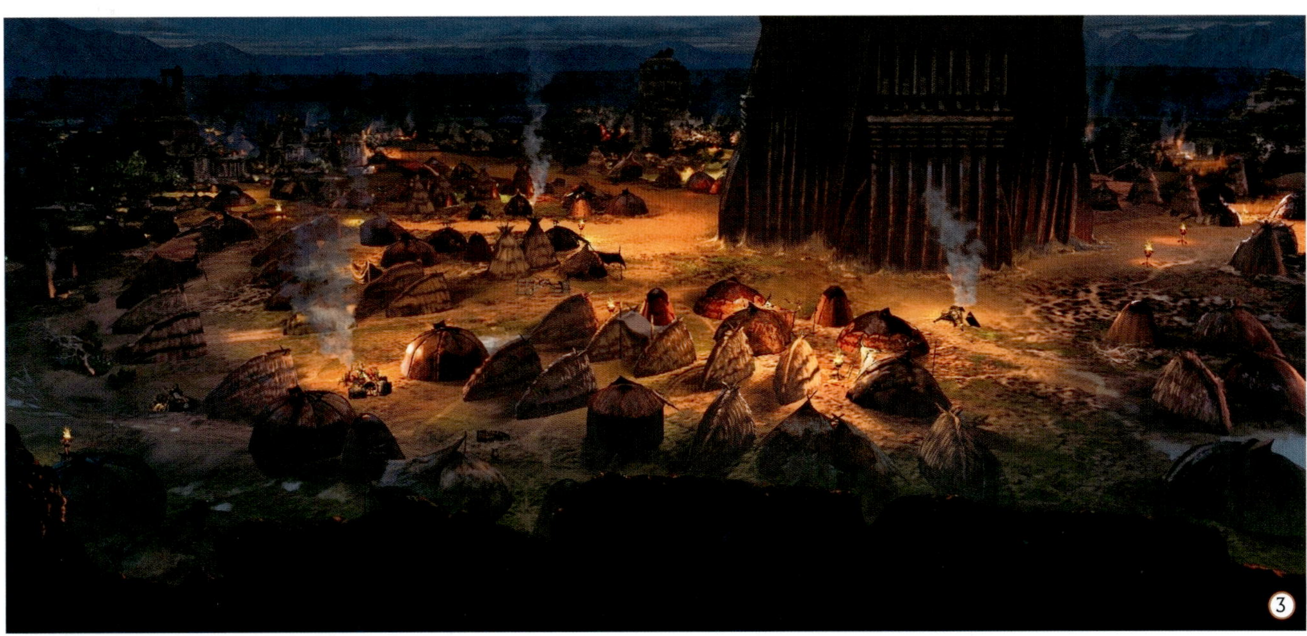

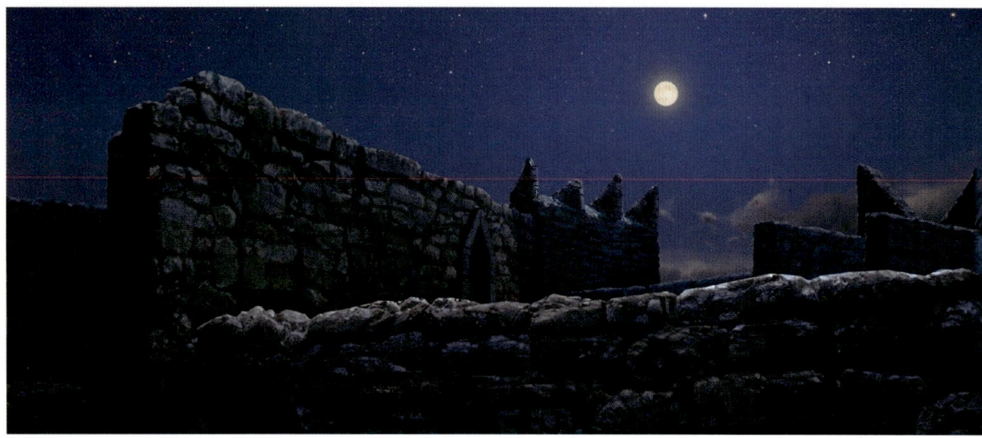

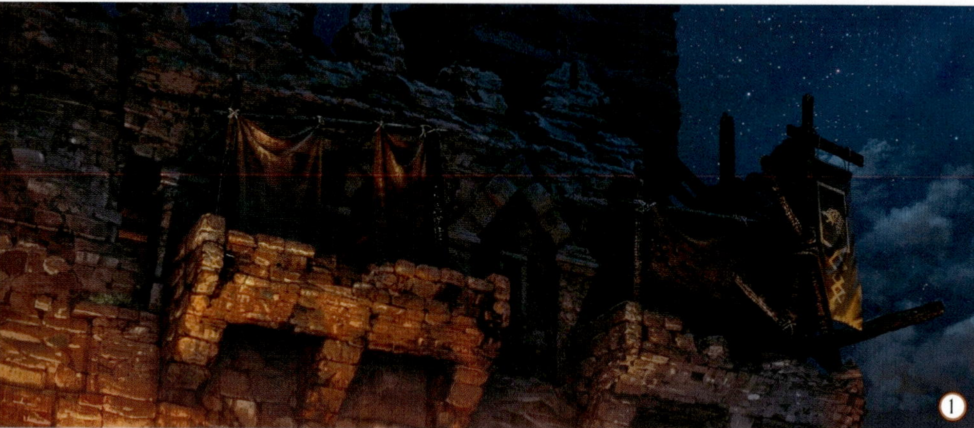

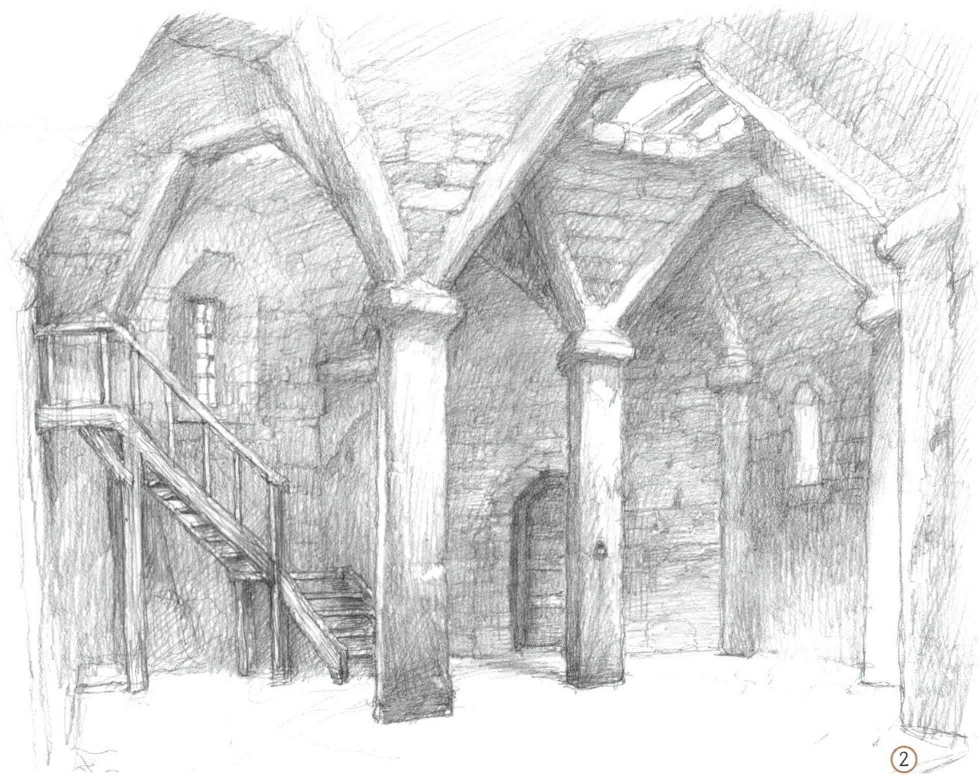

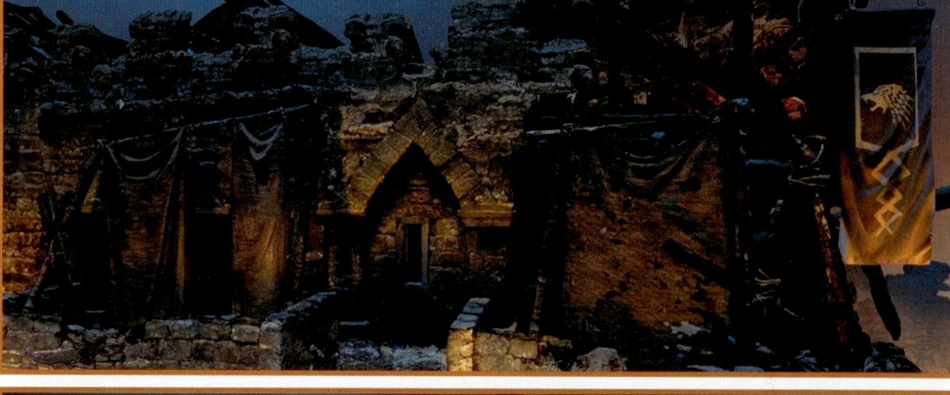

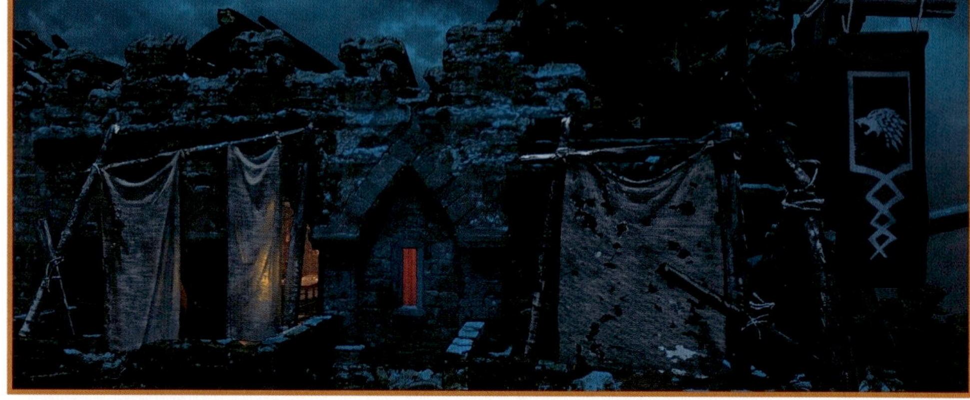

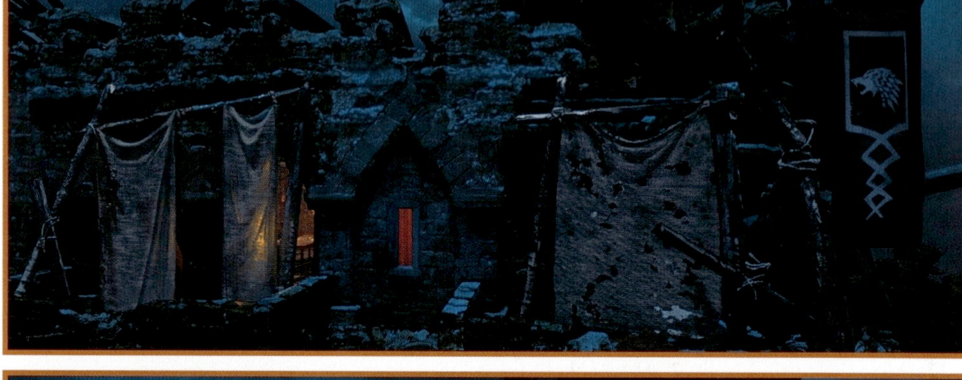

When designing the inside of the tower where Wulf has his headquarters and Héra is being held, I was inspired by Adam Middleton's windmill interior images and Alan Lee's beautiful sketches. The director explained the action that he wanted to see, and I settled on a space that would allow that to happen, incorporating ideas from Middleton and Lee's designs into the structure. I was honoured to have Alan Lee make his own corrections to the structure of the building.

A unique element that we included in Wulf's headquarters at the director's suggestion were green-flamed oil lamps. The same green flames can be seen held by Wulf's forces during the attack on Edoras, and in his tent outside the Hornburg. They created a visual connection to Wulf across the scenes. – YASUHIRO YAMANE, ART DIRECTOR

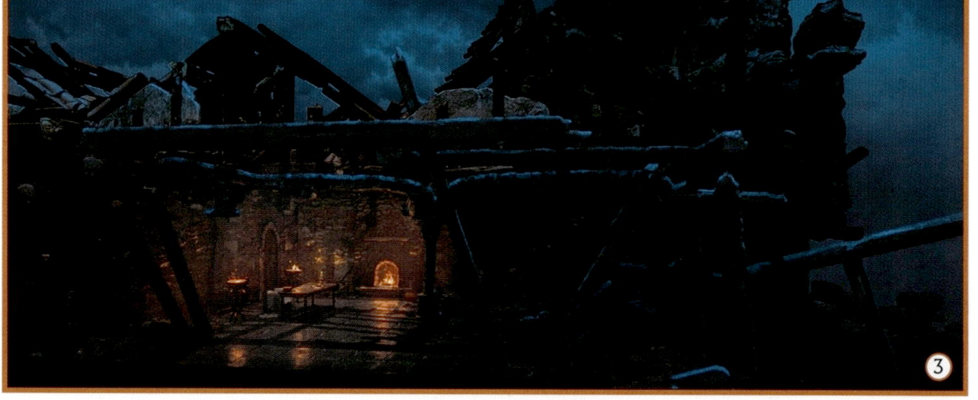

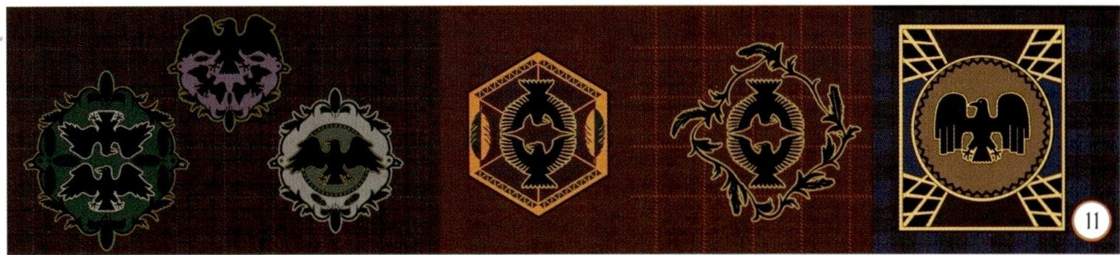

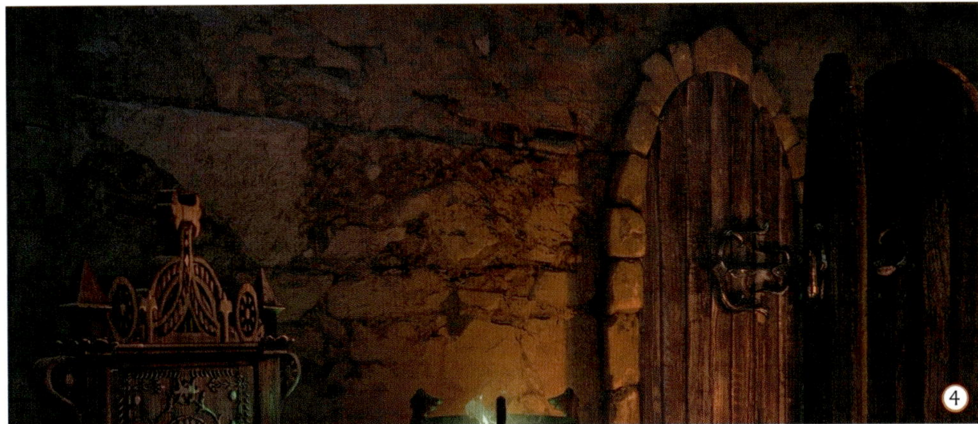

1: Tower background art. 2: Tower interior concept, AL. 3: Tower background setting art, TK. 4: Tower interior background art. 5: Wulf's Isengard map, DF. 6: Wulf's props setting art, KM. 7: Thorne's missive and seal prop setting art, KM. 8: Thorne's seal concept, JH. 9: Wulf's furniture concepts, YY. 10: Rohirrim coin concepts, DF. 11: Wulf's heraldry concepts, YY.

Hanging in Wulf's headquarters is a flag bearing Freca's sigil. If Rohan's primary animal imagery was horse inspired, then it was fitting that Freca's crest might reference his clan's Dunlending origins. There is no more famous creature of Dunland than the crebain, and this was adopted into the heraldry concepts.

On Wulf's table are hints of his plans to conquer Rohan. Most importantly there is a scroll bearing the ram and bramble seal of Thorne, the Wold's traitorous lord. While familiar to Héra, it won't be until she is home in Edoras again that she will make the connection and comprehend Thorne's treachery.

Héra also sees a map of Isengard. I offered both a clean version and an option with notes scratched over it in a 'nasty' hand. I imagined that these were Wulf's orders, hastily scrawled onto the map instructing his men to shore up the defence of their encampment.

Wulf is paying his armies with coin and the promise of spoils. When he runs out of money he lies to the Wild Men, telling them that the Hornburg is filled with gold; but what would Rohirrim coinage look like? Helm being the current king, I imagined that their coinage would be minted with his emblem, Felaróf, first of the *Mearas*. On the back we put a K-rune, which stands for *kastu*, a Rohirric word meaning 'precious thing' and related to the Westron word *castar*. We imagined it might represent a single unit of denomination.

— DANIEL FALCONER, ADDITIONAL CONCEPTS DESIGNER

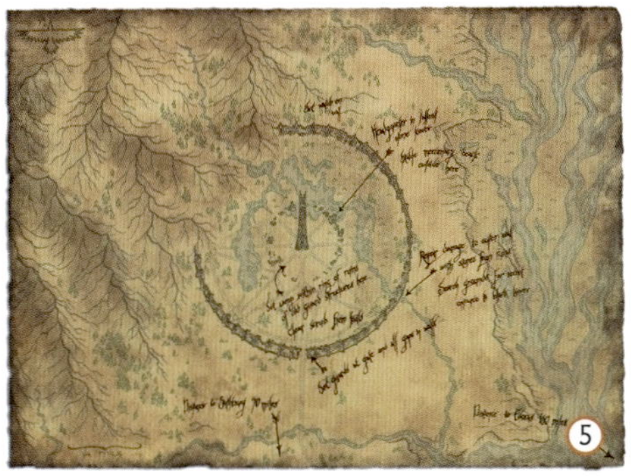

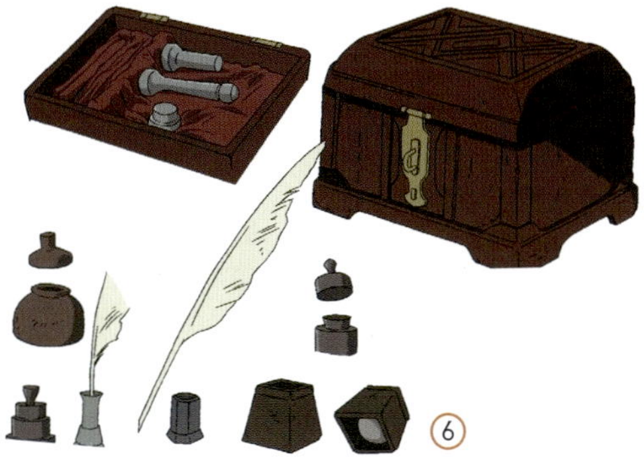

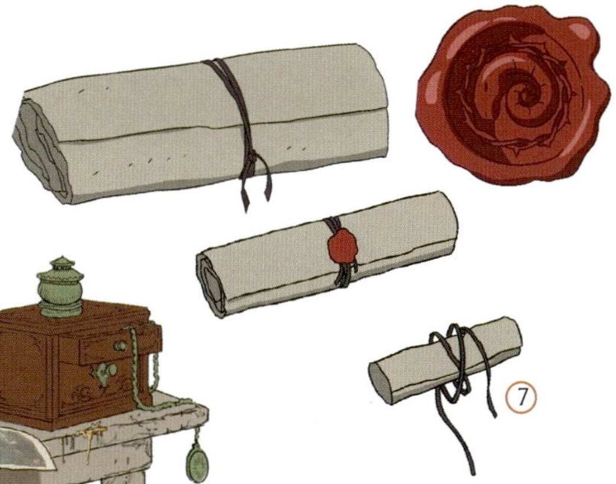

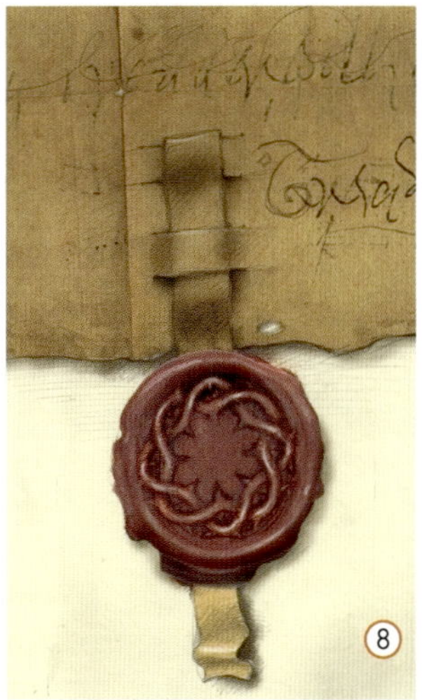

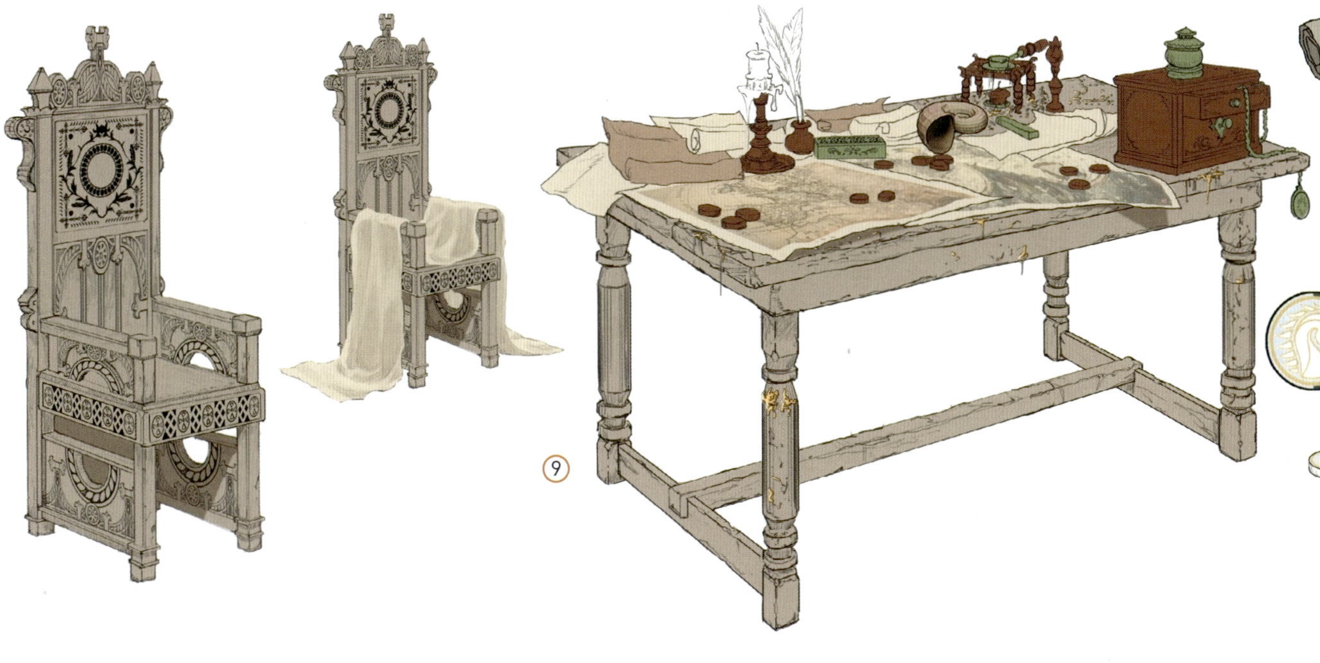

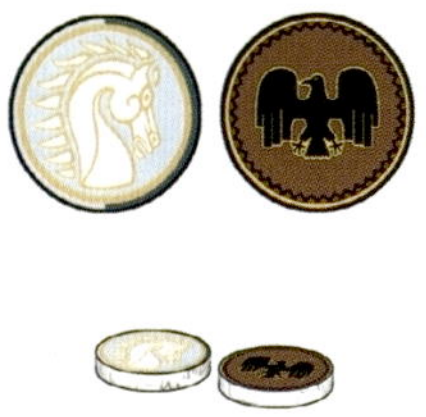

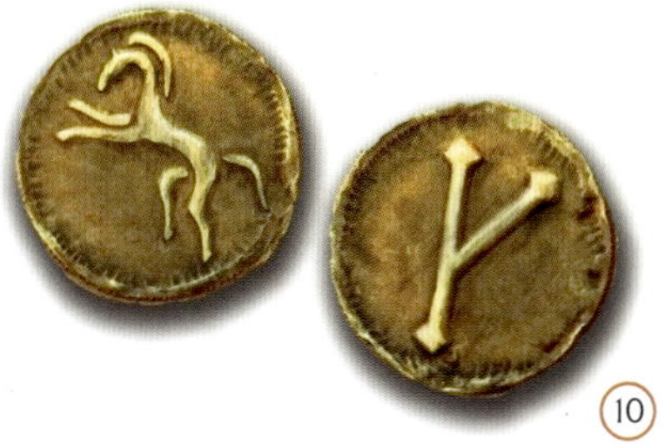

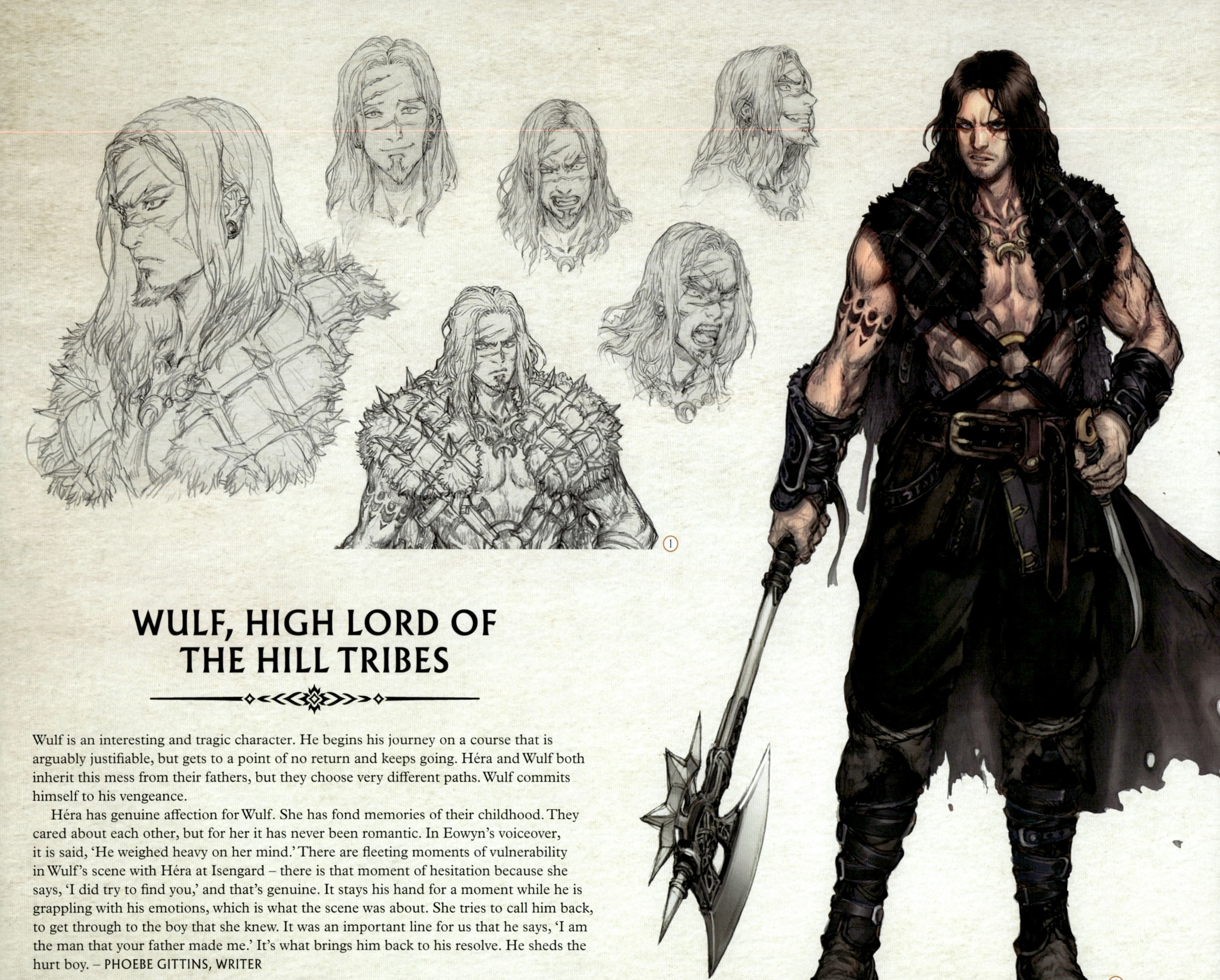

WULF, HIGH LORD OF THE HILL TRIBES

Wulf is an interesting and tragic character. He begins his journey on a course that is arguably justifiable, but gets to a point of no return and keeps going. Héra and Wulf both inherit this mess from their fathers, but they choose very different paths. Wulf commits himself to his vengeance.

Héra has genuine affection for Wulf. She has fond memories of their childhood. They cared about each other, but for her it has never been romantic. In Eowyn's voiceover, it is said, 'He weighed heavy on her mind.' There are fleeting moments of vulnerability in Wulf's scene with Héra at Isengard – there is that moment of hesitation because she says, 'I did try to find you,' and that's genuine. It stays his hand for a moment while he is grappling with his emotions, which is what the scene was about. She tries to call him back, to get through to the boy that she knew. It was an important line for us that he says, 'I am the man that your father made me.' It's what brings him back to his resolve. He sheds the hurt boy. – PHOEBE GITTINS, WRITER

For me, there is something really creepy in Wulf's marking of Héra. The slashing knife is not only violent and shocking, but there's something especially vulgar in the marking of a person, the implication of ownership. – ARTY PAPAGEORGIOU, WRITER

I think Wulf loved her, once, but it becomes about possession. I think it was his father's great mistake putting the notion in his brain that Wulf could have Héra, and that he was entitled to her. Her rejection, publicly, is humiliating. Perhaps if his father hadn't been killed by Helm as well, he might have risen above that or got over it in time, but he did genuinely have feelings for her. That's why it all gets so complicated. He could have killed her when he captured her. He says to her, 'Is there no end to the arrogance of your house?' They have always looked down on him for his Dunlending blood. Héra does care about Wulf, but not that way. – PHILIPPA BOYENS, PRODUCER

Presented with this mess of their parents' making, it's the choices that our young characters make that define them and ultimately settle who we should sympathize with. Wulf and Héra's different paths lead them to different endings. Héra becomes an obsession for Wulf, especially after her escape. It's an unanswered question, what he would have done with her when Tarrg captured her, had she not gotten away. It wasn't necessarily his plan to take her, and there's some hesitation when they're together. At this stage on his journey, he hadn't yet reached the point of no return. – PHOEBE GITTINS, WRITER

Our story is about choices, who has the right to make them and who truly has to live by the consequences once they are made. Héra and Wulf both inherit the fallout from bad decisions made by their fathers. Despite their similar circumstances the choices each makes lead them down very different moral paths, that naturally clash – the scene in Isengard is their first, mostly emotional duel,

before a second, fully combative duel at the Hornburg. At that point they are both attempting to break free from the metaphorical and physical siege that keeps them captive, and are about to experience the reckoning of their choices. – ARTY PAPAGEORGIOU, WRITER

Wulf's character goes through two visual stages: purity and vengeance. In his vengeance mode he is wearing his father's animal hide. I also initially imagined him carrying an axe to help make him look more aggressive. – STATO, ORIGINAL CHARACTER DESIGNER

Wulf had a wide range of facial expressions for those moments when he let his inner emotions come out. I think that such an emotional personality makes him more human in a good way. It definitely made drawing him so very worthwhile. His twisted expression of love towards Héra is also a part of his personality. – MIYAKO TAKASU, ANIMATION CHARACTER DESIGNER & KEY ANIMATION SUPERVISOR

'THE BOY YOU KNEW IS GONE, HÉRA. I AM THE MAN YOUR FATHER MADE ME.'

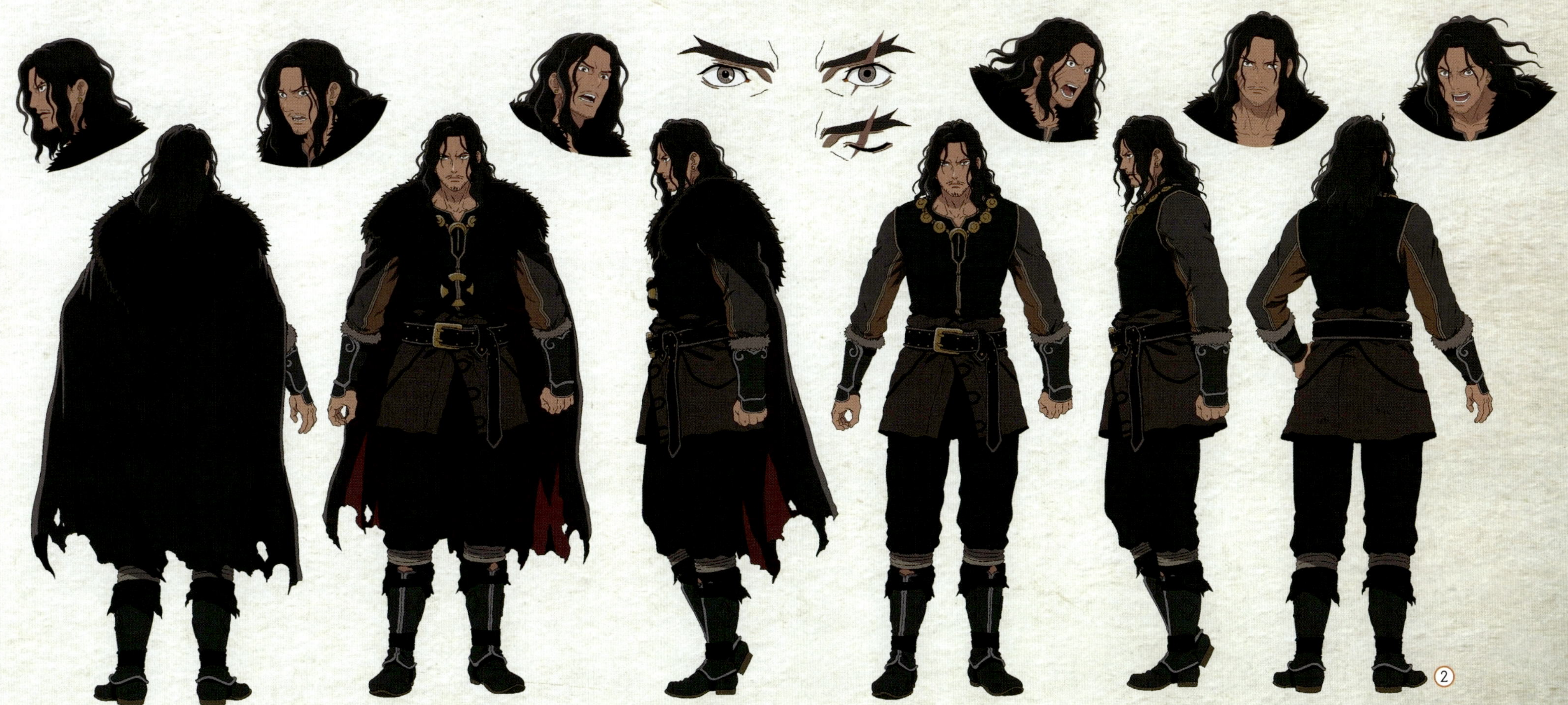

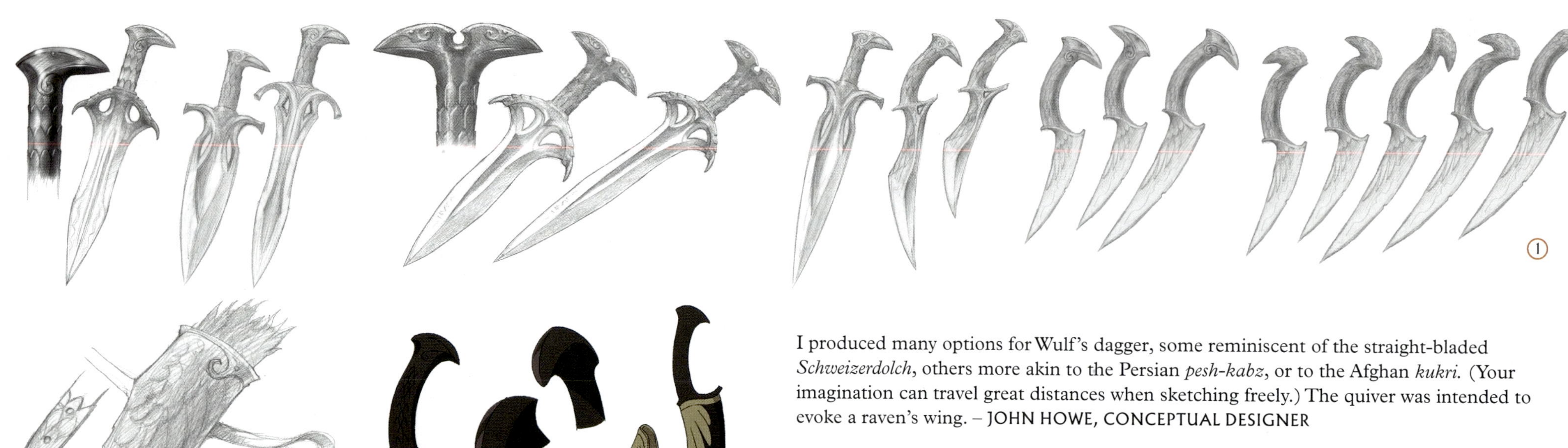

I produced many options for Wulf's dagger, some reminiscent of the straight-bladed *Schweizerdolch*, others more akin to the Persian *pesh-kabz*, or to the Afghan *kukri*. (Your imagination can travel great distances when sketching freely.) The quiver was intended to evoke a raven's wing. – JOHN HOWE, CONCEPTUAL DESIGNER

In contrast to Héra's slender, pale courser, Ashere, Wulf rides a broad, dark horse with a thick black mane, shaggy fetlocks and bone mask. Wulf has this signature tussled black hair and shaggy mantle. His horse simply had to match! – DANIEL FALCONER, ADDITIONAL CONCEPTS DESIGNER

'FIRST, I WILL KILL YOUR BROTHERS. THEN I WILL KILL YOUR FATHER. AND THEN I WILL TAKE THE THRONE.'

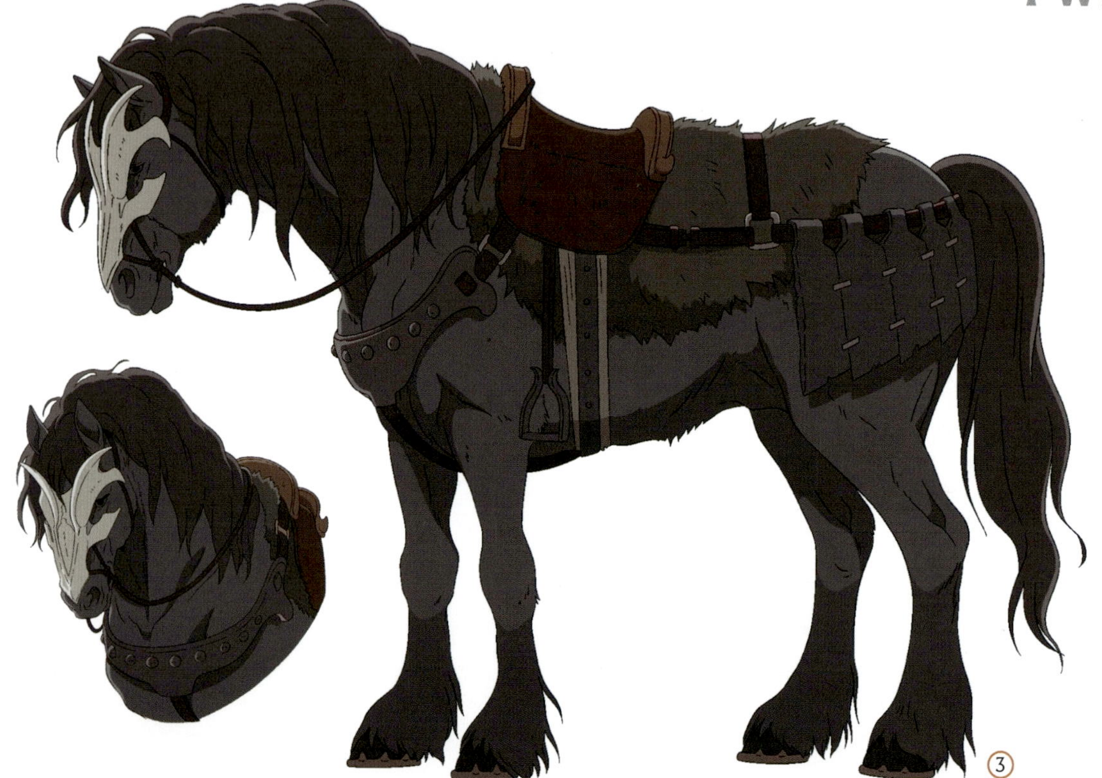

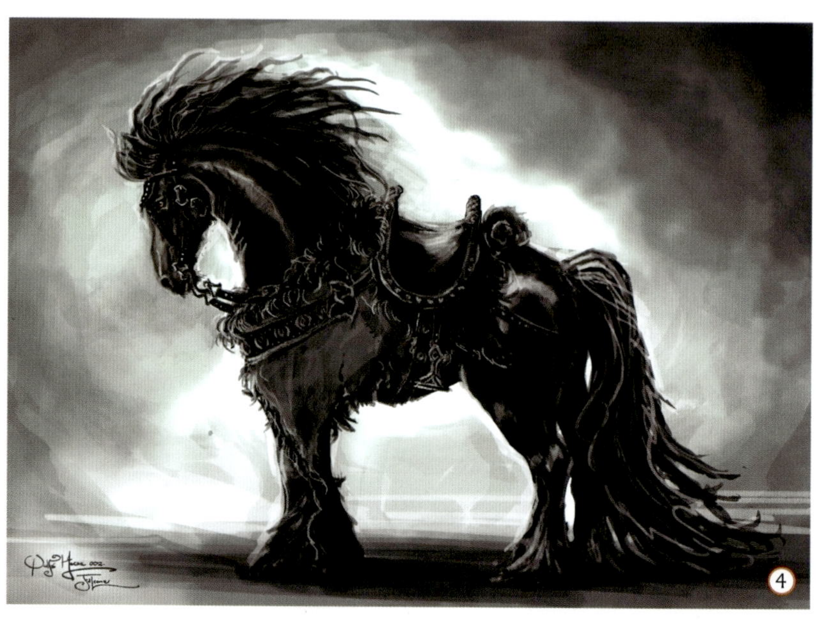

1: Wulf's dagger concepts, JH. **2:** Wulf's dagger prop setting art, KM. **3:** Wulf's horse setting art, MT. **4:** Wulf's horse concept, DF.

HÉRA'S RESCUE

Olwyn bursts into the guard tower to rescue Héra, blade in hand, revealing herself to be a warrior of considerable capability. With a buckler shield that bears the scars and shattered edge of a former battle, she deflects Wulf's blows and drives him back, buying Héra's escape. Together they leap from the tower to freedom.

The shieldmaidens were the last line of defence, which women often were in history. It came from the idea that among early Brythonic tribes the women would encourage their fighting men in battle. Standing on the perimeter of the battlefield, they would push any who fled back into the fight. When all the men were dead, the women would take up their swords and fight on. The exact nature of what a shieldmaiden is remained undefined in Tolkien's writing, so our idea of what shieldmaidens might be in Middle-earth was based on that legend. The shield also represents the notion of being protected. Of course, ultimately Héra kills Wulf with Olwyn's broken shield. There are layers to that symbolism. – PHILIPPA BOYENS, PRODUCER

We wanted Olwyn's shield to be something special and different from the shields you would usually see in *The Lord of the Rings*. The director got an idea from a shield called a buckler, which we used as a reference. Initially, it was red, but was changed to blue, which is less common in Rohirrim designs and would look more special. The shield has fissures large and small, telling the story of Olwyn's past life as a fighter. – KENJI MASUDA, PROP DESIGNER

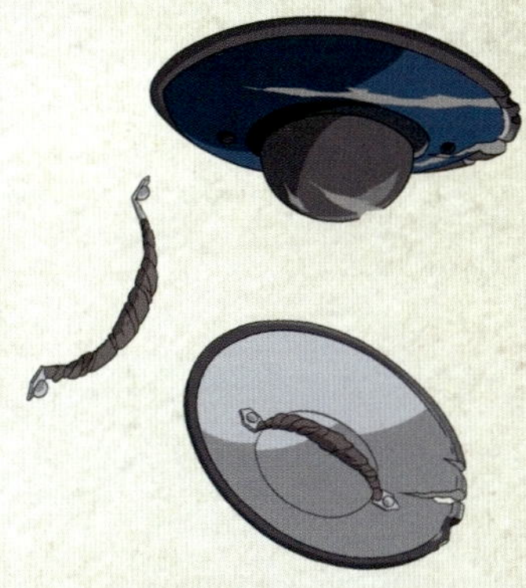
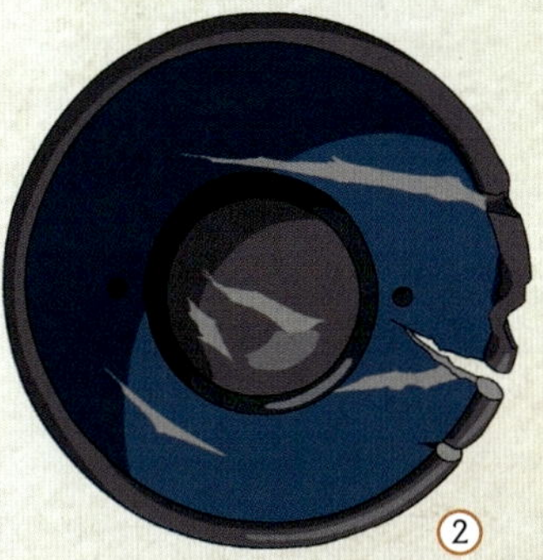

'WHAT HAVE WE HERE? A SHIELDMAIDEN. YOUR FIGHTING DAYS ARE OVER, OLD WOMAN.'

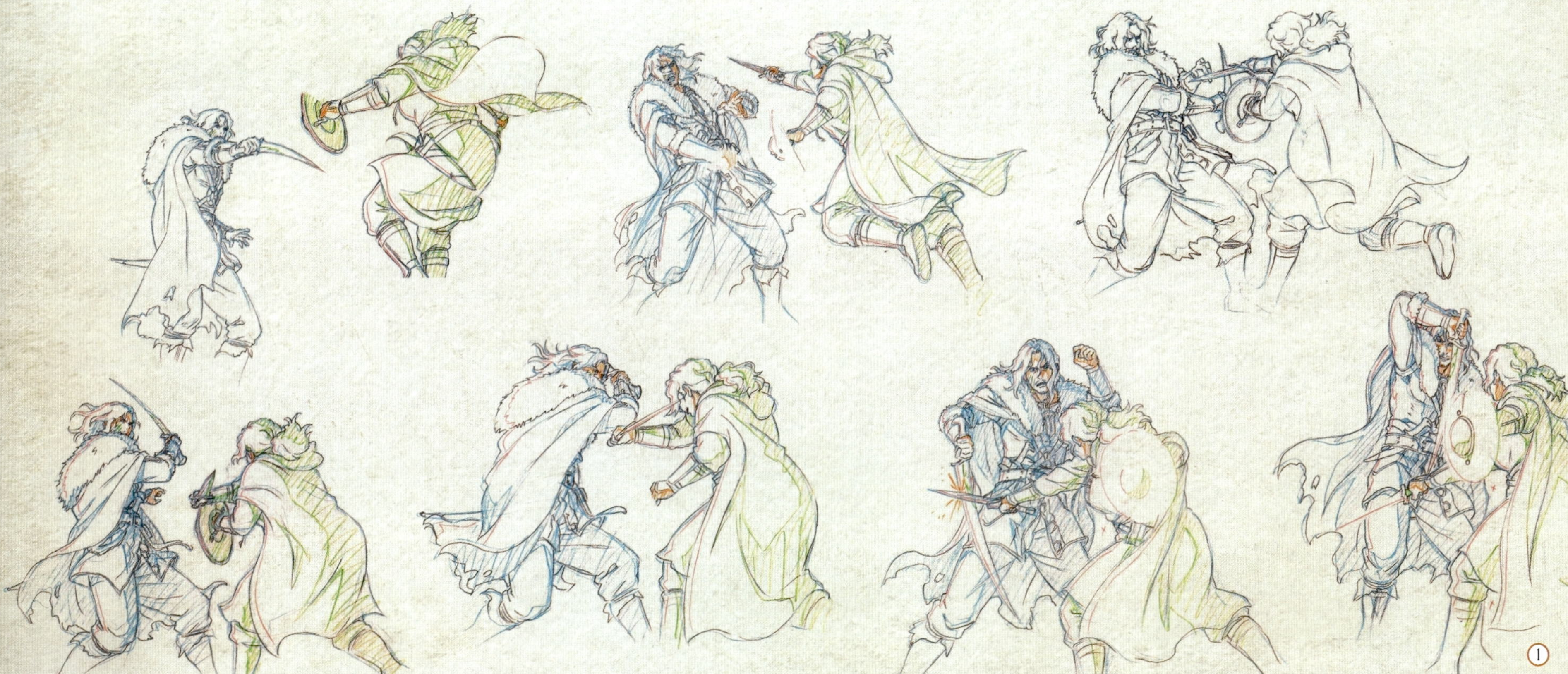

1: Animation key frames, MT . 2: Olwyn's shield prop setting art, KM.

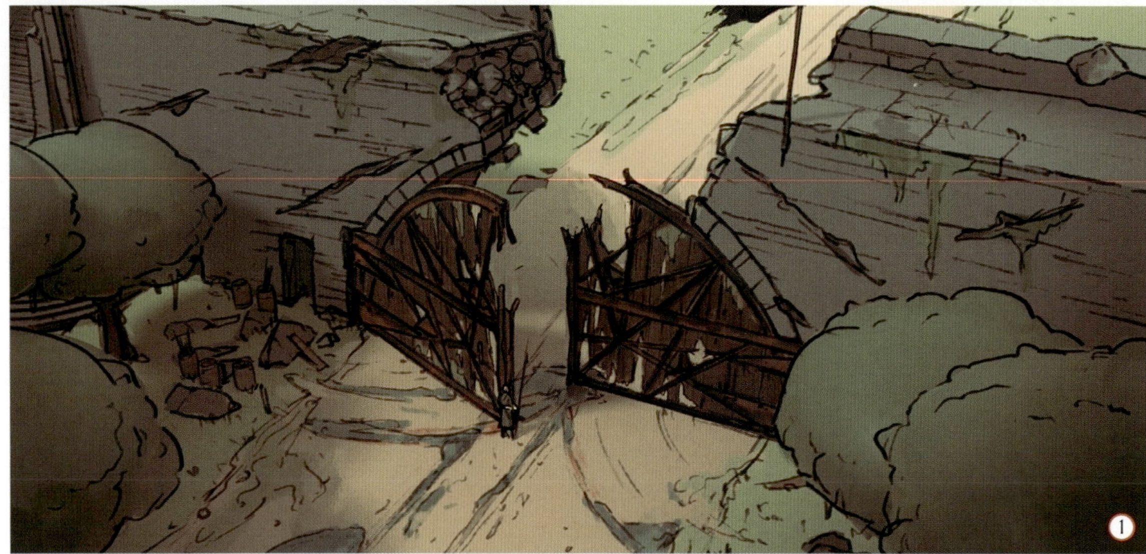

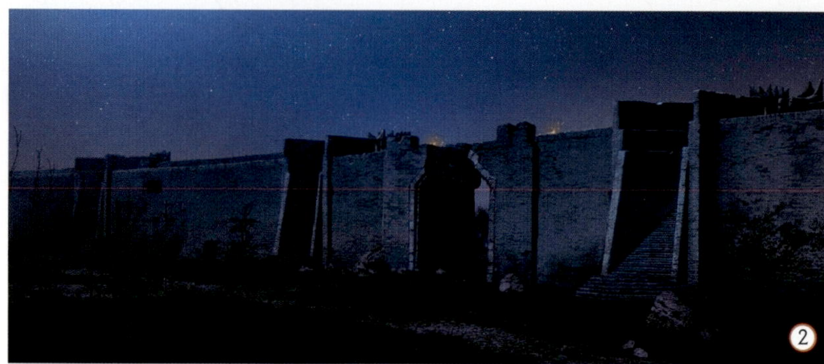

1: Isengard wall and gate concepts, AM. 2: Isengard wall and gate background art, TK. 3: Final film frame (LOTR trilogy). 4: Animation key frames, MT. 5: Wild Man bow prop setting art, KM. 6: Isengard wall and gate background art.

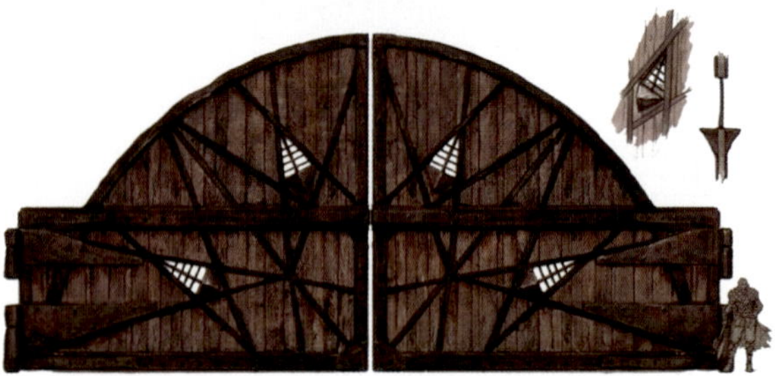

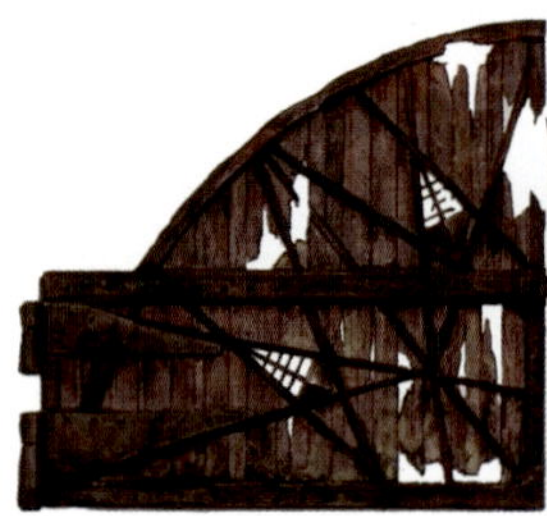

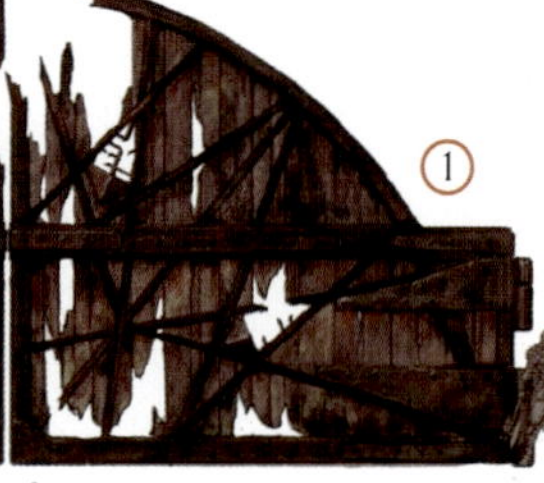

ISENGARD WALL AND GATE

Coming up with a suggestion for Isengard's gate, I took the empty gateway that we saw in the trilogy and worked backwards, imagining what might fit into that. The reinforcing metal bands in its structure form a star-shape that is repeated in the roadways within the grounds that you would see in an aerial view, which were originally designed by Alan Lee for the trilogy. Those shapes look creepy and aggressive with the wood eroded, jagged and broken, which was the feeling I wanted to get across with the gate. In the other films, a very similar motif is carved into the floor of the top of Orthanc's tower and the plinth on which Saruman has his palantír. It's a little nod to that and ties together the design elements of

the ring wall and central tower. You can even see where the hinges would have gone in the original archway. – ADAM MIDDLETON, WĒTĀ WORKSHOP ART DIRECTOR & SENIOR CONCEPT ARTIST

The final design of Isengard's gateway differed from what had been established in the Lord of the Rings *trilogy, setting up the notion that at some point after Saruman took possession it was rebuilt. In Helm's time the gateway has angular geometry rather than an arch, and is broken. While the central tower of Orthanc stands immutable, Isengard's walls are crumbling after many centuries of neglect.*

The top of the gateway is broken away, allowing *mûmakil* to pass through and enter the courtyard. We piled up soil on the outside so that Fréaláf could slide down during the action of the rescue and escape. – TAMIKO KANAMORI, ART DIRECTOR

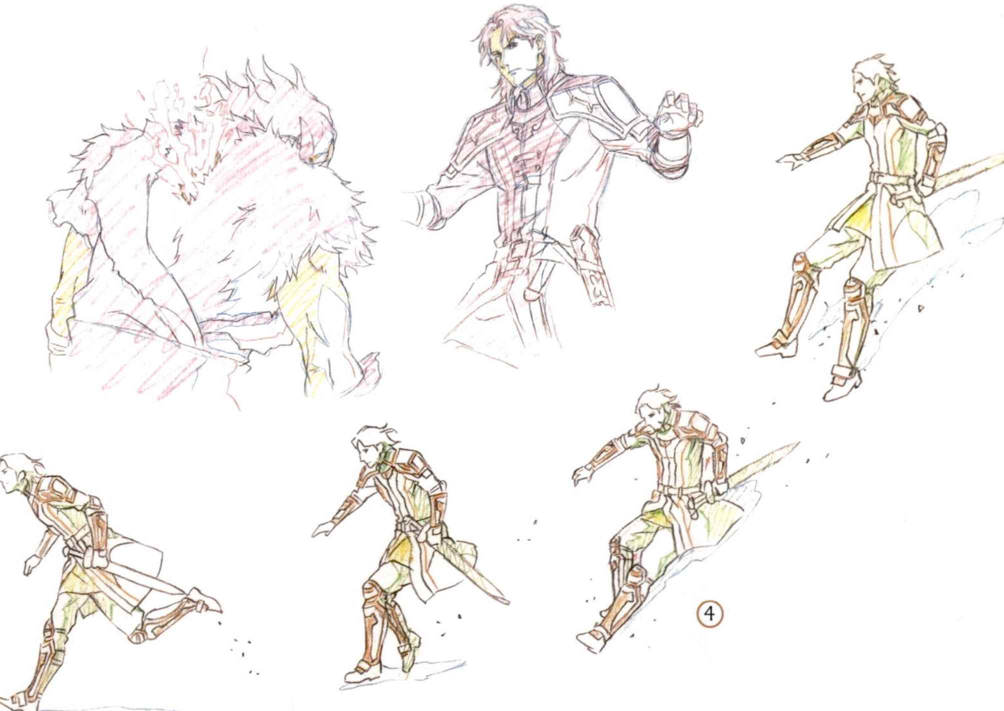

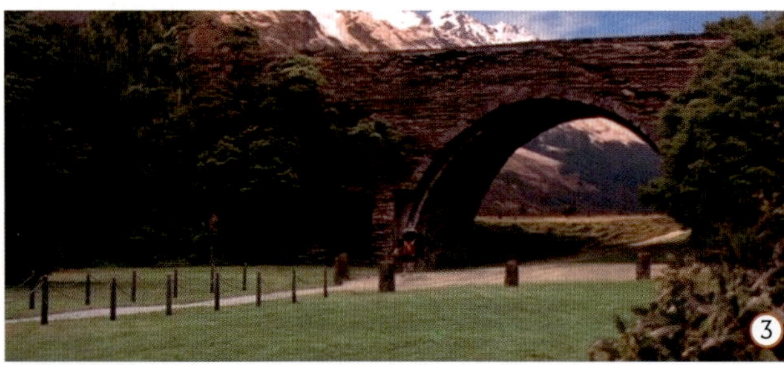

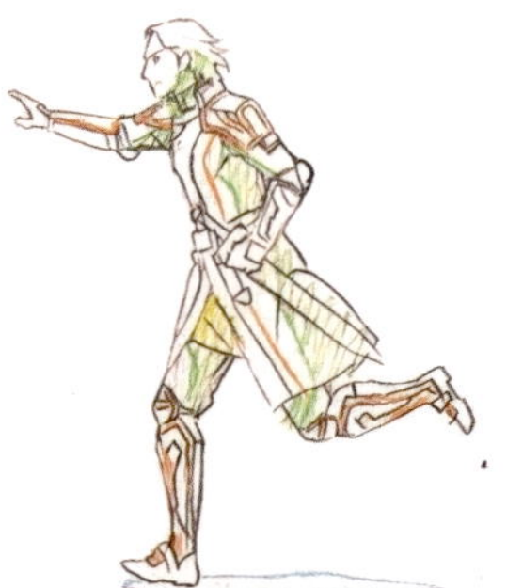

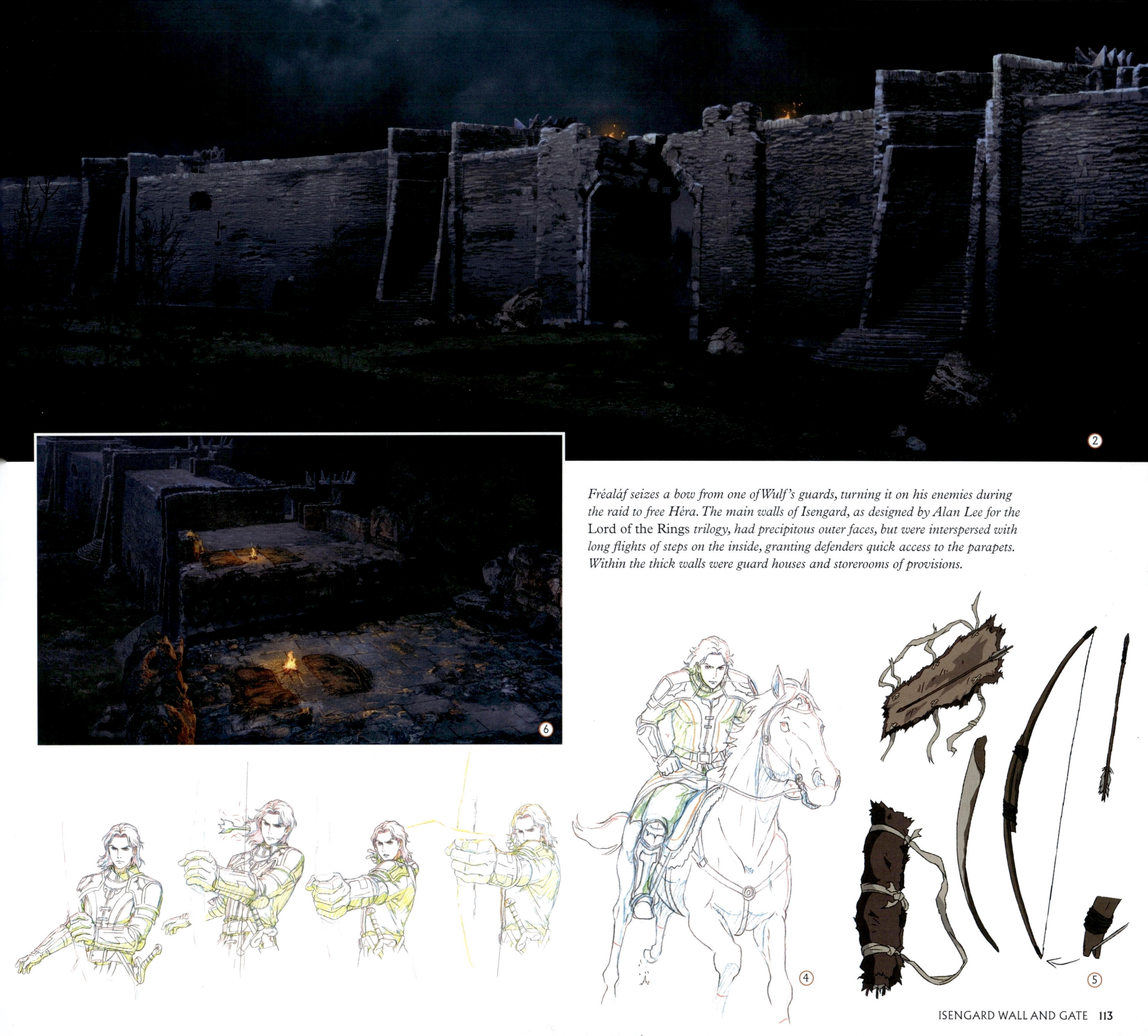

Fréaláf seizes a bow from one of Wulf's guards, turning it on his enemies during the raid to free Héra. The main walls of Isengard, as designed by Alan Lee for the Lord of the Rings *trilogy*, had precipitous outer faces, but were interspersed with long flights of steps on the inside, granting defenders quick access to the parapets. Within the thick walls were guard houses and storerooms of provisions.

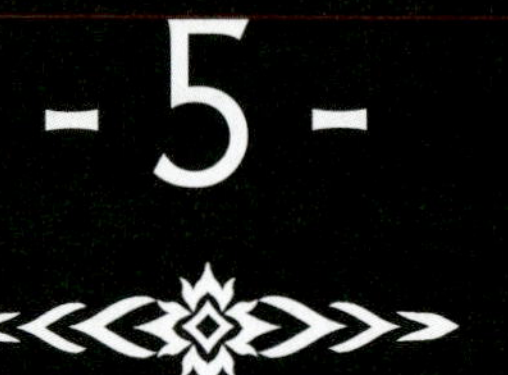

- 5 -

THE BATTLE OF EDORAS

A war council is called as the Rohirrim prepare to meet Wulf's invasion. Fréaláf counsels a withdrawal and is rebuked by Helm, who blames him for Héra's capture. Helm will meet Wulf's armies in the saddle, riding out to attack them upon the braided river valley before Edoras. Héra is commanded to remain in the city, but she perceives treachery, recognizing the seal she saw on a scroll in Wulf's possession as that of Lord Thorne, on whom Helm is counting to defend the city.

On the plain Helm engages Wulf's forces, a combined army of Dunlendings from the West-march, Wild Men of the Hill Tribes, and mercenary Southrons riding three great mûmakil, armoured for war. The trap is sprung, and Thorne betrays the king. In the royal stables he waylays Héra, but is kicked by Ashere, and killed. Fire erupts as the city is breached, and Héra uses it to her advantage in bringing down one of the mûmakil at the gate, though invaders now run through Edoras, making for the summit. Héra hurries her people to fly for the mountains.

Before the doors of Meduseld, Héra's brother Haleth falls, slain by Wulf's arrow after taking down another mûmak. Helm is overcome by the sight of his son's death as fire tears through his home. The Rohirrim are routed and flee Edoras. Háma, Héra's remaining brother, guards the rear of the retreat but gradually falls further behind upon his tiring old grey mare.

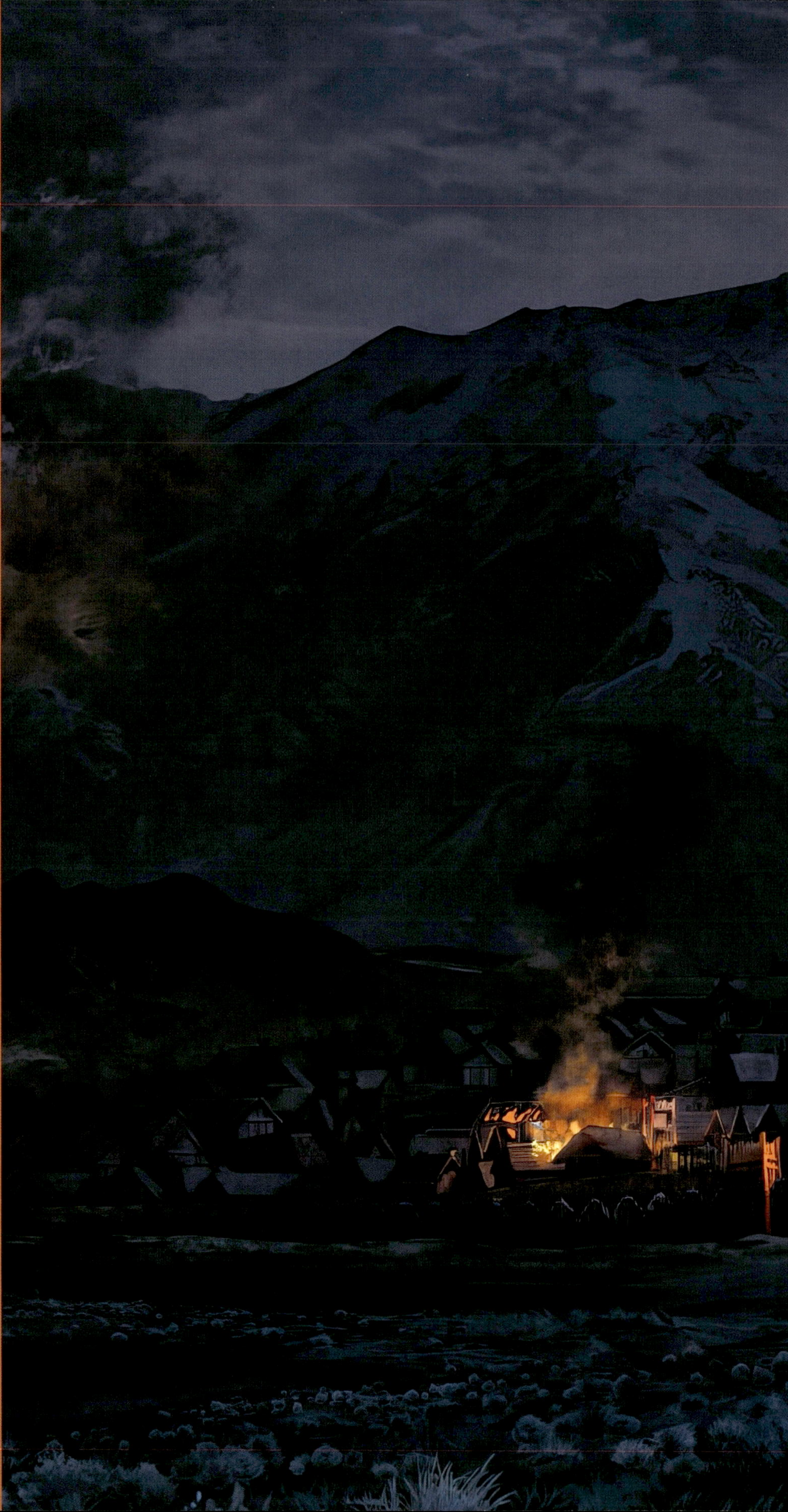

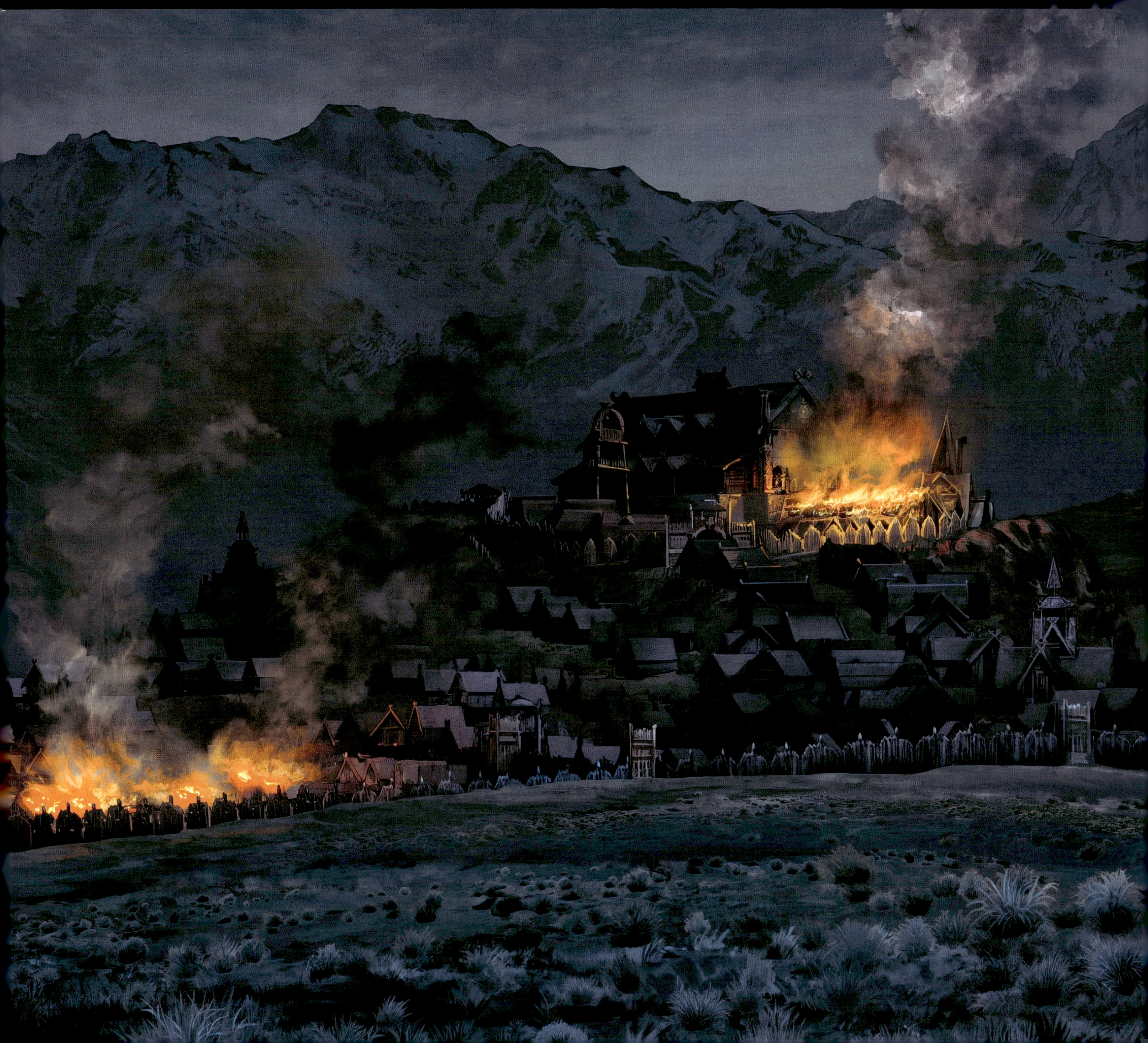

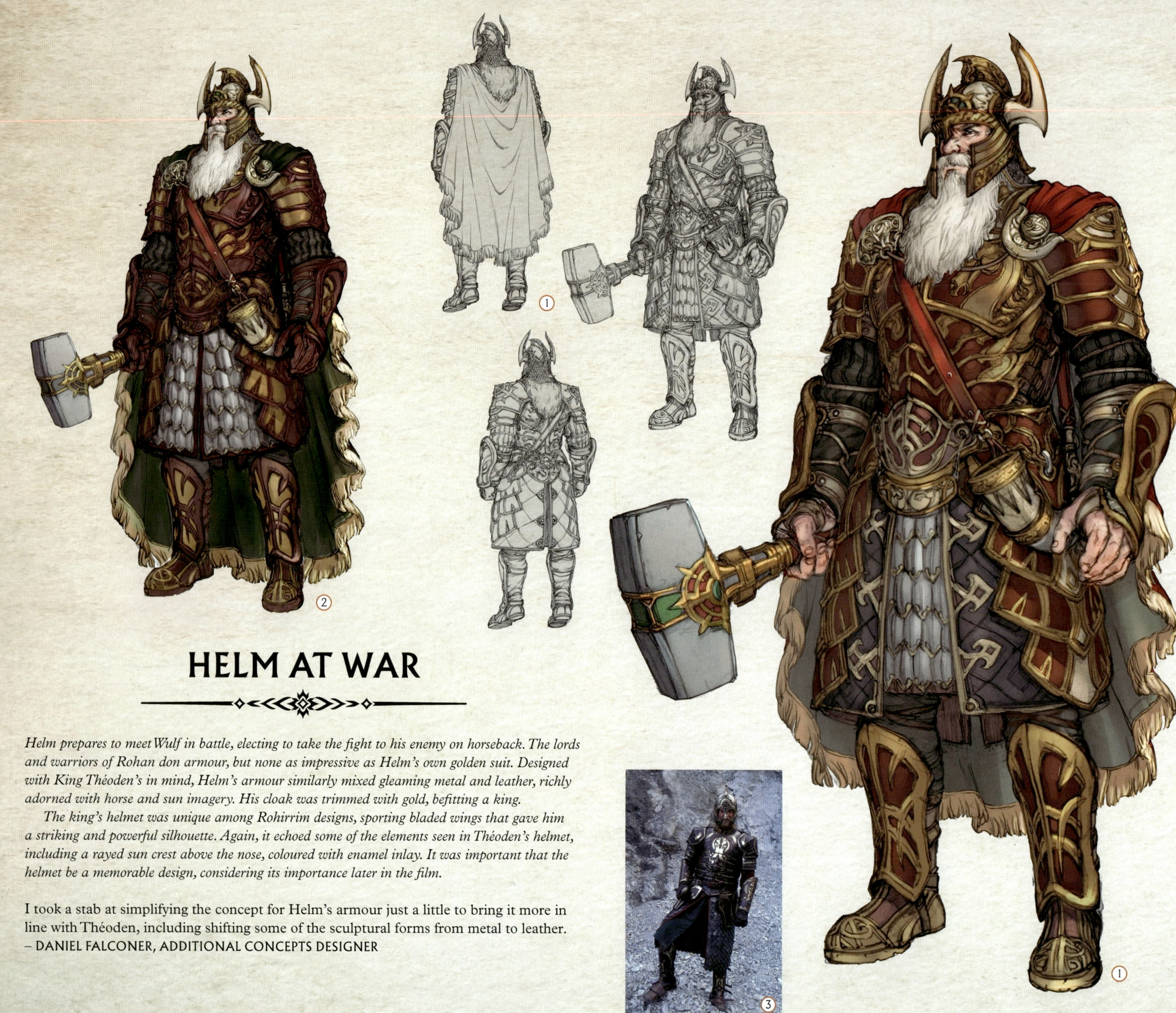

HELM AT WAR

Helm prepares to meet Wulf in battle, electing to take the fight to his enemy on horseback. The lords and warriors of Rohan don armour, but none as impressive as Helm's own golden suit. Designed with King Théoden's in mind, Helm's armour similarly mixed gleaming metal and leather, richly adorned with horse and sun imagery. His cloak was trimmed with gold, befitting a king.

The king's helmet was unique among Rohirrim designs, sporting bladed wings that gave him a striking and powerful silhouette. Again, it echoed some of the elements seen in Théoden's helmet, including a rayed sun crest above the nose, coloured with enamel inlay. It was important that the helmet be a memorable design, considering its importance later in the film.

I took a stab at simplifying the concept for Helm's armour just a little to bring it more in line with Théoden, including shifting some of the sculptural forms from metal to leather.
– DANIEL FALCONER, ADDITIONAL CONCEPTS DESIGNER

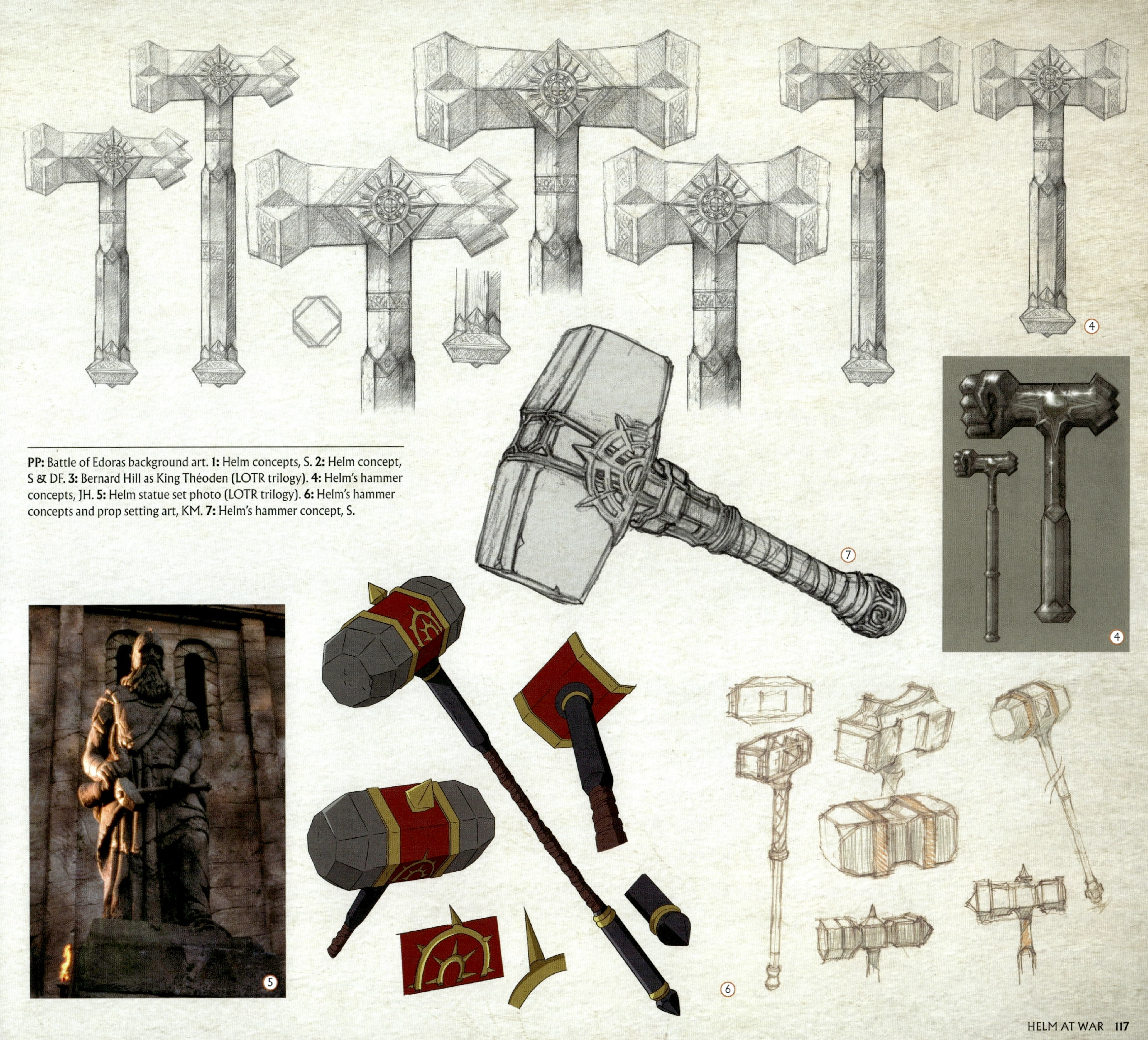

PP: Battle of Edoras background art. **1:** Helm concepts, S. **2:** Helm concept, S & DF. **3:** Bernard Hill as King Théoden (LOTR trilogy). **4:** Helm's hammer concepts, JH. **5:** Helm statue set photo (LOTR trilogy). **6:** Helm's hammer concepts and prop setting art, KM. **7:** Helm's hammer concept, S.

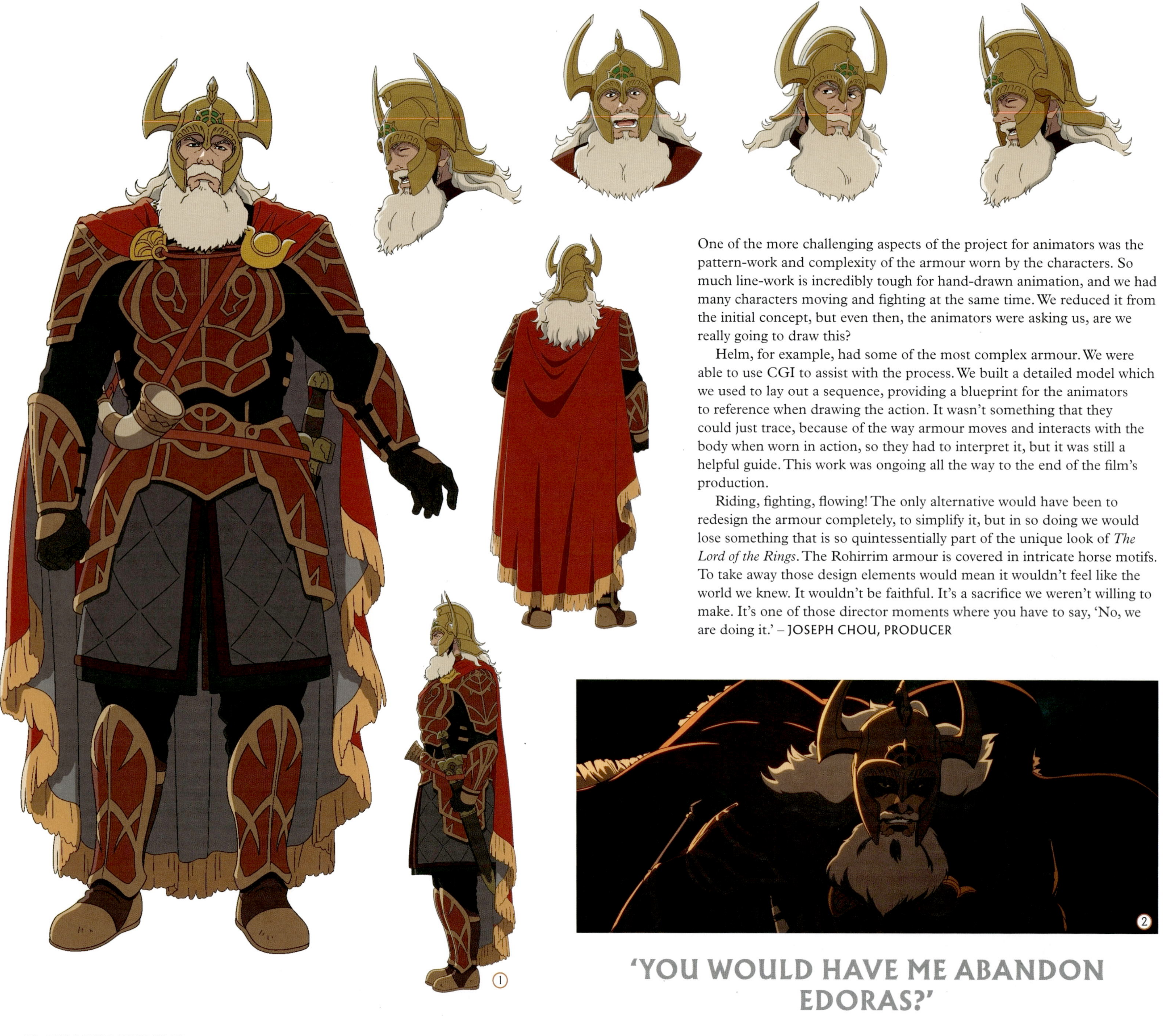

One of the more challenging aspects of the project for animators was the pattern-work and complexity of the armour worn by the characters. So much line-work is incredibly tough for hand-drawn animation, and we had many characters moving and fighting at the same time. We reduced it from the initial concept, but even then, the animators were asking us, are we really going to draw this?

Helm, for example, had some of the most complex armour. We were able to use CGI to assist with the process. We built a detailed model which we used to lay out a sequence, providing a blueprint for the animators to reference when drawing the action. It wasn't something that they could just trace, because of the way armour moves and interacts with the body when worn in action, so they had to interpret it, but it was still a helpful guide. This work was ongoing all the way to the end of the film's production.

Riding, fighting, flowing! The only alternative would have been to redesign the armour completely, to simplify it, but in so doing we would lose something that is so quintessentially part of the unique look of *The Lord of the Rings*. The Rohirrim armour is covered in intricate horse motifs. To take away those design elements would mean it wouldn't feel like the world we knew. It wouldn't be faithful. It's a sacrifice we weren't willing to make. It's one of those director moments where you have to say, 'No, we are doing it.' – JOSEPH CHOU, PRODUCER

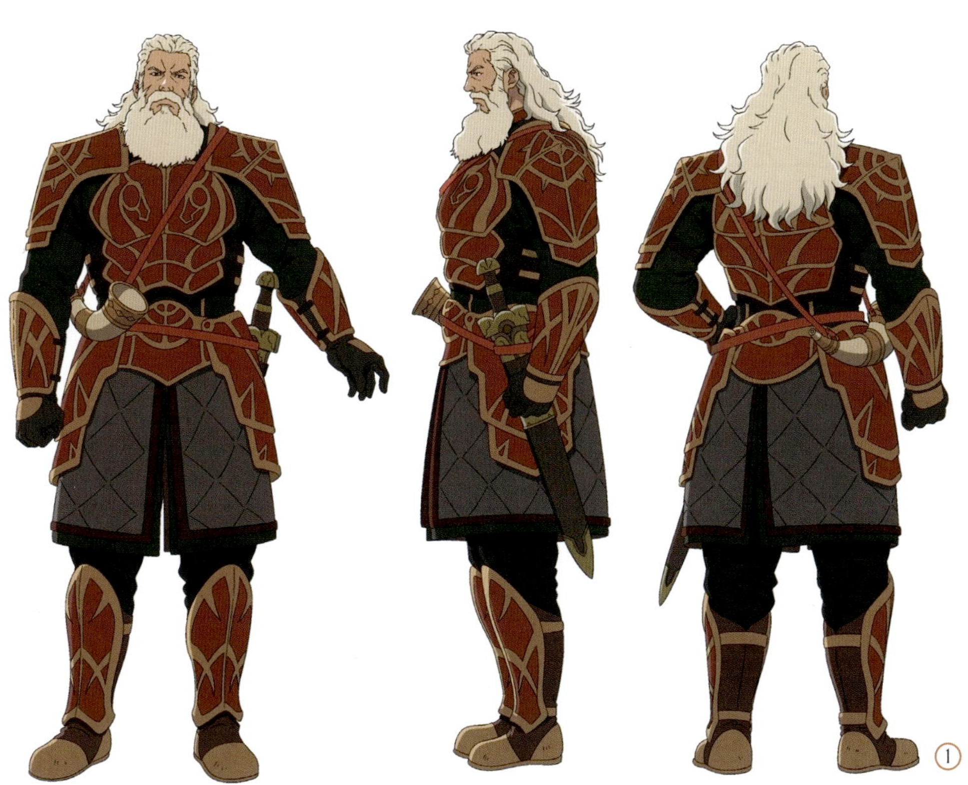

As Wulf advances on Edoras, Fréaláf urges Helm to light the beacons and call Gondor for aid, but Helm won't do it. He's too proud. It's the opposite of what we saw with Théoden.
– PHILIPPA BOYENS, PRODUCER

One of my favourite scenes between Héra and Helm takes place before the battle, in the stables. Héra asks her father if it would please him to have her gone. Héra is Helm's Achilles' heel; 'Yes, it would please me, because you would be safe.' He takes away her choice out of love. He's got it all wrong, but it shows what is most important to him, which is her safety. – PHOEBE GITTINS, WRITER

Helm's hammer was conceived as a large weapon, but it was made smaller to conform to the design held by Helm's statue in *The Two Towers*. The handle was elongated to allow him to wield it more effectively as a weapon. – STATO, ORIGINAL CHARACTER DESIGNER

Given Helm's legendary strength, a weightier hammer seemed possible. I offered concepts in which the iron head was offset by 45 degrees to make the silhouette more interesting; the whole hammer, handle and all, being forged of one piece, rather than assembled, with a leather-sheathed grip and brass inlays.
   Helm's sword was a more traditional Rohirrim design, though much stockier, with more sheer punching power. – JOHN HOWE, CONCEPTUAL DESIGNER

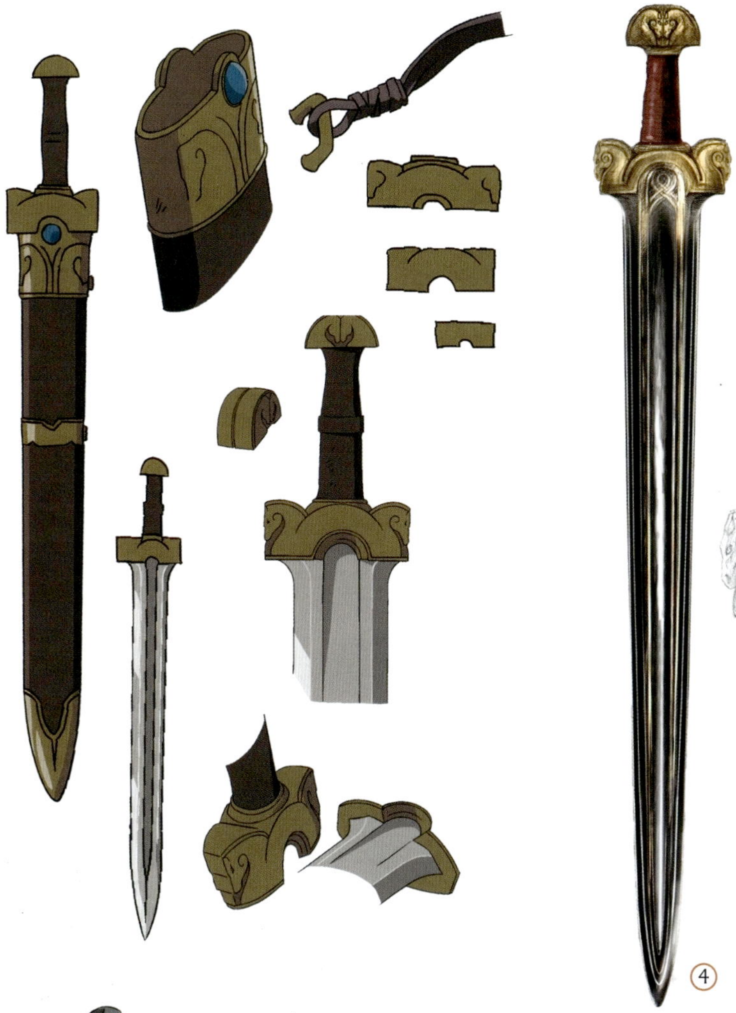

1: Helm character and expressions setting art, MT. 2: Final film frame. 3: Helm's sword and horn prop setting art, KM. 4: Helm's sword concept, JH & DF. 5: Helm's sword hilt concept, JH.

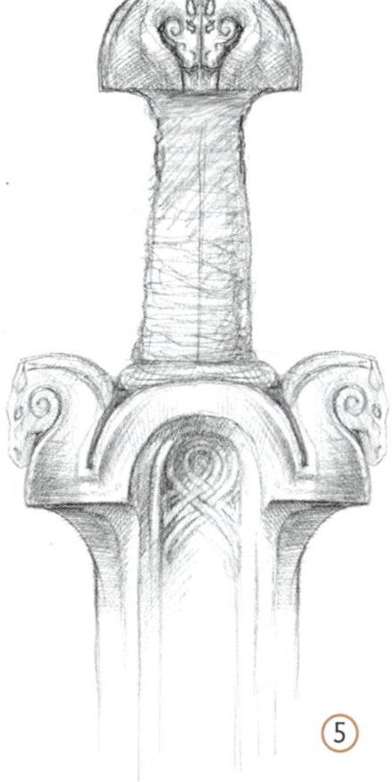

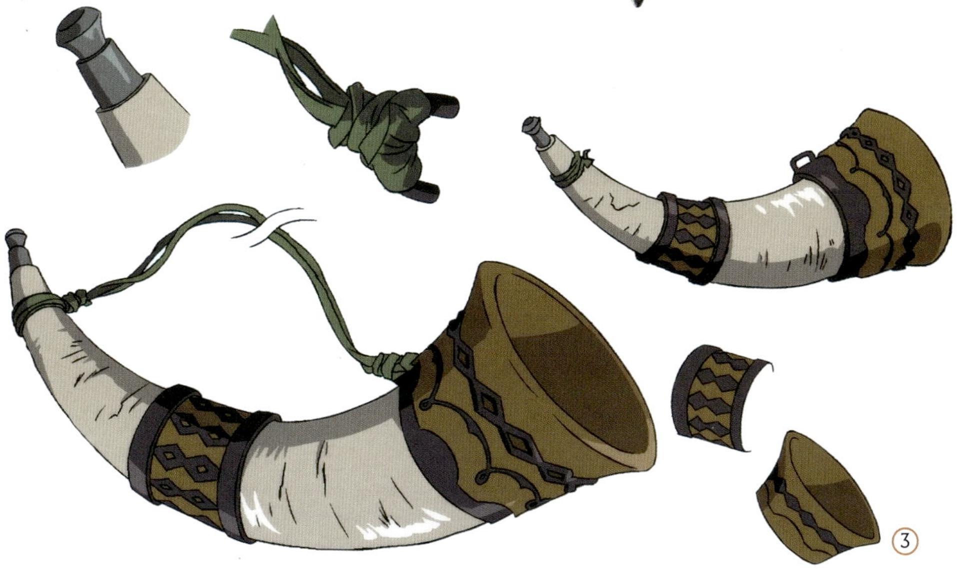

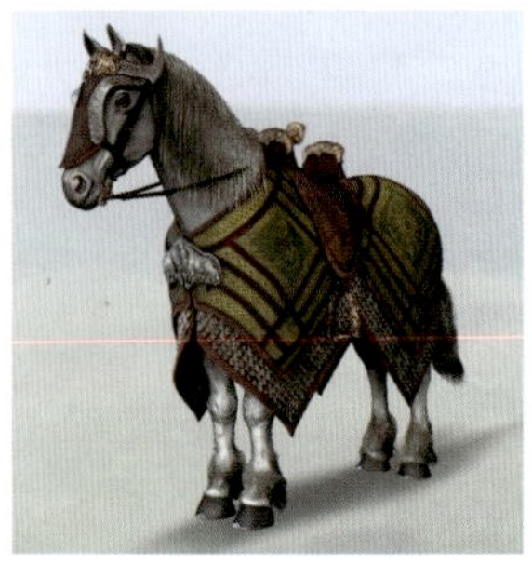 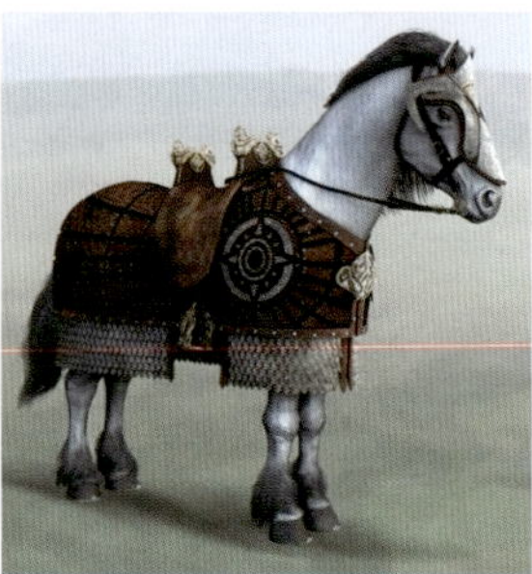 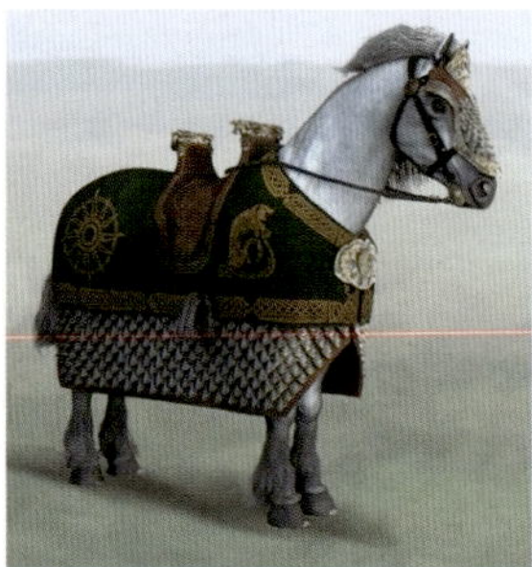 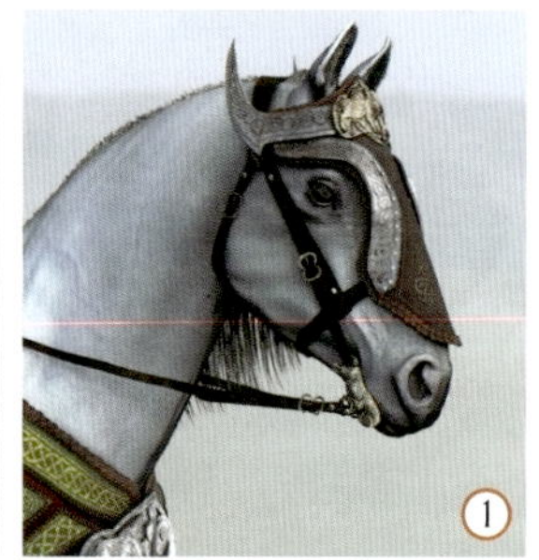

1: Helm's horse concepts, WW. 2: Helm's horse concepts, JD. 3: Helm's horse setting art and colour concept, MT.

'WHAT DO YOU SAY, OLD FRIEND? WILL YOU CARRY ME ONCE MORE?'

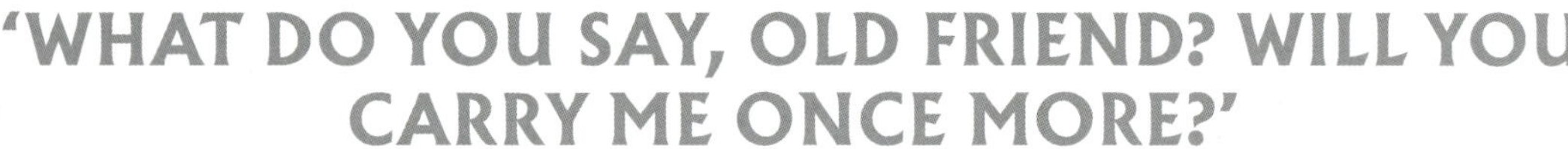

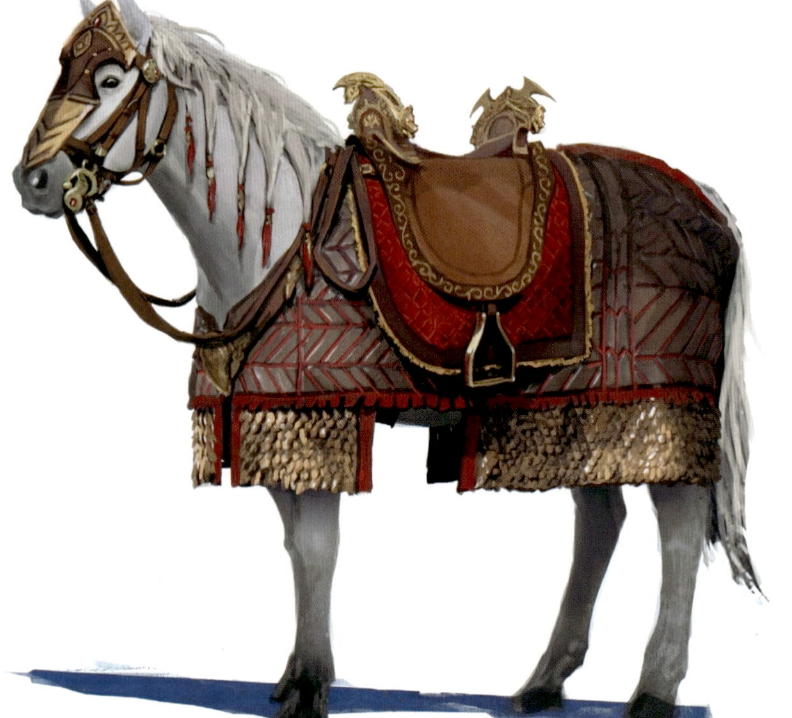

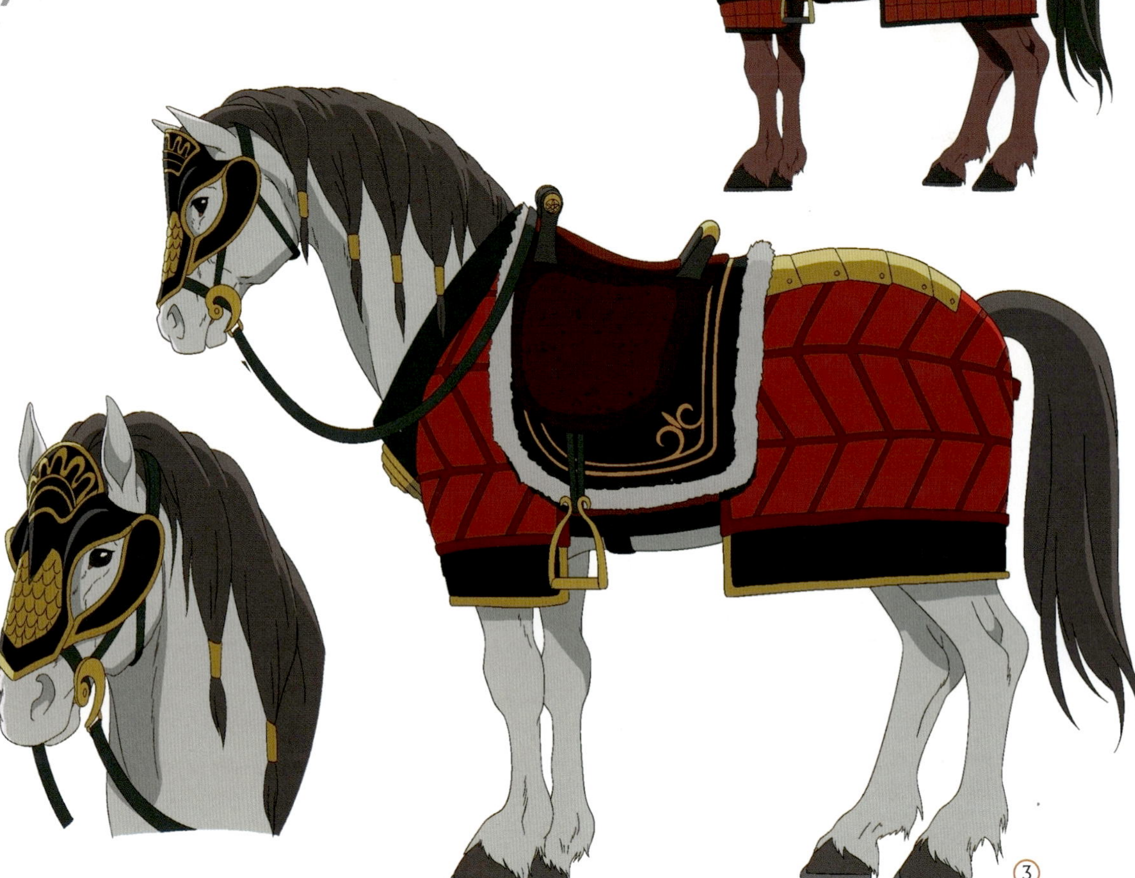

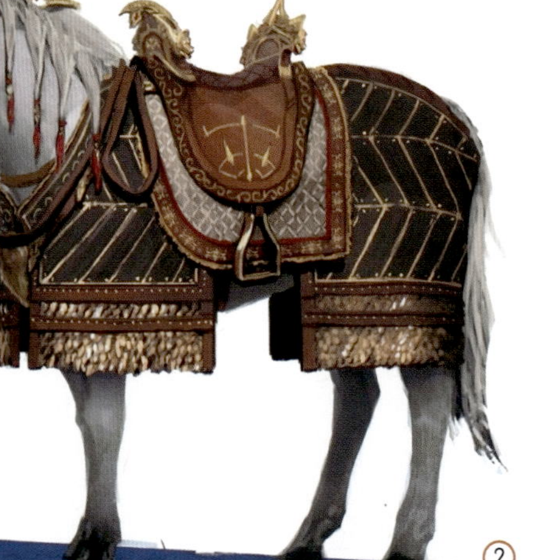

In the Wētā Workshop Design Studio, work on concepts for Helm's steed began with the artists looking back at King Théoden's warhorse, Snowmane. Although not stated in the films, Snowmane was one of the Mearas, the great horses of Middle-earth, whose ancestry reached deep into the past. So too, was Shadowfax, whom Gandalf rode and described as the Lord of all Horses. This same regal power and intelligence elevated the Mearas above ordinary horses and, by legend, they would suffer only the kings of Rohan to ride upon their backs. Gandalf was the exception.

Helm's horse, while not named, was almost certainly of the same lineage, so it was a conscious choice to keep him in the grey or white colour scheme already established in the films. The designers also looked to Snowmane for inspiration for Helm's horse's armour and saddlery. Helm being a larger than average man, his horse was also imagined as powerfully built. The designers sought to visually link the great stallion to Helm with colour and also shapes, incorporating elements of his armour and helmet into the concepts for the horse's chamfron (face-plate) and leather cowl.

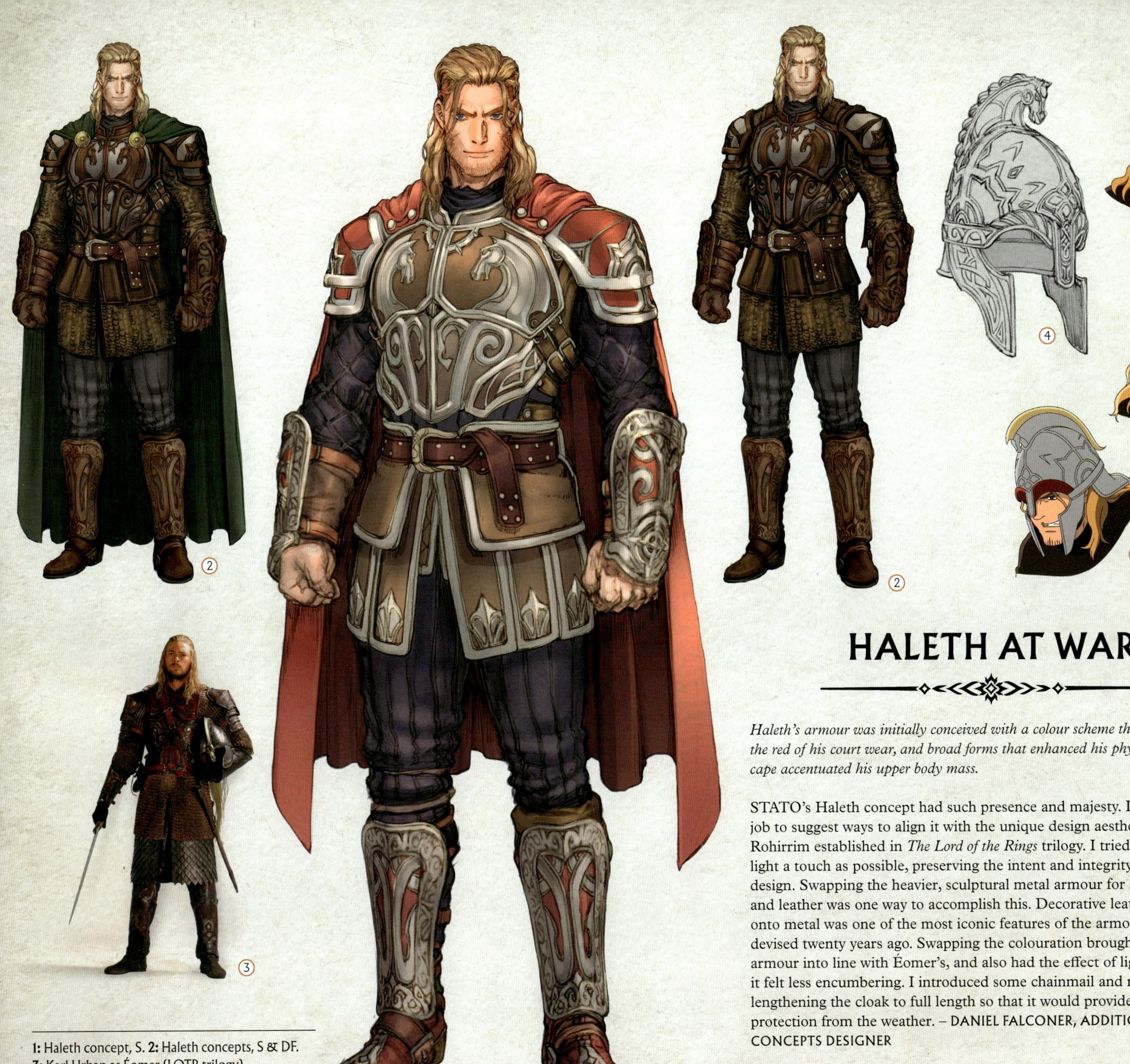

HALETH AT WAR

Haleth's armour was initially conceived with a colour scheme that closely recalled the red of his court wear, and broad forms that enhanced his physique. The short cape accentuated his upper body mass.

STATO's Haleth concept had such presence and majesty. It was my job to suggest ways to align it with the unique design aesthetics of the Rohirrim established in *The Lord of the Rings* trilogy. I tried to apply as light a touch as possible, preserving the intent and integrity of STATO's design. Swapping the heavier, sculptural metal armour for a mix of steel and leather was one way to accomplish this. Decorative leather laminated onto metal was one of the most iconic features of the armour that we had devised twenty years ago. Swapping the colouration brought Haleth's armour into line with Éomer's, and also had the effect of lightening it, so it felt less encumbering. I introduced some chainmail and recommended lengthening the cloak to full length so that it would provide practical protection from the weather. – DANIEL FALCONER, ADDITIONAL CONCEPTS DESIGNER

1: Haleth concept, S. 2: Haleth concepts, S & DF.
3: Karl Urban as Éomer (LOTR trilogy).
4: Haleth's helmet concept, S. 5: Haleth character and expressions setting art, MT.

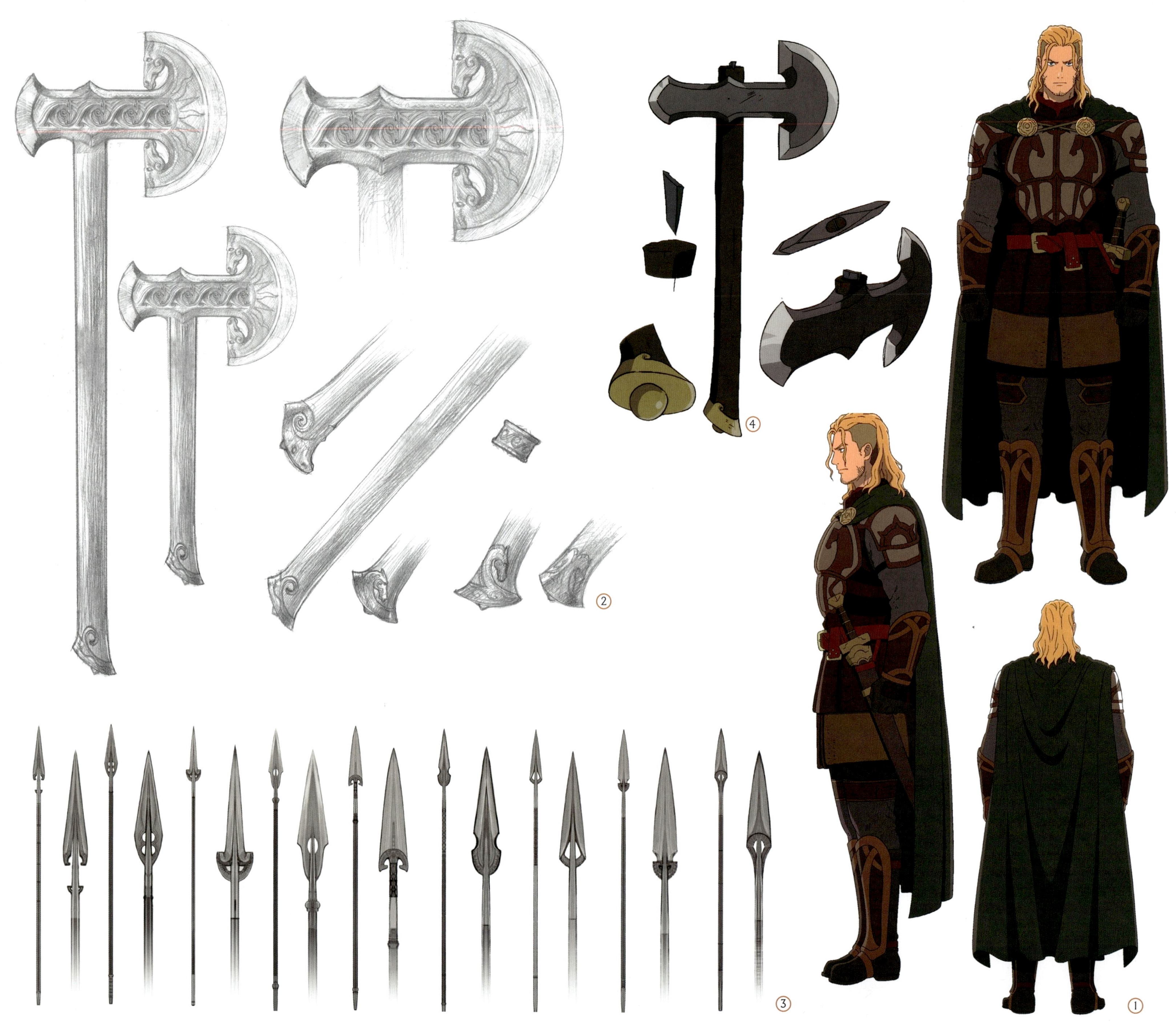

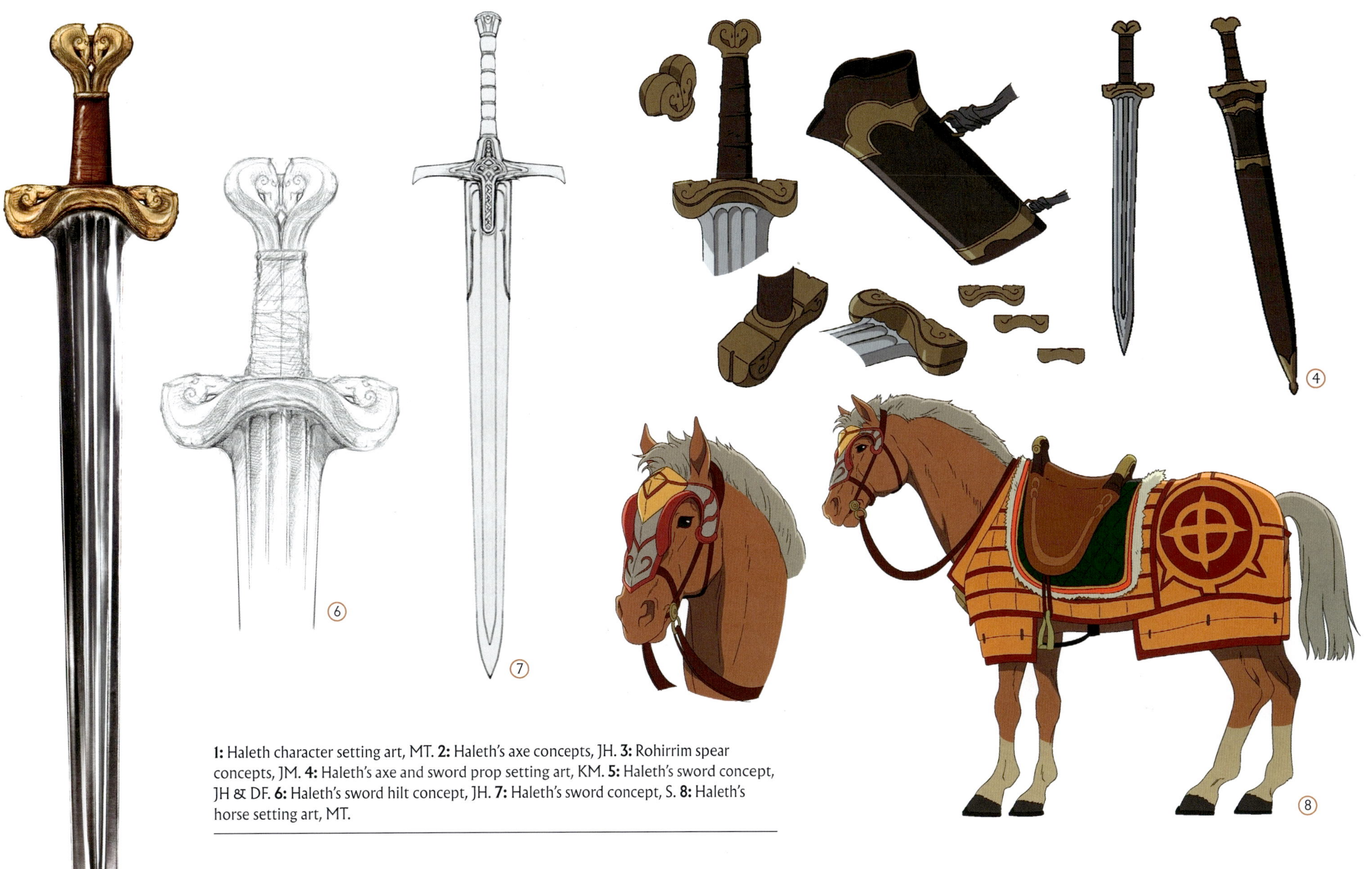

1: Haleth character setting art, MT. 2: Haleth's axe concepts, JH. 3: Rohirrim spear concepts, JM. 4: Haleth's axe and sword prop setting art, KM. 5: Haleth's sword concept, JH & DF. 6: Haleth's sword hilt concept, JH. 7: Haleth's sword concept, S. 8: Haleth's horse setting art, MT.

Stepping away from the Viking axe shapes generally associated with the Rohirrim, my concepts for Haleth's axe favoured a more formally shaped axe head, affixed to a tapering handle with a figurative end cap. I imagined that the sun motif would have been inlaid brass or copper. – JOHN HOWE, CONCEPTUAL DESIGNER

I had drawn a sword with a wider blade which was selected for Haleth. It was reminiscent of the Italian *cinquedea*, with a brass pommel and guard, and cord and leather-wrapped grip. – JOHN HOWE, CONCEPTUAL DESIGNER

Haleth's sword closely matched John Howe's concept with its distinctive three fullers, the channels running down the middle of the blade. It has the widest crossguard of any Rohirrim sword. As established in the trilogy, Rohirrim swords were similar in design to viking or Roman blades, lacking the cruciform shape and wide crossguards of many later, iconic medieval blades.

Haleth's horse matched him in physicality and colour, a visual shorthand that not only tied the character and horse together but kept both in proportion on screen; an important consideration, given characters like Helm and Haleth were depicted as physically large. Had their horses not been similarly powerful they might have seemed odd looking or even comical when drawn riding astride horses too small for them. Prominent on the horse's flank is the rayed sun emblem of Rohan reversed in the same hues as it appears on the shoulder of Haleth's cloak.

Just as all the Rohirrim care for their mounts, I imagined Haleth looking after his tall horse. The mane has been trimmed short in a wild style, which I liked to think was something that Haleth has done himself.
– MIYAKO TAKASU, ANIMATION CHARACTER DESIGNER & KEY ANIMATION SUPERVISOR

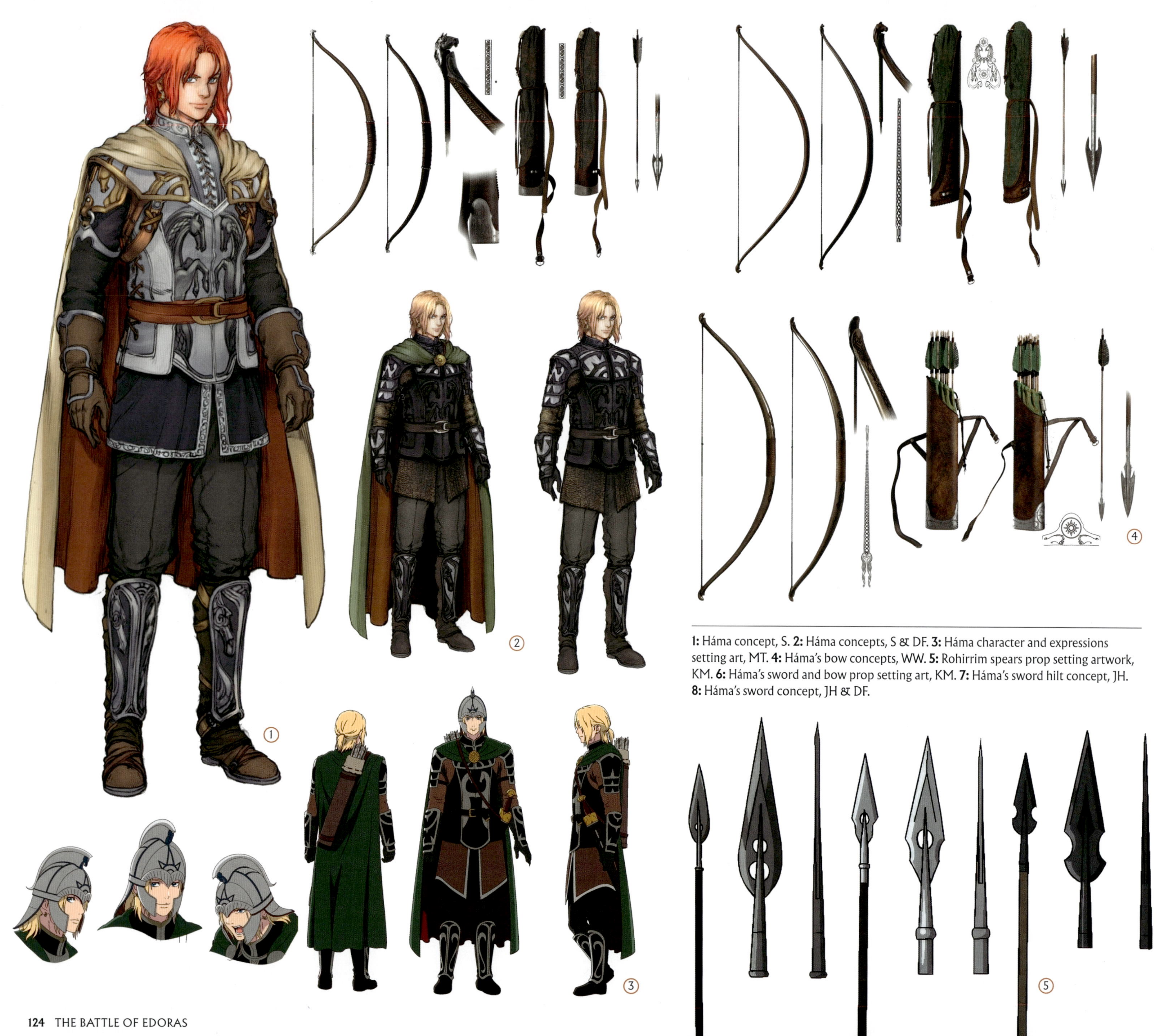

1: Háma concept, S. 2: Háma concepts, S & DF. 3: Háma character and expressions setting art, MT. 4: Háma's bow concepts, WW. 5: Rohirrim spears prop setting artwork, KM. 6: Háma's sword and bow prop setting art, KM. 7: Háma's sword hilt concept, JH. 8: Háma's sword concept, JH & DF.

HÁMA AT WAR

Some of the elements in the concept art for Háma's armour leaned a bit more into high fantasy than the established Rohirrim feel, but it was undeniably beautiful. We needed to get a little bit more of the classic *Rings* movie DNA in there, so I suggested some subtle edits to nudge it back into the Rohirrim design world, while hopefully maintaining the integrity of STATO's original concept. – DANIEL FALCONER, ADDITIONAL CONCEPTS DESIGNER

In contrast with his brother, Haleth, Háma projects a gentleness and serenity that is unusual for a warrior. I thought at first that he had a more effeminate personality, but I came to understand the character much better once I was drawing him in the production phase of the film. He may not be as big and strong as Haleth, but Háma too had the blood of a warrior of Rohan within him. He expresses himself in song, but he has a great respect for the warrior tradition of his people and a dignified way of supporting them that complements his father's style of leadership. – MIYAKO TAKASU, ANIMATION CHARACTER DESIGNER & KEY ANIMATION SUPERVISOR

Háma's weapons were original, but firmly based in the established Rohirrim aesthetic. The sword, which began as a sketch by John Howe, was embellished in colour and simplified for animation. The red leather hilt followed the theme of royal blades seen in the blades of King Théoden, Éomer, and Éowyn.

The favoured sword for Háma was one-handed. I suggested multiple fullers in my drawing, tapering quickly to a long point. – JOHN HOWE, CONCEPTUAL DESIGNER

Háma's bow, arrows and quiver were conceived as slightly more decorated variations on the standard Rohirrim versions seen in the earlier films, featuring quivers with cloth arrow bags supported in leather tubes.

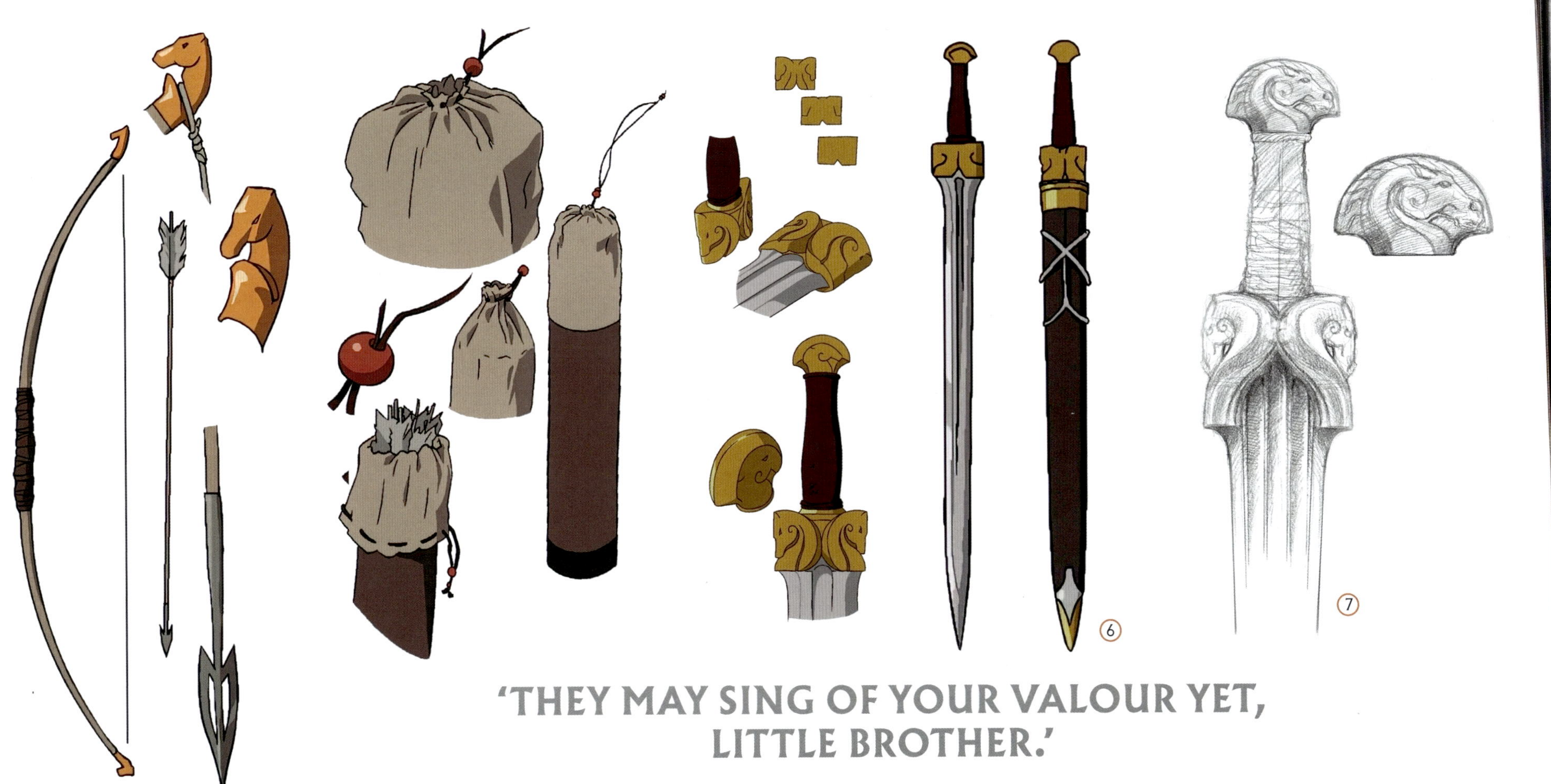

'THEY MAY SING OF YOUR VALOUR YET,
LITTLE BROTHER.'

FRÉALÁF AT WAR

Wulf and his army advance on Edoras, moving south along the River Snowbourn. At Helm's war council Fréaláf speaks against his uncle's plan to ride out and attack Wulf's forces head-on. The king rebukes him and casts him out.

Helm puts a great deal of trust in Fréaláf. We learn in Éowyn's voiceover that after the death of Freca the king would no longer let Héra ride out alone. Fréaláf was her guard. So, when Héra is kidnapped by Wulf, Helm blames him, and I think Fréaláf blames himself as well. – PHILIPPA BOYENS, PRODUCER

Fréaláf is the cool to Helm's hot, he's always level-headed. We see that here, Fréaláf knows his uncle all too well, he knows that his harsh words and choices are a knee-jerk reaction to the threat made against Héra - 'She could have died!' Despite his hurt, he is able to act rationally in the face of Helm's wrath, where a pettier man would break ties, Fréaláf is not so easily deterred. – PHOEBE GITTINS, WRITER

Fréaláf would have been the loyal lieutenant to his lord for the rest of his life, so Helm's rebuke wounds him deeply. – PHILIPPA BOYENS, PRODUCER

All of the blades wielded by the Rohirrim characters are new designs, with one exception: Fréaláf's sword bears a striking resemblance to Éowyn's. While Théodred's funeral in the trilogy set a precedent for Rohirrim royalty being buried with their swords, it is also possible that sometimes they are passed down. The intentional similarities between Fréaláf and Éowyn's weapons underscore their familial link, whether they are the exact same sword, or one was fashioned from, or in the likeness of, the other.

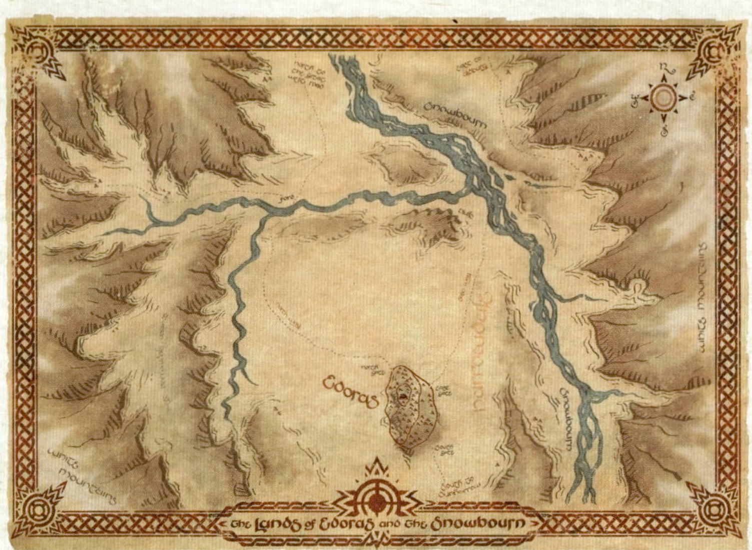

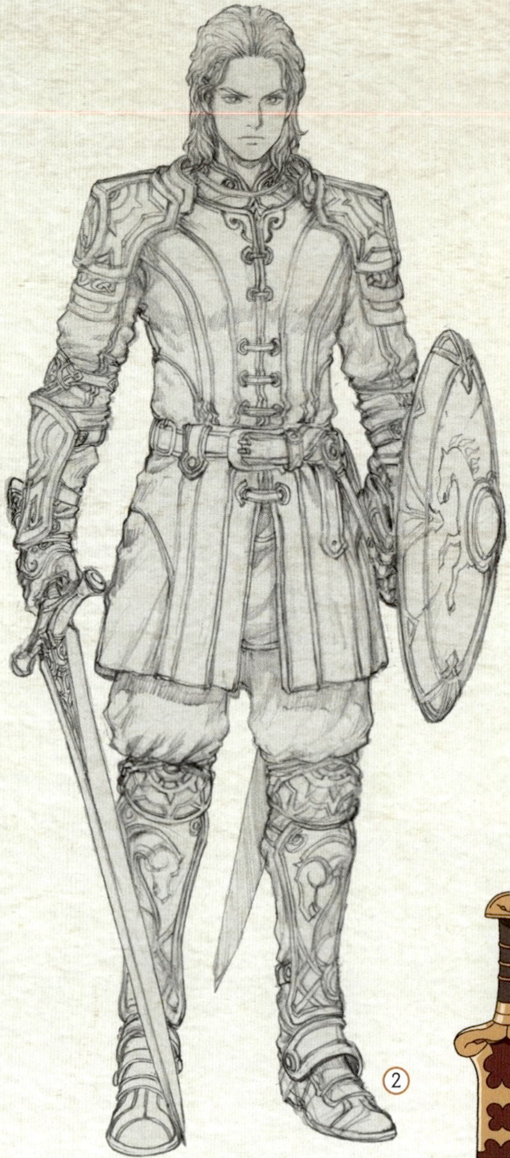

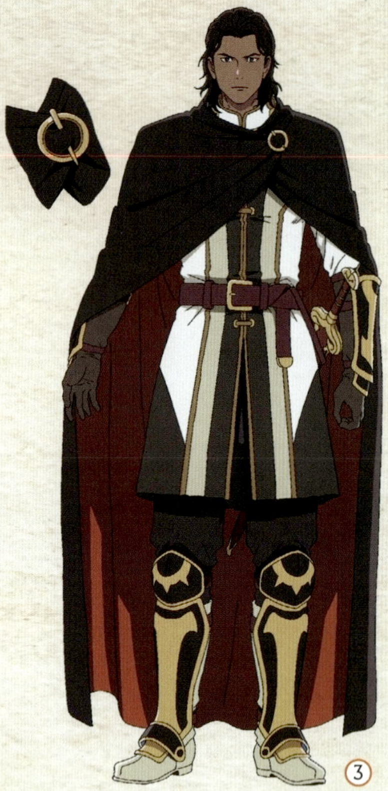

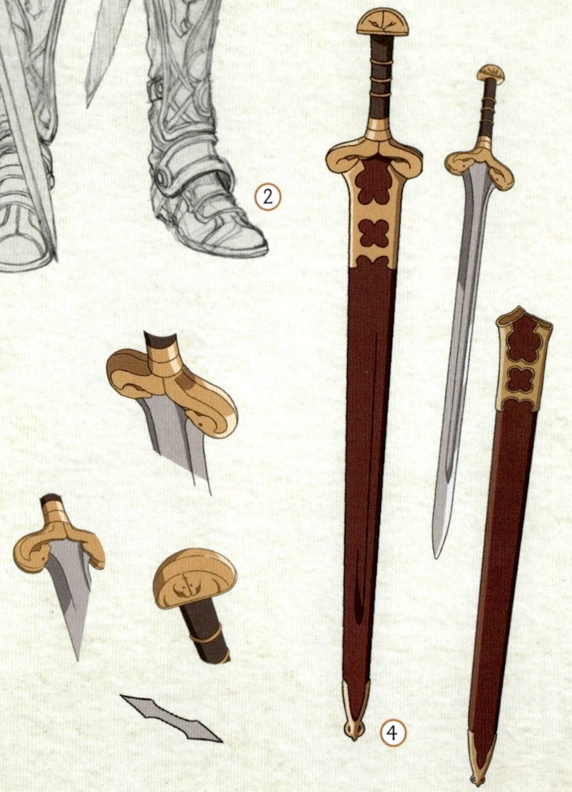

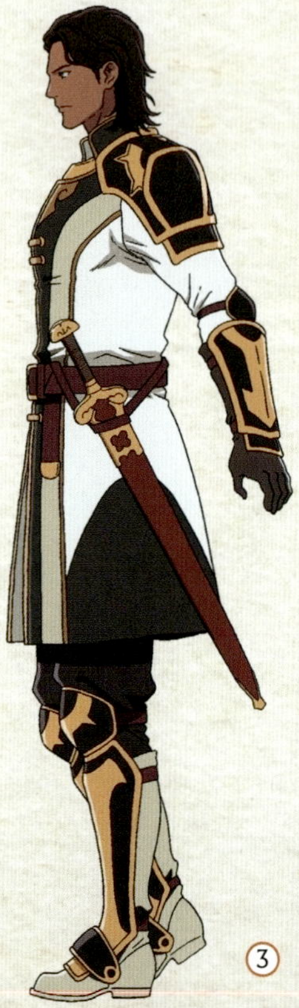

'YOU WILL ALWAYS HAVE MY SWORD, UNCLE, WHETHER YOU VALUE IT OR NOT.'

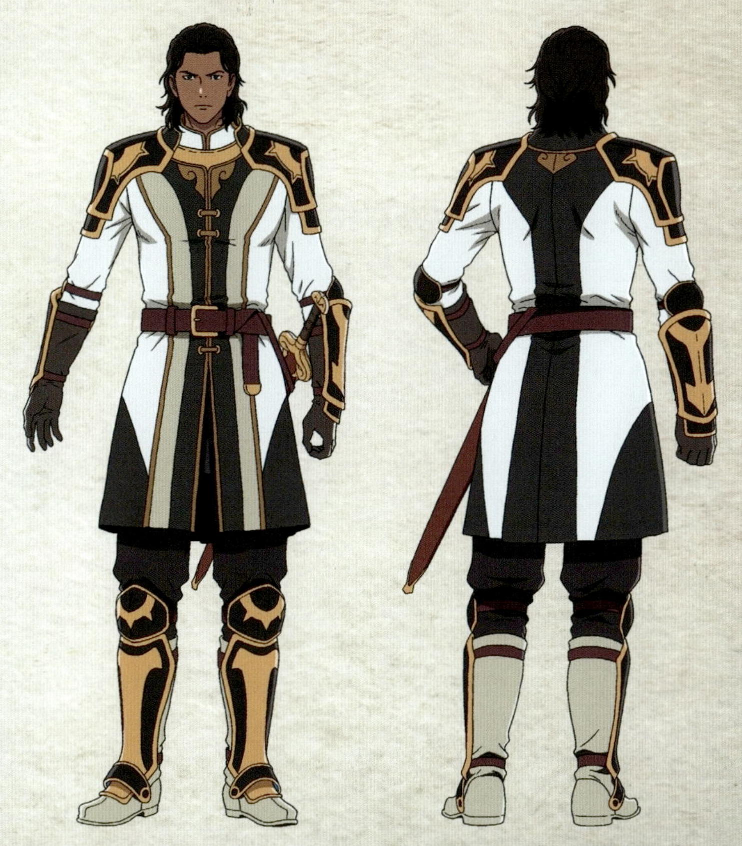

1: Snowbourn valley map, DF. 2: Fréaláf concept, S. 3: Fréaláf character setting art, MT. 4: Fréaláf's sword prop setting art, KM.

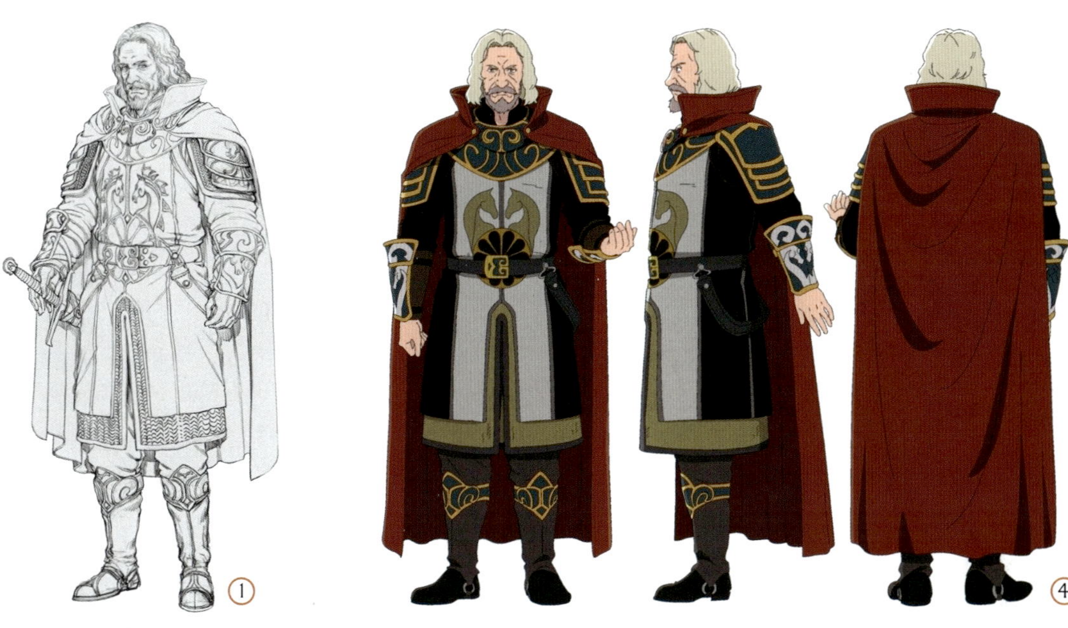

THORNE AT WAR

Thorne dons armour and a sword, joining the rest of the Lords of Rohan, though in secret he has made a pact with Wulf to betray Helm. The early concepts for Thorne's sword stayed within the bounds of the established Rohirrim aesthetic, but folded in iconography based on the barbed brambles and ram's head of the character's sigil. The final design leaned more heavily into the ram motif, eschewing the spiky thorns in favour of a silhouette more friendly to animation. Instead, the rams on the crossguard seem to devour the sun emblem of Rohan, subtly foreshadowing Thorne's betrayal.

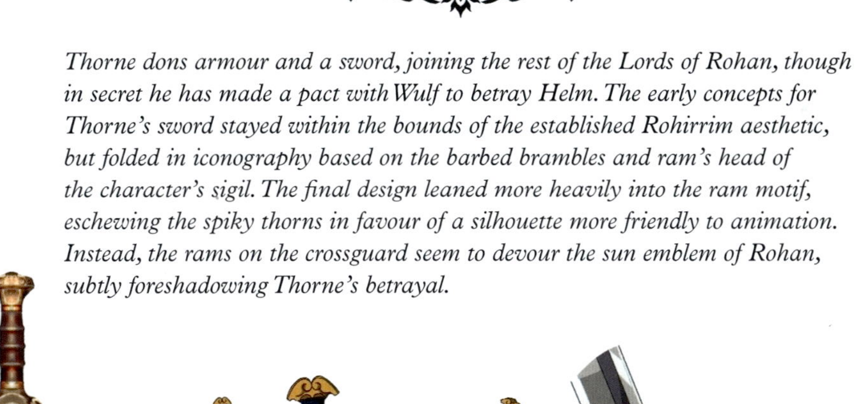

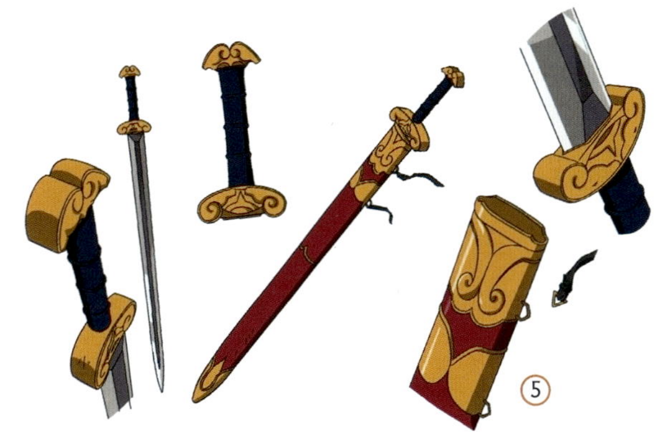

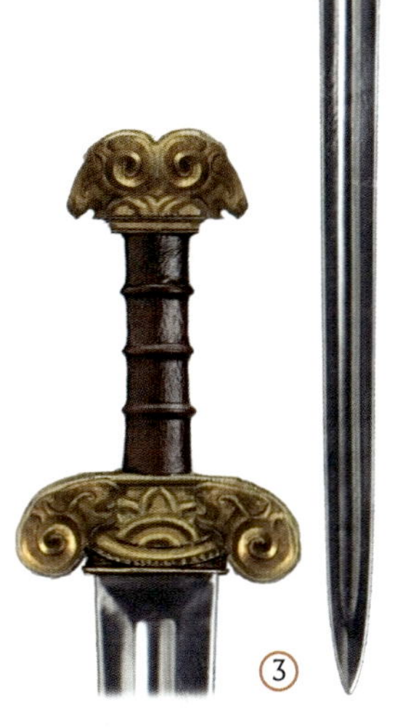

1: Thorne concept, S. 2: Thorne's sword concepts, TO. 3: Thorne's sword concepts, GH. 4: Thorne character setting art, AT. 5: Thorne's sword prop setting art, KM.

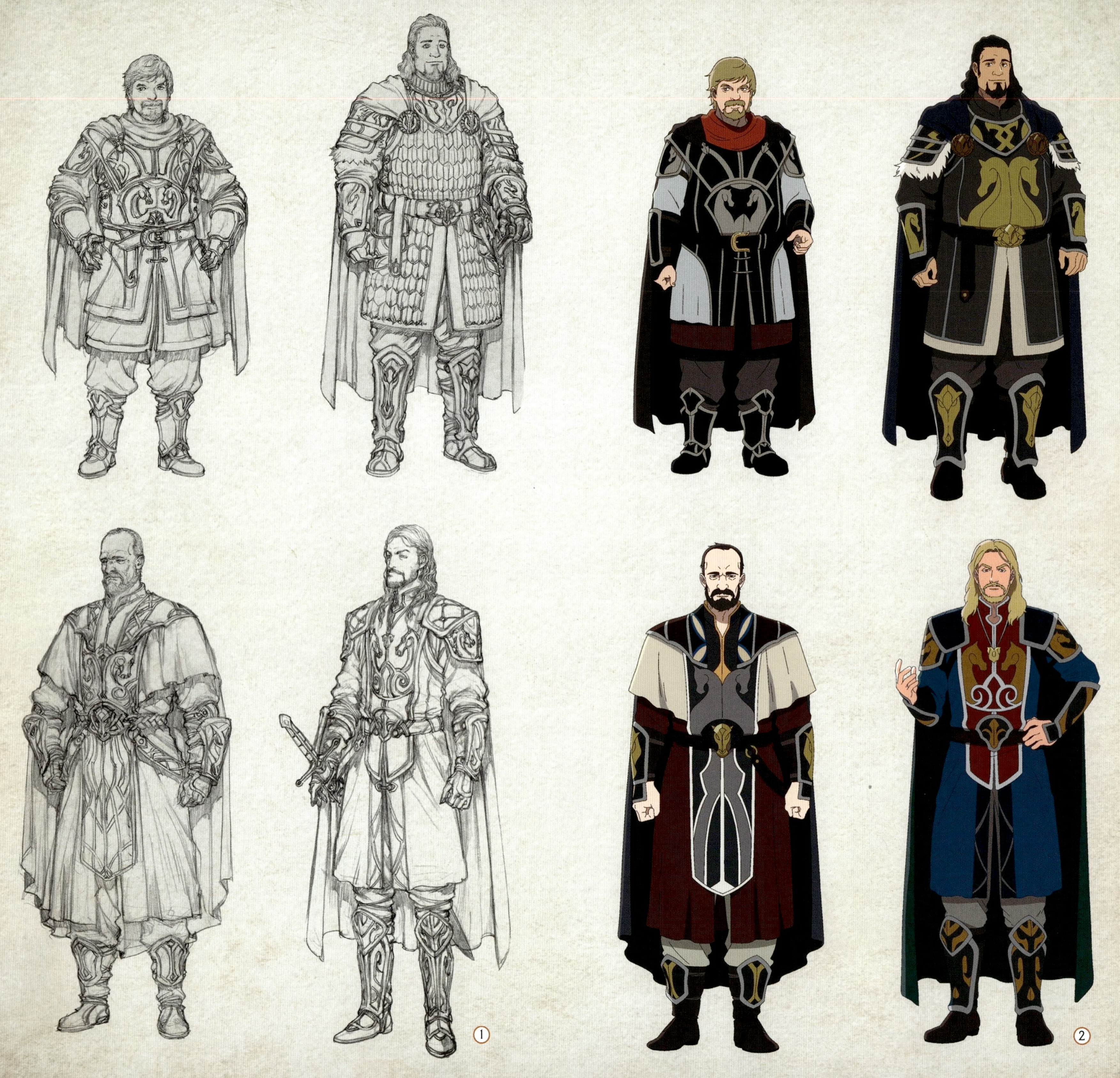

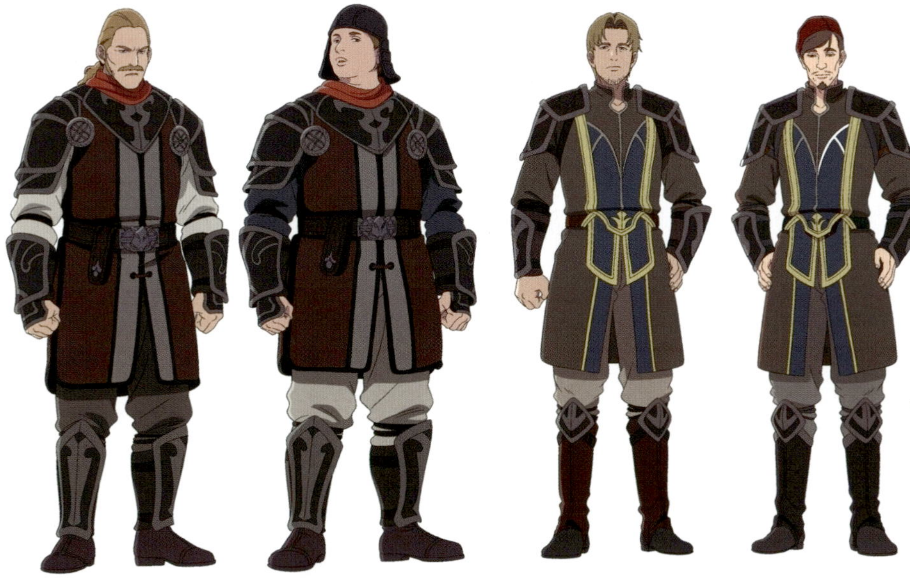

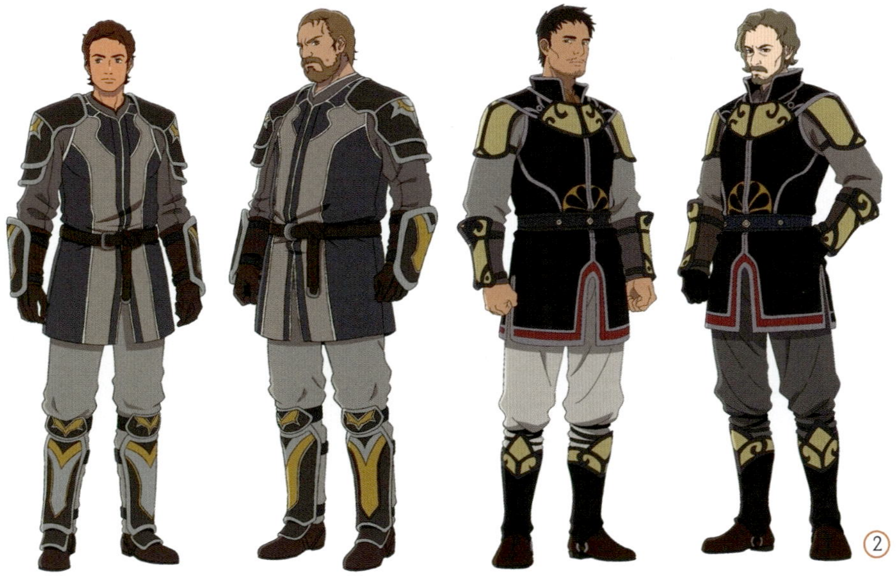

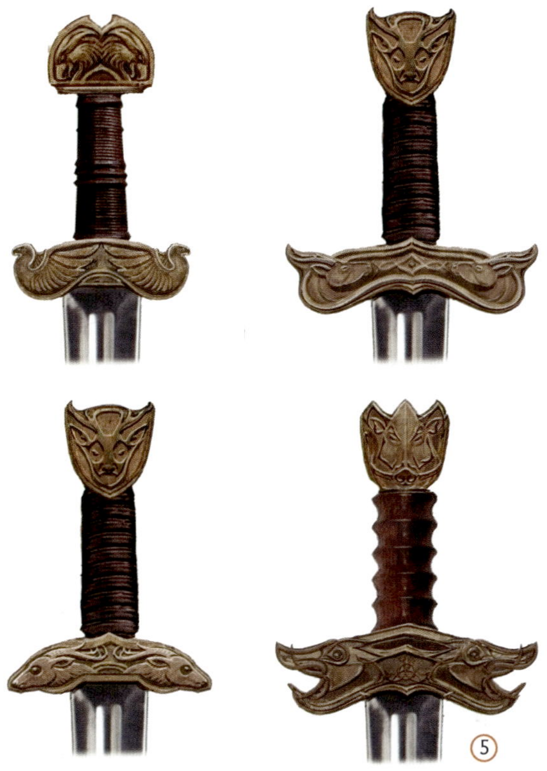

ROHIRRIM LORDS AT WAR

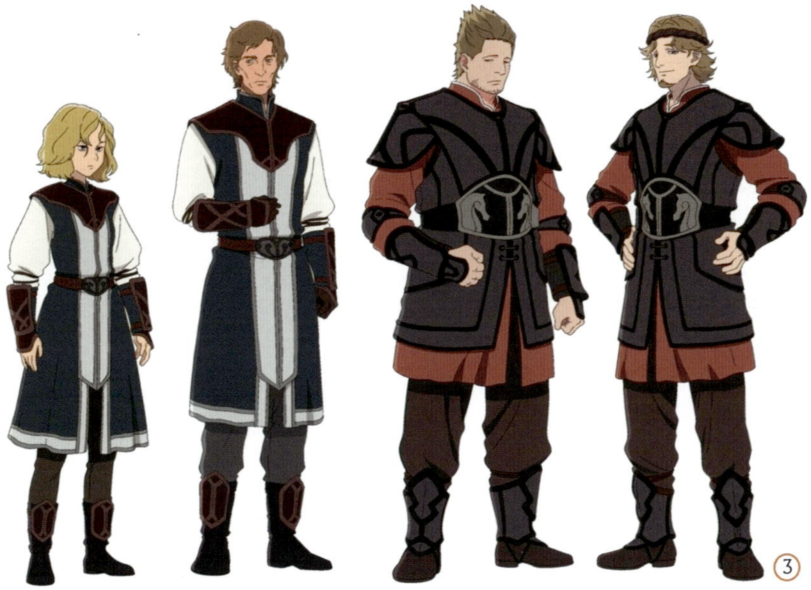

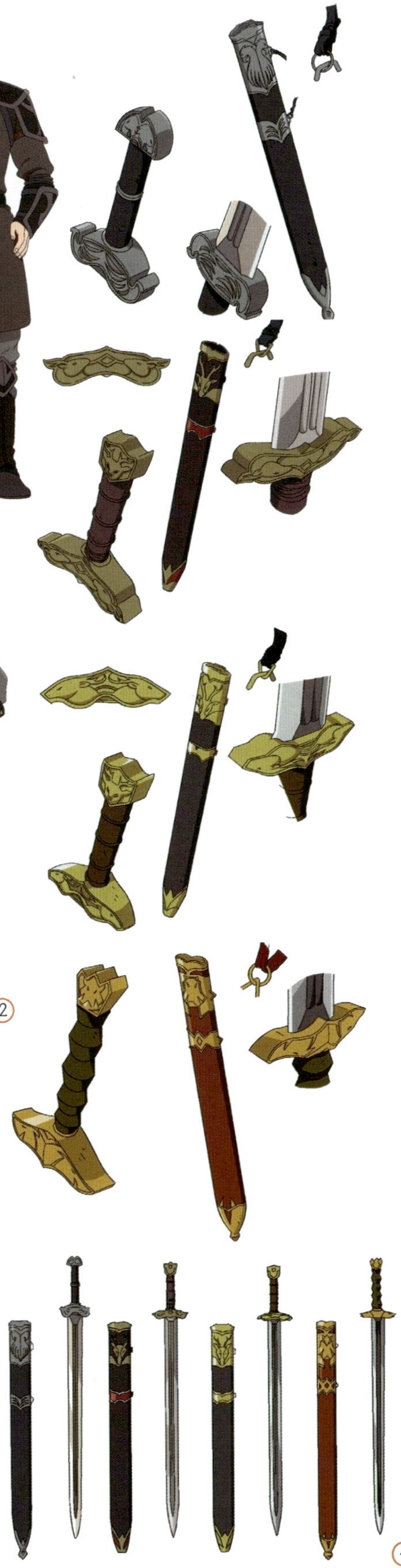

◆—≪◆≪◆≫◆≫—◆

Lords Fryght, Pryme and the others answer their king's call, taking up arms to fight, along with their staff. Each lord had his own colour palette, carried over into the armour and garments worn by his followers.

The brief for the swords carried by the various Rohirrim lords was that they should incorporate some animalistic heraldic elements. Overall, there should be a similarity in their appearance, so they all have a good basic sword blade in common, but then differ in the motifs, which correlate to their heraldry. – GUS HUNTER, WĒTĀ WORKSHOP SENIOR CONCEPT ARTIST

1: Rohirrim Lords concepts (from top left, Fryght, Everbrand, Pryme & Gramhere), S. 2: Rohirrim Lords staff character setting art, AS. 3: Rohirrim Lords and staff character setting art, AT. 4: Rohirrim Lords' swords prop setting art, KM. 5: Rohirrim Lords' swords concepts, GH.

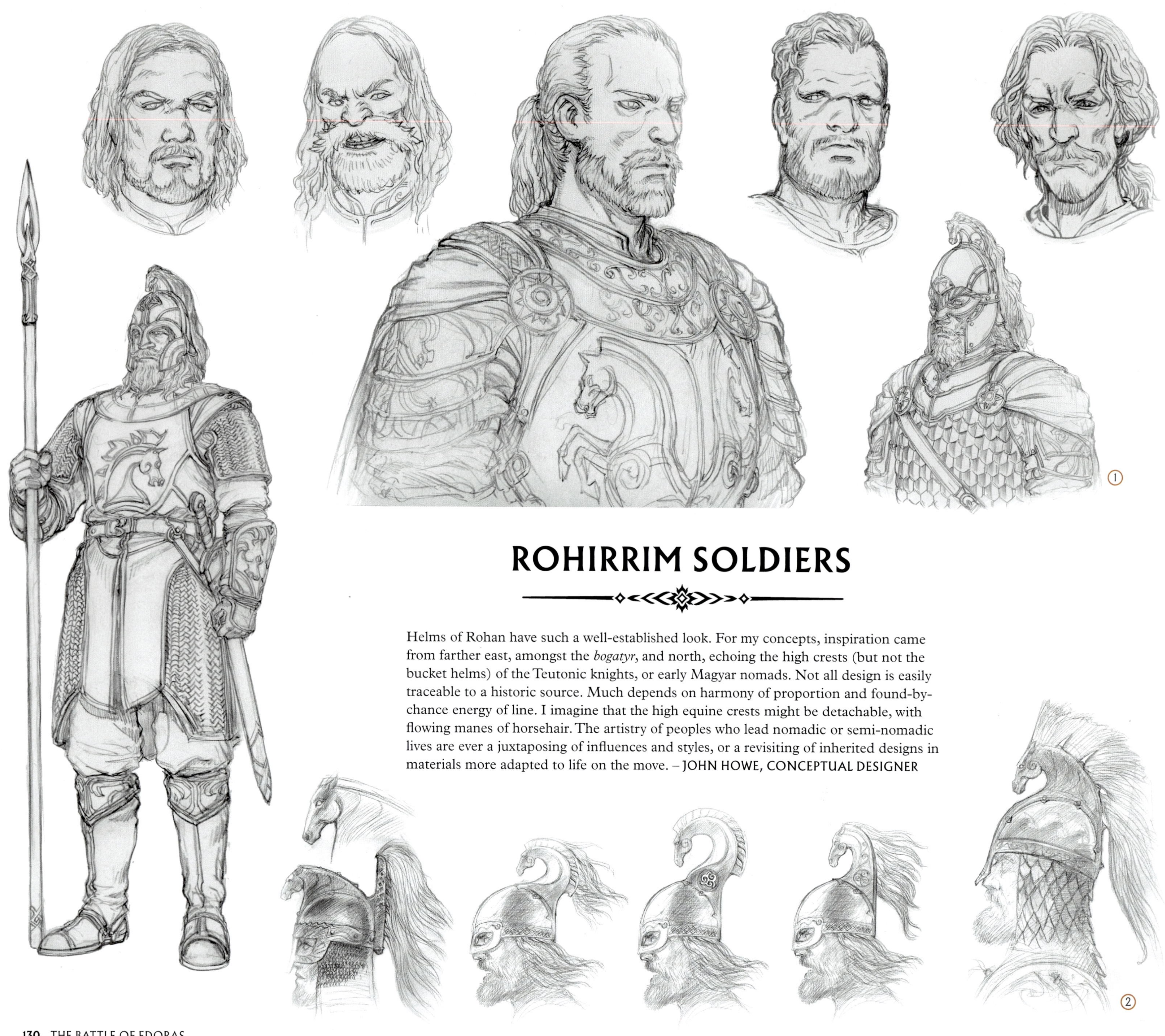

ROHIRRIM SOLDIERS

Helms of Rohan have such a well-established look. For my concepts, inspiration came from farther east, amongst the *bogatyr*, and north, echoing the high crests (but not the bucket helms) of the Teutonic knights, or early Magyar nomads. Not all design is easily traceable to a historic source. Much depends on harmony of proportion and found-by-chance energy of line. I imagine that the high equine crests might be detachable, with flowing manes of horsehair. The artistry of peoples who lead nomadic or semi-nomadic lives are ever a juxtaposing of influences and styles, or a revisiting of inherited designs in materials more adapted to life on the move. — JOHN HOWE, CONCEPTUAL DESIGNER

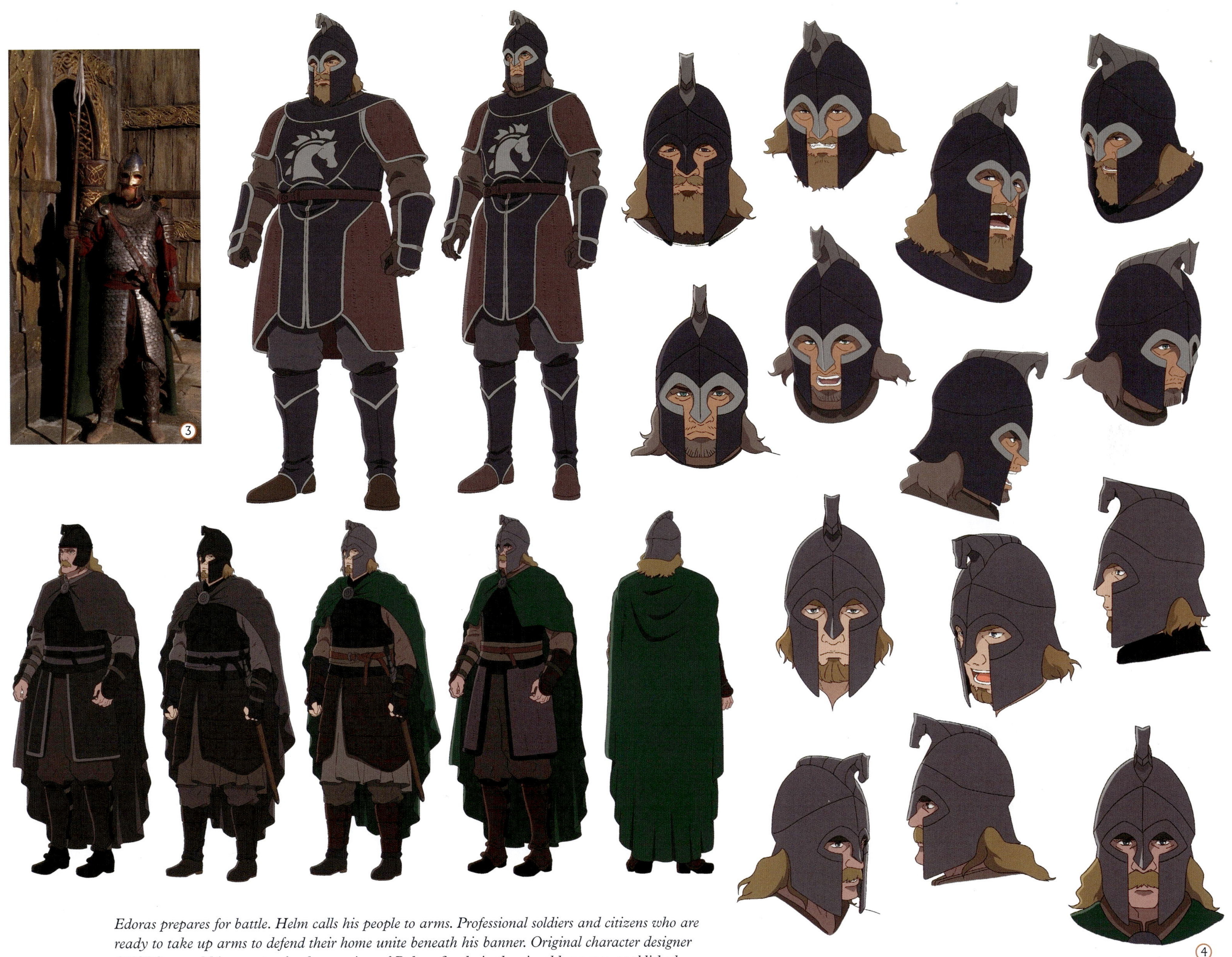

Edoras prepares for battle. Helm calls his people to arms. Professional soldiers and citizens who are ready to take up arms to defend their home unite beneath his banner. Original character designer STATO rooted his concepts for the warriors of Rohan firmly in the visual language established by prior films, but also introduced relatively simple surcoats covering some of the more complex armour, which would make animating hundreds of them much more achievable.

Animation Character Designer Miyako Takasu further simplified the designs for production. When seen in motion and in the haze of battle the stripped detail would not be missed.

1: Rohirrim soldier concepts, S. **2:** Rohirrim helmet concepts, JH. **3:** Rohirrim royal guard on-set still (LOTR trilogy). **4:** Rohirrim soldiers character setting art, AS.

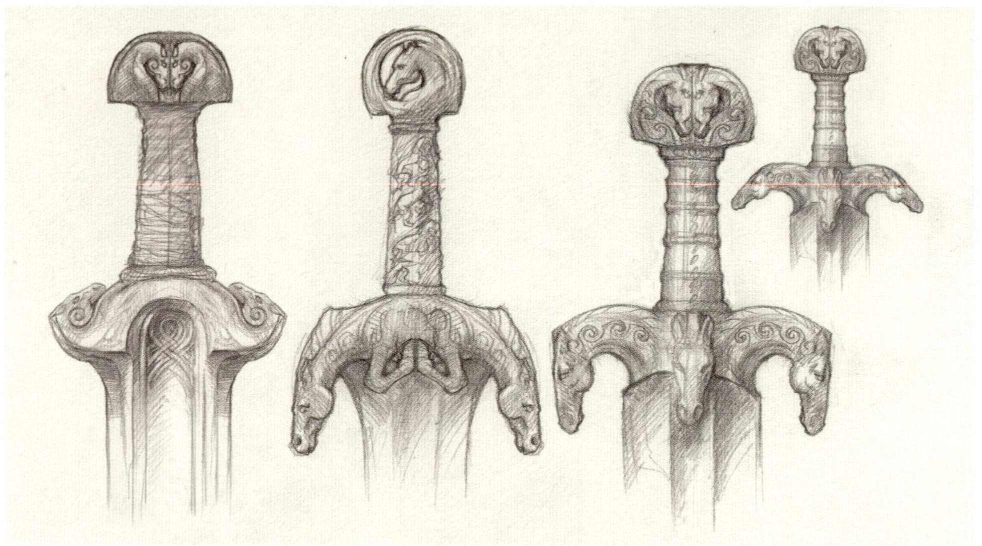
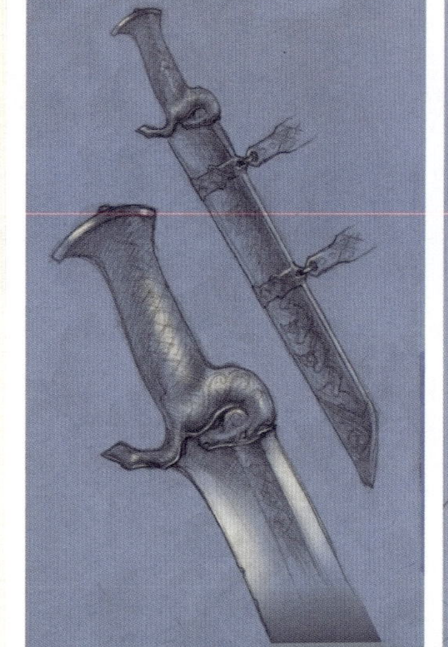
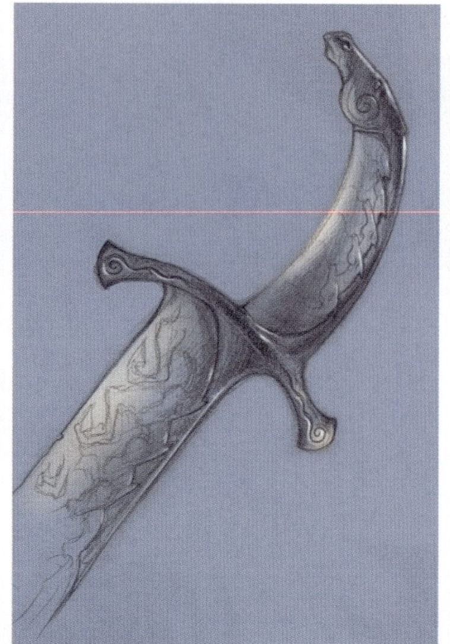
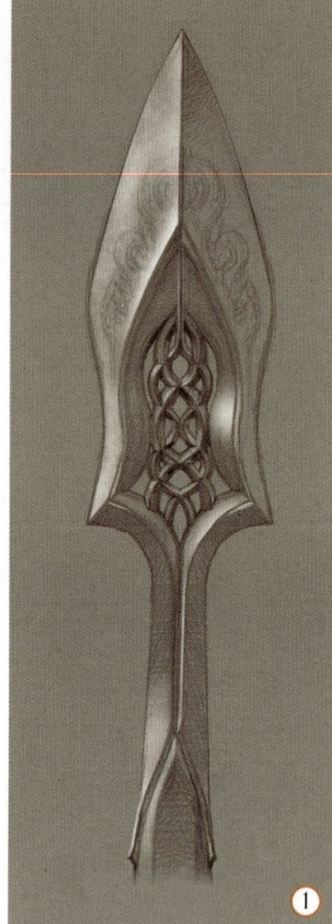

1: Rohirrim weapon concepts, JH. **2:** Rohirrim bow concepts, AA. **3:** Final film frame.

Form and function, combined with cultural preferences and choice of materials, will determine the nature of weapons in a pre-industrial society. The materials and techniques used to fashion them will determine the forms, guided by the necessities of attack and defence; the purely decorative element can be predominant or minimal, largely depending on rank and how serviceable a weapon must be.

These considerations do not, of course, constitute an infallible recipe for weapons design but can serve as reminders while searching for the most important element: energy of line and harmony of proportion, best uncovered when you simply do not overthink, just let the pencil draw freely. – JOHN HOWE, CONCEPTUAL DESIGNER

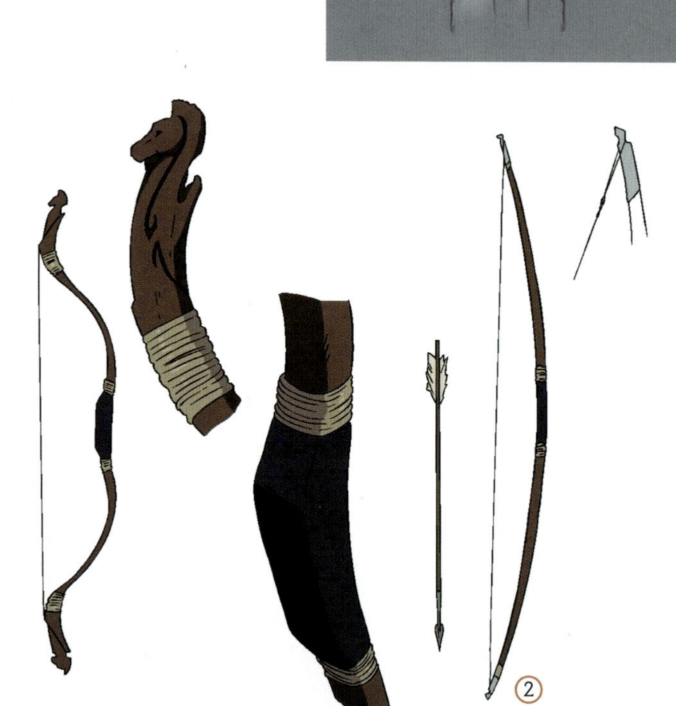
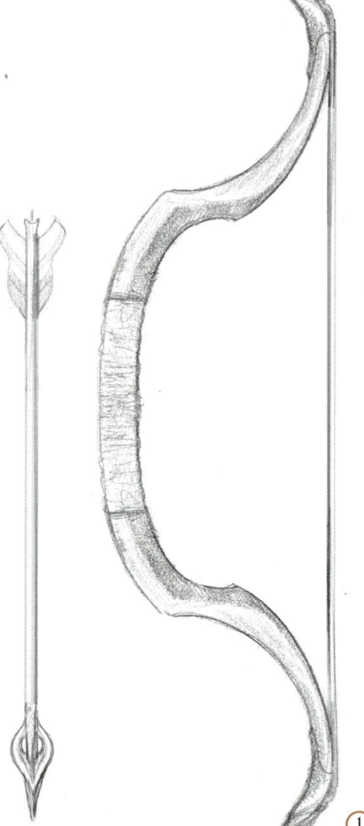

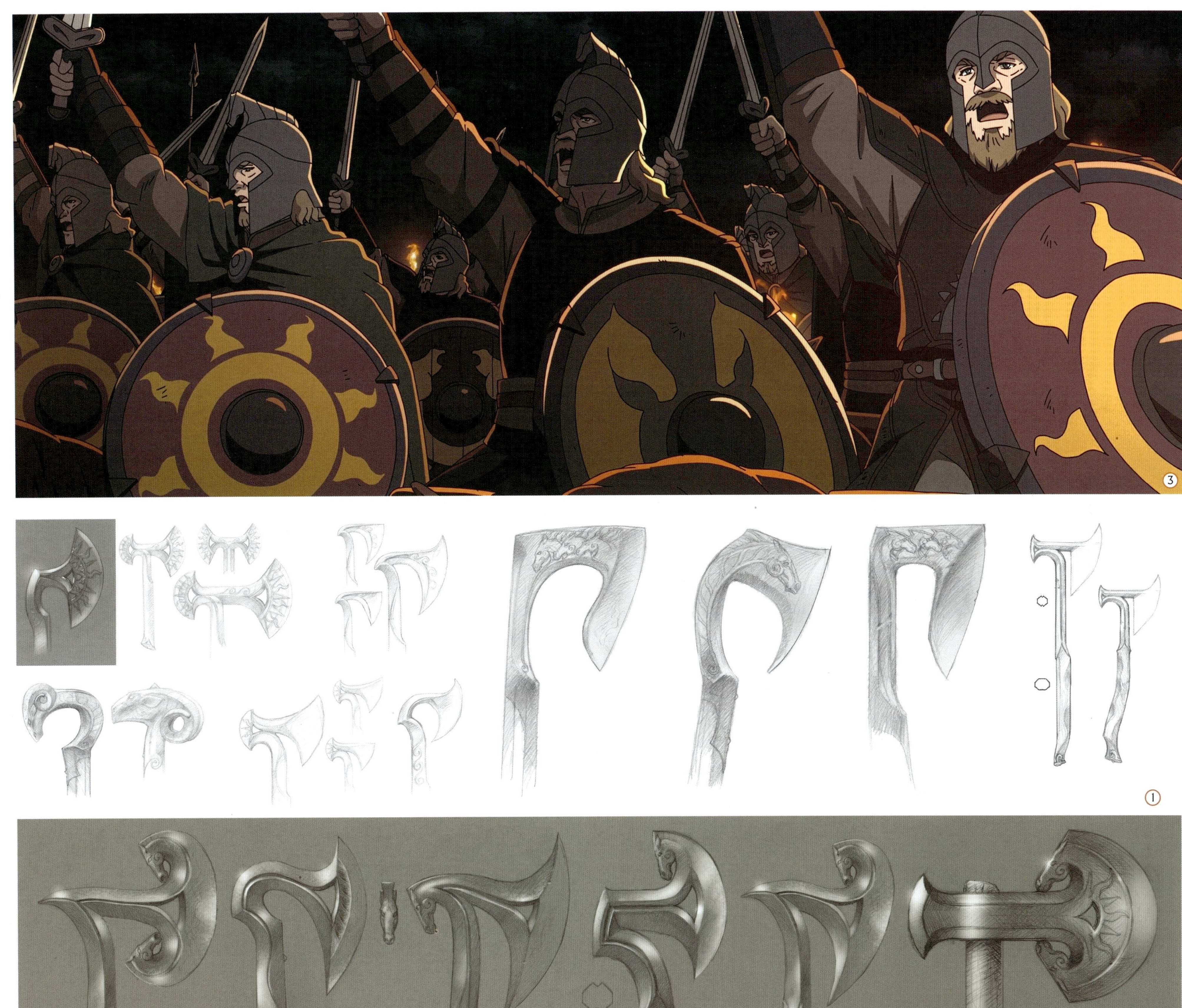

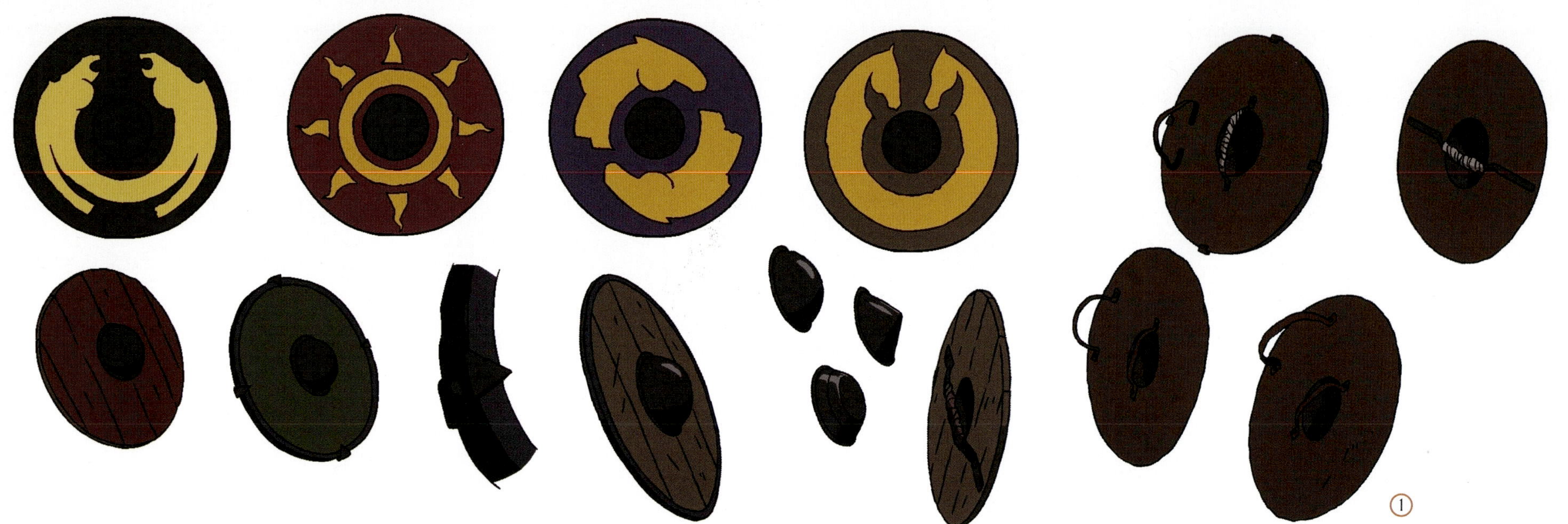

'RIDERS OF THE MARK! BROTHERS OF ROHAN! ARISE! ARISE NOW! WE WILL PAINT THE DAWN RED WITH THE BLOOD OF MY FOES!'

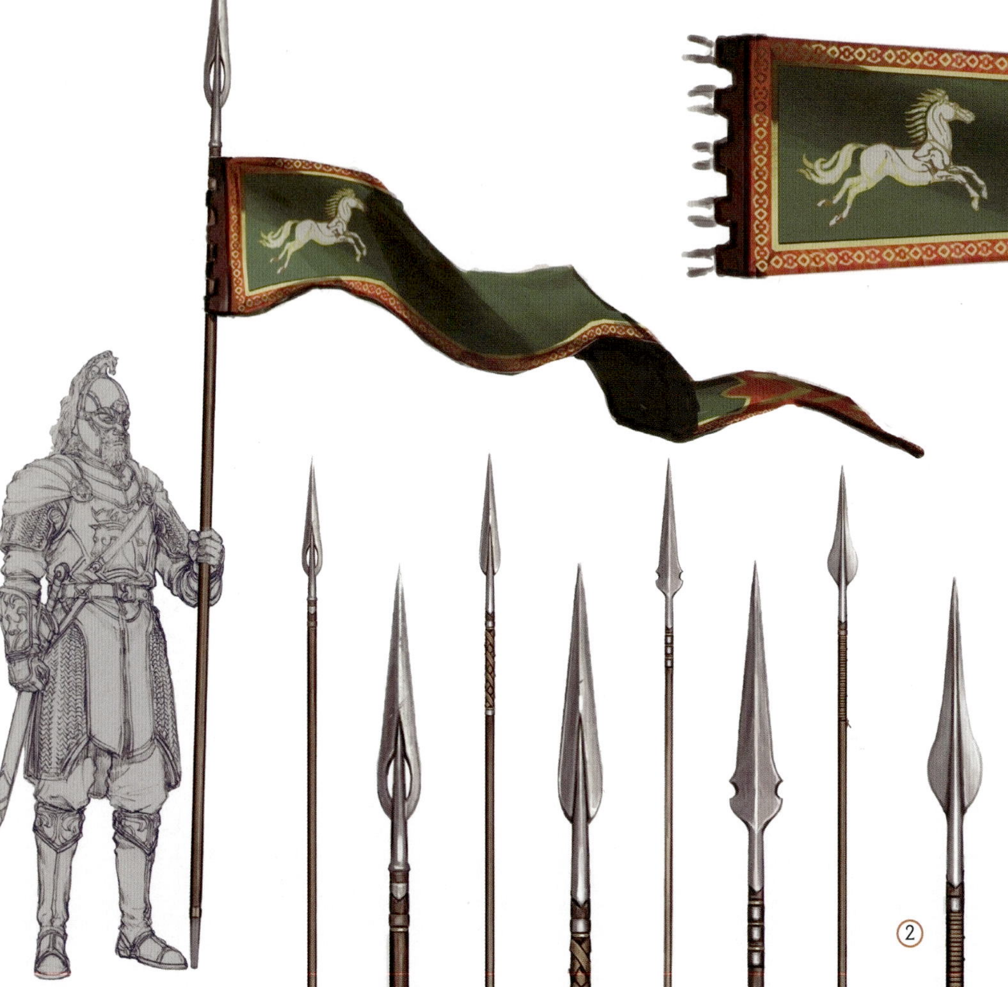

Following the convention established in the Lord of the Rings trilogy, the Rohirrim are depicted carrying mid-sized round shields with circular, steel bosses. Most are wooden, bound in steel frames, with some laminated with leather. Stylized horses and the rayed sun that is Rohan's emblem emblazon those bearing devices on faces of earthen hues.

For the Rohirrim spears, I looked at those made for the live-action movies and tried to simplify them as much as possible, chipping away until we had a simple shape that still read as from Rohan. While we could put lots of detail into them, it would be pointless because that's the first thing that's going to be lost when it's animated.

I love anime, so it was wonderful to know that what we were producing would be translated into that style by anime artists. – JOSHUA DAMIAN, WĒTĀ WORKSHOP JUNIOR CONCEPT ARTIST

1: Rohirrim shields prop setting art, KM. **2:** Rohirrim spear and heraldry concepts, JD.

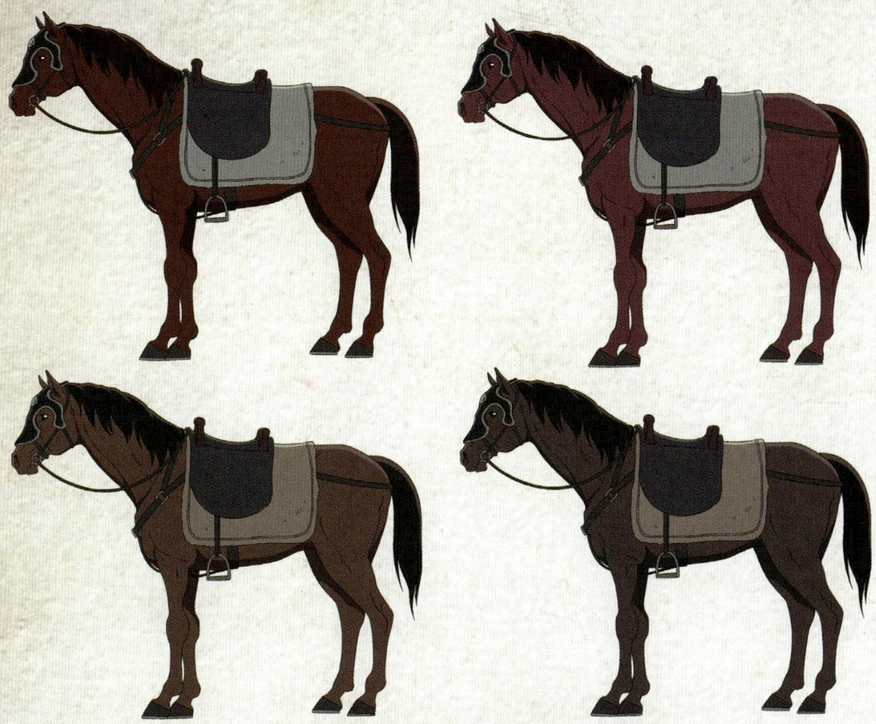

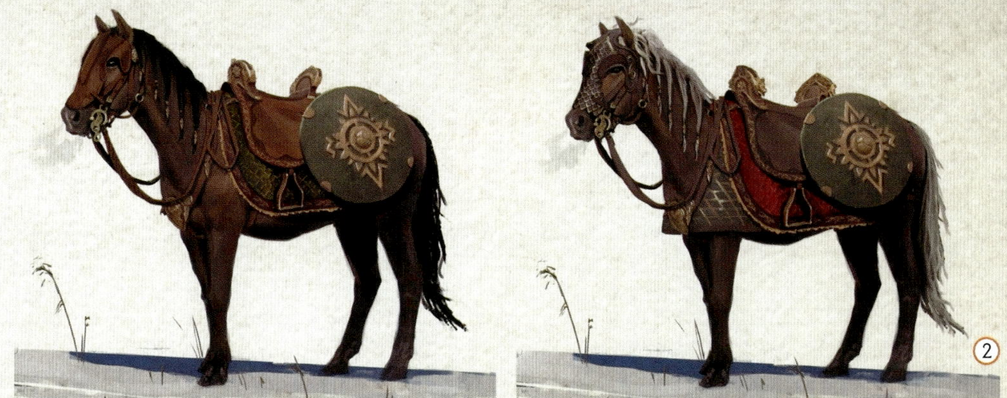

ROHIRRIM HORSES

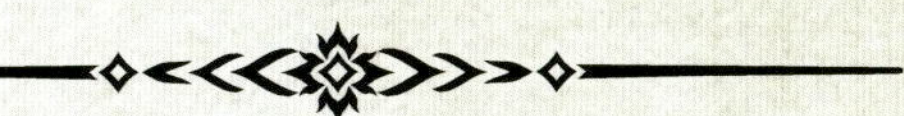

It is very difficult to draw a horse from scratch, let alone animate one, and we were going to have scenes involving hundreds of them galloping.

One of the things we did early on was send our team of animators to visit a stables. Many of them had never had the chance to see or interact with a horse in person. Being able to observe them moving up close provided a better understanding of their muscle and skeletal movement, and also what it feels like to ride one. That included understanding the size relationship between horse and rider, and how their movements were interconnected. To see all that, to experience it, have a professional demonstrate riding, and have footage of it that they could use as reference, was so valuable.

We also made use of computer-generated horses to help provide a basis for the animation. Multiple tries are possible with CGI; we can try different options and improve with trial and error. Traditional 2D animation doesn't really permit that. Redoing animation is expensive and time consuming. For shots involving hundreds of horses and riders, CG presented clear efficiencies. – JOSEPH CHOU, PRODUCER

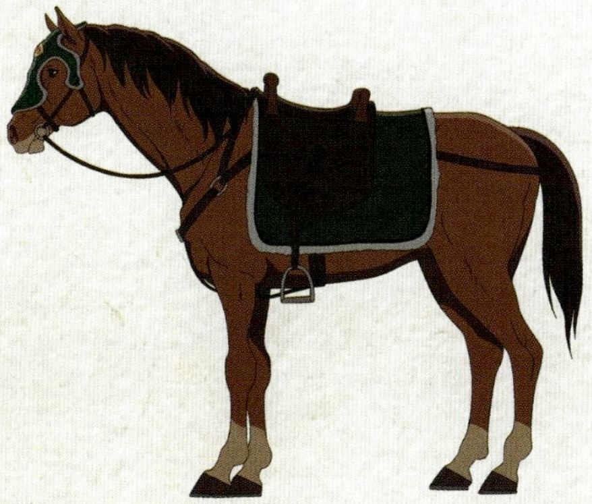

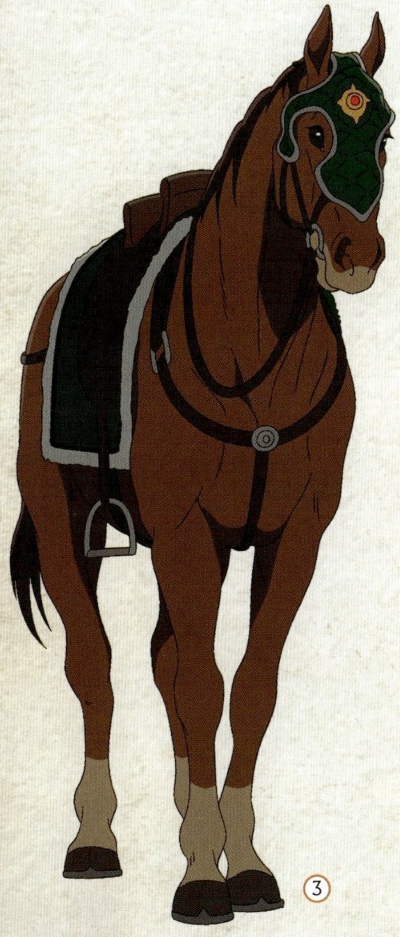

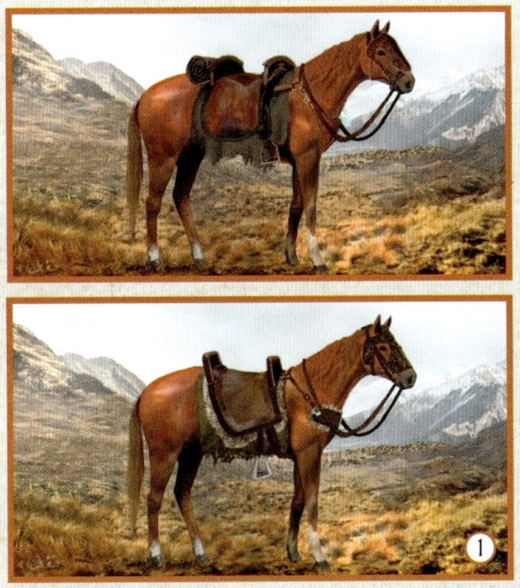

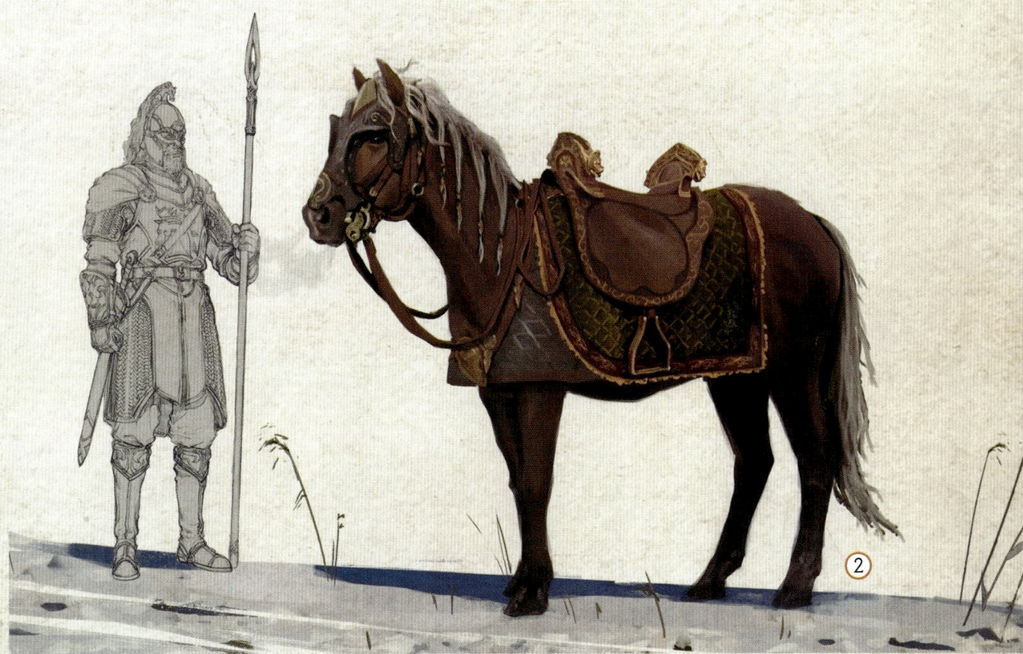

1: Rohirrim horse concepts, CG. 2: Rohirrim horse concepts, JD. 3: Rohirrim horse setting art, MT.

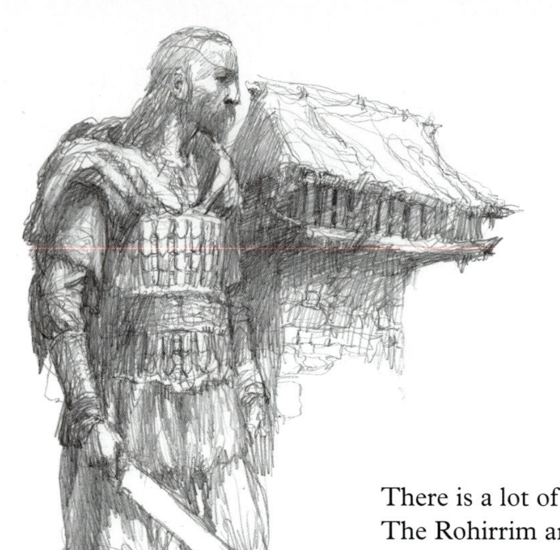

DUNLENDINGS

There is a lot of history there, between the Dunlendings and the Rohirrim. The Rohirrim are certainly not without flaw, their arrogance can get the better of them and Helm does look down on the Dunlendings. To me, it felt like another fork in the road. Wulf and Héra were genuine friends, their backgrounds never mattered to one another as children. Had things gone differently, they could have been a natural bridge towards repairing some of that bad blood for future generations. But because of the exploitation and perversion of their relationship, initially Freca's doing, it instead becomes a rift that further tears them and their people apart. – PHOEBE GITTINS, WRITER

The Dunlendings and the hill tribes are peoples who have been treated badly for such a long time that when Wulf calls for them, they do not need much convincing to take up arms. There are generations of grievances, so while there's also the promise of money and riches, it's an old enmity that Wulf exploits. There's a reason why there has been a period of relative peace in Rohan and its surrounding lands – force. Helm and his forefathers have ensured, through any means necessary, a status quo that benefits them. So it was only a matter of time before someone said, 'You know what? It doesn't need to be like this, remember there was a time when it wasn't!' The difference is that for Wulf, it is more about revenge than ideology. For him it is deeply personal, he uses the ideology to raise an army to wage his own private war. – ARTY PAPAGEORGIOU, WRITER

The first Dunlending concepts were quite orderly looking, but the feedback we got was that they looked too much like the Rohirrim, so the colours and amount of armour we put on them changed to create more of a contrast. Making an interesting silhouette is always important, so the barbs on the weapons, the horns, and shaggy animal fur cloaks were all about that. The shield idea incorporating a deer's face was a contrast to the horses of the Rohirrim and suggested something a bit wilder. – GUS HUNTER, WĒTĀ WORKSHOP SENIOR CONCEPT ARTIST

As the only entirely new people introduced in the film, I wish we had had more time to really dive deep into Dunlending culture, but we still got to have some fun trying to define them. The first concepts suggested historical kinship with the oath-breakers of the Dimholt and borrowed elements from the costume designs done for the Army of the Dead, but the colour scheme and forms were too similar to the Rohirrim, so we

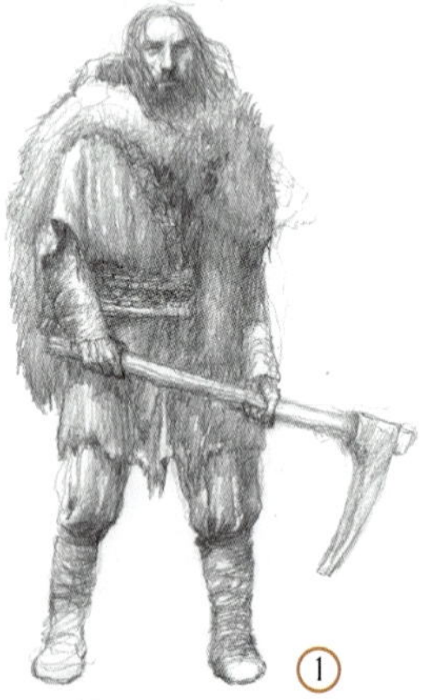

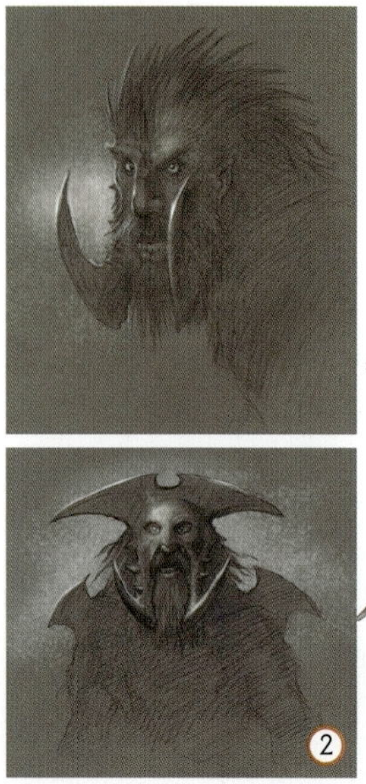

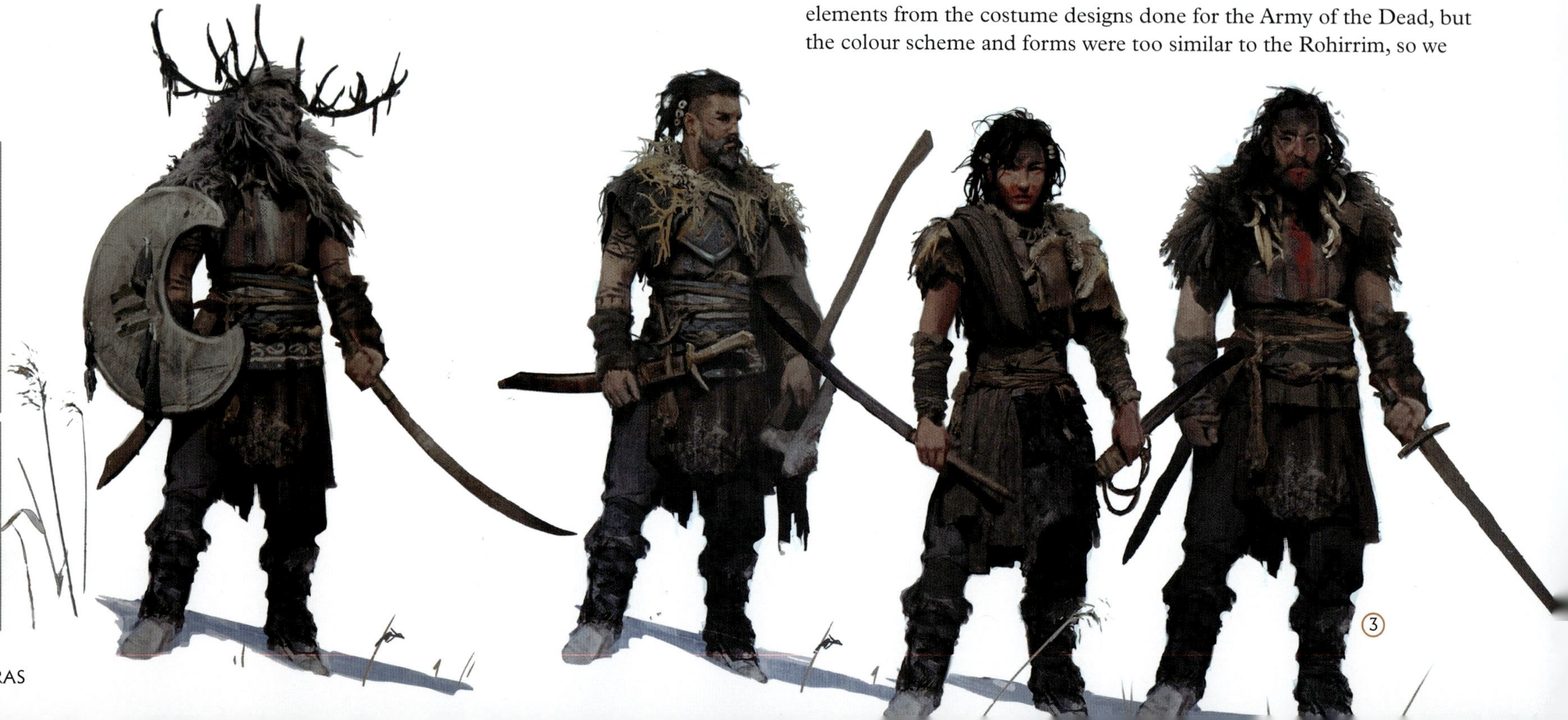

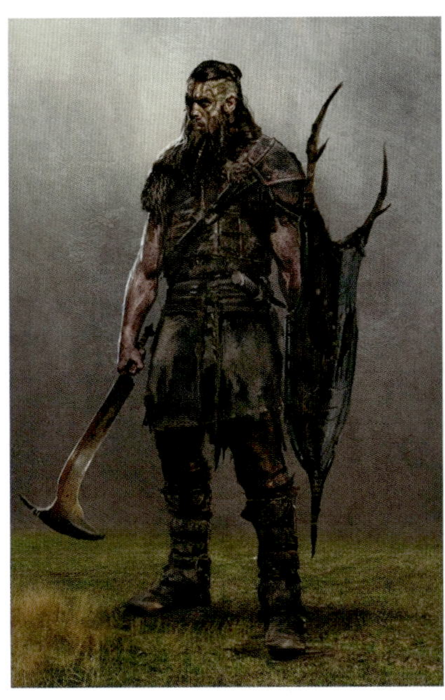 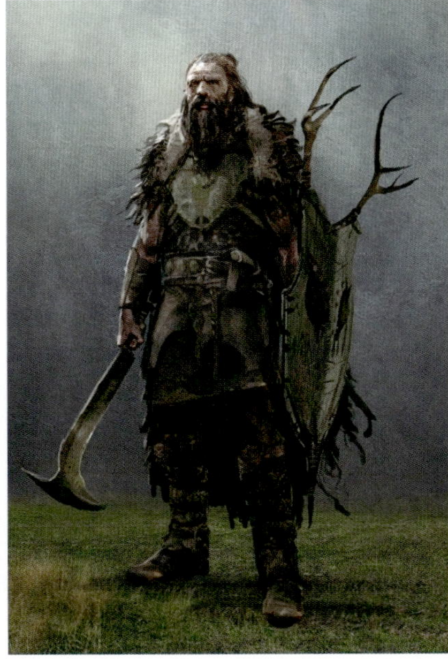 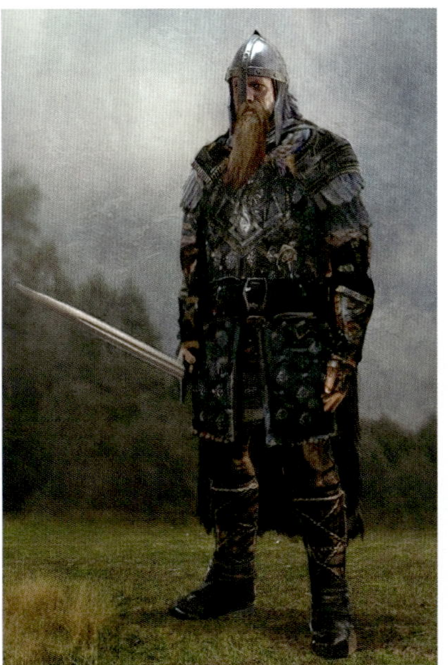 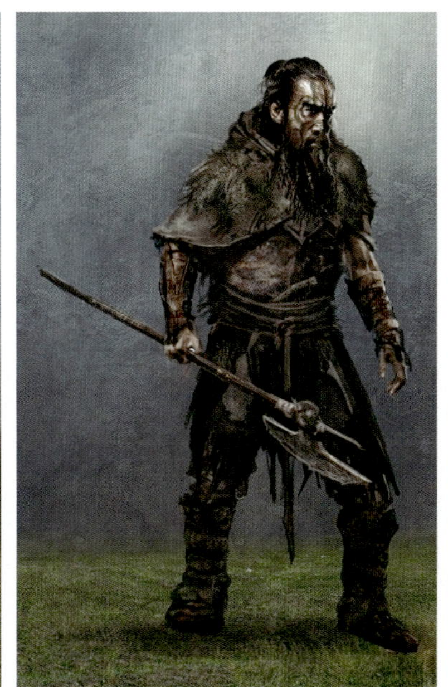 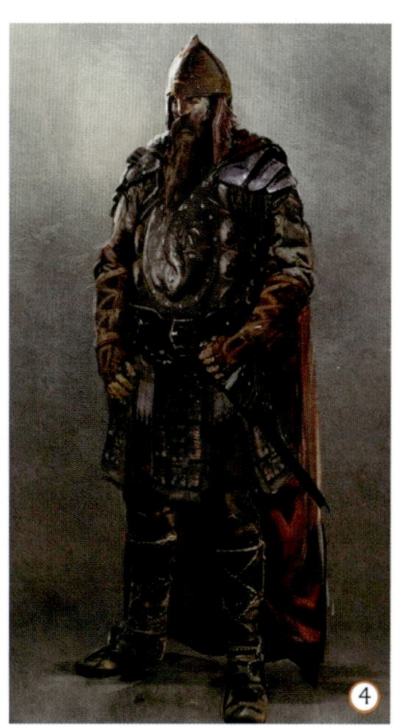

1: Dunlending concepts, AL. 2: Dunlending concepts, JH. 3: Dunlending concepts, JD.
4: Dunlending concepts, GH. 5: Dunlending concepts, IB.

pivoted away from that. For research and inspiration, we looked at the ancient Viking and Pict peoples, the Celts, Ainu people of Japan, and many others, trying to understand how the lifestyles and landscapes shaped the clothing and artifacts of these cultures. I really, really wanted the Dunlendings to wear some sort of Middle-earth version of tartan, but it turns out it's not something that translates well to hand-drawn animation! The final designs were very much a blend of ideas and sources, coming together to form something new. – DANIEL FALCONER, ADDITIONAL CONCEPTS DESIGNER

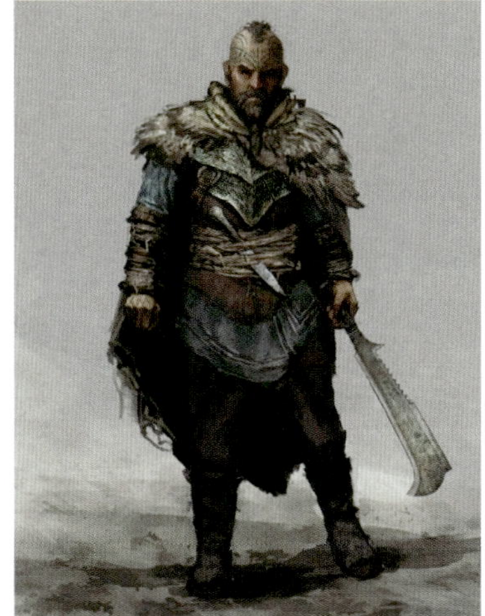 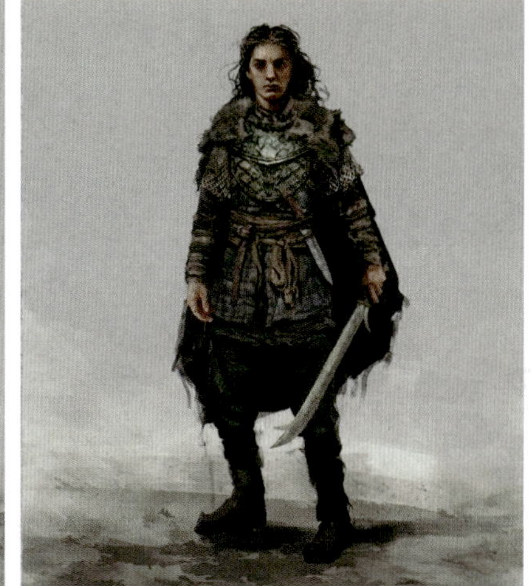

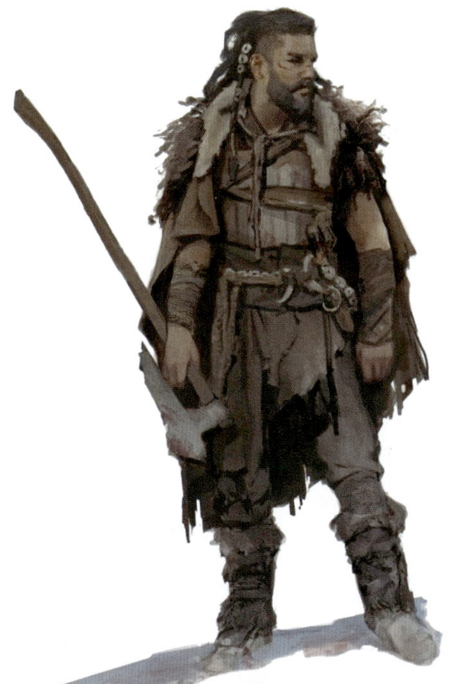

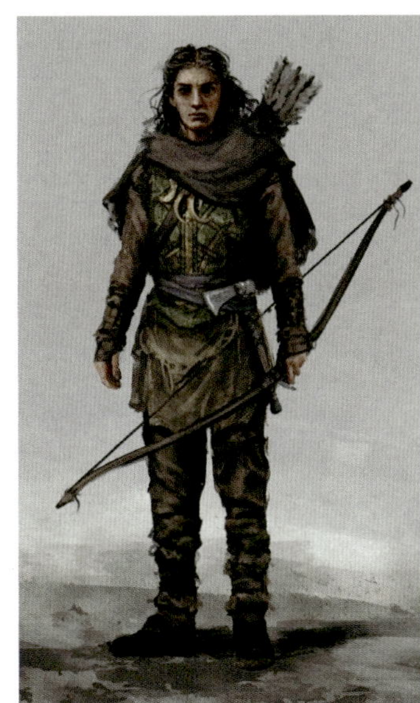 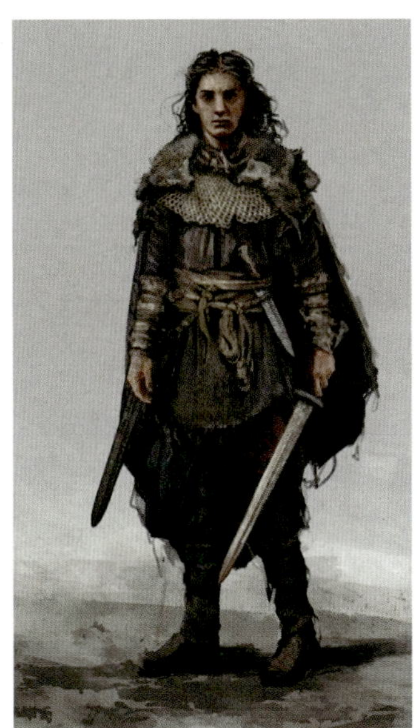 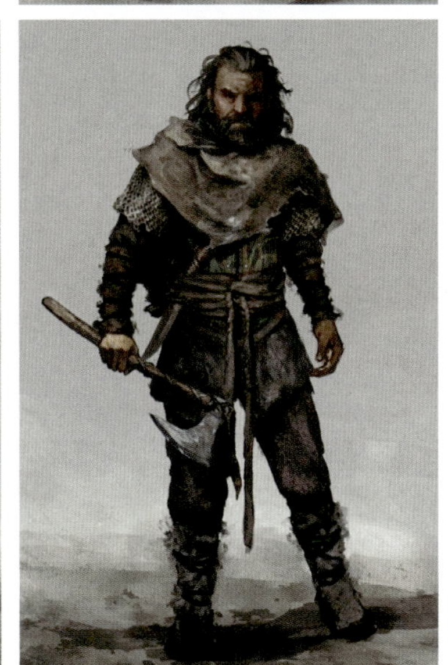 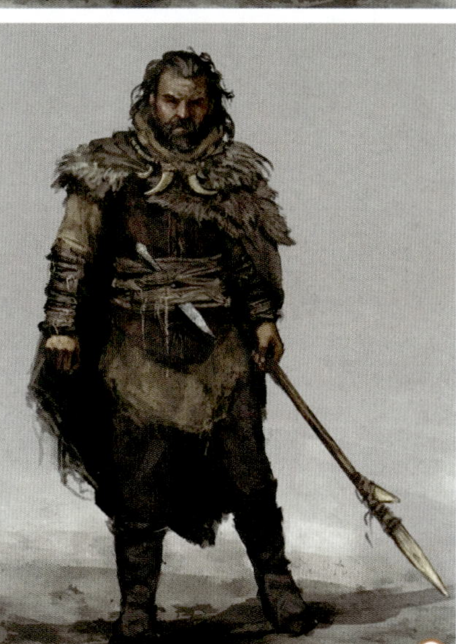

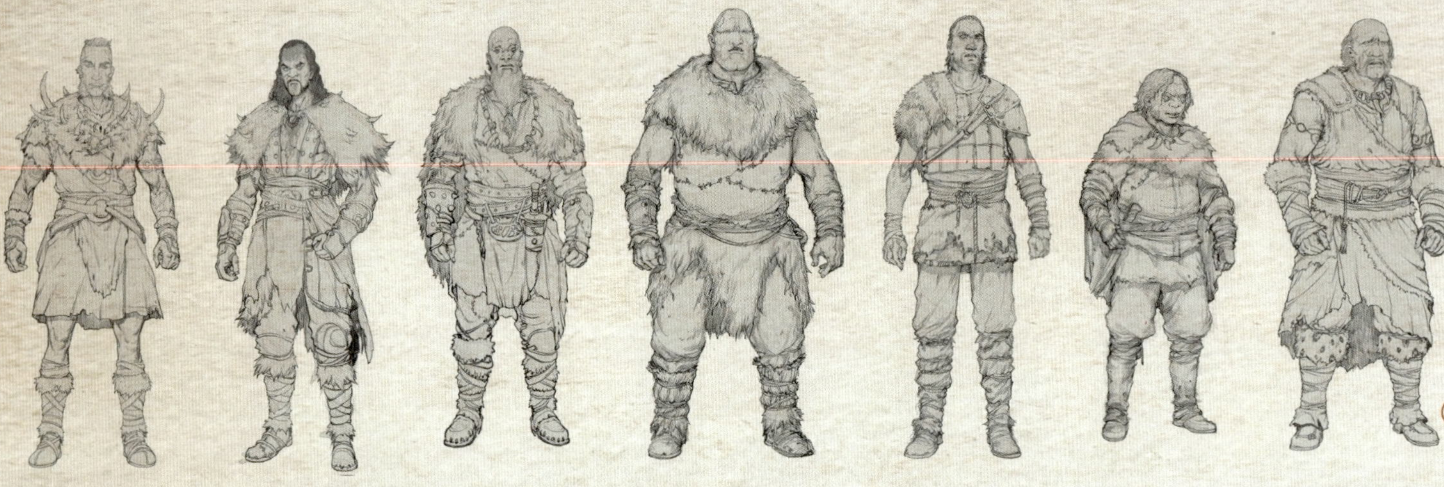

I love fantasy and researching it, so it was fun to do a deep dive into the lore and find out who these characters were. Historical illustrator Angus McBride's art helped me to understand how armour was made, and here was the perfect opportunity to put it into practice.

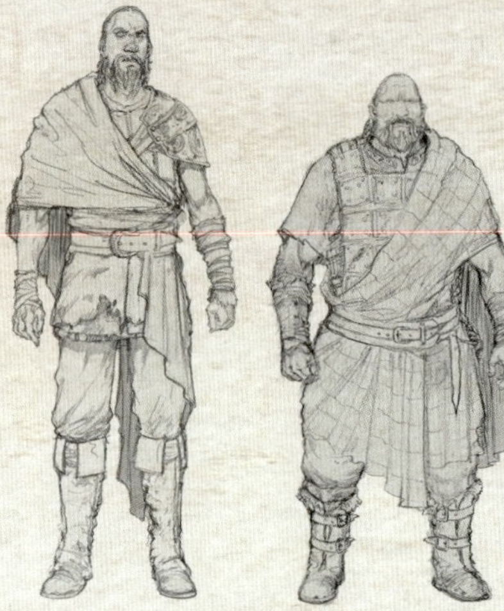

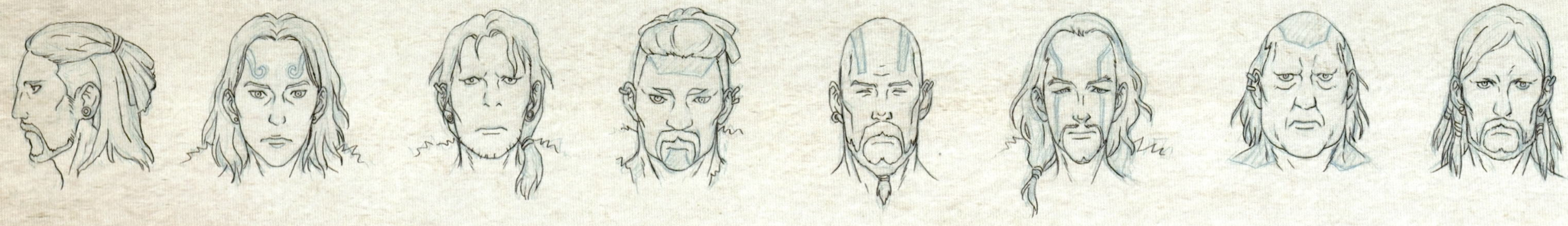

I got a lot of inspiration from nomadic Indo-Thracian culture, and saw similarities with the Dunlendings. Pushed out of their homelands, they would take armour from battlefields and mend and modify it to their needs. The Mongolian people were another inspiration. This all got melded together and put through a Middle-earth lens in my mind.

I imagined the Dunlendings might be a proud and rugged people. Their way of life is closely tied to the harsh terrain where they live. Each tribe might have its own traditions and language. Their attire might be a mixture of sturdy fibre and animal hides, with intricate leatherwork adorned with symbols representing their clan and achievements. – JOSHUA DAMIAN, WĒTĀ WORKSHOP JUNIOR CONCEPT ARTIST

It was winter in the story, so I included lots of layers and furs. The colour scheme was earthy with the idea that it might help camouflage the Dunlendings within their wintery surroundings, but with little pops of colour showing through to keep it interesting. We looked at different hairstyles with shaved sections, and tattoos. I drew both men and women warriors, because I thought that it would be interesting and a contrast for the army to have both. – IONA BRINCH, WĒTĀ WORKSHOP CONCEPT ARTIST

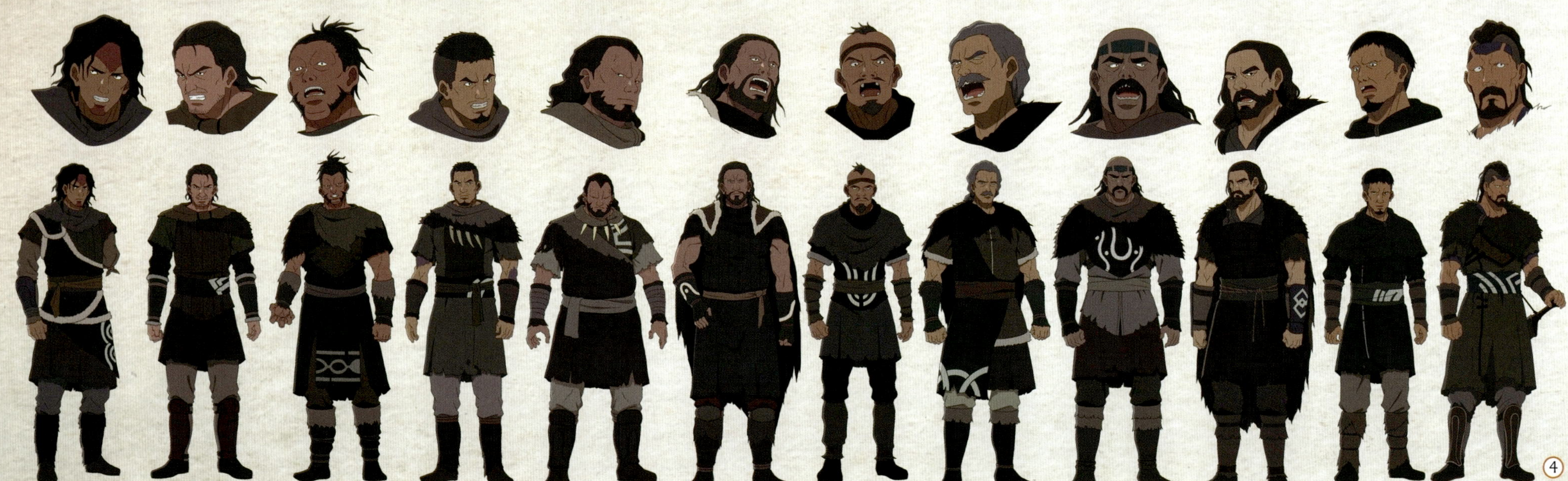

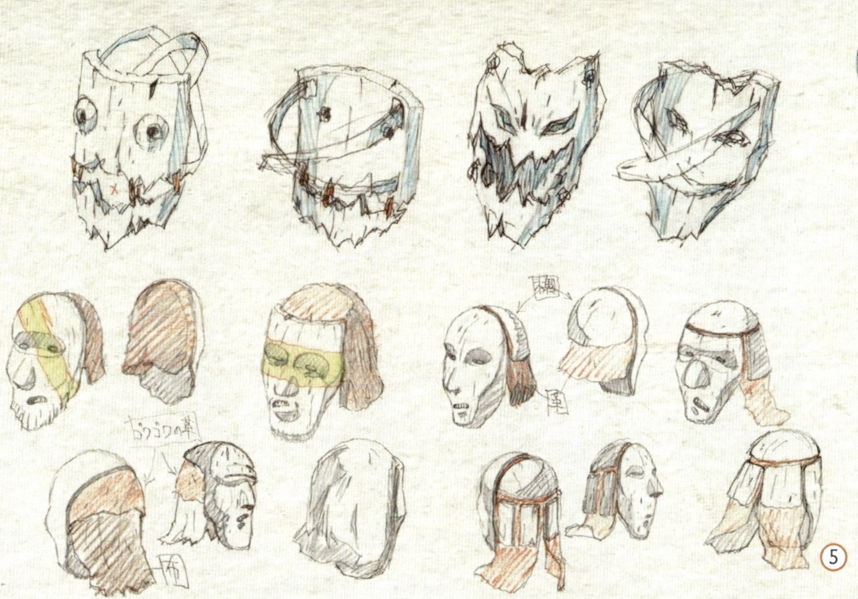

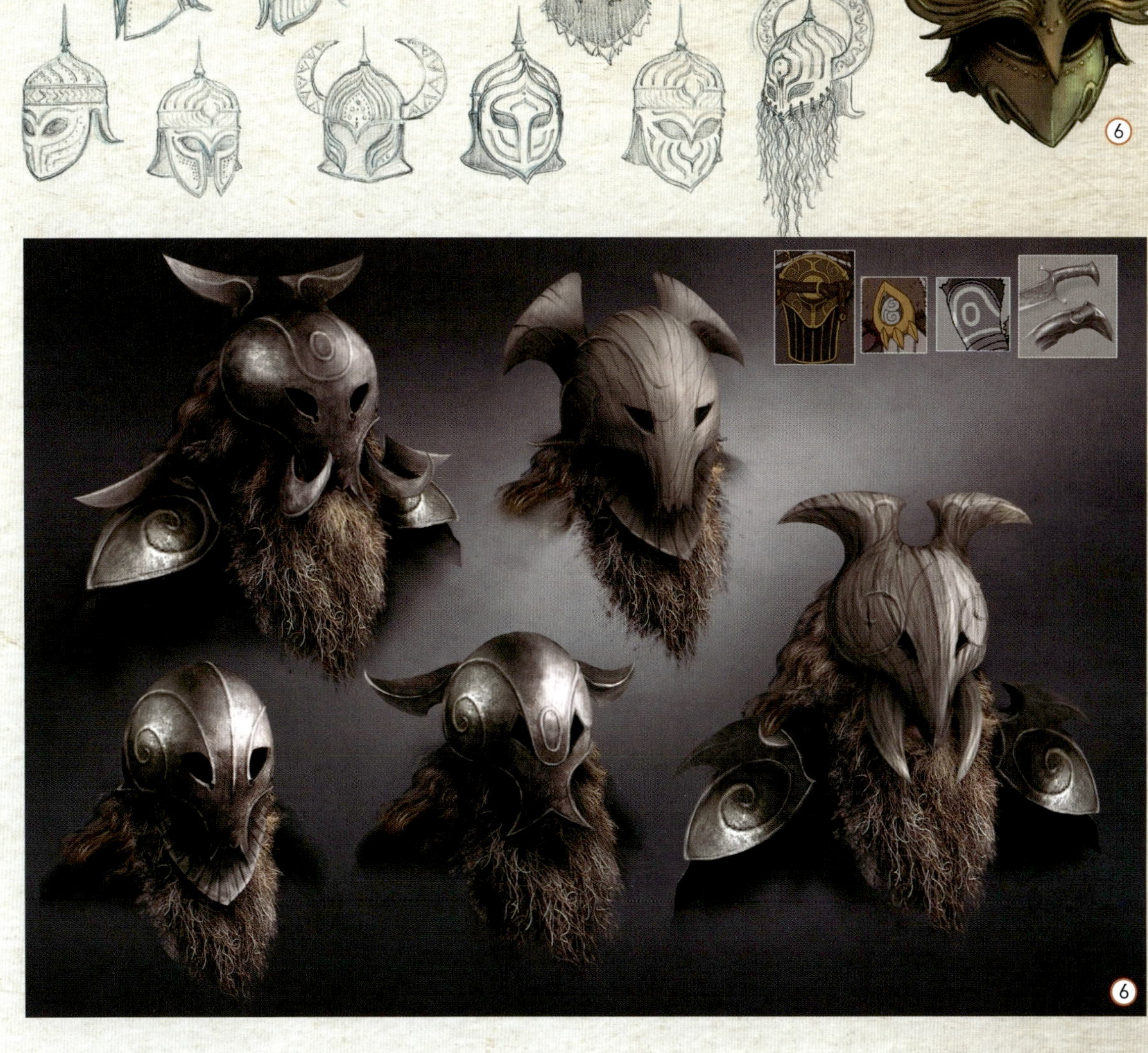

The notion of facial tattoos on the Dunlendings sprouted independently in both the New Zealand and Japanese teams. Curliform white glyphs also emerged as something that would repeat across their dark costuming. As the designs were refined it became clear that Wulf's warriors would be less uniform in appearance than the Rohirrim soldiers, requiring more variation in the ranks.

In contrast to the Rohirrim, we imagined the Dunlendings lived in colder conditions. We see them dressed in layers and furs, all of it darker by default. In more mountainous terrain it might even serve as camouflage.
– JOSEPH CHOU, PRODUCER

Anticipating that we'd see our heroes cutting their way through swathes of Dunlending warriors, I thought it would be useful to have helmets for some of Wulf's forces. Masked, villainous henchmen are less empathetic, so an audience might be less inclined to balk at seeing them slain by the good guys. I imagined that simple helmets might be less time-consuming to animate than expressive human faces, but was also thinking of how distinctive helmets offer a very quick and easy way for an audience to distinguish between armies. Each of the different peoples seen in *The Lord of the Rings* trilogy are readily identified by their helmet shapes and colours. There hadn't been as much visual development done for the Dunlendings up to this point, so I pulled shapes from the favoured Dunlending costume and weapon drawings to try to craft a suite of helmet concepts that were unlike any others we had seen in Middle-earth. – DANIEL FALCONER, ADDITIONAL CONCEPTS DESIGNER

For practical purposes, only two patterns each were used for the helmets or masks of both the Dunlendings and Wild Men, but they had to cover entire armies. I was relieved to hear that there were enough interesting shapes and silhouettes in both pairs of designs that we didn't fall into copy-and-paste monotony. – KENJI MASUDA, PROP DESIGNER

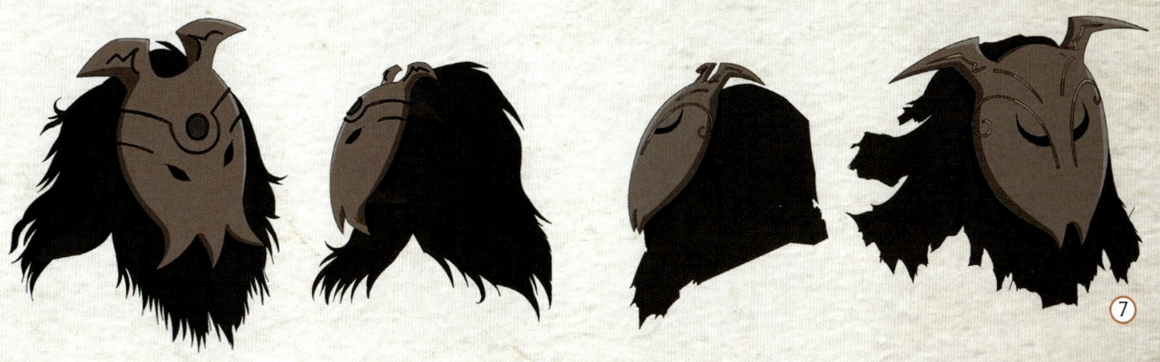

1: Dunlending concepts, S. 2: Dunlending concepts, S & DF. 3: Dunlending concepts, MT. 4: Dunlending character setting art, AS. 5: Dunlending mask concepts, KM. 6: Dunlending helmet concepts, DF. 7: Dunlending mask setting art, KM.

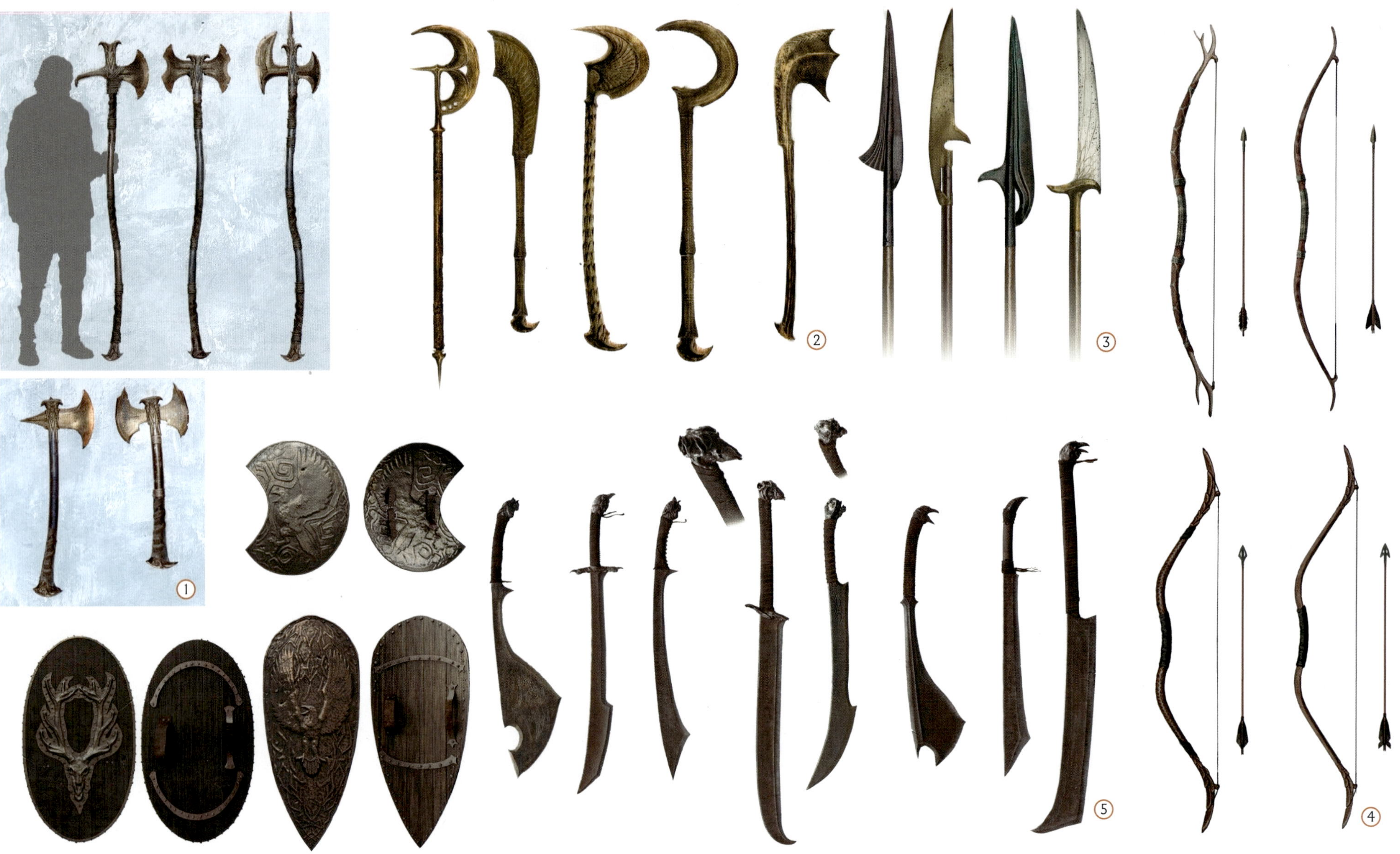

Contrasting the straight, refined forms of the Rohirrim swords, Dunlending blades were imagined as heavy-headed, cleaver or axe-like weapons, and in some instances curved. Inspiration was found in real-world blades like the Egyptian khopesh or gunstock war club of Indigenous American tradition. The Dunlending shields were also conceived to differ from their Rohirrim counterparts, with longer forms versus the circular shields of Rohan, and beaten metal surfaces and detailing over wooden backs. Sculptural, totemic forms based on corvids, deer and wolves adorned the pommels of the blades and faces of the shields in the Wētā Workshop concepts, although these would be too detailed to include in the final onscreen animated designs.

1: Dunlending halberd and axe concepts, GH. 2: Dunlending halberd concepts, DF.
3: Dunlending spear concepts, JM. 4: Dunlending bow concepts, IB. 5: Dunlending shield and sword concepts, WW. 6: Dunlending weapons prop setting art, AAH.
7: Dunlending weapons prop setting art, KM.

If the Rohirrim design language was all about horses, then perhaps for the Dunlendings we could find a different animalistic association? I liked the idea of leaning into the talons and feathers of crows, or, more specifically, crebain. My weaponry concepts for the Dunlendings were entirely inspired by wing and claw shapes, but I also liked the notion of their weapons being bronze, if only for the contrast in colour to the steel blades of the Rohirrim. – DANIEL FALCONER, ADDITIONAL CONCEPTS DESIGNER

When drawing bows, I thought in terms of the silhouette, because you might not see much more than that in a scene. They are fairly simplistic, and not too heavily decorated like something the Elves might have made. For materials, I imagined that wood, animal bones, antlers, and maybe some metal, were what they would have to work with. I also looked at the costumes we had been designing and tried to imagine what would look good together. – IONA BRINCH, WĒTĀ WORKSHOP CONCEPT ARTIST

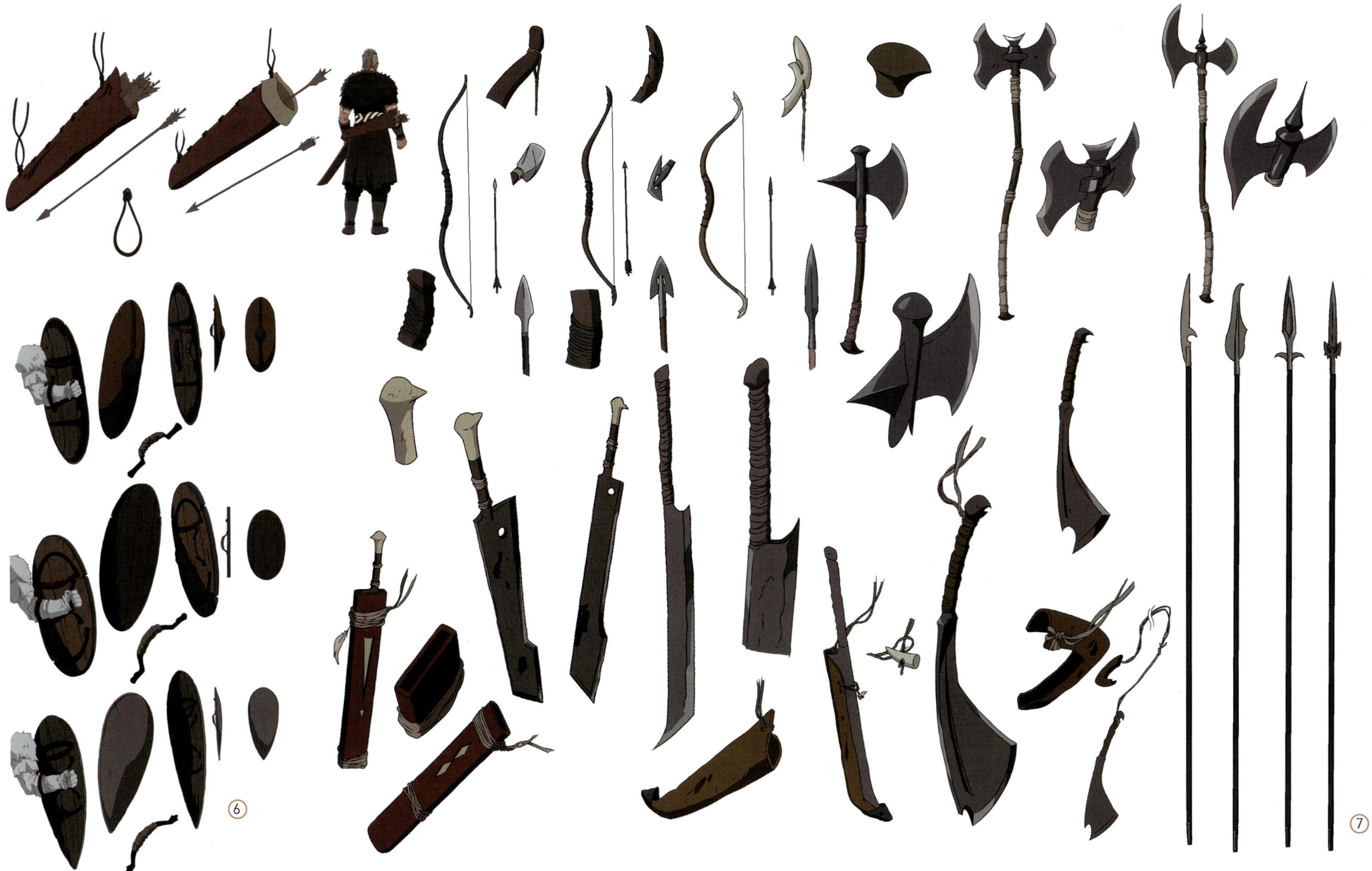

Since this film had live-action antecedents, my visual goal as prop designer was quite clear from the beginning. The director wanted to see weapons and props that could exist in the real world, with earthiness and weight. This was a fantasy world, but the artifacts that appeared in it had to feel like they were achievable in civilizations roughly analogous with our own Middle Ages.

While wood products were the main focus, we carefully considered to what extent metal or other materials like glass might be used, in line with our worldview. Some tribes, like the Dunlendings and Wild Men, included symbolic bone and ivory elements, which helped illustrate differences in their civilization level and focus.

One of the hardest parts of the work was the sheer quantity of things I had to design. For instance, just a sword for a certain tribe would need several different variations. I was surprised at how high the total count would be and struggled with it, but looking back now, it was also a lot of fun.

Of the concept art that was produced, I was particularly impressed by the Dunlending swords and the weapons of the Southrons. It was interesting to see unique weapons that had shapes I had not seen before. – KENJI MASUDA, PROP DESIGNER

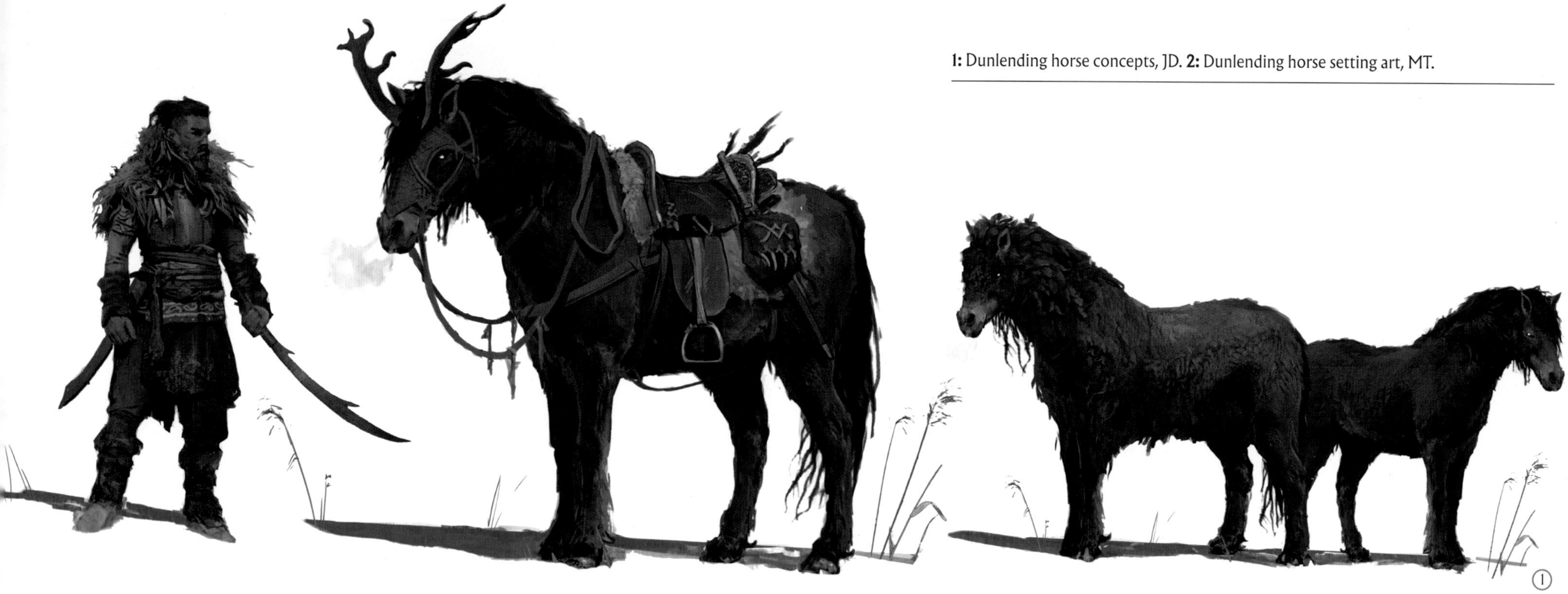

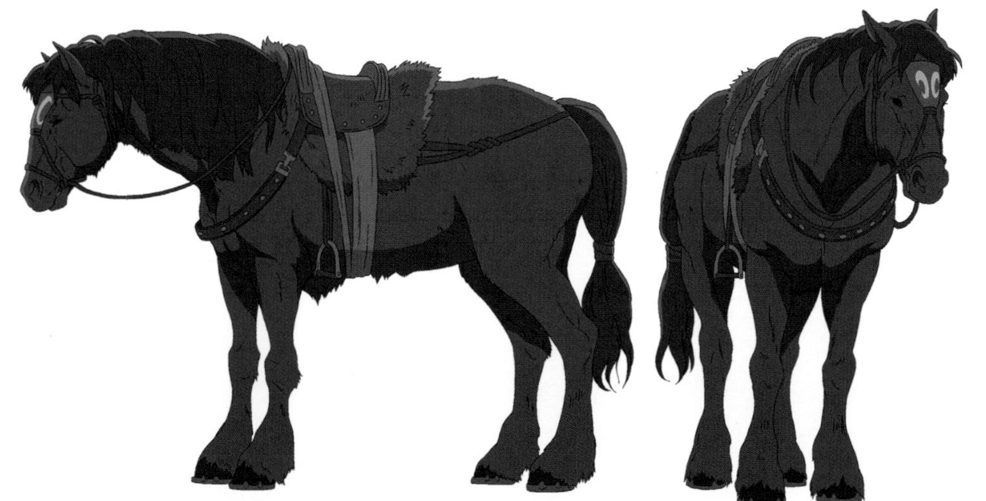

Thinking about how the Dunlendings might treat their horses, I was inspired by traditional Mongolian culture and the relationships they had with theirs, but reinterpreted through the lens of the film and the references that were provided. I imagined that they might groom their horses' hair and use it to entwine and repair their armour.

World-building a culture is so much fun. I had the idea that maybe Dunland horses live in rougher, colder places than the Rohirrim horses on the plains. Maybe the males were bigger and really shaggy, harder to tame and lived higher in the mountains? Maybe the Dunlendings might prefer females as mounts, generally, because they are more practical? Their riders could milk them for sustenance, they might be better groomed, and I liked the idea that maybe Dunlending riders drank the blood of their mares for strength or to bond them to their horses, and the blood of the females might be seen as cleaner. We might see one stallion who was the chief's, almost legendary in status, but then twenty mares. It could be a glimpse at their culture and how they also revere horses, but in a different way to the Rohirrim. I also just loved drawing horses. There's something romantic and magical about them. They're spiritual beings and if you take care of them, they will take care of you. – JOSHUA DAMIAN, WĒTĀ WORKSHOP JUNIOR CONCEPT ARTIST

I was very excited when I received the Wētā Workshop Dunlending horse suggestions. We had imagined the Dunlendings might move about in a colder landscape than the Rohirrim, which is why they wear more furs and dress in layers of darker clothing, so for the horses to be heavier, stronger, thicker in the legs, and shaggier, made sense to us and we paid attention to it. – KENJI KAMIYAMA, DIRECTOR

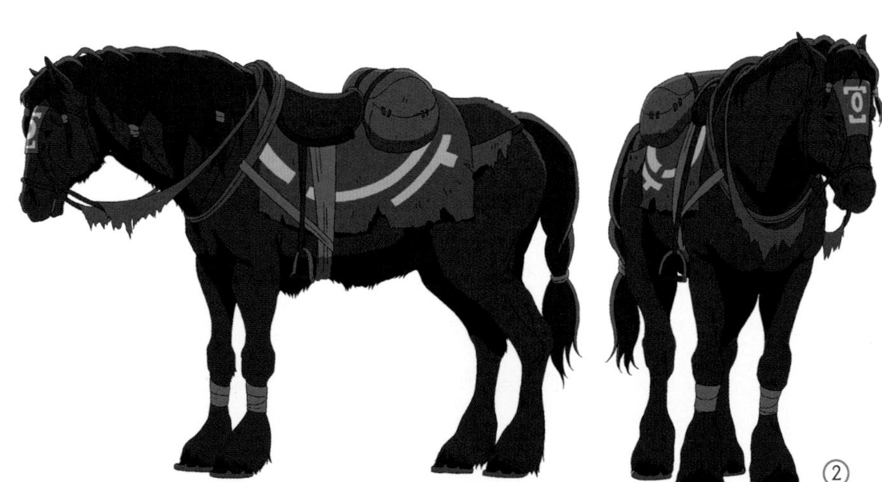

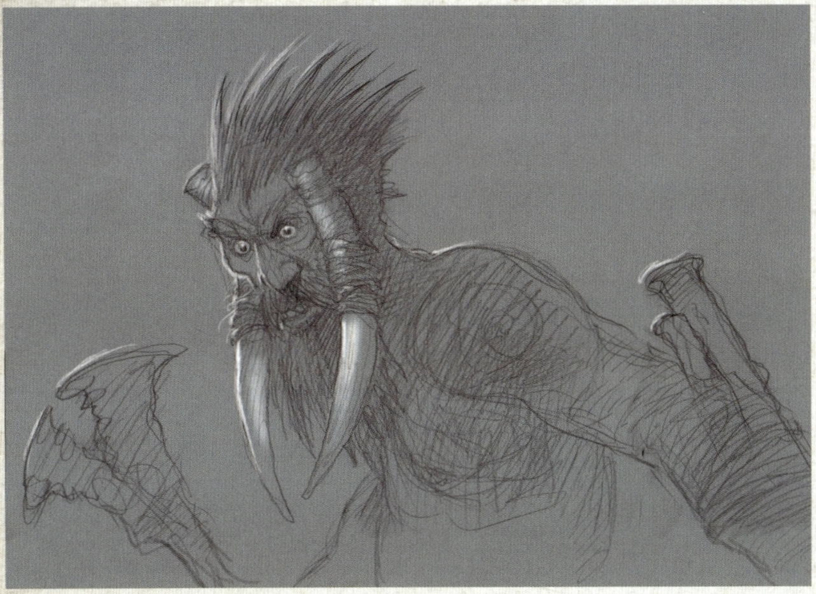

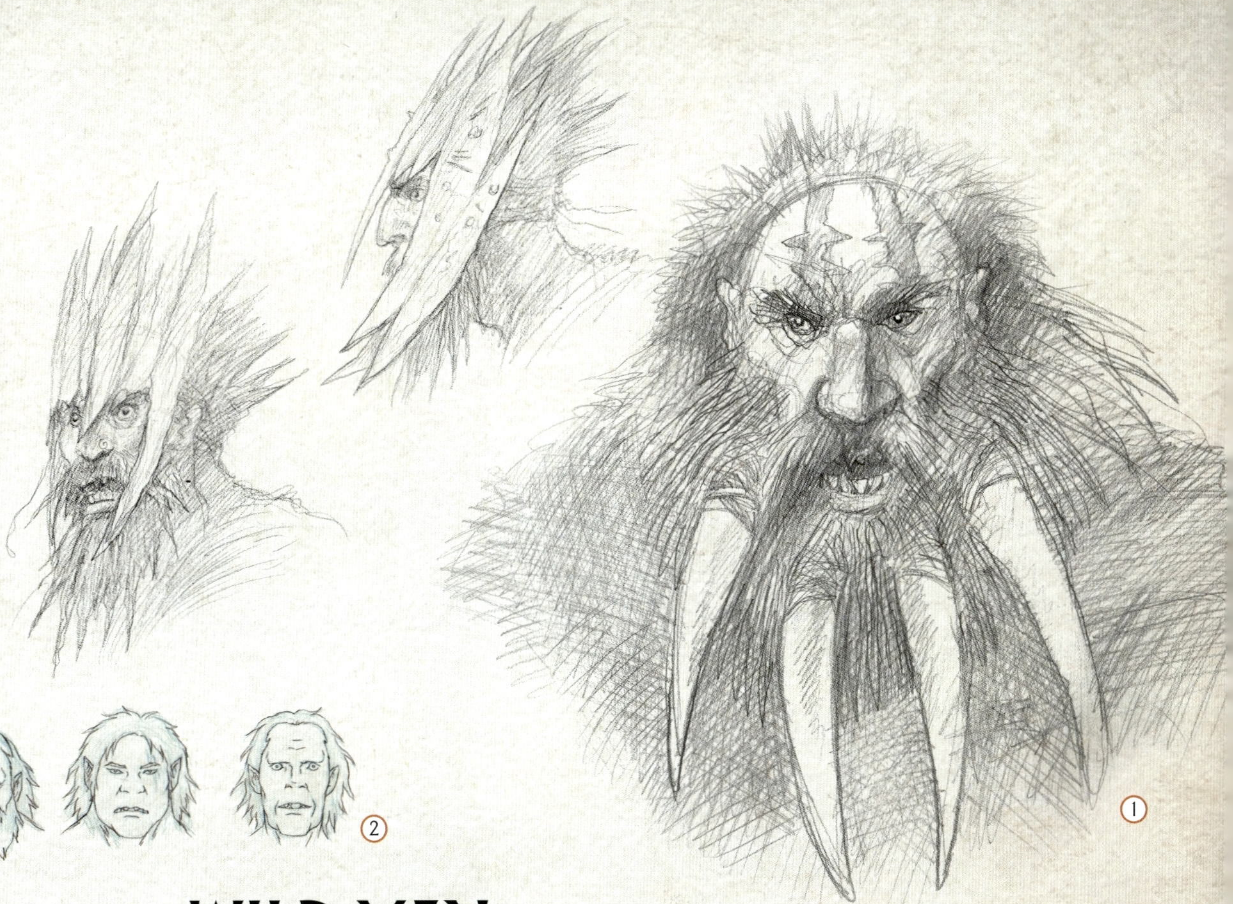

WILD MEN

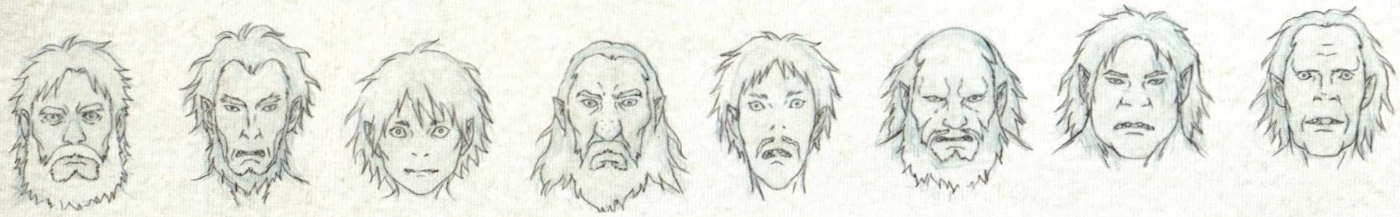

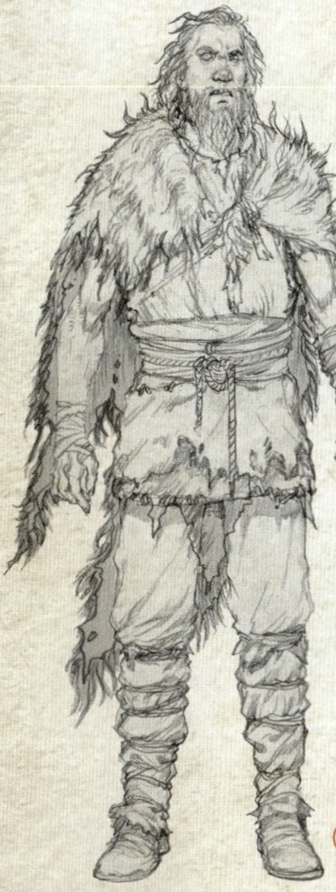

The *Wild Men* of The Lord of the Rings *trilogy return in* The War of the Rohirrim, *enlisted by Wulf to bolster his numbers in the campaign against Edoras. Just as Saruman the White incited the Hill Tribesmen to wage war on the Westfold during his attack upon Rohan, Wulf takes advantage of ancient grievances and good old-fashioned greed to direct the Wild Men to do his bidding.*

The choice was made in The War of the Rohirrim *to differentiate between the more culturally sophisticated Dunlendings, and what the filmmakers were calling the Wild Men of the Hill Tribes. The Dunlendings were Freca and Wulf's people, originating in Dunland, but also dwelling in the West-marches of Rohan where Freca claimed lordship. They are depicted as the technological equals of the Helm's people. In contrast, the Wild Men were a remnant of a more ancient people who once occupied a larger territory, who during the reign of Helm are restricted to the barren hills of Dunland. They are a primitive, under-resourced culture ripe for Wulf's exploitation as foot soldiers. The Wild Men were first seen in* The Two Towers. *For* The War of the Rohirrim, *the designers sought to maintain visual continuity with their previous depiction, but with a slightly expanded palette of materials and colour.*

The accoutrements of the Wild Men evoke the beasts with which they are familiar, reminiscent of tusks and fangs, as well as protective assemblages of iron strips or bone shards, braided into their hair and beards. Perhaps they are intended to confer on their wearers the power and ferocity of boars and even *mûmakil*. – JOHN HOWE, CONCEPTUAL DESIGNER

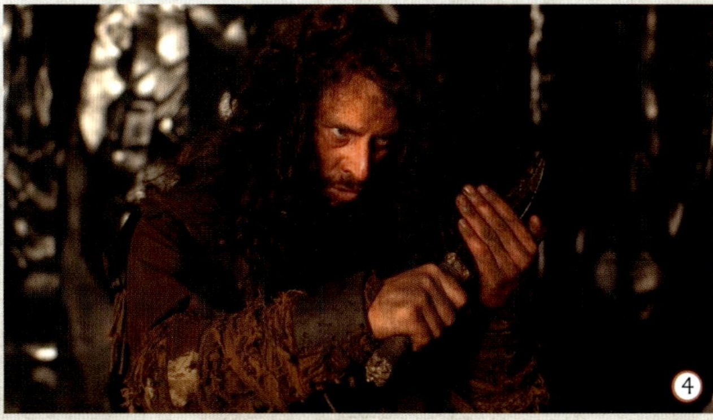

'THE HILL TRIBES HAVE SWORN AN OATH TO ME, EVERY LAST ONE.'

1: Wild Men concepts, JH. 2: Wild Men concepts, MT. 3: Wild Man concept, S & DF.
4: Wild Man on-set still (LOTR trilogy).

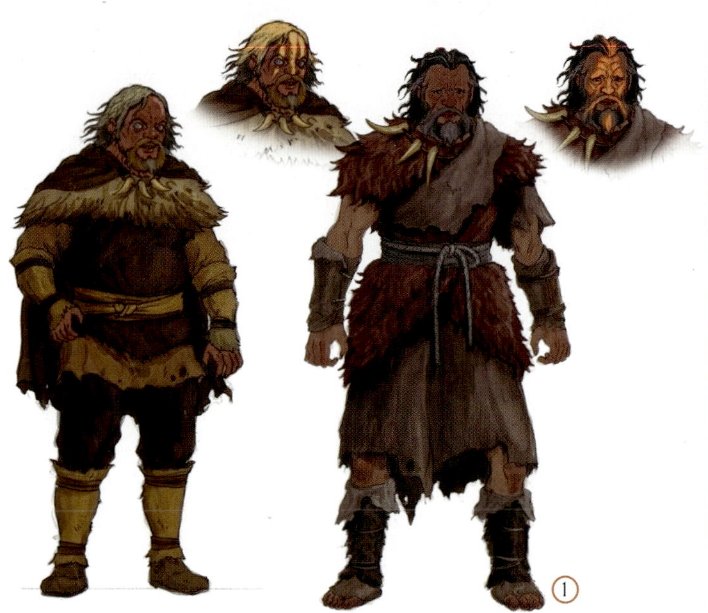

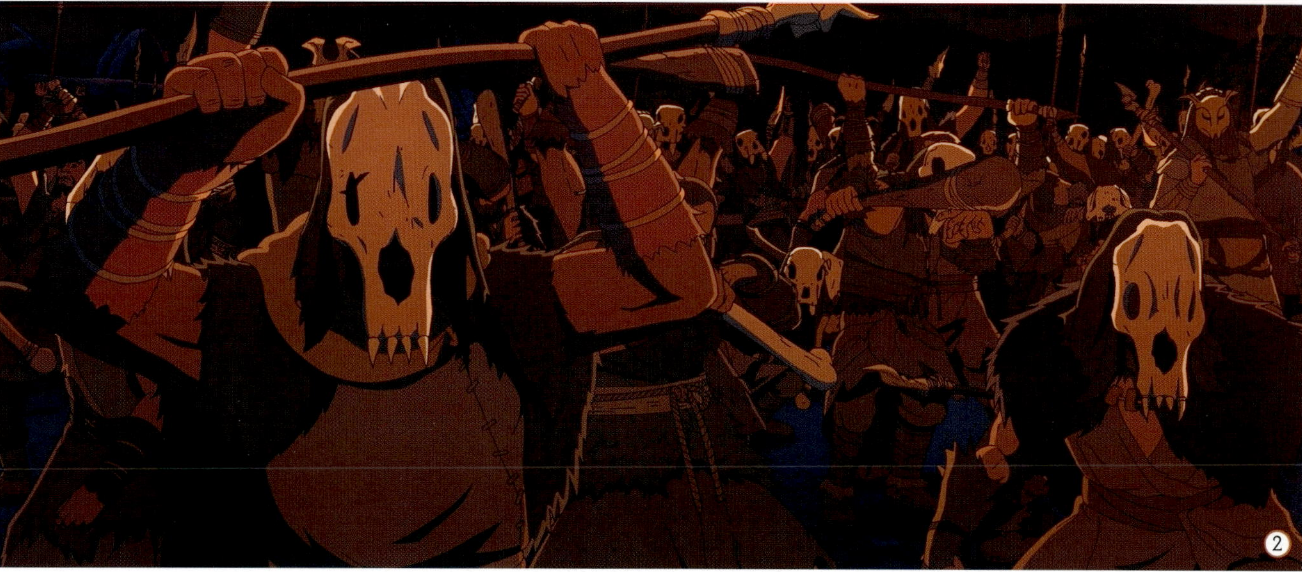

During work on *The Lord of the Rings* films there was an awareness that we had to overcome certain preconceptions about fantasy as a marginal genre. We consciously avoided some of the tropes that had perhaps become clichés. Bones and skulls as armour we employed only sparingly. It would have been easy for every Orc to be clad in fantastical skulls, but we held back from that indulgence.

By the time of *The Hobbit*, that had been relaxed somewhat, in part because a decade on fantasy movies had become more mainstream, but also because it was fresh territory for us to explore.

We had seen very little of the Wild Men in the Jackson films, so their culture remained relatively undefined. The filmmakers on *The War of the Rohirrim* were keen to expand the visual identity of the Hill Tribes, and employing bones to create fearsome war masks was something they specifically asked for. Bone doesn't necessarily make great armour, but it can look scary and intimidating, so I played with war masks that included elements from animals that the Wild Men would have had easy access to: cattle, sheep, goats, even maybe some bear and wolf skulls. Antlers and horns could give the Wild Men distinctive and cool silhouettes, but I shied away from making up skulls based on hitherto unseen monsters. That's not really the Middle-earth that we know. – DANIEL FALCONER, ADDITIONAL CONCEPTS DESIGNER

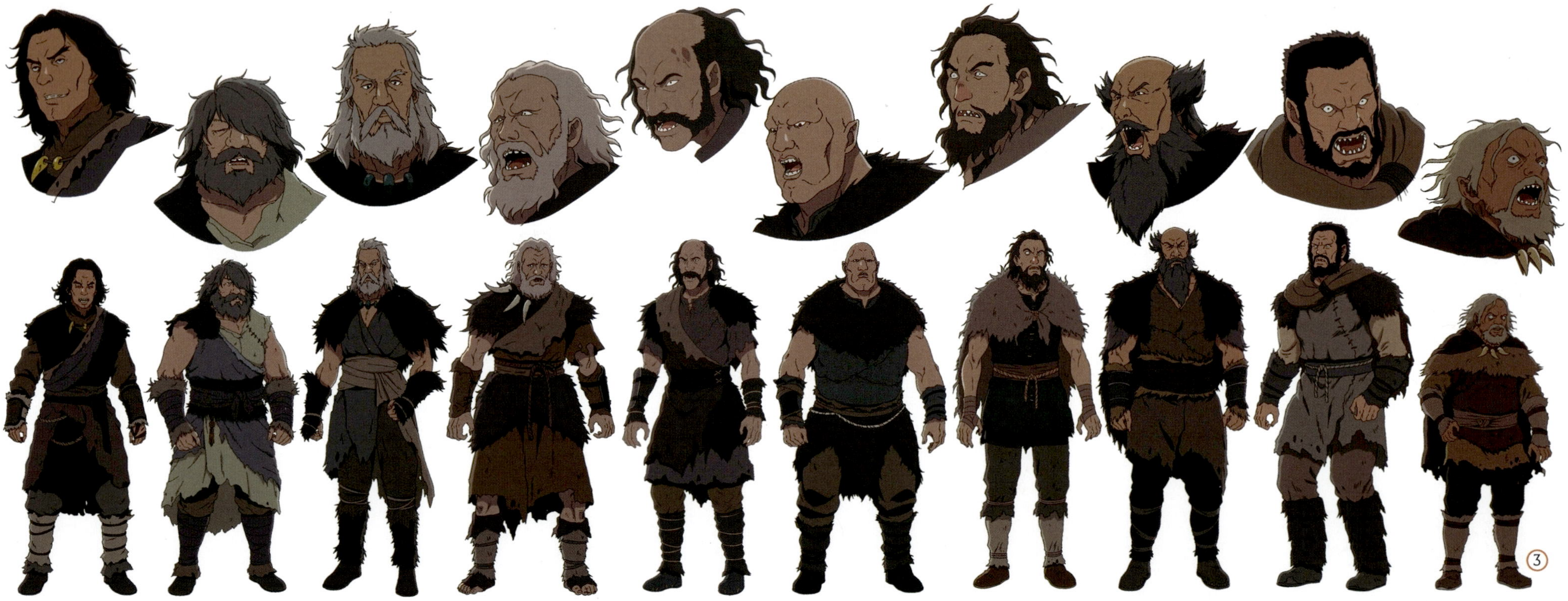

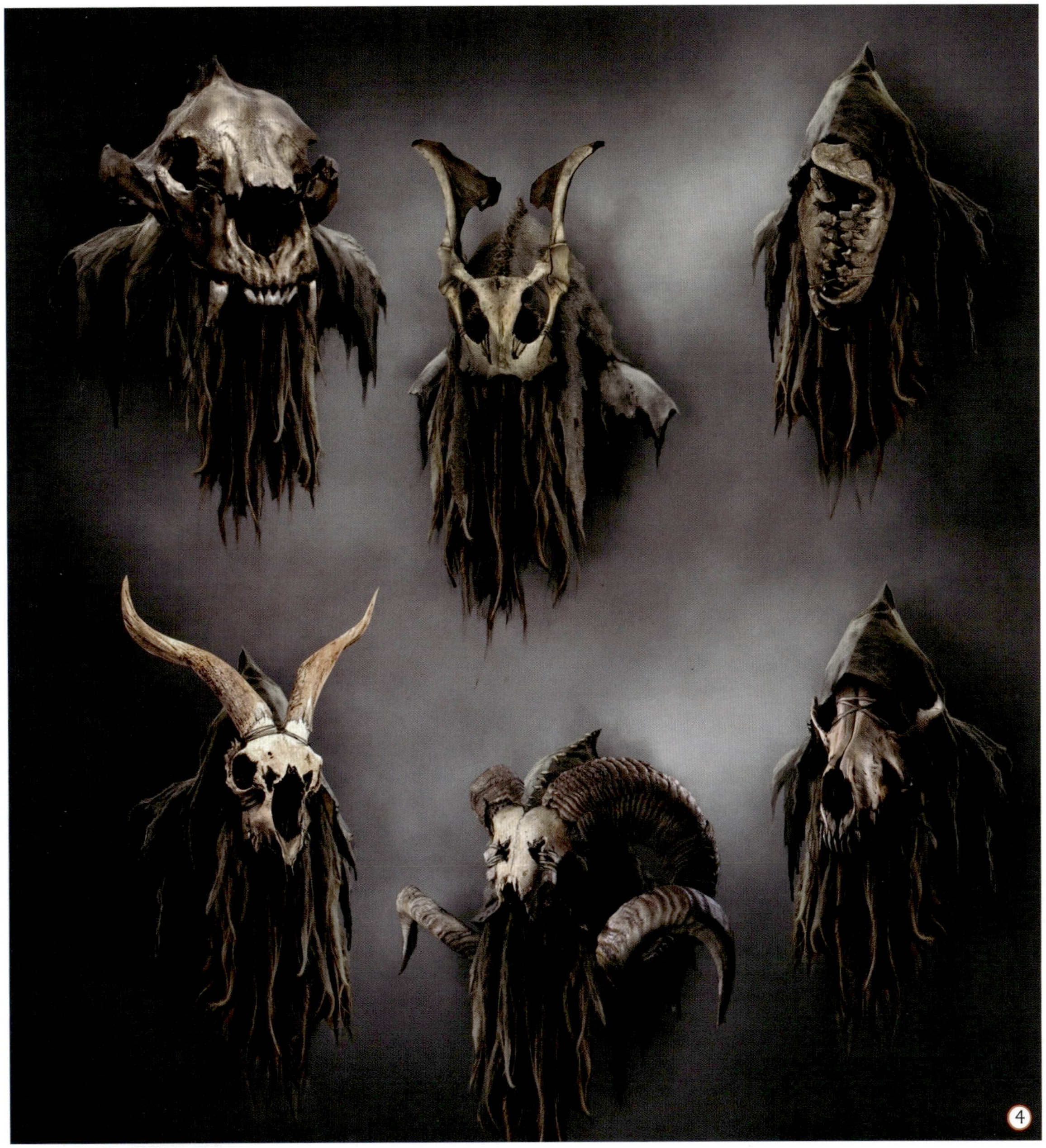

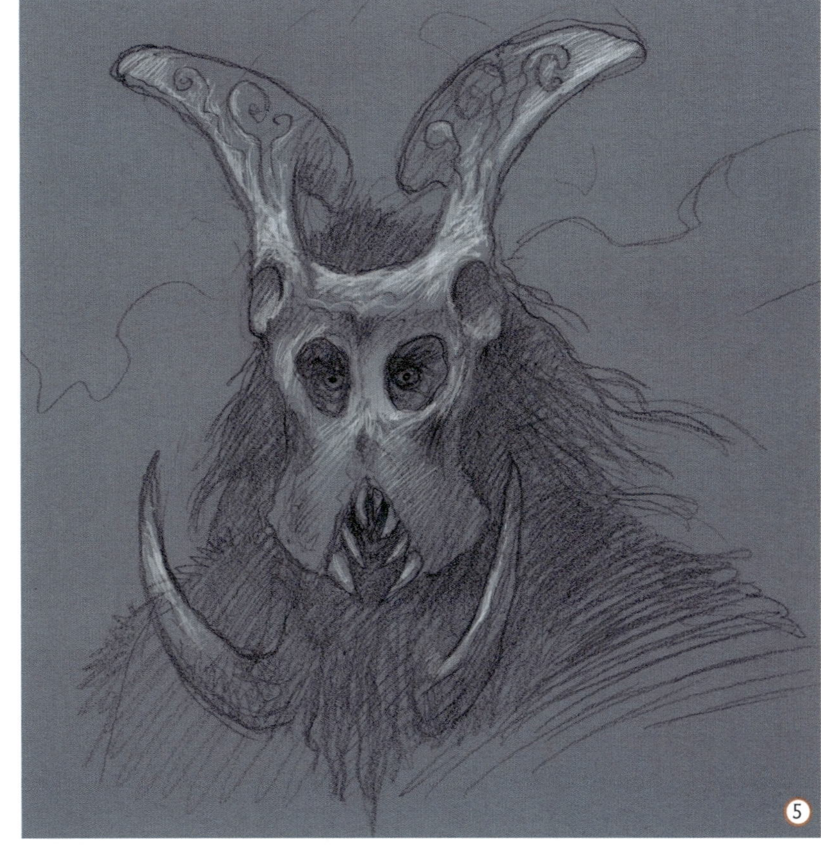

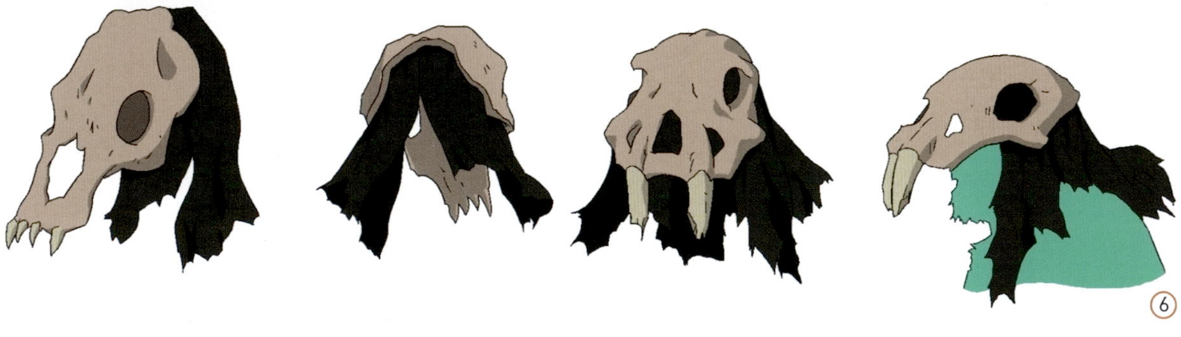

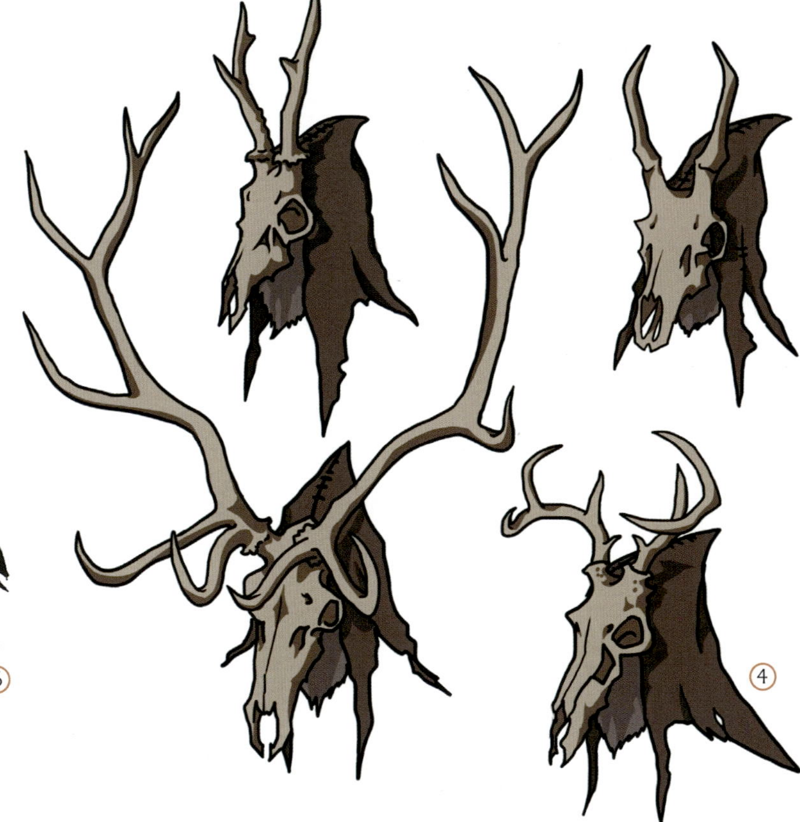

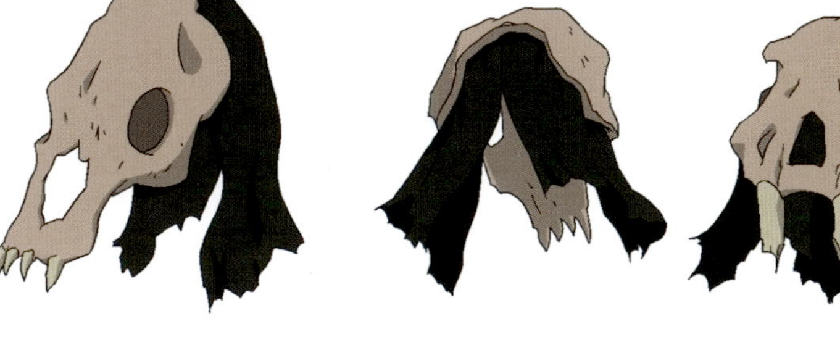

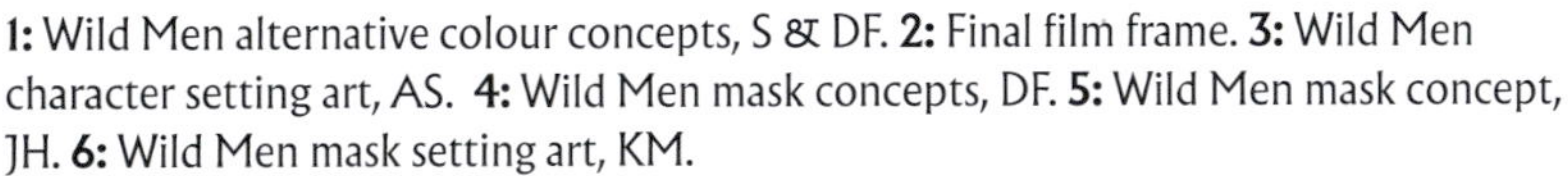

1: Wild Men alternative colour concepts, S & DF. 2: Final film frame. 3: Wild Men character setting art, AS. 4: Wild Men mask concepts, DF. 5: Wild Men mask concept, JH. 6: Wild Men mask setting art, KM.

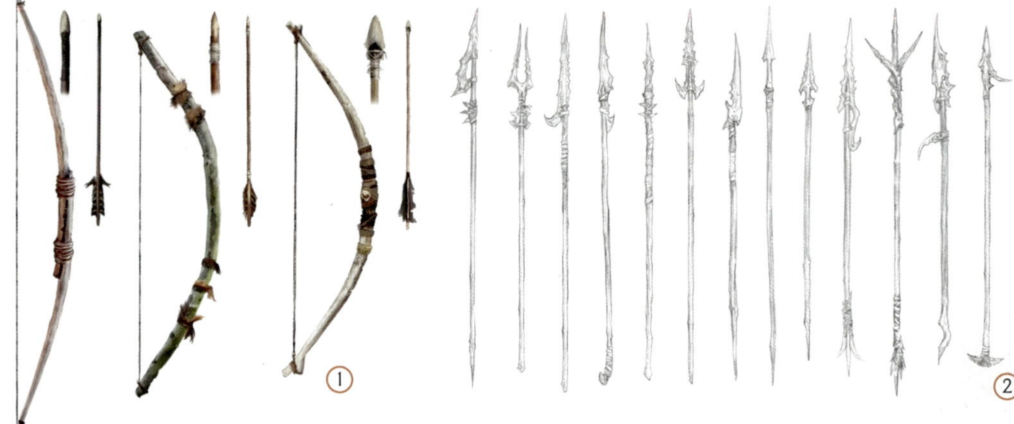

Of the cultures depicted in the film, the Wild Men have the simplest weaponry. In the live-action films Orc weapons were repurposed, but for The War of the Rohirrim *a suite of unique weapons was designed for them, relatively crudely fashioned from wood, bone, or found objects.*

For the Wild Men, I offered concepts of weapons reminiscent of carnivores' open jaws, roughed out of raw iron and riveted to sturdy wooden handles. Only the points of the 'teeth' would be filed and polished. The rest would remain sanguined (allowed to rust, then oiled) or black from the forge. – JOHN HOWE, CONCEPTUAL DESIGNER

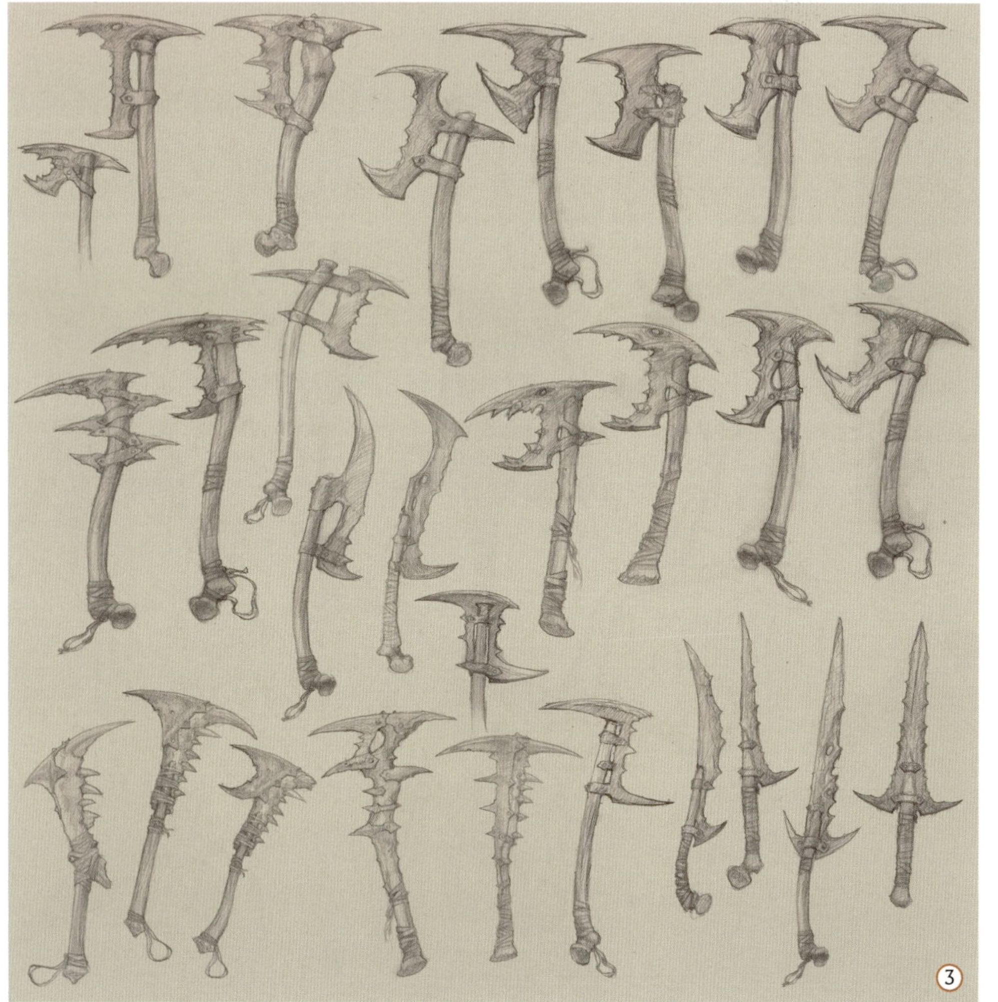

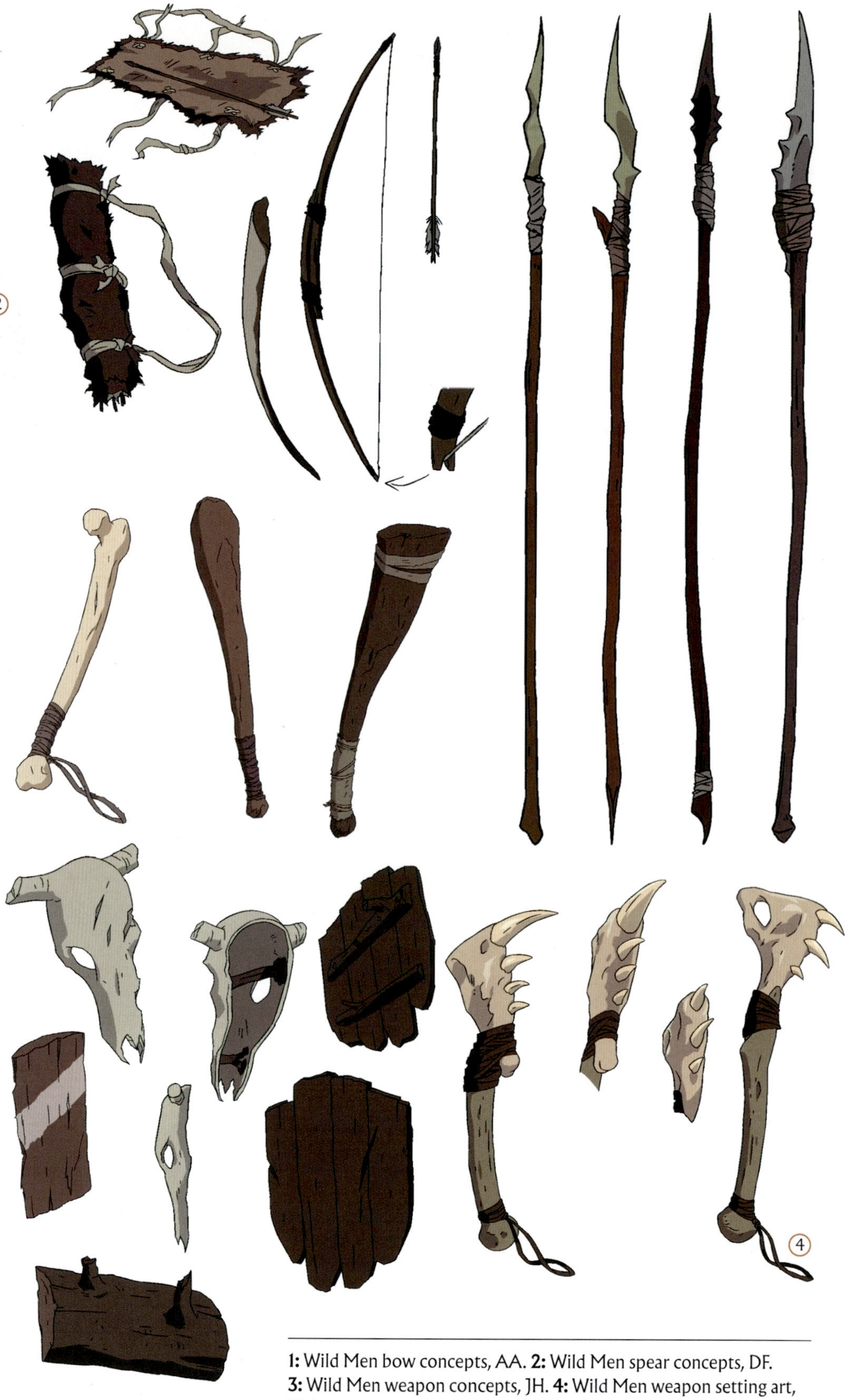

1: Wild Men bow concepts, AA. **2:** Wild Men spear concepts, DF. **3:** Wild Men weapon concepts, JH. **4:** Wild Men weapon setting art, KM.

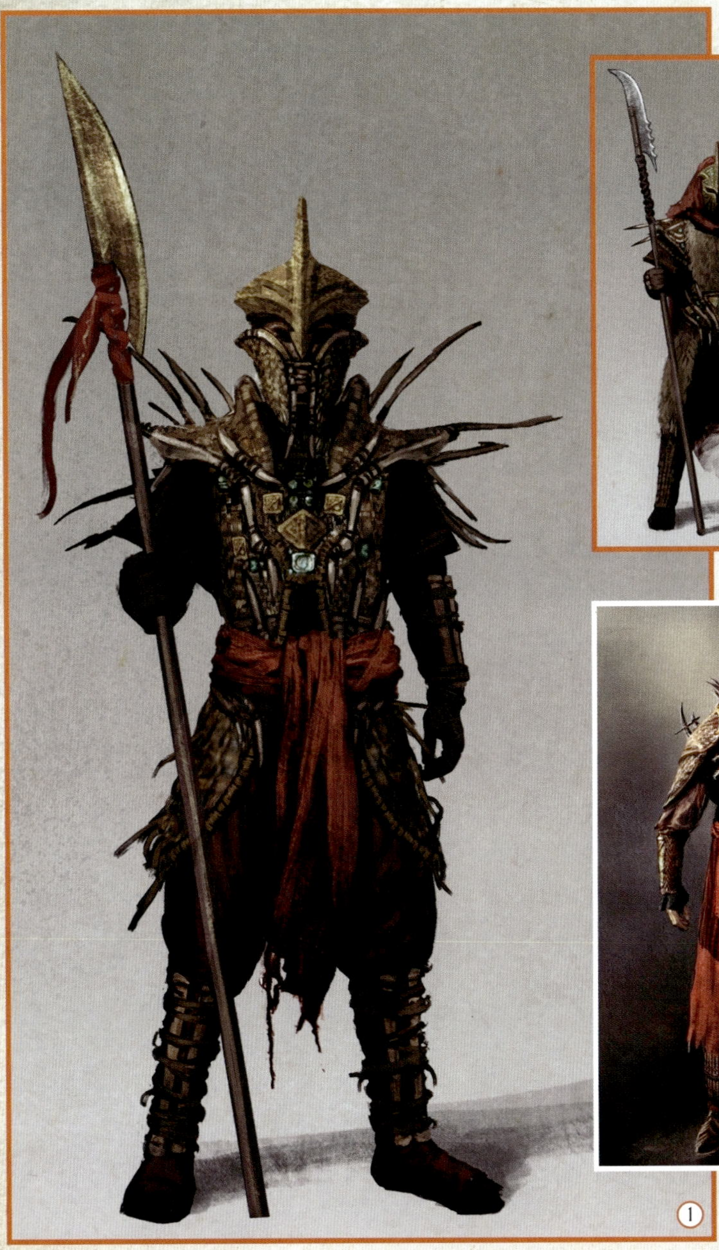

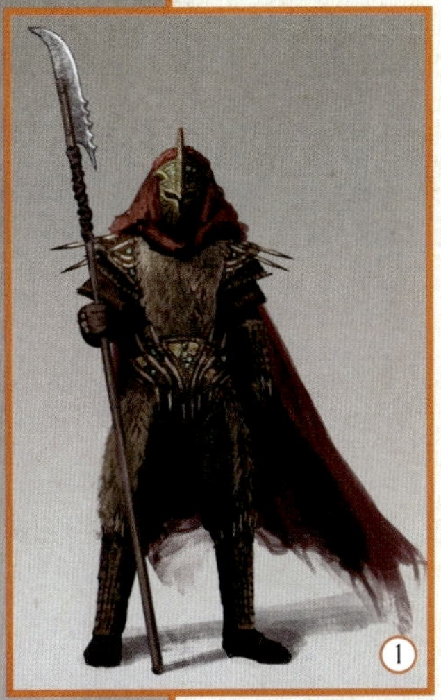

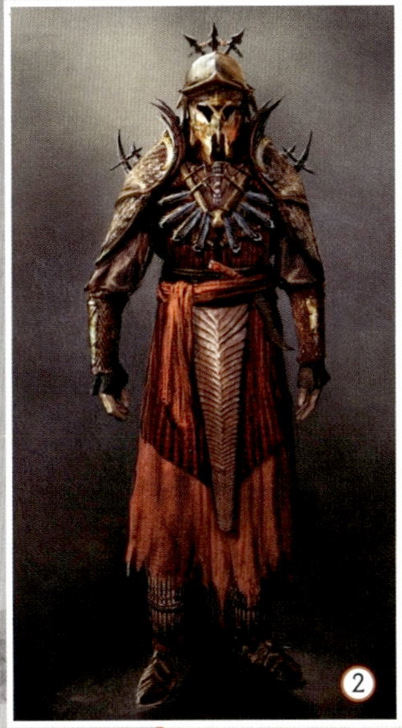

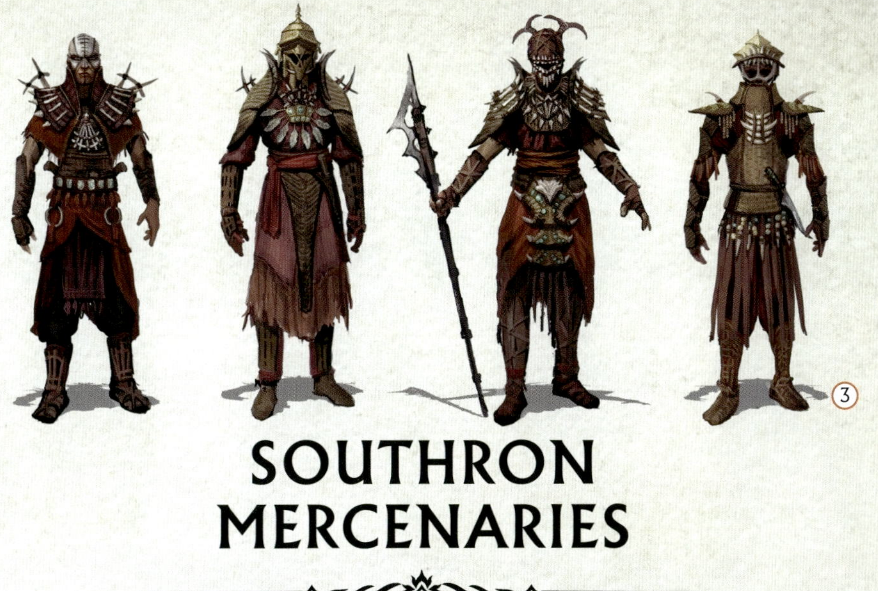

SOUTHRON MERCENARIES

The war in Rohan is not occurring in isolation. There is a larger game being played in Middle-earth geopolitics and we are given glimpses and hints of it. In the book, Tolkien tells us that corsairs have been striking targets on Gondor's south coast, which is why Rohan's traditional allies are nowhere to be seen. Wulf has bolstered his own forces with hired mercenaries from the south. Tolkien describes him being joined by enemies of Gondor landing in the mouths of the rivers that flow through his father's lands. While we don't see them land, these are the Southrons of our movie, the Haradrim, or Variags, as Haleth calls them, with their *mûmak* mounts, hired (or perhaps sent?) to help Wulf destroy Rohan. – DANIEL FALCONER, ADDITIONAL CONCEPTS DESIGNER

The possibility of showing the corsairs attacking Gondor on screen was something that we discussed, but the director presented us with the choice of seeing ocean battles or having armies of soldiers fighting on horseback. Both are incredibly complex to create in anime, and we simply couldn't practically accomplish them with the time and money that we had. It was clear that the horseback battles were the priority for our story, so we let the corsairs go. – JASON DEMARCO, PRODUCER

When I was drawing the Haradrim, I was having flashbacks to when I was working in the leather room back in *The Lord of the Rings* trilogy days and seeing the materials that their costumes were being made with. I tried to figure out a new 'shape language', but using those same materials, because the characters in the new film were supposed to be related. These are bad guys, so there's a certain spikiness that seemed appropriate and would give them aggressive silhouettes. The colours and textures were all intended to help make them stand out as distinct from the Rohirrim.

The helmet concepts were inspired by birds of prey and even Sauron, who had one of my favourite helmet designs. The Rohirrim base their aesthetic on horses, so I was trying to imagine a different animal for these guys; maybe something vicious like a predatory bird? – CHRIS GUISE, WĒTĀ WORKSHOP SENIOR CONCEPT ARTIST

Ken Samonte produced some rough concepts that I worked over and added more details to. We were inspired by the original movie designs, but to make them look a bit fancier we added more metals, stones and jewels. We also introduced fur as a new element. Some of the shapes in the helmets and armour were inspired by Middle-eastern architecture and desert cultures. It helped give us very distinct silhouettes. – IONA BRINCH, WĒTĀ WORKSHOP CONCEPT ARTIST

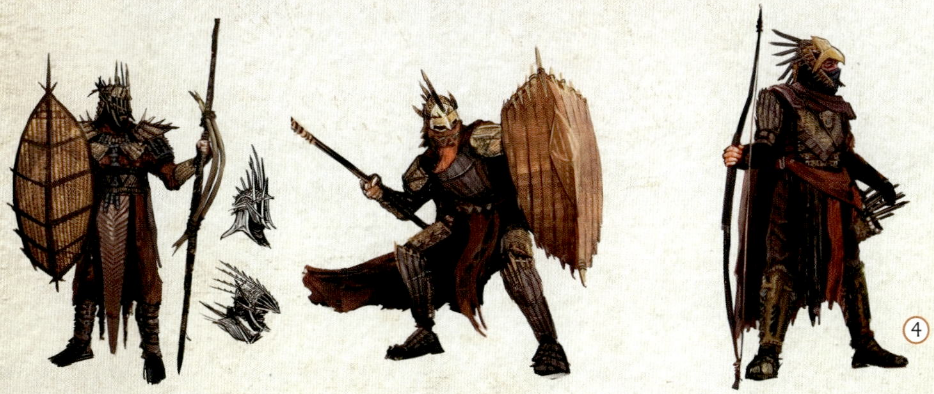

1: Southron mercenary concepts, IB. 2: Southron mercenary concepts, GH. 3: Southron mercenary concepts, KSa & IB. 4: Southron mercenary concepts, CG.

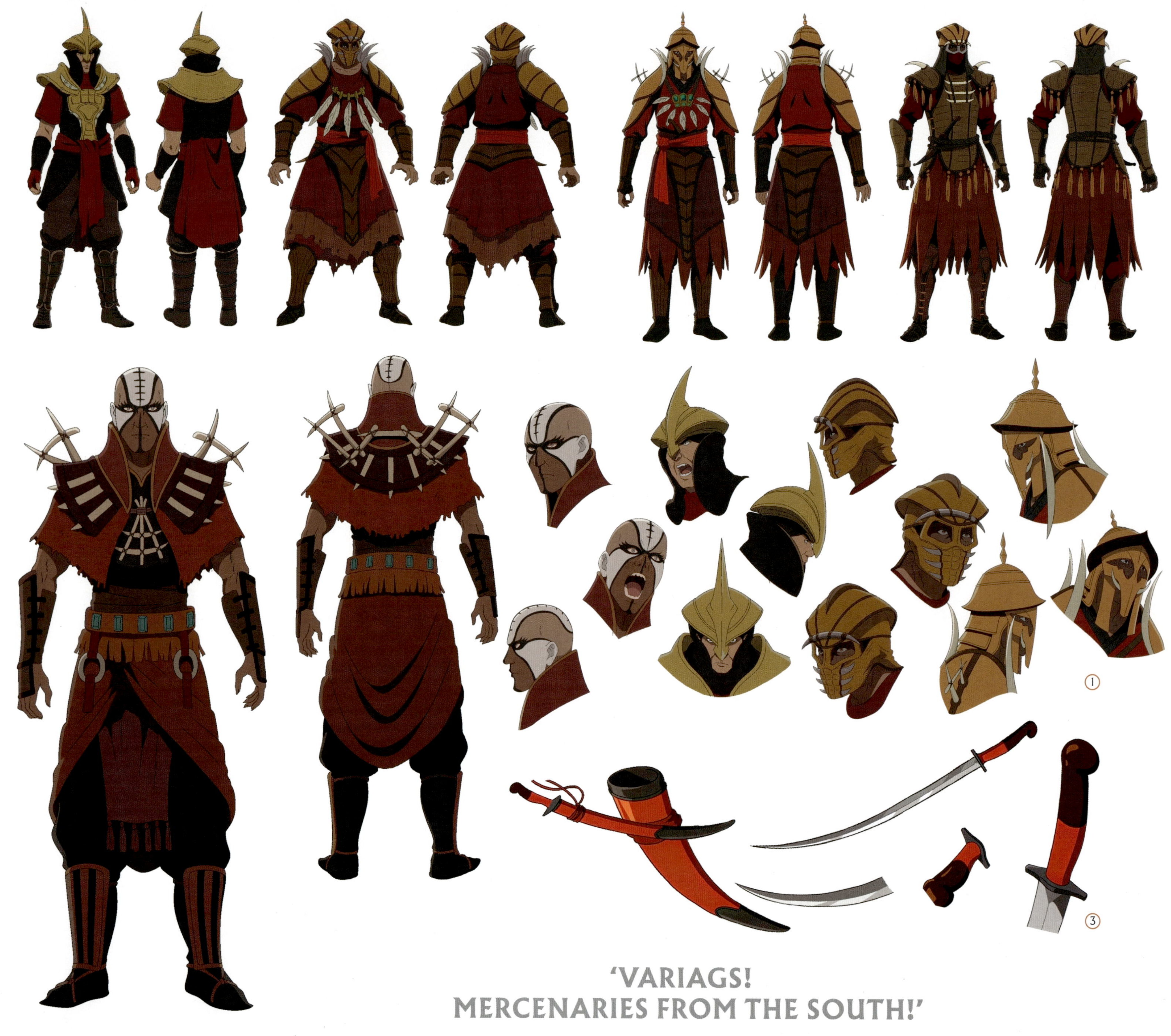

'VARIAGS!
MERCENARIES FROM THE SOUTH!'

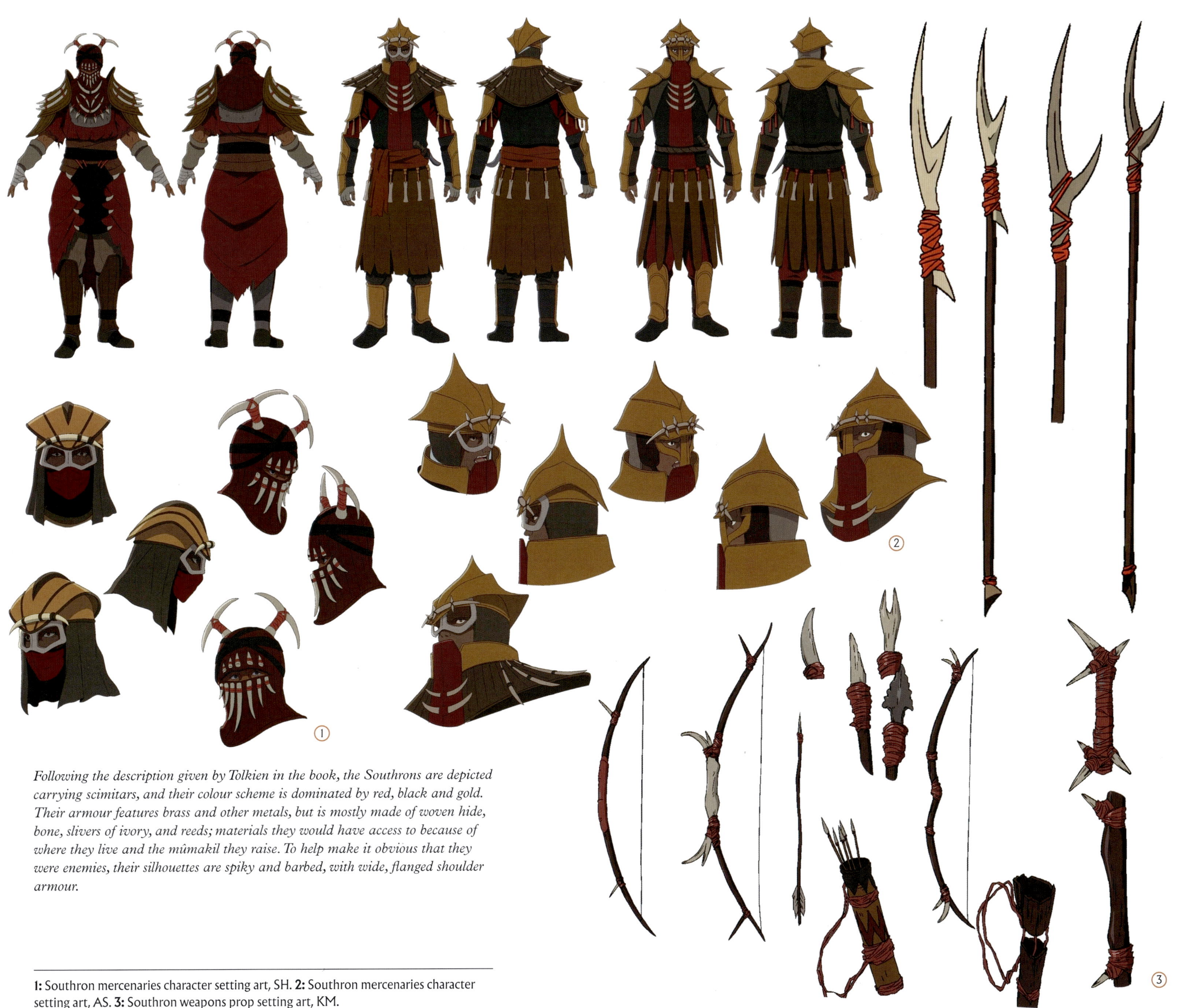

Following the description given by Tolkien in the book, the Southrons are depicted carrying scimitars, and their colour scheme is dominated by red, black and gold. Their armour features brass and other metals, but is mostly made of woven hide, bone, slivers of ivory, and reeds; materials they would have access to because of where they live and the mûmakil they raise. To help make it obvious that they were enemies, their silhouettes are spiky and barbed, with wide, flanged shoulder armour.

1: Southron mercenaries character setting art, SH. **2:** Southron mercenaries character setting art, AS. **3:** Southron weapons prop setting art, KM.

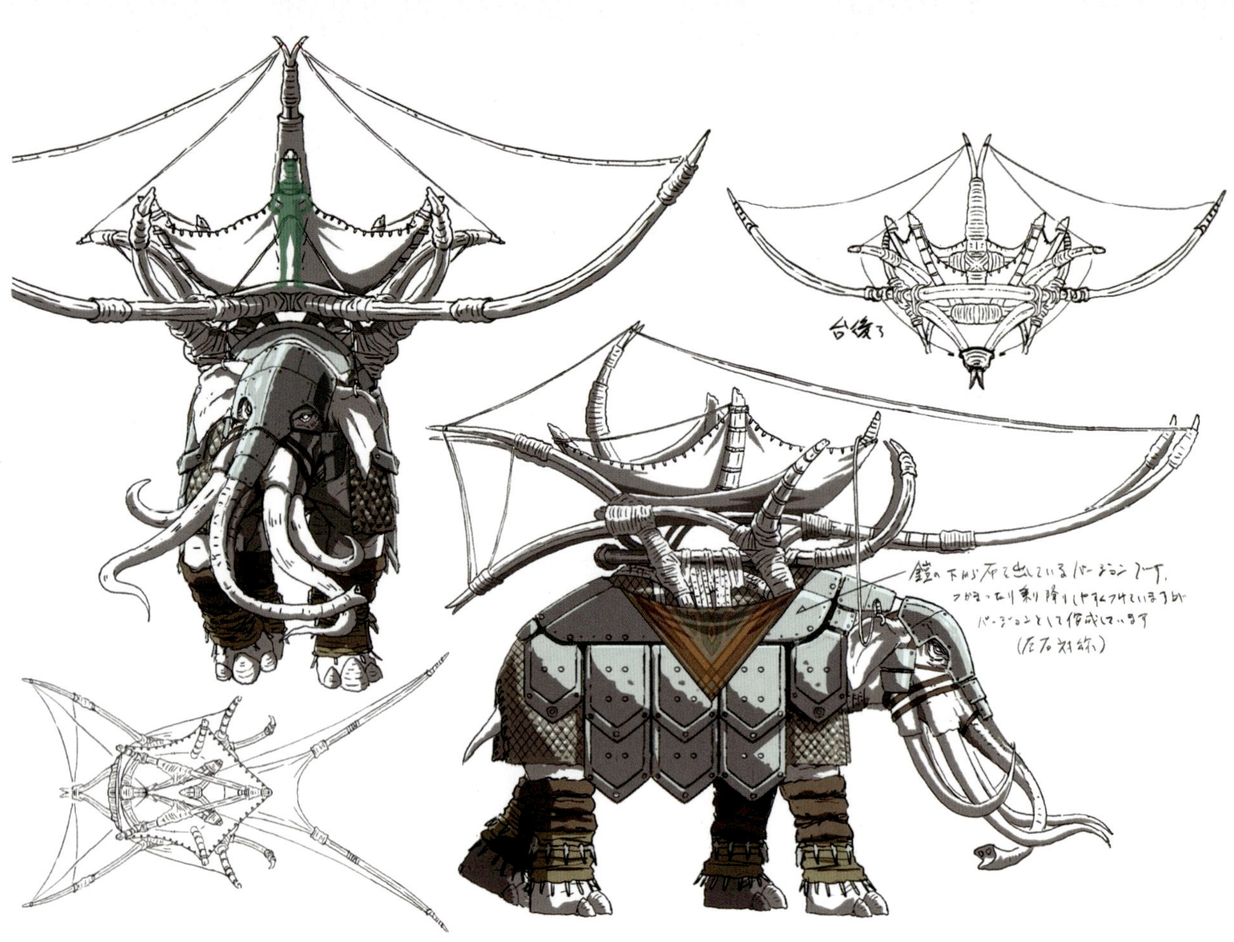

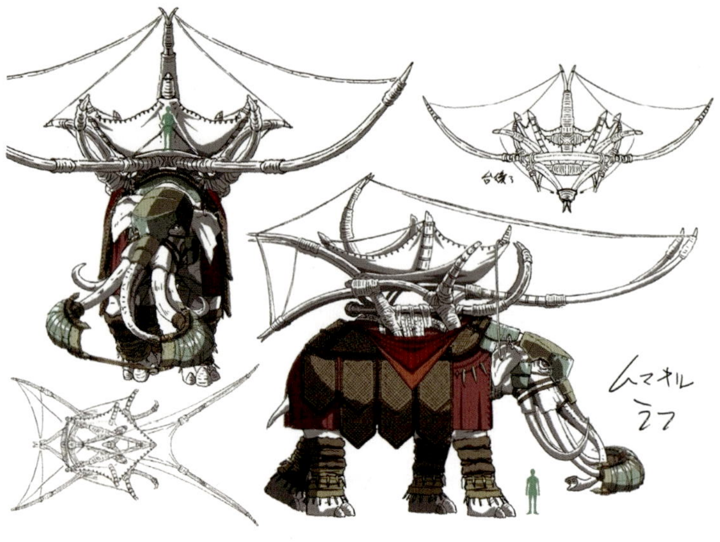

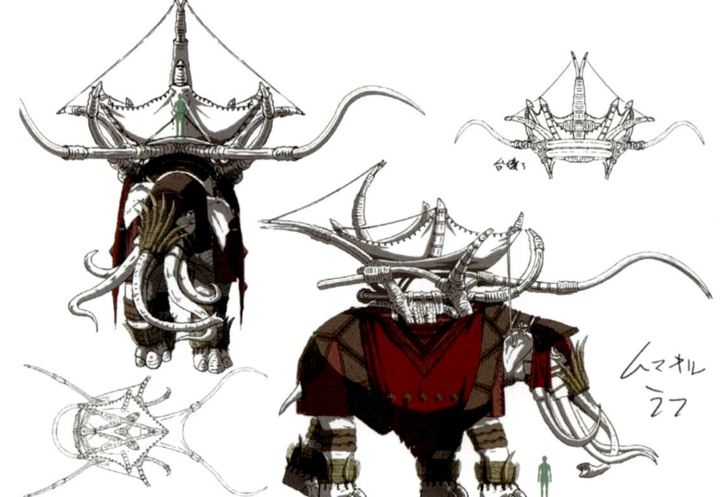

ARMOURED MÛMAKIL

The mûmakil in Wulf's army are outfitted for war with rigs on their backs to bear warriors, armoured sides and legs, and weaponry strapped to their tusks. Among the first concepts explored were some much heavier, steel-plated versions, but introducing these elements moved the mûmakil too far from what had already been established for Southron culture. Subsequent rounds of concepts explored ideas that remained within the material bounds of what had been done before, but sought to find new combinations and configurations to help make these new mûmakil distinctive.

Sporting war paint, it was imagined that each mûmak might belong to a different tribe or unit of warriors and be decorated to reflect their individuality. The more unique each was, the easier it would be for audiences to track what was originally going to be half a dozen animals engaged on different fronts of the battle. This was eventually reduced to three as the battle was rewritten.

It was cool to be seeing mûmakil again, and also exciting that these were not the same ones we had met in the trilogy. My assumption was that they were a related variety, but that their masters were from mercenary clans separate from the Haradrim that we had seen before. The designs should have something in common and it should be evident that they come from the same region, but we had license to introduce new things. I loved that Joshua Damian at Wētā Workshop had introduced the idea of some even having burning elements. Painting into the Wētā images, I had a lot of fun coming up with unique riffs on the established mûmak war rig and weaponry designs, really leaning into the spiky, threatening vibe. – DANIEL FALCONER, ADDITIONAL CONCEPTS DESIGNER

1: Armoured mûmakil concepts, MS. 2: Armoured mûmakil concepts, JD. 3: Armoured mûmakil concepts, JD & DF.

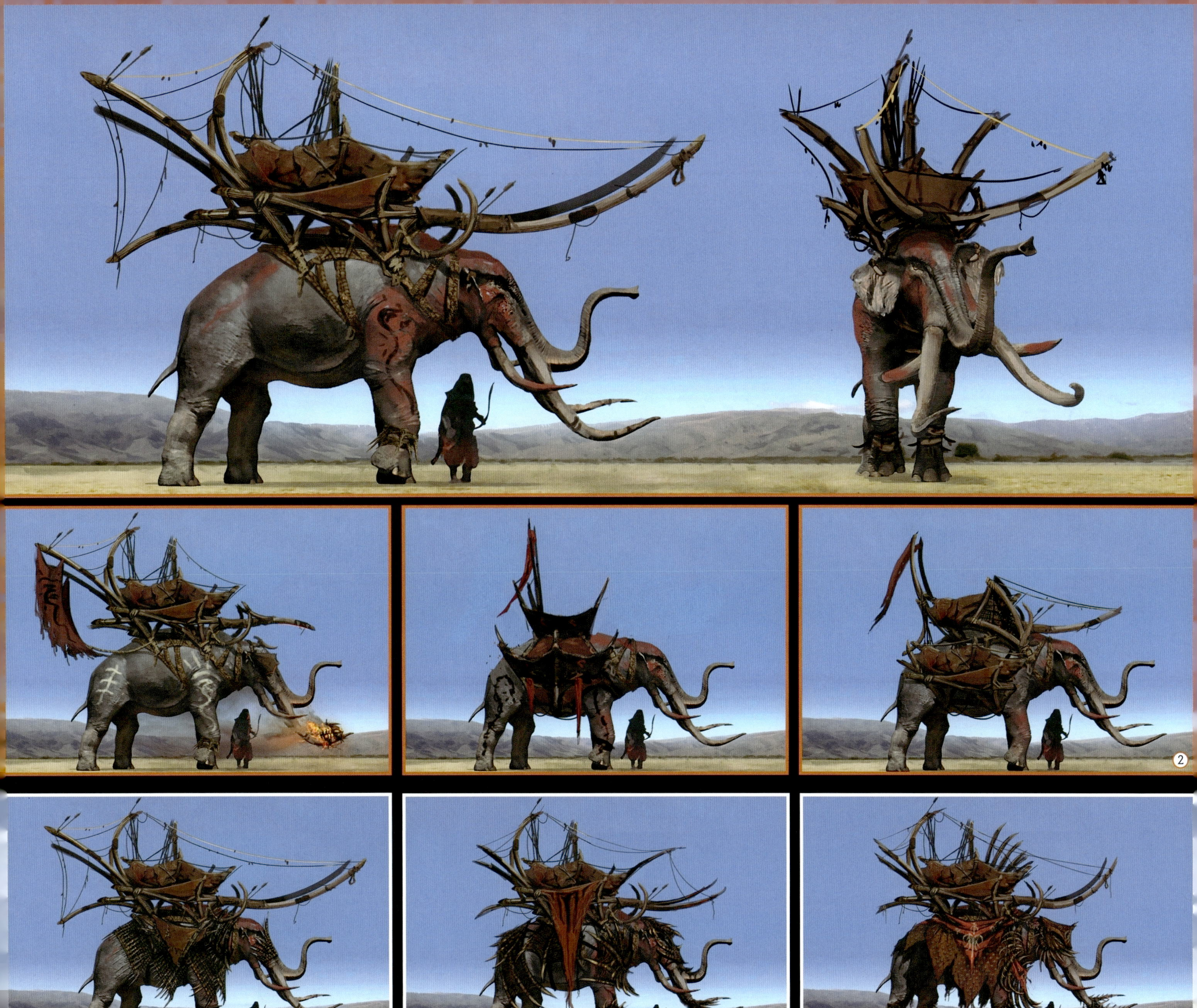

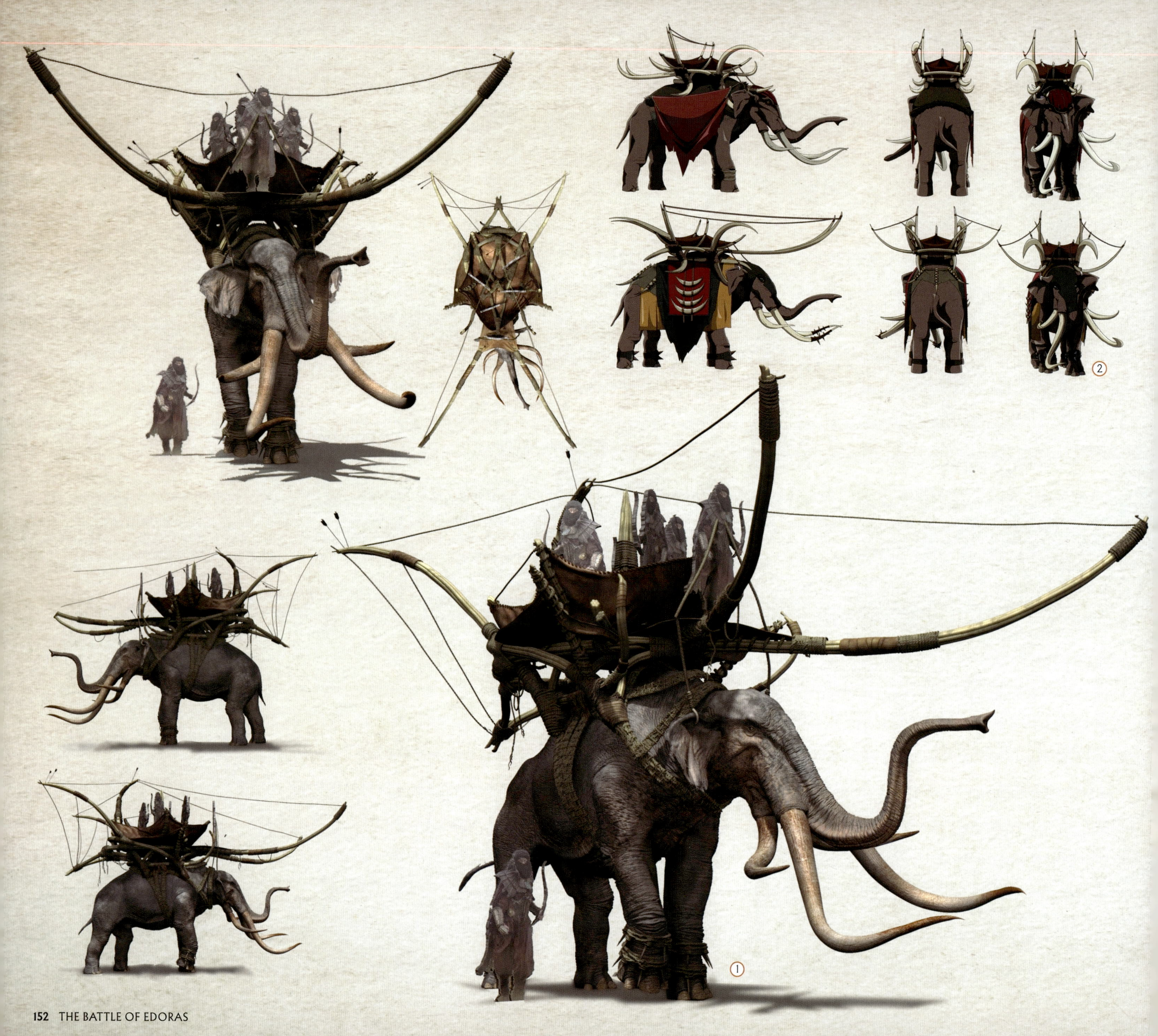

2
1

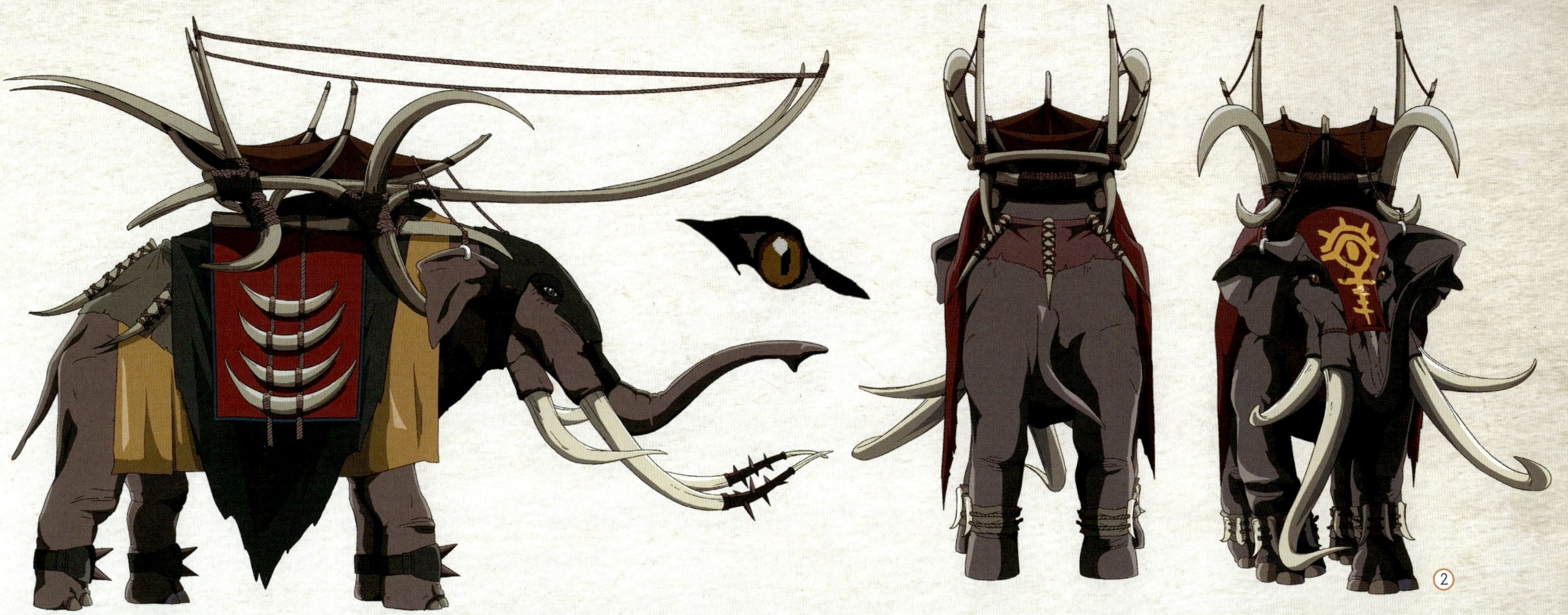

1: Armoured mûmakil concepts, WW. **2:** Armoured mûmakil creature setting art, YA. **3:** Final film frame.

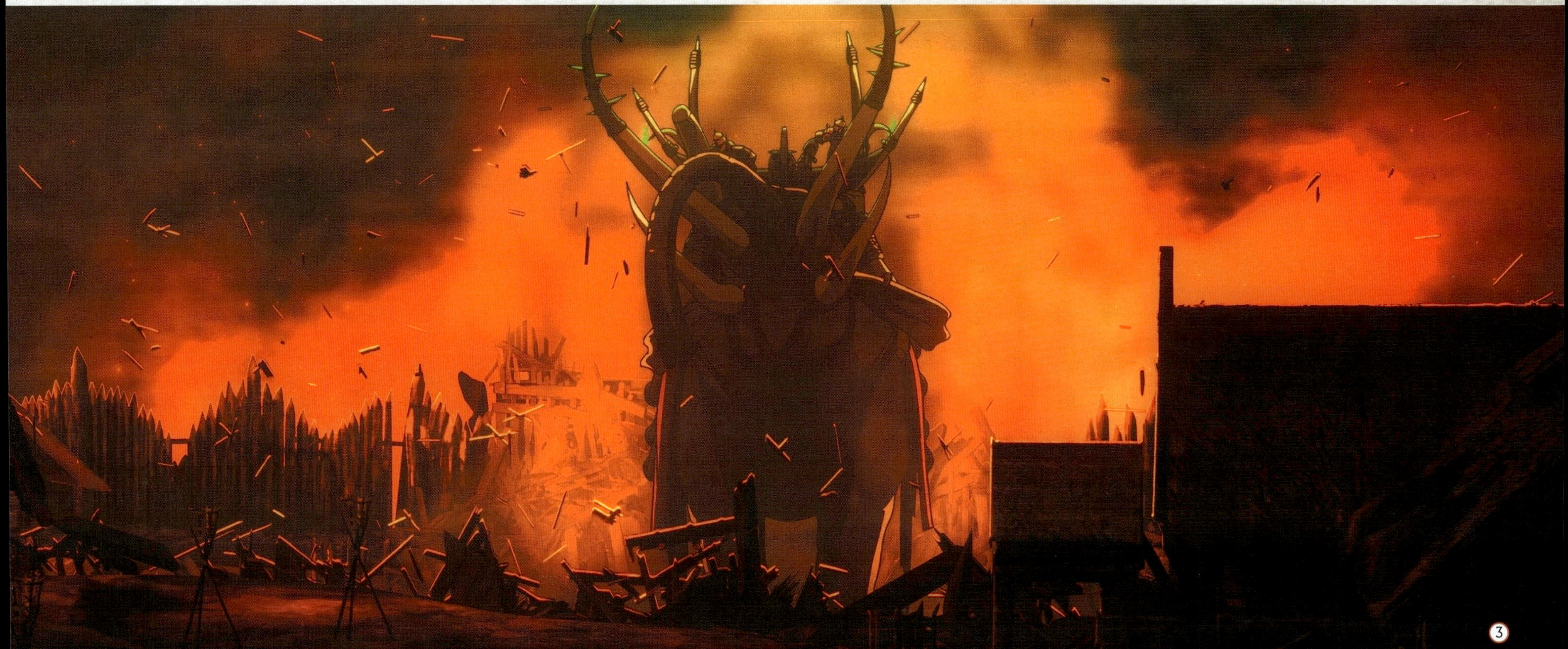

THE BATTLE OF EDORAS

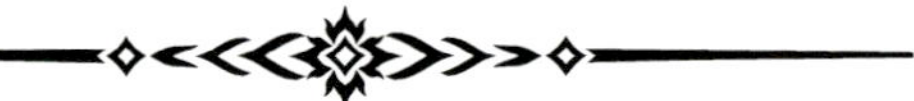

Wulf brings his forces to Edoras, counting on Helm and his riders to charge upon his position, thereby drawing them away from the city. In addition to Dunlendings and Wild Men, the vengeful would-be conqueror has hired mercenaries from the hot lands of the distant south to swell his ranks, bringing with them towering mûmakil, an enemy the Rohirrim have neither the experience nor fortifications to deal with.

The *mûmakil* breach the city, destroying the wall next to the East Gate, which allows Wulf to invade and head toward Meduseld. Meanwhile, the people of Edoras secretly escape through the South Gate. – TAMIKO KANAMORI, ART DIRECTOR

The battle began as something much more involved. The director plotted the flow of the action using a map of Edoras with the defending army and various attacking armies. As scripted originally, Wulf had split his forces and had a smaller army to use as a feint. In that plan *mûmakil* were coming in from three different directions: there was one with Wulf, one with Tarrg, and one which Helm would have encountered. But then they also attack different parts of Edoras and come into the city. All of it had to make sense, and it was meticulously planned and timed using the map, but how the audience perceives it is entirely dependent on how you frame it. What's in shot helps you understand where you are, but not everyone watching knows the layout of Edoras, and even if they do, it can still become confusing. How accurate do you want to get and what's the order? We plotted the whole thing, but even people inside the production could find it confusing, so it was clear that we needed to make it simpler to follow. It was very hard to do, especially because the attack takes place in the dark of night. – JOSEPH CHOU, PRODUCER

We broke down the battle in ways that could give each character their own action, including giving Héra the opportunity to show that she could fight. She is the lead, so it was important to see that she could do this because she is smart and capable. Everyone is having a hard time taking down the *mûmakil*, but Héra understands what she is facing and figures out a way to do it using fire to scare the beast. She takes it out with one shot from a ballista on the Edoras palisade. It was a moment conceived to demonstrate her qualities and capabilities, because they would become even more important later in the film when she has to lead her people. – KENJI KAMIYAMA, DIRECTOR

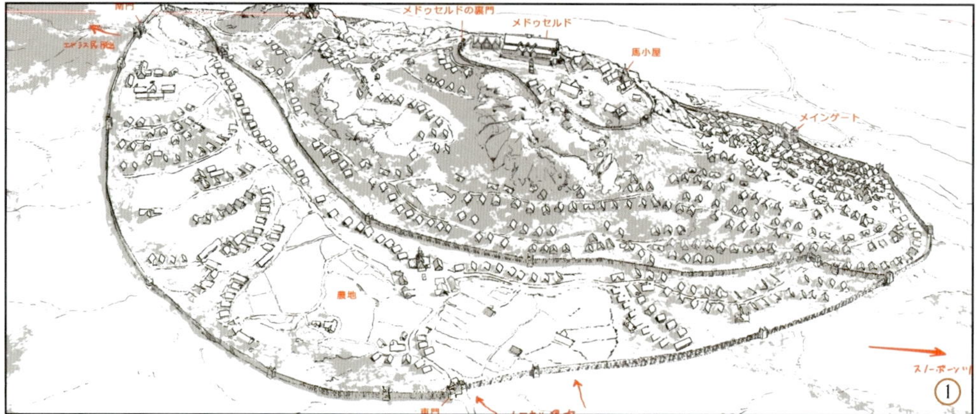

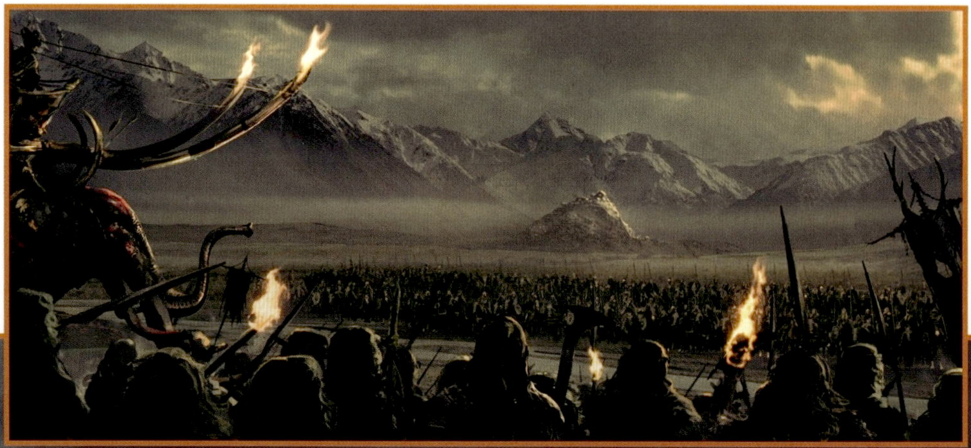

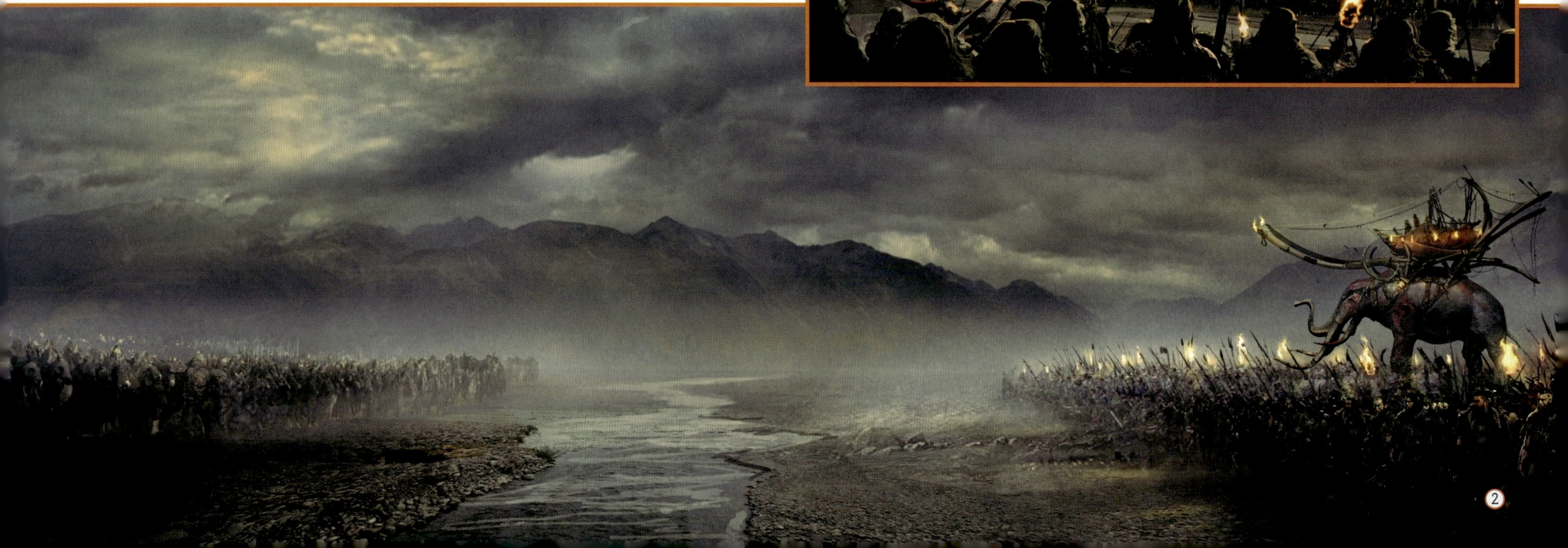

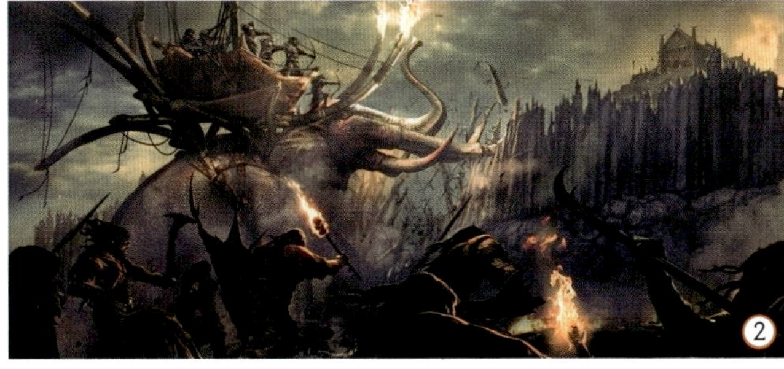

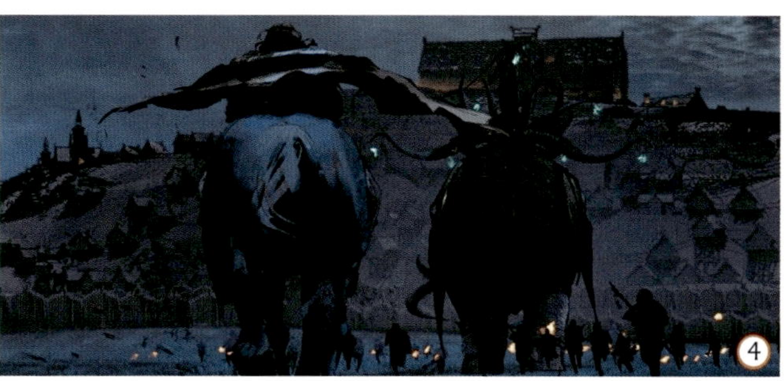

Tolkien's account of Helm is only a couple of pages long. He didn't go into detail about the battle, saying only that Rohan was overrun and Wulf took Edoras, so we had to answer how Wulf did that. If we're telling the story of the defeat of one of Rohan's greatest kings, who has been undefeated until this point, we had to make it a big event. Helm would not have neglected his defences, but he loses his city, his kingdom and his son, and orders his people to flee to the Hornburg. Whatever force Wulf brought to bear therefore had to be significant. There was no way we could depict this as a skirmish. It demanded a big battle and we had to deliver.

That was where the idea of the *mûmakil* came in – an ace up Wulf's sleeve – something that no one would have expected him to have access to. Even if Helm had seen this move coming, his defences were made of wood. What could he do?

It meant we had a huge task to animate all of this. The battle was by far the most complex sequence in the entire film and the last one to be delivered, involving multiple charging *mumakil*, armies of men and animals clashing, Edoras on fire, walls broken down, horses, intercutting between the field of battle and Héra evacuating the city, and geography that must be presented in a way that audiences can follow.

Part of the sheer weight of the animation was due to the fact that everyone was in motion: fighting, running, yelling, crashing into one another, blood flying; chaos in motion. Everyone was in armour, much of it unique. Even the enemies had variety in their ranks, including recognizable individuals, lieutenants, senior officers and juniors. None of that is easy to do in animation. – JASON DEMARCO, PRODUCER

As originally planned, Wulf and Helm's armies faced off against each other across the shallow river. I followed some familiar shots from the trilogy as a starting point and created a similar composition with the elements from our new story in my key scene artwork. Part of the goal was to set the action of the armies against the beautiful environment behind them, with the mountains, ominous clouds in the sky and dramatic lighting. The city is picked out in light. – GUS HUNTER, WĒTĀ WORKSHOP SENIOR CONCEPT ARTIST

Tolkien says that the Rohirrim would sing when riding out to war, which led to us talking about having all of the riders singing as they ride out of Edoras. – PHOEBE GITTINS, WRITER

For key scene battle images, I was trying to capture everything that's going on in one snapshot, so there were lots of elements to balance: the *mûmak* crashing through the palisade wall, the guys on top of its back, the army following them into the city, and the Golden Hall they're trying to get to shining on the hill. There were a couple of ways to do it, so I provided options; either looking at the *mûmak* coming through from inside the city with the defenders in the foreground watching it come, or from the defenders in the foreground watching it come, or from

'WAR IS UPON US.'

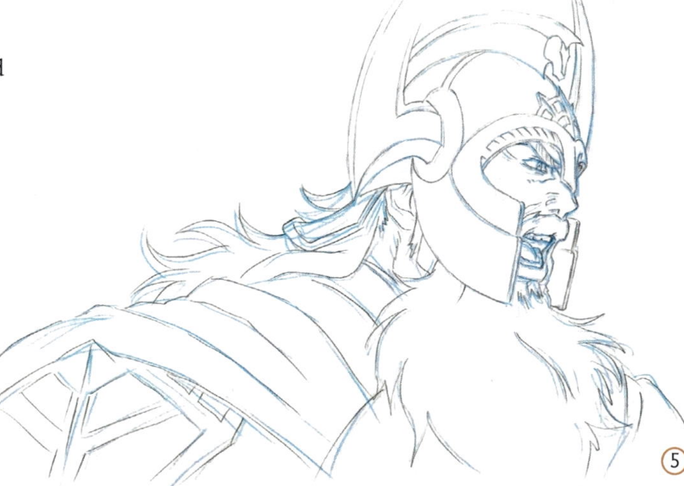

1: Edoras battle map, TK. 2: Battle of Edoras key scene art, GH. 3: Battle of Edoras background setting art, TK 4: Battle of Edoras key scene art, TK. 5: Animation key frame, MT.

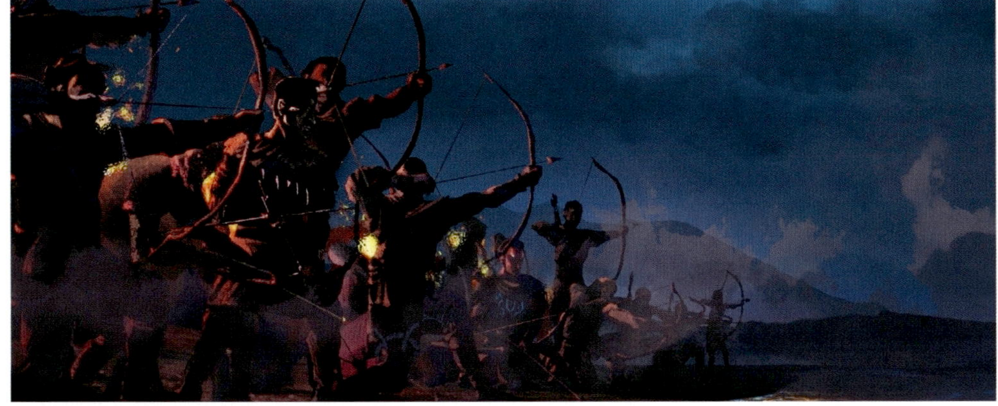

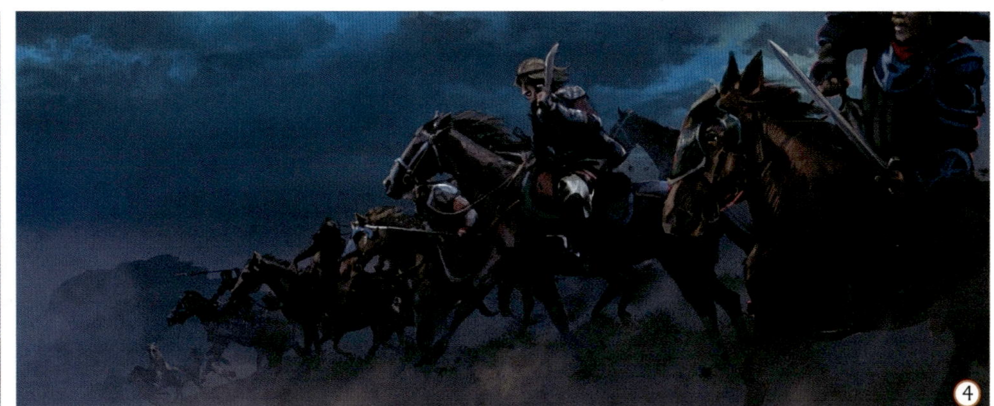

behind, from the point of view of the attackers, which I thought gave more of the gist of the whole scene and meant we could include Meduseld. There's a lot to include in one frame, while also capturing the mood with fire and dynamic poses for all the participants. – GUS HUNTER, WĒTĀ WORKSHOP SENIOR CONCEPT ARTIST

While *The War of the Rohirrim* is a hand-drawn 2D animated feature, CGI references were used in almost every part of the production process. CGI played an extremely important role in clarifying the director's intentions for each shot, including background art elements, layout and lighting.

As a CGI/composite director, I was involved in everything to do with the look of the film. This included the early previsualization stages, which allowed us to work on developing the CGI look in parallel with the art team, aiming for anything CGI in the film to have the texture of hand-drawn animation.

Similarly, by lighting and compositing CGI materials, we were able to work on creative tasks such as developing the look of the movie, from the earliest stages, bringing with it important efficiencies. These results were reviewed and finalized in the presence of the animation director, art director, colour designer, and director.

My work on the Battle of Edoras began with creating and lighting the CG background assets. They were essential in showing the size and scope of the battle, as well as the tactics being employed by the different combatants. We also created CG background assets to give the look of hand-drawn animation to the vast plains of Rohan, with camera mapping for each shot.

We had our CG animators create key animation for the horses and armies as a reference base. The hand-drawn animation teams then drew over the top, using our CG animation as reference, but correcting costumes, expressions, and other subtle actions to bring the battle to life.

The final step in the process of creating the battle scenes was to use the camerawork from the CGI key animation to composite VFX such as fire, smoke, and sparks. – SHUNSUKE WATANABE, SANKAKU STUDIO, CG/COMPOSITE DIRECTOR

The battle brings several simultaneous realizations for Helm; Wulf's Wild Men and Dunlendings are not fleeing when they see Helm's cavalry coming down on them, Lord Thorne's men are not on the western flank where they should be, and he should have listened to Fréaláf's warnings about the *mûmakil*, and now he and his forces are too far away to help. The enemy has laid a trap for him and now they have weapons of mass destruction on the field, heading for Edoras. Helm realizes that he doesn't have enough men to split his forces and deal with all of these threats. He has been outmanoeuvred, and he is going to lose the city. It's a shocking revelation for the king who has never lost a battle. – JASON DEMARCO, PRODUCER

Battle of Edoras key scene art, GH.

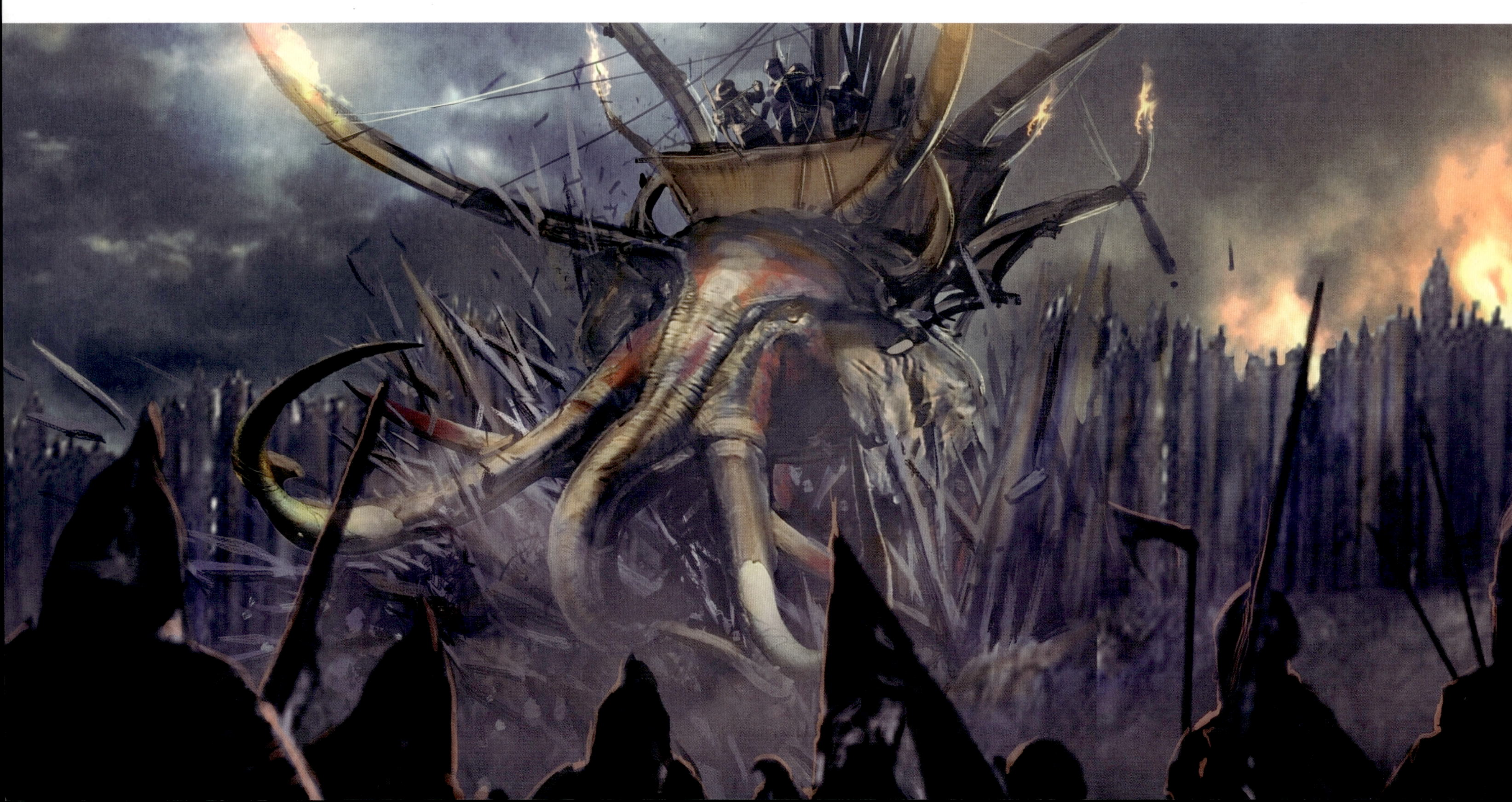

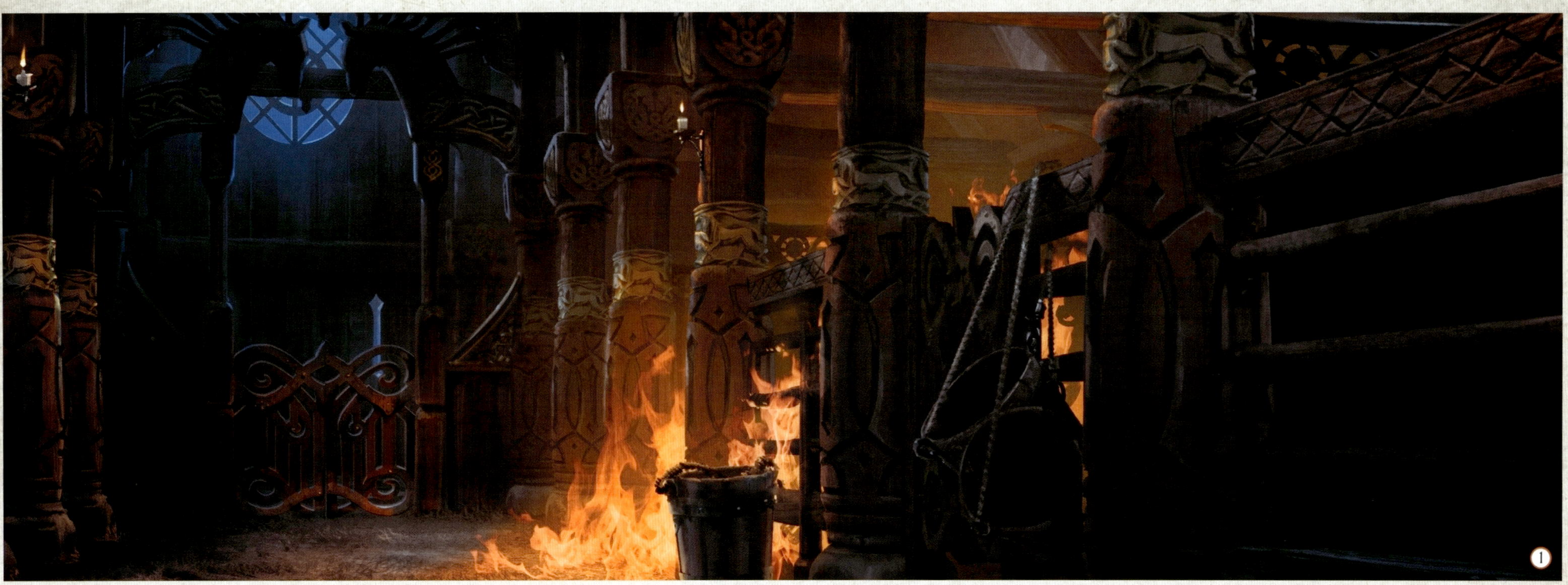

THORNE'S TREACHERY

Helm and his sons ride out to meet Wulf's forces in battle, leaving Héra behind in Edoras, but there she uncovers Thorne's treachery. We seeded that in Isengard when she first saw the crest of Thorne upon a parchment. Héra discovers the betrayal and acts to get her people out of the city. For her, it is always about the people.

Thorne's double-cross served multiple story functions – while it is a critical moment in Helm's arc, that he has been outmanouvered, it also allowed us to keep our heroine active in the storytelling during a battle that she is not a part of. Héra is the one who has the realization that Thorne is in league with Wulf, which allows her to take decisive action – she evacuates the city without hesitation. In another demonstration of the tight bond between the Rohirrim and their horses, Ashere fights to defend Héra when Thorne attacks her in the stables. Having Ashere step in also meant we could have Héra fight defensively rather than aggressively, which was an important part of who we envisioned her to be. – PHOEBE GITTINS, WRITER

The fire in the stables begins where Lord Thorne and Héra fight, but I made sure to show how and where it was spreading rather than just having the whole space in flames. – TAMIKO KANAMORI, ART DIRECTOR

When creating light-emitting fire effects we used Unreal Engine to check the lighting and layout of each scene. The amount of light and the depth of the shadows was always checked against directorial vision and the results communicated to the animators and background artists. – SHUNSUKE WATANABE, SANKAKU STUDIO, CG/COMPOSITE DIRECTOR

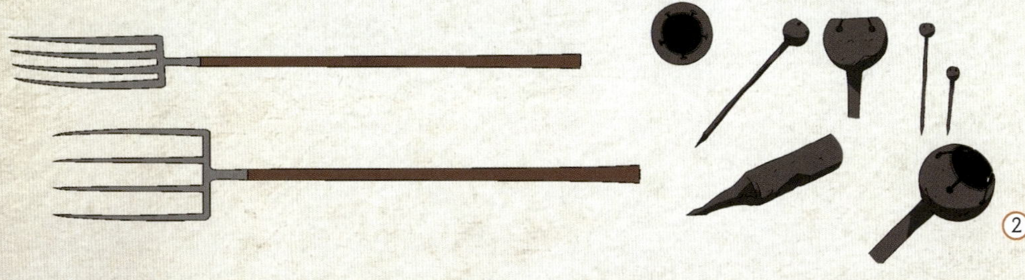

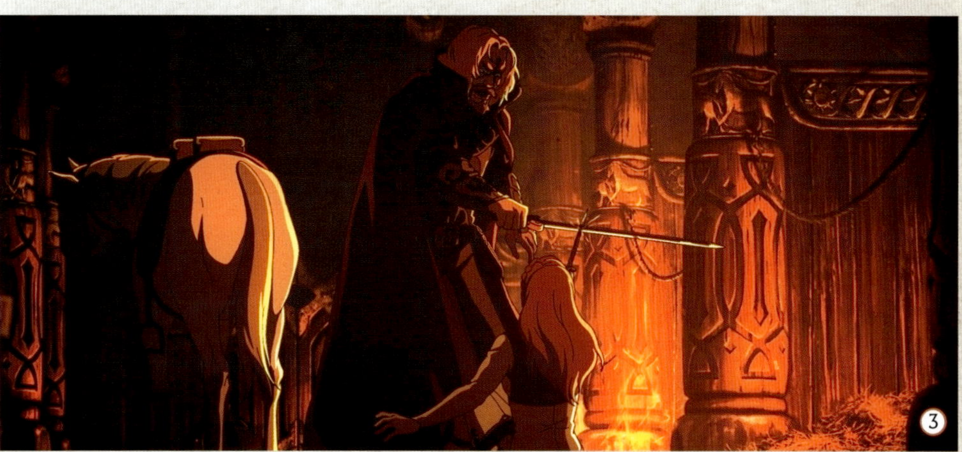

1: Edoras stables background setting art, TK. 2: Fork and torch prop setting art, KM. 3: Final film frame.

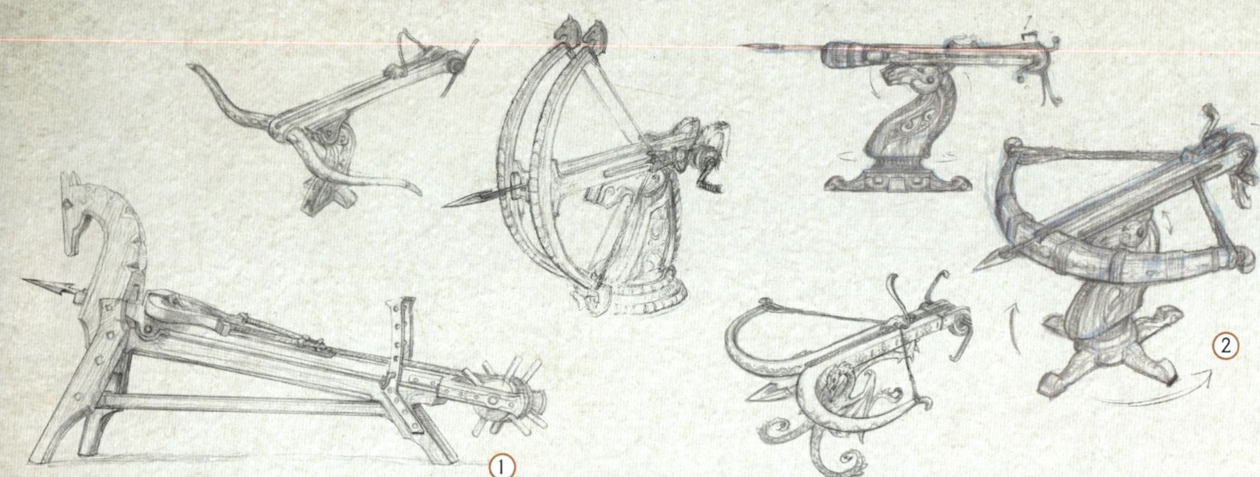

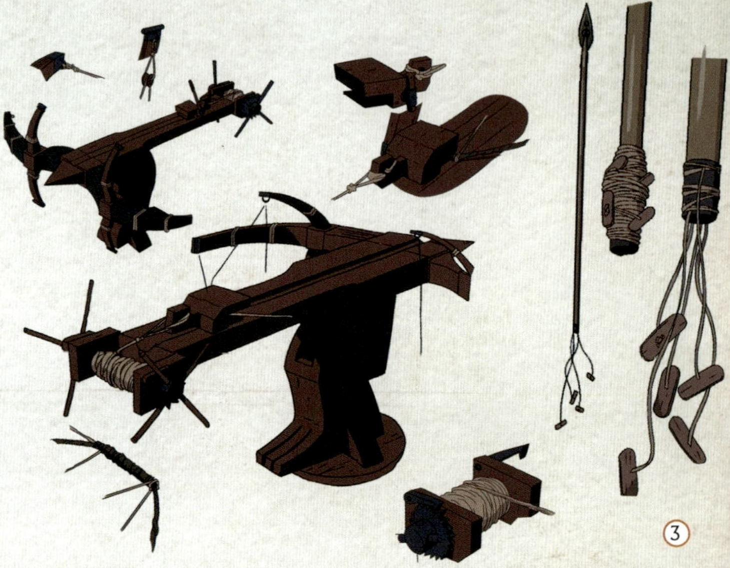

DEFENDING THE EAST GATE

I thought it might add interest to the look of the city if the fortifications weren't necessarily exactly the same as we saw in the live-action films. Adding a ditch and embankment to the outer wall in the previously unexplored part of the city might make the battle more interesting. Perhaps there might be a second gate, of a different design, on the newly created side of the town? The buildings might vary in design, with some perhaps being storage barns or larger houses, more stables, an armoury, or a blacksmith's forge. – ALAN LEE, CONCEPTUAL DESIGNER

Edoras has a number of gates along its walls, with differing defences. Héra identifies a threat at the previously unseen eastern gate and mounts a desperate defence to stall the advance of the Southrons and their mûmak. Part of her plan involves using a spear-hurling ballista, a new weapon in the Rohirrim arsenal.

Given the relative meagreness of the Edoras palisade, mobile ballistae might be moved between key defensive sites along the wall, such as the gatehouses. I imagined the vertical angle could be adjusted like a medieval cannon, though to change direction laterally it would have to be shifted by hand. – JOHN HOWE, CONCEPTUAL DESIGNER

We hadn't previously seen any evidence of the Rohirrim using mechanized weaponry. In fact, it had been a design choice to give the Uruk-hai crossbows and ballistae while the Rohirrim were depicted with short bows to underscore the industrialized nature of Saruman's army; but in this instance the action called for Héra to use a ballista to impale a *mûmak* with a spear. While we hadn't seen the Rohirrim employ such a weapon before, there were other examples of their use in the films, so it wasn't out of the question. What then, might a Rohirrim ballista look like? Might it be richly carved or ornamented with horse, sun, or bird imagery? Perhaps it wasn't originally from Rohan? Was it Dwarven, or from Dale, like the wind-lances we had seen in *The Hobbit*? – DANIEL FALCONER, ADDITIONAL CONCEPTS DESIGNER

For the final ballista design, we went for a realistic-looking weapon that possessed a solid structure, felt weighty, and had a contraption powerful enough to take down a charging *mûmak*. – KENJI MASUDA, PROP DESIGNER

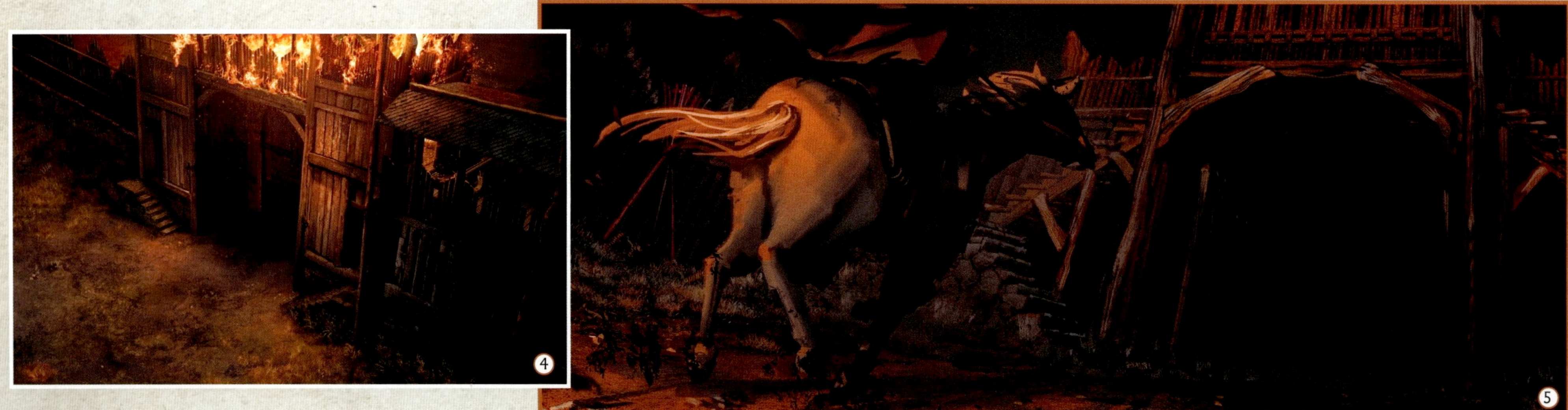

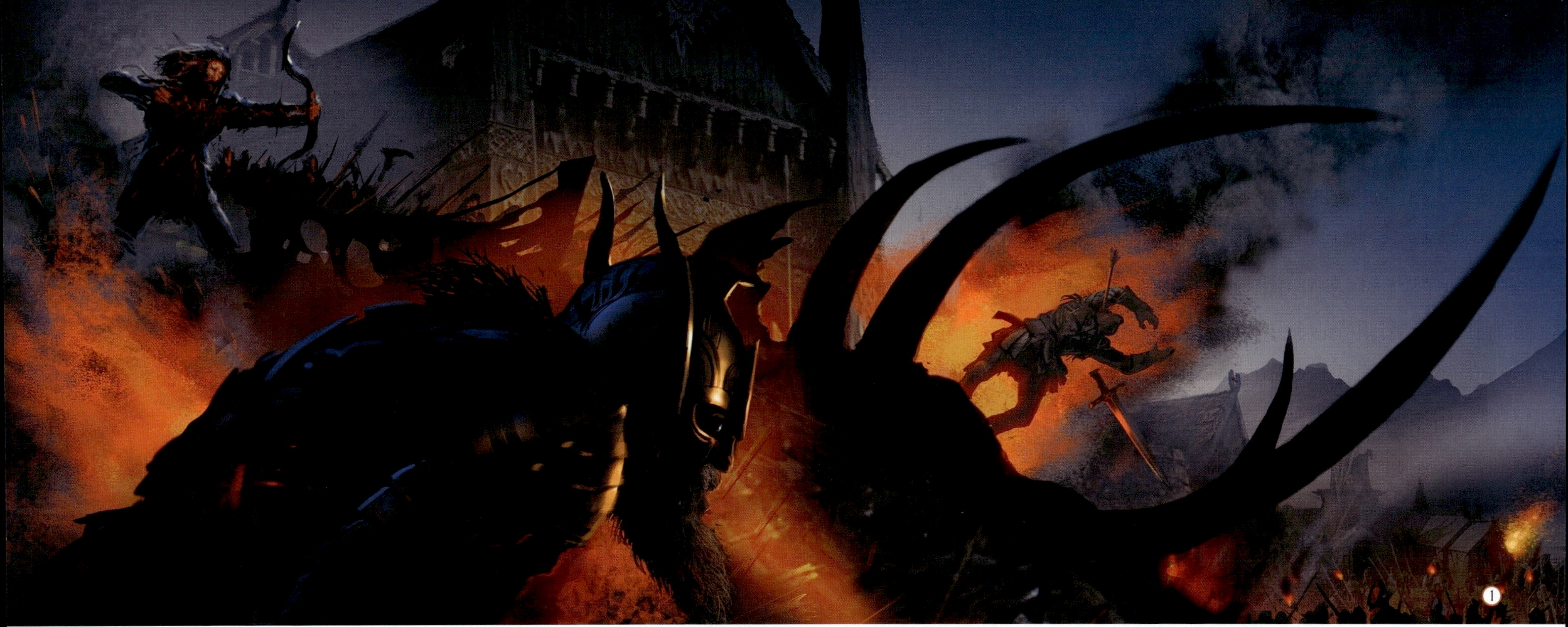

THE FALL OF HALETH

Haleth slays the *mûmak* charging towards the doors of Meduseld, and technically it is an epic, heroic act, but watching this majestic beast being hacked into is also savage and brutal. The line between noble prince and feral warrior is blurred and we get to see the type of leader Rohan would've had in Haleth after Helm's passing. – ARTY PAPAGEORGIOU, WRITER.

Haleth is not in the film for long so we had very few opportunities to demonstrate his valour. It was important that he had an epic moment, so in a feat of heroism Haleth defends Meduseld from a charging *mûmak* and singlehandedly slays the beast. But his victory is short lived, for Wulf has set a trap. He wants to destroy Meduseld – the home of the Rohirrim and symbol of Helm's power – but he also wants to wipe away Helm's legacy, including his sons. It all serves his need for revenge. The arrow that kills Helm's heir tears right through his throat. Haleth's victory and subsequent death had to be dramatic, a moment that begins as a triumph but is in fact the beginning of the end. – KENJI KAMIYAMA, DIRECTOR

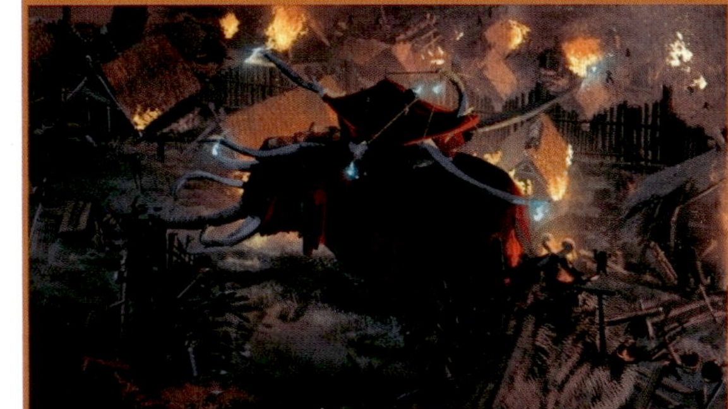

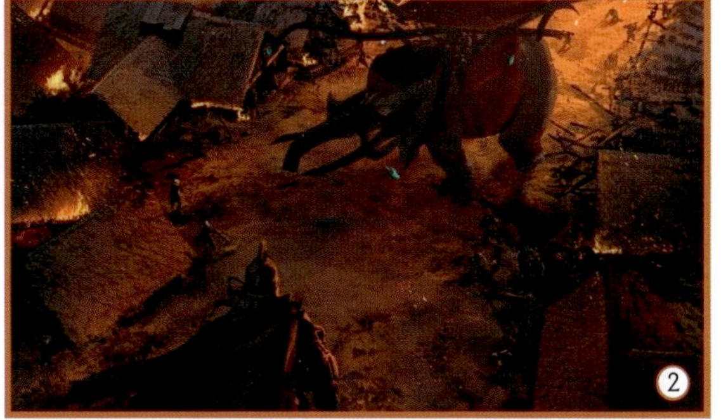

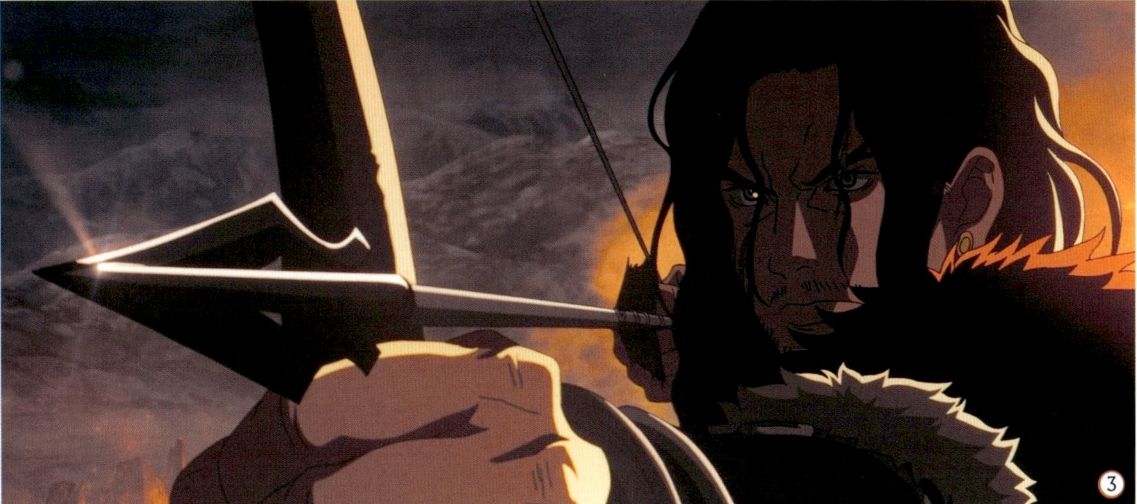

1: Battle of Edoras key scene art, JH. 2: Battle of Edoras key scene art, TK. 3: Final film frame.

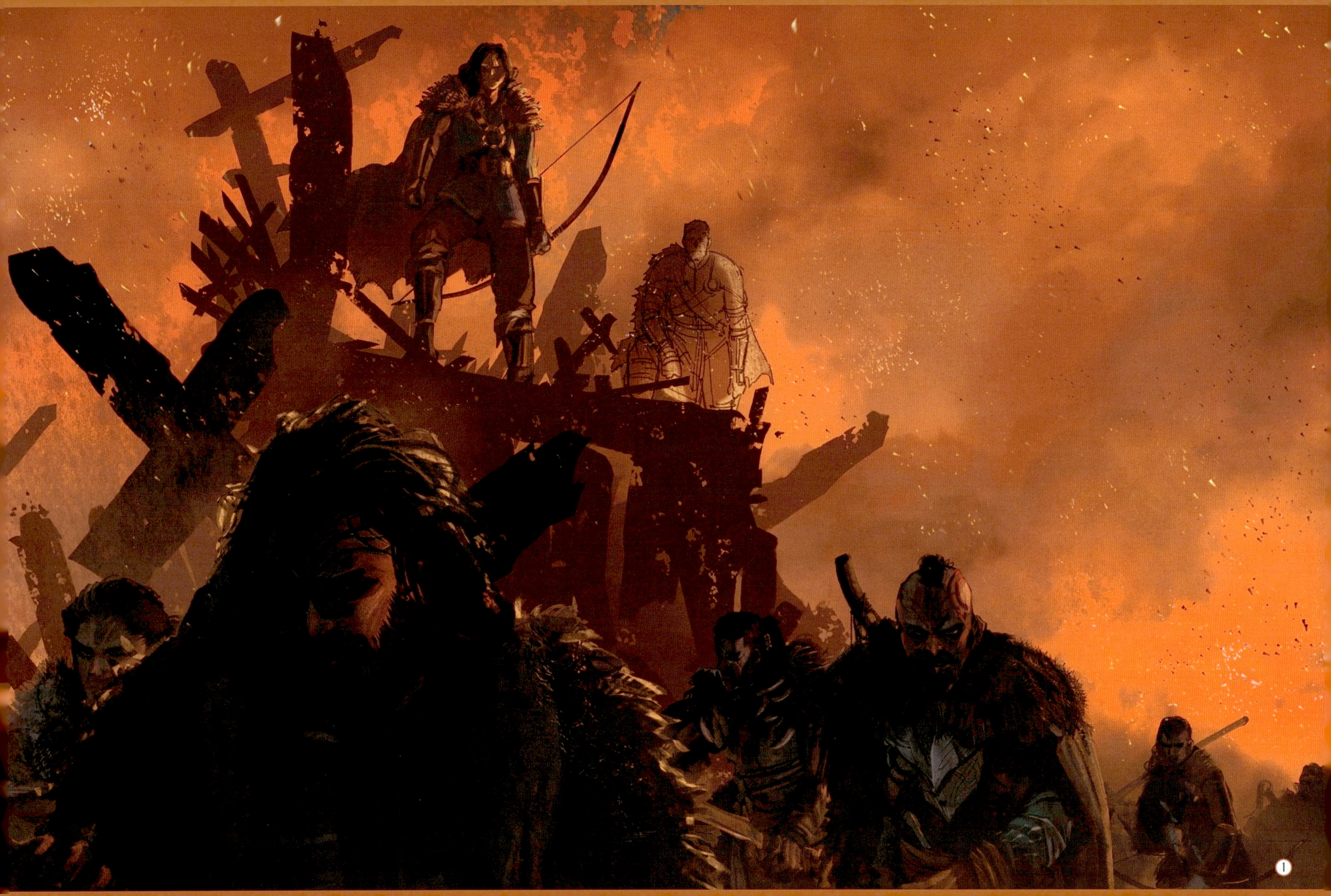

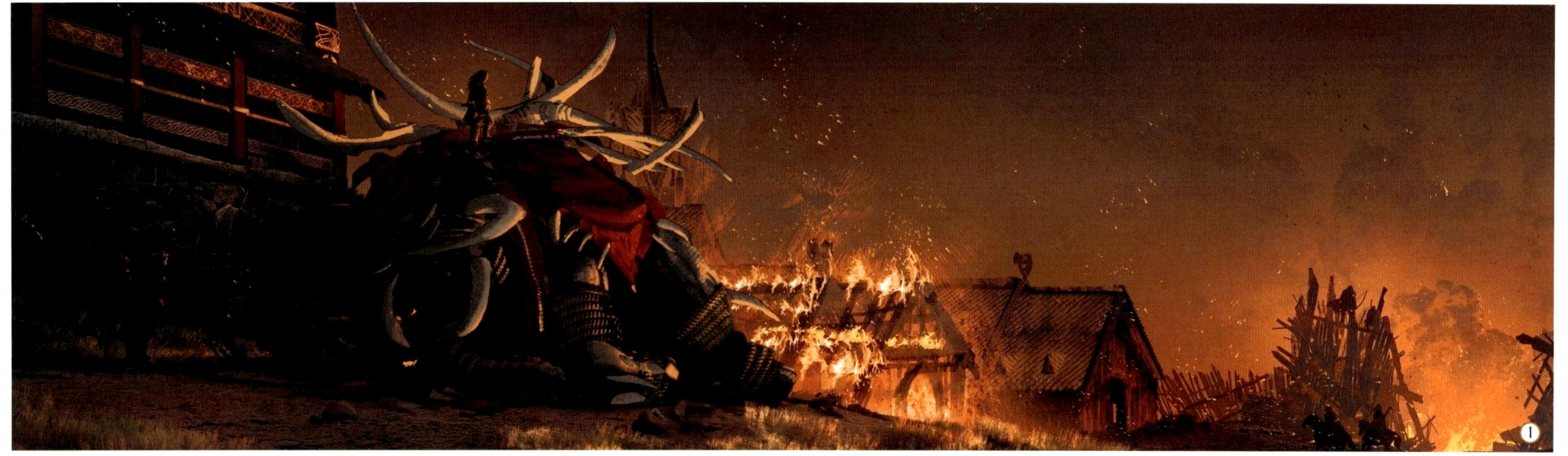

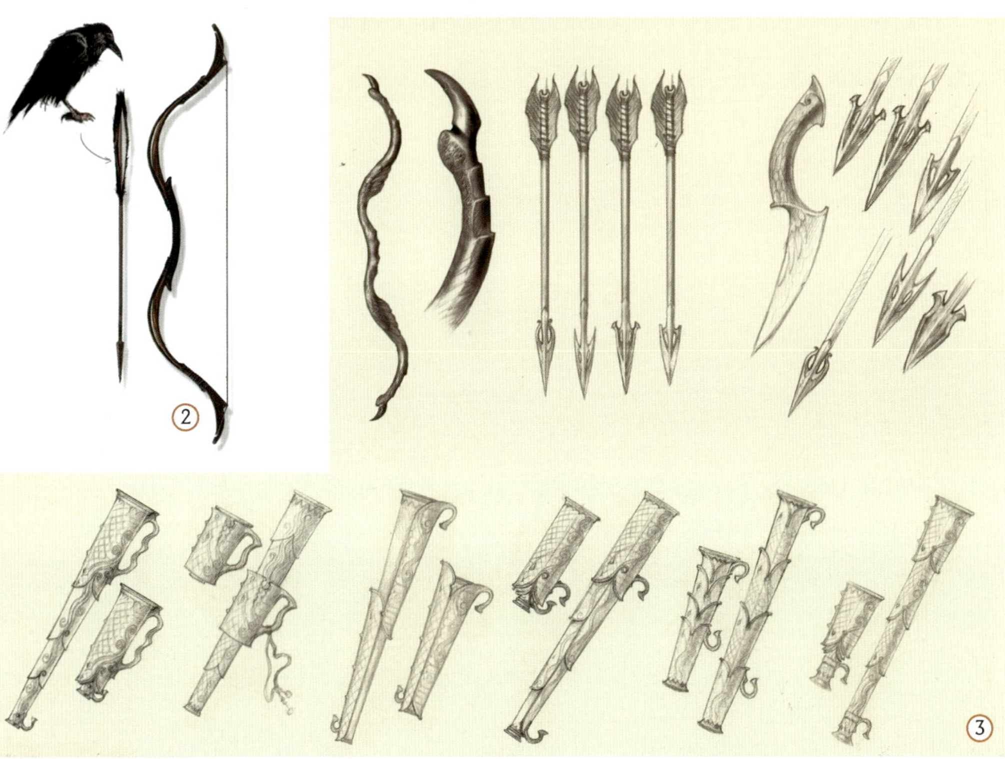

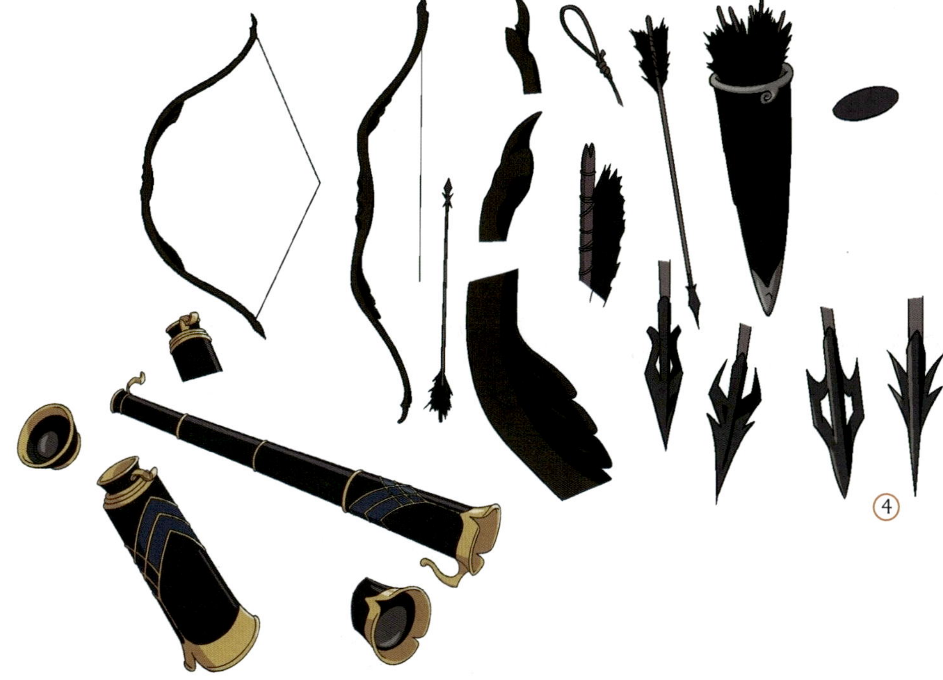

1: Battle of Edoras key scene art, TK. 2: Wulf's bow concept, DF. 3: Wulf's bow and spyglass concepts, JH. 4: Wulf's bow and splyglass prop setting art, KM. 5: Animation key frame, MT.

Continuing with the crebain theme for Wulf, I designed a short double-curved bow sculpted to resemble ravens' claws, possibly a dark wood and horn lamellate. The arrows had rough fletching, but well-forged points, difficult to pull out of a wound. – JOHN HOWE, CONCEPTUAL DESIGNER

Originally conceived as options for Héra's spyglass, conceptual designer John Howe's additional drawings were repurposed when Wulf needed his own telescoping device.

Reinventing the wheel, in a sense, I was trying to find other options for the telescoping function of the spyglass, with interlocking half-cylinders, and the addition of small handles to hook thumb and finger through to adjust and focus. I imagined that it was perhaps fashioned of boiled leather, with brass fittings. – JOHN HOWE, CONCEPTUAL DESIGNER

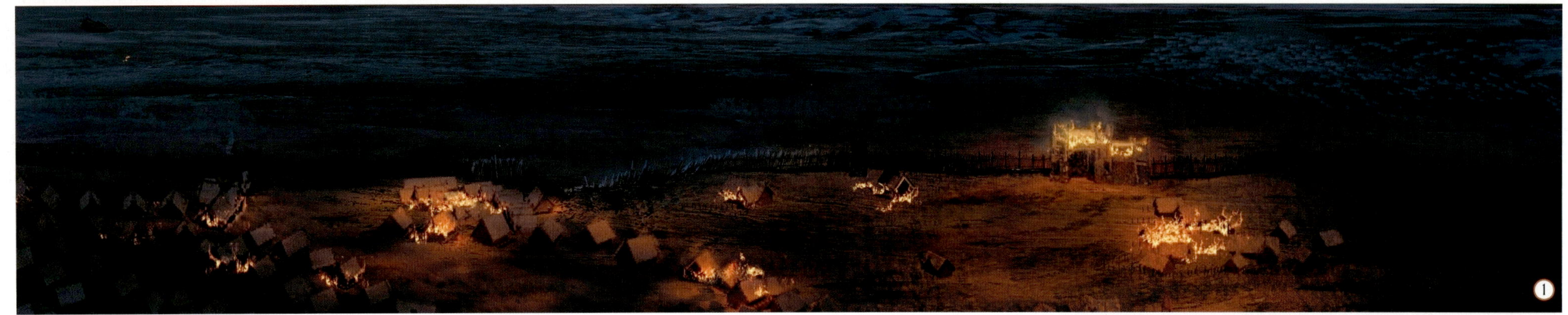

EDORAS IN FLAMES

On this film, fire was mostly achieved with visual effects, but to provide a guide for their size and colour we created temporary artwork for every shot of the battle, which was a lot of work. Usually flames and their effect on their surroundings are taken into account during compositing, when they are brightened, but on this project the exposure was also taken into account, making the result more realistic. It was good to be able to do this without relying on 3D lighting. – YASUHIRO YAMANE, ART DIRECTOR

Having artwork which was shared with everyone to guide the way in which all the elements came together was of critical importance. We had fire and smoke, and since it was a nighttime battle, it was very dark. It was very important that everything made sense for the artists working on the shots, but also that they communicated what was necessary to the audience. – TAMIKO KANAMORI, ART DIRECTOR

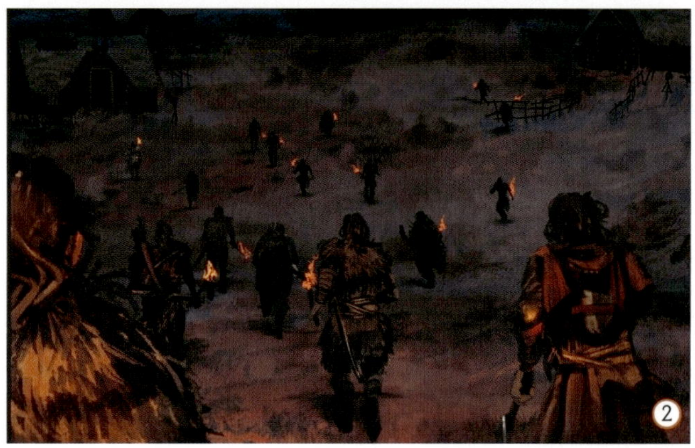

1: Battle of Edoras background setting art, TK. 2: Battle of Edoras key scene art, TK.

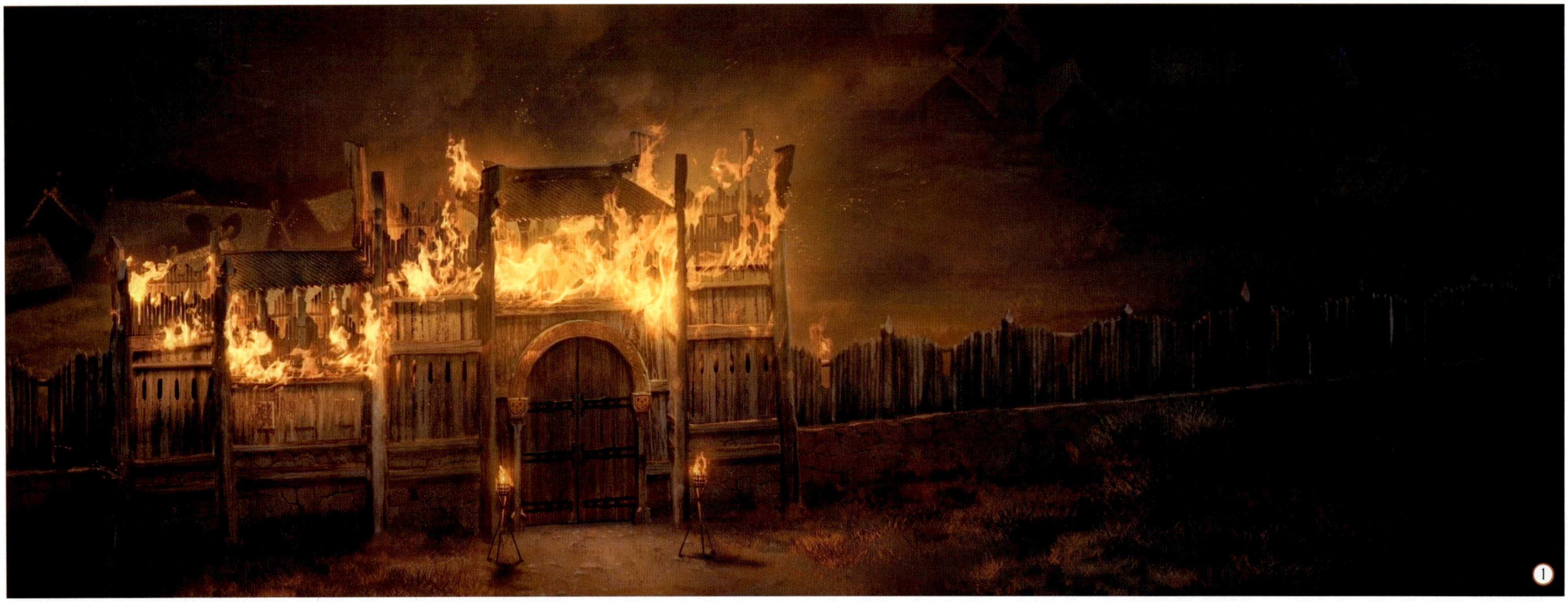

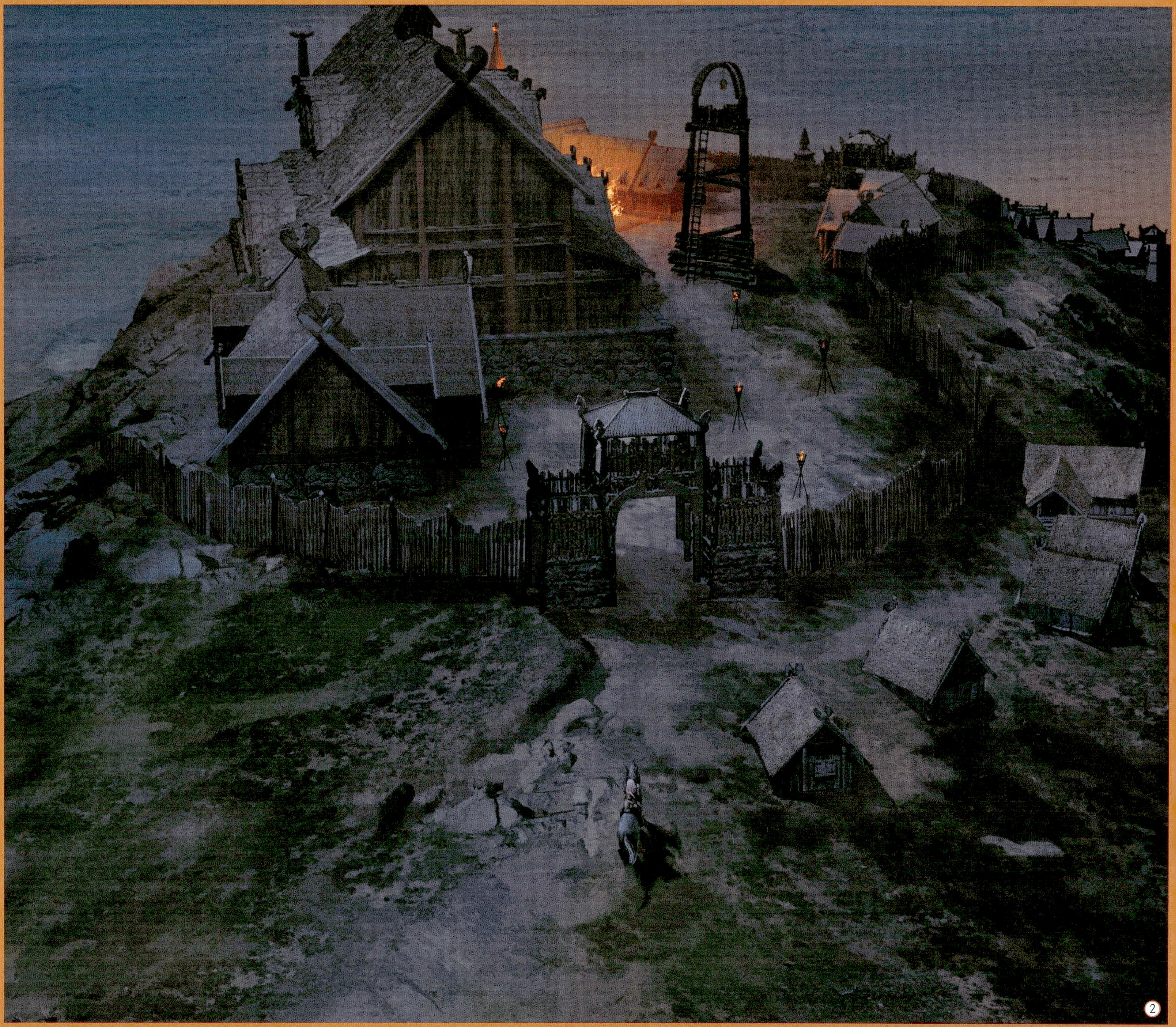

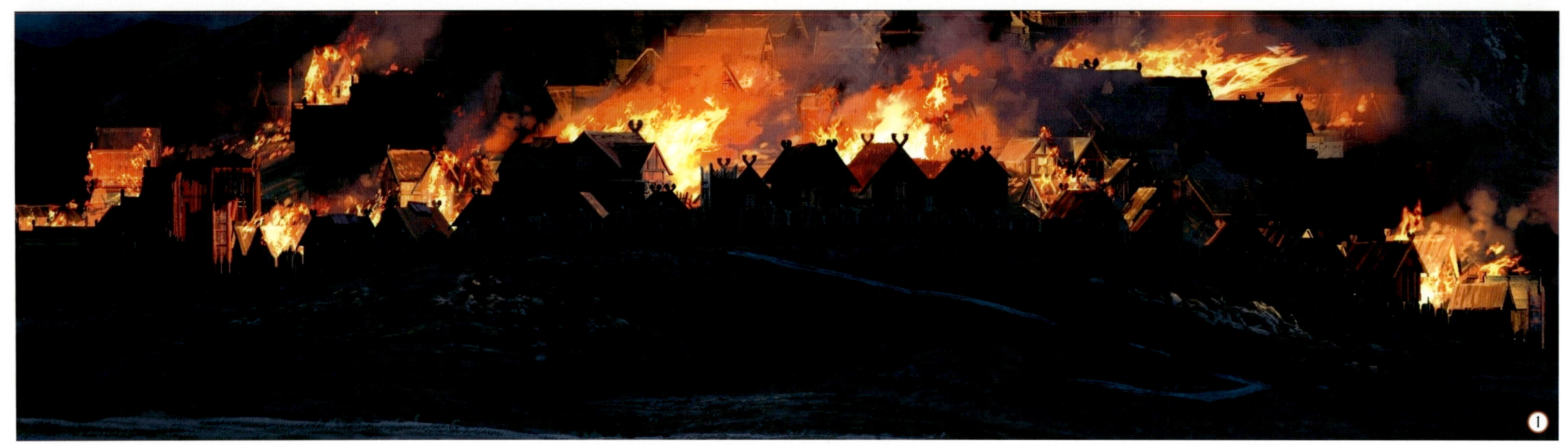

FLEEING EDORAS

The people of Edoras escape Wulf's attack and flee through the South Gate. This was a new part of the city not seen before, but we designed it to be in keeping with the gates and buildings of the rest of Edoras. – TAMIKO KANAMORI, ART DIRECTOR

Rohan's capital is emptied, but its people are saved, for the time being. With Wulf in pursuit, they must now embark on a long and difficult march toward the Hornburg. An impressive diversity of citizenry was designed by Miyako Takasu, ranging in age, gender, and station. While beasts of burden and livestock were talked about, the realities of production meant they wouldn't make it into the film, so the final carts and wagons were designed to be hauled by humans.

I had the task of coming up with concepts for various wagons and carts for the Rohirrim evacuees to use to carry their belongings. It was an enjoyable challenge to come up with different designs that shared a similar aesthetic, within the already established boundaries of what made sense for the culture of Rohan. It's always fun to try to find the right balance of cool and functional with a brief that is for a more everyday item or prop. – ADAM ANDERSON, WĒTĀ WORKSHOP SENIOR CONCEPT ARTIST

Háma's horse, described in the script as his faithful old grey mare, cannot keep pace with the retreat and is lost in the rout. Unwilling to leave her, the prince resigns himself to being left behind, buying time for his loved ones' escape at his own expense.

Given his nature, I found it easy to imagine Háma caring deeply for his horse. I could picture him combing her mane. – MIYAKO TAKASU, ANIMATION CHARACTER DESIGNER & KEY ANIMATION SUPERVISOR

The loyalty between horse and rider is so important to the Rohirrim. It's at the heart of their culture, and it goes both ways, as Háma demonstrates when he won't abandon his horse. He grew up with her as a young boy. 'I trust the old girl.' he says, and they stick together during the retreat, despite falling behind. That part breaks my heart. – PHOEBE GITTINS, WRITER

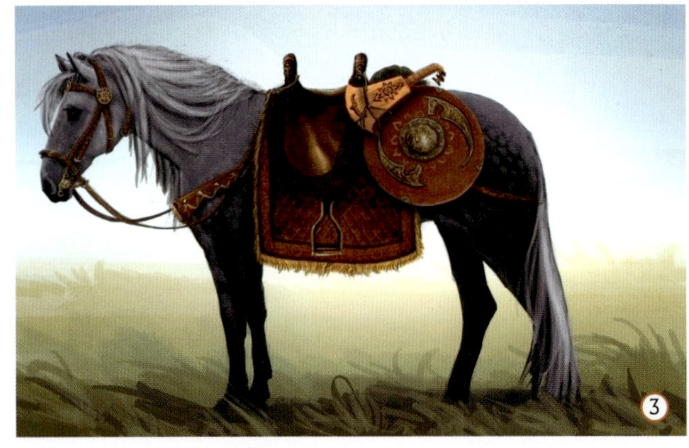

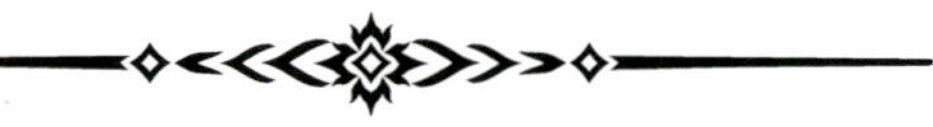

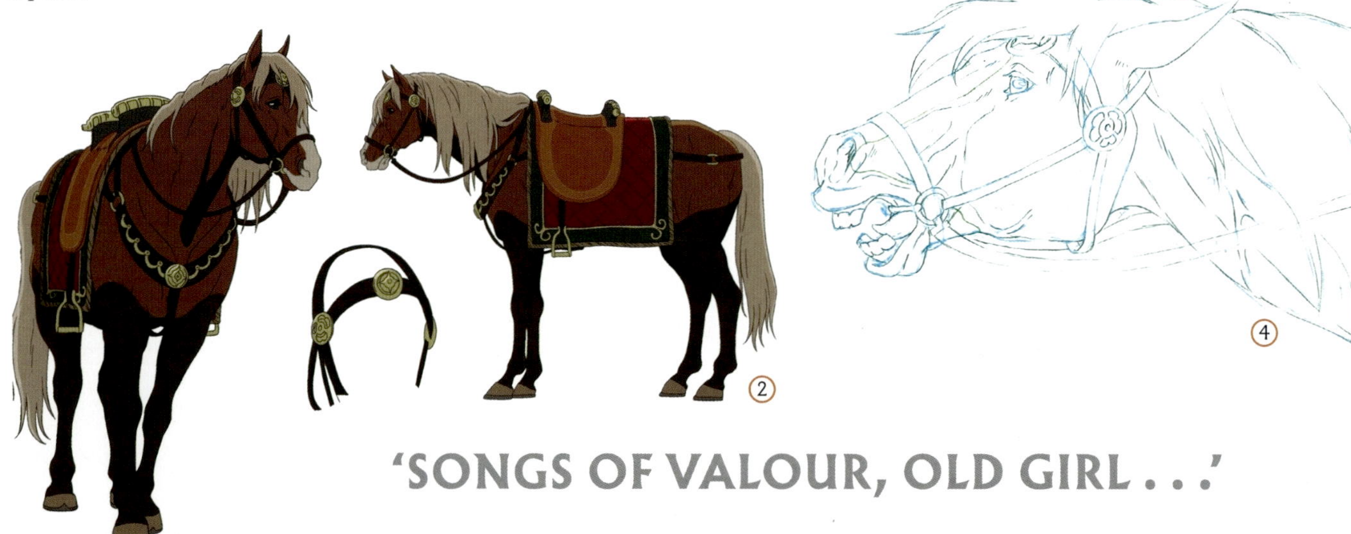

'SONGS OF VALOUR, OLD GIRL . . .'

1: Battle of Edoras background art. 2: Háma's horse setting art, MT. 3: Háma's horse concept, DF.
4: Animation key frame, MT. 5: Rohirrim cart concepts, AAH. 6: Rohirrim cart prop setting art, AAH.
7: Rohirrim refugees character setting art, MT. 8: Rohirrim refugees character setting art, SH & AS.

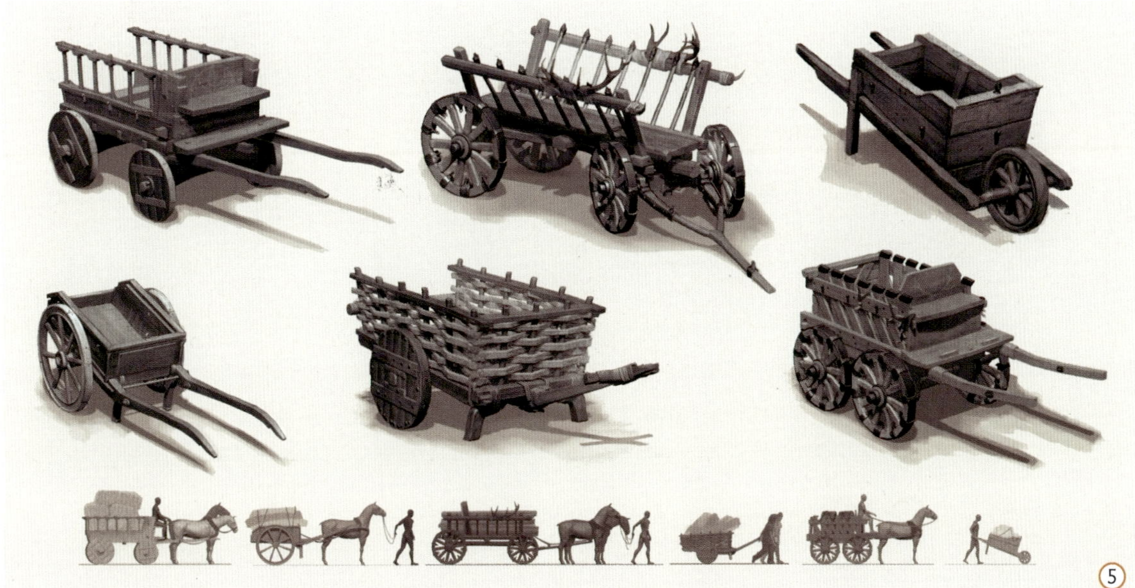

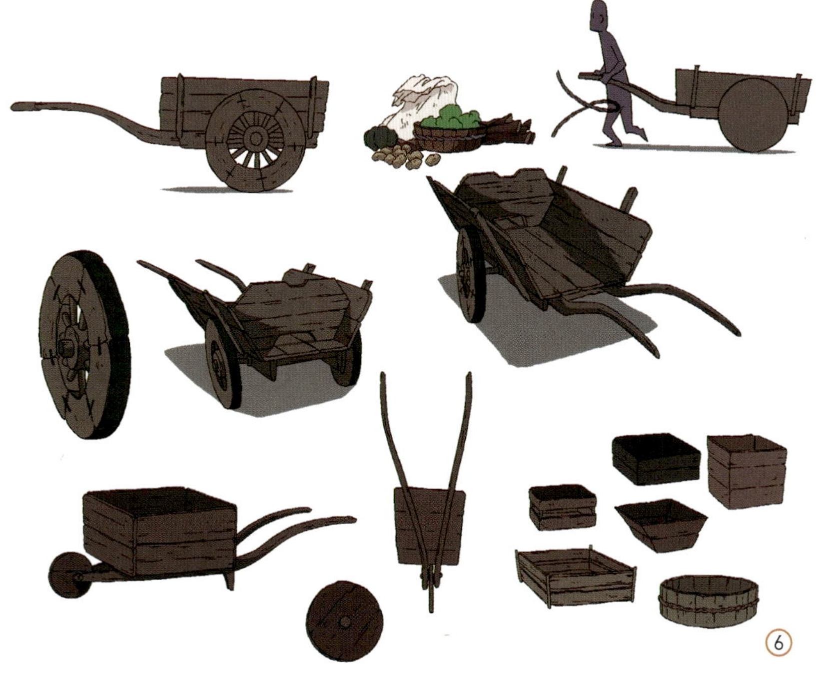

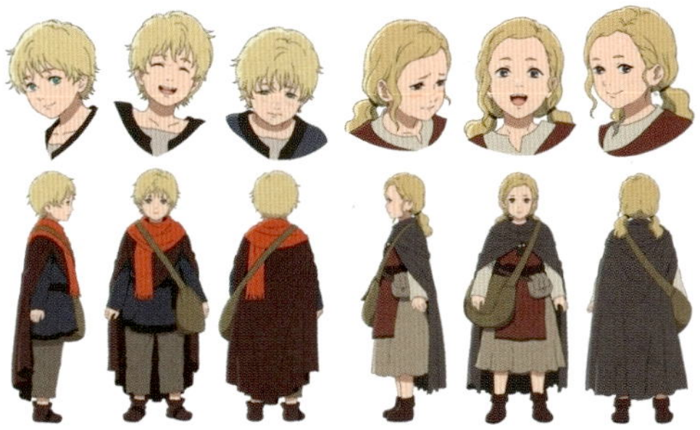

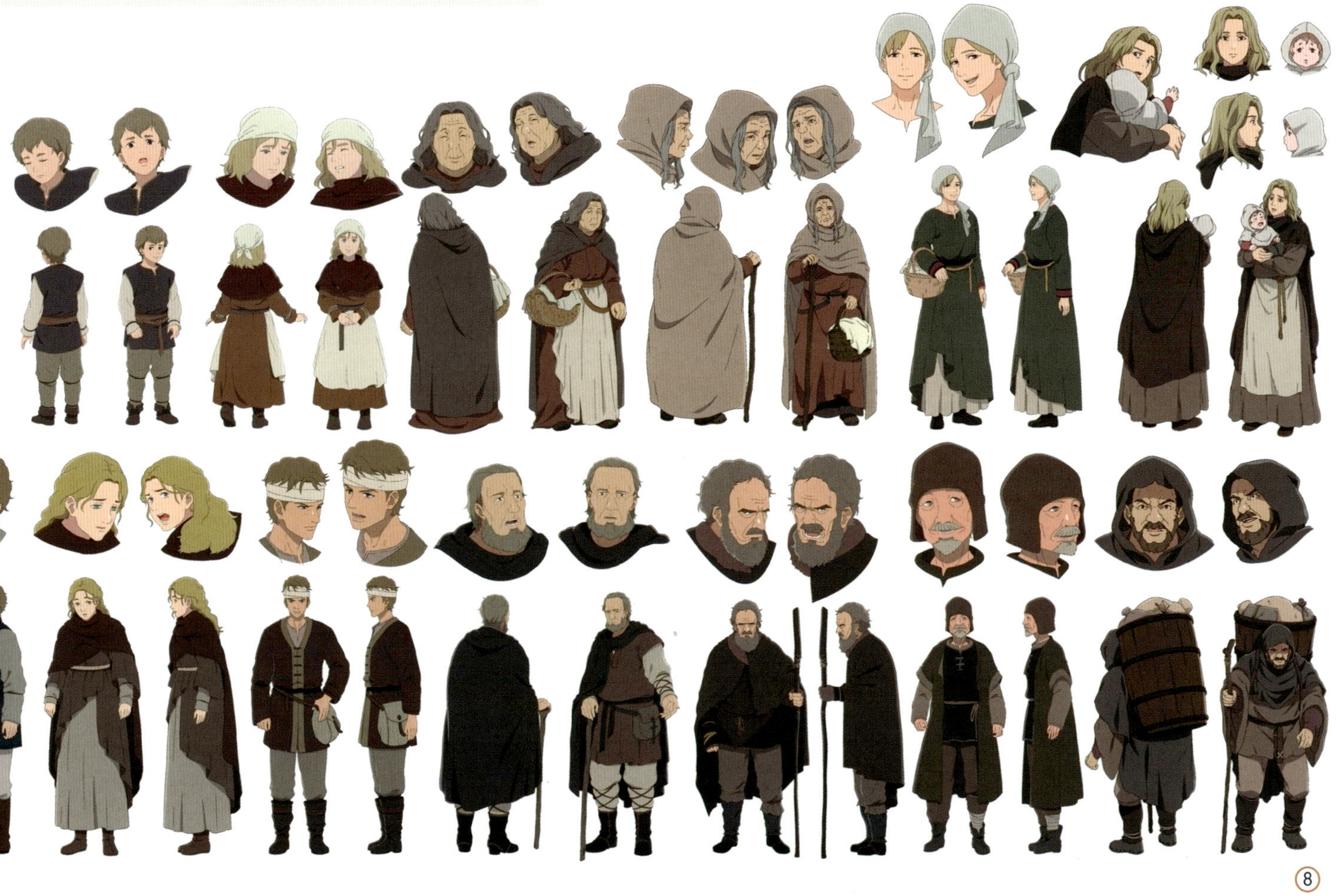

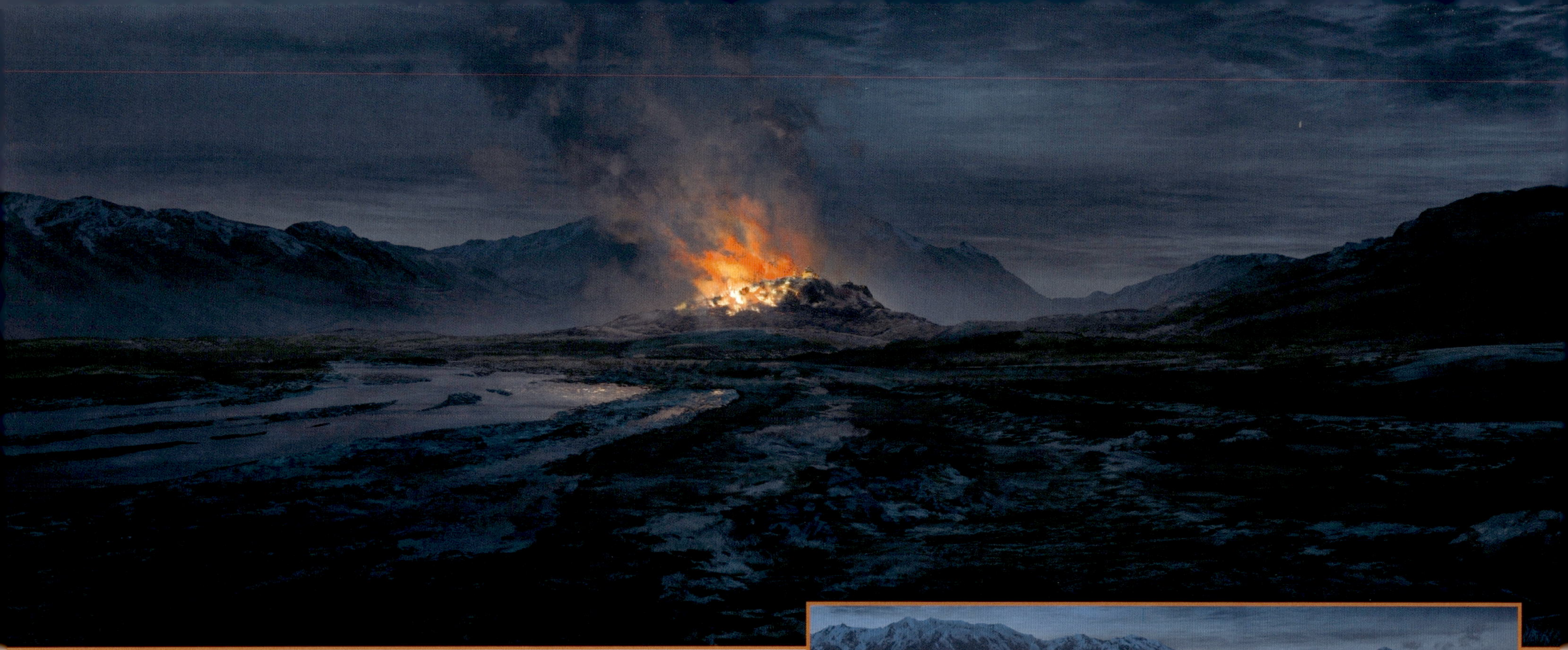

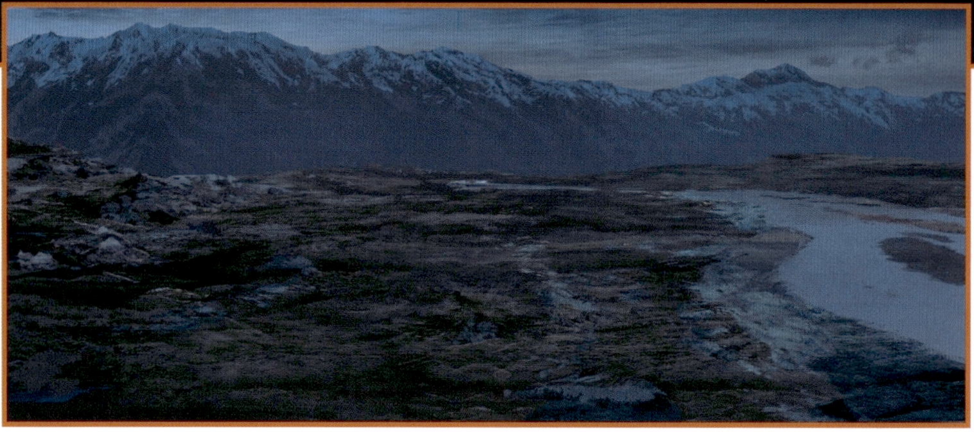

We designed the plains upon which Héra and the others flee based on careful study of photography and landscapes from the live-action films. We looked at the scenes in which King Théoden led his people from Edoras to the Hornburg in *The Two Towers*, imagining that our characters probably took a similar path, but in the end this did not appear in the finished film. – TAMIKO KANAMORI, ART DIRECTOR

I thought Kamiyama san made a powerful choice in showing the burning of Edoras from the perspective of the fleeing refugees, turning back from afar to see their home in flames and realizing they may never return – it's such a gut punch. – PHOEBE GITTINS, WRITER

Flight from Edoras background setting art, TK.

'RUN THEM DOWN!'

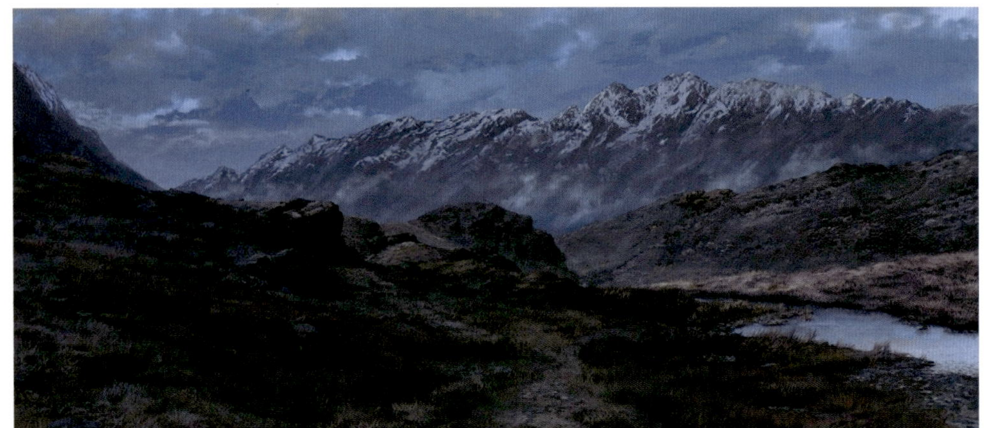

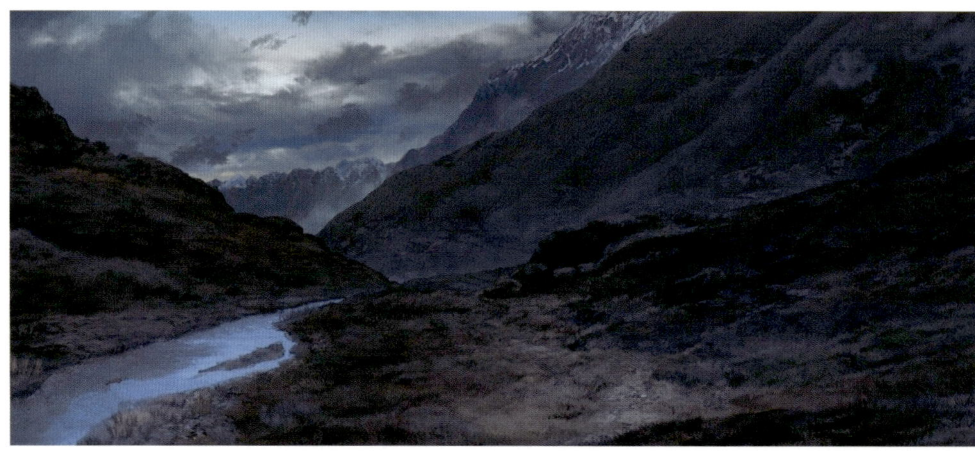

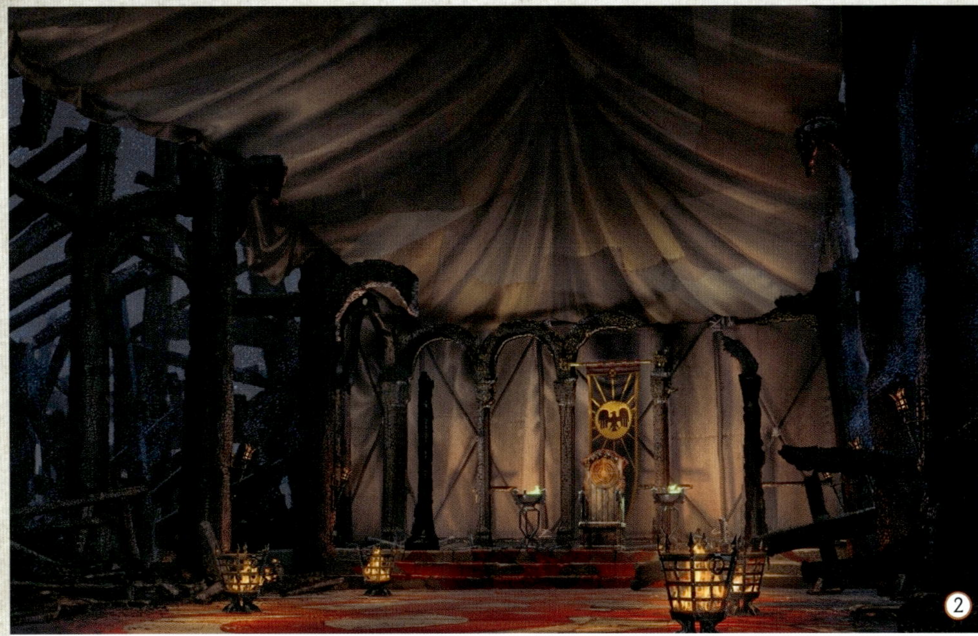

THE ASHES OF MEDUSELD

Wulf is not thinking about being a king; his thinking only takes him as far as what he can take from his enemies; what he can destroy. He wants revenge. He wants to hurt Helm. We thought, if he is willing to allow *mûmakil* smashing into Edoras and setting the city aflame, then he doesn't really care what happens to Meduseld. Kamiyama san thought it would be a powerful image to see him sitting in the wreckage of Meduseld. It wasn't in the script, but when you think about any important, old structure in our own world, so many of them have been through trials, been damaged and rebuilt or repaired. They carry that history. — JASON DEMARCO, PRODUCER

Photographs of burnt-out structures were our primary reference for the burned husk of Edoras, especially the remains of ruined temples and churches. We were told that they wanted the centre of Meduseld to be cleaned up for Wulf, so that's the only place that's free of rubble. — TAMIKO KANAMORI, ART DIRECTOR

We wanted the remains of Meduseld to give the impression of a carcass of some large animal. The model was designed and built at Sankaku Studio. — YASUHIRO YAMANE, ART DIRECTOR

It will be a shock to fans who know and love this place, given how iconic it is, but we knew that we had to burn down the Golden Hall. It is a dramatic representation of what is at stake and a metaphor for what Wulf has done to the Rohirrim. It was also ironic to show Wulf pretending to be a king within a burned-out palace. — KENJI KAMIYAMA, DIRECTOR

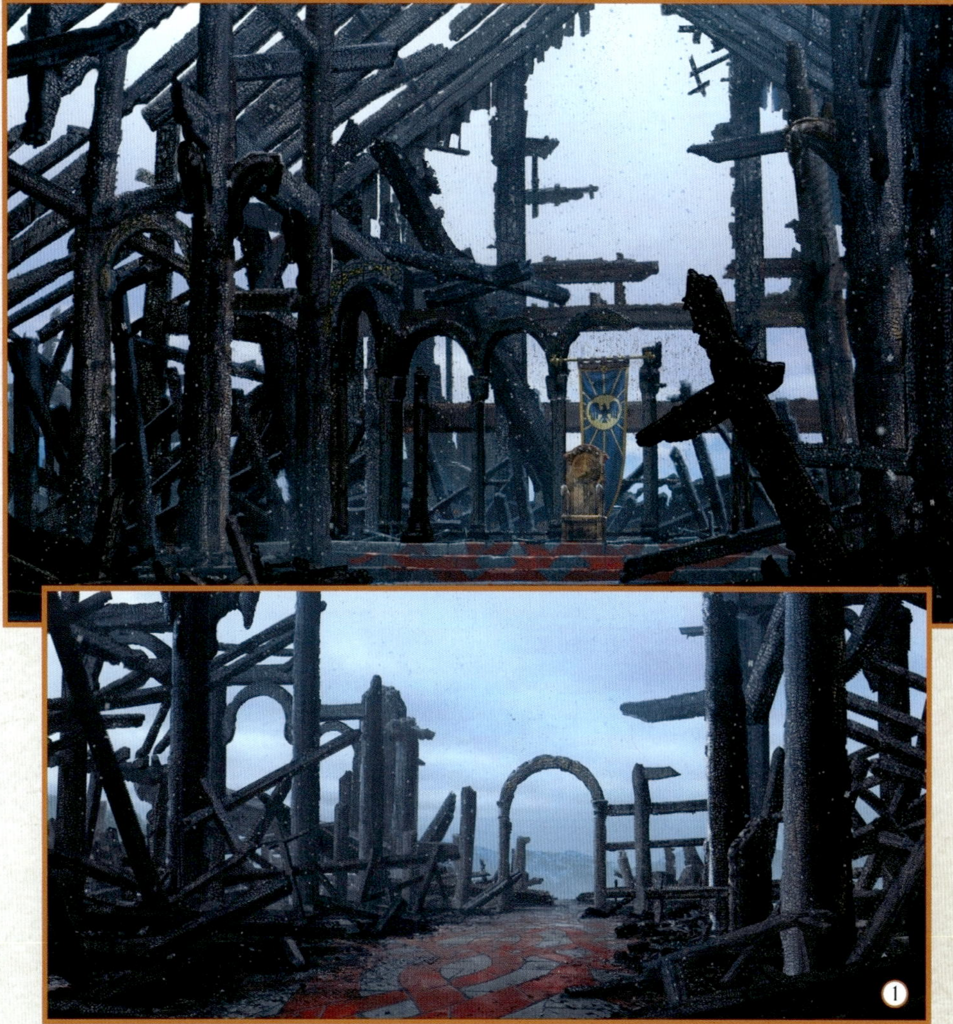

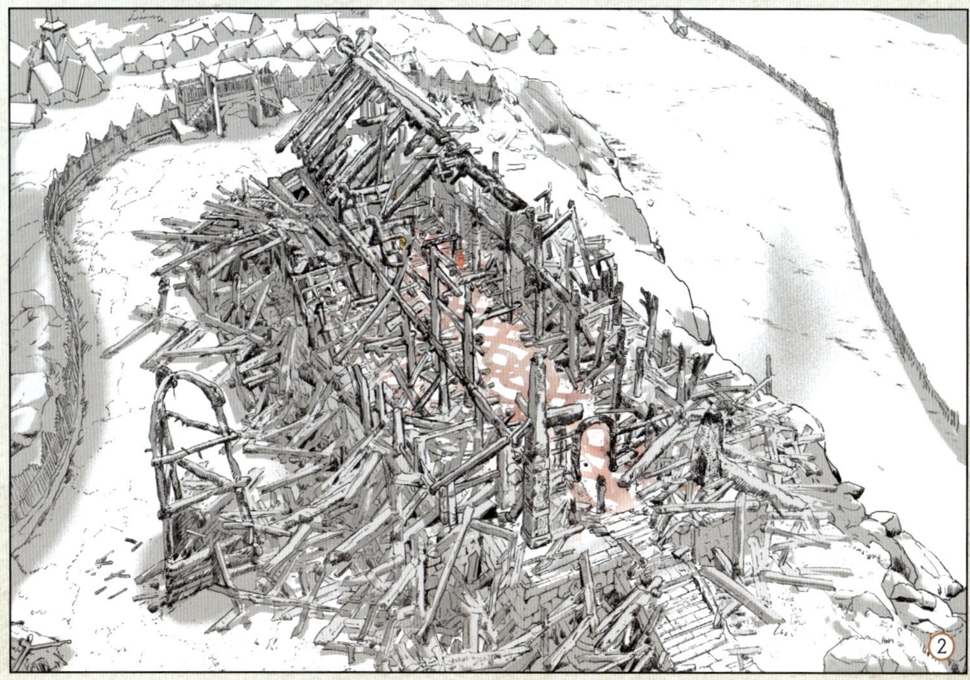

1: Burnt Meduseld background setting art, TK. 2: Burnt Meduseld concepts, TK.

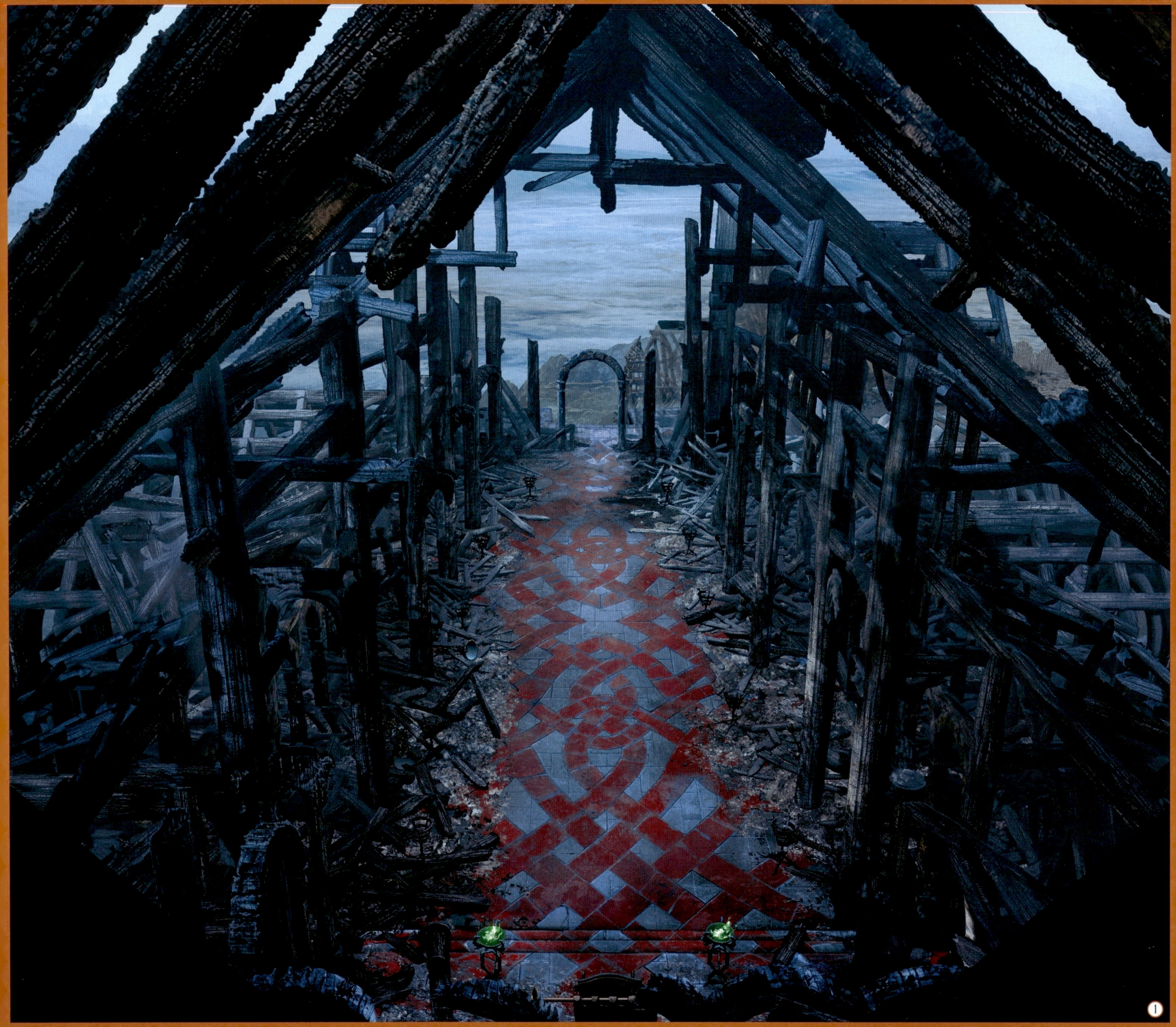

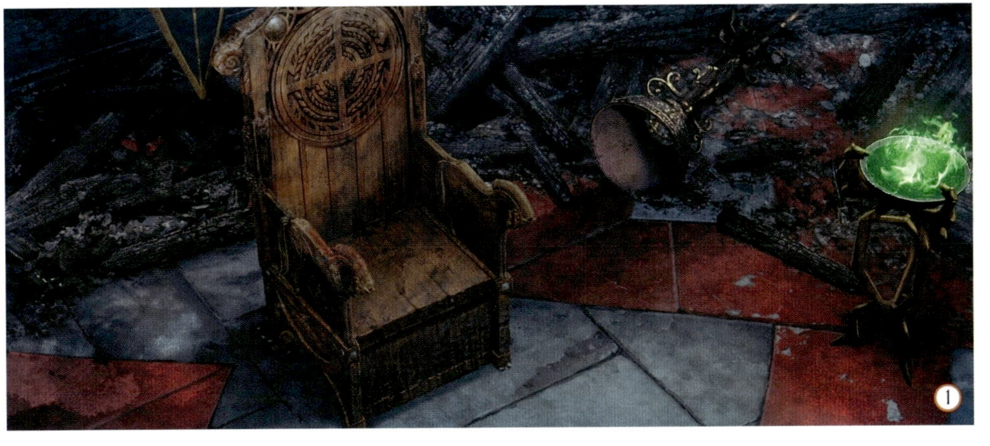

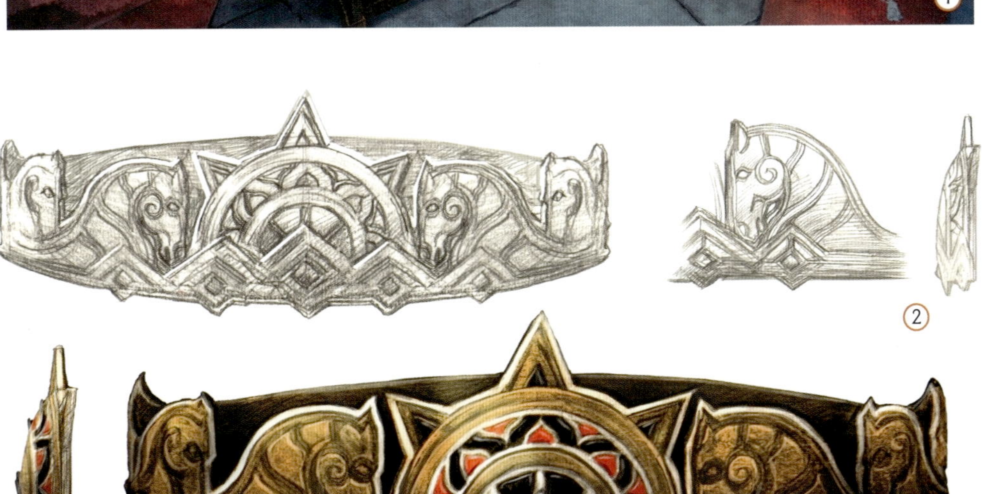

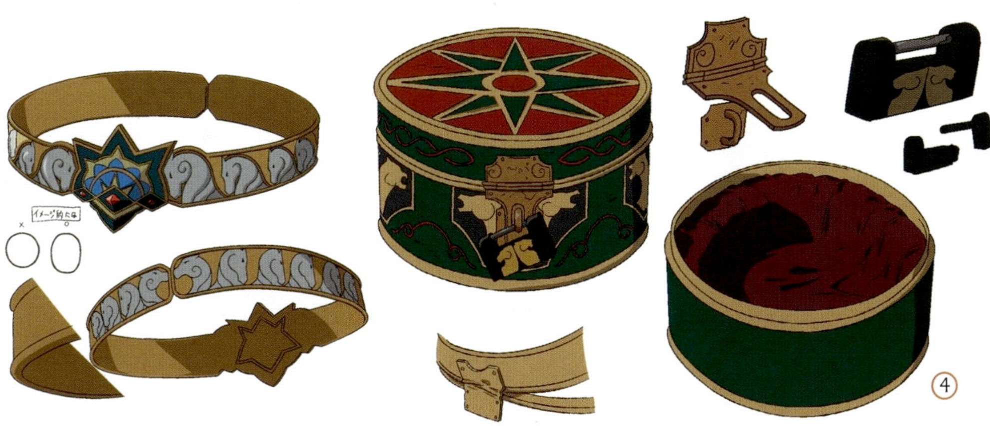

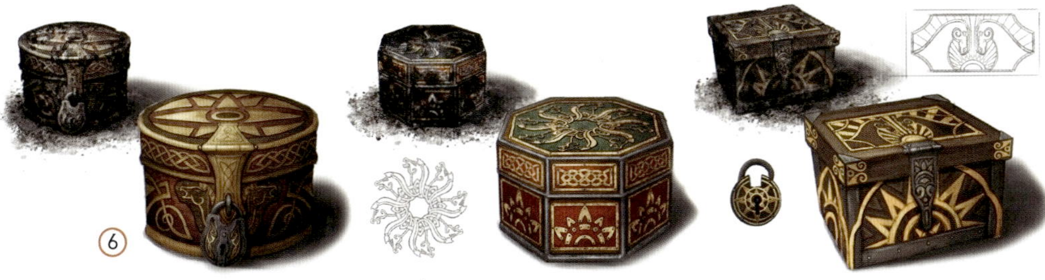

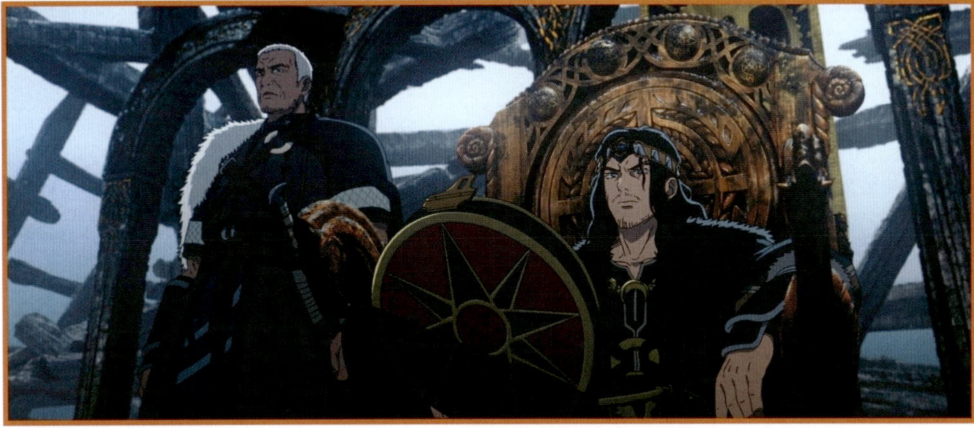

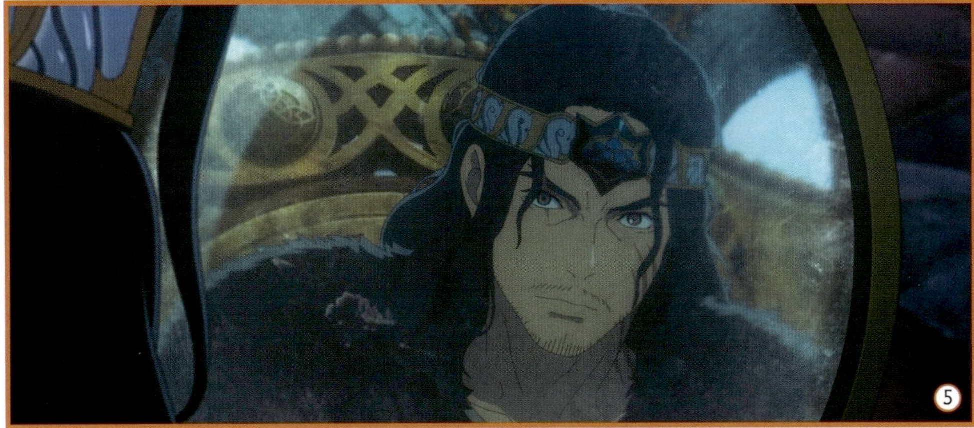

THE CROWN OF ROHAN

Helm's was more a sturdy circlet than a traditional crown. It combined equine motifs with the sun symbol of Rohan, evoking the vitality of their people (and their attachment to freedom), and the eternally renewed dawn over the land of the Rohirrim. – JOHN HOWE, CONCEPTUAL DESIGNER

For the final animation design of the crown, I used the ones that we saw in the live-action films as reference. I wondered if it would work because of the thinness, but it turned out okay as a realistic accessory for Helm, Wulf, and Fréaláf to wear in succession. I think it was difficult for the animators, because of the confusing number of horse patterns they had to draw on it. – KENJI MASUDA, PROP DESIGNER

For the case that housed the crown of Rohan, I tried to include iconic Rohan imagery, such as the horse heads and sun, or Celtic-inspired knotwork that swirls all over both their armour and Meduseld. The earthy green and brown with gold accents were also drawn from the established aesthetic. – IONA BRINCH, WĒTĀ WORKSHOP CONCEPT ARTIST

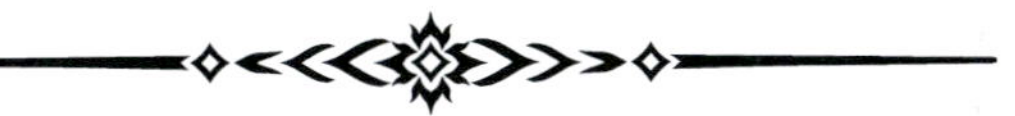

1: Burnt Meduseld background art. 2: Crown of Rohan concepts, JH. 3: Crown of Rohan concept, JH & DF. 4: Crown of Rohan and crown case prop setting art, KM. 5: Final film frames. 6: Crown case concepts, IB.

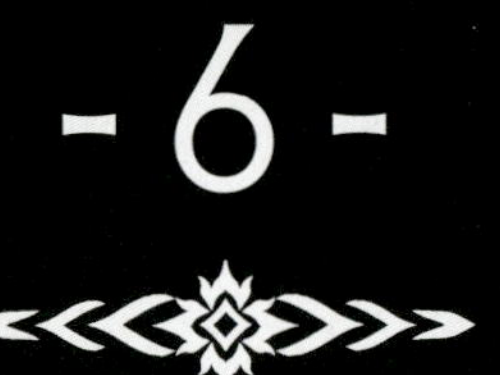

- 6 -

THE HORNBURG

Héra leads her people west to the Hornburg, an ancient fortress where they can find shelter behind tall stone walls. Wulf catches up with them as she helps Helm to the gate. The vengeful leader of the Dunlendings has Háma captive. Helm offers his own life for his son's, but Wulf is consumed by wrath and grievance, and brutally kills the youth before his father's eyes. As the last of the Rohirrim retreat inside the enemy makes camp before the walls, settling in for a siege.

A savage winter sets in, driving the Rohirrim deep into the carved passageways of their fortress. The old keeper of the keys tells tales of ghosts and darkness when Héra finds a dusty wedding dress as she takes stock of their provisions. The mood in the keep is somber. This place may yet be their tomb.

Helm is overcome by the death of his sons. Wounded and heartsick, he falls into a swoon and is attended by Héra and Olwyn at his bedside, but hope is fading with the king.

Then one night Héra is surprised when she awakens by her father's bed to find him gone. Searching the room, she finds a secret passageway that leads deep beneath the fortress, eventually joining a natural cavern system and emerging on the snowy slopes of the mountainside beyond the wall.

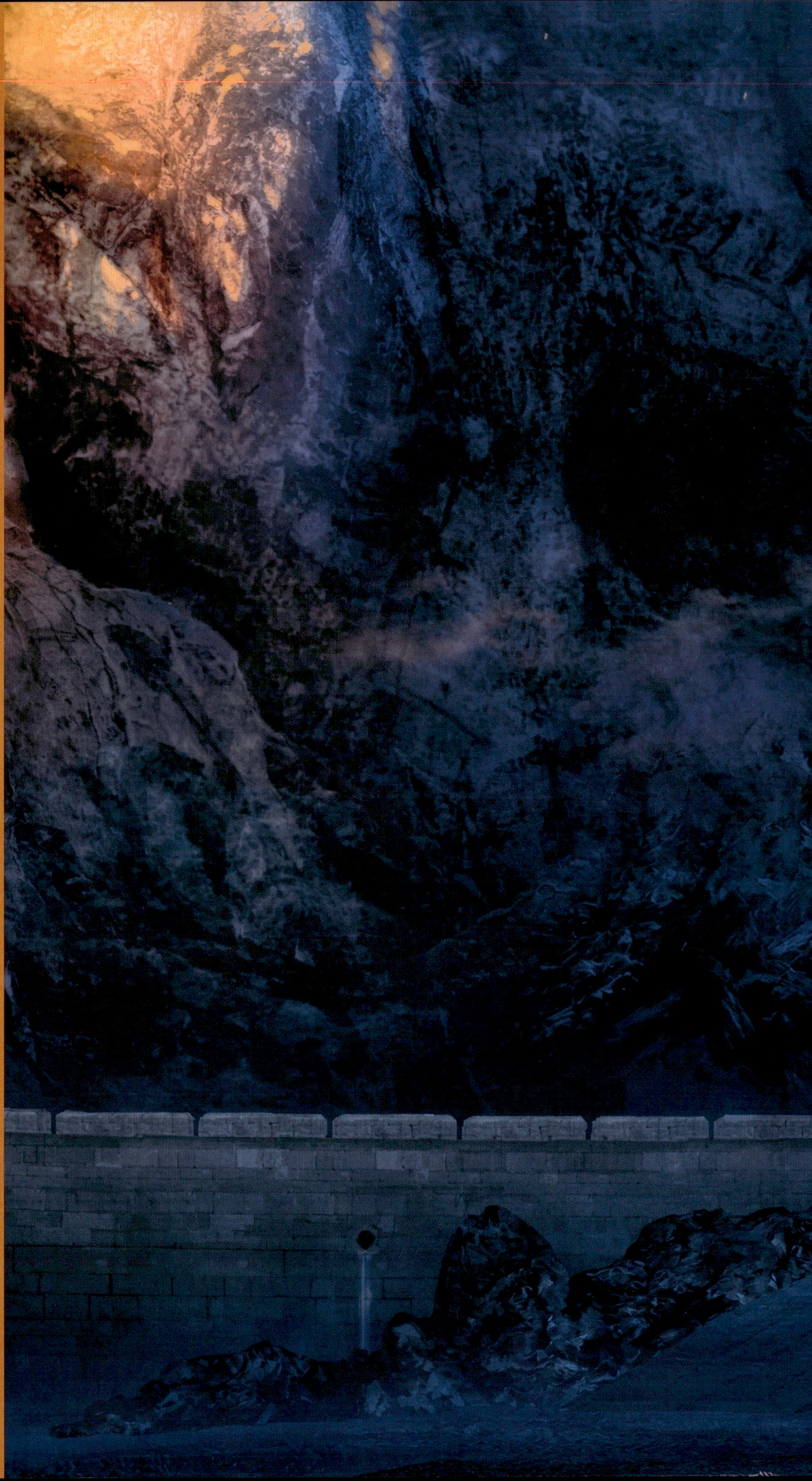

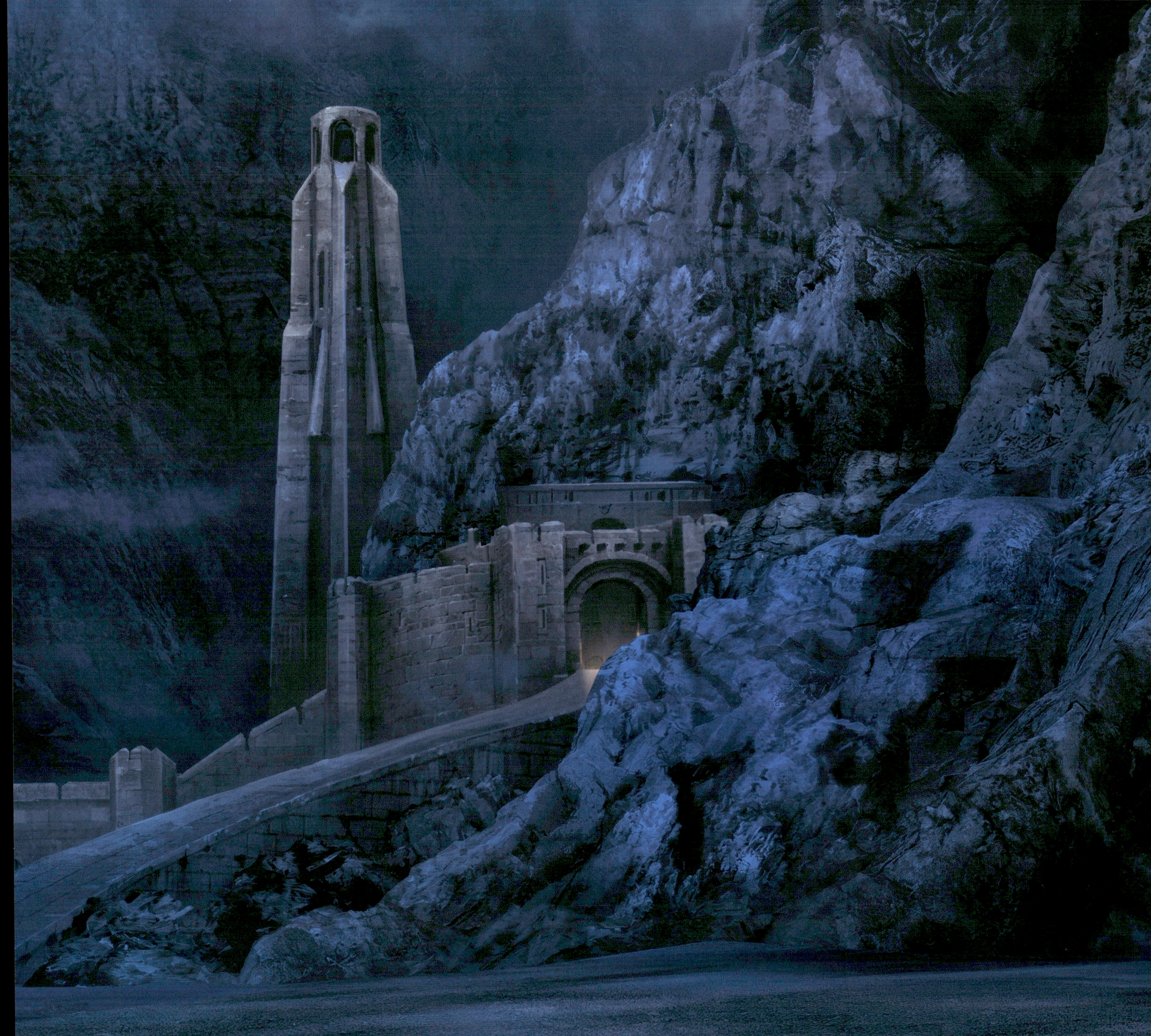

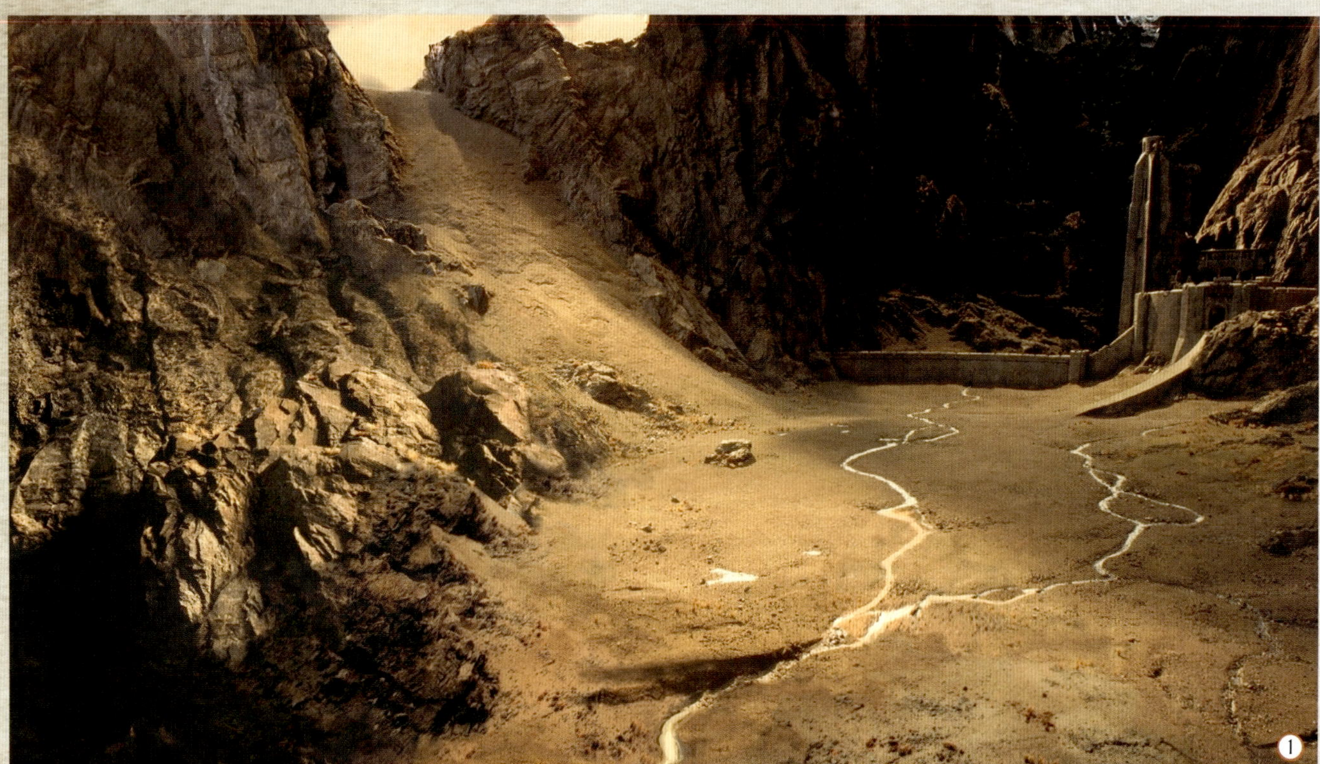

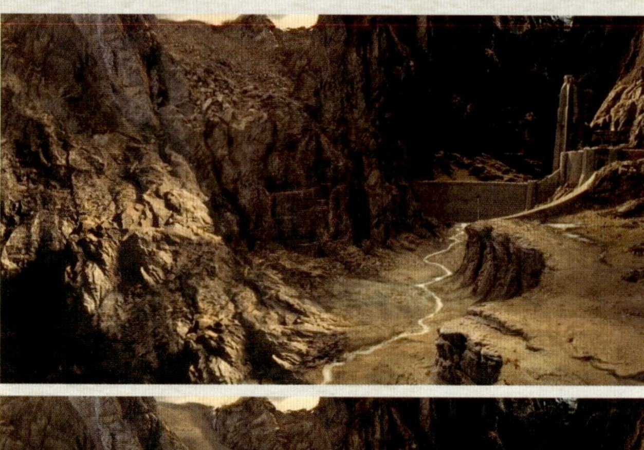

THE HORNBURG

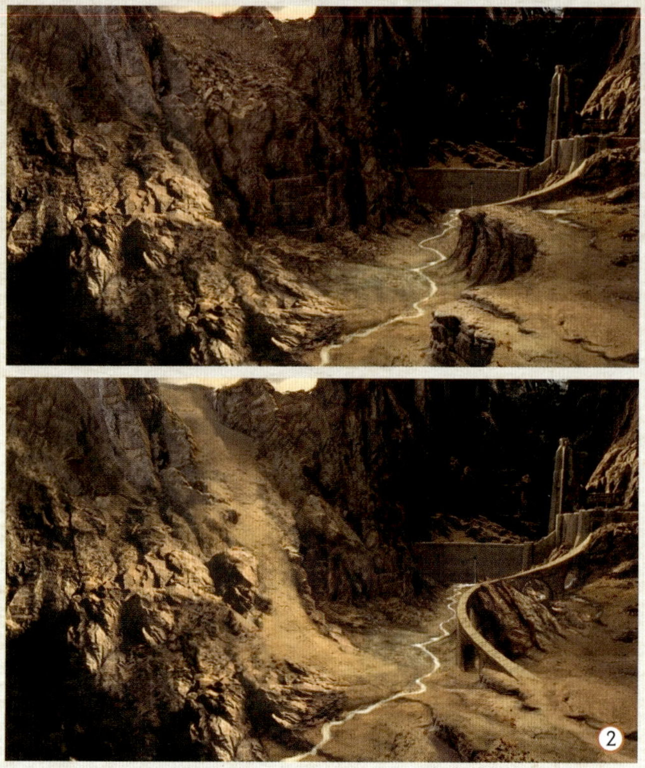

Situated within a narrow valley and carved into the roots of the White Mountains beneath the soaring peaks of the Thrihyrne, an ancient Númenórean fortress has long stood. Now an outpost of Rohan, the Hornburg is a refuge in times of war. A central keep sits atop a network of halls, stables, storerooms and barracks hewn from the rock. Beneath and beyond lies a network of glittering caves. Spanning the Coomb is the Deeping Wall, while an elevated causeway snakes from the gate to the valley floor. Rising above all is a tall tower, wherein a mighty horn is set. In times to come this place will be called Helm's Deep, but that name it has yet to earn.

Helm's Deep was the first thing I started working on when arriving in New Zealand in 1998, following Peter Jackson's invitation to help design his film adaptation of *The Lord of the Rings*. Peter knew that the battle there would be a dramatic highlight and he wanted to start planning it at an early stage; having a miniature built to populate with toy soldiers would be a major part of that. My drawings for Peter were based loosely on original illustrations I had produced for the book, adapted to accommodate particular moments that he wanted to achieve, such as the breach of the Deeping Wall and the cavalry charge from the hall.

Having devoted much of my childhood to building fortifications for my plastic knights, the exercise was hugely satisfying. Peter always takes great care that the battle scenes he is filming are more than just a confusing melee; he wanted to establish the whole environment in the viewer's mind before the battle began. Building a 1/72nd scale miniature that would later be shot for the film was very useful in his planning of the scenes, and helped me appreciate the part that miniatures would play in the trilogy. – ALAN LEE, CONCEPTUAL DESIGNER

Our story takes us to the Hornburg two centuries prior to the events seen in *The Lord of the Rings* film trilogy. While the same place, this interval afforded the Kamiyama san flexibility to make changes to suit the purposes of his story; the environment would not look identical in both time periods, and some of the events that transpire might even cause these differences. We would see the Hornburg in the grip of an exceptionally brutal winter, so it became a fun design challenge to envision an earlier version of this iconic location while still honouring the integrity of what had been established by the book and film trilogy. – DANIEL FALCONER, ADDITIONAL CONCEPTS DESIGNER

PP: Hornburg background art. **1:** Helm's Deep shooting miniature with digital landscape extension (LOTR trilogy). **2:** Hornburg concepts, DF. **3:** Final film frame (LOTR trilogy). **4:** Hornburg concept, AM.

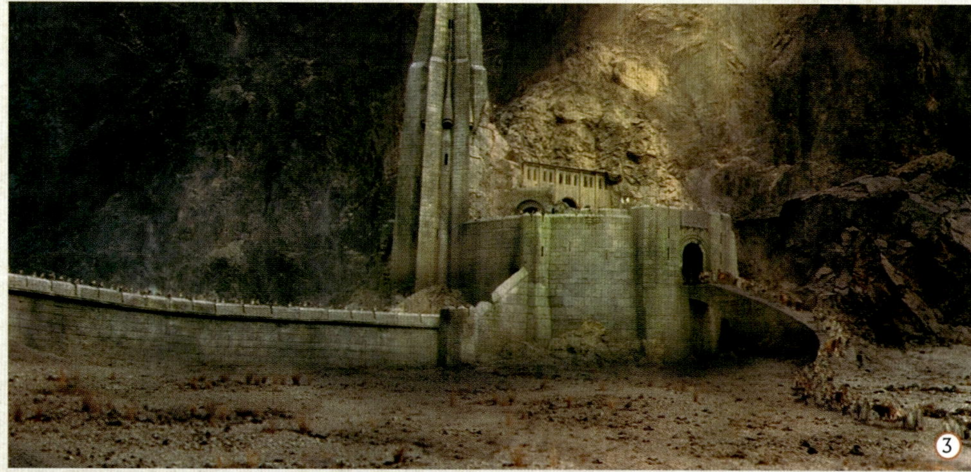

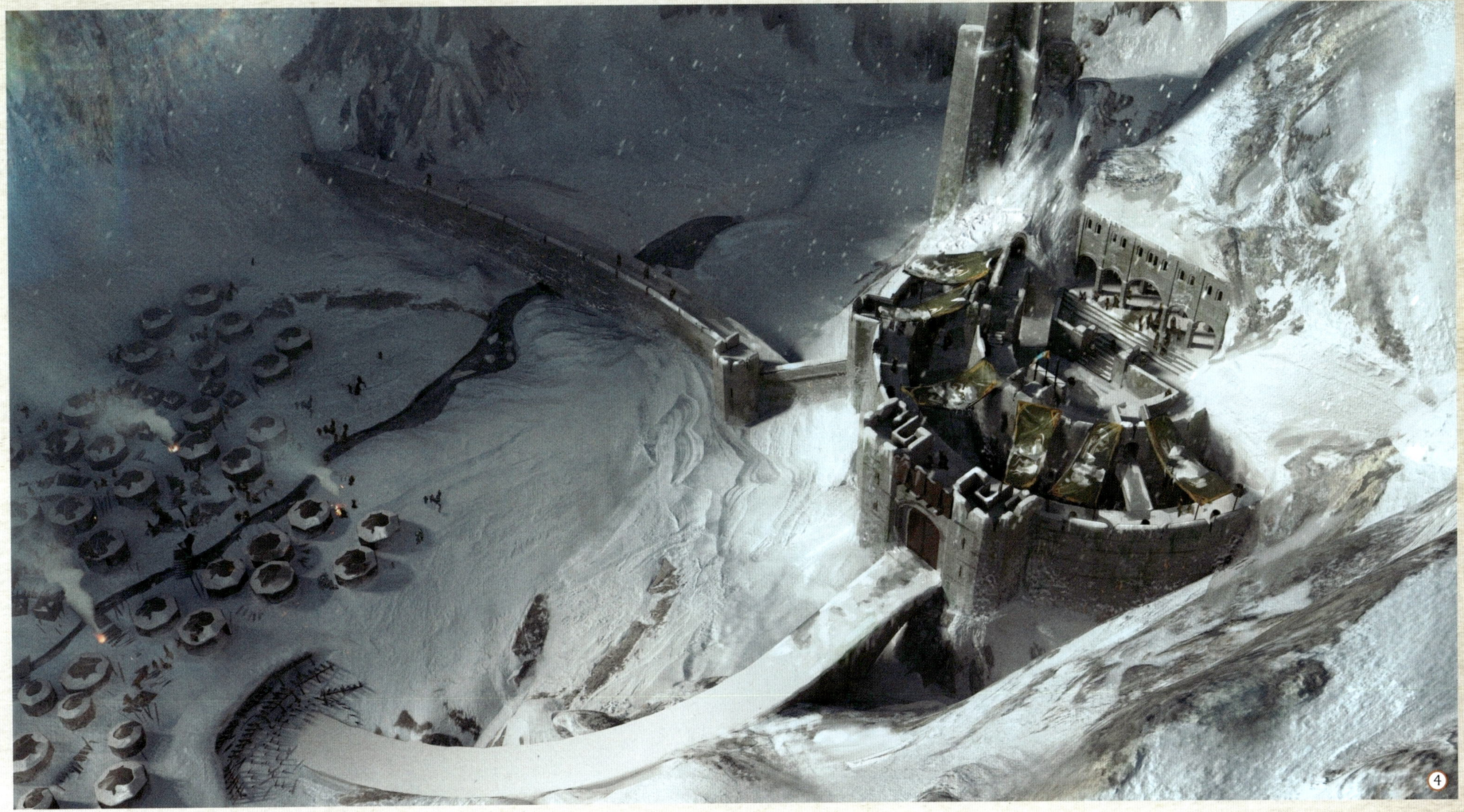

I love Helm's Deep and I love anything to do with wintery settings, so it was a pinch-me moment to get to visualize the iconic location in a snowscape. My concepts were produced before the notion of dropping the valley floor had been suggested. Their main purpose was to portray the sense that the refugees were cornered with no way out.

It was interesting to explore how the snow might fall across the architecture of the Hornburg, building up on the surfaces where flurries had heaped it against the walls. Covering the ramp with snow also showed that no one was coming in or out.

I liked the idea of emulating the composition of shots from the trilogy in my concepts. I had built a digital model of the fortress, and the thing I discovered when flying a camera around it was that Peter Jackson had already found all the best angles and used them in *The Lord of the Rings*.

When you try to do it yourself, it's obvious why he made those choices!

Among the changes that I suggested to show the passage of time was restoring some of the broken parts of the fortress. There were fortifications that were smashed in *The Two Towers*, which I fixed in my concepts. The process was about finding ways to make the place look different without changing the underlying architecture. Flags hung like awnings added a pop of colour to the bleak landscape and were an example of a significant visual difference achieved without adding permanent structures. – ADAM MIDDLETON, WĒTĀ WORKSHOP ART DIRECTOR & SENIOR CONCEPT ARTIST

One of the challenges we faced with the Hornburg concerned its depiction in the middle of a fearsome winter. Kamiyama san was worried that once the valley was piled with snow, the Deeping Wall would appear too short to present a formidable obstacle to the besiegers. He specifically asked us to make it taller. I was worried, because this was a difficult change to rationalize within canon. Could it have been rebuilt? That seemed extreme, but it occurred to me that the landscape might offer a solution. In the climax to *The Two Towers*, Gandalf and Éomer heroically rode to the rescue down a huge slope of loose shale. Perhaps over time the Deeping-coomb had filled with loose rock and silt from slips, floods and natural erosion. The wall might not be taller in times past, but maybe the valley floor was deeper? – DANIEL FALCONER, ADDITIONAL CONCEPTS DESIGNER

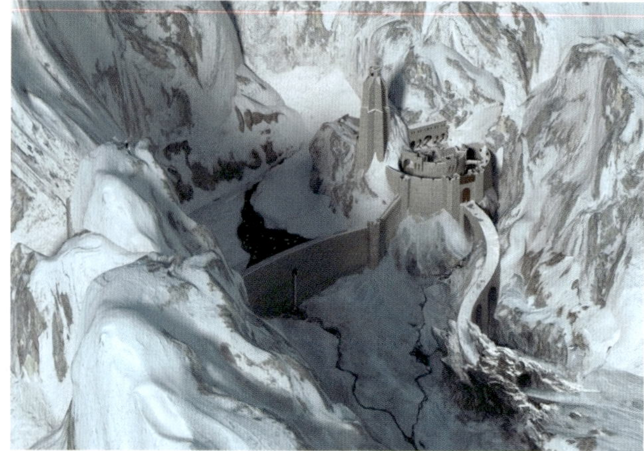

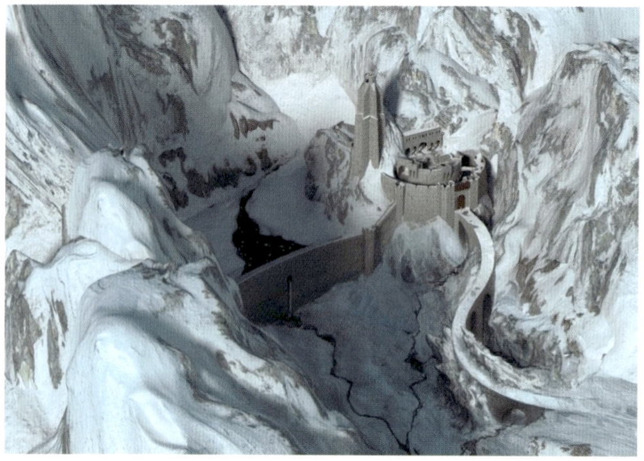

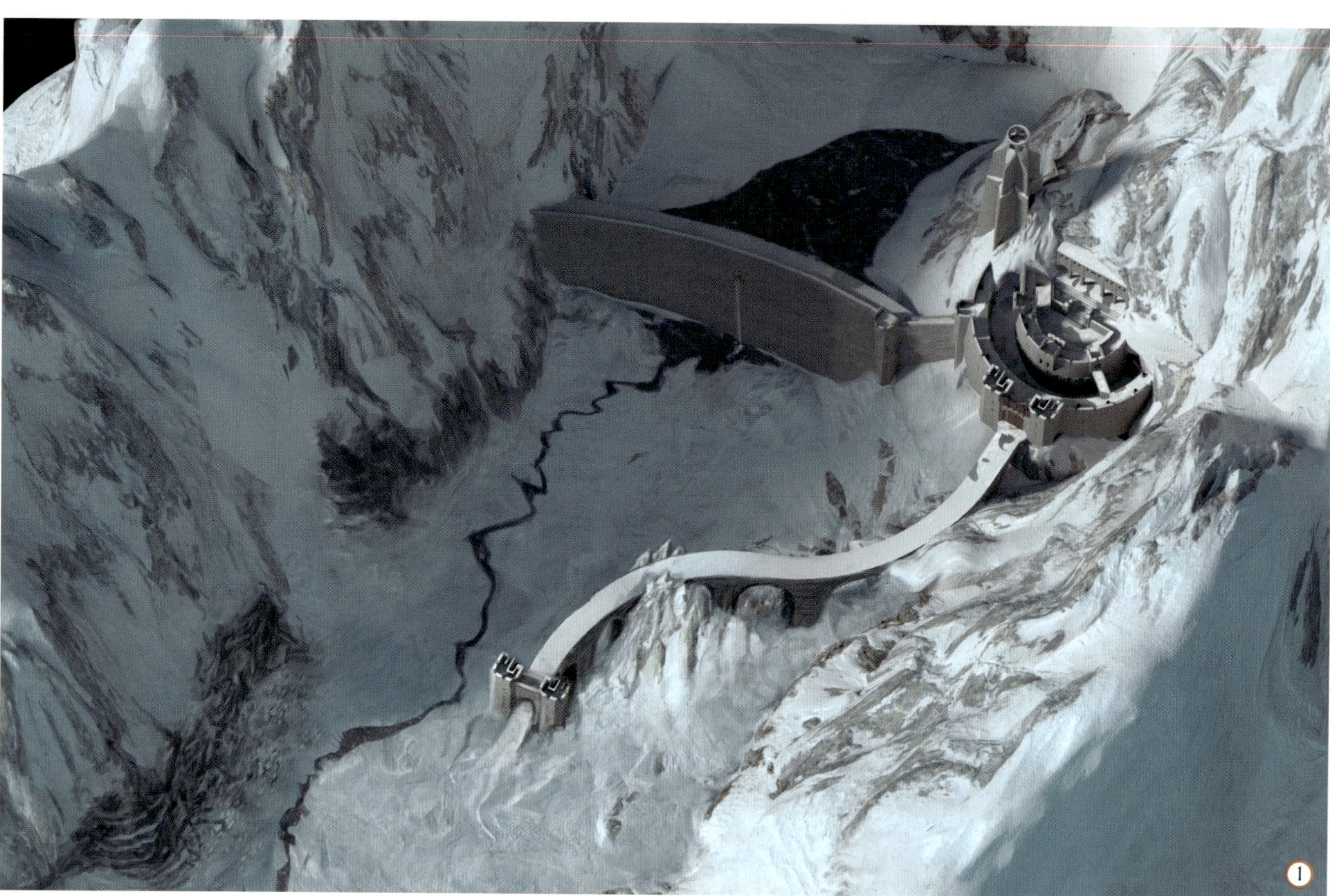

'THESE WALLS WERE BUILT BY GIANTS. THEY HAVE NEVER BEEN BREACHED.'

One of the most attractive things about the premise of the valley floor being lower in Helm's time was that it lifted the culvert, in which Saruman's forces planted their incendiaries in *The Two Towers*, halfway up the wall. Perhaps this was the spillover channel of a reservoir behind the wall? Dammed fresh water would certainly be advantageous for those occupying the fortress, and the frozen water trickling from the culvert in winter was a visual I instantly fell in love with. Luckily, the director liked the idea.

Excavating the valley also meant we could add other new features, later buried. Sharp-eyed viewers might have detected signs of quarrying on the rockface behind the Hornburg in the trilogy, but I thought it would be cool to see more of it in front of the tower, and it might also give us a jumbled, broken environment in which to hide the exit of Helm's secret tunnel.

The one tricky thing about a deeper floor was that it meant we needed to double the length of the causeway. Without railings, it was always a precipitous ramp for horses to traverse, but now, being even taller and longer, it would be a death trap! It's fortunate the Rohirrim and Númenóreans before them were such skilled riders.

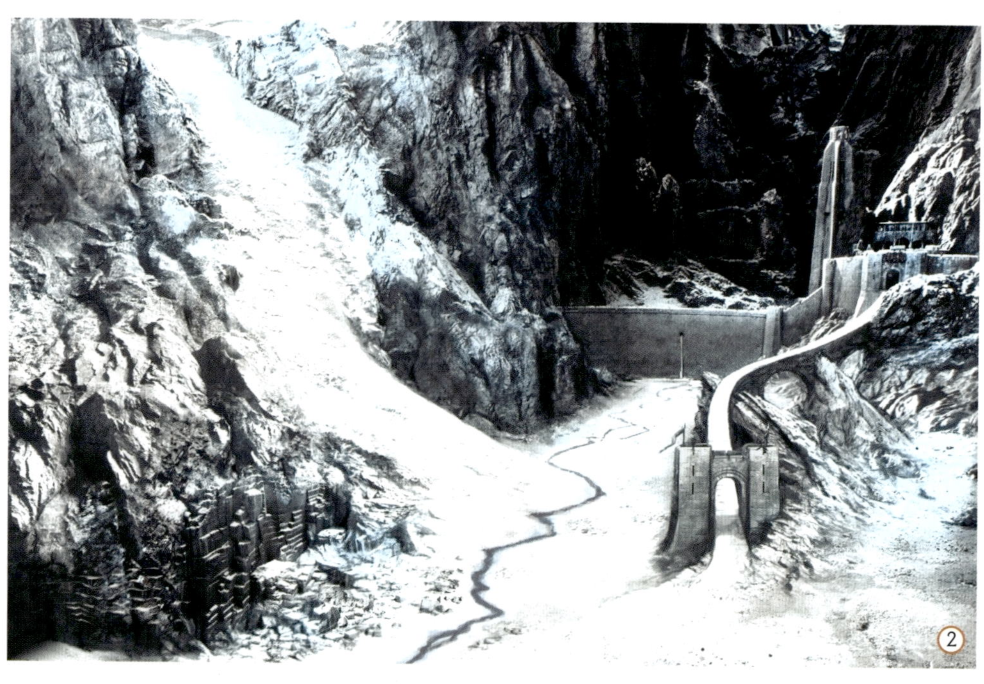

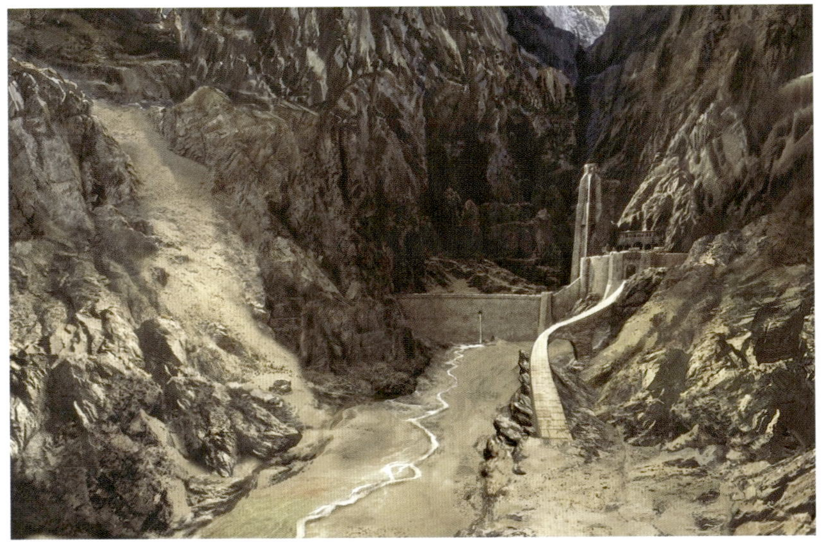

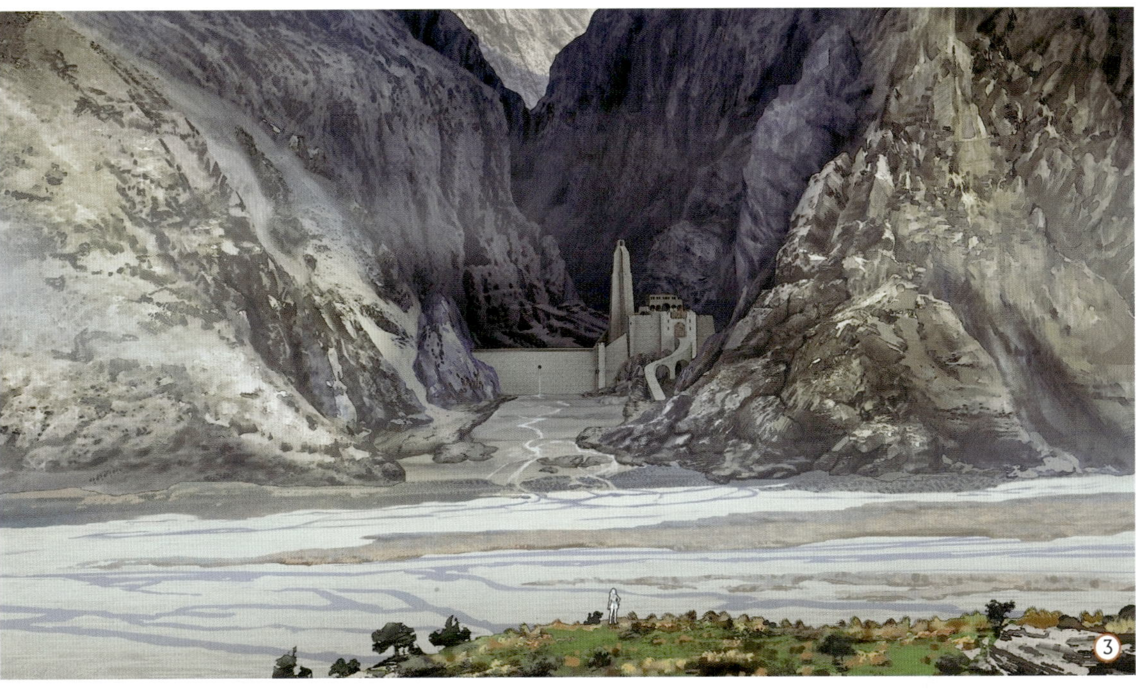

I played with different courses for the lengthened causeway, spiralling or snaking, intersecting with rocky features or cutting through to form a tunnel. Perhaps it meets a small cliff? I even suggested a guardhouse at the mouth, but it wasn't chosen. In the end, it's just a long, dangerous ride from the gate to the streambed. Hold fast! – DANIEL FALCONER, ADDITIONAL CONCEPTS DESIGNER

1: Hornburg concepts, DF & AM. 2: Hornburg concept, DF. 3: Hornburg concepts, YY. 4: Final film frame.

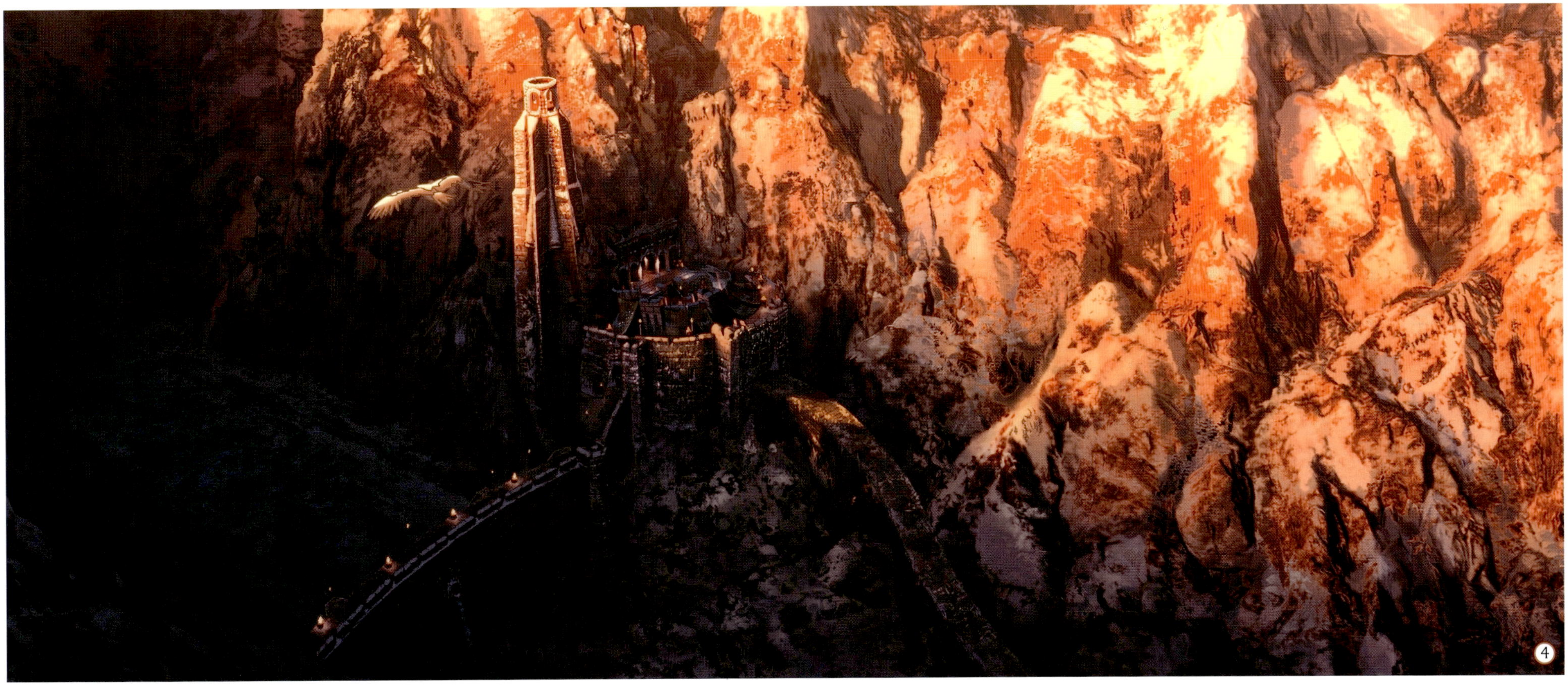

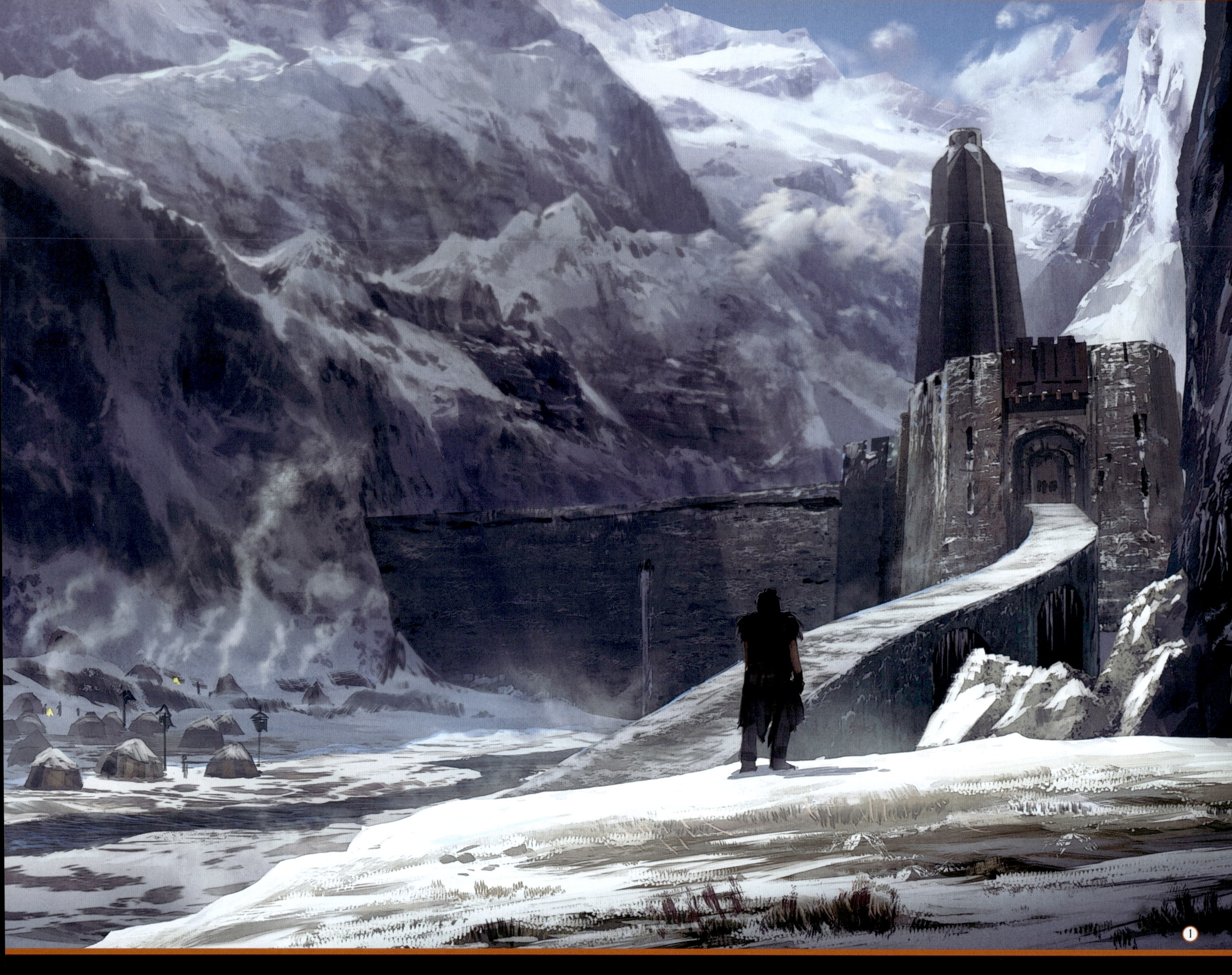

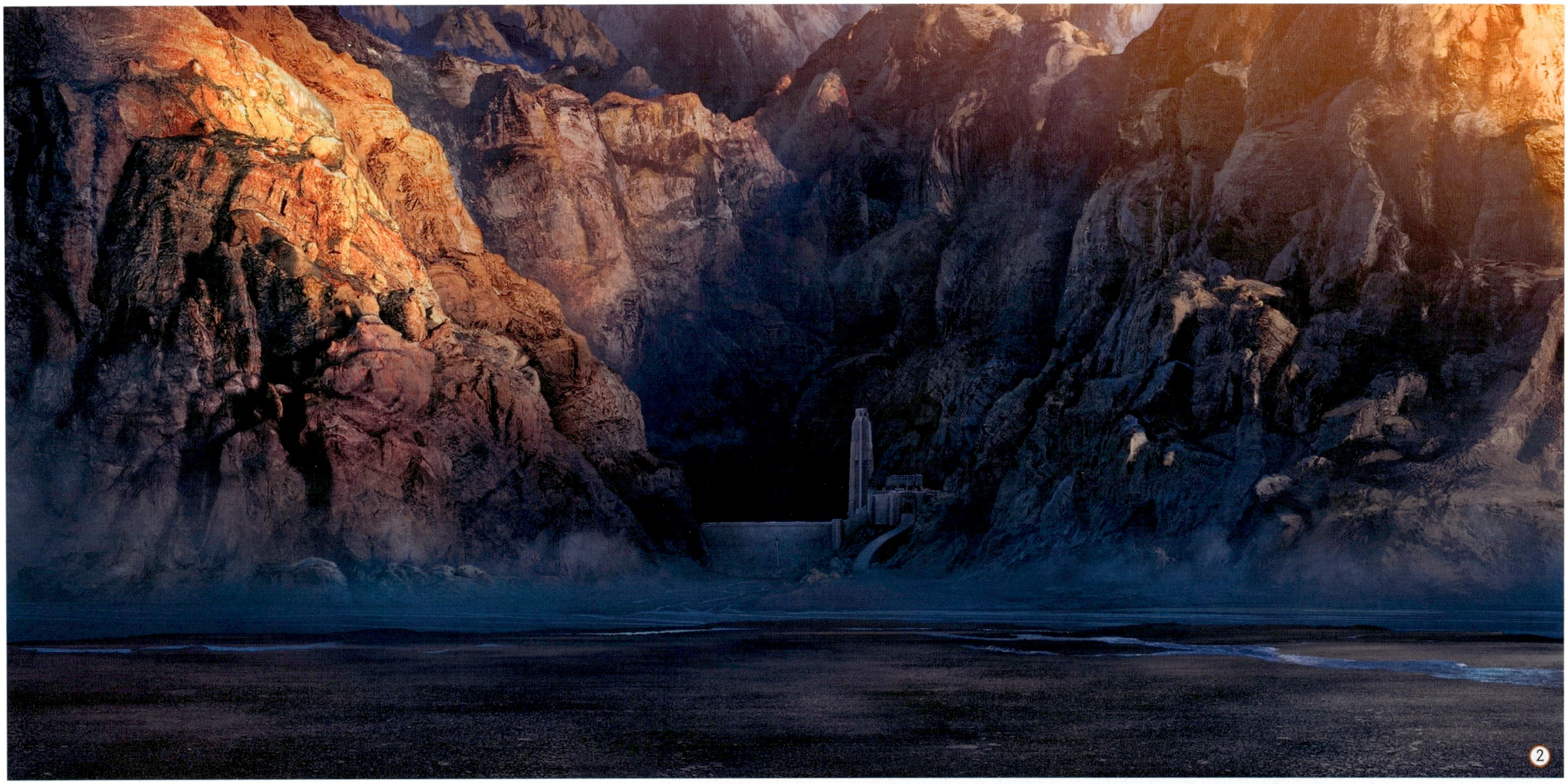

The visual backdrop of the Long Winter was something that we tried to use to our advantage to heighten what's going on in the story. You have this girl, Héra, who is the adventurer, wild and free, and now she is effectively shackled in a cold, dark place, a stone box. It served us well to invoke the imagery of the Hornburg as a dark, icy, confining tomb in which we are trapped. – PHOEBE GITTINS, WRITER

Visually I love the idea that Héra goes from the open and beautiful golden plains in the beginning of the film, to now where she is cornered under siege – strangled by the cold tones and darkness of this fortress. – ARTY PAPAGEORGIOU, WRITER

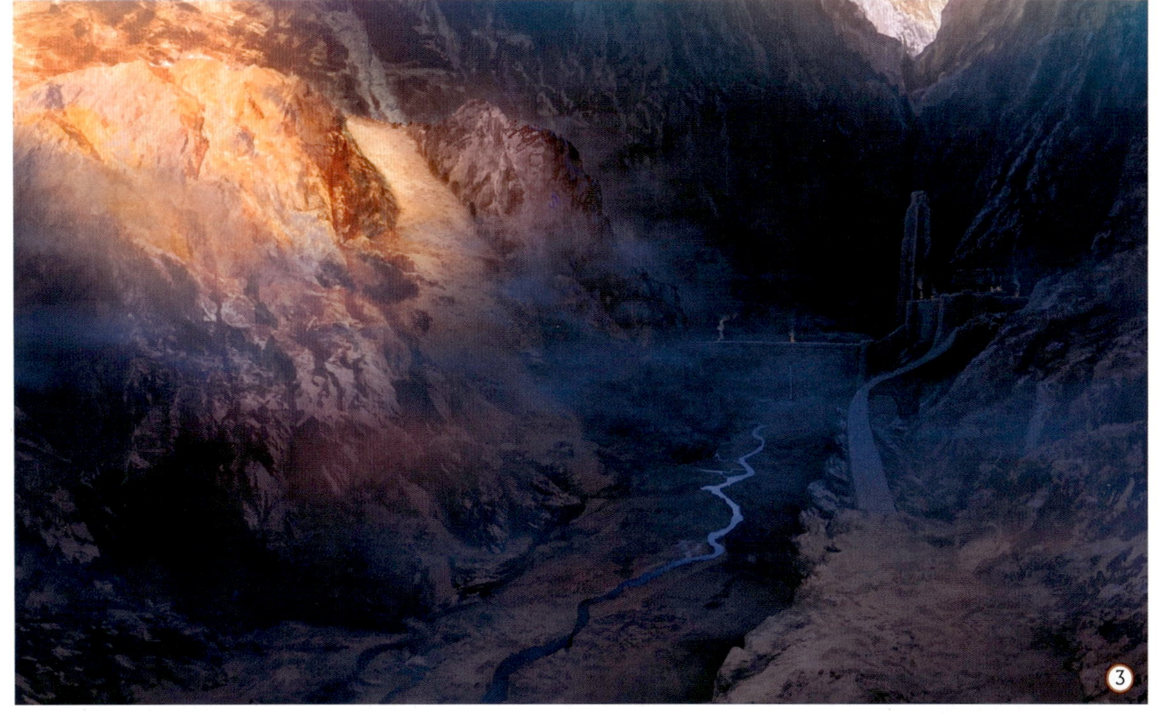

1: Hornburg concept, KS. 2: Hornburg background art. 3: Hornburg background setting art, KS.

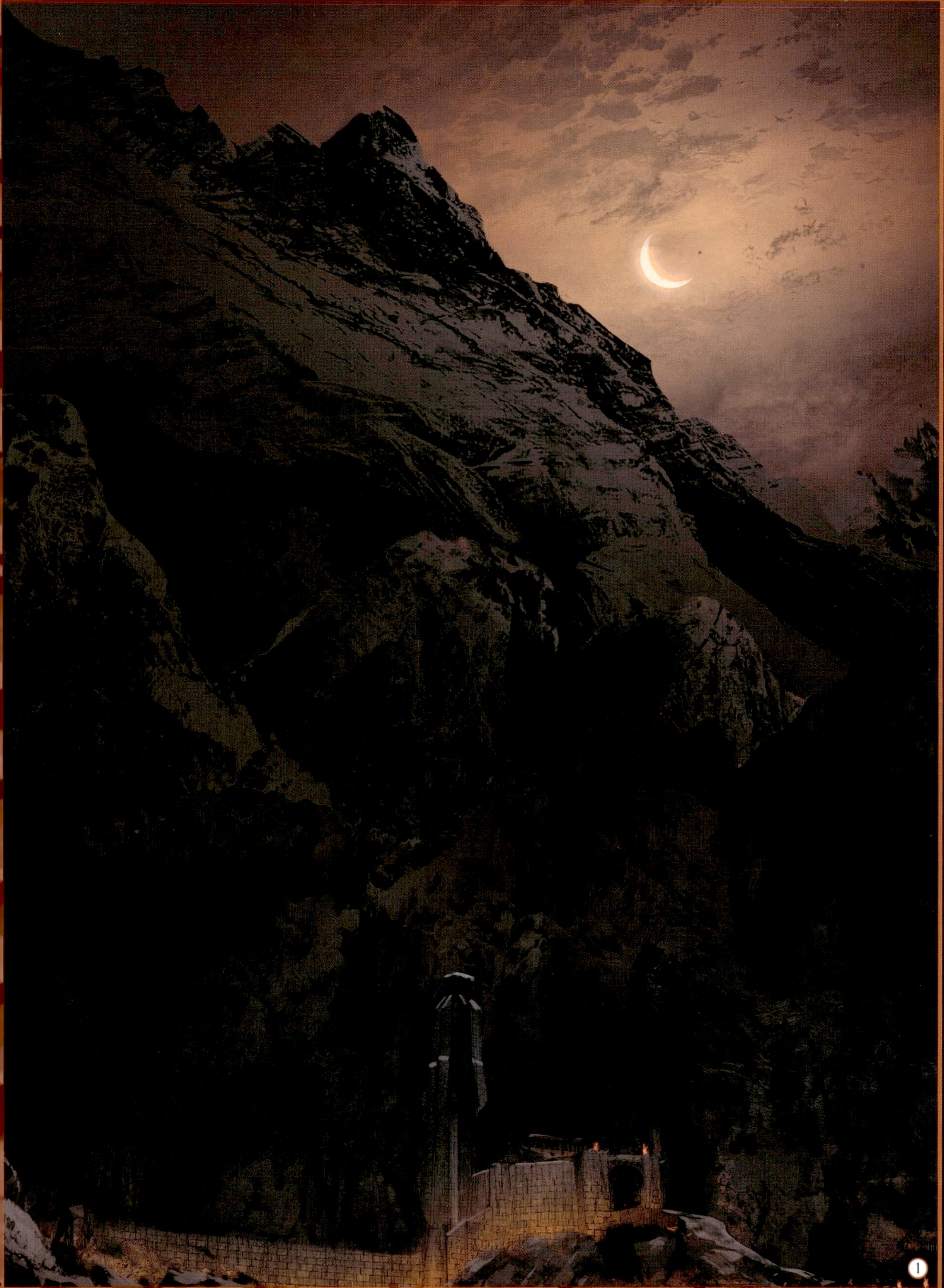

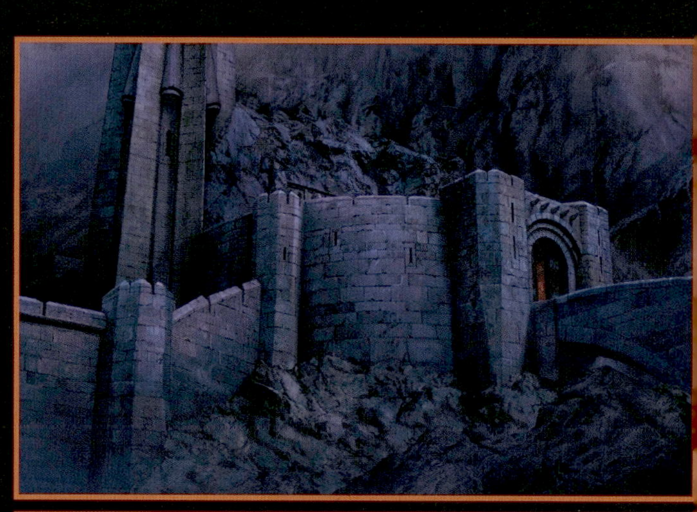

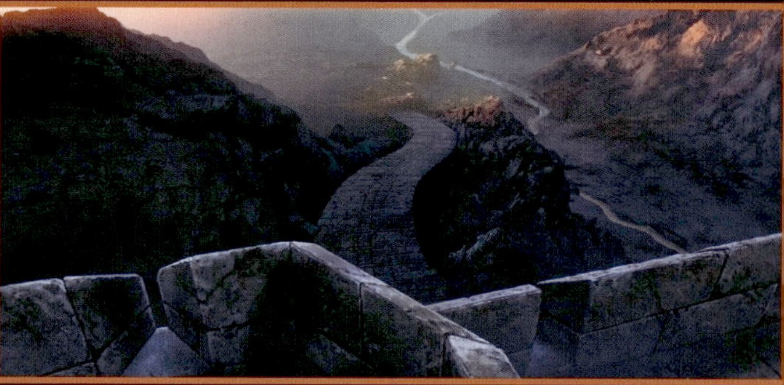

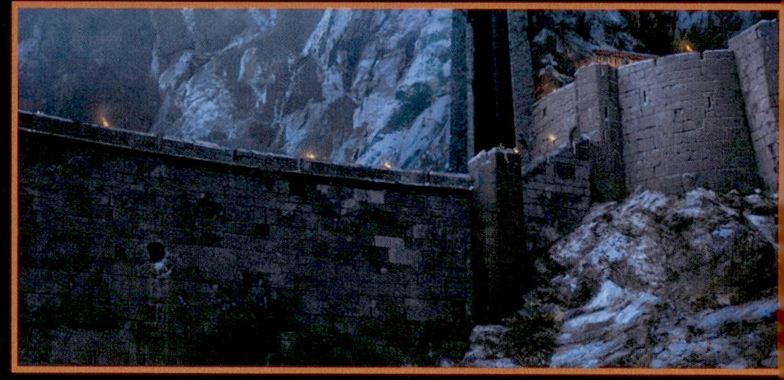

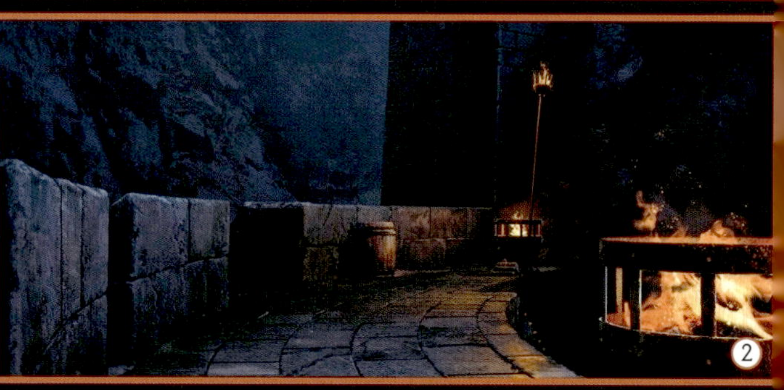

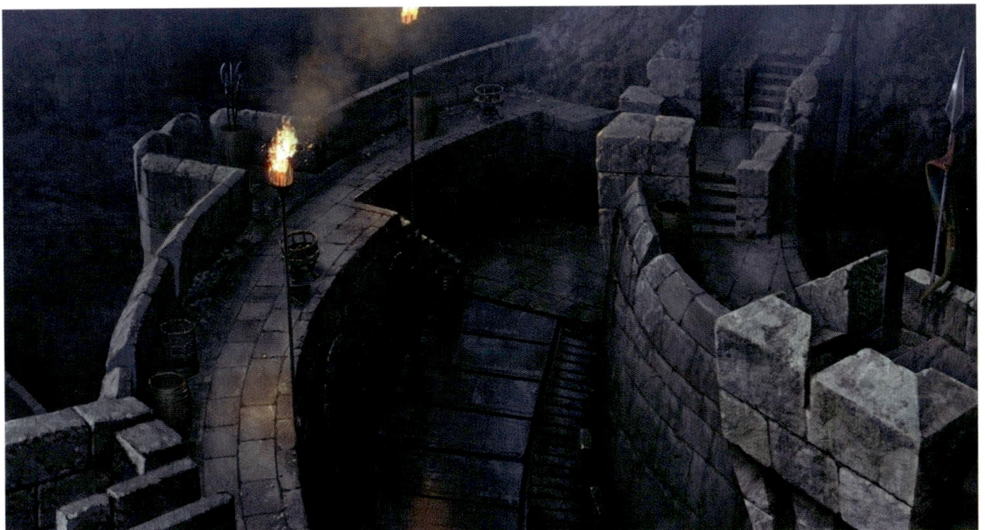

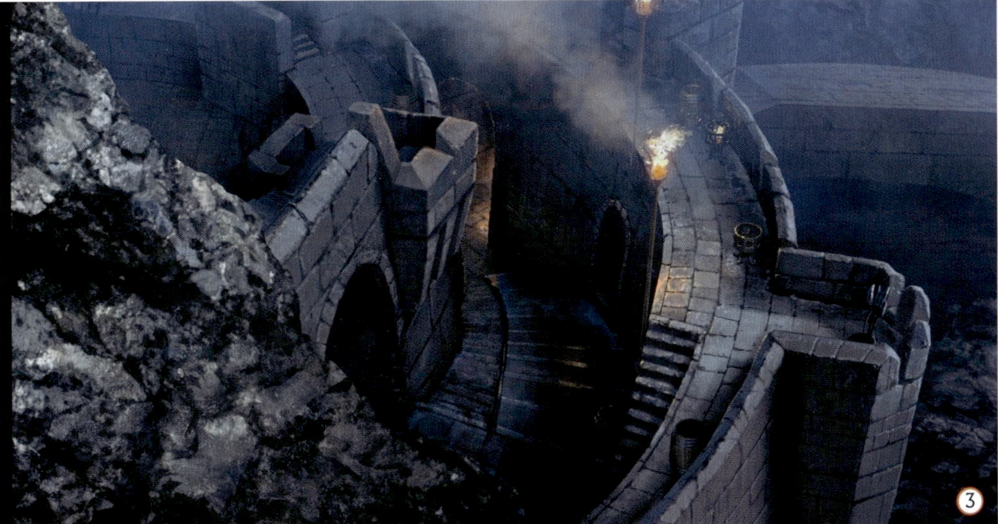

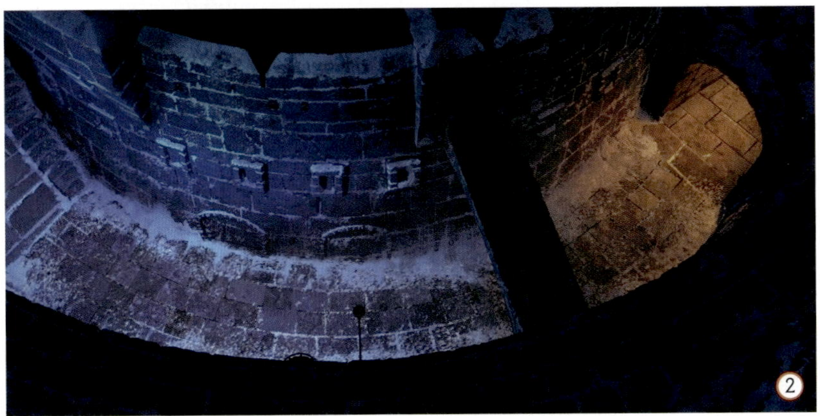

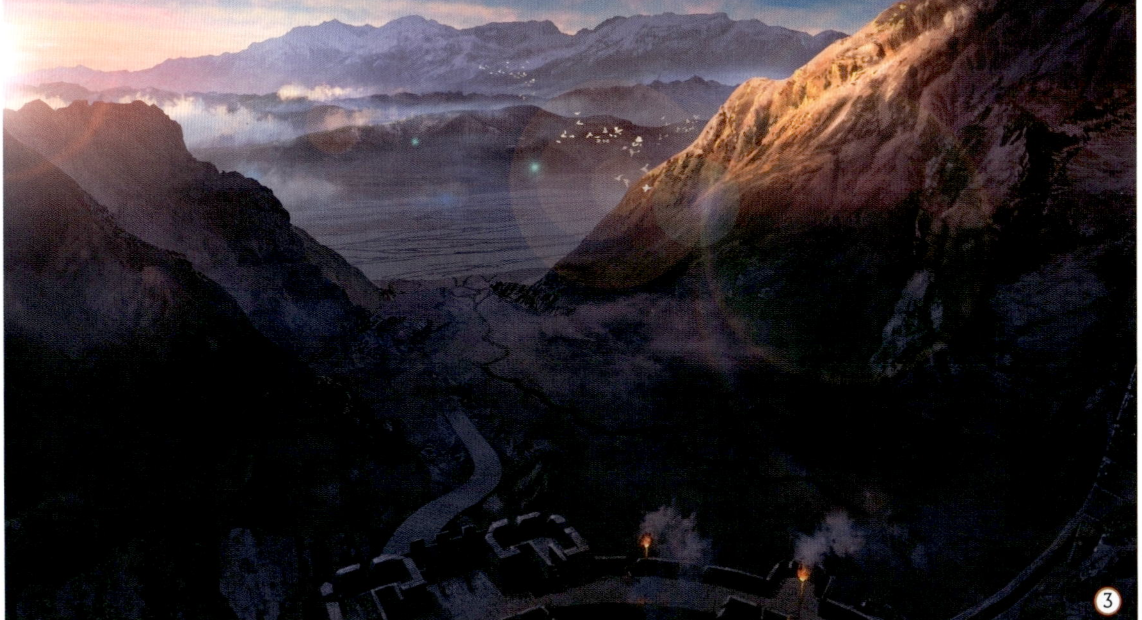

Because we are in an earlier time, I was careful not to make the Hornburg look too shabby. The stones of the castle were very large, a characteristic of its design, so I was very mindful to pay close attention to these sorts of details when recreating it in animated form.

I tried to stay as faithful to the original design as possible, but one of the differences between the trilogy and our version was the absence of Helm's statue in the courtyard. This would be added later, in remembrance of Helm's sacrifice.

It is late autumn when Héra and her people arrive. In winter the snows pile up, supplies become scarce, and the atmosphere becomes dark and lonely. It was difficult to paint the snowy, stormy night scenes and the underground where the refugees were because there were so few sources of light. The backgrounds were sometimes hard to see, but visual effects brought the snowstorm to life and looked very cool. – TAMIKO KANAMORI, ART DIRECTOR

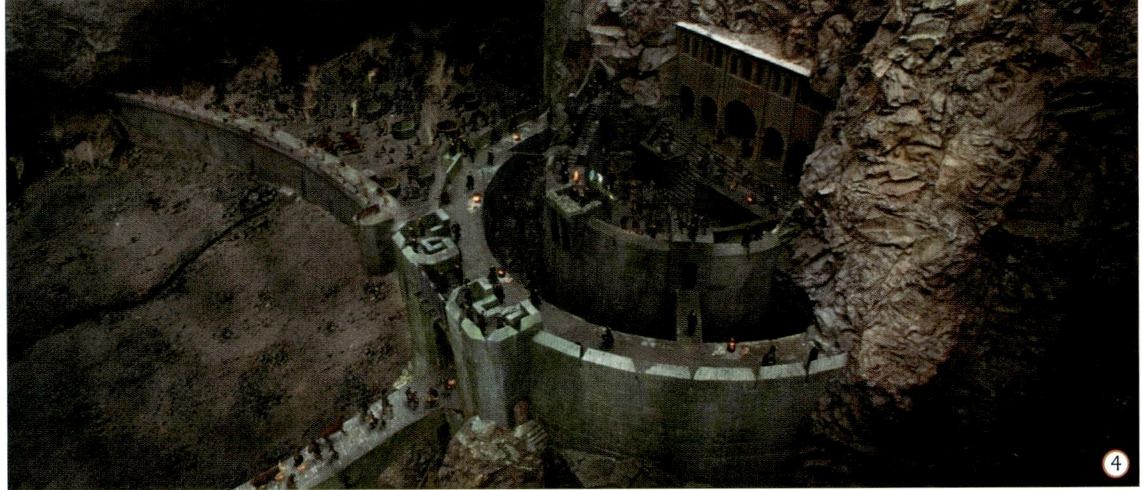

1: Hornburg background setting art, TK. 2: Hornburg background art. 3: Hornburg background setting art, KS. 4: Final film frame (LOTR trilogy).

HÁMA'S DEATH

Háma is not a great warrior like his brother Haleth, but he is still of the bloodline of Helm Hammerhand. We wanted to depict him as someone who faces the moment when the time comes to protect his family. It was important to show that Háma stops and tries to change the situation to save those he loves, and that he has courage. He won't desert his horse. He doesn't complain or cry, and even though he knows death may come his way, in the end, he isn't scared. – KENJI KAMIYAMA, DIRECTOR

The way Háma died was different in the book. During the siege he went out into the snow on a sortie and never returned. We spent a lot of time discussing whether we could honour that detail, but ultimately determined it was a story element that could be adapted with greater purpose – to serve as a pivotal moment of choice for our antagonist. Wulf follows the Rohirrim to the Hornburg, and stands before the walls with Háma as his captive. Up to this point, it's arguable that Wulf has genuine grievance against Helm, that everything has been 'above board' as far as warfare goes. The slaughtering of Háma, however, is the point of no return; an utterly dishonorable act in the face of Helm's surrender for the love of his son. Wulf has the chance to end the war, but the choice he makes here gives him away, it gets at the heart of what his whole campaign is really about; the personal pain he is carrying. It will never be enough. – PHOEBE GITTINS, WRITER

Tarrg is witness to Wulf's descent, and it begins to erode his belief. To Tarrg, the fight is about ideology. He is very hopeful that in supporting Wulf he is backing the right horse. As events unfold, Tarrg sees things in Wulf as the mask slips away that undermine his confidence. During the siege, Wulf tells him, 'Do you think I want to be here? I have nothing else.'

He has nothing but revenge. Ultimately, it will mean his defeat. If Wulf had made different choices, the Dunlendings could probably have kept Edoras. – PHOEBE GITTINS, WRITER

Final film frame.

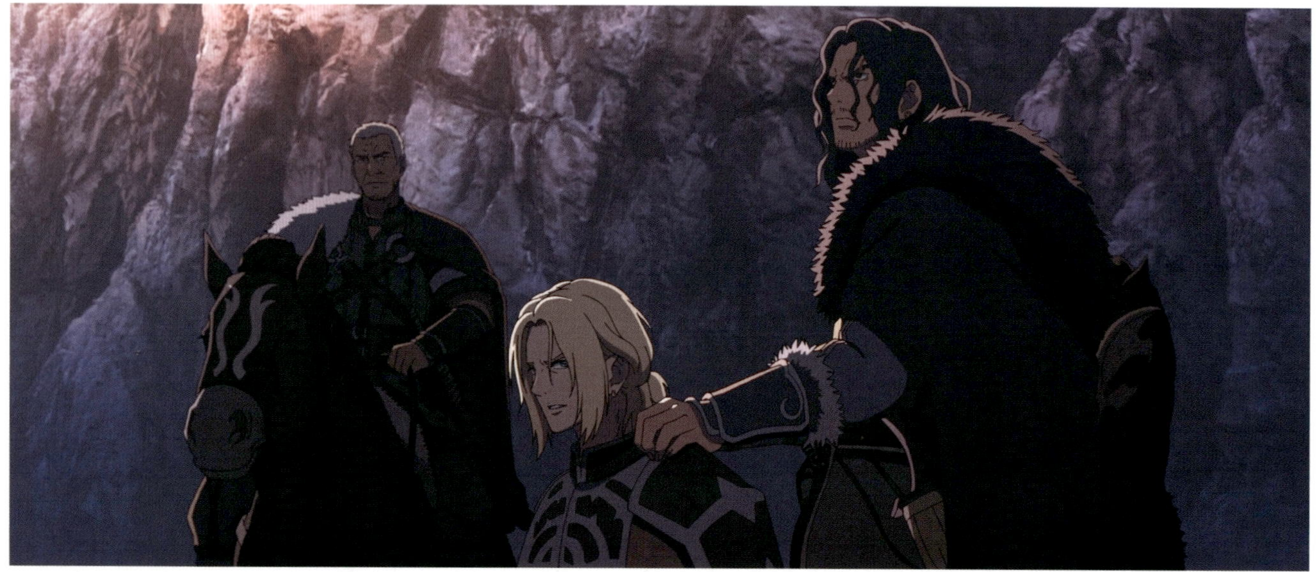

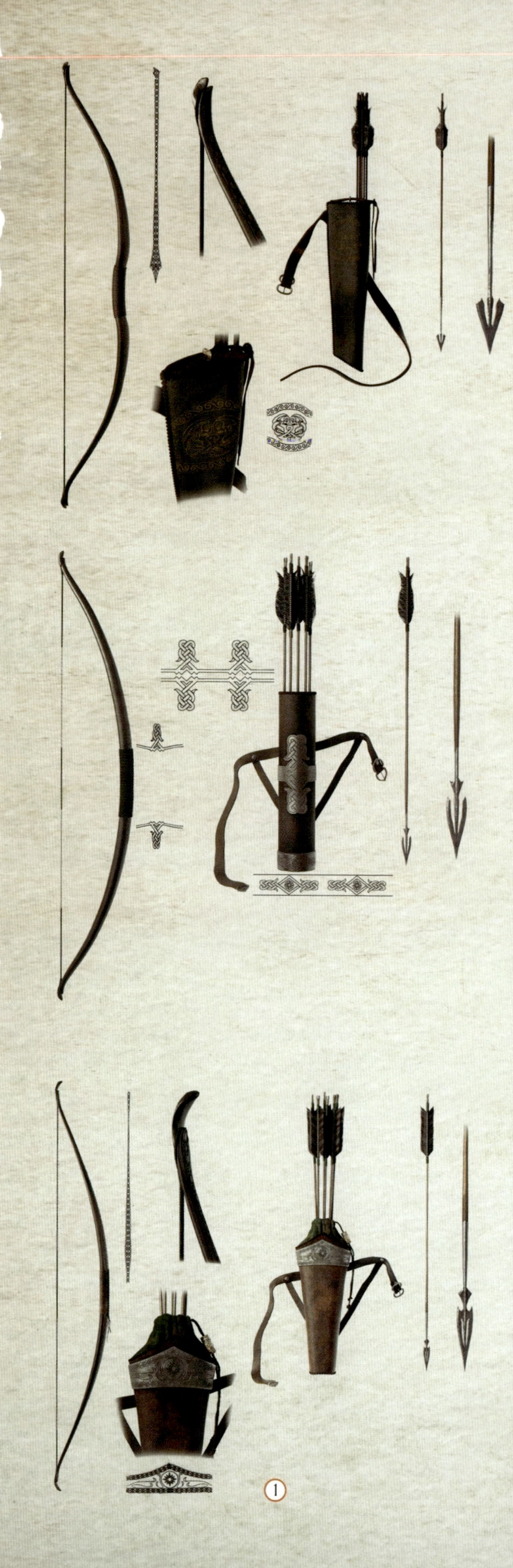

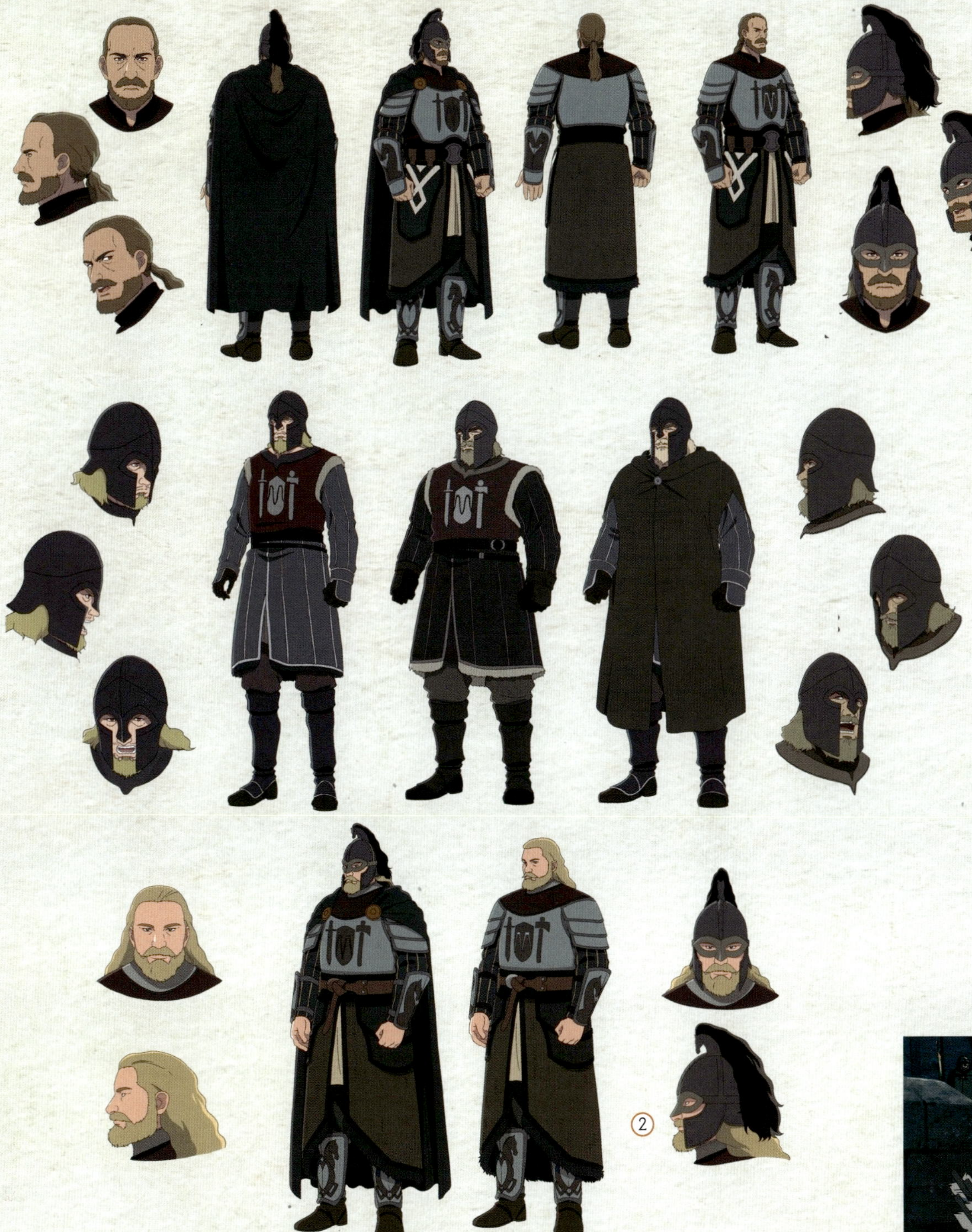

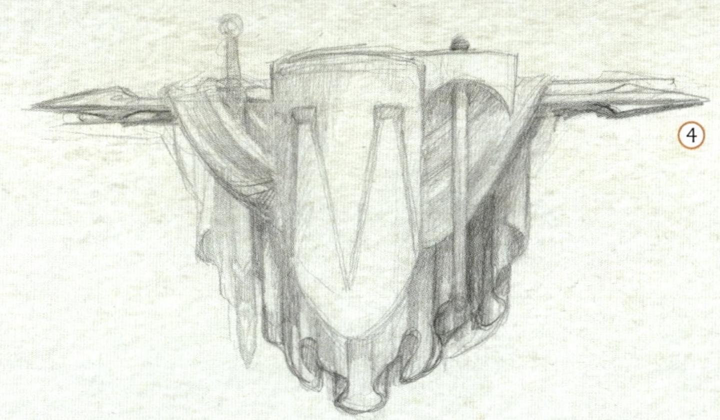

THE HORNBURG GARRISON

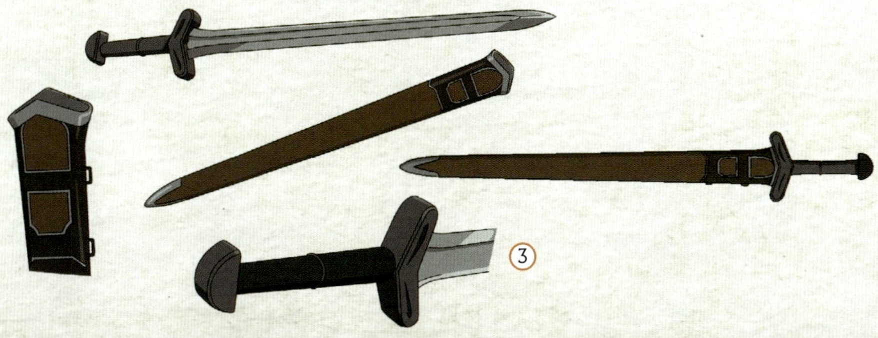

Soldiers fleeing the sack of Edoras join a force already stationed at the Hornburg outpost. The Hornburg's garrison may be small, but it is composed of broad-shouldered, battle-hardened troops, dedicated to making any attacker pay a high price for assaulting the Keep. The director specifically asked for the Hornburg's troops to be imposing, weathered warriors with their own livery and a colour palette matching the location.

The Hornburg was originally built by exiles of Númenor. There is a crest of arms carved on the wall of the keep, heraldry of a people long gone. We needed unique livery for the Rohirrim stationed at the outpost. Even if not Rohirrim in origin, it made sense that they might have incorporated this crest into their armour. – DANIEL FALCONER, ADDITIONAL CONCEPTS DESIGNER

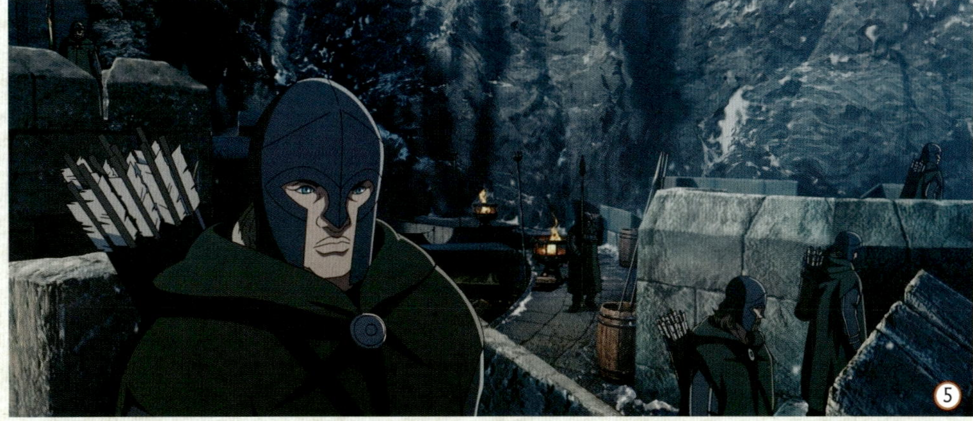

1: Rohirrim bow concepts, WW. 2: Rohirrim soldiers character setting art, AS. 3: Rohirrim sword prop setting art, KM. 4: Hornburg heraldry concept (LOTR trilogy), AL. 5: Final film frame.

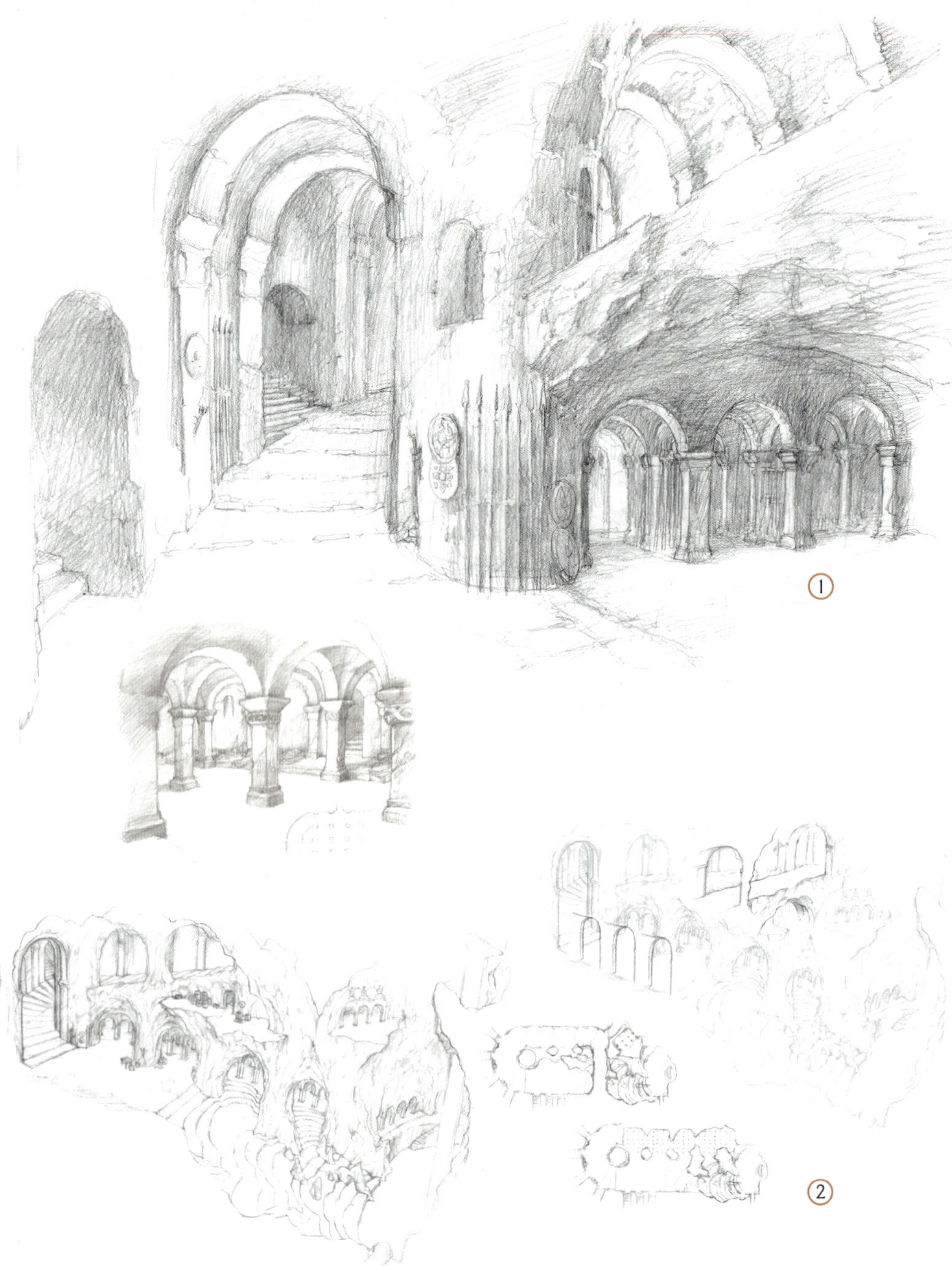

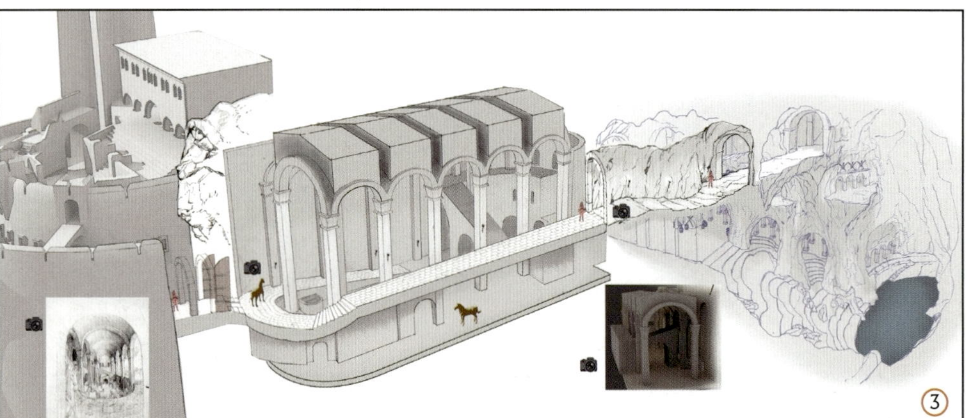

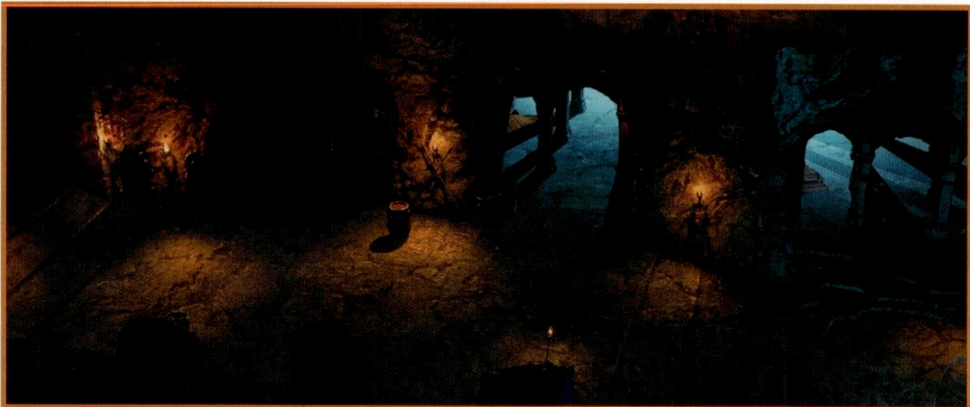

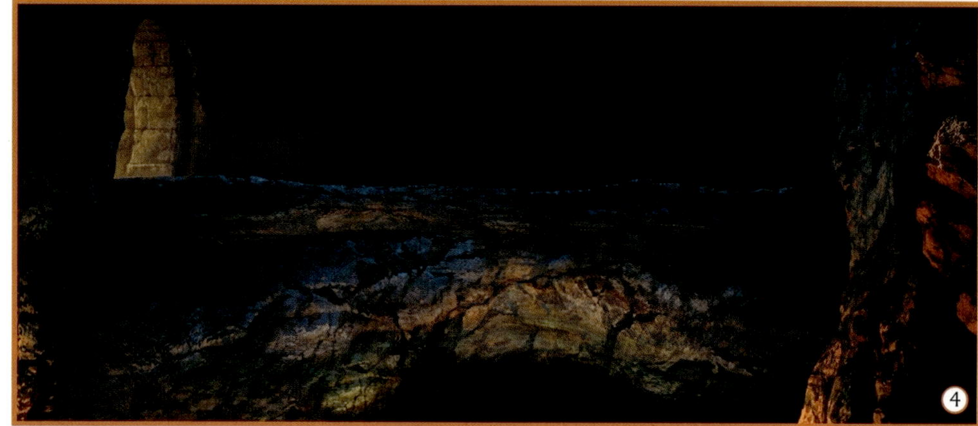

THE HORNBURG BARRACKS

Adapting Helm's Deep for the new film was an interesting exercise. We have to assume that we didn't see all of it in the trilogy. Of course there would have to be space for a garrison, as well as for the horses, and burrowing into the mountainside there would be plenty of space for rock tunnels and additional rooms. – ALAN LEE, CONCEPTUAL DESIGNER

The refugees of Edoras take shelter in this place. Using Alan's concepts as a starting point, I expanded the garrison hall, transitioning from carved architectural forms to a natural cavern, perhaps connected by tunnels to the Glittering Caves? It is multi-tiered, with a stone bridge linking to the upper halls. It was fun to explore beyond the spaces established twenty years ago. I added an underground pool and waterfall that I imagined might slowly freeze as winter progressed. – DANIEL FALCONER, ADDITIONAL CONCEPTS DESIGNER

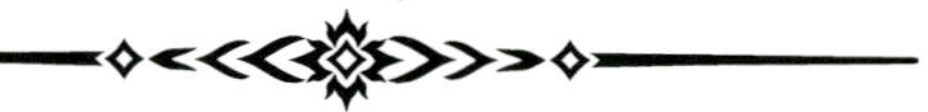

1: Barracks concepts, AL. 2: Barracks concepts, DF. 3: Barracks concepts. 4: Barracks background art.
5: Barracks background setting art, YY.

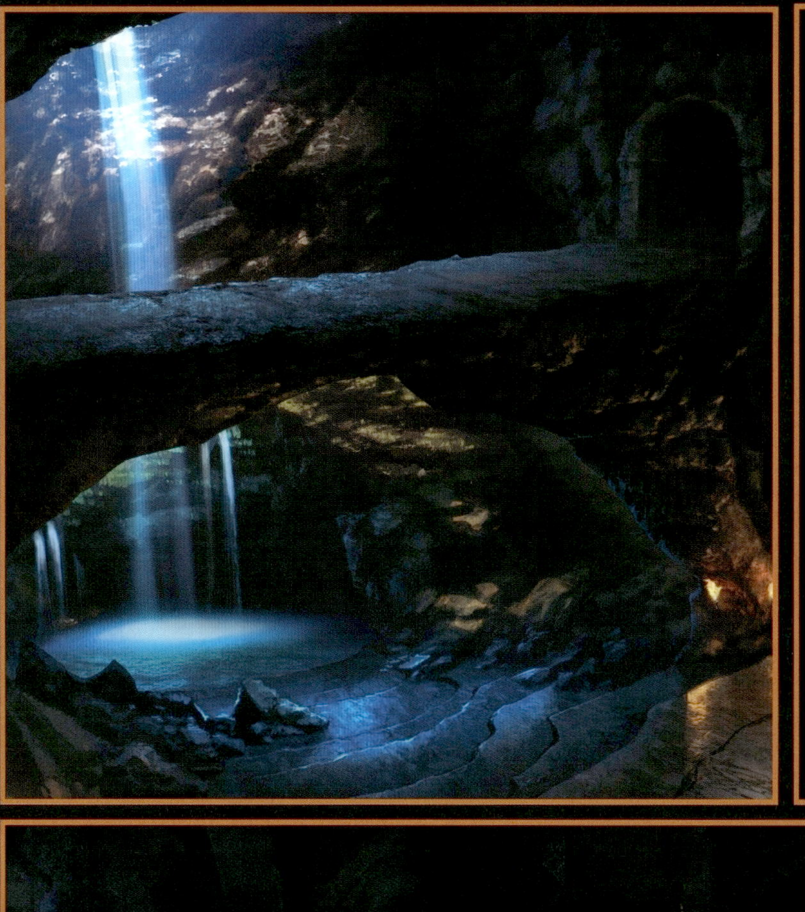
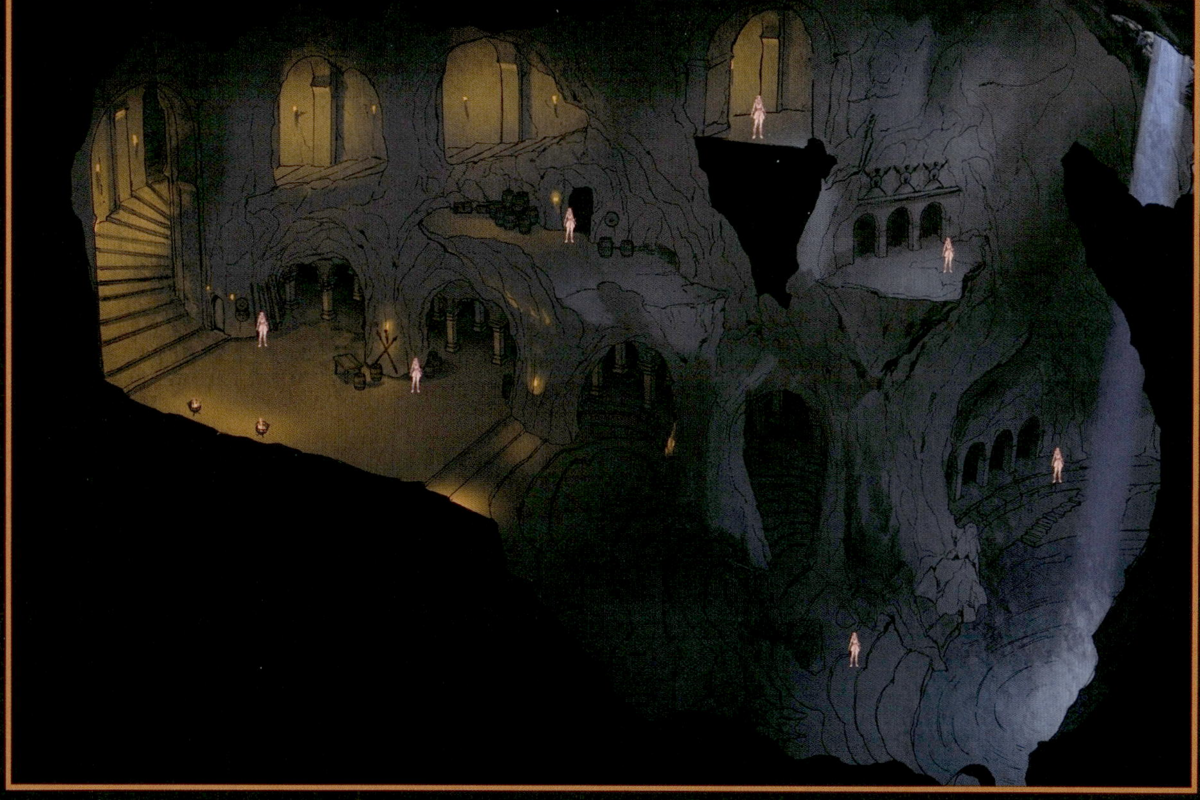
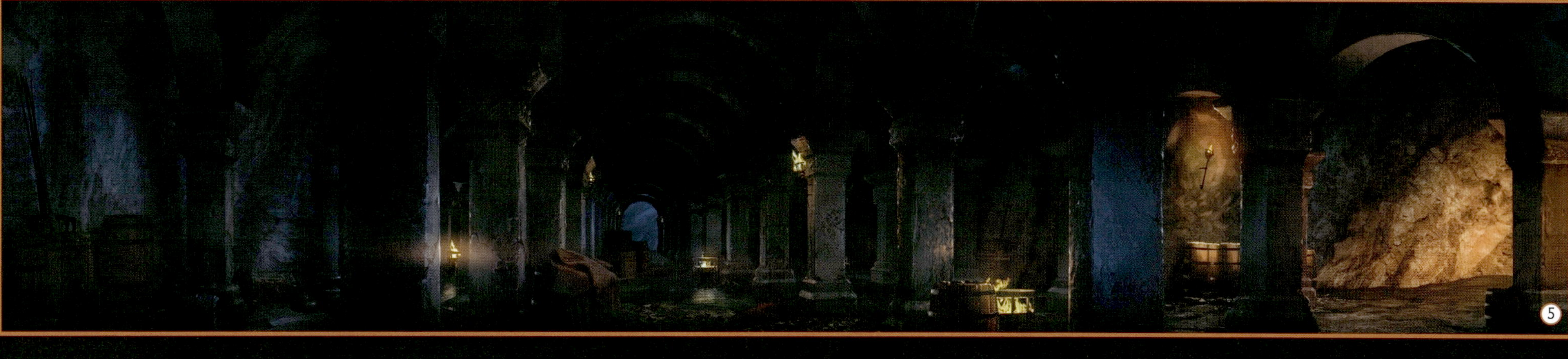

5

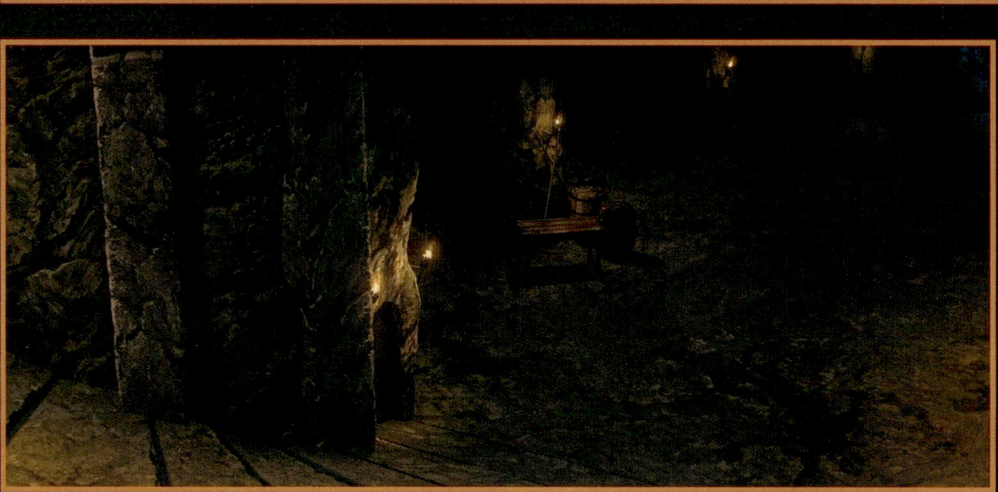

4

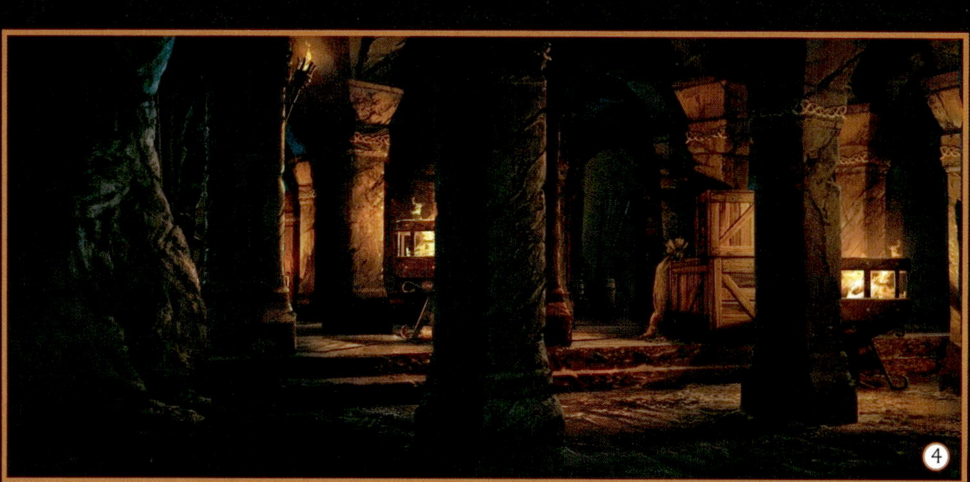

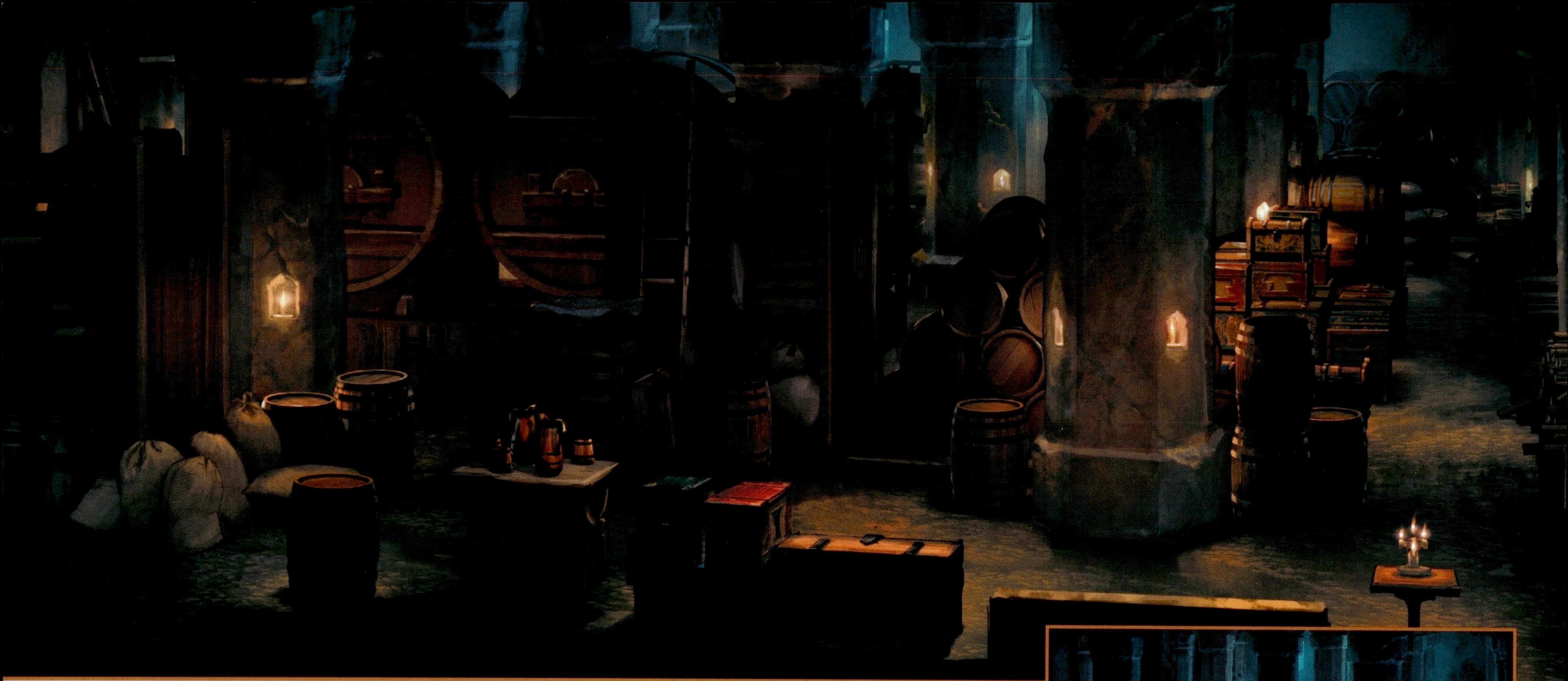

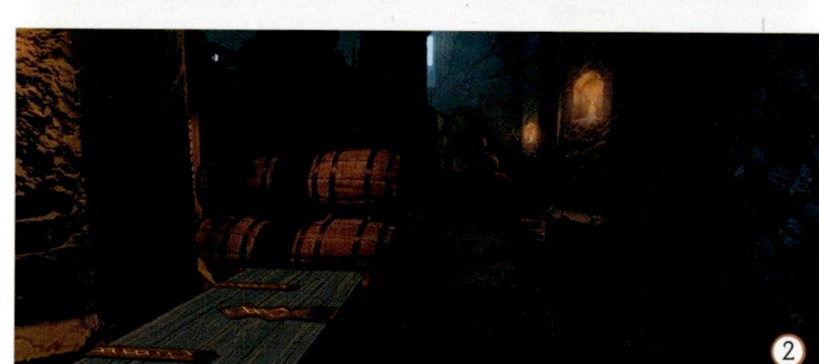

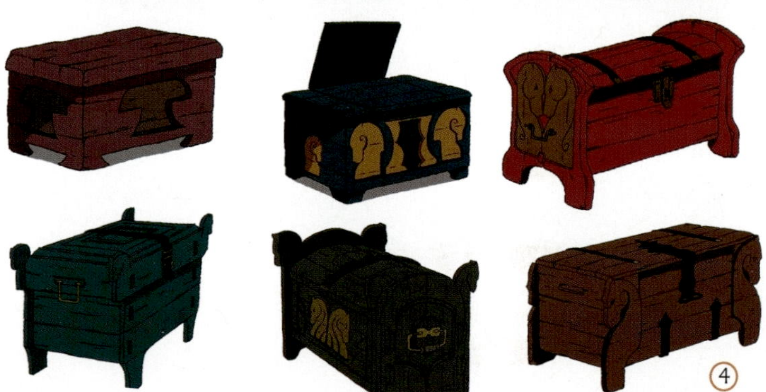

THE HORNBURG
STOREROOM

I drew a large space with lots of firewood and barrels to make it look like there was an abundance of supplies in the storeroom at first, but with so many refugees, supplies quickly begin to disappear. As firewood and oil become scarce, there are fewer torches lit. Cold colours became more prominent in the artwork, making the Hornburg appear less and less hospitable. – TAMIKO KANAMORI, ART DIRECTOR

It was very exciting to dabble (far too briefly) in Rohan furniture: sturdy, mobile, with endless possibilities to decorate. *Kerbschnitte*, or chip-carving, is a long-standing alpine tradition, in this case transposed to a more nomadic grasslands culture, necessitating no more complicated tools than chisel, saw and knife. The chests are of a purely medieval construction with tall legs to keep the body of the chest clear of the ground and damp. – JOHN HOWE, CONCEPTUAL DESIGNER

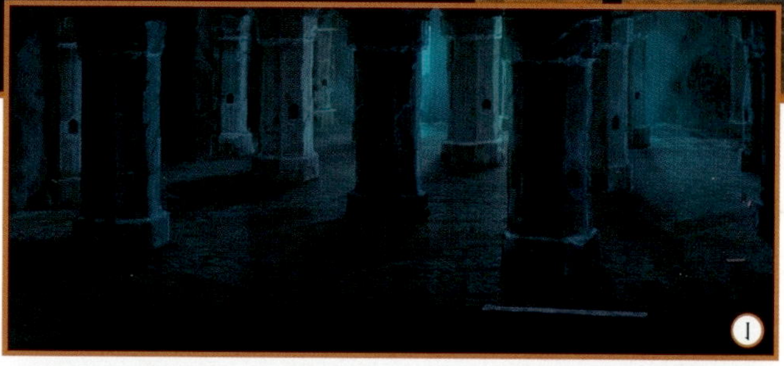

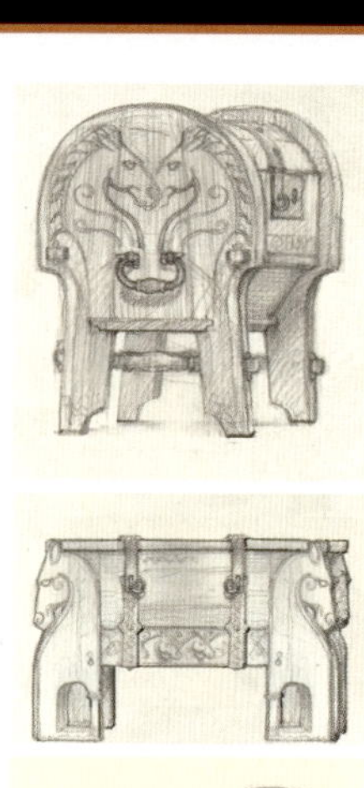

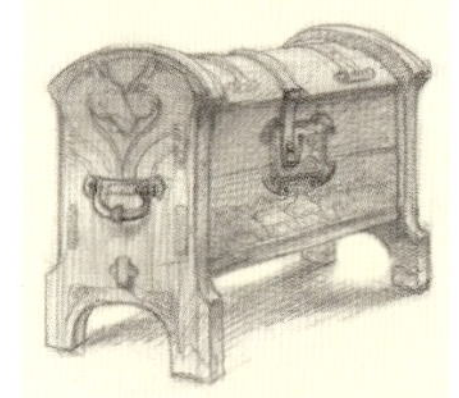

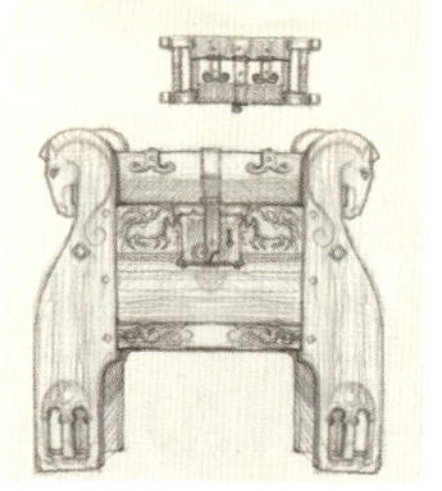

1: Storeroom background setting art, TK. 2: Storeroom background art. 3: Trunk prop setting art, KM. 4: Trunk concepts, JH.

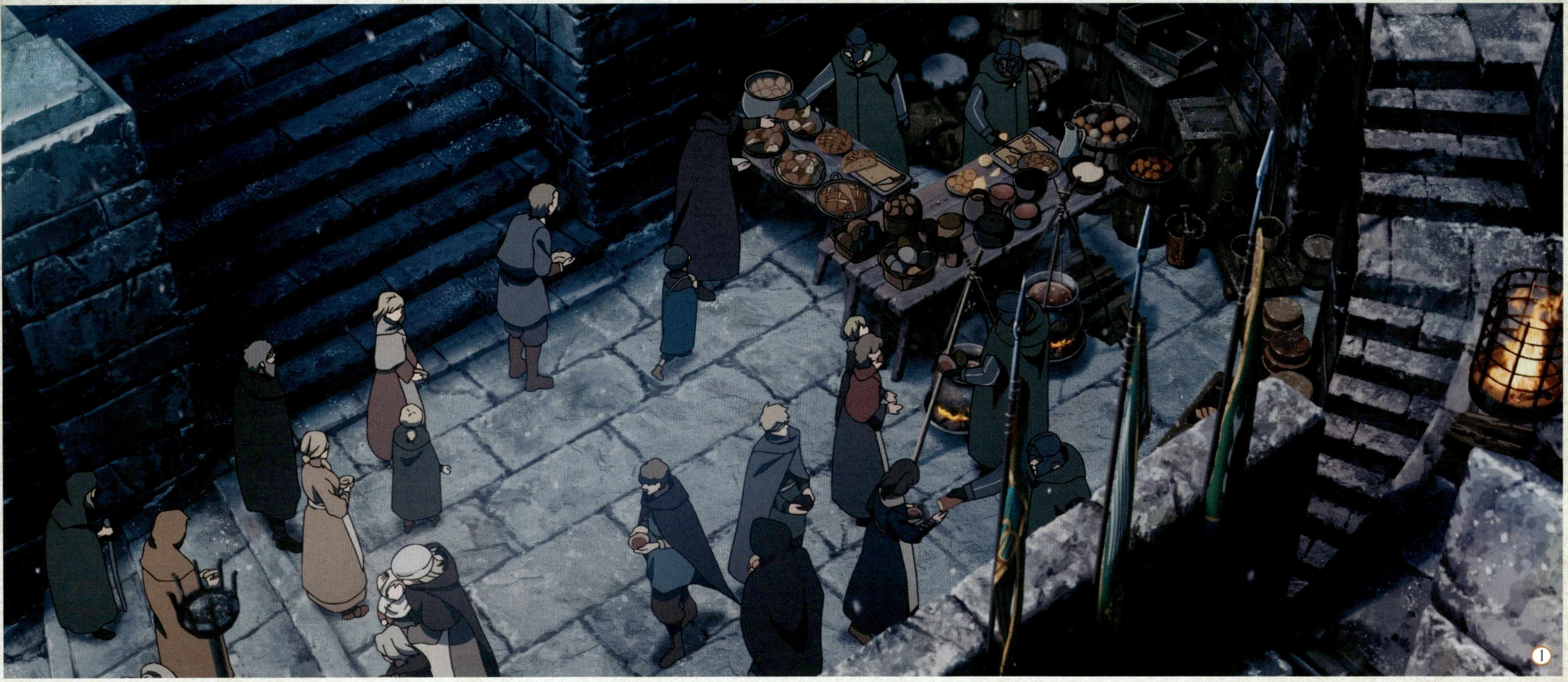

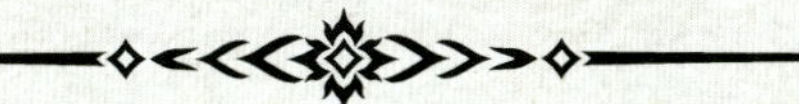

PROVISIONS

To give the props I was drawing the handmade quality of an era predating mass production, I avoided perfectly straight lines, maintaining a hand-drawn touch. My preference has always been for the rougher, less-refined-but-still-interesting lines rather than uniform drafting – a great fit for this assignment.

I design props with a care to make each item recognizable, even when it is reproduced hundreds of times in hand-drawings by dozens of different animators depicting it from various angles.

The design assignments were divided into two segments, household goods, and later weapons and other individualized items. To make them reproduceable in animation, we were conscious to limit the number of lines used to draw each object, including weathering such as scratches and dirt. Looking back, I am glad that I began with common, realistic objects, as they offered a smooth way into this imagined world. – KENJI MASUDA, PROP DESIGNER

'I NEVER THOUGHT I WOULD SEE SUCH TIMES . . .'

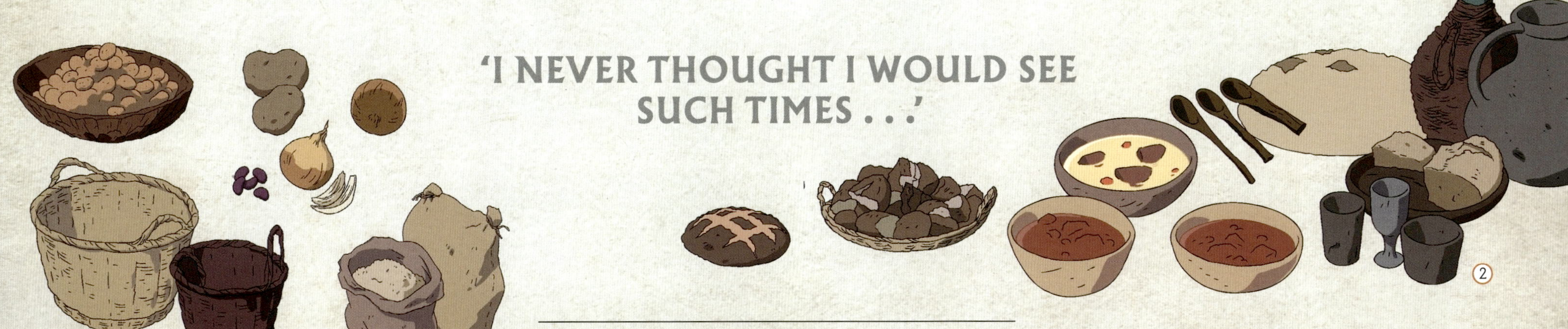

1: Final film frame. 2: Provisions prop setting art, KM.

OLD PENNICRUIK

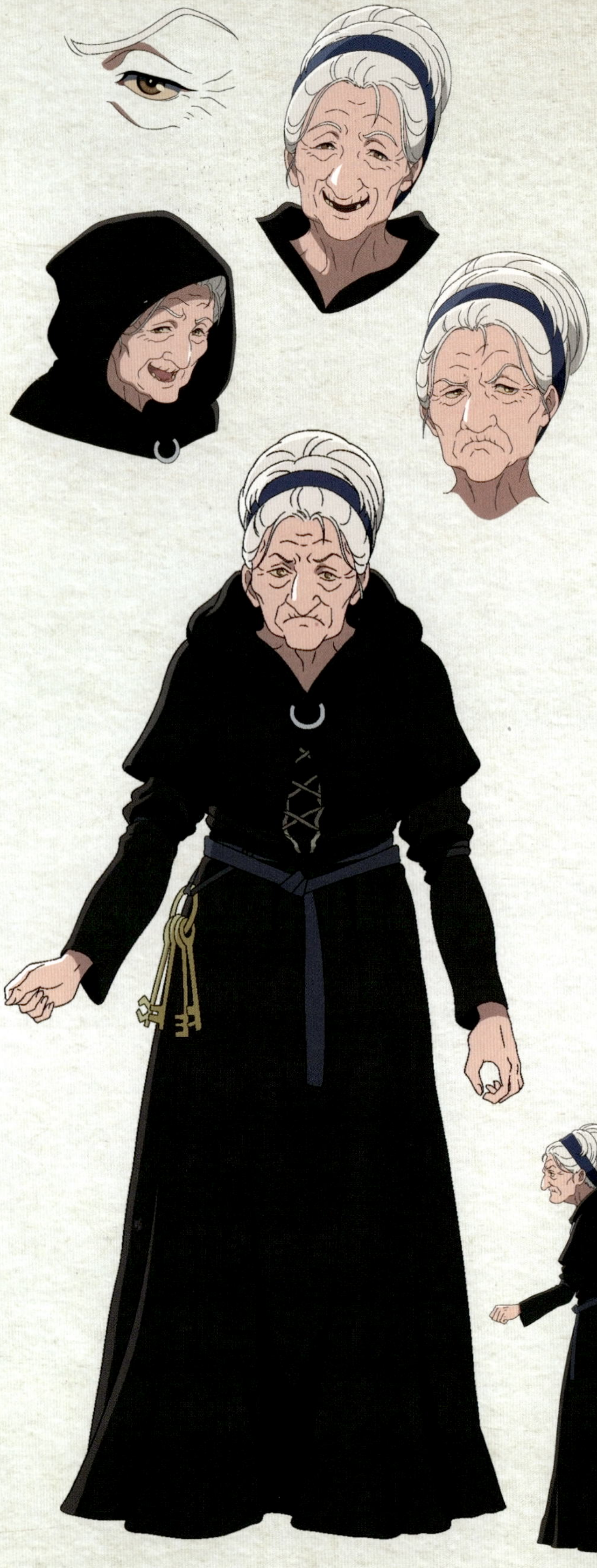

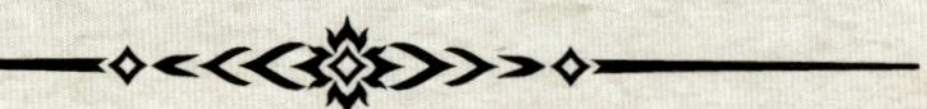

Within the darkness of the Hornburg's deepest chambers Héra meets Old Pennicruik, the ancient Keeper of the Halls, who manages the stores. Among the trunks of supplies Héra stumbles upon a tattered wedding dress, which the crone dramatically proclaims as haunted!

Pennicruik is a great hybrid of a traditional anime archetype and *The Lord of the Rings*, and especially the way that Kamiyama san realized her. I love the jangle of the keys as she moves. It's beautiful. – PHOEBE GITTINS, WRITER

As a character, she comes across in a few different ways. Sometimes it can be difficult to balance the horror and comedy elements. Philippa and I went back and forth on Pennicruik together to find what we both felt was the right balance. – KENJI KAMIYAMA, DIRECTOR

Through Pennicruik we get to see the importance of history and memories to the Rohirrim – the wedding dress; the haunted fortress; the idea of Helm as a wraith – she gives context to, and feeds these stories, passing them on to Héra. The memory of Háma and Haleth becomes like a ghost haunting Helm and Héra. That's why we have the thread of the lyre woven through the story. Háma is gone, but there is this object, which is kept, that represents his memory and the way in which these people will keep him alive – through song, through sharing his story. And it is Pennicruik who passes the lyre on to one of the children for safe keeping. – ARTY PAPAGEORGIOU, WRITER

Pennicruik is a gossip! She lives for this, but importantly, she also chooses not to burn Háma's lyre when Héra gives it to her. She hands it off to the little boy; 'Our people have a song or two left in them yet.' She is keeping the tradition alive. – PHOEBE GITTINS, WRITER

We wanted this section of the film to take on the feel of a classic Gothic ghost story … even if it is Pennicruik who, having lived alone in this dank place for so long, is the true ghost haunting the Keep! – ARTY PAPAGEORGIOU, WRITER

Since they're for a big stone fortress, I thought the keys should feel large and heavy. I imagined them going into doors that were quite thick, so the stems would be long. I tried to subtly include some of the themes and shapes of the architecture in the concepts so that they felt like they were part of the same world. – CHRIS GUISE, WĒTĀ WORKSHOP SENIOR CONCEPT ARTIST

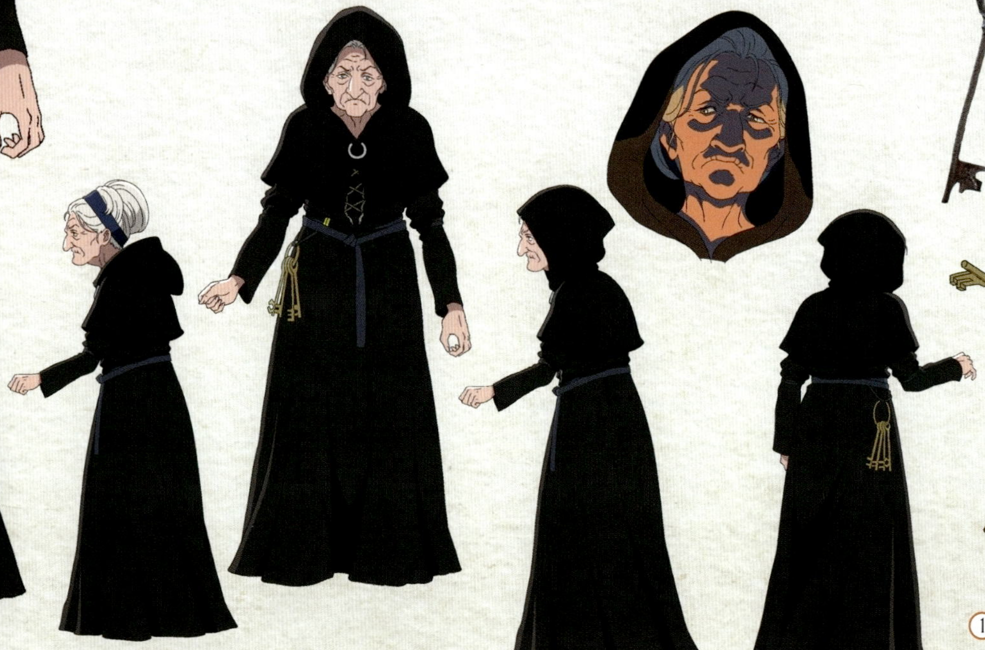

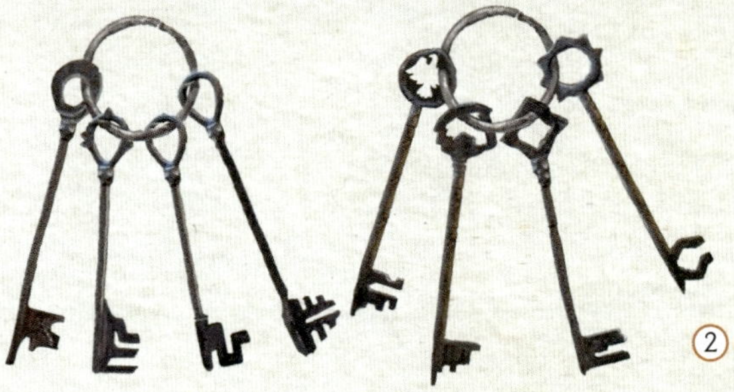

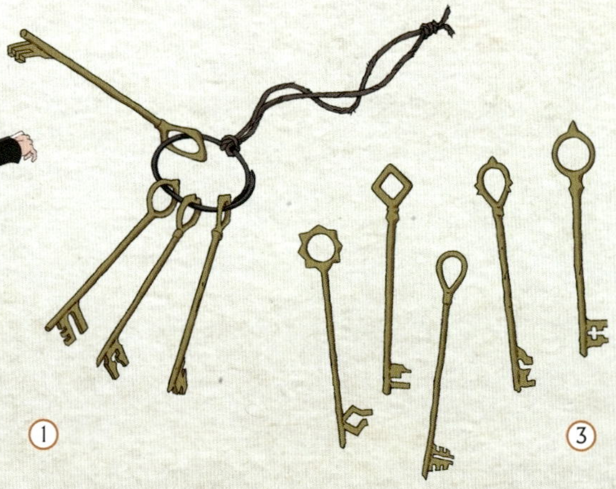

When she makes her entrance, it is with a mysterious, witch-like air, but once the hood is removed, it turns out Old Pennicruik is a kind-hearted, old lady. She is an interesting contrast, being an older female character who retains a certain innocence about her. As with Olwyn, I wanted to convey hints of the beauty and handsomeness of younger days in her present incarnation.

There are challenges in portraying older characters in animation. When drawing wrinkles, for example, we need to think about how to balance looking age-appropriate with the appeal of the character. – MIYAKO TAKASU, ANIMATION CHARACTER DESIGNER & KEY ANIMATION SUPERVISOR

The ragged wedding gown was great fun to draw, with its decayed cloth and bedraggled finery; echoes of a Vendel-era Miss Havisham, ghost-like and ethereal, but grim and portentous. – JOHN HOWE, CONCEPTUAL DESIGNER

It's not explicitly said, but the whole thing with the wedding dress is also layered with the idea that it was perhaps Pennicruik's own daughter's dress. – PHOEBE GITTINS, WRITER

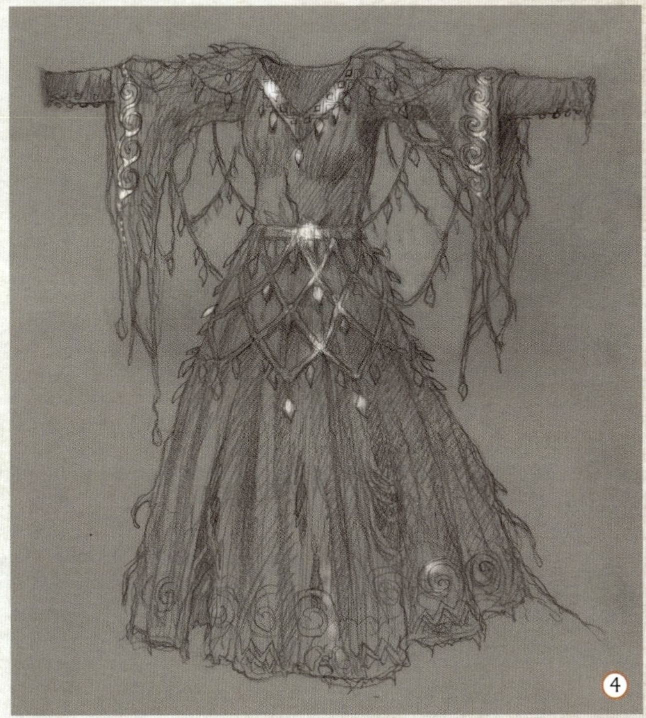

1: Pennicruik character and expressions setting art, MT. 2: Key ring concepts, CG. 3: Key ring prop setting art, KM. 4: Tattered wedding dress concept, JH.

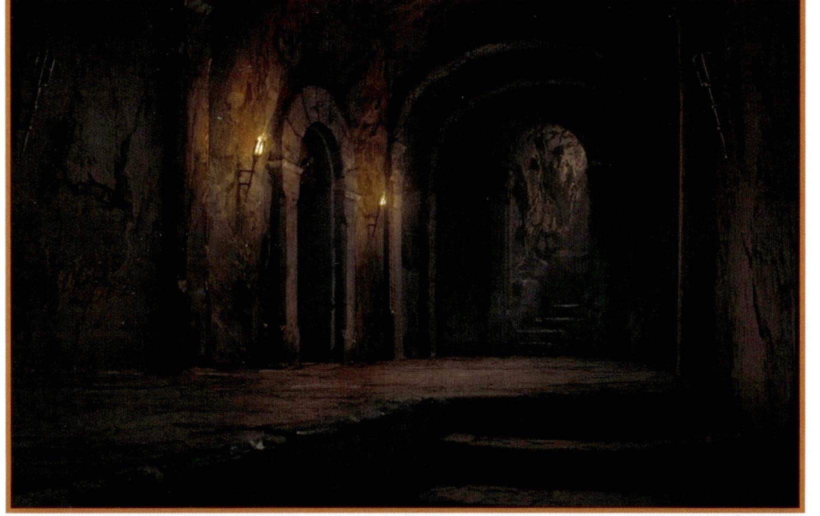

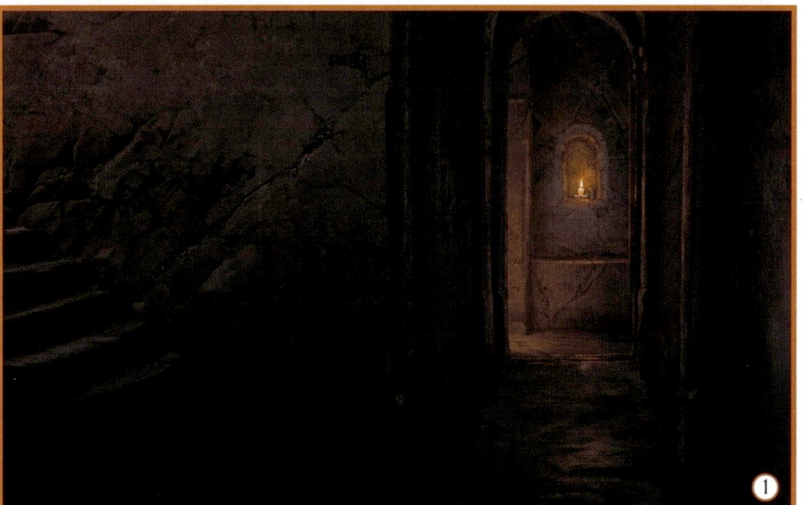

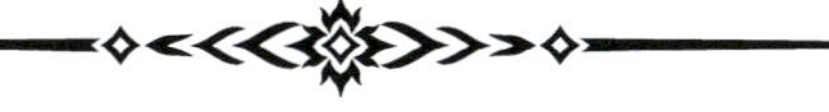

HORNBURG PASSAGES

Behind the cliffs and beneath the surface structures there are many chambers in the Hornburg, connected by passageways, vaulted ramps and stairs. While those above ground were built with great quarried blocks of stone, beneath the surface they were carved and hewn from the heart-rock.

There are simple passageways carved into the stone. To maintain the characteristic feel of the Hornburg, we tried to avoid cylindrical pillars as much as possible. – TAMIKO KANAMORI, ART DIRECTOR

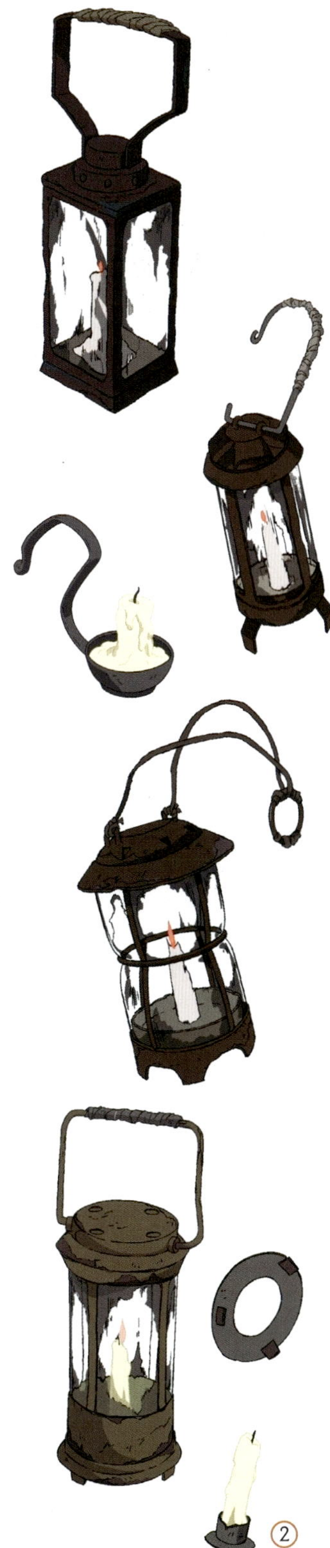

1: Hornburg interiors background art. 2: Lantern and candle prop setting art, KM.

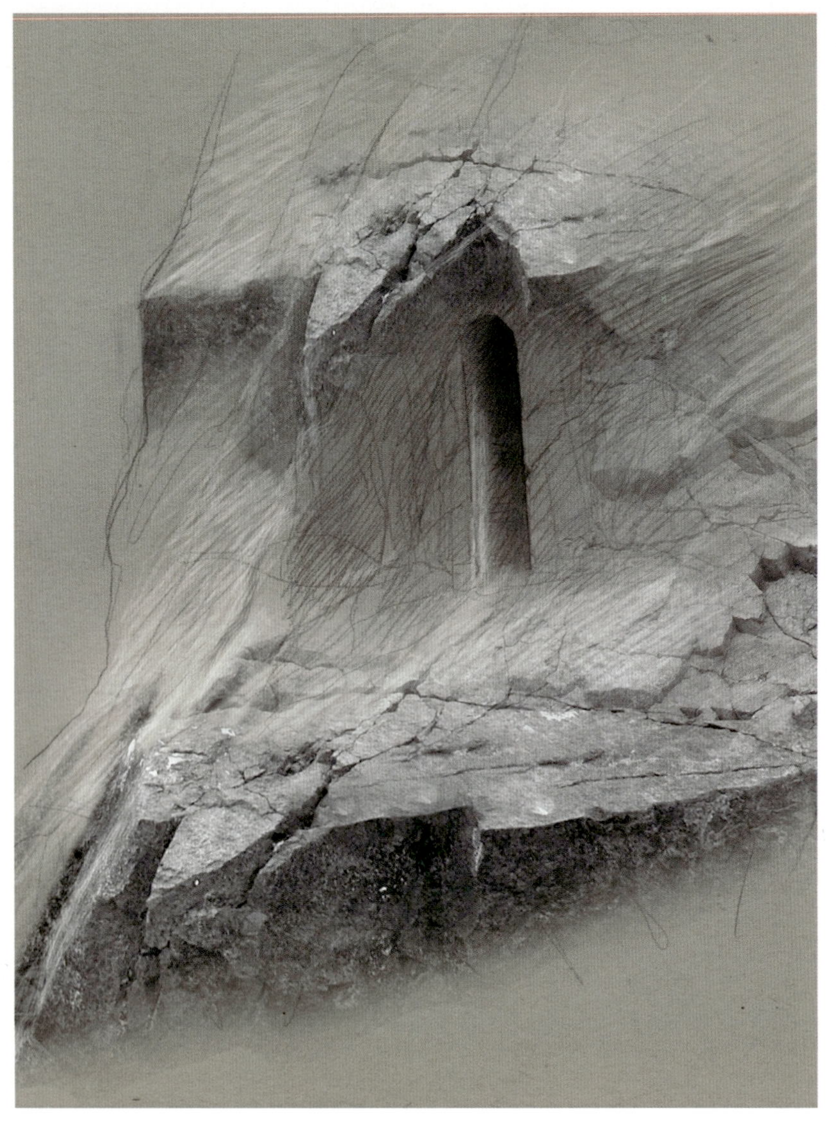

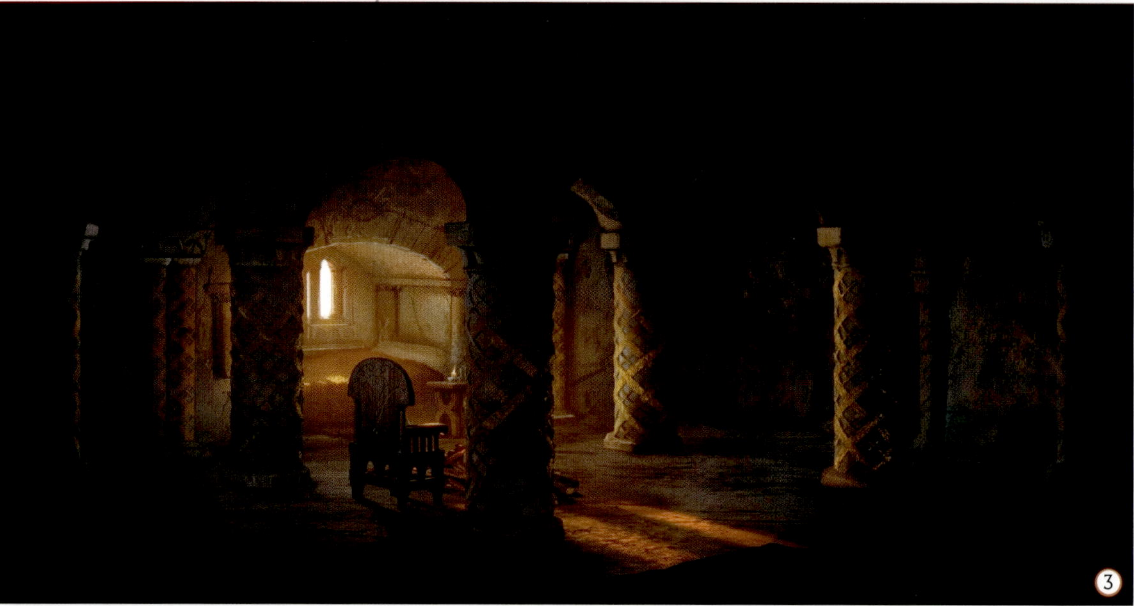

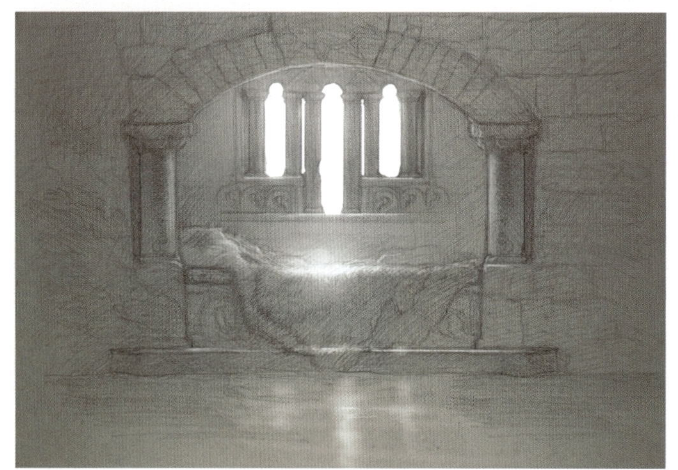

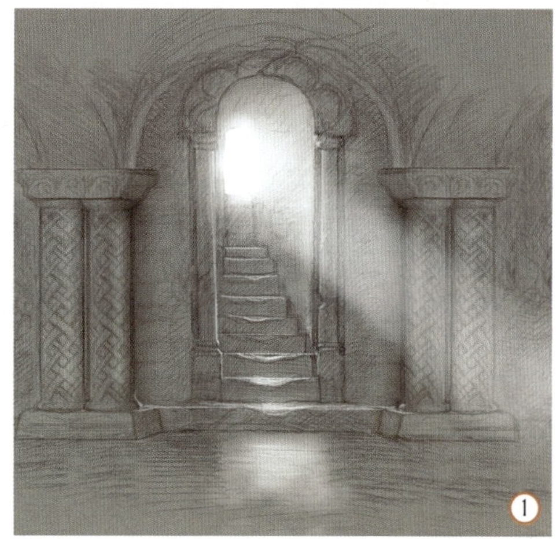

1: Helm's chamber and prop concepts, JH. 2: Helm's chamber concept, TK. 3: Helm's chamber background setting art, TK. 4: Helm's chamber background art.

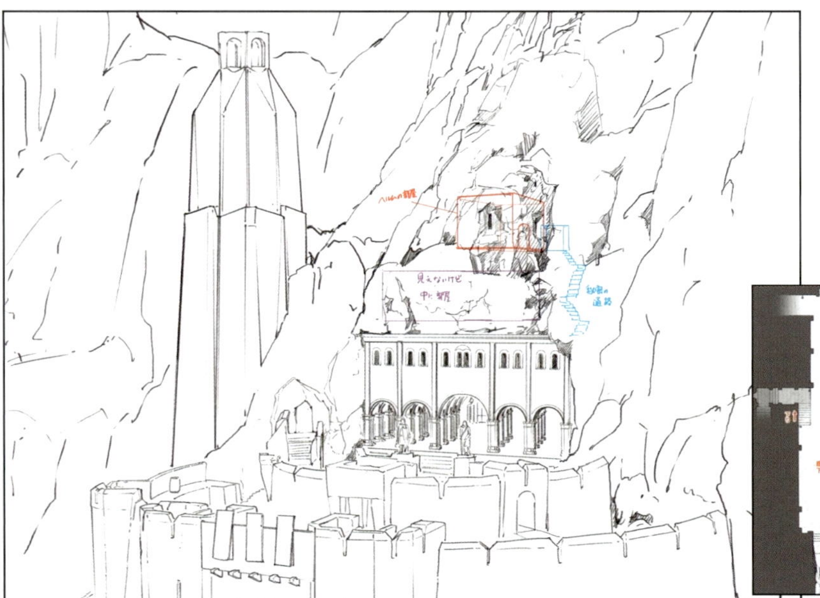

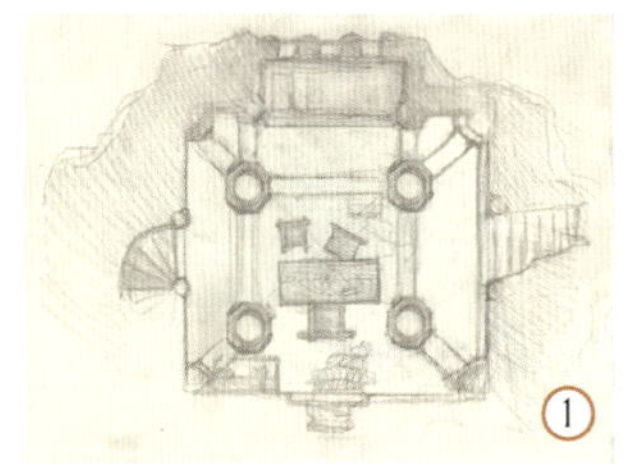

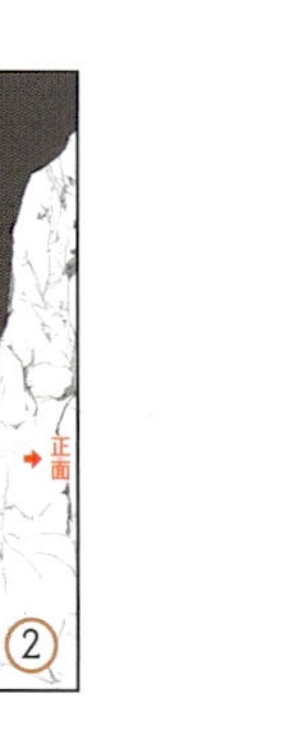

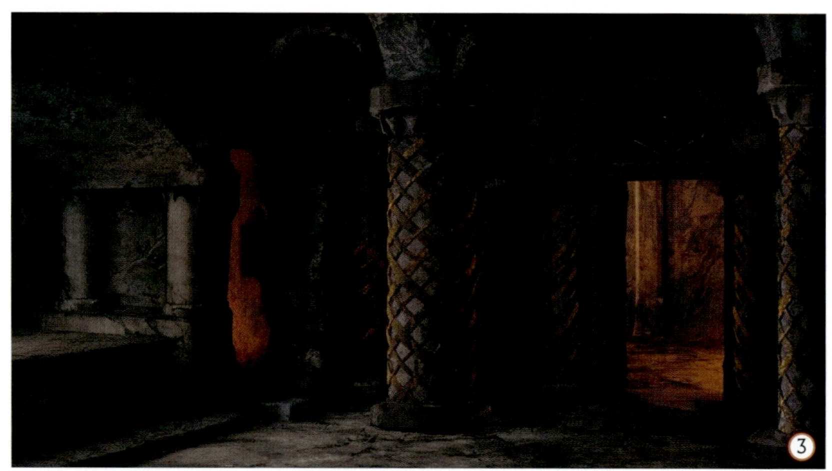

HELM'S CHAMBER

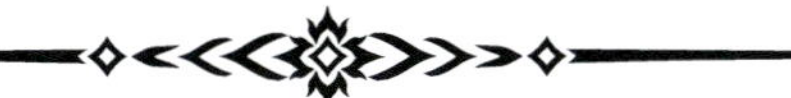

The king's personal chamber presented a new design opportunity, but where would it be located? The room was not accounted for in the original design. Several positions were considered, including behind the row of windows arrayed above the Keep's main doors, but a more intimate space was sought. The choice was made to nest it in the crumpled rockface above the Keep, where its windows on two sides were hidden in cracks overlooking the courtyard and the walled valley.

Helm's chamber might be one of those marvellous interior spaces that can occasionally be found when masonry and natural rock meet and mix, leading to endless design possibilities. Much of the decoration, in low relief, evokes Second Age Gondorian; single, doubled or recessed pillars with diagonal checkerboard interlace, Romanesque arches or low spans; a floor of simple flagstones and smoothed rock (we are inside a mountain, after all) and perhaps, here and there, a few more recently chiselled decorations done by a Rohirrim stonemason.

The view outside can be reached by climbing up a short flight of steps to a seat just behind the viewing slit, partly hidden under an overhang. The fireplace is built into a natural fissure. A sleeping alcove is framed with more elaborate and columned windows looking into the Keep's interior.

The furniture itself is simple but rich, as befits a king: a Savonarola folding chair with removable back rest, a sturdy throne-like seat, trestle table and an easily moveable double-lidded chest with carrying handles. The design of the campaign throne is more architectural, intended to evoke stability and solidity, while remaining relatively easy to disassemble and transport. The furnishings – aquamaniles, rhyton, jug and cups, candlestick and brazier are intended to show the diversity of provenance inherent to royalty on the move. The pottery aquamanile, for example, might be found in a modest household, the other, cast in bronze, is fit for a king's banquet hall. The ceramic lamp is unadorned and unglazed, but the *Krautstrunk* beaker and the rhyton are hardly everyday items. – JOHN HOWE, CONCEPTUAL DESIGNER

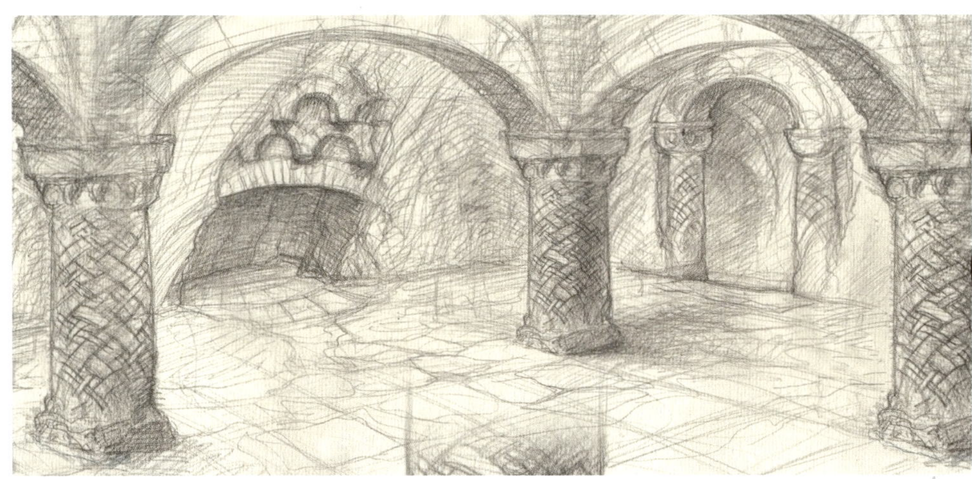

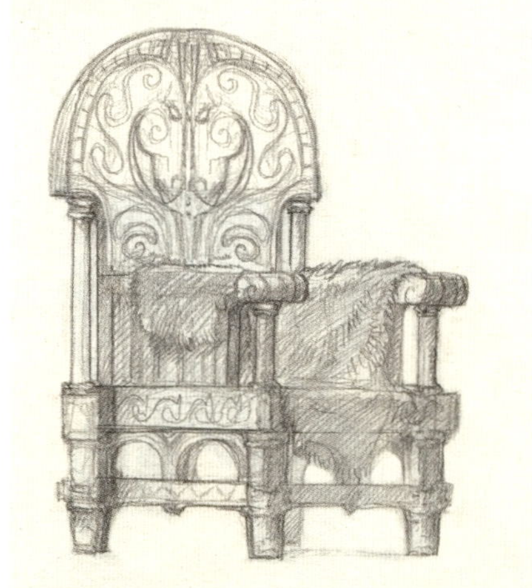

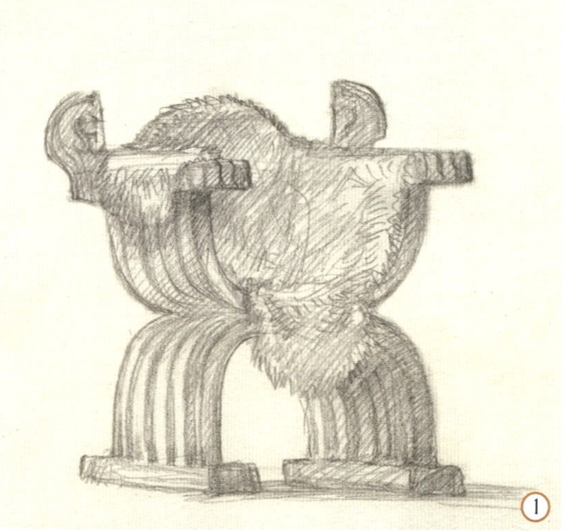

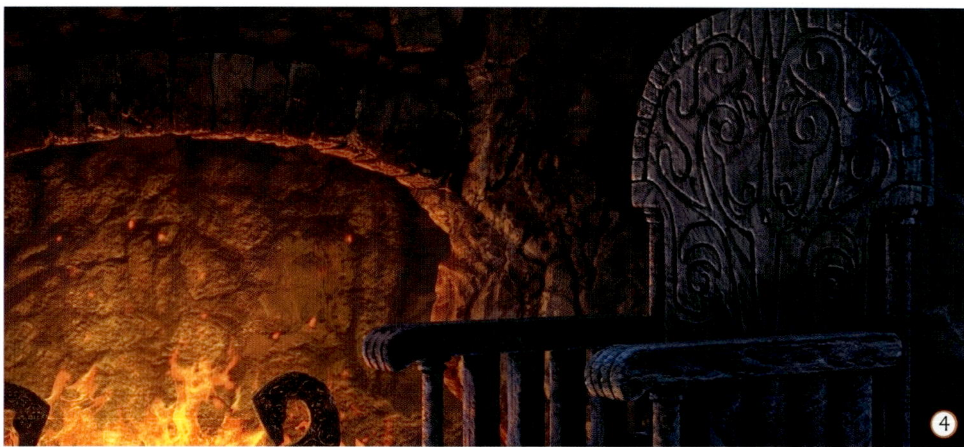

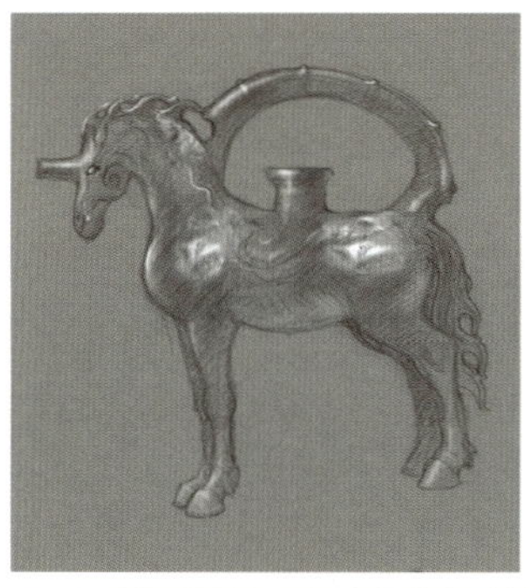

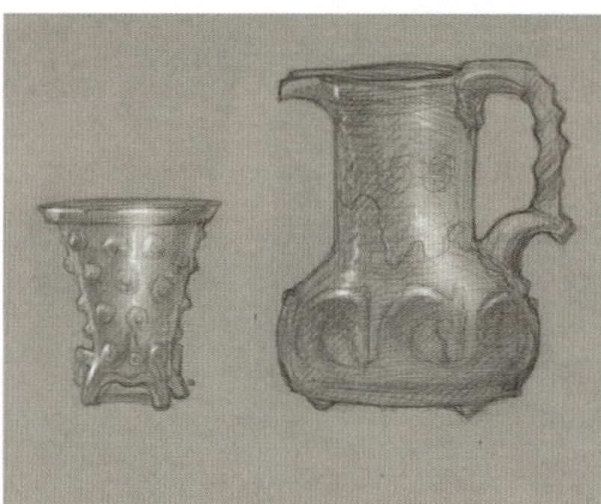

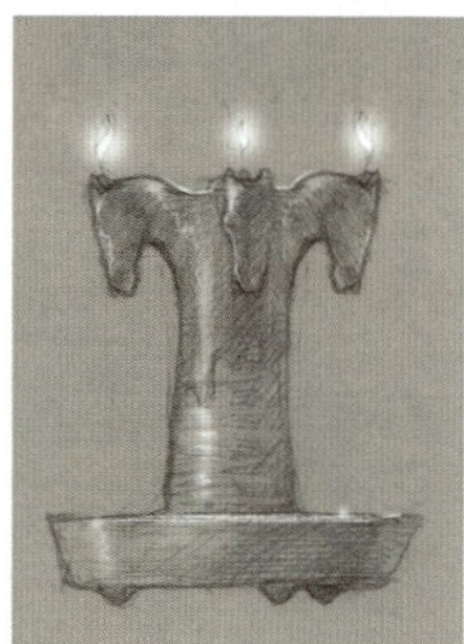

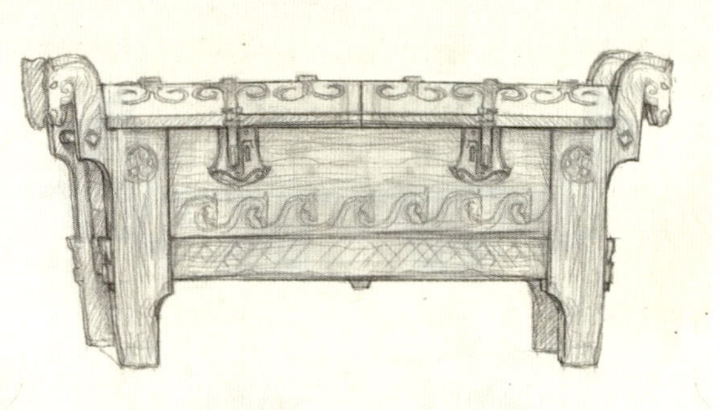

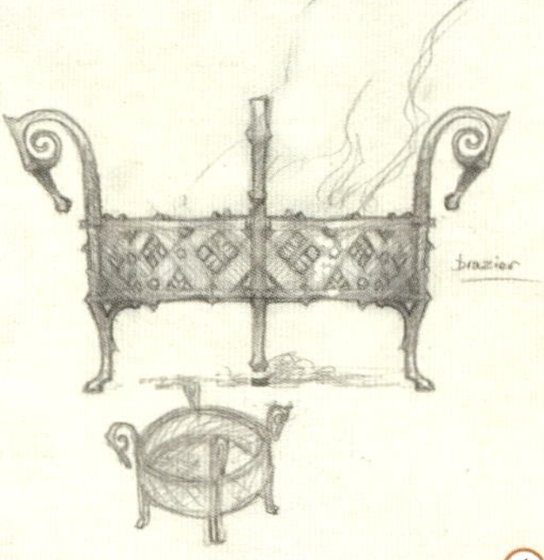

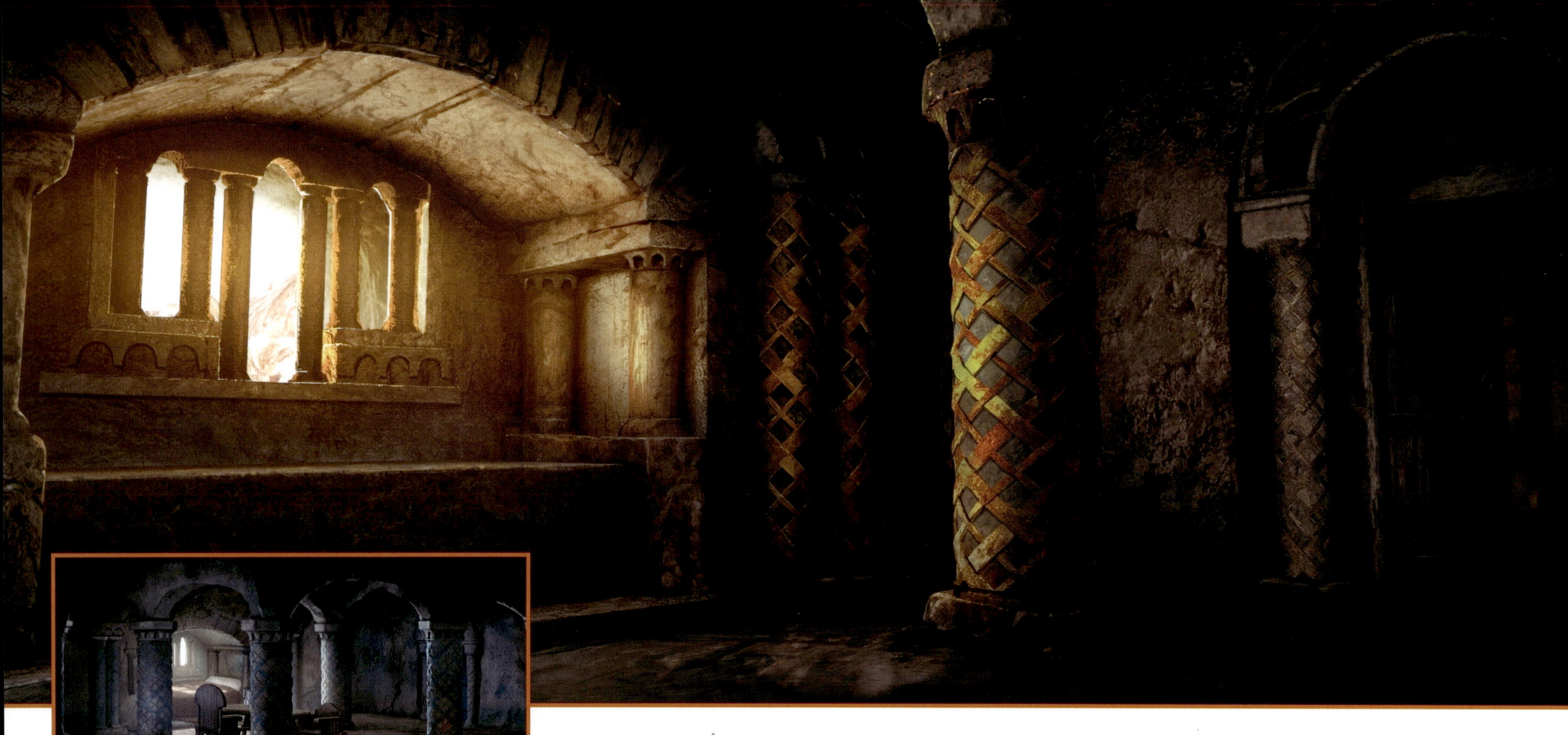

John Howe's concepts were very beautiful, so we tried to be as faithful to them as possible. We adjusted the furniture placement based on where characters needed to interact in certain scenes. We were mindful of the fact that the room was carved from stone, so even if there are block forms, they are superficial and aesthetic rather than structural.

I thought it would be sad if the only colour was the natural grey of the stone, so I initially painted the decorative banding on the pillars blue. Gold was suggested as an alternative. It stood out in the cold stone room, looked beautiful, and was appropriate for the king's room, so we ran with it. It was fun to depict how it might sparkle in dim light or night scenes. – TAMIKO KANAMORI, ART DIRECTOR

Characters' colours vary according to the environments that they appear in. Evenings, mornings, and shadowy scenes are generally simple because they have a single light source, but on this film there were many night and underground scenes with multiple lights requiring distinct colour schemes corresponding to each source. There was a lot of coordination between animation, colour design and photography, and some trial and error before shots were finalized. Ultimately, multiple different coloured materials were composited together, taking lighting and other effects into account. Compositing processes played a very important role in shot construction. – OSAMA MIKASA, COLOUR DESIGNER

The Hornburg serves as a refuge of last resort for the Rohirrim, so Helm's chamber in the Hornburg was not his actual bed chamber but instead a place he inhabits out of need. It had to look makeshift, but still kingly. It had to be roomy enough to include a nook that could hide a secret escape route, but not too cavernous or grand. When Helm was dying, it had to be able to look bleak and sad, but the space also had to change character and appearance. A lot of that came down to how it could be lit, where changing the lighting could alter it from cosy to forbidding or creepy. It had to look spooky when the film becomes more of a ghost story, during Helm's episodes of slipping out at night to raid and the resulting rumours of a stalking wraith. – JASON DEMARCO, PRODUCER

1: Helm's chamber background setting art and colour concepts, TK.
2: Helm's chamber concept, JH. 3: Helm's chamber background art.

'SOME SAY . . . THIS PLACE DOES STRANGE THINGS TO A MAN . . . IT CAN DRIVE HIM MAD.'

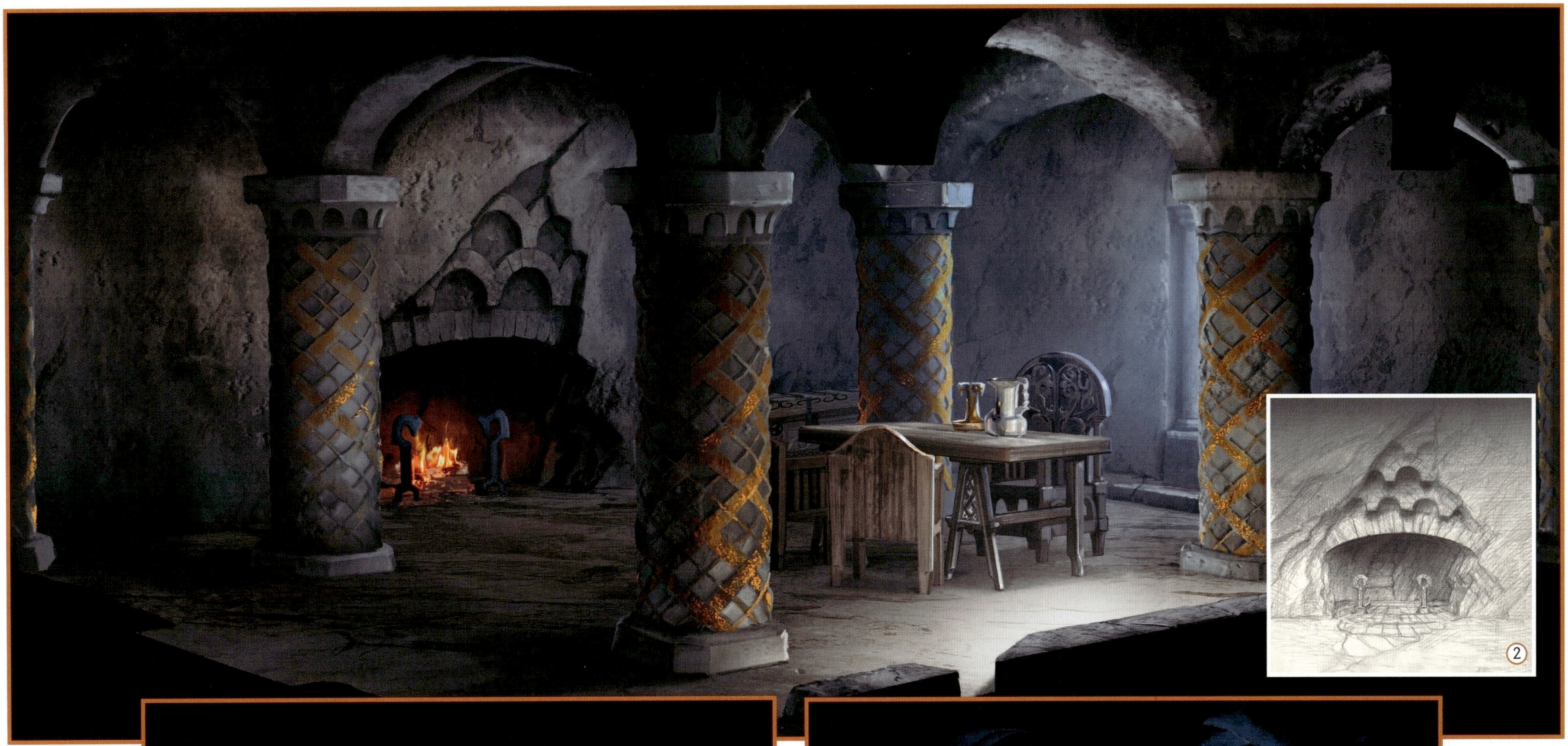

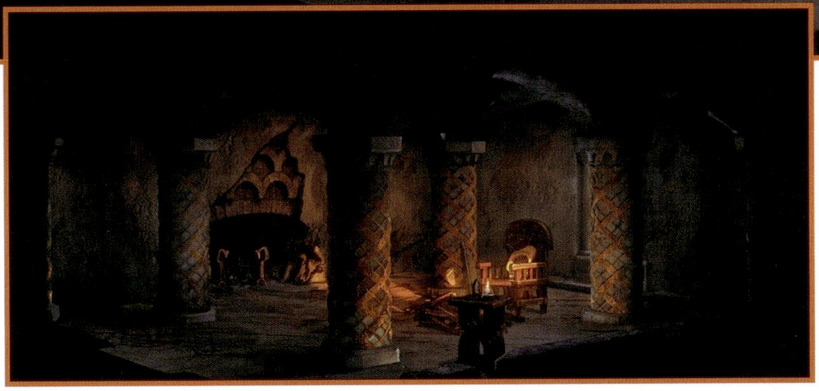

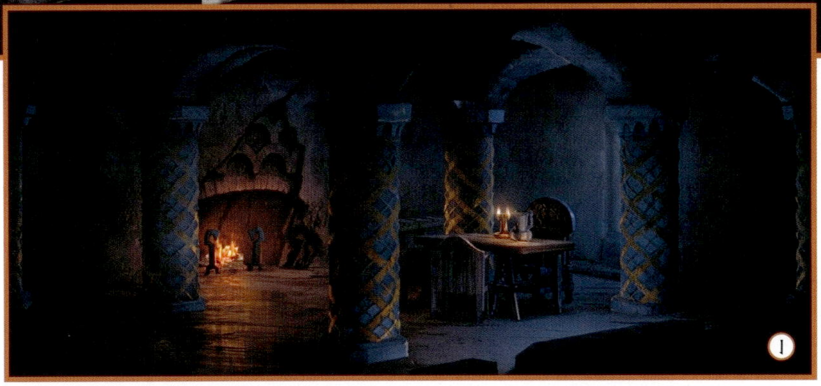

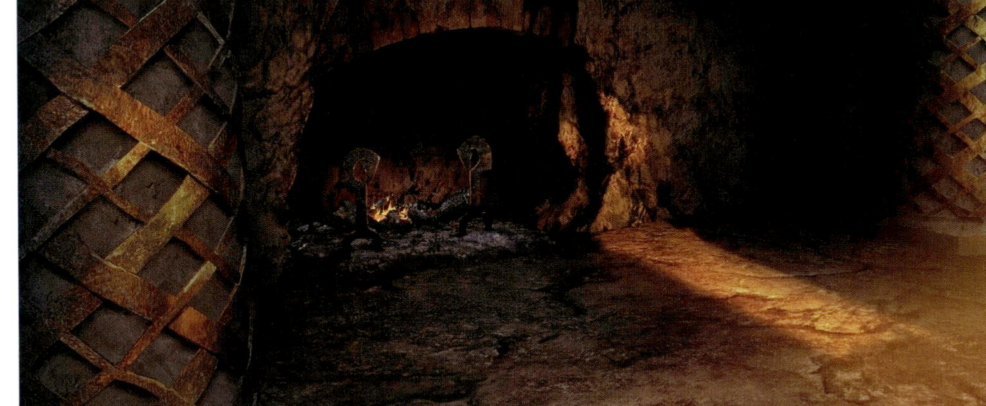

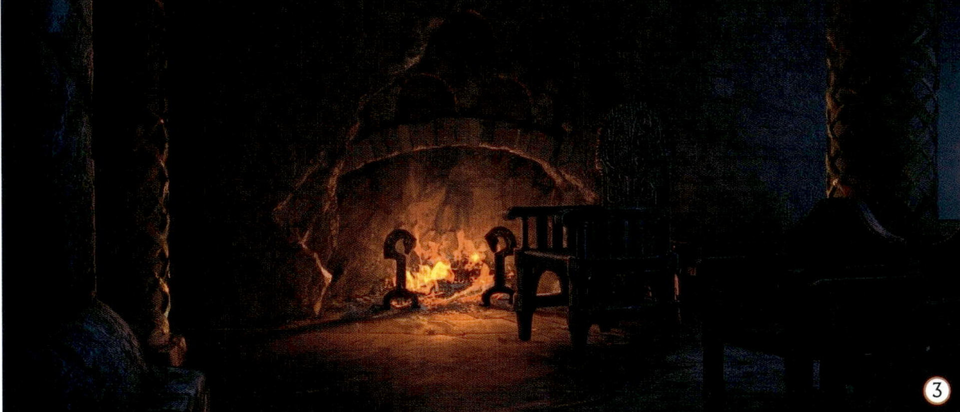

HELM ABED

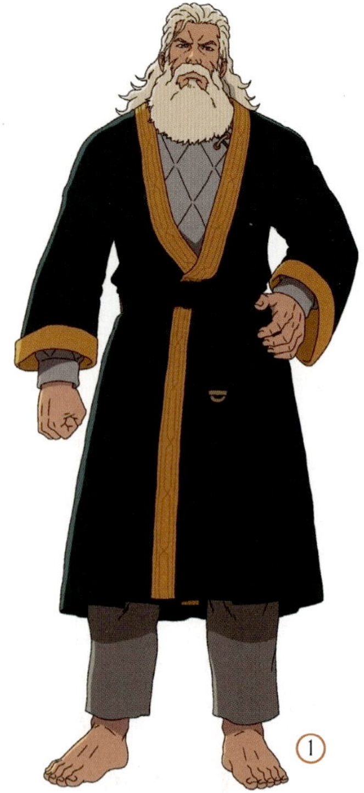

Helm is at his lowest point. He has not only lost his kingdom, but more tragically, he has lost his sons. Even Fréaláf has been banished. And Helm blames himself for it all; he knows it has come to this because of his choices, his actions. – ARTY PAPAGEORGIOU, WRITER

Helm's body is mending, and yet he does not wake. He is trapped in his mind; the madness of Helm. Héra comes to his bedside to say that she knows it is grief that pulls him under, but reminds him that all is not lost, she is still there and she still needs him. Some part of this reaches Helm, that drive to protect his child, it's what spurs him to disappear; to go out and kill, lost in the madness. What is he seeking? Redemption? Revenge? It's all that he can do. – PHOEBE GITTINS, WRITER

Helm's vengeful, hunting Wraith look was designed first. His bed clothes were imagined as the original versions of those garments, including gown and quilted undergarments.

1: Helm character setting art, MT. **2:** Helm's chamber background art. **3:** Animation key frames, MT.

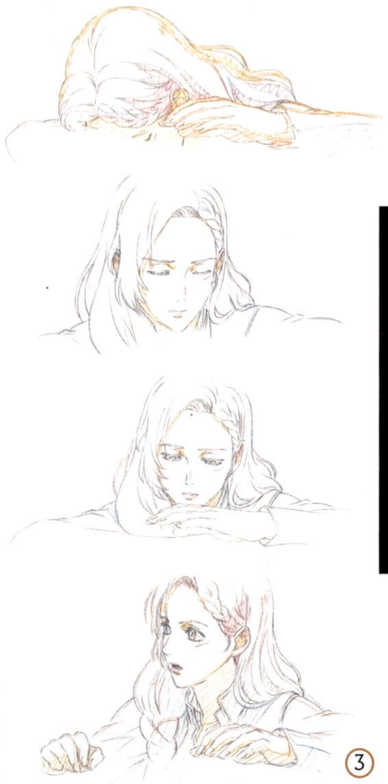

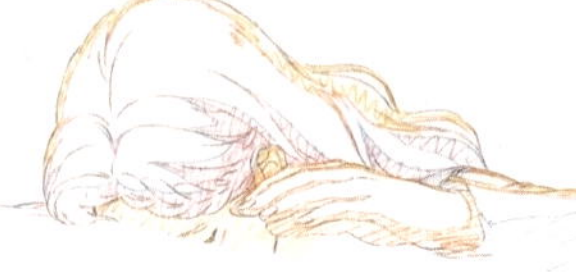

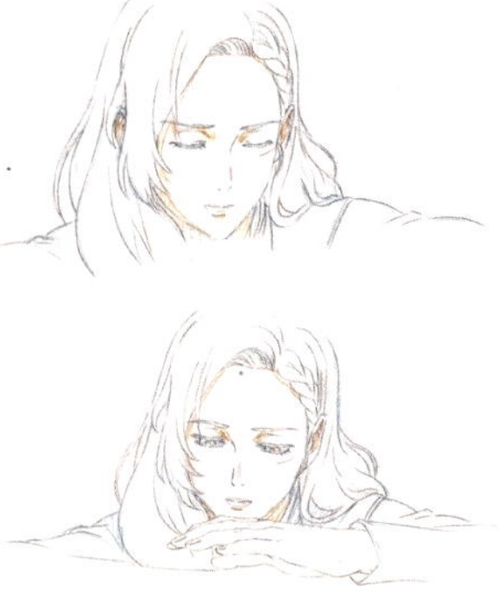

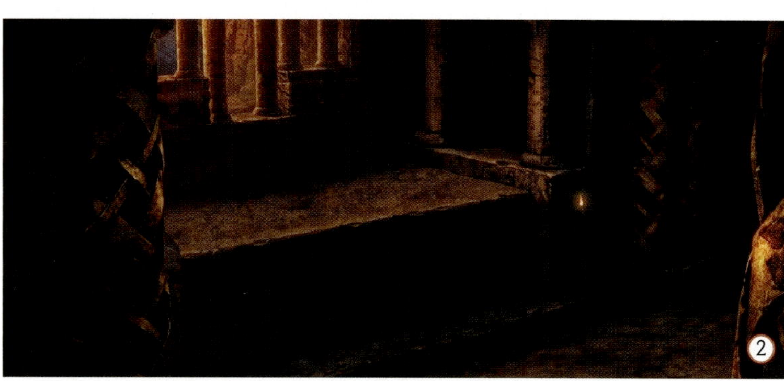

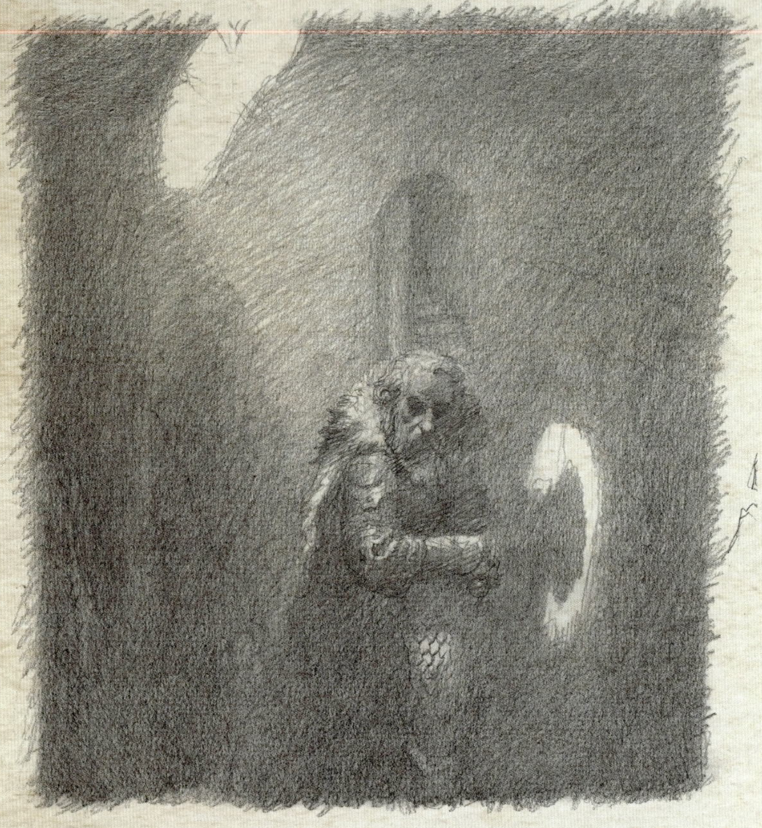

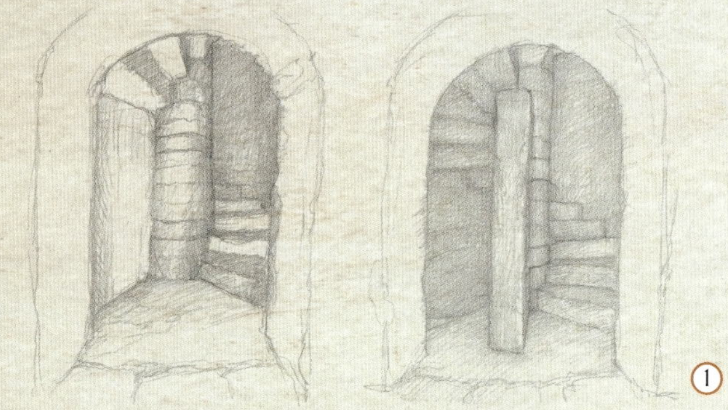

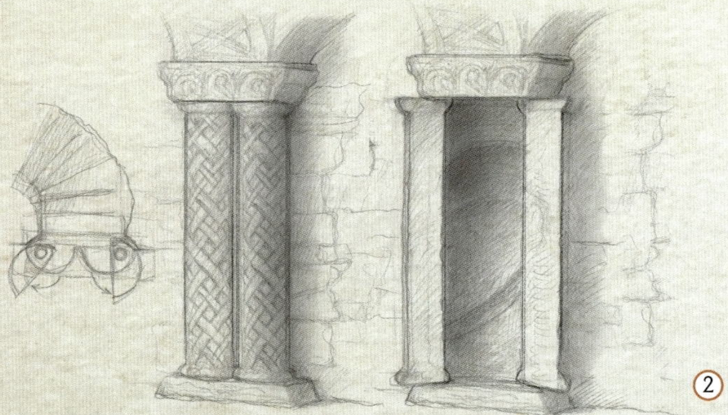

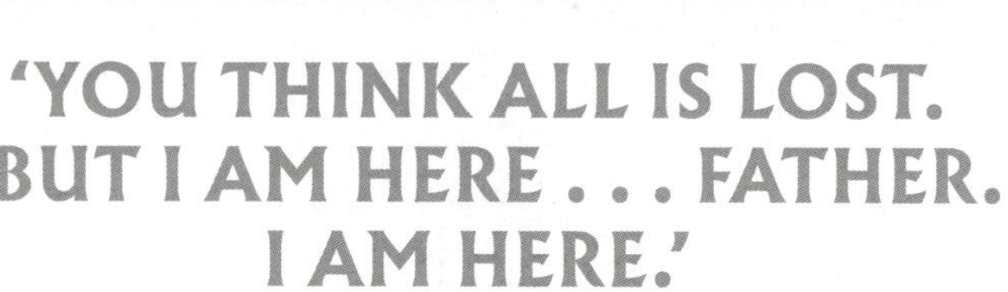

1: Secret passage concepts, AL. 2: Secret passage concepts, JH. 3: Secret passage concepts, TK. 4: Secret passage concepts, YY. 5: Final film frame.

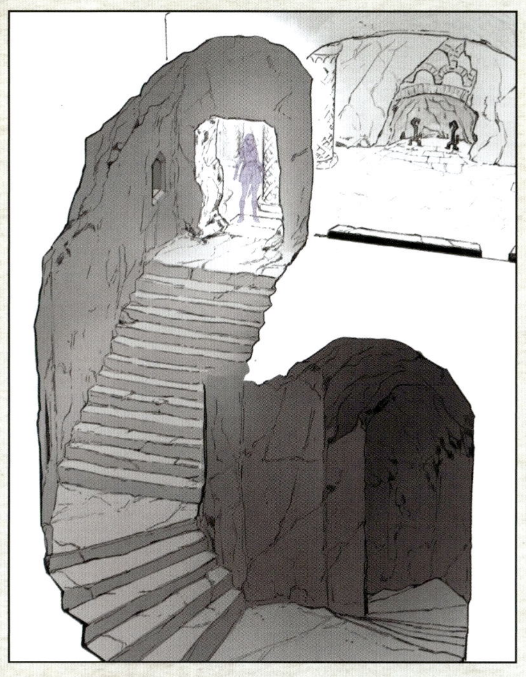

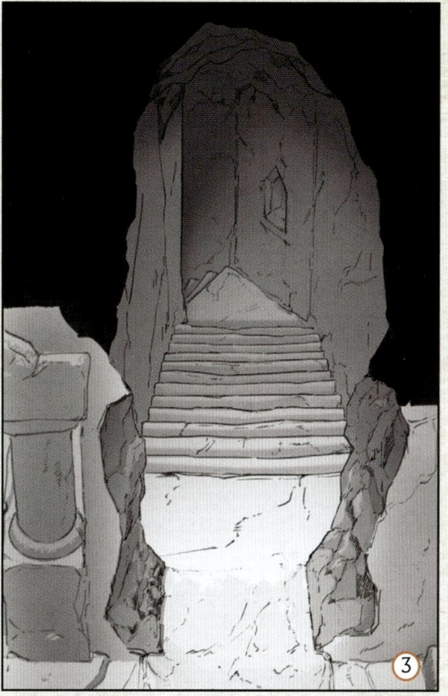

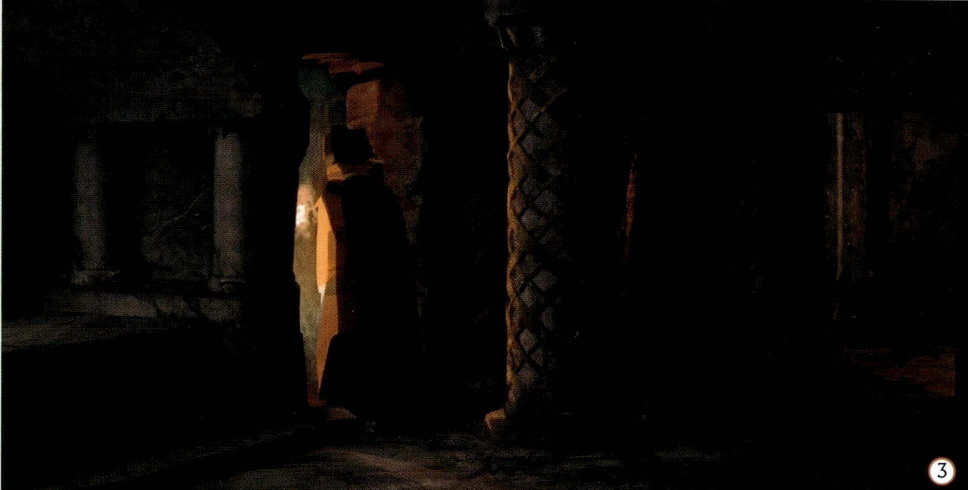

THE SECRET PASSAGE

We needed a way for Helm to sneak out at night with no one seeing his coming or going. We imagined that, as a king, his chamber probably had a secret door which might give him access to an escape route – something that you might see in medieval castles.
– JASON DEMARCO, PRODUCER

My initial idea for the secret entrance in Helm's chamber was to conceal the hinges in open sight by being two of the courses of stone at the centre of a spiral staircase. When swung, they revealed another flight of stairs curving deeper into the mountainside.
– ALAN LEE, CONCEPTUAL DESIGNER

I provided a number of drawings for Hornburg's secret tunnels and hidden entrance. We had taken a cue from the book in implying the idea of tunnels for refugees in *The Two Towers*, though they headed back further into the Coomb and into the Glittering Caves. It is logical that this defensive cave network could also be utilized as a means of escaping behind enemy lines.

The idea made me think of the secret tunnel below Dover Castle, which I visited as a child. It was built to be able to keep the defenders supplied during sieges, and had some ingenious defences. – ALAN LEE, CONCEPTUAL DESIGNER

The secret passage changes in character as we move through it. The lower you go, the darker it gets. We designed a gazebo-like space halfway down the stairs. The only light source in this section is a handheld lamp, so the colours change little by little, but they were able to control it well during the compositing stage. – YASUHIRO YAMANE, ART DIRECTOR

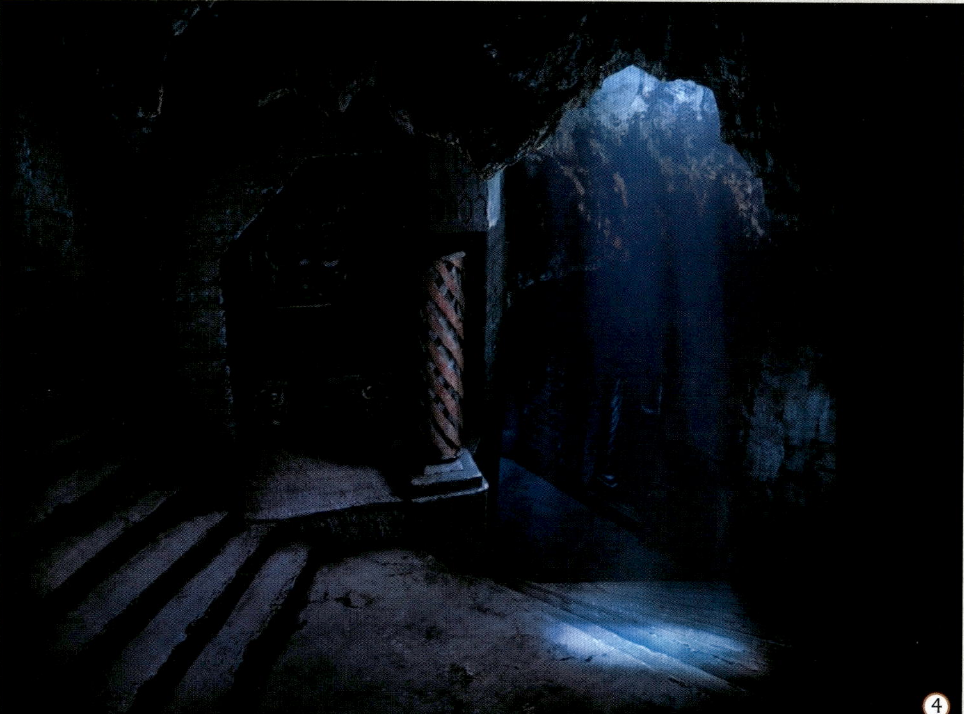

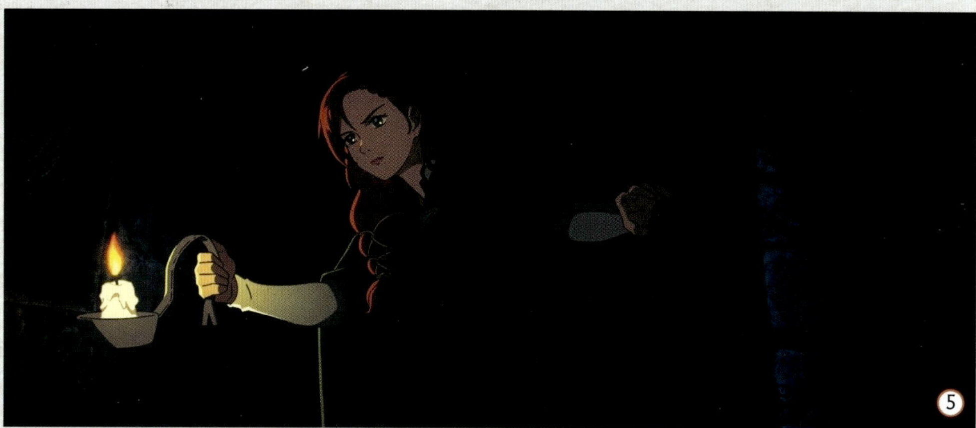

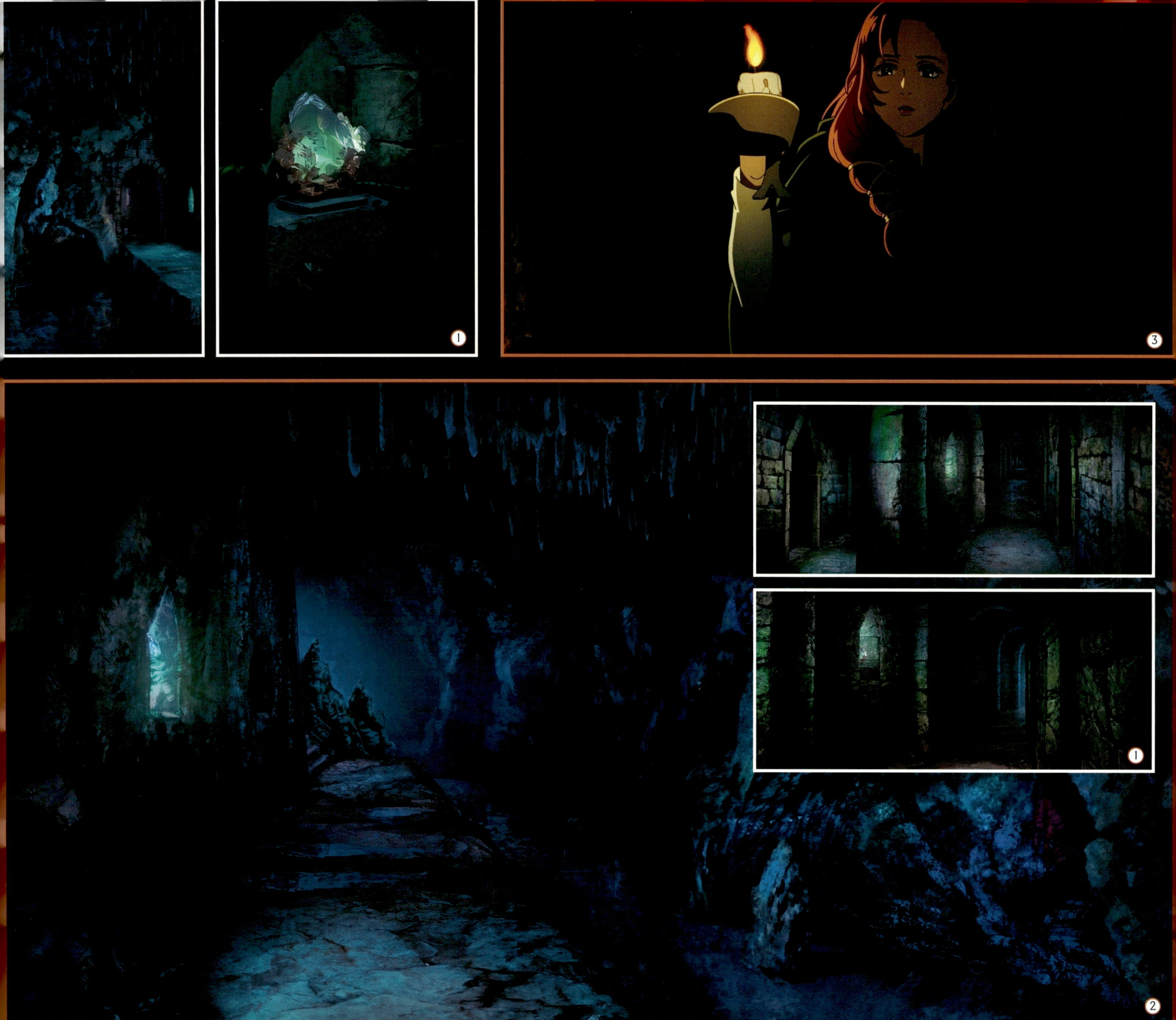

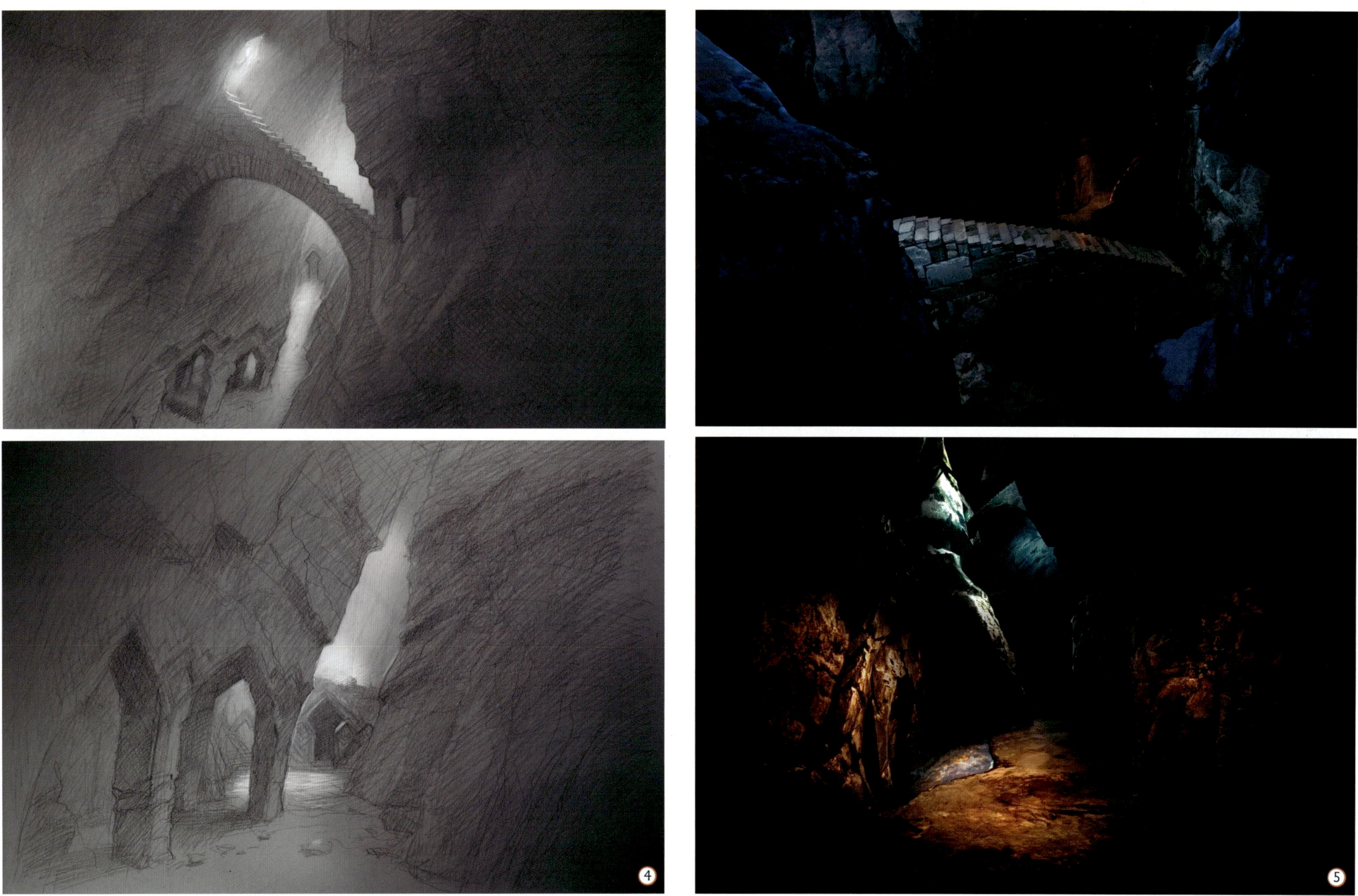

As Héra explored the passageway beneath the Hornburg we leaned fully into the ghost story vibe. With a candle in her hand, she begins to investigate where her father has gone. What is this creepy, empty passageway that she didn't know existed? Where does it lead? Where is the eerie wind blowing from? Who else is down here? – JASON DEMARCO, PRODUCER

A lot of thought was put into charting the winding course of the secret passageway. It would begin in the heart-rock of the mountain, behind Helm's chamber, curling as it descended behind the Keep. Far beneath, it would turn to run through the Deeping Wall to the far side of the valley, illuminated by eldritch crystals rather than torchlight. Penetrating the far slope, it would rise, wind, twist and fall through a labyrinth of natural and cut fissure, eventually joining caves of dripping minerals and a sheltered exit. – DANIEL FALCONER, ADDITIONAL CONCEPTS DESIGNER

The space had scant light sources and could have ended up being entirely monochromatic, so we looked for ways to add colour to prevent monotony. – YASUHIRO YAMANE, ART DIRECTOR

Such a propitious location as the Hornburg might well have been occupied before it was constructed in the Second Age. Perhaps deeper and long-abandoned delvings of Dwarves might be hinted at, overlaid with Gondorian improvements and additions? – JOHN HOWE, CONCEPTUAL DESIGNER

1: Secret passage background art. 2: Secret passage background setting art, KS. 3: Final film frame. 4: Secret passage concepts, JH. 5: Secret passage background setting art, YY.

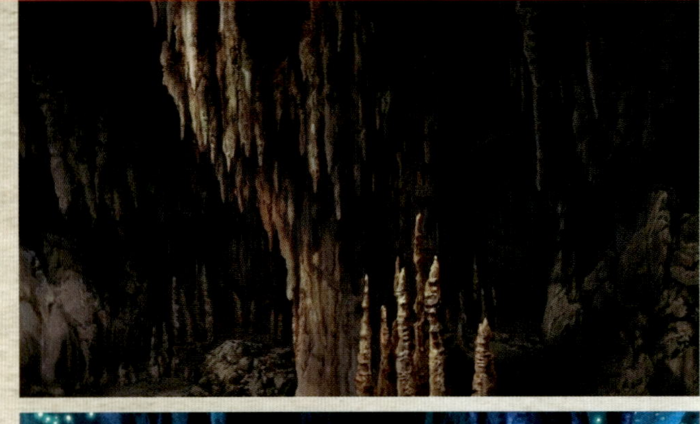

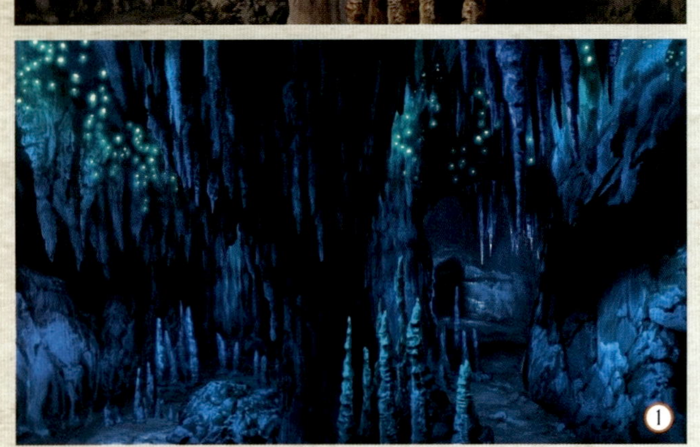

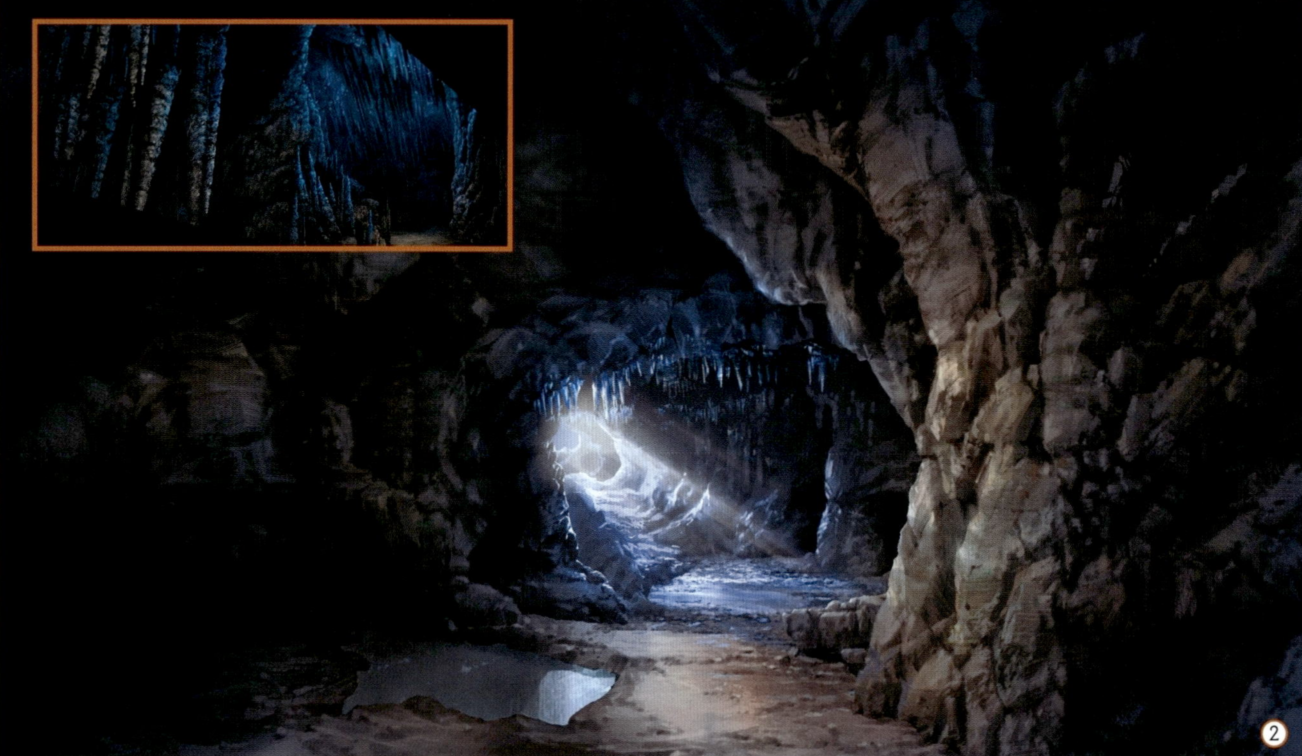

THE CAVES

Exploring the tunnels, Héra enters a cavern of glittering stone pillars and twinkling lights, eventually emerging on the icy slope beyond the Deeping Wall.

In *The Two Towers* we saw people escaping into the caves behind the Hornburg, so we knew that the mountains were threaded with tunnels. Helm would certainly be aware, so we reasoned that he might make use of them. We had discussions about where the natural caverns were, how they might connect with carved tunnels, and where they might lead. After figuring out the layout, things began to make sense. – KENJI KAMIYAMA, DIRECTOR

During the War of the Ring the Rohirrim took shelter in these Glittering Caves, but in addition to those vaulted caverns we imagined there might be other, smaller passageways threading the mountainsides bounding the valley. The script required Helm to travel via tunnel between the fortress and the Dunlending camp. We hypothesized that such a passage might have been carved as a bolt hole by the Hornburg's builders, taking advantage of natural fissures; this visually connected viewers with the Glittering Caves of the trilogy, even if they weren't the exact same places. – DANIEL FALCONER, ADDITIONAL CONCEPTS DESIGNER

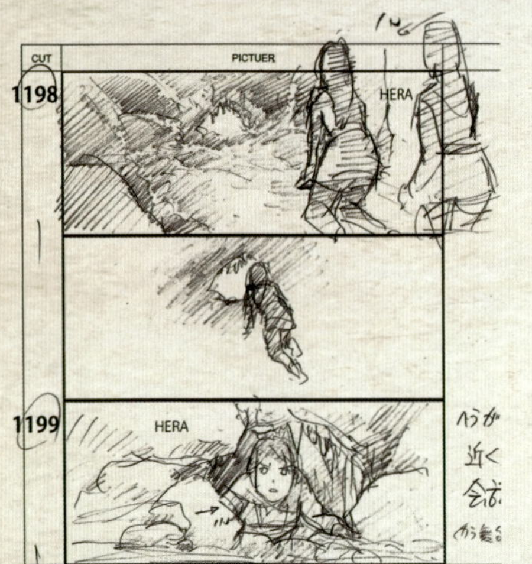

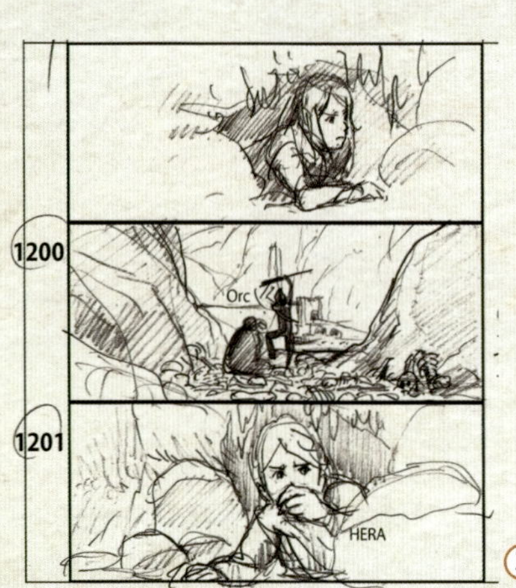

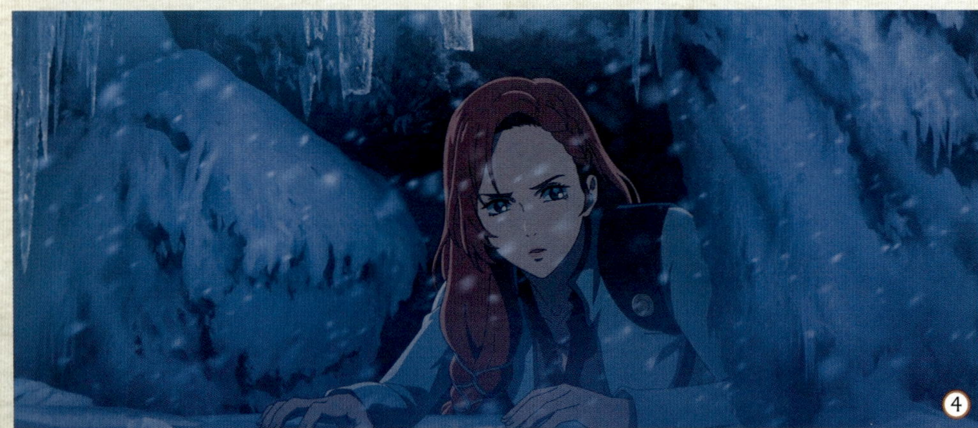

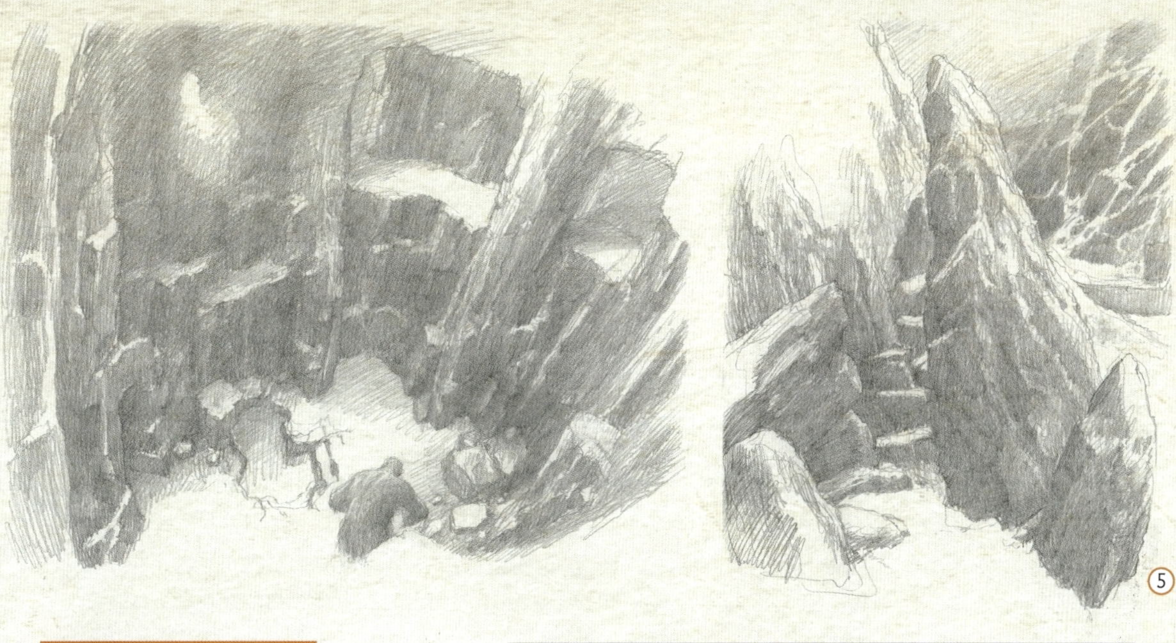

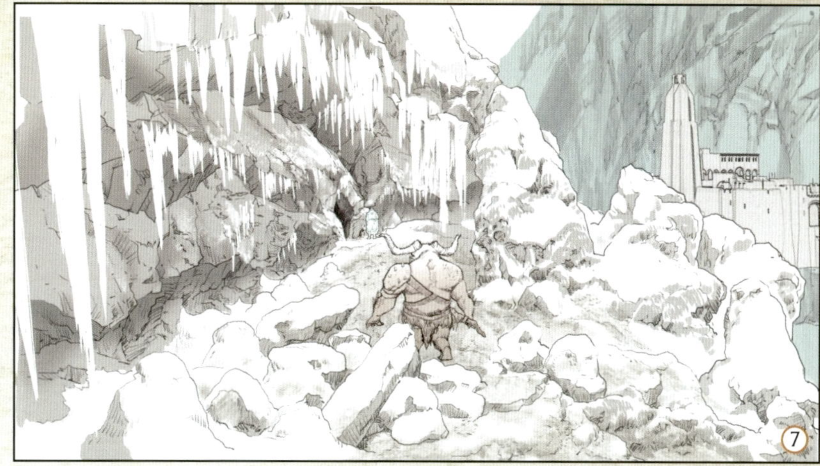

1: Cave background setting art, YY. 2: Cave background art.
3: Storyboards, KK. 4: Final film frame. 5: Secret exit concepts, AL.
6: Secret exit concept, DF. 7: Secret exit concept, YY. 8: Secret exit
background setting art, YY.

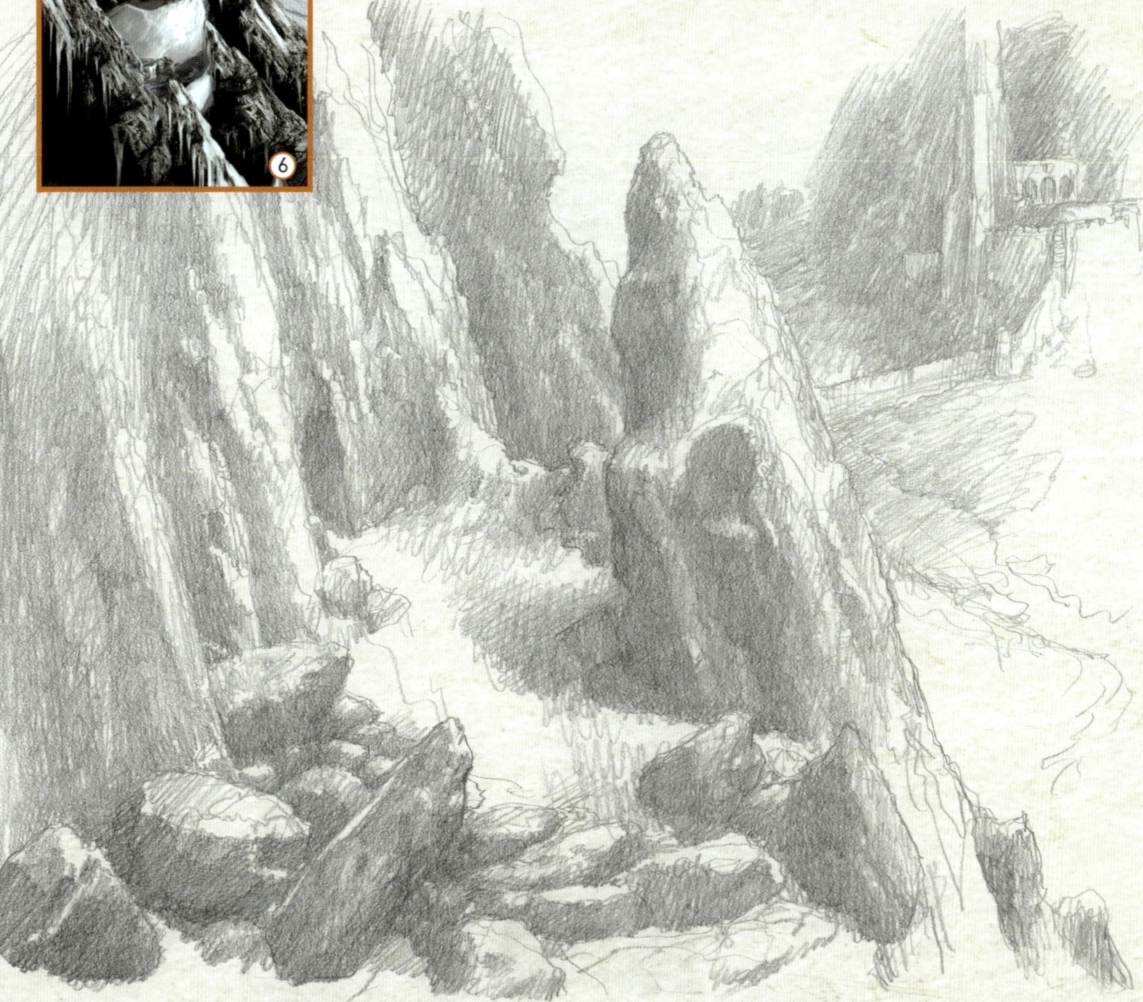

What Héra finds as she moves through the passages is a secret way out of the fortress that opens onto the broken mountainside. Unfortunately, this isn't all that she finds. There are Orcs out here, too. 'Is my father going down here and if so, why? What else is down here?' As it turns out, it's nothing good, so we needed to design a space that felt like somewhere where bad things were happening. – JASON DEMARCO, PRODUCER

One of the challenges of the tunnel exit was how had it remained secret all these years? Héra and the audience would need to be able to orient themselves in the geography when she emerged, so the exit needed a view of the valley. We tried to come up with compositions that hid the exit in or behind broken rock. Perhaps it was part of a quarry area, or a jagged cliff edge? – DANIEL FALCONER, ADDITIONAL CONCEPTS DESIGNER

There were some very cool designs for the cave exit area produced by Alan Lee and Daniel Falconer. In the end, its shape was dictated by the action that had to take place there, so it ended up being a bit flatter than some of the early concepts. – YASUHIRO YAMANE, ART DIRECTOR

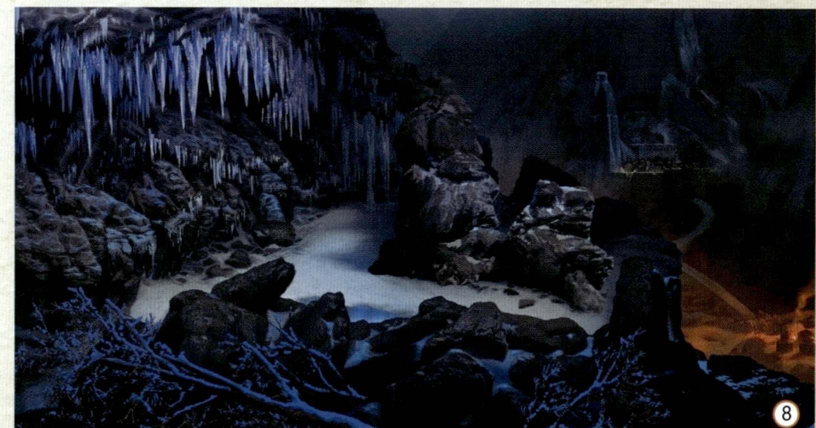

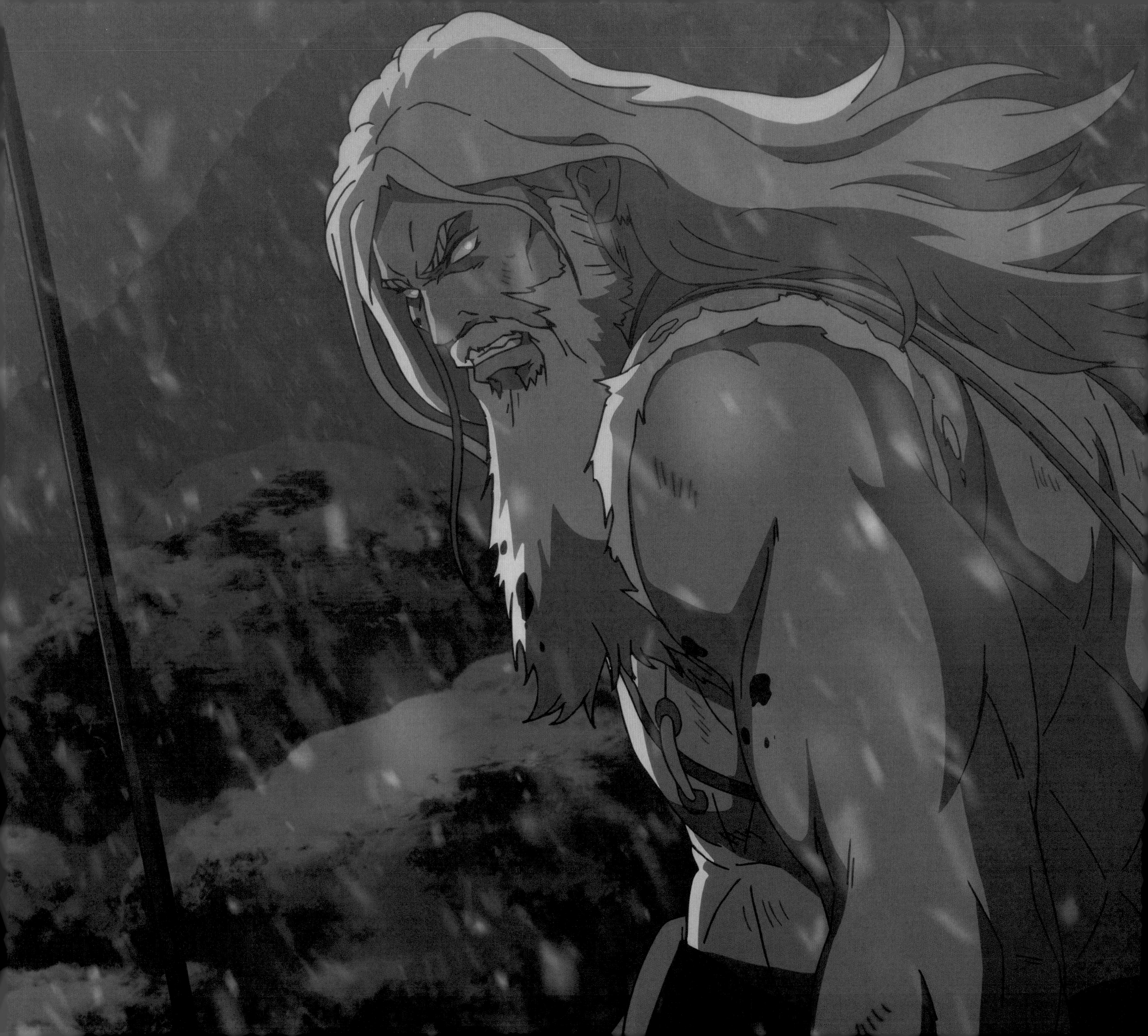

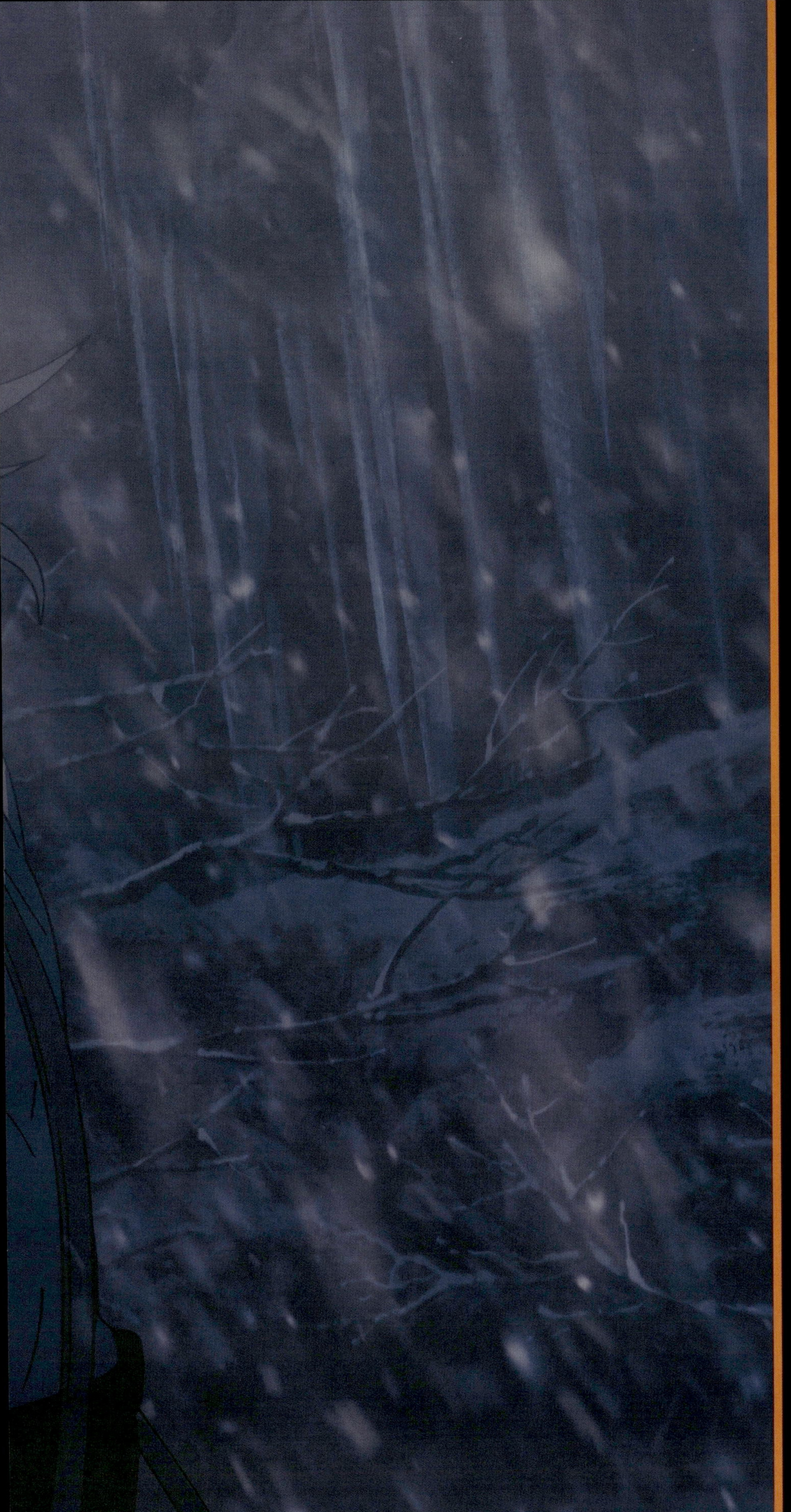

- 7 -

⟨⟨⟨◆⟩⟩⟩

THE WRAITH
OF HELM
HAMMERHAND

Mad with grief, Helm stalks the snowy wastes beyond the Deeping Wall, killing enemies with his bare hands. The Dunlendings and Wild Men fear him as a wraith that comes in the night to grab men, one at a time.

Seeking her father, Héra discovers a pit where the enemy has been dumping their fallen. Winter has not been kind to either side, but she is not alone in her grim discovery. A pair of Orcs scavenges among the dead, collecting rings for their master in the east. They seize Héra, but Helm comes flying to her rescue out of the snowstorm. The mad king battles a Snow-troll hand to hand, crushing the beast's skull, and he and Héra flee through the snow, across the enemy encampment and up the causeway toward the Hornburg's front gate.

Wulf's men pursue them, but thrusting his daughter through a narrow gap in the doorway, Helm entrusts the safety of his people to her, pulling closed the fortress doors. Alone in the blizzard, the king protects the gate, slaying every warrior who charges up the ramp toward him.

Morning finds Helm standing frozen outside the doors, his fists raised, dead enemies strewn about him, triumphant even in death.

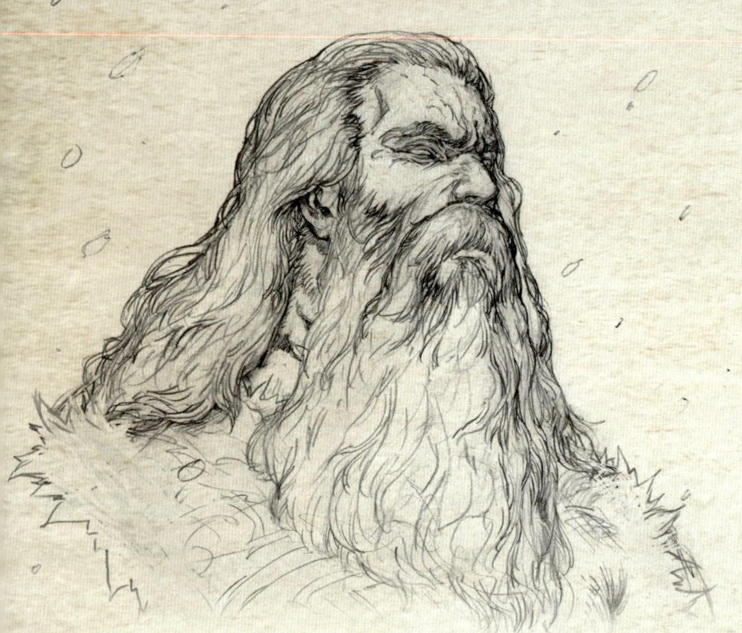

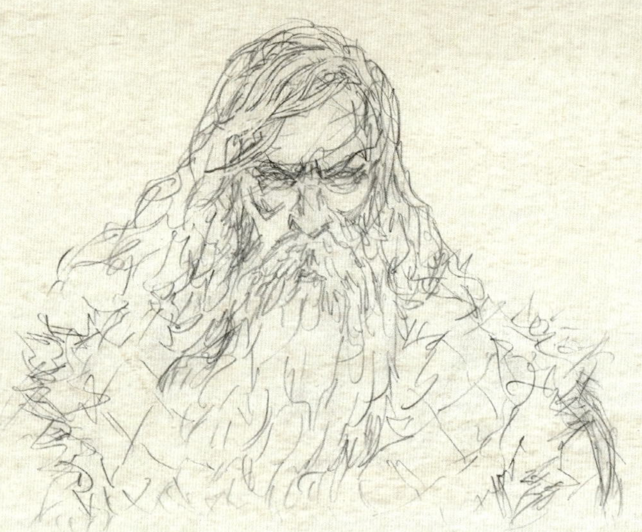

THE WRAITH OF HELM HAMMERHAND

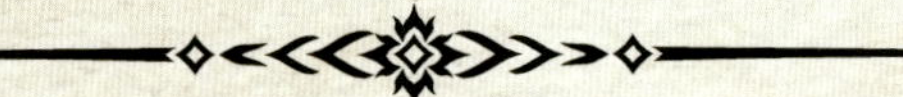

Ragged and wild-haired, Helm stalks the snowy wastes, striking terror into the encamped besiegers, who think him the wraith of their dead foe, dispensing vengeance from beyond the grave.

This was surprisingly tricky to get right. What does becoming a wraith mean and how do you show it? How do you make it convincing, but also clear that he is not? He might go out there and kill people, and perhaps he might pretend to be a wraith, or be feared as one, but what should that look like? How would he dress? How dishevelled is he? – KENJI KAMIYAMA, DIRECTOR

Even in the throes of his insanity, for Helm it is all about his people. He'll go out with nothing more than his own two hands and do whatever he can to protect them, but he doesn't know how, any more. Seeing Héra again, seeing the fear in her eyes – realizing in that moment it is him she fears – that's what pulls Helm back. – PHOEBE GITTINS, WRITER

It was Helm Hammerhand that got them into this mess, and it is Helm Hammerhand that is trying to get them out - with his fists. But it's a different type of leadership that his people need. That's what Héra can give them, and that is what Helm eventually comes to understand. Héra's temperament, her way of thinking, steeped in the tradition of the shieldmaidens, means she reaches for a different type of solution. – ARTY PAPAGEORGIOU, WRITER

Helm's tattered costume when in 'berserker mode' was an expression of his inner rage and grief. – STATO, ORIGINAL CHARACTER DESIGNER

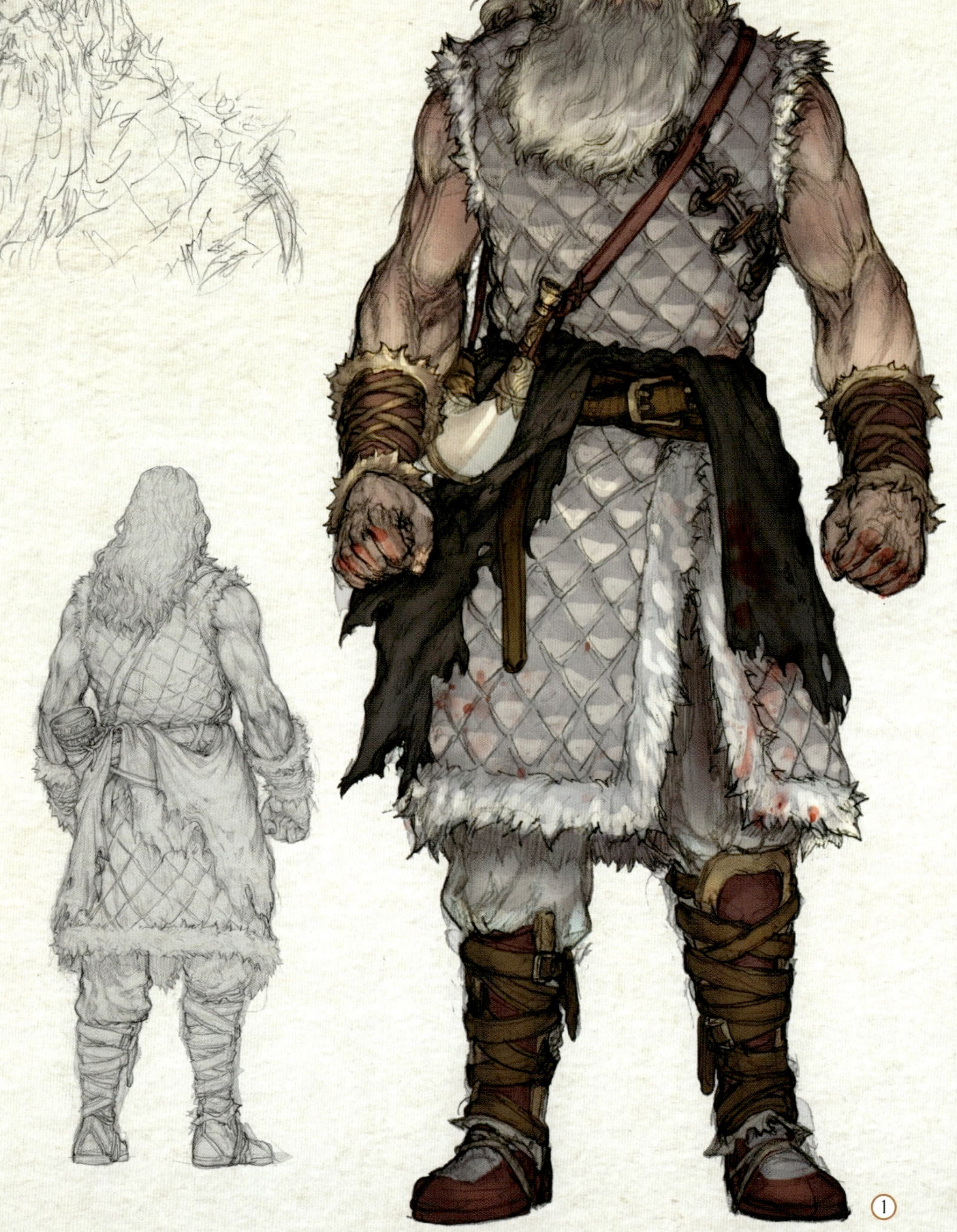

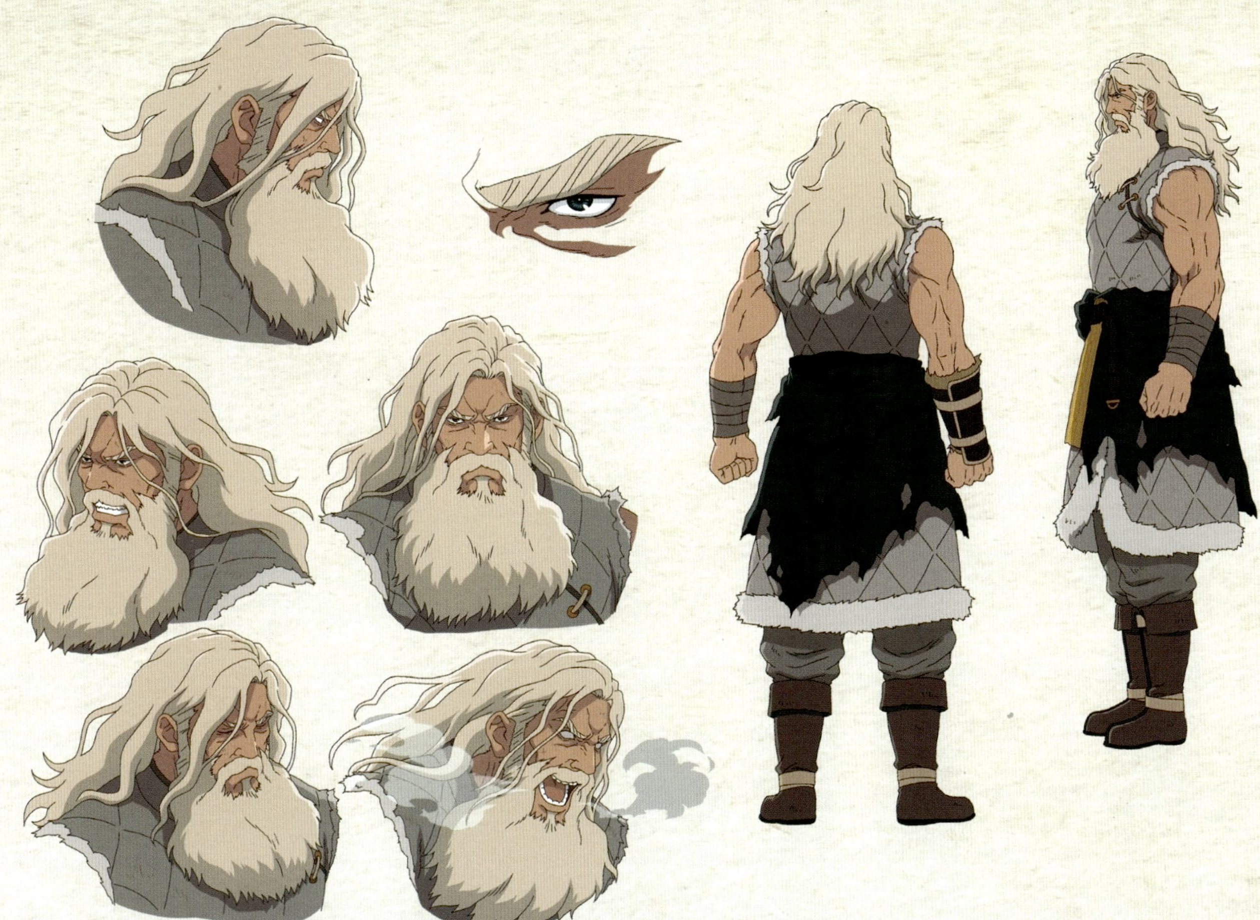

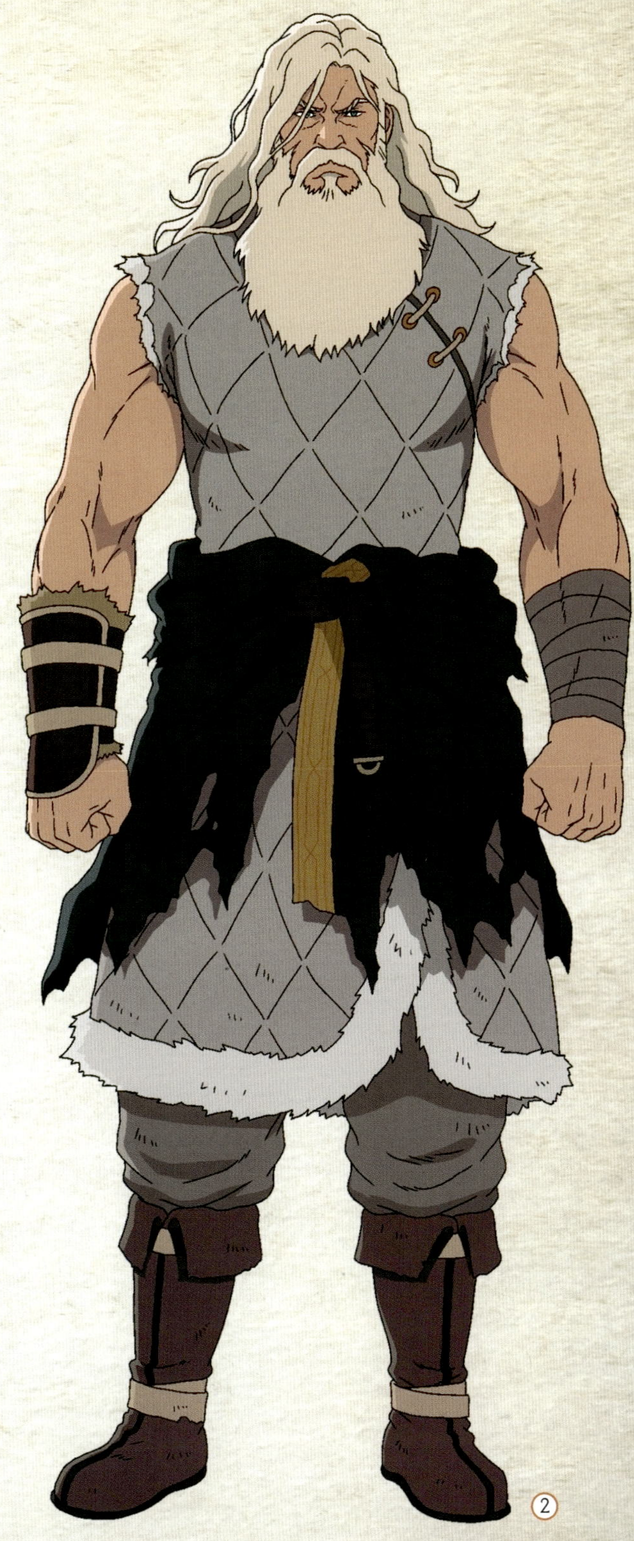

'HE KILLED THEM ALL! I SAW – HE TORE THEM APART WITH HIS BARE HANDS.'

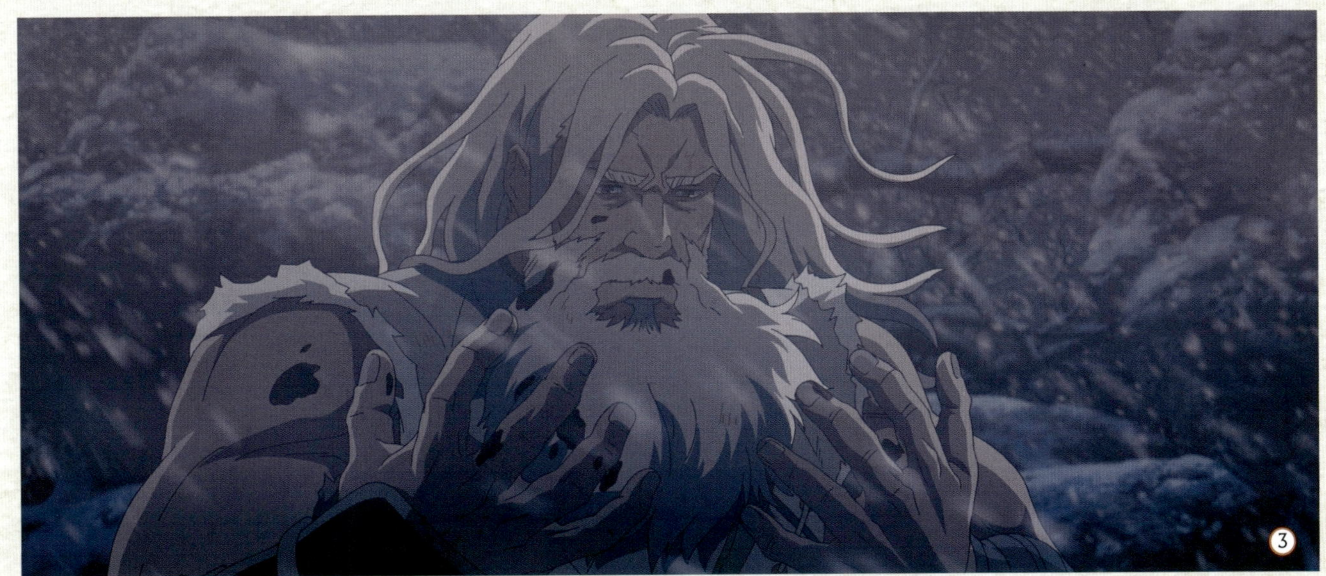

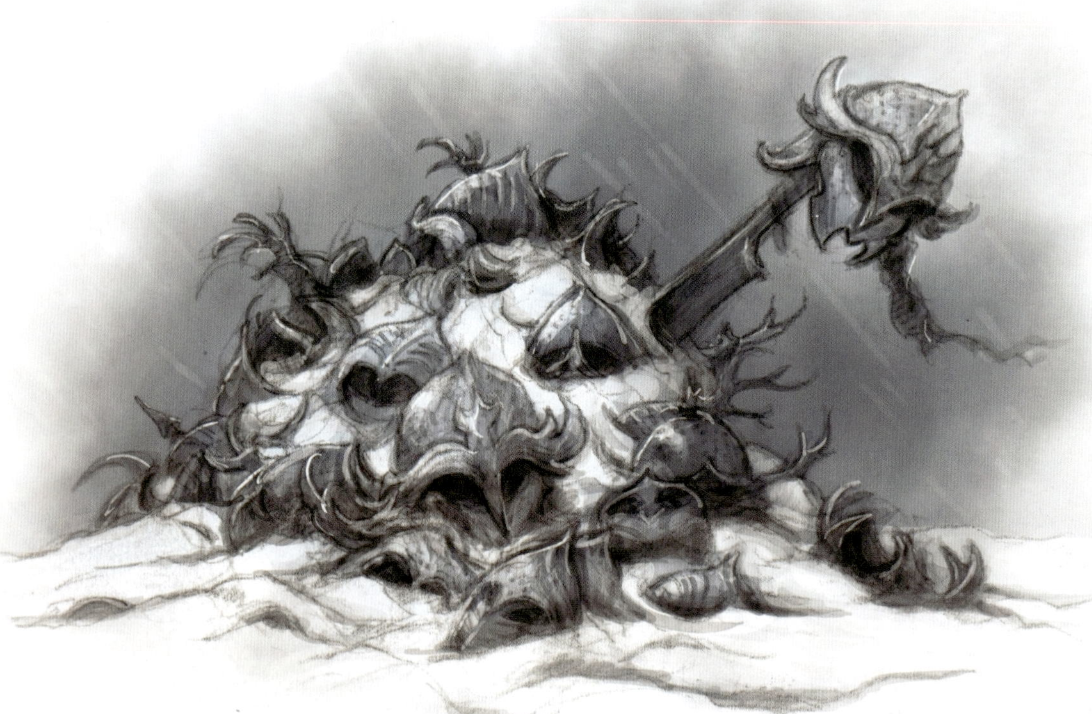

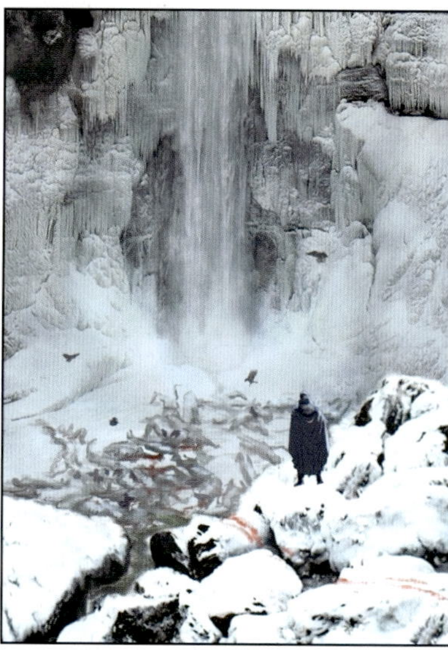

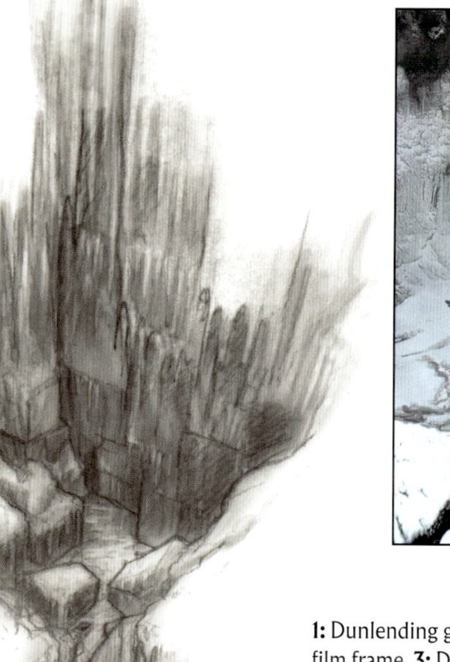

DUNLENDING BODY DUMP

—◆≺≺◆◆≻≻◆—

The bitter siege is exacting a toll from both sides. Wulf's men have been disposing of their dead in an open grave of some kind, but the exact nature of this site was not explicit in the script, so it went through a few conceptual iterations.

The first ideas for the body dump I pitched were of a frozen pond at the base of an icy cliff face, either natural or perhaps where rock had been quarried to build the Hornburg. One of the questions was, how might Wulf's men mark the mass grave of their comrades in this frozen landscape, where scraping the icy ground would be so challenging? Might they pile up helmets, or stand blades or shields in the snow? Perhaps they scored marks into a stone? The favoured idea was that they would hang flags in remembrance … or perhaps in warning. – DANIEL FALCONER, ADDITIONAL CONCEPTS DESIGNER

The pit itself was a macabre sight, made especially grisly by the unwholesome attention of the Orcs it attracted.

1: Dunlending grave concepts, DF. **2:** Final film frame. **3:** Dunlending grave concepts and background setting art, YY.

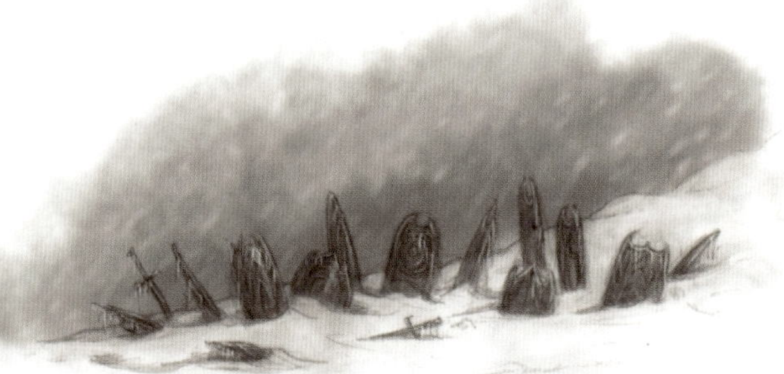

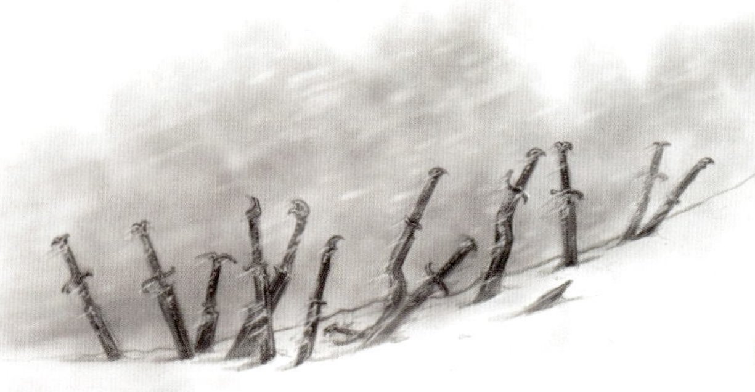

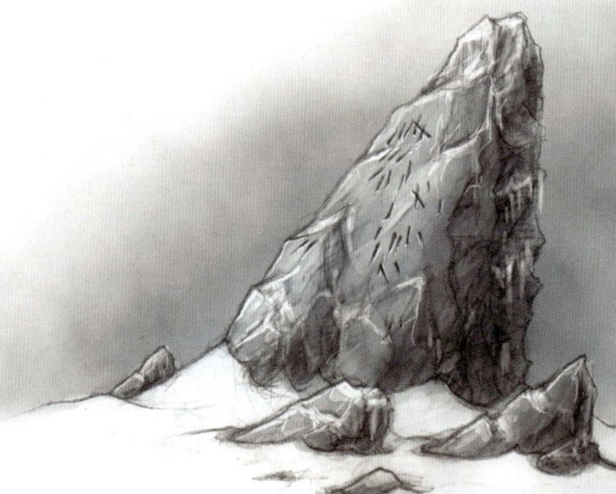

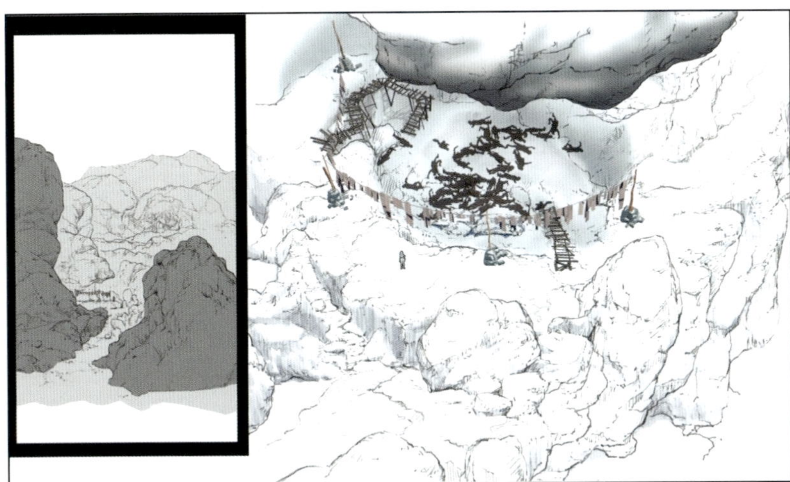

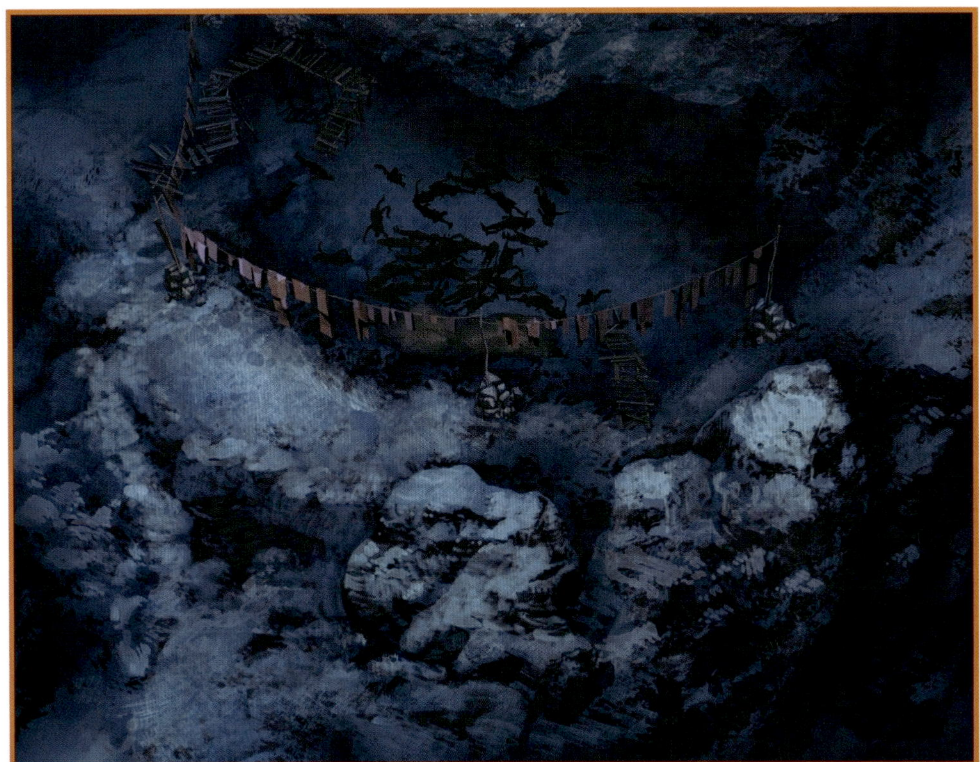

We originally placed the open grave at the bottom of the cave. Personally, I liked it better that way, giving off an image of claustrophobia and smelly decay.

In the end, it shifted to be outdoors, but I still wanted to evoke an eerie, altar-like atmosphere, so I imagined it as semi-subterranean, tucked under an overhang of rock and ice. I attached strips of fabric to ropes to create a cordon, and I think the fabric blowing in the wind helped bring a sense of bleakness and cold. – YASUHIRO YAMANE, ART DIRECTOR

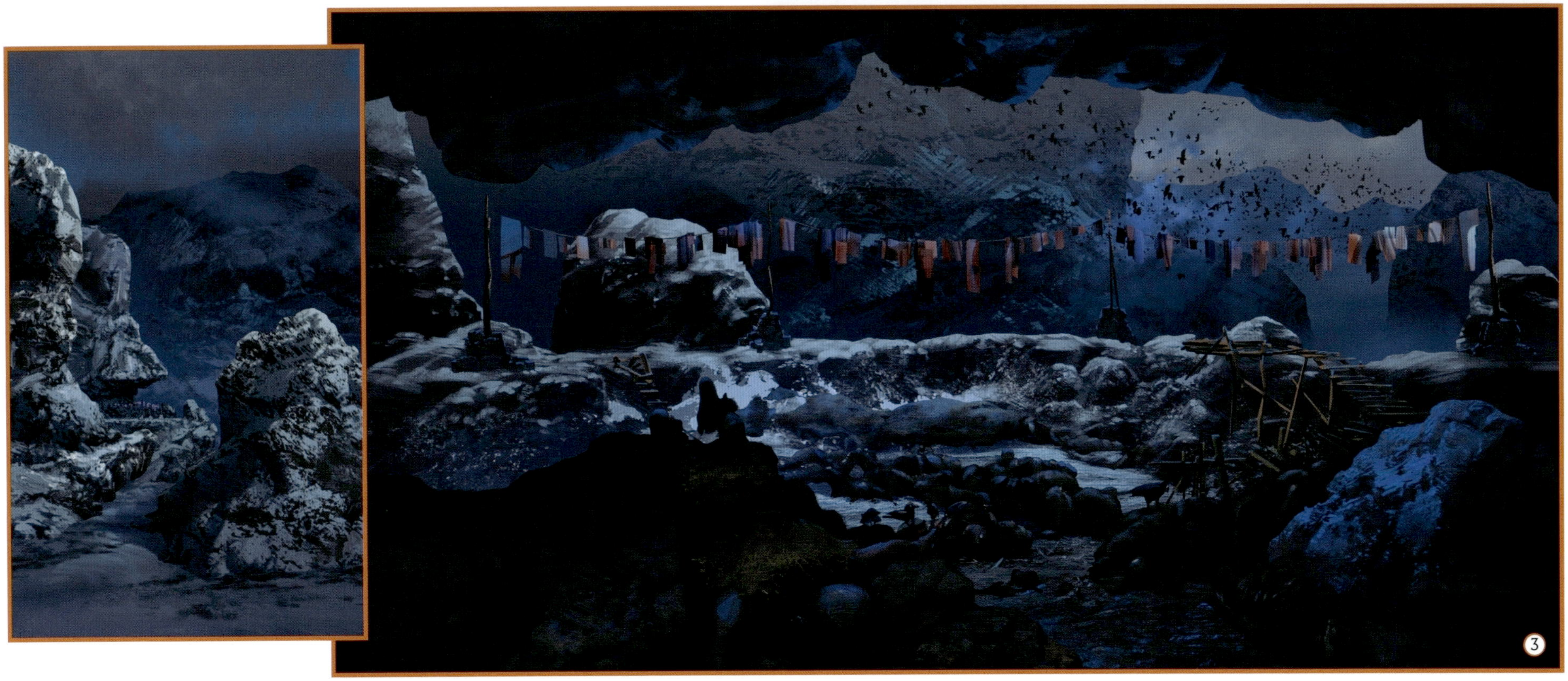

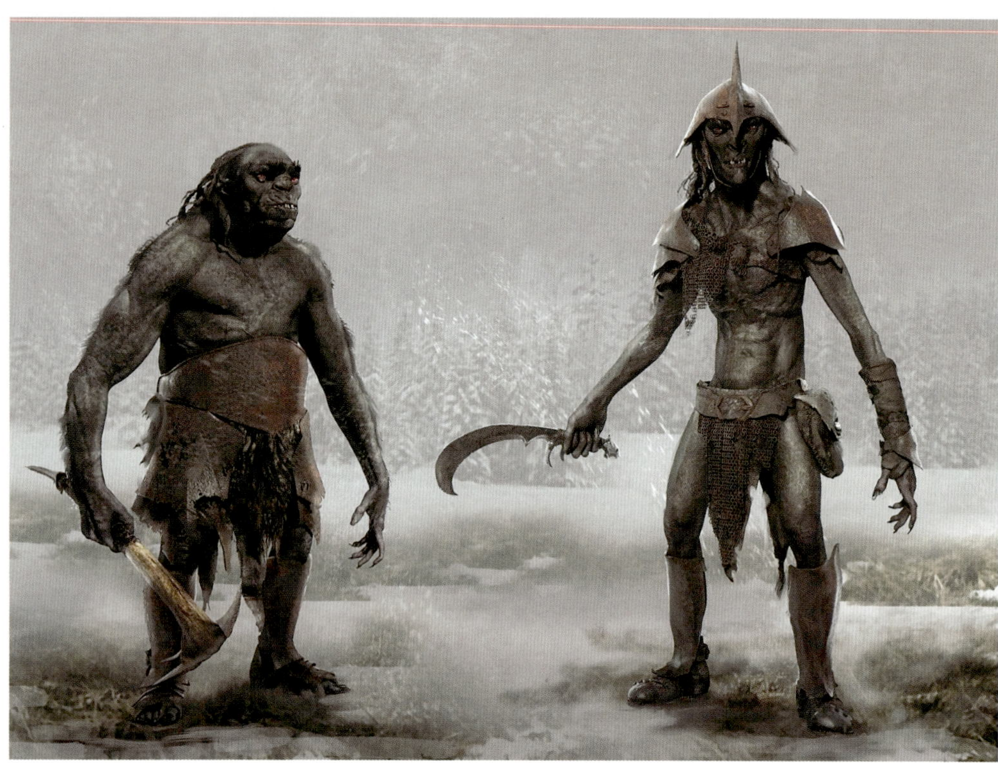

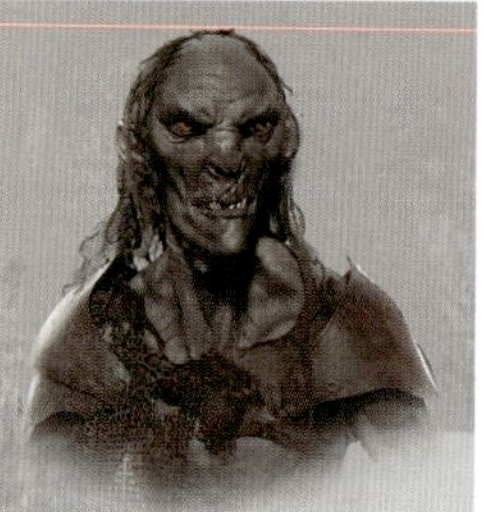

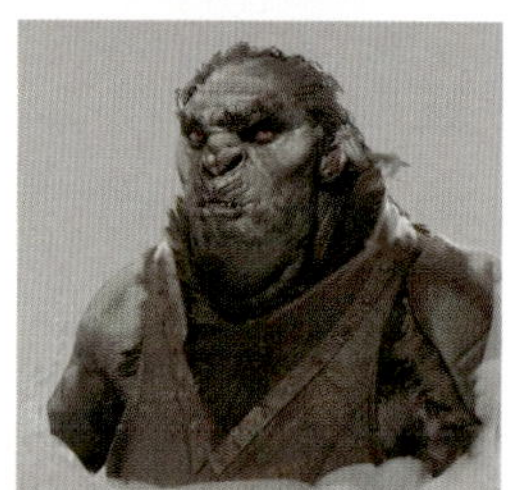

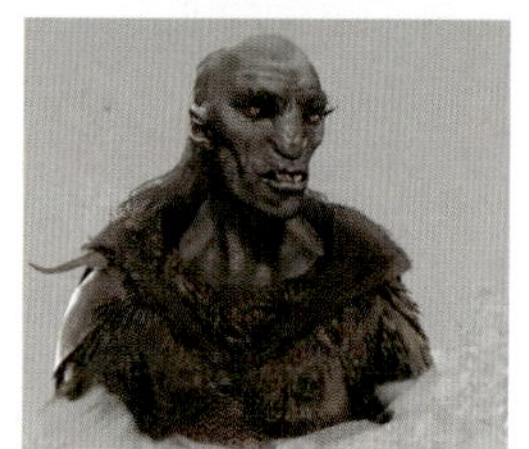

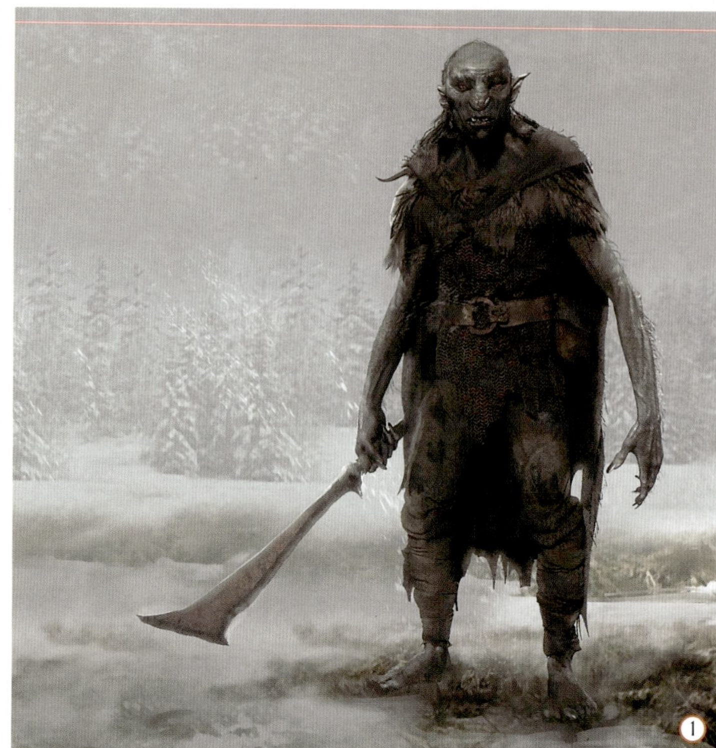

'YOU SMELL THAT?'
'THEY CAN SMELL YOU FROM MOUNT DOOM.'

SHANK AND WROT

Lurking amid the boulders and fissures of the mountainside are two wretched Orcs. Conducting their grisly business hidden from the armies in the valley below, Shank and Wrot are retrieving rings from the conflict's dead. The pair gleefully raid the Dunlending grave, eagerly partaking in the delights of free food during lean times.

Shank and Wrot don't even know why they're doing it. They're following orders and having a little lunch at the same time. Speaking of fun, we also have the Easter egg of Billy Boyd and Dominic Monahan returning to Middle-earth to voice them, which was such a joy. – PHOEBE GITTINS, WRITER

The presence of the Orcs hints at the wider story unfolding in Middle-earth; it is lurking, building in the shadows. Pragmatically, at this point in the story, the Orcs help inform what is happening with the Dunlending bodies and Helm, but I have to admit there's also an element of, 'We're in Middle-earth. I want to see some Orcs!' If you like this genre, then you like what comes with it. Orcs are part of the unique DNA of Middle-earth, and sometimes it is just fun to indulge in that. – ARTY PAPAGEORGIOU, WRITER

Tolkien spent so much time having fun with bickering Orcs in his books. It gets very tense with Frodo and Sam on their way into Mordor, but amidst all that, he gives us a scene of Orcs bickering like Felix and Oscar in *The Odd Couple*. – ARTY PAPAGEORGIOU, WRITER

Wētā Workshop's artists returned to descriptions in the book to develop the look of the Orcs, giving them a shadowy palette and red eyes like glowing coals.

They're Orcs, so they should look mean, but they're also characters with individual personalities and quirks. They were supposed to be a bit comical, so I thought that making one bulky and stumpy, while the other was very, very skinny, would create some humorous contrast. – GUS HUNTER, WĒTĀ WORKSHOP SENIOR CONCEPT ARTIST

Tolkien described Orcs as makers of many clever things, but none beautiful. They didn't lack intelligence or the ability to make more refined things; they simply didn't care to. Hooked weapons with nasty, jagged shapes, and pitted metal surfaces and rough leather wrappings characterize Orc weaponry and were staples of the established Orc aesthetic. For one of the Orcs apprehending Héra, the director asked to see a long weapon with a savagely scalloped blade and backward curving barbs. A warmer, rusty palette for the Orcs' armour and wrappings contrasted with the cold, bluish environment in which they appeared.

1: Orc concepts, WW. **2:** Orc concepts, GH. **3:** Shank and Wrot character setting art, MT. **4:** Orc weapons prop setting art, KM. **5:** Final film frame.

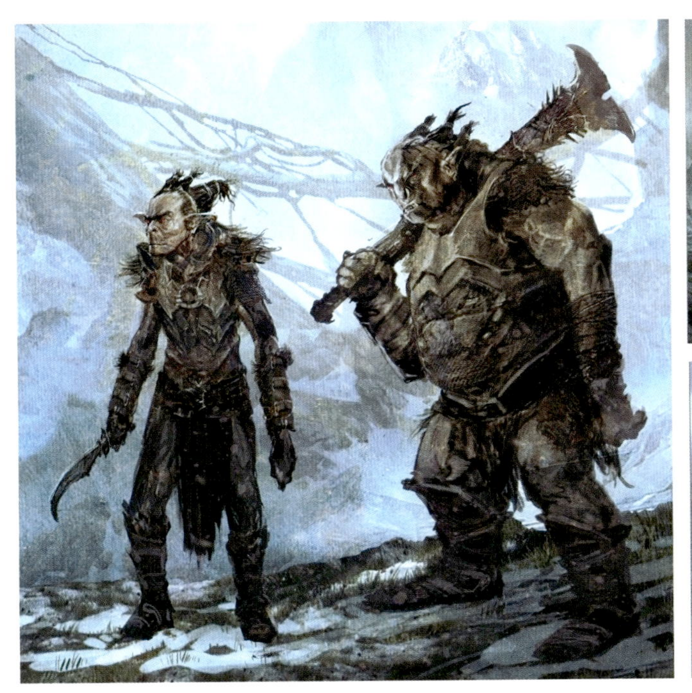
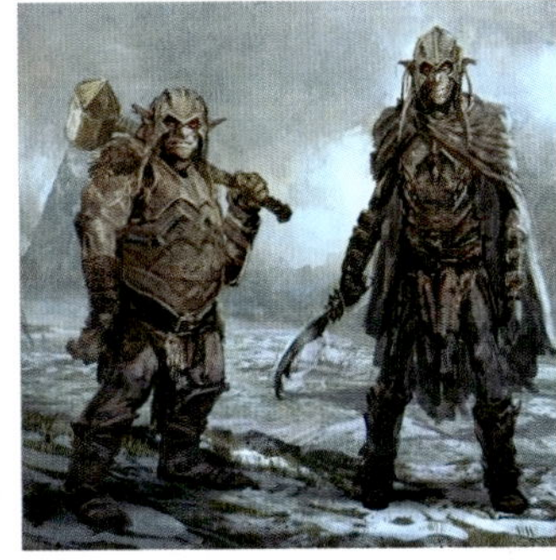
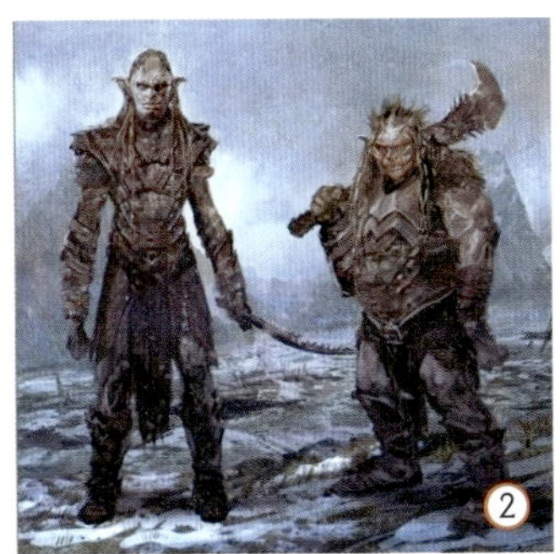
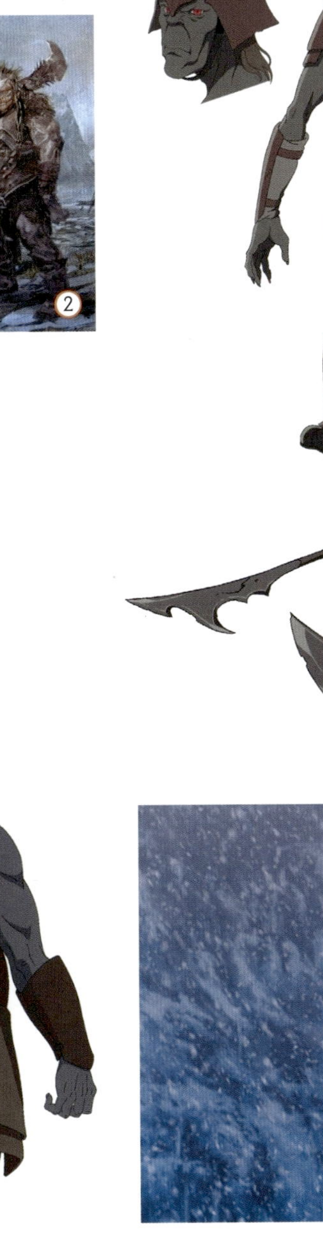
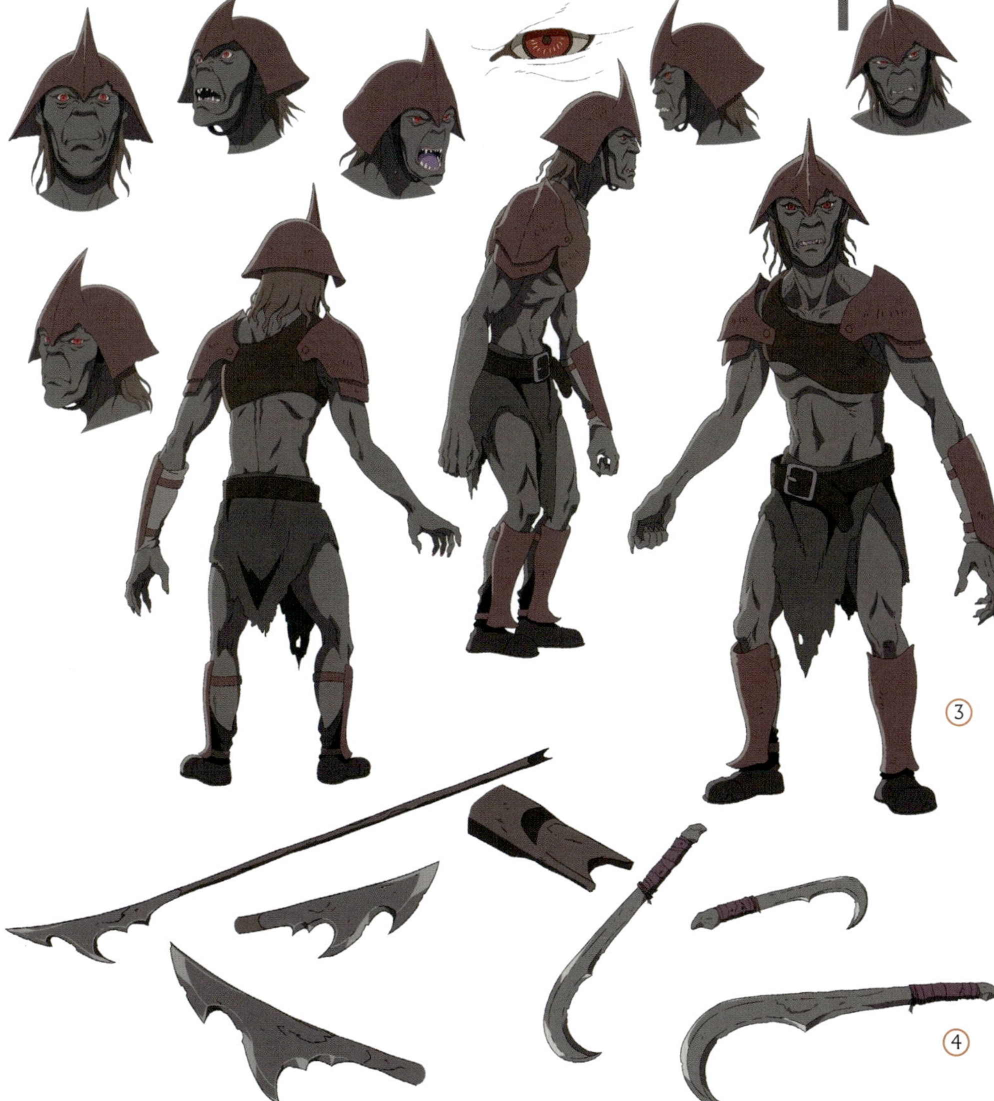
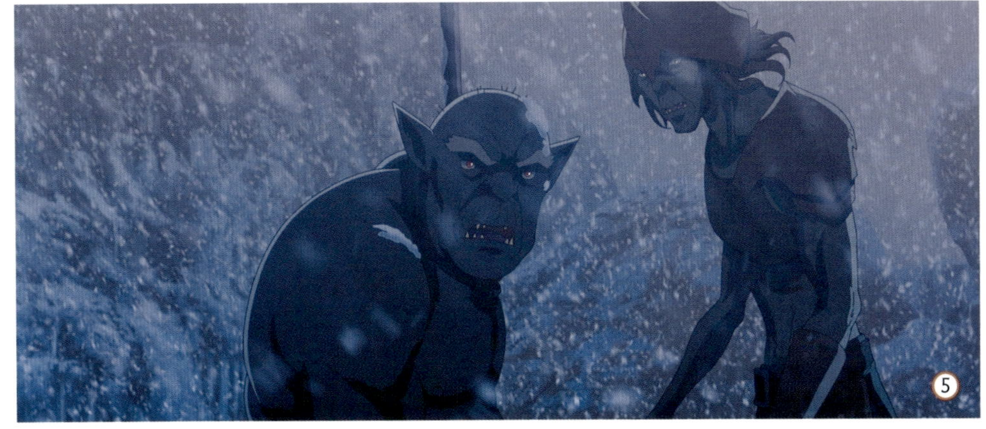
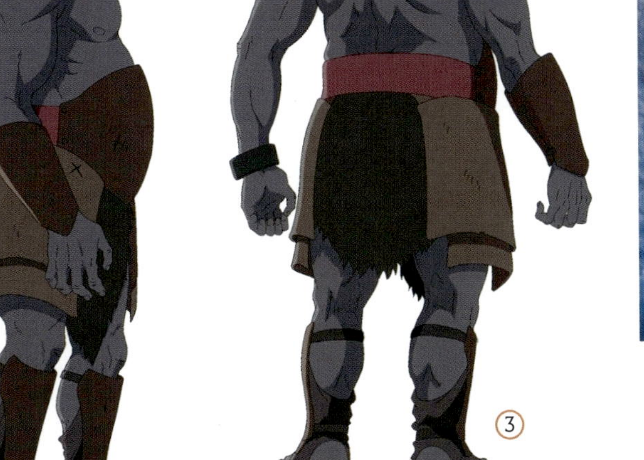

'WHAT DOES MORDOR WANT WITH
RINGS ANYWAYS?'

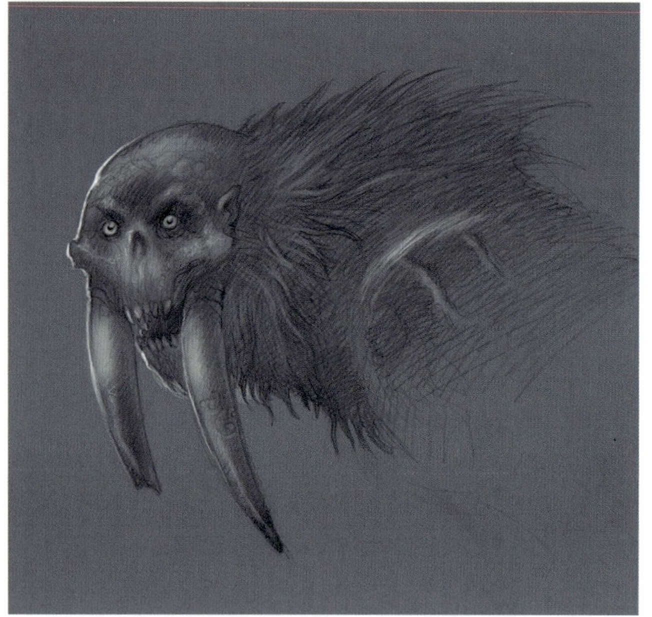

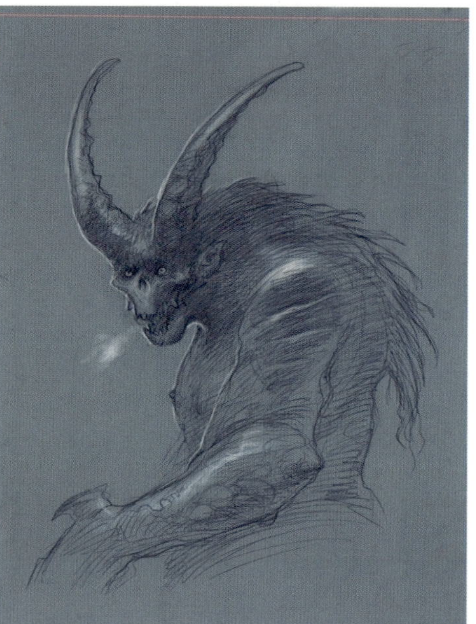

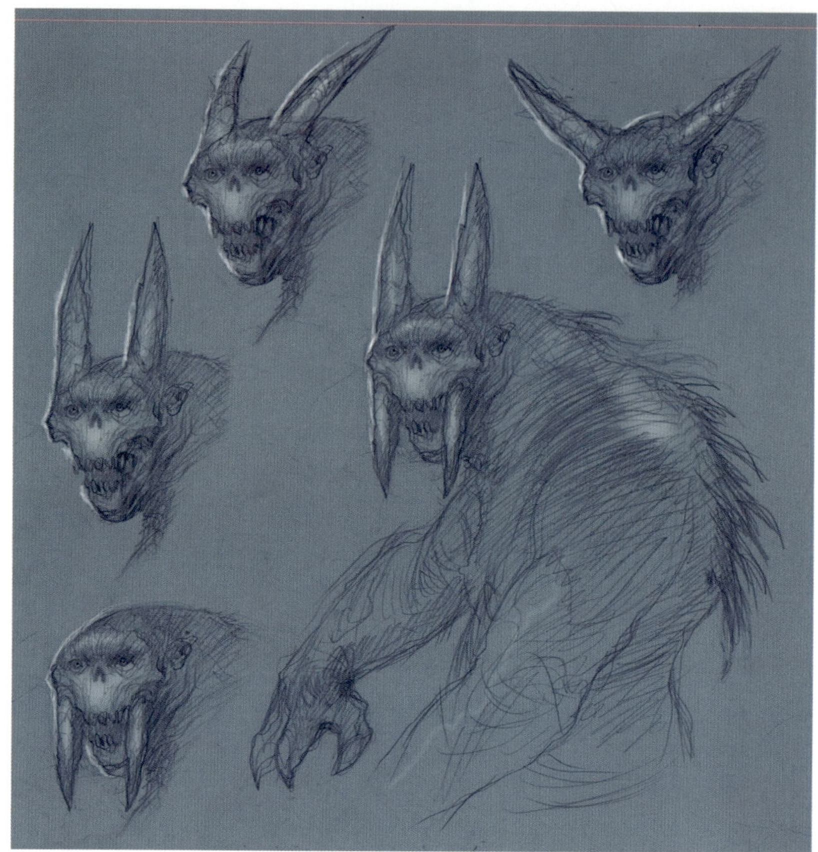

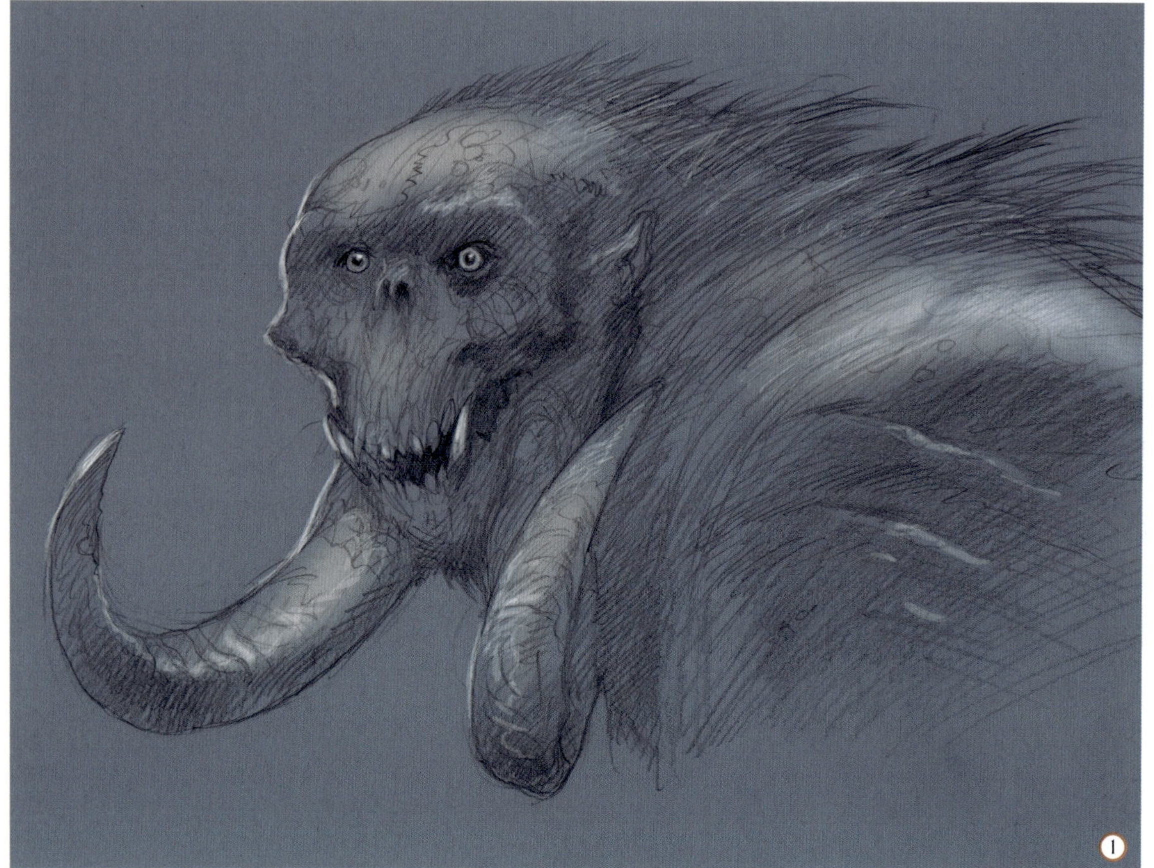

SNOW-TROLL

We know Helm is a warrior king; his first instincts will be to solve his problems by punching his way out of them. So, if he is going to have this big moment in the film, where you have him saving his beloved daughter from the danger he has put her in, what do you put him up against? A huge Snow-troll, of course! – ARTY PAPAGEORGIOU, WRITER

Trolls are some of the more diverse races of Middle-earth. Originally bred by Morgoth in the First Age, Tolkien mentions several types: Hill-trolls, mountain-trolls and Cave-trolls. It's unclear if the taxonomy indicates race or simply preferred habitat.

There is a single mention in the book of Snow-trolls, in relation to Helm being described as being 'like a Snow-troll' when, white-clad, he would lay in wait for his enemies in the blinding snowstorms of the Long Winter.

Of course, one solitary mention is all that's needed to set the imagination alight. Tusks, horns and manes (in one case, all three together) characterize these Troll designs. – JOHN HOWE, CONCEPTUAL DESIGNER

The Troll was something that producer Jason DeMarco had been fantasizing about. He would say things like, 'Wouldn't it be amazing to see the toughest human warrior in the Tolkien universe battling a Snow-troll hand-to-hand?'

It made sense to me, because Helm's actions drive so much of the story. We needed a big scene to cement him as this legendary character who his people would remember and revere, despite his faults. He kills this insane foe unarmed to defend Héra, so it reinforces what he cares most about when everything else is stripped away. Helm's last scenes had to be epic; a Troll was a fitting choice. It was one of the sequences in the film that I most looked forward to doing. – KENJI KAMIYAMA, DIRECTOR

The Snow-troll was imagined as a character in his own right, with an agenda and personality, an approach in harmony with the how the Cave-troll was designed two decades earlier. Orc manacles tethering both Trolls hint at untold back-stories. While an adversary for the heroes, in another context they might almost be sympathetic characters.

Helm's hand-to-hand victory had to be an epic feat, but also believable, so the assumption was this Snow-troll might be a little bit smaller than some of the enormous individuals seen in the other films.

I kept the same basic body shape of the Cave-troll from *The Fellowship of the Ring* but looked for ways to change his silhouette. The wide, curved horns and spiky weapon were designed to be things that would give this Troll an interesting shape. Making it hairy was cool because it could sway when he moved, and having snow clump and settle in the hair was something new and different. The chains dangling off its arms further enhanced that silhouette and would fly around when he was fighting. I gave it protruding callouses of bone or horn on its elbows for an even more aggressive outline and to stand out against the snow. – GUS HUNTER, WĒTĀ WORKSHOP SENIOR CONCEPT ARTIST

Whether they were part of his helmet or skull, those horns in Gus's design just begged for icicles! – DANIEL FALCONER, ADDITIONAL CONCEPTS DESIGNER

1: Snow-troll concepts, JH. 2: Snow-troll concepts, WW.

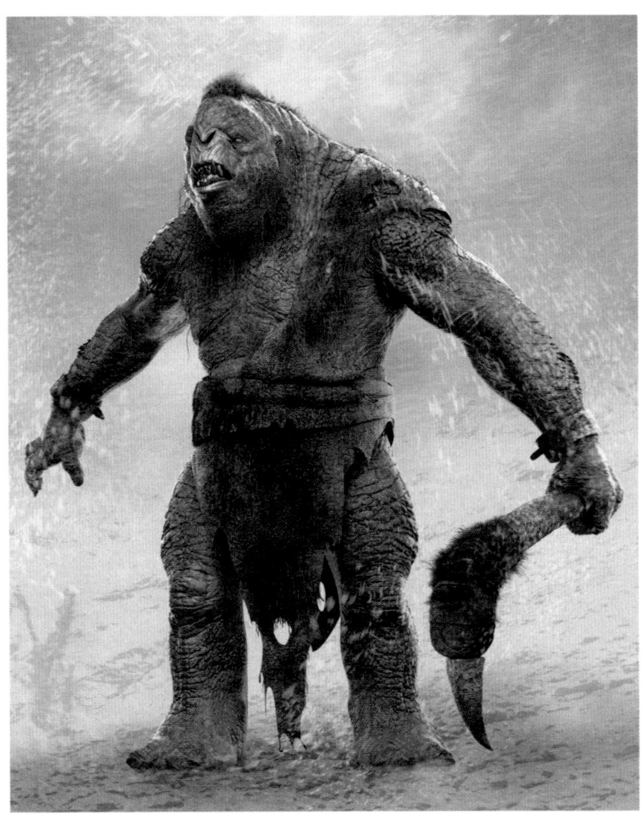

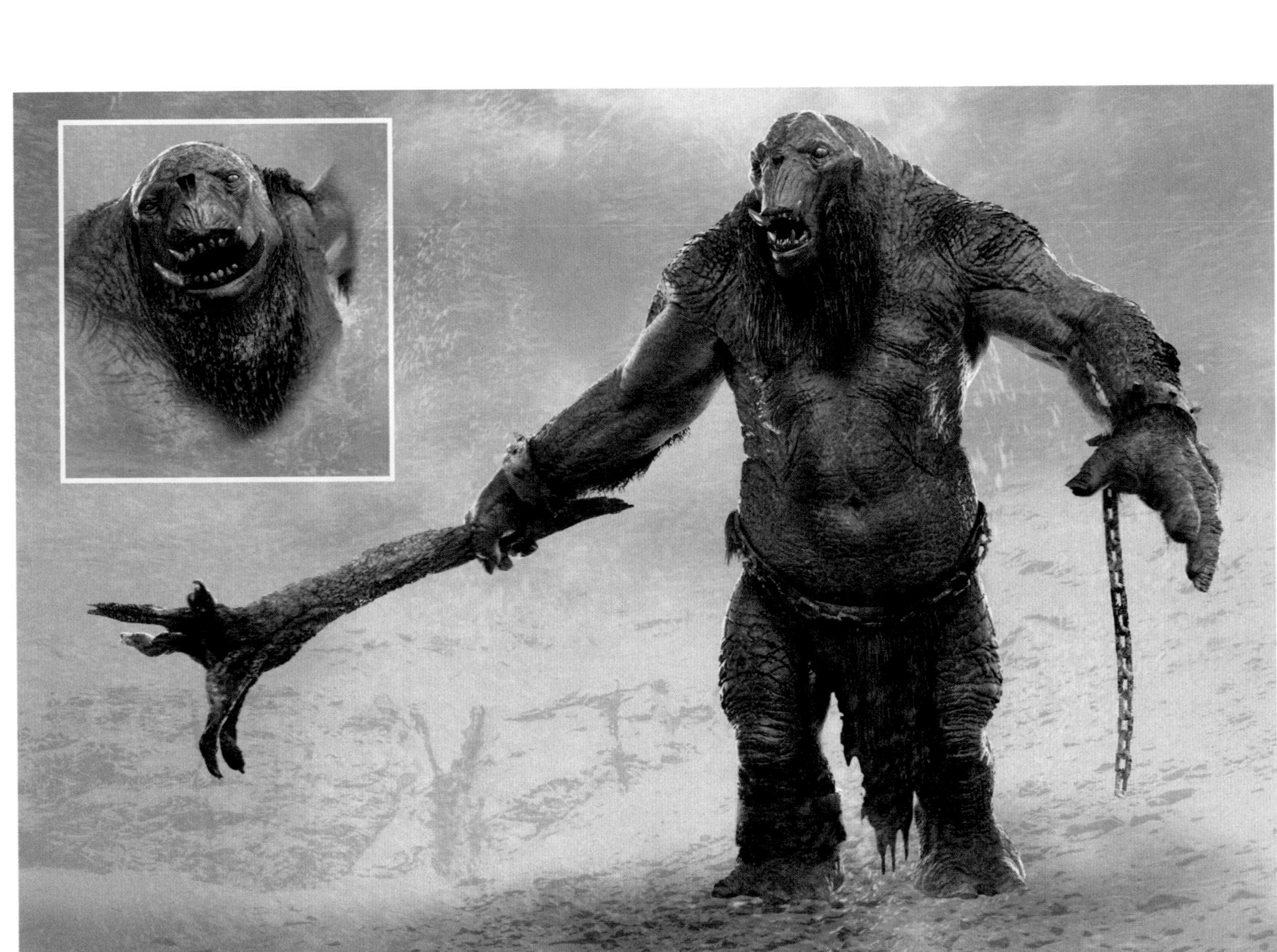

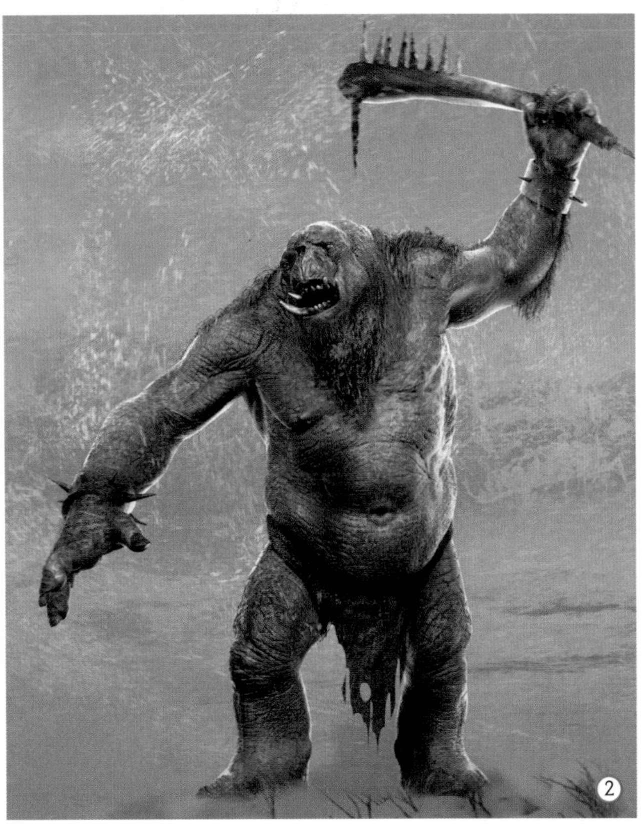

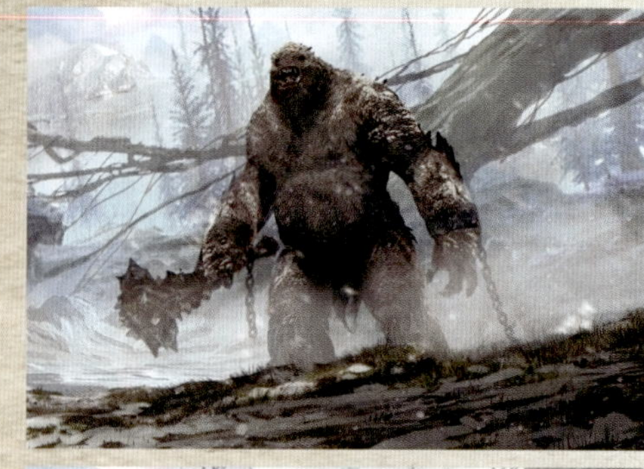

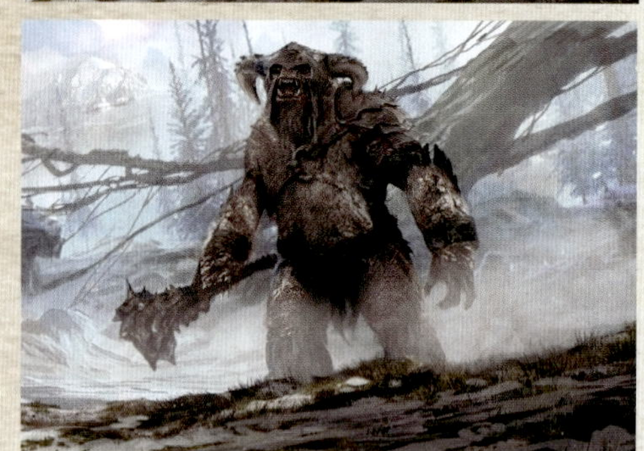

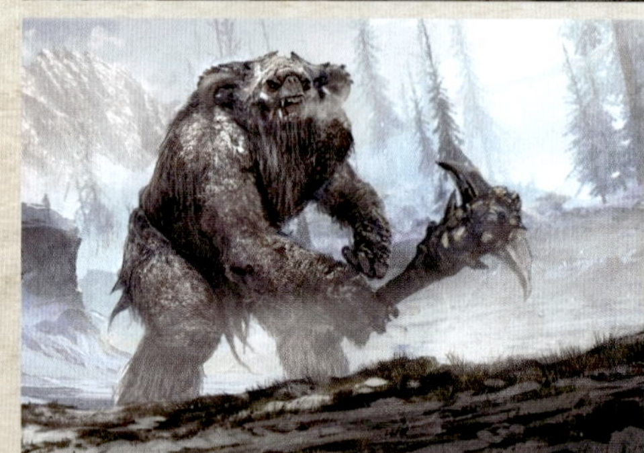

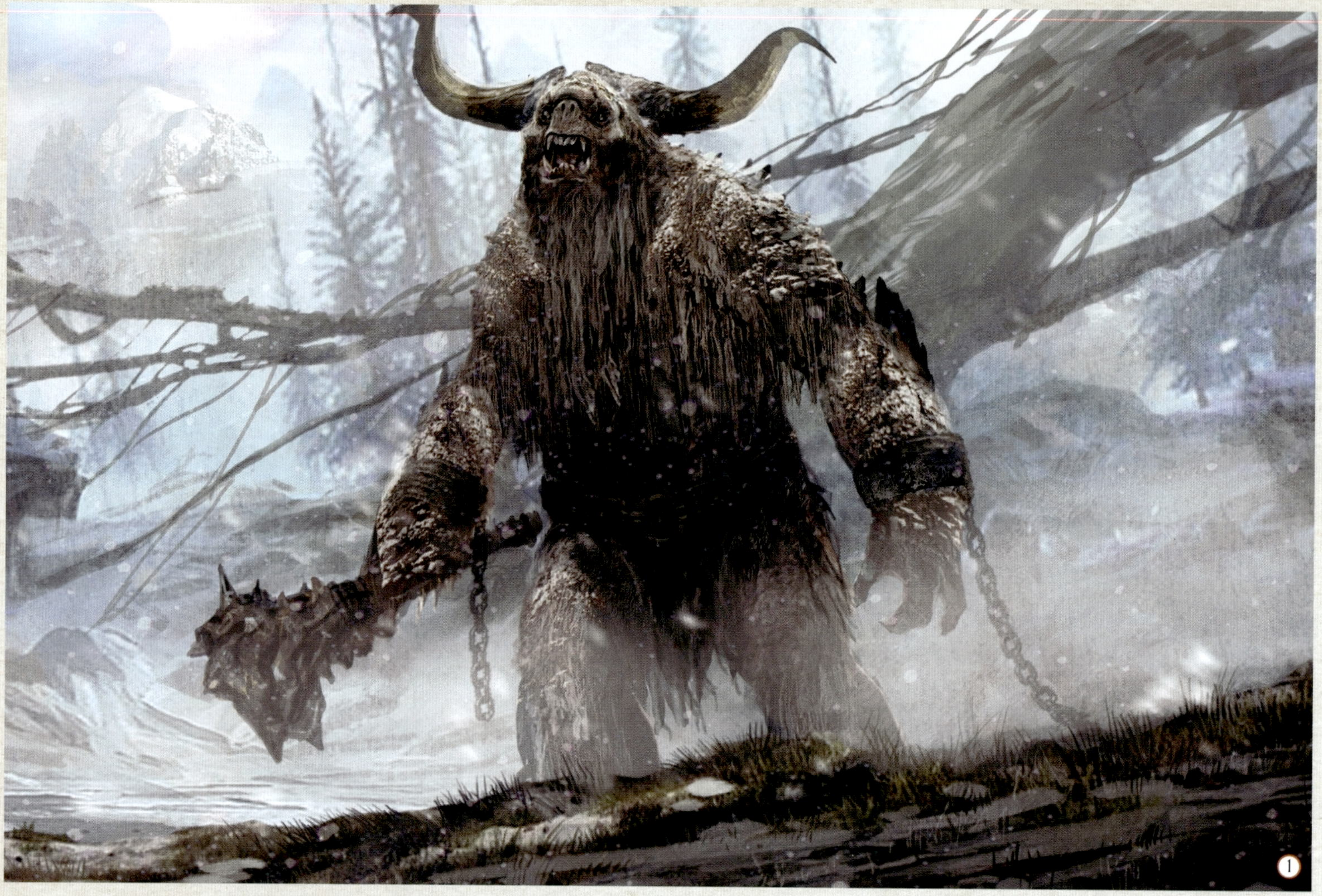

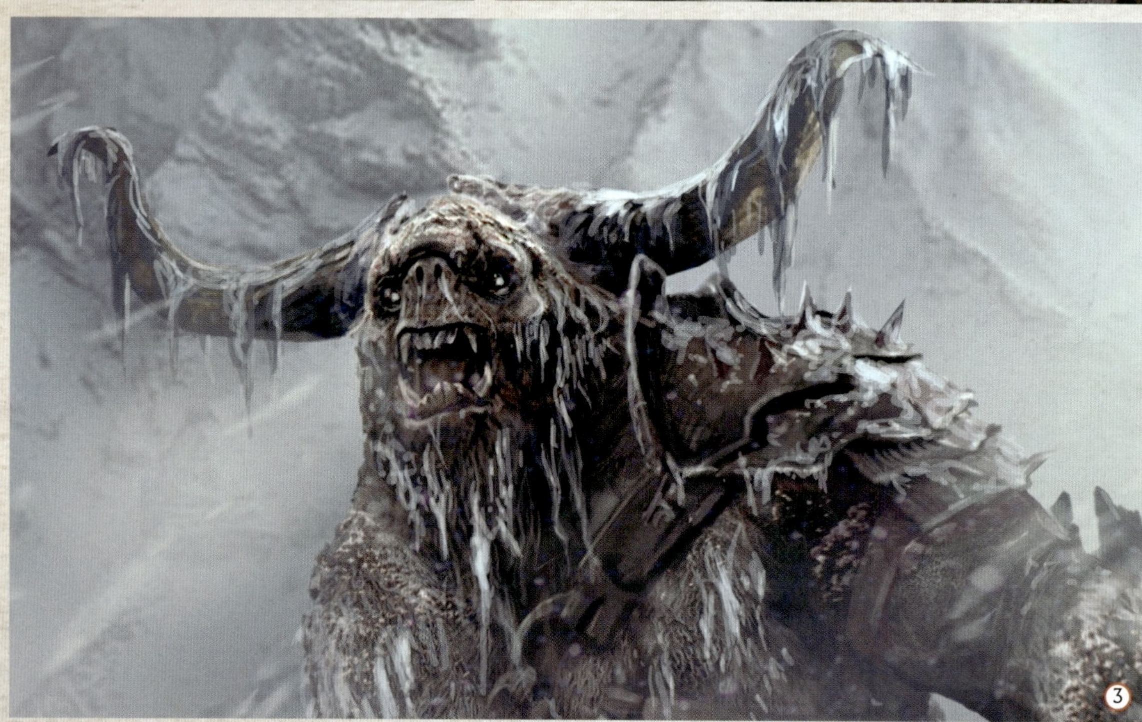

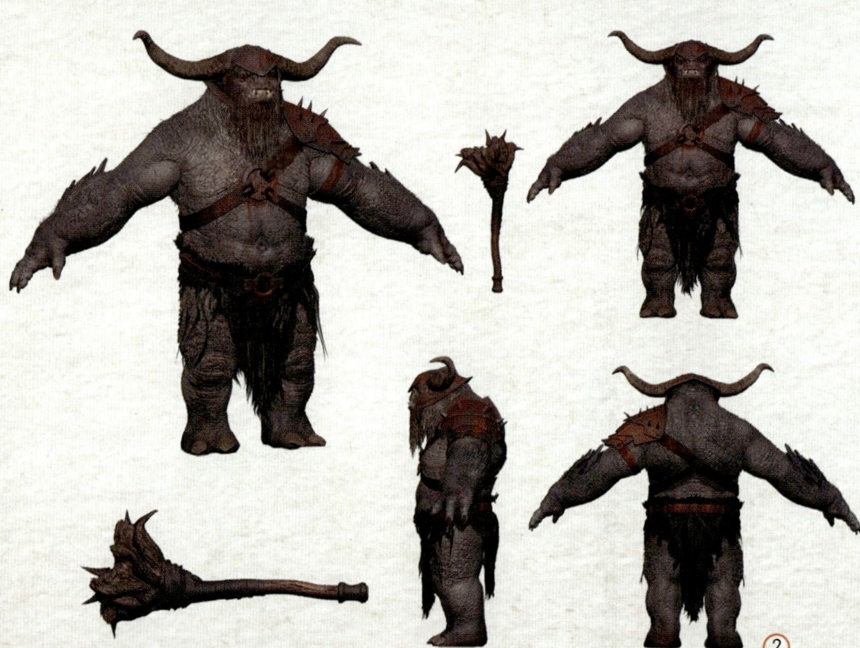

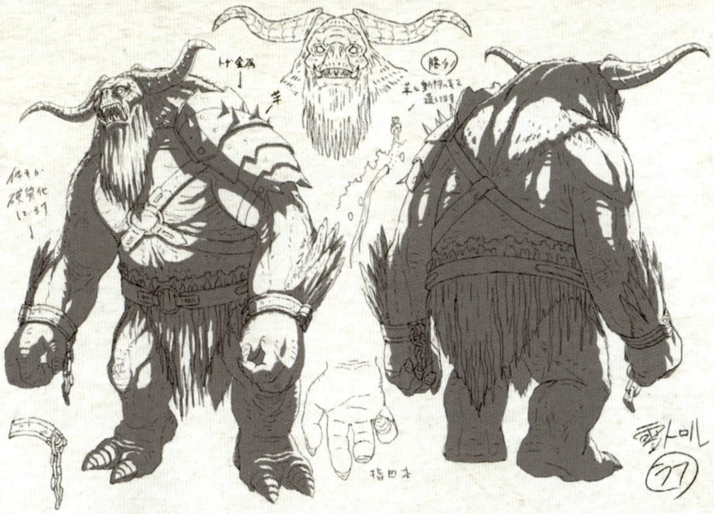

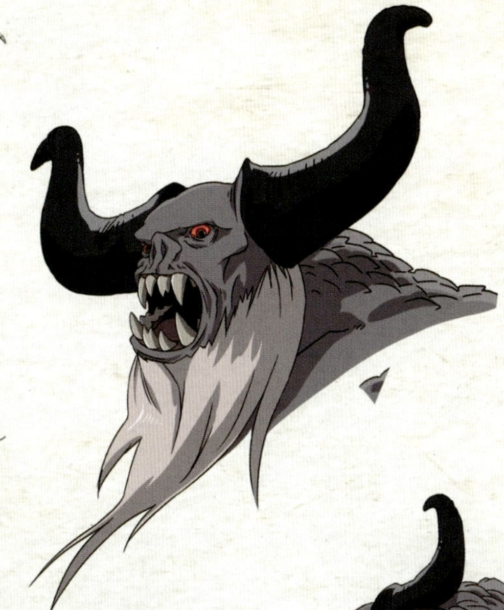

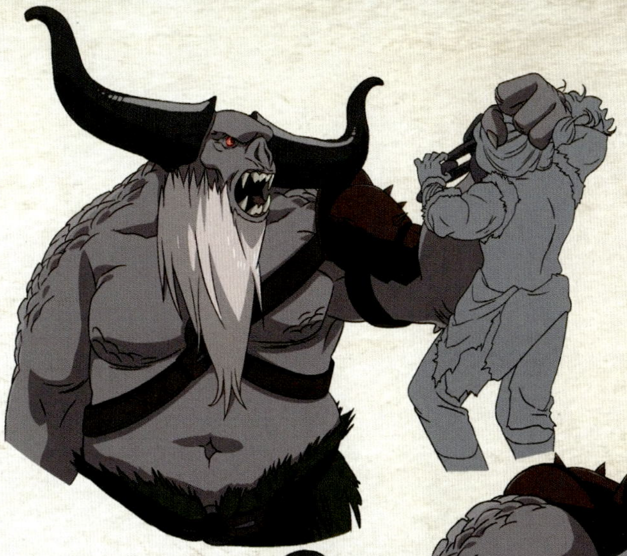

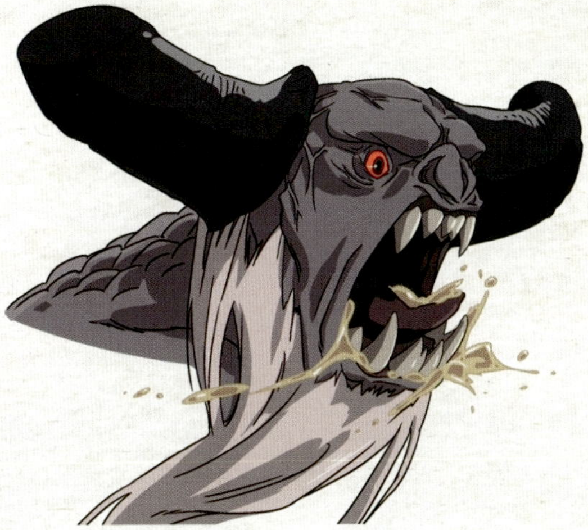

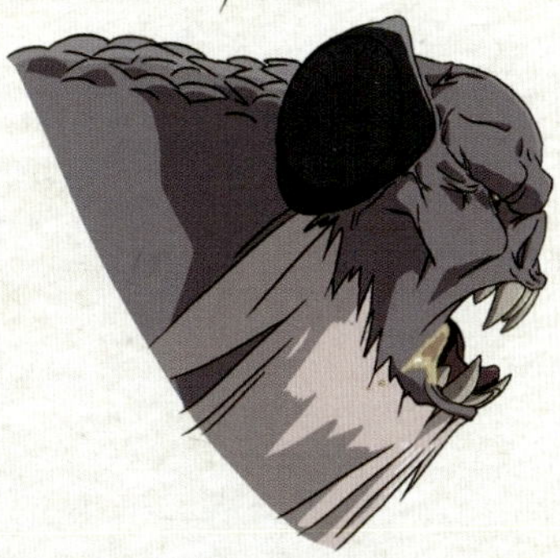

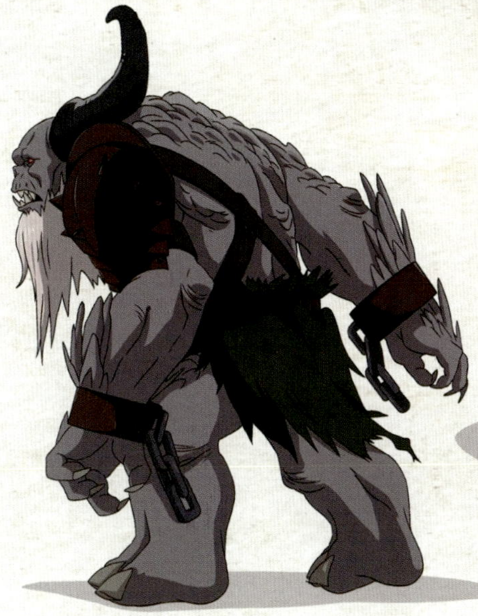

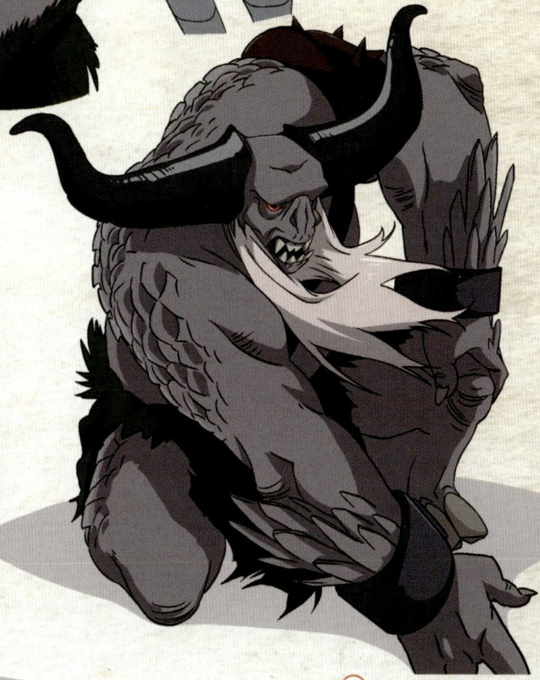

Unlike some of the other creatures, the Troll had a well-defined original design, but it proved to be difficult to adapt for animation. If overly packed with information, linework can require too much effort to animate. Conversely, being too simple isn't ideal, either. It was very difficult to achieve the right balance.

The Troll appears in a major fight scene, so fewer lines would have been easier to draw. But could deprive it of its impact and make the creature look less powerful. That would undermine Helm's accomplishment in defeating it, and this was precisely the scene in which we should witness the majesty and madness of Helm on display! Weighing these factors and knowing the challenge for the animators, I kept as much detail as I could. A strong and vicious looking creature was essential in making Helm look cool! – AISHA ARI HAGIWARA, ANIMATION CREATURE DESIGNER

I used gorillas as my primary reference for the Troll's form and movement. A gorilla's muscularity and power were perfect, but I also referenced bulls, and the skin texture of reptiles and dragons to embed the creature in the realm of fantasy. The director asked me to make its hide feel as tough as steel, so I designed the hairs on its forearm to look like armoured scales. – AISHA ARI HAGIWARA, ANIMATION CREATURE DESIGNER

1: Snow-troll concepts, GH. 2: Snow-troll concepts, WW. 3: Snow-troll concept, GH & DF. 4: Snow-troll concepts and creature setting art, AAH. 5: Final film frame.

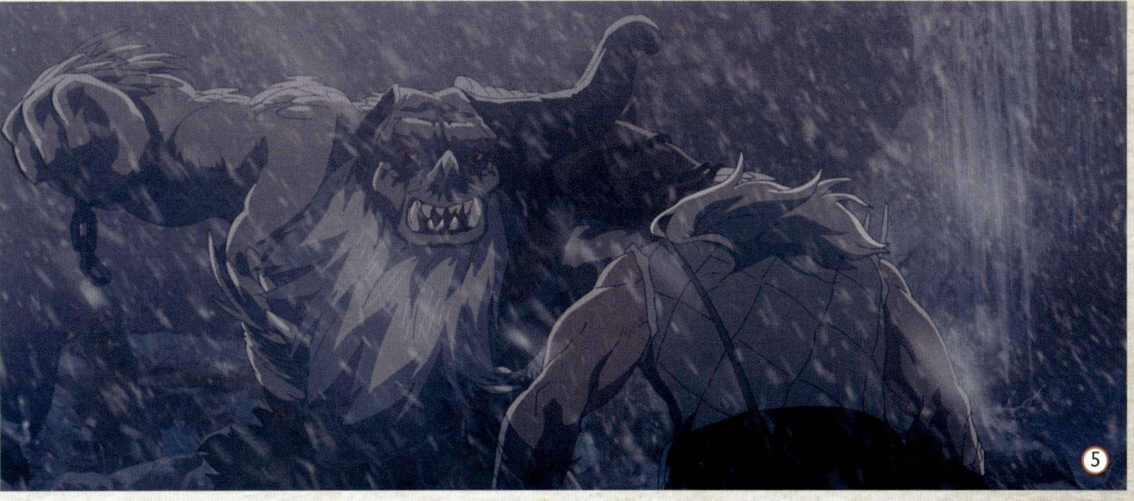

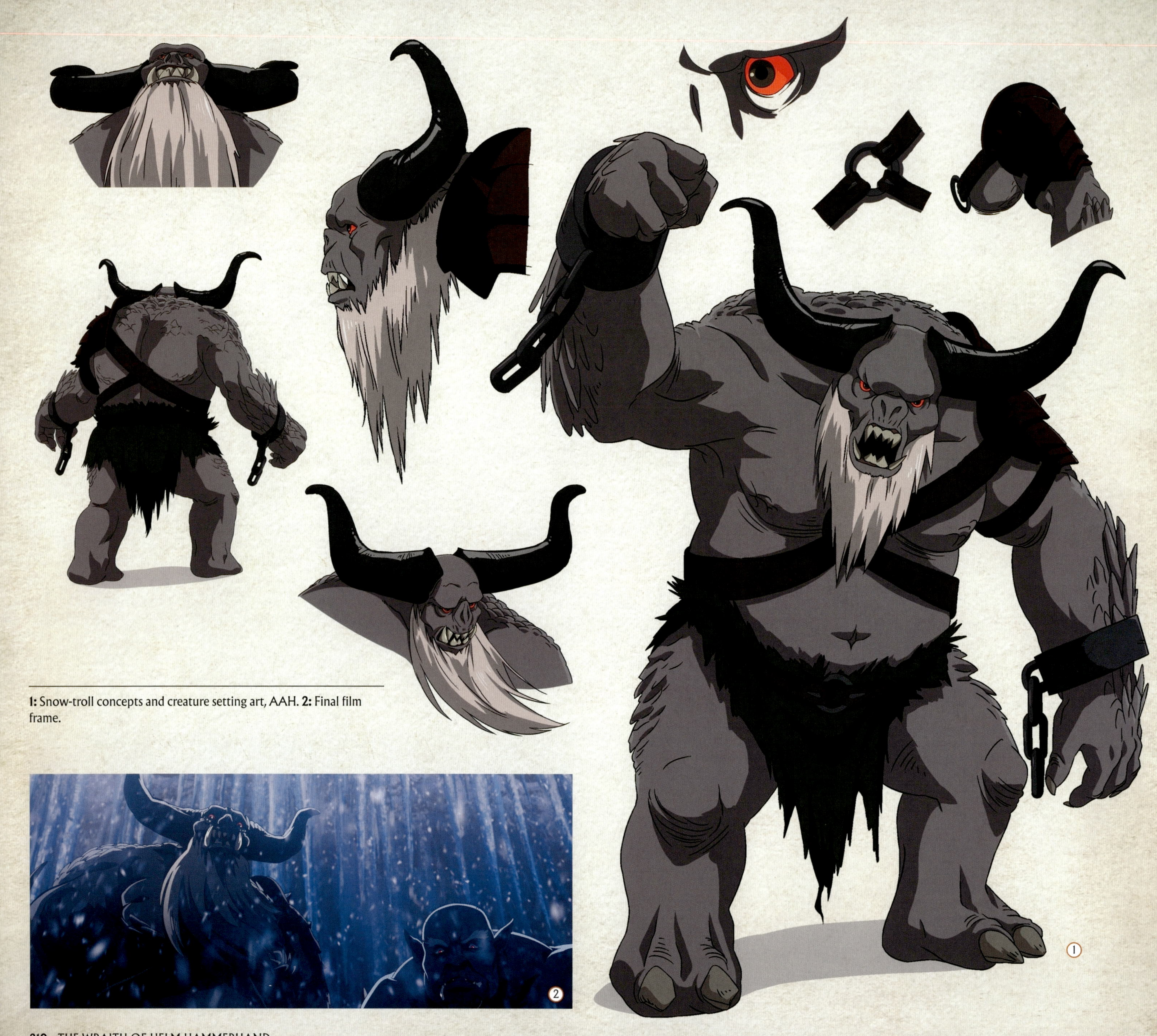

1: Snow-troll concepts and creature setting art, AAH. 2: Final film frame.

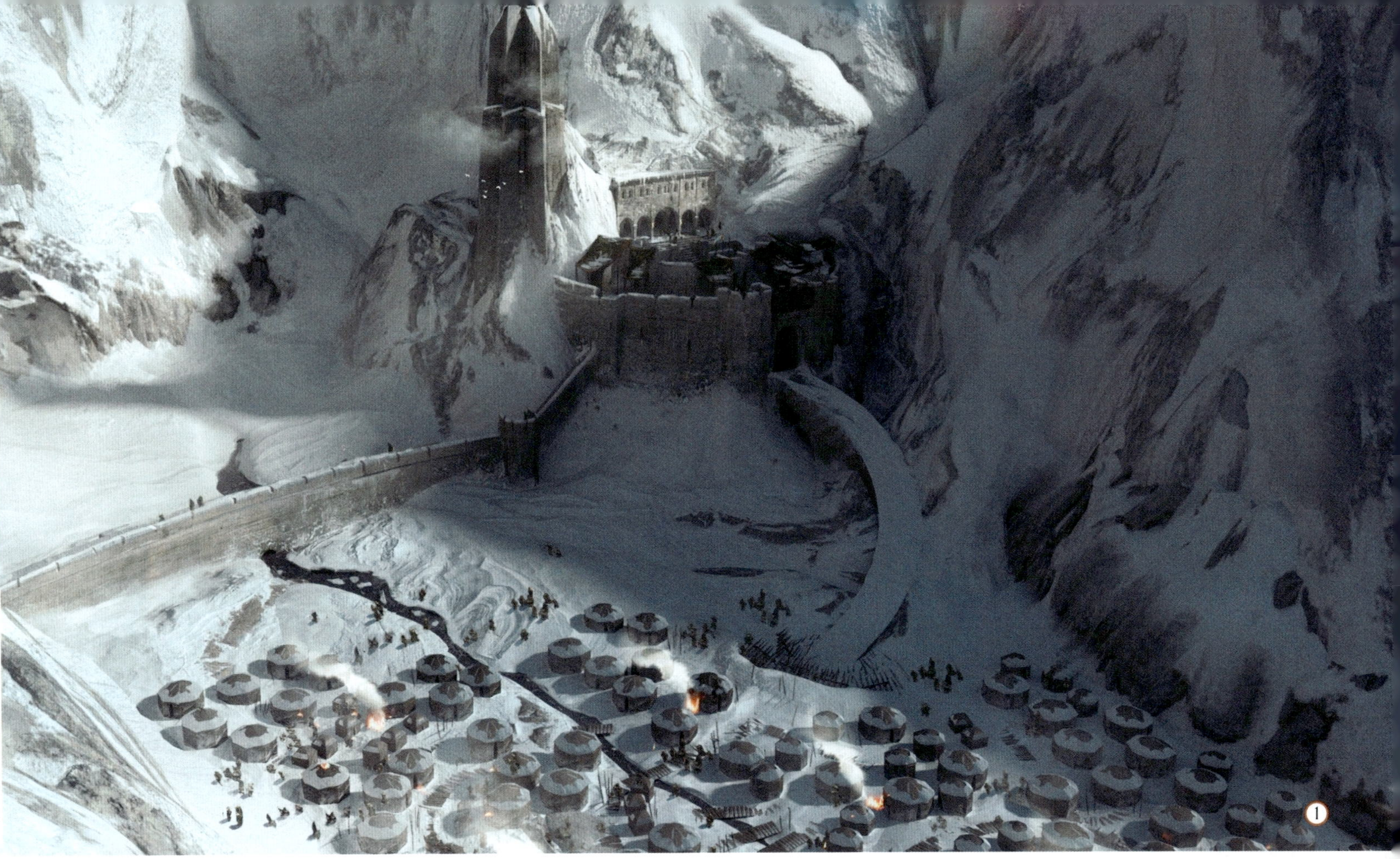

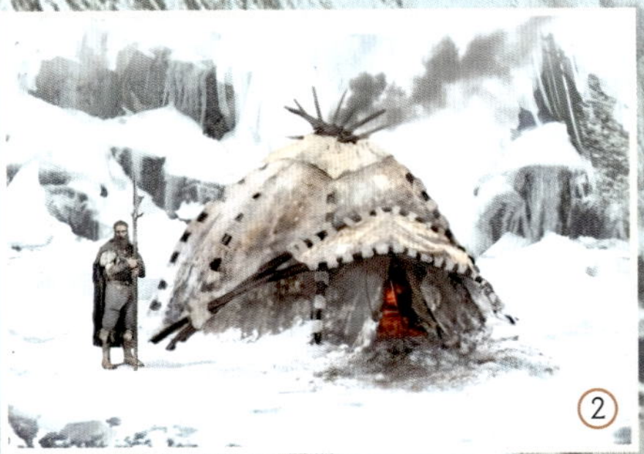

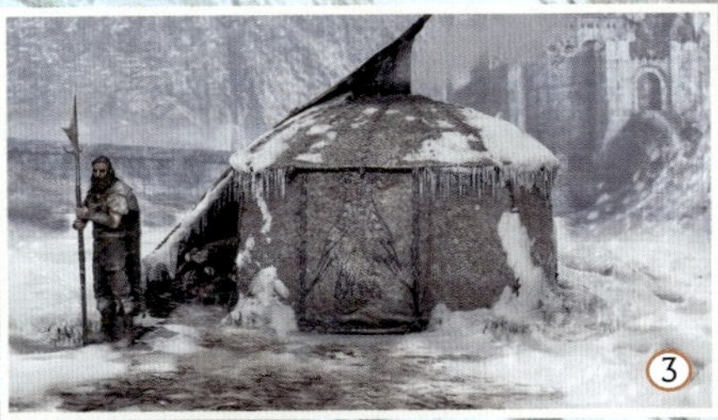

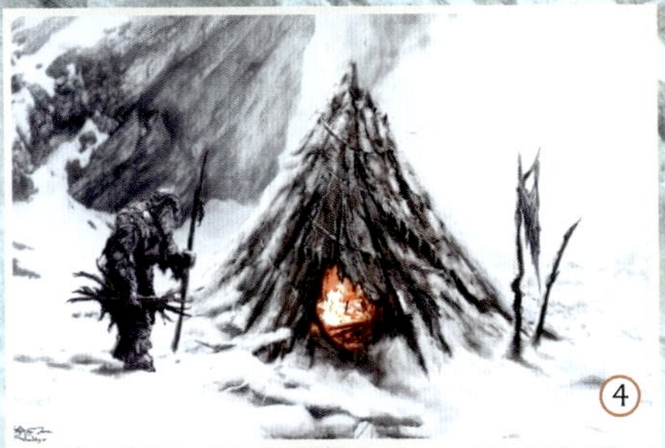

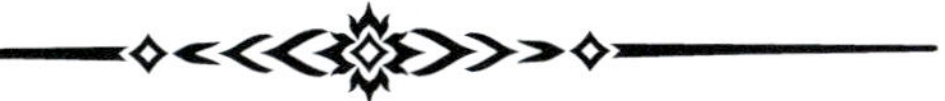

WULF'S ENCAMPMENT

The besiegers' camp would be a very cold and inhospitable environment. The icy stream is still running, and little walkways have been built to bridge it, but the camp is ramshackle and not planned with any great thought. It just fills the valley in front of the fortress to show how outnumbered the Rohirrim are. – ADAM MIDDLETON, WĒTĀ WORKSHOP ART DIRECTOR & SENIOR CONCEPT ARTIST

A conscious effort was made to differentiate between Dunlending and Hill Tribesmen shelters. While Dunlending tents were uniform and sophisticated in construction, the Wild Men had basic lean-tos or huts with found materials. Larger Dunlending tents were mostly cured hide and wood with decorative bones and antlers, whereas concepts for the Wild Men's huts suggested bark, rough-hewn timbers, reeds, and unrefined skins.

I imagined shelters made from materials the besiegers would have ready access to. The construction isn't delicate. They're utilitarian, and practical; erected and taken down as quickly as possible. The wood would be bent so that the shelter was rounded, allowing snow to fall off the sides. – CHRIS GUISE, WĒTĀ WORKSHOP SENIOR CONCEPT ARTIST

The enemy camp was a mixture of North African-inspired desert tribe tents and the Dunlending style. Wulf had his own command tent. The items inside, such as the candelabra, were brought from his former Isengard headquarters. We included the green oil lamps that we had established earlier in association with the character. – YASUHIRO YAMANE, ART DIRECTOR

It's not visible in the final film, but we included a little sleeping nook for Wulf at the back of his tent. – YASUHIRO YAMANE, ART DIRECTOR

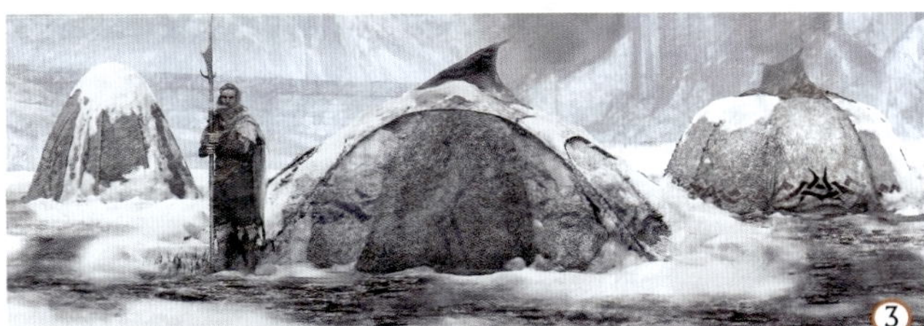

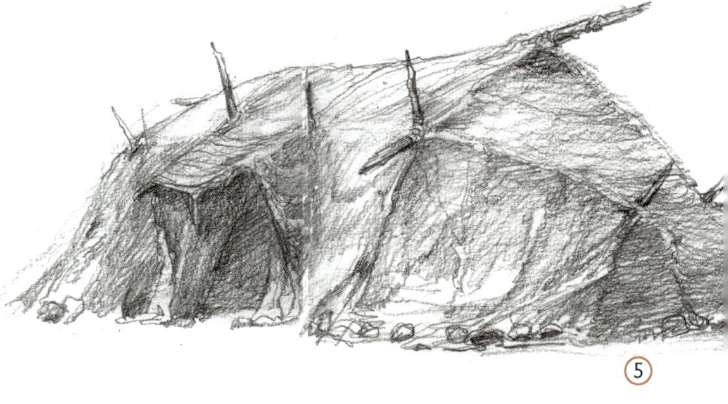

1: Hornburg concept, AM. 2: Dunlending shelter concept, CG. 3: Dunlending shelter concepts, WW. 4: Wild Man shelter concepts, DF. 5: Dunlending shelter concept, AL.

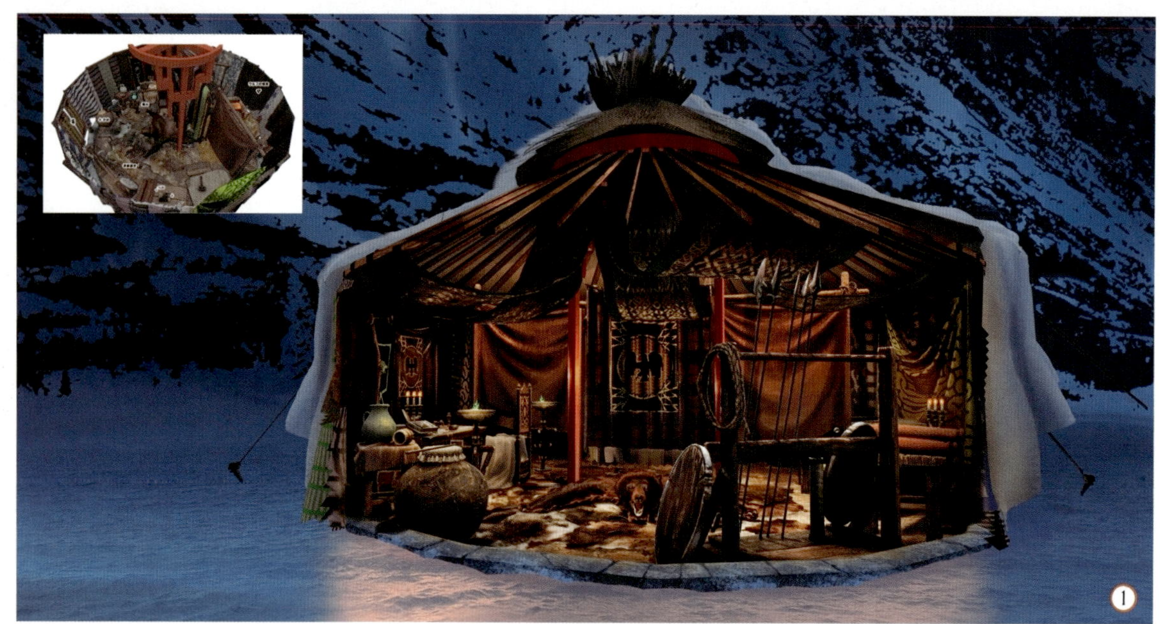

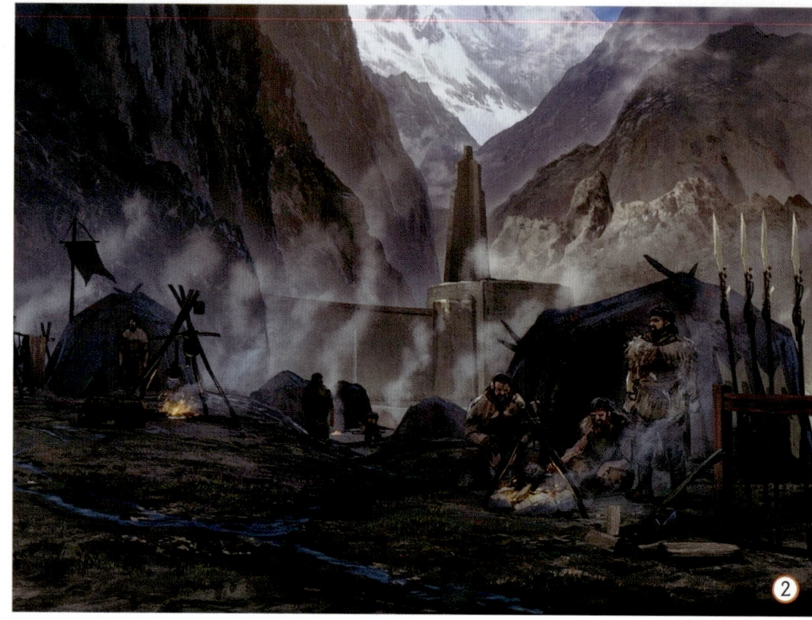

'NIGHT AFTER NIGHT, DEATH STALKED WULF'S CAMP.'

1: Wulf's tent concepts, YY. **2:** Wulf's encampment concept, KS. **3:** Wulf's camp background art.

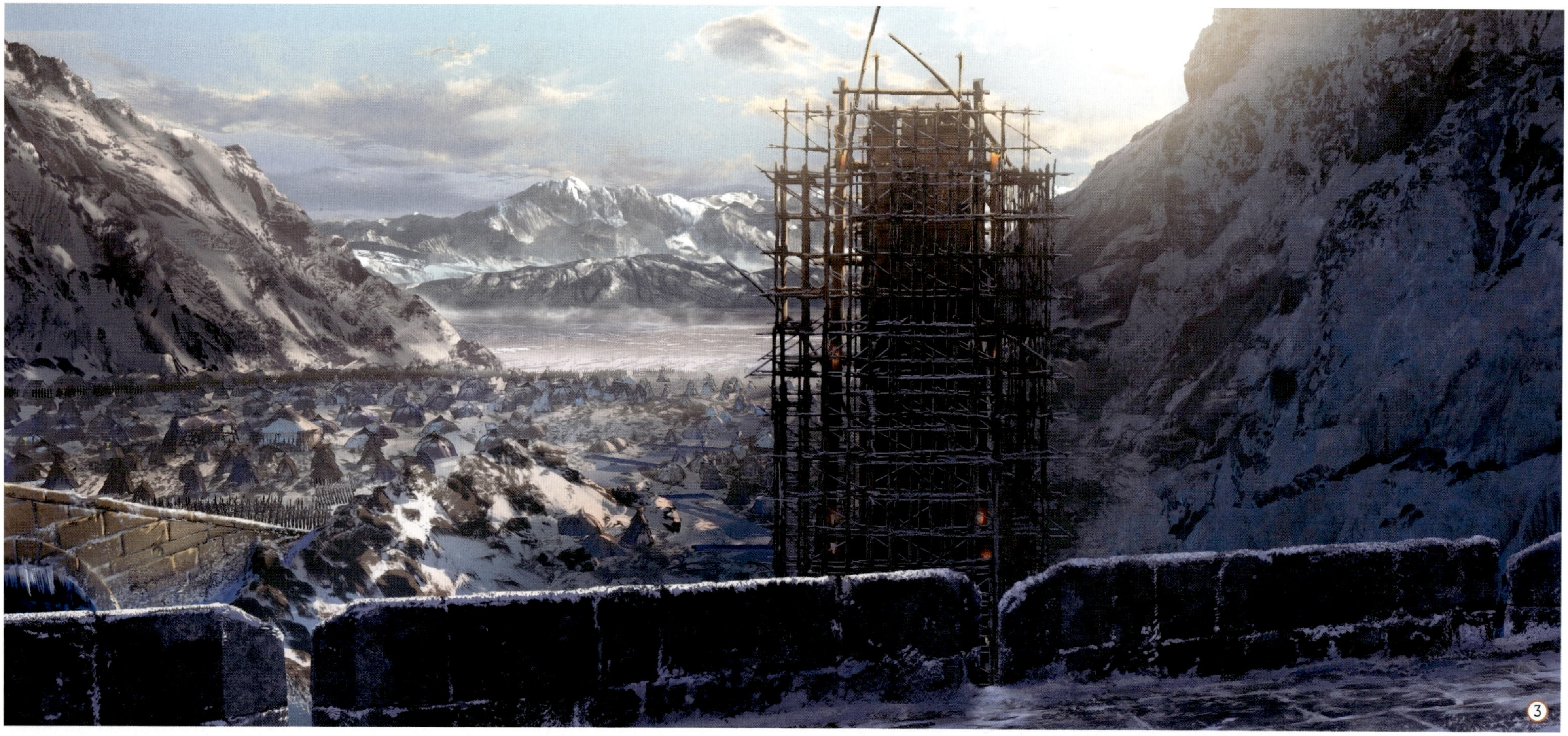

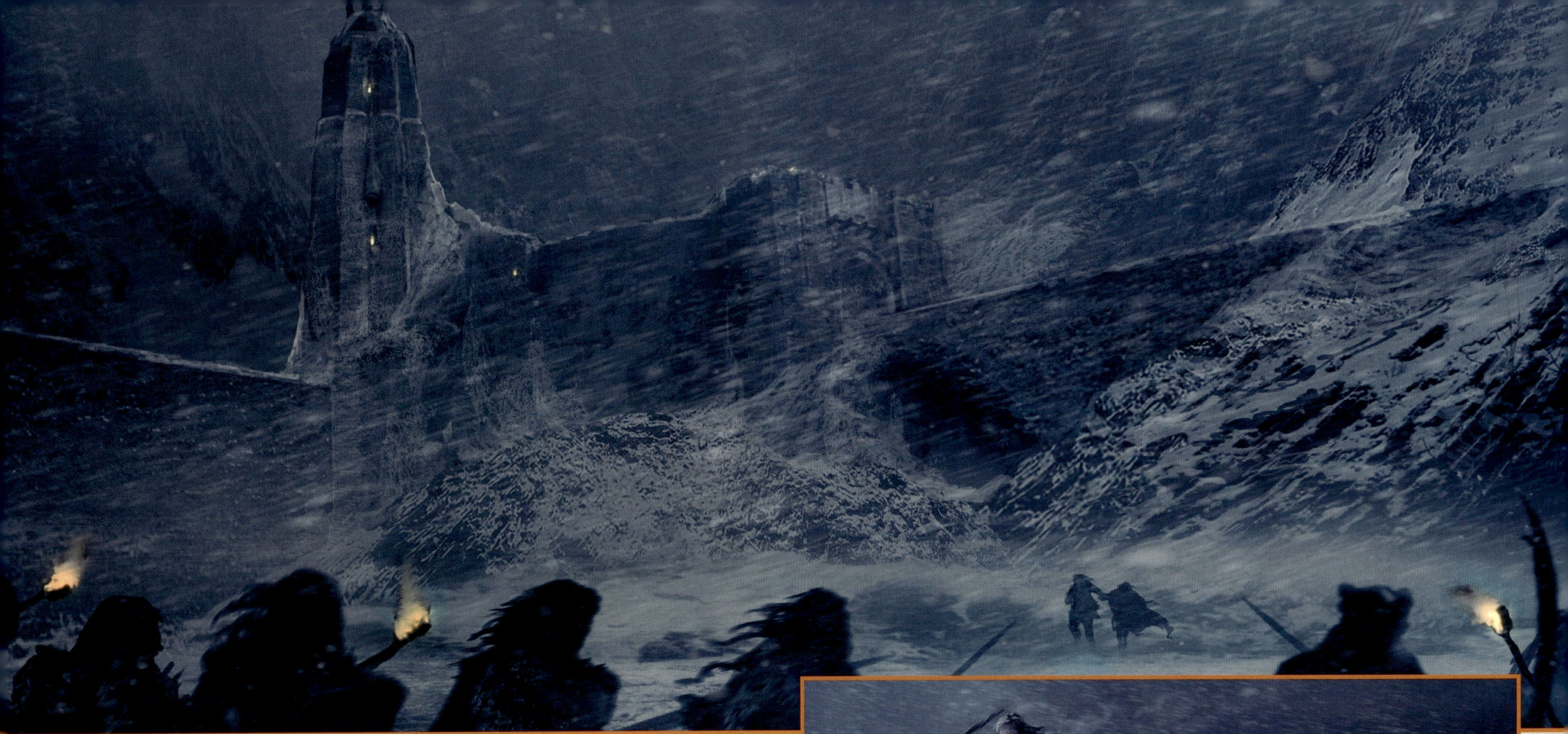

HELM AND HÉRA'S FLIGHT

A 3D model of Helm's Deep was of great help when I was producing the artwork of their pursuit through Wulf's camp. I used snapshots of the model to help achieve the right perspective and painted into them, adding the textures, snow, rocks and characters.

I tilted the reverse view, which heightened the drama and made the scene feel more dynamic. The spears created a triangular composition with the fleeing characters in the middle, Helm's face being the focal point. Misted breath helped to make it feel cold. – GUS HUNTER, WĒTĀ WORKSHOP SENIOR CONCEPT ARTIST

I knew this feature would involve a lot of snow and blizzard shots. The director told me that the snow was more expressive of the characters' emotions and the story moments than realistic weather, so rather than using CGI assets, we chose to create and add these effects when compositing. This allowed us to adjust each shot in line with the director's intent. – SHUNSUKE WATANABE, SANKAKU STUDIO, CG/COMPOSITE DIRECTOR

'THEY'RE MAKING FOR THE GATE!'

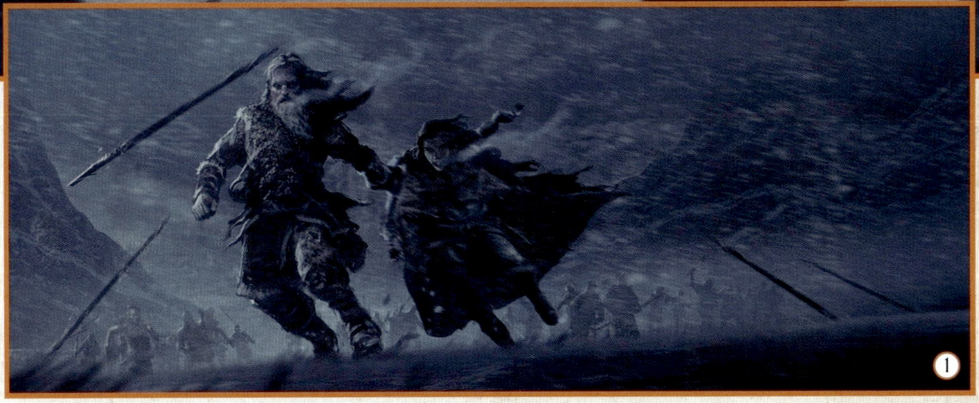

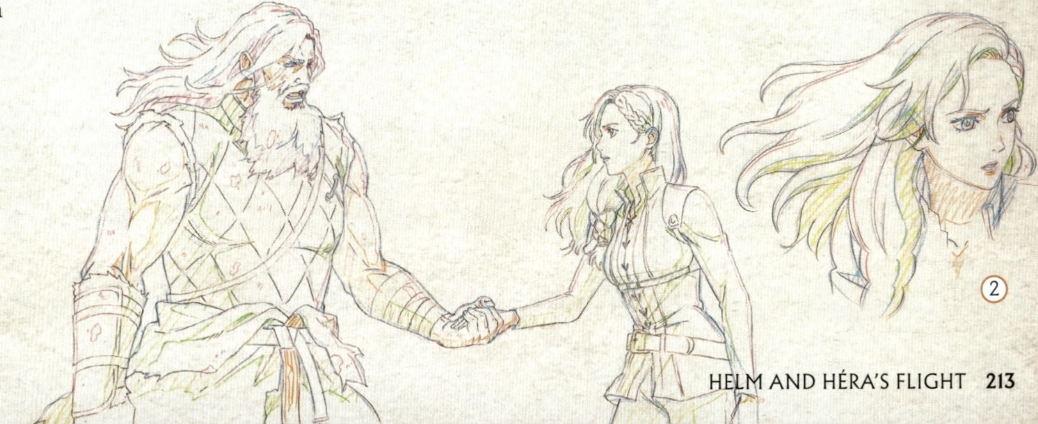

1: Helm and Héra's flight key scene art, GH. 2: Animation key frames, MT.

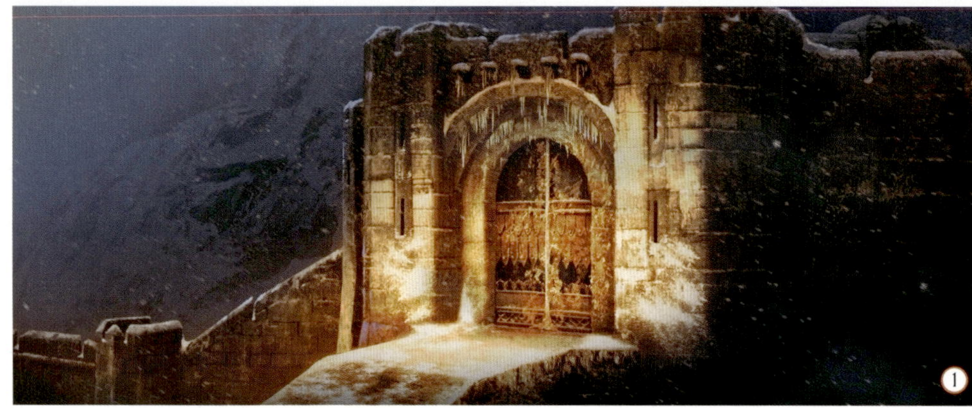

THE HORNBURG GATE

—◆◂◂◆▸◆▸◆—

While similar to the live-action version, some details of the Hornburg's gate were altered to suit the action and director's preferences. Proportions and features were tweaked as part of the anime design filter, and the door mechanism was changed. The side sallyport that Gimli and Legolas would use two centuries later is also absent, the conceit being that some alterations will be made between now and then, perhaps in reaction to the events of the siege.

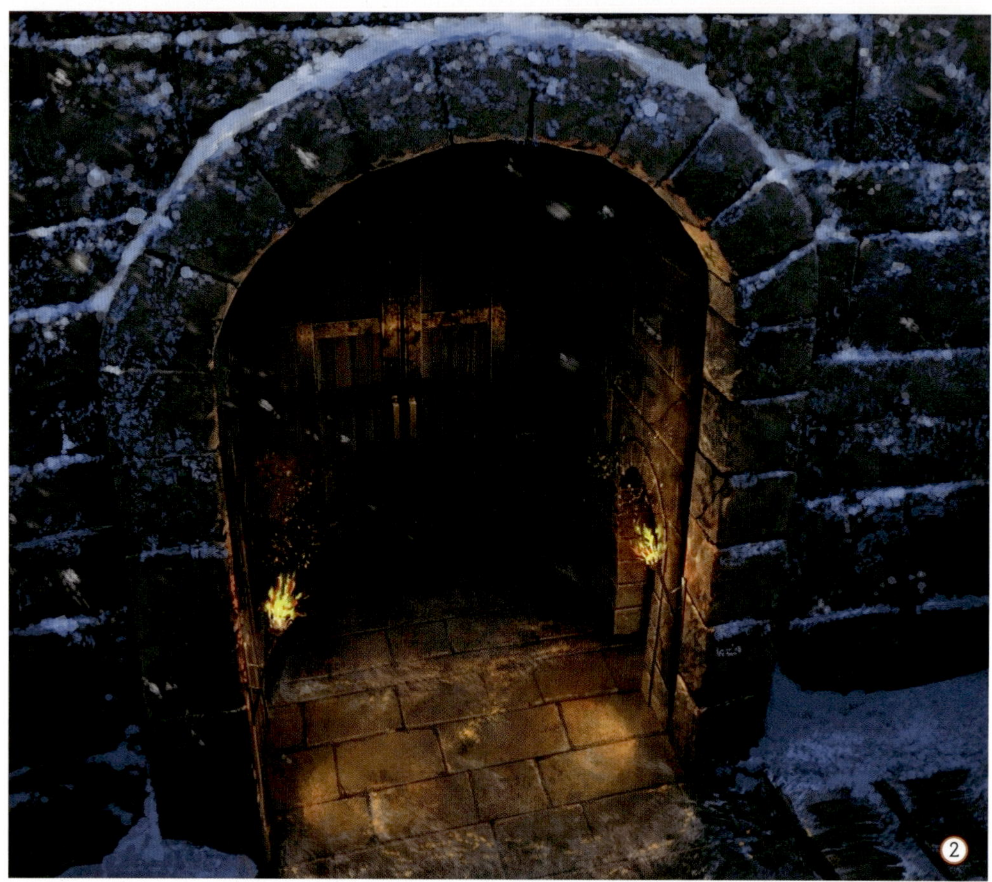

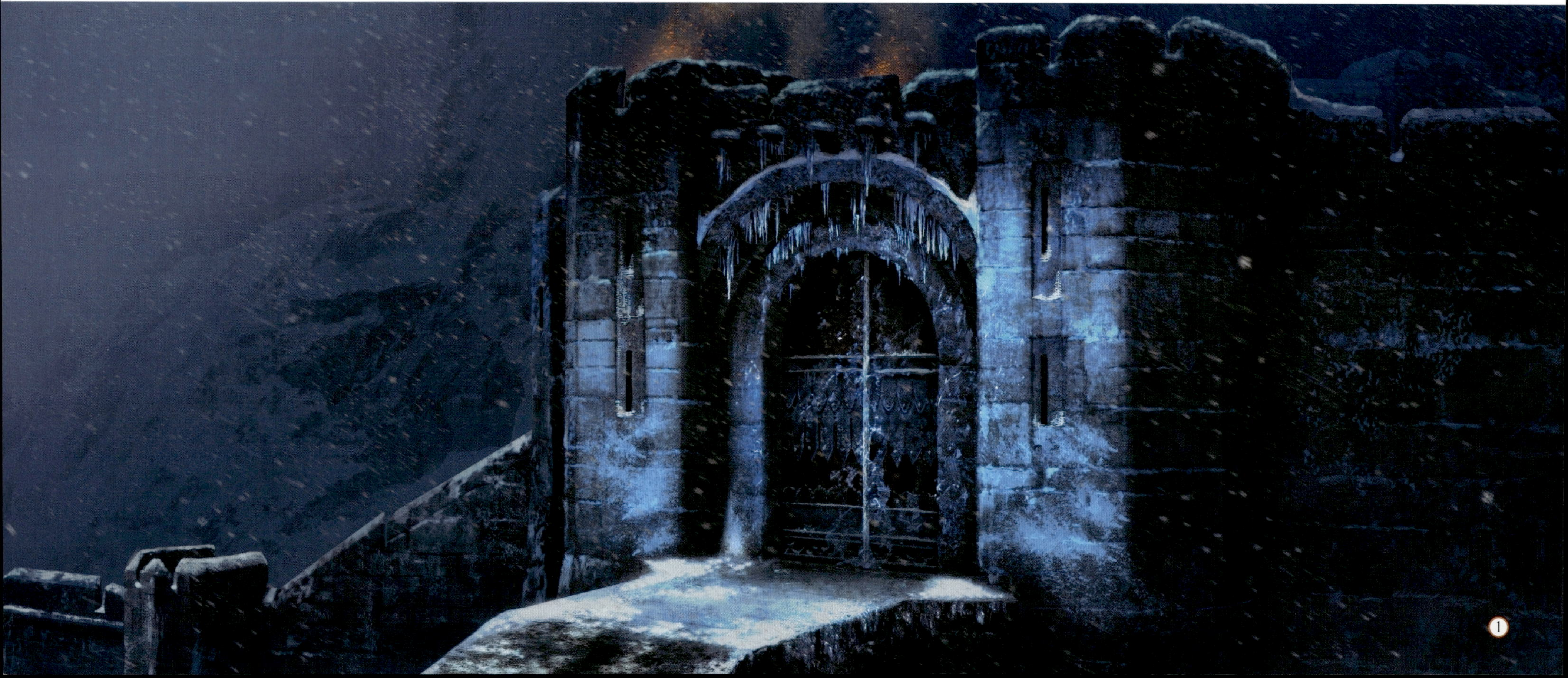

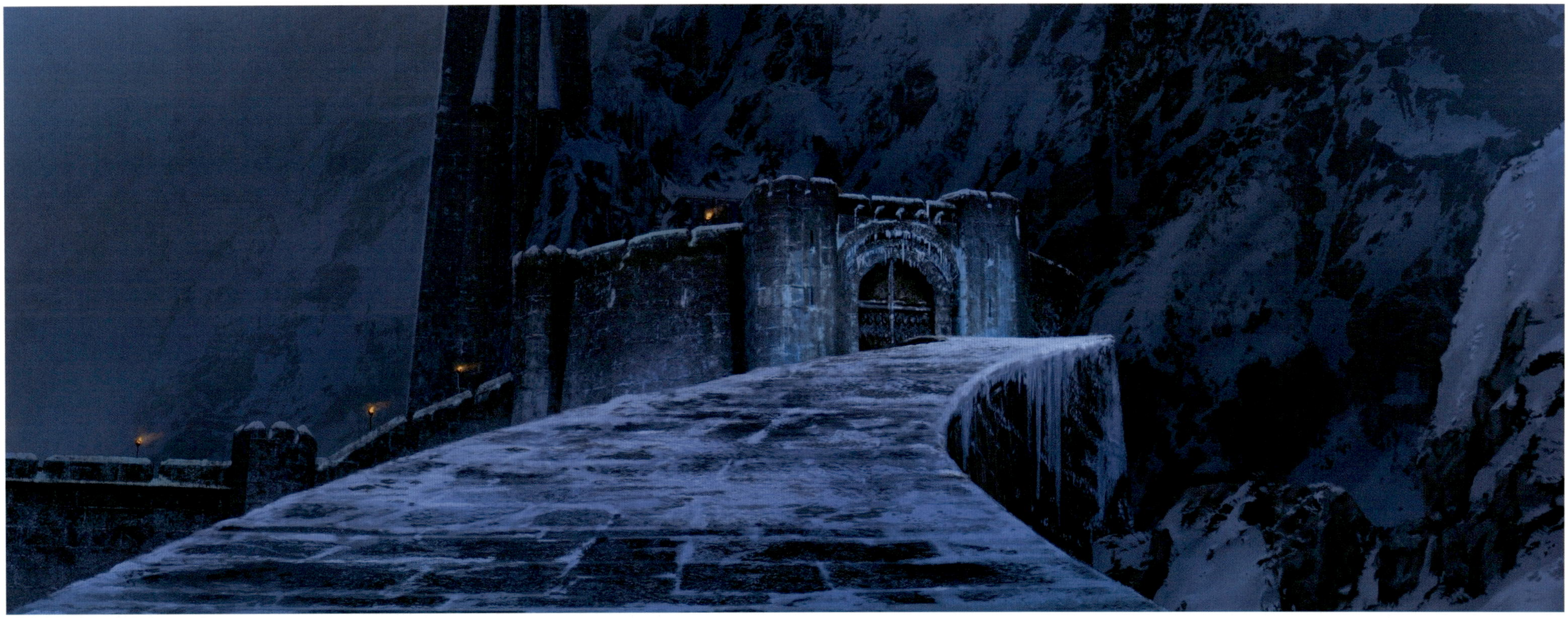

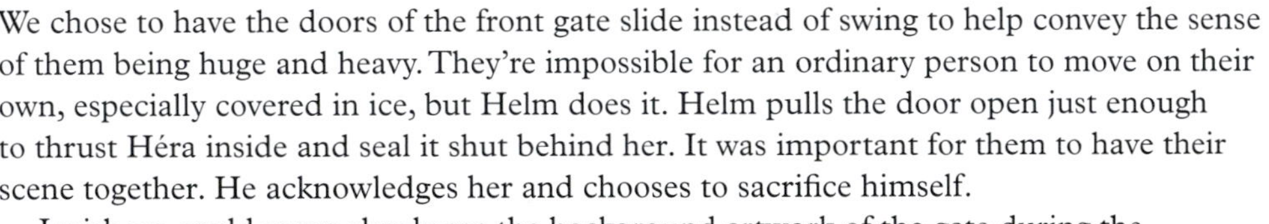

We chose to have the doors of the front gate slide instead of swing to help convey the sense of them being huge and heavy. They're impossible for an ordinary person to move on their own, especially covered in ice, but Helm does it. Helm pulls the door open just enough to thrust Héra inside and seal it shut behind her. It was important for them to have their scene together. He acknowledges her and chooses to sacrifice himself.

I wish we could more clearly see the background artwork of the gate during the snowstorm, because the art staff did such a great job with it. It's covered in icicles and frozen shut. – TAMIKO KANAMORI, ART DIRECTOR

1: Hornburg gate background art, KS. 2: Hornburg gate background art.

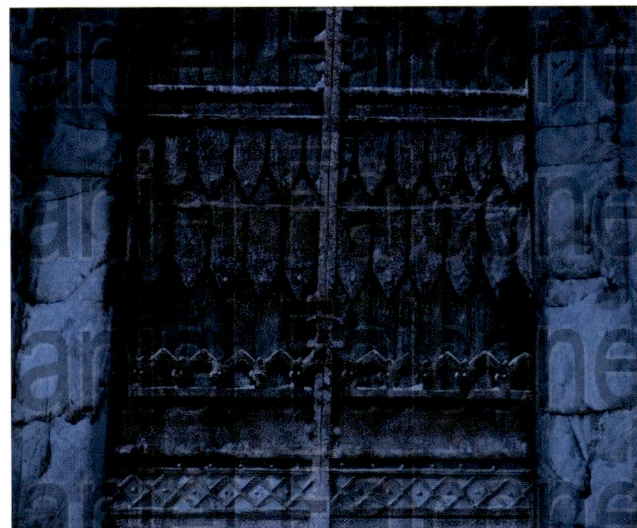

②

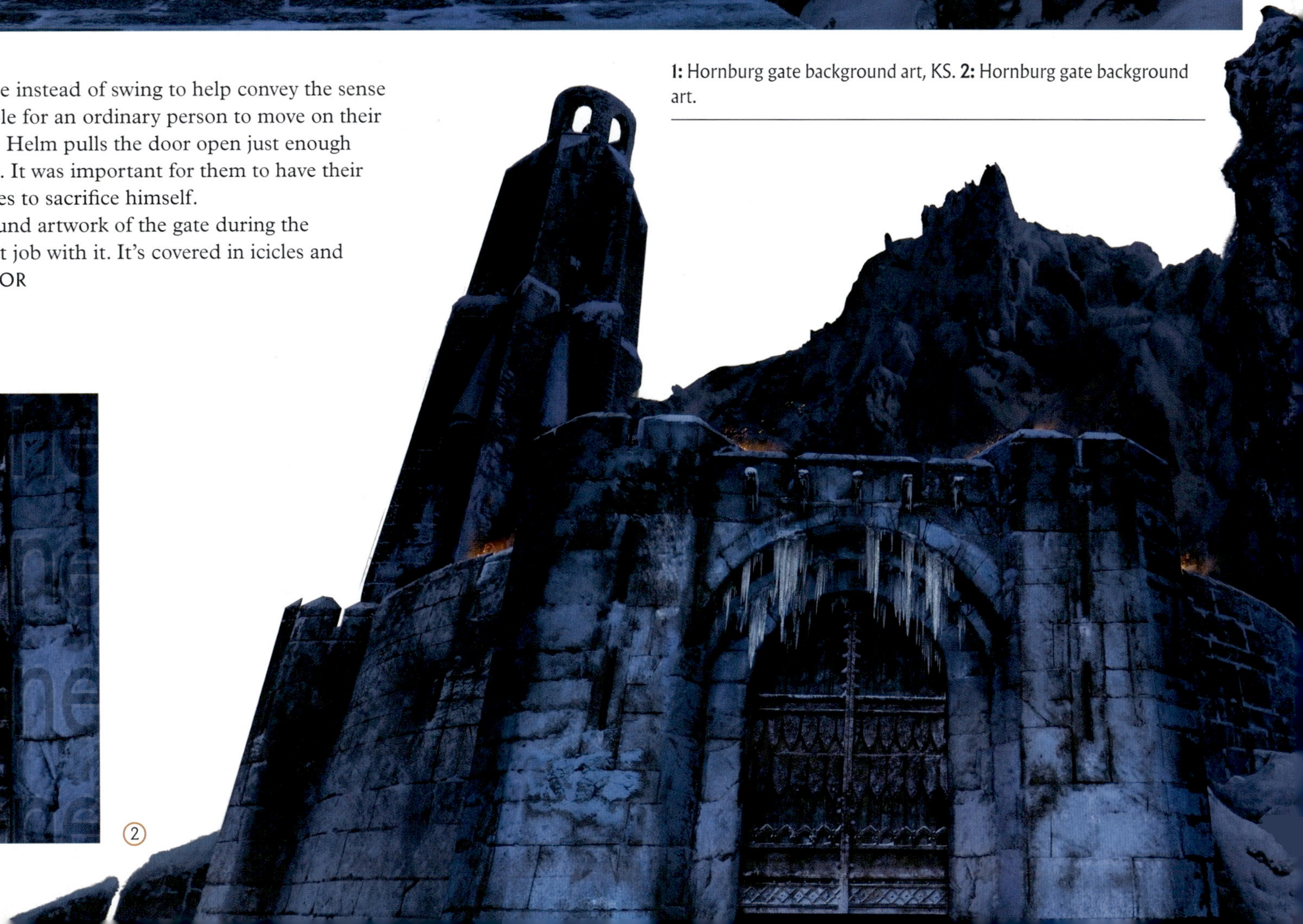

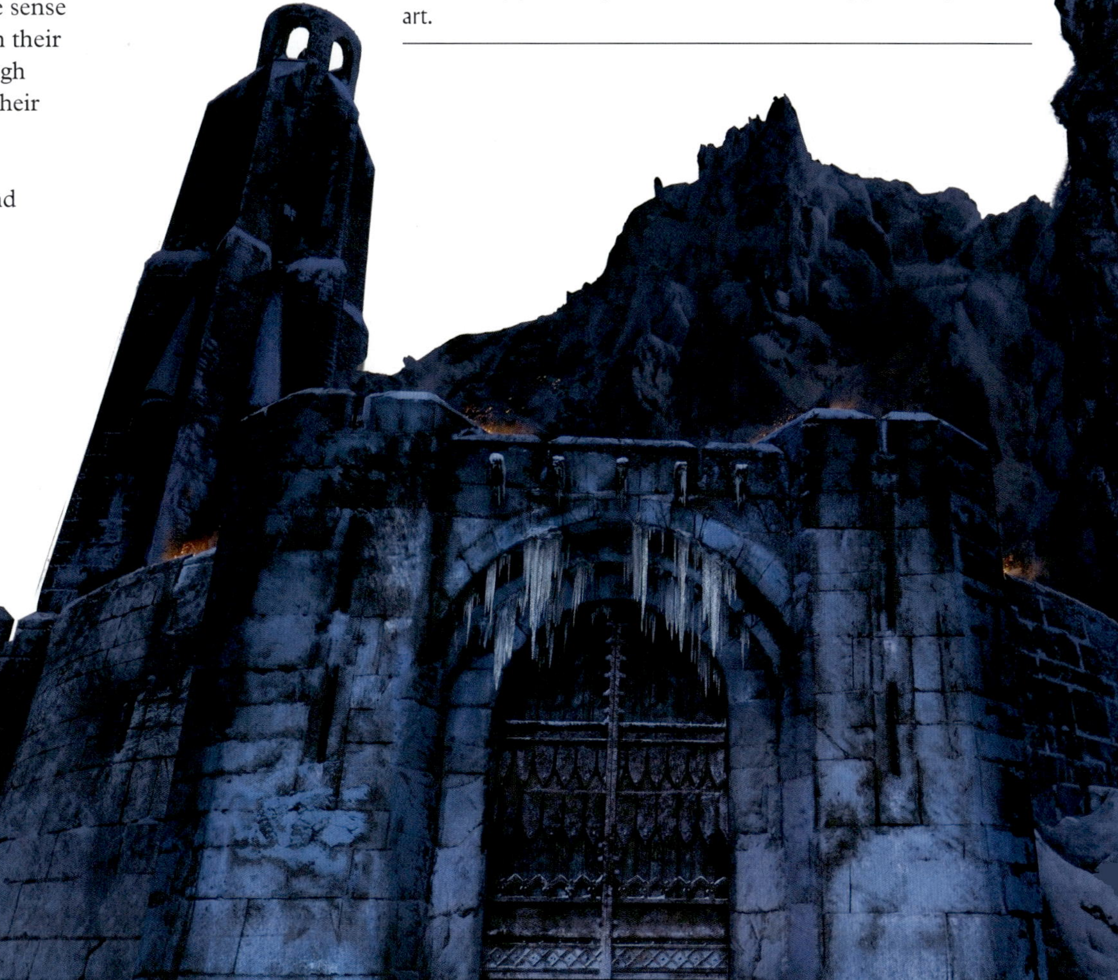

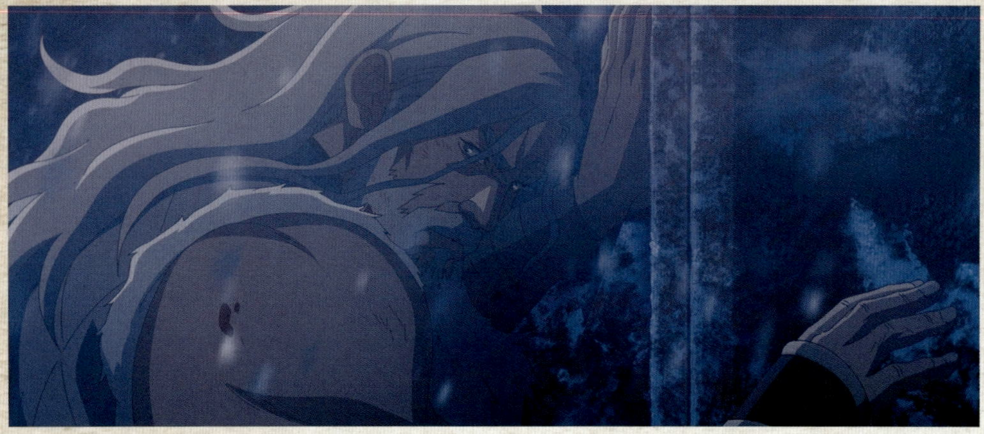

HELM'S LAST STAND

My favourite scenes in the film are between Helm and Héra. The first is in the stables of Edoras – he wants to protect her, but in doing so he takes away her choices. Their moment at the gate is the mirror to that scene, in which we see the progression of Helm's character and what he has come to understand. We wrote so many iterations, trying to get the words right.

'You are the daughter of kings,' he tells her. It's beautiful, but we wanted to be careful that this statement wasn't the sum of it; 'You are my daughter and thus…' It's not solely about Helm, so we have, 'The day you were born I was brought to my knees.' Essentially, he's saying to her, 'You are the daughter of kings, but you are your own person.' – PHOEBE GITTINS, WRITER

One of the biggest challenges of the scene was shaping it so it wasn't just Helm handing Héra the mantle of leadership, but showing him empowering his daughter to believe in herself, to be brave enough to make and see through the tough decisions that are coming her way. Helm is eerily calm before sacrificing himself outside the gates, but it's because he can die in peace, knowing that he has done all that he can to put right his mistakes, because if there is a way his people can survive, it will be Héra's way. – ARTY PAPAGEORGIOU, WRITER

Helm recognizes in Héra that 'They need you.' He is acknowledging that brute strength isn't going to be the solution here, and he believes that she will find another way to save their people. He trusts that she will lead them, and that she will do it her way; the way that is needed in this moment. – PHOEBE GITTINS, WRITER

Helm frozen before the gate is so iconic and important. It's something straight out of the book, I couldn't wait to see that realized visually and I think they did a beautiful job. – PHOEBE GITTINS, WRITER

'COME AWAY CHILD, COME AWAY BEFORE YOU FREEZE TO DEATH.'

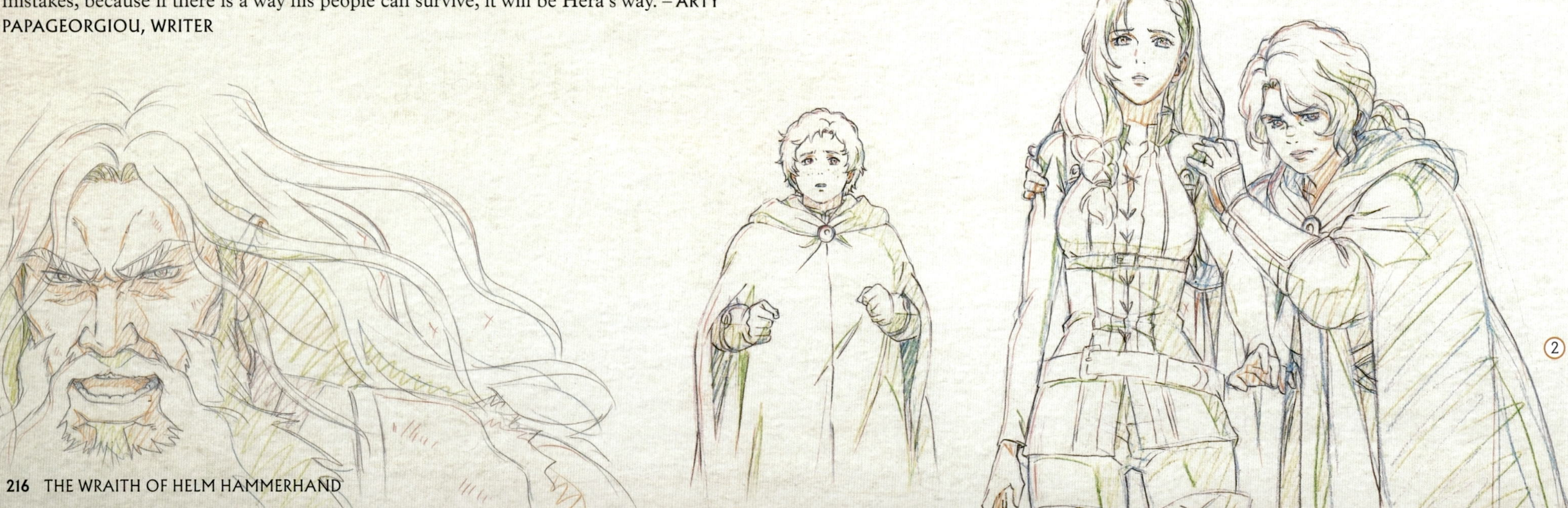

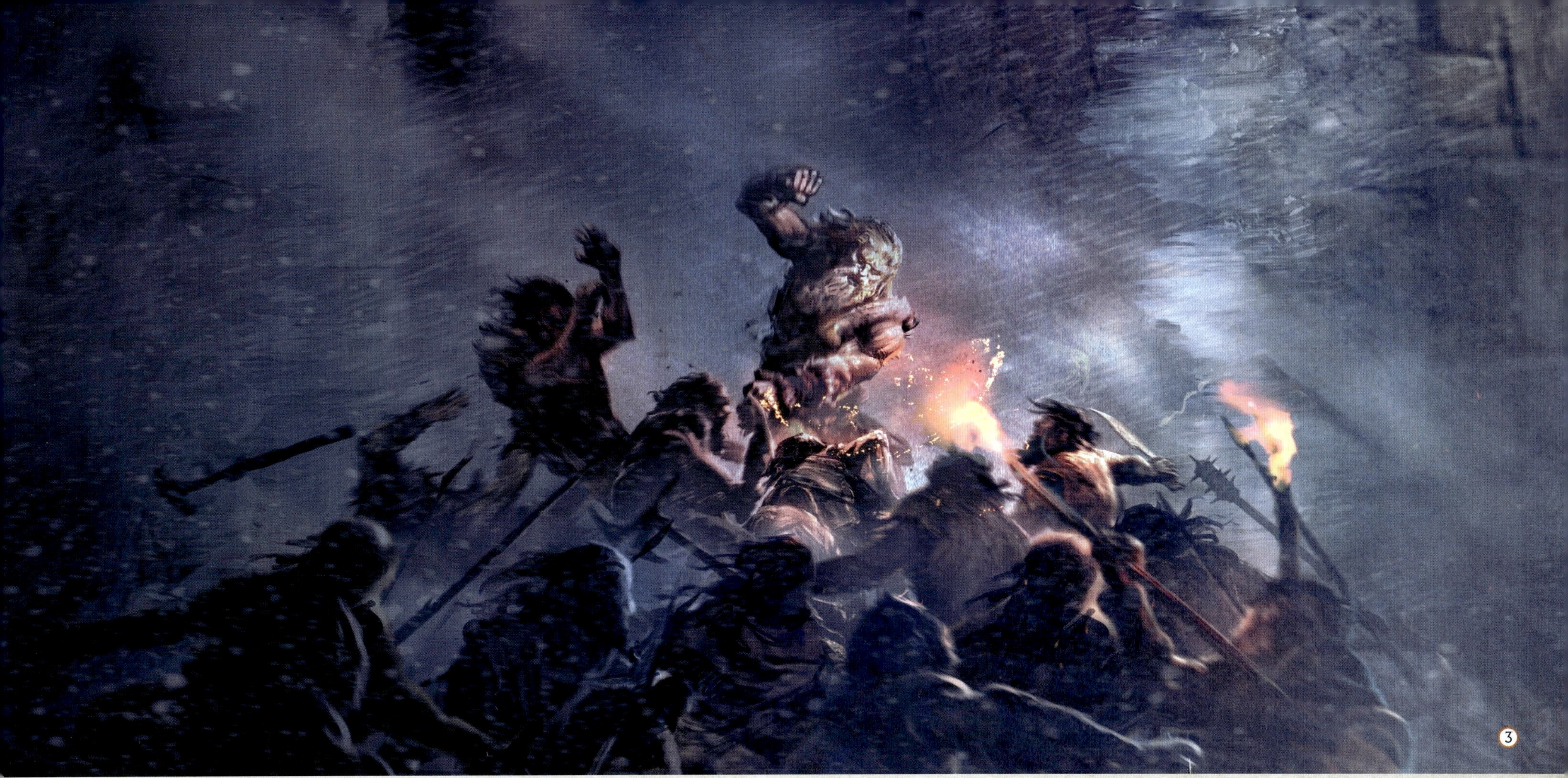

'IS THERE NO ONE LEFT TO FACE ME?'

The scene of Helm being found frozen exists in the book, but the question for us was how to backfill that ending with a dramatic scene that connects him with Héra? How do we pass the baton to her to finish the story? How do we stage this character's end in a proper way?

We were inspired by the incredible image of Helm fighting that Gus Hunter at Wētā Workshop produced. It helped us figure out what to do. Helm is not just fighting, but guarding the Hornburg, his people and his daughter. And of course, the result will be that this place will be called Helm's Deep by the generations that follow. – KENJI KAMIYAMA, DIRECTOR

I am a huge fan of Frank Frazetta, so there was definitely a Frazetta influence in my key scene art of Helm's last fight. I wanted to make this climactic scene very dynamic. Helm is taking all of his enemies on with just his fists and he's destroying them! To make him the focal point I lit Helm with firelight and composed the shot with him at the top of a triangle of foes. Motion blurring the closest enemies also helped make him stand out. – GUS HUNTER, WĒTĀ WORKSHOP SENIOR CONCEPT ARTIST

1: Final film frames. **2:** Animation key frames, MT **3:** Helm's last stand key scene art, GH.

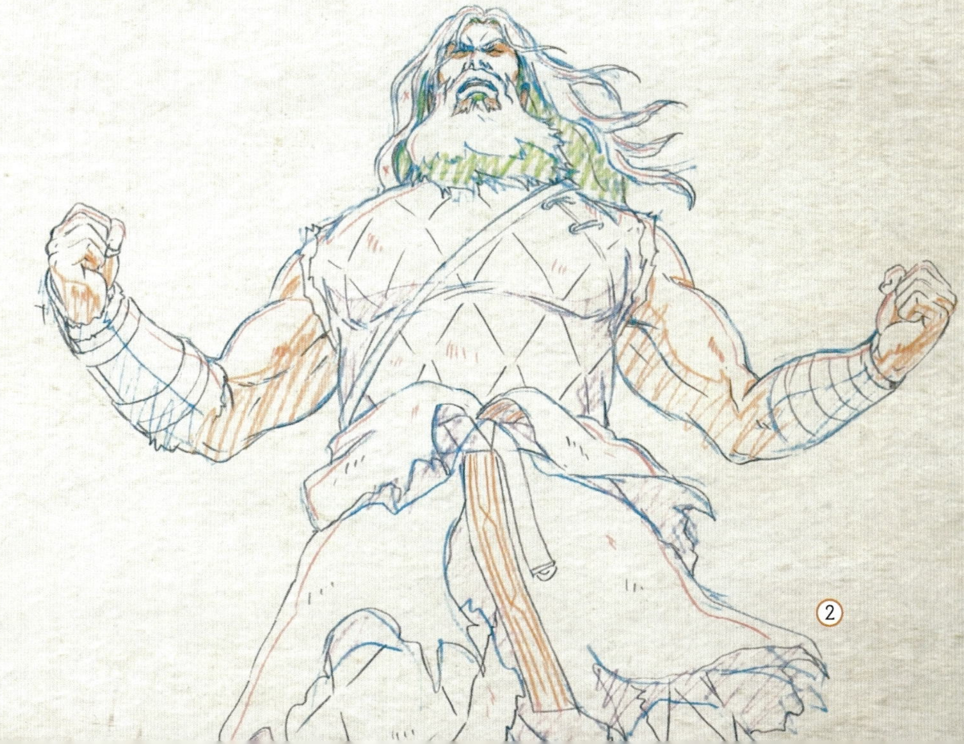

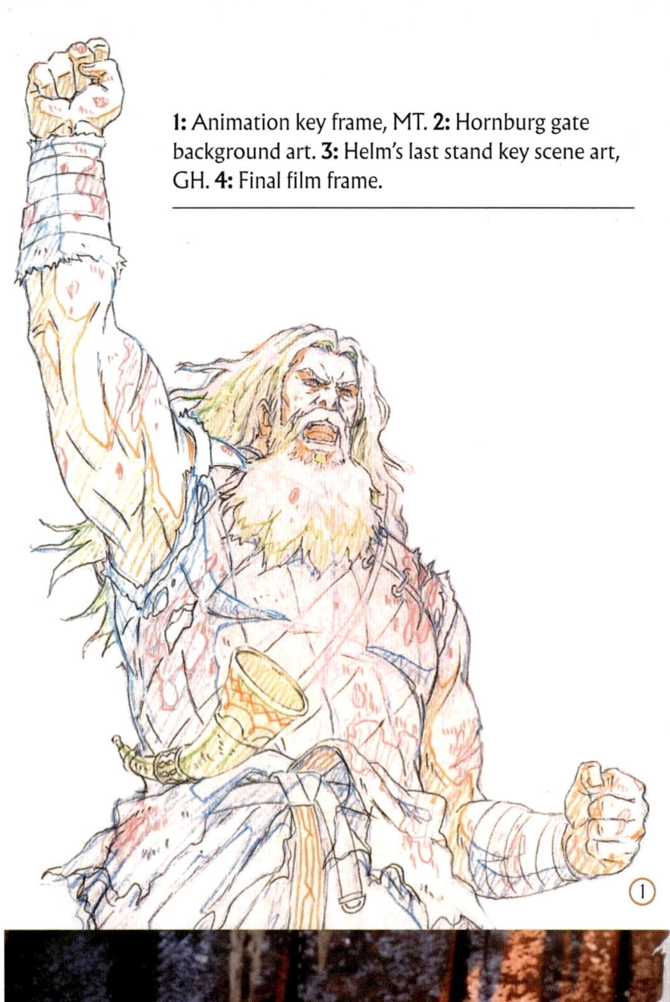

1: Animation key frame, MT. 2: Hornburg gate background art. 3: Helm's last stand key scene art, GH. 4: Final film frame.

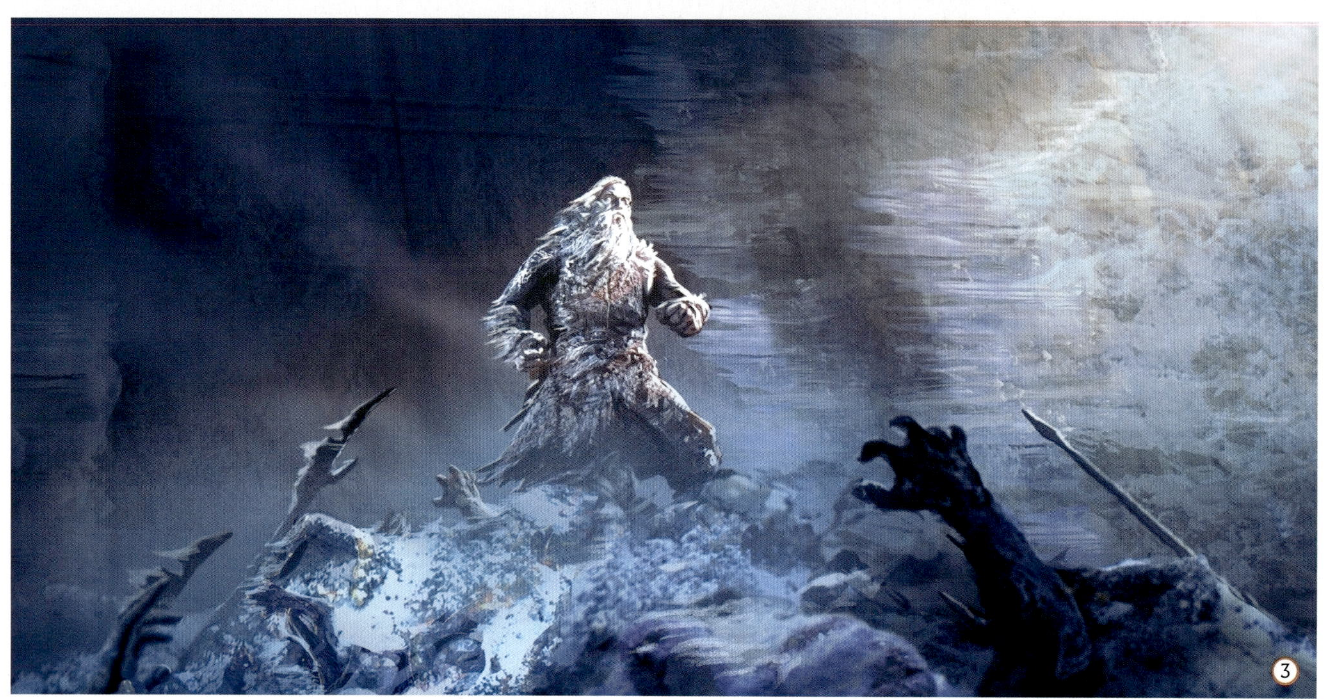

'BY MY LIFE – ROHAN STILL STANDS! HELM HAMMERHAND STILL STANDS!'

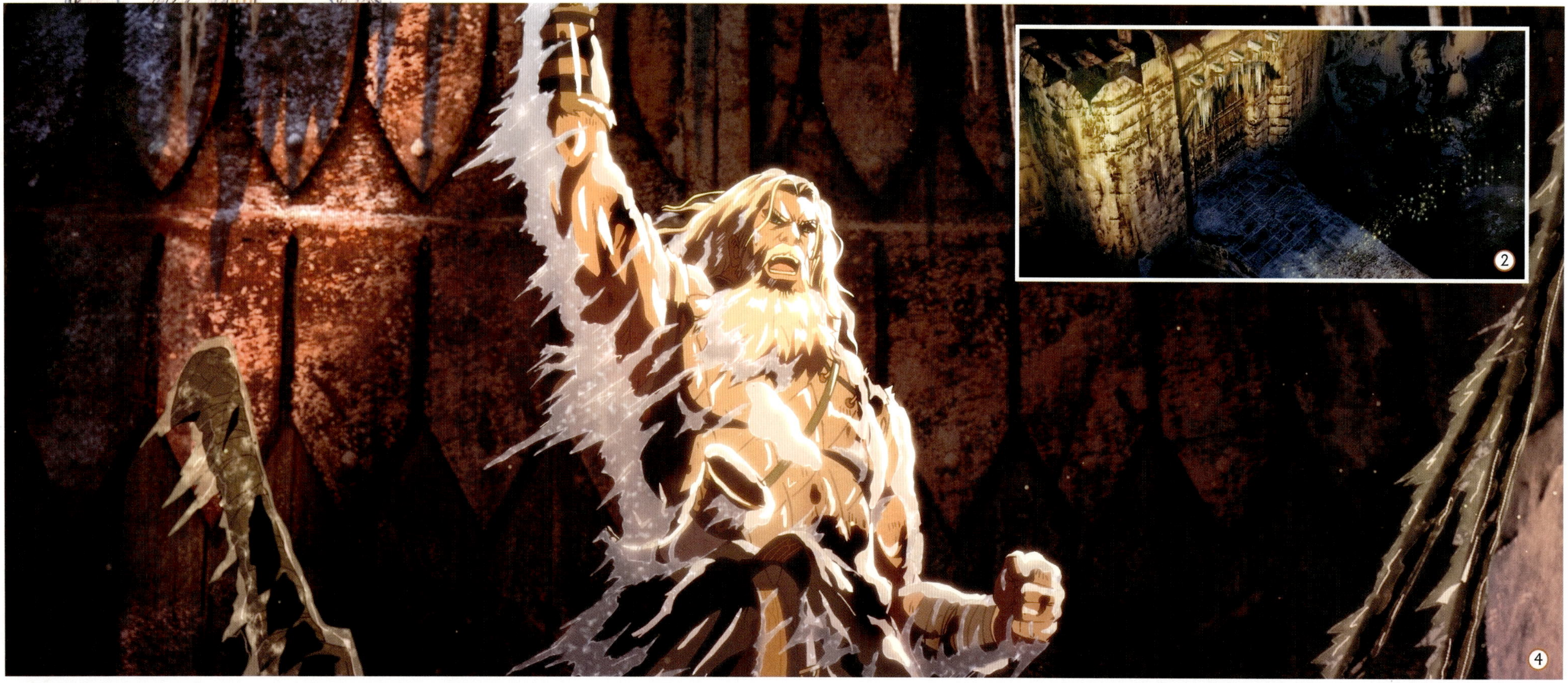

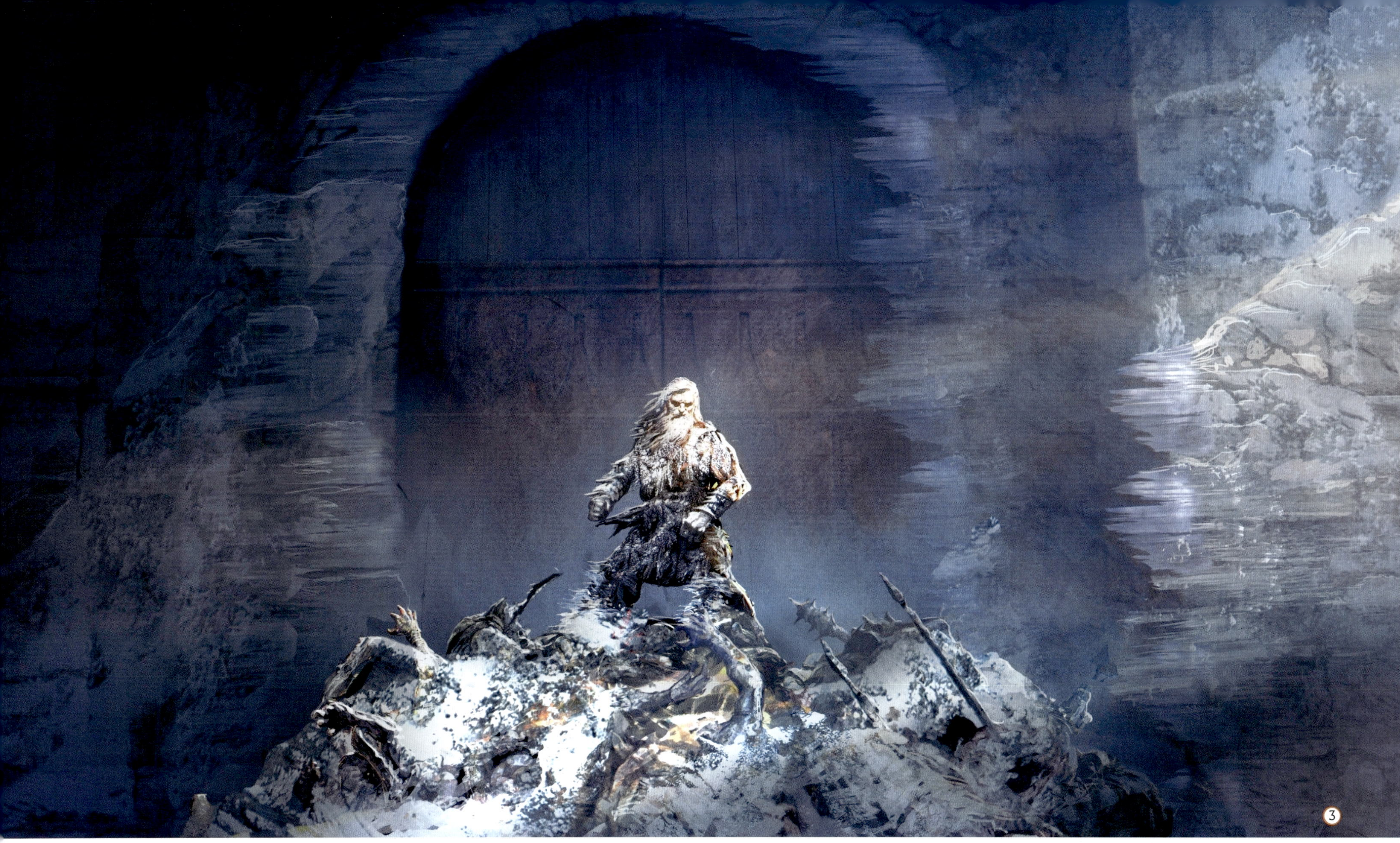

'There stood Helm, dead as stone, but his knees were unbent.' Philippa would quote this line from the book to us. It was the moment we were building to, so we had the end scenario first and had to work backwards. When you read that Helm froze to death outside and you start thinking about it practically, you have to ask, how does that work? How does he stand frozen on his feet? As a grounded filmmaker, our director's challenge was to figure out how to create a scenario in which it felt believable that Helm would save Héra but that he would be trapped outside.

There were certain things that we knew we would be doing from the outset. We staged him in front of the gates. His will would be unbroken, enemies lying dead around him, and we wanted him to be standing as if he were ready to drop the next person to try to take him on. We knew it would be happening in a blizzard and that Helm would be fighting multiple bad guys as they charge at him, and that eventually the blizzard would obscure what we would see. The next vision of him would be in the morning afterwards, caught by the first light to break through the gloom, just as Tolkien describes in the book, when the people would see him frozen and dead.

The task was to build to this moment in a way that felt believable within the context of our story and make it a key emotional moment for Héra and Helm both. – JASON DEMARCO, PRODUCER

Helm standing frozen was fun to illustrate in key scene art. He is the focal point in the image. The dawn light picks him out of the dark background. The storm has passed, but you can feel its intensity, even in this moment of stillness, by the exaggerated, horizontal icicles on the stone. – GUS HUNTER, WĒTĀ WORKSHOP SENIOR CONCEPT ARTIST

Helm's nighttime fight in the blizzard was blue-tinged, but we contrasted that with a shift to a warm palette when we cut to the morning after. The wind has dropped, the sun has come out and we are in a moment of calm. – YASUHIRO YAMANE, ART DIRECTOR

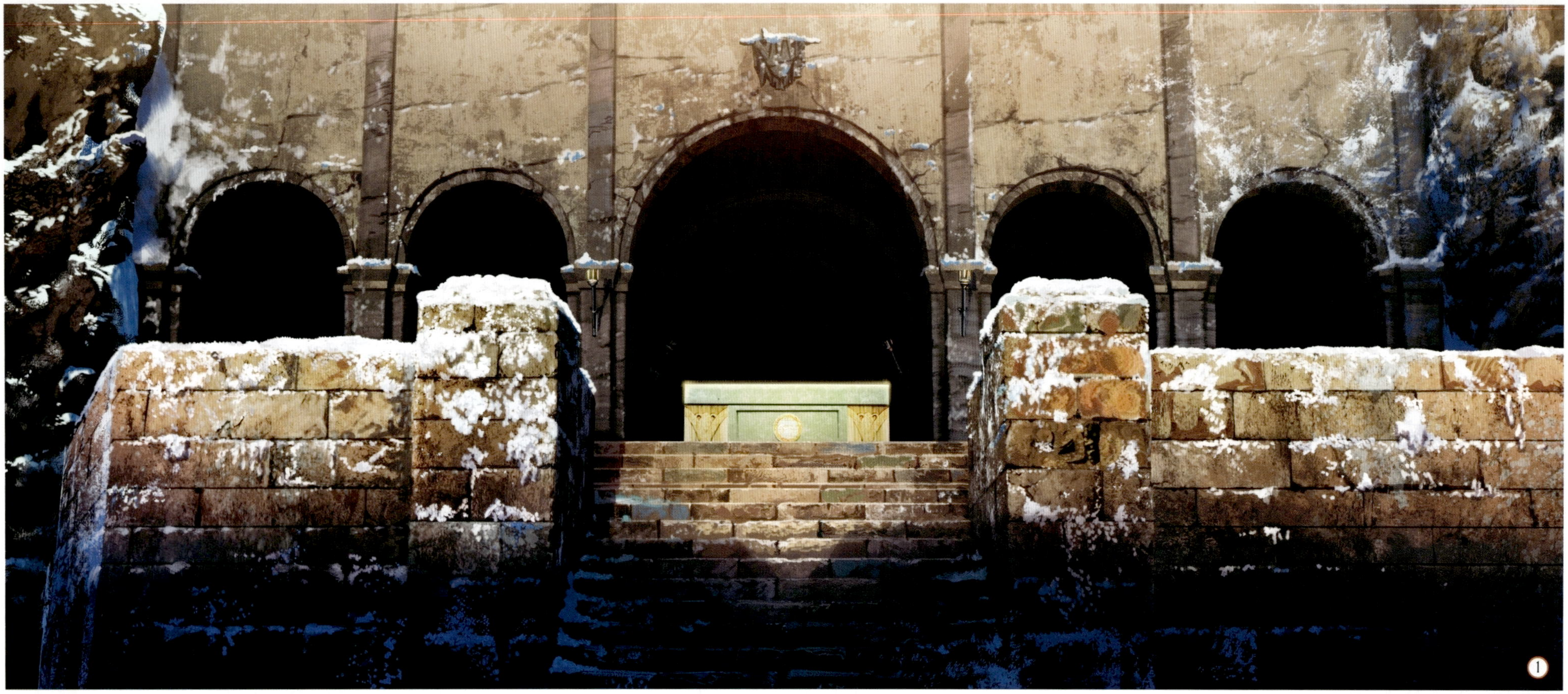

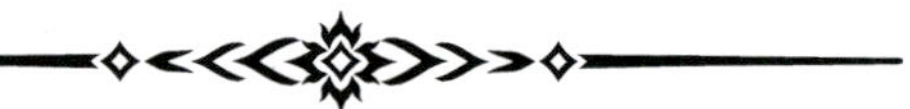

HELM'S FUNERAL

The funeral marks the passing of a character with a huge presence. From this point on, Héra must carry everything forward, so this was the passing of the torch. It needed to be symbolic in many ways, and to be emotional; to be sad, but also evoke a sense of achievement.

Imagining the scene, I started with designing the shot from inside, looking out past the silhouette of Helm and Héra, with direct light. We experimented with many different angles, but once we got that image right, it gave us the visual on which to hang the scene and everything else was designed around it. – KENJI KAMIYAMA, DIRECTOR

The kings of Rohan are buried in mounds outside the gates of Edoras, so it's a big deal that Helm can't be taken back there for his funeral. – ARTY PAPAGEORGIOU, WRITER

The palette throughout the funeral was so beautiful, and the lament. Lorraine Asbourne, who plays Olwyn, has the most brilliant, emotive voice. She sings the lament, which is a nod to the Lament for Théodred, sung by Éowyn in the extended editions, but Philippa tweaked the lyrics for specificity. The Rohirrim are a people of song, so these would be passed down, keeping them alive through the generations. – PHOEBE GITTINS, WRITER

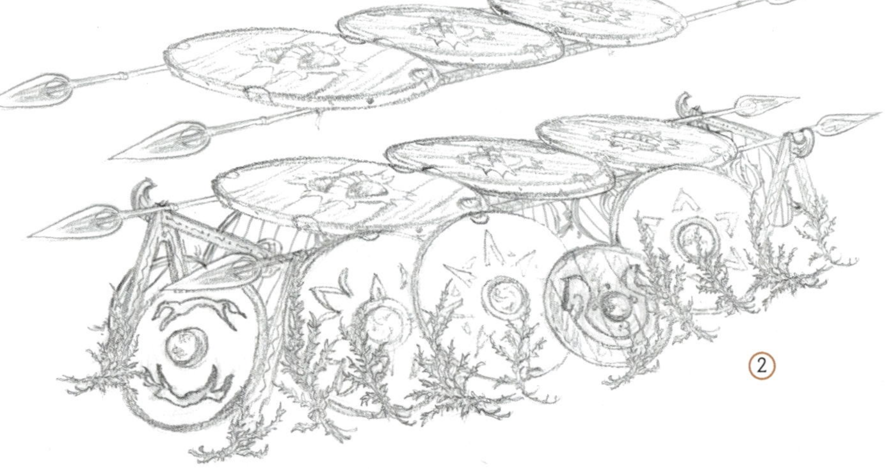

1: Helm's funeral background art. 2: Helm's bier concept, DF.
3: Helm's funeral background setting art, YY. 4: Animation key frame, MT.

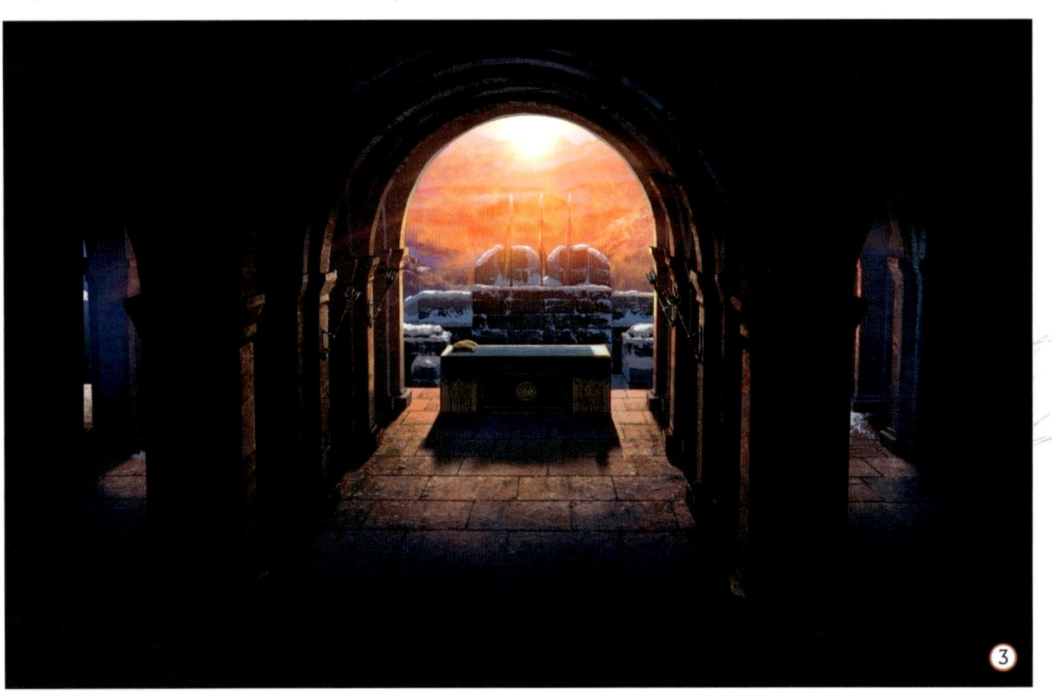

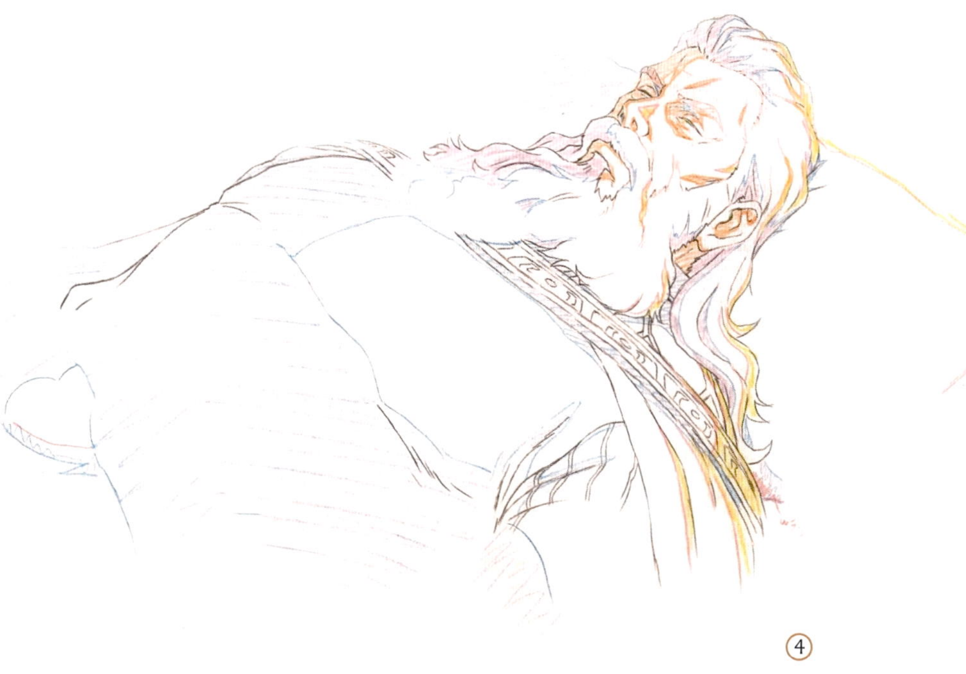

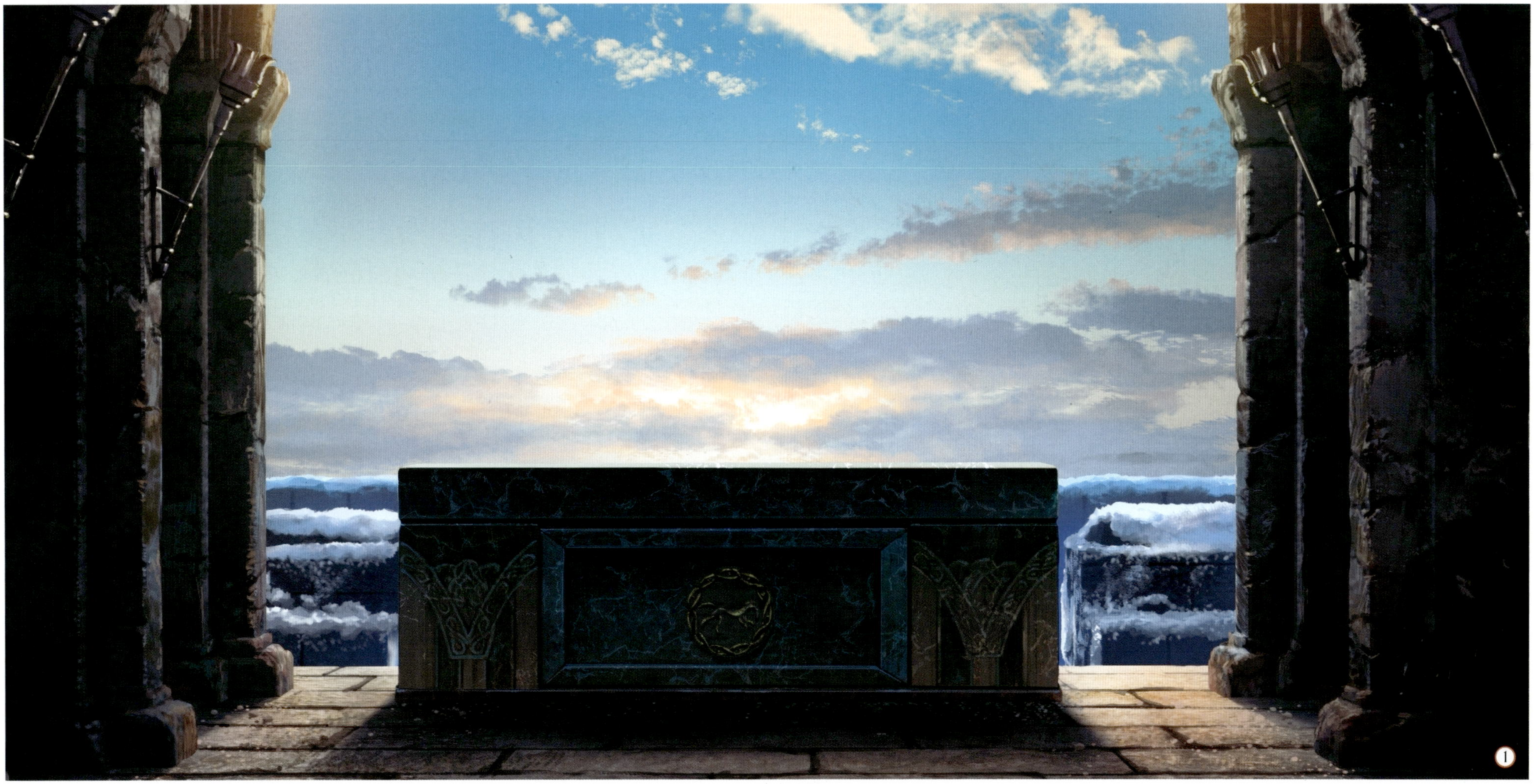

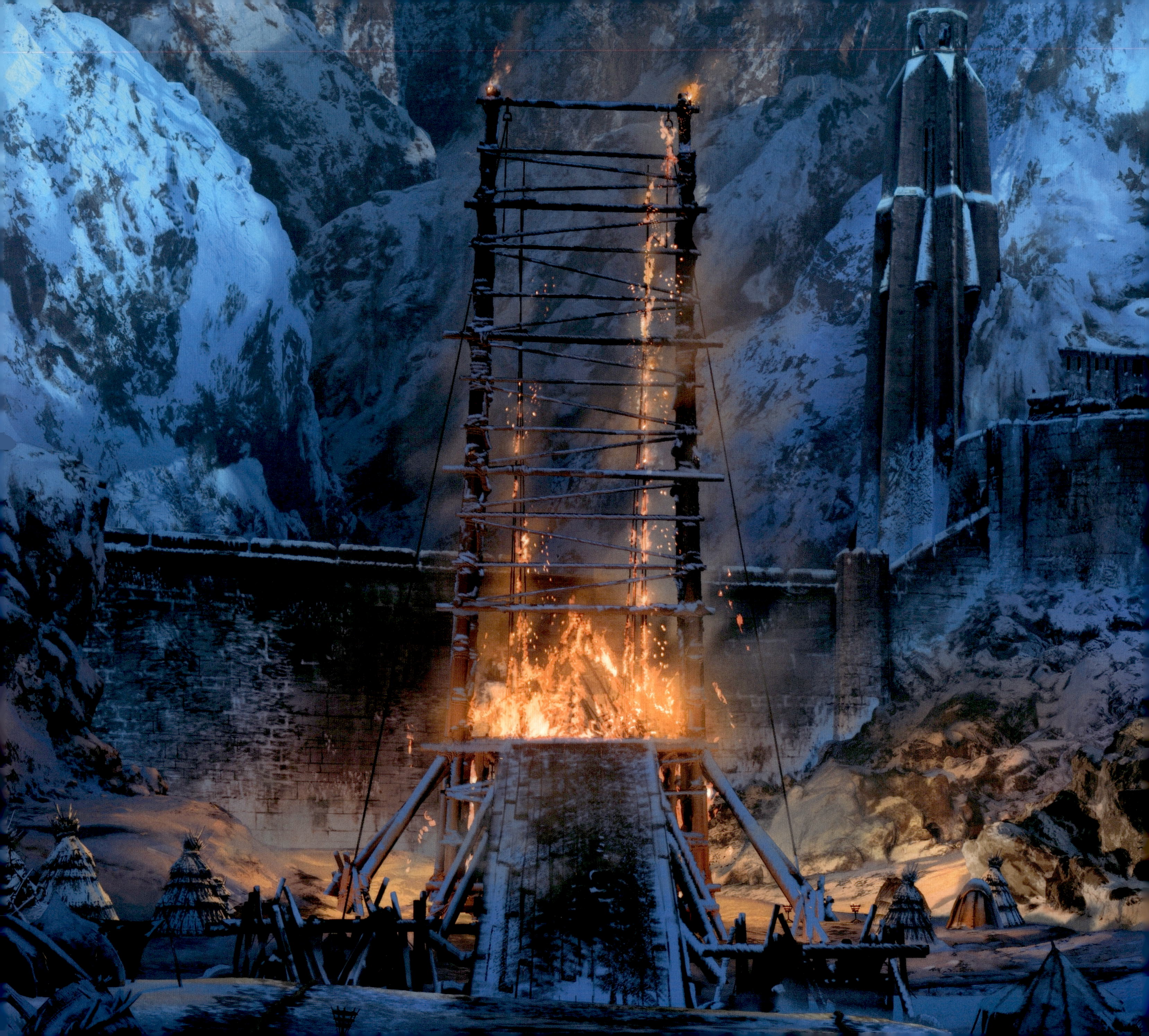

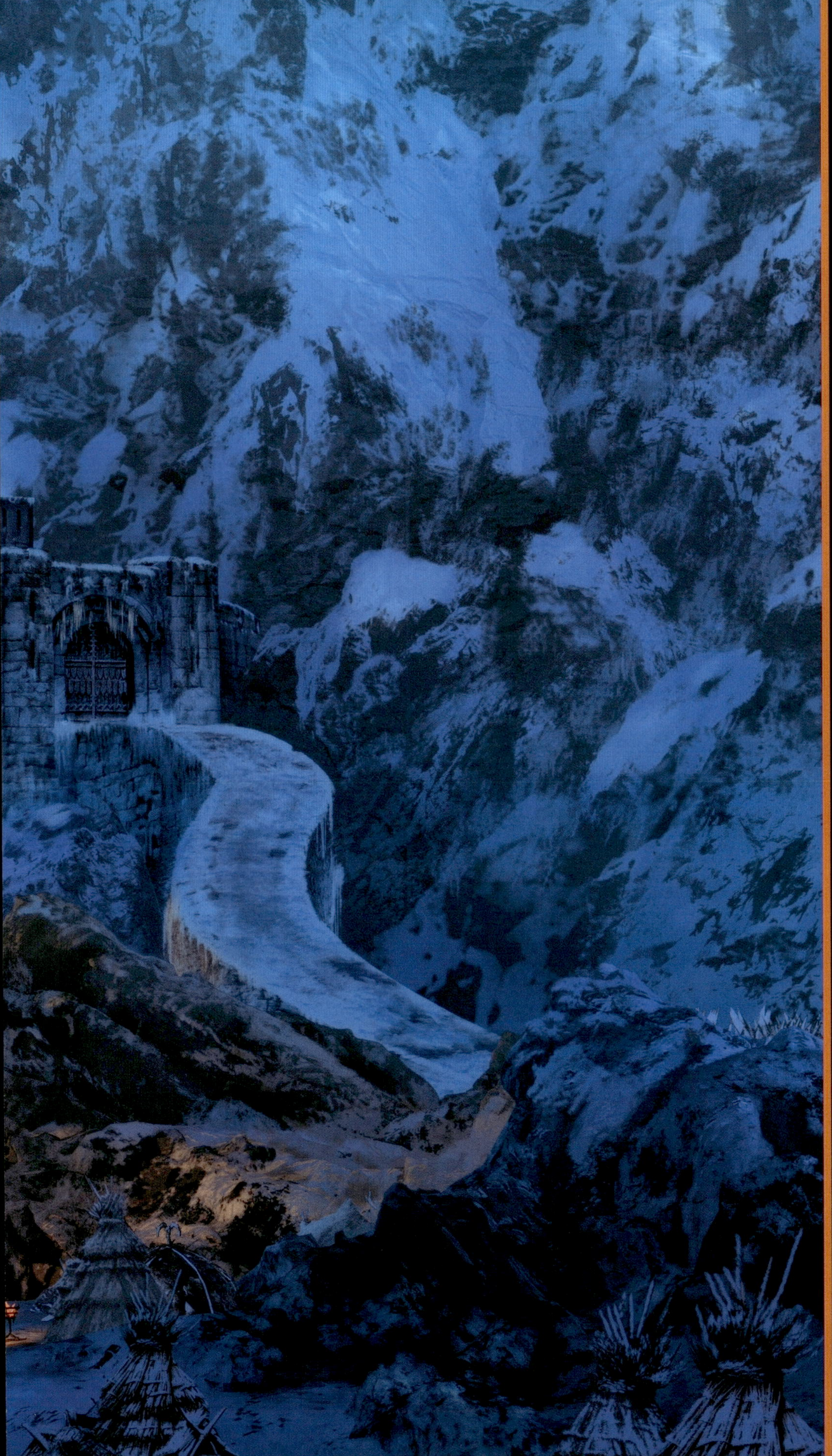

- 8 -

THE SIEGE

Helm is farewelled by his people, as food and fuel run short and the Dunlendings and Wild Men begin building some kind of siege tower to gain the walls. Héra must find a way to save them before it is completed. She turns her eyes to the mountains above.

Donning climbing gear, and giving special orders concerning Helm's armour to Lief, Héra begins a dangerous ascent of the icy cliffs behind the Keep. Her object is an eyrie, far above, where she finds the very same white-feathered Great Eagle from her days on the golden plains, so long ago. Héra knows that the Great Eagles understand the speech of men, and she begs the mighty bird for help.

Returning to the Hornburg, Héra now takes charge as the enemy completes construction of their war tower. While Héra remains behind to distract Wulf, Lief will lead the people by Helm's passageway beyond the enemy encampment. She dons the moth-eaten wedding gown and takes up sword and shield, riding out to meet her former suitor.

Héra and Wulf duel as the attackers hurl themselves upon the Keep. Fréaláf appears, clad in Helm's armour, and the Dunlendings and Wild Men are terrified by what they believe to be Helm returned from the dead. They flee in a panic. As victory slips from his grasp, in the red fog of his rage Wulf miscalculates and dies upon the broken edge of Héra's shield.

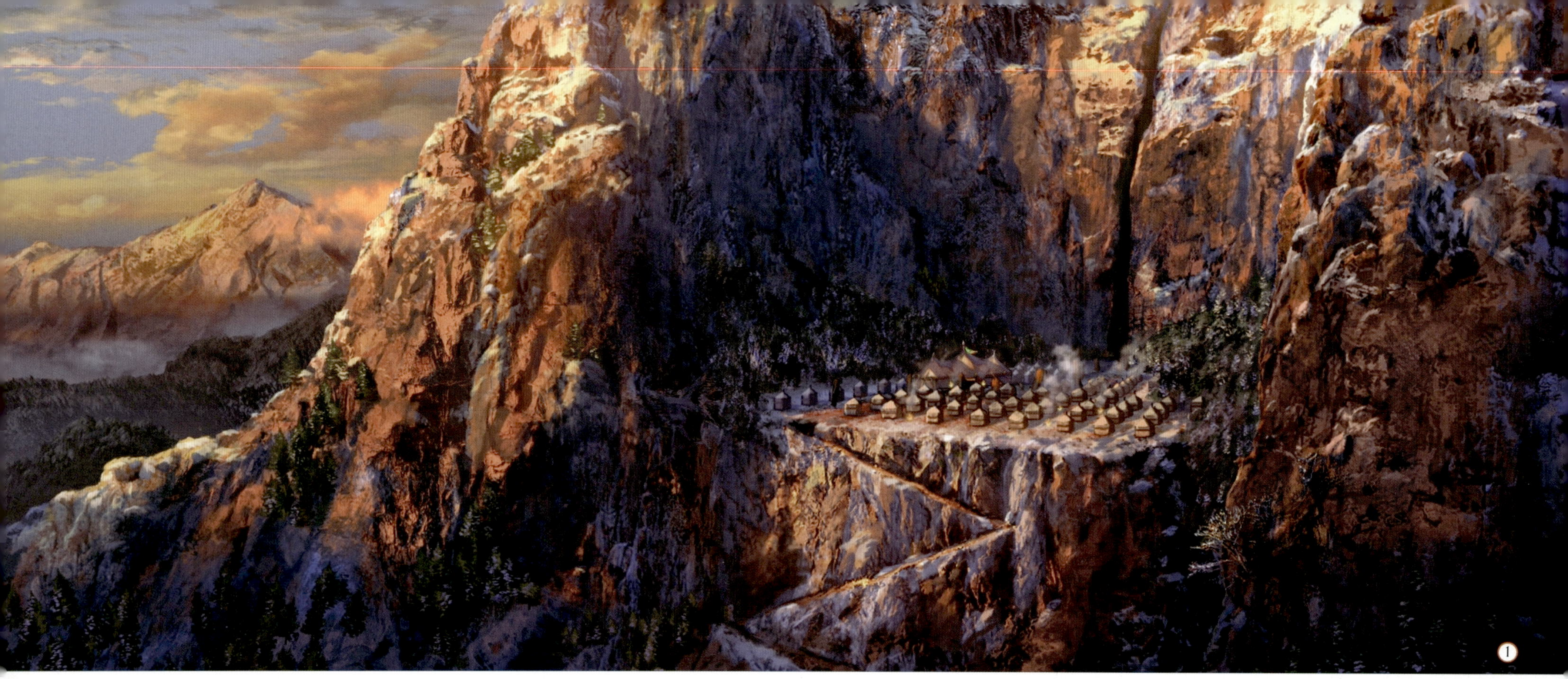

THE HOLD OF DUNHARROW

Tracing a path south from Edoras toward the headwaters of the River Snowbourn at the far end of the vale of Harrowdale, Fréaláf led his men to the ancient Hold of Dunharrow. Cut into the steep sides of the White Mountains by a long-forgotten people, the Firienfeld was a green terrace, reachable only by a steep, switchback way known as the Stair of the Hold. So situated, Dunharrow was near impossible to assail by force. Here Fréaláf and his Éored encamped, pitching tents and setting a watch to wait for word of Helm as the snow began to fall.

Dunharrow was an interesting one to pull off. We didn't want to imply that Fréaláf was just hanging out in Dunharrow while there was a siege going on at the Hornburg. We had to make it clear that he did not know the state of things and was waiting to learn the fate of his kin. Were they alive or buried in the ashes of Edoras? All of the messenger birds were shot down, but Héra knows there's one bird they can't shoot down. – PHOEBE GITTINS, WRITER

One of the most fun aspects of this project was what I liked to call the Middle-earth archaeology. In recreating environments previously visited in the original films, we had to scour multiple archives for reference, sometimes piecing things together from many sources. For Dunharrow, I found myself scrambling around the original filming locations, trying to document as many angles as I could without going over a cliff. Although seamlessly interwoven, what we saw in the films was not one place, but many, with wide-shot plate photography having been obtained near Queenstown and at least two different sites within Wellington providing locations for filming of the Firienfeld on which Théoden's command tent was pitched. One of my tasks was to help come up with a blueprint for the reconstruction of Dunharrow, folding the varied imagery of the movies into a consistent suite of reference. – DANIEL FALCONER, ADDITIONAL CONCEPTS DESIGNER

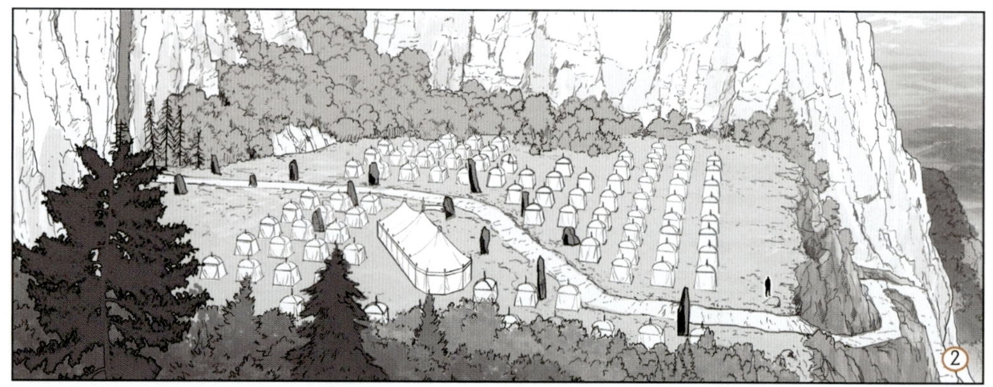

PP: Hornburg siege background art. 1: Dunharrow background setting art, TK. 2: Dunharrow concept art, KS. 3: Dunharrow concept art, DF. 4: Dunharrow background art. 5: Dunharrow soldier concepts, S. 6: Captain's tent concept, KS.

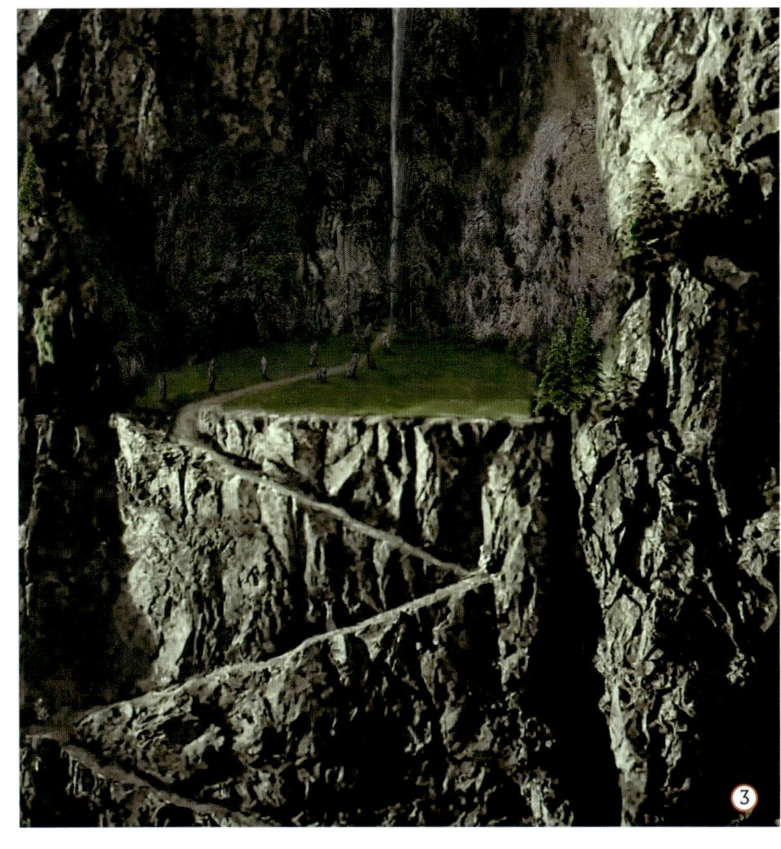

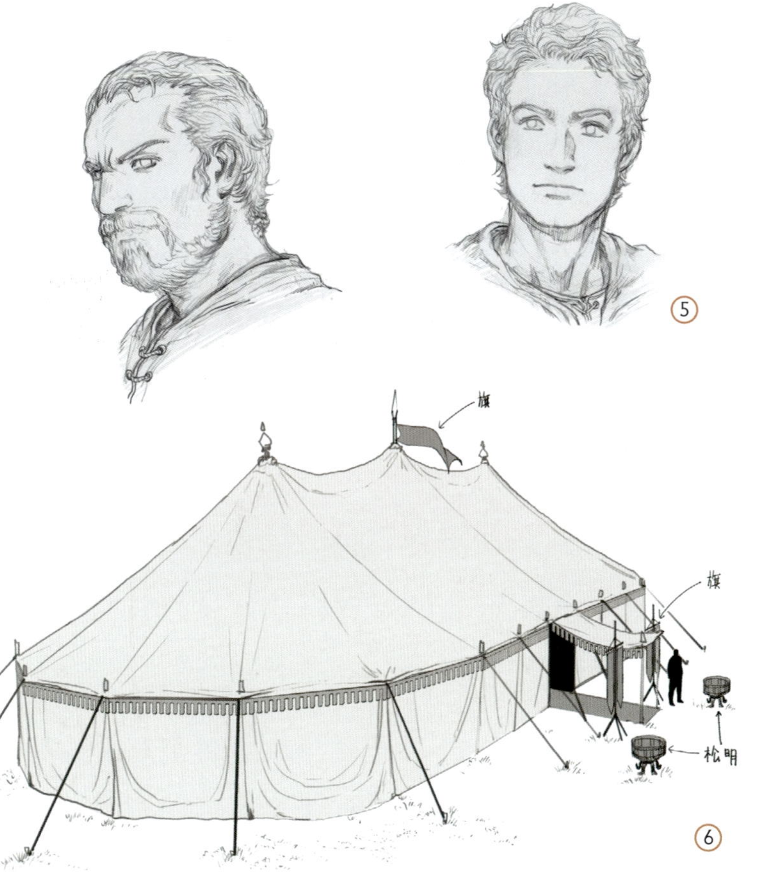

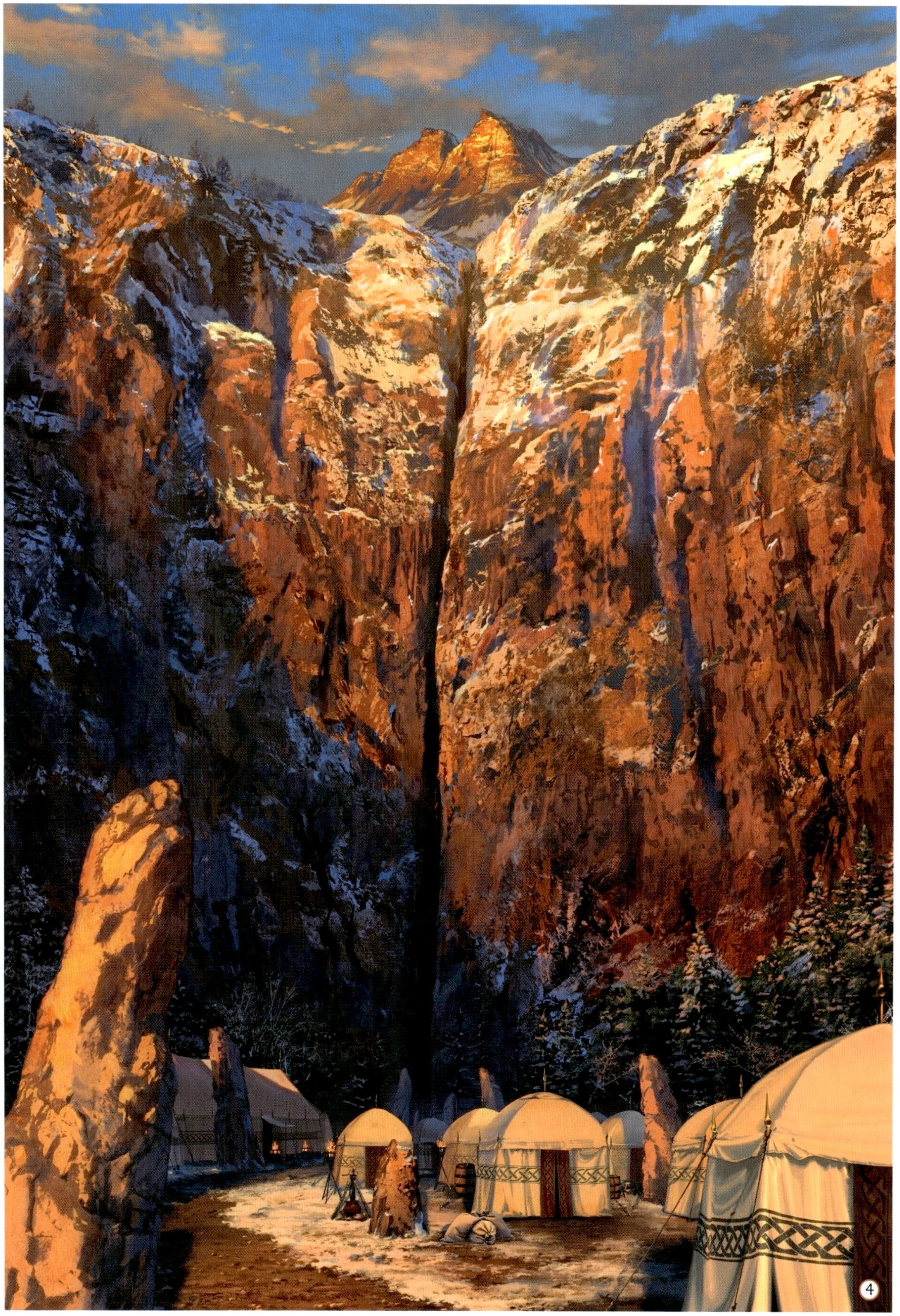

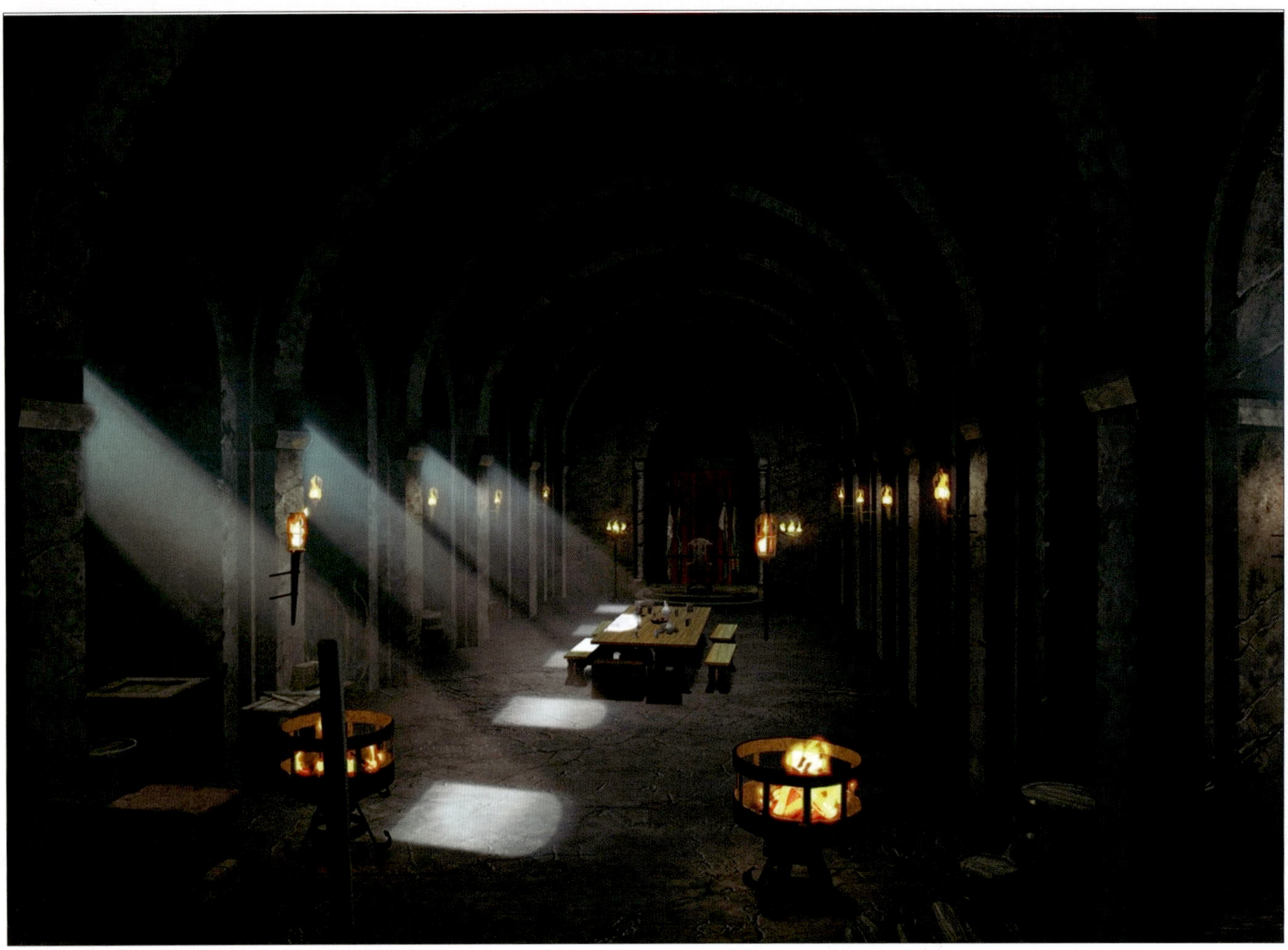

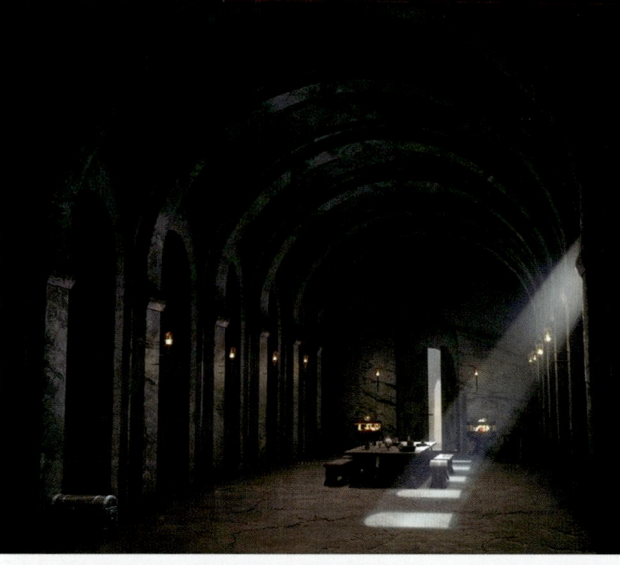

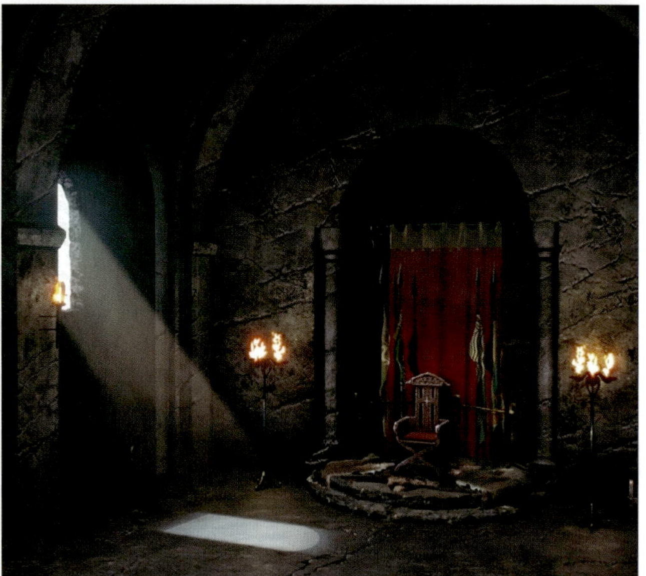

THE HORNBURG THRONE ROOM

The Hornburg presented some of the same challenges for us as Meduseld had. We were reconstructing spaces first seen in the live-action trilogy, but in both cases the interiors and exteriors were different sets, and sometimes multiple different sets. Peter Jackson told us that while he and his team knew the general geography of the Hornburg, they weren't too concerned with exactly where everything fit or connected, and when Kamiyama analyzed it, he realized there were things that didn't quite line up. The throne room, for example, didn't fit where it was located. Just like Meduseld, it was bigger on the inside than the exterior. Wherever we could we sought to replicate spaces as reverently as possible, but we also had to tweak some for our story, because it had its own needs. We spend a longer period inside the Hornburg and see more of it than we did in the trilogy. Our characters spend months there. – JASON DEMARCO, PRODUCER

In the remaining lords, Héra not only comes up against anxious and prickly personalities but also frail egos who aren't that receptive to the idea of being subservient to a young lady. – ARTY PAPAGEORGIOU, WRITER

'DESPAIR IS WULF'S GREATEST WEAPON AGAINST US.'

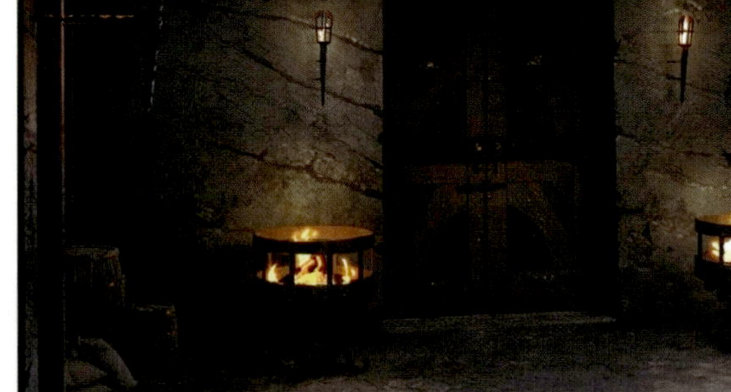

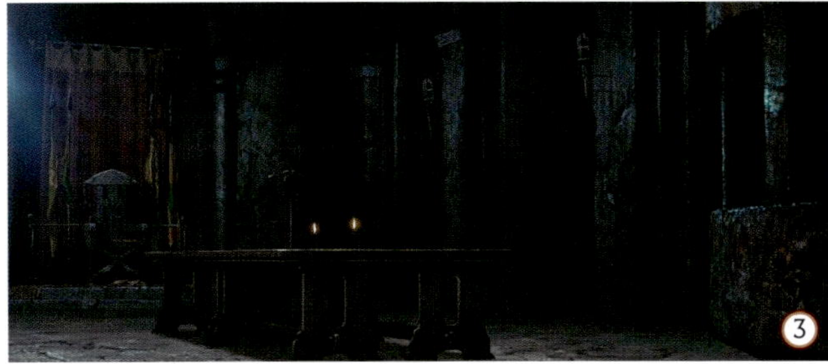

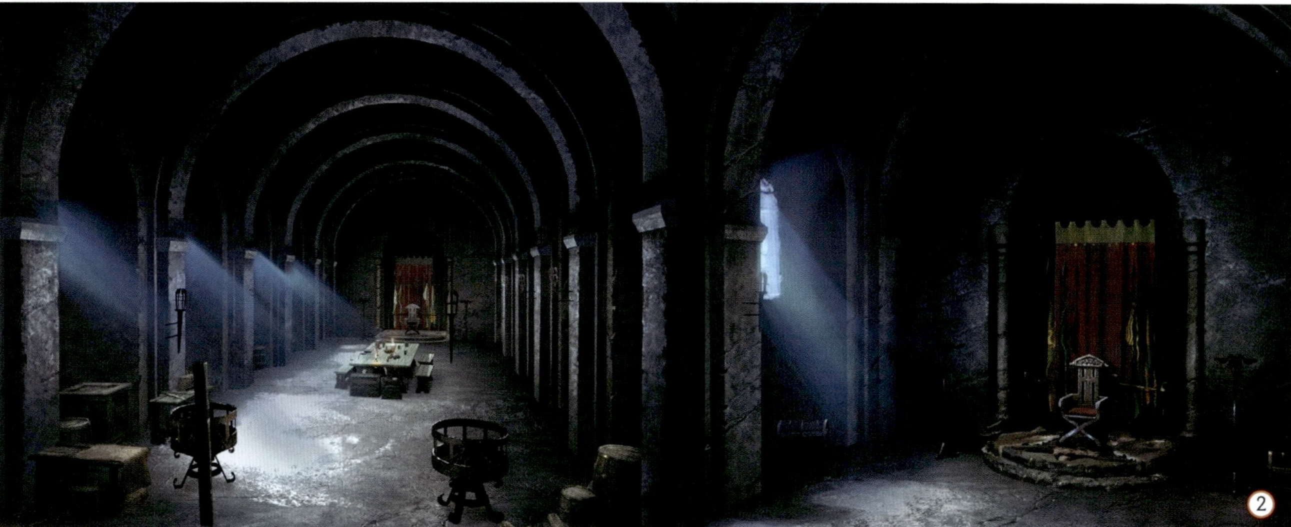

Once Helm dies, power shifts to Héra's shoulders and the clock starts ticking. Wulf knows that without Helm all he has to do is get inside that fortress and he has won. Héra knows that her people have no reason to believe that she can save them. She may be their leader by birthright, but she is not the king and only has a certain amount of time to enact a plan to save them before her people might not even remain to listen to her. Already they have doubts. She must rally them and give them a reason to trust her like Helm did, and she must act fast. – JASON DEMARCO, PRODUCER

Héra gives the equivalent of a rallying speech to the lords when she overhears their desperate quarrelling. 'We find a way, and we do it together!'

Typically, you'd expect everyone to be roused to action, but we felt it was important to hold onto the harsh reality that they are facing. 'Pretty words, but pretty words cannot save us.'

Héra is not ready yet to lead them, but they also underestimate her. Héra finds the self-belief she needs in the moment with Olwyn when she confesses that she doesn't know what to do. 'I cannot save them.'

Olwyn says, 'No, but you can choose.' Olwyn is one of my favourite characters because she is so pragmatic. She's not going to make false promises. She has seen how this goes. As a shieldmaiden, Olwyn is passing on her own experience to Héra. 'All that you can do is make your choices; you get to choose how this ends.' That's the courage that Olwyn gives her. – PHOEBE GITTINS, WRITER

Going beyond the few pages that exist in the appendices we found references and details in other parts of Tolkien's stories that inspired and informed us. Éowyn also gave us an example and tradition of who these royal women of Rohan were.

We looked at Alfred the Great's daughter, Æthelflæd. She is called the Lady of the Mercians, which is great

because Tolkien was very familiar with and almost certainly drew some inspiration from Mercia. We liked Æthelflæd's story because she was never going to be queen, and yet she led her people against the Vikings. Her father died, her husband died, and her brother was not yet schooled enough to lead, so she literally led her people, the Mercians. She was clever in her defences; building towers that stand today, and she was strategic. She wasn't a warrior in the same way as someone like Boudica, but she stepped up when they needed her and held her people together with natural authority.

Æthelflæd did all that, and yet she never tried to take the throne. Where does leadership come from? What and who is a natural leader? We wanted Héra to be that sort of hero so those Anglo-Saxon women were definitely influences.

Given where he grew up, I can't imagine that Tolkien didn't know the story of Æthelflæd, but he also said that the Rohirrim weren't the Anglo-Saxons; they were their own people, so there are echoes of them in the Rohirrim and in Héra, but they're not solely Anglo-Saxons, and nor was that the only place we went to for our reference. – PHILIPPA BOYENS, PRODUCER

'HE WILL NOT STOP UNTIL THE KEEP BECOMES OUR TOMB.'

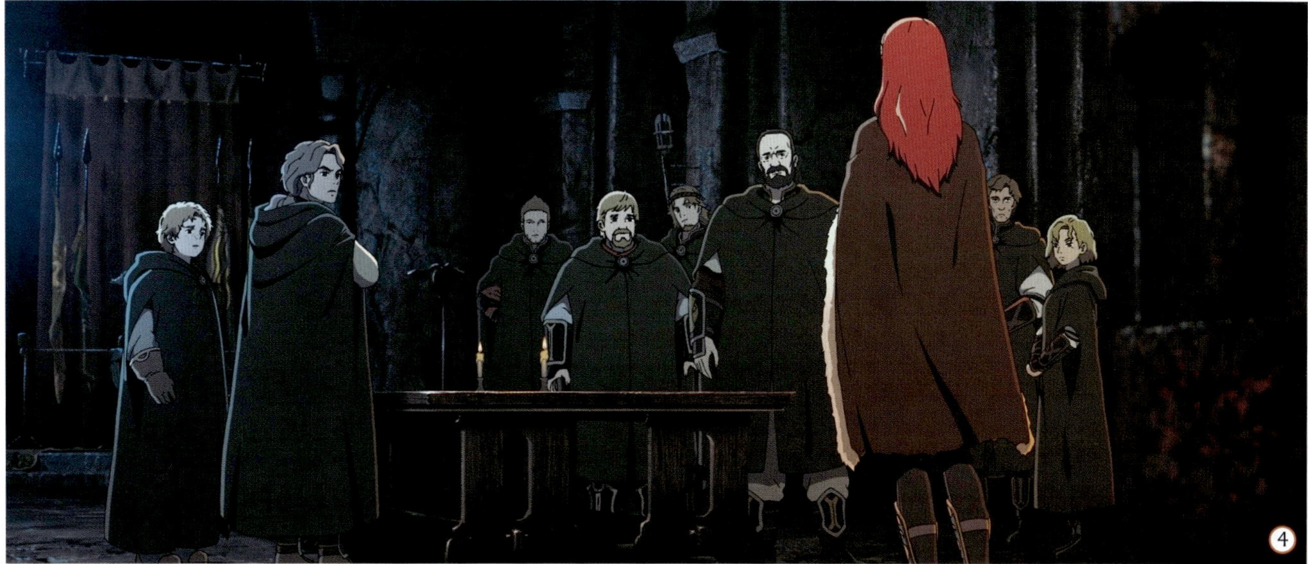

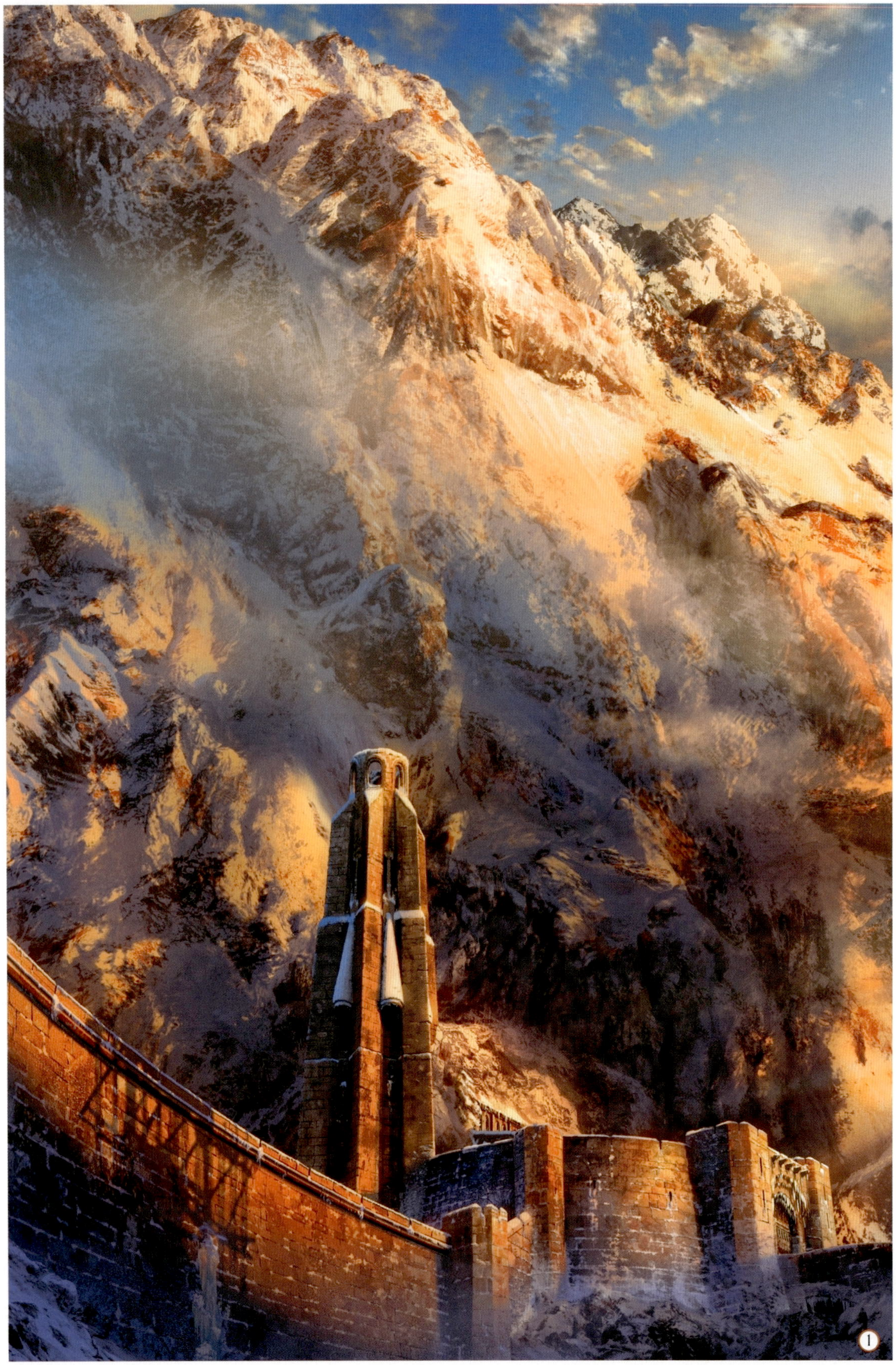

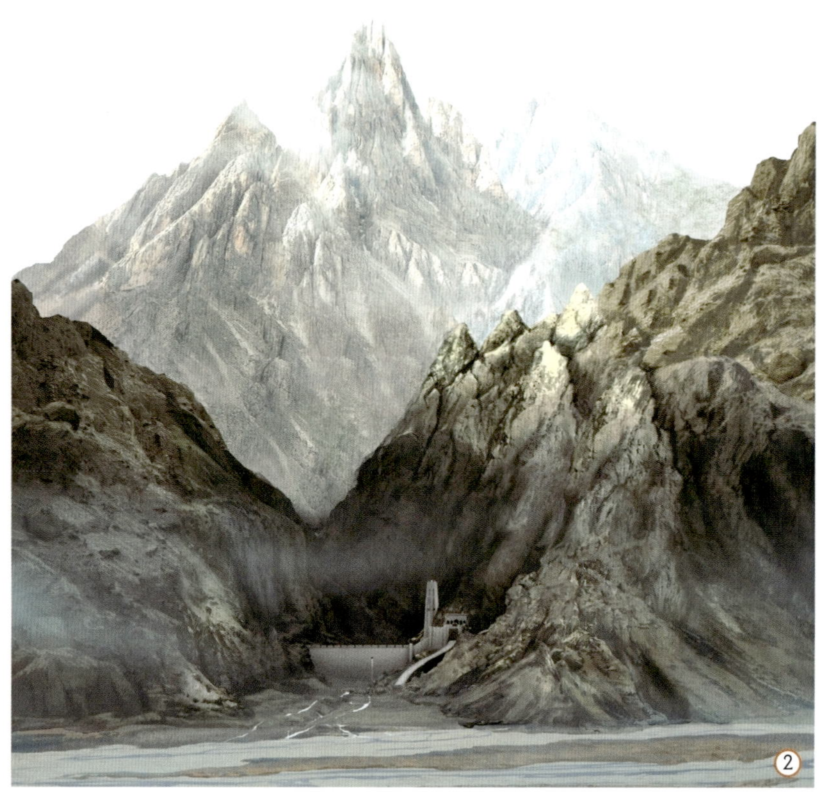

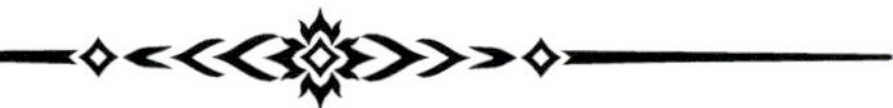

THRIHYRNE NARROWS

The Hornburg was built at the base of the Thrihyrne, a cluster of three jagged, icy peaks that loomed over the narrow terminus of the Deeping-coomb. Looking skyward for hope, Héra chooses to stake her life on a desperate climb, ascending the narrow ways behind the fortress in search on the Great Eagles.

The look of the Thrihyrne imagery that we created was not based on a single place but drew inspiration and reference from many different mountains. — KEIICHIRO SHIMIZU, BACKGROUND ARTIST

'THIS IS YOUR PLAN?' 'I NEVER SAID IT WAS A GOOD ONE.'

1: Hornburg background art. 2: Thrihyrne concept, YY. 3: Animation key frame, MT.

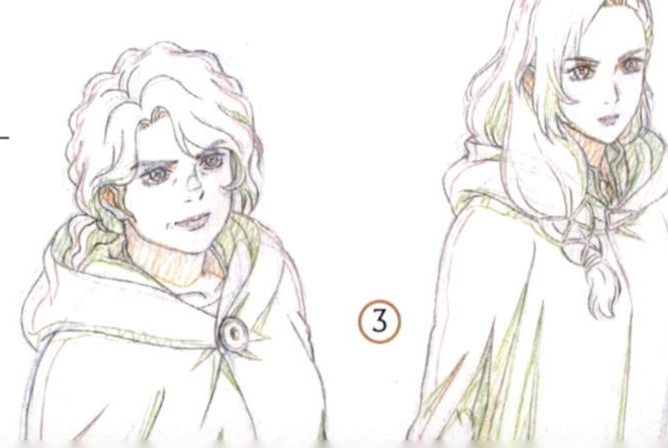

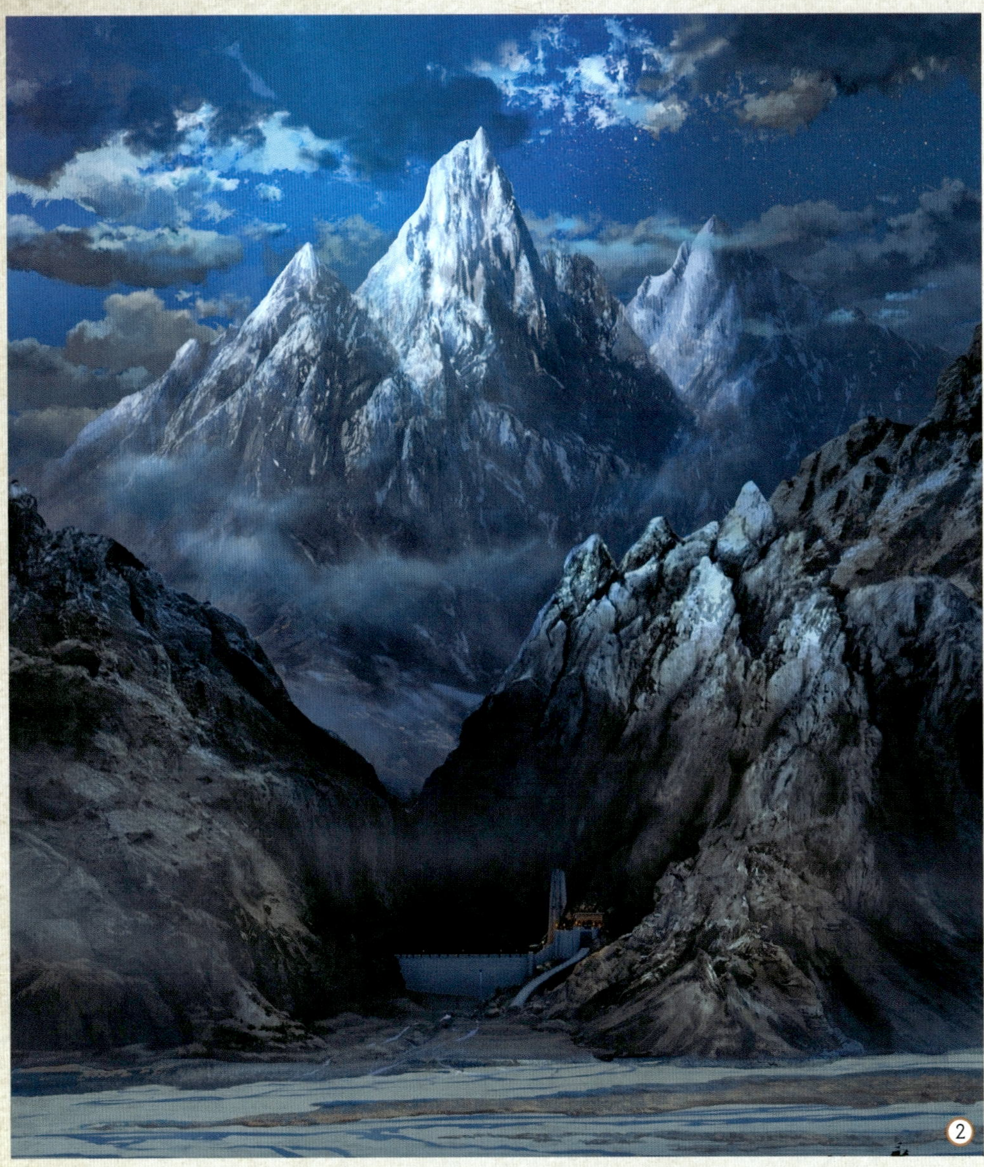

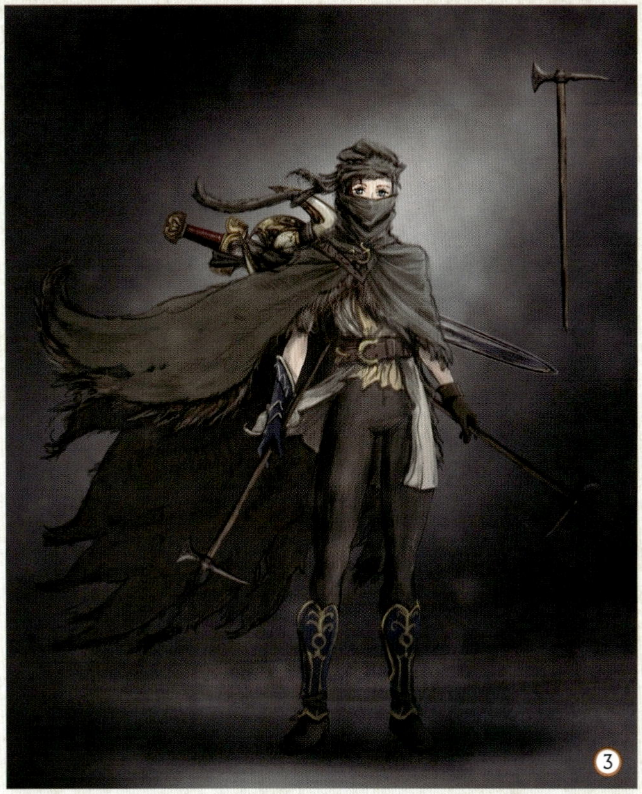

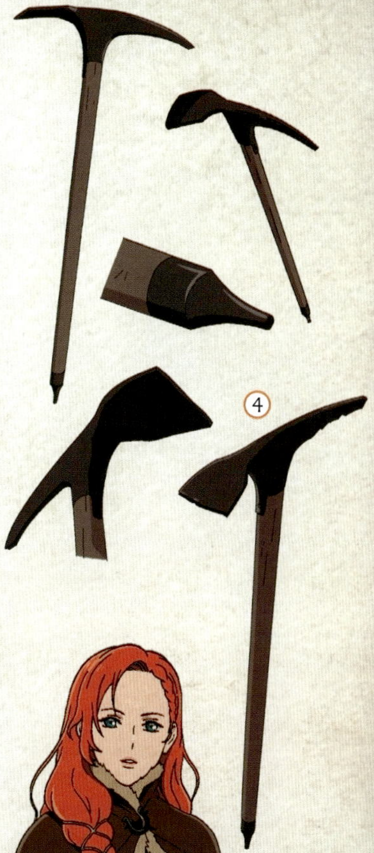

1: Héra character setting art, MT. 2: Thrihyrne concept, YY. 3: Héra concept, DF. 4: Ice axe prop setting art, KM.

HÉRA'S ASCENT

Héra knows that there are Eagles living up in the mountains. She has lived her whole life exploring Rohan, and always been fascinated by them. Being built into the base of the mountains, we imagined that the Hornburg would have had some climbing equipment that she could use. It's her epic task to complete and she is not afraid to risk her own life if it means finding a way to save everyone. – JASON DEMARCO, PRODUCER

It seemed very fitting for Héra to climb into the mountains in search of the Eagles. We had established her relationship with them. It would be within her skillset. She finds a solution that others wouldn't think of. – PHOEBE GITTINS, WRITER

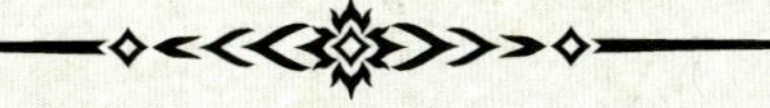

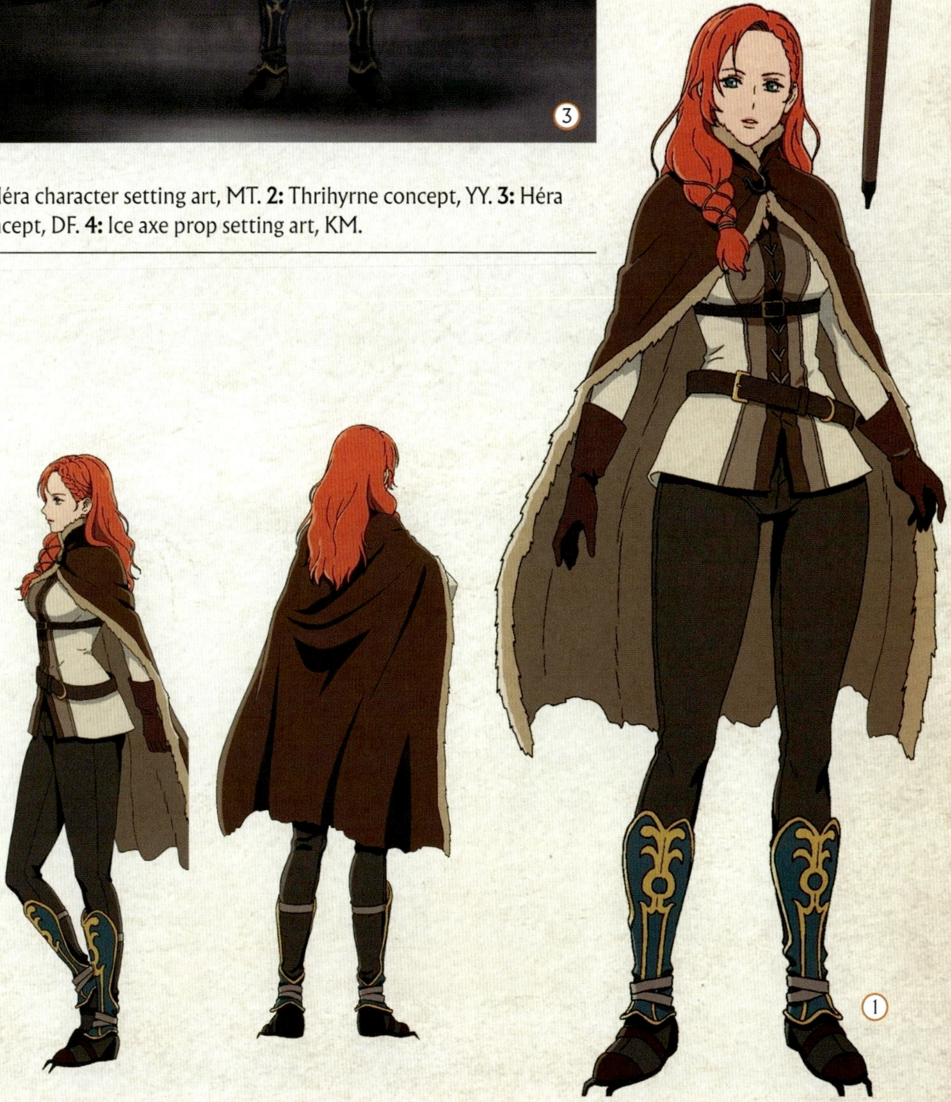

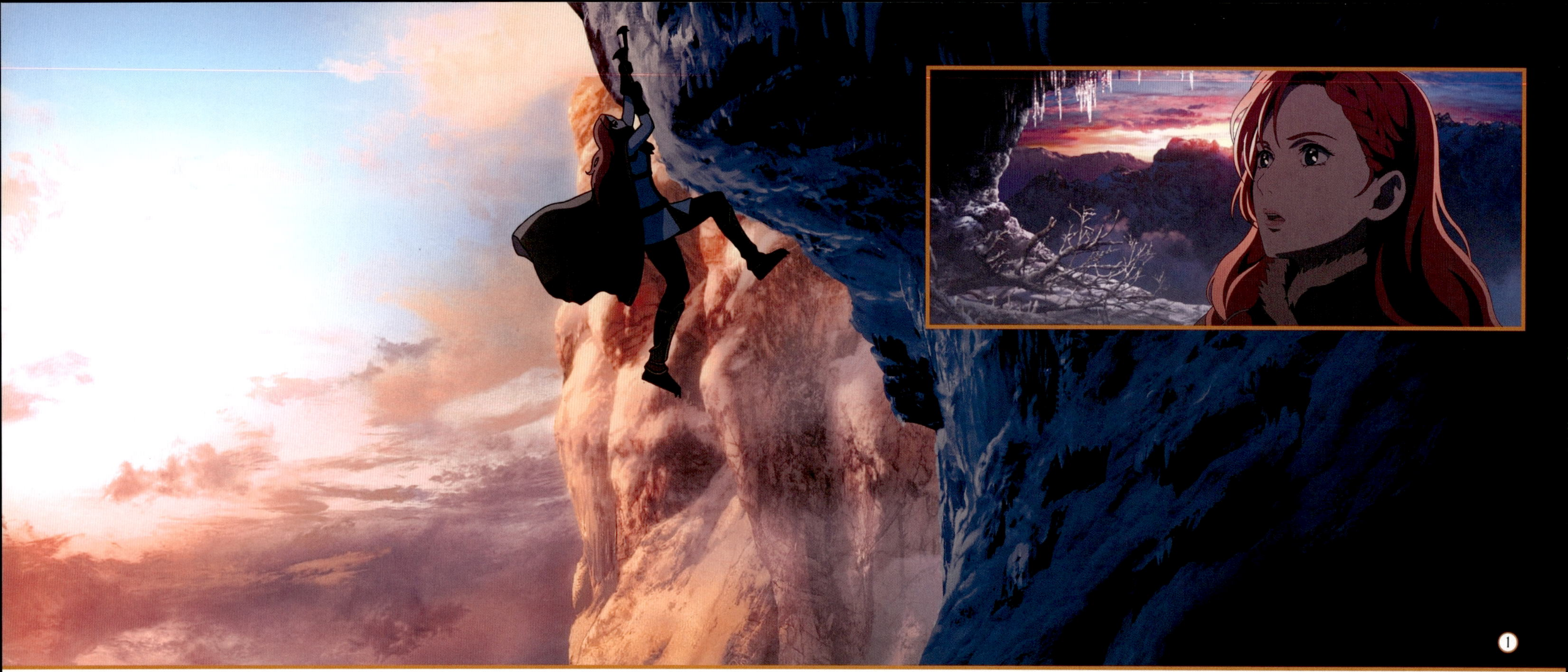

It was important that Héra rise to the challenge in this moment, but we didn't want her to run out and fight off Wulf's whole army – she isn't Glorfindel, a legendary Elven warrior of old – her heroism is of a different sort. She stakes her life on the slimmest of hopes. She puts herself at the mercy of the Eagle in an act of humility and deference and pleads for its help. – JASON DEMARCO, PRODUCER

This is something that Helm would just never do. It wouldn't occur to him. He couldn't bring himself to light the beacons and call for help when he needed to, and he wouldn't do this. But in his final realization and actions, we see that whatever shortfalls his leadership style may have he cares about his people more than anything, and he is perceptive enough to know that it's Héra and only Héra who will be able to get their people out of the trap he has ensnarled them in. – ARTY PAPAGEORGIOU, WRITER

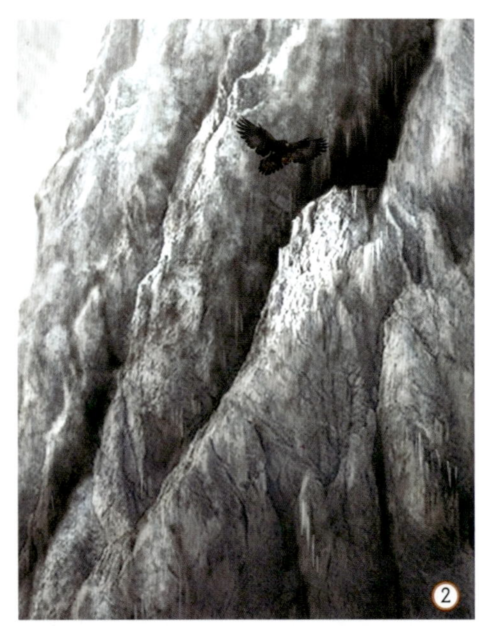

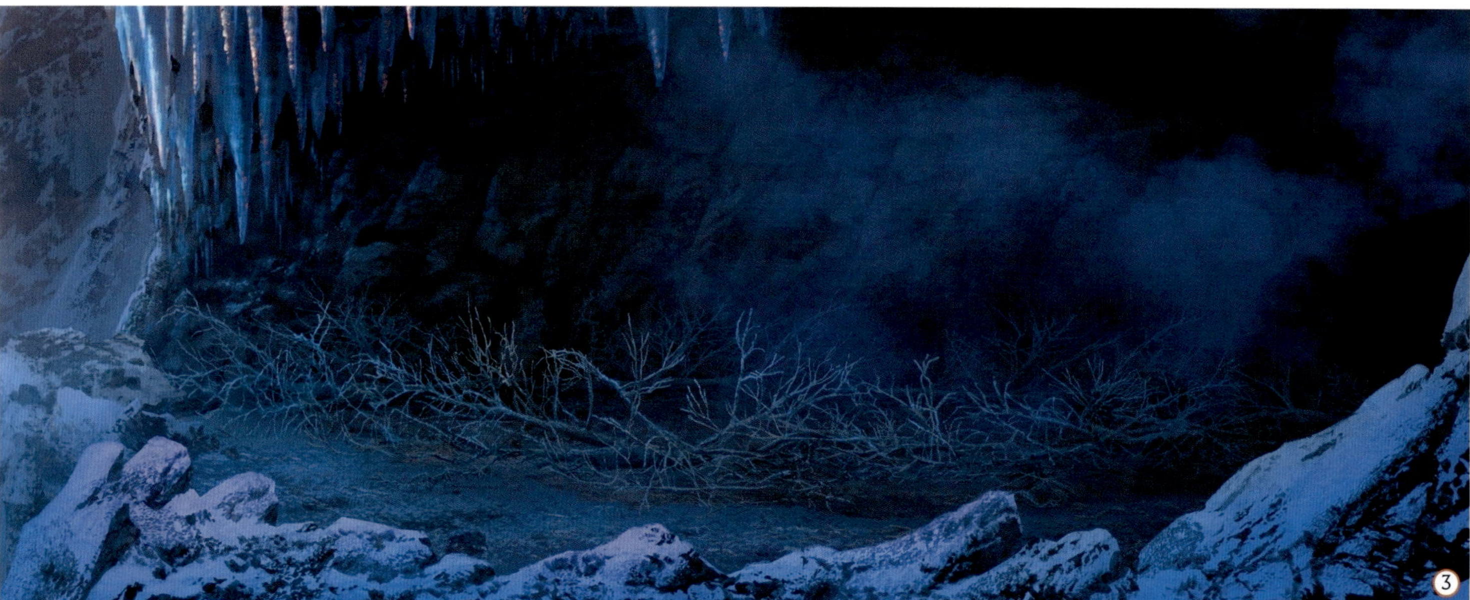

The nest was based on real eagles' nests, but massively scaled up.
I imagined what the nest might look like if it was made by a truly giant
bird. – KEIICHIRO SHIMIZU, BACKGROUND ARTIST

The director asked me to define the differences between the juvenile
Fledgling that we saw at the beginning of the film, and how it appeared
when full-grown later. It was important that the viewer be able to see the
change between its original appearance with a young face, plumage, and
patterning of small birds to look of a mature Great Eagle. – AISHA ARI
HAGIWARA, ANIMATION CREATURE DESIGNER

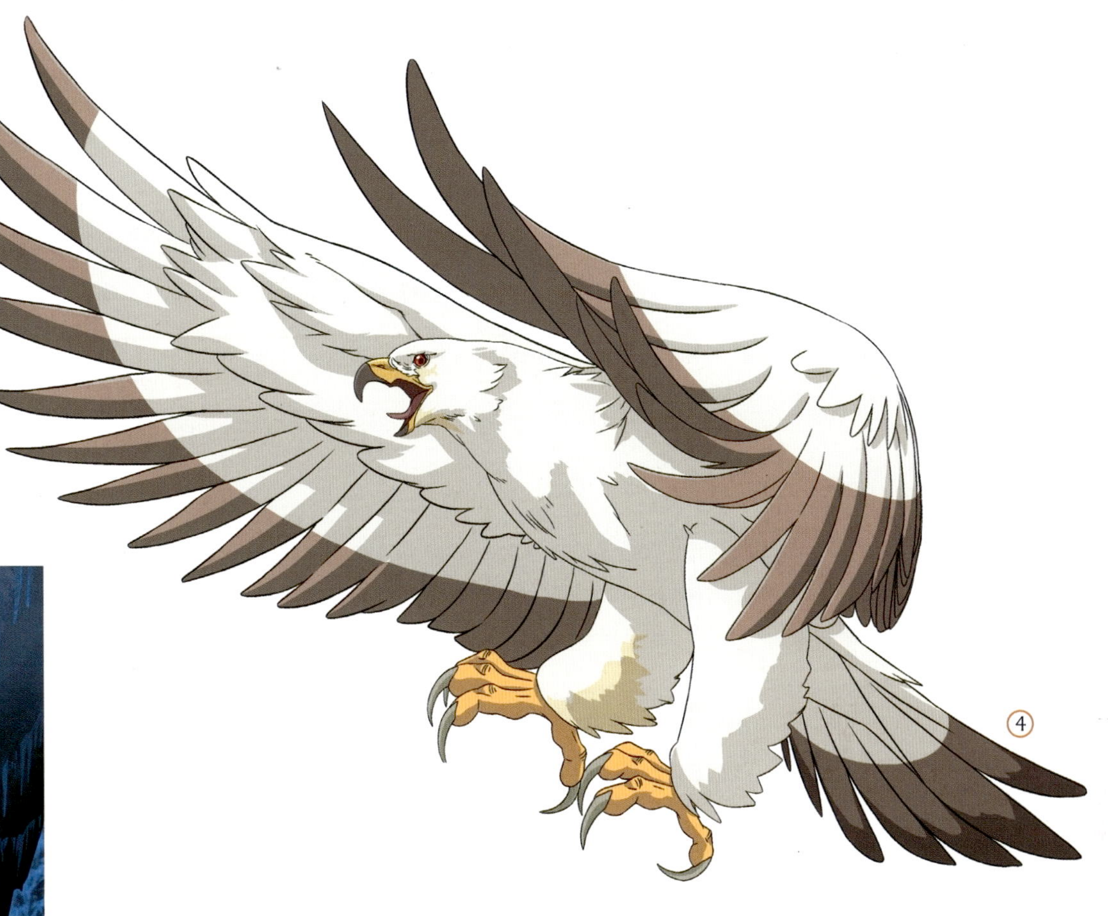

'MY PEOPLE NEED YOUR HELP . . .'

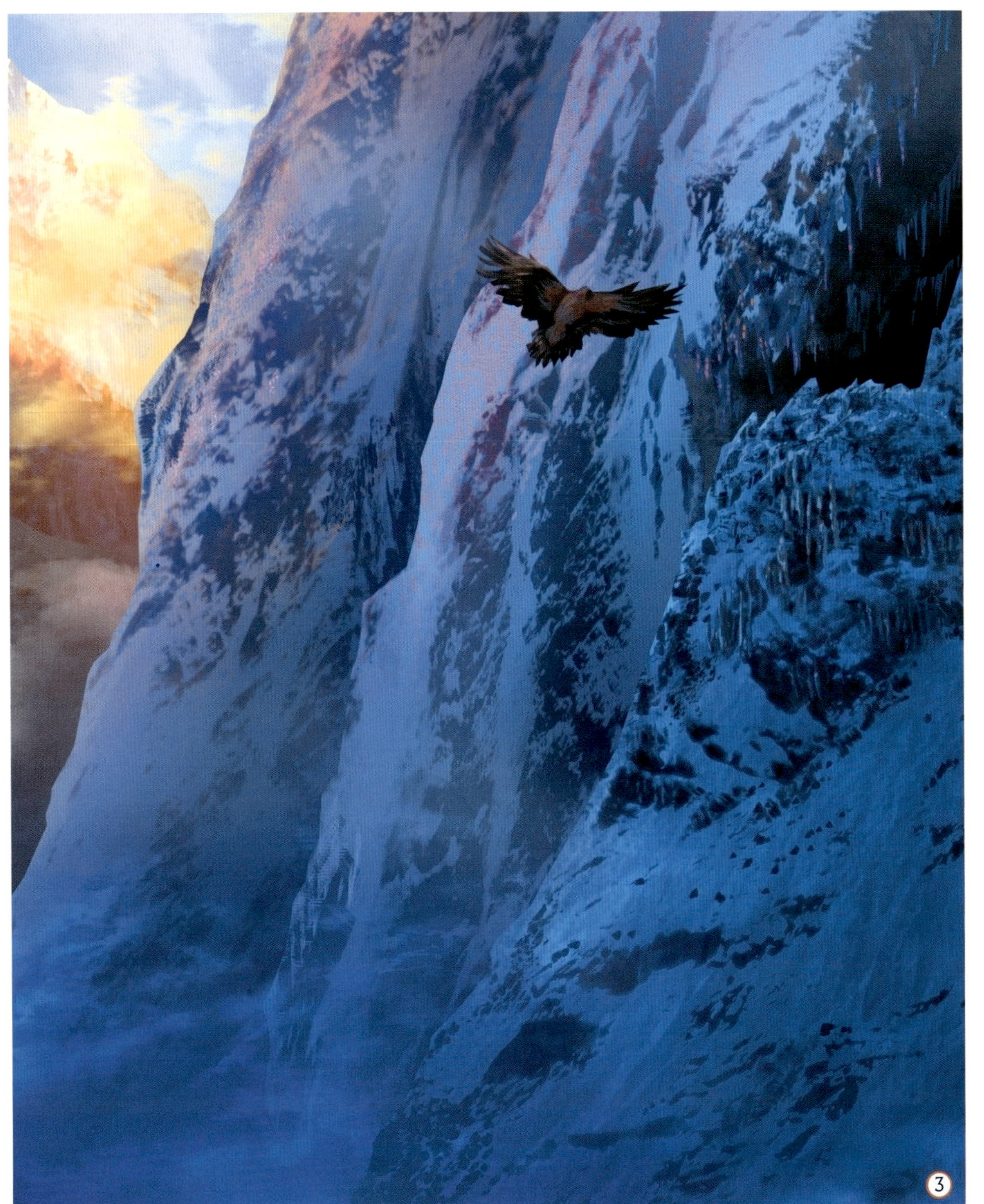

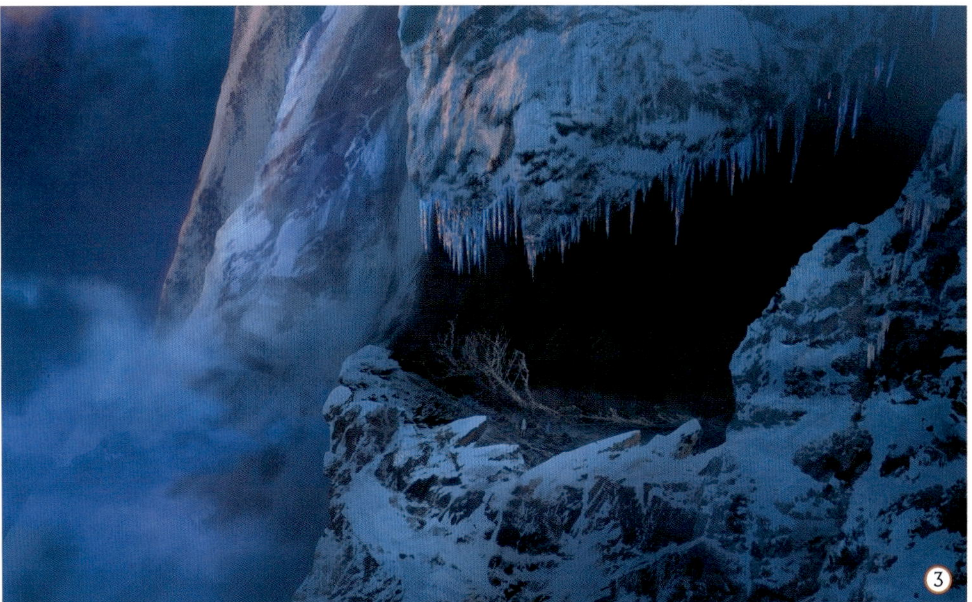

1: Final film frames. 2: Eyrie concept, DF. 3: Eyrie background setting art, KS. 4: Fledgling Great Eagle,
grown, character setting art, AAH.

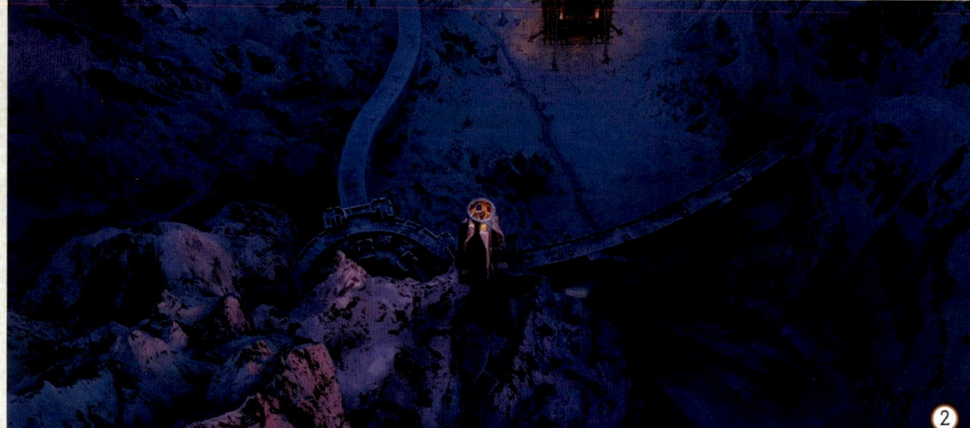

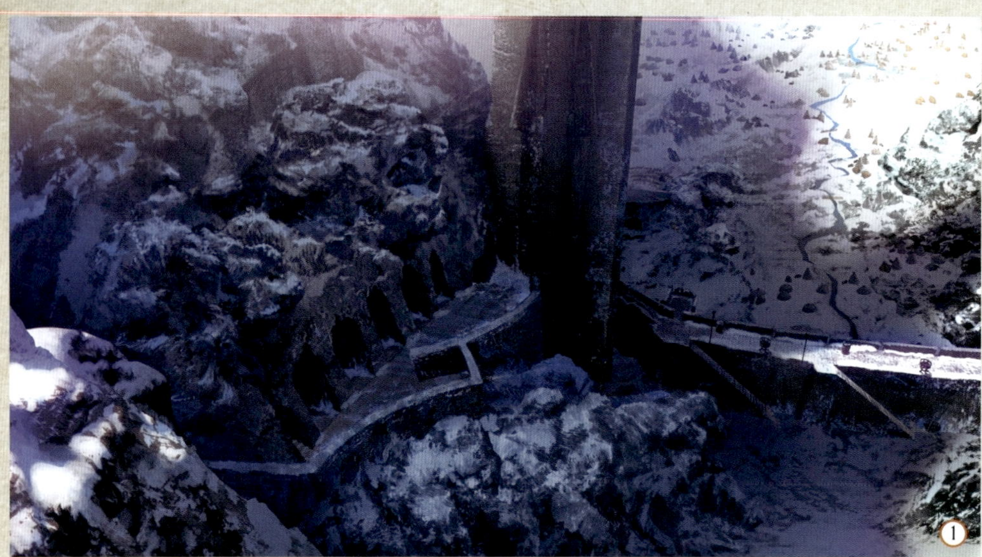

THE TOWER

—◦≪≪◆≫≫◦—

The tallest structure in the Hornburg is the tower housing the Great Horn of the Deep, first established in The Two Towers. *The horn is built into the tower itself. On the chance that her quest to seek aid from the Eagles will succeed, Héra tasks Lief with carrying Helm's armour to the top. When the Eagle swoops a block is dislodged from the apex, damage that will remain unrepaired two hundred years later, when Théoden seeks refuge in the Deep.*

I love Lief. In a film as dark as ours Kamiyama san was adamant that we needed a lighter character with a sense of innocence about him. Lief is comedic, but not in the same way as Gimli. He is a very relatable, human character who isn't a great warrior, but he is brave and hopeful. It was great that he had his opportunity to rise when called upon late in the film. – JASON DEMARCO, PRODUCER

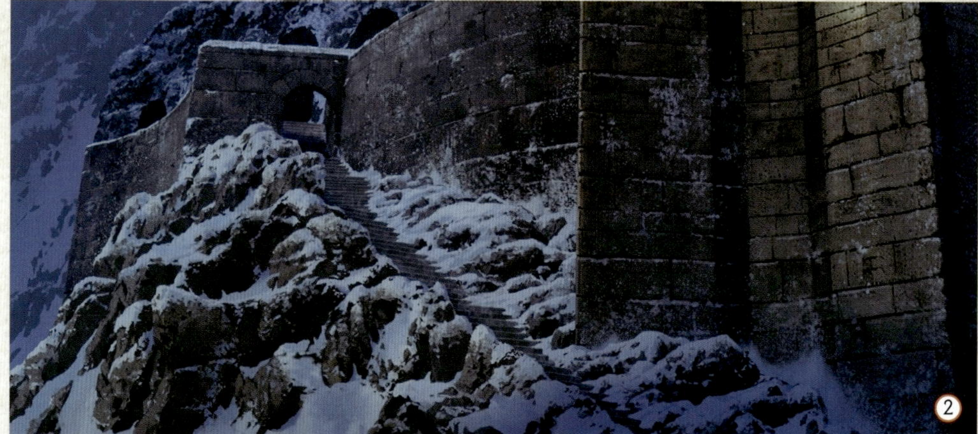

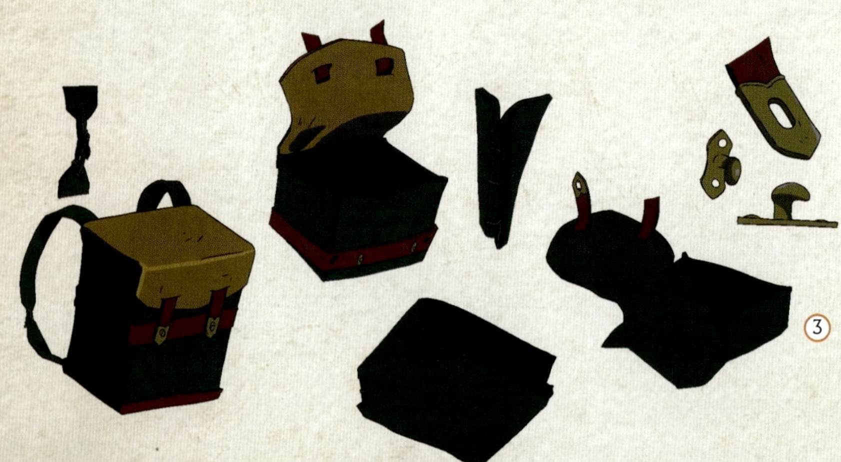

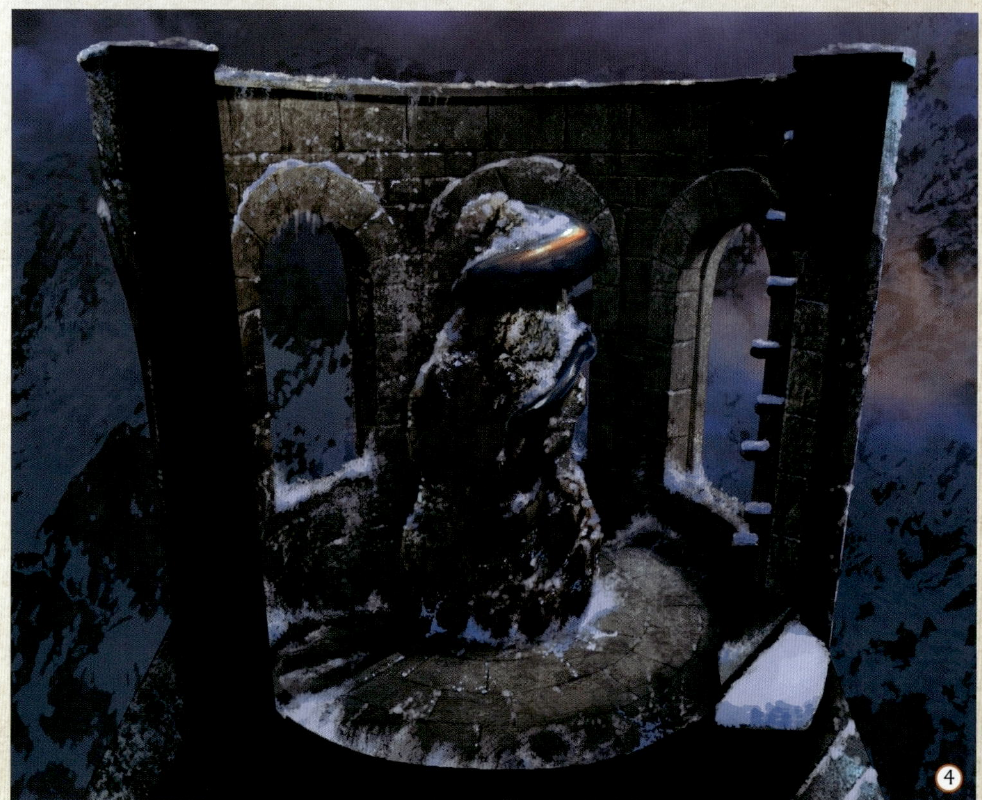

1: Hornburg background setting art, YY. **2:** Hornburg background art. **3:** Lief's pack prop setting art, KM. **4:** Hornburg tower background setting art, YY.

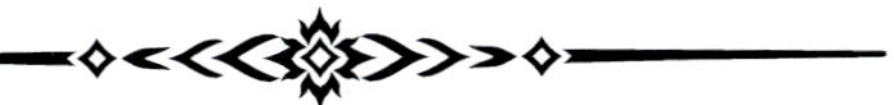

SIEGE WEAPONRY

How Wulf's forces might gain the wall was unresolved during much of the conceptual process. An array of different siege weaponry and even beasts of burden were mooted and discussed before the notion of a static tower agreed.

For years I have been seeking an excuse to depict the Kine of Araw, the near-mythical aurochs that once lived near the Sea of Rhûn. (Boromir's horn is said to have come from one of these creatures.) Perhaps their descendants haul the Dunlending siege engines?

I've always seen the *mûmakil* as distant kin of prehistoric pachyderms, much closer to them than to modern elephants.

The siege weapons themselves, principally trebuchets and ballistae, might have been highly mobile, drawn by boars or oxen, or harnessed on the wide backs of the *mûmakil*. As the siege takes place in winter, the drawn machines could be on sleds.

The ballista had one runner in front, and two at the rear, armed with giant bolts wrapped in pitch-soaked canvas, with hinged hooks that could potentially sink into masonry far enough to keep them in place as they burned. Like the Hornburg, the Deeping Wall was entirely stone, but they might have been shot at the doors, or at the wall of the keep, to lodge there and burn and blind the defenders. Admittedly, this idea is really to validate an excuse to have flaming missiles flashing across the battlefield. – JOHN HOWE, CONCEPTUAL DESIGNER

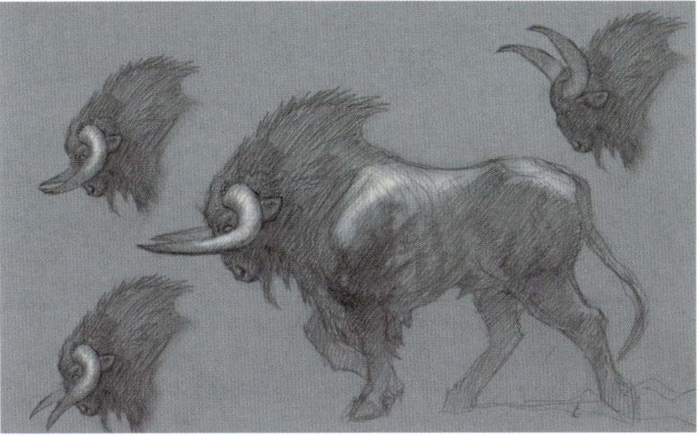

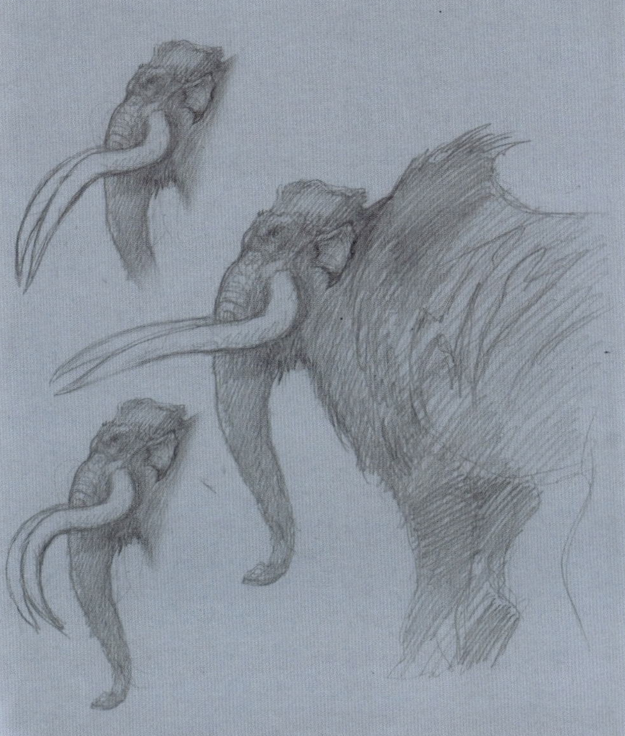

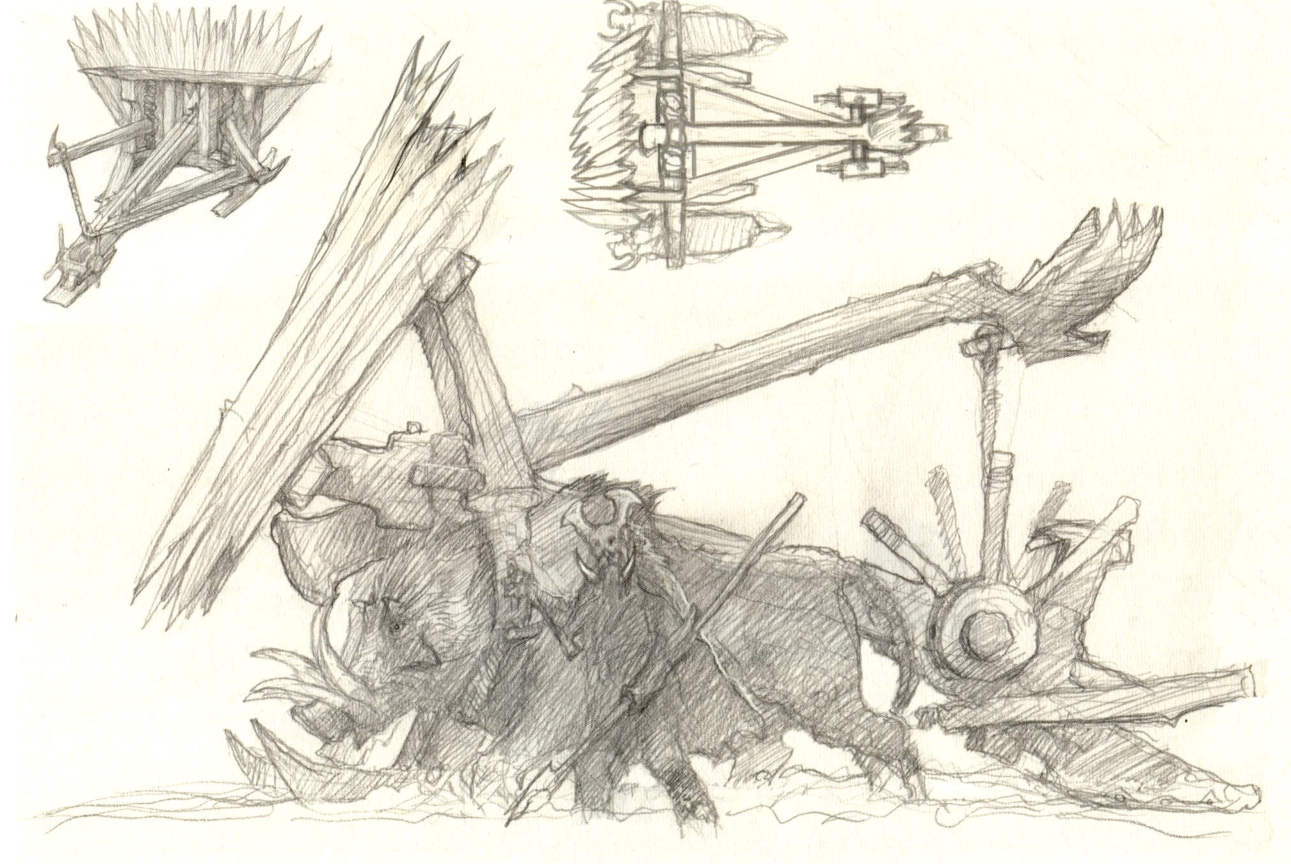

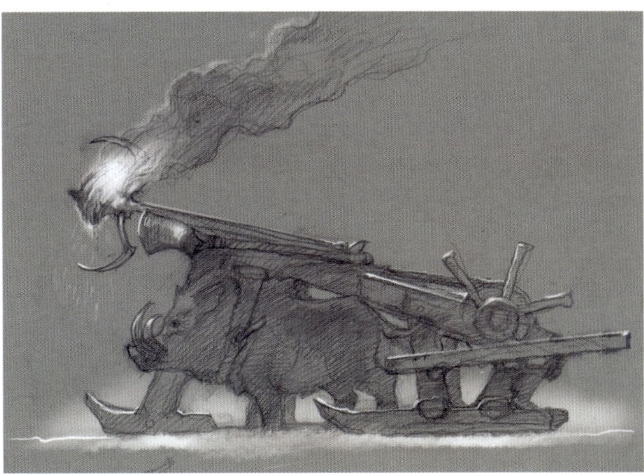

Siege equipment and beast concepts, JH.

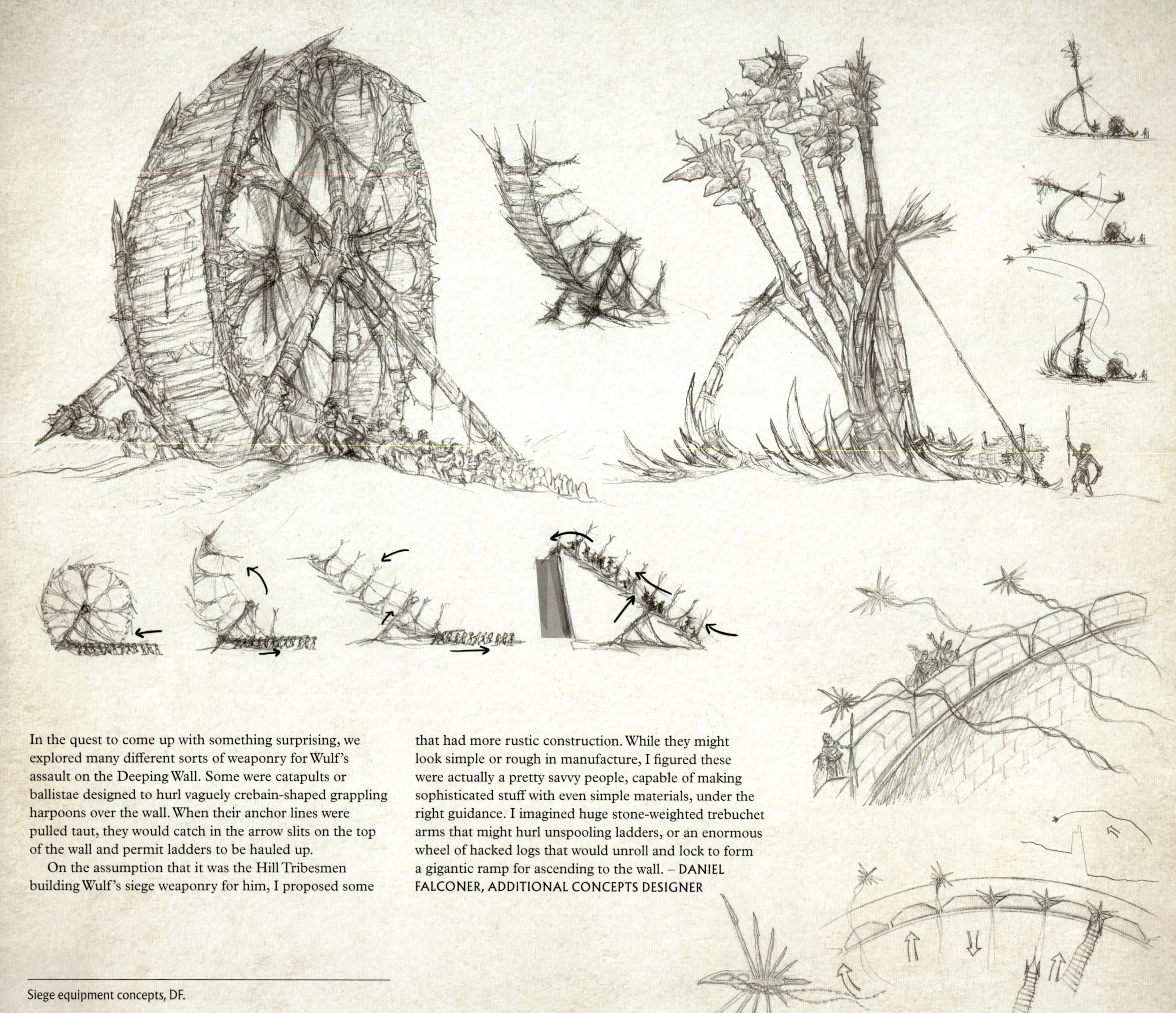

In the quest to come up with something surprising, we explored many different sorts of weaponry for Wulf's assault on the Deeping Wall. Some were catapults or ballistae designed to hurl vaguely crebain-shaped grappling harpoons over the wall. When their anchor lines were pulled taut, they would catch in the arrow slits on the top of the wall and permit ladders to be hauled up.

On the assumption that it was the Hill Tribesmen building Wulf's siege weaponry for him, I proposed some that had more rustic construction. While they might look simple or rough in manufacture, I figured these were actually a pretty savvy people, capable of making sophisticated stuff with even simple materials, under the right guidance. I imagined huge stone-weighted trebuchet arms that might hurl unspooling ladders, or an enormous wheel of hacked logs that would unroll and lock to form a gigantic ramp for ascending to the wall. – DANIEL FALCONER, ADDITIONAL CONCEPTS DESIGNER

Siege equipment concepts, DF.

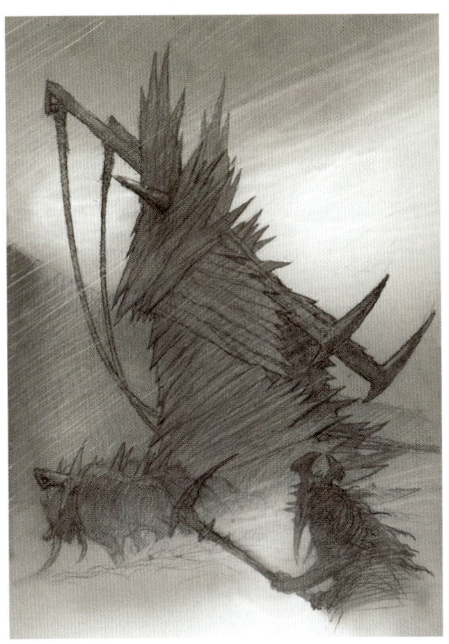

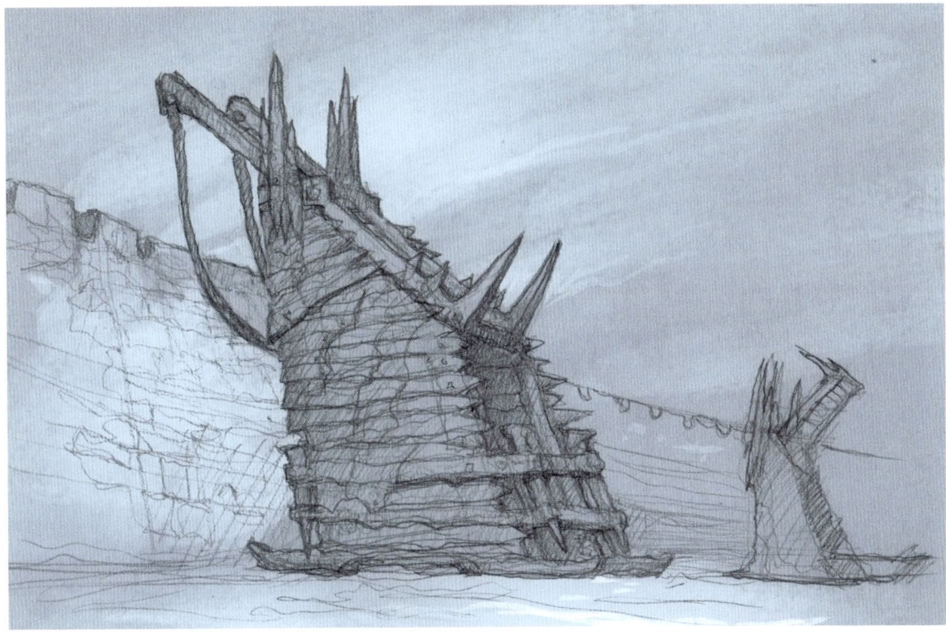

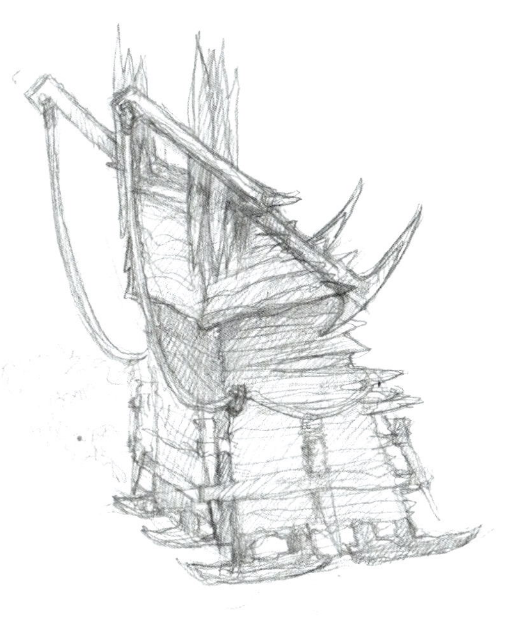

Siege equipment and tower concepts, JH.

SIEGE TOWER

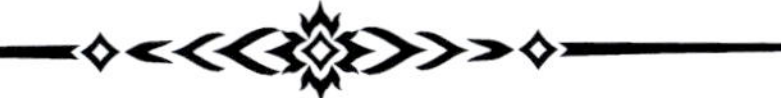

After attempting to imagine a siege tower that could be towed in pieces and quickly assembled, the idea was abandoned in favour of a lighter tower on skids or skis, with a drawbridge-like platform ending in two giant hooks, to hold fast to the parapet of the Deeping Wall. The kine were harnessed to a transversal beam, to allow the tower to closely approach the wall.

Once close enough, the release of a counterweight would cause the spiked beams at the top to swing over and crash down atop the wall, and the warriors in the tower could swarm over the ramparts.

The other odd contraption I imagined was a sort of scaling ladder with double hooks that would be fired over the wall to snag on the stone and allow the invaders to scale the wall. – JOHN HOWE, CONCEPTUAL DESIGNER

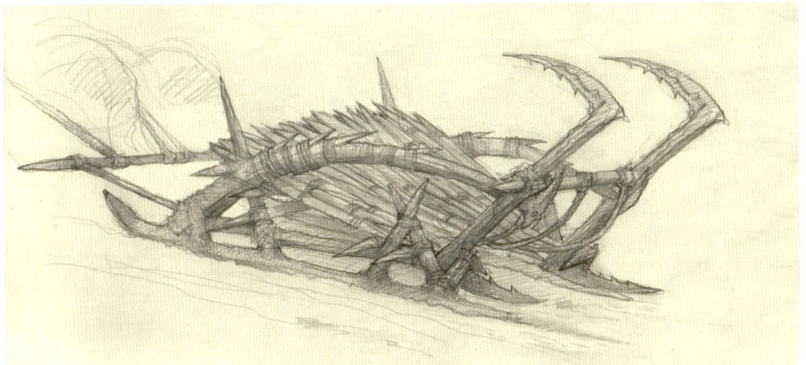

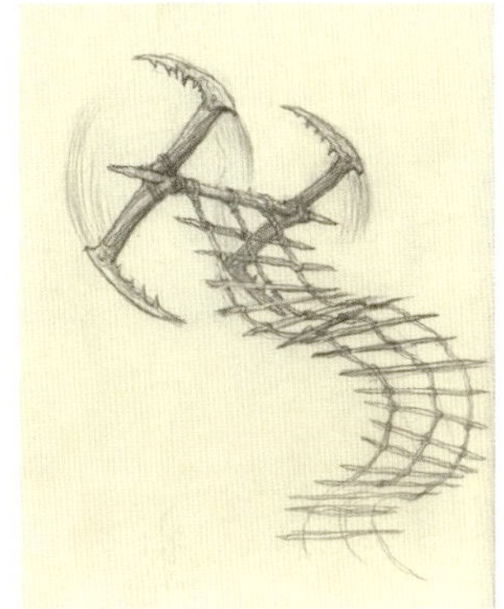

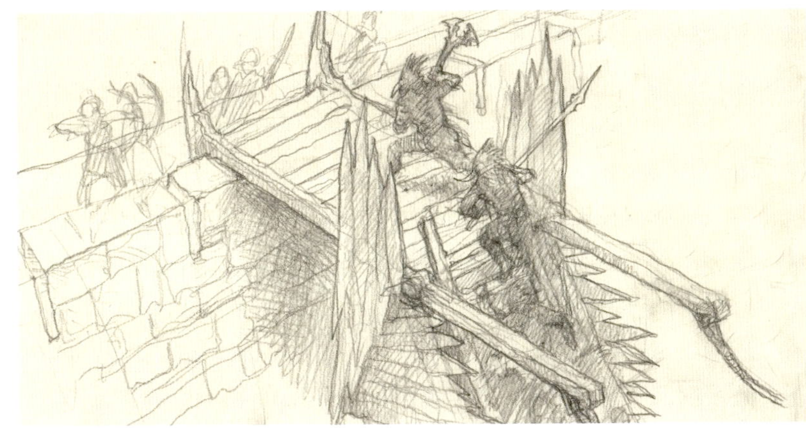

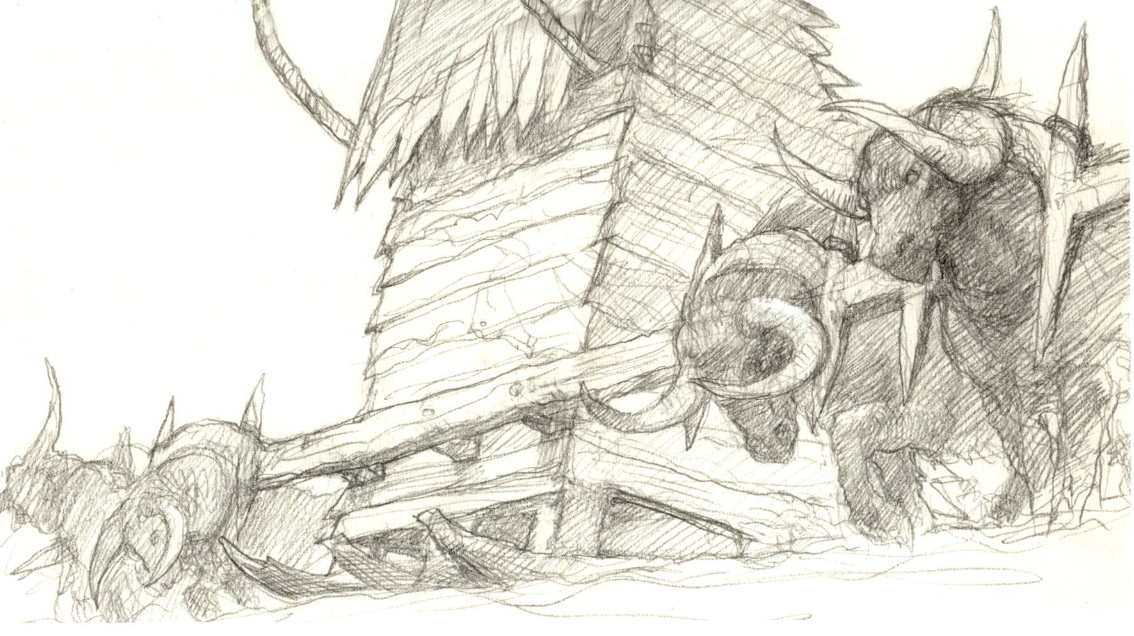

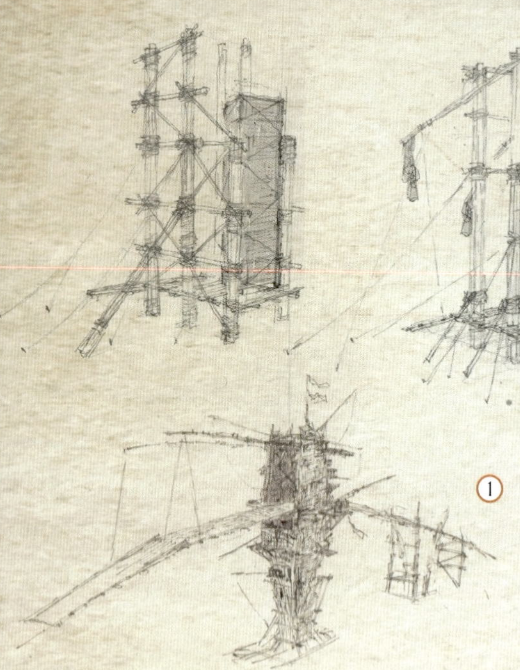

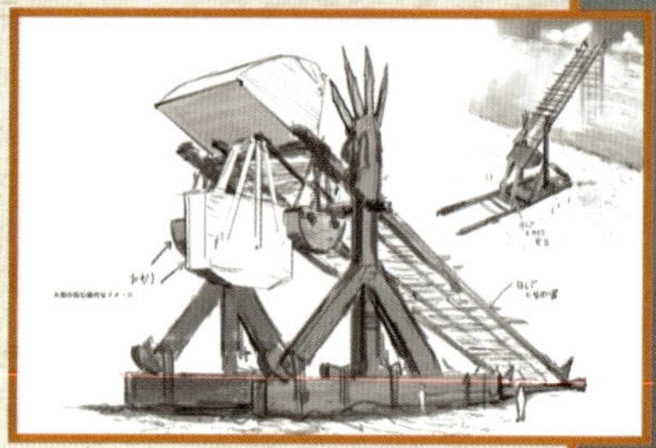

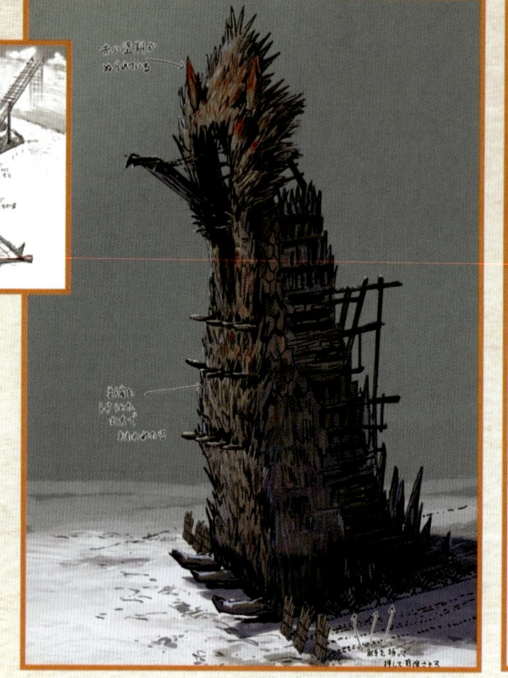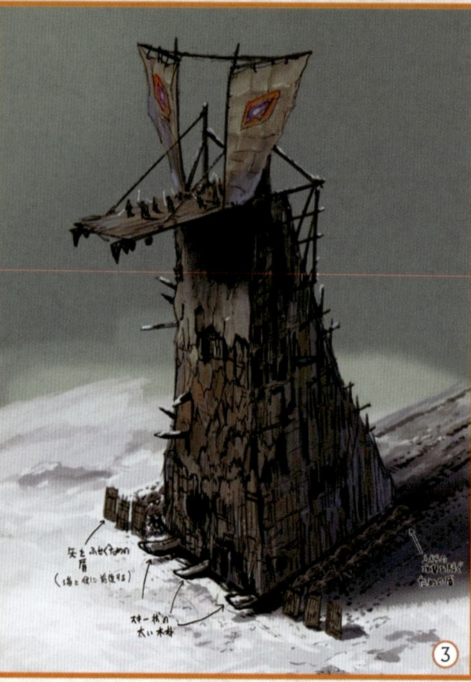

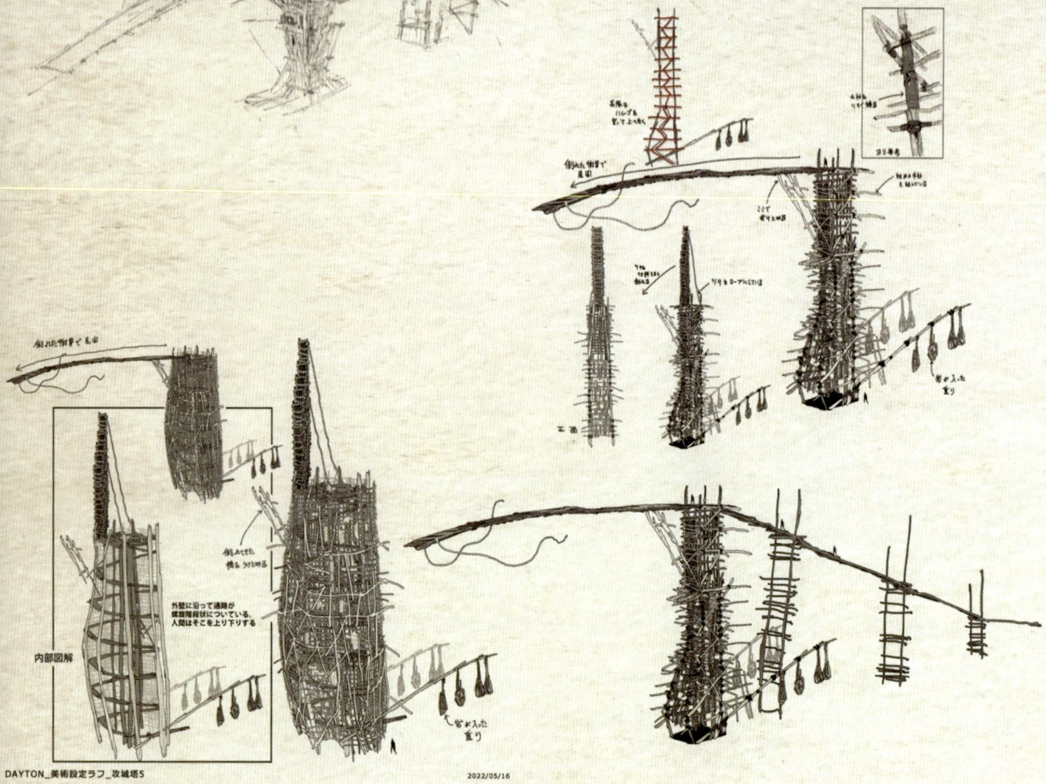

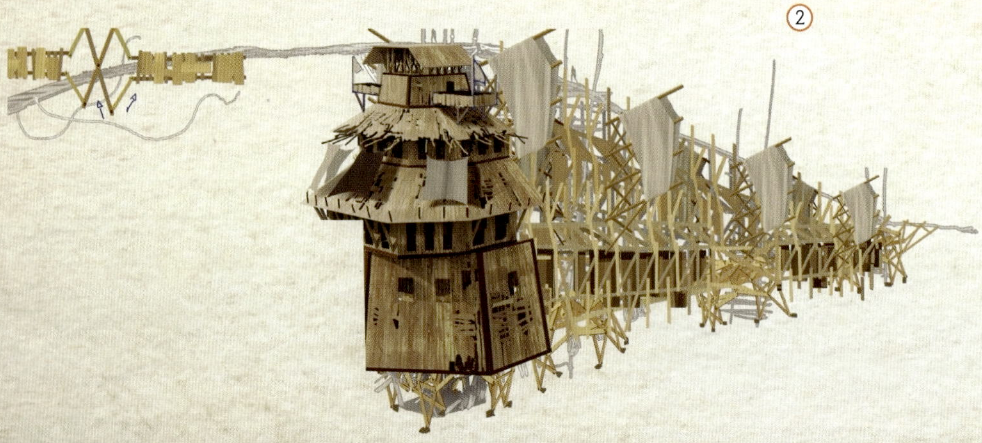

The siege tower surprised everyone when it first manifested in the director's storyboards. We all saw it there for the first time and said, 'What's this? This wasn't in the script!'

The reasons for it being introduced were manifold. For one, Kamiyama san felt that we needed to somehow be able to show the fear of Wulf and how it grows on the people in the Hornburg, visually. In addition, as originally written, the ending was a lot like *The Two Towers*, with Fréaláf riding to the rescue. We didn't want to repeat that, so we needed something new.

It also needed to be something that builds suspense: something is coming that is very big and scary, something that could be seen and would cause that feeling rather than a nebulous threat that is only talked about. Wulf no longer has his hired *mûmakil*, so what's the scary thing that he can do next? Also, without *mûmakil*, how do we pull this thing? People need to be able to handle this. Maybe it is built in place?

On top of this, if the Dunlendings are trying to breach the wall, which is very tall since we redesigned it, you can't just have an even bigger ladder than they had in the other films. All these reasons pointed to needing something like a tower, something that the Dunlendings and Wild Men could build in front of the wall.

The final argument for the structure was as a stage for Wulf and Héra's climactic confrontation. We had already used the gates of the Hornburg for Helm's last fight, so we needed a new environment for the showdown.
Kamiyama san put a lot of thought into the idea. It surprised everyone, and initially we were trepidatious, but once we came together there was the realization, 'Okay, we get it. This actually solves so many problems!' It was an ingenious solution. – JOSEPH CHOU, PRODUCER

1: Siege tower concepts, KM. 2: Siege tower concepts, YY. 3: Siege tower concepts, KS. 4: Siege tower concepts, SS.

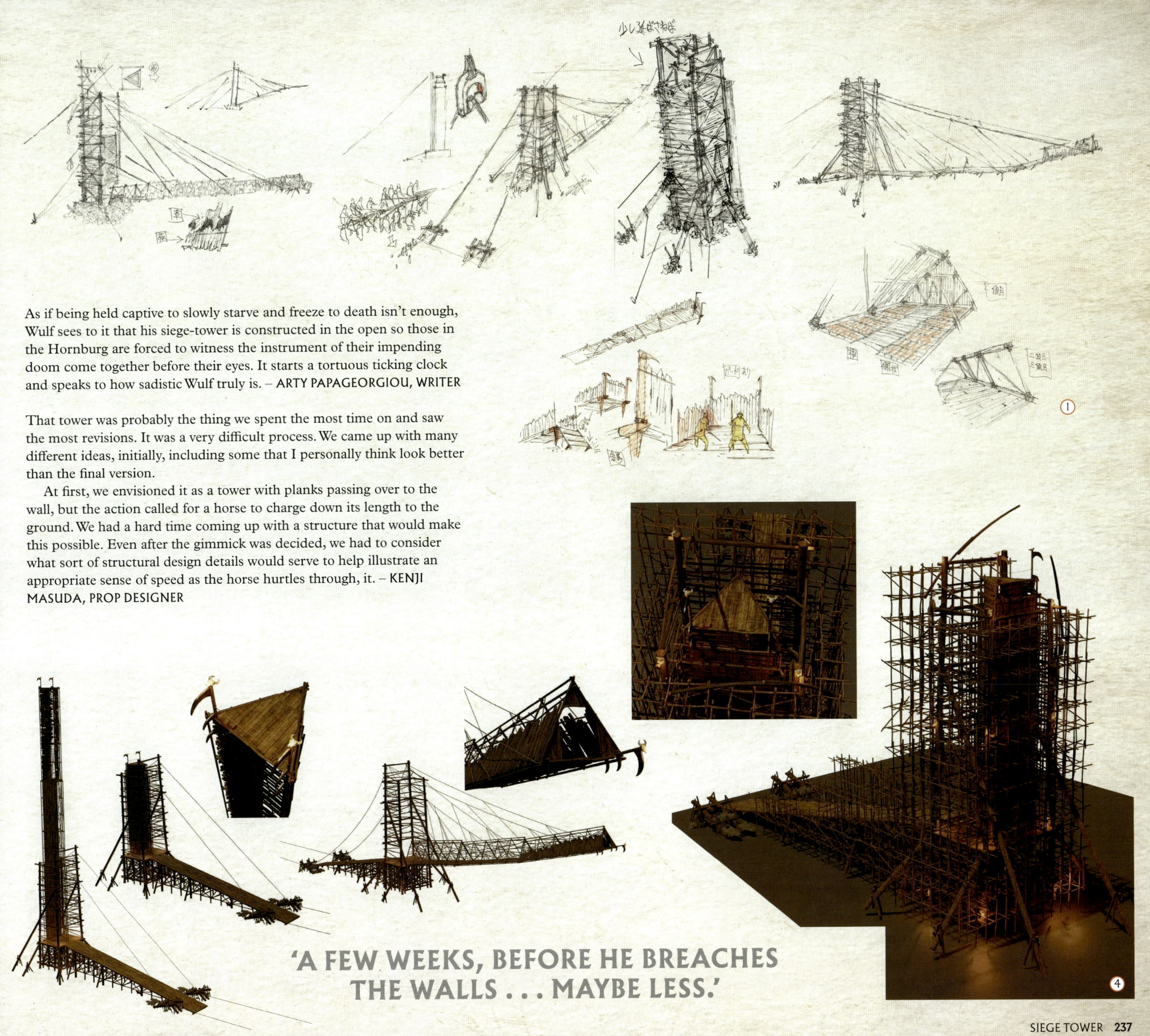

As if being held captive to slowly starve and freeze to death isn't enough, Wulf sees to it that his siege-tower is constructed in the open so those in the Hornburg are forced to witness the instrument of their impending doom come together before their eyes. It starts a tortuous ticking clock and speaks to how sadistic Wulf truly is. – ARTY PAPAGEORGIOU, WRITER

That tower was probably the thing we spent the most time on and saw the most revisions. It was a very difficult process. We came up with many different ideas, initially, including some that I personally think look better than the final version.

At first, we envisioned it as a tower with planks passing over to the wall, but the action called for a horse to charge down its length to the ground. We had a hard time coming up with a structure that would make this possible. Even after the gimmick was decided, we had to consider what sort of structural design details would serve to help illustrate an appropriate sense of speed as the horse hurtles through, it. – KENJI MASUDA, PROP DESIGNER

'A FEW WEEKS, BEFORE HE BREACHES
THE WALLS . . . MAYBE LESS.'

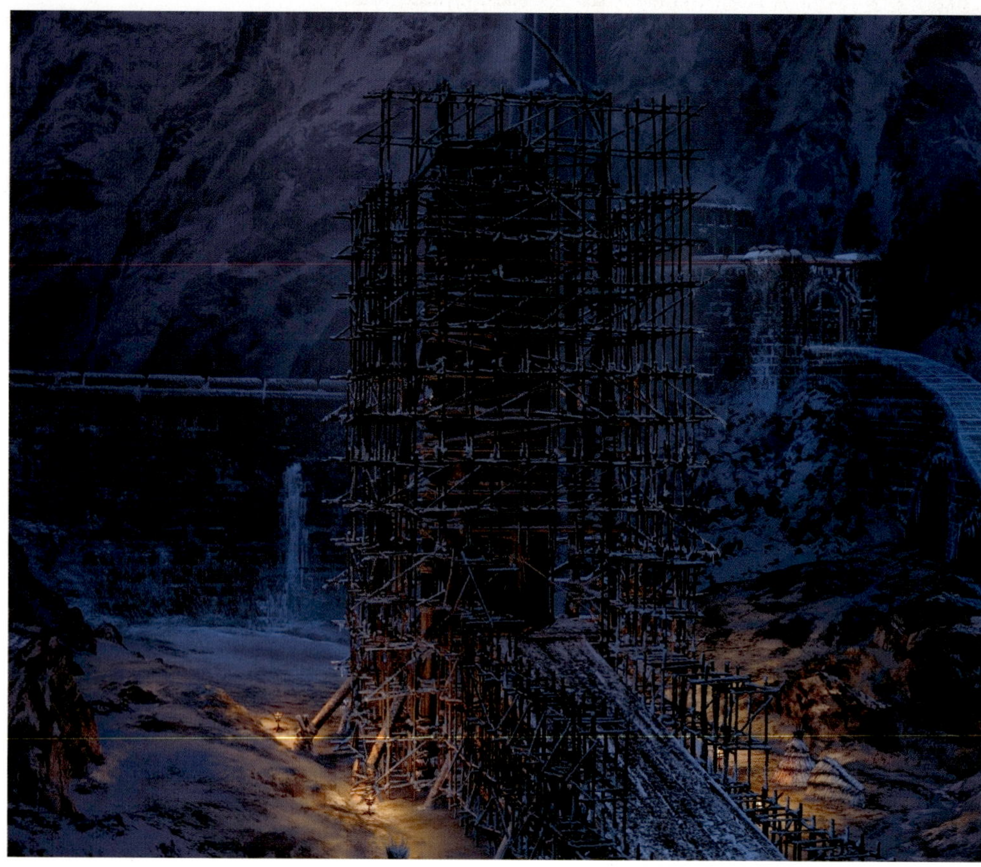

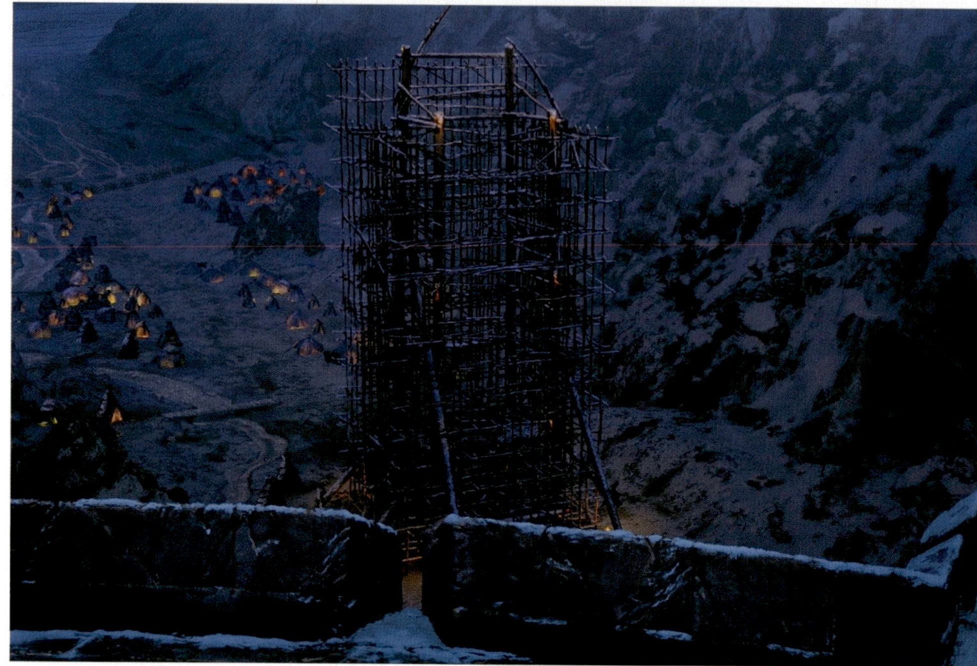

1: Siege tower background art. 2: Final film frame.

The top of the tower telescopes and then drops onto the wall, disgorging warriors. Since there needed to be enough width in the planks for soldiers to run out of the end, we calculated that the base would need to be about five times that size.

The structure had started with a square foundation, but during our consideration we found it made things too complex. It was the director's idea to change it to a more unusual and interesting triangular shape. – KENJI MASUDA, PROP DESIGNER

The siege tower was created in three different ways: hand-drawn art, camera mapping, and as a 3D computer-generated model. Without CGI, it would have been impossible to achieve uniformity in the shapes as we animated such a complex object.

The tower is lit with lamps made from cow bones attached on all sides, and the green Dunlending lamps at the top. We underlit it with fire which helped give it a sense of scale and make it feel ominous. – YASUHIRO YAMANE, ART DIRECTOR

The siege tower was built in CG with great care as we sought to give form to the director's idea. We aspired to create something that was imaginary, yet structurally convincing. As a setting for Héra and Wulf's final confrontation, I felt the unique shapes enhanced the visuals presented on screen. – SHUNSUKE WATANABE, SANKAKU STUDIO, CG/COMPOSITE DIRECTOR

'THERE WILL BE NO SURRENDER – ONLY SLAUGHTER.'

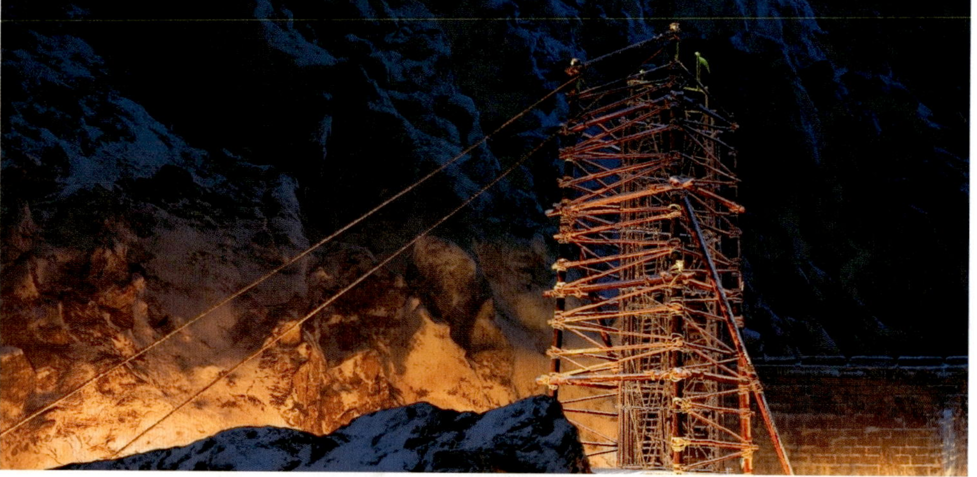

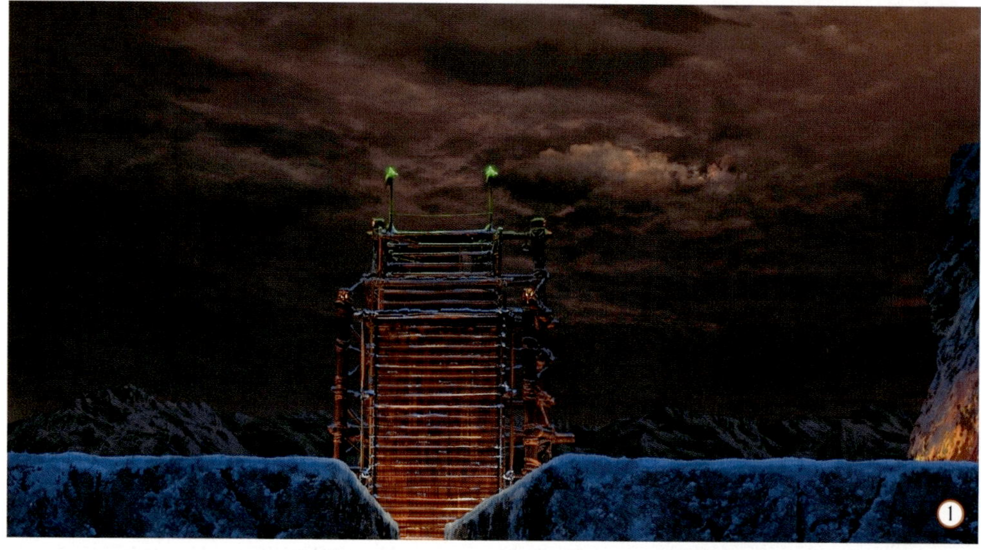

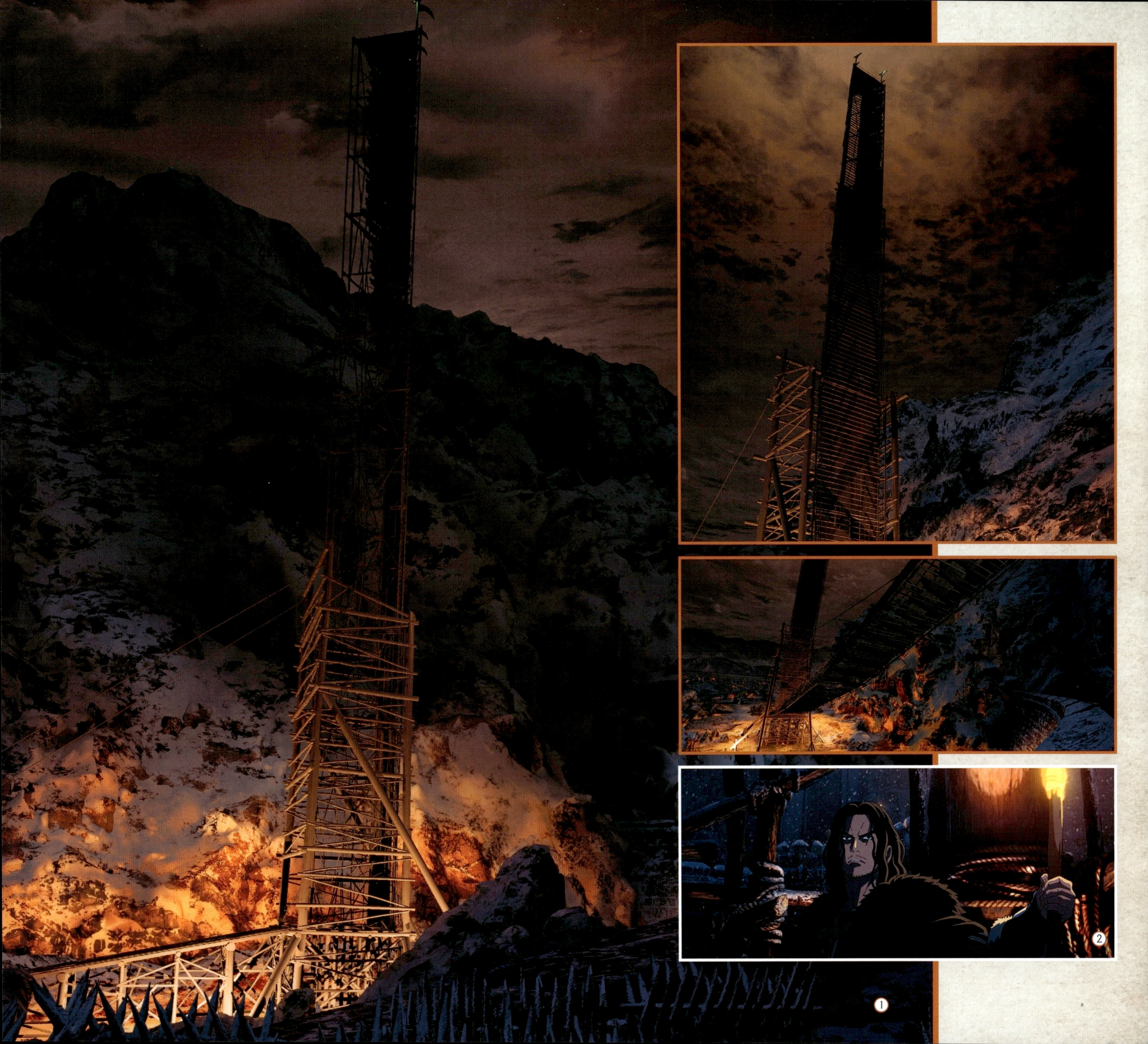

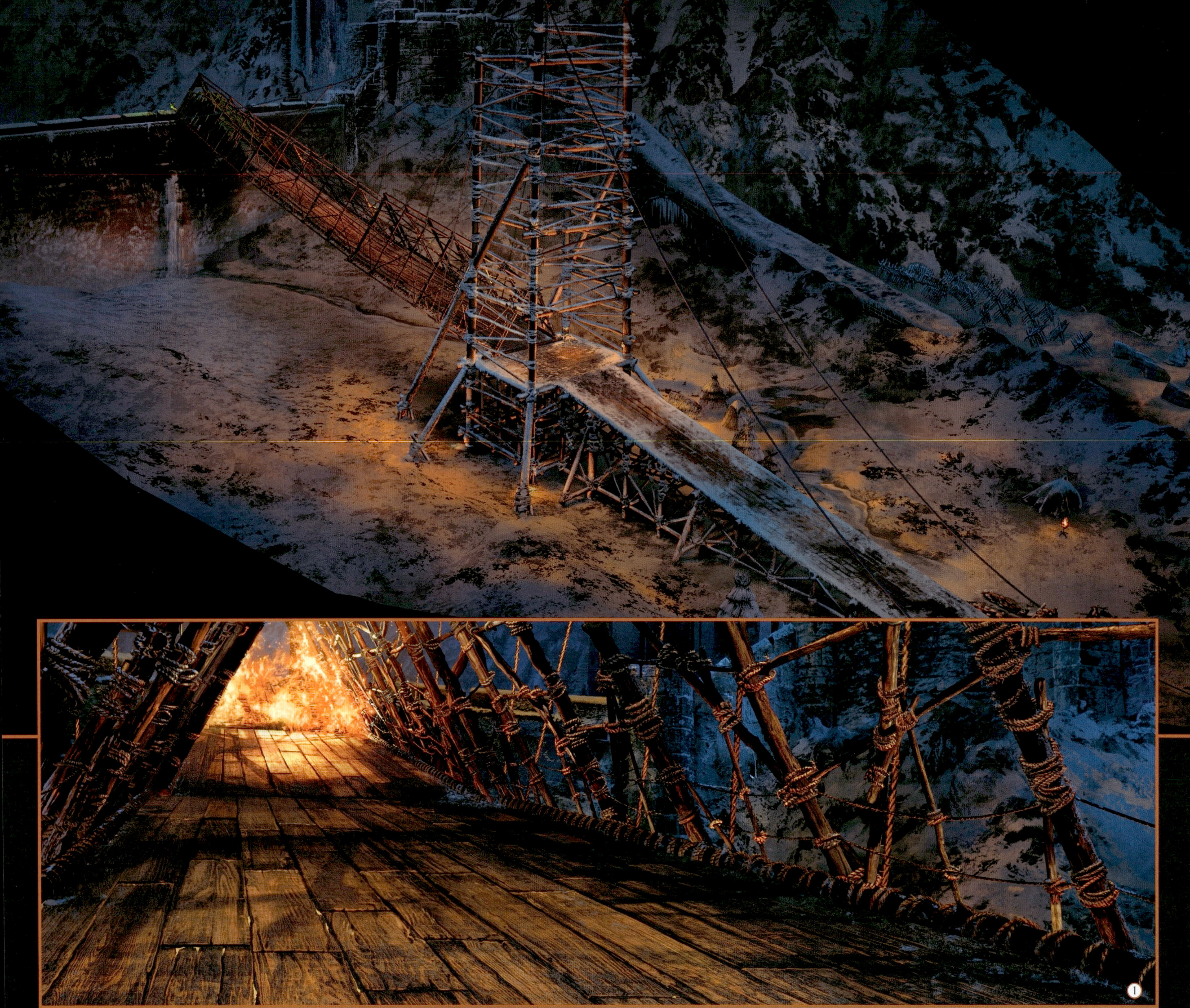

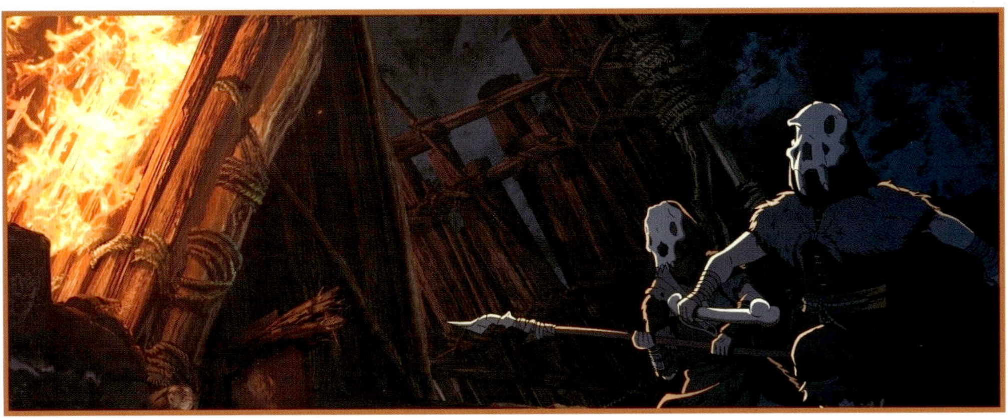

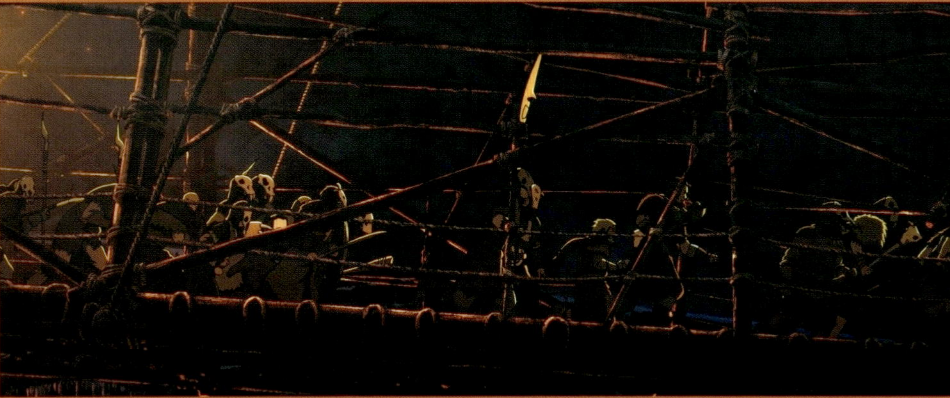

THE BATTLE OF THE DEEP

❖◀◀◆▶▶❖

Wulf's lust for revenge cannot be slaked. Driven by bloodlust, he launches his final assault on the Hornburg using his siege tower to gain the Deeping Wall. The top of the wall and deployed siege bridge become stages upon which the battle plays, with Wulf's Wild Men and Dunlending warriors hurling themselves at the defences on the promise that victory will see their long months of suffering rewarded with treasure. That is, of course, a lie, but Wulf will stop at nothing now that he senses his ultimate triumph so close at hand.

It's an incidental thing, but I passionately championed the idea of the Dunlendings carrying war horns inspired by the Celtic *carnyx*. They're so cool and feel like something that should exist in Middle-earth. I was delighted when they made it into the film. I thought Masuda san's design was very elegant and original. I hope someday someone makes a physical replica of it! – DANIEL FALCONER, ADDITIONAL CONCEPTS DESIGNER

I designed a long, slender, upward extending horn, which appears only fleetingly in the distance in the siege tower scenes. Looking at the design settings now, one wonders why there is a lamp in its mouth and why it is lit, but this is because we had an idea that it would have strong impact if it breathed fire from the horn, so I developed that image. In the event, no such action was adopted in the film. – KENJI MASUDA, PROP DESIGNER

'WE KILL THEM ALL.'

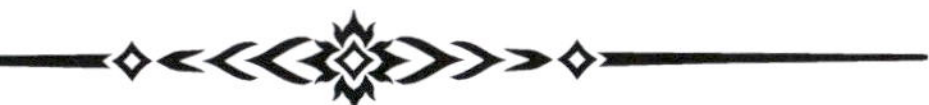

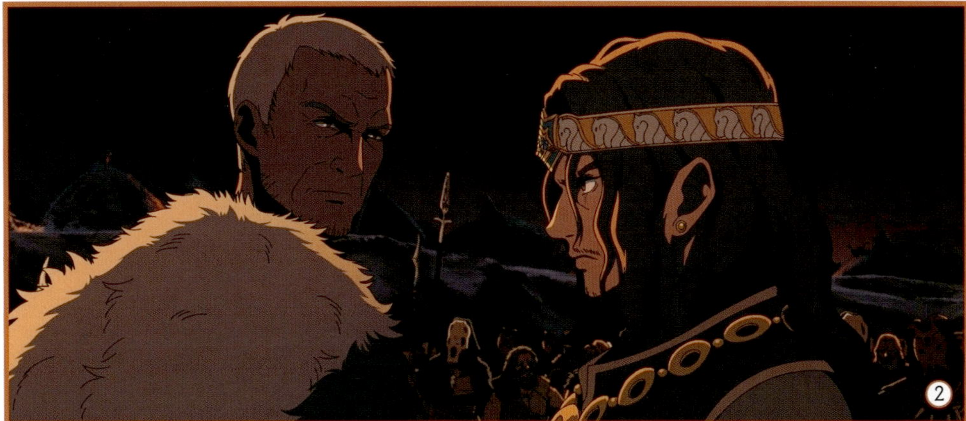

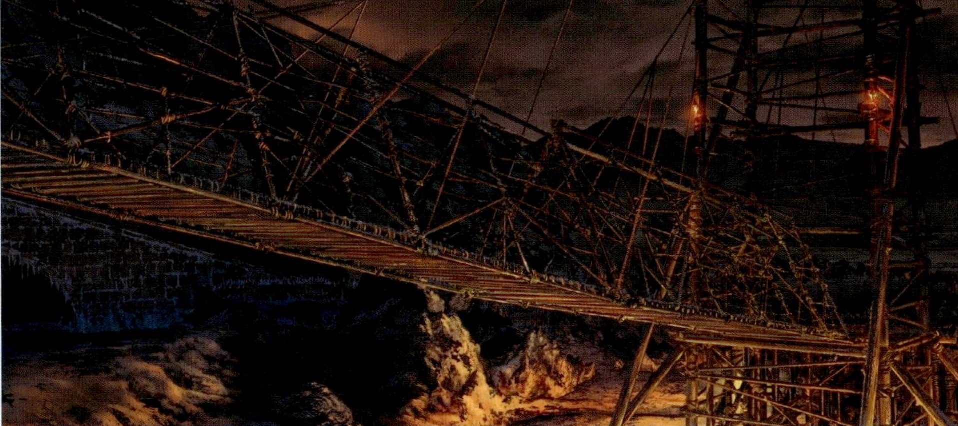

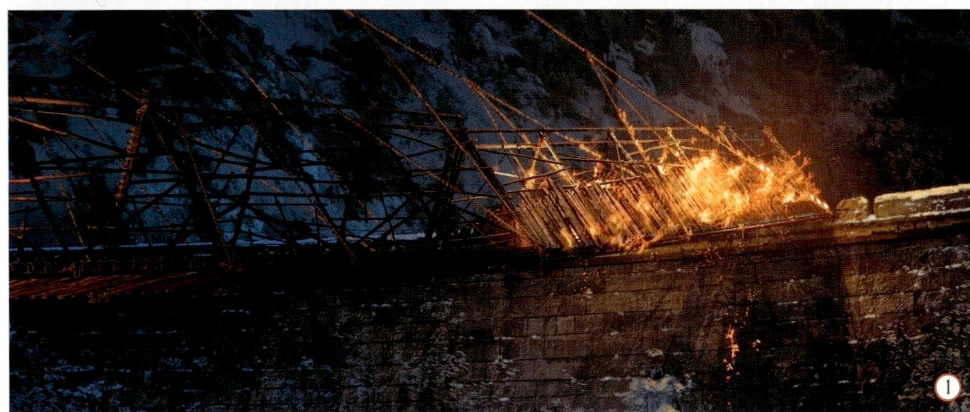

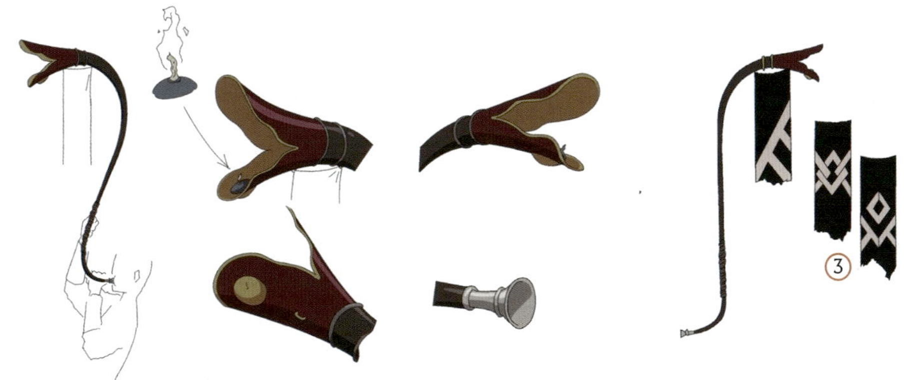

1: Siege tower background art. 2: Final film frames. 3: Dunlending carnyx prop setting art, KM.

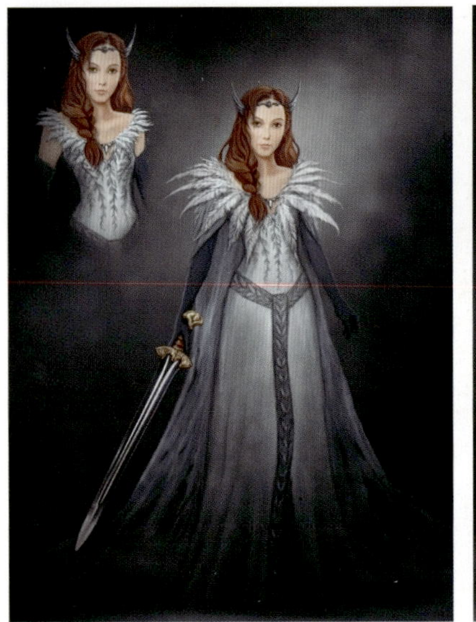
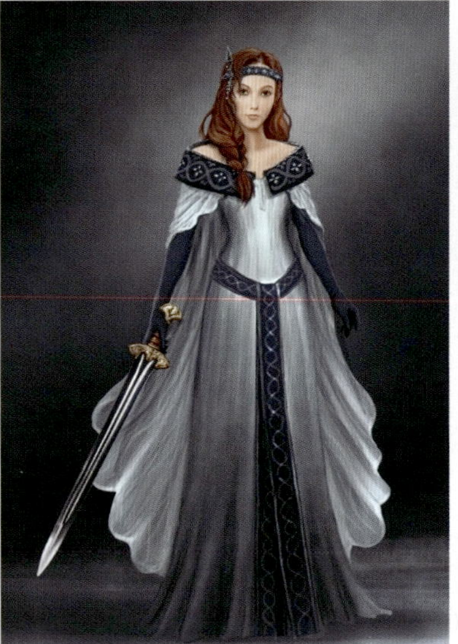
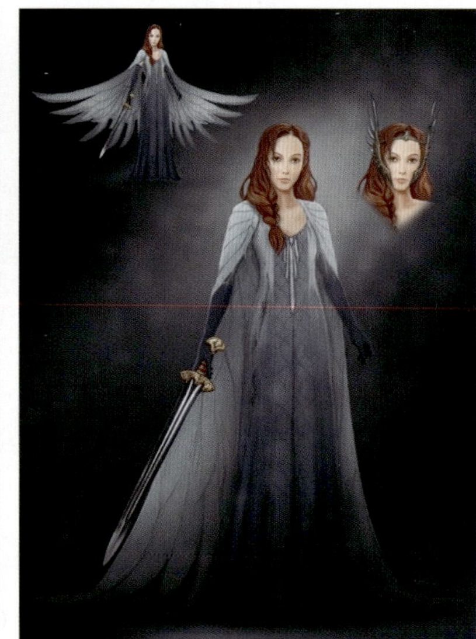
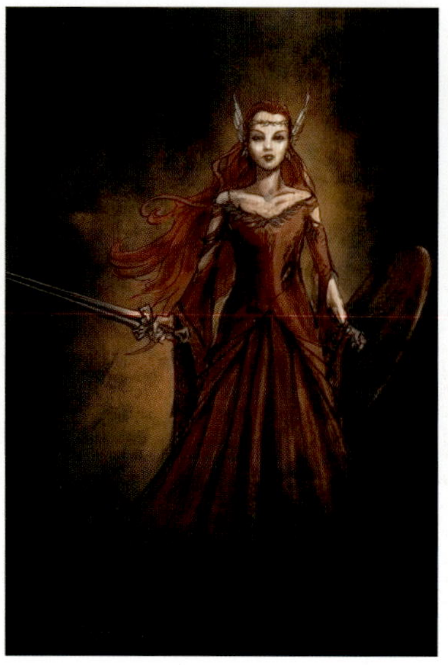
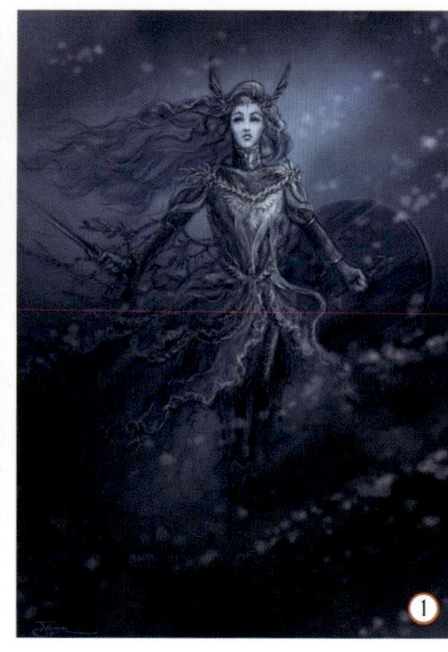

1

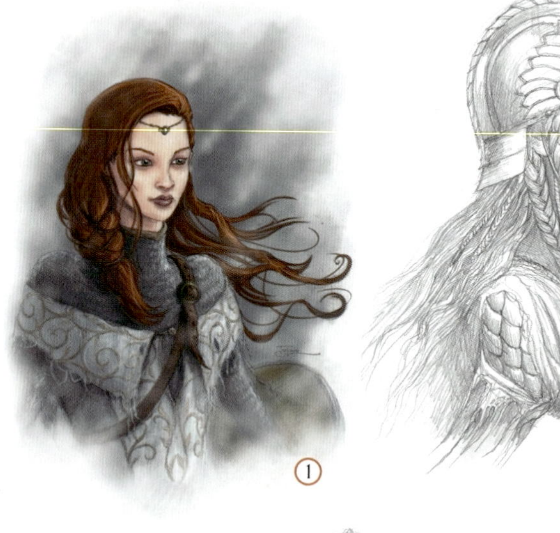

1

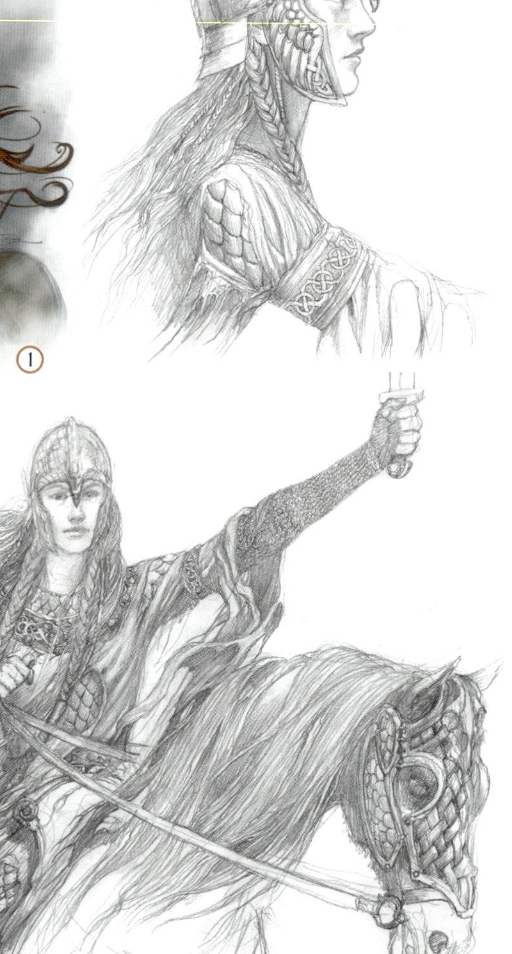

2

HÉRA, BRIDE OF DEATH

The climax of our story about choices is Héra taking ownership. She takes all of the things that were thrust upon her, or expected of her, and she takes ownership of them; 'You wanted a bride, well buckle up buddy, you're going to get a freaking bride of deaaaaaaath!'. – PHOEBE GITTINS, WRITER

In addition to the Anglo-Saxon histories, the other place we often went to for inspiration for the Rohirrim was the old Icelandic sagas. Héra's bride of death moment is a definite nod to the Valkyries. We wanted her to look slightly scary, unnatural, and vengeful, about war. The Valkyries ride on the wind, which brings us back to the beginning with Héra, and the Great Eagles. That is who she becomes.

I was inspired by an amazing sketch by Alan Lee of Kriemhild with her sword, having killed all the men. She is dressed in her feminine gown with corpses at her feet. – PHILIPPA BOYENS, PRODUCER

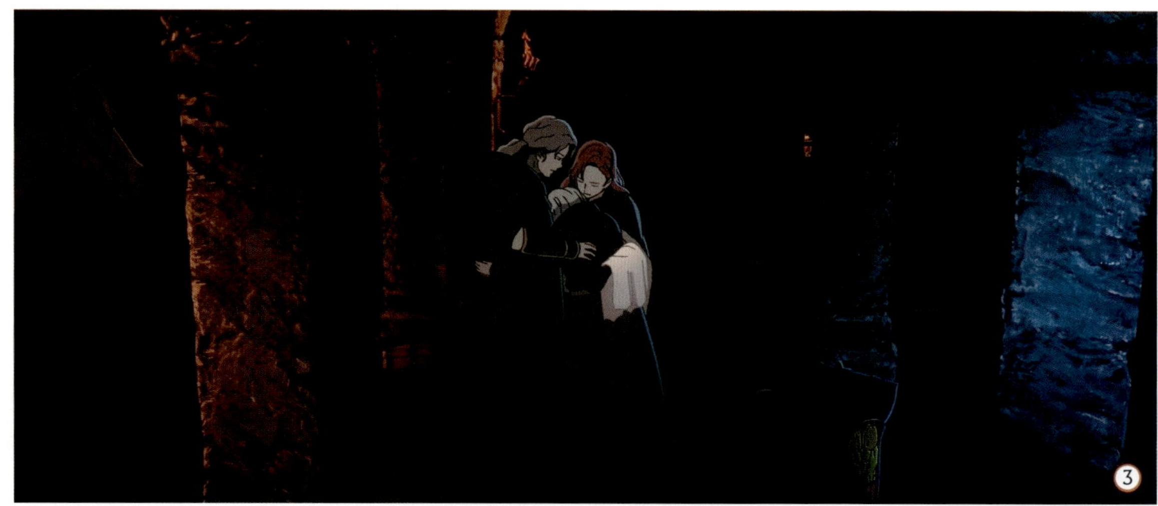

3

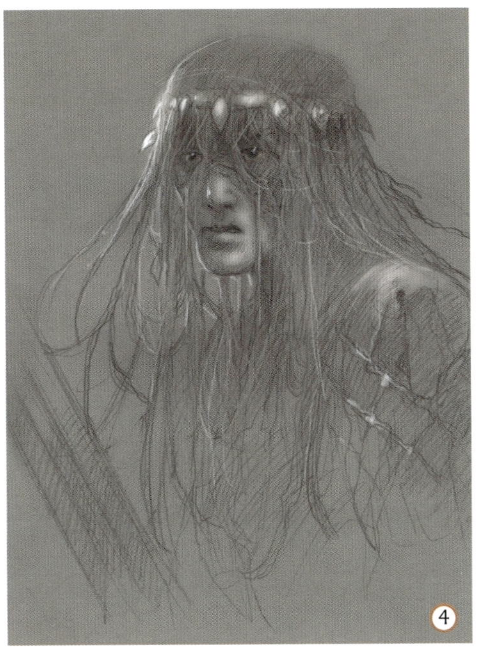

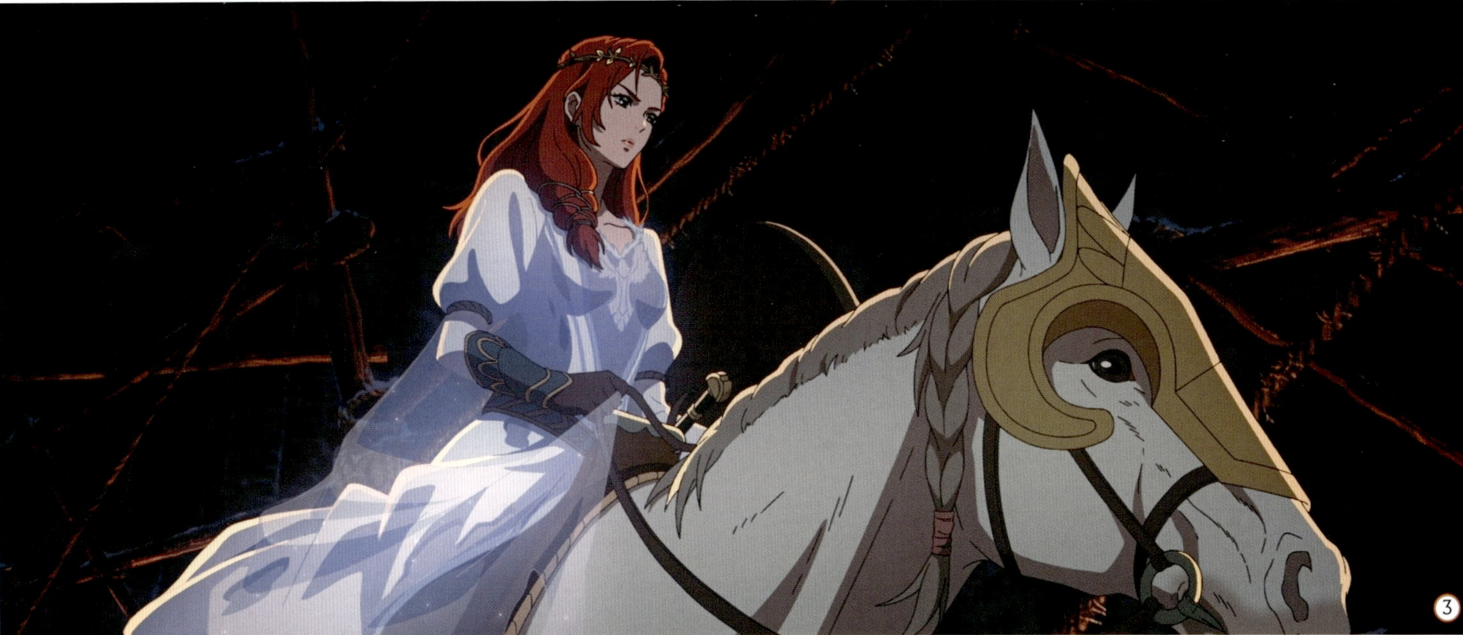

Phillippa liked a drawing that I had made for a book in the nineties: an image of Kriemhild with a bloody sword, surrounded by the bodies of Siegfried's murderers – both bride and avenger. She referenced this when writing a scene of Éowyn battling pursuing Orcs in the Glittering Caves for *The Two Towers*, and also when thinking about Héra as a warrior – a pleasing contrast between the softness and romance of a wedding gown and the fury of battle. – ALAN LEE, CONCEPTUAL DESIGNER

It was a welcome change from more military subjects to draw Rohirrim wedding dresses for a while. I tried to keep my concepts simple in construction but folded in some not-so-subtle eagle references. We didn't really get traction with the designs until Philippa talked about the Valkyrie inspiration behind the idea, the way the scene would play, and about Héra being married to Death. Then suddenly the imagery made sense. Alan understood, of course, but I hadn't been thinking in those terms. It had to be mythic! – DANIEL FALCONER, ADDITIONAL CONCEPTS DESIGNER

'YOU ARE THE WIND, CHILD. RIDE STRONG.'

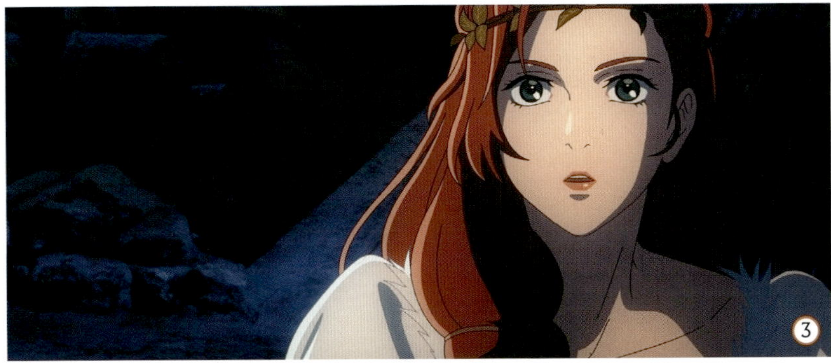

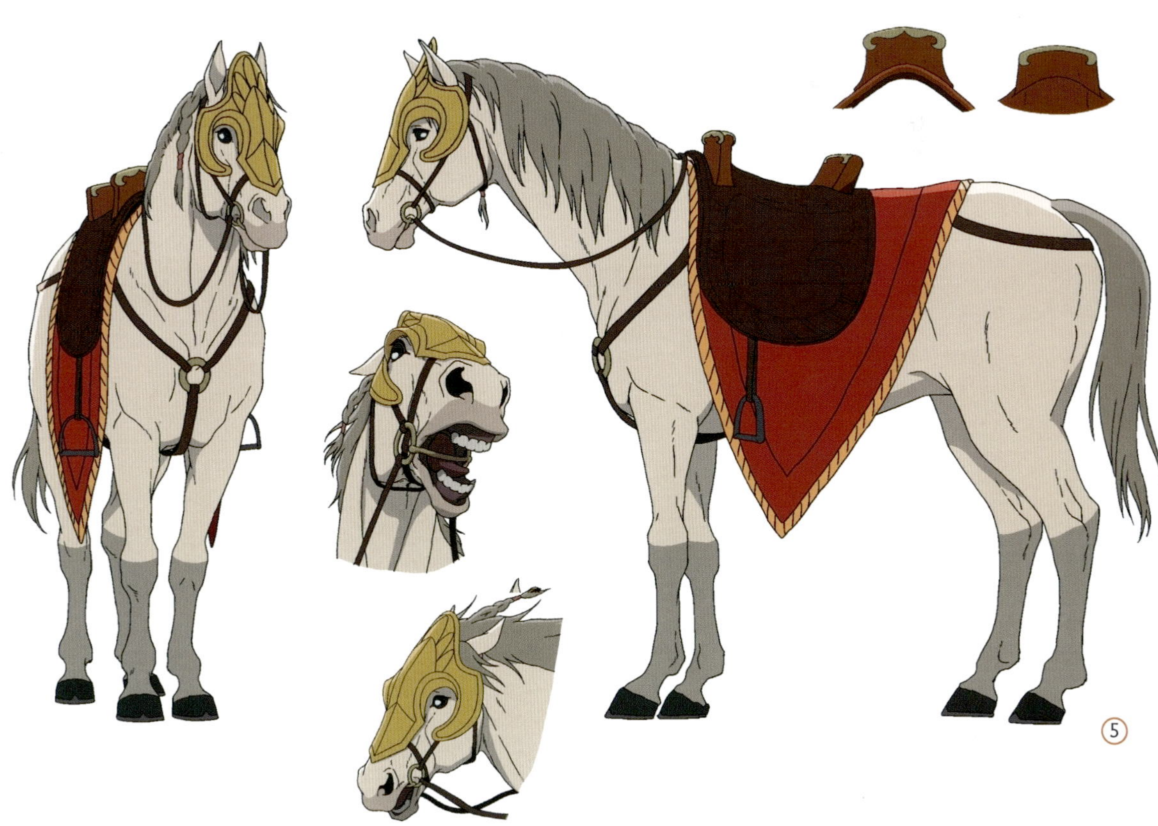

1: Héra concepts, DF. 2: Héra concepts, AL. 3: Final film frames. 4: Héra concept, JH.
5: Ashere creature setting art, MT.

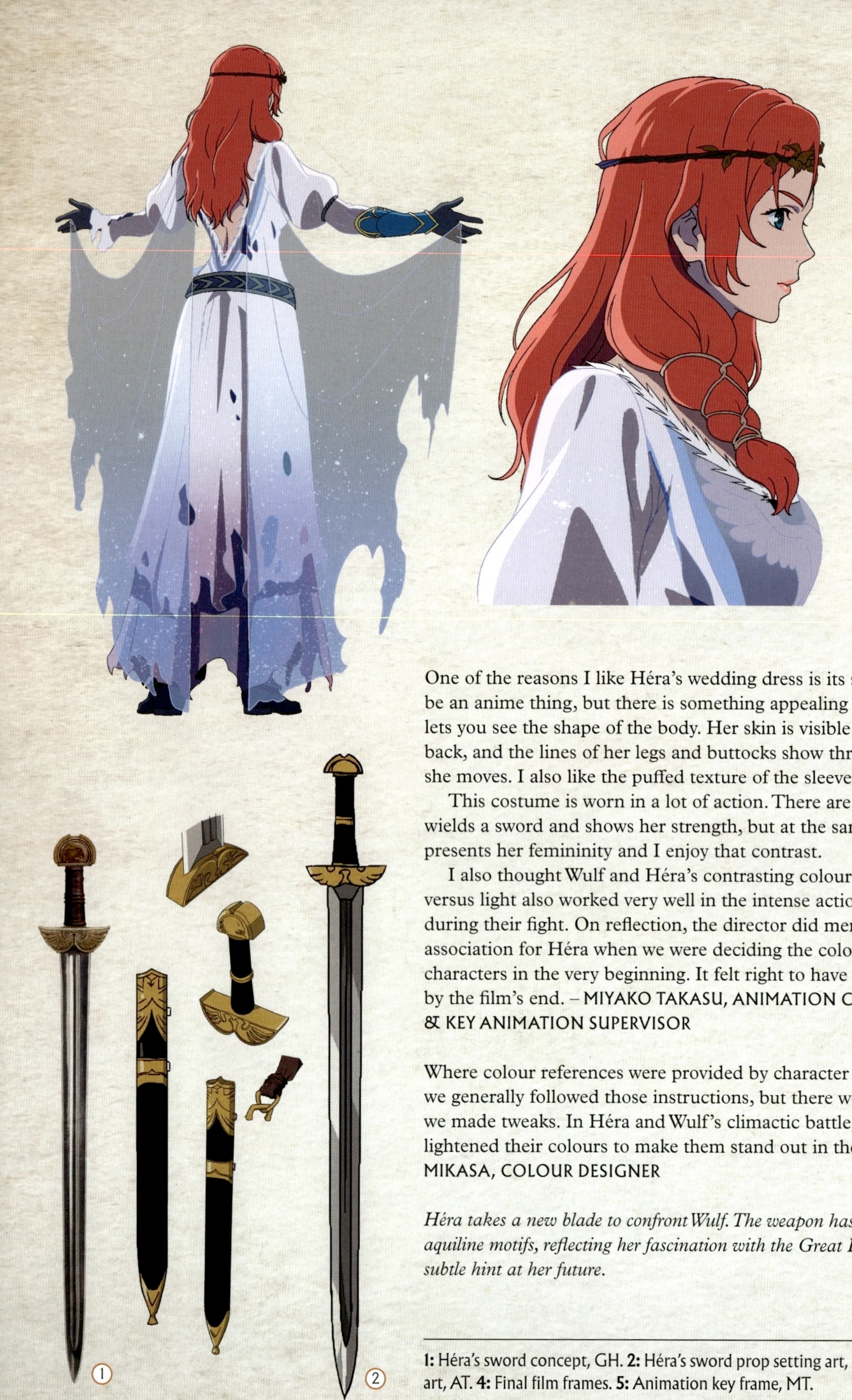

One of the reasons I like Héra's wedding dress is its silhouette. This may be an anime thing, but there is something appealing about a design that lets you see the shape of the body. Her skin is visible on the chest and back, and the lines of her legs and buttocks show through the soft fabric as she moves. I also like the puffed texture of the sleeves.

This costume is worn in a lot of action. There are shots in which she wields a sword and shows her strength, but at the same time the costume presents her femininity and I enjoy that contrast.

I also thought Wulf and Héra's contrasting colour schemes of dark versus light also worked very well in the intense action between them during their fight. On reflection, the director did mention white as his key association for Héra when we were deciding the colour schemes for the characters in the very beginning. It felt right to have returned to that place by the film's end. – MIYAKO TAKASU, ANIMATION CHARACTER DESIGNER & KEY ANIMATION SUPERVISOR

Where colour references were provided by character and prop designers, we generally followed those instructions, but there were instances when we made tweaks. In Héra and Wulf's climactic battle, for example, we lightened their colours to make them stand out in the scene. – OSAMA MIKASA, COLOUR DESIGNER

Héra takes a new blade to confront Wulf. The weapon has furniture bearing aquiline motifs, reflecting her fascination with the Great Eagles and a not-so subtle hint at her future.

1: Héra's sword concept, GH. **2:** Héra's sword prop setting art, KM. **3:** Héra character setting art, AT. **4:** Final film frames. **5:** Animation key frame, MT.

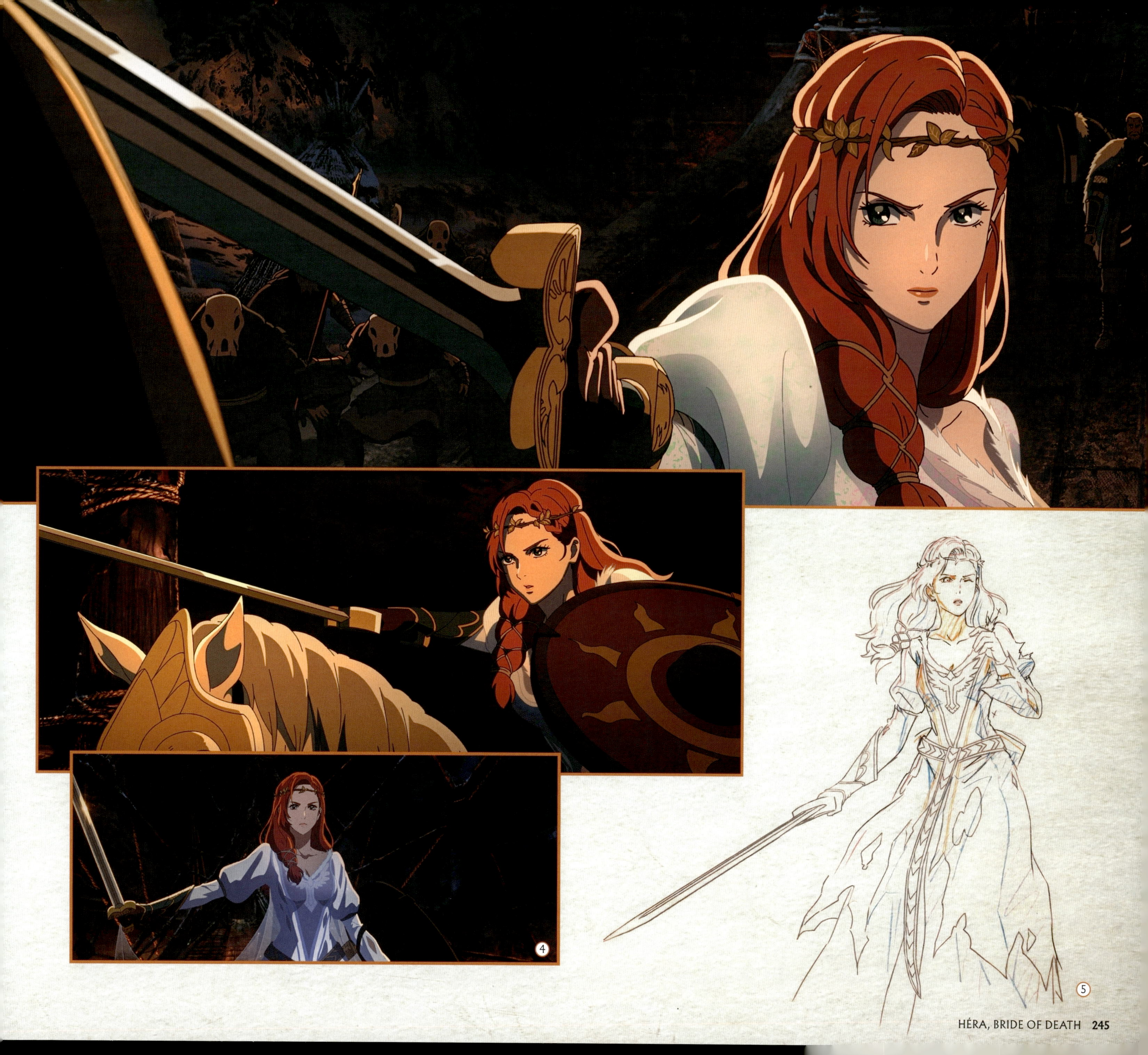

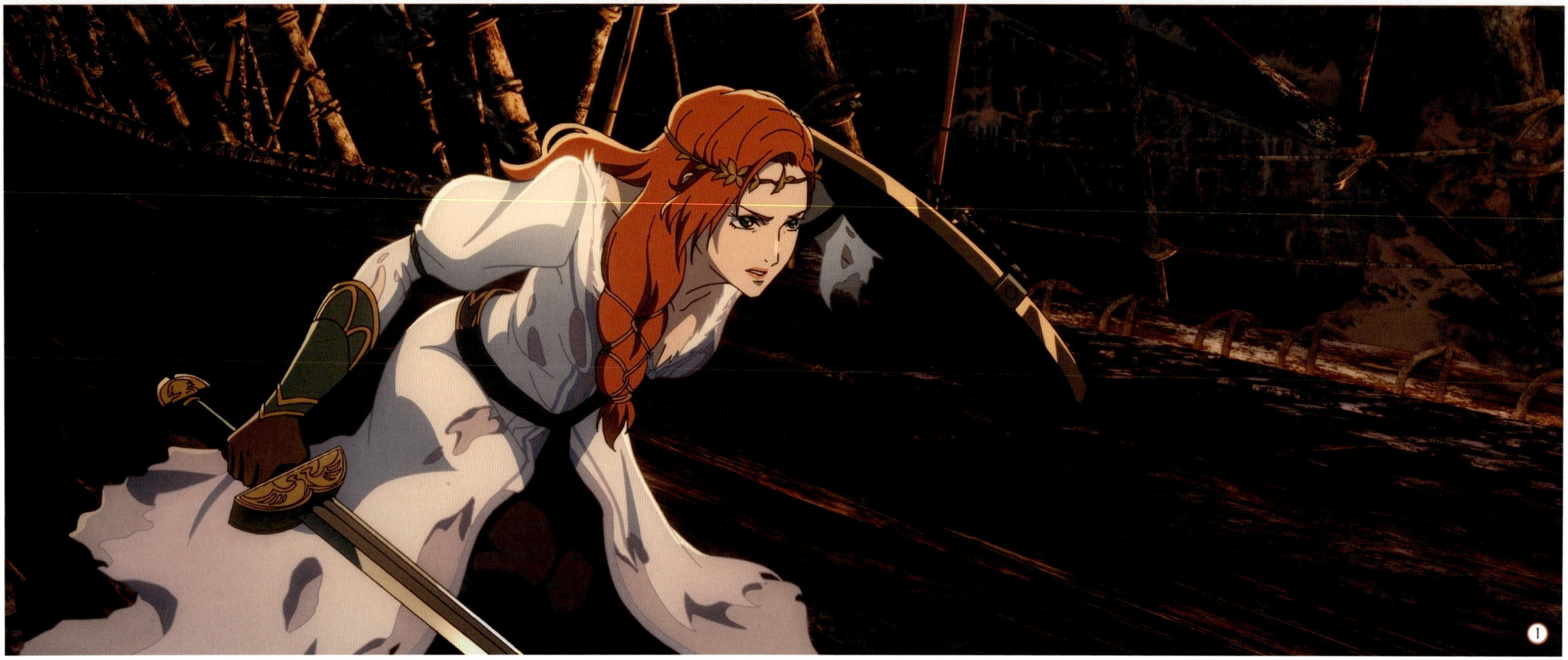

HÉRA AND WULF'S DUEL

This epic battle eventually all comes down to a one-on-one confrontation between Wulf and Héra. It comes back to the two young people we saw in the flashback holding blades.

Héra is a strategist. She uses Wulf's weakness against him, as a ploy, turning his obsession to her power. – PHOEBE GITTINS, WRITER

Essentially, the Siege of Troy grew out of the fallout between individuals and it is similar in our story. It's domestic, personal hurt, which escalates into something that involves and destroys the lives of an entire people. It begins being all about Héra and Wulf and despite everything that takes place Héra is perceptive enough to strip it back to that. She redefines the conflict and by focussing Wulf on her, she is able to give her people a chance at freedom. – ARTY PAPAGEORGIOU, WRITER

Visually, there's something exciting about seeing Héra ride out to war in a tattered wedding dress, bride to no man. Meantime, only a handful of defenders stay behind to help cover the retreat of the refugees. Among the main things that inspired Arty and me were the events of Gallipoli in World War One, and how the Anzacs, having endured such horror, eventually made their retreat without losing a soldier. When you retreat you are at your most vulnerable, but through their ingenuity in setting up self-firing guns and other tricks to cover their escape, they got away. We imagined Héra might think about how to save her people from a similar perspective. She wasn't about to send them all off to die in a hopeless battle. – PHOEBE GITTINS, WRITER

'YOU THINK I AM AFRAID OF YOU?'
'YOU SHOULD BE.'

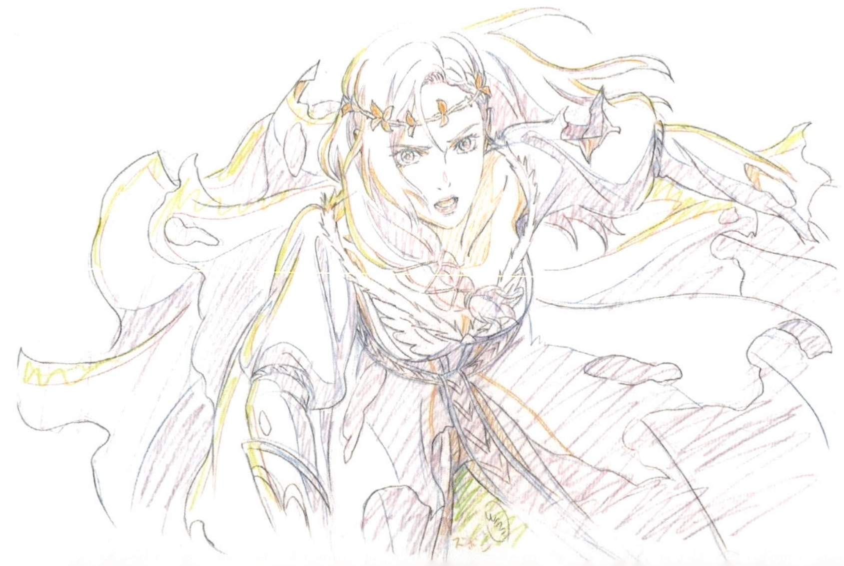

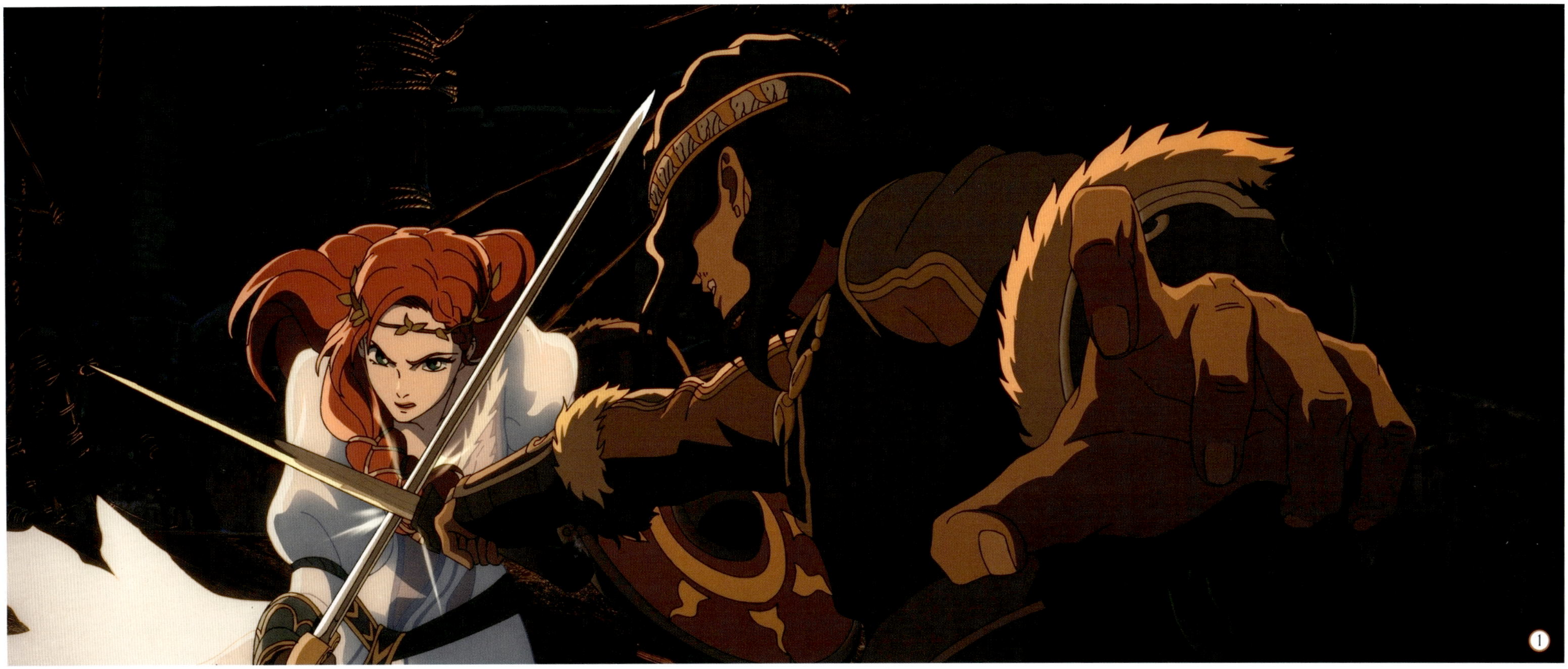

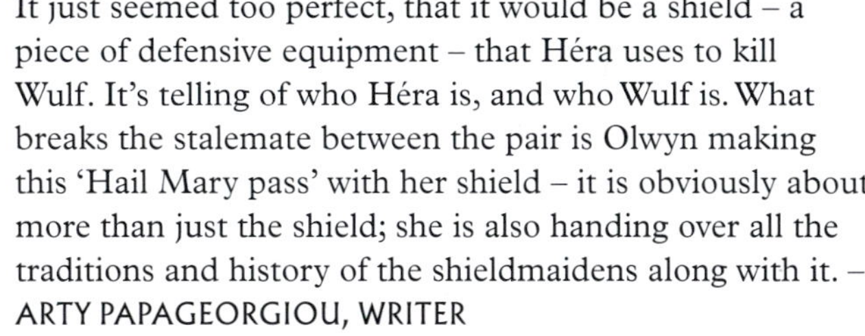

'LET US END THIS WULF, AS IT BEGAN, WITH YOU AND I.'

By embracing death themselves, the Rohirrim strip that power from their enemies.

'To whom are you pledged?' Wulf asks? 'Death.'

Héra embraces her heritage. It's a culmination of things; her heritage as one of the Rohirrim, and as a shieldmaiden, and the proposal that started it all. She takes control of it all. It felt so right. – PHOEBE GITTINS, WRITER

Olwyn's broken shield is set up earlier in our story; 'It's not broken, just broken in.' She could have had it repaired, but she chose not to, which is significant. Héra rides into battle with her own shield, but it's stripped from her during the fight, so Olwyn tosses Héra hers. That's the broken shield that Wulf eventually gets in the neck and it is because of the broken edges that it tears his jugular. It's symbolic. Wulf never broke Héra. This whole thing that he has inflicted upon them has made her more defined, stronger, and that's how he is overcome by her in the end. – PHOEBE GITTINS, WRITER

It just seemed too perfect, that it would be a shield – a piece of defensive equipment – that Héra uses to kill Wulf. It's telling of who Héra is, and who Wulf is. What breaks the stalemate between the pair is Olwyn making this 'Hail Mary pass' with her shield – it is obviously about more than just the shield; she is also handing over all the traditions and history of the shieldmaidens along with it. – ARTY PAPAGEORGIOU, WRITER

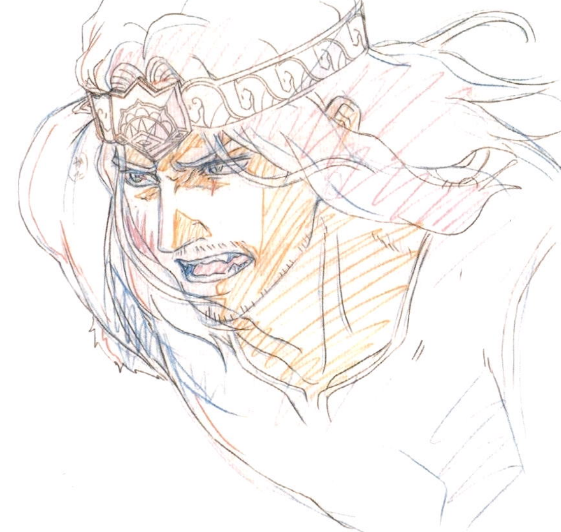

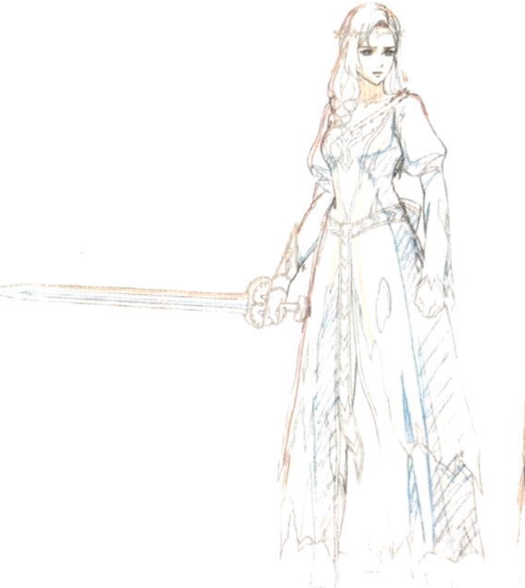

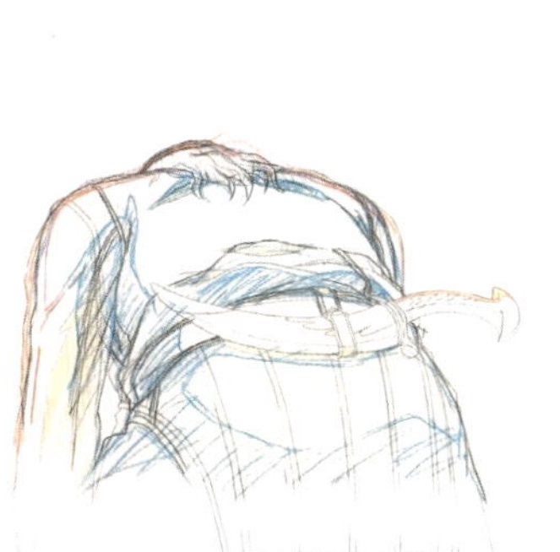

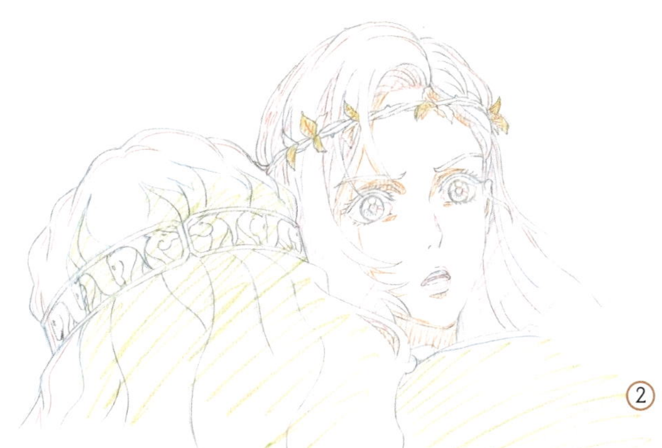

1: Final film frames. 2: Animation key frames, MT.

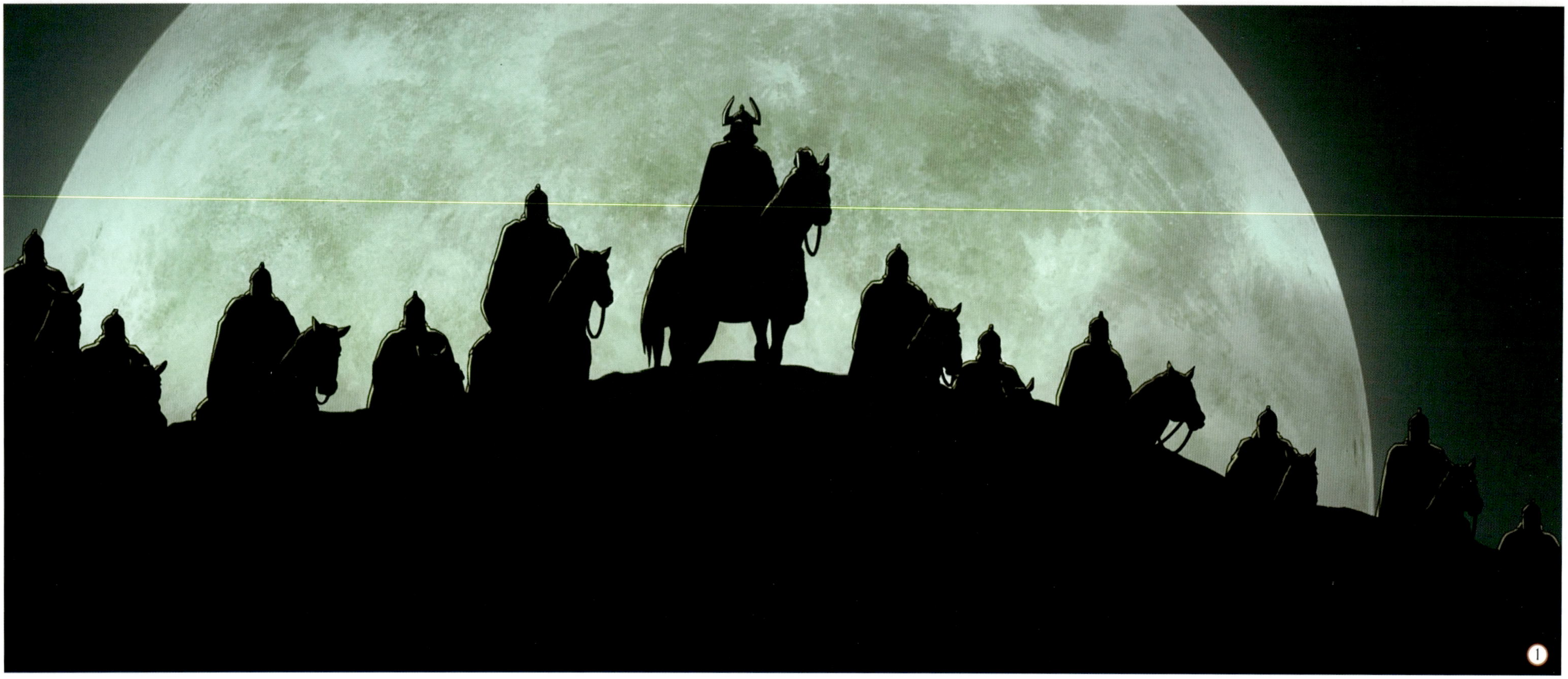

1: Final film frames. 2: Fréaláf and Fréaláf's horse setting art, including alternative colour concepts, MT.

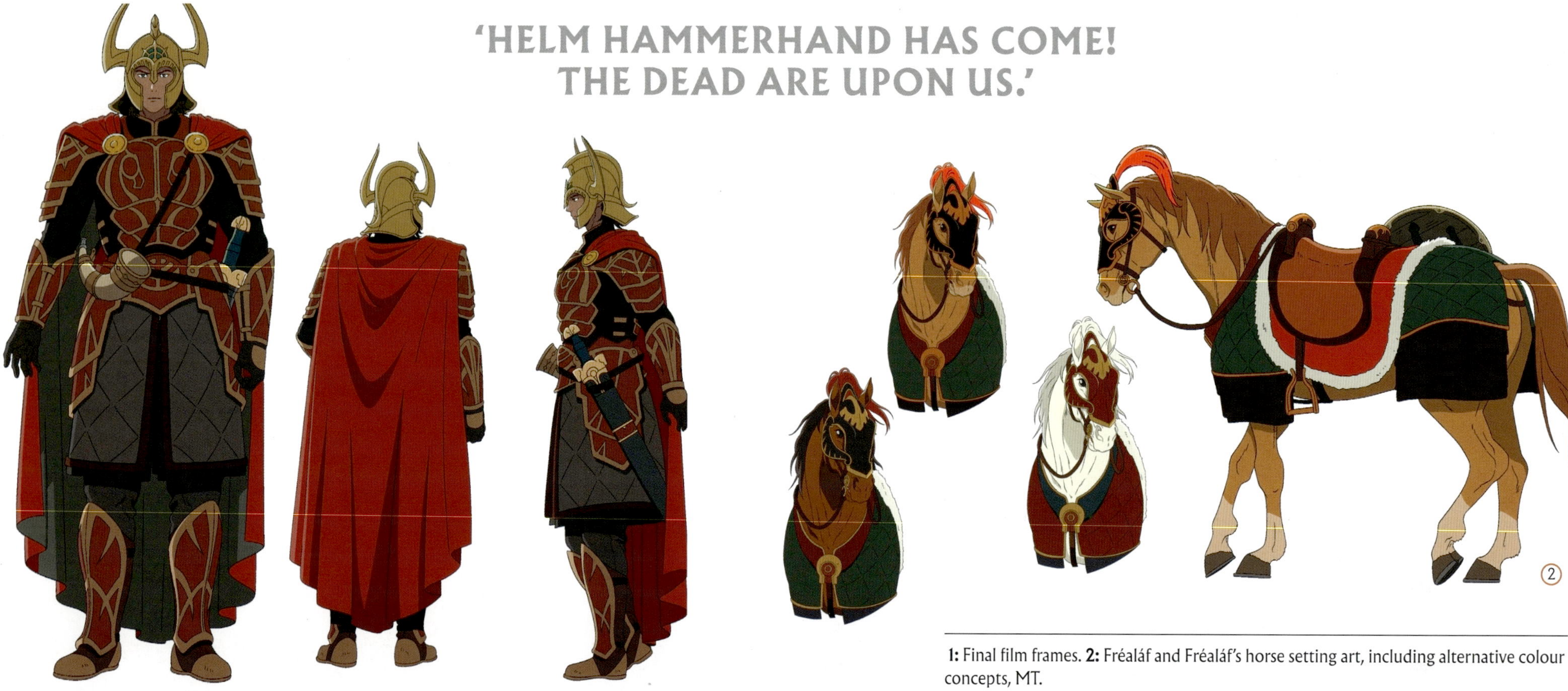

THE HAMMERHAND'S RETURN

Wulf's army is so traumatized by what they have gone through, and the myth of the wraith of Helm Hammerhand has taken root so strongly, that just the sight of him appearing on the ridge above, the thought that he had returned, sends them fleeing. The terror in the Wild Men was so deep by the end of it that the sound of Helm's horn would send them running. – PHOEBE GITTINS, WRITER

It was important to make it clear that Fréaláf was wearing Helm's armour and that Wulf's men thought it was their enemy returned from the dead. They are primed to break. They have been here for so long and it has been so miserable, so when faced with this apparition it's the last straw. Fréaláf rides down on them in a moment that echoes Éomer and Gandalf's charge in *The Two Towers*, but on a smaller scale. It's not hundreds of horses, but it's enough to win because Wulf's men are already broken. The point is that they have the numbers and could probably still take the Hornburg, but the spectre of Helm's return is too much.

Fréaláf immediately takes control. It's clear that he has kingly qualities, but he also defers to Héra when she pleads on her enemies' behalf to let them live; there has been death enough. He listens to her. It sets up Fréaláf as the kind of future king who is smart, brave, noble and fair. He stood up to Helm when he thought his uncle was wrong, and was hurt by Helm's wrath, but he was ready to come back when needed.

It's a deviation from what happened in the book, in which Fréaláf snuck in and slew Wulf in Edoras, but our movie was about the siege, and we needed the action to conclude at the Hornburg. Fréaláf still wins the war and demonstrates what kind of king he will be. – JASON DEMARCO, PRODUCER

Near the end of the film, we got to call out the naming of Helm's Deep. That was so cool. We loved having the opportunity to include that line and directly connect Héra and Helm, and the events of our film with the trilogy. – PHOEBE GITTINS, WRITER

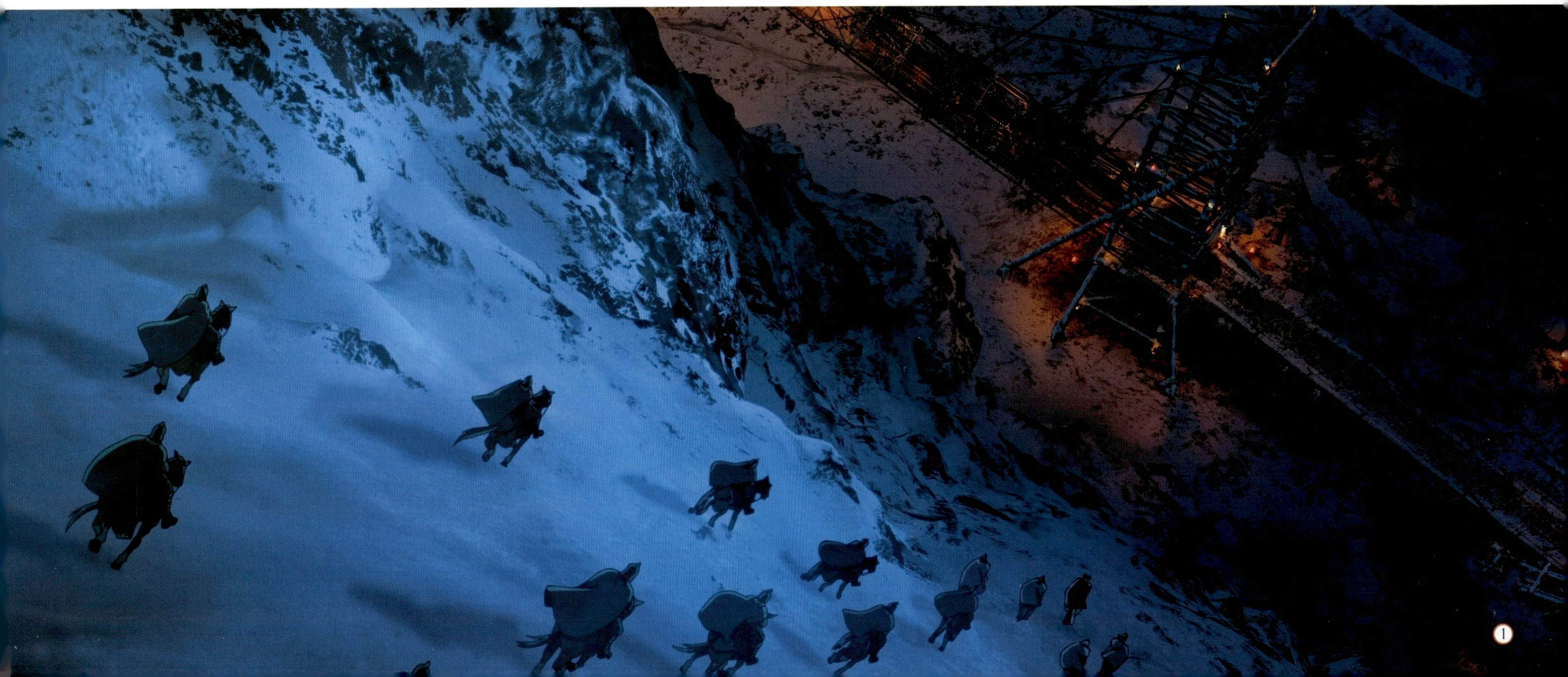

- 9 -

THE PROMISE OF SPRING

Their battles won and winter over, the people of Rohan start to rebuild. Fréaláf is crowned king in Edoras as Héra makes ready to depart. By rights, the crown should be hers, but she has other plans. A letter has come to her; an invitation of sorts, and she and Olwyn bid farewell to her cousin king, riding out to meet a wizard even as another pledges his friendship to Rohan.

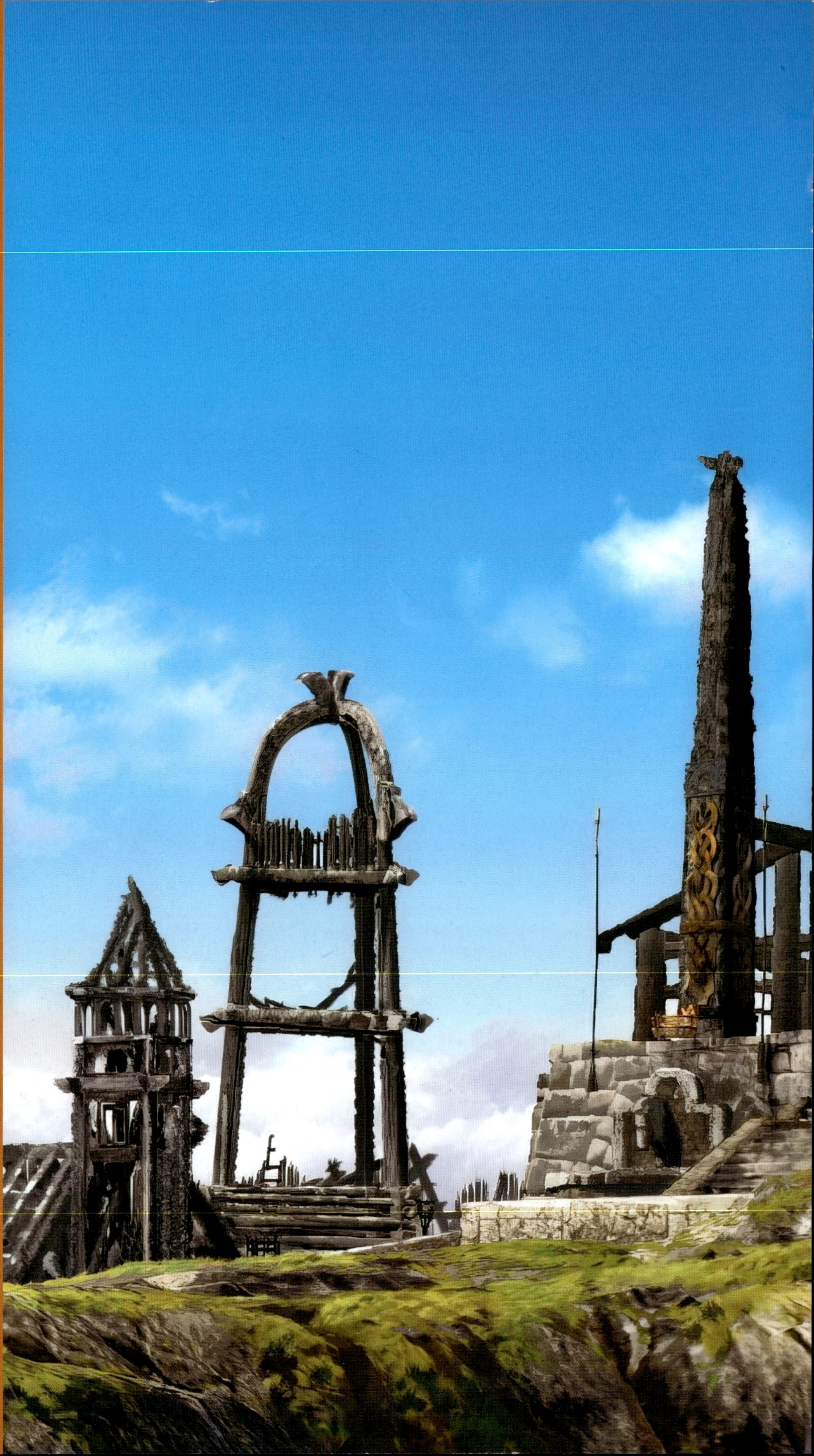

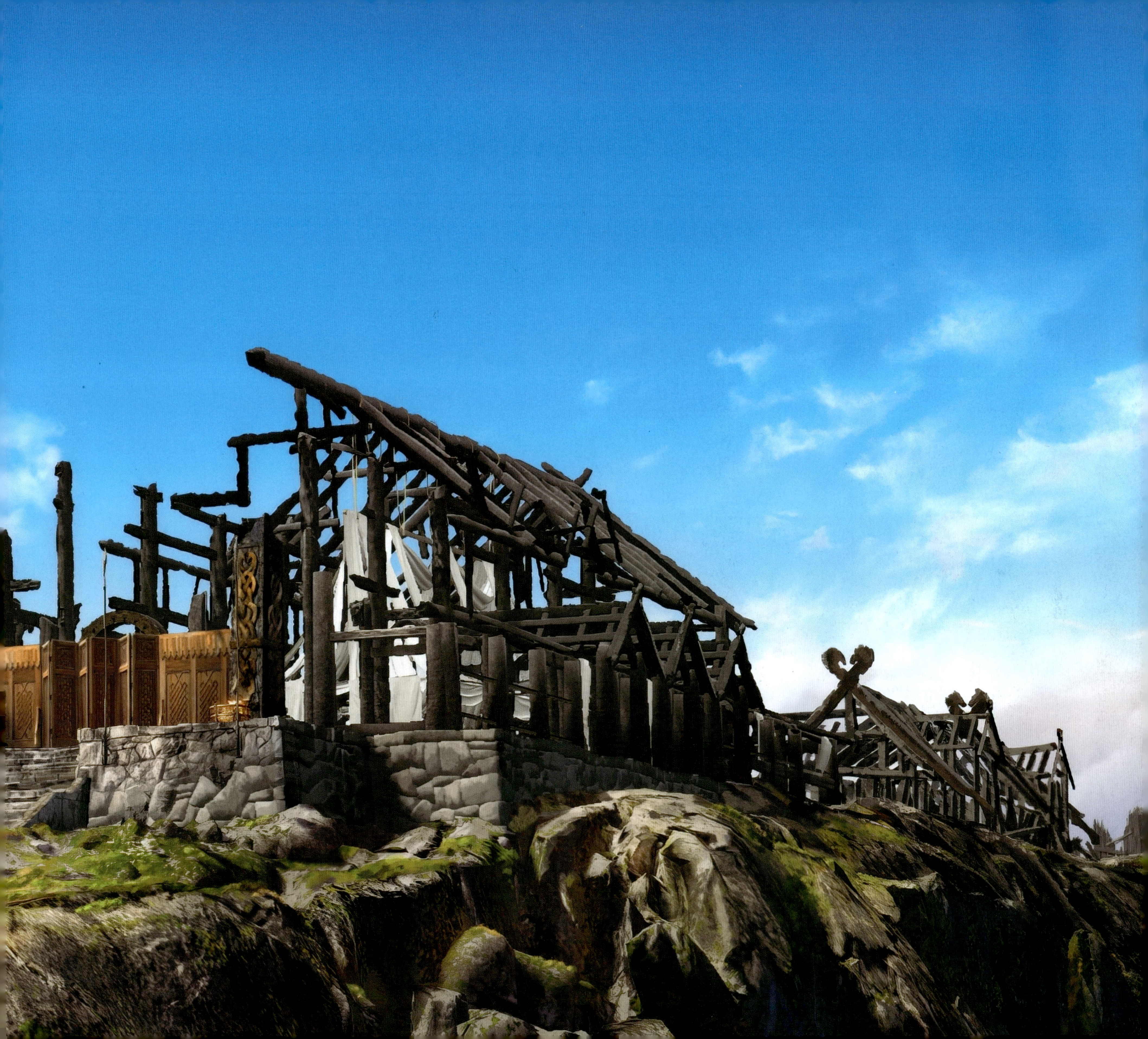

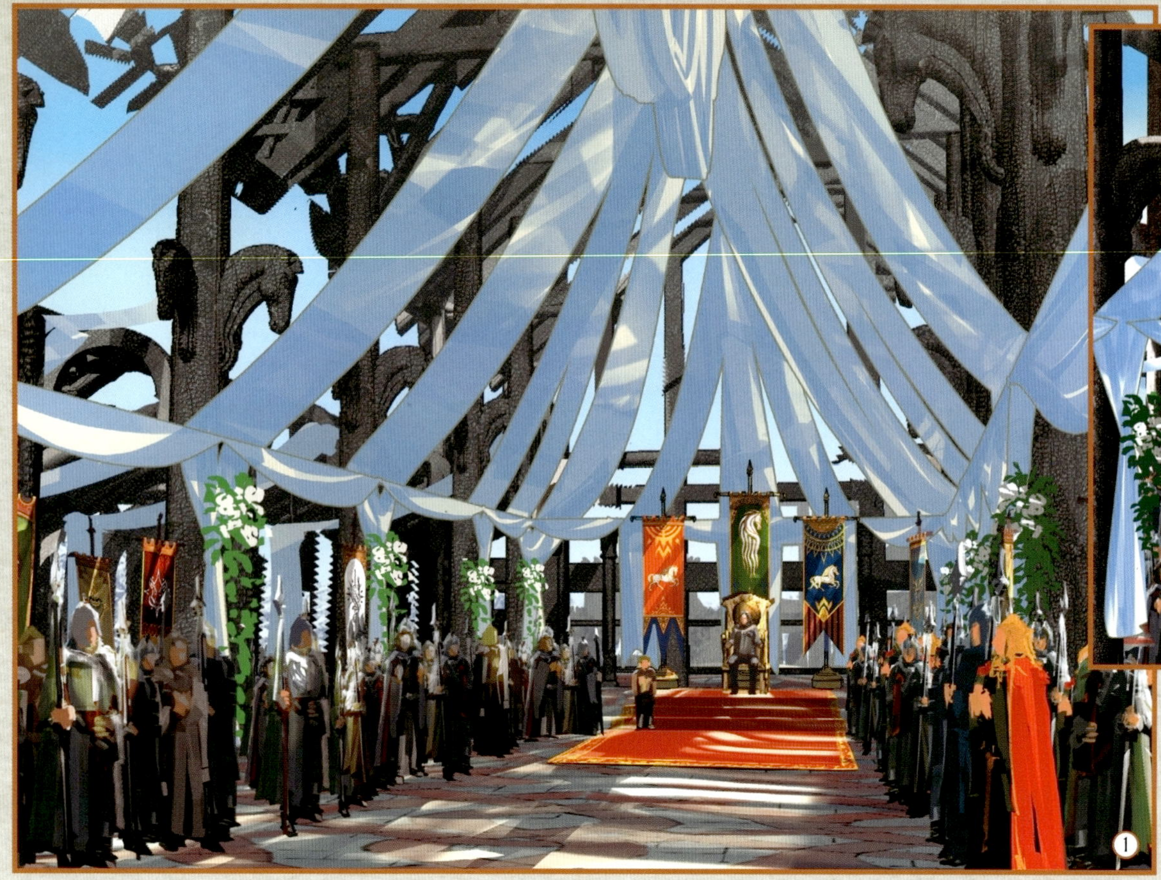

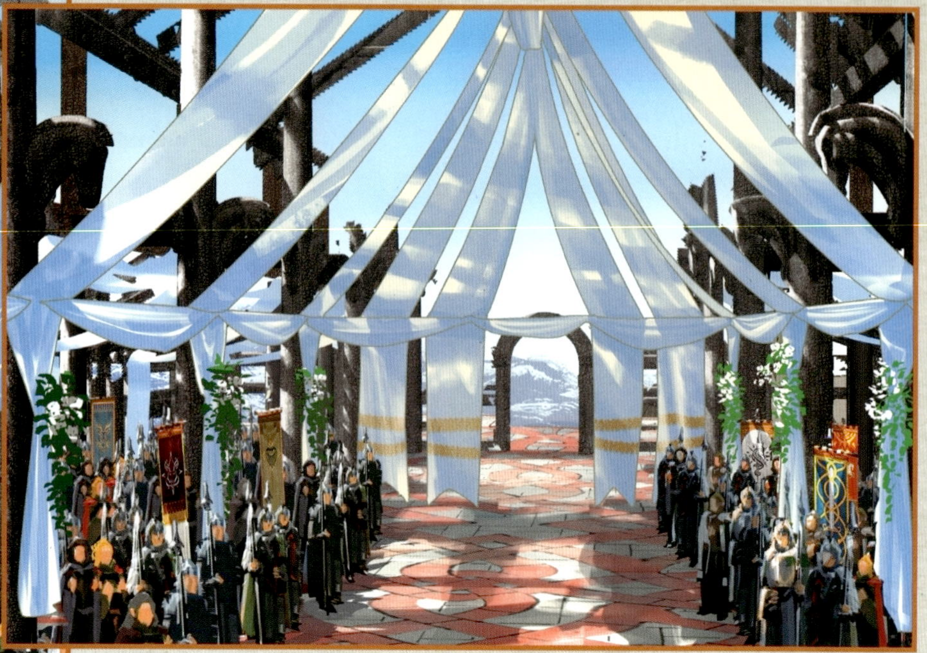

FRÉALÁF'S CORONATION

'THE LONG WINTER HAD ENDED. THE GREEN PROMISE OF SPRING HAD COME.'

The coronation scene was only a week or two after Héra and the others returned to Edoras, so we decided to leave the burnt pillars, but decorate them for the celebration. We were careful to make them look burnt, but not dirty.

It may be difficult to make out because the cityscape is seen in a wide shot, but the reconstruction of burned homes is already underway. Meduseld itself would eventually be rebuilt and come to appear the way it does in the trilogy. – TAMIKO KANAMORI, ART DIRECTOR

Returning to Meduseld for the coronation was something straight out of the text, but in crowning Fréaláf we didn't want to overlook Héra. Having the conversation between the two of them was important for us and for the rounding out of Héra's character. 'It should have been you,' he tells her. The truth is that she never wanted it, but, again, it comes back to being her choice, and she chooses not to take the throne.

'Do not look for her in the old tales, there are none.' This line about Héra opens us up to be able to tell a story about a character who makes a very different choice and doesn't end up on a throne. – PHOEBE GITTINS, WRITER

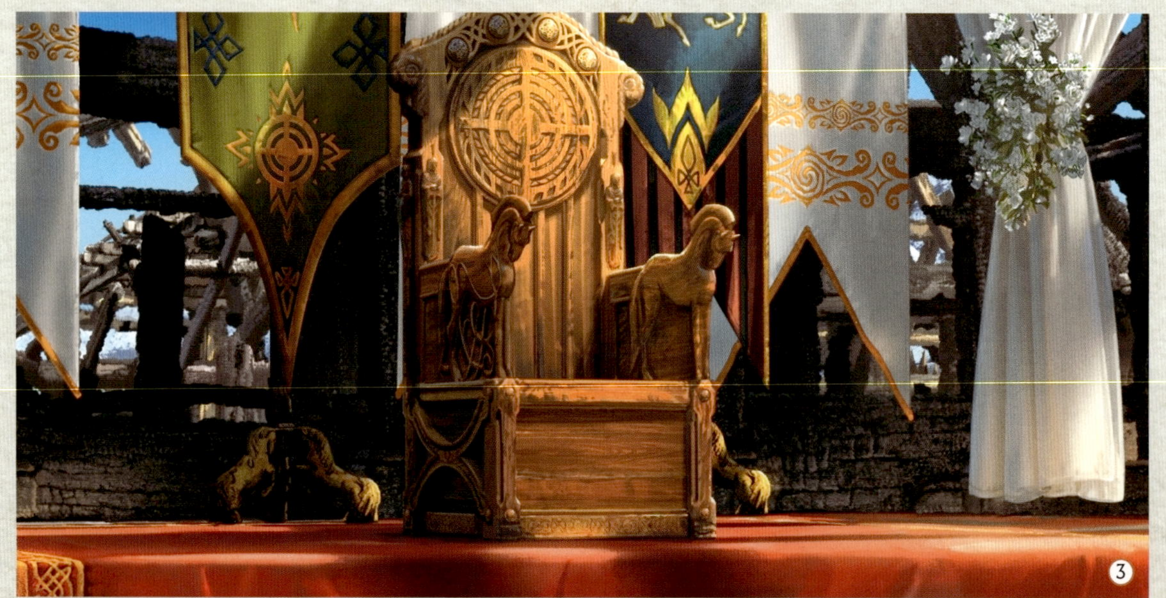

PP: Meduseld background art. 1: Coronation background setting art, TK. 2: Fréaláf character setting art, MT. 3: Coronation background art.

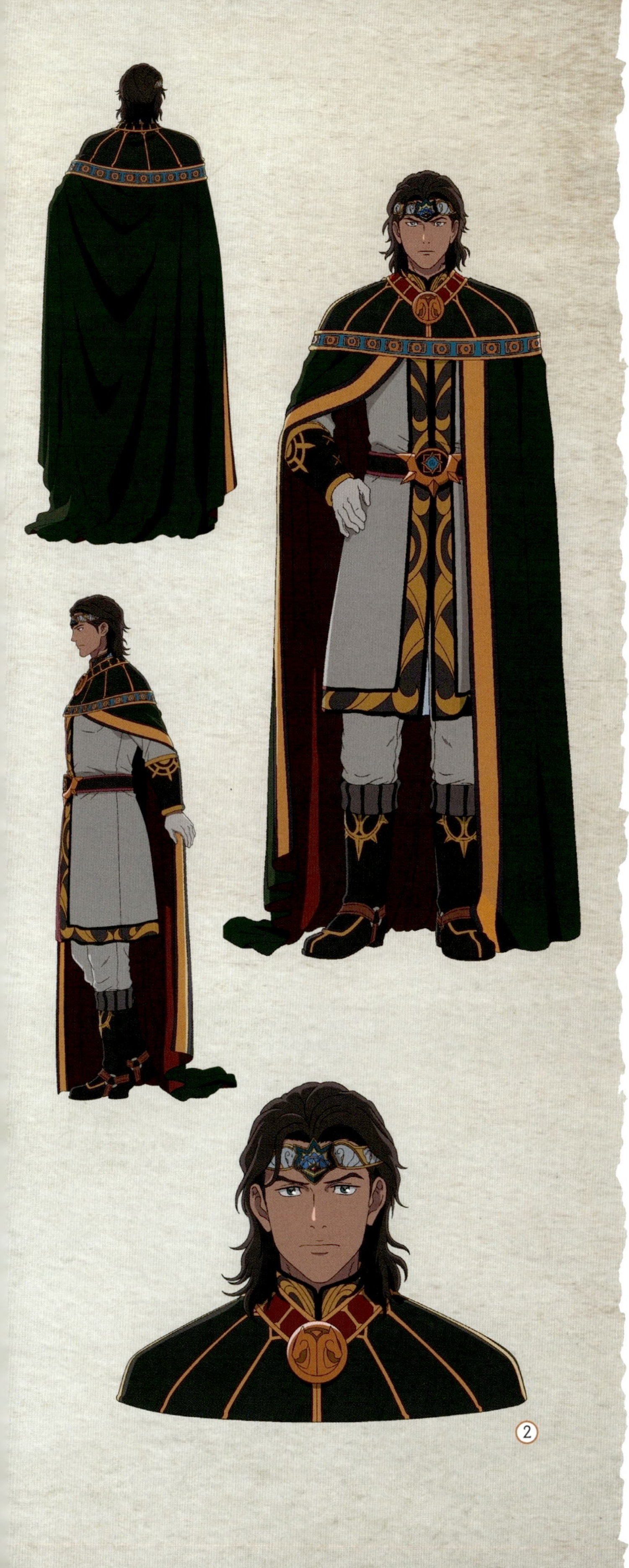

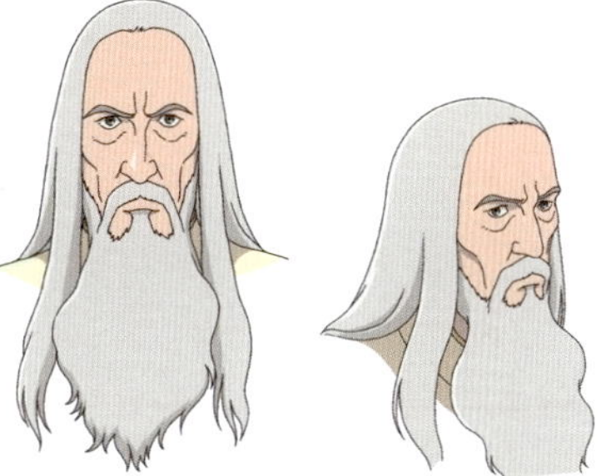

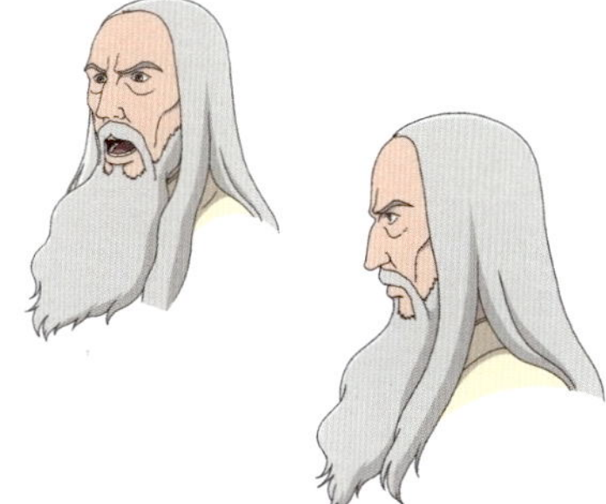

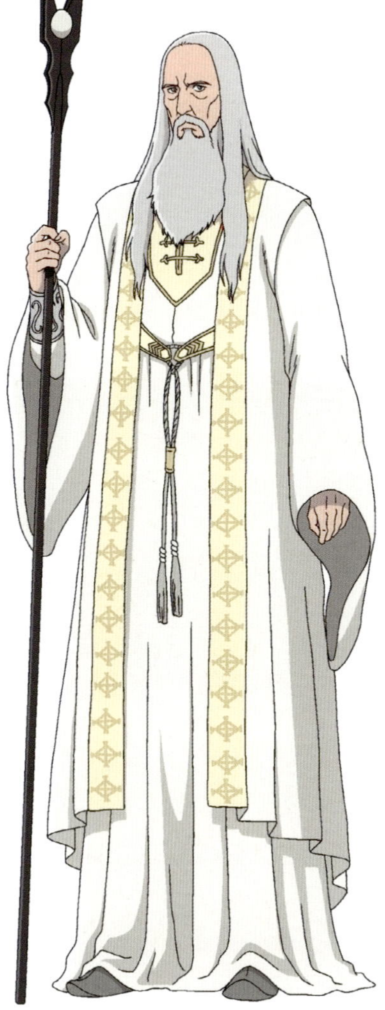

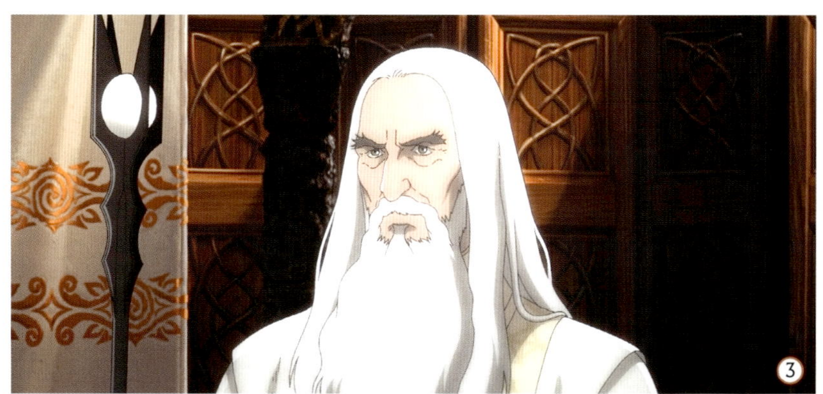

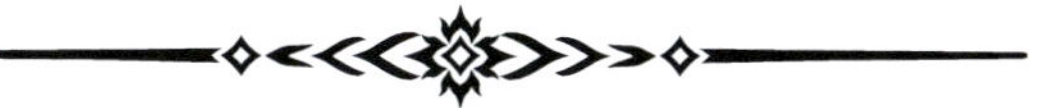

SARUMAN THE WHITE

As written by Tolkien, Saruman the White appeared at Fréaláf's coronation, after which he would be given the keys to the tower of Orthanc and take up residence there.

It was very important to us that Saruman speak with Sir Christopher Lee's voice. Thankfully we had three films' worth of recordings of Saruman, including alternate takes and lines that weren't in the final cut. Philippa has a Rolodex memory of what was recorded twenty years ago and was able to suggest things like lifting a word from this take and something else from that one, so she conceived dialogue knowing what could be constructed from what existed. Saruman's lines in our film were painstakingly pieced together and finessed from words first spoken by Sir Christopher more than two decades ago, and his wife Gitte Krøncke gave it her blessing, which was very important to all of us.

It gave me chills to hear it. – PHOEBE GITTINS, WRITER

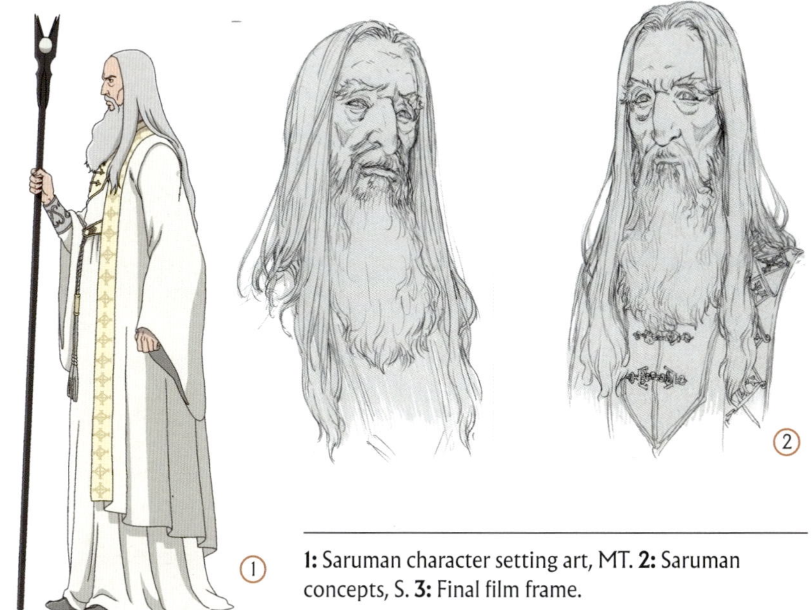

1: Saruman character setting art, MT. 2: Saruman concepts, S. 3: Final film frame.

HÉRA'S NEW PATH

The final scene of the movie after the war is won seems like it would be a happier one, but that's not the case. The director said that he envisioned a somewhat sad atmosphere.

I like to think of it in terms of it making you feel Wulf's absence. This may be a Japanese way of looking at it. – MIYAKO TAKASU, ANIMATION CHARACTER DESIGNER & KEY ANIMATION SUPERVISOR

Héra is the last of Helm's children. While Rohan has never had a queen, her claim could be argued. Nevertheless, the choice that she makes is a different one…

Héra taking the throne would not have felt authentic to Tolkien's world or history; women did not take the throne. It is about choices. Héra did not win a crown; she won her freedom. I think that is what young women watching the film will connect to more than the idea of her becoming queen. – PHILIPPA BOYENS, PRODUCER

1: Edoras stables background setting art, YY. 2: Edoras background art. 3: Edoras stables background art. 4: Character, horse and prop setting art, MT. 5: Final film frame. **Overleaf:** Final film frame.

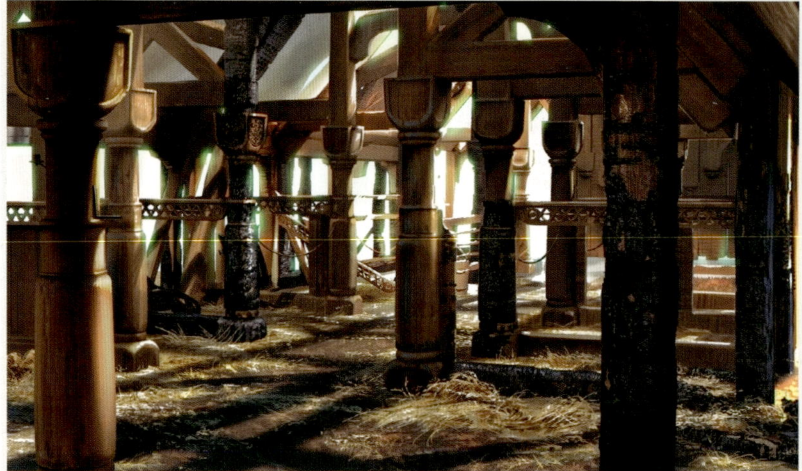

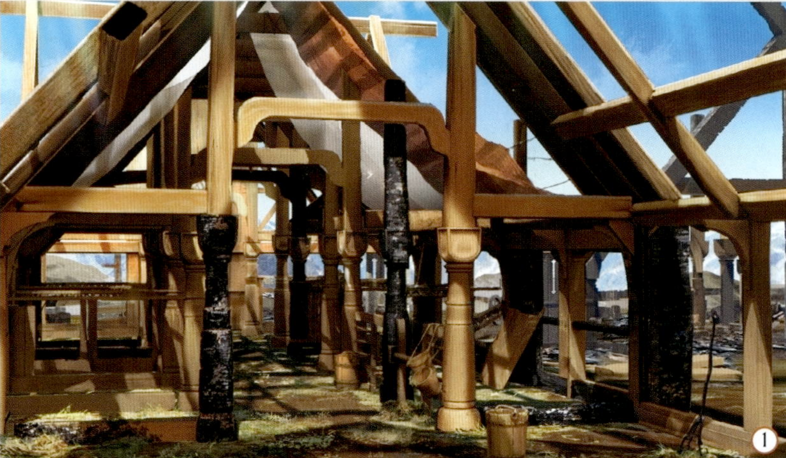

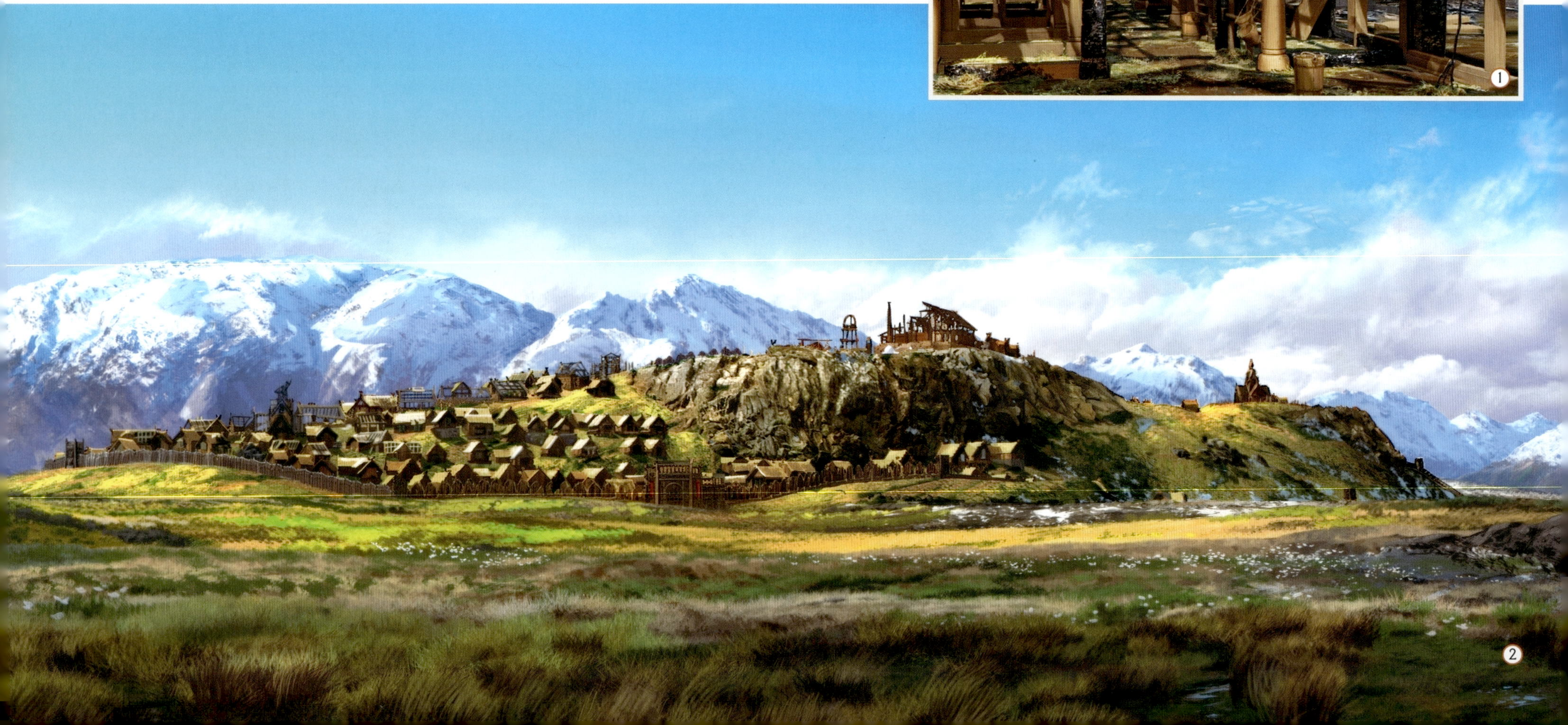

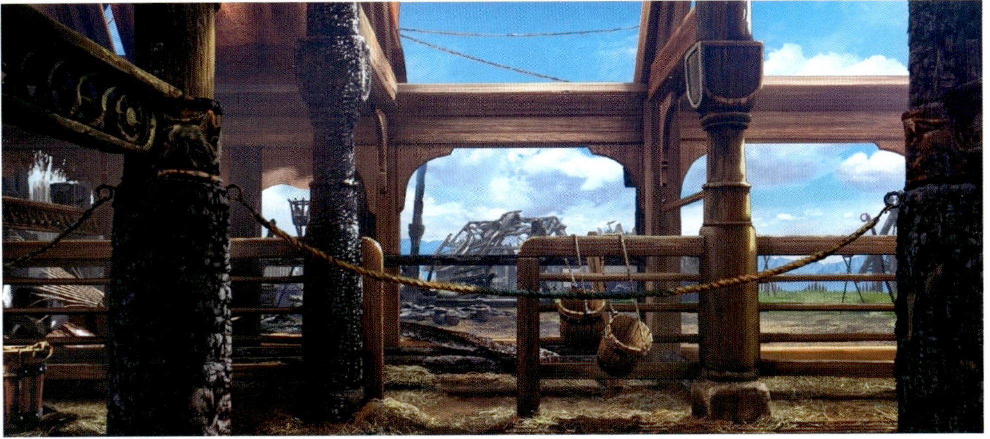

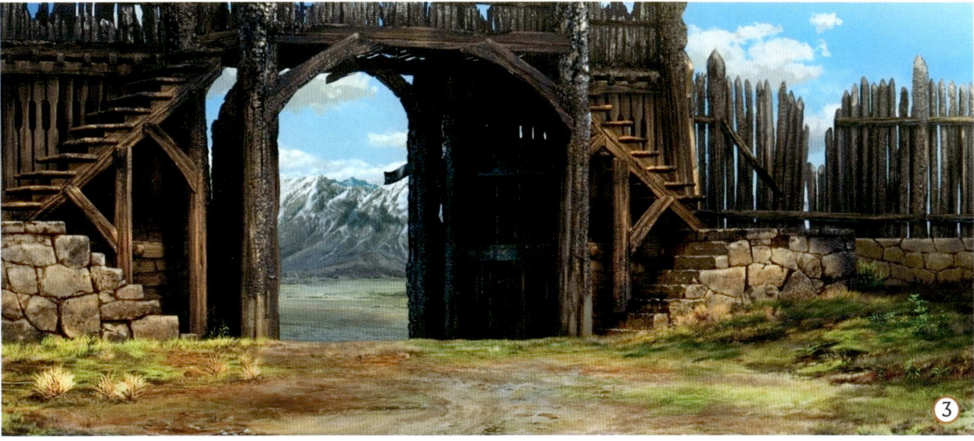

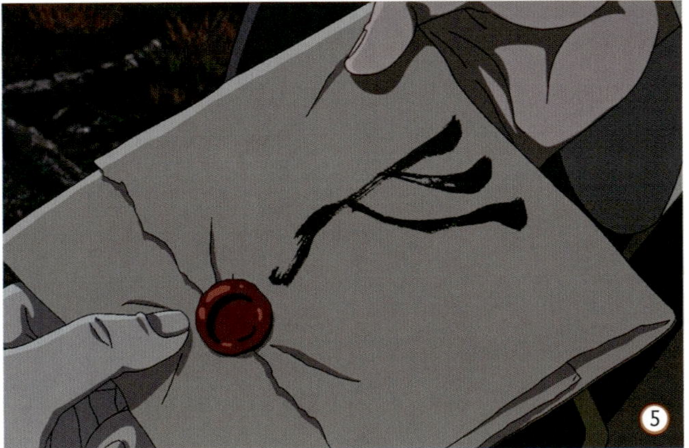

It is clear that there is no obligation for Olwyn to stay with Héra after she decides to leave Edoras, but Olwyn chooses to ride at her side; two shieldmaidens riding off to adventure. – ARTY PAPAGEORGIOU, WRITER

The hook at the end of the film furthers what we set up with what the Orcs were doing, looking for rings, and it meant we could tease Gandalf. In a way it connects with how the other films begin, with adventures coming to the Hobbits. – ARTY PAPAGEORGIOU, WRITER

Going off to meet a Wizard seemed like a fun way to end the whole thing. Adventure beckons, as Fréaláf intimates. He knows Héra too well. That is the happy ending for Héra.

'Wild, some called her, headstrong and free and so she remained to the end of her days.' – PHOEBE GITTINS, WRITER

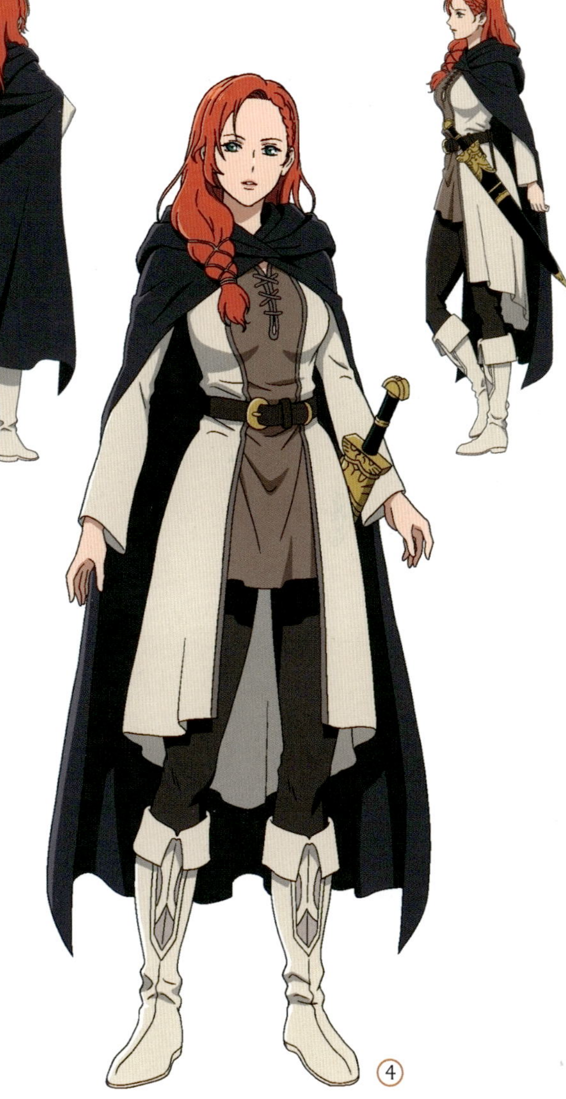

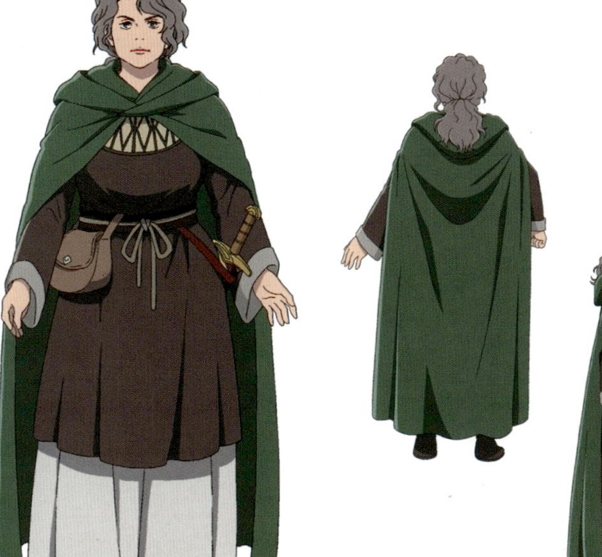

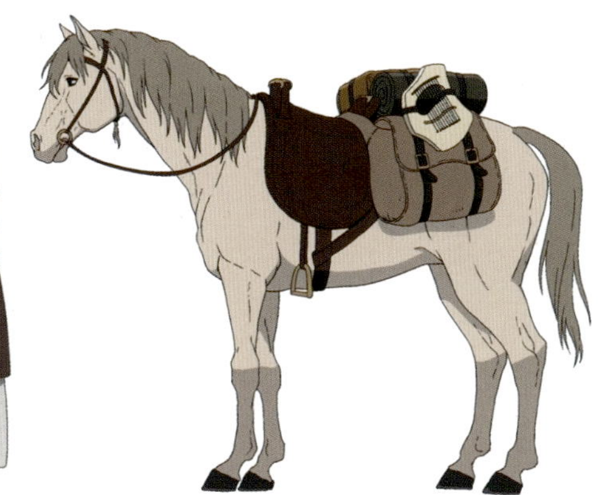

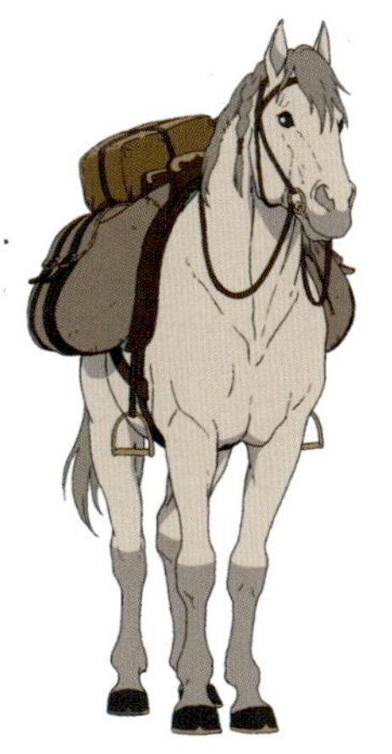

'WE RIDE FOR THE FORDS OF ISEN TO MEET A WIZARD.'

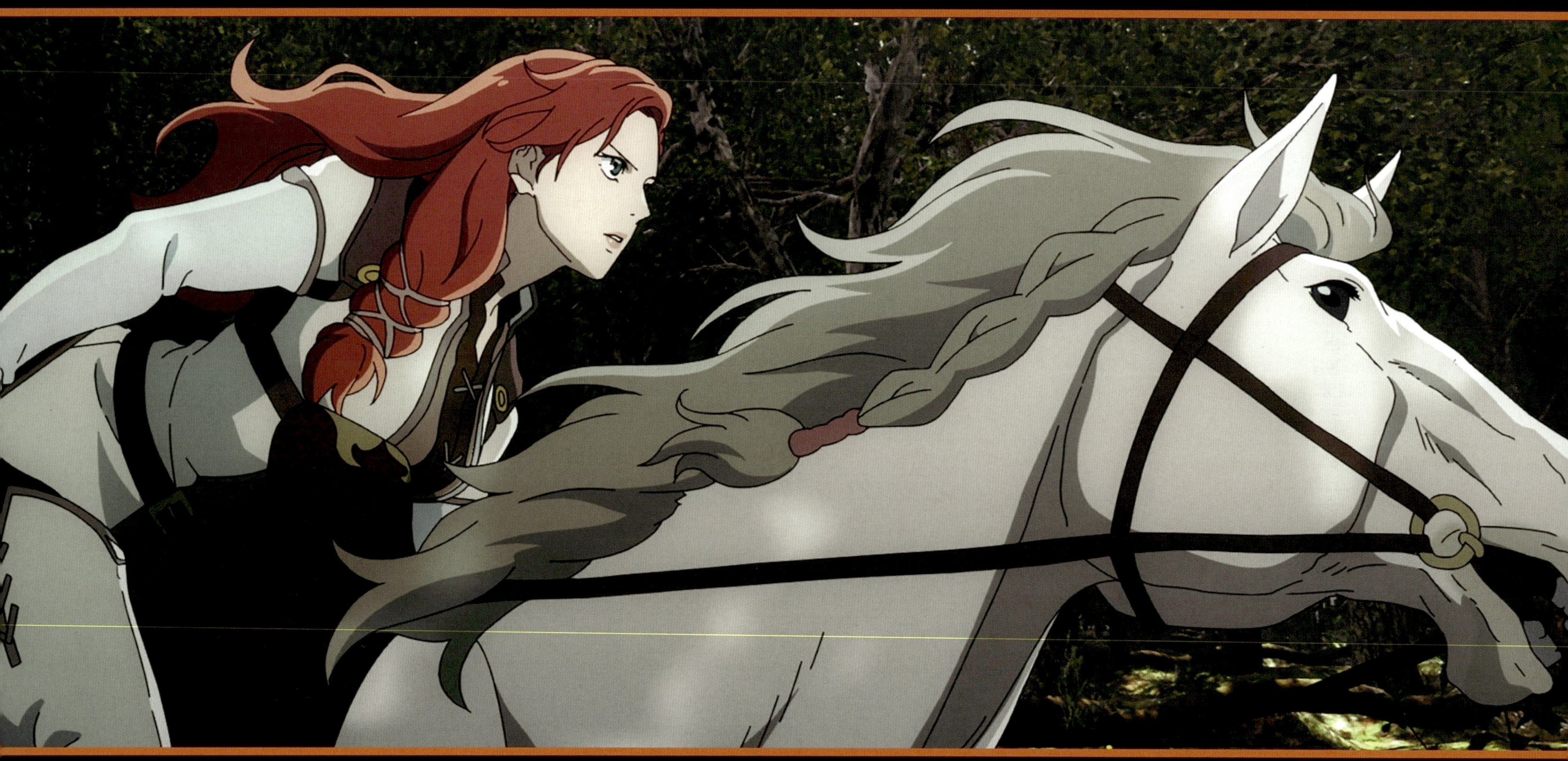

'. . . WILD, SOME CALLED HER, HEADSTRONG AND FREE . . .
AND SO SHE REMAINED, TO THE END OF HER DAYS.'

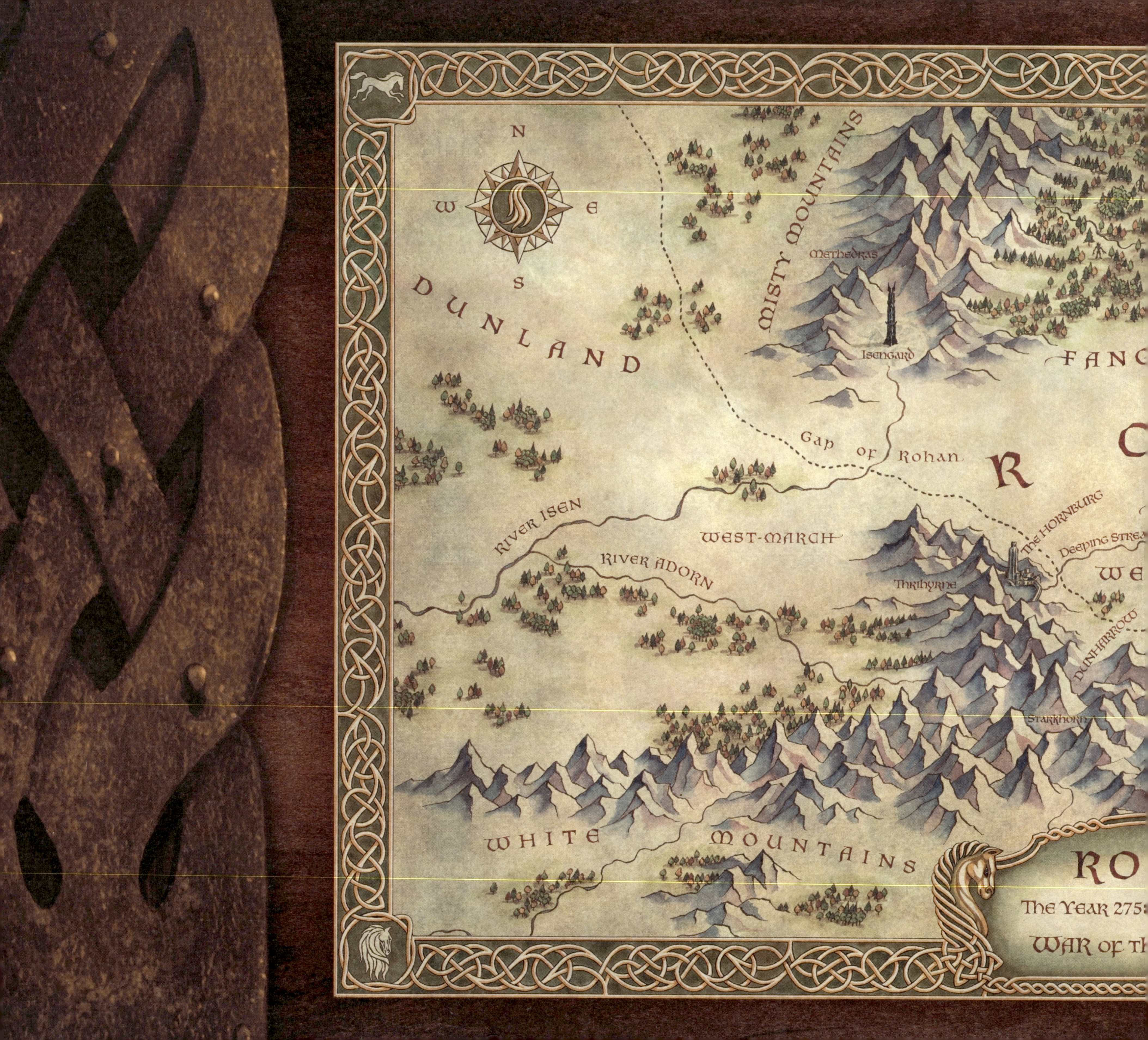

N
W E
S
DUNLAND
MISTY MOUNTAINS
METHEDRAS
ISENGARD
FANG
Gap of Rohan
R O
RIVER ISEN
WEST-MARCH
RIVER ADORN
THE HORNBURG
DEEPING STREA
THRIHYRNE
WE
DUNHARROW
STARKHORN
WHITE MOUNTAINS
RO
THE YEAR 275
WAR OF TH